MOON

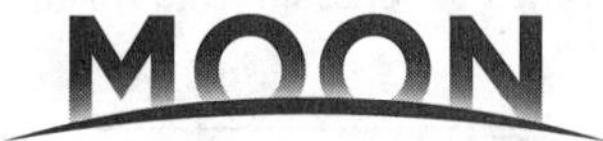

CALIFORNIA HIKING

TOM STIENSTRA • ANN MARIE BROWN

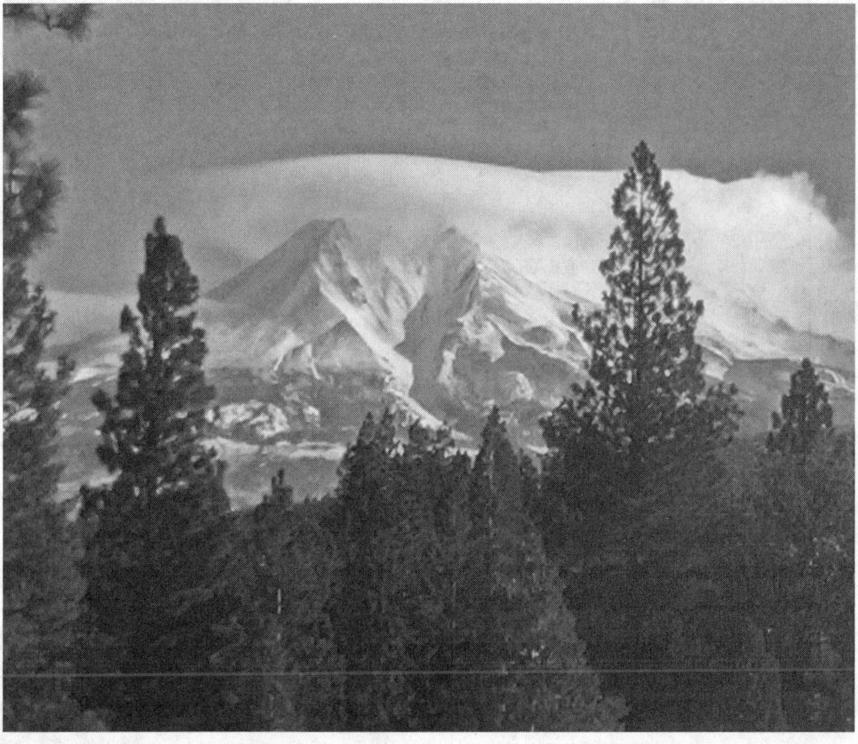

CALIFORNIA REGIONS
OREGON
IDAHO
NEVADA
ARIZONA
MEXICO
PACIFIC OCEAN
Chapter 1
REDWOOD EMPIRE
page 38
Chapter 2
SHASTA AND TRINITY
page 66
Chapter 3
LASSEN AND MODOC
page 130
Chapter 4
MENDOCINO AND WINE COUNTRY
page 172
Chapter 5
SACRAMENTO AND GOLD COUNTRY
page 198
Chapter 6
TAHOE AND NORTHERN SIERRA
page 212
Chapter 7
SAN FRANCISCO BAY AREA
page 288
Chapter 8
MONTEREY AND BIG SUR
page 438
Chapter 9
SAN JOAQUIN VALLEY
page 468
Chapter 10
YOSEMITE AND MAMMOTH LAKES
page 482
Chapter 11
SEQUOIA AND KINGS CANYON
page 558
Chapter 12
SANTA BARBARA AND VICINITY
page 640
Chapter 13
LOS ANGELES AND VICINITY
page 682
Chapter 14
SAN DIEGO AND VICINITY
page 738
Chapter 15
CALIFORNIA DESERTS
page 768
©MOON.COM

Contents

How to Use This Book

ABOUT THE TRAIL PROFILES

Each hike in this book is listed in a consistent, easy-to-read format to help you choose the ideal hike. From a general overview of the setting to detailed driving directions, the profile will provide all the information you need. Here is a sample profile:

Map number and hike number →

1 SOMEWHERE USA HIKE

Round-trip mileage (unless otherwise noted) and the approximate amount of time needed to complete the hike (actual times can vary widely, especially on longer hikes) →

9.0 mi/5.0 hrs 3 8 ← Difficulty and quality ratings

at the mouth of the Somewhere River ← General location of the trail, named by its proximity to the nearest major town or landmark

Map on which the trailhead can be found and page number on which the map can be found →

Map 1.2, page 24 BEST ← Symbol indicating that the hike is listed among the author's top picks

Each hike in this book begins with a brief overview of its setting. The description typically covers what kind of terrain to expect, what might be seen, and any conditions that may make the hike difficult to navigate. Side trips, such as to waterfalls or panoramic vistas, in addition to ways to combine the trail with others nearby for a longer outing, are also noted here. In many cases, mile-by-mile trail directions are included.

User Groups: This section notes the types of users that are permitted on the trail, including hikers, mountain bikers, horseback riders, and dogs. Wheelchair access is also noted here.

Permits: This section notes whether a permit is required for hiking, or, if the hike spans more than one day, whether one is required for camping. Any fees, such as for parking, day use, or entrance, are also noted here.

Maps: This section provides information on how to obtain detailed trail maps of the hike and its environs. Whenever applicable, names of U.S. Geologic Survey (USGS) topographic maps and national forest maps are also included; contact information for these and other map sources are noted in the Resources section at the back of this book.

Directions: This section provides mile-by-mile driving directions to the trail head from the nearest major town.

Contact: This section provides an address and phone number for each hike. The contact is usually the agency maintaining the trail but may also be a trail club or other organization.

ABOUT THE ICONS

The icons in this book are designed to provide at-a-glance information on the difficulty and quality of each hike.

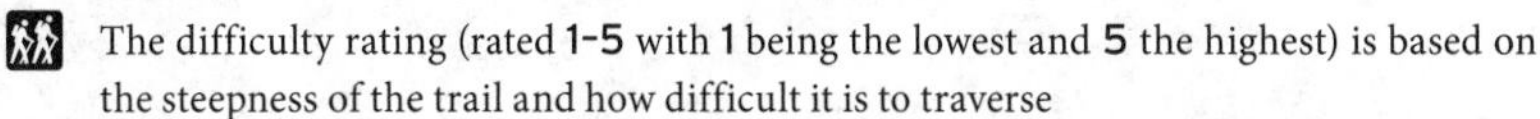

The difficulty rating (rated 1-5 with 1 being the lowest and 5 the highest) is based on the steepness of the trail and how difficult it is to traverse

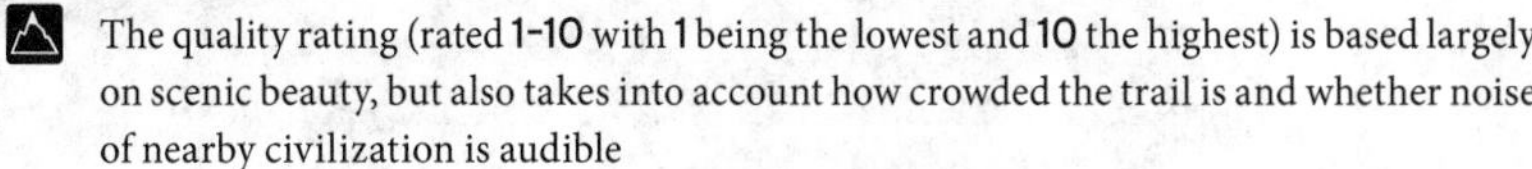

The quality rating (rated 1-10 with 1 being the lowest and 10 the highest) is based largely on scenic beauty, but also takes into account how crowded the trail is and whether noise of nearby civilization is audible

ABOUT THE DIFFICULTY RATINGS

Trails rated 1 are very easy and suitable for hikers of all abilities, including young children.

Trails rated 2 are easy-to-moderate and suitable for most hikers, including families with active children 6 and older.

Trails rated 3 are moderately challenging and suitable for reasonably fit adults and older children who are very active.

Trails rated 4 are very challenging and suitable for physically fit hikers who are seeking a workout.

Trails rated 5 are extremely challenging and suitable only for experienced hikers who are in top physical condition.

MAP SYMBOLS

Expressway	80 Interstate Freeway	Airfield
Primary Road	101 U.S. Highway	Airport
Secondary Road	21 State Highway	City/Town
Unpaved Road	66 County Highway	Mountain
Ferry	Lake	Park
National Border	Dry Lake	Pass
State Border	Seasonal Lake	State Capital

ABOUT THE MAPS

This book is divided into chapters based on major regions in the state; an overview map of these regions precedes the table of contents. Each chapter begins with a map of the region, which is further broken down into detail maps. Trailheads are noted on the detail maps by number.

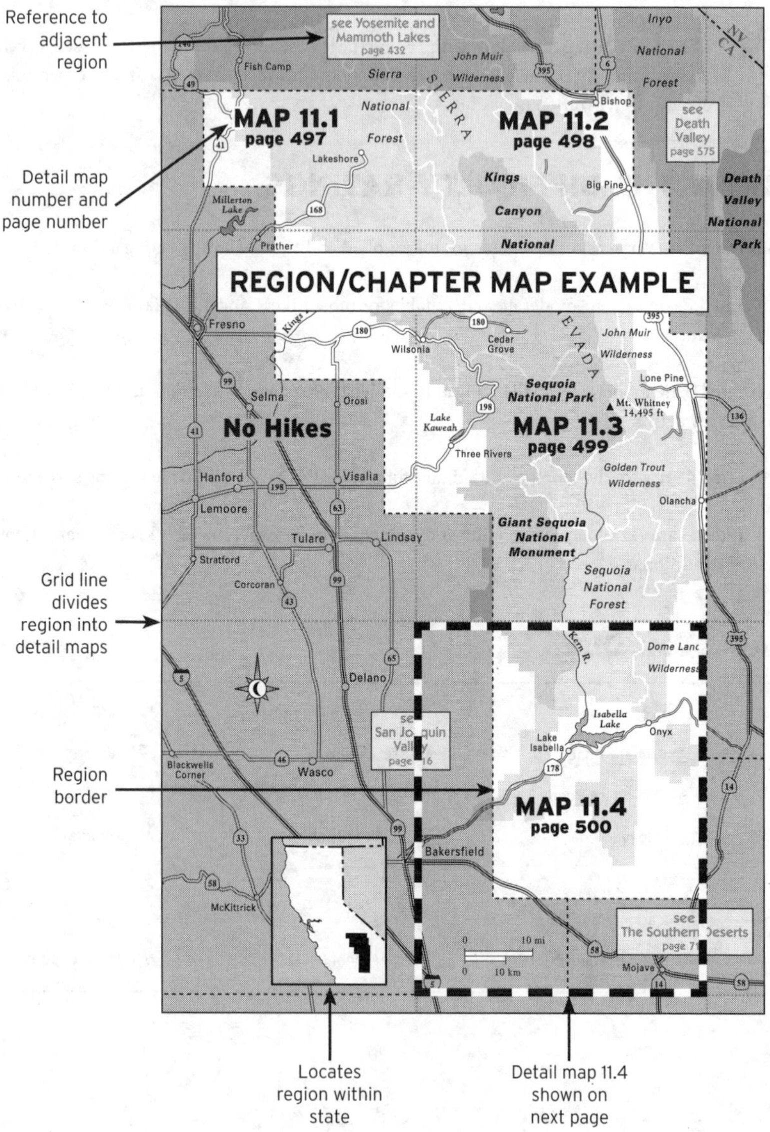

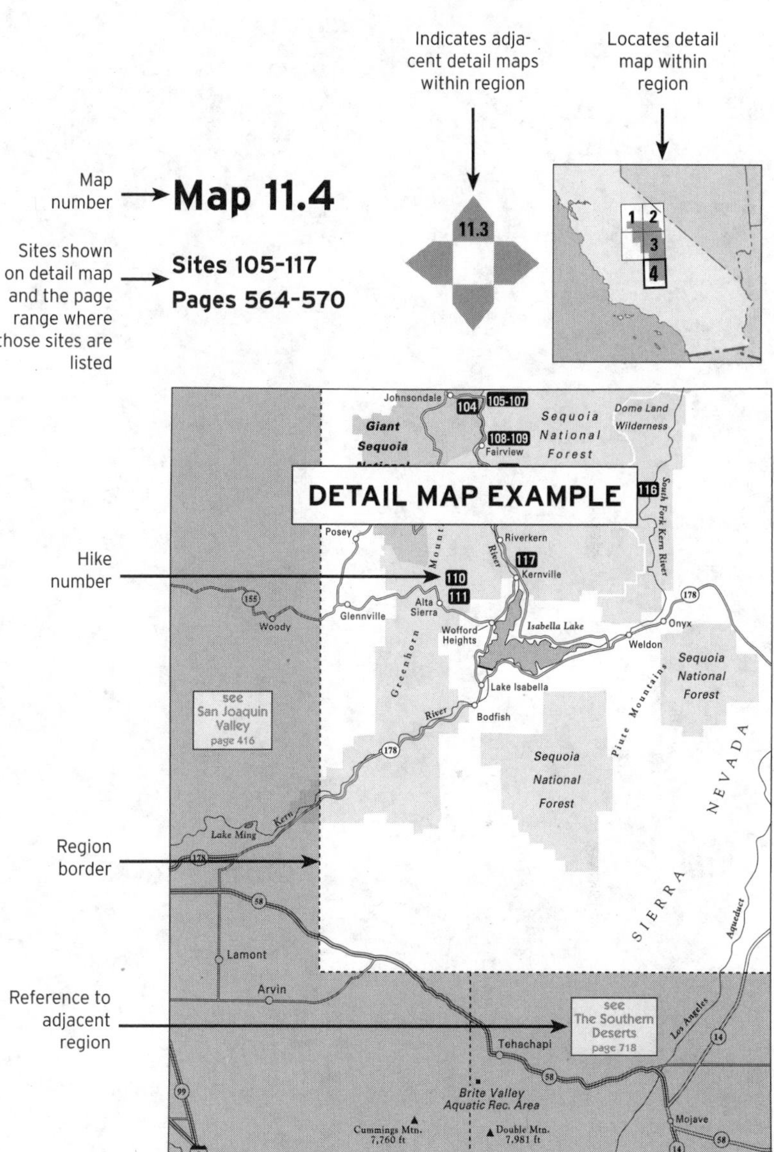
Indicates adjacent detail maps within region
Locates detail map within region
Map number
Map 11.4
Sites shown on detail map and the page range where those sites are listed
Sites 105-117
Pages 564-570
11.3
1
2
3
4
DETAIL MAP EXAMPLE
Hike number
Region border
Reference to adjacent region
see San Joaquin Valley page 416
see The Southern Deserts page 718
Johnsondale
Giant Sequoia
Sequoia National Forest
Dome Land Wilderness
Fairview
South Fork Kern River
Posey
Riverkern
Kernville
Glennville
Alta Sierra
Woody
Wofford Heights
Isabella Lake
Onyx
Weldon
Lake Isabella
Bodfish
Greenhorn
Piute Mountains
Sierra Nevada
Lake Ming
Kern
River
Lamont
Arvin
Tehachapi
Los Angeles
Aqueduct
Brite Valley Aquatic Rec. Area
Cummings Mtn. 7,760 ft
Double Mtn. 7,981 ft
Mojave

INTRODUCTION

Author's Note

If the great outdoors is so great, then why don't people enjoy it more? The answer is because of the time trap, and I will tell you exactly how to beat it.

For many, the biggest problem is finding the time to go, whether it is hiking, backpacking, camping, fishing, boating, biking, or even just for a good drive in the country. The solution? Believe it or not, the answer is to treat your fun just as you treat your work, and I'll tell you how.

Consider how you treat your job: Always on time? Go there every day you are scheduled? Do whatever it takes to get there and get it done? Right? No foolin' that's right. Now imagine if you took the same approach to the outdoors. Suddenly your life would be a heck of a lot better.

The secret is to schedule all of your outdoor activities. For instance, I go fishing every Thursday evening, hiking every Sunday morning, and on an overnight trip every new moon (when stargazing is best). No matter what, I'm going. Just like going to work, I've scheduled it. The same approach works with longer adventures. The only reason I have been able to complete hikes ranging from 200 to 300 miles was that I scheduled the time to do it. The reason I spend 125 to 150 days a year in the field is that I schedule them. In my top year, I had nearly 200 days where at least some of the day was enjoyed taking part in outdoor recreation.

If you get out your calendar and write in the exact dates you are going, then you'll go. If you don't, you won't. Suddenly, with only a minor change in your plan, you can be living the life you were previously just dreaming about.

—Tom Stienstra

Note on this Updated Edition

Many keep this book in their cars or pickup trucks at all times. It sits dog-eared, often with cryptic notes, on a seat, on the center floorboard or on the dashboard, ready for use. No matter where we each might be on our separate paths, we are both kind of like dogs: We need to go for a walk every day . . . and we share the hope that there is always a trail waiting nearby, always another hike to look forward to.

We've selected the best 1,000 trails in California for this book. We have hiked each of them. We have also involved hundreds of rangers, interpretive specialists, and field scouts across the state to review our work to make it as correct as possible as we go to press. Each word has been vetted multiple times. For this edition, we've included too many updates to count. If you run across any changes out there on the trail, feel free join our team and drop us a line.

This is the only complete guide to hiking in California. Its range and scope are unmatched. There are many excellent locally focused guidebooks. Both of us have written several. Most hikers love to range both near and far, to explore and make each day a discovery. Put no bounds on your life or what is possible. That is what this book can do for you.

You have the best of California in your hands. We've done everything possible to put it within reach.

Author's Note

A wise person once said that a culture can be measured by the resources it chooses to preserve. If that's true, then California's parks and preserve are an immense credit to our culture. The Golden State is blessed with an abundance of public land, including more than 25 units of the National Park System, 19 national forests, 137 federally designated wilderness areas, 280 state parks, and thousands of county and regional parks.

This huge mosaic of parklands celebrates California's diverse landscape, which includes the highest peak in the contiguous United States (Mount Whitney at 14,495 feet or 14,505 feet, depending on which measurement is currently in vogue) and the lowest point in the western hemisphere (Badwater in Death Valley at 282 feet below sea level). Our state contains 20,000 square miles of desert, nearly 700 miles of Pacific coastline, an unaccountable wealth of snow-capped peaks and alpine lakes, a smattering of islands, and even a handful of volcanoes.

California also boasts its share of the world's tallest living things, the towering coast redwoods. And we are the only state that is home to the world's largest living trees (by volume), the giant sequoias. Also within California's borders are groves of the planet's oldest living things, the ancient bristlecone pines.

Quite simply, we live in a land of superlatives. California's public lands are some of my favorite places on earth, and I believe that everyone should have the chance to see them and be humbled by their wonders. But this wish comes with a caveat: We must tread lightly and gently on our parks, with great respect and care for the land. And we must do whatever is required to ensure the protection of these beautiful places for future generations.

I wish you many inspiring days on the trail.

—Ann Marie Brown

Best Hikes

Can't decide where to hike this weekend? Here are our picks for the best hikes in California in 17 different categories, listed from north to south throughout the state:

BEST Beach and Coastal Walks

Rim Loop Trail, Patrick's Point State Park, Redwood Empire, page 54.

Lost Coast Trail/Mattole Trailhead, King Range National Conservation Area, Redwood Empire, page 60.

Lost Coast Trail/Sinkyone Trailhead, Sinkyone Wilderness State Park, Mendocino and Wine Country, page 177.

Coast Trail, Point Reyes National Seashore, San Francisco Bay Area, page 302.

Old Landing Cove Trail, Wilder Ranch State Park, Monterey and Big Sur, page 440.

Asilomar Coast Trail, Asilomar State Beach, Monterey and Big Sur, page 445.

Point Lobos Perimeter, Point Lobos State Reserve, Monterey and Big Sur, page 450.

Montaña de Oro Bluffs Trail, Montaña de Oro State Park, Santa Barbara and Vicinity, page 650.

Razor Point and Beach Trail Loop, Torrey Pines State Reserve, San Diego and Vicinity, page 747.

Cabrillo Tidepools, Cabrillo National Monument, San Diego and Vicinity, page 752.

BEST Bird-Watching

Arcata Marsh Trail, Arcata Marsh and Wildlife Sanctuary, Redwood Empire, page 55.

Abbotts Lagoon Trail, Point Reyes National Seashore, San Francisco Bay Area, page 294.

Martin Griffin Preserve/Audubon Canyon Ranch Trail, Martin Griffin Preserve, San Francisco Bay Area, page 316.

Arrowhead Marsh, Martin Luther King Regional Shoreline, San Francisco Bay Area, page 381.

Elkhorn Slough South Marsh Loop, Moss Landing, Monterey and Big Sur, page 443.

Chester, Sousa, and Winton Marsh Trails, San Luis National Wildlife Refuge, San Joaquin Valley, page 475.

Carrizo Plain and Painted Rock, Carrizo Plains National Monument, San Joaquin Valley, page 479.

Mono Lake South Tufa Trail, Mono Lake Tufa State Reserve, Yosemite and Mammoth Lakes, page 518.

Silverwood Wildlife Sanctuary, San Diego and Vicinity, page 760.

BEST Butt-Kickers

Devils Punchbowl (via Doe Flat Trail/Buck Lake Trail), Siskiyou Wilderness, Shasta and Trinity, page 73.

Shasta Summit Trail, Shasta-Trinity National Forest, Shasta and Trinity, page 91.

Rooster Comb Loop (Long Version), Henry W. Coe State Park, San Francisco Bay Area, page 433.

Half Dome, Yosemite Valley, Yosemite and Mammoth Lakes, page 537.

Don Cecil Trail to Lookout Peak, Kings Canyon National Park, Sequoia and Kings Canyon, page 583.

Alta Peak, Sequoia National Park, Sequoia and Kings Canyon, page 593.
Mount Whitney Trail, John Muir Wilderness, Sequoia and Kings Canyon, page 624.
Mount Baldy, Angeles National Forest, Los Angeles and Vicinity, page 716.
Vivian Creek Trail to Mount San Gorgonio, San Gorgonio Wilderness, Los Angeles and Vicinity, page 732.

BEST Desert Hikes

Ubehebe Peak, Death Valley National Park, California Deserts, page 774.
Mosaic Canyon, Death Valley National Park, California Deserts, page 775.
Wildrose Peak Trail, Death Valley National Park, California Deserts, page 780.
Ryan Mountain Trail, Joshua Tree National Park, California Deserts, page 793.
Mastodon Peak, Joshua Tree National Park, California Deserts, page 795.
Lost Palms Oasis, Joshua Tree National Park, California Deserts, page 795.
Tahquitz Canyon, Agua Caliente Indian Reservation, California Deserts, page 799.
Ladder Canyon and Big Painted Canyon, Mecca Hills Wilderness, California Deserts, page 803.
Borrego Palm Canyon, Anza-Borrego Desert State Park, California Deserts, page 804.
The Slot, Anza-Borrego Desert State Park, California Deserts, page 806.

BEST Fall Colors

Whiskeytown Falls, Whiskeytown Lake National Recreation Area, Shasta and Trinity, page 125.
American River Parkway, Sacramento and Gold Country, page 207.
Fallen Leaf Lake Trail, South Lake Tahoe, Tahoe and Northern Sierra, page 253.
Parker Lake Trail, Ansel Adams Wilderness, Yosemite and Mammoth Lakes, page 520.
Convict Canyon to Lake Dorothy, John Muir Wilderness, Yosemite and Mammoth Lakes, page 551.
McGee Creek to Steelhead Lake, John Muir Wilderness, Yosemite and Mammoth Lakes, page 552.
Blue Lake, John Muir Wilderness, Sequoia and Kings Canyon, page 570.
Tyee Lakes, John Muir Wilderness, Sequoia and Kings Canyon, page 572.
Farewell Gap Trail to Aspen Flat, Sequoia National Park, Sequoia and Kings Canyon, page 605.
Boucher Trail and Scott's Cabin Loop, Palomar Mountain State Park, San Diego and Vicinity, page 754.

BEST Hikes with a View

Mount Eddy Trail, Shasta-Trinity National Forest, Shasta and Trinity, page 103.
Lassen Peak Trail, Lassen Volcanic National Park, Lassen and Modoc, page 157.
Rubicon Trail, D. L. Bliss State Park, Tahoe and Northern Sierra, page 244.
Perimeter Trail, Angel Island State Park, San Francisco Bay Area, page 334.
Clouds Rest, Yosemite National Park, Yosemite and Mammoth Lakes, page 500.
Sentinel Dome, Yosemite National Park, Yosemite and Mammoth Lakes, page 542.
Panorama Trail, Yosemite National Park, Yosemite and Mammoth Lakes, page 544.
Moro Rock, Sequoia National Park, Sequoia and Kings Canyon, page 600.

The Needles Spires, Giant Sequoia National Monument, Sequoia and Kings Canyon, page 619.

Devils Slide Trail to Tahquitz Peak, San Jacinto Wilderness, Los Angeles and Vicinity, page 735.

Aerial Tramway to San Jacinto Peak, Mount San Jacinto State Park and Wilderness, California Deserts, page 798.

BEST Kids

Rainbow and Lake of the Sky Trails, Tahoe National Forest, Tahoe and Northern Sierra, page 250.

Angora Lakes Trail, Tahoe National Forest, Tahoe and Northern Sierra, page 254.

Tomales Point Trail, Point Reyes National Seashore, San Francisco Bay Area, page 293.

Fitzgerald Marine Reserve, Moss Beach, San Francisco Bay Area, page 350.

Año Nuevo Trail, Año Nuevo State Preserve, San Francisco Bay Area, page 368.

Pinecrest Lake National Recreation Trail, Stanislaus National Forest, Yosemite and Mammoth Lakes, page 485.

Devils Postpile and Rainbow Falls, Devils Postpile National Monument, Yosemite and Mammoth Lakes, page 526.

Tokopah Falls, Sequoia National Park, Sequoia and Kings Canyon, page 595.

Cabrillo Tidepools, Cabrillo National Monument, San Diego and Vicinity, page 752.

Lost Horse Mine, Joshua Tree National Park, California Deserts, page 793.

BEST Meadow Hikes

Haypress Meadows Trailhead, Marble Mountain Wilderness, Shasta and Trinity, page 76.

South Gate Meadows, Mount Shasta Wilderness, Shasta and Trinity, page 94.

Carson Pass to Echo Lakes Resort (PCT), Tahoe and Northern Sierra, page 268.

Grass Valley Loop, Anthony Chabot Regional Park, San Francisco Bay Area, page 384.

BEST Redwoods

Boy Scout Tree Trail, Jedediah Smith Redwoods State Park, Redwood Empire, page 42.

Tall Trees Trail, Redwood National Park, Redwood Empire, page 50.

Redwood Creek Trail, Redwood National Park, Redwood Empire, page 52.

Bull Creek Trail North, Humboldt Redwoods State Park, Redwood Empire, page 58.

Redwood Creek Trail, Muir Woods National Monument, San Francisco Bay Area, page 326.

Shadow of the Giants, Sierra National Forest, Yosemite and Mammoth Lakes, page 549.

General Grant Tree Trail, Kings Canyon National Park, Sequoia and Kings Canyon, page 577.

Redwood Canyon, Kings Canyon National Park, Sequoia and Kings Canyon, page 586.

Congress Trail Loop, Sequoia National Park, Sequoia and Kings Canyon, page 596.

Trail of 100 Giants, Giant Sequoia National Monument, Sequoia and Kings Canyon, page 619.

BEST Self-Guided Nature Walks

McCloud Nature Trail, Shasta-Trinity National Forest, Shasta and Trinity, page 115.
Rainbow and Lake of the Sky Trails, Tahoe National Forest, Tahoe and Northern Sierra, page 250.
Trail of the Gargoyles, Stanislaus National Forest, Tahoe and Northern Sierra, page 281.
Shadow of the Giants, Sierra National Forest, Yosemite and Mammoth Lakes, page 549.
Methuselah Trail, Inyo National Forest, Yosemite and Mammoth Lakes, page 556.
Unal Trail, Sequoia National Forest, Sequoia and Kings Canyon, page 635.
Piño Alto Trail, Los Padres National Forest, Santa Barbara and Vicinity, page 660.
McGrath State Beach Nature Trail, McGrath State Beach, Santa Barbara and Vicinity, page 673.
Ponderosa Vista Nature Trail, San Bernardino National Forest, Los Angeles and Vicinity, page 729.
Inaja Memorial Trail, Cleveland National Forest, San Diego and Vicinity, page 756.

BEST Short Backpack Trips

Taylor Lake Trailhead to Hogan Lake, Russian Wilderness, Shasta and Trinity, page 98.
Toad Lake Trail, Shasta-Trinity National Forest, Shasta and Trinity, page 105.
Echo and Twin Lakes, Lassen Volcanic National Park, Lassen and Modoc, page 156.
Woods Lake to Winnemucca Lake, Mokelumne Wilderness, Tahoe and Northern Sierra, page 270.
Coast Trail, Point Reyes National Seashore, San Francisco Bay Area, page 302.
Black Mountain, Monte Bello Open Space Preserve, San Francisco Bay Area, page 363.
May Lake and Mount Hoffman, Yosemite National Park, Yosemite and Mammoth Lakes, page 500.
Glen Aulin and Tuolumne Falls, Yosemite National Park, Yosemite and Mammoth Lakes, page 508.
Ladybug Trail, Sequoia National Park, Sequoia and Kings Canyon, page 612.
Gabrielino National Recreation Trail to Bear Canyon, Angeles National Forest, Los Angeles and Vicinity, page 690.

BEST Summit Hikes

Preston Peak, Siskiyou Wilderness, Shasta and Trinity, page 71.
Grizzly Lake, Trinity Alps Wilderness, Shasta and Trinity, page 86.
Shasta Summit Trail, Shasta-Trinity National Forest, Shasta and Trinity, page 91.
Lassen Peak Trail, Lassen Volcanic National Park, Lassen and Modoc, page 157.
East Peak Mount Tamalpais, Mount Tamalpais State Park, San Francisco Bay Area, page 320.
Mount Dana, Yosemite National Park, Yosemite and Mammoth Lakes, page 513.
White Mountain Peak Trail, Inyo National Forest, Yosemite and Mammoth Lakes, page 555.
Mount Whitney Trail, John Muir Wilderness, Sequoia and Kings Canyon, page 624.

Mount Williamson, Angeles National Forest, Los Angeles and Vicinity, page 712.

Vivian Creek Trail to Mount San Gorgonio, San Gorgonio Wilderness, Los Angeles and Vicinity, page 732.

BEST Swimming Holes

McClendon Ford Trail, Smith River National Recreation Area, Redwood Empire, page 45.

Deer Creek Trail, Lassen National Forest, Lassen and Modoc, page 165.

Paradise Creek Trail, Sequoia National Park, Sequoia and Kings Canyon, page 601.

Alder Creek Trail, Giant Sequoia National Monument, Sequoia and Kings Canyon, page 621.

BEST Waterfalls

Burney Falls Loop Trail, McArthur-Burney Falls Memorial State Park, Lassen and Modoc, page 140.

Feather Falls Loop, Plumas National Forest, Sacramento and Gold Country, page 202.

Grouse Falls, Tahoe National Forest, Tahoe and Northern Sierra, page 236.

McWay Falls Overlook, Julia Pfeiffer Burns State Park, Monterey and Big Sur, page 462.

Waterwheel Falls, Yosemite National Park, Yosemite and Mammoth Lakes, page 507.

Devils Postpile and Rainbow Falls, Devils Postpile National Monument, Yosemite and Mammoth Lakes, page 526.

Upper Yosemite Fall, Yosemite Valley, Yosemite and Mammoth Lakes, page 532.

Mist Trail and John Muir Loop to Nevada Fall, Yosemite Valley, Yosemite and Mammoth Lakes, page 535.

Bridalveil Fall, Yosemite Valley, Yosemite and Mammoth Lakes, page 539.

Tokopah Falls, Sequoia National Park, Sequoia and Kings Canyon, page 595.

BEST Wheelchair-Accessible Trails

Taylor Lake Trail, Russian Wilderness, Shasta and Trinity, page 98.

Kangaroo Lake Trailhead/Cory Peak, Klamath National Forest, Shasta and Trinity, page 102.

Lake Cleone Trail, MacKerricher State Park, Mendocino and Wine Country, page 179.

South Yuba Independence Trail, Nevada City, Sacramento and Gold Country, page 204.

Sierra Discovery Trail, PG&E Bear Valley Recreation Area, Tahoe and Northern Sierra, page 229.

Abbotts Lagoon Trail, Point Reyes National Seashore, San Francisco Bay Area, page 294.

McWay Falls Overlook, Julia Pfeiffer Burns State Park, Monterey and Big Sur, page 462.

Lower Yosemite Fall, Yosemite Valley, Yosemite and Mammoth Lakes, page 533.

Roaring River Falls, Kings Canyon National Park, Sequoia and Kings Canyon, page 583.

Salt Creek Interpretive Trail, Death Valley National Park, California Deserts, page 777.

BEST Wildflowers

Lake Margaret, Eldorado National Forest, Tahoe and Northern Sierra, page 263.

Chimney Rock Trail, Point Reyes National Seashore, San Francisco Bay Area, page 298.

Grass Valley Loop, Anthony Chabot Regional Park, San Francisco Bay Area, page 384.

Rocky Ridge and Soberanes Canyon Loop, Garrapata State Park, Monterey and Big Sur, page 450.

Path of the Padres, San Luis Reservoir State Recreation Area, San Joaquin Valley, page 477.

Lundy Canyon Trail, Hoover Wilderness, Yosemite and Mammoth Lakes, page 490.

Hite Cove Trail, Sierra National Forest, Yosemite and Mammoth Lakes, page 531.

Whitney Portal to Lake Thomas Edison (JMT/PCT), Sequoia and Kings Canyon, page 626.

Montaña de Oro Bluffs Trail, Montaña de Oro State Park, Santa Barbara and Vicinity, page 650.

Antelope Valley Poppy Reserve Loop, California Deserts, page 784.

BEST Wildlife

Coastal Trail Loop (Fern Canyon/Ossagon Section), Prairie Creek Redwoods State Park, Redwood Empire, page 51.

Spirit Lake Trail, Marble Mountain Wilderness, Shasta and Trinity, page 77.

Captain Jack's Stronghold, Lava Beds National Monument, Lassen and Modoc, page 135.

Tomales Point Trail, Point Reyes National Seashore, San Francisco Bay Area, page 293.

Pescadero Marsh, San Francisco Bay Area, page 366.

Año Nuevo Trail, Año Nuevo State Preserve, San Francisco Bay Area, page 368.

Carrizo Plain and Painted Rock, Carrizo Plains National Monument, San Joaquin Valley, page 479.

Tule Elk State Natural Reserve, San Joaquin Valley, page 480.

Caliche Forest and Point Bennett, Channel Islands National Park, page 675.

Desert Tortoise Discovery Loop, Desert Tortoise Natural Area, California Deserts, page 782.

A brief stop along the trail to examine a map can save you time and frustration.

Hiking Tips

HIKING ESSENTIALS

Aside from the shoes on your feet, it doesn't take much equipment to go day hiking. Whereas backpackers must concern themselves with tents, sleeping pads, pots and pans, and the like, day hikers don't have as much planning and packing to do. Still, too many day hikers set out carrying too little and get into trouble as a result. Here's our list of essentials:

Food and Water

Water is even more important than food, although it's always unwise to get caught without a picnic, or at least some edible supplies for emergencies. If you don't want to carry the weight of a couple water bottles, at least carry a purifier or filtering device so you can get water from streams, rivers, or lakes. It should go without saying, but never, ever drink water from a natural source without purifying it. The microscopic organisms *Giardia lamblia* and *Cryptosporidium* are found in backcountry water sources and can cause a litany of terrible gastrointestinal problems. Only purifying or boiling water from natural sources will eliminate giardiasis.

There are plenty of tools available to make backcountry water safe to drink. One of the most popular for day hikers and backpackers is a purifier called SteriPEN, which uses ultraviolet light rays instead of chemicals to purify water. It's small, light, runs on batteries, and purifies 32 ounces of water in about 90 seconds.

Water bottle-style filters, such as those made by Bota, Aquamira, Katadyn, or LifeStraw, are as light as an empty plastic bottle and eliminate the need to carry both a filter and a bottle. You simply dip the bottle in the stream, screw on the top (which has a filter inside it), and squeeze the bottle to drink. The water is filtered on its way out of the squeeze top.

There's even a straw that purifies water so you can drink right out of creeks and lakes, as long as you don't mind having to lie on your belly next to the water to do it. It costs about 20 bucks, fits in your pocket, and weighs almost nothing. If you carry the LifeStraw Personal Water Filter and an empty water bottle, you don't even have to lay on the ground. Just fill your empty bottle with water, then insert the LifeStraw and drink.

Of course, in desert regions and arid parts of the state, you won't find a natural water source to filter from, so carrying water may still be necessary. Remember that trails that cross running streams in the winter and spring months may cross dry streams in the summer and autumn months.

What you carry for food is up to you. Some people go gourmet and carry the complete inventory of a fancy grocery store. If you don't want to bother with much weight, stick with high-energy snacks like nutrition bars, nuts, dried fruit, turkey or beef jerky, and crackers. We like to carry a mix of salty and sweet foods, so we are always ready to accommodate any possible trail craving. Our rule is always to bring more than you think you can eat. You can always carry it out with you, or give it to somebody else on the trail who needs it.

If you're hiking in a group, each of you should carry your own supply of food and water just in case someone gets too far ahead or behind.

Trail Maps

A map of the park or public land you're visiting is essential. Never count on trail signs to get you where you want to go. Signs get knocked down or disappear with alarming frequency due to rain, wind, wildfire, or park visitors looking for souvenirs. Many hikers think that carrying a GPS device eliminates the need for a map, but this isn't always true. If you get lost, a map can show you where you are (via landmarks such as peaks, lakes, ridges, etc.) and can show you where the nearest trail or junction is located. It can also show alternate routes if you decide not to go the way you originally planned.

Always obtain a map from the managing agency of the place you're visiting. Their names and phone numbers are listed in the Resource guide in the back of this book. Most California parks and preserves have online maps that you can download for free.

Extra Clothing

On the trail, conditions can change at any time. Not only can the weather suddenly turn windy, foggy, or rainy, but your body's conditions also change: You'll perspire as you hike up a sunny hill and then get chilled at the top of a windy ridge or when you head downhill into shade. Because of this, cotton fabrics don't function well in the outdoors. Once cotton gets wet, it stays wet. Generally, polyester-blend fabrics dry faster. Some high-tech fabrics will actually wick moisture away from your skin. Invest in a few items of clothing made from these fabrics and you'll be more comfortable on the trail.

Always carry a lightweight jacket, preferably one that is waterproof and also wind-resistant. If your jacket isn't waterproof, pack along one of the $3, single-use rain ponchos that come in a package the size of a deck of cards. They're available at outdoors stores, hardware stores, and drugstores. If you can't part with three bucks, carry an extra-large garbage bag, which can be converted into a waterproof vest. In cooler temperatures, or when heading to a mountain summit (even on a hot day), carry gloves and a hat as well.

Flashlight

Just in case your hike takes a little longer than you planned, bring at least one flashlight and preferably two or three. Your cell phone light may work great, but if your battery runs out of juice, you're out of luck. Don't count on your cell phone as your only source of light. Mini flashlights are available everywhere, weigh almost nothing, and can save the day—or night. We especially like the tiny squeeze flashlights, about the size and shape of a quarter, which you can clip on to any key ring. Make sure you buy the kind with a long-lasting LED bulb and an on/off switch. Headlamps also make a great light source and will leave your hands free for other tasks. Whatever type of light sources you carry, make sure they work before you set out on the trail. Always take along an extra set of batteries and an extra bulb, or simply an extra light source or two.

Sunglasses and Sunscreen

You know the dangers of the sun. Wear sunglasses to protect your eyes and sunscreen with a high SPF rating on any exposed skin. Put on your sunscreen 30 minutes before you go outdoors so it has time to take effect. Reapply your sunscreen every two hours. In addition, protect the skin on your face with a good widebrimmed hat, and don't forget about your lips, which burn easily. Wear lip balm that has a high SPF rating.

Insect Repellent

Several kinds of insect repellent now come with sunscreen, so you can put on one lotion instead of two. Many types of insect repellent have an ingredient called DEET, which is extremely effective but also quite toxic. Children should not use repellent with high levels of DEET, although it seems to be safe for adults. Don't leave it sitting on your dashboard, though; if it spills, it can damage plastic, rubber, and vinyl. Other types of repellent are made of natural substances, such as lemon eucalyptus oil. What works best? Every hiker has his or her opinion. If you visit the High Sierra in the middle of a major mosquito hatch, it often seems like nothing works except covering your entire body in mosquito netting. For typical summer days outside of a hatch period, find a repellent you like and carry it with you. We're fond of a brand called Natrapel, which is DEET-free and available in various-sized spray bottles. It contains a 20 percent picaridin formula, which is recommended by the Centers for Disease Control and World Health Organization for insect bite protection.

First-Aid Kit

Nothing major is required here unless you're fully trained in first aid, but a few supplies for treating blisters, an antibiotic ointment, and an anti-inflammatory medicine (such as ibuprofen) can serve as valuable tools in minor and major emergencies. (For details on taking care of and preventing blisters, see *Shoes and Socks.*) If anyone in your party is allergic to bee stings or anything else in the outdoors, carry their medication.

Swiss Army-Style Pocket Knife

Be sure to carry one with several blades, a can opener, scissors, and tweezers. The latter is useful for removing slivers or ticks.

Compass

A compass can be a real lifesaver. Just be sure that you know how to use it.

Hiking Poles

Hikers are divided over the necessity of using hiking or trekking poles. They either swear by them or swear they will never carry them. We've had enough injuries over the years to know that a pair of ultra-lightweight hiking poles can come in handy, especially if you're trying to accomplish a long hike on rough, rocky trails. First, research shows that hiking poles definitely improve your speed and efficiency when walking, so if you're traveling a long distance, they'll get you where you want to go faster and with less fatigue. Secondly, poles are incredibly useful when you need to ford a creek or river (plant your poles in the streambed and they provide stability, so you have less chance of going for a swim) or when you're hiking steeply downhill on loose shale (plant your poles ahead of you and you won't topple forward). In terms of biomechanics, hiking poles transform you from a somewhat awkward twolegged human to an ultra-efficient four-legged mountain goat. Today's hiking poles are extremely lightweight and fold up into small sections, so if you don't want to use them for your entire hike, you can always strap them to your pack's exterior or stick them inside.

Emergency Supplies

Ask yourself this question: "What would I need

to have if I had to spend the night out here?" Aside from food, water, and other items previously listed, here are some basic emergency supplies that will get you through an unplanned night in the wilderness.

Lightweight tarp or sleeping bag. Get one made of foil-like mylar film, designed to reflect radiating body heat. These make a great emergency shelter and weigh almost nothing. The non-reflective side can even be used to signal a helicopter, should the need ever arise.

Fire-starting kit. A couple of packs of matches, a lighter, a candle, and some cotton balls soaked in Vaseline. Keep these in a waterproof container or sealable plastic bag, just in case you ever need to build a fire in a serious emergency.

Whistle. If you ever need help, you can blow a whistle for a lot longer than you can shout. Voices don't carry well in wind or near a running stream. A plastic whistle is a cheap investment that can save your life.

Small signal mirror. It could be just what you need to get found if you ever get lost. Or if you want to go the high-tech route, consider investing in a personal locator beacon (PLB). These are invaluable for people who hike enjoy hiking alone. If you wind up injured and your cell phone doesn't work, a PLB will let you signal for help.

HIKING GEAR

Shoes and Socks

Every hiker eventually conducts a search for the perfect boot. This means looking for something that will provide ideal foot and ankle support and won't cause blisters. Although there are dozens of possibilities—in fact so many that it can be confusing—you *can* find the perfect boot.

For advice on selecting boots, two of the nation's preeminent long-distance hikers, Brian Robinson of Mountain View (7,200 miles in 2001) and Ray Jardine of Oregon (2,700 miles of Pacific Crest Trail in three months), weighed in on the discussion. Both believe that the weight of a boot is the defining factor when selecting hiking footwear. They both go as light as possible, believing that heavy boots will eventually tire you out. Arch support is also vital, especially to people who hike less frequently and thus have not developed great foot strength.

To stay blister-free, the most important factors are clean feet, good socks, and the flexibility of a boot. If there is any foot slippage from a too-thin or compressed sock, accumulated dirt, or a stiff boot, you can rub up a blister in minutes. Wearing two pairs of socks can sometimes do the trick—try two fresh sets of SmartWool socks ($15 a pop), or try one pair over the top of a lightweight wicking liner sock. If you still get a blister or two, know how to treat them fast so they don't turn your walk into a sore-footed endurance test.

Selecting the Right Boots

In addition to finding boots with the proper flexibility, comfort, and arch support, you'll need to consider the types of terrain you'll be covering and the number of miles (or number of days) you'll be hiking. Investing in the correct shoes will take some time and research, but your feet will thank you for it.

There are three basic kinds of hiking footwear, ranging from lightweight to midweight to heavyweight. Select the right one for you or pay the consequences. One great trick when on a hiking vacation is to bring a couple different pairs, and then for each hike, wear different footwear. By changing boots, you change the points of stress on your feet and legs, greatly reducing soreness and the chance of creating a hot spot on a foot. This also allows you to go lightweight on flat trails with a hard surface, and heavyweight on steep trails with loose footing, where additional boot weight can help traction in downhill stretches.

Lightweight Hiking Boots

In the first category, lightweight hiking boots or trail-running shoes are designed for day-hiking and short and easy backpacking trips. For those with strong feet and arches, they are popular even on multiday trips. Some of the newer models are like rugged athletic shoes, designed with a Gore-Tex top for lightness and a Vibram sole for traction. These are perfect for people who like to hike fast and cover a lot of ground. Because these boots are flexible, they're easy to break in, and with fresh socks they rarely cause blister problems. Because they are lightweight and usually made of a breathable fabric, hiking fatigue is greatly reduced. For day-hiking, they are the footwear of choice for most. Many long-distance hikers also choose these.

On the negative side, because these boots are so light, traction is not always good on steep, slippery surfaces. In addition, lightweight boots provide less than ideal ankle and arch support, which can be a problem on rocky or steep trails. Turn your ankle and your trip can be ruined. Lightweight hiking boots often are not very durable, either. If you hike a lot, you may wear a pair out in one summer.

Midweight Hiking Boots or Backpacking Boots

These boots are designed for both on- and off-trail hiking, and are constructed to meet the demands of carrying a light to moderately heavy pack. They usually feature high ankle support, a deep Vibram lug sole, built-in orthotics, arch support, and often a waterproof exterior. They can stand up to hundreds of miles of wilderness use, even if they are banged against rocks and walked through streams.

On the negative side, midweight or backpacking boots can be quite hot. If the boots get wet, they can take days to dry. They weigh a fair amount and can tire you out, especially if you are not accustomed to having weight on your feet. This may reduce the number of miles you are capable of hiking in a day.

Mountaineering Boots or Heavyweight Backpacking Boots

Like midweight boots, these shoes are designed for both on- and off-trail hiking, but they can stand up to the rigors of carrying a much heavier load. They are designed to be worn on multiday backpacking trips (four days or more with substantial miles hiked each day). Mountaineering boots are identified by

Lightweight hiking shoes are perfect for short treks and day-long trips.

ADDING TO THE PACK

If you're setting out on a long-distance adventure, it pays to add these two lightweight items to your backpack: an Ace elastic bandage and a pair of gaiters.

For sprained ankles and twisted knees, an Ace bandage can be like an insurance policy to get you back on the trail and out of trouble. Many hikers with a twisted ankle or a sprained knee have relied on a good wrap with a four-inch bandage to get them home. Always buy the Ace bandage that comes with the clips permanently attached, so you don't have to worry about losing them.

Gaiters are leggings made of water-repellent fabric (Gore-Tex is a popular brand) that fit from just below your knees, over your calves, and attach under your boots. They are of particular help when walking in damp areas or in places where rain is common. As your legs brush against ferns or low-lying plants, gaiters will deflect the moisture. Without them, your pants will be soaking wet in short order.

Should your boots become wet, never try to force them to dry. Some well-meaning folks will try to dry them quickly at the edge of a campfire or actually put the boots in an oven. Although this may dry the boots, it can also loosen the glue that holds them together, ultimately weakening them until one day they fall apart in a heap. A better bet is to treat the exterior so the boots become water repellent. Silicone-based liquids are the easiest to use and the least greasy of the treatments available.

A final tip is to have another pair of lightweight shoes or moccasins that you can wear around after a trip. This will give your feet the rest they deserve.

midrange tops, laces that extend almost as far as the toes, and ankle areas that are as stiff as a board. The lack of "give" is what endears them to some mountaineers. Their stiffness is preferred when rock climbing, walking off-trail on craggy surfaces, or hiking down the edge of streambeds. Because these boots don't yield on rugged terrain, they can reduce ankle and foot injuries and provide better traction. Some are made so that they can accept crampons for travel on snow and ice.

The drawback to stiff boots is that if you don't have the proper socks and your foot starts slipping around in the boot, you will get a set of blisters that require so much tape and moleskin you will end up looking like a mummy. Also, heavyweight boots must be broken in for weeks or even months before taking them out on the trail.

At the Store

Hiking shoes come in a wide range of styles, brands, and prices. If you wander about comparing all their many features, you will get as confused as a kid in a toy store. Instead, go into the store with your mind clear about what you want. For the best quality, expect to spend $80-120 for lightweight hiking boots, $100-200 for midweight boots, and $150-250 for mountaineering boots. If you go much cheaper, the quality of the boot—and the health of your feet—will likely suffer. This is one area where you don't want to scrimp.

If you plan on using the advice of a shoe salesperson, first look at what kind of boots he or she is wearing. If the salesperson isn't even wearing boots, then take whatever he or she says with a grain of salt. Most people who own quality boots, including salespeople, will wear them almost daily if their job allows, since boots are the best footwear available.

Enter the store with a precise use and style in mind. Rather than fish for suggestions, tell the salesperson exactly what type of hiking you plan to do. Try two or three brands of the same category of shoe (lightweight, midweight, or heavyweight/mountaineering). Try on both boots in a pair simultaneously so you know exactly how they'll feel. Always try them on over a good pair of hiking socks (see *Socks*), not regular everyday socks. If possible, walk up and down a set of stairs, or up and down an incline, while wearing the boots. Your feet should not slide forward easily, and your heel should not move from side to side. Also, your heel should not lift more than one-quarter inch when you walk around. Are the boots too stiff? Are your feet snug yet comfortable, or do they slip? Do they feel supportive on the inside of your foot? Is there enough room in the toe box so that your toes can spread or wiggle slightly? If your toes touch the front of your boot, count on blisters.

Socks

People can spend so much energy selecting the right kind of boot that they virtually overlook wearing the right kind of socks. One goes with the other.

Your socks should be thick enough to cushion your feet and should fit snugly. Without good socks you might fasten the bootlaces too tight, and that's like putting a tourniquet on your feet. On long trips of a week or more, you should have plenty of clean socks on hand, or plan on washing what you have during your trip. As socks become worn, they also become compressed, dirty, and damp. If they fold over, you'll get a blister.

Do not wear cotton socks. Your foot can get damp and mix with dirt, which can cause a hot spot to start on your foot. Instead, start with a sock made of a synthetic composite, such as those made by SmartWool. These will partially wick moisture away from the skin.

If you choose to wear two pairs, or a pair of socks over a sock liner, the exterior sock should be wool or its synthetic equivalent. This will cushion your feet, create a snug fit in your boot, and provide some additional warmth and insulation in cold weather. It is critical to keep socks clean. If you wear multiple socks, you may need to go up a boot size to accommodate the extra layers around your feet.

Blisters

In almost all cases, blisters are caused by the simple rubbing of skin against the rugged interior of a boot. It can be worsened by several factors:

The key to treating blisters is to work fast at the first sign of a hot spot. If you feel a hot spot, never keep walking, figuring the problem will go away. Stop immediately and remedy the situation. Before you remove your socks, check to see if the sock is wrinkled—a likely cause of the problem. If so, either change socks or pull them tight, removing the tiny folds, after taking care of the blister.

To take care of the blister, cut a piece of moleskin to cover the offending spot, securing the moleskin with white medical tape. Even better than moleskin is a product called Spenco Second Skin, which helps to heal the blister as well as protect it, and will stick to your skin without tape.

SAFETY IN THE OUTDOORS

Insects and Plants

Ticks, poison oak, and stinging nettles can be far worse than a whole convention of snakes, mountain lions, and bears. But you can avoid them with a little common sense, and here's how:

Ticks

The easiest way to stay clear of ticks is to wear long pants and long sleeves when you hike, and tuck your pant legs into your socks. But this system isn't fail-proof. The darn things sometimes find their way on to your skin no matter what you do. Always check yourself thoroughly when you leave the trail, looking carefully for anything that's crawling on you. Check your clothes, and also your skin underneath. A good friend can be a useful assistant in this endeavor.

Remember that if you find a tick on your skin, the larger brown ones are harmless. Of the nearly 50 varieties of ticks present in California, only the tiny brown-black ones, called the western black-legged tick, can carry Lyme disease.

Most tick bites cause a sharp sting that will get your attention. But rarely, ticks will bite you without you noticing. If you've been in the outdoors, and then a few days or a week later start to experience flu-like symptoms like headaches, fever, muscle soreness, neck stiffness, or nausea, see a doctor immediately. Tell the doctor you are concerned about possible exposure to ticks and Lyme disease. Another early tell-tale symptom is a slowly expanding red rash near the tick bite, which appears a week to a month after the bite. Caught in its early stages, Lyme disease is easily treated with antibiotics, but left untreated, it can be severely debilitating.

The best way to remove a tick is by grasping it as close to your skin as possible, then pulling it gently and slowly straight out, without twisting or jerking it. Tweezers work well for the job, and many Swiss Army knives include tweezers.

Poison Oak

That old Boy Scout motto holds true: Leaves of three, let them be. Learn to recognize and avoid *Toxicodendron diversilobum,* which produces an itching rash that can last for weeks. The shiny-leaved shrub grows with maddening exuberance in California coastal and mountain canyons below 5,000 feet. If you can't readily identify poison oak, stay away from vinelike plants that have three leaves. Remember that in spring and summer, poison oak looks a little like wild blackberry bushes and often has red colors in its leaves, as well as green. In late fall and winter, poison oak goes dormant and loses its leaves, but it's still potent.

Avoid poison oak by staying on the trail and wearing long pants and long sleeves in areas that are encroached by it. If you prefer to wear shorts when you hike, try a pair of the convertible pants that are found at most outdoor stores. These are lightweight pants with legs that zip off to convert to shorts. Put the pant legs on when you come to an area that is rife with poison oak. If you accidentally touch the plant with your bare skin, wash off the area as soon as possible. Waiting until you get home five hours later may be too late, so wash as

poison oak

best as you can, using stream water or whatever is available. Hikers who are highly allergic to poison oak should consider carrying packages of Tecnu, a poison oak wash-off treatment that is sold in bottles or individual foil packs. Carrying one little package could save you weeks of scratching.

Remember that if poison oak touches your clothes, your pack, or even your dog, and then you handle any of those items, the oils can rub off onto your skin. Wash everything thoroughly as soon as you get home.

If you do develop poison oak rash, a few relatively new products on the market can help you get rid of it. One product is called Zanfel, and although it costs a small fortune ($20-40 a bottle), it is available at pharmacies without a prescription. You simply pour it on the rash and the rash vanishes, or at least greatly diminishes. Some hikers also swear by a product called Mean Green Power Hand Scrub, which costs about half what Zanfel does. No matter what you use, if you get a severe enough case of poison oak, the only recourse is a trip to the doctor for prednisone pills.

Stinging Nettles

Ouch! This member of the nettle family is bright green, can grow to six feet tall, and is covered with tiny stinging hairs. When you brush against one, it zaps you with its poison, which feels like a mild bee sting. The sting can last for up to 24 hours. Stinging nettles grow near creeks or streams, and they're usually found in tandem with deer ferns and sword ferns. If the nettles zing you, grab a nearby fern leaf and rub the underside of it against the stinging area. It sounds odd, but it sometimes helps to take the sting out. If it doesn't help, you're out of luck, and you just have to wait for the sting to go away.

Wildlife

Snakes, mountain lions, and bears—these creatures deserve your respect, and you should understand a little bit about them.

Rattlesnakes

Eight rattlesnake species are found in California. These members of the pit viper family have wide triangular heads, narrow necks, and rattles on their tales. Rattlesnakes live where it's warm, usually at elevations below 6,000 feet. Most snakes will slither off at the sound of your footsteps; if you encounter one, freeze or move back slowly so that it can get away without feeling threatened. They will almost always shake their tails and produce a rattling or buzzing noise to warn you off. The sound is unmistakable, even if you've never heard it before.

If you're hiking on a nice day, when rattlesnakes are often out sunning themselves on trails and rocks, keep your eyes open for them so you don't step on one or place your hand on one. Be especially on the lookout for rattlesnakes in the spring, when they leave their winter burrows and come out in the sun. Morning is the most common time to see them, as the midday sun is usually too hot for them.

Although rattlesnake bites are painful, they are very rarely fatal. More than 100 people in California are bitten by rattlesnakes each year, resulting in only one or two fatalities on average. About 25 percent of rattlesnake bites are dry, with no venom injected. Symptoms of bites that do contain venom usually include tingling around the mouth, nausea and vomiting, dizziness, weakness, sweating, and/or chills. If you should get bitten by a rattlesnake, your car key—and the nearest telephone—are your best first aid. Call 911 as soon as you can, or have someone drive you to the nearest hospital. Don't panic or run, which can speed the circulation of venom through your system.

Except for a handful of rattlesnake species, all other California snakes are not poisonous. Just give them room to slither by.

Mountain Lions

The mountain lion (also called cougar or puma) lives in almost every region of California but is rarely seen. Most habitats that are wild enough

FACTS ABOUT MOUNTAIN LIONS

Mountain lion expert Steve Torres of the California Department of Fish and Wildlife provided the following list of truths regarding mountain lions:

- Mountain lions are very shy and wary of humans. Attacks on people are extremely rare, which is why any threatening encounter can make the news–it is an anomaly.
- Mountain lions are rarely seen; they are masters of stealth. That is why repeat sightings are alarming and should be reported to the CDFW headquarters in Sacramento (916/445-0411).
- Mountain lions are known for their silence and are rarely vocal. If you hear the cry or roar of a lion, your experience is likely a once-in-a-lifetime event.
- Mountain lions are not threatened or endangered in any way. Populations are stable to increasing. The biggest threat to mountain lions is loss of habitat to development.
- Mountain lions are not afraid of dogs. Whereas packs of trained hounds are capable of putting a lion in a tree, solitary pets of all kinds, including dogs, are fair game for mountain lions. In areas with documented mountain lion habitat, dogs should be kept inside at night.

to support deer will support mountain lions, which typically eat about one deer per week. When the magnificent cats do show themselves, they receive a lot of media attention. The few mountain lion attacks on California hikers have been widely publicized. Still, the vast majority of hikers never see a mountain lion, and those who do usually report that the cat vanished into the brush at the first sign of nearby humans.

If you're hiking in an area where mountain lions or their tracks have been spotted, remember to keep children close to you on the trail, and your dog leashed. If you see a mountain lion and it doesn't run away immediately, make yourself appear as large as possible (raise your arms, open your jacket, wave a big stick) and speak loudly and firmly or shout. If you have children with you, pick them up off the ground, but try to do it without crouching down or leaning over. (Crouching makes you appear smaller and less aggressive, more like prey.) Don't turn your back on the cat or run from it, but rather back away slowly and deliberately, always retaining your aggressive pose and continuing to speak loudly. Mountain lions are far more likely to attack a fleeing mammal than one that stands its ground. Even after attacking, lions have been successfully fought off by adult hikers and even children who used rocks and sticks to defend themselves.

Bears

The only bears found in California are black bears (even though they are usually brown in color). A century ago, our state bear, the grizzly, roamed here as well, but the last one was shot and killed in the 1930s. Black bears almost never harm human beings—although you should never approach or feed a bear, or get between a bear and its cubs or its food. Black bears weigh between 250 and 400 pounds, can run up to 30 miles per hour, and are powerful swimmers and climbers. When they bound, the muscles on their shoulders roll like ocean breakers. If provoked, a bear could cause serious injury.

There's only one important fact to remember about bears: They love snacks. The average black bear has to eat as much as 30,000 calories a day, and since their natural diet is made up of berries, fruits, plants, fish, insects, and the like, the high-calorie food of human beings is very appealing to them. Unfortunately, too many California campers have trained our state's bears to crave the taste of corn chips, hot dogs, and soda pop.

Any time you see a bear, it's almost a given

that it is looking for food, preferably something sweet. Bears have become specialists in the food-raiding business. As a result, you must be absolutely certain that you keep your food away from them. Backpackers should always use bear-proof canisters to store their food for overnight trips. Hanging food from a tree is largely ineffective when done improperly, and the practice is now banned in most of the Sierra Nevada, where bear-proof food canisters are required by law. You can rent or buy a bear canister from most outdoor stores, or from many ranger stations in national parks and national forests. In national parks like Yosemite, Sequoia, and Kings Canyon, you can rent a bear canister for $5, then return it at the end of your trip.

At car campgrounds in bear territory, metal bear-proof food storage lockers must be used. Never leave your food unattended or in your vehicle. Rangers will ticket you for these violations. In addition, get an update from the rangers in your park about suitable bear precautions.

Bears are sometimes encountered on trails, although not as frequently as in campgrounds. If you're hiking, bears will most likely hear you coming and avoid you. If one approaches you, either on the trail or in camp, yell loudly, throw small rocks or pine cones in the vicinity, and try to frighten the bear away. A bear that is afraid of humans is a bear that will stay wild and stay alive.

If you are backpacking in an area where bear canisters are not required, or where bears aren't as bold as they are in the Sierra Nevada, you can substitute a food hang for a bear canister. This is where you place your food in a plastic or canvas garbage bag (always double-bag your food), then suspend it from a rope in midair, 10 feet from the trunk of a tree and 20 feet off the ground. Counterbalancing two bags with a rope thrown over a tree limb is very effective, but finding an appropriate limb can be difficult.

This is most easily accomplished by tying a rock to a rope, then throwing it over a high but sturdy tree limb. Next, tie your food bag to the rope and hoist it in the air. When you are satisfied with the position of the food bag, tie off the end of the rope to another tree.

Once a bear gets her mitts on your food, she considers it hers. There is nothing you can do. If this happens to you once, you will learn never to let food sit unattended.

First Aid

Hypothermia

A leading cause of death in the outdoors is hypothermia, which occurs when your body's core temperature drops low enough that your vital organs can no longer function. Most cases of hypothermia occur at temperatures in the 50s, not below freezing, as you might expect. Often the victim has gotten wet, and/or is fatigued from physical exertion.

Initial symptoms of hypothermia include uncontrollable shivering, often followed by a complete stop in shivering, extreme lethargy, and an inability to reason. A hypothermic person will often want to lie down and rest or sleep. His or her hiking partners must jump into action to get the victim warm and dry immediately. Remove all wet clothes and put on dry ones. Cover his or her head with a warm hat. If someone in the group has an emergency space blanket (see *Hiking Gear Checklist*), wrap it around the victim. Get the hypothermic person to eat some quick-energy food, even candy, and drink warm beverages—this helps the body produce heat. Do not give the person alcohol, as this encourages heat loss.

Heat Stroke

Usually the result of overexposure to the sun and dehydration, symptoms of heat stroke include headache, mental confusion, and cramps throughout the body. Immediate action must be taken to reduce the body's core temperature. Pour water on the victim's head. Have him or her sit in a cool stream if possible. Make the person drink as much liquid as possible. Heat stroke is easily avoided by staying adequately hydrated and wearing a large-brimmed hat for protection from the sun.

Altitude Sickness and Adjustment

Many hikers experience a shortness of breath when hiking only a few thousand feet higher than the elevation where they live. If you live on the California coast, you may notice slightly labored breathing while hiking at an elevation as low as 5,000 feet. As you go higher, it gets worse, sometimes leading to headaches and nausea. It takes a full 72 hours to acclimate to major elevation changes, although most people acclimatize after only 24 to 48 hours. The best preparation for hiking at a high elevation is to sleep at that elevation, or as close to it as possible, the night before. If you are planning a strenuous hike at 7,000 feet or above, spend a day or two before doing easier hikes at the same elevation. Also, get plenty of rest and drink plenty of fluids (but avoid all alcohol). Lack of sleep and dehydration can contribute to your susceptibility to "feeling the altitude."

Serious altitude sickness typically occurs above 10,000 feet. It is generally preventable by simply allowing enough time for acclimation. But how do you acclimate for a climb to the top of Mount Whitney or Shasta, at more than 14,000 feet? The answer is you can't, at least not completely. Spending a few days beforehand hiking at 10,000 feet and above will help tremendously. Staying fueled with food and fully hydrated will also help. But if you've never hiked above a certain elevation—say 13,000 feet—you don't know how you are going to feel until you get there. If you start to feel ill (nausea, vomiting, severe headache), you are experiencing altitude sickness. Some people can get by with taking aspirin and trudging onward, but if you are seriously ill, the only cure is to descend as soon as possible. If the altitude has gotten to you badly enough, you may need someone to help you walk. Fatigue and elevation sickness can cloud your judgment in the same manner that hypothermia does, so take action before your symptoms become too severe.

Rock cairns act as directional aids on the trail.

Safety on the Trail

Navigational Tools

For some hikers, it is quite easy to become lost. If you don't get your bearings, getting found is the difficult part. If you're hiking with a family or group, make sure everybody stays together. If anyone decides to split off from the group for any reason, make sure they have a trail map with them and that they know how to read it. Also, ensure that everyone in your group knows the rules regarding what to do if they get lost:

In areas above tree line or where the trail becomes faint, some hikers will mark the route with piles of small rocks to act as directional signs for the return trip. But if an unexpected snow buries these piles of rocks, or if you get well off the track, all you are left with is a moonscape. That is why every hiker should understand the concept of orienteering. In the process, you become a mountaineer.

When lost, the first step is to secure your present situation—that is, to make sure it does not get any worse. Take stock of your food, foul-weather gear, camp fuel, clothes, and your readiness to spend the night. Keep in mind that this is an adventure, not a crisis.

Then take out your topographic map, compass, and altimeter. What? Right: Never go into the unknown without them. Place the map on the ground, then set the compass atop the map and orient it north. In most cases, you will easily be able to spot landmarks, such as prominent mountaintops. In cases with a low overcast, where mountains are obscured in clouds, you can take this adventure one step further by checking your altimeter. By scanning the elevation lines on the map, you will be able to trace your near-exact position.

Always be prepared to rely on yourself, but also file a trip plan with the local ranger station, especially if hiking in remote wilderness areas. Carry plenty of food, fuel, and a camp stove. Make sure your clothes, weather gear, sleeping bag, and tent will keep you dry and warm. Always carry a compass, altimeter, and map with elevation lines, and know how to use them, practicing in good weather to get the feel of it.

With enough experience, you will discover that you can "read" the land so well that you will hardly even need to reference a map to find your way.

Lightning

If you see or hear a thunderstorm approaching, avoid exposed ridges and peaks. This is disheartening advice when you're only a mile from the summit of Half Dome, but follow it anyway. If you're already on a mountain top, stay out of enclosed places, such as rock caves or recesses. Confined areas are deadly in lightning storms; hikers seeking refuge from lightning have been killed inside the stone hut on top of Mount Whitney. Do not lean against rock slopes or trees; try to keep a few feet of air space around you. Squat low on your boot soles, or sit on your day pack, jacket, or anything that will insulate you in case lightning strikes the ground.

HIKING ETHICS

Hiking is a great way to get out of the concrete jungle and into the woods and the wild, to places of natural beauty. Unfortunately, this manner of thinking is shared by millions of people. Following some basic rules will ensure that we all get along and keep the outdoors a place we can enjoy... together.

Wilderness Ethics

Take good care of this beautiful land you're hiking on. The basics are simple: Leave no trace of your visit. Pack out all your trash. Do your best not to disturb animal or plant life. Don't collect specimens of plants, wildlife, or even pine cones. Never, ever carve anything into the trunks of trees. If you're following a trail, don't cut the switchbacks. Leave everything in nature exactly as you found it, because each tiny piece has its place in the great scheme of things.

You can go the extra mile, too. Pick up any litter that you see on the trail. Teach your children to do this as well. Carry an extra bag to hold picked-up litter until you get to a trash receptacle, or just keep an empty pocket for that purpose in your day pack or fanny sack.

If you have the extra time or energy, join a trail organization in your area or spend some time volunteering in your local park. Anything you do to help this beautiful planet will be repaid to you, many times over.

Tips for Getting Along

When hiking with others, and especially over several days, it pays to do a little planning and a lot of communicating. Here are some tips to having a successful trip:

The destination and activities must be agreed upon. A meeting of the minds gives everybody an equal stake in the trip.

If backpacking, guarantee yourself refreshing sleep. Make certain that your sleeping bag, pillow, pad, and tent are clean, dry, warm, and comfortable.

Develop technical expertise. Test all gear at home before putting it to use on the trail.

Guarantee yourself action. Pick a destination with your favorite activity: adventuring, wildlife watching, swimming, fishing...

Guarantee yourself quiet time. Savor the views and the sound of a stream running free, and reserve time with people you care for, and your soul will be recharged.

Accordance on food. Always have complete agreement on the selections for each meal, and check for allergies.

Agree on a wake-up time. Then when morning comes, you will be on course from the start.

Equal chances at the fun stuff. Many duties can be shared over the course of a trip, such as navigating and preparing meals.

Be aware, not self-absorbed. Live so there can be magic in every moment, with an awareness of the senses: sight, sound, smell, touch, taste, and how you feel inside. Have an outlook that alone can promote great satisfaction.

No whining. You can't always control your surroundings, only your state of mind.

Hiking with Dogs

Dogs are wonderful friends and great companions. But dogs and nature do not mix well. Bless their furry little hearts, most dogs can't help but disturb wildlife, given half a chance. Even if they don't chase or bark at wildlife, dogs leave droppings that may intimidate other mammals into changing their normal routine. But kept on a leash, a dog can be the best hiking companion you could ask for.

Dogs are allowed on some trails in California and not on others. For many dog owners, it's confusing. When using this book, check the *User Groups* listing under each trail listing to see whether dogs are permitted. Always call the park or public land in advance if you are traveling some distance with your dog. Here are general guidelines to park rules about dogs:

If you are visiting a national or state park, 99 percent of the time, your dog will not be allowed to hike with you. There are only a few exceptions to this rule within the national and state park systems. Dogs are usually allowed in campgrounds or picnic areas, but they are not allowed on trails in these parks. If you are planning to visit a national or state park, consider leaving your dog at home.

At other types of parks (county parks, regional parks, and so on), dogs may or may not be allowed on trails. Always follow and obey a park's specific rules about dogs. Oftentimes, if dogs are allowed, they must be on a six-foot or shorter leash. Don't try to get away with carrying the leash in your hand while your dog runs free; rangers may give you a ticket.

In national forest or wilderness lands, dogs are usually permitted off leash, except in special wildlife management areas or other special-use areas. Understand that your dog should still be under voice control—for his or her safety more than anything. The outdoors presents many hazards for dogs, including mountain lions, porcupines, black bears, ticks, rattlesnakes, and a host of other potential problems. Dogs are frequently lost in national forest areas. Keeping your dog close to your side or on a leash in the national forests will help you both have a worry-free trip and a great time.

Check to make sure your dog is allowed on a trail.

TRAIL ETIQUETTE

- **Enjoy the silence and let nature's sounds prevail.** Keep your voice low and avoid making loud noises. You will increase your chances of encountering wildlife, plus help others enjoy their quiet time in the outdoors.
- **Be aware of other trail users and yield appropriately.** If you hear someone coming up behind you who is clearly traveling faster than you, stand aside and let them pass. On narrow trails, hikers going downhill should always yield to hikers going uphill. Get out of the way so uphill hikers can keep their momentum as they climb. Also, large groups of hikers should always yield to smaller groups or solo travelers.
- **Be friendly and polite to other trail users.** A smile or a "hello" as you pass others on the trail is always a good idea. And it may seem obvious, but if someone steps aside to allow you to pass, say "thank you."
- **Obey all posted signs and trail closures.** Only hike where it's legal. Do not invent "shortcuts" or hike across private property without the express permission of the owner.
- **Hike only on established trails.** As soon as you walk off a trail, you trample vegetation. Never cut switchbacks; hillside trails are built with switchbacks to keep the slope from eroding. Just a few people cutting the switchbacks can destroy a hillside.
- **Yield to equestrians.** Horses can be badly spooked by just about anything. Always give them plenty of room. If horses are approaching you, stop alongside the trail until they pass. If horses are traveling in your direction and you need to pass them, call out politely to the rider and ask permission. If the horse and rider moves off the trail and the rider tells you it's okay, then pass.

AVOIDING THE CROWDS

Although many regions of California exist where you can hike without seeing another soul, even on holiday weekends, some of our better-known parks and public lands are notorious for crowds. No matter where in California you want to hike, there's no reason to subject yourself to packed parking lots, long lines of people snaking up and down switchbacks, and trail destinations that look like Times Square on New Year's Eve. If you take a few simple steps, you can avoid the crowds almost anywhere, even in well-traveled parks near urban areas and in our famous national parks.

Hike in the off-season. For most public lands, the off-season is any time other than summer, or any time when school is in session. Late September through mid-May is an excellent period of time for hiking trips (except during the week between Christmas and New Year's and Easter week). Try to avoid periods near holidays; many people try to beat the crowds by traveling right before or after a holiday, and the result is more crowds.

Time your trip for midweek. Tuesday, Wednesday, and Thursday are always the quietest days of the week in any park or public land.

Get up early. Even Yosemite Valley is serene and peaceful until 8 or 9am. In most parks, if you arrive at the trailhead before 9am, you'll have the first few hours on the trail all to yourself. As an insurance policy, get to the trailhead even earlier.

If you can't get up early, stay out late. When the days are long in summer, you can hike shorter trails from 4pm to 7:30pm or even later. You may see other hikers in the first hour or so, but they'll soon disperse. Trailhead parking lots are often packed at 1pm, then nearly empty at 5pm. Note that if you hike in the late afternoon or evening, you should always carry a flashlight with you (at least one per person), just in case it gets dark sooner than you planned.

Get out and hike in foul weather. Don your favorite impermeable layer, and go where fair-weather hikers dare not go. Some of the best memories are made on rainy days, cloudy days, foggy days, and days when the wind blows at gale force. The fact is, the vast majority of hikers only hike when the sun is out. Witness nature in all its varied moods, and you may be surprised at how much fun you have.

HIKING GEAR CHECKLIST

BACKPACK

- Cell phone
- Compass or navigational device
- Extra clothing (lightweight jacket, rain poncho, gloves, hat)
- First-aid kit
- Flashlight or head lamp
- Food (energy bars, nuts, dried fruit, jerky)
- Insect repellent
- Pocket knife
- Sunglasses
- Sunscreen
- Trail map
- Watch
- Water or water filter

EMERGENCY SUPPLIES

- Extra shoelaces
- Matches in a waterproof container
- Mylar blanket
- Signal mirror
- Whistle

LONG DISTANCE TRAILS

- Ace bandage
- Bandana
- Bear canister
- Extra pair of socks
- Eyeglass cleaner or saline solution (for contacts)
- Gaiters
- Lightweight shoes or moccasins
- Toilet paper and zippered plastic bags
- Trekking poles

FUN STUFF

- Binoculars
- Book, including wildflower or bird identification guides
- Camera (with extra battery and memory card)
- Deck of cards
- Fishing license and equipment
- Picnic gear

REDWOOD EMPIRE

Visitors come to the Redwood Empire for one reason: to see groves of giant redwoods, the tallest trees in the world. But the redwoods are only one of the attractions in this area. The Smith River Canyon, Del Norte and Humboldt coasts, and the remote edge of the Siskiyou Wilderness in Six Rivers National Forest all make this region like none other in the world. Three stellar areas should be on your must-see list for outstanding days of adventure: the redwood parks from Trinidad to Klamath River, the Smith River Recreation Area, and the Lost Coast. Redwood campgrounds are in high demand, and reservations are necessary in the peak vacation season. On the opposite end of the spectrum are primitive and remote settings in Six Rivers National Forest, the Lost Coast, and even a few surprise nuggets in Redwood National Park.

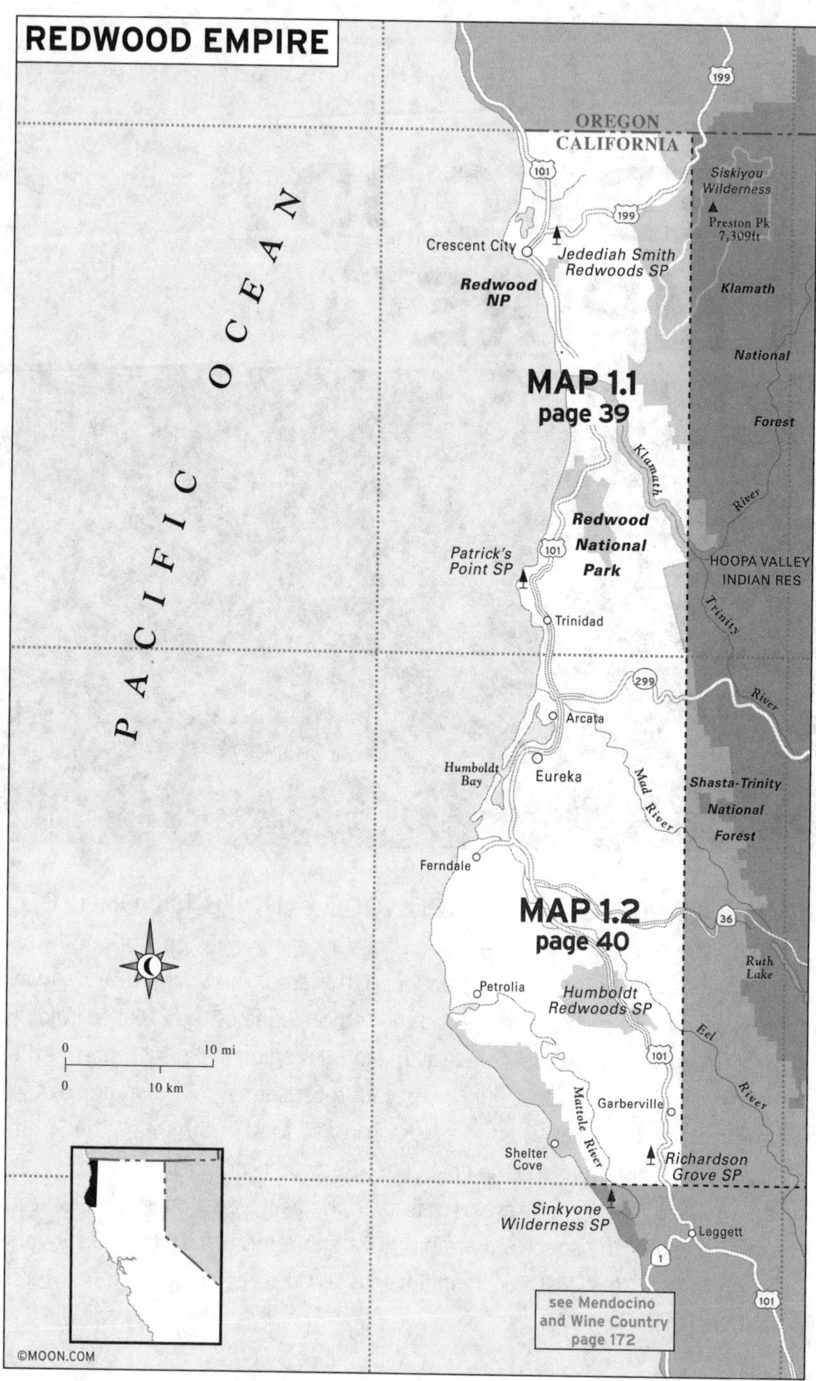
REDWOOD EMPIRE
PACIFIC OCEAN
OREGON
CALIFORNIA
199
101
Siskiyou Wilderness
Preston Pk 7,309ft
Crescent City
Jedediah Smith Redwoods SP
Redwood NP
Klamath
National
Forest
MAP 1.1
page 39
Klamath
River
Redwood National Park
Patrick's Point SP
HOOPA VALLEY INDIAN RES
Trinity
Trinidad
299
River
Arcata
Humboldt Bay
Eureka
Mad River
Shasta-Trinity National Forest
Ferndale
MAP 1.2
page 40
36
Ruth Lake
Petrolia
Humboldt Redwoods SP
Eel River
0
10 mi
0
10 km
Garberville
Mattole River
Shelter Cove
Richardson Grove SP
Sinkyone Wilderness SP
Leggett
1
see Mendocino and Wine Country page 172
©MOON.COM

Map 1.1

Sites 1-22
Pages 41-55

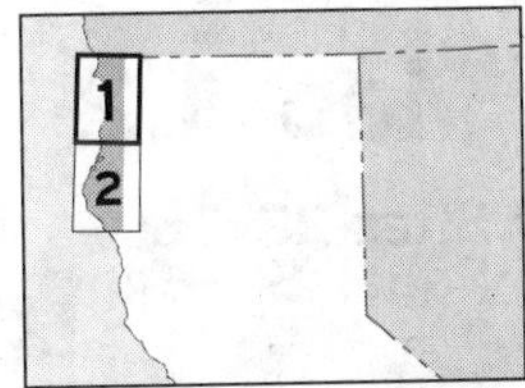

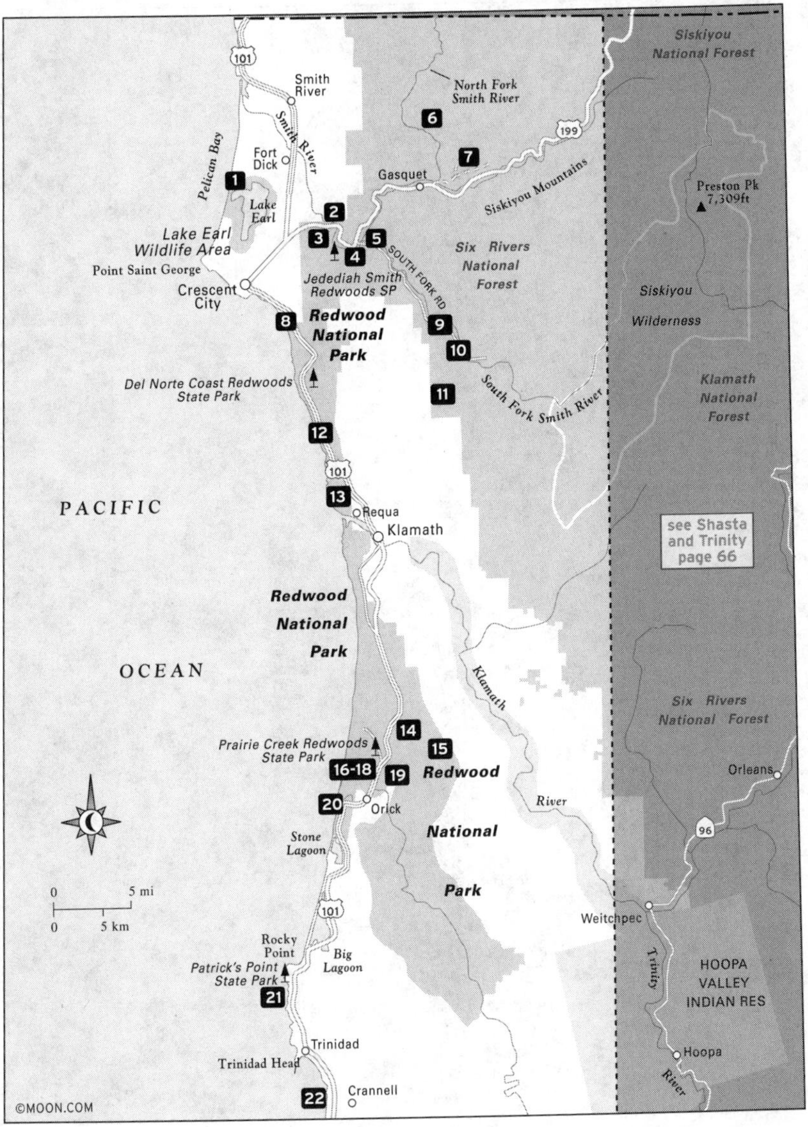

101
Smith River
North Fork Smith River
Siskiyou National Forest
6
Pelican Bay
Fort Dick
Smith River
199
7
1
Gasquet
Preston Pk 7,309ft
Lake Earl
Siskiyou Mountains
2
Lake Earl Wildlife Area
3
5
4
South Fork Rd
Six Rivers National Forest
Point Saint George
Jedediah Smith Redwoods SP
Siskiyou
Crescent City
Siskiyou Wilderness
8
Redwood National Park
9
10
Del Norte Coast Redwoods State Park
Klamath National Forest
11
South Fork Smith River
12
101
PACIFIC
13
Requa
see Shasta and Trinity page 66
Klamath
Redwood National Park
OCEAN
Klamath
Six Rivers National Forest
14
Prairie Creek Redwoods State Park
15
16-18
19
Redwood
Orleans
20
Orick
River
National
Stone Lagoon
96
Park
0 5 mi
0 5 km
101
Weitchpec
Rocky Point
Big Lagoon
Patrick's Point State Park
Trinity
HOOPA VALLEY INDIAN RES
21
Trinidad
Hoopa
Trinidad Head
River
22
Crannell

Map 1.2

Sites 23-36
Pages 55-64

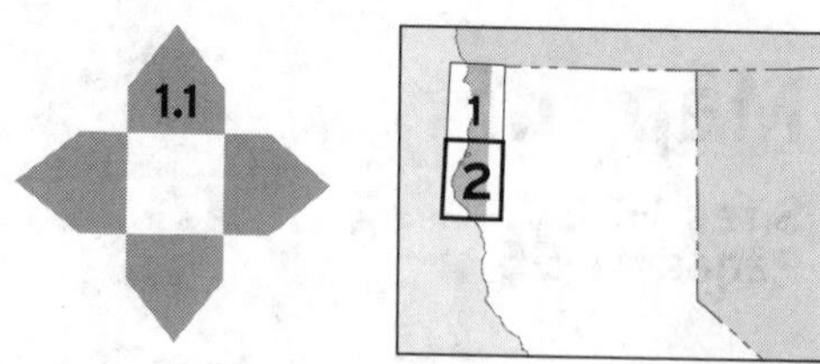

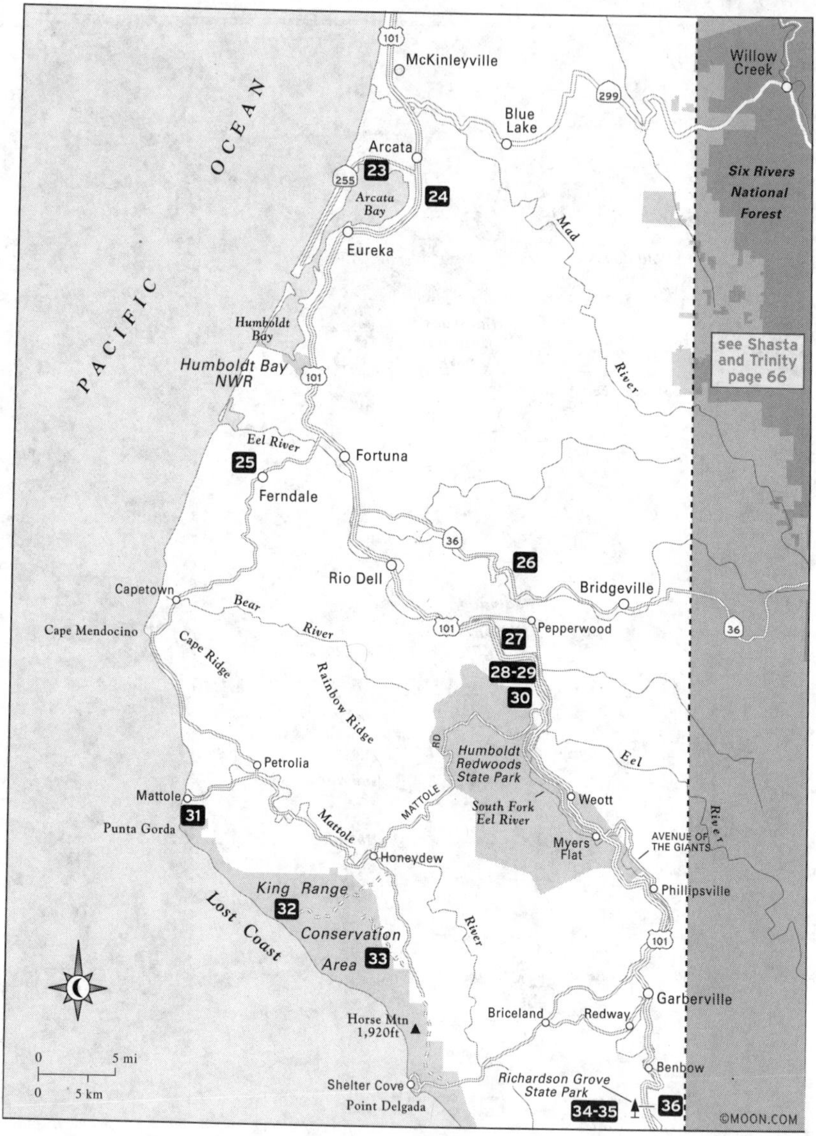

101
McKinleyville
299
Willow Creek
Blue Lake
Arcata
23
255
Arcata Bay
24
Six Rivers National Forest
PACIFIC OCEAN
Eureka
Mad River
Humboldt Bay
Humboldt Bay NWR
101
see Shasta and Trinity page 66
Eel River
25
Fortuna
Ferndale
36
26
Rio Dell
Bridgeville
Capetown
Bear River
101
Pepperwood
36
Cape Mendocino
Cape Ridge
27
28-29
Rainbow Ridge
30
MATTOLE RD
Humboldt Redwoods State Park
Eel River
Petrolia
Mattole
Weott
31
South Fork Eel River
Mattole River
Punta Gorda
Myers Flat
AVENUE OF THE GIANTS
Honeydew
King Range Conservation Area
32
33
Phillipsville
Lost Coast
101
Garberville
Briceland
Redway
Horse Mtn 1,920ft
0 5 mi
0 5 km
Benbow
Richardson Grove State Park
Shelter Cove
Point Delgada
34-35
36

1 TOLOWA DUNES

2.5 mi/1.0 hr 1 7

Tolowa Dunes State Park north of Crescent City

Map 1.1, page 39

This ancient sand dune complex seems to sweep on forever. It spans more than 10 miles from the mouth of the Smith River south along the Pacific Ocean, nearly reaching Crescent City, and is adjacent to Lake Earl to the east. After parking at Kellogg Beach, walk north or south for five minutes or five hours—take your pick. Either way, you will feel like a solitary speck against the enormous backdrop of untouched sand dunes and ocean. Only rarely will you see other people. The area is known by several names, including Fort Dick Beach, Kellogg Beach, and Pelican Bay Sand Dunes, but by any name, it's a good place to escape to nothing but wide-open beach for miles.

User Groups: Hikers, dogs, and horses. Mountain bikes permitted but not recommended. No wheelchair facilities.

Permits: No permits are required. Parking and access are free.

Maps: No map or brochure is available for this park. For topographic maps, ask the USGS for Crescent City and Smith River.

Directions: Take U.S. 101 to Crescent City and Northcrest Drive. Turn northwest on Northcrest Drive and drive 1.5 miles to Old Mill Road. Turn left on Old Mill Road and drive 1.25 miles to the end of Old Mill Road and the junction with Sand Hill Road. Turn left on Sand Hill Road (at the Department of Fish and Wildlife office) and drive 0.25 mile to the parking lot and the trailhead.

For trail and walk-in beach access: Take U.S. 101 to Crescent City and Northcrest Drive. Turn northwest on Northcrest Drive and drive six miles (it becomes Lake Earl Drive) to Lower Lake Road. Turn left on Lower Lake Road and drive 2.5 miles to Kellogg Road. Turn left and drive 0.5 mile to the trailhead.

Alternative access: Follow the above access directions, but after turning left on Lower Lake Road, drive five miles to Pala Road. Turn left and drive 0.5 mile to the trailhead.

Contact: Tolowa Dunes State Park, c/o Redwood National and State Parks, 707/465-7335, www.parks.ca.gov.

2 MYRTLE CREEK TRAIL

2.0 mi/0.75 hr 1 7

in the Smith River National Recreation Area

Map 1.1, page 39

This interpretive trail follows year-round Myrtle Creek. The stream drainage runs along a geological boundary between typical local soils (which support redwood and Douglas fir forests) and dry, reddish, iron- and magnesium-rich serpentine soil (where rarer native species grow, such as Bolander's and Vollmer's lilies). It's an easy hike with a lot to look at and learn about, including the remains of an extensive hydraulic mining operation, dating back to 1853, when gold was discovered here; 15 interpretive stops are linked to a numbered brochure. Keep to the trail. Collecting artifacts or plants is prohibited. This area receives an average of 93 inches per year of rain.

User Groups: Hikers and dogs. No horses or mountain bikes.

Permits: Campfire permits (free) are required for overnight use. Parking and access are free.

Maps: For a free brochure and hiking guide, contact Smith River National Recreation Area. For a topographic map, ask the USGS for Hiouchi.

Directions: From Crescent City, drive north on U.S. 101 for three miles to U.S. 199. Bear right (east) on U.S. 199 and drive seven miles to the parking area and trailhead. Park on the south side of U.S. 199 and cross the road to access the trailhead.

Contact: Smith River National Recreation Area, Gasquet, 707/457-3131, www.fs.usda.gov/srnf.

3 BOY SCOUT TREE TRAIL

7.0 mi/3.5 hr 2 10

in Jedediah Smith Redwoods State Park northeast of Crescent City

Map 1.1, page 39 BEST

This is the kind of place where a nature lover can find religion; where the beauty is pure and untouched. The trail is a soft dirt path—often sprinkled with redwood needles—that allows hikers to penetrate deep into an old-growth redwood forest, complete with a giant fern understory and high-limbed canopy. The trail leads 2.8 miles to Fern Falls, which makes this one of the area's better hikes in winter. The centerpiece is supposed to be the Boy Scout Tree, named after a scoutmaster, a double redwood that is located 2.5 miles in. Most people look for it and never see it. Look for a spur trail, unmarked—that's right, no sign—that leads to it.

This is an easy hike, nearly flat and with only small hills—yet it's extremely rewarding. Just walk into the forest, and a few hours later, walk out. Those few hours can change how you feel about the world. A bonus known to relatively few is Fern Falls, a 40-foot waterfall that flows in the rainy season. Reaching it requires a 3.5-mile hike one-way, making it a seven-mile round-trip hike.

User Groups: Hikers only. No dogs, horses, or mountain bikes. No wheelchair facilities.

Permits: No permits are required. The park entry fee is $8 at the main entrance.

Maps: A trail map is available for a fee from Jedediah Smith Redwoods State Park. For a topographic map, ask the USGS for Hiouchi.

Directions: From U.S. 101 in Crescent City, turn east on Elk Valley Road and drive one mile to Howland Hill Road. Turn right and drive 3.5 miles to the trailhead, on the left. The last two miles are unpaved.

If you plan to camp at Jedediah Smith Redwoods State Park, use these directions: From Crescent City, drive north on U.S. 101 for three miles to U.S. 199. Bear right (east) on U.S. 199 and drive east (past the main entrance to Jedediah Smith Redwoods State Park) and continue just past Hiouchi to South Fork Road. Turn right on South Fork Road (County Road 427) and cross two bridges (stay right at the fork). At the junction, turn right on Howland Hill Road and drive about five miles to a small parking area and the signed trailhead, on the right side of the road.

Contact: Jedediah Smith Redwoods State Park, Crescent City, 707/464-6101, www.parks.ca.gov.

4 STOUT GROVE TRAIL

0.7 mi/0.75 hr 1 8

in Jedediah Smith Redwoods State Park northeast of Crescent City

Map 1.1, page 39

The Stout Tree, a mammoth coastal redwood, used to be signed and ringed by a short fence, with a short trail directly from the parking lot to the tree. The sign and fence are gone. What you'll find now is a newer trail that is routed through the Stout Grove and beyond along the Smith River. You have to figure out on your own which tree is the Stout Tree, but most don't find that too difficult, it's that much bigger than most all the others in this grove. The trail is a 10- to 15-minute walk that takes an easy course to the Stout Grove, on to the Stout Tree (off the trail to your right as you walk in) and beyond to the Smith River. Most people take their time, absorbing the surroundings. Most everybody makes the mandatory stroll to the nearby Smith River a few minutes' walk beyond the Stout Tree.

User Groups: Hikers and wheelchairs. No dogs, horses, or mountain bikes.

Permits: No permits are required. The park entry fee is $8 at the main entrance.

Maps: A trail map is available for a fee from Jedediah Smith Redwoods State Park. For a topographic map, ask the USGS for Hiouchi.

Directions: From Crescent City, drive north on U.S. 101 for three miles to U.S. 199. Bear right (east) on U.S. 199 and drive east past the

Stout Grove, fallen redwood tree stump

main entrance to Jedediah Smith Redwoods State Park and continue just past Hiouchi to South Fork Road. Turn right on South Fork Road (County Road 427) and cross two bridges. At the junction, turn right on Howland Hill Road and drive about two miles to a small parking area (on the right) and the signed trailhead.
Contact: Jedediah Smith Redwoods State Park, Crescent City, 707/465-6101, www.parks.ca.gov.

5 CRAIG'S CREEK TRAIL

3.4 mi/2.0 hr — 2 — 8

in Smith River National Recreation Area northeast of Crescent City

Map 1.1, page 39

This is an old miners' pack route, vintage 1800s, that has been converted into this hiking trail, an obscure path that is overlooked by most visitors. It starts along the South Fork Smith River, loops up the slopes of Craig's Creek Mountain and back down to the river, and ends where Craig's Creek enters the South Fork. In the process, it rises above the river, and in 1.75 miles, reaches a lookout with a sweeping view over the South Fork Smith River and a deep river bend. Most turn around at this point. They got what they came for. You can venture on 3.7 miles one-way, where the trail is routed back down to the river, but few complete the entire route. Most of the time, you can have the entire trail to yourself. The South Fork Smith is very pretty here—a clear, free-flowing stream that drains a huge expanse of the Siskiyou Wilderness.
User Groups: Hikers, dogs, horses, and mountain bikes. No wheelchair facilities.
Permits: For overnight use, a campfire permit (free) is required. Parking and access are free.
Maps: For a free brochure and hiking guide, contact Smith River National Recreation Area. For a map, ask the U.S. Forest Service for Six Rivers National Forest. For a topographic map, ask the USGS for Hiouchi.
Directions: From Crescent City, drive north on U.S. 101 for three miles to U.S. 199. Bear right (east) on U.S. 199 and drive east past the main entrance to Jedediah Smith Redwoods State Park and continue just past Hiouchi to South Fork Road. Turn right on South Fork

Road (County Road 427) and drive approximately one-third mile and park in the signed area for river access. After parking, walk a short distance across South Fork Road to the north side of the second bridge. The trailhead is on the north side of the second bridge (called the Tryon Bridge). Park at the river access area then cross the road carefully to the trailhead.

Contact: Smith River National Recreation Area, Gasquet, 707/457-3131, www.fs.usda.gov/srnf.

6 STONY CREEK TRAIL

1.0 mi/0.5 hr — 1 — 8

in Smith River National Recreation Area northeast of Crescent City

Map 1.1, page 39

This easy walk in an unblemished river setting will take hikers to the mouth of Stony Creek, right where it pours into the North Fork Smith River. It's the kind of special place where you just sit and listen to the flow of moving water as it gurgles and pops its way over stones smoothed by years of river flows. The hike is easy, with a few ups and downs as it follows a bluff adjacent to the North Fork Smith (a designated Wild and Scenic River), then is routed right out to the mouth of Stony Creek. You're surrounded by woods, water, and in the spring, wildflowers.

For years, there has been an ongoing disagreement on how to spell it, either Stony or Stoney. The creek itself is spelled "Stony," so it only makes sense to spell it the same, and yet on some maps and guides, we've seen it as "Stoney."

User Groups: Hikers and dogs. No horses or mountain bikes. No wheelchair facilities.

Permits: Campfire permits (free) are required. Parking and access are free, but parking space is very limited.

Maps: For a free brochure and hiking guide, contact Smith River National Recreation Area. For a map, ask the U.S. Forest Service for Six Rivers National Forest. For a topographic map, ask the USGS for Gasquet.

Directions: From Crescent City, drive north on U.S. 101 for three miles to U.S. 199. Bear right (east) on U.S. 199 and drive 14 miles to Gasquet and continue a short distance to Middle Fork Road. Turn left on Middle Fork, continue a short distance and bear right on Gasquet Flat Road. Cross the bridge and stay left at the intersection of Gasquet Toll Road and continue 0.8 mile to Stony Creek Road (signed). Turn right and drive a short distance to the trailhead.

Contact: Smith River National Recreation Area, Gasquet, 707/457-3131, www.fs.usda.gov/srnf.

7 ELK CAMP RIDGE TRAIL

2-16 mi/1.0 hr-2 days — 3 — 9

in Smith River National Recreation Area northeast of Crescent City

Map 1.1, page 39

This trail is like a walk through history. It was originally part of a pack trail between Crescent City and the gold mines in southern Oregon, and the memories of the old days can shadow your hike much of the way. The trailhead is at 2,100 feet, but the route climbs right up to the ridge, reaching more than 3,000 feet. Within a mile, you'll reach excellent views of surrounding peaks (Preston Peak is the big one) and the Smith River Canyon. Just ahead is a glimpse of the ocean. For many, that's all they need. Hikers may also notice that much of the vegetation along the trail is stunted, a result of the high mineral content in the serpentine rocks. The trail keeps climbing and ends at 3,400 feet. From start to finish, the trail covers 8.2 miles, although few hikers complete the route.

This trail is often closed in the rainy season to stop the transfer of Port Orford cedar root disease.

User Groups: Hikers, dogs, horses, and mountain bikes. No wheelchair facilities.

Permits: Campfire permits (free) are required. Parking and access are free.

Maps: For a free brochure and hiking guide, contact Smith River National Recreation Area. For a map, ask the U.S. Forest Service for Six Rivers National Forest. For topographic maps, ask the USGS for Gasquet and High Plateau Mountain.

Directions: From Crescent City, drive north on U.S. 101 for three miles to U.S. 199. Bear right (east) on U.S. 199 and drive east past the main entrance to Jedediah Smith Redwoods State Park and continue just past Hiouchi to South Fork Road. Turn right on South Fork Road (County Road 427) and drive over the two bridges to a fork. Turn left on South Fork Road and drive 7.9 miles to Rock Creek Bridge and Forest Road 16N23. Turn right on Forest Road 16N23 and drive 0.9 mile (rough road, high-clearance advised). The trail begins at the creek.

This hike can also be done as a one-way trip with a shuttle. Leave second car on Howland Hill Road at a trailhead inside the park boundary for Jedediah Smith Redwoods State Park.

Contact: Smith River National Recreation Area, Gasquet, 707/457-3131, www.fs.usda.gov/srnf.

8 CALIFORNIA COASTAL TRAIL/NICKEL CREEK CAMP

3-15.0 mi one-way/1 day 3 8

in Del Norte Redwoods State Park south of Crescent City

Map 1.1, page 39

You get a little bit of heaven on this hike. It's one of the feature trips on the Del Norte coast, coursing through virgin forest and meadows (with beautiful wildflowers in the spring) and granting great coastal views in several spots. Note that in the past, some would camp at the Nickel Creek Campground, then launch from there; landslides closed Nickel Creek Campground in 2019 and the park may choose not to reopen it. The trail starts along the coast, veers up sharply into coastal spruce and fir, and then dips into dense, old-growth forest. That's the heaven. You will cross Damnation Creek, and then walk roughly parallel to U.S. 101. Most turn around at that point. You can extend the walk to make a one-way trip, with a car shuttle at your end point, with two crossings of U.S. 101 as you venture south; it's 15 miles to the second crossing of U.S 101. Note that the cutoff trail, the Damnation Trail, is another site that has been closed to the beach due to erosion and slides. Check for status before planning this section. Also note that when you cross meadows here, ticks can be a common problem.

User Groups: Hikers and mountain bikes (restricted to first six miles only). No dogs or horses. No wheelchair facilities.

Permits: No permits are required. The park entry fee is $8 at the main entrance.

Maps: A trail guide is available for a fee from Redwood National and State Parks (707/464-6101). For a topographic map, ask the USGS for Sister Rocks.

Directions: From Crescent City, drive south on U.S. 101 for about 2.5 miles to milepost 23.03 and Enderts Beach Road. Turn right (west) onto Enderts Beach Road and drive for 2.5 miles to the trailhead at the end of the road.

Contact: Del Norte Redwoods State Park, Crescent City, 707/464-6101, www.nps.gov/redw or www.parks.ca.gov.

9 MCCLENDON FORD TRAIL

3.0 mi/1.5 hr 1 8

in Smith River National Recreation Area east of Crescent City

Map 1.1, page 39 BEST

This is a perfect trail for a hot summer day, complete with a swimming hole. Hike 0.5 mile on the South Kelsey Trail, then one mile on the McClendon Ford Trail to the river. It's an easy hike through a large forest of Douglas fir. The trail crosses Horse Creek, a small tributary, and then leads to a pretty beach on the South Fork Smith River. The starting elevation is 1,000 feet, and the ending elevation is 200 feet. Get the idea? Right, this trail follows an easy descent to the river, taking about 45 minutes to get there. The swimming hole on the river is secluded and out of the way of most vacationers, so most often, you have the place completely to yourself. You end up at a bouldered beach and a beautiful pool. It's called the McClendon Ford because this is a historic river crossing, or ford, of the South Fork Smith.

This is also the trailhead for South Kelsey Trail. If you are unfamiliar with the area, be sure to have a map of Six Rivers National Forest to reach the trailhead.

User Groups: Hikers, dogs, horses, and mountain bikes. No wheelchair facilities.

Permits: No permits are required. Parking and access are free.

Maps: For a free brochure and hiking guide, contact Smith River National Recreation Area. For a map, ask the U.S. Forest Service for Six Rivers National Forest. For a topographic map, ask the USGS for Ship Mountain.

Directions: From Crescent City, drive north on U.S. 101 for three miles to U.S. 199. Bear right (east) on U.S. 199 and drive east past the main entrance to Jedediah Smith Redwoods State Park and continue just past Hiouchi to South Fork Road. Turn right on South Fork Road (County Road 427), cross two bridges and bear left on South Fork Road and drive 13.7 miles (one mile past Steven Bridge) to Forest Road 15 (locals call it the "GO Road"). Turn right on Forest Road 15 and drive 3.5 miles to Forest Road FS15N39 (signed for Kelsey Trail; road turns to gravel here). Turn left and drive two miles to trailhead. Hike on South Kelsey Trail for 0.5 mile before connecting with McClendon Ford Trail.

Contact: Smith River National Recreation Area, Gasquet, 707/457-3131, www.fs.usda.gov/srnf.

South Kelsey Trail

10 SOUTH KELSEY TRAIL

3-10.2 mi/1.5 hr-2 days 2 9

in Smith River National Recreation Area east of Crescent City

Map 1.1, page 39

Back before cars, trains, and planes, Kelsey Trail spanned 200 miles from Crescent City eastward to Fort Jones near Yreka. It was built in the mid-19th century by Chinese laborers as a mule-train route. The trail is in good shape for about 4.5 miles, then occasionally deteriorates in quality. The maintained section is on a beautiful piece of the South Fork Smith River. The trailhead is near Horse Creek, on the South Fork Smith River, at a 1,200-foot elevation. The trail initially drops down along the South Fork and continues south for 1.5 miles one-way to Buck Creek and a small waterfall that feeds into a gorgeous swimming hole, with the Buck Creek shelter, which is heaven during a heavy rainstorm. For many, this three-mile round-trip is pure heaven. If you keep on, the route then rises above the river, and at this point, can continue a total of 5.1 miles one-way (from the trailhead) with a 4,500-foot climb to 5,775-foot Baldy Peak. The payoff view is a 360 that spans 10,000 square miles. In the past few years, the Bigfoot Trail Alliance has brushed the trail from the Buck Creek Shelter to the ridge below Bald Mountain. What most backpackers do on the way in is make mental notes of potential flats for campsites along the South Fork. Some will dump their packs at a campsite, rig them in a bear-proof hang in a tree, then climb Baldy Peak and return without the burden of carrying the extra. Beyond Baldy Peak, maps show the route extending to Harrington Lake, but the trail seems to degenerate into oblivion.

User Groups: Hikers, dogs, and horses. Mountain bikes are permitted only to the wilderness boundary. No wheelchair facilities.

Permits: A campfire permit (free) is required. Parking and access are free.

Maps: For a free brochure and hiking guide, contact Smith River National Recreation Area. For a map, ask the U.S. Forest Service for Six Rivers National Forest. For a topographic map, ask the USGS for Summit Valley.

Directions: From Crescent City, drive north on U.S. 101 for three miles to U.S. 199. Bear right (east) on U.S. 199 and drive east past the main entrance to Jedediah Smith Redwoods State Park and continue just past Hiouchi to South Fork Road. Turn right on South Fork Road (County Road 427), cross two bridges and bear left on South Fork Road and drive 13.7 miles (one mile past Steven Bridge) to Forest Road 15 (locals call it the "GO Road"). Turn right on Forest Road 15 and drive 3.5 miles to Forest Road FS15N39 (signed for Kelsey Trail; road turns to gravel here). Turn left and drive two miles to trailhead.

Contact: Smith River National Recreation Area, Gasquet, 707/457-3131, www.fs.usda.gov/srnf.

11 SUMMIT VALLEY TRAIL

8.1 mi one-way/1 day 2 8

in Smith River National Recreation Area east of Crescent City

Map 1.1, page 39

The payoff here is the site of the old Summit Valley Lookout, a quarter-mile side trip from the main trail after you climb out of the valley. You get views across to the Siskiyous on one side and to the coast on the other, with a chance on stellar days to even see distant Mount Shasta. It's best done as a one-way trip with a shuttle to avoid a return climb of 3,500 feet.

The trailhead is set on a ridge at 4,600 feet, and the first mile of the hike is on an old jeep road. It then becomes a hiking path as it travels through meadows, where the wildflowers are spectacular in early summer. The trail then drops, plunging into a canyon and landing hikers along the South Fork Smith River at Elkhorn Bar, a beautiful spot at an elevation of 1,160 feet. Here it junctions with South Kelsey Trail, where you'll find a few primitive campsites along the river. You then reach your other shuttle car for the trailhead for the Kelsey Trail.

This hike is best taken in the early summer when the wildflowers are blooming; the Smith River is running with a fresh, ample flow; and the temperature is not too warm. Nobody does this trip down and back; that would be a death march.

User Groups: Hikers, dogs, and horses. Mountain bikes are permitted only to the wilderness boundary. No wheelchair facilities.

Permits: A campfire permit (free) is required. Parking and access are free.

Maps: Write to Smith River National Recreation Area for a free brochure and hiking guide. For a map, ask the U.S. Forest Service for Six Rivers National Forest. For a topographic map, ask the USGS for Summit Valley.

Directions to start of trail: From Crescent City, drive north on U.S. 101 for three miles to U.S. 199. Bear right (east) on U.S. 199 and drive east past the main entrance to Jedediah Smith Redwoods State Park and continue just past Hiouchi to South Fork Road. Turn right on South Fork Road (County Road 427), cross two bridges and bear left on South Fork Road, and drive 13.7 miles (one mile past Steven Bridge) to Forest Road 15. Turn right on Forest Road 15 and drive 15 miles to the trailhead, on the left. Park on the side of the road.

Directions to end of trail for shuttle car: From Crescent City, drive north on U.S. 101 for three miles to U.S. 199. Bear right (east) on U.S. 199 and drive east past the main entrance to Jedediah Smith Redwoods State Park and continue just past Hiouchi to South Fork Road. Turn right on South Fork Road (County Road 427), cross two bridges and bear left on South Fork Road, and drive 13.7 miles (one mile past Steven Bridge) to Forest Road 15 (locals call it the "GO Road"). Turn right on Forest Road 15 and drive 3.5 miles to Forest Road FS15N39 (signed for Kelsey Trail; road turns to gravel here). Turn left and drive two miles to trailhead.

Contact: Smith River National Recreation Area, Gasquet, 707/457-3131, www.fs.usda.gov/srnf.

12 YUROK LOOP

1.0 mi/0.5 hr 1 8

in Redwood National and State Parks south of Crescent City

Map 1.1, page 39

The Yurok Loop is a great short loop hike that starts right next to pretty Lagoon Creek Pond in Redwood National and State Parks. Here's the deal: From the trailhead, it's a 10-minute walk above a beautiful beach with lots of driftwood, and a gentle climb to a great coastal overlook. From here you can scan miles of ocean and many rocky stacks. The prettiest view spans across False Klamath Cove, one of the loveliest beaches on the Pacific Coast. After enjoying the view, head south, and when you reach a junction, turn left and enter a forest where the trail burrows almost like a tunnel, heading gently downhill. It then emerges from the forest and leads back to the parking lot, making it a delightful and easy walk that is a perfect break for highway drivers.

The Hidden Beach section of Coastal Trail (also in this chapter) junctions with this trail.

User Groups: Hikers only. No dogs, horses, or mountain bikes.

Permits: No permits are required. Parking and access are free.

Maps: A trail guide is available for a fee from Redwood National and State Parks Headquarters. For a topographic map, ask the USGS for Requa.

Directions: From Crescent City, drive south on U.S. 101 for approximately 14 miles. Turn right at the sign for the Lagoon Creek Parking Area. The trailhead is adjacent to the parking lot (on the ocean/north side).

Contact: Redwood National Park and California State Parks, Crescent City, 707/464-6101, www.nps.gov/redw or www.parks.ca.gov.

13 COASTAL TRAIL (HIDDEN BEACH SECTION)

6.4 mi/3.0 hr 2 8

in Redwood National Park south of Crescent City

Map 1.1, page 39

This trek starts at one of the greatest coastal views, at the Klamath Overlook, on California's north coast. You can scan the vast ocean-blue horizon, where it seems you can see the curvature of the earth. After parking, enjoy the view and then head off. It's a 3.2-mile trip, one-way, to Hidden Beach. Locals with two cars can set up a shuttle. Leave a vehicle at the parking area for the Yurok Loop. It's a 7.8-mile trip, one-way, with a climb of roughly 1,400 feet, excellent with a shuttle car. The trail runs along coastal bluffs and rocky cliffs, with sweeping views of the ocean. Pray for a clear day.

User Groups: Hikers only. No dogs, horses, or mountain bikes.

Permits: No permits are required. Parking and access are free.

Maps: A trail guide is available for a fee from Redwood National and State Parks Headquarters. For a topographic map, ask the USGS for Requa.

Directions: From Eureka, drive north on U.S. 101 for about 60 miles to the Klamath River. Continue two miles north of the Klamath River Bridge to Requa Road. Turn west on Requa Road and drive 2.5 miles to the Klamath Overlook, at the end of the road. The trailhead is at the south end of the parking area. Head north on Coastal Trail.

Contact: Redwood National Park and California State Parks, Crescent City, 707/464-6101, www.nps.gov/redw or www.parks.ca.gov.

14 LOST MAN CREEK TRAIL

2.0 mi/1.0 hr 1 7

in Redwood National Park south of Klamath

Map 1.1, page 39

Lost Man Creek is very pretty, with many rock pools and lots of lush vegetation. It's also a destination that is easy to reach. The trail heads southeast, the first 1.5 miles nearly flat, then starts to climb moderately, and then nearly levels out along the creek. Bring your camera, because it is rare to reach such a pristine setting with such a short walk. The trail is actually an old logging road that the park service plans on reclaiming and turning into a more low-key setting. The two-mile round-trip is as far as virtually all hikers take it; the trail actually continues for 10 miles, all the way back down to Bald Hills Road. In summer, the upper parts of this hike/bike trail (near Holter Ridge and Bald Hills Road) is closed due to forest restoration operations. The park has been restoring the rivers, second-growth forests and removing legacy logging roads in this area for more than 20 years.

User Groups: Hikers and mountain bikes. No dogs, horses, or mountain bikes.

Permits: No permits are required. Parking and access are free.

Maps: A trail guide is available for a fee from Redwood National and State Parks Headquarters. For a topographic map, ask the USGS for Orick.

Directions: From Eureka, drive north on U.S. 101 for 41 miles to Orick. Continue north for 3.5 miles just past Davison Road to Lost Man Creek Road. Turn right and drive 0.75 mile to the parking area and trailhead. Trailers and RVs are not permitted on Lost Man Creek Road.

Contact: Redwood National Park and California State Parks, Crescent City, 707/464-6101, www.nps.gov/redw or www.parks.ca.gov.

15 TALL TREES TRAIL

4.0 mi/2.25 hr 2 10

in Redwood National Park south of Klamath

Map 1.1, page 39 BEST

This trail is the paradox of the Redwood Empire. The payoff is an easy walk into a grove of tall and ancient redwoods of cathedral-like beauty, with the trail shaded and surrounded by a lush fern understory. Your mission here is to reach Tall Trees Grove, home of the Libby Tree (more about this to come). Problem is, the access road is unpaved and narrow, with no place to turn around, and the parking lot is small. So you need a permit and gate code to get past the gate; it's free at a visitors center; the main interest of rangers is the number of people with you. The hike in is an easy walk in the forest that leads to the Tall Trees Grove along Redwood Creek. In the 1960s, the Libby Tree was believed to be the tallest tree in the world and helped lead to the creation of Redwood National Park. The top of the tree, about 10 feet, broke off, and with laser-guided measuring techniques, the tree now rates 34th. Regardless, if you love big trees, this is a must-do.

User Groups: Hikers only. No dogs, horses, or mountain bikes. No wheelchair facilities.

Permits: A permit is required if you want to drive to the trailhead, with only a limited number of cars allowed per day. Permits are free and can be obtained at the Thomas H. Kuchel Visitor Center starting at 9am. Just pick it up, get the gate combination, and then enjoy your trip.

Maps: A trail guide is available for a fee from Redwood National and State Parks Headquarters. For a topographic map, ask the USGS for Orick.

Directions: From Eureka, drive north on U.S. 101 for 40 miles. About a mile before reaching Orick, stop at the Thomas H. Kuchel Visitor Center, at the west side of the highway. At the Kuchel Visitor Center, the rangers will provide accurate directions to the trailhead. Note that visitors relying on digital maps and apps have been led to the wrong place to get to the Tall Trees Grove gate. Drive north on U.S. 101 through Orick and continue 0.25 mile to Bald Hills Road. Turn right on Bald Hills Road. Look for the Tall Trees Access sign and drive seven miles to a locked gate, on the right. Open the gate, close and lock the gate, and then drive six miles down the gravel road (C-Line Road) to the trailhead. No RVs or trailers are permitted.

Contact: Redwood National Park and California State Parks, Crescent City, 707/464-6101, www.nps.gov/redw or www.parks.ca.gov.

16 JAMES IRVINE TRAIL

7.5 mi/3.0 hr 2 10

in Prairie Creek Redwoods State Park

Map 1.1, page 39

This is one of the best hikes in the Redwood Empire: This trail can be done short (just a mile out and back) or long (7.5-mile loop). The James Irvine Trail is the best walk to see "Champion Trees," which are listed among largest recorded living specimens of each tree variety. In just a mile or so, you will see world-class coastal redwoods, western hemlock, Douglas fir and Sitka spruce, all in the 300-foot range. The trailhead is located at the far end of the small parking lot for the Prairie Creek Visitor Center. From the trailhead, it's a 0.6-mile hike to the junction with the James Irvine Trail. Within a few steps, you'll know you're walking in history. The James Irvine Trail contours in and out of lush ravines filled with big trees for 2.6 miles. In one ravine, old-growth 300-foot mammoths rise up with a canopy that blots out the sky, while a sloping wall of ferns and sorrel create an understory that extends 150 yards to the canyon bottom. To complete the loop, turn left on the Clintonia Trail and hike 1.4 miles past two more groves to the Miners Ridge Trail. Follow the Miners Ridge Trail 2.7 miles back to the visitors center and enjoy the good, clean feeling that comes with hiking a few hours in a pristine landscape. The James Irvine Trail is easy enough that anyone can get a feel for ancient forest within a mile or so, yet long enough that the entire loop delivers a sense of discovery and awe with each grove.

We advise a loop hike (and then doing Fern Canyon as a separate loop hike with the Coastal Trail), but the trail can be extended to Fern Canyon and beyond to the Coastal Trail and huge expanses of wilderness beachfront.

Permits: No permits are required. There is a state park day-use fee of $8 per vehicle.

Maps: Trail maps are available at the park visitors center for a fee. For a topographic map, ask the USGS for Fern Canyon.

Directions: From Eureka, drive north on U.S. 101 for 41 miles to Orick. Continue north for five miles past Orick and exit at Newton B. Drury Scenic Parkway. Travel west on the parkway for one mile to the park entrance on left. Turn left and drive a short distance to the visitors center and trailhead on right.

Contact: Prairie Creek Redwoods State Park, Orick, 707/465-7347; Visitor Center, 707/465-7354; www.parks.ca.gov.

17 COASTAL TRAIL LOOP (FERN CANYON/ OSSAGON SECTION)

7.6 mi/3.5 hr 2 10

in Prairie Creek Redwoods State Park south of Klamath

Map 1.1, page 39 **BEST**

This is a great hike, one of my favorites, anywhere. There is a good chance of seeing Roosevelt elk (they often roam at Prairie Creek Redwoods State Park at Elk Meadow and often along Davison Road), Fern Canyon (see listing in this chapter), a dense forest (quiet and pretty), and a series of hidden waterfalls. In addition, there is a huge wilderness beach that seems to extend into infinity. From the parking area, start the trip by crossing a shallow stream; most of the year, the crossing consists of a few rock hops. If it's higher, that's good news, because it means the narrow waterfalls are running along the trail up ahead. Small temporary bridges are often provided from June through September.

Coastal Trail

Once you cross Home Creek, this trips starts off as a near-level walk. On the Coastal Trail, you walk roughly 2.5 miles north (waterfalls, wilderness beach, ocean views, coastal forest) to the West Ridge Trail. Then turn right and climb 1.8 miles (towering Sitka spruce, Douglas fir) to Friendship Ridge. Turn right again, where the trail contours south for three miles (old-growth redwoods), and then descend one mile into Fern Canyon (vertical fern walls, waterfall, stream) and then back to parking.

We often see elk on this hike. The ones to be wary of are not the big bulls with the giant racks, but the smaller females guarding their yearlings. On the Friendship Ridge Trail, on the last leg of a loop hike at dusk, we found ourselves staring into the bugged-out eyes of what appeared to be a 175-pound juvenile female, about 40 feet away. It then ran straight at us. To avoid it, we barreled over a fallen log on the right side of the trail and down about 10 feet into a fern-covered gulch, and then laughed like hell over what seemed a bizarre experience. Turns out 10 other hikers had been driven off the trail that day by female elk with young. Rangers say late fall is the most common time when the females' protective maternal instincts give rise to hiker encounters.

User Groups: Hikers and mountain bikes. No dogs or horses. No wheelchair facilities.

Permits: No permits are required. There is a state park day-use fee of $8 per vehicle. Overnight parking is not permitted.

Maps: Trail maps are available at the park visitors center for a fee. For a topographic map, ask the USGS for Fern Canyon.

Directions: From Eureka, drive north on U.S. 101 for 41 miles to Orick. Continue north for 2.5 miles to Davison Road. Turn west on Davison Road and drive eight miles to Fern Canyon trailhead. No trailers or RVs are permitted.

Contact: Prairie Creek Redwoods State Park, Orick, 707/465-7347, www.parks.ca.gov.

18 FERN CANYON LOOP TRAIL

0.8 mi/0.5 hr

in Prairie Creek Redwoods State Park south of Klamath

Map 1.1, page 39

The Fern Canyon Loop is one of the most inspiring short hikes in California. When you walk along the bottom of Fern Canyon, you'll be at the base of 50-foot-high walls covered with giant ferns. It's unique, dramatic, beautiful, and romantic. A small waterfall, which pours in through a chasm in the canyon wall and gushes into Home Creek, adds to the beauty. It is Home Creek, which runs through the bottom of the canyon, which can cause the one serious problem here for some day hikers. In winter this creek can flood, making the trail impassable. In spring, you need waterproof boots or hip waders. Bridges are sometimes provided from June through September. Come prepared to hop back and forth across the stream in order to reach the back of the canyon. Got it: wear waterproof footwear. At the end of the canyon, turn left and climb the trail to the canyon rim, and then continue through the forest back to the trailhead. A bonus is the adjacent beach to the north, which is wide open and spans for miles. It is also common to see Roosevelt elk on the drive in. This trail is well known by many, so it can get a lot of use during the summer months. Yet it is the rainy months, winter through early spring, when it glows and people are few.

User Groups: Hikers only. No dogs, horses, or mountain bikes. No wheelchair facilities.

Permits: No permits are required. There is a state park day-use fee of $8 per vehicle.

Maps: Trail maps are available at the park visitors center for a fee. For a topographic map, ask the USGS for Fern Canyon.

Directions: From Eureka, drive north on U.S. 101 for 41 miles to Orick. Continue north for 2.5 miles to Davison Road. Turn west on Davison Road and drive eight miles to Fern Canyon Trail. No trailers or RVs are permitted.

Contact: Prairie Creek Redwoods State Park, Orick, 707/465-7347, www.parks.ca.gov.

19 REDWOOD CREEK TRAIL

3.0 mi/1.25 hr 1 7

in Redwood National Park south of Klamath

Map 1.1, page 39 BEST

With easy access, a flat trail, and a great name, this has become an extremely popular trail, with high numbers of tourists in summer. It's short and pretty, with woods and water.

The trail is routed along Redwood Creek, a small stream that flows out to sea near Orick. In the first mile, there are no giant redwoods, and tourists wonder what's wrong. The enlightened few will instead notice the diversity of the forest, with spruce, alder, and maples, and a few redwoods, as well as lush blackberries and fern beds in some areas. The appeal is the riparian watershed, rather than old growth, along the stream. In summer, for hikers, there are two temporary bridges put in over Redwood Creek. The first is about 1.5 miles in. Some big redwoods are on the far side of the creek, though it is "mission accomplished" for most tourists at that point, and they turn around and head back.

There's a chance to see elk near the parking area. Stinging nettles are also abundant here, so stay on the trail. The stream attracts a diversity of wildlife, with ducks, herons, and hawks the most common sightings, and ruffed grouse and eagles are occasionally seen. Note that during the winter, the creek can flood the trail in some areas, making it impassable.

User Groups: Hikers only. No dogs, horses, or mountain bikes. No wheelchair facilities.

Permits: No permits are required. Parking and access are free.

Maps: A trail guide is available for a fee from Redwood National and State Parks Headquarters. For a topographic map, ask the USGS for Orick.

Directions: From Eureka, drive north on U.S. 101 for approximately 41 miles to Orick and then about 0.25 mile north of Orick to Bald Hills Road. Turn right on Bald Hills Road and drive 0.25 mile to the access road. Turn right and drive 0.5 mile to the parking area and trailhead.

Contact: Redwood National Park and California State Parks, Crescent City, 707/464-6101, www.nps.gov/redw or www.parks.ca.gov.

20 SKUNK CABBAGE TRAIL

5.6 mi/3.0 hr 2 9

in Redwood National Park south of Klamath

Map 1.1, page 39

Like love, it's all about timing on this trail. In the spring, when the skunk cabbage, fern, and redwood understory reaches peak growth, this trail is a sensational 10. In the fall and early winter, when the vegetation gets knocked down, well, more like a 6 or 7. Since you now know this, we rated it a 9, assuming you will go in peak season. That done, few places anywhere cast an aura such as that found here in late spring and early summer on the Skunk Cabbage Trail in Redwood National Park. Every step is filled with the sense that this is an ancient place for old souls and youthful spirits. The trail is routed 2.8 miles amid a stunning forest understory out to a coastal bluff that towers over the Pacific Ocean. Hidden in the Redwood Empire, this rainforest looks like a jungle right out of *Jurassic Park,* or at least interior Kauai. You might even swear that a T. rex must be lurking amid the massive vegetation, spruces, and redwoods. Instead of dinosaurs, you might see black bears, endangered northern spotted owls, or marbled murrelets. We've found spots where bears have chewed the bark on trees here, too.

From the parking area, the trail quickly enters a dense redwood and spruce forest, where the canopy is often completely enclosed by towering tree limbs. The trail meanders along a small watershed, Skunk Cabbage Creek; set beneath is a luxuriant forest floor filled with huge sword ferns, sorrel, and the giant skunk cabbage. Since you probably wondered, skunk cabbage is an herbaceous plant with massive stalks, a perennial that reaches its full growth from May through June. It is called skunk cabbage because of its strong scent when taken in, up close and personal; it's even considered by some to be rank. But the smell isn't a factor on this trip; rather, it's about how the lavish growth of the plant adds a sense of age-old mystery to this quiet jungle. The trail eventually winds its way through redwoods as you near the coastal bluffs. That's the spot for your trail lunch and turnaround.

User Groups: Hikers only. No mountain bikes, dogs, or horses. No wheelchair facilities.

Permits: Parking and access are free.

Maps: Trail maps are available at the park

visitors center for a fee. For a topographic map, ask the USGS for Fern Canyon.

Directions: From Eureka, take U.S. 101 north for 41 miles to the signed exit for Thomas H. Kuchel Visitor Center (if you reach Orick, you have gone one mile too far) and get in the left turn lane. Turn left and go 150 yards to the parking area. After obtaining trail and park materials at the center, turn left (north) on U.S. 101 and drive two miles (through Orick) to the trailhead entrance road on the left (comes up suddenly), signed Skunk Cabbage Trail. Turn left and drive 0.25 mile to a parking area.

Contact: Redwood National Park and California State Parks, Crescent City, 707/464-6101, www.nps.gov/redw or www.parks.ca.gov.

21 RIM LOOP TRAIL

5.0 mi/2.5 hr 1 8

at Patrick's Point State Park north of Eureka

Map 1.1, page 39 BEST

For visitors to Patrick's Point State Park, this trail is the rite of passage. Problem is, in big winters with high rainfall, there has been occasional erosion on the trail section between Agate Beach and Mussel Rock, and some other sections can need maintenance as well. That done, it is one of the best easy hikes around is yours. If not, the trail is blocked off at the closed section.

Patrick's Point is set on a coastal headland that is lush with ferns, spruce, and wildflowers. It's bordered by the Pacific, which means visitors can go tidepooling or whale-watching. That means with this trail, you can get the best of these two worlds. At times, the trail tunnels through thick vegetation, and at other times it opens up to sweeping ocean views. Along the way, several spur trails provide access to many features, including Mussel Rock, Wedding Rock, Agate Beach, Rocky Point, Patrick's Point, Abalone Point, and Palmer's Point. The views are sensational at every one of these spots. The elevation of the trail is 200 feet and nearly level its entire length. Each of the spur trails thus drops 200 feet to the beach. The spur trails, while short (they add just 1.5 miles to the hike), will make this a two- to three-hour trip, since you won't want to just rush through it. In addition, Octopus Tree Trail offers a short hike that starts just across from the northern end of Rim Loop Trail. This bonus trail provides a chance to see many spruce trees with roots that have straddled downed logs, hence the name "Octopus Trees."

User Groups: Hikers only. No dogs, horses, or mountain bikes. The best wheelchair-accessible hiking trail in this park is from the visitors center to the Sumeg Village.

Permits: No permits are required. A state park day-use fee of $8 per vehicle is charged.

Maps: A park map and brochure are available for a fee from Patrick's Point State Park. For a topographic map, ask the USGS for Trinidad.

Directions: From Eureka, drive north on U.S. 101 for 22 miles to Trinidad and continue north for 5.5 miles to Patrick's Point Drive exit. Take that exit and at the stop sign, turn left, and drive 0.5 mile to the entrance station. Continue to the Agate Beach parking area.

Contact: Patrick's Point State Park, Trinidad, 707/677-3570, www.parks.ca.gov.

22 TSURAI LOOP

1.5 mi/1.0 hr 2 9

on Trinidad Head on the Humboldt coast north of Eureka

Map 1.1, page 39

The Tsurai Loop is a great, easy walk with coastal vistas, unique terrain, and a nearby restaurant. The terrain includes the 300-foot miniature mountain at Trinidad Head, the pretty beachfront to the north of the Trinidad Head area, and the Trinidad Pier. The trip is best done in a counterclockwise loop. It starts by hiking up for beautiful views to the north, eventually reaching this perfectly situated rock lookout of the ocean. On clear days in spring and early summer it can be an ideal spot to watch for the puff-of-smoke spouts on the ocean surface made by migrating whales. The trail circles the mountain and then climbs to the top, a flat summit, where the views are only fair. The views are actually a lot better just 50 yards to the south, looking south toward Eureka and Humboldt Bay. As you head back down, you get more views of the rocky Trinidad Harbor and coast. The restaurant? It's called Seascape, and you can get a crab or shrimp omelet (always fresh crab, in season) for breakfast that'll have your mouth watering every time you start driving north of Eureka on U.S. 101. If there's a wait at the restaurant, don't hesitate to line up anyway.

User Groups: Hikers and dogs. Mountain bikes permitted but not recommended. No horses. No wheelchair facilities.

Permits: No permits are required. Parking and access are free.

Maps: For a topographic map, ask the USGS for Trinidad.

Directions: From Eureka, drive north on U.S. 101 for 28 miles to Trinidad. Take the Trinidad exit, turn left at the stop sign, and drive under the U.S. 101 overpass to Main Street. Continue on Main Street to Trinity Street. Turn left and drive a short distance to Edwards Street. Turn right on Edwards Street and drive to the parking area at the foot of the harbor.

Contact: Seascape Restaurant, Trinidad Pier, 707/677-3762, www.seascape-trinidad.com.

23 ARCATA MARSH TRAIL

2-4.5 mi/1-2.0 hr 1 8

in Arcata Marsh and Wildlife Sanctuary on the northern edge of Humboldt Bay

Map 1.2, page 40 **BEST**

The 307-acre Arcata Marsh is a great bird-watching area, a mosaic of ponds, marshes, and wetlands that border Arcata Bay. It's best explored by walking the loop. It is set on a levee above the marsh; the trail is short, flat, and routed in a loop for the best viewing possibilities. The loop is two miles, but it can be extended on other trails on levees for a longer trip. Several wooden photography blinds are available on the route, where you can hide yourself to view the ponds up close and take pictures of the birds. The setting is unique, with the coast, saltwater bay, brackish-water marsh, pond, foothills, and streams all nearby. This diversity means that an outstanding variety of species—more than 250 have been verified—are attracted to the area. Sightings can include belted kingfishers, ospreys, peregrine falcons, black phoebes, and song and savannah sparrows. In other words, birds from nearly all habitats are represented. Guided bird walks are common on Saturday mornings. One side note is that many locals eat lunch at the parking area, and just like Pavlov's dog, tons of birds show up in the parking lot daily at noon for handouts. The rangers request that you don't feed the birds (but everybody does). The Arcata Marsh Interpretive Center is open daily and has free maps, literature, and a posted list of recent bird sightings.

User Groups: Hikers, dogs, and mountain bikes. No horses.

Permits: No permits are required. Parking and access are free.

Maps: For a free, detailed trail map, contact the City of Arcata and ask for the Marsh and Wildlife Trail map. For a topographic map, ask the USGS for Arcata South.

Directions: From Eureka, drive north on U.S. 101 for five miles to Arcata and the Samoa Boulevard exit. Take that exit and turn west onto Samoa Boulevard; drive to I Street. Turn left (south) on I Street and continue to G Street, then continue straight on South I Street to a sharp right turn. Turn right and continue (around Hauser Marsh to your left) to parking and a trailhead (Arcata Bay to the west, Klopp Lake to your east).

Contact: Arcata Marsh Interpretive Center, 707/826-2359, www.cityofarcata.org.

24 NATURE TRAIL

2.0 mi/1.0 hr

in Arcata Community Forest in the Arcata foothills

Map 1.2, page 40

Arcata Community Forest provides a respite for students at nearby Humboldt State and for locals who want to wander amid a beautiful second-growth forest. A network of 18 trails covers about 10 miles and the Redwood Loop connects several of them. For newcomers a map is an absolute necessity to understand the mosaic of routes. Mountain bikes are prohibited on about 50 percent of the trails in the forest, although these rules are occasionally broken. (On weekends, kamikaze mountain bikers tearing downhill can turn this hike into an extremely unpleasant experience.)

Start this trip at Redwood Lodge (mountain bikes not allowed) and take the Nature Trail. The trail will take you by many huge stumps, a small creek, and a forest of redwoods and spruce. At one point, you will see the awesome Octopus Tree, where the roots of a Sitka spruce have grown over the top and sides of a giant stump. At the junction of two trails, turn left twice for an easy and pretty trip. Trips in the Arcata forest can be expanded to include elevation gains and losses of 1,200 feet.

User Groups: Hikers, dogs, and horses. No mountain bikes. Certain sections of the trail are off-limits to horses and mountain bikes; check the trail map for details. No wheelchair facilities.

Permits: No permits are required. Parking and access are free.

Maps: For a free, detailed trail map, contact the City of Arcata and ask for the Community Forest Trail map. A free mountain bike trail map is also available. For topographic maps, ask the USGS for Arcata North and Arcata South.

Directions: From Eureka, drive north on U.S. 101 to Arcata and the 14th Street/Humboldt University exit. Take that exit to 14th Street. Turn right on 14th and drive a short distance to Union Street. Turn right on Union and drive a short distance to 11th Street. Turn left on 11th and drive a short distance to Bayview. Turn left on Bayview and drive (road curves to the right, becomes East Peak Road) to Redwood Lodge and trailhead.

No mountain bikes are permitted. Bikers and equestrians should use the Meadow trailhead where 14th Street enters the park.

Contact: City of Arcata, Department of Parks, 707/822-8184, www.cityofarcata.org.

25 LYTEL RIDGE/ EUCALYPTUS TRAIL

1.5 mi/1.0 hr 2 7

in Russ City Park in Ferndale south of Eureka

Map 1.2, page 40

Russ City Park is like an island wilderness. It is located at the southern edge of Ferndale, covers just 105 acres, and yet retains its primitive state for wildlife, birds, and hikers. The best trip is the short 350-foot climb up Lytel Ridge. You climb up Lytel Ridge, where you pass Francis Creek, with sections routed through heavy fern beds and large firs and offering views of a small pond and the Eel River watershed and floodplain. The trip is relatively short and easy enough, yet the terrain is steep in spots, and heavy fog or rain can make it slippery. It feels quiet and secluded, and gets overlooked by out-of-towners.

User Groups: Hikers and dogs. No horses or mountain bikes. No wheelchair facilities.

Permits: No permits are required. Parking and access are free.

Maps: A free map and brochure can be obtained by contacting the City of Ferndale. For a topographic map, ask the USGS for Ferndale.

Directions: From U.S. 101, drive to the exit for Ferndale/Highway 211 (13 miles south of Eureka). Take that exit and continue to Highway 211, turn right and drive (over the Eel River Bridge) four miles to Ferndale and

Main Street. Continue on Main Street to Ocean Street. Turn left on Ocean Street and drive 0.75 mile to a gravel parking area and trailhead on the right (where Ocean Street turns into Bluff Street).

Contact: Ferndale Chamber of Commerce, 707/786-4477, www.visitferndale.com.

26 RATHERT GROVE/ MEMORIAL TRAIL LOOP

1.8 mi/1.0 hr 1 10

at Grizzly Creek Redwoods State Park near Bridgeville

Map 1.2, page 40

This pretty hike is an easy walk through the redwoods on the southern side of the Van Duzen River. Most visitors instead walk to two redwood groves from a trailhead at the visitors center. On the north side of the Van Duzen, you have a chance to have the world to yourself in Rathert Grove. The trailhead is at the bridge at the Van Duzen River, just upstream from where Grizzly Creek enters the Van Duzen. The trail then is routed, about a 10-minute walk, to a junction with the Memorial Trail Loop. Turn right. The trail then circles the beautiful Rathert Grove and then reaches a junction on the right with the Loop Trail; this is a short spur/circle at the Harriet Hunt Bard Grove. It then loops back to the Memorial Trail Loop, and you walk a short distance back to the bridge.

The Rathert Grove is one of seven relatively small yet pristine old-growth redwood groves protected in this park. There is nothing difficult about this or the other hikes in the park. In fact, stairs are provided in many of the few short, steeper spots. What makes this hike special is that on a weekday, you can have an entire old-growth redwood grove all to yourself. Where else can you do that? Grizzly Creek Redwoods State Park is one of the most overlooked redwood state parks in California, receiving fewer than 25,000 visitors per year—and most of those in July and August. It is often overlooked because it is not on U.S. 101, but rather more than 15 miles east on Highway 36, a curvy two-laner that provides access to some of the state's remotest areas. Many discover the park by accident, usually heading up to fish, canoe, or kayak the Van Duzen River; the state park provides an excellent river access point, as well as a campground.

User Groups: Hikers only. No dogs, horses, or mountain bikes are permitted. Some facilities are wheelchair-accessible, but there is no trail access for wheelchairs.

Permits: No permits are required. A fee of $8 per vehicle is charged for parking.

Maps: For a free brochure and map, contact Grizzly Creek Redwoods. For a topographic map, ask the USGS for Redcrest Quad.

Directions: From Eureka, drive south on U.S. 101 to the junction of Highway 36 at Alton. Turn east on Highway 36 and drive 17.2 miles to the park entrance, on the right.

Contact: Grizzly Creek Redwoods State Park, 707/777-3683, www.parks.ca.gov.

27 FIVE ALLENS TRAIL

2.2 mi/1.5 hr 3 8

in Humboldt Redwoods State Park south of Eureka

Map 1.2, page 40

Most of the trails into beautiful redwood groves are on flats near watersheds. The Five Allens Trail is just the opposite: up, up, and up it goes, where you climb 800 feet in 1.2 miles. The payoff is a pretty redwood grove, the Allens Grove, gorgeous and quiet, just the reason most visitors venture to the Redwood Empire. You'll see a sign at the grove that says "The Five Allens," and it refers to five redwood trees. From the trailhead near the Eel River, walk under the highway and then start the climb. As it rises up, the trail passes through a forest of mixed conifers; the tree canopy provides needed shade in the summer. A bridged creek can be very pretty. After a good climb, you'll reach a fork. Bear left for the Allens Grove. You won't see the huge mammoth-size redwoods here, but it is a quiet, peaceful spot that most tourists from out of state never see. That's why it's in the book.

User Groups: Hikers only. No dogs, horses, or mountain bikes. No wheelchair facilities.

Permits: No permits are required. The park entry fee is $8 at the main entrance.

Maps: A map can be obtained for a fee from Humboldt Redwoods State Park. For a topographic map, ask the USGS for Weott.

Directions: From Eureka, drive south on U.S. 101 to the Redcrest exit. Take that exit and turn left, drive under the overpass, and continue a short distance to Avenue of the Giants. Turn right on Avenue of the Giants and drive south three miles (past High Rock Conservation Camp) to the Maria McKean Allen marker at the pullout for trailhead parking. Cross through the pedestrian tunnel for U.S. 101.

For an alternate route from Garberville, drive north on U.S. 101 to the Founders Tree/Rockefeller Forest exit. Take that exit (north), turn right, and drive about 200 yards to Avenue of the Giants. Turn left on Avenue of the Giants, cross over the South Fork Eel River, and then bear right at the intersection in order to stay on Avenue of the Giants. Drive a short distance to the Five Allens trailhead parking.

Contact: Humboldt Redwoods State Park, Weott, 707/946-2409, www.parks.ca.gov.

28 FOUNDERS GROVE NATURE TRAIL

0.4 mi/0.3 hr 1 8

in Humboldt Redwoods State Park south of Eureka

Map 1.2, page 40

The paradox of the tourist public makes this one of the highest visited trails in the Redwood Empire. As the tourists drive U.S. 101, they'll see the off-ramp for the Avenue of the Giants, and then, in the desire for a short walk among the giant redwoods, see the parking lot and trailhead, like, right there, 100 yards away. What you get is an old-growth grove with the classic sword fern-based understory on a flat route that makes for a short, easy walk. At the far end of the loop, you can extend the walk on a 0.2-mile link to the 0.5-mile Mahan Loop Trail. It's very beautiful and the photos are classics. Problem is, you see, it's too close to the highway. You can often hear traffic. We've been here in the winter, though, and it's like a different planet: fewer people, little noise, moist and pristine. Truth is, if you want big trees—without the tourists—go instead to the next hike, just a few minutes away, the Bull Creek Trail North.

User Groups: Hikers only. There is wheelchair access, although the trail is a bit uneven. No dogs, horses, or mountain bikes.

Permits: No permits are required. There is a fee of $8 per vehicle.

Maps: A map is available for a fee from Humboldt Redwoods State Park. For a topographic map, ask the USGS for Weott.

Directions: From Garberville, drive north on U.S. 101 about 20 miles to the Founders Tree/Rockefeller Forest exit. Take that exit and drive a short distance to Avenue of the Giants. Drive 100 yards (cross Avenue of the Giants) to the Founders Grove Parking Area/Trailhead (well signed).

Contact: Humboldt Redwoods State Park, Weott, 707/946-2409, www.parks.ca.gov.

29 BULL CREEK TRAIL NORTH

7.4 mi/4.0 hr 2 10

in Humboldt Redwoods State Park south of Eureka

Map 1.2, page 40 BEST

This trail provides a walk amid the largest grove of old-growth redwood trees in the world. It's easy walking, with maybe a 200-foot rise, that's all. You are amid sorrel, sword ferns, and the redwoods with massive bases that rise up and seem to poke holes in the sky. Start at the trailhead at Bull Creek Flats (signed Lower Bull Creek Flats Trail), a short walk to the Federation Grove. The trail ventures west along Bull Creek, an easy grade as you hike upstream. All the while you're surrounded by forest, both redwoods and firs in a variety of mixes. In summer, there is a seasonal bridge at the Big Trees Area. A little over 3.5 miles in, you'll arrive at the Big Tree Area. There are many redwoods here that range from 5 to 10 feet in diameter and 30 to 40 feet around.

On-the-spot notes: The park installs summer bridges across Bull Creek in the Big Trees Area, mid-May to early October. Also: For years, a big attraction was the Flat Iron Tree, a huge leaning redwood that grew in strange dimensions in order to support itself. Well, it's not leaning anymore, because it fell down and went boom. On the broad side, the Flat Iron Tree measures more than 15 feet. An option: After the trail passes the Big Tree Area, it's routed to the mouth of Albee Creek and ends at Mattole Road. The trailhead here (at Mattole Road) provides a shorter hike of about a mile to the seasonal bridge at the Big Tree Area.

User Groups: Hikers only. No dogs, horses, or mountain bikes. No wheelchair facilities.

Permits: No permits are required. The park entry fee is $8 at the main entrance.

Maps: A map is available for a fee from Humboldt Redwoods State Park. For a topographic map, ask the USGS for Weott.

Directions: From Garberville, drive north on U.S. 101 about 20 miles to the Founders Tree/Rockefeller Forest exit. Take that exit and turn left and drive a short distance to Avenue of the Giants. Turn left and drive a short distance to Mattole Road (the sign will say Rockefeller Forest/Honeydew, not Mattole Road). Turn left and drive 1.3 miles to the Lower Bull Creek Flats trailhead.

Contact: Humboldt Redwoods State Park, Weott, 707/946-2409, www.parks.ca.gov.

30 WILLIAMS GROVE TRAIL

0.5 mi/20.5 hr 1 8

in Humboldt Redwoods State Park south of Eureka

Map 1.2, page 40

The Williams Grove is one of Humboldt's protected groves of old-growth redwoods. The launch point to enjoy this is the Williams Grove Day Use Area, which has a picnic area with barbecue grills along with restrooms. (It used to be free, but easy access and the new mission of California's Department of Parks and Recreation means there is now an $8 fee.) We've always liked to start instead at the trailhead at the Hidden Springs Campground, an easy 1.75-mile walk (one-way). The camp is set in forest just above a big bend in the South Fork Eel River. The trailhead is on the southwest side of the camp. The trail starts out nearly flat, then turns right and parallels the highway. It's easy walking all the way, amid redwoods both young and old. Then the trail crosses under the highway and goes down the hill to Williams Grove. If you camp at Hidden Springs, a short trail is also available that is routed a short distance to the Eel River and Hidden Springs Beach.

User Groups: Hikers only. No dogs, horses, or mountain bikes. No wheelchair facilities.

Permits: No permits are required. The park entry fee is $8 at the main entrance.

Maps: A map is available for a fee from Humboldt Redwoods State Park. For topographic maps, ask the USGS for Weott and Myers Flat.

Directions: From Garberville on U.S. 101, drive north for 16.4 miles to the exit for Myers Flat. Take that exit 0.2 mile to Avenue of the Giants. Turn right and drive 1.2 miles to Williams Grove parking area on the left. For Hidden Springs Campground (open only during the summer), take the same exit. At Avenue of the Giants, instead turn left and drive 0.8 mile the campground and trailhead.

Contact: Humboldt Redwoods State Park, Weott, 707/946-2409, www.parks.ca.gov.

31 LOST COAST TRAIL/ MATTOLE TRAILHEAD

25.7 mi one-way/5 days 5 10

on the Humboldt coast south of Eureka in King Range National Conservation Area

Map 1.2, page 40 **BEST**

For many, this is considered one of the greatest treks on the Pacific Coast. It spans 25 miles on some of the coast's remotest and most beautiful landscapes and beaches. Always do the trip one-way, with a second shuttle car, north-to-south. But get the challenge in focus. Even though you don't face the all-day climbs as with high Sierra passes, it can be no less difficult.

It's called the Lost Coast because of the isolation of the area, which is shielded on all sides by natural boundaries. The route is set on bluffs and beaches from the mouth of the Mattole River south to Shelter Cove. With two vehicles, one parked at each end of the trail, or a shuttle service, hikers can then hike the trail one-way. This hike is best done from north to south. That way the winds out of the north will be at your back, not in your face. Firm-fitting waterproof boots with good, gripping soles are a necessity. They should be firm fitting because some of the walking is in soft sand, waterproof because there are several small creek crossings, and good gripping because some scrambling over wet boulders is required. The trail surface, well, it often isn't much of a trail at all.

This is best way to do it, to end up at spots with good campsites available. The trip starts at the Lost Coast trailhead at the Mattole Campground:

Day 1: Mattole to (past Punta Gorda Lighthouse) Cooskie Creek (right in the middle of an impassable zone at high tide, but lots of good campsites), 6.3 miles

Day 2: To Kinsey, 5.4 miles

Day 3: To Miller Flat (best camping area by far here), 5 miles

Day 4: Gitchell Creek, 5 miles

Day 5: To Black Sands Beach (4 miles)

Note that when you start, do not take the Jeep Trail out of the campground, but rather take the signed trailhead from near the campground.

Bring a tide book. At several spots, you can only pass during low tides, and these are impassable at tides above 3 feet; never attempt when tides are above 3 feet. At high tides in winter, you can face water-covered sections where sneaker waves can carry you out to sea and kill you. In addition, in wet weather, landslides often cover the beach between Shipman and Buck Creeks. At times they are minor, but at other times, the slides can be significant. High tides and/or large swells wash against the base of these slides. During high tides and/or large swells, to pass through this landslide zone may be hazardous.

In summer, the tides, weather, slides, and creeks are far more manageable. Consult your tide book, keep an eye on ocean conditions, and plan to hike during low tides, particularly if ocean swells are large. Be cautious: This is an extremely isolated area. In many parts, there is no trail, and there is a lot of boulder hopping and walking across cobblestones that can be very tiring and tough on ankles, plus a lot of beach walking. Do not rush. Those who do can twist an ankle. In winter after heavy rain, several streams can be impassable.

For a first visit and a great day hike, take the abandoned jeep trail from the campground at Lighthouse Road and head south three miles to the Punta Gorda Lighthouse. You'll get a glimpse of the greatness here, and you might even get the inspiration to continue on Lost Coast Trail, one of California's greatest weekend trips.

User Groups: Hikers, dogs, horses. No wheelchair facilities. Mountain bikes and horses are not advised, and dogs should react to instant voice command.

Permits: Wilderness permits are required through www.recreation.gov. No walk-in permits available. Parking and access are free. Bear-proof containers are required and available for rental at headquarters for King Range National Conservation Area.

Maps: A detailed trail map is available for a fee, and a free map and brochure can be obtained from the Bureau of Land Management at headquarters for King Range National Conservation Area. For topographic maps, ask the USGS for Petrolia, Cooskie Creek, Shubrick Peak, and Shelter Cove.

Directions: Take U.S. 101 to Garberville and then Exit 639B for Redway. Follow that exit 0.2 miles to Redwood Drive. Turn left on Redwood Drive and go 2.6 miles to Briceland Road. Turn left and drive 10 miles, and continue on to Ettersburg/Honeydew Road and drive 5.8 miles (several jogs) to Wilder Ridge Road. Continue on Wilder Ridge Road and drive 13.5 miles to Mattole Road. Bear left on Mattole Road and drive 13.6 miles to Lighthouse Road. Turn left and drive 4.8 miles to the campground and trailhead.

Shuttle: Bill's Lost Coast Shuttle, 707/442-1983; Lost Coast Adventure Tours, www.lostcoastadventures.com, 707/986-9895; Mendo Insider Tours, 707/962-4131, www.mendoinsidertours.com.

Contact: King Range National Conservation Area, 707/986-5400; Bureau of Land Management, Arcata Field Office, Arcata, 707/825-2300, www.blm.gov/visit/king-range.

32 KING CREST TRAIL

12.4 mi/1 day 3 10

in King Range National Conservation Area on the Lost Coast

Map 1.2, page 40

King Peak is one of the most prized destinations in the King Range. At 4,087 feet it's the highest point on the Northern California coast, and from it you get a view that can make you feel that you're perched on top of the world. The ocean seems to stretch on forever to the west, and on a perfect day you can make out Lassen Peak behind the ridgeline of the Yolla Bolly Wilderness to the east. You can see along the Lost Coast and across the Mattole River Valley. But get this one in focus: The road in, Smith-Etter Road, requires four-wheel drive and is open in summer only. One you've arrived at the Northslide Peak trailhead, reaching King Peak requires a 6.2-mile hike. In the process, you climb about 800 feet. Making the trip on a clear day is an absolute necessity, since the climb through the fire zone is buffered by the reward of the sweeping views. Trail signs are very poor, and water supplies at trail camps are from dubious sources, so it's also essential to have a good map and a double-canteen water supply.

The entire King Crest Trail extends 11.4 miles one-way, starting from the trailhead listed in this hike to Saddle Mountain trailhead; then it descends four miles to the beach. That provides the alternative of a one-way overnight trip with a shuttle vehicle at the end of the trail. Note that the portion that heads down to the beach is called Buck Creek Trail and that it is very steep, one the steepest trails in California, with portions difficult to follow—this is considered an advanced hike; for some hikers, orienteering with a map and compass may be required.

User Groups: Hikers, dogs, horses. No mountain bikes past wilderness boundary. No wheelchair facilities.

Permits: Parking and access are free. Permits are required for overnight use through www.recreation.gov. Bear-proof containers are required and available for rental at headquarters for King Range National Conservation Area.

Maps: A detailed trail map is available for a fee, and a free map and brochure can be obtained from the Bureau of Land Management; ask for the King Range Conservation Area map. For a topographic map, ask the USGS for Shubrick Peak.

Directions: On U.S. 101, drive to the South Fork-Honeydew exit (just north of Garberville). Take that exit to Wilder Ridge Road and turn southwest. Drive one mile to Smith-Etter Road and turn west. Drive six miles to the trailhead (this is a primitive, four-wheel-drive road and closed from November 1 to March 31).

Contact: King Range National Conservation Area, 707/986-5400; Bureau of Land Management, Arcata Field Office, Arcata, 707/825-2300, www.blm.gov/visit/king-range.

33 SPANISH RIDGE TRAIL

9.6 mi/1 day 3 8

in King Range National Conservation Area south of Eureka

Map 1.2, page 40

In just a few miles, you can gain access to some of the remotest sections of the California coast. But there's a price (and we'll get to that). The payoffs are excellent views, a descent along a grassy ridge, and then down to a remote beach you'll have all to yourself. One big problem: You descend 2,400 feet to the beach. Know what that means? Right. Unless you can get a helicopter ride back, you're looking at some serious grunt work, climbing 2,400 feet to get back to your car.

To reach the Spanish Ridge trailhead requires traversing Smith-Etter Road, a rough-and-tumble four-wheel-drive route that is open only in summer. From the trailhead, hike 1.8 miles along Cooskie Creek Trail and climb an easy 300 feet before reaching the junction with Spanish Ridge Trail. You then descend 2,400 feet in three miles en route to the coast.

The King Range is very rugged, primitive, and isolated. Thanks to that bumpy access road and the climb on the return trip, it's rare to see other people here. And because there are no water sources along this trail, each hiker should carry two canteens of water. This trail is for experienced hikers only, and as with several of the hikes in the King Range, you should bring a map and a compass.

User Groups: Hikers, dogs, mountain bikes, and horses. No wheelchair facilities.

Permits: Parking and access are free. Permits are required for overnight use through www.recreation.gov. Bear-proof containers are required and available for rental at headquarters for King Range National Conservation Area.

Maps: A detailed trail map is available for a fee, and a free map and brochure can be obtained from the Bureau of Land Management; ask for the King Range Conservation Area map. For topographic maps, ask the USGS for Cooskie Creek and Shubrick Peak.

Directions: On U.S. 101, drive to the South Fork-Honeydew exit (just north of Garberville). Take that exit to Wilder Ridge Road and turn southwest. Drive one mile to Smith-Etter Road and turn west. Drive 10 miles (this is a primitive, four-wheel-drive road and closed from November 1 to March 31) to Telegraph Ridge Road. Turn northwest on Telegraph Ridge Road and drive eight miles to the trailhead gate. In summer, continue driving two miles to the trailhead. When the gate is locked, the trailhead is accessible only by a two-mile walk.

Contact: King Range National Conservation Area, 707/986-5400; Bureau of Land Management, Arcata Field Office, Arcata, 707/825-2300, www.blm.gov/visit/king-range.

34 LOOKOUT POINT LOOP TRAIL

2.6 mi/1.5 hr 2 8

in Richardson Grove State Park south of Garberville

Map 1.2, page 40

Big woods. Big water. That's what Lookout Point Loop Trail supplies, with a tour through giant redwoods culminating at the canyon rim over the South Fork Eel River. Giant redwoods approaching 300 feet tall and estimated to be 1,000 years old are the highlight of Richardson Grove, while younger redwoods, firs, and tan oaks fill out the forest. Park at the visitors center. Start by walking through the old-growth redwoods for the first half mile. The trail crosses the road at the Madrone Campground Loop. Near the restroom, there is a signed trailhead for Lookpoint. The trail then rises through hardwoods (hence the name Madrone) about 300 feet over 0.4 mile to a 0.1-mile spur for Lookout Point. You get an excellent view of the South Fork. You can also see across the river to the Oak Flat Campground. To return, the trail loops back in a short circle over 0.3 mile to the trailhead sign.

As a free-flowing river, the South Fork Eel River can seem like a small trickle in late summer or a howling torrent during peak flows in winter. When looking down from Lookout Point during summer, it may seem hard to imagine how high the Eel has risen in high-water years. In 1955, 1963, 1986, 1997, and 1998, the river actually flooded its banks and wiped out several campgrounds in the state park. This is an easy and popular hike, both for daytime park visitors and for overnighters at Madrone Campground.

User Groups: Hikers only. No dogs, horses, or mountain bikes. No wheelchair facilities.

Permits: No permits are required. A state park entrance fee of $8 is charged per vehicle.

Maps: For a trail guide and brochure (free), write Richardson Grove State Park. For a topographic map, ask the USGS for Garberville.

Directions: From Santa Rosa, drive north on U.S. 101 to Leggett. Continue north on U.S. 101 about 17 miles to the park entrance, on the west side of the highway. Park at the visitors center (for campers, Madrone Campground; trailhead near restroom).

Contact: Richardson Grove State Park, Garberville, 707/247-3318, www.parks.ca.gov.

35 WOODLANDS LOOP TRAIL

1.6 mi/1.0 hr — 1 — 7

in Richardson Grove State Park south of Garberville

Map 1.2, page 40

You want easy? You get easy. You want forest? You get forest. You want a campground trailhead? You get a campground trailhead. The Woodlands Loop, an easy, pretty trail that starts at the Huckleberry Campground, does all that and more. At the campground, the trailhead is near the ranger station. The trail crosses North Creek and then goes through both redwoods and tan oaks that are dense at times. It also includes a gentle uphill portion, rising about 250 feet. At the visitors center, get the brochure for the self-guided Quest Guide, which explains the flora you'll see along the way.

Note that this trail and camp are set on the west side of U.S. 101, and that the South Fork Eel River is on the east side of the highway. There's no direct river access from this trail or the nearby campground.

User Groups: Hikers only. No dogs, horses, or mountain bikes. No wheelchair facilities.

Permits: No permits are required. A fee of $8 per vehicle is charged for parking.

Maps: For a trail guide and brochure (free), contact Richardson Grove State Park. For a topographic map, ask the USGS for Garberville.

Directions: From Santa Rosa, drive north on U.S. 101 to Leggett. Continue north on U.S. 101 about 17 miles to the park entrance, on the west side of the highway. The trailhead is accessible from the parking lot just inside the entrance.

Contact: Richardson Grove State Park, Garberville, 707/247-3318, www.parks.ca.gov.

36 TOUMEY GROVE TRAIL

3.8 mi/2.75 hr — 2 — 9

in Richardson Grove State Park south of Garberville

Map 1.2, page 40

The Toumey Trail is one of Richardson Grove State Park's feature summer hikes (it is not accessible when the river is up in winter). As we say, "The hits just keep on coming." The trailhead is between campsite Nos. 123 and 126 at Oak Flat Campground. The trail crosses the South Fork Eel River on a summer bridge, and then enters the redwoods; take your time and enjoy the surroundings. You are routed through the redwoods. The trail climbs 300 feet, rising quickly to Panorama Point, with excellent views of the Eel River Canyon and Richardson Grove redwoods. It then is routed down, via a few switchbacks, to Kauffman Springs, and then ventures to a swimming hole on the South Fork Eel.

This trail can be accessed only in the summer months.

User Groups: Hikers only. No dogs, horses, or mountain bikes. No wheelchair facilities.

Permits: No permits are required. A fee of $8 per vehicle is charged for parking.

Maps: For a trail guide and brochure (free), contact Richardson Grove State Park. For a topographic map, ask the USGS for Garberville.

Directions: From Santa Rosa, drive north on U.S. 101 to Leggett. Continue north on U.S. 101 about 17 miles to the park entrance, on the west side of the highway. Follow the signs to Oak Flat Campground. The trailhead is between sites 123 and 126.

Contact: Richardson Grove State Park, Garberville, 707/247-3318, www.parks.ca.gov.

SHASTA AND TRINITY

At 14,179 feet, Mount Shasta rises like a diamond in a field of coal. Its sphere of influence spans a radius of 125 miles, and its shadow is felt everywhere in the region. This area has much to offer with giant Shasta Lake, the Sacramento River above and below the lake, the McCloud River, and the wonderful Trinity Divide with its dozens of pretty backcountry lakes and several wilderness areas. This is one of the best regions anywhere for outdoor adventures set near quiet wilderness. The most popular destinations are Shasta Lake, the Trinity Alps and their surrounding lakes and streams, Marble Mountain Wilderness, and the Klamath Mountains.

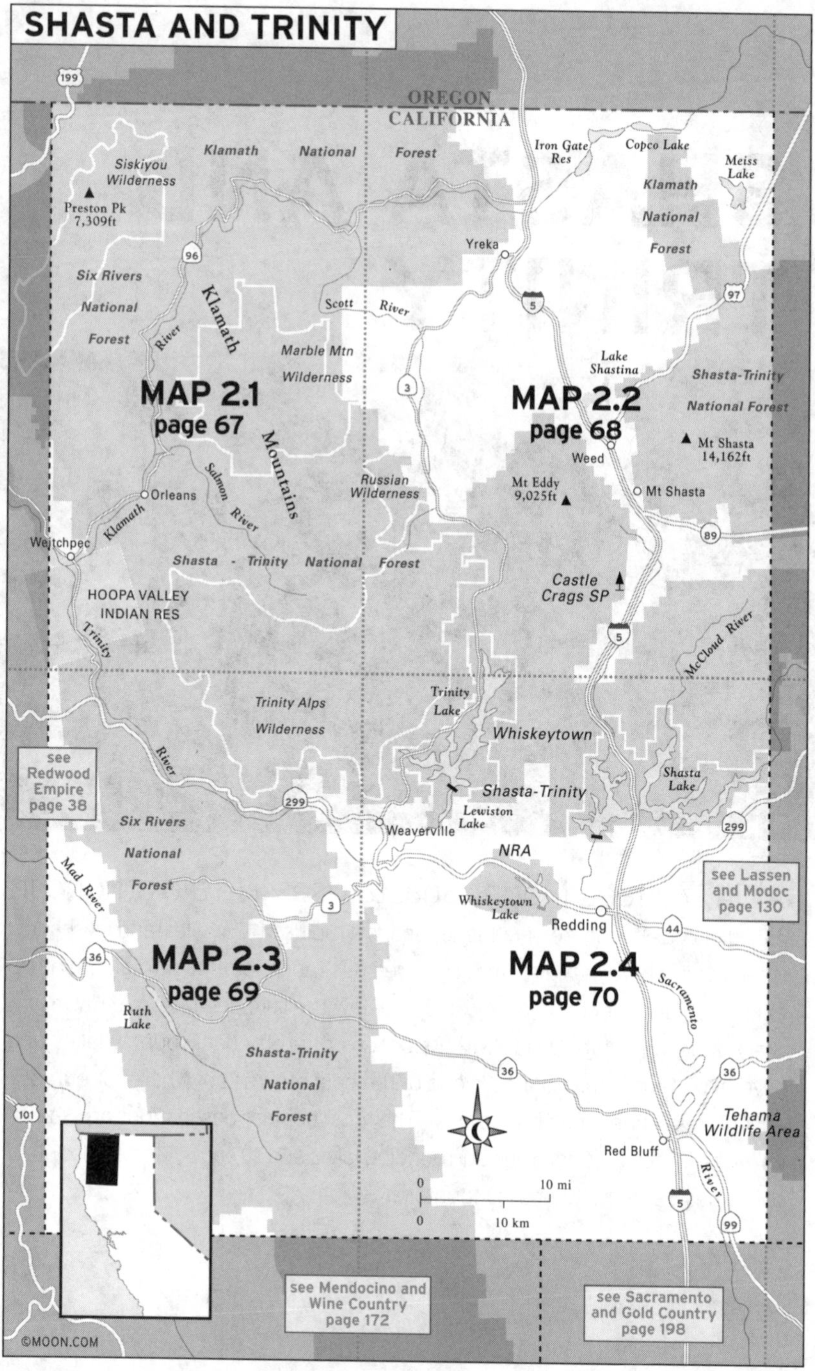

SHASTA AND TRINITY

OREGON
CALIFORNIA
Klamath National Forest
Siskiyou Wilderness
Preston Pk 7,309ft
Iron Gate Res
Copco Lake
Meiss Lake
Klamath National Forest
Yreka
Six Rivers National Forest
Klamath River
Klamath
Scott River
Marble Mtn Wilderness
Lake Shastina
Shasta-Trinity National Forest
MAP 2.1
page 67
MAP 2.2
page 68
Mountains
Weed
Mt Shasta 14,162ft
Salmon River
Russian Wilderness
Mt Eddy 9,025ft
Mt Shasta
Orleans
Klamath
Weitchpec
Shasta - Trinity National Forest
Castle Crags SP
HOOPA VALLEY INDIAN RES
Trinity
McCloud River
Trinity Alps Wilderness
Trinity Lake
Whiskeytown
River
see Redwood Empire page 38
Shasta-Trinity
Shasta Lake
Lewiston Lake
Weaverville
Six Rivers National Forest
NRA
Mad River
see Lassen and Modoc page 130
Whiskeytown Lake
Redding
MAP 2.3
page 69
MAP 2.4
page 70
Sacramento
Ruth Lake
Shasta-Trinity National Forest
Tehama Wildlife Area
Red Bluff
River
0 10 mi
0 10 km
see Mendocino and Wine Country page 172
see Sacramento and Gold Country page 198

Map 2.1

Sites 1-21
Pages 71-87

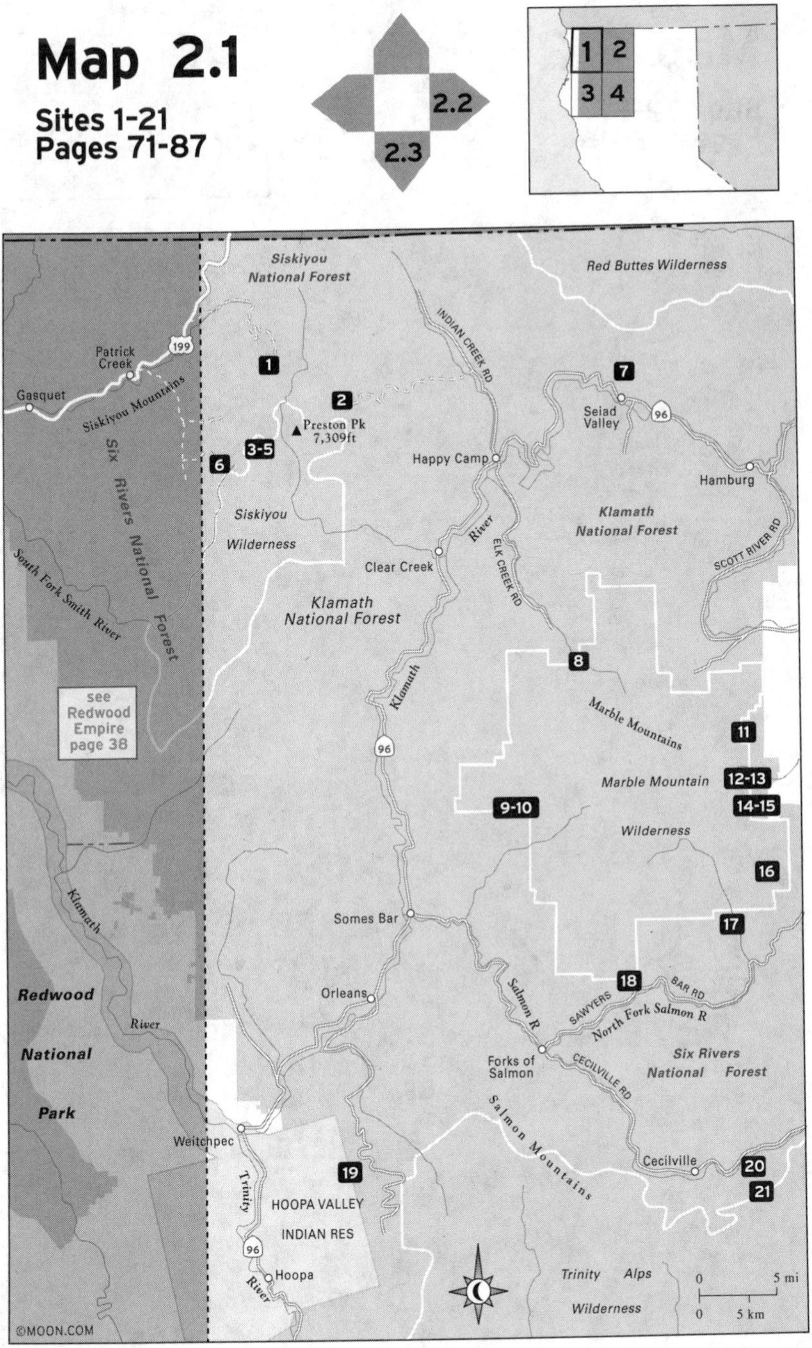

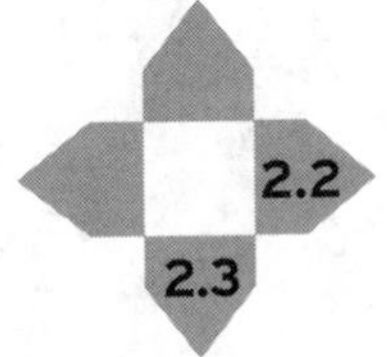

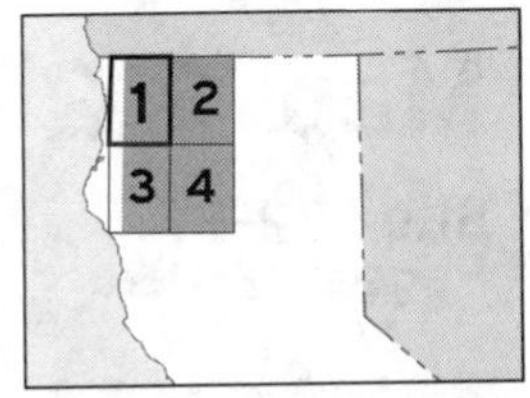

Siskiyou National Forest
Red Buttes Wilderness
INDIAN CREEK RD
199
Patrick Creek
Gasquet
Siskiyou Mountains
1
2
7
Preston Pk 7,309ft
Seiad Valley
96
3-5
6
Happy Camp
Hamburg
Six Rivers National Forest
Siskiyou Wilderness
Klamath National Forest
River
ELK CREEK RD
SCOTT RIVER RD
Clear Creek
South Fork Smith River
Klamath National Forest
8
Klamath
see Redwood Empire page 38
Marble Mountains
11
96
Marble Mountain
12-13
14-15
9-10
Wilderness
16
Klamath
Somes Bar
17
18
BAR RD
Salmon R
SAWYERS
North Fork Salmon R
Redwood
Orleans
River
National
Forks of Salmon
CECILVILLE RD
Six Rivers National Forest
Park
Salmon Mountains
Weitchpec
Cecilville
20
19
21
Trinity
HOOPA VALLEY INDIAN RES
96
Hoopa
River
Trinity Alps Wilderness
0 5 mi
0 5 km
©MOON.COM

Map 2.2

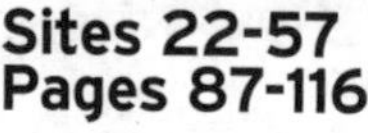

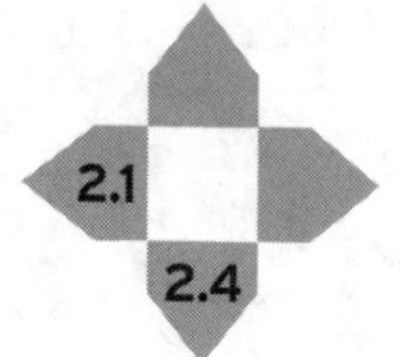

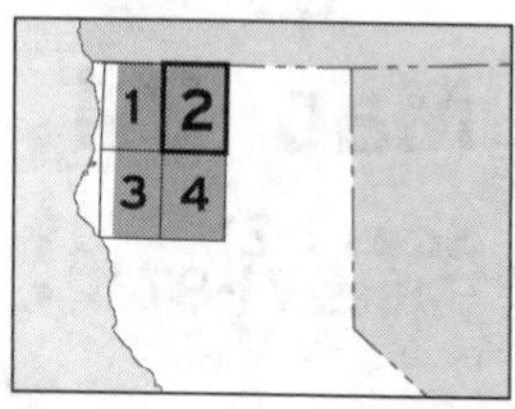

Hilt
Copco Lake
Iron Gate Reservoir
Hornbrook
Klamath River
Klamath River
Klamath National Forest
Scott Bar Mountains
Yreka
Montague
Meiss Lake
Macdoel
Mount Hebron
Grenada
Fort Jones
Deer Mtn 7,006ft
Whaleback 8,528ft
Gazelle
Lake Shastina
Shasta-Trinity National Forest
Etna
GAZELLE – CALLAHAN RD
Weed
Mt Shasta Wilderness
Mt Shasta 14,162ft
EVERETT MEMORIAL HWY
Russian Wilderness
Callahan
Mt Eddy 9,025ft
Mount Shasta
CECILVILLE RD
Klamath National Forest
Shasta-Trinity National Forest
Lake Siskiyou
McCloud
Dunsmuir
Castle Crags State Park
Castella
COFFEE CREEK RD
Trinity Alps Wilderness
Grey Rocks 7,241ft
Shasta-Trinity National Forest
Whiskeytown Shasta-Trinity NRA
Trinity Lake
0 5 mi
0 5 km

22 23 24 25 26 27 28 29 30-31 32 33 34 35 36 37 38 39 40 41 42 43 44 45 46 47 48 49 50 51 52 53-55 56 57

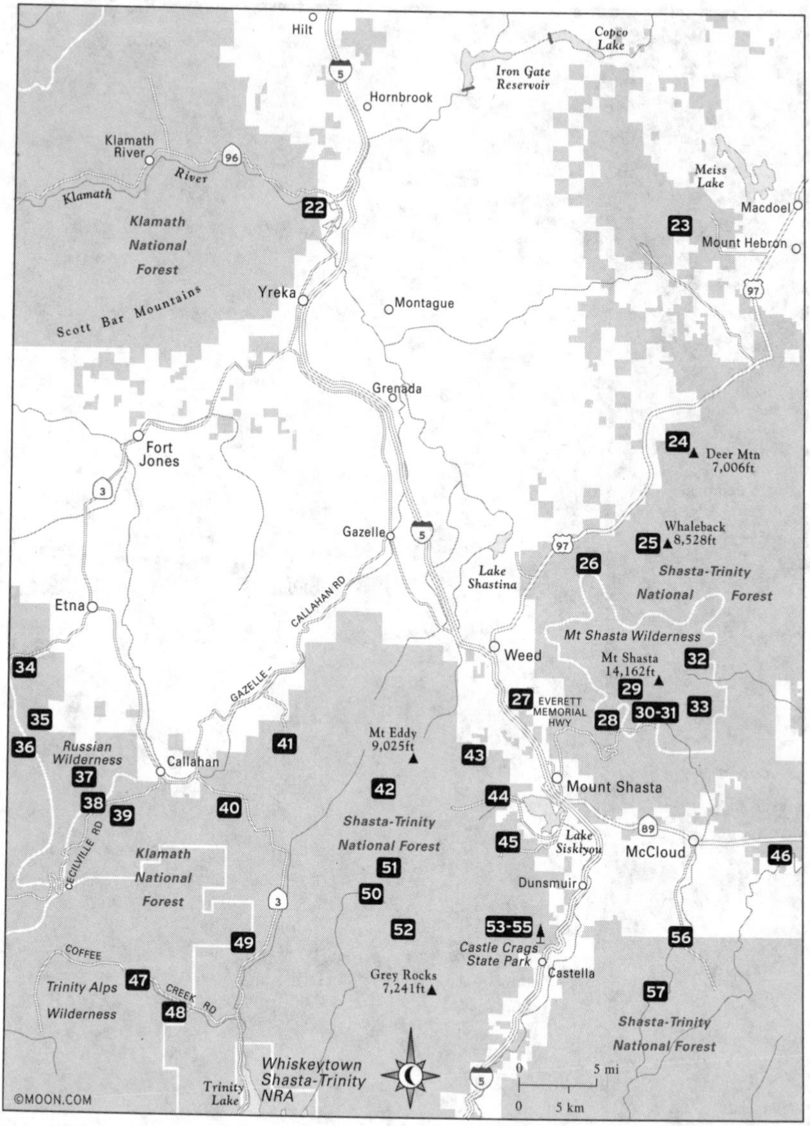

Map 2.3

Sites 58-64
Pages 116-120

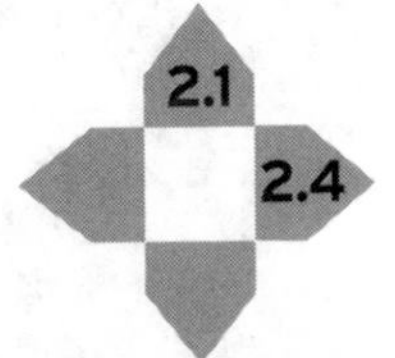

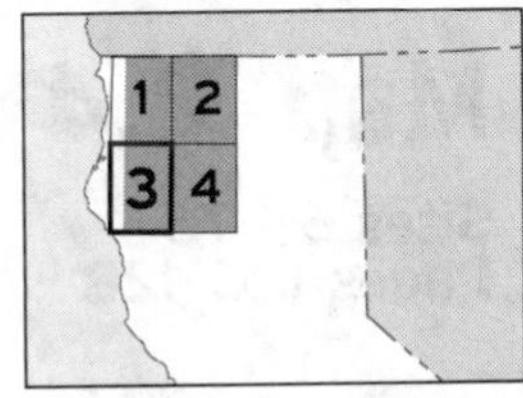

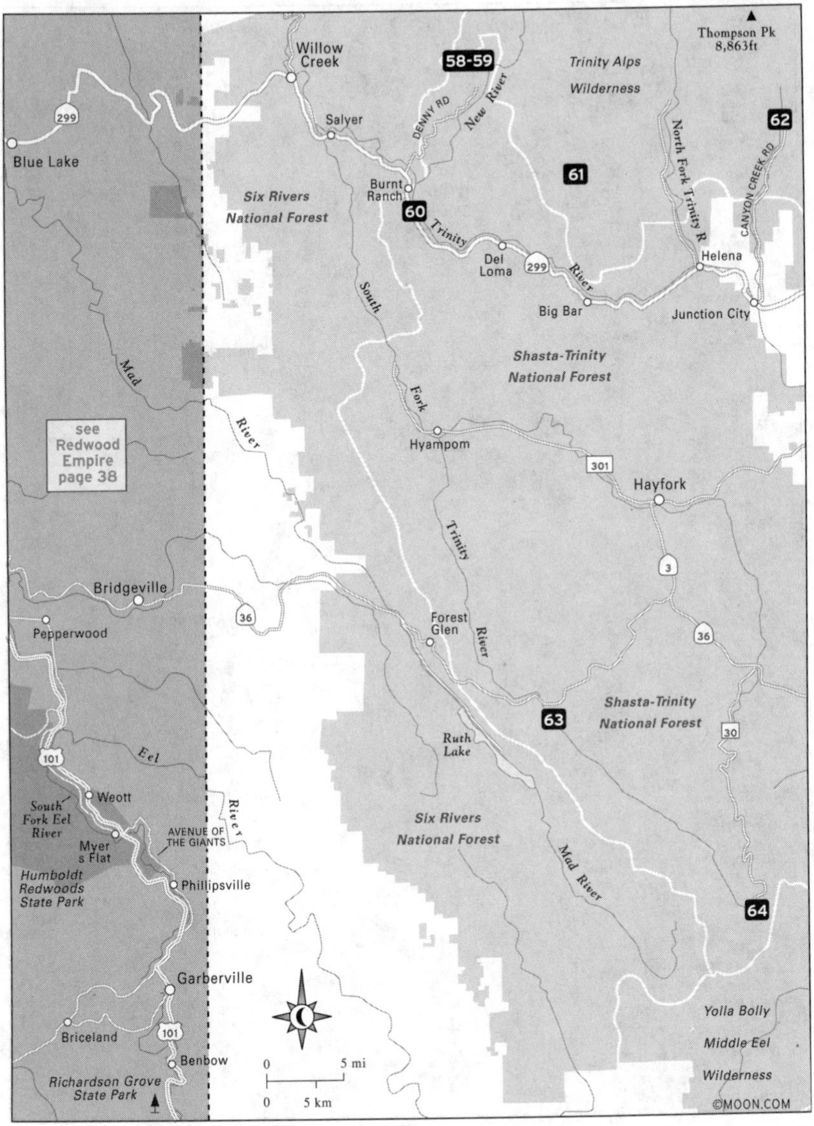

Thompson Pk
8,863ft
Willow Creek
58-59
Trinity Alps Wilderness
DENNY RD
New River
299
Salyer
62
Blue Lake
North Fork Trinity R
CANYON CREEK RD
61
Burnt Ranch
Six Rivers National Forest
60
Trinity
Del Loma
299
River
Helena
South
Big Bar
Junction City
Shasta-Trinity National Forest
Mad
Fork
River
see Redwood Empire page 38
Hyampom
301
Hayfork
Trinity
3
Bridgeville
36
Forest Glen
36
Pepperwood
River
Shasta-Trinity National Forest
63
30
Ruth Lake
101
Eel
Weott
River
South Fork Eel River
Six Rivers National Forest
Myers Flat
AVENUE OF THE GIANTS
River
Mad River
Humboldt Redwoods State Park
Phillipsville
64
Garberville
Yolla Bolly Middle Eel Wilderness
Briceland
101
Benbow
0 5 mi
0 5 km
Richardson Grove State Park

Map 2.4

Sites 65-76
Pages 120-128

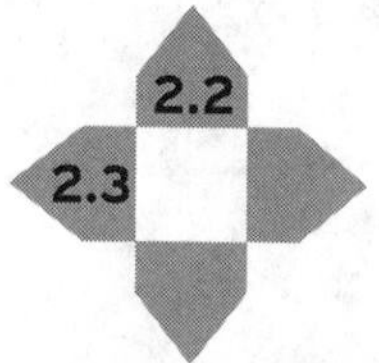

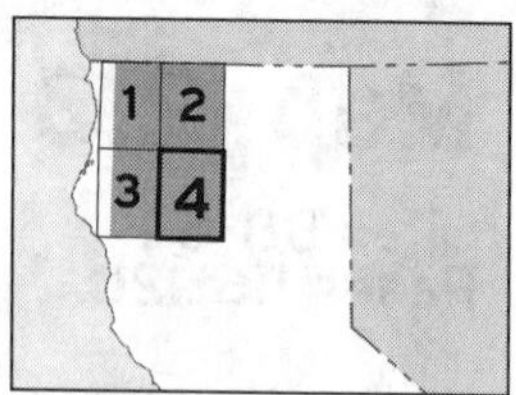

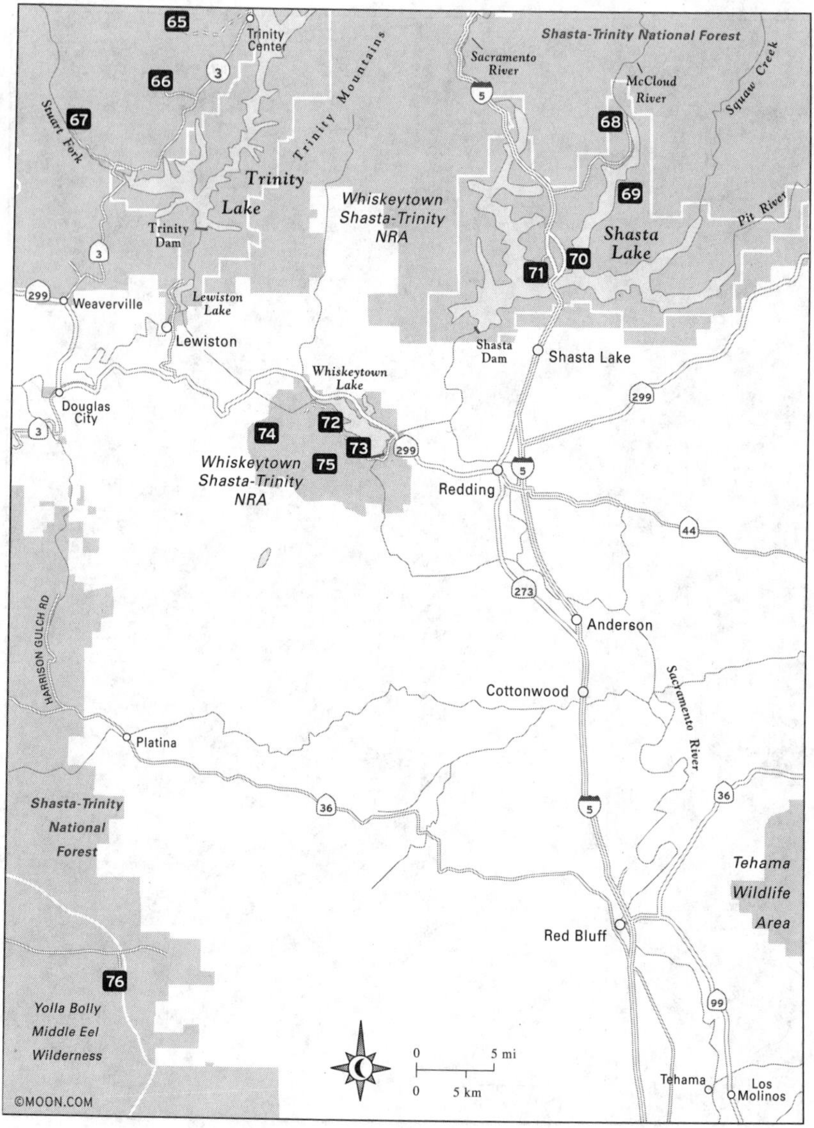

65
Trinity Center
3
66
67
Stuart Fork
Trinity Mountains
Trinity Lake
Trinity Dam
3
299
Weaverville
Lewiston Lake
Lewiston
Douglas City
3
Whiskeytown Shasta-Trinity NRA
Sacramento River
5
Shasta-Trinity National Forest
McCloud River
Squaw Creek
68
69
Pit River
Shasta Lake
70
71
Shasta Dam
Shasta Lake
299
Whiskeytown Lake
72
73
74
75
299
Whiskeytown Shasta-Trinity NRA
Redding
5
44
273
Anderson
Cottonwood
Sacramento River
HARRISON GULCH RD
Platina
36
36
5
Shasta-Trinity National Forest
Tehama Wildlife Area
Red Bluff
76
99
Yolla Bolly Middle Eel Wilderness
0 5 mi
0 5 km
Tehama
Los Molinos
©MOON.COM

1 YOUNGS VALLEY TRAIL

6.0 mi/1 day 2 8

in the Siskiyou Wilderness east of Crescent City

Map 2.1, page 67

The 6.5-mile trip from Youngs Valley down Clear Creek to Youngs Meadow is a beautiful and rewarding trip. The trailhead is at an elevation of 5,400. Youngs Meadow, set at an elevation of 4,500 feet below the western slope of Preston Peak, is very pretty and makes an excellent picnic area and campsite.

The drive to the trailhead is long and circuitous. It's long just to get to U.S. 199, and from there, you face more than an hour on forest roads. The trailhead is near Sanger Lake, and some camp there the first night in. You start the trip by hiking on a decommissioned Forest Service road; it climbs 0.8 mile to a ridge and the boundary for the Siskiyou Wilderness. It turns to trail, then you descend about 1,000 feet over two miles into Youngs Valley and to Clear Creek. Most continue along Clear Creek until they find a site for a trail lunch, and then head back. But listen up, because from here, the ambitious can take this trip farther—much farther. The Youngs Valley Trail is a great first leg of a multiday trip, ultimately where you head either down Clear Creek to Wilderness Falls, which is a very pretty setting (see the listing in this chapter), or to Rattlesnake Meadows on the slopes of Preston Peak, which requires a short but rugged climb.

User Groups: Hikers, dogs, and horses. No mountain bikes. No wheelchair facilities.

Permits: No permits are required. A campfire permit (free) is required for overnight use. Parking and access are free.

Maps: For a map, ask the U.S. Forest Service for Klamath National Forest. For a topographic map, ask the USGS for Devils Punchbowl.

Directions: From Crescent City, drive north on U.S. 101 for three miles to U.S. 199. Bear right (east) on U.S. 199 and drive 32 miles to Forest Road 18N07. Turn right and drive five miles to a signed junction for Forest Road 18N07. Continue on Forest Road 18N07 for 10 miles (slow, twisty) toward Sanger Lake. Just before Sanger Lake, bear right on Forest Road 4803 (signed Youngs Valley Trail) and drive one mile to the end of the road and the trailhead.

Contact: Smith River National Recreation Area, Gasquet, 707/457-3131, www.fs.usda.gov/srnf; Klamath National Forest, Happy Camp-Oak Knoll Ranger District, Happy Camp, 530/493-2243, www.fs.usda.gov/klamath.

2 PRESTON PEAK

19.0 mi/2 days 5 10

in the Siskiyou Wilderness east of Crescent City

Map 2.1, page 67 BEST

Preston Peak is the awesome 7,309-foot monolith that rises above forest for miles in all directions. It has the qualities of a much larger mountain, and at the peak, it feels like you're on top of the world. But a word of caution: Only mountaineers need sign up for this trip. The last mile to reach the summit of Preston Peak is steep, rough, and primitive; it can be scary and dangerous for newcomers to mountaineering. With no marked trail on top, hikers must have the ability to scramble cross-country and recognize any dangerous spots—and then avoid them. That done, you'll gain the top. It's by far the highest spot in the region, with fantastic surrounding views. Even Mount Shasta, way off to the southeast, comes clearly into view, along with the famous peaks in the Trinity Alps and Marble Mountain Wilderness.

The best route to climb Preston Peak is to hike Youngs Valley Trail (see details about Youngs Valley Trail in this chapter) to Youngs Meadow (an easy five miles). Then head down the Clear Creek Trail (another easy mile) to a somewhat faint junction with the Rattlesnake Meadow Trail. Turn left on Rattlesnake Meadow Trail, where you start to climb, including two very steep, rough, and primitive miles to the flank of Preston Peak. At the end of Rattlesnake Meadow Trail, hikers must go cross-country for another mile or so to the Preston Peak Summit. The last mile is a scramble. Pick your route very carefully and make no climbing mistakes. Although this is a nontechnical climb, there is one difficult spot that can be dangerous. You will see it: a mix of shale, loose gravel, and boulders, with no discernible route. Take your time and pick your way up one step at a time.

Note: Always stay off this mountain in wet weather, because the route near the top is very slippery. Always avoid routes that cross through loose shale, which can be extremely dangerous. A fall here can kill you.

User Groups: Hikers only. Dogs are permitted but are strongly not recommended above tree line at Preston Peak. No horses or mountain bikes. No wheelchair facilities.

Permits: A campfire permit is required for overnight use. Parking and access are free.

Maps: For maps, ask the U.S. Forest Service for Six Rivers and Klamath National Forest. For a topographic map, ask the USGS for Devils Punchbowl.

Directions: From Crescent City, drive north on U.S. 101 for three miles to U.S. 199. Bear right (east) on U.S. 199 and drive 32 miles to Forest Road 18N07. Turn right and drive five miles to Forest Road 18N07. Continue on Forest Road 18N07 for 10 (twisty) miles toward Sanger Lake. Just before Sanger Lake, bear right on Forest Road 4803 (signed Youngs Valley Trail) and drive one mile to the trailhead, at the end of the road.

Contact: Klamath National Forest, Happy Camp-Oak Knoll Ranger District, Happy Camp, 530/493-2243, www.fs.usda.gov/klamath; Smith River National Recreation Area, Gasquet, 707/457-3131, www.fs.usda.gov/srnf.

3 DOE FLAT/BUCK LAKE TRAILHEAD

3.4 mi/2.0 hr 2 8

in the Siskiyou Wilderness east of Crescent City

Map 2.1, page 67

Buck Lake is a little emerald jewel surrounded by old-growth firs. It's set in the heart of a wilderness forest at an elevation of 4,300 feet, a destination that makes for an excellent picnic, trail-style. After parking, the first 0.75 mile of this easy hike is on a closed Forest Service road. After that, a trail is routed through forest and then intersects with Buck Lake Trail. Turn right on Buck Lake Trail and hike 0.1 mile to the lake. We found three primitive campsites near the shore. There are plenty of deer and bears in the area, and the brook trout at the lake are abundant, though small. The area has beautiful meadows and forest, including Douglas, white, and red firs, along with some maples. In the fall, the changing colors of the maples add a pretty touch to the trip. The first time we saw Buck Lake was a Memorial Day weekend, the opening day of trout season here, and there were so many rising brook trout that all the dimples on the lake surface looked like raindrops.

Note: Longtime trail users will remember the days when you would drive to Doe Flat and from there hike a half mile to Buck Lake, or venture down the canyon and take a cutoff trail up to Devils Punchbowl, or even continue down the ravine to Clear Creek and Trout Camp. Those days are long gone. Though most people still refer to this trailhead as the Doe Flat trailhead, the closed road and new trail route you a half mile away from Doe Flat, and the trail now has a different route to the connection with the trail to Devils Punchbowl.

User Groups: Hikers, dogs, and horses. No mountain bikes. No wheelchair facilities.

Permits: No permits are required. A campfire permit (free) is required for overnight use. Parking and access are free.

Maps: For a free brochure and hiking guide, write to Smith River National Recreation Area. For a map, ask the U.S. Forest Service for Six Rivers and Klamath National Forest. For a topographic map, ask the USGS for Devils Punchbowl.

Directions: From Crescent City, drive north on U.S. 101 for three miles to U.S. 199. Bear right (east) on U.S. 199 and drive east (past the main entrance to Jedediah Smith Redwoods State Park) and continue just past Hiouchi to South Fork Road. Turn right on South Fork Road (County Road 427) and cross two bridges to a fork. Turn left at the fork and drive 14 miles to Forest Road 16. Turn left and drive about 15 miles (with slow, twisty climbs as the pavement turns to gravel) to the trailhead. Take Doe Flat trailhead.

Note: The former, faster way to reach this trailhead on Little Jones Creek Road/Jawbone Road (Forest Road 16) has been closed indefinitely by a slide.

Contact: Smith River National Recreation Area, Gasquet, 707/457-3131, www.fs.usda.gov/srnf.

4 DEVILS PUNCHBOWL (VIA DOE FLAT/ BUCK LAKE TRAIL)

12.2 mi/1.5 days  5 10

in the Siskiyou Wilderness east of Crescent City

Map 2.1, page 67 BEST

The Punchbowl is a drop-dead beautiful lake, nestled in a glacial cirque with high granite walls towering overhead. The hike includes a steep climb with switchbacks of roughly 1,500 feet over the course of two miles. That aside, this one is paradise found. From the Doe Flat/ Buck Lake trailhead, elevation 3,400 feet, the trip starts with a downhill glide of 0.75 mile on a closed Forest Service road. The trail is routed through forest and then intersects with Buck Lake Trail at 1.4 miles (Buck Lake is only 0.1 mile off to the right). Continue ahead and the trail descends gently through forest for another 1.8 miles to the junction with the Devils Punchbowl Trail. Turn right, and the trail climbs, steeply at times, for 1.2 miles to the lake. When you top the ridge, the route crosses Devils Creek and leaves the forest behind, crossing bare granite domes. The trail is marked by cairns. You pass a smaller lake, cross a rise, and then the beautiful, gemlike Devils Punchbowl awaits. The elevation is 4,700 feet. This place is something of a legend. It's small but pristine, set in a mountain granite bowl, framed by an imposing back wall—a shrine.

Note: The entire region surrounding Devils Punchbowl consists of sheets of bare granite. The few campsites here are merely small, flat sleeping spaces on rock. There is no firewood available, so bring a backpacking stove for cooking. Bring sealable plastic bags to carry out waste. With fresh snow, the trail cairns will be buried and low overcast will cover up landmarks; you need to be an expert with an altimeter, map, and compass to find your way back to the main trail. Guess how we know?

User Groups: Hikers and dogs. No horses or mountain bikes. No wheelchair facilities.

Permits: No permits are required. A campfire permit (free) is required for overnight use. Parking and access are free.

Maps: For a free brochure and hiking guide, write to Smith River National Recreation Area. For a map, ask the U.S. Forest Service for Six Rivers and Klamath National Forest. For a topographic map, ask the USGS for Devils Punchbowl.

Directions: From Crescent City, drive north on U.S. 101 for three miles to U.S. 199. Bear right (east) on U.S. 199 and drive east (past the main entrance to Jedediah Smith Redwoods State Park) and continue just past Hiouchi to South Fork Road. Turn right on South Fork Road (County Road 427) and cross two bridges to a fork with South Fork Road. Turn left at the fork and drive 14 miles to Forest Road 16. Turn left and drive about 15 miles (slow, twisty, climbs, pavement turns to gravel) to the trailhead. Take Doe Flat trailhead.

Note: The former, fast way to reach this trailhead on Little Jones Creek Road/Jawbone Road (Forest Road 16) has been closed indefinitely by a slide.

Contact: Smith River National Recreation Area, Gasquet, 707/457-3131, www.fs.usda.gov/srnf; Klamath National Forest, Happy Camp-Oak Knoll Ranger District, Happy Camp, 530/493-2243, www.fs.usda.gov/klamath.

5 WILDERNESS FALLS

16.0 mi/2 days 3 10

in the Siskiyou Wilderness east of Crescent City

Map 2.1, page 67

Wilderness Falls is a bubbling torrent of water created by Clear Creek. It crashes down through a narrow cascading chute about 35 feet into a boulder, and then pounds its way down into a foaming pool that's 100 feet across. If you can handle the cold water, it's a great swimming hole. Wilderness Falls is one of the great secrets of northwestern California. It's a true hidden jewel, dramatic and pure, untouched and wild.

The recommended route is to start on Clear Creek National Recreation Trail out of Youngs Valley (see *Youngs Valley Trail* in this chapter). The trailhead is at an elevation of 5,400. You start the trip by hiking on a decommissioned Forest Service road; it climbs 0.8 mile to a ridge and the boundary for the Siskiyou Wilderness. It turns to trail, then descends over two miles into Youngs Valley, at an elevation of 4,500 feet, and to Clear Creek. From here, you continue another five miles with a gentle descent the rest of the way. There is an excellent campsite about a quarter of a mile upstream from the falls. It's an easy hike to the waterfall, but the trip back is up all the way and best started very early in the morning, when the temperature is the coolest. There is also a campsite called Trout Camp near the confluence of Doe Creek.

User Groups: Hikers, dogs, and horses. No mountain bikes. No wheelchair facilities.

Permits: A campfire permit (free) is required for overnight use. Parking and access are free.

Maps: For a map, ask the U.S. Forest Service for Six Rivers and Klamath National Forest. For a topographic map, ask the USGS for Devils Punchbowl.

Directions: From Crescent City, drive north on U.S. 101 for three miles to U.S. 199. Bear right (east) on U.S. 199 and drive 32 miles to Forest Road 18N07. Turn right and drive five miles to Forest Road 18N07. Continue on Forest Road 18N07 for 10 (twisty) miles toward Sanger Lake. Just before Sanger Lake, bear right on Forest Road 4803 (signed Youngs Valley Trail) and drive one mile to the trailhead, at the end of the road.

Contact: Klamath National Forest, Happy Camp-Oak Knoll Ranger District, Happy Camp, 530/493-2243, www.fs.usda.gov/klamath; Smith River National Recreation Area, Gasquet, 707/457-3131, www.fs.usda.gov/srnf.

6 ISLAND LAKE TRAIL

13.0 mi/2 days 4 8

in Siskiyou Wilderness east of Crescent City

Map 2.1, page 67

Island Lake is a mountain bowl framed by the back wall of Jedediah Mountain, a wild, primitive area where threatened spotted owls are more common than hikers. The trailhead is now off the road to Doe Flat Road/Forest Road 16 at the Bear Basin area. The hike starts with a walk on a portion of trail (a former road) that is routed down to the South Fork Smith River, where you'll enter the untouched Siskiyou Wilderness. Enjoy the stream and tank up your water bottles. The trail then rises for about three miles. It tops a ridge and turns around a bend, where little Island Lake comes into view. A great sense of relief will wash over you.

There are two excellent camps at the lake, set in trees near the shore. The trout are eager to bite, but most are very small, dinker-size brook trout. A great afternoon side trip is to hike the rim around the lake, which is most easily done in a counterclockwise direction to the top of Jedediah Mountain—a perfect picnic site and a great lookout.

If you hiked to Island Lake back in the day, you will note that the trailhead has been moved a few miles, lengthening the distance to the lake from four miles to 6.5 miles, but easing the severity of the former climb. The former access road has been closed by a slide. In addition, this trailhead keeps vehicles away from the wilderness; a fungus that is most commonly introduced from tires on vehicles can infect Port Orford cedars.

User Groups: Hikers, dogs, and horses. No mountain bikes. No wheelchair facilities.

Permits: A campfire permit is required. Parking and access are free.

Maps: For a free brochure and hiking guide, write to Smith River National Recreation Area. For a map, ask the U.S. Forest Service for Six Rivers and Klamath National Forest. For a topographic map, ask the USGS for Devils Punchbowl.

Directions: From Crescent City, drive north on U.S. 101 for three miles to U.S. 199. Bear right (east) on U.S. 199 and drive east (past the main entrance to Jedediah Smith Redwoods State Park) and continue just past Hiouchi to South Fork Road. Turn right on South Fork Road (County Road 427) and cross two bridges to a fork with South Fork Road. Turn left at the fork and drive 14 miles to Forest Road 16. Turn left and drive about 10 miles (slow, twisty, climbs, pavement turns to gravel) to the trailhead. Note: The trailhead has been moved from its old location. Do not attempt to reach the former trailhead by Jawbone Road, closed indefinitely by a slide.

Contact: Smith River National Recreation Area, Gasquet, 707/457-3131, www.fs.usda.gov/srnf; Klamath National Forest, Happy Camp-Oak Knoll Ranger District, Happy Camp, 530/493-2243, www.fs.usda.gov/klamath.

7 SEIAD VALLEY TO OREGON BORDER (PCT)

36.0 mi one-way/3 days 

in Klamath National Forest from Seiad Valley to the Siskiyou Mountains

Map 2.1, page 67

The few people you see on this section of the Pacific Crest Trail (PCT) are through-hikers heading to Canada. It is the northernmost segment of the PCT in California. But it's a memorable chunk of trail, whether for a day hike or for the whole duration, all the way to Wards Fork Gap, on the edge of the Rogue Wilderness in southern Oregon. The ambitious few will head up from the trailhead to the junction of the Boundary National Recreation Trail, a seven-mile trip one-way. From Seiad Valley, elevation 1,443 feet, the first five miles are a steep climb out of the Klamath River Valley. You climb 4,600 feet to Upper Devils Peak at an elevation of 6,040 feet. This features sensational views to the south of 14,179-foot Mount Shasta.

This hike marks the final steps of the 1,700-mile Pacific Crest Trail in California, an epic journey for all, but always classic, even if only sections are enjoyed. If you decide to attempt the south-to-north route, see the *Grider Creek to Seiad Valley (PCT)* hike in this chapter.

User Groups: Hikers, dogs, and horses. No mountain bikes. No wheelchair facilities.

Permits: No permits are required. Parking and access are free. A single permit is required to hike the Pacific Crest Trail. Contact the national forest, Bureau of Land Management (BLM), or national park office at your point of entry for a combined permit that is good for traveling through multiple-permit areas during your dates of travel.

Maps: A trail information sheet can be obtained by contacting the Happy Camp-Oak Knoll Ranger District. For a map, ask the U.S. Forest Service for Klamath National Forest. For a topographic map, ask the USGS for Seiad Valley.

Directions: From Yreka, take I-5 north to

Highway 96. Turn west on Highway 96 and drive approximately 50 miles to Seiad Valley. Continue another mile west on Highway 96 to the trailhead, on the north (right) side. Parking is minimal; park across the highway.

Contact: Klamath National Forest, Headquarters, Yreka, 530/842-6131, www.fs.usda.gov/klamath.

8 GRIDER CREEK TO SEIAD VALLEY (PCT)

7.0 mi one-way/1 day 

in Klamath National Forest, southeast of Happy Camp to the Grider Creek Trailhead

Map 2.1, page 67

Most hikers use this trailhead to head south into the Marble Mountain Wilderness, not north. For PCT hikers heading south to north, the trail is seven miles one-way, with an additional five miles of road to Seiad Valley on Highway 96. This is an excellent place for PCT hikers to pick up a food stash and dump garbage. You could walk the road, but most try to hitch a ride. The trail here follows Grider Creek, an easy descent northward as the stream pours toward the Klamath River. The only downer is that the last three miles are on a dirt Forest Service road, but for PCT hikers, it's a sign that the next restaurant is not far off. The area features magnificent stands of virgin timber—a mixed conifer forest of cedar, pine, and fir. A good Forest Service campground (Grider Creek Camp) is available about three miles before reaching Seiad Valley.

To pick up the next trail heading for the Oregon border, see the *Seiad Valley to Oregon Border (PCT)* hike in this chapter. If you are hiking this trail in reverse, see the *Etna Summit to Grider Creek (PCT)* hike in this chapter to continue south.

User Groups: Hikers, dogs, and horses. No mountain bikes. No wheelchair facilities.

Permits: A campfire permit (free) is required. Parking and access are free. A single permit is required to hike the Pacific Crest Trail. Contact the national forest, Bureau of Land Management (BLM), or national park office at your point of entry for a combined permit that is good for traveling through multiple-permit areas during your dates of travel.

Maps: A trail information sheet can be obtained by contacting the Happy Camp-Oak Knoll Ranger District. For a map, ask the U.S. Forest Service for Klamath National Forest. For a topographic map, ask the USGS for Seiad Valley.

Directions: From Yreka, take I-5 north to Highway 96. Turn west on Highway 96 and drive approximately 40 miles to Walker Creek/Grider Creek Road (Forest Road 46N64) one mile before Seiad Valley. Turn left on Walker Creek Road and drive about 50 feet (staying to the left as it runs adjacent to the Klamath River) to Grider Creek Road. Turn right and drive two miles to the trailhead.

Contact: Klamath National Forest, Headquarters, Yreka, 530/842-6131, www.fs.usda.gov/klamath.

9 HAYPRESS MEADOWS TRAILHEAD

29.0 mi/3 days 

in the Marble Mountain Wilderness near Somes Bar

Map 2.1, page 67 BEST

The Cuddihy Lakes basin is one of the prettiest sections of the Marble Mountain Wilderness. It also is home to one of the largest concentrations of bears anywhere in California. This is a great trip, leading out to One Mile Lake and the Cuddihy Lakes. This area is perfect for backpacking, with beauty, lookouts, and good trail access. You'll see some remnants of past forest fires, but much of the area is a mix of high-country granite and sparse conifers that burned in a mosaic, so the impact is often fleeting and passing.

Park at the trailhead (at 4,500 feet), then

Monument Lake out of Haypress Meadows trailhead

begin the first two miles of trail, up and across a fir-covered slope of a small peak (a little butt-kicker of a climb). Then the trail descends into Haypress Meadows, a major junction. Turn right and head up Sandy Ridge, which is a long, steady climb. Plan to top the ridge and then camp at Monument Lake, Meteor Lake, One Mile Lake, or Cuddihy Lakes. The view from Sandy Ridge is a sweeping lookout of the Marble Mountains to the east and the Siskiyous to the west, with mountaintop glimpses of Mount Shasta and the Marble Rim. You can often see elk at Monument Lake and the meadow just beyond the lake.

User Groups: Hikers, dogs, and horses. No mountain bikes. No wheelchair facilities.

Permits: A campfire permit (free) is required for overnight use. Parking and access are free.

Maps: A trail information sheet can be obtained by contacting the Ukonom Ranger District. For a map, ask the U.S. Forest Service for Klamath National Forest or Marble Mountain Wilderness. For a topographic map, ask the USGS for Somes Bar.

Directions: From Willow Creek, at the junction of Highways 299 and 96, take Highway 96 north (twisty at first) for 42 miles to Orleans. Continue eight miles to Somes Bar and Salmon River Road. Turn right on Salmon River Road (Highway 93) and drive 100 feet to a sign that says Camp 3/Haypress Trailhead and Forest Road 15N17 (Offield Mountain Road). Turn left and drive 14.6 miles to Forest Road 15N17E. Turn left and drive 1.5 miles to the access road for Haypress trailhead. Turn left and drive one mile to the trailhead.

Contact: Six Rivers National Forest, Orleans/Ukonom Ranger District, Orleans, 530/627-3291, www.fs.usda.gov/srnf.

10 SPIRIT LAKE TRAIL

34.0 mi/4 days 3 10

in the Marble Mountain Wilderness near Somes Bar

Map 2.1, page 67 **BEST**

We've hiked to hundreds and hundreds of mountain lakes, and Spirit Lake is one of the prettiest we've ever seen. It sits at the bottom of a mountain bowl encircled by old-growth trees, with a few campsites set at the side of the lake. Spirit Lake can be the feature destination for a weeklong backpack loop. Start your trek at the Haypress Meadows trailhead, which is routed up to Sandy Ridge. Most hikers will stop for the night at One Mile or the Cuddihy Lakes on the way out, and that is why those two areas get so much use. On the second or third day, continue to Spirit Lake, about 17 miles one-way. Spirit Lake is best visited in June, when the nights are still cold, the people are few, and the area abounds with fish and deer.

The Karuk Tribe considers Spirit Lake a sacred place, and visit as such. The abundance of wildlife can be remarkable. The far side of the lake is a major deer migration route, ospreys make regular trips to pluck trout out of the lake for dinner, and the fishing is quite good, especially early in the summer.

User Groups: Hikers, dogs, and horses. No mountain bikes. No wheelchair facilities.

Permits: A campfire permit (free) is required for overnight use. Parking and access are free.

Maps: A trail information sheet can be obtained by contacting the Orleans/Ukonom Ranger District. For a map, ask the U.S. Forest Service for Klamath National Forest or Marble Mountain Wilderness. For a topographic map, ask the USGS for Somes Bar.

Directions: From Willow Creek, at the junction of Highways 299 and 96, take Highway 96 north (twisty at first) for 42 miles to Orleans. Continue eight miles to Somes Bar and Salmon River Road. Turn right on Salmon River Road (Highway 93) and drive 100 feet to a sign that says Camp 3/Haypress Trailhead and Forest Road 15N17 (Offield Mountain Road). Turn left and drive 14.6 miles to Forest Road 15N17E. Turn left and drive 1.5 miles to the access road for Haypress trailhead. Turn left and drive one mile to the trailhead.

Contact: Six Rivers National Forest, Orleans/Ukonom Ranger District, Orleans, 530/627-3291, www.fs.usda.gov/srnf.

11 KELSEY CREEK TRAIL

18.0 mi/2 days 3 9

in the Marble Mountain Wilderness west of Yreka

Map 2.1, page 67

This section of the Kelsey Creek Trail offers many miles of beautiful streamside travel. For most hikers on the "Old Kelsey Trail," as we call it, the Paradise Lake basin is the intended destination. The trailhead for this section is set near the confluence of Kelsey Creek and the Scott River, and from there, the trail follows Kelsey Creek upstream. Wildflowers are abundant in the meadows. After four miles and two creek crossings, you'll reach Maple Falls, one of the few waterfalls in the region. The trail continues up the canyon, finally rising to intersect with the Pacific Crest Trail, just below Red Rock. From this junction, hikers have many options. The closest lake is secluded Bear Lake, a pretty spot with a nice campsite, but, alas, with some tules and mosquitoes; to reach it from the junction requires a short but steep drop into the basin to the immediate west. For Paradise Lake, actually a small, shallow lake that is meadowing out, turn left on the PCT.

User Groups: Hikers, dogs, and horses. No mountain bikes. No wheelchair facilities.

Permits: A campfire permit (free) is required for overnight use. Parking and access are free.

Maps: A trail information sheet can be obtained by contacting the Scott River Ranger District. For a map, ask the U.S. Forest Service for Klamath National Forest or Marble Mountain Wilderness. For topographic maps, ask the USGS for Scott Bar and Grider Valley.

Directions: From Redding, take I-5 to Yreka and the exit for Highway 3/Fort Jones. Take that exit to the stop sign, turn left, and drive a short distance to the lighted intersection. Turn left on Highway 3 and drive 16.5 miles to Fort Jones and Scott River Road. Turn right on Scott River Road and drive 16.8 miles to the Scott River Bridge. Cross it and then turn left immediately, following the road for 0.3 mile.

Bear right on another dirt road (do not continue to a second bridge) and drive 0.25 mile to the trailhead.

Contact: Klamath National Forest, Salmon/Scott River Ranger District, Fort Jones, 530/468-5351, www.fs.usda.gov/klamath.

12 PARADISE LAKE TRAIL

4.0 mi/2.75 hr

in the Marble Mountain Wilderness west of Yreka

Map 2.1, page 67

This trail takes you on a climb through forest, where you pop out at the PCT and nearby Paradise Lake at the foot of Kings Castle. The first two miles climb 1,300 feet, with only occasional switchbacks to ease the gradient. The shade is a relief, even on a cool mountain morning, and you pass a mixed forest with hardwoods that transitions into conifers as you rise up, with occasional lush beds of bracken ferns. You then emerge from forest and hit the Pacific Crest Trail. It feels like you are walking through a door into a special world. You turn right for a break at Paradise Lake, a small shallow lake, just five acres, that is slowly filling in this century to a meadow. Kings Castle, a massive outcrop with a vertical face, looms directly above. A small spring, a steady trickle of cold, clean water, is just above the head of the lake in a tiny ravine, a must-know for PCT hikers and as sweet-tasting as anywhere in the world. The lake has a few shaded campsites. This is the shortest hike to a lakeside campsite in the Marble Mountain Wilderness, with many excellent side trips, including climbing Kings Castle (see the following hike).

User Groups: Hikers, dogs, and horses. No mountain bikes. No wheelchair facilities.

Permits: No permits are required. A campfire permit (free) is required for overnight use. Parking and access are free.

Maps: A trail information sheet can be obtained by contacting the Scott River Ranger District. For a map, ask the U.S. Forest Service for Klamath National Forest or Marble Mountain Wilderness. For topographic maps, ask the USGS for Scott Bar and Marble Mountain.

Directions: From Redding, take I-5 north for 95 miles to Yreka and the exit for Highway 3/Fort Jones-Etna. At the stop sign, turn left and drive 0.1 mile (beneath underpass) to the intersection at Highway 3. Turn left and drive 15.4 miles to Fort Jones and Scott River Road. At Scott River Road, turn right and drive 14 miles to Indian Scotty Campground Road/Forest Road 44N45. Turn left to drive over the Scott River Bridge, and continue on Forest Road 44N45 for about five miles to a signed turn for Paradise Lake Trailhead. Bear right, and follow the dirt road for six miles to the parking area.

Contact: Klamath National Forest, Salmon/Scott River Ranger District, Fort Jones, 530/468-5351, www.fs.usda.gov/klamath.

13 KINGS CASTLE TRAIL

7.0 mi/1 day 5 10

in the Marble Mountain Wilderness west of Yreka

Map 2.1, page 67

Kings Castle is the awesome crag that towers over Paradise Lake. To claim it, your mission is to ascend 2,500 feet over 3.5 miles, with the last mile or so a faint route, steep and rocky, not marked on maps. Your reward is a world-class view: To the south, you can see 6,990-foot Marble Mountain, a megalith of white, marbleized limestone. Nearby is Black Marble. In the distance is Boulder Peak, 8,220 feet, the highest point in the Marbles. It can feel like a kill-me, eat-me trek, but is short enough to do round-trip in a day. The first section is from the trailhead to Paradise Lake (the previous hike, this chapter). At the Pacific Crest Trail, turn right for a short distance to a spur for adjacent Paradise Lake on your left. From the campground, walk toward the head of the lake and you'll find a spring with sweet, cold, pure water. Tank up. The route to Kings Castle is right there. Cross that little creek and start on a clear route through vegetation. It emerges in rock, where a faint route arcs around the southern side of the lake and then up a steep canyon. Every step of the way, Kings Castle looms ahead. At times, the trail disappears in rock and the hike becomes an act of faith. Then you'll see a trail cairn and realize you're on course after all. A towering escarpment rises up to your left. As you emerge from the canyon, you'll arrive at a saddle below the final ridge. The final push is up the back of the Castle. En route, you pass the blackened remains of a pine turned into charcoal from a lightning strike. From the top, you can see across the interior of the Marble Mountain Wilderness and to a half dozen significant mountain peaks. Directly across is a full frontal view of Marble Mountain and adjacent Black Marble. Spectacular! Below, Paradise Lake looks like an emerald pond. The trip passed our test: more bears than people.

User Groups: Hikers only. No dogs, horses, or mountain bikes. No wheelchair facilities.

Permits: No permits are required. A campfire permit (free) is required for overnight use. Parking and access are free.

Maps: A trail information sheet can be obtained by contacting the Scott River Ranger District. For a map, ask the U.S. Forest Service for Klamath National Forest or Marble Mountain Wilderness. For topographic maps, ask the USGS for Scott Bar and Marble Mountain.

Directions: From Redding, take I-5 north for 95 miles to Yreka and the exit for Highway 3/Fort Jones-Etna. At the stop sign, turn left and drive 0.1 mile (beneath underpass) to the intersection at Highway 3. Turn left and drive 15.4 miles to Fort Jones and Scott River Road. At Scott River Road, turn right and drive 14 miles to Indian Scotty Campground Road/Forest Road 44N45. Turn left to drive over the Scott River Bridge, and continue on Forest Road 44N45 for about five miles to a signed turn for Paradise Lake Trailhead. Bear right, and follow the dirt road for six miles to the parking area.

Contact: Klamath National Forest, Salmon/Scott River Ranger District, Fort Jones, 530/468-5351, www.fs.usda.gov/klamath.

14 MARBLE MOUNTAIN RIM

14.0 mi/2 days 3 10

in the Marble Mountain Wilderness west of Yreka

Map 2.1, page 67

Marble can seem like a gemstone for hikers on this trail. The trek to the Marble Mountain Rim is an off-trail side trip from the Pacific Crest Trail. You end up walking along the top of this wide-topped megalith of marbleized limestone with a variety of shades, white to black, with black marble at the summit. It tops out at 6,990 feet. The trailhead at Lovers Camp, elevation 4,300 feet, is one of the most popular in the wilderness, with the road paved, ideal for packers going by horse into Marble Mountain Wilderness (corrals and a campground are available near the trailhead). The route heads up Canyon Creek, a moderate climb of 1,200 over four miles, past several creeks and a waterfall, and continues on to the junction with the Pacific Crest Trail. Turn north on the PCT for a short distance, about 10 minutes, and look for a route on the left. This spur climbs steeply up to Marble Gap, and mountaineers can trek to the Marble Rim. (The late, great Foonsky led our trip here to the rim.) With a topo map, it is not difficult to figure your route along the rim. The views are stunning, sweeping in both directions, with steep drop-offs adding to the quiet drama. The rock itself is unlike anything else in Northern California—a mix of white, black, red, and tan marble, something you'll never forget. To extend your trip by several days, venture to the Sky High Lakes, Little Elk Lake, Deep Lake, or Rainy Lake.

User Groups: Hikers only. No dogs, horses, or mountain bikes. No wheelchair facilities.

Marble Mountain from Kings Castle Trail

Permits: A campfire permit (free) is required for overnight use. Parking and access are free.
Maps: A trail information sheet can be obtained by contacting the Scott River Ranger District. For a map, ask the U.S. Forest Service for Klamath National Forest or Marble Mountain Wilderness. For topographic maps, ask the USGS for Scott Bar and Marble Mountain.
Directions: From Redding, take I-5 north for 95 miles to Yreka and the exit for Highway 3/Fort Jones-Etna. At the stop sign, turn left and drive 0.1 mile (beneath underpass) to the intersection at Highway 3. Turn left and drive 15.4 miles to Fort Jones and Scott River Road. At Scott River Road, turn right and drive 14 miles to Indian Scotty Campground Road/Forest Road 44N45 for eight miles to the campground spur on left. Continue a short distance to the end of the road, signed Lovers Camp Trailhead.
Contact: Klamath National Forest, Salmon/Scott River Ranger District, Fort Jones, 530/468-5351, www.fs.usda.gov/klamath.

15 SKY HIGH LAKES

13.1 mi/2 days 3 10

in the Marble Mountain Wilderness west of Yreka

Map 2.1, page 67

The Sky High Lakes make for a great overnighter, roughly a 6.5-mile hike each day, or an inspired one-day in-and-outer. From the Lovers Camp trailhead, elevation 4,300 feet, you take the Canyon Creek Trail (the creek is far below you on the left) for four miles with a 550-foot climb to a junction (a short distance past a small waterfall). Turn left (if you instead turn right, you will be routed past the Marble Valley and up to the east foot of Marble Mountain) and the trail is routed through forest and climbs over a sub-ridge, and then descends to beautiful Lower Sky High Lake. Just above is Upper Sky High Lake, connected by a small stream, and nearby is little Frying Pan Lake. Just to the south, a massive rock wall and outcrop provide a gorgeous backdrop. This is one of the prettiest settings in the Marbles.

User Groups: Hikers, dogs, and horses. No mountain bikes. No wheelchair facilities.
Permits: A campfire permit is required only for hikers planning to camp in the wilderness. Parking and access are free.
Maps: A trail information sheet can be obtained by contacting the Scott River Ranger District. For a map, ask the U.S. Forest Service for Klamath National Forest or Marble Mountain Wilderness. For a topographic map, ask the USGS for Marble Mountain.
Directions: From Redding, take I-5 north for 95 miles to Yreka and the exit for Highway 3/Fort Jones-Etna. At the stop sign, turn left and drive 0.1 mile (beneath underpass) to the intersection at Highway 3. Turn left and drive 15.4 miles to Fort Jones and Scott River Road. At Scott River Road, turn right and drive 14 miles to Indian Scotty Campground Road/Forest Road 44N45 for eight miles to the campground spur on left. Continue a short distance to the end of the road, signed Lovers Camp Trailhead.
Contact: Klamath National Forest, Salmon/Scott River Ranger District, Fort Jones, 530/468-5351, www.fs.usda.gov/klamath.

16 SHACKLEFORD CREEK TRAIL

13.0 mi/2 days — 4 — 8

in the Marble Mountain Wilderness west of Yreka

Map 2.1, page 67

Campbell, Cliff, and Summit Lakes are three pretty lakes in the Marble Mountain Wilderness. The trailhead elevation is 4,400 feet. It is 5.5 miles to Campbell Lake, your first destination. You reach Campbell Lake via the Shackleford Trail, close enough for an ambitious day hike. That makes this a popular destination all summer long for those who know about it. The trail is routed up Shackleford Creek to a basin set just below the Pacific Crest Trail. Here you'll find the series of small mountain lakes.

There is no direct connection to the Pacific Crest Trail. Note that trekkers traveling off-trail, cross-country style, can then create routes to little Gem, Jewel, and Angel Lakes. Trekking is not for everybody, however, which is why this trip rates a 4 out 5 in difficulty. If you want to extend the trip into a loop, you can hike up to the rim of the Pacific Crest Trail, then turn right and go three miles to the Sky High Lakes. Excellent.

User Groups: Hikers, dogs, and horses. No mountain bikes. No wheelchair facilities.
Permits: A campfire permit is required only for hikers planning to camp in the wilderness. Parking and access are free.
Maps: A trail information sheet can be obtained by contacting the Scott River Ranger District. For a map, ask the U.S. Forest Service for Klamath National Forest or Marble Mountain Wilderness. For a topographic map, ask the USGS for Boulder Peak.
Directions: From Redding, take I-5 to Yreka and the exit for Highway 3/Fort Jones. Take that exit to the stop sign, turn left, and drive a short distance to the lighted intersection. Turn left on Highway 3 and drive 16.5 miles to Fort Jones and Scott River Road. Turn right on Scott River Road and drive seven miles to Quartz Valley Road. Turn left on Quartz Valley Road and drive about four miles to the sign for Shackleford trailhead and Forest Road 43N21. Turn right and drive 6.5 miles to the trailhead, at the end of the road.
Contact: Klamath National Forest, Salmon/Scott River Ranger District, Fort Jones, 530/468-5351, www.fs.usda.gov/klamath.

17 MULE BRIDGE TRAILHEAD

28.0 mi/4 days — 5 — 8

in the Marble Mountain Wilderness west of Etna

Map 2.1, page 67

The trailhead at Mule Bridge is set alongside the Salmon River; once you've tightened your backpack, get ready for a long climb up the river drainage. The trailhead elevation is only 2,800 feet. Afternoons are hot and the climb sticky. The trail follows the Salmon River all the way up to its headwaters, and in the process, you gain nearly 3,500 feet. Plan on climbing for 14 or 15 miles along the river until you reach the higher country where there are many lakeside camps. The trail forks eight miles from the trailhead. The right-hand fork leads to Shelly Meadows and the Pacific Crest Trail.

The main trail continues north for access to Upper Abbotts Camp and many lakes in the upper drainage. This trail ties in with Little North Fork Trail near Hancock Lake. The prettiest glacial-formed lakes in this region are Lake of the Island (12-mile hike), Abbott Lake (13-mile hike), and Lake Ethel (14-mile hike). Even remoter lakes are Wooley Lake, Milne Lake, and Osprey Lake. All of these are hard to reach and require cross-country travel. Several other lakes are in the region, allowing this trek to be extended by several days. The long, hot climb out of Quartz Valley, compared to the steady and shorter climbs from Lovers Camp and Paradise Lake trailhead, is why few use this trailhead.

User Groups: Hikers, dogs, and horses. No mountain bikes. No wheelchair facilities.

Permits: A campfire permit (free) is required for campfires and stoves. Parking and access are free.

Maps: A trail information sheet can be obtained by contacting the Salmon Ranger District. For a map, ask the U.S. Forest Service for Klamath National Forest or Marble Mountain Wilderness. For a topographic map, ask the USGS for Sawyers Bar.

Directions: From Redding, take I-5 to Yreka and the exit for Highway 3/Fort Jones. Take that exit to the stop sign, turn left, and drive a short distance to the lighted intersection. Turn left on Highway 3 and drive southwest 28 miles to Etna. Turn west on Etna-Somes Bar Road (which is Main Street in town) and drive 21 miles to Idlewild Campground. As you enter the campground, take the left fork in the road and continue two miles to the trailhead.

Contact: Klamath National Forest, Salmon/Scott River Ranger District, Fort Jones, 530/468-5351, www.fs.usda.gov/klamath.

18 LITTLE NORTH FORK TRAILHEAD

16.0 mi/2-3 days

in the Marble Mountain Wilderness near Sawyers Bar

Map 2.1, page 67

In the shadow of so many easier hikes to stellar destinations in the region, this trail is bypassed by most. Your destination options from this trailhead? There are many: Chimney Rock, Clear Lake, Lily Lake, and Chimney Rock Lake. Take your pick. Or devise a route where you hop from one to another. It starts where you face a long grind of a climb to reach the lakes. Like a lot of trails on the edge of the wilderness, this one starts with a long haul out of a river canyon. From the Little North Fork trailhead, start by climbing out toward Chimney Rock, grunting out a rise of about 4,000 feet as you leave the river lowlands and reach the Marble Mountain Wilderness. It's about an eight-mile trip to Clear Lake, a good first day's destination. Although you can simply return the next day, most people will take several days to venture deeper into the wilderness, with 13 lakes and 20 miles of stream in the Upper Abbotts Camp and English Peak areas.

User Groups: Hikers, dogs, and horses. No mountain bikes. No wheelchair facilities.

Permits: A campfire permit (free) is required for campfires and stoves. Parking and access are free.

Maps: A trail information sheet can be obtained by contacting the Salmon Ranger District. For a map, ask the U.S. Forest Service for Klamath National Forest or Marble Mountain Wilderness. For a topographic map, ask the USGS for Sawyers Bar.

Directions: From Redding, take I-5 to Yreka and the exit for Highway 3/Fort Jones. Take that exit to the stop sign, turn left, and drive a short distance to the lighted intersection. Turn left on Highway 3 and drive southwest 28 miles to Etna at Sawyers Bar Road. Turn right on Sawyers Bar Road and drive about 25 miles to Sawyers Bar. Continue west on the same road for four miles to Little North Fork Road (Forest Road 40N51). Turn right (north) and drive two miles to the trailhead at the end of the road.
Contact: Klamath National Forest, Salmon/Scott River Ranger District, Fort Jones, 530/468-5351, www.fs.usda.gov/klamath.

19 HORSE TRAIL RIDGE NATIONAL RECREATION TRAIL

15.0 mi one-way/2 days 

in Six Rivers National Forest east of Hoopa

Map 2.1, page 67

This is one of the lesser-known national recreation trails in the western United States, but it has many excellent features, and, alas, a few negative ones as well. The six-mile trip to Mill Creek Lakes is set in the least-explored western sector of the Trinity Alps. Although some of the region has been burned severely by wildfire, the Mill Creek Lakes area remains untouched, like an island of green, and makes for a good overnighter.

From the trailhead (at 4,800 feet), the grades are gradual, with relatively easy elevation climbs and descents. A majority of the forest along the trail was burned in forest fires. While there are many continuous stretches of burned areas, there are also pockets of greenery that the fire missed and ground-level vegetation is making a good comeback. In all, the fire affects 10 miles of this route. There are also some areas where the trail needs to be brushed near Devils Hole and Lipps Camp.

Note: Do not drink the water available here without first treating it with the best filtration system you can afford.
User Groups: Hikers, dogs, and horses. No mountain bikes. No wheelchair facilities.
Permits: A wilderness permit is required for hikers planning on camping. Parking and access are free.
Maps: For a map, ask the U.S. Forest Service for Six Rivers National Forest. For topographic maps, ask the USGS for Tish Tang Point and Trinity Mountain.
Directions: From the Arcata area, take Highway 299 east to Willow Creek and Highway 96. Turn north on Highway 96 and drive about 12 miles into Hoopa Valley to Big Hill Road. Turn right (east) on Big Hill Road and drive 11 miles to the Six Rivers National Forest border (the road becomes Forest Road 8N01). Continue for 4.5 miles (the road becomes Forest Road 10N02) to the Redcap trailhead (once off Hoopa reservation land, stay on the chip-seal road).
Contact: Six Rivers National Forest, Lower Trinity Ranger District, Willow Creek, 530/629-2118, www.fs.usda.gov/srnf.

20 LITTLE SOUTH FORK LAKE TRAIL

13.0 mi/2 days 

in the Trinity Alps Wilderness near Cecilville

Map 2.1, page 67

You have to be a little bit crazy to try this trip, and like my late pal Waylon Jennings said—I miss him every day—"I've always been crazy 'cause it's kept me from going insane." This is one of the most difficult lakes to reach in California. Yet Little South Fork Lake has two idyllic campsites, excellent swimming and good trout fishing. This route is largely off-trail and requires skirting around a big waterfall, but there's no better way in—we've tried all three different routes. If you want an easy, clearly marked trail, this is not the hike for you. If you want a challenge with a payoff, this is it. Over the years, enough people have taken the challenge to create somewhat of a route to get there.

From the South Fork trailhead, the trip starts out easy enough on a route. Start by hiking four miles along the Salmon River until reaching the Little South Fork Creek. Turn up the trail upstream along Little South Fork Creek. The trail quickly becomes faint and starts to resemble a game trail. The route eventually dead-ends into Little South Fork Creek. (A faint route on the other side of the creek, the north side, climbs through brush and up the canyon, and we came in that way once from the Caribou Lakes; it is like trying to make your way through a spiderweb of brush and should be avoided.) From here, with no apparent route up Little South Fork Creek or out of the canyon, the best route, though still steep and very difficult, is to lateral across the slope on the right side of the stream. It is 1.25 miles upstream to a beautiful, pristine waterfall. Michael Furniss, the renowned hydrologist from Humboldt, named it Crystal Falls.

To get around the waterfall, loop back until you can project a safe route up the slope to the right, and trek with no trail in an arc around and above the waterfall; if you go to the left (which we've tried), you'll add several dreadful hours to the trip scrambling on all fours straight up the slope (plus we got stung by bees in a ground nest we accidentally disturbed). Remember that there is no trail and no marked route; this is a cross-country scramble and very slow going. It's another 1.5 miles to the lake, which can take hours of scrambling up and across the wooded slope until you emerge from the forest onto granite plates. Ahead is the lake, beautifully set in a rock bowl framed by a high back wall. There are excellent campsites at each end of the lake. When you arrive, you will collapse, believe me, or jump in the lake for a swim.

We hiked into this lake once from Caribou Lakes by climbing the Sawtooth Ridge and dropping down into the basin—the entire route, also off-trail, but that creates a potentially hazardous proposition, with some rock climbing and having rope packs going either up or down. On another trip from Caribou Lakes, we dropped down into Little South Fork Canyon, losing thousands of feet in altitude and in the process getting caught in a brush field like bugs in a spiderweb. Neither of these other two routes is recommended. In fact, the suggested route we detailed is not recommended either. During reviews of the book, rangers have twice said we were crazy to include it and they would never recommend such a thing. They are right, of course. You need to be a little crazy to get membership to the Little South Fork Club. Just like my old pal Waylon.

User Groups: Hikers only. Dogs are permitted but are strongly advised against. No horses or mountain bikes. No wheelchair facilities.

Permits: A free wilderness permit is required for hikers planning to camp.

Maps: For a map, ask the U.S. Forest Service for Klamath National Forest or Trinity Alps Wilderness. For a topographic map, ask the USGS for Thompson Peak.

Directions: From Redding, drive north on I-5 for 70 miles past Weed to the exit for Edgewood. At the stop sign, turn left and drive through the underpass to another stop sign to Old Highway 99. Turn right on Old Highway 99 and drive about six miles to Gazelle. Turn left on Gazelle-Callahan Road and drive 27 (twisty) miles to Callahan and continue a short distance to Cecilville Road. Turn left (west or right if coming from Yreka) on Cecilville Road and drive 28 miles to Caribou Road/County Road 1E003 (across from East Fork Campground). Turn left (south) on Caribou Road and drive 3.5 miles to a fork. Bear left at the fork and drive 2.5 miles to the South Fork trailhead. Bring detailed maps, not a GPS.

Contact: Klamath National Forest, Salmon/Scott River Ranger District, Fort Jones, 530/468-5351, www.fs.usda.gov/klamath.

21 GRIZZLY LAKE

12.0 mi/2 days or 38.0 mi/5 days

5 10

in the Trinity Alps Wilderness north of Junction City

Map 2.1, page 67 BEST

This hike is a butt-kicker climb to Grizzly Lake, the signature lake in the Trinity Alps. A friend of ours, Bob Winston, calls it a "Kill-me, eat-me hike." By the time you get here, you might be thinking the same thing. The lake is gorgeous (and we'll get to that), the trek is just plain hard (we'll get to that, too), but the surprise is that despite the extreme difficulty there always seem to be folks here in the summer. You only seem to get it to yourself in the fall, when the nights are cold.

Grizzly Lake is set below awesome Thompson Peak (8,863 feet). One of the most beautiful wilderness waterfalls, 80-foot Grizzly Falls, flows at the lake's cliff outfall. The lake is so pristine against the backdrop of the rising flank of Thompson that you can spend hours just looking at it.

There are two ways to get in. Take your pick: From the China Creek trailhead, a butt-kicking six-mile climb with a 5,000-foot elevation gain (with a 1,500-foot canyon descent included on the way); or from the Hobo Gulch trailhead, a moderate grade over the course of 19 miles to make the lake.

Given a choice, most people take the short, butt-kicker route, then cuss at themselves the whole way in for doing so. There is almost nothing rewarding about it. Most complete the trip with head down, trying to think about something else. Before you race off to this destination, think long and hard about whether you are ready to pay a terrible physical toll to get there. Surprisingly, many do this regardless of the price, and the place gets fairly heavy use. It's one of the marquee destinations in the north state.

On the other hand, you could take the longer but more gradual climb from the Hobo Gulch trailhead, set deep in the national forest along Backbone Ridge. On this route, Grizzly Lake is 19 miles away. There's also a fair amount of forest fire damage along the way. So instead of camping along lakes, hikers camp along pretty streams and flats, taking days to reach the promised land at Grizzly Lake. The trail from Hobo Gulch starts by heading straight north about five miles along the North Fork Trinity River to Rattlesnake Camp, climbing very gently. Cross Rattlesnake Creek, and continue another three miles past the Morrison Cabin (from the mining days) and on to Pfeiffer Flat. Here the North Fork Trinity is joined by Grizzly Creek, an attractive backpacking destination. From Pfeiffer Flat, the trail follows Grizzly Creek, rising high toward the Trinity Sawtooth Ridge and requiring an uphill pull to beautiful Grizzly Meadows and then to Grizzly Lake; the final mile is a scramble over a clear hiking route amid rock.

For rock climbers, climbing the lake bowl in a clockwise direction makes for an exciting scramble to Thompson Peak and a perch just below the rock summit; to reach the tip-top of the mountain requires a technical climb, dangerous for most.

User Groups: Hikers, dogs, and horses. No mountain bikes. No wheelchair facilities.

Permits: A wilderness permit is required for hikers planning to camp.

Maps: For a map, ask the U.S. Forest Service for Shasta-Trinity National Forest or Trinity Alps Wilderness. For a topographic map, ask the USGS for Thurston Peaks.

Directions: To reach the China Creek trailhead from Redding, drive north on I-5 for 70 miles. Just past Weed, take the Edgewood exit. At the stop sign, turn left and drive through the underpass to another stop sign. Turn right on Old Highway 99 and drive about six miles to Gazelle. Turn left on Gazelle-Callahan Road and drive 27 miles to Callahan and Cecilville Road. Turn west on Cecilville Road and drive 27 miles to Forest Road 37N24. Turn south and drive 3.8 miles to Forest Road 37N07 (well signed). Take Forest 37N07 and drive six miles to the trailhead.

To reach the Hobo Gulch trailhead from Weaverville, drive 13 miles west on Highway 299 to Helena and East Fork Road. Turn north on East Fork Road (County Road 421) and drive 3.9 miles to Hobo Gulch Road. Turn left on Hobo Gulch Road (Forest Road 34N07Y) and drive 12 miles to the Hobo Gulch trailhead, located at Hobo Gulch Campground at the end of the road.

Contact: Shasta-Trinity National Forest, Weaverville Ranger Station, Weaverville, 530/623-2121, www.fs.usda.gov/stnf.

22 TREE OF HEAVEN TRAIL

0.5 mi/0.5 hr 1 8

on the Klamath River in Klamath National Forest northwest of Yreka

Map 2.2, page 68

The trail out of the Tree of Heaven Campground provides one of the few streamside trails anywhere along the Klamath River. This is a level, wheelchair-accessible trail that heads downstream along the Klamath and also an interpretive trail on neotropical bird migrations. Visit in fall for berry picking. The Tree of Heaven River access is also a good take-out point for drift boaters and rafters who make the easy all-day run, often with good fishing in the fall from half-pounders, down from Iron Canyon Dam. Note that this trail once extended 2.5 miles to a good fishing spot at the west end of the campground, but the trail is largely overgrown, with poor access; anglers should instead wear waders to get out in the stream a bit and steer well clear of the shoreline brush.

User Groups: Hikers, dogs, horses, and mountain bikes. No wheelchair facilities.

Permits: No permits are required. Parking and access are free.

Maps: For a map, ask the U.S. Forest Service for Klamath National Forest. For a topographic map, ask the USGS for Badger Mountain.

Directions: From Yreka, drive north on I-5 for 10 miles to the Highway 96 exit. Turn west on Highway 96 and drive about five miles. Look for the Tree of Heaven Campground on the left. The trailhead is at the west end of the campground.

Contact: Klamath National Forest, Headquarters, Yreka, 530/842-6131, www.fs.usda.gov/klamath.

23 JUANITA LAKE TRAIL

1.75 mi/1.0 hr 1 7

in Klamath National Forest east of Yreka

Map 2.2, page 68

Not many people know about Juanita Lake, including many Siskiyou County residents. Once they find it, most will take at least a portion of this easy loop trail around the lake to get a feel for the place. The lake is set in a mixed, sparse conifer forest, though few trees here are large. In the last hour of light during summer, both osprey and bald eagles occasionally make fishing trips to the lake. Juanita Lake is a small lake that provides lakeside camping and fishing for brook trout. The small fishing piers are wheelchair-accessible.

A good side trip is driving on the forest road up to Ball Mountain, about two miles southwest of the lake, for great views of Mount Shasta from the 7,786-foot summit.

User Groups: Hikers and leashed dogs. No mountain bikes or horses. The fishing piers are wheelchair-accessible.

Permits: No permits are required. Parking and access are free.

Maps: For a map, ask the U.S. Forest Service for Klamath National Forest. For a topographic map, ask the USGS for Panther Rock.

Directions: From Redding, take I-5 north for 68 miles to the exit for Central Weed/Klamath Falls (Highway 97). Take that exit to the stop sign, turn right and drive 0.5 mile (through town) to the lighted intersection with Highway 97. Bear right (north) on Highway 97 and drive

35 miles to Ball Mountain Road/Little Shasta Road. Turn left and drive two miles to a signed turnoff for Juanita Lake. Turn right and drive 2.7 miles to Forest Road 46N04. Bear right and drive 3.2 miles to the lake and campground. Start near the boat dock.

Contact: Klamath National Forest, Goosenest Ranger District, Macdoel, 530/398-4391, www.fs.usda.gov/klamath.

24 DEER MOUNTAIN

4.0 mi/2.25 hr

in Klamath National Forest north of Mount Shasta

Map 2.2, page 68

Deer Mountain is the second in a line of small peaks set on the north side of Mount Shasta that extend all the way to the Medicine Lake wildlands. North from Shasta, the first peak is the Whaleback, at an elevation of 8,528 feet, and the second is Deer Mountain, at 7,006 feet. Starting elevation at the parking area is 6,200 feet, and from here you climb 800 feet through forest consisting of various pines and firs to gain the summit. This route gets very little use, even though it's easy to reach and the destination is a mountaintop. Most out-of-towners visiting this area are attracted to the trails on Mount Shasta instead, and most locals just plain overlook it. The one exception is in late summer and early fall, when it gets use by hunters. Deer numbers are decent here, but many seem very small, like 90 to 100 pounds. and scant few of the bucks have three-point or better.

User Groups: Hikers, dogs, horses, and mountain bikes. No wheelchair facilities.

Permits: No permits are required. Parking and access are free.

Maps: For a map, ask the U.S. Forest Service for Klamath National Forest. For a topographic map, ask the USGS for Whaleback.

Directions: From Redding, take I-5 north for 68 miles to the exit for Central Weed/Klamath Falls (Highway 97). Take that exit to the stop sign, turn right and drive 0.5 mile (through town) to the lighted intersection with Highway 97. Bear right (north) on Highway 97 and drive 16.8 miles to Deer Mountain Road/Forest Road 19 (Forest Road 42N12). Turn right and drive 3.8 miles to Deer Mountain Snowmobile Park and Forest Road 44N23. Turn left on Forest Road 44N23 and drive 2.3 miles. There is no designated trailhead; park off road and hike cross-country to the top of the mountain.

Note that Forest Road 43N69 loops around the base of the mountain; you may also hike from anywhere along that road. Forest Road 43N69 continues through remote forest to Highway 89.

Contact: Klamath National Forest, Goosenest Ranger District, Macdoel, 530/398-4391, www.fs.usda.gov/klamath.

25 THE WHALEBACK

3.0 mi/2.5 hr

in Klamath National Forest north of Mount Shasta

Map 2.2, page 68

After you pass Mount Shasta on I-5, driving north on Highway 97, look off to your right and you'll see a large, humplike mountain that sits north of Shasta. It looks like a huge volcanic bump that was born when Shasta was active. That's because it is. This is the Whaleback, 8,528 feet high. It provides a hike with a payoff view at the top, and a surprise: a large crater. The Whaleback Summit is actually a volcanic cinder cone with a collapsed center. This interesting geology, along with the panorama of Mount Shasta to the south, makes this a first-rate hike. Yet almost nobody tries it, most likely because they don't realize how near you can drive to the top, or because there is no formal trail. After parking at the gate, you just hike cross-country style up to the rim; it's steep all the way. The 1.5-mile hike is a scramble only in a few places. In the process, you'll climb 1,100 feet, from a starting elevation of 7,400 feet, to Whaleback Rim.

User Groups: Hikers, dogs, horses, and mountain bikes. No wheelchair facilities.

Permits: No permits are required. Parking and access are free.

Maps: For a map, ask the U.S. Forest Service for Klamath National Forest. For a topographic map, ask the USGS for Whaleback.

Directions: From Redding, take I-5 north for 68 miles to the exit for Central Weed/Klamath Falls (Highway 97). Take that exit to the stop sign, turn right and drive 0.5 mile (through town) to the lighted intersection with Highway 97. Bear right (north) on Highway 97 and drive 15 miles to Deer Mountain Road. Turn right on Deer Mountain Road and drive four miles to Deer Mountain Snowmobile Park. Drive east on Deer Mountain Road/Forest Road 19 (Forest Road 42N12) for three miles to Forest Road 42N24. Turn right on Forest Road 42N24 and drive three miles to a gate. Park and hike in. There is no designated trail; you must hike cross-country from the road. The peak is about 1.5 miles from the gate.

Contact: Klamath National Forest, Goosenest Ranger District, Macdoel, 530/398-4391, www.fs.usda.gov/klamath.

26 WHITNEY FALLS TRAILHEAD

3.4 mi/2.5 hr  

on the northwest slope of Mount Shasta

Map 2.2, page 68

For years, this was a great, easy hike. No more. The first mile of this trail is buried under a flow of mud and debris, the results of a flash flood released upslope from the Whitney Glacier. Enough hikers have traversed it to create a route through and past it. Regardless, there are still short stretches where you have to negotiate rocks, boulders, logs, and deep erosion channels. It takes a mile of scrambling to intersect the former trail. If you feel a bit confused here (there is no such as lost, according to Davy Crockett), get higher, on one of the volcanic crags, and look ahead for the faint trail on the right side of the flow and a small gorge. That's the way.

The Whitney Falls trail then rises from about 5,600 feet uphill out of the drainage. The trail spans 1.6 miles to an unsigned fork at 6,400 feet. Take the right fork, a spur trail to an overlook at a deep gorge. On the far uphill side is hidden Whitney Falls, a 250-foot waterfall, with its thin, silvery wisp tumbling through a narrow chute in a dramatic ashen gorge. It takes perfect timing during late spring snowmelt to see this waterfall at anything more than a trickle. The view to the north of Shasta Valley is outstanding, highlighted by the series of hummocks and vast volcanic formations. Geologists have identified this as from a catastrophic debris avalanche produced from the ancestral Mount Shasta volcano, roughly 350,000 years ago.

Special notes: If you turn left at the fork instead, you'll venture through forest, then up through another gutted stream drainage. The trail ends, and mountaineers will have to pass Coquette Falls, and then near the peak at the Bolam Glacier, in order to make the summit. Safety gear and expert climbing skills are required. Stay off the Whitney Glacier. It has a crevasse that can be camouflaged with snow in spring and early summer; it is possible to plunge through the snowbridge and fall deep into the crevasse—it is the Venus flytrap of Mount Shasta.

User Groups: Hikers only. No dogs, horses, or mountain bikes. No wheelchair facilities.

Permits: Parking and access are free. A free wilderness permit is required for both day use and overnight use. The Forest Service requires a Summit Pass, available for 3 days for $25, and $30 for the year, for hikers climbing over 10,000 feet in elevation. All climbers are required to pack out waste and must bring a pack-out bag.

Maps: For a map, ask the U.S. Forest Service for Shasta-Trinity National Forest or Mount

Shasta Wilderness. For a topographic map, ask the USGS for Mount Shasta.

Directions: From Redding, take I-5 north for 68 miles to the exit for Central Weed/Klamath Falls (Highway 97). Take that exit to the stop sign, turn right and drive 0.5 mile (through town) to the lighted intersection with Highway 97. Bear right (north) on Highway 97 and drive 12 miles to Bolam Road (Forest Road 43N21), which is usually unsigned. (If you reach County Road A12 on the left, you have gone 0.25 mile too far.) Turn right on Bolam Road for four miles (you'll cross railroad tracks) to the end of the road. A high-clearance vehicle is required.

Contact: Shasta-Trinity National Forest, Mount Shasta Ranger District, Mount Shasta, 530/926-4511, www.fs.usda.gov/stnf; Fifth Season Climbing Report, 530/926-5555; Shasta Mountain Guides, 530/926-3117, www.shastaguides.com; Avalanche Center Climbing Report, 530/926-9613.

27 BLACK BUTTE TRAIL

5.0 mi/3.5 hr 5 8

in Shasta-Trinity National Forest between I-5 and Mount Shasta

Map 2.2, page 68

Anybody who has cruised I-5 north to Oregon and gawked in astonishment at Mount Shasta has inevitably seen Black Butte right alongside the highway. That's right, it's that barren "cinder cone" set between the highway and Mount Shasta, and it can pique a traveler's curiosity. Technically, it is a dome composed of hornblende andesite, not cinders. The trail is routed right to the top and can answer all of your questions. But you may not like all of the answers. Over the course of 2.5 miles, you'll climb 1,845 feet—much of it steep, most of it rocky, and in the summer, all of it hot and dry. Shade is nonexistent. There are only two rewards. One is claiming the summit, at 6,325 feet, where you'll find the foundation of an old U.S. Forest Service lookout and great 360-degree views; the other is that the hike is an excellent warm-up for people who are planning to climb Mount Shasta. (That is, providing you don't need a week to recover.) This trip is actually best done on a warm summer night under a full moon. From the summit, you'll also see that the top is a series of volcanic crags, each unique.

User Groups: Hikers and dogs. No horses or mountain bikes. No wheelchair facilities.

Permits: No permits are required.

Maps: A trail information sheet is available by contacting the Mount Shasta Ranger District. For a map, ask the U.S. Forest Service for Shasta-Trinity National Forest. For a topographic map, ask the USGS for Mount Shasta city.

Directions: From Redding, take I-5 north to the exit for Central Mount Shasta. Follow that exit to the stop sign at Lake Street. Turn right and drive one mile east (through town) on Lake Street, and then bear left as it merges with Washington Drive (and becomes Everitt Memorial Highway). Continue on Washington/Everitt Memorial Highway (past the high school on the right) for about two miles, and look for the sign for Spring Hill Plantation (on the right) and Forest Road 41N18 (on the left). Turn left on Forest Road 41N18/Ash Flat (a gravel road), drive about 200 yards, and bear right, continuing on Forest Road 41N18 for 2.5 miles. After the road crosses under the overhead power line, turn left on Forest Road 41N18A (Black Butte Road) and drive 0.75 mile to the trailhead. Parking is limited; be sure to park off the road.

Contact: Shasta-Trinity National Forest, Mount Shasta Ranger District, Mount Shasta, 530/926-4511, www.fs.usda.gov/stnf.

28 SAND FLAT TRAILHEAD

3.4 mi/2.75 hr 3 8

on the southern slope of Mount Shasta

Map 2.2, page 68

The hike from Sand Flat to Horse Camp, a

distance of 1.7 miles with a climb of 1,000 feet, will give you a good taste of the Mount Shasta experience, and you're likely to savor the flavors. Many who make this day hike are compelled to return to climb all the way to the top.

Sand Flat provides a shaded parking area to start from, away from all the people in summer at the primary Bunny Flat trailhead. The elevation is 6,800 feet. The trail immediately takes off uphill. The climb is gradual at first, but then it becomes quite steep. At 7,360 feet, it intersects with Bunny Flat Trail and then continues to rise through the forest. Along the way are amazing examples of how avalanches and windstorms have knocked down entire sections of forest. When you reach Horse Camp, at 7,800 feet, nearing timberline, you'll find many rewards. The first is spring water flowing continuously out of a piped fountain near the Sierra Hut; it's perhaps the best-tasting water in the world. A solar-powered composting toilet is also available. The second reward is the foreboding view of Red Bank, which forms the mountain rim above Horse Camp. The third is the opportunity to hike up a short way above tree line for the sweeping views to the south of Castle Crags and Lake Siskiyou. After taking the first steps on Summit Trail, you'll likely yearn to keep going all the way to the very top of this magic mountain. If you wish to hike Summit Trail, see the following hike out of Bunny Flat trailhead.

User Groups: Hikers only. No dogs, horses, or mountain bikes. No wheelchair facilities.

Permits: Parking and access are free. A free wilderness permit is required for both day use and overnight use. The Forest Service requires a Summit Pass, available for 3 days for $25, and $30 for the year, for hikers climbing over 10,000 feet in elevation. All climbers are required to pack out waste and must bring a pack-out bag.

Maps: For a map, ask the U.S. Forest Service for Shasta-Trinity National Forest or Mount Shasta Wilderness. For a topographic map, ask the USGS for Mount Shasta.

Directions: From Redding, take I-5 north to the exit for Central Mount Shasta. Follow that exit to the stop sign. Turn right and drive one mile east on Lake Street, and then bear left on Washington Drive (it merges, and then Washington Drive becomes Everitt Memorial Highway). Continue on Washington/Everitt Memorial Highway (past the high school) for 9.7 miles to Sand Flat Road. Turn left and drive 0.4 mile to parking and the trailhead.

Contact: Shasta-Trinity National Forest, Mount Shasta Ranger District, Mount Shasta, 530/926-4511, www.fs.usda.gov/stnf; Fifth Season Climbing Report, 530/926-5555; Shasta Mountain Guides, 530/926-3117, www.shastaguides.com; Avalanche Center Climbing Report, 530/926-9613.

29 SHASTA SUMMIT TRAIL

14 mi/1.5 days 5 10

on the southern slope of Mount Shasta in the Shasta-Trinity National Forest

Map 2.2, page 68 **BEST**

The hike to the top of 14,179-foot Mount Shasta is one of America's epic treks. Your challenge is to climb 7,229 feet over ice, snow, and rock while trying to suck what little oxygen you can out of the thin air. It may be the greatest adventure in the West that most hikers in good condition have an honest chance of achieving. Timing is everything. Plan your trip for when the wind is down on top, the summit is clear, no thunderstorms, and the route has plenty of snow, which provides an excellent climbing surface (where you wear crampons) and acts as a mortar for holding boulders in place.

The trip starts out of Bunny Flat at 6,950 feet, leads through a forest of Shasta red firs, climbs to where the trail intersects with the route out of Sand Flat, then turns right and rises to Horse Camp, at an elevation of 7,800 feet and a distance of 1.8 miles. There's a hiker's cabin, called the Sierra Club Hut, on the left, an incredible spring with sweet-tasting water on the right—it's a must to fill up your water bottles here—and a short walk to environmental toilets to your right. Most people camp one night at Horse Camp and then leave very early the next morning for the summit.

After filling your canteens at the spring, start hiking the Summit Trail. Make your first steps across a series of large stones called Olberman's Causeway. From here, the trail quickly rises above timberline, gaining 1,000 feet per mile for six miles, and after a short time, it becomes a faint path. One route ventures to your left and is routed, including a span of switchbacks, up to Helen Lake, a flat spot for a trail camp. Another route crosses a sub-ridge to your right and then you are routed up Avalanche Gulch, with Red Bank looming directly overhead.

Expect snow and ice, that's when the climbing is best, and you will stop and strap your crampons onto your boots. The walking is easy with crampons. The trail climbs up Avalanche Gulch, and some people stop to make trail camps at a flat spot called Helen Lake at 10,440 feet. Hikers not acclimated to high altitudes may begin experiencing some dizziness, but there's no relief in sight. At this point, the hike gets steeper (about a 35-degree slope), and some give up before reaching Red Bank—a huge, red, volcanic outcrop at about 12,500 feet. In periods of low snow, a narrow and steep rock/ice chute emerges at Red Bank. I prefer this route, though you'll need your ice ax in order to pull your way through and a slip is certain without crampons; often there is a stream of melting water where you can fill your water bottle. In high snow years, on the other hand, the chute is filled with snow and the climb continues ahead at steep grade. There are two other routes as well: one very steep ascent to your left, another that circles The Thumb to your right, but in the latter, you will pass a crevasse that should not be circumvented without an experienced guide to keep you safe.

When you emerge atop Red Bank, you are nearly 13,000 feet high, at the foot of Misery Hill, so named because it's a long, slow climb through snow in spring and scree in summer. It's a myth that a lot of people actually mistake

Shasta Summit Trail

it for the peak—if you were that off base, you'd never make it this far. Once atop Misery Hill, you'll see the true Shasta Summit, a massive pinnacle of lava that seems to jut straight up into the air. Cross a sun-cupped glacier field to reach the pinnacle and there you will see the trail routed up to the top. With a final push, follow the trail, grabbing rocks to help pull you up and sucking the thin air, and with a few last steps, you'll be on top, at 14,179 feet. On clear days you can see hundreds of miles in all directions, and the sky is a deeper cobalt blue than you ever imagined. On top, you'll sign your name in a logbook in an old rusted metal box, then take in the grand wonders surrounding you. It's a remarkable trip, one that can inspire some people to keep their bodies in good enough shape to make it every year.

About half the people who try to climb Mount Shasta don't make it. The number one reason is because they are stopped by bad weather. High winds above 12,000 feet are common in May and June. In late summer, typically mid-August through early October, there is a danger from tumbling boulders. Snow acts as a mortar and holds the volcanic landscape together. Most hikers in good condition who start the trip very early and have the proper equipment can summit, especially in July, when the weather and climbing conditions are often best. Early? You should depart from Bunny Flat by 3am, or hike in a day early, set up a base camp at Horse Camp (at tree line), and start no later than 4am. Another strategy that works is to set up a base camp higher on the mountain, at Helen Lake, or in high snow years at the flat spot on Green Butte to climb Green Butte Ridge (it is not passable is low snow years). For equipment, you'll need a day pack with warm clothes, a windbreaker, two canteens of water, food, and an ice ax and crampons are mandatory. Refill your canteen wherever you find a rivulet of water (it's occasionally possible at Red Bank); rangers recommend using a water filter.

It's an absolute must to make an early start. In the hot summer months, towering cumulus clouds sometimes form on Mount Shasta during the afternoon, and by then you'll want to be making the trip down. If towering cumulonimbus begin forming by noon, intense thunderstorms are possible by midafternoon.

All hikers must pack out their waste. Special waste pack-out bags are available at no charge at the trailhead and at the Mount Shasta Ranger Station in Mount Shasta.

The biggest danger and largest number of injuries on Mount Shasta come not from falling, but from being hit by tumbling boulders. In fact, our former research assistant, Robyn Brewer, was struck in the foot by a boulder in her first attempt at climbing Shasta. She was hit so hard that it knocked her hiking boot off, breaking her foot and requiring an emergency helicopter airlift out for medical treatment. Always keep a good distance between you and your hiking partners, don't hike in a vertical line, and if a rock comes bouncing down, always shout, "Rock! Rock!" Some guides recommend wearing helmets. By the way, Robyn returned to Mount Shasta the following two years and made it to the top on both trips.

The mountain is best hiked when it still has a good coating of snow and ice, which provide excellent footing with crampons. When the snow and ice melt off in late fall, tromping through the small volcanic rocks is like slogging in mushy sand, and there is the additional problem of boulder falls.

Drink lots of water. In high altitudes, dehydration is a common problem and can result in early exhaustion and extreme vulnerability to mountain sickness.

When you drive into the town of Mount Shasta, at the corner of Lake and Main Street, the main intersection downtown, you'll see Shasta Mountain Guides on the right and the Fifth Season, which provides rental equipment, on the left.

User Groups: Hikers only. No dogs, horses, or mountain bikes. No wheelchair facilities.

Permits: Parking and access are free. A free wilderness permit is required for both day use and overnight use. The Forest Service requires a Summit Pass, available for 3 days for $25, and $30 for the year, for hikers climbing over 10,000 feet in elevation. All climbers are required to pack out waste and must bring a pack-out bag.

Maps: For a map, ask the U.S. Forest Service for Shasta-Trinity National Forest or Mount Shasta Wilderness. For a topographic map, ask the USGS for Mount Shasta.

Directions: From Redding, take I-5 north to the exit for Central Mount Shasta. Take that exit to the stop sign at Lake Street. Turn right and drive one mile east (through town) on Lake Street, and then bear left as it merges with Washington Drive (and becomes Everitt Memorial Highway). Continue on Washington/Everitt Memorial Highway (past the high school on the right) and drive 11.1 miles to Bunny Flat. As you drive in, the trailhead is on the left, next to the restroom.

Contact: Shasta-Trinity National Forest, Mount Shasta Ranger District, Mount Shasta, 530/926-4511, www.fs.usda.gov/stnf; Fifth Season Climbing Report, 530/926-5555; Shasta Mountain Guides, 530/926-3117, www.shastaguides.com; Avalanche Center Climbing Report, 530/926-9613.

30 SOUTH GATE MEADOWS

4.0 mi/3.0 hr 2 10

from Ski Bowl on the southern slope of Mount Shasta in Mount Shasta Wilderness

Map 2.2, page 68 BEST

This is a great day hike. It's easy, unique, and with a great payoff with a view perch and trail lunch site that overlooks miles. There is a stellar lookout to the south with Castle Crags, Mount Lassen, and the drop-off in the Sacramento Valley, all prominent. Start at the old Ski Bowl, on the right of the road at the sign for Gray Butte/South Meadows Trail. This trailhead sign may confuse those long familiar with the area. It used to be called Squaw Creek trailhead and Squaw Meadows, but it has been renamed. From the trailhead, head east on a clear trail routed amid volcanic scree, just above tree line. You'll see a sculpted volcanic valley called The Gate. Some visitors consider this to be the mountain's sacred portal to the spiritual dimension. Gray Butte looms above to your right (reaching the top at 8,119 feet requires a scramble over sharp-edged volcanic rock; if you wear rings on your fingers, they will scuff the exposed bottom side). It can touch the heart when you arrive at South Gate Meadows and the headwaters of Squaw Valley Creek. This is a pristine meadow that is not in a valley, but rather rises up the slope of Shasta, and cut by a thin streaming cascade. Along the upper reaches, a few flat sites are available for small campsites.

User Groups: Hikers only. Dogs are not advised. No horses or mountain bikes. No wheelchair facilities.

Permits: Parking and access are free. A free wilderness permit is required for both day use and overnight use. The Forest Service requires a Summit Pass, available for 3 days for $25, and $30 for the year, for hikers climbing over 10,000 feet in elevation. All climbers are required to pack out waste and must bring a pack-out bag.

Maps: For a map, ask the U.S. Forest Service for Shasta-Trinity National Forest or Mount Shasta Wilderness. For a topographic map, ask the USGS for Mount Shasta.

Directions: From Redding, take I-5 north to the exit for Central Mount Shasta. Follow that exit to the stop sign at Lake Street. Turn right and drive one mile east (through town) on Lake Street, and then bear left as it merges with Washington Drive (and becomes Everitt Memorial Highway). Continue on Washington/Everitt Memorial Highway (past the high school on the right) and drive 11.1 miles to Bunny Flat (restroom available), and then continue 2.5 miles (past the entrance spur to Panther Meadows) to the trailhead on the right.

Contact: Shasta-Trinity National Forest, Mount Shasta Ranger District, Mount Shasta, 530/926-4511, www.fs.usda.gov/stnf; Fifth

Season Climbing Report, 530/926-5555; Shasta Mountain Guides, 530/926-3117, www.shastaguides.com; Avalanche Center Climbing Report, 530/926-9613.

31 GREEN BUTTE RIDGE

4.4 mi/4.0 hr 

on the southern slope of Mount Shasta

Map 2.2, page 68

In the big snow years, this is our favorite trek on Mount Shasta. You have a towering view down into canyons on each side of you and beyond to Castle Crags and miles of wildlands. Yet it is also one of the most overlooked. Green Butte, a huge rock outcrop set at 9,200 feet, is your destination. From Bunny Flat at 6,950 feet, it means a climb of 2,250 feet in a little over two miles. In the big snow years, a climber's route will be available across the top of the knife-edge ridge, a great route to The Thumb and beyond to the summit.

From the Bunny Flat trailhead, just about everybody hikes to Horse Camp. Instead, there is an unsigned cutoff to the right that climbs through forest and connects to Green Butte Ridge. You end up with a towering view over Lake Siskiyou and beyond to the top of Castle Crags. From here, in winter, many will snowboard back down. Most use split boards. This one is a 10, an unforgettable trek, and though you earn every step, the payoffs are world-class in scope.

In big snow years, this is a great route to summit. As you climb on the ridge, you will tower over Avalanche Gulch to your left, the old Mount Shasta Ski Bowl to your right. It leads up to The Thumb, where you cross above Red Bank and join the main route up Misery Hill.

The route is well protected from spring winds. It can blow 80 mph across Misery Hill and you'll feel only a light breeze here until you top 10,000 feet.

User Groups: Hikers only. No dogs. No horses or mountain bikes. No wheelchair facilities.

Permits: Parking and access are free. A free wilderness permit is required for both day use and overnight use. The Forest Service requires a Summit Pass, available for 3 days for $25, and $30 for the year, for hikers climbing over 10,000 feet in elevation. All climbers are required to pack out waste and must bring a pack-out bag.

Maps: For a map, ask the U.S. Forest Service for Shasta-Trinity National Forest or Mount Shasta Wilderness. For a topographic map, ask the USGS for Mount Shasta.

Directions: From Redding, take I-5 north to the exit for Central Mount Shasta. Take that exit to the stop sign at Lake Street. Turn right and drive one mile east (through town) on Lake Street, and then bear left as it merges with Washington Drive (and becomes Everitt Memorial Highway). Continue on Washington/Everitt Memorial Highway (past the high school on the right) and drive 11.1 miles to Bunny Flat. As you drive in, the trailhead is on the left, next to the restroom.

Contact: Shasta-Trinity National Forest, Mount Shasta Ranger District, Mount Shasta, 530/926-4511, www.fs.usda.gov/stnf; Fifth Season Climbing Report, 530/926-5555; Shasta Mountain Guides, 530/926-3117, www.shastaguides.com; Avalanche Center Climbing Report, 530/926-9613.

32 BREWER CREEK TRAILHEAD

4.2 mi/3.0 hr 

on the northeast slope of Mount Shasta

Map 2.2, page 68

It's so quiet here that you can practically hear the wildflowers bloom. We've hiked the north slope of Shasta out of the Brewer Creek trailhead several times and often not seen another person. The trip makes for a good day hike in the Mount Shasta Wilderness. The trailhead is set near Brewer Creek (at 7,200 feet), hence the name. The drive in is long, and because of that, many prefer Clear Creek trailhead and its views of Mud Creek Falls and Ash Creek Falls to this trailhead.

After a short walk through a section of forest that was selectively logged many years ago, you'll enter the Shasta Wilderness and be surrounded by old-growth firs, many scraggly from enduring harsh winters and the short growing season. Here the trail climbs more. It's a steady ascent through forest, with gradual switchbacks as it goes. When you near tree line, at 7,700 feet, the trail turns to the left and begins to lateral across the mountain. It's 2.1 miles to timberline from the trailhead, and most people hike to this point, then turn back. The trail becomes a route, and at times seems to disappear. You can add a mile or two by climbing a wide, volcanic slope with good footing all the way, and rise to 9,500 feet. This is a great spot for a picnic, provides sweeping views, and may inspire dreams of the day you'll next climb all the way to the top of Shasta.

Note: Mountaineers who try to climb Shasta from this trailhead have only one good route from the point where the trail meets tree line, which is to head to the right up and over Hotlum-Wintun glaciers. This has become one of the most popular routes up the mountain. It is especially attractive for skiers and boarders since it has a descent of about 7,000 feet off the top of the summit block. Also note that this route is extremely difficult, steep and dangerous. Only mountaineers with guides or considerable experience glacier-trekking should attempt it.

User Groups: Hikers only. No dogs, horses, or mountain bikes. No wheelchair facilities.

Permits: Parking and access are free. A free wilderness permit is required for both day use and overnight use. The Forest Service requires a Summit Pass, available for 3 days for $25, and $30 for the year, for hikers climbing over 10,000 feet in elevation. All climbers are required to pack out waste and must bring a pack-out bag.

Maps: For a map, ask the U.S. Forest Service for Shasta-Trinity National Forest or Mount Shasta Wilderness. For a topographic map, ask the USGS for Mount Shasta.

Directions: From Redding, take I-5 north for 58 miles to the Highway 89/McCloud-Reno exit. Bear right on Highway 89 and drive nine miles to McCloud, then continue for another 2.8 miles to Pilgrim Creek Road. Turn left on Pilgrim Creek Road and drive 5.3 miles (becomes Forest Road 13) and continue another two miles to Forest Road 19. Continue on Forest Road 19/Military Pass Road for seven miles to Forest Road 42N02. Turn left on 42N02 and drive four miles (signed, stay on 42N02 at junctions) to trailhead parking area. High-clearance vehicles are recommended; four-wheel drive is helpful.

Contact: Shasta-Trinity National Forest, Mount Shasta Ranger District, Mount Shasta, 530/926-4511, www.fs.usda.gov/stnf; McCloud Ranger District, 530/964-2184; climbing report 530/926-5555.

33 CLEAR CREEK TRAILHEAD/MUD CREEK FALLS

4.0 mi/2.5 hr 3 9

on the southeast slope of Mount Shasta

Map 2.2, page 68

A short walk on the remote southeast flank of Mount Shasta can provide entry to a land of enchantment. From Clear Creek Trail, you get a great day hike that features an overlook of deep canyons, views of glaciers, and Mount Shasta's prettiest waterfall, Mud Creek Falls (and for those with the zest for it, nearby Ash Creek Falls). The drive in is well signed and much closer from Highway 89 than the drive to the distant Brewer Creek trailhead.

At the parking area, the trail starts just to the left of the restroom (many years ago, the trail instead followed an old overgrown jeep road from the upper end of the parking area; that is now reclaimed by a young forest and the going is very slow, where you must pass many downed trees). The trail is routed along a ridge as you climb on an even grade through forest. As you near tree line, you'll see the edge of a canyon rim to your left. At a break in the trees on your left, look up the canyon, you'll see the sensational Mud Creek Falls, roughly 125 feet high, directly ahead, though from a distance. This is the payoff for day hikes.

If you want more, you can continue upslope about a mile to a meadow, creek, and campsite that summit hikers use as a base camp. This is a launch point, not an end point. The route here includes an open crossing on the side of the Wintun Glacier, scary for most, where a slip means a long fall. Only mountaineers with guides or considerable experience glacier-trekking should attempt this route to the summit.

There's another option for those who want to trek the subalpine region of giant Shasta. With a topo map, the ambitious can venture off-trail to find and see nearby Ash Creek Falls. Mud Creek Falls and Ash Creek Falls are best viewed in early summer, when snowmelt is peaking and runoff is high. They are both gorgeous.

This area is rich in natural history. The canyon was carved by a glacier and is still fed with water from the towering, fractured Konwakiton Glacier, which runs the color of volcanic silt. There are several glaciers directly above your vantage point, which feed the canyon's erosive silt into Mud Creek.

User Groups: Hikers only. No dogs, horses, or mountain bikes. No wheelchair facilities.

Permits: Parking and access are free. A free wilderness permit is required for both day use and overnight use. The Forest Service requires a Summit Pass, available for 3 days for $25, and $30 for the year, for hikers climbing over 10,000 feet in elevation. All climbers are required to pack out waste and must bring a pack-out bag.

Maps: For a map, ask the U.S. Forest Service for Shasta-Trinity National Forest or Mount Shasta Wilderness. For a topographic map, ask the USGS for Mount Shasta.

Directions: From Redding, take I-5 north for 47 miles to the Highway 89/McCloud-Reno exit. Bear right on Highway 89 and drive nine miles to McCloud, then continue for another 2.8 miles to Pilgrim Creek Road. Turn left on Pilgrim Creek Road (Forest Road 13) and drive five miles (paved) to Widow Springs Road (Forest Road 41N15). Turn left and drive about five miles to Forest Road 31. Cross this road (still Forest Road 31) for 0.1 mile to a junction, stay left, and continue 0.5 mile to Forest Road 4N125. Turn left on Forest Road 4N125 and drive 2.2 miles to the parking area and trail. The road is well signed. High-clearance, four-wheel-drive vehicles are recommended. Note: As you drive in near the trailhead, the road becomes steep with long ruts, often with deep dust in late summer that can feel like snow under your tires. Vehicles not suited for it can get stuck.

Contact: Shasta-Trinity National Forest, Mount Shasta Ranger District, Mount Shasta, 530/926-4511, www.fs.usda.gov/stnf; McCloud Ranger District, 530/964-2184; climbing report 530/926-5555.

34 ETNA SUMMIT TO GRIDER CREEK (PCT)

49.0 mi one-way/4 days 3 10

from Etna Summit into the Marble Mountain Wilderness west of Etna

Map 2.2, page 68

The Etna Summit is one of the major access points for the Pacific Crest Trail in Northern California. There is a good, safe parking area (with a nice view), and at an elevation of 5,492 feet, you don't have to start your hike with a wicked climb that is demanded at so many other PCT trailheads. From Etna Summit, the trail starts by crossing rugged, dry, and often hot terrain that is best dealt with in the morning. You'll reach Shelly Lake about eight miles in. Note that there is no water available along this route until Shelly Lake. The campground at Shelly Meadows is a good first-night stopover. From there, an excellent second-day destination is the Marble Valley, about another 10 miles north, with camping in the nearby Sky High Lakes Basin. The next 20 miles of trail cross through and out of the Marble Mountains. You'll pass Marble Mountain (a side trip to the Marble Rim is mandatory), Paradise Lake (many visitors will make camp here), and Kings Castle. As you face the lake, a spring is to the left of the campsites in a small ravine at the head of the lake. Most of the trail here is above tree line, with outstanding lookouts at several points, including a great vista from Marble Rim. Moving onward, the trail follows Big Ridge to Buckhorn Mountain (6,908 feet), continues past Huckleberry Mountain (6,303 feet), and then drops down to the headwaters of Grider Creek, the next major trailhead access point. As you head north, the trail becomes less and less traveled.

To pick up the next trail heading north, see the *Grider Creek to Seiad Valley (PCT)* hike in this chapter. If you are walking this trail in reverse, see the *Cecilville Road to Russian Wilderness (PCT)* hike in this chapter to continue south.

User Groups: Hikers, dogs, and horses. No mountain bikes. No wheelchair facilities.

Permits: Campfire permits (free) are required for campfires and stoves. Parking and access are free. A single permit is required to hike the Pacific Crest Trail. Contact the national forest, Bureau of Land Management (BLM), or national park office at your point of entry for a combined permit that is good for traveling through multiple-permit areas during your dates of travel.

Maps: A trail information sheet can be obtained by contacting the Salmon River Ranger District. For a map, ask the U.S. Forest Service for Klamath National Forest or Marble Mountain Wilderness. For a topographic map, ask the USGS for Eaton Peak.

Directions: From Redding, take I-5 to Yreka and the exit for Highway 3/Fort Jones. Take that exit to the stop sign, turn left, and drive a short distance to the lighted intersection. Turn left on Highway 3 and drive 28 miles to Etna. Turn west on Etna-Somes Bar Road (called Main Street in town) and drive 10.5 miles to Etna Summit. The parking area is on the left.

Contact: Klamath National Forest, Salmon/Scott River Ranger District, Fort Jones, 530/468-5351, www.fs.usda.gov/klamath.

35 TAYLOR LAKE TRAILHEAD TO HOGAN LAKE

7.4 mi/4.0 hr 3 8

from Etna Summit into the Russian Wilderness west of Etna

Map 2.2, page 68 **BEST**

Taylor Lake, a gorgeous lake at 6,400 elevation, is proof that wilderness-like lakes can be accessible by wheelchair. The trail is made of hard-packed dirt and wheelchair-accessible, though wheelchairs with wide wheels are recommended. For those with boots instead of wheels, it's about a 10-minute walk to Taylor Lake, a long, narrow lake set on the northern end of the Russian Wilderness. A high back wall completes the setting. Trout fishing is often very good here, and the walk is short enough for hikers to bring along a small raft or float tube.

Just before you reach the foot of Taylor Lake, there is a signed-cutoff (posted on a tree) for Hogan Lake. It picks up a trail on the right side of Taylor Lake. The route climbs a mile to a ridge at 7,000 feet, laterals across the divide, and then sails down the other side 1,000 feet. As you near Hogan, you cross a meadow and the trail disintegrates into a mosaic of faint routes. The lake is nestled at 5,950 feet, emerald green and against a high back wall, with a great campsite. From Hogan, a route to Big Blue Lake (6,800 feet) is available up a drainage that climbs 1,000 feet to the outlet at the rim (no marked trails). This hike is already rated high, an 8, and if you make it to Big Blue, make it a 10.

User Groups: Hikers, wheelchairs, dogs, and horses. No mountain bikes.
Permits: No permits are required for day use. A campfire permit (free) is required for campfires and stoves. Parking and access are free.
Maps: A trail information sheet can be obtained by contacting the Salmon Ranger District. For a map, ask the U.S. Forest Service for Klamath National Forest or Marble Mountain Wilderness. For a topographic map, ask the USGS for Eaton Peak.
Directions: From Redding, take I-5 to Yreka and the exit for Highway 3/Fort Jones. Take that exit to the stop sign, turn left, and drive a short distance to the lighted intersection. Turn left on Highway 3 and drive 28 miles southwest to Etna. Turn west (right) on Etna-Somes Bar Road (called Main Street in town) and drive 10.25 miles (over the top of the Etna Summit and down the other side) to Forest Road 41N18 (a signed access road). Turn left and continue to the trailhead.
Contact: Klamath National Forest, Salmon/Scott River Ranger District, Fort Jones, 530/468-5351, www.fs.usda.gov/klamath.

36 STATUE LAKE

6.0 mi/4.0 hr 

in the Russian Wilderness west of Etna

Map 2.2, page 68

Statue Lake earned its name from the unique granite sculptures that frame its back wall. When you first arrive at the small lake, it's a gorgeous yet solemn sight, one of nature's mountain temples. No place else looks like this. Some of the granite outcrops look like fingers sculpted with a giant chisel. There is a small primitive campsite on a granite overlook, from which you can often see small brook trout rising to feed in the lake.

After parking at the Music Creek trailhead, start the trip by hiking up a moderate grade and climbing about a mile through burned-out forest to the Pacific Crest Trail. It's black and burned for more than a mile. At the PCT, turn right and hike for about 1.5 miles, an easy walk in the forest. When you reach a small spring creek, stop and fill your canteens, then leave the trail and head uphill. There is no trail or sign. This is an off-trail trek where you read a topo map and match it up with the landscape. Well worth it. It's about a 30-minute, cross-country hike to the lake, and the last 10 minutes is over a large field of boulders. Pick your route carefully; some are difficult, some are easy. While much of the region shows evidence of a significant forest fire burn, Statue Lake itself is untouched.
User Groups: Hikers only. Dogs are permitted but not advised because of the route crossing a boulder field. No horses or mountain bikes. No wheelchair facilities.
Permits: No permits are required for day use. A campfire permit (free) is required for campfires and stoves. Parking and access are free.
Maps: A trail information sheet can be obtained by contacting the Salmon Ranger District. For a map, ask the U.S. Forest Service for Klamath National Forest or Marble Mountain Wilderness. For a topographic map, ask the USGS for Sawyers Bar.
Directions: From Redding, take I-5 to Yreka and the exit for Highway 3/Fort Jones. Take that exit to the stop sign, turn left, and drive a short distance to the lighted intersection. Turn left on Highway 3 and drive 28 miles southwest to Etna. Turn west on Etna-Somes Bar Road (called Main Street in town), drive over Etna Summit, and continue down the other side to Forest Road 40N54 (just before the Salmon River Bridge). Turn left on Forest Road 40N54 and drive eight miles to the Music Creek trailhead. (A sign that says Pacific Crest Trail is usually posted. The sign for Music Creek trailhead is repeatedly stolen.)
Contact: Klamath National Forest, Salmon/Scott River Ranger District, Fort Jones, 530/468-5351, www.fs.usda.gov/klamath.

37 TRAIL CREEK ROUTE

7.0 mi/2 days  4 6

in the Russian Wilderness west of Callahan

Map 2.2, page 68

The Trail Creek "Trail" is no longer an official trail. Outside of us, few have done this. The Forest Service has decommissioned it, which means no trail maintenance is performed. It is now more of a route, one that leads into the Russian Wilderness. We found it a quick, yet very steep, way to gain access to Syphon Lake and the Russian Wilderness. From Trail Creek Campground to the PCT, you are unlikely to see anybody else, and that's a plus. Because you won't see a soul, this is also a good route with dogs. The trailhead is a short distance up a gravel road across from Trail Creek Campground (located along Cecilville-Callahan Road). For the first 1.5 miles, the trail ventures steeply up on an old fire road (when you finish, you could always write the book, *My Life as a Jeep*). It continues to climb, and as you near the crest, you'll junction with the Pacific Crest Trail. Turn left on the PCT, and then just five minutes later, turn at a signed junction to Syphon Lake. This is a good first night's camp. Russian or Waterdog Lakes are good second-day destinations.

Once you hit the high country, the lakes are very beautiful, especially Russian Lake, which is excellent for swimming. Because the wilderness here is small, it does not take many people hiking in to take up the campsites. Expect occasional cow sightings in midsummer near Syphon Lake. The Russian Wilderness is a place so pristine and so small that it just can't handle many visitors (and the cows shouldn't be here either). If you go, walk softly, and treat the fragile area with care.

Note that the trailhead for the Pacific Crest Trail off the Cecilville-Callahan Road is by far preferable. This provides a much *easier* route into the southern portion of the Russian Wilderness, but it will add 10 miles to your round-trip. So it's your choice: easier and longer, shorter or harder?

User Groups: Hikers, dogs, and horses. Mountain bikes allowed only outside of the wilderness border. No wheelchair facilities.

Permits: A wilderness permit is required for hikers planning to camp. Parking and access are free.

Maps: For a map, ask the U.S. Forest Service for Klamath National Forest. For topographic maps, ask the USGS for Deadman Peak and Eaton Peak.

Directions: From Redding, drive north on I-5 for 70 miles. Just past Weed, take the Edgewood exit. At the stop sign, turn left and drive through the underpass to another stop sign. Turn right on Old Highway 99 and drive six miles to Gazelle. Turn left at Gazelle on Gazelle-Callahan Road and drive about 20 miles to Callahan. From Callahan on Highway 3, turn west on County Road 402 (Cecilville Road) and drive 17 miles to Trail Creek Campground. The trail has been decommissioned. Across from the campground, a route heads north from a gravel road.

Contact: Klamath National Forest, Salmon/Scott River Ranger District, Fort Jones, 530/468-5351, www.fs.usda.gov/klamath.

38 CECILVILLE ROAD TO RUSSIAN WILDERNESS (PCT)

3.0 mi one-way/1 day  3  7

from Cecilville Road west of Callahan to the southern border of the Russian Wilderness

Map 2.2, page 68

Most hikers use this as a jumping-off spot to the Russian Wilderness. This involves a long, steady climb up to the southern border of the Russian Wilderness. A good destination to the south is the short hike to Hidden Lake or South Fork Lakes. Those venturing onward along the PCT will then enter a complex landscape matrix that includes the headwaters of the Scott,

Salmon, and Trinity Rivers, along with the beautiful scenery that such diversity creates. Either way, you start from the bottom of the canyon at the North Fork Scott River, so you'll face a climb no matter what your destination.

To pick up the next trail heading north (actually, in this case, heading west), see the *Etna Summit to Grider Creek (PCT)* hike in this chapter. If you are walking this trail in reverse, see the *Scott Mountain to Cecilville Road (PCT)* hike in this chapter to continue east.

User Groups: Hikers, dogs, and horses. No mountain bikes. No wheelchair facilities.

Permits: No permits are required for this section. Parking and access are free. A single permit is required to hike the Pacific Crest Trail. Contact the national forest, Bureau of Land Management (BLM), or national park office at your point of entry for a combined permit that is good for traveling through multiple-permit areas during your dates of travel.

Maps: For topographic maps, ask the USGS for Deadman Peak and Eaton Peak.

Directions: From Redding, drive north on I-5 for 70 miles. Just past Weed, take the Edgewood exit. At the stop sign, turn left and drive through the underpass to another stop sign. Turn right on Old Highway 99 and drive six miles to Gazelle. Turn left at Gazelle on Gazelle-Callahan Road and drive about 20 miles to Callahan. From Callahan, turn west on Cecilville Road (County Road 402, narrow at times) and drive 11.5 miles to the Cecilville Summit. Parking is limited here; a larger parking area is just past Cecilville Summit at the Carter Meadows trailhead (it will add 0.25 mile to your hike).

Contact: Klamath National Forest, Salmon/Scott River Ranger District, Fort Jones, 530/468-5351, www.fs.usda.gov/klamath.

39 TRAIL GULCH LAKE/ LONG GULCH LAKE LOOP

9.1 mi/2 days 3 9

in the Trinity Alps Wilderness west of Callahan

Map 2.2, page 68

This is a beautiful weekend trek with two gorgeous lakes as your destinations in the Trinity Alps. It's a nine-mile round-trip with an elevation gain of roughly 2,400 feet. When you look at the map, you might think it makes more sense to do Long Gulch Lake first, then Trail Gulch, but we have recommended this route for many years and it still works the best.

The Trail Gulch Trail rises along Trail Gulch Creek, steeply at times, but in just 2.25 miles, you'll arrive at Trail Gulch Lake. That makes it close enough to go in and out in a day, or better yet, you can make it a good weekend overnighter without tremendous strain. Trail Gulch Lake is 14 acres and 21 feet deep. It is set northeast of Deadman Peak (7,741 feet). The fishing at Trail Gulch Lake is often good for small trout. Long Gulch Lake is just another three miles from Trail Gulch Lake, another gorgeous lake nestled in forest and backed on its far side by a towering sloped wall.

User Groups: Hikers, dogs, and horses. No mountain bikes. No wheelchair facilities.

Permits: A wilderness permit is required for hikers planning to camp. Parking and access are free.

Maps: For a map, ask the U.S. Forest Service for Klamath National Forest or Trinity Alps Wilderness. For topographic maps, ask the USGS for Deadman Peak and Billys Peak.

Directions: From Redding, drive north on I-5 for 70 miles. Just past Weed, take the Edgewood exit. At the stop sign, turn left and drive through the underpass to another stop sign. Turn right on Old Highway 99 and drive about six miles to Gazelle. Turn left on Gazelle-Callahan Road and drive about 20 miles to Callahan. From Callahan, turn west on County Road 402 (Cecilville Road) and drive 11 miles.

Turn left on Forest Road 39N08 and drive 1.5 miles to the trailhead.

Contact: Klamath National Forest, Salmon/Scott River Ranger District, Fort Jones, 530/468-5351, www.fs.usda.gov/klamath.

40 SCOTT MOUNTAIN TO CECILVILLE ROAD (PCT)

18.0 mi one-way/2 days 4 10

from Highway 3 at Scott Mountain Campground

Map 2.2, page 68

A number of wilderness lakes in the Trinity Alps that can that can be reached by side-trip hikes make this section of the PCT appealing. It draws many for trips of a weekend up to a week. From the camp at Scott Mountain, the trail is routed west for five miles, where the first of a series of lakes is within 0.5 mile of the trail. They include Upper Boulder, East Boulder, Mid Boulder, and Telephone Lakes—all quite pretty and accessible from the main trail. After hiking past Eagle Peak, set at 7,789 feet, you'll pass additional short cutoffs that are routed to West Boulder, Mavis, and Fox Creek Lakes. Hikers often camp at one of these lakes before the steep drop down to the South Fork Scott River and heading north into the Russian Wilderness.

To pick up the next trail heading north (actually, in this case, heading west), see the *Cecilville Road to Russian Wilderness (PCT)* hike in this chapter. If you are walking this trail in reverse, see the *Mumbo Basin to Scott Mountain (PCT)* hike in this chapter to continue south.

User Groups: Hikers, dogs, and horses. No mountain bikes. No wheelchair facilities.

Permits: A wilderness permit is required for camping in the Trinity Alps Wilderness. Contact the Weaverville Ranger District for information. A single permit is required to hike the Pacific Crest Trail. Contact the national forest, Bureau of Land Management (BLM), or national park office at your point of entry for a combined permit that is good for traveling through multiple-permit areas during your dates of travel.

Maps: For topographic maps, ask the USGS for Scott Mountain, Tangle Blue Lake, Billys Peak, and Deadman Peak.

Directions: From Callahan, drive south on Highway 3 about seven miles to the trailhead at Scott Mountain Campground.

Contact: Shasta-Trinity National Forest, Weaverville Ranger Station, Weaverville, 530/623-2121, www.fs.usda.gov/stnf.

41 KANGAROO LAKE TRAILHEAD/CORY PEAK

3.0 mi/2.25 hr 3 9

in Klamath National Forest east of Callahan

Map 2.2, page 68 BEST

From the lake, a spur trail rises steeply to the south and quickly intersects the Pacific Crest Trail. Turn left and the PCT rises steeply to the rim overlooking the lake. You climb about 800 feet in 1.5 miles. A nearby scramble to Cory Peak, at 7,737 feet, provides a 360-degree view. This is a great trail-style picnic site. All of Northern California's prominent mountain peaks are in view here, and immediately below you, to the west, is Kangaroo Lake, like a large sapphire. Backpackers can extend this trip eastward four miles on the Pacific Crest Trail past Robbers Meadow to Bull Lake, a small lake in a remote, sparse setting. Note that the early section of this trail is called the Fen Trail, but most use it to get to the rim above the lake for the big views.

Kangaroo Lake is one of the most easily reached pristine mountain lakes, with a campground, wheelchair-accessible fishing, and PCT trailhead located near the campground. Getting here may feel remote, but the road, Rail Creek Road, is paved all the way. It leads to a parking area set adjacent to the walk-in campground and trailhead for the short walk to the lake. The trailhead is just downhill from the parking area. Some will start at the campground and then intersect it, and make a left turn toward Cory Peak. The lake covers only 21 acres, but often produces large brook trout. In an unsolved conflict, most hikers call this the Kangaroo Lake trailhead, while some Forest Service rangers refer to it as the Fen trailhead.

User Groups: Hikers, dogs, horses, and mountain bikes. Fishing is wheelchair-accessible.

Permits: No permits are required. Parking and access are free.

Maps: A trail guide can be obtained by contacting Klamath National Forest. For a map, ask the U.S. Forest Service for Klamath National Forest. For a topographic map, ask the USGS for Scott Mountain.

Directions: From Redding, drive north on I-5 for 70 miles. Just past Weed, take the Edgewood exit. At the stop sign, turn left and drive through the underpass to another stop sign. Turn right on Old Highway 99 and drive about six miles to Gazelle. Turn left on Gazelle-Callahan Road and drive over the summit. Continue down the other side of the mountain about five miles to Rail Creek Road. Turn left on Rail Creek Road and drive seven miles to where the road dead-ends, at the parking area for Kangaroo Lake. As you drive up, look for the trail to the right of the campground.

Contact: Klamath National Forest, Salmon/Scott River Ranger District, Fort Jones, 530/468-5351, www.fs.usda.gov/klamath.

42 MOUNT EDDY TRAIL

10.3 mi/5 hr 5 10

Parks Creek Trailhead in Shasta-Trinity National Forest west of Mount Shasta

Map 2.2, page 68 BEST

The trip to the top of Mount Eddy is one of the best one-day mountain climbs in California. It requires a round-trip of about 10 miles, with a climb of 2,200 feet. Though most of it is rhythmic, there are two steep sections, including a long stretch of switchbacks to make the summit. Just as you gain the summit, a surreal moment arrives with the view of 14,179-foot Mount Shasta revealed all in that one moment. Giant Shasta looms over everything for a radius of 100 miles. Yet it is the summit of Mount Eddy where you get the best view of giant Shasta. Mount Eddy is directly to the west of Mount Shasta in Siskiyou County, with I-5 running down the valley between them. If you've ever cruised I-5, you've probably already seen it, even if it barely registered in the shadow of nearby Shasta.

The trip starts at a trailhead for the Pacific Crest Trail (known locally at the Parks Creek trailhead) with an easy hike to Deadfall Lakes. The walking starts off as easy and rhythmic, where you poke in and out of forest of mostly Douglas fir, with occasional visits from golden-mantled ground squirrels. It stays like this for just under three miles, gaining just 450 feet, when you reach a junction with the Mount Eddy Trail on your left and the Pacific Crest Trail on your right, at the foot of Middle Deadfall Lake (set just over a short rise). Turn left and start to climb. Once you pass Middle Deadfall Lake (7,300 feet), the climb becomes steeper, where you rise up 600 feet past the Upper Deadfall Lakes. The trail skirts the upper lake, nestled against the back face of Mount Eddy, and climbs to the ridge that overlooks the Deadfall Lakes Basin. The long-distance views to the west are breathtaking, and to soak them up, the ridge top makes for a natural rest stop.

From here the trail rises above tree line, and then climbs another 900 feet in less than a mile, with seven switchbacks routed up a barren slope. In the process, there is no hint of the coming view of Mount Shasta. Then, suddenly, just as you gain the top of Mount Eddy, the entire western exposure of Mount Shasta comes into view, a stunning moment with an additional 125 miles of scenic points stretching into the distance. Looking down to the east, you can see how the giant Shasta rises 11,000 feet from

Mount Eddy Trail

the 3,000-foot elevations of the valley below, a euphoric moment.

To turn this into an overnighter, there are several backpacking sites at Middle Deadfall Lake, both at the foot of the lake (popular with locals) and at the far end of the lake. A better choice is to climb up to the Upper Deadfall Lake, where there are a few pristine sites at the far end of the lake, to the left of the Mount Eddy Trail.

There is one continuing problem on this route. For years, and at times it can even seem routine, mountain bikers illegally ride the Pacific Crest Trail here. Bikes are banned from the entire length of the PCT, of course. I bike a lot, hit about 1,000 miles a year, and respect the PCT and wilderness and rules that ban any form of mechanization from the trail. That's how you step back in time.

User Groups: Hikers, dogs, and horses. No mountain bikes. No wheelchair facilities.

Permits: A campfire permit (free) is required for overnight use. Parking and access are free.

Maps: For a map, ask the U.S. Forest Service for Shasta-Trinity National Forest. For a topographic map, ask the USGS for Mount Eddy.

Directions: From Redding, drive north on I-5 for 70 miles. Just past Weed, take the Edgewood exit. At the stop sign, turn left and drive through the underpass to another stop sign. Turn right on Old Highway 99 and drive 0.5 mile to Stewart Springs Road. Turn left on Stewart Springs Road and drive to the road's end, at Stewart Springs Resort. Bear right on Forest Road 17 (Parks Creek Road) and drive nine miles to the Deadfall Lakes parking area at the summit. The trailhead is at the south side of the parking area. Take the Pacific Crest Trail, heading south.

Contact: Shasta-Trinity National Forest, Mount Shasta Ranger District, Mount Shasta, 530/926-4511, www.fs.usda.gov/stnf.

43 TOAD LAKE TRAIL

1.5 mi/2 days 1 8

in Shasta-Trinity National Forest west of Mount Shasta

Map 2.2, page 68 BEST

You might be wondering why a 1.5-mile round-trip hike, with a difficulty rating of only 1, is projected as a two-day trip. The reason is the drive to the trailhead. It's an endless, twisting road that winds its way up the Middle Fork drainage of the Sacramento River, rising up along the east flank of the Trinity Divide. It's too much driving, for most, to go up and back in a day (and on the way in, keep your tongue in your mouth, because the ride is so jarring that you might bite off the end of it when you hit a big pothole). Once parked, you'll immediately notice the perfect calm, and then, with a 15-minute walk to the lake (at 6,950 feet), you'll be furnished with a picture-perfect lakeside campsite. The lake covers 23 acres, provides excellent swimming, fair fishing for small trout (sometimes a bit weedy in late summer), and great side trips.

Side trip: The best side trip is the one-mile hike from Toad Lake to Porcupine Lake, an idyllic, pristine small lake near the PCT. To get there from Toad Lake, first walk to the back end of Toad Lake. Then look for an unsigned route (it looks kind of like a game trail) that is routed up the slope at the back of the lake. That route ventures upslope and, on top, junctions with the Pacific Crest Trail. Turn left and then walk south for 0.25 mile on the PCT to the Porcupine Lake cutoff, on the right. Gorgeous.

User Groups: Hikers, dogs, and horses. No mountain bikes allowed on the Pacific Crest Trail. No wheelchair facilities.

Permits: No permits are required. Parking and access are free.

Maps: For a map, ask the U.S. Forest Service for Shasta-Trinity National Forest. For a topographic map, ask the USGS for Mount Eddy.

Directions: From Redding, take I-5 north to the exit for Central Mount Shasta. Follow that exit to the stop sign. At the stop sign, turn left and drive 0.5 mile to Old Stage Road. Turn left on Old Stage Road and drive 0.25 mile to a fork with W. A. Barr Road. Stay to the right at the fork and drive two miles, cross Box Canyon Dam at Lake Siskiyou, and continue around the lake on W. A. Barr Road (which becomes Forest Road 26/South Fork Road). Continue past the turnoff for Lake Siskiyou Camp resort and then continue four miles, cross an unnamed concrete bridge, and look for a dirt road (Forest Road 41N53) on the right (signed Toad Lake/Morgan Meadows). Turn right and drive 0.2 mile to the first fork, bear left (on Forest Road 40N64), and drive 11 miles to the lake trailhead parking area. The road is very rough and twisting, and for the last 0.5 mile, a high-clearance, four-wheel-drive vehicle is recommended. It is a 0.5-mile walk from the parking area to the lake.

Contact: Shasta-Trinity National Forest, Mount Shasta Ranger District, Mount Shasta, 530/926-4511, www.fs.usda.gov/stnf.

44 SISSON-CALLAHAN

14.0 mi one-way/2 days 5 8

in Shasta-Trinity National Forest near Lake Siskiyou west of Mount Shasta

Map 2.2, page 68

The Sisson-Callahan Trail is something of a legend in the Mount Shasta area. For many years, few made this trek. It is getting revived by locals with an interest in history and unique hikes. This route is long, steep, and hot, climbing 5,000 feet over the course of nine miles to the top of Mount Eddy (at 9,025 feet), then heading down nearly 2,000 feet in two miles to Deadfall Lakes for the nearest campsite. Long ago, it was a well-traveled route up the east flank of Mount Eddy, over the top (through a saddle below the summit), and down to Deadfall Lakes. But with a much easier route available from the other side of Mount Eddy from the Deadfall Lakes trailhead, this trail is passed over. It is now something of a historic landmark.

The Sisson-Callahan Trail starts as an old logging road on the back side of Lake Siskiyou, not far from the mountain bike route that circles the lake (with a jog at the campground). The trail climbs up a canyon past meadows, then gains a ridge. It is not designated as wilderness, but after an hour, you will not see another soul and the land takes on a wilderness feel. The great scenic beauty doesn't start until you've climbed several thousand feet, and by then you'll care more about how much water is left in your canteen than about the incredible sweeping view of Mount Shasta to the east. As you get near the Trinity Divide, you'll face some killer switchbacks to reach the Eddy Ridge. As you come to the Eddy crest, look close and you will find an old metal sign for a former route for the Pacific Crest Trail; it might be 50 or 60 years old (and perhaps far older, as best we could gauge).

From here it is mandatory to detour and hike the switchbacks up to the Mount Eddy Summit. After that, it's a 1,750-foot descent to Middle Deadfall Lake, where you make camp. Your hiking reward comes the next morning, when, after lounging around at the lake, you walk out three nearly level miles to the Park Creek/PCT trailhead, then catch your shuttle ride back to Mount Shasta. All in all, this is a genuine butt-kicker of a trail. Unless you want to do a hike that no one else does, a much better route to the Deadfall Lakes and Mount Eddy is from the Parks Creek trailhead. On the other hand, you will be hiking in shadows of the pioneers that created this route more than a century ago.

User Groups: Hikers, dogs, horses, and mountain bikes. This is very difficult for mountain bikes, yet technically legal for trail if you stay off the PCT on the route out. No wheelchair facilities.

Permits: No permits are required. Parking and access are free.

Maps: For a map, ask the U.S. Forest Service for Shasta-Trinity National Forest. For topographic maps, ask the USGS for Mount Shasta city and Mount Eddy.

Directions: From Redding, take I-5 north to the exit for Central Mount Shasta city. Take that exit to the stop sign. Turn left and drive 0.5 mile to Old Stage Road. Turn left on Old Stage Road and drive 0.25 mile to a fork with W. A. Barr Road. Stay to the right at the fork and drive two miles to North Shore Road (if you cross the dam at Lake Siskiyou, you have gone too far). Turn right on North Shore (which becomes Forest Road 40N27/Deer Creek Road) and drive four miles, across the bridge on Deer Creek to the next major junction, Forest Road 40N27C. Turn left on Forest Road 40N27C and park along the edge of the road before the ford on the North Fork Sacramento. (The water here is sometimes deeper than it looks; don't be tempted to drive it.) The Sisson-Callahan Trail (which first appears as a road) starts on the other side of the ford, on an old logging skid road that goes to the right. Within 0.5 mile, it turns into a trail.

Contact: Shasta-Trinity National Forest, Mount Shasta Ranger District, Mount Shasta, 530/926-4511, www.fs.usda.gov/stnf.

45 HEART LAKE TRAIL

3.0 mi/2.25 hr 2 10

at Castle Lake in Shasta-Trinity National Forest west of Mount Shasta

Map 2.2, page 68

This is the best site for a photo of Mount Shasta. If you want a calendar-quality photograph, trek to Heart Lake. Then scramble up the back wall and you'll get a breathtaking view of Mount Shasta with this heart-shaped alpine pond in the foreground. (Also note that the best drive-to spot anywhere for photographs of Mount Shasta is on Castle Lake Road at a turnout about one mile downhill from the Castle Lake parking area.) For years, this route crossed a section of private property, but the local Siskiyou Land

Trust helped arrange the purchase of it in 2019 and the route is protected forever.

To start, at the parking area for pretty Castle Lake, look for the trailhead on the left side of the lake. You will cross the outlet stream. The trail then rises up along the slope just left of the lake. Below to your right is Castle Lake, a pretty sight that's set in a rock bowl with a high back wall. The trail rises up, steep in a few spots, to a saddle at 5,900 feet. At the saddle, bear uphill to the right on the faint trail. If you have the ability to envision wild landscapes, look for the wall and terrace above you, a bit to the right. The hike then becomes an easy scramble. Keep an eye out for faint routes and rock cairns that lead the way to the lake. It is nestled over a lip at 6,050 feet, tucked away in a pocket. Because the lake is small, the water warms up by midsummer, making it great for wading, a quick dip or short swims. The view is a real stunner.

The tale of Castle Lake, set at an elevation of 5,450 feet, is that the water is like none other in the world, which has led some people to jump into the lake for complete renewal. In reality, the water is so pure, containing few nutrients of any kind, that UC Davis has a water-sampling station here in an ongoing comparison study with Lake Tahoe.

User Groups: Hikers and dogs. Not suitable for horses or mountain bikes. No wheelchair facilities.

Permits: No permits are required. Parking and access is free.

Maps: For a map, ask the U.S. Forest Service for Shasta-Trinity National Forest or Castle Crags Wilderness. For a topographic map, ask the USGS for Mount Shasta city.

Directions: From Redding, take I-5 north to the exit for Central Mount Shasta city. Follow that exit to the stop sign. Turn left and drive 0.5 mile to Old Stage Road. Turn left on Old Stage Road and drive 0.25 mile to a fork with W. A. Barr Road. Stay to the right at the fork and drive two miles, cross Box Canyon Dam at Lake Siskiyou, and continue 0.5 mile to Castle Lake Road. Turn left and drive 7.5 miles to the parking area at the end of the road at Castle Lake. The trailhead begins on the eastern end of the parking lot.

Contact: Shasta-Trinity National Forest, Mount Shasta Ranger District, Mount Shasta, 530/926-4511, www.fs.usda.gov/stnf.

46 MCCLOUD RIVER WATERFALL TRAIL

3.8 mi/2.0 hr

at Fowler's Camp in Shasta-Trinity National Forest east of McCloud

Map 2.2, page 68

Middle Falls on the McCloud River is one of the prettiest waterfalls in Northern California. After a photo of it appeared on the cover of *Sunset* in 2019, it has become one of the most popular go-to spots in the north state. It is a wide and tall curtain-like cascade of water that pours over a 50-foot cliff into a deep pool in a rock bowl. A spur from a paved road leads to an overlook, but a better trip is to hike the McCloud River Waterfall Trail, where you not only get a better view from the plunge pool, but see three waterfalls in the process of a 3.8-mile round-trip. Start at the parking area for Lower Falls. Lower Falls is a chute-type waterfall, visible with a short walk from the paved parking area. The trail starts down a rock staircase on the left and then picks up as a paved pathway. You skirt above the McCloud River to your right, pass Fowler's Campground on your left, and then come to a junction with the dirt Middle Falls Trail. The trail is routed into forest, with the gorgeous river off to your right for 0.8 mile. You'll round a bend, probably hearing the waterfall before you see it, and then suddenly, there it is, this wide sheet. It's something like a miniature Niagara Falls. The trail runs near a boulder field on the outer reaches of the plunge pool. On summer weekends, teenagers climb to the rim above the falls, then plunge 50 feet into the pool like human missiles. It's a dangerous venture that we don't recommend. A friend tried it and broke his leg.

The trail then cuts to your left and switchbacks up to the rim overlooking Middle Falls. Though not signed, the route is clear extending upstream to staircase-like Upper Falls. The trail runs near the brink of the falls, where water shoots past. It is also possible to drive to a parking area near the brink of the falls, reducing the hike to about 50 yards. A restroom is available at the parking area. There is one frustrating element. Because the falls have become easy to reach with a paved service road, you get the bad with the good—visitors litter this spot, or worse, they discard cigarette butts on the trail. We try to reverse this violation of nature by packing out any trash that we see.

User Groups: Hikers and dogs. No horses or mountain bikes. The paved path from Lower Falls to Middle Falls is wheelchair-accessible.

Permits: No permits are required. Parking and access are free.

Maps: For a map, ask the U.S. Forest Service for Shasta-Trinity National Forest. For a topographic map, ask the USGS for McCloud.

Directions: From Redding, take I-5 north for 47 miles to the Highway 89/McCloud-Reno exit. Bear right on Highway 89 and drive nine miles to McCloud. Continue southeast on Highway 89 for five miles to the sign for Fowler's Campground and Forest Road 39N28. Turn right and drive one mile to a fork.

To reach Lower Falls: At the fork, turn right and drive to the parking area and overlook.

To reach Middle Falls Trailhead: Bear left at the fork for Fowler's Campground, drive through the campground to the restroom, and park. The trailhead is across the road from the restroom.

Contact: Shasta-Trinity National Forest, McCloud Ranger District, McCloud, 530/964-2184, www.fs.usda.gov/stnf.

Middle Falls Trail

47 CARIBOU LAKES TRAIL

18.0 mi/2 days 3 9

in the Trinity Alps Wilderness northwest of Trinity Lake

Map 2.2, page 68

The Caribou Lakes Basin provides the classic Trinity Alps scene: three high-mountain lakes, beautiful and serene, with the back wall of the Sawtooth Ridge casting a monumental backdrop on one side, and on the other side, a drop-off and great views of a series of mountain peaks and ridgelines. Sunsets are absolutely remarkable when viewed from here. The centerpiece is Caribou Lake, the largest lake in the Trinity Alps Wilderness. Because it's a nine-mile hike to the Caribou Lakes Basin, this often makes for a first night's camp for week-long treks into this section of the Trinity Alps Wilderness.

The trail starts at the bottom of the Salmon River, however, and like all trails that begin at the bottom of canyons, it means you set out with a terrible climb that never seems to end, especially on hot summer afternoons. Plan on drinking a full canteen of water, and be certain not to miss the natural spring near the crest, just off to the right (look for the spur-like footpath that leads to it). After reaching the crest, the trail travels counterclockwise around the mountain for several hours en route, then drops into the Caribou Lakes Basin. Ignore your urge to stop at the first lake, because the best campsites, swimming, and views are from last lake of the circuit, Caribou Lake. Because this is a popular destination, fishing is often poor.

User Groups: Hikers and dogs. Horses are permitted but not recommended. No mountain bikes. No wheelchair facilities.

Permits: A wilderness permit is required for camping.

Maps: For a map, ask the U.S. Forest Service for Klamath National Forest or Trinity Alps Wilderness. For a topographic map, ask the USGS for Caribou Lakes.

Directions: From Weaverville, take Highway 3 north past Trinity Lake and continue to Coffee Creek Road/County Road 104 (near the Coffee Creek Ranger Station). Turn left and drive 17 miles to the trailhead at the end of the road at Big Flat Campground.

Contact: Shasta-Trinity National Forest, Weaverville Ranger Station, Weaverville, 530/623-2121, www.fs.usda.gov/stnf; Klamath National Forest, Salmon/Scott River Ranger District, Fort Jones, 530/468-5351, www.fs.usda.gov/klamath.

48 UNION LAKE TRAIL

12.0 mi/2 days

in the Trinity Alps Wilderness northwest of Trinity Lake

Map 2.2, page 68

Union Lake is a blue gem nestled in a granite basin below sloped alpine granite Red Rock Mountain. The hike in and out is a good weekend affair, but most visitors are backpackers who are using the camp at the lake as a first-day destination for a multiday trip. It's one of several good trailheads on (or near) Coffee Creek Road. The trail starts near an old sawmill along Coffee Creek, heads south (to the left), and in less than a mile starts the climb adjacent to Union Creek (on your right). Like most hikes that start at a streambed, you pay for your pleasure, going up, not down. After about two miles, the trail crosses Union Creek and continues on for a few miles, now with the stream on the left. Most of the walk is in forest with good shade. You'll pass a trail junction for Bullards Basin, and about 0.5 mile later, turn right on the cutoff trail to Union Lake. The lake is long and shallow, with good swimming in summer. With Union Lake as a base camp, other lakes within range by day hikes are Landers and Foster Lakes.

User Groups: Hikers, dogs, and horses. No mountain bikes. No wheelchair facilities.

Permits: A wilderness permit is required for hikers planning to camp.

Maps: For a map, ask the U.S. Forest Service for Shasta-Trinity National Forest or Trinity Alps Wilderness. For a topographic map, ask the USGS for Caribou Lakes.

Directions: From Weaverville, take Highway 3 north past Trinity Lake and continue to Coffee Creek Road/County Road 104 (near the Coffee Creek Ranger Station). Turn left and drive about 10 miles to the trailhead, on the left.

Contact: Shasta-Trinity National Forest, Weaverville Ranger Station, Weaverville, 530/623-2121, www.fs.usda.gov/stnf.

49 BIG BEAR LAKE TRAIL

10.0 mi/2 days 3 8

in the Trinity Alps Wilderness south of Callahan

Map 2.2, page 68

The five-mile hike up to Big Bear Lake, a large lake by wilderness standards, beautiful by anybody's standards, can make for a weekend backpack trip. The hike is steep, with little shade. The trail ends at the lake, so if the lakeside campsites are already taken when you arrive, you're out of luck for a quality place to camp. The trailhead is easy to reach just off Highway 3 north of Trinity Lake. The route is simple but not easy. It follows Bear Creek for the entire route, with one stream crossing, and climbs all the way. The trail is steep and beautiful. Once you reach the lake, a bonus is the side trip to the Wee Bear Lakes. From the outlet of Big Bear, take the easterly ridge, which takes about a mile of scrambling cross-country to reach the basin with the Wee Bears, as we call them. Big Bear has become popular in peak summer.

User Groups: Hikers and dogs. Horses are allowed but not recommended. No mountain bikes. No wheelchair facilities.

Permits: A wilderness permit is required for hikers planning to camp in the wilderness.

Maps: For a map, ask the U.S. Forest Service for Shasta-Trinity National Forest. For a topographic map, ask the USGS for Tangle Blue Lake.

Directions: From Redding, take I-5 to Yreka and the exit for Highway 3/Fort Jones. Take that exit to the stop sign, turn left, and drive a short distance to the lighted intersection. Turn left on Highway 3 and drive about 40 miles to Callahan. Continue south on Highway 3 for about 13 miles to Bear Creek Loop Road. Turn right and drive a short distance (on an unpaved road) to the signed trailhead (located near the Bear Creek road crossing).

Contact: Shasta-Trinity National Forest, Weaverville Ranger Station, Weaverville, 530/623-2121, www.fs.usda.gov/stnf.

50 MUMBO BASIN TO SCOTT MOUNTAIN (PCT)

35.0 mi one-way/4 days 3 10

in Shasta-Trinity National Forest from Gumboot trailhead to Scott Mountain

Map 2.2, page 68

This section of the PCT starts at a popular trailhead and quickly jumps northward into remote, beautiful country. The first highlight, only a mile up the trail, is the view below, to the left of secluded Picayune Lake (there are no trails to it). The PCT then heads on, passing little yet pristine Porcupine Lake (you don't see it from the trail, but access is easy from the PCT on a short spur trail). The trail then heads over the rim and skirts below Middle Deadfall Lake (just over the rise to your right), a popular site for easy backpack trips (plan on company). From Deadfall Lakes, the trail continues as an easy jaunt to the Parks Creek trailhead and crosses a paved road. It then eventually descends and curves around the headwaters of the Trinity River, then climbs back up Chilcoot Pass and past Bull Lake. No more people. From here, it's a 10-mile pull to the Scott Mountain Summit trailhead (see the *Cecilville Road to Russian Wilderness (PCT)* hike in this chapter).

If you are walking this trail in reverse, see

the *Castle Crags to Mumbo Basin (PCT)* hike in this chapter to continue south.

User Groups: Hikers, dogs, and horses. No mountain bikes. No wheelchair facilities.

Permits: No permits are required. Parking and access are free. A single permit is required to hike the Pacific Crest Trail. Contact the national forest, Bureau of Land Management (BLM), or national park office at your point of entry for a combined permit that is good for traveling through multiple-permit areas during your dates of travel.

Maps: For topographic maps, ask the USGS for Mumbo Basin, South China Mountain, and Scott Mountain.

Directions: From Redding, take I-5 north to the exit for Central Mount Shasta city. Follow that exit to the stop sign. Turn left and drive 0.5 mile to Old Stage Road. Turn left on Old Stage Road and drive 0.25 mile to a fork with W. A. Barr Road. Stay to the right at the fork and drive two miles, cross Box Canyon Dam at Lake Siskiyou, and continue around the lake on W. A. Barr Road (which becomes Forest Road 26/ South Fork Road). Continue four miles past the Lake Siskiyou Camp resort and continue up the canyon for 12.5 miles to Gumboot Lake Road. Bear right, staying on Forest Road 26, and continue 2.5 miles to the ridge and the parking area and trailhead.

Contact: Shasta-Trinity National Forest, Mount Shasta Ranger District, Mount Shasta, 530/926-4511, www.fs.usda.gov/stnf.

51 GUMBOOT OVERLOOK CRAG

1.5 mi/1.5 hr 4 10

in Shasta-Trinity National Forest west of Mount Shasta

Map 2.2, page 68

This is an off-trail trek for people who like to scramble to ridges for views. If you must always have a trail to hike on, well, this trip is not for you. But if you don't mind a little cross-country scramble to a mountain rim, then a short cutoff to a peak with spectacular views of Gumboot Lake and Mount Shasta beyond, sign up for this hike.

The trip starts at Gumboot Lake (6,050 feet elevation), a pretty lake in the Trinity Divide. As you face the lake, look for an anglers' trail on the right. It leads in a half circle around the lake. At the back of the lake, break off to the right of the trail and start climbing the slope, where you head up toward the ridge that is a backdrop for the basin. A little less than halfway to the top, you'll pass Little Gumboot Lake and after that, you will scramble your way to the ridge, where you'll intersect with the Pacific Crest Trail. If you are comfortable off-trail, the difficulty is a 3; if not, a 5. Head to the left for a short distance, then break off the trail again, this time to the left, where you head on the mountain spine toward the peak that towers over Gumboot Lake, with Mount Shasta as the backdrop off to the east. This is Gumboot Overlook Crag, your destination. The world may not be perfect, but from this lookout, it comes close.

User Groups: Hikers and dogs only. No horses or mountain bikes. No wheelchair facilities.

Permits: No permits are required. Parking and access are free.

Maps: For a map, ask the U.S. Forest Service for Shasta-Trinity National Forest. For a topographic map, ask the USGS for Mumbo Basin.

Directions: From I-5 at Mount Shasta city, take the Central Mount Shasta exit. At the stop sign, turn west and drive 0.5 mile to Old Stage Road. Turn left on Old Stage Road and drive 0.25 mile to a fork with W. A. Barr Road. Stay to the right at the fork and drive two miles, cross Box Canyon Dam at Lake Siskiyou, and continue around the lake on W. A. Barr Road (which becomes Forest Road 26/South Fork Road). Continue four miles past the Lake Siskiyou Camp resort and continue up the canyon to Gumboot Lake Road (Forest Road 40N37). Bear left on Gumboot Lake Road and drive 0.5 mile to the parking area near the shore of the lake.

Contact: Shasta-Trinity National Forest, Mount Shasta Ranger District, Mount Shasta, 530/926-4511, www.fs.usda.gov/stnf.

52 TAMARACK LAKE TRAILHEAD

5.0 mi/4.0 hr

in Shasta-Trinity National Forest southwest of Mount Shasta

Map 2.2, page 68

Tamarack Lake is a beautiful alpine lake and a place of remarkable serenity so pretty that it can feel sacred. Set high in the Trinity Divide at 6,000 feet, this jewel sits nestled in a high basin and backed by a mountain wall. The route in is on an old jeep road. From the trailhead at 5,232 feet, you are routed south up to a subridge at 5,600 feet, then past a meadow. At the first of two smaller lakes, the Twin Lakes, bear left past both lakes. The route then climbs another short ridge to arrive at Tamarack Lake at 5,962 feet. From the back (southern) side of Tamarack, there is a great view of Grey Rocks, a series of dark, craggy peaks. Hit it right, with nobody else around, and this place will have you thanking a higher power for the privilege of breathing the air here. This is where my lifetime friend John Reginato, a north state legend voted into the California Outdoors Hall of Fame, told me he wanted his ashes scattered; his family chose otherwise.

User Groups: Hikers and dogs. Not suitable for horses or mountain bikes. No wheelchair facilities.

Permits: No permits are required.

Maps: For a map, ask the U.S. Forest Service for Shasta-Trinity National Forest. For a topographic map, ask the USGS for Chicken Hawk Hill.

Directions: From Redding, take I-5 north for about 50 miles to the exit for Castella/Castle Crags State Park. Take that exit to the stop sign, turn left and drive west on Castle Creek Road. Continue past the park (the road becomes Forest Road 25/Whalen Road) and continue 12.5 miles on to Forest Road 38N17 (Tamarack Road). Turn left on Forest Road 38N17 and drive about three miles (near the second crossing of Twin Lakes Creek) to a very rough jeep road on your right. The jeep road is the trailhead. Park on the shoulder in the vicinity; do not block the road. Note: A handful of off-road drivers with specialized vehicles occasionally drive the jeep road to Tamarack Lake.

Contact: Shasta-Trinity National Forest, Mount Shasta Ranger District, Mount Shasta, 530/926-4511, www.fs.usda.gov/stnf.

53 ROOT CREEK TRAIL

2.3 mi/1.75 hr 1 7

in Castle Crags State Park south of Mount Shasta

Map 2.2, page 68

Castle Crags State Park features a series of huge granite spires that tower over the Sacramento River Canyon, the kind of sight that can take your breath away the first time you see it from I-5. That sight inspires a lot of people to take one of the hikes at the park, and while most don't have the time, energy, or body conditioning to complete Castle Crags Trail, Root Creek Trail is a good second choice.

As you drive up the access road, look for the signed trailhead to the left, just as you arrive at the parking area. The elevation is 2,500 feet at the trailhead. Start at this trailhead, which is signed for Castle Crags Trail, and walk 0.25 mile to a trail junction. Turn right on Root Creek Trail. From here, the trail is routed through a thick, cool forest, an easy walk that most visitors overlook. It continues to Root Creek, a pretty, babbling stream. You'll eventually see some vintage pipes, valves, and infrastructure from when this was the water intake for a small settlement down the canyon below. Those with canyoneering skills should trek upstream; on the right side of the stream, look for a series of small pool-and-drop waterfalls that few know about.

User Groups: Hikers only. No dogs, horses, or mountain bikes. No wheelchair facilities.

Permits: No permits are required. A state park entrance fee of $8 is charged for each vehicle.

Maps: A trail map can be obtained for a fee by contacting Castle Crags State Park. For a topographic map, ask the USGS for Dunsmuir.

Directions: From Redding, take I-5 north for 46 miles to the exit for Castella/Castle Crags State Park. Take that exit to the stop sign, turn left and drive west on Castle Creek Road. Continue (past a gas station and store on the left) for 0.25 mile to the park entrance on the right. Turn right and drive to the kiosk. Just past the kiosk, bear right and drive two miles (past the campground) to the parking area for Vista Point. From the parking area, walk a short distance west down the entrance road to the signed trailhead on the north side (right side, when walking back).

Contact: Castle Crags State Park, Castella, 530/235-2684, www.parks.ca.gov.

54 CASTLE CRAGS TO MUMBO BASIN (PCT)

25.0 mi one-way/2 days 

from Castle Crags State Park west into Shasta-Trinity National Forest

Map 2.2, page 68

This is a key juncture for the PCT, where the trail climbs out of a river canyon and back to high ridgelines. It's in a classic region, the Trinity Divide, known for lakes sculpted in granite and sweeping views of Mount Shasta. From the start, the trail runs beneath the spires of Castle Crags, a setting that can astonish newcomers. From the Sacramento River at Castle Crags, at an elevation of 2,000 feet, the trail laterals up the north side of Castle Creek Canyon, rising just below the base of the awesome crags. In wet years, you will pass beautiful Burstarse Falls on the right. The trail finally hits the rim at the back of Castle Ridge. Then it follows the rim in a half circle to the west to the Seven Lakes Basin and beyond to the Mumbo Basin and the Gumboot Lake trailhead. The final five miles of this segment pass by a dozen pristine mountain lakes, but most are well off the trail.

To continue north on the PCT, see the *Mumbo Basin to Scott Mountain (PCT)* hike in this chapter. If you are walking this trail in reverse, see the *Ash Camp to Castle Crags Wilderness (PCT)* hike in this chapter to continue south.

User Groups: Hikers only. No dogs, horses, or mountain bikes. No wheelchair facilities.

Permits: No permits are required. A state park entrance fee of $8 is charged for each vehicle if you drive through the park entrance. A single permit is required to hike the Pacific Crest Trail. Contact the national forest, Bureau of Land Management (BLM), or national park office at your point of entry for a combined permit that is good for traveling through multiple-permit areas during your dates of travel.

Maps: A trail map can be obtained for a fee by contacting Castle Crags State Park. For topographic maps, ask the USGS for Dunsmuir, Seven Lakes Basin, and Mumbo Basin.

Directions: From Redding, take I-5 north for 46 miles to the exit for Castella/Castle Crags State Park. Take that exit to the stop sign, turn left and drive west on Castle Creek Road. Continue (past a gas station and store on the left) for 0.25 mile to the park entrance on the right. Turn right and drive to the kiosk. Just past the kiosk, bear right and drive two miles (past the campground) to the parking area for Vista Point. From the parking area, walk a short distance west down the entrance road to the signed trailhead on the north side (right side, when walking back).

Contact: Castle Crags State Park, Castella, 530/235-2684, www.parks.ca.gov.

55 CRAGS TRAIL TO CASTLE DOME

6.5 mi/4.0 hr 5 10

in Castle Crags State Park south of Mount Shasta

Map 2.2, page 68

From Vista Point in Castle Crags State Park, hikers can gaze up at the fantastic crags and spot Castle Dome (at 4,966 feet), the leading spire on the crags' ridge. This high, rounded, missile-shaped piece of rock is your destination on Castle Crags Trail. If you're out of shape, be warned: This climb is a butt-kicker, where you climb all the way, often like a workout on a Stairmaster, until you reach the ridge.

As you drive up to the parking area, you will see the signed trailhead on your left (just before the parking lot). The elevation is 2,500 feet. Start by taking Castle Crags Trail for 0.25 mile; when you reach a three-trail junction, continue ahead on the Castle Crags Trail. Here the trail launches off, rising through a thick forest. It climbs steeply at times before eventually turning to the right. It emerges from the forest. Once above tree line, the views of the Sacramento River Canyon far below get better with each rising step. In spring, snow and ice fields are common this high. The trail goes onward, always climbing, and eventually you will reach a saddle at the foot of Castle Dome, where a few trees have somehow gained toeholds (you cannot climb Castle Dome without ropes and high-level rock-climbing skills). Continue on, the best is just ahead. The trail wends its way into the ridge interior of the crags. To your right, you can scramble off-trail up to a notch, where you get a divine perch to gaze north at Mount Shasta. You don't actually climb the dome, but rather this perch in the notch for a view. It will be a moment you'll prize forever.

The views and photographs are eye-popping, making it a must-do for those who rate their hikes based on the lookouts. However, not all of the trip is pristine; unfortunately, highway noise emerges from the canyon, as well as that of the inevitable freight train. Once you gain the interior of the near the summit rim, there isn't a hint of extraneous noise.

User Groups: Hikers only. No dogs, horses, or mountain bikes. No wheelchair facilities.

Permits: No permits are required. A state park entrance fee of $8 is charged for each vehicle.

Maps: A trail map can be obtained for a fee by contacting Castle Crags State Park. For a topographic map, ask the USGS for Dunsmuir.

Directions: From Redding, take I-5 north for 46 miles to the exit for Castella/Castle Crags State Park. Take that exit to the stop sign, turn left and drive west on Castle Creek Road. Continue (past a gas station and store on the left) for 0.25 mile to the park entrance on the right. Turn right and drive to the kiosk. Just past the kiosk, bear right and drive two miles (past the campground) to the parking area for Vista Point. From the parking area, walk a short distance west down the entrance road to the signed trailhead on the north side (right side, when walking back).

Contact: Castle Crags State Park, Castella, 530/235-2684, www.parks.ca.gov.

56 ASH CAMP TO CASTLE CRAGS WILDERNESS (PCT)

30.0 mi one-way/2 days 4 10

from Ash Camp on the McCloud River west into Castle Crags State Park

Map 2.2, page 68

Of the hundreds of rivers along the Pacific Crest Trail, the McCloud River is one of the most prized. Yet this segment of the PCT is largely high above the river, not right next to it, and except for one spot, you have to scramble down the canyon on anglers' trails to get to water. The starting point for this segment is right alongside the lush McCloud River at Ash Camp, set at about 3,000 feet (note that the road in from McCloud to this access point has been blocked by a landslide, and most PCT hikers now continue to Castella for supplies and to pick up food drops). From Ash Camp, the trail is routed downstream above the McCloud River for 2.5 miles, then is routed away from it. Eventually you cross Squaw Valley Creek (gorgeous, be sure to fill your water bottles) and then climb steeply to top Girard Ridge (at 4,500 feet), a long and dry climb. But when you top the final ridge above the Sacramento River Canyon, Mount Shasta, Black Butte, and Castle Crags suddenly emerge into view. After traversing the ridge for a few miles, the trail suddenly drops and cascades down to the Sacramento River Canyon at Soda Creek. Your toes will be jamming into your boots as you head downhill. At the river you might stop to soak your feet before picking up and heading west to start the climb into Castle Crags State Park. A small store, bar, and resupply point is nearby in Castella at Ammirati's.

To continue north on the PCT, see the *Castle Crags to Mumbo Basin (PCT)* hike in this chapter. If you are walking this trail in reverse, see the *McArthur-Burney Falls Memorial State Park to Ash Camp (PCT)* hike, in the *Lassen and Modoc* chapter, to continue south.

User Groups: Hikers, dogs, and horses. No mountain bikes. No wheelchair facilities.

Permits: Wilderness permits are required only in Castle Crags Wilderness. A single permit is required to hike the Pacific Crest Trail. Contact the national forest, Bureau of Land Management (BLM), or national park office at your point of entry for a combined permit that is good for traveling through multiple-permit areas during your dates of travel.

Maps: For topographic maps, ask the USGS for Shoeinhorse Mountain, Yellowjacket Mountain, and Dunsmuir.

Directions: From Redding, take I-5 north for 47 miles to the Highway 89/McCloud-Reno exit. Bear right on Highway 89 and drive nine miles to McCloud and Squaw Valley Road. Turn right on Squaw Valley Road, and drive about five miles (Squaw Valley Road becomes Forest Road 11/Hawkins Creek Road). Continue on Forest Road 11, keeping right past the McCloud boat ramp, and continue over the McCloud Dam. Turn right (still Forest Road 11) and drive down the canyon for one mile. At the turnoff for Ash Camp, bear right and drive a short distance to the parking area.

Note: A slide has blocked the access road to Ash Camp; it's unlikely to be re-opened before 2022.

Contact: Shasta-Trinity National Forest, McCloud Ranger District, McCloud, 530/964-2184, www.fs.usda.gov/stnf.

57 MCCLOUD NATURE TRAIL

5.0 mi/2.5 hr 1 9

at Nature Conservancy on the McCloud River south of McCloud

Map 2.2, page 68 **BEST**

Have you ever yearned for a place where old trees are left standing, deer and bobcats roam without fear, and a crystal-perfect river flows free in an untouched canyon? The McCloud River Preserve is such a place, and because it's managed by the Nature Conservancy, it will always remain that way. Although the lower McCloud River is best known for its fly-fishing for trout, there's an excellent hiking trail that runs alongside the river that spans 2.5 miles from the parking area on downstream. After parking, the trail is routed along the river, with a rocky path for 100 yards, and then ventures into forest and emerges at a cabin managed for the McCloud River Preserve for the Nature Conservancy. The trail then runs along the river, with one climb and drop, for 2.25 miles. A highlight, about two miles in, is where the river plunges into a series of deep holes and gorges. Few go past this point. At the end of the trail, the river is blocked by a yellow nylon rope, with some poison oak in the vicinity here, to indicate the end of the property owned by the Nature Conservancy.

If you camp at nearby Ah-Di-Na Campground, another trail runs upstream along the McCloud River, but does not connect to this featured stretch. The McCloud Nature Trail starts a full mile downstream by road from Ah-Di-Na.

User Groups: Hikers only. No dogs, horses, or mountain bikes. No wheelchair facilities.

Permits: No permits are required. Parking and access are free. If you fish, access is limited to no more than 10 rods at a time, the use of artificials with single barbless hooks, and catch-and-release only.

Maps: For a map, ask the U.S. Forest Service for Shasta-Trinity National Forest. For a topographic map, ask the USGS for Lake McCloud.

Directions: From Redding, take I-5 north for 47 miles to the Highway 89/McCloud-Reno exit. Bear right on Highway 89 and drive nine miles to McCloud at Squaw Valley Road. Turn right on Squaw Valley Road and drive 11.5 miles (at five miles, the road passes from Siskiyou County into Shasta County and becomes Forest Road 11. It then crosses a cattle guard and continues to McCloud Reservoir. At the reservoir, turn right and continue) to Battle Creek Cove and Forest Road 38N53/Ah-Di-Na Road (a dirt road) on the right. Turn right and drive seven miles (dusty, often bumpy, continue past Ah-Di-Na Campground) to the road's end at Fisher Creek and trailhead. The Nature Conservancy boundary is 0.5 mile downstream.

Contact: McCloud River Preserve, The Nature Conservancy, 415-777-0487, www.nature.org.

58 NEW RIVER TRAILHEAD

24.0 mi/3 days 3 6

in the Trinity Alps Wilderness east of Willow Creek

Map 2.3, page 69

This route is a little-used rarity in the Trinity Alps Wilderness: a trail that features small streams, not high-mountain lakes. In addition, there is damage from forest fires in the area. But if you want to be by yourself, this is the place. The highlights are the headwaters of the New River (a tributary to the Trinity River), the history of the area, and Mary Blaine Meadow.

The trail starts right along the New River, the site of one of California's last runs of summer steelhead. You'll hike about three miles before the junction with the Slide Creek Trail. Slide Creek Trail is 9.5 miles and passes Mary Blaine Meadow, the final destination of this hike (just a half mile before Slide Creek Trail ends at Salmon Summit Trail). The meadow is set below Mary Blaine Mountain and, to the north, Dees Peak. The whole region is cut with small streams in crevices and canyons. You want a hike with no people? You just found it.

User Groups: Hikers, dogs, and horses. No mountain bikes. No wheelchair facilities.

Permits: A wilderness permit is required for hikers planning to camp.

Maps: For a map, ask the U.S. Forest Service for Shasta-Trinity National Forest or Trinity Alps Wilderness. For topographic maps, ask the USGS for Jim Jam Ridge, Dees Peak, and Trinity Mountain.

Directions: From Weaverville, take Highway 299 west 45 miles to Denny Road. Turn north (right) on County Road 402 (Denny Road) and drive about 21 miles. Turn left on Forest Road 7N15 and drive four miles north to the trailhead parking area. The trailhead is at Hawkins Bar.

Contact: Shasta-Trinity National Forest, Weaverville Ranger Station, Weaverville, 530/623-2121, www.fs.usda.gov/stnf.

59 EAST FORK LOOP

20.0 mi/3 days 3 7

in the Trinity Alps Wilderness east of Willow Creek

Map 2.3, page 69

Where else can you hike 20 miles with a chance of not seeing anybody? The East Fork trailhead provides access to one of the more primitive, less-traveled regions of the Trinity Alps Wilderness. It's an area known for streams and forests in the lower reaches and bare limestone ridges in the higher reaches, with a mosaic of forest fire damage in the region from several fires. The trip starts at East Fork trailhead, adjacent to the East Fork New River. It climbs along this watershed and, after two miles, turns before coming to Pony Creek. In the next six miles, which include sections that are quite steep, the trail climbs to Limestone Ridge, near little Rattlesnake Lake. At Limestone Ridge, turn right on New River Divide Trail and head south for six miles, passing Cabin Peak at 6,870 feet and arriving at White Creek Lake.

To complete the loop, turn right on the trail at White Creek Lake and start the trip back, descending most of the way. The trail goes past Jakes Upper Camp and Jakes Lower Camp before linking up again with East Fork Trail for the jog back to the parking area.

User Groups: Hikers, dogs, and horses. No mountain bikes. No wheelchair facilities.

Permits: A wilderness permit is required for hikers planning to camp.

Maps: For a map, ask the U.S. Forest Service for Shasta-Trinity National Forest or Trinity Alps Wilderness. For a topographic map, ask the USGS for Jim Jam Ridge.

Directions: From Weaverville, turn west on Highway 299 and drive 45 miles to Denny Road. Turn north on County Road 402 (Denny Road) and drive 22 miles (the last four miles of the road become unpaved Forest Road 7N01) to the trailhead parking area. The trailhead is at Hawkins Bar.

Contact: Shasta-Trinity National Forest, Weaverville Ranger Station, Weaverville, 530/623-2121, www.fs.usda.gov/stnf.

60 BURNT RANCH FALLS

1.25 mi/1.0 hr 1 8

in Shasta-Trinity National Forest on Highway 299 east of Willow Creek

Map 2.3, page 69

Burnt Ranch Falls isn't a spectacular cascade of water like other, more famous waterfalls, but it is the center of a very pretty, easy-to-reach scene on the Trinity River. It's a relatively small but wide waterfall, composed of about 10 feet of rock that creates a natural barrier for migrating salmon and steelhead during low-water conditions. Thus the highlight comes when river flows rise a bit in the fall, so that you can watch the spectacular sight of salmon and steelhead jumping and sailing through the air to get over and past the falls. Timing is best in fall and early winter, when the season's first rains attract the fish upstream.

The trip starts at the Burnt Ranch Campground. The trail is a short but steep 0.75-mile jaunt. When you arrive at the river, walk out a short way on the rocky spot to watch the fish jump. The setting, in an area along Highway 299, has a magnificent natural landscape. When you look up from the river, the Trinity Canyon walls look like they ascend into the sky. Unlike most waterfalls, Burnt Ranch Falls is a far less compelling scene at high water. During high, turbid flows, it becomes much more difficult to see fish jumping past the falls. See a fish and this one is a 10.

User Groups: Hikers and dogs. No horses or mountain bikes. No wheelchair facilities.

Permits: No permits are required.

Maps: For a map, ask the U.S. Forest Service for Shasta-Trinity National Forest. For a topographic map, ask the USGS for Ironed Mountain.

Directions: From Weaverville, drive west on Highway 299 to Burnt Ranch. From Burnt Ranch, continue 0.5 mile west on Highway 299 to Burnt Ranch Campground and the trailhead, on the right.

Contact: Shasta-Trinity National Forest, Weaverville Ranger Station, Weaverville, 530/623-2121, www.fs.usda.gov/stnf.

61 NEW RIVER DIVIDE TRAIL

30.0 mi/3 days 

in the Trinity Alps Wilderness north of Trinity River's Big Bar

Map 2.3, page 69

The New River Divide Trail provides access to the Limestone Ridge of the Trinity Alps, taking a ridgeline route most of the way. This is an area known for having lookouts from mountain rims, the headwaters of many small feeder streams, and few people. The trip starts at the Green Mountain trailhead, at an elevation of 5,052 feet, and in the first three miles, the route skirts the southern flank of Brushy Mountain, past Panther Camp and Stove Camp, and along the eastern flank of Green Mountain. As the trail climbs toward the Limestone Ridge, you'll find yourself perched on a divide, where the streams on each side pour into different watersheds. Eventually the trail rises all the way to Cabin Peak (at 6,870 feet) and beyond to little Rattlesnake Lake, a one-way distance of about 15 miles. Some of the area, especially off to the north, has evidence of past forest fires.

User Groups: Hikers, dogs, and horses. No mountain bikes. No wheelchair facilities.

Permits: A wilderness permit is required. Parking and access are free.

Maps: For a map, ask the U.S. Forest Service for Shasta-Trinity National Forest or Trinity Alps Wilderness. For a topographic map, ask the USGS for Del Loam.

Directions: From Weaverville, drive west on Highway 299 for 28 miles to French Creek Road (Forest Road 5913). Turn north (right) and drive seven miles (the road becomes Forest Road 5N04). Continue straight for four miles to the trailhead, at the Green Mountain parking area.

Contact: Shasta-Trinity National Forest, Weaverville Ranger Station, Weaverville, 530/623-2121, www.fs.usda.gov/stnf.

62 CANYON CREEK LAKES TRAILHEAD

16.0 mi/2 days 

in the Trinity Alps Wilderness north of Weaverville

Map 2.3, page 69

This is the kind of place where wilderness lovers think they can find religion. But what they find, guaranteed, are tons of other people: Expect about 50 other hikers on weekdays and 200 to 300 on weekends. The Forest Service is reluctant to establish trailhead quotas for overnight use, but each visitor would benefit with that approach. The destination is Canyon Creek Lakes, set high in a mountain canyon, framed by Sawtooth Mountain to the east and a series of high granite rims to the north. The route in is no mystery; it's a climb of 3,100 feet over the course of eight miles. The trail heads straight upstream along Bear Creek for about 0.25 mile, crossing Bear Creek before continuing along Canyon Creek. Four miles out, you'll reach the first of four waterfalls. The first is the smallest, then they get progressively taller, and all are gorgeous. After the last waterfall, walk 0.5 mile to reach Lower Canyon Creek Lake (5,600 feet), seven miles out from the trailhead. From this place, which is now largely above tree line, cross Stonehouse Gulch to reach the first of two lakes. The trail skirts the left side of the first of the Canyon Creek Lakes, then in 0.5 mile, it arrives at the head of the larger one. From Lower Canyon Creek Lake, the trail turns to the right away from the lake. Follow the cairns to bear to the right, rather than the trail that runs along the shore of Lower Lake and ends in brush.

These lakes are like jewels set in the bottom of a gray, stark, high-mountain canyon, and once you've seen them, you'll have their picture branded permanently in your mind. This has become a special weekend favorite for hikers from Eureka and Redding. It's got it all. Literally.

User Groups: Hikers, dogs, and horses. No mountain bikes. No wheelchair facilities.

Permits: A wilderness permit is required for hikers planning to camp.
Maps: For a map, ask the U.S. Forest Service for Shasta-Trinity National Forest or Trinity Alps Wilderness. For a topographic map, ask the USGS for Dedrick.
Directions: From Weaverville, drive west on Highway 299 for eight miles to Junction City and Canyon Creek Road. Turn north on Canyon Creek Road and drive 13 miles to the trailhead, at the end of the road (0.75 mile past Ripstein Campground).
Contact: Shasta-Trinity National Forest, Weaverville Ranger Station, Weaverville, 530/623-2121, www.fs.usda.gov/stnf.

63 SOUTH FORK NATIONAL RECREATION TRAIL

5.0 mi/2.5 hr 2 6

in Shasta-Trinity National Forest east of Ruth Lake on Highway 36

Map 2.3, page 69

This remote trail is best known for following along the South Fork Trinity River and heads south toward the Yolla Bolly Wilderness. This is best accessed as an early-season trail, when so many other mountain routes are still snowbound. There are no lakes anywhere near the trail, and for the most part, the trail just meanders along, with that stream nearby providing a constant point of reference.

Even the trailhead, a short drive out of the Hell Gate Campground, is remote and obscure. Immediately, the trail picks up the stream, and in less than an hour, you might even feel as if you've discovered your own private little universe. How far might you go? For many, an hour in, an hour out is plenty. Locations along the creek include Collins Creek (0.3 mile), Farley Creek (0.9), Marie Creek (2.5), Steel Mule Bridge (2.8), Silver Creek (6.2), and Smokey Creek and the site of an old ranger station (7.2). Hikers can keep going about 10 miles farther one-way to the trail's end at Double Cabin site, where you can leave a shuttle car and make this a one-way trip. In summer, the temperatures can really smoke out here and the stream is your savior. Note that the trail crosses private property several times; stay on the trail, respect property rights, and help keep this trail open.
User Groups: Hikers and dogs. No horses or mountain bikes. No wheelchair facilities.
Permits: Campfire permits are required for overnight use. Parking and access are free.
Maps: For a map, ask the U.S. Forest Service for Shasta-Trinity National Forest. For a topographic map, ask the USGS for Forest Glen.
Directions: From Red Bluff, take Highway 36 (very twisty) west and drive 47 miles to Platina and continue to the junction with Highway 3. Continue west on Highway 36 for 10 miles to the Hell Gate Campground (on the left) and Forest Road 1526. Turn left on Forest Road 1526 and drive to the trailhead.
Contact: Shasta-Trinity National Forest, Hayfork Ranger Station, Hayfork, 530/628-5227, www.fs.usda.gov/stnf.

64 BLACK ROCK LAKE TRAIL

4.5 mi/3.0 hr 2 8

on the northern boundary of the Yolla Bolly Wilderness west of Red Bluff

Map 2.3, page 69

This 2.25-mile hike from the Stuart Gap trailhead to Black Rock Lake is one of the best day hikes in the Yolla Bolly Wilderness. One of the highlights comes in mid- to late June, when the wildflower blooms are absolutely beautiful. From the trailhead at 5,600 feet at the northern tip of the wilderness, start by hiking about a mile on the Pettyjohn Trail. It is set along the northwestern flank of North Yolla Bolly Mountain (7,863 feet) and is routed toward Pettyjohn Basin. When you reach the Black Rock Lake Trail, turn right on it and tromp another 1.25 miles to the lake. The trail contours through open stands of pine and fir and some small meadows. Small Black Rock Lake is set just below Black Rock Mountain (7,755 feet) and ideal for swimming.

There are many other excellent day hikes from this trailhead: Yolla Bolly Lake, Black Rock Mountain (great views), North Yolla Bolly Mountain (more sweeping vistas), and Cedar Basin (several creeks). Any of these make for good days, remote and quiet. The trailhead can also be used as a jumping-off spot for a hike straight south on Pettyjohn Trail into the wilderness interior.

User Groups: Hikers, dogs, and horses. No mountain bikes. No wheelchair facilities.

Permits: A campfire permit is required for hikers planning to camp.

Maps: For a map, ask the U.S. Forest Service for Shasta-Trinity National Forest or Yolla Bolly Wilderness. For a topographic map, ask the USGS for North Yolla Bolly.

Directions: From Red Bluff, take Highway 36 (very twisty) west and drive 47 miles to Platina. Continue west on Highway 36 for 11 miles to Forest Road 30 (Wildwood-Mad River Road). Turn left (south) and drive nine miles to Forest Road 35. Turn left (east) on Forest Road 35 and drive 10 miles to the intersection of several roads. Take the signed fork for Stuart Gap trailhead and drive 1.8 miles (unpaved) to the trailhead parking area. Hike on Pettyjohn Trail for one mile to reach Black Rock Lake Trail.

Contact: Shasta-Trinity National Forest, Yolla Bolly and Hayfork Ranger Station, Hayfork, 530/628-5227, www.fs.usda.gov/stnf.

65 SWIFT CREEK TRAIL GRANITE LAKE

12.0 mi/2 days 4 0

in the Trinity Alps Wilderness west of Trinity Center

Map 2.4, page 70

The trip in to Granite Lake is about six miles, and it's anything but easy. From the trailhead, start by tracing the right side of Swift Creek. One mile in, the Granite Lake Trail splits off. Just beyond the confluence of Swift and Granite Creeks, you cross the stream to the left. This trail runs along the right side of Granite Creek for four miles and includes a very steep section in the final mile that will have you wondering why you ever thought this was going to be such a short, easy trip. Four miles in, you'll get your sighting of Bear Basin. Finally you'll rise to Gibson Meadow and just beyond, Granite Lake, at 6,000 feet, a gorgeous sight below Gibson Peak. For a natural mountain lake, it's a fair size, with good swimming during the day and trout fishing in the evening. This is a popular spot, so plan on company.

One important note on the way in: For the most part, the creek is not accessible as a water source, so monitor your canteen level.

User Groups: Hikers, dogs, and horses. No mountain bikes. No wheelchair facilities.

Permits: A wilderness permit is required for hikers planning to camp.

Maps: For a map, ask the U.S. Forest Service for Shasta-Trinity National Forest or Trinity Alps Wilderness. For topographic maps, ask the USGS for Covington Mill and Trinity Center.

Directions: From Weaverville, take Highway 3 north for 28 miles to Trinity Center and Swift Creek Road. Turn left and drive 6.8 miles to the parking area at the wilderness border.

Contact: Shasta-Trinity National Forest, Weaverville Ranger Station, Weaverville, 530/623-2121, www.fs.usda.gov/stnf.

66 LONG CANYON TRAILHEAD

16.0 mi/2 days 4 9

in the Trinity Alps Wilderness northwest of Trinity Lake

Map 2.4, page 70

Your mission, should you choose to accept it, is the 6.5-mile, largely uphill hike to the west side of Gibson Peak, where Deer Lake, Summit Lake, Luella Lake, Diamond Lake, and Siligo Peak can provide days of side-trip destinations.

From the trailhead, the trip starts by tracing along the East Fork Stuart Fork, a feeder creek to Trinity Lake. After two miles you'll arrive at a fork in the trail. Take the right fork (the left fork is routed to Bowerman Meadows and little Lake Anna), which climbs farther along the stream and then traces the southern flank of Gibson Peak. At times the trail is steep in this area, but finally you'll pass Gibson Peak, and Siligo Peak will come into view. The trail also intersects a loop trail that circles Siligo Peak and provides access to four high-mountain lakes. Summit Lake (7,350 feet) is the favorite. Spring wildflowers are spectacular.

User Groups: Hikers, dogs, and horses. No mountain bikes. No wheelchair facilities.

Permits: A wilderness permit is required for hikers planning to camp.

Maps: For a map, ask the U.S. Forest Service for Shasta-Trinity National Forest or Trinity Alps Wilderness. For a topographic map, ask the USGS for Covington Mill.

Directions: From Weaverville, take Highway 3 north to Covington Mill and Forest Road 115. Turn left and drive for 2.5 miles to the trailhead.

Contact: Shasta-Trinity National Forest, Weaverville Ranger Station, Weaverville, 530/623-2121, www.fs.usda.gov/stnf.

67 STUART FORK TRAILHEAD

28.0 mi/4 days 

in the Trinity Alps Wilderness northwest of Trinity Lake

Map 2.4, page 70

Don't say we didn't warn you: This trail doesn't have a difficulty rating of five for nothing. The hike requires an endless climb—very steep at times, particularly as you near the Sawtooth Ridge—spanning nearly 14 miles to Emerald Lake. The first nine miles are easy, and it will have you thinking that this hike is a piece of cake—long, but easy. But surprise! The last five miles from Morris Meadows are the killer. But after arriving and resting up for a night, you'll find that ecstasy follows. Emerald Lake is one of three lakes set in line in a canyon below the Sawtooth Ridge; the others on this side of the ridge are Sapphire and Mirror. The surroundings are stark and prehistoric, and the lakes are gemlike, blue, and clear, with big rainbow trout and water that is perfect for refreshing swims. From Emerald Lake, the trail continues a mile to Sapphire Lake. From Sapphire, it's an off-trail scramble, often across big boulders, as you climb another mile to reach Mirror Lake. The entire scene is surreal.

Note: On the way to Emerald Lake, you might notice a cutoff trail to the right. On your trail map, you'll see it crosses the Sawtooth Ridge and leads into the acclaimed Caribou Lakes Basin. On the map it appears to be a short, easy trip, but in reality, it involves a terrible climb with more than 100 switchbacks. Don't say you weren't warned.

User Groups: Hikers, dogs, and horses. No mountain bikes. No wheelchair facilities.

Permits: A wilderness permit is required for hikers planning to camp.

Maps: For a map, ask the U.S. Forest Service for Shasta-Trinity National Forest or Trinity Alps Wilderness. For a topographic map, ask the USGS for Covington Mill.

Directions: From Weaverville, take Highway 3 north to Trinity Lake and Trinity Alps Road. Turn left on Trinity Alps Road and drive 2.5 miles to the trailhead at Bridge Camp.

Contact: Shasta-Trinity National Forest, Weaverville Ranger Station, Weaverville, 530/623-2121, www.fs.usda.gov/stnf.

68 HIRZ BAY TRAIL

3.2 mi/1.75 hr 

on the McCloud arm of Shasta Lake north of Redding

Map 2.4, page 70

This trail, along a remote section of Shasta

Lake, is best in spring when the temperatures are ideal, the lake is highest, the oaks are budding, and wildlife is abundant. Start at Dekkas Rock day-use area on the upper McCloud River Arm of Shasta Lake, near Hirz Bay. From Dekkas Rock, the trail traces the shoreline of the lake, in and out along small coves and creek inlets. Straight across the lake are pretty views of the deep coves at Campbell Creek and Dekkas Creek, of unique limestone outcrops, and of Minnesota Mountain (at 4,293 feet). Note that the forest slopes directly above the Hirz Bay Campground were burned in a fire.

User Groups: Hikers and leashed dogs. No mountain bikes or horses. No wheelchair facilities.

Permits: No permits are required. Free at Dekkas Rock day-use area. A parking fee of $10 per vehicle is charged if parking at the Hirz Bay boat launch.

Maps: For a map, ask the U.S. Forest Service for Shasta-Trinity National Forest. For a topographic map, ask the USGS for O'Brien.

Directions: From Redding, take I-5 north to Shasta Lake and the exit for Salt Creek/Gilman Road. Take that exit and drive east on Gilman Road/County Road 7H009 for 10 miles (past the access road for Hirz Bay boat launch and campground) and then continue two miles to the Dekkas Rock day-use area.

Contact: Shasta-Trinity National Forest, Shasta Lake Ranger District, Redding, 530/275-1587; Shasta Lake Visitors Center, 530/275-1589, www.fs.usda.gov/stnf.

69 GREENS CREEK BOAT-IN TRAIL

1.0 mi/1.0 hr 3 8

on the McCloud arm of Shasta Lake north of Redding

Map 2.4, page 70

Your reward is a towering view of Shasta Lake, unique and special. Even with two million people estimated to visit Shasta Lake every year, the only way to access this trail is from a boat-in campsite at Greens Creek, on the east side of the McCloud arm of the lake. At the back of the cove at Greens Creek, you'll find a small U.S. Forest Service billboard posted with recreation guide sheets, and behind it are the campground and trailhead. Yet it is one of our favorites. Some spots are a bit overgrown, but for most, the route up to the viewpoint is clear enough.

The trail enters an oak and madrone forest that is interspersed with limestone formations. There are many fascinating side trips on the steep climb up toward a saddle between Town Mountain, at 4,325 feet, and Horse Mountain, at 4,025 feet. These are worth exploring, and if you spend enough time hiking and investigating, you may find some small caves. Most people are inspired to hike just high enough to get a good clear view of the lake below.

User Groups: Hikers and leashed dogs. No horses or mountain bikes. No wheelchair facilities.

Permits: No permits are required. A parking fee of $10 per vehicle is charged at boat ramps.

Maps: For a map, ask the U.S. Forest Service for Shasta-Trinity National Forest. For a topographic map, ask the USGS for O'Brien.

Directions: First, load your boat. From Redding, take I-5 north to Shasta Lake and the exit for Salt Creek/Gilman Road. Take that exit and drive east on Gilman Road/County Road 7H009 for 10 miles to the access road for Hirz Bay boat launch. Launch your boat and drive out in the McCloud arm of Shasta Lake toward the Shasta Caverns. Turn left at Greens Creek Cove and land your boat at Greens Creek Boat-In Campground. A billboard is at the back of the cove near the trailhead.

Nearby boat ramps: Bailey Cove (lake must be 73 percent full or higher).

Contact: Shasta-Trinity National Forest, Shasta Lake Ranger District, Redding, 530/275-1587; Shasta Lake Visitors Center, 530/275-1589, www.fs.usda.gov/stnf.

70 BAILEY COVE LOOP TRAIL

2.8 mi/1.5 hr 2 7

on the McCloud arm of Shasta Lake north of Redding

Map 2.4, page 70

The McCloud River arm is the prettiest part of giant Shasta Lake. The mountain canyon features towering limestone formations and the lake's clear, emerald waters. This trail provides a great view of these phenomena, as well as a close-to-the-water loop hike on one of the lake's peninsulas.

From the trailhead, start by hiking on the left fork, which travels out along Bailey Cove. As you continue, the trail is routed in a clockwise direction, first along the McCloud arm of the lake, then back to the parking area along John's Creek Inlet. When you reach the mouth of Bailey Cove, stop and enjoy the view. Directly across the lake are the limestone formations, featuring North Gray Rocks (at 3,114 feet) and topped by Horse Mountain (at 4,025 feet). The famous Shasta Caverns are located just below North Gray Rocks. This hike is best done in April and May, when the lake is at its highest levels and hot weather has yet to arrive. In late summer or fall, when the levels are down, you'll be looking out at a lot of red dirt. Watch out for the poison oak just off the trail.

User Groups: Hikers and leashed dogs. No mountain bikes or horses. No wheelchair facilities.

Permits: No permits are required. A parking fee of $7 per vehicle is charged.

Maps: For a map, ask the U.S. Forest Service for Shasta-Trinity National Forest. For a topographic map, ask the USGS for O'Brien.

Directions: From Redding, take I-5 north to Shasta Lake and the exit for O'Brien/Shasta Caverns. Take that exit and turn east on Shasta Caverns Road and drive 0.1 mile to the sign for Bailey Cove Boat Ramp. Bear right at the sign and drive 0.5 mile to the day-use parking area.

Contact: Shasta-Trinity National Forest, Shasta Lake Ranger District, Redding, 530/275-1587; Shasta Lake Visitors Center, 530/275-1589, www.fs.usda.gov/stnf.

71 WATERS GULCH OVERLOOK

3.8 mi/2.0 hr

at Packers Bay on Shasta Lake north of Redding

Map 2.4, page 70

Shasta Lake is so big—the biggest reservoir in California—that it can be difficult to know where to start in your mission to explore it. A good answer is right here on the Waters Gulch Loop. It connects to the Overlook Trail, a cutoff of 0.8 mile that climbs atop a small mountain and furnishes a view of the main lake. The trailhead is at Packers Bay, which is easily accessible off I-5. From the trailhead at the parking area, walk down the road and start hiking the trail from the Packers Bay boat-ramp parking lots, and then finish back at the trailhead parking areas. This provides the best loop hike for this site. Highlights of this trip include a route that extends onto one of the lake's peninsulas, Waters Gulch, a cove on the main Sacramento River arm of the lake, and several lookout points.

User Groups: Hikers and leashed dogs. No horses or mountain bikes. No wheelchair facilities.

Permits: No permits are required. Parking and access are free.

Maps: For a map, ask the U.S. Forest Service for Shasta-Trinity National Forest. For a topographic map, ask the USGS for O'Brien.

Directions: From Redding, take I-5 north to Shasta Lake and the exit for Packers Bay. Take the exit and drive southwest on Packers Bay Road for one mile to the trailhead, on the right (0.25 mile before the boat ramp).

Contact: Shasta-Trinity National Forest, Shasta Lake Ranger District, Redding, 530/275-1587; Shasta Lake Visitors Center, 530/275-1589, www.fs.usda.gov/stnf.

72 BOULDER CREEK FALLS

2.0 mi/1.0 hr 1 10

at Whiskeytown Lake National Recreation Area west of Redding

Map 2.4, page 70

Note: In the aftermath of the 2018 Carr Fire, which burned 98 percent of Whiskeytown National Recreation Area, several roads and all the trails in burn areas were closed. That includes the hikes to the park's waterfalls, including to Whiskeytown Falls, Boulder Creek Falls, and Brandy Creek Falls, as well as to trail camps and access to former renowned mountain biking trails. Those will not be reopened until hazard trees are removed and the routes are classified as safe. Call before planning a trip to any of the waterfalls.

Boulder Creek Falls is a 138-foot tall waterfall set in a deep ravine. At the top, the waterfall starts as a narrow cascade where the water builds speed. It then widens into a 28-foot cataract, a gentler rush of water over boulders. You get a full frontal view for great photos. There are two ways to get here, and, of course, we picked the short, easier hike with the more difficult drive to the trailhead. At the parking area, the trailhead is well signed. The route starts on dirt, a former logging road, and is routed into a hardwood forest. It's an easy walk to a creek with a well-signed spur to the waterfall. Turn right at the spur, and it's another 0.1 mile along the creek to the plunge pool. A four-wheel-drive vehicle is advised to reach this trailhead. If you do not have an aggressive vehicle, another trailhead to Boulder Creek Falls is available along the lake on South Shore Drive; from there, it is a 5.5-mile round-trip.

User Groups: Hikers, mountain bikes, dogs, and horses. No wheelchair facilities.

Permits: A parking fee of $25 per vehicle, good for a week, is charged.

Maps: For a detailed trail map, contact Whiskeytown National Recreation Area. For a topographic map, ask the USGS for Igo.

Directions: Take I-5 to Redding and the exit for Highway 44 West. Take that exit, merge onto 44W and drive 1.2 miles (into town) to Highway 273/N. Pine Street (large signs for 299/Weaverville-Eureka). Turn right on North Pine and drive 500 feet to the first left, for Eureka Way (signed for 299/Weaverville-Eureka). Turn left on Eureka Way and drive 7.7 miles (becomes Highway 299) to Whiskeytown Lake (signed for Visitor Center) on left.

To the waterfall: From the Whiskeytown Visitors Center, return to the junction with Highway 299. Turn left and drive 7.1 miles to a left turn for South Shore Drive/Carr Powerhouse. Turn left and drive 0.5 mile to Mill Creek Road (a steep dirt road on right). Turn right (four-wheel drive advised) and drive 1.8 miles to the end of the road. A parking area and the signed trailhead are on the gated road on the right.

Option: For another trailhead with a paved road, from the turnoff on South Shore Drive, drive 5.3 miles to Brandy Creek; requires a 5.5-mile round-trip hike.

Contact: Whiskeytown National Recreation Area, Whiskeytown, 530/246-1225, www.nps.gov/whis.

73 DAVIS GULCH TRAIL

3.3 mi one-way/3.5 hr 1 7

at Whiskeytown Lake National Recreation Area west of Redding

Map 2.4, page 70

This area avoided damage from the Carr Fire. The Davis Gulch Trail is Whiskeytown Lake's easiest hike that you can do as a one-way descent, with a shuttle car at the end. Or you can drop off your kids, go have fun with something more serious, and pick them up later at the end. This meandering route along the southwest end of the lake starts out at 1,414 feet (at an information billboard along an access road) and winds its way down to the Brandy Creek Picnic Area, at 1,240 feet. It is a moderate descent on a wide, flat footpath surrounded mostly by oak and manzanita. Along the way, there are many good views of Whiskeytown Lake. The trail spans 3.3 miles and dead-ends. With two vehicles, it is possible to make it a one-way hike with a shuttle and then (better yet) hike the whole route downhill.

User Groups: Hikers and dogs. No horses or mountain bikes. No wheelchair facilities.

Permits: A parking fee of $25 per vehicle, good for a week, is charged.

Maps: For a detailed trail map, contact Whiskeytown National Recreation Area. For a topographic map, ask the USGS for Igo.

Directions: Take I-5 to Redding and the exit for Highway 44 West. Take that exit, merge onto 44W, and drive 1.2 miles (into town) to Highway 273/N. Pine Street (large signs for 299/Weaverville-Eureka). Turn right on North Pine and drive 500 feet to first left, for Eureka Way (signed for 299/Weaverville-Eureka). Turn left on Eureka Way and drive 7.7 miles (becomes Highway 299) to Whiskeytown Lake (signed for Visitor Center) on left. From the visitors center, continue on J. F. Kennedy Memorial Drive for three miles to the Davis Gulch trailhead on the right. To reach the Brandy Creek Picnic Area (and end of the trail), continue three more miles on J. F. Kennedy Memorial Drive.

Contact: Whiskeytown National Recreation Area, Whiskeytown, 530/246-1225, www.nps.gov/whis.

74 WHISKEYTOWN FALLS

3.4 mi/2.5 hr 3 10

at Whiskeytown Lake National Recreation Area west of Redding

Map 2.4, page 70 BEST

Note: In the aftermath of the 2018 Carr Fire, which burned 98 percent of Whiskeytown National Recreation Area, several roads and all the trails in burn areas were closed. That includes the hikes to the park's waterfalls, including to Whiskeytown Falls, Boulder Creek Falls, and Brandy Creek Falls, as well as to trail camps and access to former renowned mountain biking trails. Those will not be reopened until hazard trees are removed and the routes are classified as safe. Call before planning a trip to any of the waterfalls.

The viewing areas for Whiskeytown Falls are set in a rock staircase, with a railing for safety, just to the left of the cascades. You rise up to a series of perches, including Photographer's Ledge and, above that, Artist's Ledge. These are among the best waterfall views in the state, so close you can often taste the water as it surges past. The waterfall is estimated at 220 feet tall, top to bottom. You can feel a rush of cool air pushed by the blast of water.

From the metal railing, the water sails past you just a few feet distant and then rockets over a brink into a foaming white cascade. It thunders down the canyon. Above you are a series of four giant steps where the water carves mosaics down the rock faces. Below you, a white torrent pounds to the final ledge—and then over the top and pours like an angled fountain into the final plunge pool. Whiskeytown Falls is the prettiest waterfall in California that relatively few have seen.

It's only a 1.7-mile hike one-way, a short yet aerobic climb most of the way, where you arrive at the final cascade and a staircase built into the rock just to the left of the waterfall. The moments here, one after another, are touched by how this place makes you feel as much as what you see. It starts out as a mild walk on a trail over a sandstone-based terrain. The route leads to Crystal Creek, over a bridge, and beyond to a junction (with the Mill Creek Trail). You bear right, signed for Whiskeytown Falls, and you're on your way. From the junction, it's about a half-hour aerobic climb, with several concrete benches positioned as rest stops, past a picnic area and then into the canyon. The first view is of the lower cascade. This seems to be the most popular site for a photo, but it represents only a small piece of the entire falls. If you own a quality camera, bring a tripod and set a slow shutter speed to capture the soft, blurred rush of moving water down the falls.

User Groups: Hikers, mountain bikes, and horses are permitted up to picnic area. Hikers only allowed after this point. No dogs. No wheelchair facilities.

Permits: A parking fee of $25 per vehicle, good for a week, is charged. A self-pay station is available at the trailhead.

Maps: For a trail map/brochure, contact Whiskeytown National Recreation Area. For a topographic map, ask the USGS for Igo.

Directions: Take I-5 to Redding and the exit for Highway 44 West. Take that exit, merge onto 44 West and drive 1.2 miles (into town) to Highway 273/N. Pine Street (large signs for 299/Weaverville-Eureka). Turn right on North Pine and drive 500 feet to first left for Eureka Way (signed for 299/Weaverville-Eureka). Turn left on Eureka Way and drive 7.7 miles (becomes Highway 299) to Whiskeytown Lake (signed for Visitor Center) on left.

From visitors center, return a short distance to Highway 299. Turn left on 299 and drive west 8.4 miles to Crystal Creek Road. Turn left and drive 3.7 miles (paved) to parking and trailhead on left.

Contact: Whiskeytown National Recreation Area, Whiskeytown, 530/246-1225, www.nps.gov/whis.

75 BRANDY CREEK FALLS

3.0 mi/2.0 hr 3 9

at Whiskeytown Lake National Recreation Area west of Redding

Map 2.4, page 70

Note: In the aftermath of the 2018 Carr Fire, which burned 98 percent of Whiskeytown National Recreation Area, several roads and all the trails in burn areas were closed. That includes the hikes to the park's waterfalls, including to Whiskeytown Falls, Boulder Creek Falls, and Brandy Creek Falls, as well as to trail camps and access to former renowned mountain biking trails. Those will not be reopened until hazard trees are removed and the routes

lower cascade of Whiskeytown Falls

are classified as safe. Call before planning a trip to any of the waterfalls.

Brandy Creek Falls is a cascade chute with a series of pool-and-drops that pour into a big pool. It is spectacular at high water, a cataract where all the waterfall pools are connected into a massive white-water flow. At low water, it splits into two thin cascades with a series of small drops. This is not a Yosemite-like free fall, and the trailhead is still fairly obscure. It's a 1.5-mile hike to get there, with a 500-foot climb.

From the trailhead, you'll cross a creek in 0.5 mile. There is a large debris field of logs and boulders in the creek, the result of the 1977 flood. Continue on and in another 0.25 mile, you will reach a junction with the Rich Gulch Trail. Though you pass this by and continue ahead, note that the trail narrows here and is accessible only for hikers. From here to the falls, the trail enters the Brandy Creek Canyon with fern grottoes and cliff-like drop-offs. It can be slippery, but the route heads right along the cascade. As you forge on, you will find steps cut in rock that will lead you past five pools and falls that run about 50 feet. Very special stuff.

User Groups: Hikers only. No mountain bikes, dogs, or horses. No wheelchair facilities.

Permits: A parking fee of $25 per vehicle, good for a week, is charged.

Maps: For a detailed trail map, contact Whiskeytown National Recreation Area. For a topographic map, ask the USGS for Igo.

Directions: Take I-5 to Redding and the exit for Highway 44 West. Take that exit, merge onto 44W and drive 1.2 miles (into town) to Highway 273/N. Pine Street (large signs for 299/Weaverville-Eureka). Turn right on North Pine and drive 500 feet to first left for Eureka Way (signed for 299/Weaverville-Eureka). Turn left on Eureka Way and drive 7.7 miles (becomes Highway 299) to Whiskeytown Lake (signed for Visitor Center) on left.

From the visitors center, continue south on Kennedy Memorial Drive to a fork. Bear right at the fork, cross over the dam, and continue past the Brandy Creek area to Shasta Bally Road. Turn left and drive 2.5 miles on the dirt road to a junction. Turn left and drive 0.75 mile to a small parking area. The signed trailhead is 150 feet up the road.

Contact: Whiskeytown National Recreation Area, Whiskeytown, 530/246-1225, www.nps.gov/whis.

76 SYD CABIN RIDGE TRAIL

8.0 mi/2 days 3 7

on the eastern boundary of the Yolla Bolly Wilderness west of Red Bluff

Map 2.4, page 70

Not many people hike into the Yolla Bolly Wilderness, set up a camp, then hike back out the next day. But here is a chance to do exactly that. The trailhead is at the Tomhead Saddle, located just west of Tomhead Mountain, at an elevation of 6,757 feet. From here, hike past Tomhead Spring on Syd Cabin Ridge Trail, then drop down into Hawk Camp. Set just below the confluence of three feeder streams, Hawk Camp is a spot to overnight. On the way back, expect a steady climb with no water between Tomhead Spring and Hawk Camp. If you plan on extending your trip for several days into the wilderness, a network of trails intersects just beyond Hawk Camp, but note that a stream crossing is required. The Yolla Bolly Wilderness is one of the least-used significant wilderness areas in California.

User Groups: Hikers, dogs, and horses. No mountain bikes. No wheelchair facilities.

Permits: A campfire permit is required for hikers planning to camp.

Maps: For a map, ask the U.S. Forest Service for Shasta-Trinity National Forest or Yolla Bolly Wilderness. For a topographic map, ask the USGS for North Yolla Bolly.

Directions: From Red Bluff, turn west on Highway 36 (twisty) and drive about 13 miles to Cannon Road. Turn left (south) on

Cannon Road and go approximately five miles to Pettyjohn Road. Turn right (west) on Pettyjohn Road and drive to Forest Road 27N06. Turn left (south) on Forest Road 27N06 and continue three miles to the parking area at Tomhead Saddle Campground. From Highway 36, this route is a dirt road all the way in. A high-clearance vehicle is recommended. In storms, it can also be slippery when wet.

Contact: Shasta-Trinity National Forest, Yolla Bolly and Hayfork Ranger Station, Hayfork, 530/628-5227, www.fs.usda.gov/stnf.

LASSEN AND MODOC

At 10,457 feet, Lassen Peak's cragged plug-dome summit is visible for more than 100 miles. Lassen blew its top in 1914, with continuing eruptions through 1918. Now dormant, the volcanic-based geology—pumice boulders, volcanic rock, and spring-fed streams from underground lava tubes—dominates this landscape. Lassen Volcanic National Park is one of the few national parks where you can enjoy the wilderness in relative solitude. The best hikes are the Summit Climb and Bumpass Hell. Highlights include canoeing and fly-fishing at Fall River, Big Lake, and Ahjumawi State Park. McArthur-Burney Falls State Park, along with the Pit River and Lake Britton, make the best destinations for families. In remote Modoc County, Lava Beds National Monument boasts caves and lava tubes, including the 6,000-foot Catacomb Tunnel. Nearby is pretty Medicine Lake, formed in a caldera, which provides good exploring.

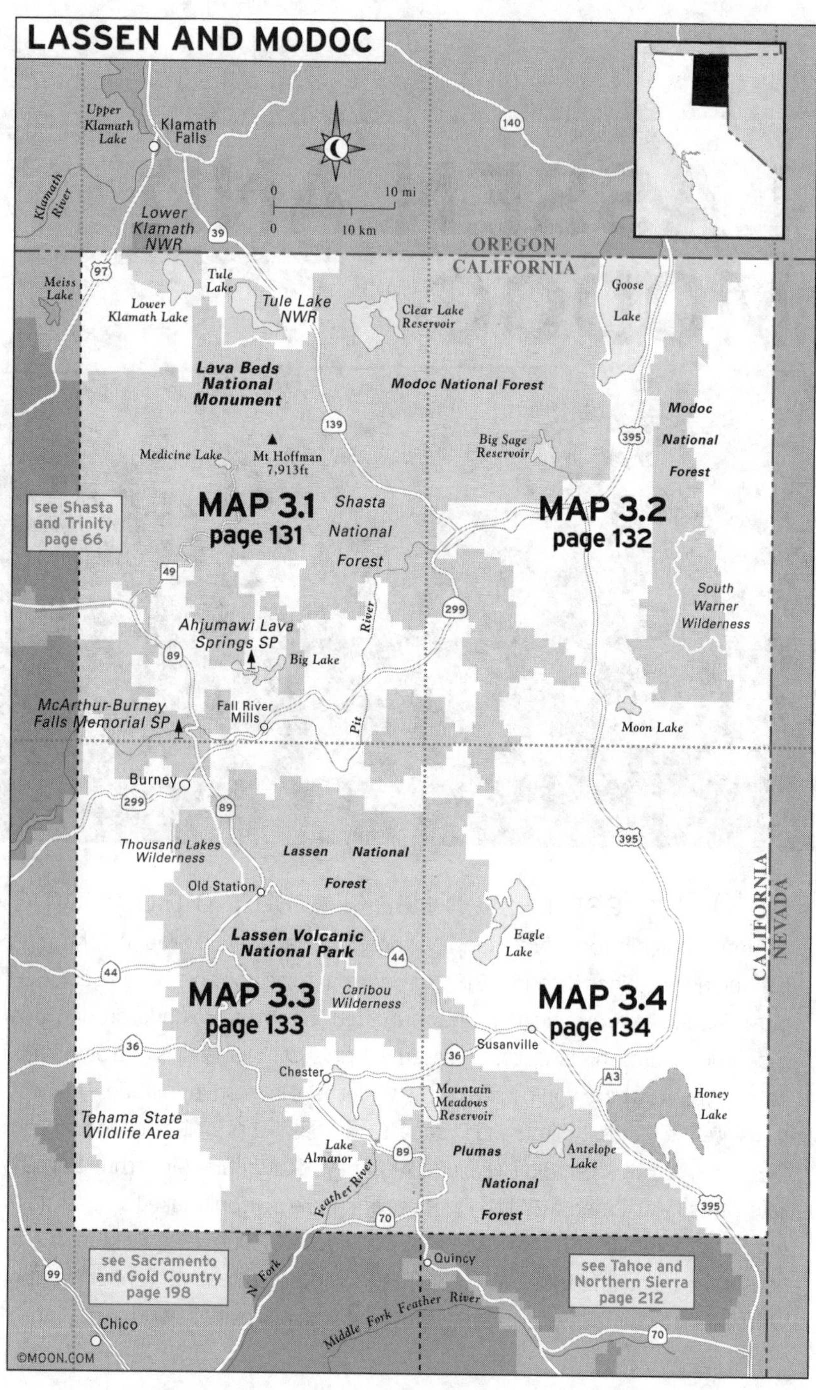
LASSEN AND MODOC
Upper Klamath Lake
Klamath Falls
Klamath River
Lower Klamath NWR
0 10 mi
0 10 km
OREGON
CALIFORNIA
Meiss Lake
Lower Klamath Lake
Tule Lake
Tule Lake NWR
Clear Lake Reservoir
Goose Lake
Lava Beds National Monument
Modoc National Forest
Modoc National Forest
Medicine Lake
Mt Hoffman 7,913ft
Big Sage Reservoir
see Shasta and Trinity page 66
MAP 3.1 page 131
Shasta National Forest
MAP 3.2 page 132
South Warner Wilderness
Ahjumawi Lava Springs SP
Big Lake
Pit River
McArthur-Burney Falls Memorial SP
Fall River Mills
Moon Lake
Burney
Thousand Lakes Wilderness
Lassen National Forest
Old Station
Lassen Volcanic National Park
Eagle Lake
CALIFORNIA
NEVADA
MAP 3.3 page 133
Caribou Wilderness
MAP 3.4 page 134
Susanville
Chester
Mountain Meadows Reservoir
Honey Lake
Tehama State Wildlife Area
Lake Almanor
Feather River
Plumas National Forest
Antelope Lake
Quincy
see Sacramento and Gold Country page 198
N Fork
Middle Fork Feather River
see Tahoe and Northern Sierra page 212
Chico
©MOON.COM
140
39
97
139
395
49
299
89
44
36
A3
70
99

Map 3.1

Sites 1-11
Pages 135-143

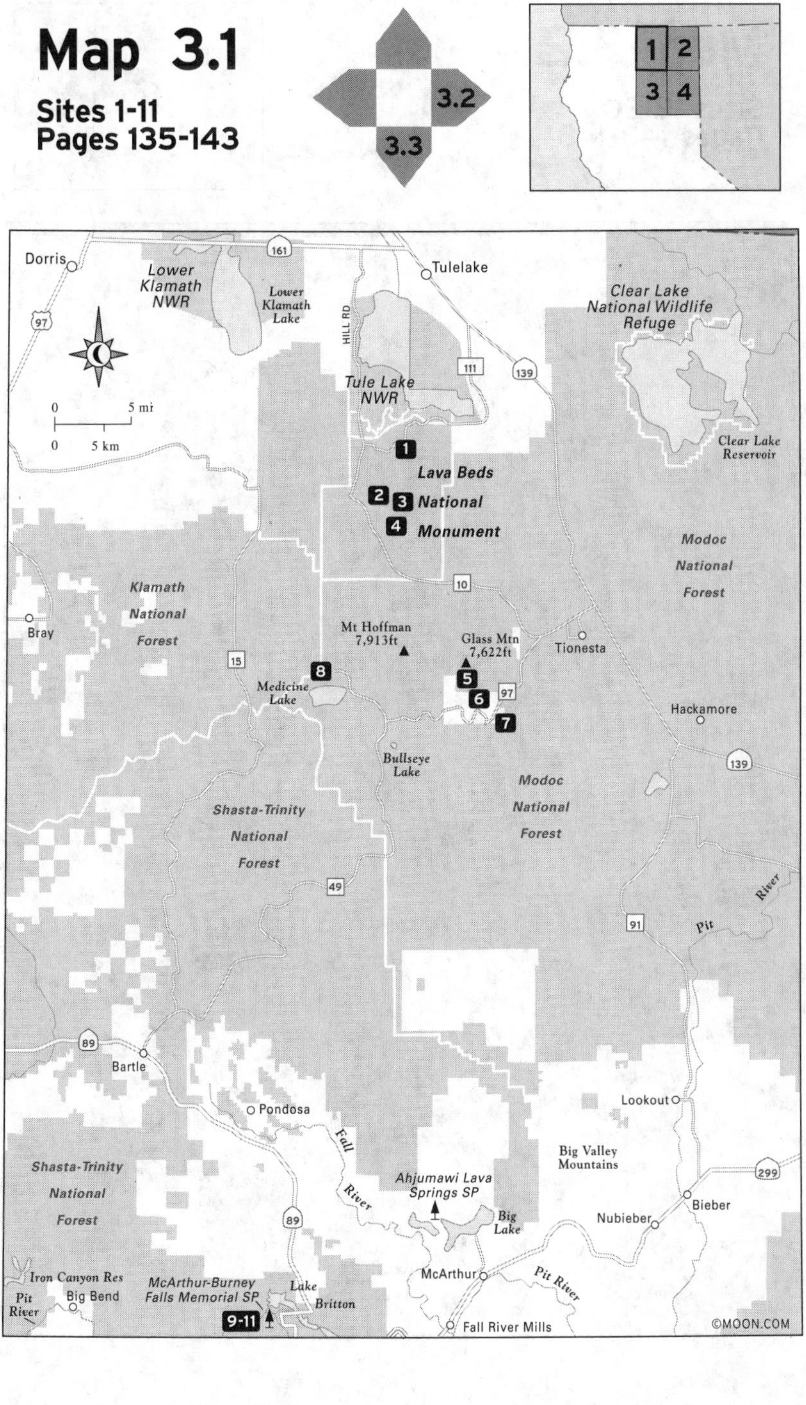

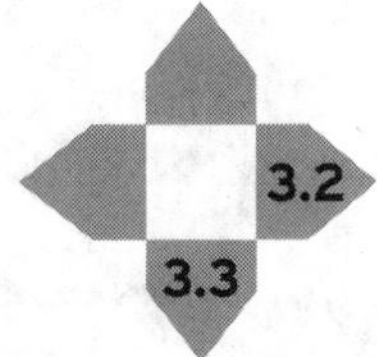

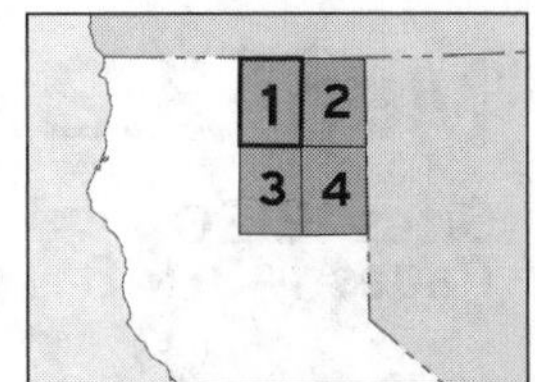

Dorris
Lower Klamath NWR
161
Lower Klamath Lake
Tulelake
Clear Lake National Wildlife Refuge
HILL RD
97
111
139
Tule Lake NWR
0 5 mi
0 5 km
1
Lava Beds
2 3 National
4 Monument
Clear Lake Reservoir
Modoc National Forest
Klamath National Forest
10
Bray
Mt Hoffman 7,913ft
Glass Mtn 7,622ft
Tionesta
15
8
Medicine Lake
5
6
97
7
Hackamore
Bullseye Lake
139
Shasta-Trinity National Forest
Modoc National Forest
49
91
Pit River
89
Bartle
Lookout
Pondosa
Fall River
Big Valley Mountains
Shasta-Trinity National Forest
Ahjumawi Lava Springs SP
299
Bieber
89
Big Lake
Nubieber
Iron Canyon Res
McArthur-Burney Falls Memorial SP
Lake Britton
McArthur
Pit River
Pit River
Big Bend
9-11
Fall River Mills
©MOON.COM

Map 3.2

Sites 12-20
Pages 143-148

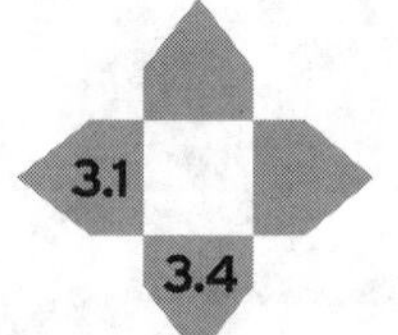

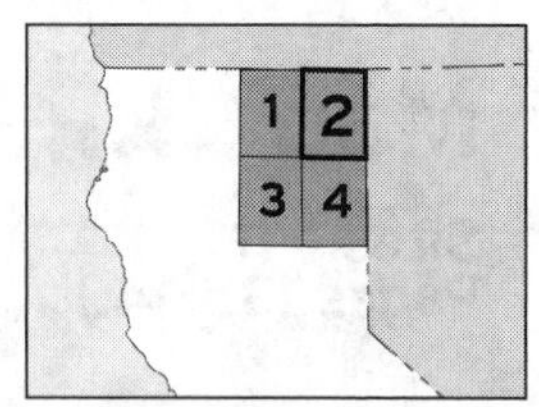

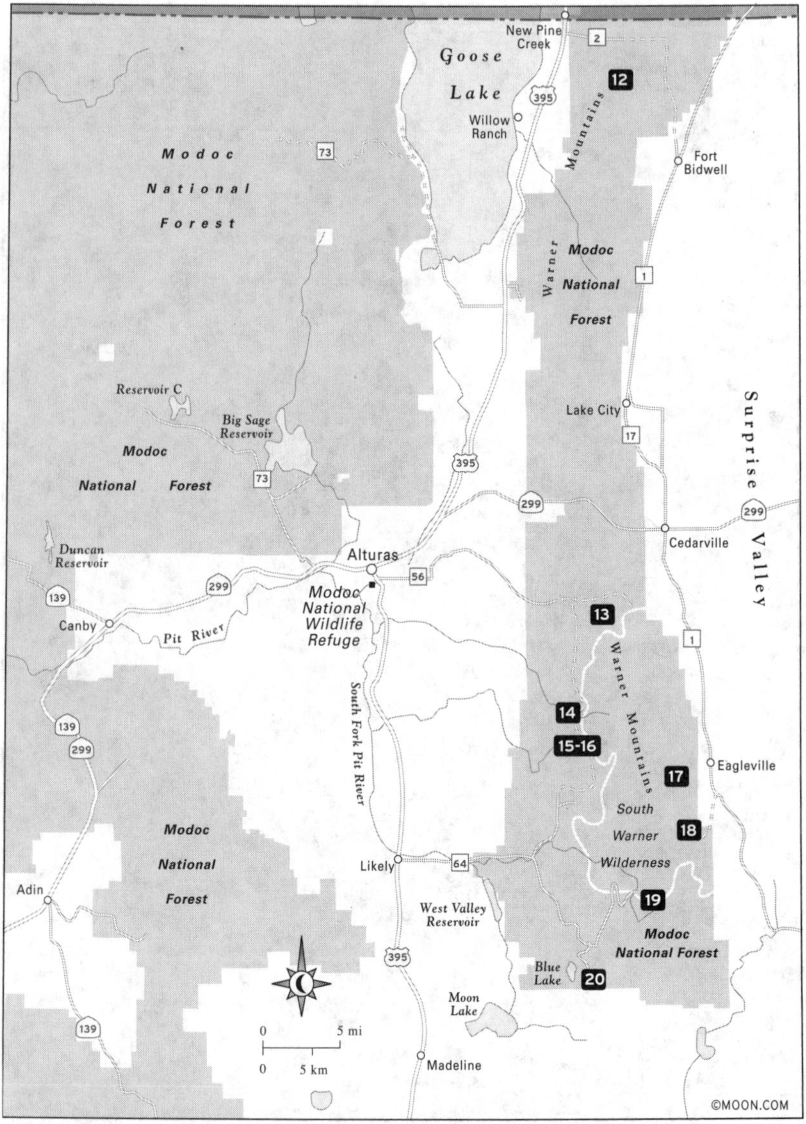

New Pine Creek
2
Goose Lake
12
395
Willow Ranch
Mountains
73
Fort Bidwell
Modoc National Forest
Warner
Modoc National Forest
1
Reservoir C
Big Sage Reservoir
Lake City
17
Surprise Valley
Modoc National Forest
395
73
299
299
Cedarville
Duncan Reservoir
Alturas
56
299
Modoc National Wildlife Refuge
139
13
Canby
Pit River
1
Warner Mountains
South Fork Pit River
14
15-16
139
299
Eagleville
17
South Warner Wilderness
18
Modoc National Forest
Likely
64
Adin
West Valley Reservoir
19
Modoc National Forest
395
Blue Lake
20
Moon Lake
139
0 5 mi
0 5 km
Madeline
©MOON.COM

Map 3.3

Sites 21-52
Pages 148-170

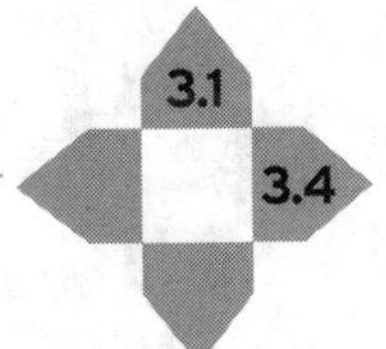

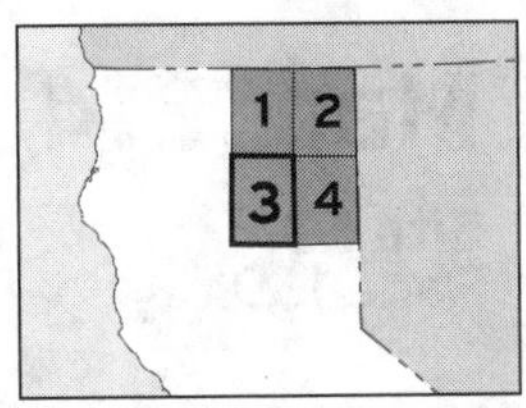

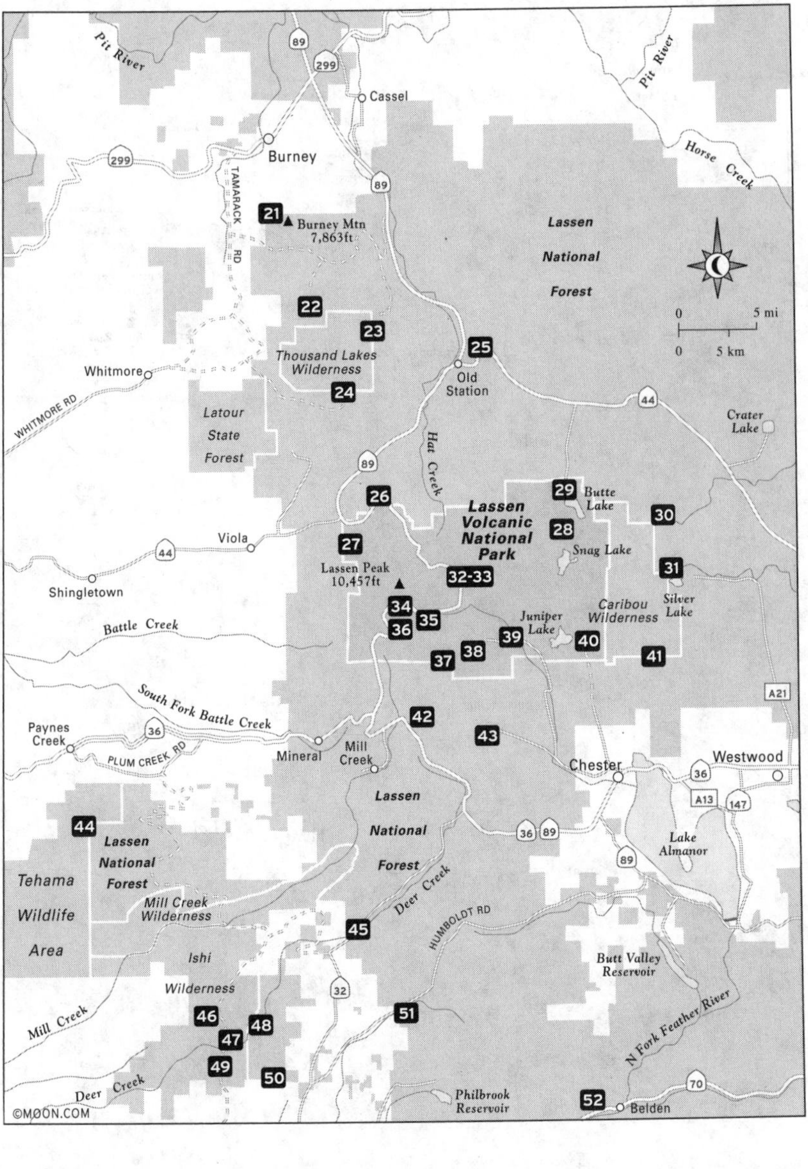

Pit River
Cassel
Burney
Horse Creek
TAMARACK RD
Burney Mtn 7,863ft
Lassen National Forest
Thousand Lakes Wilderness
Whitmore
WHITMORE RD
Old Station
Latour State Forest
Hat Creek
Crater Lake
Lassen Volcanic National Park
Butte Lake
Snag Lake
Viola
Shingletown
Lassen Peak 10,457ft
Caribou Wilderness
Silver Lake
Juniper Lake
Battle Creek
South Fork Battle Creek
Paynes Creek
PLUM CREEK RD
Mineral
Mill Creek
Chester
Westwood
Lake Almanor
Tehama Wildlife Area
Mill Creek Wilderness
Deer Creek
HUMBOLDT RD
Ishi Wilderness
Butt Valley Reservoir
N Fork Feather River
Philbrook Reservoir
Belden
0 5 mi
0 5 km

Map 3.4

Site 53
Page 169

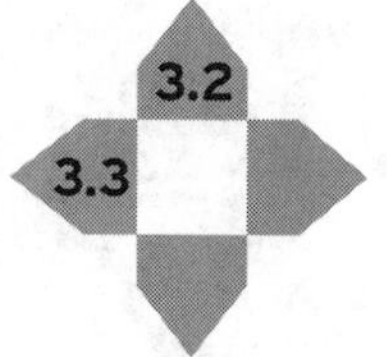

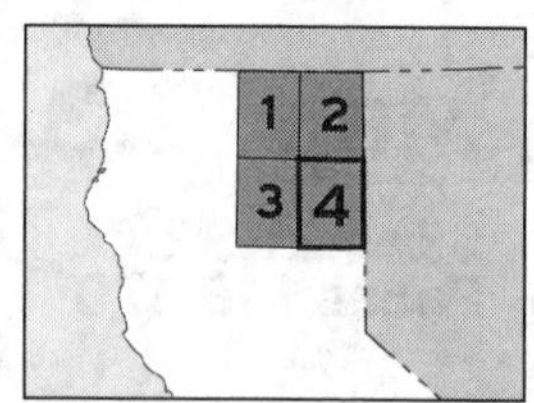

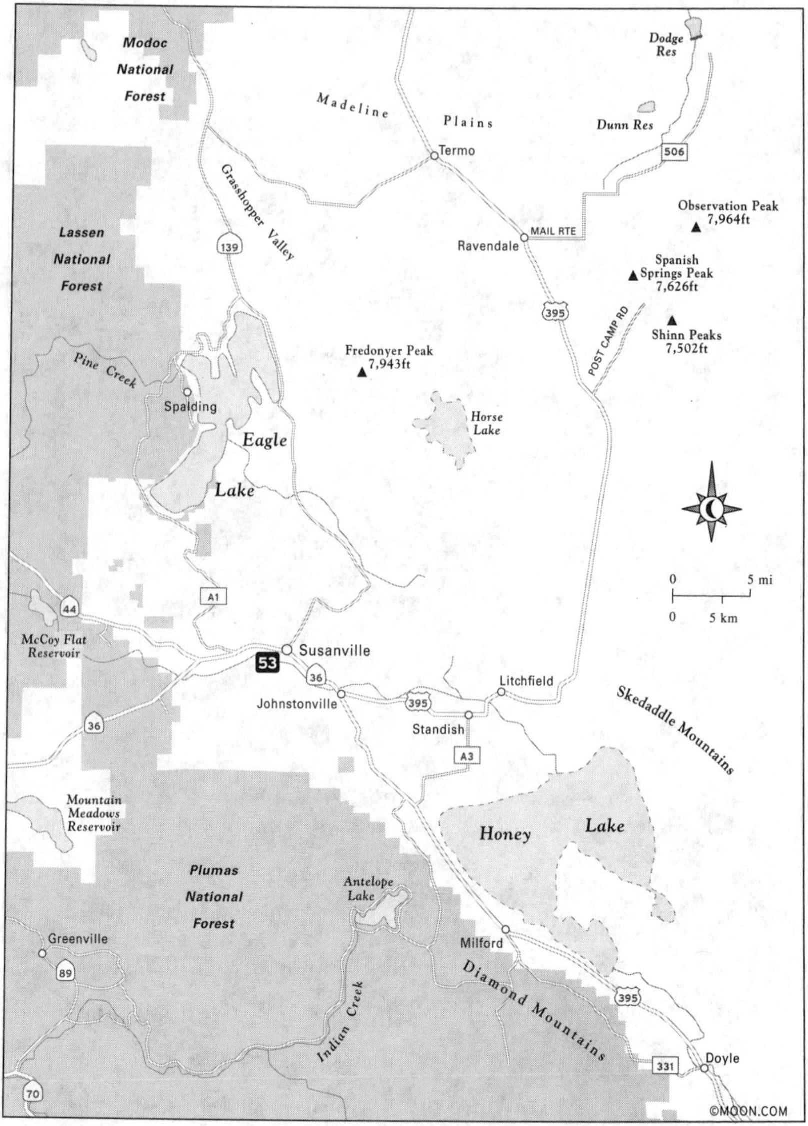

1 CAPTAIN JACK'S STRONGHOLD

2.0 mi/1.5 hr 1 8

in Lava Beds National Monument south of Klamath Basin Wildlife Refuge Complex

Map 3.1, page 131 BEST

Captain Jack's Stronghold provides a history lesson and an introduction to the Lava Beds National Monument. It's an easy walk on a clear trail amid a volcanic plateau, with a few trenches, dips, and rocks. From this trailhead, there are actually two loop trails available. From the trailhead, you start out on a half-mile route toward the Stronghold to a junction. The shorter route then leads to the inner Stronghold. The other trail is routed around the outside of the Stronghold. The walks are short but rocky. The general terrain is level, with a trailhead elevation of 4,047 feet and a high point of 4,080 feet. Captain Jack was a Modoc warrior who fought U.S. troops attempting to relocate Native Americans off their lands and onto a reservation. His hiding place was in this natural lava fortress, but in 1873, Captain Jack was finally captured and hanged, and this site was later named for him.

Note that during the winter, this is an outstanding area to see mule deer. Many of the famous photographs of big bucks in California were taken in this area. The wildlife viewing is best at the onset of winter, after the first inch or two of snow has fallen. In addition, a good nearby side trip is Tule Lake, a favorite wintering area for waterfowl and bald eagles.

User Groups: Hikers only. No dogs, horses, or mountain bikes. No wheelchair access.

Permits: No permits are required. A park entrance fee of $25, good for seven days, is charged per vehicle. A free Cave Permit and screening for white-nose syndrome, which can be devastating to bats, is required before entering any cave at Lava Beds.

Maps: A free brochure is available by contacting Lava Beds National Monument. For a topographic map, ask the USGS for Captain Jack's Stronghold.

Directions: From Redding, take I-5 north for 68 miles to the exit for Central Weed/Highway 97-Klamath Falls. Follow that exit to the stop sign, turn right and drive one mile through town to the junction with Highway 97. Bear right on Highway 97 and drive 54 miles to Highway 161. Turn right (east) on Highway 161 and drive 20 miles to Hill Road. Turn right (south), drive 18 miles to the visitors center, and look for the main road of the Lava Beds National Monument (it's unnamed). Turn north and drive 13 miles on the main monument road to the Captain Jack's Stronghold access road. Turn right and drive to the trailhead.

Contact: Lava Beds National Monument, Tulelake, 530/667-8113, www.nps.gov/labe.

2 WHITNEY BUTTE TRAIL

3.3-6.6 mi/2-4.0 hr 2 8

in Lava Beds National Monument south of Klamath Basin Wildlife Refuge Complex

Map 3.1, page 131

The Whitney Butte Trail is one of four wilderness trails in Lava Beds National Monument, and for many, it's the best of the lot. From the top of Whitney Butte, a cinder cone of 5,004 feet, the views are spectacular across the volcanic landscape. The trailhead, 4,880 feet, is at Merrill Ice Cave. The trail goes west for two miles near the edge of the butte. You then bear left and walk 1.2 miles to the end of the trail at the edge of the Callahan Lava Flow. Be sure to climb Whitney Butte. There is no official trail to the top. Leave no trace, of course. This area bears a resemblance to the surface of the moon, and skilled photographers who know how to use sunlight to their advantage can take black-and-white pictures that can fool most people into thinking they are looking at a lunar surface. Most people arrive just to see the Merrill Ice Cave (which is actually a lava tube) at the beginning of the hike. If you plan to explore the

Catacombs Cave on the Cave Loop Road

cave, bring plenty of flashlight power, a hard hat, and kneepads. The views are often spectacular across the volcanic landscape to 14,179-foot Mount Shasta.

User Groups: Hikers and horses. No dogs or mountain bikes. No wheelchair facilities.

Permits: No permits are required. A park entrance fee of $25, good for seven days, is charged per vehicle.

Caving notes: A free Cave Permit and screening for white-nose syndrome, which can be devastating to bats, is required before entering any cave at Lava Beds. All visitors who enter caves need a hard hat (available for purchase at the visitors center) and flashlight (available for purchase or loan); to keep your hands free, most prefer a headlamp strapped on a hard hat.

Maps: A free brochure is available by contacting Lava Beds National Monument. For a topographic map, ask the USGS for Schonchin Butte.

Directions: From Redding, take I-5 north for 68 miles to the exit for Central Weed/Highway 97-Klamath Falls. Follow that exit to the stop sign, turn right and drive one mile through town to the junction with Highway 97. Bear right on Highway 97 and drive 54 miles to Highway 161. Turn right (east) on Highway 161 and drive 20 miles to Hill Road. Turn right (south), drive 18 miles to the visitors center, and look for the main road of the Lava Beds National Monument (it's unnamed). From the visitors center, turn north on the monument main road and drive 1.2 miles north to the turnoff for Merrill Ice Cave. Turn left and drive 0.7 mile to the parking lot and trailhead at the end of the road.

Contact: Lava Beds National Monument, Tulelake, 530/667-8113, www.nps.gov/labe.

3 THOMAS WRIGHT BATTLEFIELD TRAIL/ BLACK CRATER

2.2 mi/1.0 hr 1 8

in Lava Beds National Monument south of Tulelake Wildlife Refuge

Map 3.1, page 131

One trail, two payoffs. After just 0.25 mile on

this trail, hikers reach a short spur to the awesome Black Crater. In the world of volcanic geology, this is a spatter cone. It feels as if you are looking into the bowels of the earth. When ready, return to the main trail. It's an easy glide along lava fields. At the end of the trail are interpretive signs that explain the Thomas Wright battlefield site. For an excellent side trip from here, continue off trail, clambering up to the Hardin Butte, a 130-foot climb, for a view. The butte sits on the western edge of the huge Schonchin Lava Flow.

User Groups: Hikers only. No dogs, horses, or mountain bikes. No wheelchair facilities.

Permits: No permits are required. A park entrance fee of $25, good for seven days, is charged per vehicle.

Caving notes: A free Cave Permit and screening for white-nose syndrome, which can be devastating to bats, is required before entering any cave at Lava Beds. All visitors who enter caves need a hard hat (available for purchase at the visitors center) and flashlight (available for purchase or loan); to keep your hands free, most prefer a headlamp strapped on a hard hat.

Maps: A free brochure is available by contacting Lava Beds National Monument. For a topographic map, ask the USGS for Captain Jack's Stronghold.

Directions: From Redding, take I-5 north for 68 miles to the exit for Central Weed/Highway 97-Klamath Falls. Follow that exit to the stop sign, turn right and drive one mile through town to the junction with Highway 97. Bear right on Highway 97 and drive 54 miles to Highway 161. Turn right (east) on Highway 161 and drive 20 miles to Hill Road. Turn right (south) and drive five miles to the trailhead on the left (the visitors center is another five miles south).

Contact: Lava Beds National Monument, Tulelake, 530/667-8113, www.nps.gov/labe.

4 SCHONCHIN BUTTE TRAIL

1.4 mi/1.0 hr 3 8

in Lava Beds National Monument south of Tulelake Wildlife Refuge

Map 3.1, page 131

This is a short hike, but for many, it's a butt-kicker. A portion of it is quite steep—enough to get most folks wheezing like old steam locomotives. The trail climbs 600 feet, from a trailhead elevation of 4,700 feet to the lookout at 5,300 feet. There are benches along the trail in case you need to catch your breath. Schonchin Butte has an old fire lookout, and the views are spectacular, of course, especially of the Schonchin Lava Flow to the northeast. Because of the proximity to the visitors center, as well as the short distance involved, many visitors make the tromp to the top. After completing this trip, always explore some of the caves in the matrix of underground lava tubes. You need a hard hat and flashlight to do it (available for a fee at the visitors center). For extensive caving, always wear kneepads. There are more than 700 caves in a five-mile radius, including 15 with signed entrances on the Cave Loop.

User Groups: Hikers only. No dogs, horses, or mountain bikes. No wheelchair facilities.

Permits: No permits are required. A park entrance fee of $25, good for seven days, is charged per vehicle.

Caving notes: A free Cave Permit and screening for white-nose syndrome, which can be devastating to bats, is required before entering any cave at Lava Beds. All visitors who enter caves need a hard hat (available for purchase at the visitors center) and flashlight (available for purchase or loan); to keep your hands free, most prefer a headlamp strapped on a hard hat.

Maps: A free brochure is available by contacting Lava Beds National Monument. For a topographic map, ask the USGS for Schonchin Butte.

Directions: From Redding, take I-5 north for 68 miles to the exit for Central Weed/Highway 97-Klamath Falls. Follow that exit

to the stop sign, turn right and drive one mile through town to the junction with Highway 97. Bear right on Highway 97 and drive 54 miles to Highway 161. Turn right (east) on Highway 161 and drive 20 miles to Hill Road. Turn right (south), drive 18 miles to the visitors center, then look for the main (unnamed) road for the Lava Beds National Monument. Turn north and drive 2.3 miles to the turnoff for Schonchin Butte. Turn right at the sign for Schonchin Butte and drive about one mile on a gravel road to the trailhead.
Contact: Lava Beds National Monument, Tulelake, 530/667-8113, www.nps.gov/labe.

5 MEDICINE LAKE SHORELINE

1.0 mi/1.0 hr 1 8

in Modoc National Forest northeast of Mount Shasta

Map 3.1, page 131

When you stand on the shore of Medicine Lake, it might be difficult to believe that this was once the center of a volcano. The old caldera is now filled with water and circled by conifers, and the lake is clear and crisp. Set at 6,700 feet, it's a unique and popular destination for camping, boating, and fishing. At some point in their stay, most campers will take a morning or afternoon to walk around part of the lake. Although there is no specific trail, the route is clear enough. From the campgrounds, facing the lake, routes are available to the beach and beyond to the campground to the left and to the head of the lake to your right. There is a sense of timelessness here. Although its geology is comparable to Crater Lake in Oregon, Medicine Lake is neither as deep nor as blue. But a bonus here is the good shore fishing for large brook trout, often in the 12- to 14-inch class, buoyed by the large stocks of trout. There are also many excellent nearby side trips. They include the ice caves (along the access road on the way in); a great mountaintop lookout from Little Mount Hoffman (available for overnight rental), Little Medicine Lake (very deep, good fishing), and nearby Bullseye and Blanche Lakes.
User Groups: Hikers, dogs, horses, and mountain bikes. There are wheelchair facilities at the beach and the boat ramp.
Permits: No permits are required. Parking and access are free unless you're camping.
Maps: A free brochure on the Medicine Lake Highlands is available by contacting the Doublehead Ranger District. For a map, ask the U.S. Forest Service for Modoc National Forest. For a topographic map, ask the USGS for Medicine Lake.
Directions: From Redding, take I-5 north for 58 miles to the exit for Highway 89. Bear right at that exit and drive 26.5 miles to Harris Springs Road (just past Bartle). Turn left on Harris Springs Road and drive 4.4 miles to Medicine Lake Road. Turn right on Medicine Lake Road and drive 27.5 miles (paved, but narrow at times) to the turnoff for Medicine Lake. Turn left and drive 0.3 mile to a T. Turn left at the T for beach and boat ramp. Turn right at the T for campgrounds, Little Medicine Lake, and Hoffman Lookout. For a shoreline walk, turn left to the boat ramp, and then walk to the right along the swimming beach.
Contact: Modoc National Forest, Doublehead Ranger District, Tulelake, 530/667-2246, www.fs.usda.gov/modoc.

6 LITTLE GLASS MOUNTAIN

0.5 mi/2.0 hr 3 10

in Modoc National Forest east of Medicine Lake

Map 3.1, page 131

Little Glass Mountain is a spectacular volcanic "glass flow" that covers a square mile in the Medicine Lake Highlands. It was created when glassy dacite and rhyolitic obsidian flowed from the same volcanic vent without mixing, creating a present-day phenomenon that exhibits no modification from weather, erosion, or vegetation. It's about 100 feet high. There are no designated trails on Glass Mountain, so visitors just wander about, inspecting the geologic curiosities as they go. Take care to stay clear of the obsidian, which is slippery and can have arrowhead-sharp edges. Don't walk on it, and don't handle it. Be sure to stay on the gray-colored dacite instead. Got it? Stay on the gray stuff. Stay off the black stuff. The mountain was formed 1,000 years ago as a lava flow. If you wear rings, you will scuff the bottom of the ring with lava when you grab for handholds. A panoramic view of Little Glass Mountain backed by Mount Shasta is available at the Little Mount Hoffman Lookout near Medicine Lake.

User Groups: Hikers and dogs. The terrain is not suitable for horses or mountain bikes. No wheelchair facilities.

Permits: No permits are required. Parking and access are free.

Maps: A free brochure on the Medicine Lake Highlands is available by contacting the Doublehead Ranger District. For a map, ask the U.S. Forest Service for Modoc National Forest. For a topographic map, ask the USGS for Medicine Lake.

Directions: From Redding, take I-5 north for 58 miles to the exit for Highway 89. Bear right at that exit and drive 26.5 miles to Harris Springs Road (just past Bartle). Turn left on Harris Springs Road and drive 4.4 miles (continue straight past the turnoff to Medicine Lake Road on right), and continue on Harris Spring Road for 7.9 miles to Forest Road 44N05. Turn right and drive 0.6 miles to Forest Road 43N77 and continue for 0.5 mile to the foot of Little Glass Mountain. Park and trek in the volcanic landscape.

Contact: Modoc National Forest, Doublehead Ranger District, Tulelake, 530/667-2246, www.fs.usda.gov/modoc.

7 BURNT LAVA FLOW

1.0 mi/1.5 hr

in Modoc National Forest south of Medicine Lake

Map 3.1, page 131

The Burnt Lava Flow is called a land of "rocks that float and mountains of glass." It may seem as if you're exploring some prehistoric area that resembles the moon. But get this: The lava formation is only a few hundred years old, the youngest flow in the Medicine Lake Highlands. It's located south of Glass Mountain and covers some 8,760 acres, with little islands of forest amid the bare, jet-black lava flow. High Hole Crater at the north end rises up 386 feet above the base layer of the flow and is about 150 feet deep. There is no trail, so pick any direction—most visitors go from what appears a sprinkling of what look like tree islands. There are a few weird spots where the ground can be like quicksand when dry and like wet concrete when wet. Just walk around those spots, staying on the hard, black lava flow. When we took an aerial survey of the area, the Burnt Lava Flow was one of the most fascinating portions of the entire region. On foot, it's even stranger.

User Groups: Hikers and dogs. The terrain is not suitable for mountain bikes or horses. No wheelchair facilities.

Permits: No permits are required. Parking and access are free.

Maps: For a map, ask the U.S. Forest Service for Modoc National Forest. For a topographic map, ask the USGS for Porcupine Butte.

Directions: From Redding, take I-5 north for 58 miles to the exit for Highway 89. Bear right at that exit and drive 26.5 miles to Harris Springs Road (just past Bartle). Turn left on Harris Springs Road and drive 4.4 miles to Medicine Lake Road. Turn right on Medicine Lake Road and drive 19.6 miles (paved, but narrow at times) to the turnoff for Burnt Lava Flow (straight would instead take you to Medicine Lake). Turn right and drive 4.1 miles to Forest

Road 43N17. Turn right and drive 1.7 miles to the foot of the Burnt Lava Flow Geologic Area.
Contact: Modoc National Forest, Doublehead Ranger District, Tulelake, 530/667-2246, www.fs.usda.gov/modoc.

8 MEDICINE LAKE GLASS FLOW

1.0 mi/1.0 hr

in Modoc National Forest north of Medicine Lake

Map 3.1, page 131

First, a good story: In 1965, the Medicine Lake Glass Flow was selected by the Manned Spacecraft Center for study by astronauts preparing for the first manned trip to the moon. It feels much the same today as you make your visit. The Medicine Lake Glass Flow Geologic Area covers 570 acres. It has no designated trails. You can explore in any direction you wish, where you probe about the stony-gray dacite, which runs 50-150 feet deep. This part of the Medicine Lake Highlands is about a mile north of Medicine Lake. It is set within the caldera of the Medicine Lake Volcano. Before the first lunar landing, many originally believed this area to resemble the surface of the moon. Most people will just poke around for an hour or two, take a few pictures, and leave, saying they've never seen anything like it.
User Groups: Hikers and dogs. The terrain is not suitable for mountain bikes or horses. No wheelchair facilities.
Permits: No permits are required. Parking and access are free.
Maps: A free brochure on the Medicine Lake Highlands is available by contacting the Doublehead Ranger District. For a map, ask the U.S. Forest Service for Modoc National Forest. For a topographic map, ask the USGS for Medicine Lake.
Directions: From Redding, take I-5 north for 58 miles to the exit for Highway 89. Bear right at that exit, merged with Highway 89, and drive 26.5 miles to Harris Springs Road (just past Bartle). Turn left on Harris Springs Road and drive 4.4 miles to Medicine Lake Road. Turn right on Medicine Lake Road and drive 27.5 miles (paved, but narrow at times) to the turnoff for Medicine Lake. Turn left and drive 0.3 mile to a T. At the T, turn right and drive (slowly) past the campgrounds and Little Medicine Lake for 1.5 miles to a junction with Lava Beds/Forest Road 44N75. Turn right on Forest Road 44N75 and drive 1.2 miles to the foot of the Medicine Lake Glass Flow on the right. There are no designated trailheads or trails.
Contact: Modoc National Forest, Doublehead Ranger District, Tulelake, 530/667-2246, www.fs.usda.gov/modoc.

9 BURNEY FALLS LOOP TRAIL

1.2 mi/0.5 hr

in McArthur-Burney Falls Memorial State Park north of Burney

Map 3.1, page 131 BEST

Spectacular Burney Falls is one of the prettiest waterfalls in the north state. The trip starts by taking in Burney Falls at a lookout point for the full frontal. This is the eye-popping 129-foot waterfall. If you look close, you will see that the surrounding moss-covered canyon wall is a mosaic of oozing water. That is because lava tubes feed underground water through the basalt rock: 100 million gallons a day, year-round—making it an endless freshwater fountain. The waterfall plunges over the brink in two pieces, split at the rim by a small bluff, where two trees have managed toeholds (although the river flows over the top of them during high water from the spring snowmelt). From a parking lot, it's a 100-foot walk to the overlook. This spot also marks the start of Burney Falls Loop Trail, an easy 1.2-mile loop around the waterfall and back.

At the start of the trail, you descend 200 feet

and skirt the plunge pool of the waterfall. Then the trail is routed downstream along Burney Creek and crosses a wood bridge. You then hike upstream back to the waterfall for more fantastic views. At one spot, you are situated directly adjacent to the water's cascade and midlevel curtains. The trail climbs up past the brink of the falls and continues upstream along Burney Creek. It then crosses another bridge. Look up to your left here to the treetops, where a mated pair of bald eagles often tend a nest atop a towering pine. The trail then returns to the falls overlook. It's also a self-guided nature trail, but rather than having to carry a brochure with you, you can just read the small signs that explain the featured sites. The trail was renovated in 2019.

User Groups: Hikers only. No dogs, horses, or mountain bikes. There is paved wheelchair access at the falls overlook point at the beginning of the trail.

Permits: No permits are required. A state park day-use fee of $8 is charged for each vehicle.

Maps: A trail guide is available for a fee at the state park. For a topographic map, ask the USGS for Burney Falls.

Directions: From Redding, take Highway 299 east for 50 miles to Burney and continue five miles to the junction with Highway 89. Turn left (north) and drive 5.8 miles to the state park entrance on the left. At the entrance station, continue straight for a short distance and park in the main lot on the right. The trailhead is across the road at the falls overlook.

Contact: McArthur-Burney Falls Memorial State Park, Burney, 530/335-2777, www.parks.ca.gov.

10 RIM TRAIL

3.0 mi/1.75 hr — 1 — 7

at Lake Britton in McArthur-Burney Falls Memorial State Park north of Burney

Map 3.1, page 131

The Rim Trail provides an easy walk at McArthur-Burney Falls Memorial State Park. It doesn't get the numbers of the Burney Falls

Burney Falls Loop Trail

Loop; for some, that brings an appeal all its own. The trail starts at the campground and is routed to the rim of Lake Britton, a distance of 1.5 miles. It's an easy walk, and pretty too, heading first through forest, then emerging in a pretty cove, with PG&E's Camp Britton across the water. From here, the trail traces the shore of Lake Britton, a sheltered area of the lake, and leads to the road. It's another minute to the little marina, with kayak and paddleboat rentals, or to the adjacent swimming beach. The lake is kept full nearly year-round, even in drought years. In recent summers, algae amounts have been a problem for swimmers.

User Groups: Hikers only. No dogs, horses, or mountain bikes. No wheelchair facilities.

Permits: No permits are required. A state park day-use fee of $8 is charged for each vehicle.

Maps: A trail guide is available for a fee at the state park. For a topographic map, ask the USGS for Burney Falls.

Directions: From Redding, take Highway 299 east for 50 miles to Burney and continue five miles to the junction with Highway 89. Turn left (north) and drive 5.8 miles to the state park entrance on the left. At the entrance station, continue straight for a short distance and park in the main lot on the right. The trailhead is across the road at the falls overlook.

Contact: McArthur-Burney Falls Memorial State Park, Burney, 530/335-2777, www.parks.ca.gov.

11 MCARTHUR-BURNEY FALLS MEMORIAL STATE PARK TO ASH CAMP (PCT)

52.0 mi one-way/4 days 5 5

from McArthur-Burney Falls Memorial State Park west into Ash Camp in Shasta-Trinity National Forest

Map 3.1, page 131

For PCT hikers, it may be difficult to leave the woods, waters, and aura of McArthur-Burney Falls Memorial State Park, but off you go, facing dry country and some of Northern California's least-used portions of the Pacific Crest Trail. Typically the only hikers who complete this section are the ones hiking the entire route from Mexico to Canada; they're virtually forced to endure it.

From Burney Falls, the PCT heads west, touching the Pit River arm of Lake Britton, and then continues forward into Lassen Volcanic National Park, crossing into Shasta-Trinity National Forest and up to Grizzly Peak. Much of this route is across dry, hot, exposed slopes, where the trail has deteriorated in many spots due to the encroachment of brush and the zero trail maintenance by the U.S. Forest Service. Fire damage is a problem too in Lassen Volcanic National Park and the vicinity. Knowing you're smack between the lush beauty of Burney Falls (behind you) and the McCloud River (ahead of you) can make dealing with the present landscape a frustrating encounter. Always fill your canteens with water wherever you find it, and don't hesitate to make a camp if, late in the day, you find even a small flat spot with water nearby. In extremely dry years it's possible to travel this entire stretch without finding any water.

After the hot climb near Grizzly Peak, make the short side trip up to Grizzly Peak. You get a world-class view of Mount Shasta and the McCloud Flats. It's then a high-speed descent to the "Eden" of the McCloud River at Ash Camp. Considering the PCT is the feature national recreation trail in America, this stretch from Burney Falls to the McCloud River, both world-class in beauty, is an embarrassment to the U.S. Forest Service and an abomination to hikers. It's almost as bad as their choice to route the PCT on the Hat Creek Rim instead of along Hat Creek.

To continue north on the PCT, see the *Ash Camp to Castle Crags Wilderness (PCT)* hike in the *Shasta and Trinity* chapter. If you are walking this trail in reverse, see the *Hat Creek Rim to McArthur-Burney Falls Memorial State Park (PCT)* hike in this chapter to continue south.

User Groups: Hikers, dogs (except in the state park boundaries), and horses. No mountain bikes. No wheelchair facilities.
Permits: A campfire permit (free) is required. A fee of $8 is charged per vehicle at the state park. A single permit is required to hike the Pacific Crest Trail. Contact the national forest, Bureau of Land Management (BLM), or national park office at your point of entry for a combined permit that is good for traveling through multiple-permit areas during your dates of travel.
Maps: For USGS topographic maps, ask for Burney Falls, Skunk Ridge, and Grizzly Peak.
Directions: From Redding, take Highway 299 east for 50 miles to Burney and continue five miles to the junction with Highway 89. Turn left (north) and drive 5.8 miles to the state park entrance on the left. At the entrance station, continue straight for a short distance and park in the main lot on the right.
Contact: McArthur-Burney Falls Memorial State Park, Burney, 530/335-2777, www.parks.ca.gov.

12 HI GRADE NATIONAL RECREATION TRAIL

1.1 mi/0.5 hr 2 7

in Modoc National Forest east of Goose Lake

Map 3.2, page 132

The Hi Grade National Recreation Trail is actually 5.5 miles long, but only 1.1 miles are specifically designed for hiking. The remainder of this trail is an old jeep road designated for four-wheel-drive use, one of the only national four-wheel-drive trails in the state. Of course, you can still hike all of it, but it's better to use four-wheeling to get out there, then hike the final mile to get way out there. As you go, watch for signs of old, abandoned mining operations, because gold was discovered here. They never found enough to cause any outpouring of gold miners, though, and the result is a sparsely populated county, with this area being abandoned completely. The surrounding habitat is a mix of high desert and timber, although the trees tend to be small.

History stranger than fiction: A good side trip from the nearby Buck Creek Ranger Station is to Fandango Pass, where there are nice views to the east of Surprise Valley and the Nevada Mountains. This is where a group of immigrants arrived, topped the ridge, looked west, saw Goose Lake, and shouted, "Aha! The Pacific Ocean! We have arrived!" So they started dancing the fandango. That's how the mountain pass got its name. As lore has it, the local natives then massacred them.
User Groups: Hikers, dogs, horses, and mountain bikes. No wheelchair facilities.
Permits: No permits are required. Parking and access are free.
Maps: For a map, ask the U.S. Forest Service for Modoc National Forest. For topographic maps, ask the USGS for Mount Bidwell and Willow Ranch.
Directions: From Redding, take Highway 299 east for 146 miles to Alturas and the junction with U.S. 395. Turn north on U.S. 395 and drive about 35 miles to Forest Road 9. Turn right on Forest Road 9 and drive 4.5 miles to Buck Creek Ranger Station. At the Buck Creek Ranger Station, turn left on Forest Road 47N72 and drive about six miles to the trailhead. Four-wheel-drive vehicles are required.
Contact: Modoc National Forest, Warner Mountain Ranger District, Cedarville, 530/279-6116, www.fs.usda.gov/modoc.

13 PEPPERDINE TRAILHEAD

12.0 mi/2 days 3 9

on the northern boundary of the South Warner Wilderness east of Alturas

Map 3.2, page 132

The six-mile trip on Summit Trail to Patterson Lake is the most popular hike in the South Warner Wilderness. That still doesn't mean you'll run into other people or horses, because the Warners are a remote, lonely place rarely visited by hikers from the Bay Area, Sacramento, or Los Angeles. Patterson Lake is set in a rock basin at 9,000 feet, just below Warren Peak (9,718 feet), the highest lake in the wilderness and the highlight destination for most visitors. The Pepperdine trailhead (at 6,900 feet) is just beyond Porter Reservoir, where a primitive campground and a horse corral are available. The hike is a sustained climb, gaining 2,100 feet, passing to the right of Squaw Peak (8,646 feet) and then tiny Cottonwood Lake. From Squaw Peak, looking east, you'll feel as if you're casting your eyes across hundreds of miles of a stark, uninhabited landscape.

User Groups: Hikers, dogs, and horses. No mountain bikes. No wheelchair facilities.

Permits: A campfire permit (free) is required for overnight use. Parking and access are free.

Maps: For a map, ask the U.S. Forest Service for Modoc National Forest or South Warner Wilderness. For a topographic map, ask the USGS for Warren Peak.

Directions: Take U.S. 395 to the south end of Alturas and to County Road 56. Turn east on County Road 56 and drive 13 miles to the Modoc National Forest boundary and Parker Creek Road/Forest Road 31. Turn left and drive six miles on Parker Creek Road, to the sign for Pepperdine Campground on the right. Turn right and drive to the trailhead.

Contact: Modoc National Forest, Warner Mountain Ranger District, Cedarville, 530/279-6116, www.fs.usda.gov/modoc.

14 PINE CREEK TRAILHEAD

2-11.0 mi/2.0-5.0 hr 3 8

on the northwestern boundary of the South Warner Wilderness east of Alturas

Map 3.2, page 132

This is one of the great short hikes anywhere. The Pine Creek Trail is a magnificent traipse into the beautiful South Warner Wilderness.

The trail starts along the south fork of Pine Creek, about 6,800 feet in elevation, then heads straight east into the wilderness, climbing the lush western slopes. In the course of 4.64 miles, the trail rises 1,000 feet to the Pine Creek Basin. Along the trail are several small lakes, the largest being the two set right along the trail as you enter the basin. Above you is a stark, volcanic-faced rim with few trees, where the headwaters of eight small creeks start from springs, pour down the mountain, join, and then flow into several small lakes. To lengthen the hike, go on to Patterson Lake, a gorgeous mountain lake surrounded by towering rock walls; the round-trip is 11 miles.

Modoc County is the least-populated and least-known region of California, with only 10,000 residents sprinkled across a huge area. Yet there are many outstanding adventures available here.

User Groups: Hikers, dogs, and horses. No mountain bikes. No wheelchair facilities.

Permits: A campfire permit (free) is required for overnight use. Parking and access are free.

Maps: For a map, ask the U.S. Forest Service for Modoc National Forest or South Warner Wilderness. For a topographic map, ask the USGS for Eagle Peak.

Directions: Take U.S. 395 to the south end of Alturas and to County Road 56. Turn east on County Road 56 and drive 13 miles to the Modoc National Forest boundary and West Warner Road. Turn right (south) on West Warner Road and go about 10 miles to the sign for the Pine Creek trailhead. Turn left (east) and head 1.75 miles to the parking area. The road is unpaved for the last 12 miles.

Contact: Modoc National Forest, Warner Mountain Ranger District, Cedarville, 530/279-6116, www.fs.usda.gov/modoc.

15 SOUP SPRINGS TRAILHEAD

3.0 mi/2.0 hr

on the western boundary of the South Warner Wilderness east of Alturas

Map 3.2, page 132

Upper Mill Creek is a small, pristine trout stream that brings the lonely Warner Mountains to life. It's a short hike to get here, up a hill and then down, heading into a valley. On this valley floor, you'll find Mill Creek, only a 1.5-mile walk out of the Soup Springs trailhead. The trailhead is a short distance from the Soup Springs Campground (drinking water available in summer). Your hiking destination is Mill Creek. Mill Creek is a great spot for a picnic lunch or a high-finesse fishing trip. The trout are extremely sensitive, so anything unnatural—like letting your shadow hit the water or clanking your boots on the shore—will spook them off the bite. The trout are small, dark, and chunky, unlike any seen elsewhere.

Some hikers use Slide Creek Trail as a way of climbing up near the Warner Rim and to the intersection with the Summit Trail, a feature hike in the South Warner Wilderness. That makes sense, as there is a primitive campground and corral at the trailhead; then it's a four-mile romp uphill to the Summit Trail junction. It includes a 1,000-foot climb on the way, with the trail routed up the Slide Creek Canyon over the last two miles.

User Groups: Hikers, dogs, and horses. No mountain bikes. No wheelchair facilities. Horse corrals are available near the trailhead and campground.

Permits: No permits are required. Parking and access are free. A campfire permit (free) is required for overnight use.

Maps: For a map, ask the U.S. Forest Service for Modoc National Forest or South Warner Wilderness. For a topographic map, ask the USGS for Eagle Peak.

Directions: From Alturas, take U.S. 395 south for 18.5 miles to Likely and Jess Valley Road (County Road 64). Turn east on Jess Valley Road/County Road 64 and drive 3.2 miles to Blue Lake Road and West Warner Road. Turn left on West Warner Road (Forest Road 5) and drive five miles to Soup Loop Road (Forest Road 40N24). Turn right and drive 4.5 miles (a gravel road) to the campground parking lot, on the right.

Contact: Modoc National Forest, Warner Mountain Ranger District, Cedarville, 530/279-6116, www.fs.usda.gov/modoc.

16 MILL CREEK FALLS TRAILHEAD

1 mi/1 hr

on the southwestern boundary of the South Warner Wilderness east of Alturas

Map 3.2, page 132

The short, easy walk from the Mill Creek Falls trailhead to Clear Lake leads to one of the prettiest spots in Modoc County. It's 0.5 mile to Mill Creek Falls and another 0.5 mile to Clear Lake. At the fork, bear left for the waterfalls or right for the lake. Most hikers will take in both. The trailhead is near the Mill Creek Falls Campground (drinking water available in summer). The trail skirts along the perimeter of a pretty lake set at 6,000 feet. Of the lakes and streams in the Warners, it's Clear Lake that has the largest fish, with brown and rainbow trout ranging to more than 10 pounds. There just aren't many of them. Backpackers can head onward from Clear Lake on Poison Flat Trail, but expect a very steep howler of a climb before intersecting with Mill Creek Trail.

User Groups: Hikers, dogs, and horses. Some wheelchair-accessible facilities are available at the nearby campground, but there is no wheelchair access on this trail. No mountain bikes.

Permits: No permits are required. Parking and access are free.

Maps: For a map, ask the U.S. Forest Service for Modoc National Forest or South Warner

Wilderness. For a topographic map, ask the USGS for Eagle Peak.

Directions: From Alturas, take U.S. 395 south for 18.5 miles to Likely and Jess Valley Road (County Road 64). Turn east on Jess Valley Road/County Road 64 and drive 3.2 miles to Blue Lake Road and West Warner Road. Turn left on West Warner Road (Forest Road 5) and drive 2.5 miles to Forest Road to Mill Creek Road/40N46. Turn right and drive two miles to the campground and trailhead.

Contact: Modoc National Forest, Warner Mountain Ranger District, Cedarville, 530/279-6116, www.fs.usda.gov/modoc.

17 SOUTH EMERSON TRAILHEAD

7.0 mi/2 days 5 9

on the eastern boundary of the South Warner Wilderness east of Alturas

Map 3.2, page 132

Don't be yelpin' about the dreadful climb up to North Emerson Lake, because we're warning you right here, loud and clear, that it qualifies as a first-class butt-kicker. A kill-me, eat-me kind of hike. If you choose to go anyway, well, you asked for it. The trail climbs 2,000 feet in 3.5 miles, but much of that is in a hellish 0.5-mile stretch that'll have you howling for relief. Your reward is little North Emerson Lake at 7,800 feet, a wonderland in a rock bowl with a high sheer back wall.

The South Emerson trailhead, the remotest of those providing access to the Warners, is located on the east side of the mountain rim, near stark, dry country. A primitive campground is available at the trailhead. Out of camp, take the South Emerson Trail for 1.5 miles to the North Emerson Trail. You then connect with the Bear Camp Flat Trail/Emerson Trail. You climb to South Emerson Lake, and for those who want a multiday backpack trek, junction with the Summit Trail. North Emerson Lake is worth every step. You also get incredible long-distance views across the desert to the east.

User Groups: Hikers, dogs, and horses. No mountain bikes. No wheelchair facilities.

Permits: A campfire permit (free) is required for overnight use. Parking and access are free.

Maps: For a map, ask the U.S. Forest Service for Modoc National Forest or South Warner Wilderness. For a topographic map, ask the USGS for Emerson Peak.

Directions: From Alturas, take Highway 299 east for 22 miles to Cedarville and County Road 1. Turn right (south) on County Road 1 and go about 16 miles to Eagleville and continue another 1.5 miles south on County Road 1 to Emerson Road. Turn right on Emerson Road and go three miles to the trailhead. Emerson Road is very steep and is slippery when wet or icy. Four-wheel drive advised.

Contact: Modoc National Forest, Warner Mountain Ranger District, Cedarville, 530/279-6116, www.fs.usda.gov/modoc.

18 PATTERSON/EAST CREEK LOOP

15.0 mi/2 days 3 7

on the southern boundary of the South Warner Wilderness east of Alturas

Map 3.2, page 132

The East Creek Loop is a favorite loop hike in the Warner Mountains. It can be completed in a weekend, not including driving time, and provides a capsule look at the amazing contrasts of the Warners. The hike includes small, seemingly untouched streams, as well as high, barren mountain rims. The trailhead is at the Patterson Campground (no horses); horses are allowed a mile to the west at the East Creek Campground. The highlight of this hike is access to the Summit Trail, the renowned hike in the South Warners.

To start this trip, take the East Creek Trail, elevation 7,100 feet. It is routed 5.5 miles north into the wilderness. Just before the junction with Poison Flat Trail, a spring is on the left side of the trail. Don't miss it—you'll need the water for the upcoming climb. Turn right at the junction with Poison Flat Trail to make the 800-foot climb above tree line, and turn right again on Summit Trail. The loop is completed by taking Summit Trail back south, crossing high, stark country—most of it more than 8,000 feet in elevation. In the last two miles, the trail drops sharply, descending 1,000 feet on the way to Patterson Campground, which marks the end of the loop trail. Reaching the parking area at the East Creek trailhead requires a 0.5-mile walk on the forest road.

User Groups: Hikers, dogs, and horses. No mountain bikes. No wheelchair facilities.

Permits: A campfire permit (free) is required for overnight use. Parking and access are free.

Maps: For a map, ask the U.S. Forest Service for Modoc National Forest or South Warner Wilderness. For a topographic map, ask the USGS for Emerson Peak.

Directions: From Alturas, take U.S. 395 south for 18.5 miles to Likely and Jess Valley Road (County Road 64). Turn east on Jess Valley Road/County Road 64 and drive 3.2 miles to Blue Lake Road. Turn right on Blue Lake Road (still County Road 64) and drive seven miles to the signed turnoff for Blue Lake. Turn left (a right goes to Blue Lake) and drive eight miles (becomes slow and curvy) to the Patterson Campground and nearby trailhead for East Creek Trail.

Contact: Modoc National Forest, Warner Mountain Ranger District, Cedarville, 530/279-6116, www.fs.usda.gov/modoc.

19 SUMMIT LOOP

45.0 mi/4 days

on the southern boundary of the South Warner Wilderness east of Alturas

Map 3.2, page 132

The Summit Loop is the backpacking trek that the few hikers who know of the South Warners will yearn to take someday. If you are one of the lucky few to make the time, you'll find this hike traverses both sides of the Warner ridge, providing an intimate look at a diverse place. The west side of the Warner Mountains is a habitat filled with small pine trees, meadows, and the headwaters of many small streams. The east side, however, is stark and rugged, with great long-distance lookouts to the east across high desert and miles of sagebrush and juniper. The trail runs the entire length of the South Warner Wilderness, from the Patterson Campground to the south extending to the Pepperdine Campground at the north.

Start the trip at the Patterson Camp trailhead (at 7,200 feet). From here the trail climbs quickly, rising to 8,200 feet in two miles, accessing high, barren country. Great views abound from here as hikers head north. Then, to reach the north end of the wilderness, take the turn at Owl Creek Trail and hike to Linderman Lake, set at the foot of Devils Knob (8,776 feet). Continue past Squaw Peak (8,646 feet). To return in a loop, make the hairpin left turn at Summit Trail and walk back on the mostly lush western slopes of the Warners. Highlights on the return loop segment include Patterson Lake, 9,000 feet, the headwaters of Mill Creek and North Fork East Creek, and many beautiful and fragile meadows. The trail ends at the East Creek parking area, a 0.5-mile walk from the Patterson Camp trailhead.

Savor every moment of this trip—it's one of the greatest little-known hikes anywhere in America. The Warner Mountains have a mystique about them, a charm cultivated by the thoughts of hikers who dream of an area where the landscape is remote and untouched and the trails are empty. However, only rarely do they get around to it. For most, the Warners are just too remote and too far away, and the trip requires too much time.

User Groups: Hikers, dogs, and horses. No mountain bikes. No wheelchair facilities.

Permits: A campfire permit (free) is required for overnight use. Parking and access are free.

Maps: For a map, ask the U.S. Forest Service for Modoc National Forest or South Warner Wilderness. For a topographic map, ask the USGS for Emerson Peak.

Directions: From Alturas, take U.S. 395 south for 18.5 miles to Likely and Jess Valley Road (County Road 64). Turn east on Jess Valley Road/County Road 64 and drive 3.2 miles to Blue Lake Road. Turn right on Blue Lake Road (still County Road 64) and drive seven miles to the signed turnoff for Blue Lake. Turn left (a right goes to Blue Lake) and drive eight miles (becomes slow and curvy) to the Patterson Campground and nearby trailhead for East Creek Trail.

Contact: Modoc National Forest, Warner Mountain Ranger District, Cedarville, 530/279-6116, www.fs.usda.gov/modoc.

20 BLUE LAKE LOOP NATIONAL RECREATION TRAIL

2.0 mi/1.25 hr — 1 — 7

at Blue Lake in Modoc National Forest southeast of Alturas

Map 3.2, page 132

Blue Lake is the prettiest lake you can reach with a car in Modoc County. The Blue Lake Loop National Recreation Trail is simply a trail around the lake. With a campground at the lake, this trail makes a good side trip for overnight visitors. In addition, a fishing pier and wheelchair-accessible restroom are available. Most visitors are here to camp, boat, and fish. Some of the surrounding forest has evidence of a past fire in the area. Though most fish for rainbow trout, which are stocked, large and often elusive brown trout provide a trophy fishery.

User Groups: Hikers and dogs. The fishing pier and restroom are wheelchair-accessible. No horses or mountain bikes.

Permits: No permits are required. Parking and access are free.

Maps: For a map, ask the U.S. Forest Service for Modoc National Forest. For a topographic map, ask the USGS for Jess Valley.

Directions: From Alturas, take U.S. 395 south for 18.5 miles to Likely and Jess Valley Road (County Road 64). Turn east on Jess Valley Road (County Road 64) and drive nine miles to Blue Lake Road. Turn right on Blue Lake Road and drive seven miles to Forest Road 39N30 (signed for Blue Lake). Turn right and drive to the parking area.

Contact: Modoc National Forest, Warner Mountain Ranger District, Cedarville, 530/279-6116, www.fs.usda.gov/modoc.

21 BURNEY MOUNTAIN SUMMIT

0.25-8.0 mi/0.25-3.0 hr — 1 — 9

in Lassen National Forest south of Burney

Map 3.3, page 133

The view is just so good from the top of Burney Mountain (elevation 7,863 feet) that the trip had to be included in this book. If you show up in the winter or after 6pm, when the access road is gated, or if you simply want the exercise, it's a four-mile hike up the road to the top of the mountain. Otherwise you can drive right to the top. If you drive to the summit, the "hike" consists of just moseying around and gazing off in all directions. There is a fire lookout on top of the mountain. Burney Mountain often gets lost in the shadow of its big brothers, Lassen Peak and Mount Shasta, but of the three, the view just might be best from Burney. That's because you can see both Lassen and Shasta from the top of Burney. You need a swivel instead of a neck.

User Groups: Hikers, dogs, horses, and mountain bikes. No wheelchair facilities.

Permits: No permits are required. Parking and access are free.

Maps: For a map, ask the U.S. Forest Service for Lassen National Forest. For topographic maps, ask the USGS for Burney Mountain West and Burney Mountain East.

Directions: From Redding, take Highway 299 east for 50 miles to Burney and continue five more miles east to Highway 89. Turn south (right) on Highway 89 and drive 10.5 miles to Forest Road 26/Forest Road 34N19 (signed). Turn right on Forest Road 26 and drive 10 miles to Forest Road 34N23 (known locally as Burney Mountain Road). Turn right and drive seven miles to the mountain summit.

Burney Mountain Road is blocked at 6pm each day and throughout winter by a locked gate. You can park at the gate and hike to the top.

Contact: Lassen National Forest, Hat Creek Ranger District, Falls River Mills, 530/336-5521, www.fs.usda.gov/lassen.

22 CYPRESS TRAILHEAD TO LAKE EILER

6.0 mi/1 day 

on the north boundary of the Thousand Lakes Wilderness north of Lassen Volcanic National Park

Map 3.3, page 133

Before the relocation of the Tamarack trailhead (see next hike listing), the Cypress trailhead was the primary launch point to reach beautiful Lake Eiler, a round-trip of six miles with a climb of 1,000 feet on the way in. Nowadays, with a large parking area here and the required climb to reach Eiler, it is favored by the backcountry horse set and not so much hikers. The Cypress trailhead provides the best access for backcountry riding in the Thousand Lakes Wilderness. From the trailhead, you climb 1,000 feet over three miles to a ridge, then drop down to Lake Eiler. A great side trip for the ambitious is to take a well-worn route, another three miles one-way, to Magee Peak for its sweeping view across the wilderness. Eiler is the largest lake in this region, set just below Eiler Butte. Many small lakes are sprinkled in a radius of just two miles. A network of trails here connects to other lakes, so an option is to keep on going for an overnighter. From the south side of Eiler, the trail loops deeper into the wilderness in a clockwise arc. It passes near several other lakes, including Box and Barrett Lakes. Both of these provide good fishing for small trout.

This wilderness is not called "Thousand Lakes" because there are a lot of lakes. After heavy rains or snowmelt, there are thousands of little pockets of water-breeding mosquitoes here in spring. And *that* is how it was named.

User Groups: Hikers, dogs, and horses. No mountain bikes. No wheelchair facilities.

Permits: No permits are required. Self-registration requested. Parking and access are free.

Maps: For a map, ask the U.S. Forest Service for Lassen National Forest. A wilderness trail map is available for a fee from the Hat Creek Ranger District. For topographic maps, ask the USGS for Thousand Lakes Valley and Jacks Backbone.

Directions: From Redding, take Highway 299 east for 50 miles to Burney and continue east five miles to Highway 89. Turn right (south) on Highway 89 and drive 10.5 miles to Forest Road 26 (Forest Road 34N19). Turn west on Forest Road 26 (Forest Road 34N19) and drive 8.5 miles to Forest Road 34N60. Turn left and drive 2.5 miles to the parking area (large).

Contact: Lassen National Forest, Hat Creek Ranger District, Falls River Mills, 530/336-5521, www.fs.usda.gov/lassen.

23 TAMARACK TRAILHEAD/ LAKE EILER

7.0 mi/3.5 hr 

on the east boundary of the Thousand Lakes Wilderness north of Lassen Volcanic National Park

Map 3.3, page 133

From the Tamarack trailhead, it's a 3.5-mile walk with a 400-foot climb to Lake Eiler. The lake is gorgeous, but note that the Eiler fire burned much of the national forest in the vicinity. Most visitors will do this as a weekend trip, or locals will venture in as a day trip; have a picnic, swim, or fish, and then return. If you are setting out on a multiday backpacking trek, then go onward to several other wilderness lakes. The trail is then routed into the northwestern interior of the Thousand Lakes Wilderness. After two miles, you'll reach a fork in the trail; turn left (south) to reach Barrett Lake in just another mile of hiking. Note that there is a complex trail network in this area with many junctions, creating a situation in which backpackers can invent their own multiday route. From Barrett Lake, other attractive destinations include Durbin Lake, 0.5 mile to the south, and Everett and Magee Lakes, another (very challenging) 2.7 miles away.

User Groups: Hikers, dogs, and horses. No mountain bikes. No wheelchair facilities.

Permits: No permits are required. Self-registration requested. Parking and access are free.

Maps: For a map, ask the U.S. Forest Service for Lassen National Forest. A wilderness trail map is available for a fee from the Hat Creek Ranger District. For topographic maps, ask the USGS for Thousand Lakes Valley and Jacks Backbone.

Directions: From Redding, take Highway 299 east for 50 miles to Burney and continue east five miles to Highway 89. Turn right (south) on Highway 89 and drive about 14 miles to Forest Road 33N25. Turn west on Forest Road 33N25 and drive 7.5 miles to a Y junction. Turn right and drive just about 1.5 miles to the trailhead (the new route is well signed).

Contact: Lassen National Forest, Hat Creek Ranger District, Falls River Mills, 530/336-5521, www.fs.usda.gov/lassen.

24 BUNCHGRASS TRAILHEAD

8.0 mi/2 days

on the south boundary of the Thousand Lakes Wilderness north of Lassen Volcanic National Park

Map 3.3, page 133

This trailhead is obscure and difficult to reach, and because of that, few visitors choose it as a jumping-off spot for their treks. The trailhead is the southernmost access point to the Thousand Lakes Wilderness. The destination is Durbin Lake, a four-mile hike one-way, which can make for a destination for a weekend backpack trip. The trailhead elevation is 5,680 feet, and from here, it's a fair walk in, up and down. The landscape is a mix of lodgepole pine and open terrain. If you're not in shape, you'll know it well before you reach the lake. You'll come to Hall Butte (at 7,187 feet) and then Durbin Lake. A side-trip option is to climb Hall Butte. Break off the trail at three miles in, for a 0.5-mile tromp to the top with no trail.

User Groups: Hikers, dogs, and horses. No mountain bikes. No wheelchair facilities.

Permits: A campfire permit (free) is required. Parking and access are free.

Maps: For a map, ask the U.S. Forest Service for Lassen National Forest. A wilderness trail map is available for a fee from the Hat Creek Ranger District. For topographic maps, ask the USGS for Thousand Lakes Valley and Jacks Backbone.

Directions: From Redding, take Highway 299 east for 50 miles to Burney and continue east five miles to Highway 89. Turn right (south) on Highway 89 and drive 31 miles to Forest Road 16 (Forest Road 33N16). Turn right on Forest Road 16 and drive seven miles to Forest Road 32N45. Turn right on Forest Road 32N45 and drive two miles to Forest Road 32N42Y (very steep, four-wheel drive recommended). Turn left and head to the parking area, at the end of the road.

Contact: Lassen National Forest, Hat Creek

Ranger District, Falls River Mills, 530/336-5521, www.fs.usda.gov/lassen.

25 HAT CREEK RIM TO MCARTHUR-BURNEY FALLS MEMORIAL STATE PARK (PCT)

40.0 mi one-way/3 days 

from the Highway 44 parking area north to McArthur-Burney Falls Memorial State Park

Map 3.3, page 133

This section of the PCT includes the infamous 27-mile section without water. Unless you are through-hiking the entire PCT, there is no reason to suffer this ignominy. In recent years, a trail angel has stocked a water cache for hikers where the trail crosses a Forest Service road about halfway in. When my son Jeremy hiked the entire PCT, I ferried his (and companions) gear with my truck from Old Station to the Baum Lake/Crystal Lake Hatchery, and with a lightweight pack, he did the 27-mile stretch in one day, 7 a.m. to 6 p.m., aided by that water cache. We've seen many PCT hikers cheat by hitchhiking past this section on Highway 89, but with a water cache, there is no reason to do that, as it defeats the purpose of the challenge of a through-hike on the PCT.

This 40-mile section also features Hat Creek, Baum Lake, Crystal Lake, and spectacular Burney Falls. From the trailhead at Highway 44, the trail passes through the wooded watershed of Hat Creek to a long, shadeless section that will have you counting the drops of water in your canteen. This is the Hat Creek Rim section of the PCT, the roughest section of the entire route from Mexico to Canada, with no water available for 27 miles of trail. A single drop of water will be valued more than a $10,000 bill.

After departing from Hat Creek, the PCT heads past Baum and Crystal Lakes. You cross Highway 299, and from there, it's an eight-mile romp to McArthur-Burney Falls State Park and its breathtaking 129-foot waterfall.

To continue north on the PCT, see the *McArthur-Burney Falls Memorial State Park to Ash Camp (PCT)* hike in this chapter. If you are walking this trail in reverse, see the *Lassen Volcanic National Park to Highway 44 (PCT)* hike in this chapter to continue south.

User Groups: Hikers, dogs (except in the state park boundaries), and horses. No mountain bikes. No wheelchair facilities.

Permits: A campfire permit (free) is required. A state park entrance fee of $8 is charged per vehicle. A single permit is required to hike the Pacific Crest Trail. Contact the national forest, Bureau of Land Management (BLM), or national park office at your point of entry for a combined permit that is good for traveling through multiple-permit areas during your dates of travel.

Maps: For topographic maps, ask the USGS for Cassel, Dana, Old Station, Murken Bench, Hogback Ridge, and Burney Falls.

Directions: From Redding, take Highway 44 east for 60 miles to Highway 89/44. Turn left (north) on Highway 89/44 and drive 13 miles to Old Station and continue a short distance to Highway 44. Turn right (east) on Highway 44 and drive 0.25 mile beyond the Old Station Post Office to Forest Road 32N20. Turn right on Forest Road 32N20. The trail crosses the road about 0.5 mile from the junction of Highway 44 and Forest Road 32N20. If you have horses and need to park a horse trailer, use Mud Lake trailhead three miles from the junction of Highway 89 and Highway 44.

Contact: Lassen National Forest, Hat Creek Ranger District, Falls River Mills, 530/336-5521, www.fs.usda.gov/lassen.

26 NOBLES EMIGRANT TRAIL

7.0 mi/4.0 hr 

from the Manzanita Lake Trailhead in Lassen Volcanic National Park east of Red Bluff

Map 3.3, page 133

The trail, with its easy, moderate grade, passes first through an old forest with towering firs, cedars, and pines. About 2.5 miles in, you'll arrive at Lassen's strange Dwarf Forest. Not only will you be surrounded by stunted trees, but you also get views of Chaos Crags, a jumble of pinkish rocks that resulted from an avalanche hundreds of years ago. Many visitors hike to this point, then turn around and return to the campground.

The most difficult part of this hike is the first two steps. Why? Because the trailhead is set near the northern park entrance amid a number of small roads and a maintenance area, and despite a trail sign, many visitors don't see it. It's a great day hike for campers staying at Manzanita Lake.

It's a historic trail, of course, that follows part of a historical route that was originally an east-west portion of the California Trail, used by emigrants in the 1850s. There is no water available on the trail, so be sure to have at least one filled canteen per hiker. Because of the moderate slope, this trail is an ideal cross-country ski route in the winter months.

User Groups: Hikers and horses. No dogs or mountain bikes. No wheelchair facilities.

Permits: A park entrance fee of $30, good for a week, is charged for each vehicle.

Maps: Trail maps are available for free from park visitors and entrance centers and Lassen Park Foundation.

Directions: From Redding, take Highway 44 east for 46 miles to the junction with Highway 89. Turn right (south) on Highway 89 and drive one mile to the park entrance station. Continue on the main park road (Lassen Park Highway/Highway 89) for 0.5 mile to the turnoff for Manzanita Lake. The trailhead is just past the entrance station at a service road (ask the attendant at the kiosk).

Contact: Lassen Volcanic National Park, Visitor Center, 530/595-4480; headquarters, 530/595-4444, www.nps.gov/lavo; Lassen Park Foundation, Mineral, www.lassenparkfoundation.org.

27 MANZANITA LAKE TRAIL

1.5 mi/1.0 hr 1 8

at the northern entrance to Lassen Volcanic National Park on Highway 44

Map 3.3, page 133

There's no prettier lake that you can reach by car in Lassen Volcanic National Park than Manzanita Lake. That is why many consider the campground here an ideal destination. With 179 sites, it's the largest camp in the park, and it's easy to reach, located just beyond the entrance station at the western boundary of the park. The trail simply traces the shoreline of this pretty lake at a 5,950-foot elevation and is easily accessible from either the parking area just beyond the entrance station or from the campground. Rental park model-style camping cabins are available in forest near the lake, and along the shore below the cabins are kayak rentals. Nearby Reflection Lake, just across the park's entrance road, provides a side trip; that adds about a half mile. Note that the fishing at Manzanita Lake is catch-and-release only, where anglers must use artificials; that is, do not use bait, and pinch down your barbs.

User Groups: Hikers only. No dogs, horses, or mountain bikes. No wheelchair facilities.

Permits: A park entrance fee of $30, good for a week, is charged for each vehicle.

Maps: Trail maps are available for free from park visitors and entrance centers and Lassen Park Foundation.

Directions: From Redding, take Highway 44 east for 46 miles to the junction with Highway 89. Turn right (south) on Highway 89 and drive one mile to the park entrance station. Continue on the main park road (Lassen Park Highway/Highway 89) for 0.5 mile, to the turnoff for Manzanita Lake Campground. Turn right and drive 0.5 mile to the day-use parking area.

Contact: Lassen Volcanic National Park, Visitor Center, 530/595-4480; headquarters, 530/595-4444, www.nps.gov/lavo; Lassen Park Foundation, Mineral, www.lassenparkfoundation.org.

28 CINDER CONE TRAIL

4.0 mi/3.0 hr — 3 — 10

from Butte Lake Trailhead in Lassen Volcanic National Park

Map 3.3, page 133

The Cinder Cone Trail provides one of the most unique views from its rim of anywhere in California. You can see inside the collapsed center of the caldera of this mini volcano, beyond across wilderness with two gorgeous lakes, and on the nearby horizon just 10 miles away, Lassen Peak. The Cinder Cone Trail (and the next hike, the Prospect Peak Trail) gets overlooked because it is set in the northeastern corner of the park, with the trailhead near Butte Lake and its campground. When you arrive by car, you'll find a pretty campground on your right, then Butte Lake on your left, and just beyond, the end of the road and the trailhead. The trailhead for Nobles Emigrant Trail/Cinder Cone Trail is set at an elevation of 6,100 feet. The trail starts out easy, and for a few stretches in the first half mile, the surface can have short stretches of volcanic sand rubble. It heads southwest through forest. At 1.5 miles, you'll reach the Cinder Cone cutoff, and there, everything suddenly changes. The last 0.5 mile rises to the top of the Cinder Cone (6,907 feet), a short but very intense climb of 800 feet to the summit rim at 6,907 feet. You slog through the volcanic scree the whole way up. Once on top, you can hike the rim of the caldera, with cutoffs that plummet inside the collapsed volcano. The views are unforgettable, especially south to the Painted Dunes and Fantastic Lava Beds. This

Cinder Cone Trail

is a classic volcanic landscape. The cinder cone itself looks like a moon crater.

User Groups: Hikers only. No dogs, horses, or mountain bikes. No wheelchair facilities.

Permits: No permits are required. A park entrance fee of $30, good for a week, is charged for each vehicle.

Maps: Trail maps are available for free from park visitors and entrance centers and Lassen Park Foundation.

Directions: From Redding, take Highway 44 east for 60 miles to Highway 89/44. Turn left (north) on Highway 89/44 and drive 13 miles to Old Station and continue a short distance to Highway 44. Turn right (east) on Highway 44 and drive 10 miles to Butte Lake Road (Forest Road 32N21). Turn right (south) on Butte Lake Road (Forest Road 32N21) and drive six miles to Butte Lake (pass the campground on the right, boat ramp on the left) and continue to the end of the road, parking, and trailhead.

Contact: Lassen Volcanic National Park, Visitor Center, 530/595-4480; headquarters, 530/595-4444, www.nps.gov/lavo; Lassen Park Foundation, Mineral, www.lassenparkfoundation.org.

29 PROSPECT PEAK TRAIL

7.0 mi/4.5 hr

at Butte Lake in Lassen Volcanic National Park

Map 3.3, page 133

Your rewards on this trail are a series of great views in Lassen Volcanic National Park and a trail that gets little use. We've never seen anybody else here or a single piece of litter. The trailhead (Nobles Emigrant Trail), at 6,100 feet, is past Butte Lake. After less than 0.5 mile (flat, wide, and sandy), you'll turn right at the junction with Prospect Peak Trail. The trail immediately starts to climb. Get used to it, because there's no respite. It climbs more than 2,200 feet over the course of just 3.3 miles. Views emerge below of Butte Lake, Snag Lake, the Fantastic Lava Beds, Cinder Cone, and then to the volcanic rim on the horizon crowned by 10,457-foot Lassen Peak. It finally tops the summit at 8,338 feet. It's a flat-top summit, not a peak, which never fails to disappoint. The best views are on the way up, across the Cinder Cone and beyond, and from the left edge of the flat-topped summit where you can find a spot to see Lassen Peak, Mount Hoffman, and Crater Butte, along with thousands and thousands of acres of national forest to the north. Since the snowmelt occurs earlier here than in the rest of the park, this trip makes a perfect hike in the early to mid-spring, when the air is still cool. If you wait until summer, you'll find this a dry, forsaken place. Hiking to the top of most mountains requires a long, grinding climb. Gaining the summit of Prospect Peak is somewhat different. Long? No. Grinding? Yep.

User Groups: Hikers and horses. No dogs or mountain bikes. No wheelchair facilities.

Permits: No permits are required. A park entrance fee of $30, good for a week, is charged for each vehicle.

Maps: Trail maps are available for free from park visitors and entrance centers and Lassen Park Foundation.

Directions: From Redding, take Highway 44 east for 60 miles to Highway 89/44. Continue north on Highway 89/44 and drive 13 miles to Old Station and continue a short distance to Highway 44. Turn right (east) on Highway 44 and drive 10 miles to Forest Road 32N21. Turn right (south) on Forest Road 32N21 and drive seven miles to Butte Lake (pass the campground on the right, boat ramp on the left) and continue to the end of the road, parking, and trailhead.

Contact: Lassen Volcanic National Park, Visitor Center, 530/595-4480; headquarters, 530/595-4444, www.nps.gov/lavo; Lassen Park Foundation, Mineral, www.lassenparkfoundation.org.

30 CONE LAKE TRAILHEAD

4.0 mi/2.5 hr 2 8

on the boundary of Caribou Wilderness east of Lassen Volcanic National Park

Map 3.3, page 133

Triangle Lake is the prize destination of this trek, after only a two-mile hike in the northern Caribou Wilderness near Black Butte. The trailhead is at tiny Cone Lake just outside the wilderness. From here, you walk for nearly a mile before passing the wilderness boundary, which is clearly marked. At that point, you can sense the change in features, as the land becomes wild and untouched. Continue one mile south to Triangle Lake, which provides good fishing during the evening for pan-size trout. If you want more, you can get more. For an overnighter, the best campsites are on the west side of the lake.

At Triangle Lake, the trail forks and you can continue your adventure. The right fork is routed right into Lassen Volcanic National Park, a distance of only 1.5 miles, from which you can access Widow Lake. A free wilderness permit is required from Lassen Volcanic National Park for overnight use. The left fork, on the other hand, leads to Twin Lakes over the course of just 0.5 mile.

User Groups: Hikers, dogs, and horses. No mountain bikes. No wheelchair facilities.

Permits: No permits are required for day use. Campfire permits are required for overnight use. Parking and access are free.

Maps: A trail map is available for a fee from the Almanor Ranger District. For a map, ask the U.S. Forest Service for Lassen National Forest or Caribou Wilderness. For a topographic map, ask the USGS for Bogard Buttes.

Directions: From Redding, take Highway 44 east for 60 miles to Highway 89/44. Turn left (north) on Highway 89/44 and drive 13 miles to Old Station and continue a short distance to Highway 44. Turn right (east) on Highway 44 and drive 30 miles to Bogard Work Station and continue a short distance to Forest Road 10 on the right. Turn right on Forest Road 10 and drive 5.9 miles to Forest Road 32N09. Turn right (still Forest Road 32N09) and drive one mile to Cone Lake Road. Turn left on Cone Lake Road (still Forest Road 32N09) and drive 1.7 miles to the Cone Lake trailhead. Note that from Highway 44, the roads are unpaved to the trailhead.

Contact: Lassen National Forest, Almanor Ranger District, Chester, 530/258-2141, www.fs.usda.gov/lassen.

31 CARIBOU LAKE LOOP

7.0 mi/3.5 hrs 3 9

on the boundary of Caribou Wilderness east of Lassen Volcanic National Park

Map 3.3, page 133

From the Caribou Lake trailhead, you get wilderness access to an array of pretty mountain lakes and often no people. Rarely are so many wilderness lakes this close to a trailhead. The trip starts at Caribou Lake. The trail heads west, and in no time, you pass all kinds of tiny lakes. The first one, Cowboy Lake, is only 0.25 mile down the trail. It's another two miles, with an easy 400-foot climb, you will arrive at beautiful Jewel Lake on your left. Then, past just Jewel Lake, gorgeous Eleanor Lake is on your right. From Eleanor, the trail continues another hour up to a trail junction. For the day-hike Caribou Loop, turn left. In minutes you skirt Black Lake on your right. By now, you're expecting the beauty. The trail continues south for a mile to another junction, where you turn left and skirt the left side of narrow North Divide Lake. The trail then heads downhill (at a mile, there's a spur trail on the left to Gem Lake, a must-do) and then further down the trail a mile to Emerald Lake. Just beyond Emerald, you reach the first junction, just above Caribou Lake, not far from the start.

The Caribou Wilderness is quite small, just nine miles from top to bottom, and only five miles across, with elevations ranging

5,000-7,000 feet. This trip provides a visit to the best of it.

User Groups: Hikers, dogs, and horses (a horse corral is available at the trailhead). No mountain bikes. No wheelchair facilities.

Permits: A campfire permit (free) is required. Parking and access are free.

Maps: A trail map is available for a fee from the Almanor Ranger District. For a map, ask the U.S. Forest Service for Lassen National Forest or Caribou Wilderness. For a topographic map, ask the USGS for Red Cinder.

Directions: From Red Bluff, take Highway 36 east and drive 82 miles to Westwood (east of Lake Almanor) and Mooney Road/County Road 21. Turn left on Mooney Road/County Road A21 and go 13.9 miles to Silver Lake Road. Turn left on Silver Lake Road and drive five miles to a Y with Forest Road 10. Bear right on Forest Road 10 and drive 0.25 mile to a fork with Forest Road 31N18. Turn right on Forest Road 31N18 and drive 0.8 mile (at 0.2 mile, requires a left turn, same road) to Caribou Lake and the trailhead.

Contact: Lassen National Forest, Almanor Ranger District, Chester, 530/258-2141, www.fs.usda.gov/lassen.

32 ECHO AND TWIN LAKES

8.0 mi/5.5 hr — 2 — 10

in Lassen Volcanic National Park east of Red Bluff

Map 3.3, page 133 — BEST

You get it all on this hike to Lower Twin Lake: beautiful lakes, forest, meadows, and wildflowers. The route provides testimony to the beauty of the Lassen Wilderness. The trailhead elevation is 6,720 feet. The trail starts on the north side of Summit Lake near the ranger station and connects in 0.4 miles to the Summit Lake Trail. The trail to Echo Lake then branches off on the far- east side of the lake. Then the trail climbs 500 feet in about a mile. After this climb, the rest of the hike will be a breeze. You'll arrive at Echo Lake in just another mile and at Upper Twin and Lower Twin in the next two miles, dropping 500 feet on your way. Views of Lassen Peak are spectacular. It's all very pretty and a great bonus for Summit Lake campers. For campers staying at one of the Summit Lake campgrounds, it makes an outstanding day hike or an easy overnighter for backpackers. If you are not camping, start at the day-use area near the North Summit Lake Campground.

User Groups: Hikers and horses. No dogs or mountain bikes. No wheelchair facilities.

Permits: No permits are required. A park entrance fee of $30, good for a week, is charged for each vehicle.

Maps: Trail maps are available for free from park visitors and entrance centers and Lassen Park Foundation.

Directions: From Redding, take Highway 44 east for 46 miles to the junction with Highway 89. Turn right (south) on Highway 89 and drive one mile to the park entrance station. Continue on the main park road (Lassen Park Highway/Highway 89) for 12 miles to the turnoff for Summit Lake North Campground. Turn left and park in the day-use area near the lake. Look for the boardwalk that leads to a trail sign, then turn left and start your hike.

Contact: Lassen Volcanic National Park, Visitor Center, 530/595-4480; headquarters, 530/595-4444, www.nps.gov/lavo; Lassen Park Foundation, Mineral, www.lassenparkfoundation.org.

33 SUMMIT LAKE LOOP

0.5 mi/0.5 hr — 1 — 8

in Lassen Volcanic National Park east of Red Bluff

Map 3.3, page 133

Summit Lake is a beautiful spot where deer visit almost every summer evening. Nearby campgrounds on both sides of the lake (north and south) are set in conifers, with a pretty meadow just south of the lake along Kings Creek. This hike is a simple walk around Summit Lake. From the South Summit Lake Campground, the trail starts next to a day-use parking area, near the campground entrance road, and leads a short distance to the shore of the lake and the trail. From the North Summit Lake Campground, there is an area for kayak launching along the shore, and from there, you can walk to your right. The pretty walk is best taken at dusk, when the changing evening colors reflect a variety of tints across the lake surface. The best place to see wildlife, especially deer, is in the meadow adjacent to Kings Creek, the lake's outlet stream. The elevation is 7,000 feet. This trail was once an anglers' trail. No more. No lakes in Lassen Volcanic National Park are stocked with trout, and the fishing is terrible.

User Groups: Hikers and horses. No dogs or mountain bikes. No wheelchair facilities.

Permits: No permits are required. A park entrance fee of $30, good for a week, is charged for each vehicle.

Maps: Trail maps are available for free from park visitors and entrance centers and Lassen Park Foundation.

Directions: From Redding, take Highway 44 east for 46 miles to the junction with Highway 89. Turn right (south) on Highway 89 and drive one mile to the park entrance station. Continue on the main park road (Lassen Park Highway/Highway 89) for 12 miles to the turnoff for Summit Lake North Campground. Turn left and park in the day-use area near the lake.

Contact: Lassen Volcanic National Park, Visitor Center, 530/595-4480; headquarters, 530/595-4444, www.nps.gov/lavo; Lassen Park Foundation, Mineral, www.lassenparkfoundation.org.

34 LASSEN PEAK TRAIL

5.0 mi/4.0 hr 4 10

in Lassen Volcanic National Park east of Red Bluff

Map 3.3, page 133 BEST

When you gain the rim of the caldera at Lassen

Summit Lake Loop

Peak and then make the final trek to the top of the crag summit, you will feel a sense of exhilaration, relief, and history merged all into one. There is nothing quite like it: Exhilaration over the view, relief that you have made it, and a sense of the volcano's past. As you top the rise, hardened lava flows extend in the caldera in front of you, a jumble of crags and craters crowned by the plug-dome summit at 10,457 feet. The air is cool and clear, the sky cobalt blue. About 100 miles to the north, Mount Shasta rises like a diamond in a field of coal. Far below to the southeast, giant Lake Almanor looks like a sapphire nestled in a sea of conifers. To get there is a 2.5-mile hike one-way with a 2,000-foot elevation gain, five miles in all.

The trailhead starts you at an elevation of 8,500 feet along the Lassen Park Highway, with a large parking lot and several restrooms. The first 1.3 miles are routed up the back of a sub-ridge up to Grandview, where you can see Lake Helen below to the south and across to the southeast to Lake Almanor. The route follows the ridge, and in several sections, the rock stairs and reinforcement walls are now in place. You occasionally pass interpretive signs.

With each step you climb, the views get better. You get a lookout for nearby 9,239-foot Mount Brokeoff, a panorama of the scope of the caldera of the giant 600,000-year-old Tehama Volcano, and to the north, across the vast burn zones of the Eiler Fire and Reading Fire. In the caldera of Lassen Peak, the volcanics span more than a quarter mile. You could explore for hours in the volcanic crags.

The must-do is to walk north across a snowfield (that hangs around, most years, through summer) toward the summit peak. At the foot of the plug dome, the trail then forks. The right fork leads to several perches near the top with fantastic views toward Almanor. The left fork is routed around the back of the summit, where you can then rock climb to gain a perch on one of the pinnacles. Lassen Peak is a huge volcanic flume with hardened lava flows, craters, outcrops, and extraordinary views in all directions. I'd rate this as a world-class, one of the greatest day hikes on the planet.

Winds are common at Lassen Peak, especially on summer afternoons. Hikers should stash a windbreaker in their daypacks. In addition, if you see cumulus clouds starting to form on the rim, common on summer afternoons, don't go. Quick-forming thunderstorms with lightning are also common on hot afternoons. It's always a mistake to suddenly climb the summit without planning the trip. Stay at lower elevations if there's any chance of lightning activity.

User Groups: Hikers only. No dogs, horses, or mountain bikes. No wheelchair facilities.

Permits: No permits are required. A park entrance fee of $30, good for a week, is charged for each vehicle.

Maps: Trail maps are available for free from park visitors and entrance centers and Lassen Park Foundation.

Directions: From Red Bluff, take Highway 36 east and drive 47 miles to the junction with Highway 89. Turn north (left) on Highway 89 and continue 4.5 miles to the park entrance. Continue seven miles on the main park road (Lassen Park Highway/Highway 89) to the parking area on the left. The trailhead is at the west end of the parking lot.

Contact: Lassen Volcanic National Park, Visitor Center, 530/595-4480; headquarters, 530/595-4444, www.nps.gov/lavo; Lassen Park Foundation, Mineral, www.lassenparkfoundation.org.

35 SHADOW LAKE TRAIL

4.0 mi/2.0 hr 2 9

in Lassen Volcanic National Park east of Red Bluff

Map 3.3, page 133

A hike of less than a mile on this trail will take you past little Terrace Lake (7,800 feet) and then, at 1.6 miles, to Shadow Lake (7,600 feet). It's rare to reach such a pretty lake surrounded by wildlands in such a short distance. From Shadow Lake, the views are excellent of Lassen Peak. The trail is routed through the large basin nestled between Reading Peak and Lassen Peak. You make a short, steep climb to Terrace Lake, and then a 0.25-mile junket to skirt the southeast shoreline of Shadow Lake (which is at least three times the size of Terrace Lake). The lakes are set just north of Reading Peak, 8,701 feet. From Shadow Lake, add 0.75 mile to reach Cliff Lake (7,250 feet), another beautiful spot.

User Groups: Hikers only. No dogs, horses, or mountain bikes. No wheelchair facilities.

Permits: No permits are required. A park entrance fee of $30, good for a week, is charged for each vehicle.

Maps: Trail maps are available for free from park visitors and entrance centers and Lassen Park Foundation.

Directions: From Red Bluff, take Highway 36 east and drive 47 miles to the junction with Highway 89. Turn north (left) on Highway 89 and continue 4.5 miles to the park entrance. Continue nine miles on the main park road (Lassen Park Highway/Highway 89) to the parking area and trailhead, on the left (two miles past the parking area for Lassen Summit).

Contact: Lassen Volcanic National Park, Visitor Center, 530/595-4480; headquarters, 530/595-4444, www.nps.gov/lavo; Lassen Park Foundation, Mineral, www.lassenparkfoundation.org.

36 BUMPASS HELL TRAIL

3.0 mi/2.0 hr 2 10

in Lassen Volcanic National Park east of Red Bluff

Map 3.3, page 133

This is the most popular trail in Lassen Volcanic National Park. Bumpass Hell is like a walk into a prehistoric past, complete with steam vents, boiling mud pots, and natural furnaces. It's all set amid volcanic rock in a large basin, and for some, it might feel as if, at any moment, a T. rex might charge around the bend and munch a few tourists. It's the park's largest thermal area. The trail and boardwalks were rebuilt and renovated in 2019 and reopened for 2020. The area near the trailhead gets a lot of snow in winter, and the trail usually opens each summer in late June or early July.

The elevation at the trailhead is 8,200 feet. The trail starts with a gradual 500-foot climb. You pass an excellent interpretive sign at an overlook that explains the geological origins of the landscape in front of you. The trail continues in the first mile to a ridge that overlooks the thermal area, an excellent lookout for a photo. You then descend 250 feet into the thermal basin. Wood walkways are routed past the best sites, with several platform decks. Exhibits explain the area. There are usually large numbers of tourists at Bumpass Hell, but it works. The basin sits in a pocket just below Bumpass Mountain (8,753 feet).

It is called "Bumpass" Hell because back in the old days, a guy named Bumpass slipped into the boiling water, scalded his feet, and in the ensuing newspaper report, the writer called the place "Bumpass's Hell," and the name stuck.

User Groups: Hikers only. No dogs, horses, or mountain bikes. No wheelchair facilities.

Permits: No permits are required. A park entrance fee of $30, good for a week, is charged for each vehicle.

Maps: Trail maps are available for free from park visitors and entrance centers and Lassen Park Foundation.

Directions: From Red Bluff, take Highway 36 east and drive 47 miles to the junction with Highway 89. Turn north (left) on Highway 89 and drive 4.5 miles to the park entrance. Continue six miles on the main park road (Lassen Park Highway/Highway 89) to the trailhead, on the right.

Contact: Lassen Volcanic National Park, Visitor Center, 530/595-4480; headquarters, 530/595-4444, www.nps.gov/lavo; Lassen Park Foundation, Mineral, www.lassenparkfoundation.org.

37 DRAKE LAKE TRAIL

4.5 mi/2.75 hr  3 6

at Drakesbad in Lassen Volcanic National Park

Map 3.3, page 133

The appeal of Drake Lake is that it is the closest lake to Drakesbad. If you're camping or staying at the lodge, you'll see the lake on the map and might wonder what it's like. Drake Lake is a somewhat swampy subalpine lake that brightens a largely dry hillside, where deer are often more plentiful than people. It is set in a remote forested pocket, very secluded. From the trailhead at Drakesbad, at about 5,650 feet, it's about an 800-foot climb over the course of two miles to Drake Lake (6,482 feet). Midway up the grade, the hike becomes steep and stays that way for nearly 45 minutes.

The lake is the payoff, emerald green and circled by firs. After you catch your breath, you may feel like jumping in and cooling off, particularly if it's a hot summer day. Well, we've got news for you: In early summer, the water is still ice-cold, and just when you realize that, a battalion of mosquitoes will show up and start feasting on all your bare, sumptuous flesh. Then what? Jump in and freeze your buns? Stand there and get devoured? Heck no, you'll have your clothes back on in record time.

User Groups: Hikers only. Horses are allowed on a portion of the trail. No dogs or mountain bikes. No wheelchair facilities.

Permits: No permits are required. A park entrance fee of $30, good for a week, is charged for each vehicle.

Maps: Trail maps are available for free from park visitors and entrance centers and Lassen Park Foundation.

Directions: From Red Bluff, take Highway 36 east and drive 47 miles to the junction with Highway 89. Do not turn. Continue east on Highway 36 toward Lake Almanor and to Chester and Feather River Drive. Turn left on Feather River Drive and drive 0.75 mile. Bear left for Drakesbad and Warner Valley, and drive six miles to Warner Valley Road. Turn right and drive 11 miles to Warner Valley Campground. Continue for 0.5 mile to the trailhead, on the left. The last 3.5 miles is unpaved, and there is one steep hill that can be difficult for trailers or RVs.

Contact: Lassen Volcanic National Park, Visitor Center, 530/595-4480; headquarters, 530/595-4444, www.nps.gov/lavo; Lassen Park Foundation, Mineral, www.lassenparkfoundation.org.

38 DEVILS KITCHEN TRAIL

4.4 mi/2.5 hr  2 8

at Drakesbad in Lassen Volcanic National Park

Map 3.3, page 133

Drakesbad, the hidden resort and the nearby environs, is the undiscovered Lassen. It's beautiful, wild, and remote. The area gets missed by many because access is obscure and circuitous: out of Chester en route to the Warner Valley Campground and nearby trailhead, and not from the Lassen's Park Highway. There's no way to get here when entering from either of the main Lassen park entrances. But those who persevere will find a quiet paradise, along with this easy trip to Devils Kitchen, a geologic thermal area. The trail is an easy hike, heading west above Hot Springs Creek. The elevation at the trailhead is 5,650 feet, with a gradual climb of 300 feet. After two miles it ventures into this barren pocket of steaming vents, boiling mud pots, and fumaroles. You'll immediately see why it was tagged Devils Kitchen. It is not as dramatic as Bumpass Hell, but you have a chance here of getting it to yourself. Stay on the trail, of course. Do not fall in.

User Groups: Hikers only. Horses are allowed on a portion of the trail. No dogs or mountain bikes. No wheelchair facilities.

Permits: No permits are required. A park entrance fee of $30, good for a week, is charged for each vehicle.

Maps: Trail maps are available for free from

park visitors and entrance centers and Lassen Park Foundation.

Directions: From Red Bluff, take Highway 36 east and drive 47 miles to the junction with Highway 89. Do not turn. Continue east on Highway 36 toward Lake Almanor and to Chester and Feather River Drive. Turn left on Feather River Drive and drive 0.75 mile. Bear left for Drakesbad and Warner Valley, and drive six miles to Warner Valley Road. Turn right and drive 11 miles to Warner Valley Campground. Continue 0.5 mile to the trailhead, on the left. The last 3.5 miles are unpaved, and there is one steep hill that can be difficult for trailers or RVs.

Contact: Lassen Volcanic National Park, Visitor Center, 530/595-4480; headquarters, 530/595-4444, www.nps.gov/lavo; Lassen Park Foundation, Mineral, www.lassenparkfoundation.org.

39 LASSEN VOLCANIC NATIONAL PARK TO HIGHWAY 44 (PCT)

32.0 mi one-way/3 days 3 9

in Lassen Volcanic National Park

Map 3.3, page 133

Start at Warner Valley (at 5,680 feet) at Hot Springs Creek, and then head north into mostly remote terrain in Lassen Volcanic National Park. The trail is routed across Grassy Swale, past Swan Lake, and on to Lower Twin Lake (seven miles in), a pretty lake circled by conifers.

From here, the trail heads north through a strange but compelling volcanic area. It skirts the western flank of Fairfield Peak (7,272 feet) and then heads onward. It turns west past Soap Lake and Badger Flat, and continues out past the park's boundary. The area in the northeast region of the park has significant forest fire damage that extends north toward Burney.

As you hike toward Highway 44, you'll be lateraling Badger Mountain (6,973 feet) to your right, with the Hat Creek drainage off to your immediate left. In this latter stretch of trail, you'll cross no major lakes or streams (plan your water well). You forge on through the national forest, which is mostly second growth, crossing a few roads along the way. In the spring, wildflowers are exceptional near the Hat Creek area. Several primitive U.S. Forest Service campgrounds are sited on the trail about 10 miles north of the border of Lassen Volcanic National Park.

To continue north on the PCT, see the *Hat Creek Rim to McArthur-Burney Falls Memorial State Park (PCT)* hike in this chapter.

User Groups: Hikers and horses. No dogs or mountain bikes are allowed in the Lassen Volcanic National Park section of the hike. No wheelchair facilities.

Permits: A wilderness permit (free) is required for hikers planning to camp in the Lassen Volcanic National Park backcountry and for equestrians. You may not camp with horses in the national park's backcountry, but a horse corral is available by reservation for overnighters at Summit Lake and Juniper Lake, and a small corral is located near the park's northern boundary for exclusive use by those on the Pacific Crest Trail. A park entrance fee of $30, good for a week, is charged for each vehicle.

For PCT hikers: A single permit is required to hike the Pacific Crest Trail. Contact the national forest, Bureau of Land Management (BLM), or national park office at your point of entry for a combined permit that is good for traveling through multiple-permit areas during your dates of travel.

Maps: Trail maps are available for free from park visitors and entrance centers and Lassen Park Foundation.

Directions: From Red Bluff, take Highway 36 east and drive 47 miles to the junction with Highway 89. Do not turn. Continue east on Highway 36 toward Lake Almanor and to Chester and Feather River Drive. Turn left (north) and drive 0.75 mile to Warner Valley Road (signed to Juniper Lake and Drakesbad).

Turn left and drive six miles to Warner Valley Road. Turn right and drive 11 miles (on an improved dirt road) to the Warner Valley Campground and trailhead on the right.

Contact: Lassen Volcanic National Park, Visitor Center, 530/595-4480; headquarters, 530/595-4444, www.nps.gov/lavo; Lassen National Forest, Hat Creek Ranger District, Falls River Mills, 530/336-5521, www.fs.usda.gov/lassen.

40 JUNIPER LAKE TRAILHEAD/ INSPIRATION POINT

1.4 mi/2.0 hr 3 10

in Lassen Volcanic National Park north of Lake Almanor

Map 3.3, page 133

Your payoff is 7,200-foot Inspiration Point for panoramic views across the park's backcountry to Lassen Peak. The trailhead is 50 feet east from the parking area at the Juniper Lake picnic area. The trail is steep. It climbs 400 feet in 0.7 mile through both forest and patches of meadow to the summit. Your reward is spectacular views: Lassen Peak, flat-topped Prospect Peak, below to the Cinder Cone, and Mount Harkness. Juniper Lake is one of the prettiest campsites you can reach by car. And here, right next door, is the trailhead for a short, steep hike for a jaw-dropping 360.

User Groups: Hikers and horses. No dogs or mountain bikes. No wheelchair facilities.

Permits: For overnight use, a wilderness permit (free) is required. A park entrance fee of $30, good for a week, is charged for each vehicle.

Maps: Trail maps are available for a fee from park visitors centers and at Lassen Loomis Museum Association. For a topographic map, ask the USGS for Mount Harkness.

Directions: From Red Bluff, take Highway 36 east and drive 47 miles to the junction with Highway 89. Do not turn. Continue east on Highway 36 toward Lake Almanor and to Chester and Feather River Drive. Turn left on Feather River Drive and drive 0.75 mile to a Y. Bear right at the Y to Juniper Lake Road and drive 13 miles to the Snag Lake trailhead, near the ranger station. The access road is rough. Trailers and RVs are not recommended.

Contact: Lassen Volcanic National Park, P.O. Box 100, Mineral, CA 96063, 530/595-4480, www.nps.gov/lavo; Lassen Loomis Museum Association, P.O. Box 220, Mineral, CA 96063, www.lassenassociation.org.

41 HAY MEADOWS TRAIL TO LONG LAKE

8.0 mi/1-2 days 2 10

on the boundary of Caribou Wilderness north of Lake Almanor

Map 3.3, page 133

You get an easy walk in beautiful country that passes one little lake after another until your payoff destination for your camp or day hike with a picnic, Long Lake. What you'll find is that nestled between South Caribou Peak and Black Cinder Rock is a little alpine pocket where dozens of small lakes are sprinkled about the southern Caribou Wilderness. It's a slice of paradise. The trail out of Hay Meadows is a loop that crosses right through these lakes: They include Beauty, Long, Posey, and Evelyn.

After arriving at the trailhead at Hay Meadows, the trip starts easily enough, first crossing Hay Meadows. In another mile, you'll reach Beauty Lake, the first of the four lakes on this loop hike. They are all good for swimming, although a bit cold, and Beauty and Posey have the best trout fishing.

For backpackers, you can extend your trek by venturing up to Hidden Lakes, a series of several small but pretty waters, set just below South Caribou Mountain.

User Groups: Hikers, dogs, and horses (a horse corral is available at the trailhead). No mountain bikes. No wheelchair facilities.

Permits: A campfire permit (free) is required. Parking and access are free.
Maps: A trail map is available for a fee from the Almanor Ranger District. For a map, ask the U.S. Forest Service for Lassen National Forest or Caribou Wilderness. For a topographic map, ask the USGS for Red Cinder.
Directions: From Red Bluff, take Highway 36 east and drive 47 miles to the junction with Highway 89. Do not turn. Continue east on Highway 36 toward Lake Almanor and to Chester. In Chester, continue east on Highway 36 for five miles to Forest Road 10. Turn north on Forest Road 10 and drive 9.5 miles to Forest Road 30N25. Turn left on Forest Road 30N25 and drive to the trailhead.
Contact: Lassen National Forest, Almanor Ranger District, Chester, 530/258-2141, www.fs.usda.gov/lassen.

42 SPENCER MEADOW TRAIL/CANYON CREEK FALLS

10.8 mi/1 day 4 8

in Lassen National Forest south of Lassen Volcanic National Park

Map 3.3, page 133

This hike has national park-like wilderness qualities, yet it is neither. The trail is routed through forests and across meadows to a waterfall and with a spot that provides big-time views. Yet it is outside the nearby Lassen Volcanic National Park and for that reason overlooked by tourists. The trailhead is right along Highway 36. The route climbs 2,000 feet.

Start the trip by taking the trail straight north toward Lassen on the Spencer Meadow Trail. At 2.3 miles, you'll reach a fork (for an all-day loop hike); turn left. When the forest breaks into meadow, you get a view of Mount Brokeoff. Roughly three miles from the turn at the fork, map in hand, you'll find a spur on the left (there is no trail sign), which leads to an overlook of 50-foot Canyon Creek Falls. For waterfall lovers, this is the destination.
User Groups: Hikers, dogs, horses, and mountain bikes. No wheelchair facilities.
Permits: No permits are required for day use. Campfire permits are required for overnight use. Parking and access are free.
Maps: A trail map is available for a fee from the Almanor Ranger District. For a map, ask the U.S. Forest Service for Lassen National Forest. For a topographic map, ask the USGS for Childs Meadows.
Directions: From Red Bluff, take Highway 36 east for 43 miles to Mineral, then continue east on Highway 36 for about seven miles to the trailhead parking area on the left.
Contact: Lassen National Forest, Almanor Ranger District, Chester, 530/258-2141, www.fs.usda.gov/lassen.

43 DOMINGO SPRING CAMPGROUND TO WARNER VALLEY (PCT)

11.0 mi one-way/1 day 2 7

at the Domingo Spring Trailhead in Lassen National Forest west of Lake Almanor

Map 3.3, page 133

From Domingo Spring, the Pacific Crest Trail runs north through Lassen National Forest and into Lassen Volcanic National Park. As you enter the park boundary, you'll pass Little Willow Lake (not much to it) on the left. In two miles, you'll reach Boiling Springs Lake with the Warner Valley Campground (on the right) and the Drakesbad Guest Ranch (on the left). This part of the trail is short, fast, and ends with a campsite and launch point into Lassen Volcanic National Park.

To continue north on the PCT, see the *Lassen Volcanic National Park to Highway 44 (PCT)* hike in this chapter.
User Groups: Hikers and horses. No mountain bikes or dogs (in a national park). No wheelchair facilities.

Permits: A campfire permit (free) is required. Parking and access are free. A single permit is required to hike the Pacific Crest Trail. Contact the national forest, Bureau of Land Management (BLM), or national park office at your point of entry for a combined permit that is good for traveling through multiple-permit areas during your dates of travel.
Maps: For a map, ask the U.S. Forest Service for Lassen National Forest. For a topographic map, ask the USGS for Stover Mountain.
Directions: From Red Bluff, take Highway 36 east and drive 47 miles to the junction with Highway 89. Do not turn. Continue east on Highway 36 toward Lake Almanor and to Chester and Feather River Drive. Turn left (north) and drive 0.75 mile to Warner Valley Road (signed Juniper Lake and Drakesbad). Turn left and drive to Old Red Bluff Road (County Road 311) and go three miles to the parking area at Domingo Spring Campground.
Contact: Lassen National Forest, Almanor Ranger District, Chester, 530/258-2141, www.fs.usda.gov/lassen.

44 MCCLURE TRAIL

9.0 mi/1 day 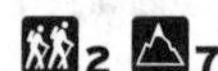

in the Tehama Wildlife Area east of Red Bluff

Map 3.3, page 133

If you love oak wildlands in the foothills above the Sacramento Valley, this is the trek for you. In spring, when the oaks first bud and the hills are glowing, the Tehama Wildlife Area is at its prettiest. The landscape includes a stream, abundant vegetation, and at times, plenty of birds and animals.

This trail accesses the best of the wildlife area. From the McClure trailhead, hike down a steep canyon to Antelope Creek. The canyon is buffered by riparian vegetation. In late winter and spring, the canyon's adjoining hillsides come alive in green, and all wildlife seems to prosper. The stream is very pretty, and fishing is catch-and-release only with the use of artificials. The hike can be cut short, of course, and you do not need to walk the entire 4.5 miles out and back.

The area is huge, covering 44,500 acres, and popular in the fall during hunting season for deer and wild pigs, but to be truthful, the odds of bagging a pig is less than 1 percent. Deer are abundant in late fall and often migrate in after the hunting season is over. There are also lots of squirrels, hawks, and rattlesnakes. Low numbers of wild pigs roam the canyons but are never seen from trails. This area is also very popular with turkey hunters in season. In summer and early fall, forget it. It's too hot, too brown.

User Groups: Hikers and dogs. Mountain bikes and horses permitted but not recommended because of terrain. No wheelchair facilities.
Permits: A campfire permit (free) is required for overnight use. Parking and access are free.
Maps: For a free map, contact the Tehama Wildlife Area. For a map, ask the U.S. Forest Service for Lassen National Forest. For a topographic map, ask the USGS for Dewitt Peak.
Directions: From Red Bluff, take Highway 36 east and drive 20 miles to Paynes Creek and Plum Creek Road. Turn right (south) on Plum Creek Road and go to Ishi Conservation Camp and continue about 2.5 miles south to High Trestle Road and follow it to Hogsback Road. Park across from the intersection of High Trestle and Hogsback Roads, and walk about 0.25 mile on the dirt road to the trailhead.
Access: Access to the Tehama Wildlife Area is closed to the public from February to the first Saturday in April. Access is also restricted for a short period during deer season in late September.
Contact: California Department of Fish and Wildlife, Tehama Wildlife Area, Paynes Creek, 530/597-2201; California Department of Fish and Wildlife, Region 1 Headquarters, 530/225-2300, www.wildlife.ca.gov.

45 DEER CREEK TRAIL (OUT OF CHICO)

1.0-8.0 mi/1 day 2 9

in Lassen National Forest west of Lake Almanor

Map 3.3, page 133 BEST

The Deer Creek Trail has all the ingredients for a trout angler, an explorer, or somebody just looking for a dunk on a hot day. The gorgeous stream runs right alongside the trail with good access throughout and fish (often plenty of them) in the summer months.

From the parking area, look for the trail on the left side of the road. Start by hiking downstream. The trail is routed downstream along the river for about 10 miles. Rarely does anybody ever walk all the way to the end. Instead they take their time, perhaps fishing at dawn or dusk or wading and floating around in the afternoon along the way.

In summer, Deer Creek is cold and clear, tumbling its way over rocks and into pools, with trout seemingly in every one. California Department of Fish and Wildlife rules mandate catch-and-release fishing with artificials with a single barbless hook for most of the river. This trail has also become popular among mountain bikers. Most are courteous to hikers, and on a single-track, that's important. An interesting note is that the canyon rim is made up of a series of volcanic crags and basalt spires. For swimmers, the cold water can provide a rush on summer days where temperatures commonly reach the 90s and 100s.

User Groups: Hikers, dogs, and horses. Mountain bikes aren't advised. No wheelchair facilities.

Permits: No permits are required. Parking and access are free.

Maps: A trail map is available for a fee from Almanor Ranger District. For a map, ask the U.S. Forest Service for Lassen National Forest. For a topographic map, ask the USGS for Onion Butte.

Directions: From Chico, take Highway 32 northeast for 40 miles (it becomes narrow and twisty). Just after crossing a small, red, metal bridge (locals call it the Red Bridge) that crosses Deer Creek, park on the right (south) side of the road, where there's a dirt pullout. The trailhead is just up from the bridge, on the left (north) side of the road.

Contact: Lassen National Forest, Almanor Ranger District, Chester, 530/258-2141, www.fs.usda.gov/lassen.

46 RANCHERIA TRAIL TO MILL CREEK

4.0 mi/2.75 hr 4 9

in the Ishi Wilderness east of Red Bluff

Map 3.3, page 133

The payoff is Mill Creek, a gorgeous foothill stream set at the bottom of a deep foothill canyon in the Ishi Wilderness. The trail starts by following an old jeep road, then leaves the road at a fence line off to the right. If it's hot, which is typical here most of the year, you'll already be reaching for your canteen. The trail then drops like a cannonball for 1,000 feet into the Mill Creek Canyon. This canyon is a surprising and awesome habitat with some of the prettiest areas of the Ishi Wilderness. Some of the volcanic rock formations and canyon rims are awesome. The fishing is also often good. Rules mandate catch-and-release with the use of artificials.

There is a problem, of course, and this is it: Shadowing your trek and enjoyment of the Mill Creek Canyon is the knowledge that you have to climb back out. To make it out before sunset, that climb will likely be during the late afternoon, the hottest part of the day. By the time you reach the car, your butt will be thoroughly kicked.

Also note that the trailhead access road is quite rough, impassable for most cars, and that's just a prelude to what lies ahead.

User Groups: Hikers, dogs, and horses. No mountain bikes. No wheelchair facilities.

Permits: A campfire permit (free) is required for overnight use. Parking and access are free.
Maps: A trail map is available for a fee from Almanor Ranger District. For a map, ask the U.S. Forest Service for Lassen National Forest or Ishi Wilderness. For topographic maps, ask the USGS for Panther Spring and Butte Meadows.
Directions: From Red Bluff, take Highway 36 east and drive 20 miles to Paynes Creek and continue to Little Giant Mill Road. Turn right (south) on Little Giant Mill Road (Road 202) and drive seven miles to Ponderosa Way. Turn south and drive about 10 miles to Forest Road 28N57. Turn right (west) and follow the Peligreen Jeep Trail for two miles to the Rancheria trailhead. The last two miles of road are suitable only for four-wheel-drive vehicles.
Contact: Lassen National Forest, Almanor Ranger District, Chester, 530/258-2141, www.fs.usda.gov/lassen.

47 LOWER MILL CREEK

13.0 mi/1 day 2 9

in the Ishi Wilderness east of Red Bluff

Map 3.3, page 133

If you have time for only one trail in the Ishi Wilderness, the trail to Lower Mill Creek is the one to pick. That goes whether you want to invest just an hour or a full day, because any length of trip can be a joy here. The trail parallels Mill Creek for 6.5 miles to its headwaters at Papes Place. You get magnificent scenery in this foothill canyonland and many good fishing and swimming holes along the way. This is a dramatic foothill canyon, and as you stand along the stream, the walls can seem to ascend into heaven. It's a land shaped by thousands of years of wind and water. In winter, this habitat provides wintering grounds for the largest migratory deer herd in California.

Directly across from the trailhead, on Ponderosa Way, is another trailhead, this one for a route that follows Upper Mill Creek into Lassen National Forest. Although not as spectacular as Lower Mill Creek, it provides a good option for hiking, fishing, and swimming. Note that fishing is restricted to catch-and-release and the use of artificials.
User Groups: Hikers, dogs, and horses. No mountain bikes. No wheelchair facilities.
Permits: A campfire permit (free) is required for overnight use. Parking and access are free.
Maps: A trail map is available for a fee from Almanor Ranger District. For a map, ask the U.S. Forest Service for Lassen National Forest or Ishi Wilderness. A trail map is strongly advised for anyone hiking in the Ishi Wilderness. For topographic maps, ask the USGS for Panther Spring and Butte Meadows.
Directions: From Red Bluff, take Highway 36 east and drive 20 miles to Paynes Creek, and continue to Little Giant Mill Road. Turn right (south) on Little Giant Mill Road (Road 202) and drive seven miles to Ponderosa Way. Turn south at Ponderosa Way and drive about 17 miles to the Mill Creek trailhead. The access road is a slow go.
Contact: Lassen National Forest, Almanor Ranger District, Chester, 530/258-2141, www.fs.usda.gov/lassen.

48 MOAK TRAIL

14.0 mi/1.5 days  

in the Ishi Wilderness east of Red Bluff

Map 3.3, page 133

In the spring in the Ishi, the foothill country is loaded with wildflowers and tall, fresh grass. The views of the Sacramento Valley are spectacular. The Moak Trail on the eastern border of the Ishi Wilderness is routed into the wilderness center. The trail includes a poke-and-probe section over a lava-rock boulder field, and there are good trail camps at Deep Hole (2,800 feet) and Drennan. It's an excellent weekend trip, including a loop route by linking Moak Trail with Buena Vista Trail, most of it easy walking. Hit it right in the spring, and

Moak Trail could be the best overnight hike in California's foothill country. Hit it wrong in the summer, and you'll wonder what you did to deserve such a terrible fate. If you try this trip in the summer or fall, you'll need to have your gray matter examined at Red Bluff General. No wildflowers, no shade, 100-degree temperatures, and as for water, you're dreamin'.

User Groups: Hikers, dogs, and horses. No mountain bikes. No wheelchair facilities.

Permits: A campfire permit (free) is required for overnight use. Parking and access are free.

Maps: A trail map is available for a fee from Almanor Ranger District. For a map, ask the U.S. Forest Service for Lassen National Forest or Ishi Wilderness. A trail map is strongly advised for anyone hiking in the Ishi Wilderness. For topographic maps, ask the USGS for Panther Spring and Butte Meadows.

Directions: From Red Bluff, take Highway 36 east and drive 20 miles to Paynes Creek, and continue to Little Giant Mill Road. Turn right (south) on Little Giant Mill Road (Road 202) and drive seven miles to Ponderosa Way. Turn south at Ponderosa Way and drive about 24 miles to the Moak trailhead.

Contact: Lassen National Forest, Almanor Ranger District, Chester, 530/258-2141, www.fs.usda.gov/lassen.

49 DEER CREEK TRAIL (IN THE ISHI)

1-14.0 mi/1.5 days 

in the Ishi Wilderness east of Red Bluff

Map 3.3, page 133

This section of the Deer Creek Trail, remote, located deep in the Ishi Wilderness, has a campground (Black Rock Campground) and requires a 4-wheel drive to get there. Even if you walk only 100 yards to put your feet in the stream, plan on overnighting it at the small (6 sites), primitive (no developed water) campgrounds. Your reward is a beautiful section of Deer Creek at the southeast border of the Ishi Wilderness. Right from the start, it's routed along the north shore of Deer Creek. Iron Mountain (at 3,274 feet) is to the immediate north. The trail continues along the stream into the wilderness interior. It skirts past the northern edge of what is called the Graham Pinery, a dense island of ponderosa pine growing on a mountain terrace. A bonus is good bird-watching for hawks, eagles, and falcons at the rock cliffs and looking for a large variety of wildlife, including rattlesnakes (here's your warning) and lots of squirrels and quail. Trout fishing can be decent near Potato Patch and Alder Creek Campgrounds. Below Potato Patch Campground, fishing is catch-and-release only with the use of artificials.

User Groups: Hikers, dogs, and horses. No mountain bikes. No wheelchair facilities.

Permits: A campfire permit (free) is required for overnight use. Parking and access are free.

Maps: A trail map is available for a fee from Almanor Ranger District. For a map, ask the U.S. Forest Service for Lassen National Forest or Ishi Wilderness. A trail map is strongly advised for those hiking in the Ishi Wilderness. For topographic maps, ask the USGS for Panther Spring and Butte Meadows.

Directions: From Red Bluff, take Highway 36 east and drive 20 miles to Paynes Creek, and continue to Payne Creek Loop. Turn right on Paynes Creek Loop/Plum Creek Road and drive 0.3 miles to Plum Creek Road. Turn right on Plum Creek Road and drive 10.4 miles (becomes Ponderosa Way). Continue straight Ponderosa Way and drive 17.2 miles to Black Rock Campground and the Deer Creek trailhead.

Contact: Lassen National Forest, Almanor Ranger District, Chester, 530/258-2141, www.fs.usda.gov/lassen.

50 DEVILS DEN TRAIL

1-9.0 mi/1.5 day  

in the Ishi Wilderness east of Red Bluff

Map 3.3, page 133

The Devils Den trailhead is on the south side of Deer Creek, just across the bridge from Black Rock Campground and the Deer Creek Trail detailed in the previous listing. The two trailheads are less than a half mile from each other, but that is where the similarities end. From the Devils Den trailhead, you are routed along Deer Creek for the first mile (trout fishing here is restricted to catch-and-release and the use of artificials). Enjoy yourself, because what follows is not exactly a picnic. The trail turns left and climbs up Little Pine Creek all the way to the ridge top, with the last mile on an old, hot, and chunky abandoned road. Along the way, the vegetation changes from riparian along the creek to woodland on the slopes, then chaparral on the ridge. A series of small volcanic spires and formations spike the Deer Creek Rim; in some cases, they look like they are from another planet. In addition, an island of conifers, the Graham Pinery, is available for viewing with a 0.25-mile side trip.

Always bring a water filtration pump to fill your canteen at Deer Creek.

The top 10 attractions here: 1) nobody else is usually around; 2) Deer Creek and trout fishing; 3) nobody else is usually around; 4) the Graham Pinery; 5) nobody else is usually around; 6) the volcanic rim; 7) nobody else is usually around; 8) the small, primitive Black Rock Campground; 9) nobody else is around; 10) nobody else is around.

User Groups: Hikers, dogs, and horses. No mountain bikes. No wheelchair facilities.

Permits: A campfire permit (free) is required for overnight use. Parking and access are free.

Maps: A trail map is available for a fee from Almanor Ranger District. For a map, ask the U.S. Forest Service for Lassen National Forest or Ishi Wilderness. For topographic maps, ask the USGS for Panther Spring and Butte Meadows.

Directions: From Red Bluff, take Highway 36 east and drive 20 miles to Paynes Creek, and continue to Payne Creek Loop. Turn right on Paynes Creek Loop/Plum Creek Road and drive 0.3 miles to Plum Creek Road. Turn right on Plum Creek Road and drive 10.4 miles (becomes Ponderosa Way). Continue straight Ponderosa Way and drive 17.2 miles to Black Rock Campground. Continue a short distance over the bridge at Deer Creek and continue to the Devils Den trailhead on the southern side of Deer Creek.

Contact: Lassen National Forest, Almanor Ranger District, Chester, 530/258-2141, www.fs.usda.gov/lassen.

51 HUMBOLDT SUMMIT TO DOMINGO SPRINGS (PCT)

28.0 mi one-way/2 days 3 6

at Humboldt Summit in Lassen National Forest

Map 3.3, page 133

The idea of back-to-back 14-mile days to get through this chunk of trail may not appeal to weekend hikers, especially while carrying full-weight expedition packs. But that's standard for most hikers on this stretch of PCT. Some may even try to do it in a day, with little here to tarry for and with Lassen Volcanic National Park beckoning ahead. The trail starts just below Humboldt Peak, at 7,087 feet, and heads north along the ridgeline. For the most part, the trail is routed past Butt Mountain (7,866 feet) and down to Soldier Meadows. A spring and stream make this a delightful stop before crossing Highway 36, forging onward another three miles to the Stove Springs Campground. The trail then skirts around the western flank of North Stover Mountain and drops down to Domingo Springs, where another campground is available.

If you are walking this trail in reverse, see

the *Feather River to Humboldt Summit (PCT)* hike in this chapter to continue south.

User Groups: Hikers, dogs, and horses. No mountain bikes. No wheelchair facilities.

Permits: A campfire permit (free) is required. Parking and access are free. A single permit is required to hike the Pacific Crest Trail. Contact the national forest, Bureau of Land Management (BLM), or national park office at your point of entry for a combined permit that is good for traveling through multiple-permit areas during your dates of travel.

Maps: For a map, ask the U.S. Forest Service for Lassen National Forest. For topographic maps, ask the USGS for Humboldt Peak and Stover Mountain.

Directions: From Red Bluff, take Highway 36 east and drive 47 miles to the junction with Highway 89. Turn south on Highway 89 and drive four miles to County Road 308 (Humboldt Road). Turn right and drive 15 miles to the trailhead parking area.

Contact: Lassen National Forest, Almanor Ranger District, Chester, 530/258-2141, www.fs.usda.gov/lassen.

52 FEATHER RIVER TO HUMBOLDT SUMMIT (PCT)

26.0 mi one-way/2 days

at the Belden Trailhead on Highway 70 in Plumas National Forest

Map 3.3, page 133

The trail is not only rough from Belden to Humboldt Summit, it's not particularly pretty either, especially compared to the nearby wilderness. The climb is a dry slice of rattlesnake country. From the North Fork Feather River at Belden (elevation 2,310 feet), the PCT climbs 4,777 feet over the course of this two-day thumper to Humboldt Summit, at 7,087 feet. There are no lakes along this trail, only a few small water holes requiring short side trips. Instead, the prettiest sections are along streams, the first being Chips Creek, which runs adjacent to the trail for eight miles. Then later, there's a short crossing over the headwaters of Willow Creek. Some might prefer to take three days instead of two to hike this section, but with the stunning Lassen Volcanic National Park looming ahead, most hikers are willing to put in long days to get through this area.

To continue north on the PCT, see the *Humboldt Summit to Domingo Springs (PCT)* hike in this chapter. If you are walking this trail in reverse, see the *Bucks Summit to Feather River (PCT)* hike, in the *Sacramento and Gold Country* chapter, to continue south.

User Groups: Hikers, dogs, and horses. No mountain bikes. No wheelchair facilities.

Permits: A campfire permit (free) is required. Parking and access are free. A single permit is required to hike the Pacific Crest Trail. Contact the national forest, Bureau of Land Management (BLM), or national park office at your point of entry for a combined permit that is good for traveling through multiple-permit areas during your dates of travel.

Maps: For a map, ask the U.S. Forest Service for Plumas National Forest. For topographic maps, ask the USGS for Belden and Humboldt Peak.

Directions: From Quincy, drive west on Highway 70 about 26 miles to the trailhead at the roadside rest area at Belden.

Contact: Plumas National Forest, Mount Hough Ranger District, Quincy, 530/283-0555, www.fs.usda.gov/plumas.

53 BIZZ JOHNSON

1.0-25.4 mi one-way/0.5 hr-3 days

1 7

west of Susanville

Map 3.4, page 134

This is the best mountain bike trail in California that nobody knows about: the 25.4-mile Bizz Johnson Trail, most of it along the gorgeous Susan River Canyon. For biking, it's a 10. For hiking, it's OK for short day trips, in and out. As a bike ride with a shuttle, it can be euphoric with views, tunnels, trestles, forest, and a 1 percent grade. Trailhead access is spaced five to seven miles apart, and for some, that makes it decent for day-trip walks, and as with cyclists, you can set up a shuttle with a partner or hike or bike different portions of the trail. The seven-mile stretch west of Susanville is the most popular of the 25-mile route. The biggest problem is your trip can feel like the endless hike to nowhere.

The trailhead is at 4,200 feet, and the high point of the route is at 5,600 feet at Westwood Junction. The trail traces the old Fernley and Lassen railroad line, a branch line of the South Pacific Railroad. It is routed in the Susan River Canyon along the Susan River for 15 miles, then from the Susanville Railroad Depot to the Mason Station trailhead five miles north of Westwood. The surface is a mixture of compacted dirt and small gravel. The trail features beautiful views in many areas and passes through two old railroad tunnels and 11 old railroad bridges. You won't cross any developed areas.

In the 1960s, when Shasta legend John Reginato heard that Southern Pacific was going to abandon the rail line between Westwood and Susanville, he urged that it be converted to a hiking trail. It took many years, but the idea eventually struck home, and the Bureau of Land Management worked with the U.S. Forest Service to develop and refine it.

The one negative: Like most rails-to-trails projects, it's way too wide. As a bike ride, though, it works. In the winter, it can make a great trip on cross-country skis or on a snowmobile (snowmobiling is allowed on the western half of the trail, from Mason Station to just beyond Westwood Junction). On foot, not so much, but is too significant of a route to not include among California's 1,000 best trails.

User Groups: Hikers, dogs (must be leashed near Susanville), horses, and mountain bikes. Wheelchair-accessible from Susanville and Hobo Camp trailhead.

Permits: No permits are required. Parking and access are free.

Maps: For a free brochure, contact the Bureau of Land Management. For a map, ask the U.S. Forest Service for Lassen National Forest. For topographic maps, ask the USGS for Westwood East, Fredonyer Pass, and Susanville.

Directions: From Susanville, take Highway 36 to Weatherlow Street. Turn on Weatherlow (it becomes Richmond Road) and drive 0.5 mile to the Susanville Depot visitors center and the trailhead, on the right.

Alternate trailhead: From Westwood, take Highway 36 to County Road A21. Turn north and drive three miles to a signed trailhead access road (dirt). Turn right and drive 0.4 mile to the trailhead, on the left.

Contact: Lassen Land & Trails Trust, 530/257-3252, www.lassenlandandtrailstrust.org; Lassen National Forest, Eagle Lake Ranger District, Susanville, 530/257-4188, www.fs.usda.gov/lassen; Bureau of Land Management, Eagle Lake Field Office, Susanville, 530/257-0456, www.blm.gov/california.

MENDOCINO AND WINE COUNTRY

The Mendocino coast is dramatic and remote with several stellar state parks, while Sonoma Valley produces some of the most popular wines in the world. The Mendocino coast features a series of romantic hideaways and excellent adventuring and hiking. The Fort Bragg area has three state parks, with outstanding recreation, including several easy hikes, many amid redwoods and along pretty streams. (For overnight hikes in a state park on a summer weekend, campsite reservations are required far in advance.) A driving tour of Highway 1 along this section of the coast is the fantasy of many. Along the twists and turns of the road are dozens of hidden beaches and untouched coastline to stop and explore. The prize spots are MacKerricher State Park, Salt Point State Park, and Anchor Bay. Inland, you'll find pockets of redwoods near Guerneville, Philo, and Calistoga.

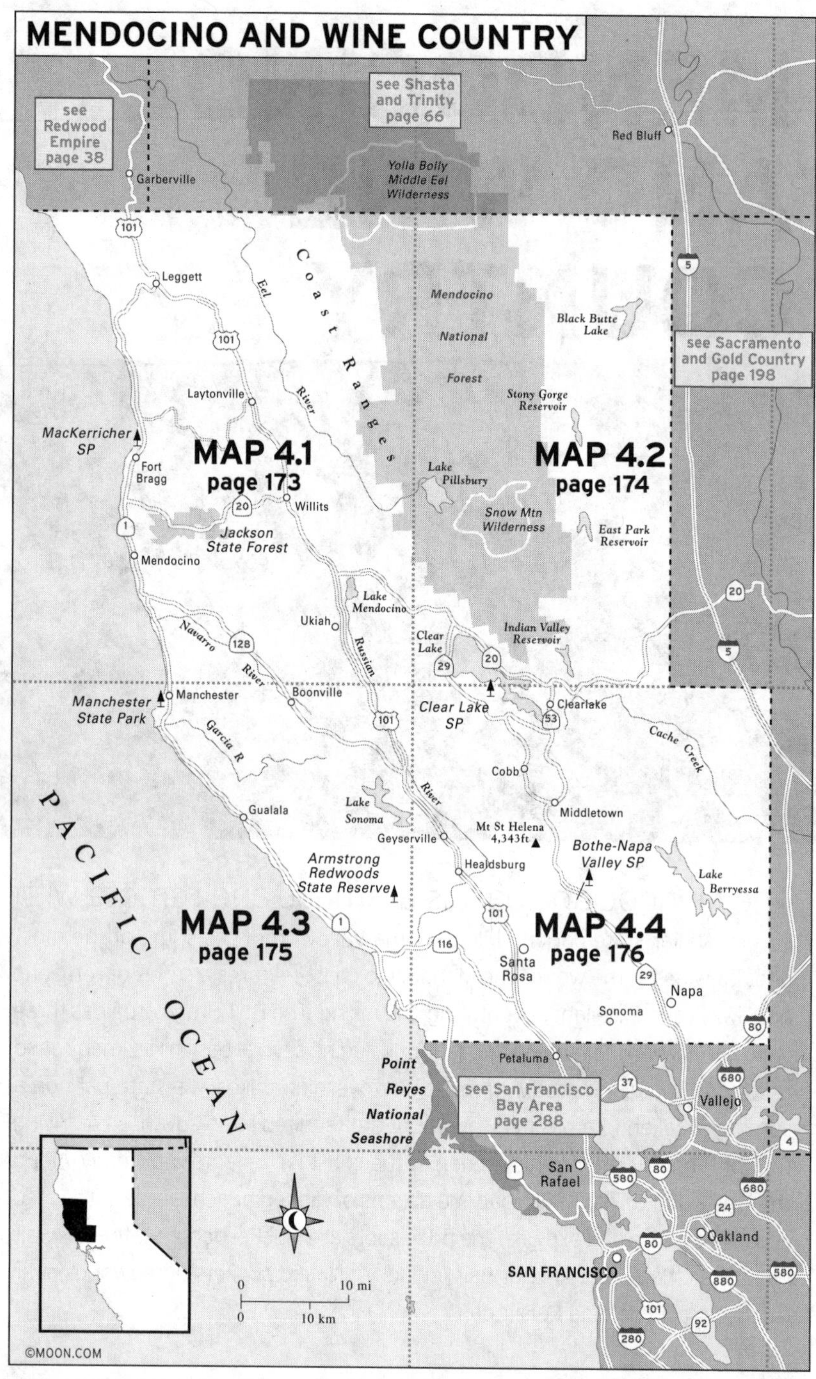
MENDOCINO AND WINE COUNTRY
see Redwood Empire page 38
see Shasta and Trinity page 66
see Sacramento and Gold Country page 198
see San Francisco Bay Area page 288
MAP 4.1
page 173
MAP 4.2
page 174
MAP 4.3
page 175
MAP 4.4
page 176
Red Bluff
Yolla Bolly Middle Eel Wilderness
Garberville
Leggett
Coast Ranges
Eel River
Mendocino National Forest
Black Butte Lake
Stony Gorge Reservoir
Laytonville
MacKerricher SP
Fort Bragg
Lake Pillsbury
Snow Mtn Wilderness
East Park Reservoir
Willits
Jackson State Forest
Mendocino
Lake Mendocino
Ukiah
Indian Valley Reservoir
Clear Lake
Navarro River
Russian River
Manchester State Park
Manchester
Boonville
Clear Lake SP
Clearlake
Cache Creek
Garcia R
Cobb
Middletown
PACIFIC OCEAN
Gualala
Lake Sonoma
Geyserville
Mt St Helena 4,343ft
Bothe-Napa Valley SP
Healdsburg
Armstrong Redwoods State Reserve
Lake Berryessa
Santa Rosa
Napa
Sonoma
Petaluma
Point Reyes National Seashore
Vallejo
San Rafael
Oakland
SAN FRANCISCO
0 10 mi
0 10 km
©MOON.COM

Map 4.1

Sites 1-9
Pages 177-182

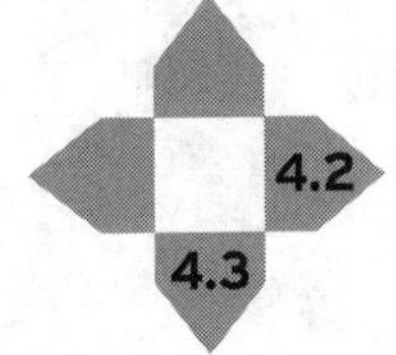

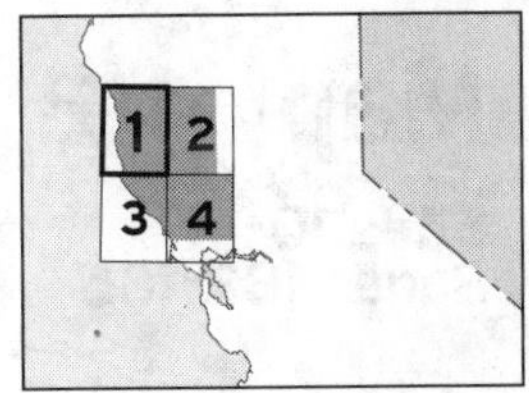

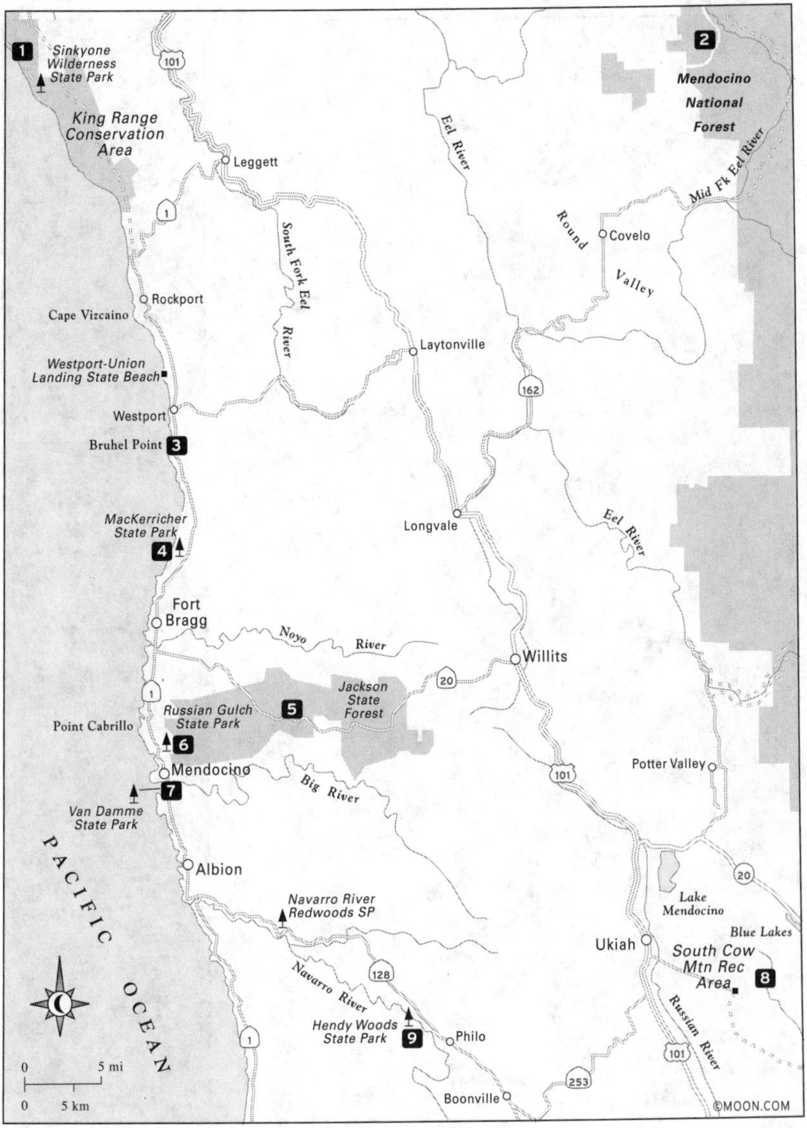

1 Sinkyone Wilderness State Park
King Range Conservation Area
101
Leggett
1
South Fork Eel River
Eel River
2 Mendocino National Forest
Mid Fk Eel River
Round Valley
Covelo
Rockport
Cape Vizcaino
Laytonville
Westport-Union Landing State Beach
162
Westport
3 Bruhel Point
Longvale
Eel River
MacKerricher State Park
4
Fort Bragg
Noyo River
Willits
20
1
Jackson State Forest
Russian Gulch State Park
5
Point Cabrillo
6
Mendocino
7
Big River
101
Potter Valley
Van Damme State Park
PACIFIC OCEAN
Albion
20
Lake Mendocino
Navarro River Redwoods SP
Blue Lakes
Ukiah
South Cow Mtn Rec Area
8
128
Navarro River
Hendy Woods State Park
9
Philo
Russian River
1
101
0 5 mi
0 5 km
253
Boonville
©MOON.COM

Map 4.2

Sites 10-14
Pages 182-185

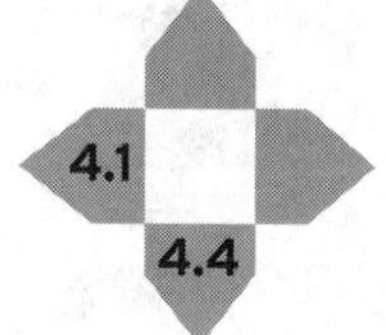

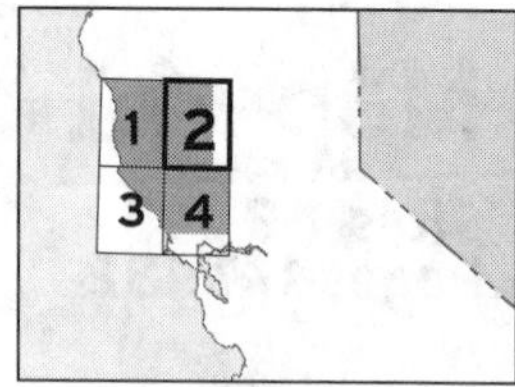

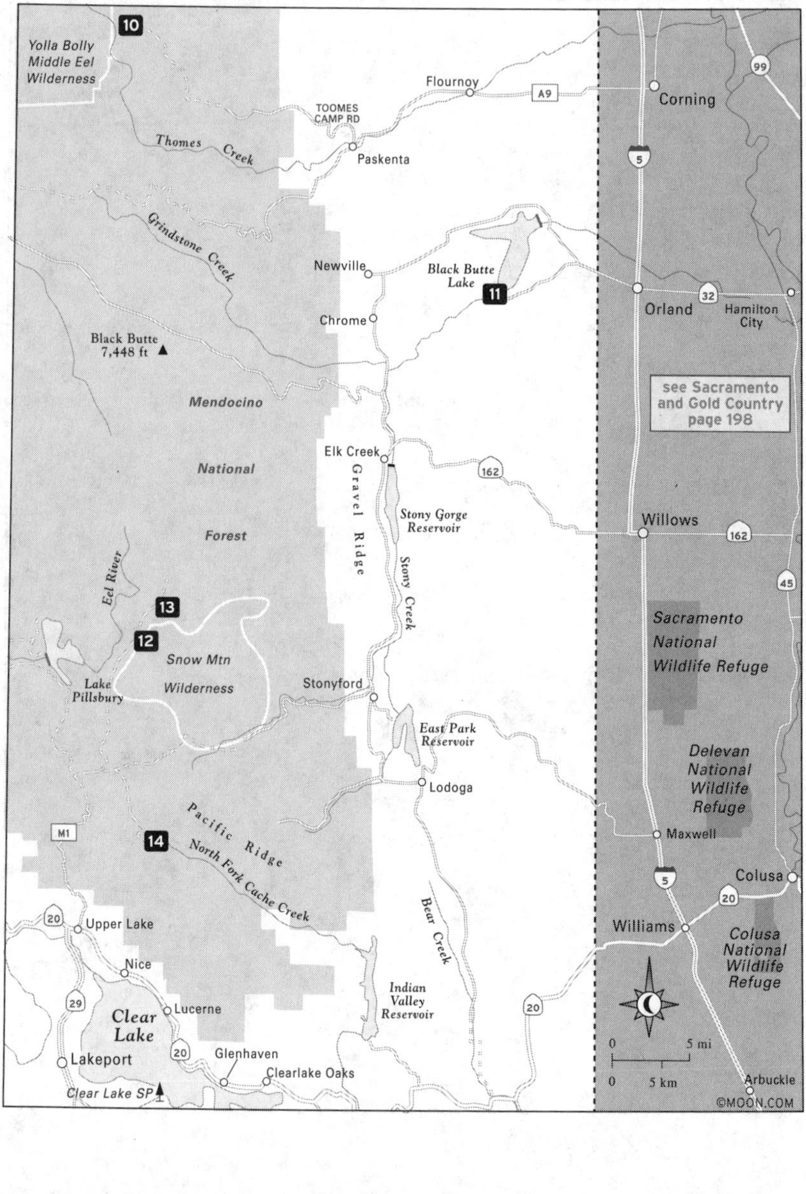

10
Yolla Bolly Middle Eel Wilderness
Flournoy
A9
Corning
99
TOOMES CAMP RD
Paskenta
Thomes Creek
5
Grindstone Creek
Newville
Black Butte Lake
11
Orland
32
Hamilton City
Chrome
Black Butte 7,448 ft
see Sacramento and Gold Country page 198
Mendocino National Forest
Elk Creek
Gravel Ridge
162
Stony Gorge Reservoir
Willows
162
Stony Creek
45
Eel River
13
12
Sacramento National Wildlife Refuge
Snow Mtn Wilderness
Lake Pillsbury
Stonyford
East Park Reservoir
Delevan National Wildlife Refuge
Lodoga
Pacific Ridge
M1
14
Maxwell
North Fork Cache Creek
Colusa
5
20
Bear Creek
20
Upper Lake
Williams
Colusa National Wildlife Refuge
Nice
29
Clear Lake
Lucerne
Indian Valley Reservoir
20
Lakeport
20
Glenhaven
Clearlake Oaks
Clear Lake SP
0 5 mi
0 5 km
Arbuckle

Map 4.3

Sites 15-21
Pages 185-190

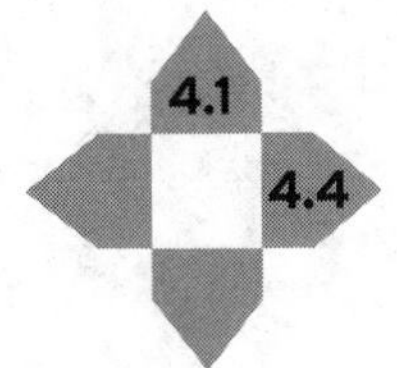

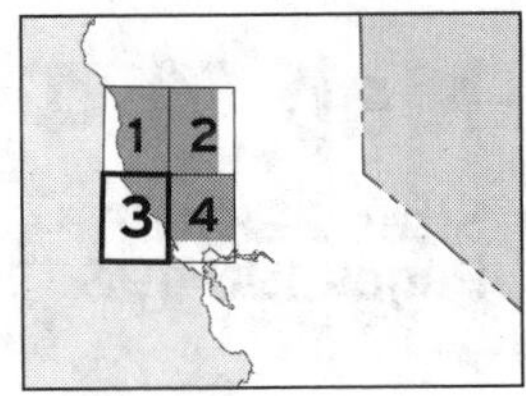

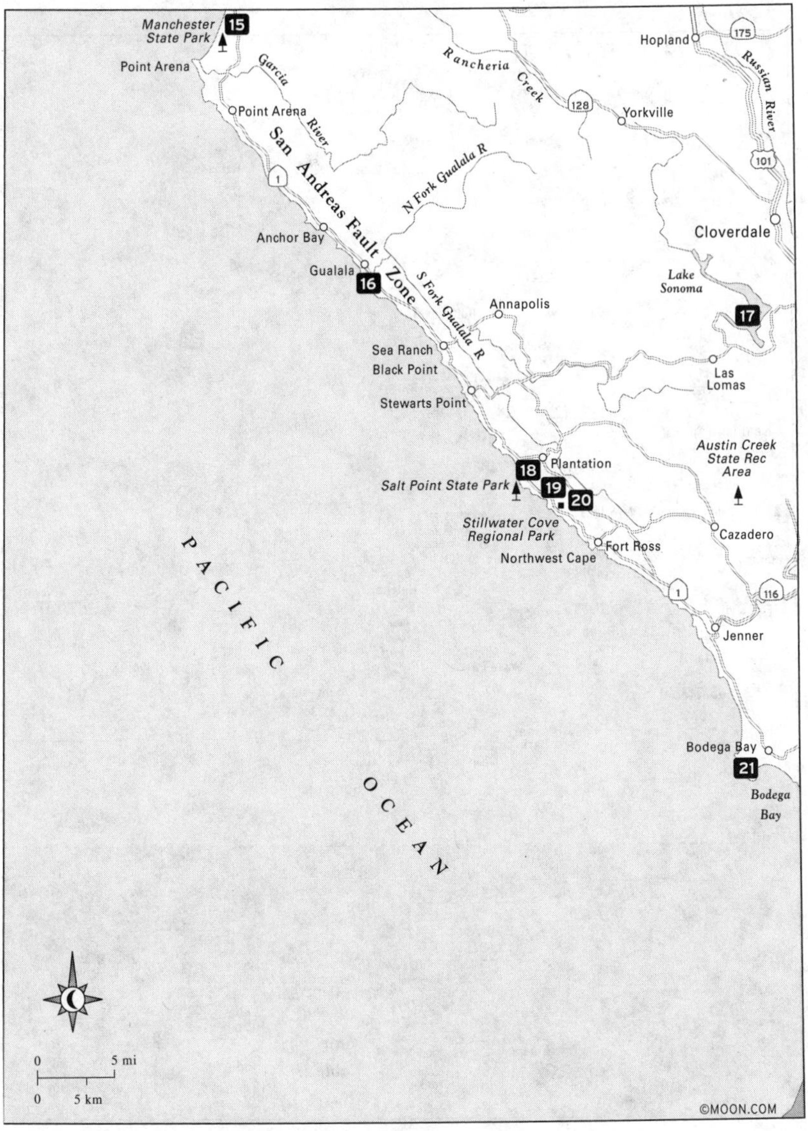

Manchester State Park
15
Point Arena
Garcia River
Rancheria Creek
128
Yorkville
Hopland
175
Russian River
101
Point Arena
San Andreas Fault Zone
N Fork Gualala R
1
Anchor Bay
Gualala
16
Cloverdale
Lake Sonoma
17
S Fork Gualala R
Annapolis
Sea Ranch
Black Point
Stewarts Point
Las Lomas
Plantation
18
19
20
Salt Point State Park
Austin Creek State Rec Area
Stillwater Cove Regional Park
Fort Ross
Northwest Cape
Cazadero
1
116
Jenner
PACIFIC OCEAN
Bodega Bay
21
Bodega Bay
0 5 mi
0 5 km

Map 4.4

Sites 22-30
Pages 190-196

4.2
4.3

1
2
3
4

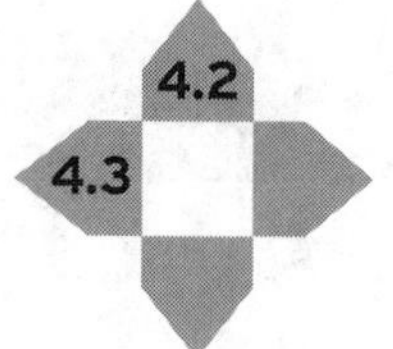

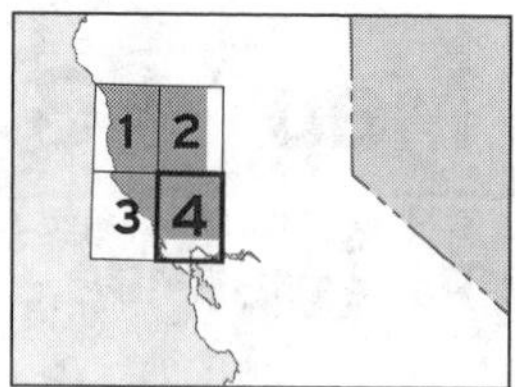

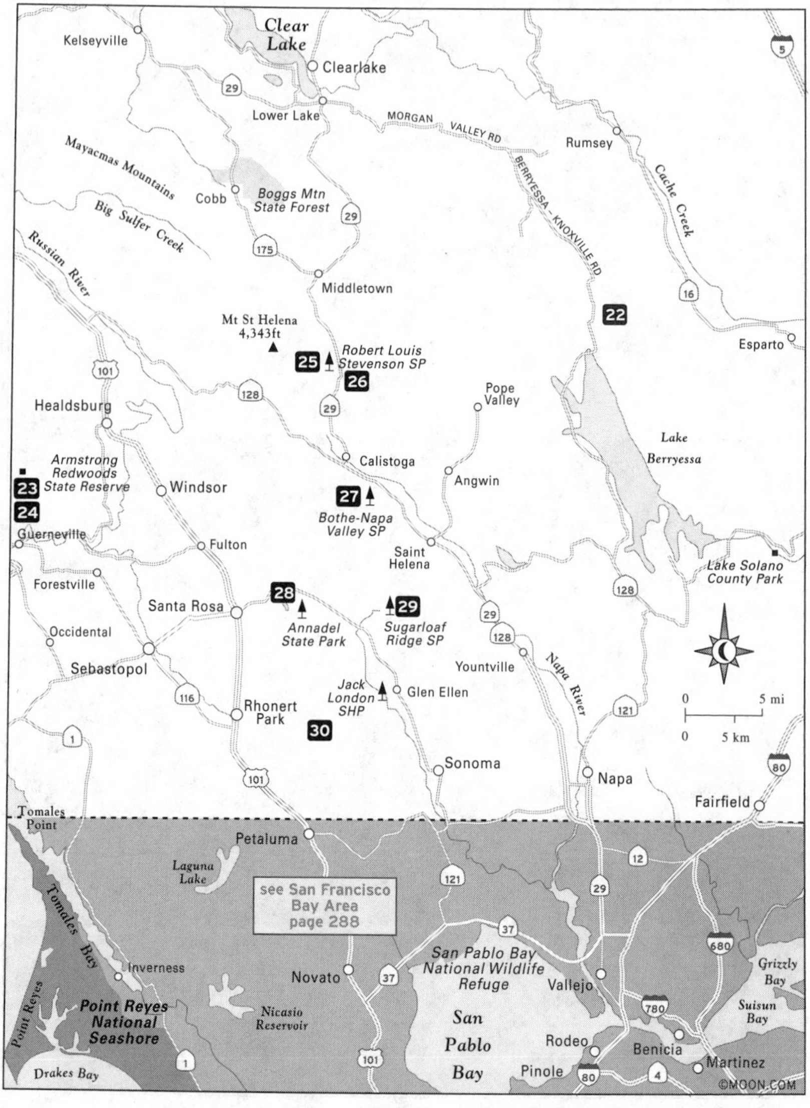

Clear Lake
Kelseyville
Clearlake
29
Lower Lake
MORGAN VALLEY RD
Rumsey
Mayacmas Mountains
Cobb
Boggs Mtn State Forest
BERRYESSA - KNOXVILLE RD
Cache Creek
Big Sulfer Creek
29
175
Russian River
Middletown
16
22
Mt St Helena 4,343ft
Robert Louis Stevenson SP
25
26
Esparto
101
128
Pope Valley
Healdsburg
29
Lake Berryessa
Calistoga
Armstrong Redwoods State Reserve
23
24
Windsor
27
Angwin
Bothe-Napa Valley SP
Guerneville
Fulton
Saint Helena
Lake Solano County Park
Forestville
128
Santa Rosa
28
29
Annadel State Park
Sugarloaf Ridge SP
29
128
Occidental
Sebastopol
Yountville
Napa River
Jack London SHP
Glen Ellen
116
Rhonert Park
30
121
0
5 mi
0
5 km
1
Sonoma
Napa
80
101
Fairfield
Tomales Point
Petaluma
12
Laguna Lake
see San Francisco Bay Area page 288
121
29
Tomales Bay
37
680
San Pablo Bay National Wildlife Refuge
Grizzly Bay
Inverness
Novato
37
Vallejo
Point Reyes
Point Reyes National Seashore
Nicasio Reservoir
San Pablo Bay
780
Suisun Bay
Rodeo
Benicia
1
101
Pinole
80
4
Martinez
Drakes Bay
©MOON.COM

1 LOST COAST TRAIL/ SINKYONE TRAILHEAD

17 mi one-way/2 days 3 10

in Sinkyone Wilderness State Park

Map 4.1, page 173 BEST

This remote and rugged wilderness of Northern California coastline, covering more than 7,000 acres, is protected forever as Sinkyone Wilderness State Park. It has become popular for trekkers looking for the wild side, despite few directional signs along roads, no highways leading here, and virtually no park promotion.

This is the southern section of the Lost Coast Trail, which starts out at Orchard Camp and heads south to Usal Campground (do not confuse this with the northern section, of course, which starts near the mouth of the Mattole River and south to Black Sands Beach, listed in the Redwood Empire chapter). The best way to explore this trip is with a one-way hike with a shuttle car, and best hiked north to south to keep the north winds out of your face. The primitive, steep, and unforgiving terrain provides a rare coastal wilderness experience.

Day 1: From the northern trailhead at Orchard Camp, Lost Coast Trail starts out flat and pleasant, arcing around Bear Harbor Cove. From here the trail climbs 800 feet and then back down, passing through a redwood grove and also breaking out for sweeping coastal views. Enjoy them, because the hike gets more difficult, including a steep climb up, over, and down a mountain. The trail finally descends into Little Jackass Creek Camp, which is set beside a small stream 10.5 miles from your start.

Day 2: The closeout of a two-day hike should always be as enjoyable as possible, and so it is here, with divine views in many spots along the 6.5-mile route. Alas, there's usually payment for views, and that comes in the form of several rugged climbs in the park's remotest sections. After climbing to nearly 1,000 feet, the trail ends with an 800-foot downgrade over the last mile, descending to the Usal Campground parking area.

Notes: All food must be bear-proofed. Dogs are permitted only at car camps. At the northern boundary of the Sinkyone Wilderness, this trail continues north into the King Range National Conservation Area, where it's routed for another 30 miles to the mouth of the Mattole River (see the listing for *Lost Coast Trail/Mattole Trailhead* in the *Redwood Empire* chapter).

User Groups: Hikers only. Horses allowed only on the section of trail between the trailhead at the park entrance and Wheeler Camp. No dogs or mountain bikes. No wheelchair facilities.

Permits: No permits are required. Parking and access are free unless you plan to camp.

Maps: A trail map and brochure are available for a fee from Sinkyone Wilderness State Park. For topographic maps, ask the USGS for Petrolia, Cooskie Creek, Shubrick Peak, Bear Harbor, and Shelter Cove.

Access Note: Briceland Road at the north end of the Sinkyone and Usal Road at the south end are subject to flooding and slides. For current conditions, phone for Mendocino County road conditions at 707/463-4363 or go to www.mendocinocounty.org. Shuttle services are expensive and they seem to come and go; for the latest, call the Southern Humboldt Chamber of Commerce in Garberville at 707/923-2613.

Directions: From Garberville, take U.S. 101 north to the exit for Redway. Follow that exit to Briceland Road. Turn left (west) on Briceland Road and drive 17 miles to Whitethorn. Continue six miles to the Four Corners Fork, then go another six miles (the road turns to gravel) to the Needle Rock Ranger Station. Continue past the ranger station to the visitors center and park at Orchard Camp. Be aware that the access road is unpaved, it may close unexpectedly in the winter, and four-wheel-drive vehicles are often required in wet weather. There are few signs pointing the way to the

park, and when they are posted, they are often stolen. Trailers and RVs are not recommended.
Contact: Sinkyone Wilderness State Park, c/o Richardson Grove, 707/247-3318, www.parks.ca.gov

2 ROCK CABIN TRAIL/ MIDDLE EEL

8.0 mi/4.5 hr 

on the boundary of Yolla Bolly Wilderness west of Red Bluff

Map 4.1, page 173

The Rock Cabin Trail (also known as the River Trail) extends north into the Yolla Bolly Wilderness and up, over, and down a short ridge before pouring into Wrights Valley. About halfway in, the River Trail jumps to Wrights Valley Trail. It's about a four-mile trip one-way to your destination. Here you'll find the headwaters of the Middle Fork Eel River, one of the prettiest streams in the wilderness. The trail is well marked and includes two creek crossings and a pretty waterfall. The Yolla Bollys provide few lakes, but the Middle Fork awaits you. In order to protect steelhead, no fishing is allowed. You won't see any evidence of fire until well into Wrights Valley, where it did a lot of good, not bad, by clearing a lot of impenetrable undergrowth.
Note: Little Henthorne Lake, complete with two wilderness cabins, is located 2.5 miles from the Rock Cabin trailhead. Resist the urge to visit. This is maintained as private property. Hikers are often tempted to walk in via a very faint cowboy trail (with a river crossing) and camp here illegally.
User Groups: Hikers, dogs, and horses. No mountain bikes. No wheelchair facilities.
Permits: A campfire permit is required for hikers planning to camp. Parking and access are free.
Maps: For a map, ask the U.S. Forest Service for Mendocino National Forest or Yolla Bolly Wilderness. For a topographic map, ask the USGS for South Yolla Bolly.
Directions: From Willits, drive north on U.S. 101 for 13 miles to Longvale and Highway 162. Turn east on Highway 162 and drive 30 miles to the turnoff for Highway 162 East. Turn right and drive nine miles to the Eel River Bridge and Forest Road M1 (Indian Dick Road). At the bridge, turn left (north) onto Forest Road M1 and drive 24 miles to Forest Road 25N15C. Turn left on Forest Road 25N15C and drive 0.75 mile to the turnoff for the Rock Cabin trailhead. Turn left and drive 0.25 mile to the trailhead, at the end of the road.
Contact: Mendocino National Forest, Covelo Ranger District, Covelo, 707/983-6118, www.fs.usda.gov/mendocino.

3 BRUHEL POINT TIDEPOOLS

0.5 mi/0.5 hr 1 10

on the Mendocino coast north of Fort Bragg

Map 4.1, page 173

Some of the best tidepools on the Pacific Coast can be found in Mendocino. One of the best of the best is here, located just south of Bruhel Point. When you first arrive, you'll find a Caltrans roadside vista point (no overnight parking), restrooms, and a beach access trail. This is your calling. The trail is routed north toward Bruhel Point, and much of it is set along the edge of ocean bluffs. Do not make your own descent down the bluff. Instead take only the cutoff trails, which lead to the best tidepool areas. Time your trip during a low tide or, better yet, a minus low tide. That is when the ocean pulls back, leaving a series of holes and cuts in a rock basin that remain filled with water, providing the perfect habitat and viewing areas for all kinds of tiny marinelife.
User Groups: Hikers and dogs. Not suitable for mountain bikes or horses. No wheelchair facilities.
Permits: No permits are required. Parking and access are free.

Maps: For a topographic map, ask the USGS for Inglenook.

Directions: From Westport, drive south on Highway 1 about two miles to milepost marker 74.09 and park at the Caltrans Vista Point parking lot. The tidepools are a short walk.

Contact: None.

4 LAKE CLEONE TRAIL

1.2 mi/0.5 hr 1 9

in MacKerricher State Park north of Fort Bragg

Map 4.1, page 173 BEST

The loop trail around Lake Cleone is not only easy but also something special. Mrs. MacKerricher named the trail Cleone, which means "gracious" or "beautiful" in Greek. The route includes several sections on raised wooden walkways, which provide routes through marshy areas. In the winter months, the southern part of the trail (without the boardwalk) can be flooded. Be sure to wear your high boots in the rainy season.

In some spots, the trail burrows like a tunnel through a variety of trees and lush vegetation. At others, it provides many glimpses of pretty Lake Cleone. It loops all the way around the lake, which is almost always full. The beautiful Pacific Ocean looms just beyond to the west, a cypress grove is to the south, and a marsh is to the east. The boardwalk is wheelchair-accessible. MacKerricher State Park is filled with many enticing highlights. It is also one of the few state parks with free day-use access.

Side trip: From the parking lot adjacent to the lake, you can walk under the built-up foundation of an old railroad line (now a bicycle trail called Old Haul Road) and connect to Headlands Trail. This is a must-do. It's an easy short walk, much of it on a raised walkway that leads to a series of tidepools and the best seal- and whale-watching station on the coast.

User Groups: Hikers, leashed dogs, and wheelchairs (the trail is partially wheelchair-accessible). No horses or mountain bikes. Horse trails and mountain bike routes are available elsewhere in the state park.

Permits: No permits are required. Parking and access are free for day use.

Maps: A brochure and trail map are available for a fee at MacKerricher State Park. For a topographic map, ask the USGS for Inglenook.

Directions: From Fort Bragg drive north on Highway 1 for three miles to the park entrance. Turn left and drive to the parking area beside the lake. The trailhead is on the east side of the parking lot.

Contact: MacKerricher State Park, Mendocino, 707/964-9112, www.parks.ca.gov.

5 CHAMBERLAIN CREEK WATERFALL TRAIL

0.5 mi/0.5 hr 2 10

in Jackson State Forest east of Fort Bragg

Map 4.1, page 173

Chamberlain Creek Falls is a surprise 50-foot waterfall set in a canyon framed by redwoods, well secluded in Jackson State Forest. Time it in the spring after a period of heavy rain and this one is a 10, where you'll find a silvery stream emerging from the greenery in a chute-like cataract over the brink. It's off the Mendocino grid and set back off an old logging road. The trail is short, little known to outsiders, and beautiful. This access road (gravel/dirt), by the way, can get muddy in the winter and extremely dusty in the summer. After parking, you'll find the trail routed a short distance down the canyon to the stream, starting with a short series of steps. The trail simply heads down the canyon directly to the base of the waterfall. Jackson State Forest is overlooked by most visitors, despite the beauty of the area and the popularity of the Mendocino coast. That means you'll most likely have the place to yourself. Jackson State Forest, at 48,652 acres, is the largest of Cal Fire's eight demonstration state forests.

User Groups: Hikers and dogs. No horses or mountain bikes. No wheelchair facilities.

Permits: No permits are required. Parking and access are free.
Maps: For a free trail map, contact Jackson Demonstration State Forest. For a topographic map, ask the USGS for Northspur.
Directions: From Willits, take Highway 20 west for 17 miles to Forest Road 200, a dirt road just before the Chamberlain Creek Bridge. Turn right on Road 200 and drive one mile to a fork. Bear left and drive 3.5 miles. Look for a parking pullout and park on the side of the road. The trailhead is on the left. In the heaviest rainy season, note that State Forest Road 200 is sometimes closed due to weather; call ahead for the status.
Contact: Jackson Demonstration State Forest, Fort Bragg, 707/964-5674, www.fire.ca.gov.

6 FALLS LOOP TRAIL

5.1 mi/2.5 hr 2 10

in Russian Gulch State Park south of Fort Bragg

Map 4.1, page 173

A 35-foot waterfall in deep forest makes this walk one of the prettiest on the Mendocino coast. Most of the year, this waterfall is a narrow silvery stream that pours atop and across a boulder. In winter it can build into more powerful multiple chutes and curtains and land in the rock basin with surging splashes. It's way better at high flows, of course. You get a full frontal of the cascade. You then descend a short distance to the foot of the plunge pool and a bridge over the creek for another angle. Although a lot of the old growth was taken a long time ago, much is still divine.

The route is simple. The trailhead is just beyond the campground, where you can park adjacent to a restroom. The first two miles are just about flat, once paved for bikes but today eroded into a pocked surface. You pass bracken ferns and sword ferns and enter redwoods with an understory of ferns, wild blackberries, and sorrel. At 2.3 miles, you arrive at the junction for the Waterfall Loop Trail. Turn left, expect a short climb, and hike out the final 0.7 miles to the waterfall. Even in the summer months, this is a pretty, if narrow, silver cascade, streaming 20 feet across a granite boulder and down into a pool. The entire trip has very little elevation gain.
Note: This used to be one of the best easy bike-and-hikes in Northern California, where youngsters and their families could ride out on a paved trail, lock up at the trail fork, and hike the final 15 minutes to the falls. The eroded patchwork surface ended that.

User Groups: Hikers only. No mountain bikes, dogs, or horses. However, a paved trail for bicycles and wheelchairs is routed 2.5 miles to the trailhead of Falls Loop Trail.
Permits: No permits are required. A state park entrance fee of $8 is charged for each vehicle.
Maps: A brochure and trail map are available for a fee at Russian Gulch State Park. For a topographic map, ask the USGS for Mendocino.
Directions: From Fort Bragg, take Highway 1 south for six miles to the Russian Gulch State Park entrance. Turn right and drive a very short distance to the state park entrance. After passing the kiosk, travel down the hill and to the bridge. Turn left and drive past the campsites to the trailhead.
Contact: Russian Gulch State Park, Mendocino, 707/937-5804, www.parks.ca.gov.

7 FERN CANYON TRAIL

8.1 mi/5.0 hr 1 10

in Van Damme State Park south of Mendocino

Map 4.1, page 173

This beautiful streamside walk amid coastal redwoods is one of the most popular trails on the Mendocino coast. In spring, this one is a 10. The trail starts at the bottom of a canyon along the Little River and heads upstream, rising gently along the way, with a series of little bridges that crisscross the water. The creek is pretty and often clear, the forest canopy towers, and the understory of fern and sorrel is lush. Most people hike 2.3 miles (paved all the way) out to the junction of Loop Trail and then turn around and head back. Visitors can add on a three-mile loop, climbing up and out of the canyon to a terrace to visit the Pygmy Forest (largely disappointing). Another option we like is to start at the Pygmy Forest and descend into Fern Canyon, continue downstream along the creek, then turn left and climb out of the canyon to create a pretty loop hike with few people.

Note that heavy rains can flood out the trail and wash out the bridges.

Note: This Fern Canyon Trail is not to be confused with the Fern Canyon Loop Trail on the Humboldt coast in the *Redwood Empire* chapter.

User Groups: Hikers only. No dogs or horses. Wheelchairs and mountain bikes are allowed only on the first 2.3 miles of the trail.

Permits: No permits are required. A state park entrance fee of $8 is charged for each vehicle. Beach parking is free.

Maps: A brochure and trail map are available for a fee at Van Damme State Park. For a topographic map, ask the USGS for Mendocino.

Directions: From Mendocino, take Highway 1 south for 2.5 miles to the park entrance. Turn left and drive 0.75 mile (signed) to the trailhead parking near the campground. The trail is just beyond the campground and restroom.

Contact: Van Damme State Park, Mendocino, 707/937-5804, www.parks.ca.gov.

Fern Canyon Trail

8 BIG HENDY GROVE/ HERMIT'S HUT TRAIL

1.0 mi/0.5 hr 1 7

in Hendy Woods State Park near Philo

Map 4.1, page 173

This easy and short walk through an ancient redwood forest can have you smiling for days. Hendy Woods is located in the redwood-filled canyon of the Navarro River, which flows to the sea on the Mendocino coast. The park covers 845 acres, and the two old-growth redwood groves, Little Hendy (20 acres) and Big Hendy (80 acres), are the most compelling sites.

When you first arrive, there is a sudden transition interface of the foothill grasslands to redwoods. At Big Hendy, start by taking the 0.5-mile Discovery Trail, which leaves the grasslands and enters the redwood grove on a dirt path. Suddenly you'll be walking among towering redwoods, moss-covered stumps, and a sprinkling of giant fallen trees, all set amid ferns and sorrel. A great side trip is to walk uphill on the cutoff trail to the old hermit's hut in a hollowed-out tree stump, where one of the last of the real hermits lived for years. No, it wasn't me, but there have been a few years where I considered it.

User Groups: Hikers and wheelchairs. No dogs, horses, or mountain bikes.

Permits: No permits are required. A state park entrance fee of $8 is charged for each vehicle.

Maps: A brochure and trail map are available for a fee at Hendy Woods State Park. For a topographic map, ask the USGS for Philo.

Directions: From Mendocino, take Highway

1 south for about five miles to Highway 128. Turn east on Highway 128 and drive about 20 miles to Philo Greenwood Road. Turn south (right) and drive 0.5 mile to the entrance of Hendy Woods State Park on the left. The trailhead begins just off the parking area.
Contact: Hendy Woods State Park, Mendocino District, Mendocino, 707/895-3141, www.parks.ca.gov.

9 GLEN EDEN TRAIL

3.0-10.5 mi/1.0-5.0 hr 2 7

in Cow Mountain Recreation Area east of Ukiah

Map 4.1, page 173

Hit it right in spring, and the Glen Eden Trail will surprise you with its foothill/oak woodland greenery and long-distance views of Clear Lake and the Mayacamas Range. The trailhead is Lake County's only access point to North Cow Mountain where no motorized vehicles are allowed, and no mountain bikes too for the first 2.5 miles. You start out on a dirty pathway, not a road, that is routed in and out of oak woodlands into the interior of the recreation land. As you go, there is a series of climbs, some steep, and falls. The Glen Eden Trail eventually crosses Mendo Rock Road (this provides another trailhead possibility) and continues up to a series of great overlooks of Clear Lake. The views of Clear Lake and the Mayacamas Range are outstanding. To return, retrace your route. Few make the entire trip, but instead they just hike out to a good lookout and then return. The chaparral-covered slopes are peppered with pine and oak, with many miles of trails and fire roads.

The 52,000-acre Cow Mountain Recreation Area is named for the longhorn cattle that once roamed wild in this area.

User Groups: Hikers, dogs, and horses. Mountain bikes are prohibited on the first 2.5 miles of trail, after which public property starts and bicycles are allowed. Cyclists should access Glen Eden Trail from other trailheads on Bureau of Land Management land.
Permits: No permits are required. Parking and access are free.
Maps: For a free trail map of the Cow Mountain Recreation Area, contact the Bureau of Land Management. For a topographic map, ask the USGS for Cow Mountain.
Directions: From Ukiah, take U.S. 101 north for five miles to Highway 20. Turn east on Highway 20 and drive 14.6 miles (past Blue Lakes) to Scotts Valley Road. Turn right and drive 2.6 miles to the trailhead and parking.
Contact: Bureau of Land Management, Ukiah Field Office, Ukiah, 707/468-4000, www.ca.blm.gov.

10 IDES COVE NATIONAL RECREATION TRAIL

10.5 mi/5.5 hr 3 7

on the boundary of Yolla Bolly Wilderness west of Red Bluff

Map 4.2, page 174

At 8,092 feet, South Yolla Bolly Mountain is the highest point in this wilderness. The Ides Cove National Recreation Trail skirts this mountain as part of one of the top one-day loop trails available in the Yolla Bollys. A bonus is that a shorter loop hike (3.5 miles) is also available. From the Ides Cove trailhead, the trail drops down to the headwaters of Slide Creek and heads out to the foot of Harvey Peak, at 7,361 feet. This is the halfway point and a good spot for lunch. The trail turns sharply and is routed back along the flank of the South Yolla Bolly Mountains. On the way, it passes both Long and Square Lakes, which are both tiny water holes with small brook trout.

A free, primitive campground with two sites is available at the trailhead. Horse facilities are nearby, but not at the trailhead. The trail gets only light use.

User Groups: Hikers, dogs, and horses. No mountain bikes. No wheelchair facilities.

Permits: A campfire permit is required for hikers planning to camp.
Maps: For a map, ask the U.S. Forest Service for Mendocino National Forest or Yolla Bolly Wilderness. For a topographic map, ask the USGS for South Yolla Bolly.
Directions: From Redding, take I-5 south to Corning and the exit for Corning Road/Paskenta Road. Take that exit, turn west on Paskenta Road and drive about 20 miles to Paskenta. In the town of Paskenta, Corning/Paskenta Road will split, becoming Round Valley Road on the left and County Road M2/Toomes Creek Road straight ahead. Continue straight on County Road M2/Toomes Creek Road for 20 miles to Cold Springs Ranger Station and County Road M22. Turn right on County Road M22 and drive about 15 miles to the trailhead.
Contact: Grindstone Ranger Station, 530-934-3316; Mendocino National Forest, Stonyford Work Center, Stonyford, 530/963-3128, www.fs.usda.gov/mendocino.

11 BIG OAK TRAIL

1.0 mi/0.5 hr

at the head of Black Butte Reservoir west of Orland

Map 4.2, page 174

The Big Oak Trail is routed through a riparian area in the Stony Creek drainage above the head of Black Butte Reservoir. The habitat is constantly changing here based on creek flows and temperatures. The route is an easy jaunt. The riparian habitat can make it an area to see wildlife in the foothills above the Sacramento Valley. It has become part of California's Watchable Wildlife system. The best chance to sight wildlife is at dusk and dawn in late spring through summer, when the temperatures are moderate and water are abundant.
User Groups: Hikers, dogs, and mountain bikes. No horses. No wheelchair facilities.
Permits: No permits are required. Parking and access are free.
Maps: For a topographic map, ask the USGS for Julian Rocks.
Directions: Take I-5 to Orland and the exit for Black Butte Lake. Take that exit, turn west on Newville Road (County Road 200) and drive 10 miles to County Road 206. Turn left on County Road 206 and drive to County Road 200A. Bear left on County Road 200A and drive to the lake and trailhead.
Contact: Buckhorn Recreation Area, U.S. Army Corps of Engineers, Black Butte Lake, Orland, 530/865-4781, www.spk.usace.army.mil.

12 WEST CROCKETT TRAILHEAD/MIDDLE FORK FALLS LOOP

4.4 mi/3.0 hr 3 9

on the boundary of Snow Mountain Wilderness in Mendocino National Forest

Map 4.2, page 174

This loop trail traverses the region's most treasured areas. Double-peaked Snow Mountain itself is the big ridge about midway between I-5 at Willows and U.S. 101 at Willits. This trail starts on I-5 at the northern boundary of the wilderness at the West Crockett trailhead (just west of Crockett Peak). Start by hiking two miles to get into Middle Fork Creek. The trail connects there with a spur trail to the waterfall. Take that spur 0.2 mile to the waterfall. In late spring and early summer, it's short, pretty and fun.

To turn this into a major loop, take the main trail uphill, a significant climb, to reach a small loop set between East Snow Mountain (7,056 feet) and West Snow Mountain (7,038 feet). To return, take North Ridge Trail, which drops down from Snow Mountain and traces the Middle Fork of Stony Creek for a good portion of the route back to the parking area; it's 13 miles.

This is a good hike in late winter or spring,

but much of this area can be quite dry and hot in midsummer, especially on the North Ridge. From late spring through fall, rattlesnakes are common. Hikers should always be certain to carry a lot of water here, twice as much as usual.

User Groups: Hikers, dogs, and horses. No mountain bikes. No wheelchair facilities.

Permits: A campfire permit is required for hikers planning to camp. Parking and access are free.

Maps: For a map, ask the U.S. Forest Service for Mendocino National Forest. For topographic maps, ask the USGS for Crockett Peak and St. John Mountain.

Directions: Take I-5 to Willows and the exit for Highway 162. Take that exit, turn west on Highway 162 and drive 21 miles to a T junction (signed Elk Creek). Turn left and drive one mile through the town of Elk Creek to Ivory Mill Road. Turn right on Ivory Mill Road (Road 308) and drive 15 miles to Forest Road M3. Turn left on Forest Road M3 and drive 15.5 miles to the signed turnoff for West Crockett trailhead. Turn left and drive 0.5 mile to the trailhead.

Contact: Mendocino National Forest, Stonyford Work Center, Stonyford, 530/963-3128, www.fs.usda.gov/mendocino.

13 BEAR WALLOW TRAILHEAD

3.25 mi/1.75 hr

on the boundary of Snow Mountain Wilderness in Mendocino National Forest

Map 4.2, page 174

Every wilderness has secret spots. So it is here in the Snow Mountain Wilderness. On a hot summer day when every drop of water is counted as if it were liquid gold, you'll find a simple paradise on this short walk to the headwaters of a tiny fork of Bear Wallow Creek. The trail was brushed and also cleared of downed trees in 2019.

Your destination is a pretty section of Bear Wallow Creek, a small feeder stream to the middle fork of Stony Creek. The hike starts at the Bear Wallow trailhead near the Windy Point Campground. The trail is routed straight east on Bear Wallow Trail for a little more than a mile. About 1.5 miles in, start looking for a spur trail on the right side, and when you see it, take it. This spur drops a short distance down to the source of the north fork of Bear Wallow Creek. If you think there are too many people in the world, just come here and look around.

User Groups: Hikers, dogs, and horses. No mountain bikes. No wheelchair facilities.

Permits: A campfire permit is required for hikers planning to camp. Parking and access are free.

Maps: For a map, ask the U.S. Forest Service for Mendocino National Forest. For topographic maps, ask the USGS for Crockett Peak and St. John Mountain.

Directions: Take I-5 to Willows and the exit for Highway 162. Follow that exit, turn west on Highway 162 and drive 21 miles to a T junction (signed Elk Creek). Turn left and drive 1.3 miles through the town of Elk Creek to Road 308/Ivory Mill Road. Turn right on Ivory Mill Road (Road 308) and drive 15 miles to Forest Road M3 (well signed). Turn left on Forest Road M3 and drive 13.4 miles to the trailhead.

Contact: Mendocino National Forest, Stonyford Work Center, Stonyford, 530/963-3128, www.fs.usda.gov/mendocino.

14 SUMMIT SPRINGS TRAILHEAD/WEST SNOW MOUNTAIN LOOP

12 mi/1 day

on the boundary of Snow Mountain Wilderness in Mendocino National Forest

Map 4.2, page 174

This trail includes two killer climbs, a wonderful little spring along the trail, and the ascent of West Snow Mountain, at 7,038 feet, for a panorama. Still interested? Then read on. The trail starts at the Summit Spring trailhead (there's a small, primitive trailhead camp with a pit toilet, an unreliable spring, and three campsites). In the first two miles, you get a no-fun clamber up to High Rock. At the trail junction here, turn right on Box Spring Loop Trail and hike past the headwaters of Trout Creek to Box Spring, located just to the right of the trail, near another trail junction. In hot weather (typically all summer), this spot is paradise. Turn left and make the three-mile climb up West Snow Mountain. You will grunt and thump it out every step of the way. At the top, enjoy this victory for a while before dropping back down for the final three miles to the trailhead and parking area.

Do you yearn for the passion of the mountain experience? Do you crave the zest of life when you have a bad case of dry mouth and discover a mountain spring? Is the price of a climb worth it for the mountaintop payoff? Are you nuts? You need to answer yes, yes, yes, and yes to be ready for this loop hike.

User Groups: Hikers, dogs, and horses. No mountain bikes. No wheelchair facilities.

Permits: A campfire permit is required for hikers planning to camp. Parking and access are free.

Maps: For a map, ask the U.S. Forest Service for Mendocino National Forest. For a topographic map, ask the USGS for Fouts Springs.

Directions: Take I-5 to the exit for Maxwell (north of Williams, south of Willows). Follow that exit to Maxwell-Sites Road, turn west, and drive to Sites and Sites-Lodoga Road. Turn left on Sites-Lodoga Road and drive to Lodoga and Lodoga-Stonyford Road. Turn left and loop around East Park Reservoir to reach Stonyford and Fouts Spring Road (Road M10). Turn west and drive 25 miles to a signed access road for Summit Spring trailhead. Turn right and drive 1.5 miles to the parking area and trailhead, at the end of the road.

Contact: Mendocino National Forest, Stonyford Work Center, Stonyford, 530/963-3128, www.fs.usda.gov/mendocino.

15 ALDER CREEK TRAIL

4.0 mi/1.75 hr

in Manchester State Park north of Point Arena

Map 4.3, page 175

The Alder Creek Trail starts by the park headquarters for Manchester State Park. The trail is routed past Lake Davis to the beach, then continues north along the beach to the mouth of Alder Creek. This is a coastal lagoon that attracts many species of shorebirds, including, though rarely, whistling swans. It's also the area where the San Andreas Fault heads off from land into the sea.

Time it right here and all can seem perfect. Manchester State Park has two moods: one is sweet and one is foul. In late summer, fall, and late winter, radiant sunbeams set the Mendocino coast aglow, making for flawless beach walks. But in early summer, winds often blast out of the northwest, and it can feel as if your head could blow off. Good thing it's attached at the neck (well, at least for most people). In midsummer, fog smothers the coast about every morning.

User Groups: Hikers and horses. No dogs. The terrain isn't suitable for mountain bikes. No wheelchair facilities.

Permits: No permits are required. Parking and access are free.

Maps: A brochure and trail map are available for a fee at Manchester State Park. For a topographic map, ask the USGS for Point Arena.

Directions: From Point Arena, take Highway 1 north for five miles to Kinney Lane. Turn left and drive one mile to the park entrance, on the right.

Contact: Manchester State Park, 707/882-2463, www.parks.ca.gov.

16 HEADLANDS LOOP

1.5 mi/0.75 hr  

in Gualala Point Regional Park on the Sonoma coast

Map 4.3, page 175

The Headlands (to beach) Loop is an easy, short walk. It provides coastal views with a short cutoff on a spur trail. It also furnishes a lookout over the Gualala River and a route amid giant coastal cypress trees. From the visitors center, the trail is routed along the Gualala River and then turns and loops to the left. Here you can take the short cutoff trail that leads to the beach. On the way back, the trail traces the ocean bluffs for a short spell. For coastal views, take the spur trail to a lookout. Then the main trail turns inland and returns to the visitors center. Bonuses here include excellent whale-watching during the winter and good wildflower blooms on the grassy hillsides in spring. It is mostly level. The trailhead elevation is 250 feet.

User Groups: Hikers and dogs. No horses.

Permits: No permits are required. There is a parking fee of $7 per vehicle.

Maps: For a topographic map, ask the USGS for Gualala.

Directions: From Gualala, drive south on Highway 1 for 0.25 mile (over the Gualala River) and turn west into the park entrance. Continue to the visitors center.

Contact: Gualala Point Regional Park, Gualala, 707/785-2377, http://parks.sonomacounty.ca.gov.

17 LAKE SONOMA SOUTHLAKE TRAIL

5.2 mi/2.0 hr 

at Lake Sonoma northwest of Healdsburg

Map 4.3, page 175

This trail provides the best introduction to Lake Sonoma, unless, that is, you have a boat and take advantage of the boat-in campsites. The Southlake Trail starts off of Stewart's Point Road below the Overlook. The short trail at the Overlook provides spectacular views of the lake. That's the payoff. The trail then winds along the southwestern portion of Warm Springs Arm through gray pine and madrone woodlands. It traces alongside the lake, enters and exits a series of small groves, and extends along the lake's fingers. At 2.7 miles, you'll reach Quicksilver Campground. Campers often take this trail out for the views of Lake Sonoma. A few trails bisect the route and extend into the remoter surrounding country. When you've had enough, just turn back. The trail is not very steep, but does have some changes in elevation. It features sun exposure, making it great for wildflowers in the spring but very hot on summer afternoons. Most of the habitat is oak grasslands, and on rare occasion you may see deer and, in summer, rattlesnakes.

User Groups: Hikers, dogs, and horses. No mountain bikes. No wheelchair facilities.

Permits: No permits are required. Parking and access are free.

Maps: For a free map, go to the visitors center or contact the U.S. Army Corps of Engineers. For a topographic map, ask the USGS for Warm Springs Dam.

Directions: From Santa Rosa, take U.S. 101 north for 12 miles to the exit for Healdsburg and Dry Creek Road. Follow that exit, turn left on Dry Creek Road, and drive about 11 miles (crossing Dry Creek; Dry Creek Road becomes Skaggs Springs Road; continue past visitors center) to Skaggs Springs-Stewarts Point Road. Turn left and drive 0.25 mile to a trailhead spur road. Turn right and drive a short distance to the trailhead on the left.

Contact: Lake Sonoma Visitor Center, 707/431-4533; U.S. Army Corps of Engineers, Lake Sonoma, Geyserville, 707/431-4590; www.spn.usace.army.mil.

Salt Point Bluff Trail

18 SALT POINT BLUFF TRAIL

3.5 mi/1.5 hr 1 10

in Salt Point State Park north of Jenner

Map 4.3, page 175

The dramatic, rocky shoreline of Salt Point State Park is memorable to anyone who has seen it. This trail provides the best look at it, including some simply awesome views from a 100-foot-high ocean bluff. The trailhead is at the parking area set near the tip of Salt Point. From here, hike north over Warren Creek, a seasonal stream, and then continue across the bluffs. You can practically feel the crashing of ocean breakers below you, the spray rocketing skyward. The trail eventually winds around and down to Stump Beach Cove, a pretty, sandy beach where the calm waters are in sharp contrast to the nearby breakers. The payoff on the Bluff Trail is the Sentinel Rock Viewing Platform and the overlook of Fisk Mill Cove. This park is stellar.

Note: At the north end of Salt Point State Park, a parking lot with a short spur to the Sentinel Rock Viewing Platform was closed due to the chance of dead and falling trees. A project to clear the hazard trees and reopen the parking lot is scheduled to be complete between 2020 and 2022; Salt Point State Park provides a marine reserve, Gerstle Cove, where no form of marinelife may be taken or disturbed.

User Groups: Hikers only. Horses are allowed on designated trails only, and mountain bikes are allowed only on fire roads. One trail (Gerstle Cove) is paved for wheelchairs for 100 yards out to Salt Point. No dogs.

Permits: No permits are required. A state park day-use fee of $8 is charged per vehicle.

Maps: A trail map is available for a fee from Salt Point State Park. For a topographic map, ask the USGS for Plantation.

Directions: From Santa Rosa, take U.S. 101 north to the exit for River Road. Follow that exit, turn left on River Road and drive 13 miles to Highway 116 and Guerneville. Turn right on Highway 116 and drive to Highway 1 at Jenner. Turn north on Highway 1 and drive 20 miles (nine miles past Fort Ross) to the park entrance. Turn left (west) and drive to the entrance kiosk. The trailhead is at the Salt Point parking area.

Mendocino shoreline

Contact: Salt Point State Park, Jenner, 707/847-3221, www.parks.ca.gov.

19 SENTINEL ROCK/ FISK MILL COVE

4.0 mi/2.5 hr 1 10

in Salt Point State Park north of Jenner

Map 4.3, page 175

Fisk Mill Cove is a beautiful spot at Salt Point State Park. It provides a great whale-watching spot. The best strategy is to enter the trail at the north end and then venture to the wooden deck at Sentinel Rock. Take in the sweeping views across the ocean and below to Fisk Mill Cove. From here, the trail ventures south two miles to Stump Beach Cove. When you roam about at the park, always keep an eye out. On the coastal bluffs, this is one of the better locations anywhere for a chance to see a badger.

User Groups: Hikers only. Horses are allowed on designated trails only, and mountain bikes are allowed only on fire roads. No dogs.

Permits: No permits are required. A state park day-use fee of $8 is charged per vehicle.

Maps: A trail map is available for a fee from Salt Point State Park. For a topographic map, ask the USGS for Plantation.

Directions: From Santa Rosa, take U.S. 101 north to the exit for River Road. Take that exit, turn left on River Road and drive 13 miles to Highway 116 and Guerneville. Turn right on Highway 116 and drive to Highway 1 at Jenner. Turn north on Highway 1 and drive 20 miles (nine miles past Fort Ross) to the park entrance. Continue north (past main park entrance on your left) for about three miles to signed parking area on left for Sentinel Rock (and on right for Kruse Rhododendron State Natural Reserve). Turn left to parking and trailhead.

Contact: Salt Point State Park, Jenner, 707/847-3221, www.parks.ca.gov.

20 STOCKOFF CREEK LOOP

1.25 mi/0.75 hr 1 8

in Stillwater Cove Regional Park north of Jenner

Map 4.3, page 175

The trailhead is located at the day-use parking lot, and after starting the walk, you'll enter a gorgeous forest of firs and redwoods. You then come to the Loop Trail junction, where you turn right. The trail is routed along the creek, crosses a few bridges, and eventually rises above the watershed and loops back through forest to the parking area. It's an easy, pretty, and secluded loop hike.

Must-do side trip: Cross Highway 1 to see Stillwater Cove, a dramatic rock-strewn shore. Highway 1 is one of the top tourist drives in the United States, which explains why the coastal state parks get such heavy use in the summer months.

User Groups: Hikers and dogs. No horses or mountain bikes. No wheelchair facilities.

Permits: No permits are required. A day-use fee of $7 is charged for each vehicle.

Maps: For a free brochure, contact Stillwater Cove Regional Park. For a topographic map, ask the USGS for Plantation.

Directions: From Santa Rosa, take U.S. 101 north to the exit for River Road. Take that exit, turn left on River Road and drive 13 miles to Highway 116 and Guerneville. Go right on Highway 116 and drive to Highway 1. Turn right and head north, past the town of Jenner, for 16 miles to the park entrance, on the right at mile marker 37.01.

Contact: Stillwater Cove Regional Park, County of Sonoma, Santa Rosa, 707/847-3245; Regional Parks Department, 707/565-2041, http://parks.sonomacounty.ca.gov.

21 BODEGA HEAD LOOP

1.5 mi/1.0 hr 1 9

on the Sonoma coast west of Bodega Bay

Map 4.3, page 175

Pick a calm, clear evening with scarcely a breeze. The view here at sunset can be so poignant that it can touch your heart at the memories of all the things you've let slip through your fingers. It's that kind of place. The short loop hike at Bodega Head will provide an introduction to one of California's great coastal areas for an easy hike and views that can set off feelings that you will never forget. The trail starts at the east parking lot. In just 1.5 miles, you get views of cliffs, untouched beaches, and the sea beyond. For a side trip, take a short tromp on a spur trail to the tip-top of Bodega Head for 360-degree views. Rarely does the ocean seem so vast as it does here. The North Farallon Island looks like you could reach it with a running leap. A few notes about the weather: In spring and early summer, the wind can really howl out of the northwest. In late summer, fall, or late winter, between storms, Bodega Bay gets its warmest, and often most wind-free, weather. Scanning for whale spouts is great from January through April. But it's the sunsets here that you'll never forget.

User Groups: Hikers only. No horses, dogs, or mountain bikes. No wheelchair facilities.

Permits: No permits are required. Parking and access are free.

Maps: A trail map and brochure are available for a fee from Sonoma Coast State Beach.

Directions: Take U.S. 101 to Petaluma and the exit for East Washington. Follow that exit to East Washington. Turn west and drive through Petaluma (the road becomes Bodega Avenue) for about 10 miles to Valley Ford Road. Bear right and drive 7.5 miles to Highway 1. Turn north on Highway 1 and drive nine miles to Bodega Bay and continue to East Shore Road. Turn left on East Shore Road and drive less than 0.5 mile to a stop sign at Bay Flat Road. Turn right and drive five miles around Bodega Bay (the road turns into West Side Road). Continue past Spud Point Marina and drive to the Bodega Head parking area.

Contact: Sonoma Coast State Beach, Bodega Bay, 707/875-3483, www.parks.ca.gov.

22 BERRYESSA PEAK TRAIL

14.5 mi/1 day 5 10

Berryessa-Snow Mountain National Monument

Map 4.4, page 176

The payoff is a sensational view from bare, flat-topped Berryessa Peak at 3,057 feet. Lake Berryessa below spans for miles, and what seems like an endless array of hilltops, valleys, and ridges extend to the coast, often fronted by a distant low-lying wall of fog on the western horizon. To the east, you also get a great view of the Sutter Buttes, and in the spring on clear days, a clear view of the snow-packed west flank of the Sierra Crest. This view is the centerpiece of the newly created Berryessa-Snow Mountain Wilderness. The trek is a 7.25-mile climb with a cumulative elevation gain of 3,500 feet to get there. Got that? You pay for your pleasure. The trailhead is remote, and at one time, very difficult to find. Now there are a few signs, and a few posts with the letters "BPT." Only nearby transmitters on the top mar a foothill-country wilderness-like experience.

The trip starts off Knoxville Road; look for mile marker 20 and the sign. The trail climbs up a former dirt road, and 1.5 miles in, you'll arrive at a junction. Turn south and the climb takes on butt-kicker proportions to a fence crossing. The road turns then turns to trail, where to your disbelief, you will then descend (!) into Green Valley. So frustrating. Finally, you start to climb again to the ridge. The last mile is on the service road built for the transmitter stations. Most credit the organization Tuleyome (www.tuleyome.org), which helps gets youth outdoors, for the trail construction. In spring, wildflowers are ablaze and bushes and trees in full bloom, and clear skies provide long-distance views. You'll see songbirds, swallows, falcons, and eagles flitting, hovering, and soaring. There is also a good share of lizards and rattlesnakes.

User Groups: Hikers and dogs (not advised, no water in summer). Horses and mountain bikes, while allowed, aren't recommended because of the steep, rocky terrain. No wheelchair facilities.

Permits: No permits are required. Parking and access are free.

Maps: For a topographic map, ask the USGS for Glascock.

Directions: From Sacramento or the Bay Area, drive to Lake Berryessa and continue to Berryessa-Knoxville Road that runs above the western shore of the lake. Continue north on Berryessa-Knoxville Road past Lake Berryessa (past the bridge over Putah Creek) and continue north as the road turns to dirt, narrows, gets rough, and becomes Knoxville Road (pay attention to mile marker signs). Continue to mile marker 20.00 and park on the road's shoulder. The trailhead is on the right.

Contact: Bureau of Land Management, Ukiah Field Office, Ukiah, 707/468-4000, www.ca.blm.gov.

23 GILLIAM CREEK TRAIL

8.9 mi/1 day 3 8

in Austin Creek State Recreation Area north of Guerneville

Map 4.4, page 176

The Gilliam Creek Trail is very pretty in late winter and spring. For much of the route, the trail parallels Gilliam Creek amid shaded oak woodlands. The area has more of a wilderness feel than most parks in this habitat because you drive through redwoods to get here, and in addition, the final 2.5 miles of access road are narrow and twisty. The trailhead elevation is 1,100 feet. You contour across the slope, then drop down to the headwaters of Schoolhouse Creek, at 400 feet. The trail then follows the stream, past the confluence with Gilliam Creek, and extends 3.7 miles into the backcountry, all the way down to an elevation of 200 feet. At the confluence of East Austin Creek, the best way to do it is to turn right and hike deeper into wild, hilly country along the stream. Then return on the loop with East Austin Creek Trail, a fire road with a—yep, by now you should have figured this out—long climb. At this point, you may ask, "Are we having fun yet?"

Visitors who love Armstrong Redwoods tend not to speak of the adjoining Austin Creek Recreation Area with any terms of endearment. The rolling hills, open forests, and streamside riparian habitat in Austin Creek State Recreation Area can seem a million miles away from the forests of Armstrong Redwoods. Yet the two parks together actually form 6,488 acres of contiguous parkland. While most tourists are walking around the redwoods at Armstrong, this trail offers a quiet and ambitious alternative.

User Groups: Hikers and horses (no horses permitted during wet weather). Mountain bikes permitted on fire roads. No dogs. No wheelchair facilities.

Permits: No permits are required. A state park day-use fee of $10 is charged for each vehicle. A senior discount is available.

Maps: A trail map is available for a fee from Armstrong Redwoods State Reserve. For a topographic map, ask the USGS for Guerneville.

Directions: From Santa Rosa, take U.S. 101 north to the exit for River Road. Follow that exit, turn left on River Road, and drive 13 miles to Highway 116 and Guerneville. Turn right on Highway 116 and drive a short distance to Armstrong Woods Road. Turn right (north) on Armstrong Woods Road and drive into Armstrong Redwoods State Reserve entrance, then continue about four miles into adjoining Austin Creek Recreation Area and to the trailhead. The last 2.5 miles are twisty and narrow; no trailers or vehicles more than 20 feet long are permitted.

Contact: Austin Creek State Recreation Area, c/o Armstrong Redwoods State Reserve, Guerneville, 707/869-2015, www.parks.ca.gov.

24 EAST RIDGE TRAIL

6.8 mi/4.0 hr

in Armstrong Redwoods State Natural Reserve north of Guerneville

Map 4.4, page 176

The East Ridge Trail rises 1,400 feet over the course of 3.4 miles. Your reward is a series of lookouts over the top of a sea of redwoods below. The trailhead is at an elevation of 200 feet, adjacent to Fife Creek. The route climbs gradually at first, then in the first 0.5 mile rises to cross the headwaters of Fife Creek, at an elevation of 600 feet. Your climb has only just begun, and if you're already running out of gas, you'd best head back. The trail continues climbing all the way, contouring its way up toward McCray Mountain (1,940 feet), and tops out at a service road at 1,600 feet.

For short strolls through the park's redwoods, take the Discovery Trail or Armstrong Nature Trail in Armstrong Redwoods.

User Groups: Hikers and horses. No dogs or mountain bikes. No wheelchair facilities.

Permits: No permits are required. A state park day-use fee of $10 is charged for each vehicle. A senior discount is available.

Maps: A trail map is available for a fee from Armstrong Redwoods State Reserve. For a topographic map, ask the USGS for Guerneville.

Directions: From Santa Rosa, take U.S. 101 north to the exit for River Road. Take that exit, turn left on River Road and drive 13 miles to Highway 116 and Guerneville. Go right on Highway 116 and drive a short distance to Armstrong Woods Road. Turn right (north) on Armstrong Woods Road and drive 2.5 miles to the Armstrong Redwoods State Reserve entrance. The trailhead is adjacent to the visitors center.

Contact: Armstrong Redwoods State Natural

Reserve, Guerneville, 707/869-2015, www.parks.ca.gov.

25 MOUNT ST. HELENA TRAIL

10.2 mi/4.5 hr 

in Robert Louis Stevenson State Park north of Calistoga

Map 4.4, page 176

Mount St. Helena is Sonoma County's highest mountain, the peak that strikes such a memorable silhouette when viewed from the Bay Area. This trail climbs to the 4,343-foot summit and requires an ascent of 2,068 feet over the course of five miles. On the crystal days of early spring, the views can make life seem complete. On the best days, 150 miles to the east, you can see the snow glisten white on the Sierra Crest. To the south, Mount Tamalpais and Mount Diablo rise up above the Bay Area. Lake Berryessa is below to the east, and the Napa Valley plunges to the south. Several times in the spring, we've seen the clear outline of Lassen Peak to the northeast. Of similar interest is the view of the fire damage, rapidly returning to life with greenery amid tree skeletons, where wildfires burned below on southern flank of St. Helena and beyond so much of the foothill country extending to Santa Rosa.

The Mount St. Helena Trail starts along Highway 29 at the ridge above the Calistoga Valley. From the trailhead, the route emerges from oak woodlands on a dirt service road. The climb is a steady pull, with two steep spots. Four miles in, continue straight at a junction to the North Peak (a left will take you instead to 4,003-foot South Peak). Strong hikers will make the summit in about 2.5 to 3 hours, with the last half hour strenuous, and then for the easy return trip, sail down in about 1.5 to 2 hours. In spring, bring a windbreaker for often chilly breezes out of the north on top and a change of shirt; you will likely sweat through whatever you are wearing on the climb, especially if you carry a pack.

Visibility is best in spring, when north winds clear the air, showcasing remarkable views in all directions. Bill Grummer, a ranger pal, claims that on the best days visitors can see Mount Shasta (192 miles away), but so far we haven't had that experience. However, it is documented that in the late 19th century, surveyors sent signals back and forth between here and Mount Shasta, setting a record for longest signal distance. On other stellar days, you can see the Farallon Islands, 25 miles offshore from San Francisco, and a glimpse of the city itself (but not the Golden Gate Bridge).

History lesson: The park is named "Robert Louis Stevenson State Park" because in 1880, this is where Stevenson, the author of *Treasure Island,* spent his summer honeymoon in a cabin (long since gone). The cabin site is off a spur (hikers only), 1.5 miles in, marked along the trail to the top.

In the summer, the hike can be pure hell: Much of the trail is actually a fire road with little shade, there's no water anywhere along the route, and the heat commonly blazes in the 90s and 100s out here. After logging weather records for years, we have found the most likely time for Mount St. Helena to receive snow is just before a full moon in February.

User Groups: Hikers only on single-track trail. Mountain bikes allowed on a nearby fire road 0.25 mile north on Highway 29. No dogs or horses. No wheelchair facilities.

Permits: No permits are required. Parking and access are free.

Maps: A brochure and map are available at the park for a fee. For topographic maps, ask the USGS for Detert Reservoir and Mount St. Helena.

Directions: From Calistoga, take Highway 29 north for eight miles to the parking area at the highway summit, signed Robert Louis Stevenson State Park. The trailhead is next to the parking area. You can park on the east or west side of the road. The trail is located on the west side of the road (the trailhead is not signed from the road).

Contact: Robert Louis Stevenson State Park, c/o Bothe-Napa Valley State Park, 707/942-4575; www.parks.ca.gov; Calistoga info, 866/306-5588, www.visitcalistoga.com.

26 TABLE ROCK/ PALISADES TRAIL

4.0-8.0 mi/2.0-4.0 hr 3 9

near Calistoga

Map 4.4, page 176

This trip can be done two ways: a four-mile round-trip to Table Rock and back or an eight-mile round-trip to the southern edge of the Palisades and back (recommended). The Palisades? Aren't the Palisades a glacier-carved series of 14,000-foot peaks in the Sierra Nevada? Well, yep, but Napa County's Palisades are nearly as dramatic and accessible year-round: This is a stunning, mile-long volcanic wall set along a ridge that overlooks Calistoga and the Napa Valley. You also get gorgeous long-distance views. In addition, this trail is one of the best near Calistoga for seeing raptors, including a chance to spot peregrine falcons, and also for wildflowers, with bitterroot the most prevalent.

From Calistoga, it's a twisty, eight-mile drive up Highway 29 to the parking area and trailhead, the same staging area used for the Mount St. Helena Trail. It is signed Robert Louis Stevenson State Park. To hike to Table Rock and the Palisades, the trailhead is on the right (southeast) side of the road (elevation 2,250 feet). Start this hike on the Table Rock Trail. It's about two miles to Table Rock (2,465 feet), just enough of a climb to get you above the canyon woodlands. Some enjoy the views from atop Table Rock, have a picnic, and then head back to the car. But the trip gets better by continuing on the Palisades Trail. This drops down to Lasky Point (2,045 feet), and then climbs back up for about two miles along the base of the Palisades (2,930 feet). The trail is spectacular, set just beneath the sheer volcanic cliffs along the ridge. At 3.9 miles in, you will reach the junction of Historic Oat Hill Mine Road, a long-abandoned, rocky jeep road. Most people turn around and head back from here.

Note than Oat Hill Mine Road is the route down to the valley for a one-way hike with a shuttle. But it plummets 2,000 feet over 4.5 miles, some of it rocky, and can be a thigh-burning, knee-wrenching, toe-jamming experience that's only for the deranged (like us, for instance).

The best time for this getaway is from mid-March through mid-May, when the foothills are green, the skies are often crystal clear, and the morning air is still cool. There is no drinking water available anywhere on the trail. Rangers warn not to leave valuables in your car (covering them with a jacket or blanket isn't enough, either). Calistoga is one of the best decompression chambers designed by humankind. But after a day or two of getting turned into Jell-O by soaks in steaming mineral water, massages, and mud baths, you can be brought back to life by the electrifying hike to the Palisades.

User Groups: Hikers only. No dogs, horses, or mountain bikes. No wheelchair facilities.

Permits: Parking and access are free.

Maps: A brochure and map are available for a fee at the park or by mail. For topographic maps, ask the USGS for Detert Reservoir and Mount St. Helena.

Directions: From Calistoga, take Highway 29 north for eight miles to the parking area at the highway summit, signed Robert Louis Stevenson State Park. The trailhead is on the right (southeast) side of the road.

Contact: Robert Louis Stevenson State Park, c/o Bothe-Napa Valley State Park, Calistoga, 707/942-4575, www.parks.ca.gov.

27 COYOTE PEAK/ REDWOOD TRAIL LOOP

4.4 mi/3.0 hr 2 8

in Bothe-Napa Valley State Park south of Calistoga

Map 4.4, page 176

The best way to see the surprise redwoods and pretty creek at Bothe-Napa Valley State Park is on the Coyote Peak/Redwood Trail Loop. Start just past the Ritchey Creek Campground turnoff, near the picnic area. The first 0.5 mile is on the Ritchey Canyon Trail, a very pretty stretch of trail along beautiful Ritchey Creek. Then bear left on the Redwood Trail. You'll be surrounded by some of the park's highest stands of redwoods. The trail continues along Ritchey Creek for 0.25 mile, then connects to the Coyote Peak Trail. Ritchey Creek is one of our favorite stretches of the trail in the region, always good for a snack and a moment in time. Then continue on the Coyote Peak Trail, which rises quickly, skirting the northern flank of Coyote Peak. (A short spur trail will take you all the way to the top, elevation 1,170 feet.) Then the trail drops down the other side of the hill and intersects with South Fork Trail, which heads all the way back down to Ritchey Creek. From the trailhead to the end of the hike, the elevation gain is roughly 800 feet, totaling the up-and-downs.

Who ever heard of redwoods in the Napa Valley? Who ever heard of a mountain peak there, too? Only those who also know of Bothe-Napa Valley State Park, which is like an island of wildland in a sea of winery tourist traffic. Bothe-Napa has some of the most easterly stands of coastal redwoods, plus Douglas fir and an excellent lookout from Coyote Peak, all quite a surprise for newcomers. Note that temperatures can be extremely hot in the summer—as high as 105 degrees in unshaded areas—but you'll find a cool paradise along Ritchey Creek.

User Groups: Hikers only. Horses permitted on some designated trails. Mountain bikes allowed on fire roads and designated trails but not on most of this described loop. No dogs. No wheelchair facilities.

Permits: No permits are required. A state park fee of $8 is charged per vehicle.

Maps: A brochure and trail map are available for a fee. For a topographic map, ask the USGS for Calistoga.

Directions: From Calistoga, take Highway 29 south for about five miles to the park entrance on the right side of the road. Turn right and drive past the entrance station to just past the Ritchey Creek Campground turnoff (near the picnic area), where there is trailhead parking.

Contact: Bothe-Napa Valley State Park, Calistoga, 707/942-4575, www.parks.ca.gov; park operated by Napa County Regional Park & Open Space District, https://napaoutdoors.org.

28 SPRING LAKE TRAIL

2.0 mi/1.0 hr 1 6

in Spring Lake Regional Park in Santa Rosa

Map 4.4, page 176

Spring Lake is Santa Rosa's backyard fishing hole, a popular place for trout fishing, an evening picnic, or a short hike. For newcomers, we suggest you take the walk along the west shore of Spring Lake. From the parking area, start this trip by walking along the shore to Spring Lake's west dam. Then turn left and head into adjoining Howarth Park and on to Lake Ralphine. It's an easy, enjoyable stroll. The lake is stocked with trout in winter and spring, and it provides a fair fishery for bass in the summer. The water is fun and quiet, with boats restricted to electric motors; no gas motors are allowed. The elevation is 300 feet, and the trail is mostly level.

User Groups: Hikers and dogs. Horses are allowed only on designated trails. The park has 2.3 miles of trail that are paved for wheelchair and bicycle use.

Permits: No permits are required. There is a parking fee of $7 per vehicle.

Maps: A free trail map is available from Spring Lake Regional Park. For a topographic map, ask the USGS for Santa Rosa.

Directions: From Santa Rosa, take Highway 12 east (it becomes Hoen Avenue) to Newanga Avenue. Turn left on Newanga Avenue and drive 0.5 mile to the park entrance. The various trailheads are well marked and easily accessible from the parking area at the lake.

Contact: Spring Lake Regional Park, c/o Sonoma County Regional Parks, Santa Rosa, 707/539-8092; Sonoma County Regional Parks Department, 707/565-2041, http://parks.sonomacounty.ca.gov.

29 BALD MOUNTAIN LOOP

8.2 mi/1 day 3 8

in Sugarloaf Ridge State Park north of Sonoma

Map 4.4, page 176

Bald Mountain, elevation 2,729 feet, overlooks the Napa Valley, with Mount St. Helena to the north. This old mountain is the centerpiece of Sugarloaf Ridge State Park, a 4,020-acre expanse featuring redwoods in the Sonoma Creek watershed, open meadows peppered with oaks on the hilltops, and some chaparral on ridges. On clear days from the summit, you can see portions of the San Francisco Bay Area and then be thankful you're here instead.

The most ambitious hike in the park is the Bald Mountain Loop, an 8.2-mile trek. The trail starts at the parking lot and then is routed into a loop by linking the Bald Mountain, Gray Pine, Brushy Peaks, and Meadow Trails. Many less-demanding hikes are available in the park, but this route will give hikers the greatest sense of the park's wildest lands. It's best hiked in the spring, when the air is still cool, the hills are green, and the wildflowers are in bloom.

There's a bonus as well: When Sonoma Creek is really flowing, a 25-foot waterfall set in a wooded canyon tumbles downstream from the campground; a short trail is available from the park's entrance road, located at an unsigned turnout on the road's shoulder. A more formal route to the waterfall is on Canyon Trail.

User Groups: Hikers only. Horses are allowed on trails in summer and on fire roads in the park in winter. No dogs. No wheelchair facilities.

Permits: No permits are required. A state park day-use fee of $8 is charged for each vehicle.

Maps: A trail map and brochure are available for a fee from Sugarloaf Ridge State Park. For a topographic map, ask the USGS for Kenwood.

Directions: From Santa Rosa, take Highway 12 east through Kenwood to Adobe Canyon Road. Turn left on Adobe Canyon Road and drive 3.5 miles to the main park entrance at the end of the road.

Contact: Sugarloaf Ridge State Park, 2605 Adobe Canyon Rd., Kenwood, CA 95452, 707/833-5712, www.parks.ca.gov.

30 RIDGE TRAIL/NORTH SONOMA MOUNTAIN

7.0 mi/3.5 hr 3 9

in Sonoma Mountain Regional Park east of Rohnert Park

Map 4.4, page 176

From the Ridge Trail on North Sonoma Mountain, you will discover why this trek can appeal to anybody. A Gunsight Rock, at 2,500 feet, you emerge above a hardwood forest for a towering view across the Sonoma Valley and to the west to the coast. The trailhead for Hood Mountain is the Goodspeed Trail on the main road to Sugarloaf Ridge State Park. In the first mile, you cross Bear Creek, and then climb about 400 feet, with switchbacks to ease the grade, to reach a sub-ridge. You then continue 2.5 miles on the flank of Mount Hood and into Hood Mountain Regional Park to the turnoff to Gunsight Rock. A spur leads 0.2 to this lookout. Back on the main trail, it's just another 0.2 miles (with a 200-foot climb) to Mount Hood Summit. You tower over Kenwood and above the Sonoma Valley.

User Groups: Hikers and horses only. No dogs or mountain bikes. No wheelchair facilities.
Permits: It is $8 per vehicle at the iron ranger (bring exact cash) at Goodspeed trailhead; automated pay station at upper park entrance (credit card, exact cash); kiosk staffed most weekends and all holidays.
Maps: Small map available at trailhead kiosk; PDF online at http://parks.sonomacounty.ca.gov/.
Directions: From the Golden Gate Bridge, take U.S. 101 north for 20 miles (stay right) to Exit 460A for Highway 37. Follow that exit and merge with Highway 37 and drive 7.2 miles (stay left) to the lighted intersection of Highway 121. Turn left on Highway 121 and drive 6.6 miles, then continue onto Highway 116W and drive 1.6 miles to Arnold Drive. Bear right on Arnold and drive five miles to a traffic circle. Take the first exit onto Agua Caliente Road and drive 0.8 miles to Highway 12. Turn left on 12 and drive 8.1 miles to Adobe Canyon Road. Turn right and drive 2.3 miles to the boundary for Sugarloaf Ridge State Park and parking for Goodspeed trailhead on the left.
Note: Park headquarters is 1.1 miles farther up Adobe Canyon Road.
Contact: Sonoma County Regional Parks, 707/565-2041, http://parks.sonomacounty.ca.gov; Sugarloaf Ridge State Park, 707-833-5712, www.parks.ca.gov.

SACRAMENTO AND GOLD COUNTRY

The Sacramento Valley is a landscape filled with rivers—the Sacramento, Feather, Yuba, American, and Mokelumne—providing both recreation and habitat for wildlife refuges. This is an area for California history buffs, with Placerville KOA and nearby Malakoff Diggins State Historic Park in the center of some of the state's most extraordinary history: the gold rush era. The highlight of foothill country is its series of great lakes—Camanche, Rollins, Oroville—for water sports, fishing, and recreation. In the Mother Lode country, three lakes—Camanche, Amador, and Pardee—are outstanding for fishing. Spring and fall are gorgeous, as are summer evenings, but there are always periods of 100°F-plus temperatures in the summer. But that's what gives these lakes and rivers such appeal. On a hot day, jumping into a cool lake is more valuable than gold.

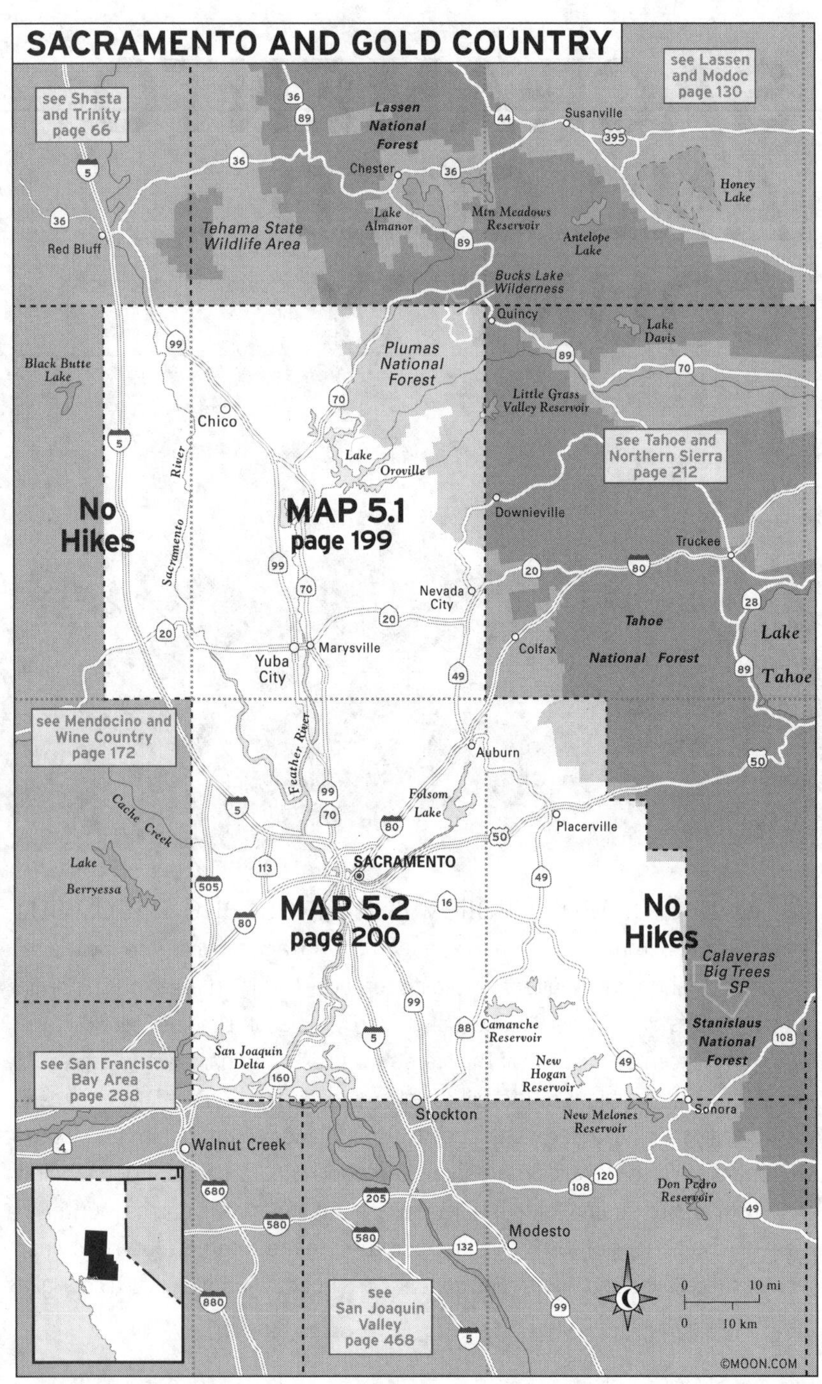
SACRAMENTO AND GOLD COUNTRY
see Shasta and Trinity page 66
see Lassen and Modoc page 130
Lassen National Forest
Susanville
Chester
Honey Lake
Red Bluff
Tehama State Wildlife Area
Lake Almanor
Mtn Meadows Reservoir
Antelope Lake
Bucks Lake Wilderness
Quincy
Lake Davis
Black Butte Lake
Plumas National Forest
Little Grass Valley Reservoir
Chico
Lake Oroville
see Tahoe and Northern Sierra page 212
Sacramento River
No Hikes
MAP 5.1 page 199
Downieville
Truckee
Nevada City
Lake Tahoe
Tahoe National Forest
Colfax
Yuba City
Marysville
see Mendocino and Wine Country page 172
Feather River
Auburn
Cache Creek
Folsom Lake
Placerville
Lake Berryessa
SACRAMENTO
MAP 5.2 page 200
No Hikes
Calaveras Big Trees SP
Stanislaus National Forest
Camanche Reservoir
San Joaquin Delta
New Hogan Reservoir
see San Francisco Bay Area page 288
Stockton
Sonora
New Melones Reservoir
Walnut Creek
Don Pedro Reservoir
Modesto
see San Joaquin Valley page 468
0 10 mi
0 10 km
©MOON.COM

Map 5.1

Sites 1-8
Pages 201-206

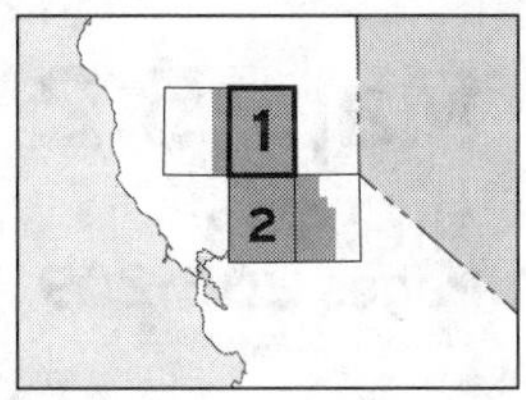

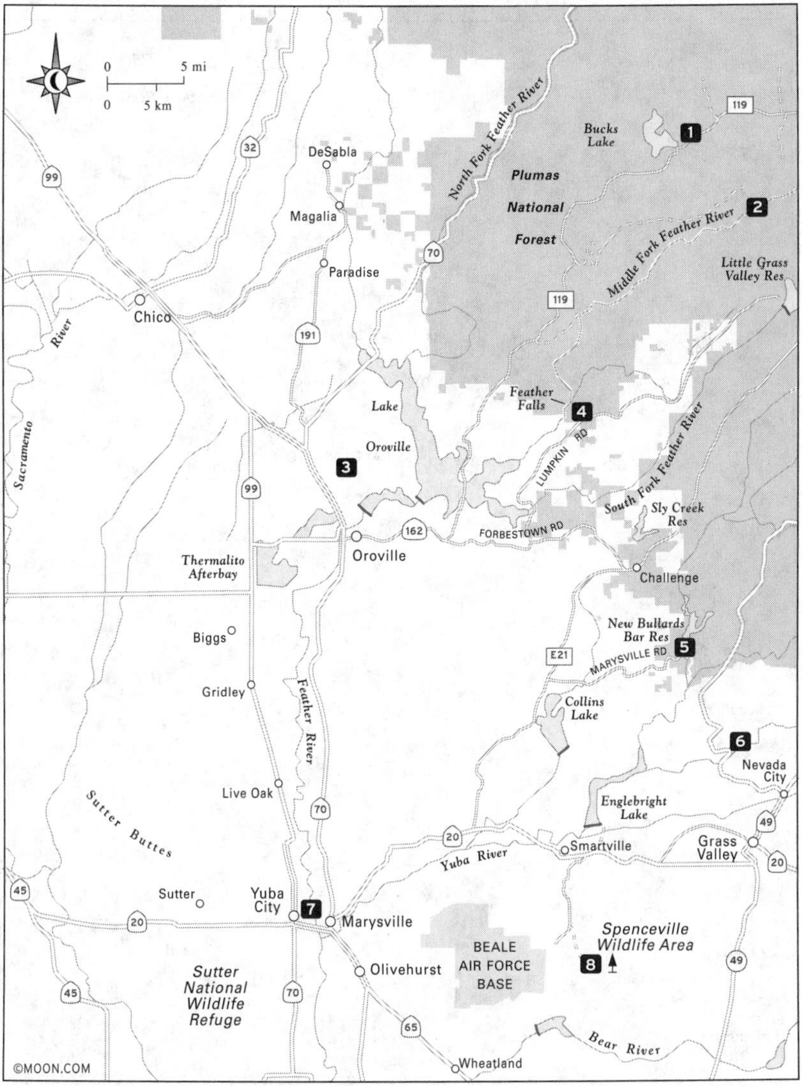

0 5 mi
0 5 km
119
Bucks Lake
1
North Fork Feather River
Plumas National Forest
2
Middle Fork Feather River
Little Grass Valley Res
32
DeSabla
99
Magalia
70
Paradise
119
Chico
River
191
Sacramento
Feather Falls
4
Lake Oroville
LUMPKIN RD
3
South Fork Feather River
99
Sly Creek Res
162
FORBESTOWN RD
Oroville
Thermalito Afterbay
Challenge
Biggs
New Bullards Bar Res
5
E21
MARYSVILLE RD
Gridley
Feather River
Collins Lake
6
Nevada City
Live Oak
Englebright Lake
Sutter Buttes
70
49
20
Smartville
Grass Valley
Yuba River
20
45
Sutter
Yuba City
7
Marysville
Spenceville Wildlife Area
20
BEALE AIR FORCE BASE
8
Sutter National Wildlife Refuge
Olivehurst
49
45
70
65
Bear River

Wheatland

Map 5.2

Sites 9-13
Pages 206-209

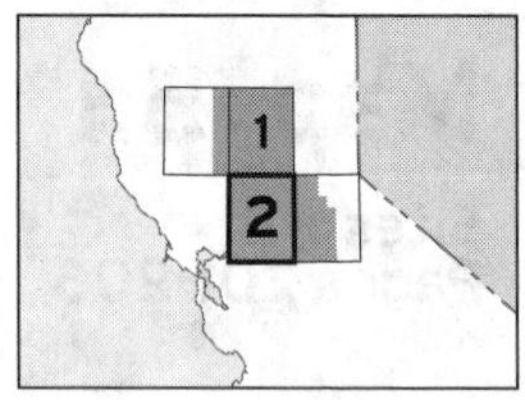

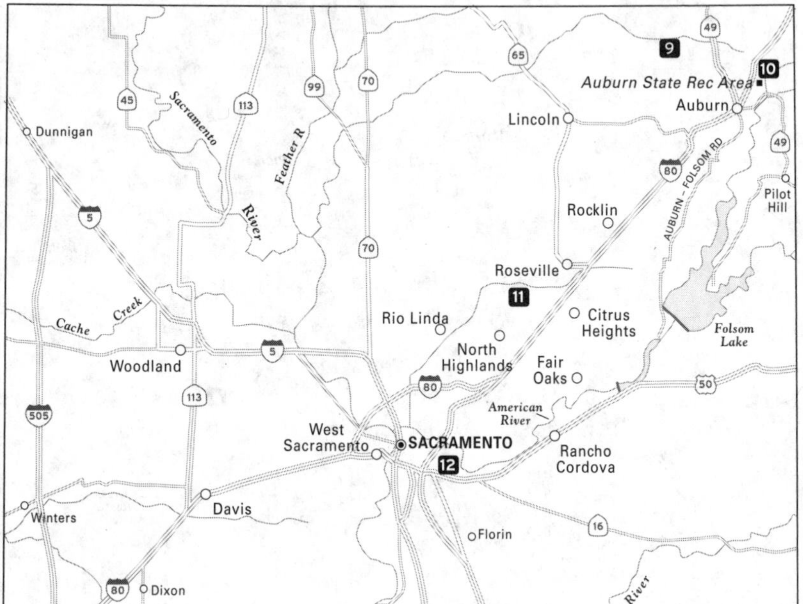

49
9
65
10
Auburn State Rec Area
Auburn
70
99
113
45
Sacramento
Lincoln
Dunnigan
Feather R
49
80
AUBURN - FOLSOM RD
Pilot Hill
River
Rocklin
5
70
Roseville
11
Cache Creek
Rio Linda
Citrus Heights
Folsom Lake
North Highlands
Woodland
5
Fair Oaks
80
50
113
505
American River
West Sacramento
SACRAMENTO
Rancho Cordova
12
Davis
Winters
16
Florin
80
Dixon
Cosumnes River
Elk Grove
5
113
Sacramento River
Vacaville
104
13
160
TWIN CITIES RD
88
Galt
Camanche Reservoir
Mokelumne River
12
12
Rio Vista
Isleton
Woodbridge
Lockeford
0 5 mi
0 5 km
12
Lodi
88
160
99
Pittsburg
4
Antioch
Frank's Tract State Rec Area
Linden
26
©MOON.COM

1 BUCKS SUMMIT TO FEATHER RIVER (PCT)

20.0 mi one-way/2 days 3 8

at Bucks Summit Trailhead at the southern boundary of the Bucks Lake Wilderness west of Quincy

Map 5.1, page 199

It's 20 miles from Bucks Summit to Belden on the Pacific Crest Trail through the Bucks Lake Wilderness. The trailhead is at Bucks Summit (elevation 5,531 feet). From here, the route generally follows the ridgeline, climbing to the southern flank of Mount Pleasant (at 6,924 feet). Along the way, you'll see a short spur trail to little Rock Lake. The trail then heads past Three Lakes, where another spur trail provides another option, this one to Kellogg Lake. In this section, the trail passes across a granitic-based alpine area, where forest is interspersed with glacier-smoothed rock peaks. The trail then descends and, at one point, drops very sharply all the way down to 2,310 feet to the North Fork Feather River at Belden.

To continue north on the Pacific Crest Trail (PCT), see the *Feather River to Humboldt Summit (PCT)* hike, in the *Lassen and Modoc* chapter. If you are walking this trail in reverse, see the *Fowler Peak to Bucks Summit (PCT)* hike, in the *Tahoe and Northern Sierra* chapter, to continue south.

User Groups: Hikers, dogs, and horses. No mountain bikes. No wheelchair access.

Permits: A wilderness permit (free) is required. Parking and access are free.

Maps: For a map, ask the U.S. Forest Service for Plumas National Forest. For a topographic map, ask the USGS for Bucks Lake.

Directions: Take Highway 89 to Quincy and Bucks Lake Road. Turn west on Bucks Lake Road and drive about 11 miles to the trailhead, at Bucks Summit.

Contact: Plumas National Forest, Mount Hough Ranger District, Quincy, 530/283-0555, www.fs.usda.gov/plumas.

2 HARTMAN BAR NATIONAL RECREATION TRAIL

4.4 mi/3.0 hr 5 8

in Plumas National Forest northeast of Lake Oroville

Map 5.1, page 199

Hikers often pay for their pleasure. This hike involves two installments. The trail descends from the Hartman Ridge down the canyon to Hartman Bar on the Middle Fork Feather River. Going down will have your toes jamming into your boots, and the trip back can have your heart firing off like cannon shots. But waiting for you is the Middle Fork Feather, one of the prettiest streams around and with some of the best trout fishing as well. In fact, of the hundreds of trout streams in California, the Middle Fork Feather is clearly in the top five. If you don't like to fish but would rather explore farther, a footbridge crosses the stream and climbs the other side of the canyon, meeting Catrell Creek at 0.5 mile. If you want to split the trip into two days and camp, the primitive Dan Beebe Camp is available along the river.

User Groups: Hikers, dogs, and horses. A horse corral is at the trailhead. Mountain bikes not recommended. No wheelchair facilities.

Permits: No permits are required. Parking and access are free.

Maps: For a map, ask the U.S. Forest Service for Plumas National Forest. For topographic maps, ask the USGS for Cascade and Haskins Valley.

Directions: From Oroville, drive east on Highway 162 for eight miles to Highway 174/Forbestown Road (and a junction signed Challenge/LaPorte). Turn right on Forbestown Road and drive east to Highway 120 (Quincy-LaPorte Road). Turn left and drive past LaPorte to Little Grass Valley Road. Turn left and drive a short distance to Black Rock Campground. Turn left on Forest Road 94 and drive 10 miles to Forest Road 22N42Y. Turn right and drive 0.25 mile to the parking area, at the end of the road.

Contact: Plumas National Forest, Feather

River Ranger District, Oroville, 530/534-6500, www.fs.usda.gov/plumas.

3 NORTH TABLE MOUNTAIN

3.2 mi/2.5 hr 

near Lake Oroville

Map 5.1, page 199

Table Mountain, with its amazing chasms and canyon, is not a mountain at all. It is a flat-topped ridge splayed by a series of dramatic gorges and a deep canyon. In spring after a heavy rain, the aquifer here can pump enough water to create a series of waterfalls in the gorges. The trail starts from the northwest corner of the Table Mountain trailhead then travels 1.6 miles to a rim. You get a sweeping view of Mill Creek and the surrounding Land of Ishi. The top of Table Mountain is on private property and you'll see the markers. We've flown it and hiked it. If you hit it right in spring after a fresh rain, it's amazing.

User Groups: Hikers, dogs, and horses. No mountain bikes. No wheelchair facilities.

Permits: Parking and access are free.

Maps: A trail map is available for a fee from Almanor Ranger District. For a map, ask the U.S. Forest Service for Lassen National Forest or Ishi Wilderness. For topographic maps, ask the USGS for Panther Spring and Butte Meadows.

Directions: From Sacramento, take Highway 70 north to Oroville and the exit for Grand Avenue. Turn right (east) and drive one mile to Table Mountain Boulevard. Turn left on Table Mountain Boulevard and go 0.1 mile to Cherokee Road. Turn right on Cherokee Road and drive 6.3 miles to reserve. Formal access is through a small parking lot on the western side of Cherokee Road.

Contact: North Table Mountain Ecological Reserve, Department of Fish and Wildlife, Lands Program, 916/445-0411, www.wildlife.ca.gov.

4 FEATHER FALLS LOOP

9.5 mi/4.0 hr 

in Plumas National Forest east of Lake Oroville

Map 5.1, page 199 BEST

From the viewing deck, perched on a knife-edge outcrop, you can take in a full frontal of 410-foot Feather Falls. Pounding water reverberates against the high walls and thunders down the canyon. It's so perfect that it can seem surreal, like you're in a movie. The side trip to the brink of the waterfall can then snap you back into the moment. From a boulder near the rim, you can watch a churning fountain of white water surge past you through a rocky gorge, pound down a chute, and then pour over the top.

The hike is not steep or hard, just long. Right from the start, the walking is easy and rhythmic. From the trailhead, you start by sailing a short distance to a fork. Take the left fork. Just above the trail on your left, explorer types will find Indian grinding mortars in the large sandstone outcrops. You then head down the canyon, in forest, for a mile to the bridge at Frey Creek. In winter, there can be unbelievable millions of migratory ladybugs at the creek (and none the rest of the year). You then climb out of the canyon and hit the main trail. Turn left.

In short order, across the main canyon, Bald Rock Dome emerges into view. It towers over the canyon like a monolith out of Yosemite. Then ahead, you will hear the thundering crash of water before you see it. At a signed cutoff, you turn left, and ahead, can see how a bridged catwalk leads out to the viewing deck, perched on an outcrop. Then, from the platform, you get the full view of Feather Falls, top to bottom. You can see straight across the canyon and watch a silver chute gush through a gorge to the brink, then sail over the top into a white plume, feathered at the edges. Awesome.

Always go "the extra mile." From the deck, you return to the main trail. Turn left and it's a half-mile hike to the brink. Above the waterfall and along the feeder stream, you'll find several short, unsigned cutoffs down to view spots. The river pours clear and swirling through a series of pools. On a rock that overlooks the brink, the Forest Service has put up a high cyclone fence to keep people from falling over the side.

On the return trip to the parking lot, to complete the loop, stay left on the main trail at the fork (right will head down to the bridge at Frey Creek). This is an easy leg-stroker, with a pretty vantage point of upper Frey Cascade, just long.

For many years, Feather Falls was reported as 640 feet, the sixth-highest waterfall outside of Yosemite, according to an information sheet published by the U.S. Forest Service. Several waterfall hunters, including Bryan Swan, Dean Goss, and Leon Turnbull, measured it using a laser rangefinder and clinometer and verified it at 410 feet.

User Groups: Hikers and dogs. Horses and mountain bikes permitted but not recommended. No wheelchair facilities.

Permits: No permits are required. Parking and access are free.

Maps: For a map, ask the U.S. Forest Service for Plumas National Forest or Middle Fork Feather River. For a topographic map, ask the USGS for Brush Creek.

Directions: Drive to Oroville and the exit for Oro Dam Blvd./Highway 162. Take that exit and turn east on Oro Dam Blvd./Olive Highway and drive for 1.7 miles to a stoplight (signed for Olive Highway). Turn right (still Olive Highway) and drive 6.6 miles to Forbestown Road. Turn right on Forbestown Road and go 6.2 miles to Lumpkin Road. Turn left on Lumpkin and drive 11.3 miles to signed turn for Feather Falls. Turn left and drive 1.5 miles to parking, trailhead, and campground.

Contact: Plumas National Forest, Feather River Ranger District, Oroville, 530/534-6500, www.fs.usda.gov/plumas.

Feather Falls Loop

5 BULLARDS BAR TRAIL/ VISTA POINT

2 mi/1 hr 

on New Bullards Bar Reservoir in Tahoe National Forest

Map 5.1, page 199

The trailhead for Vista Point is on Vista Point Road, a short, signed spur off Marysville Road above the eastern shore of the lake. If you are driving north from the dam, you'll see it on your left. You get a pretty view across the lower end of the lake to Emerald Cove. The New Bullards Bar Trail then extends along the eastern shore of the lake. Most hike a short distance and then return. Yet get this: The Bullards Bar Trail continues and a series of trails intersect it from other access points along Marysville Road. These include Rebel Ridge Trail, 7-Ball Trail, and 8-Ball Trail.

User Groups: Hikers, dogs, horses, and mountain bikes. No wheelchair facilities.

Permits: No permits are required. Parking and access are free.

Maps: For a map, ask the U.S. Forest Service for

Tahoe National Forest. For topographic maps, ask the USGS for Camptonville and Challenge.
Directions: From Marysville, take Highway 20 east for 12 miles to Marysville Road. Turn left on Marysville Road (signed for Bullards Bar Reservoir) and drive 10 miles to Old Marysville Road. Turn right and drive 14 miles, over the dam, and continue about two miles on Marysville Road to the signed turnoff on the left for Vista Point.
Contact: Tahoe National Forest, Yuba River Ranger District, Camptonville, 530/288-3231, www.fs.usda.gov/tahoe.

6 SOUTH YUBA INDEPENDENCE TRAIL

1.0-9.0 mi/0.5-3.0 hr 1 8

near Nevada City

Map 5.1, page 199 BEST

This is a pretty river trail that is routed for 4.5 miles in and out of forest and riparian habitat with views of the Yuba River Canyon and the South Yuba River. In spring, wildflower blooms are often excellent. There are multiple trailheads for the park and trail, and the recommended trailhead is set at mid-trail along Highway 49. That gives you the option of hiking either direction. From the trailhead, hike to the west to visit Rush Creek Falls and spectacular Flume 28, one mile from the trailhead. The path was originally a canal route, built in 1859 to carry water from the Yuba to a hydraulic mining site in Smartville.

This is considered the nation's first wheelchair-accessible wilderness trail; the wheelchair-accessible portion is a seven-mile round-trip. Occasionally, guided walks and gold panning demonstrations are available.
User Groups: Hikers, dogs, and wheelchairs. No horses or mountain bikes.
Permits: No permits are necessary. Parking and access are free at this access point; $10 in season at Bridgeport; $5 in off-season.
Maps: A brochure and map are available at the trailhead or from the Bridgeport Ranger Station. For a topographic map, ask the USGS for Nevada City.
Directions: From Auburn, drive north on Highway 49 for 27 miles to Nevada City. Continue on Highway 49 for six miles past Nevada City to the trailhead parking area, along the highway on the right, located just before the South Yuba River Bridge. If you reach the bridge, you have gone too far.
Contact: South Yuba River State Park, 530/432-2546, www.parks.ca.gov.

7 NORTH BUTTE/ SUTTER BUTTES

3.0 mi/2.0 hr 3 10

at Sutter Buttes near Yuba City

Map 5.1, page 199

From a lava pinnacle atop the Smallest Mountain Range in the World, you get a hawk's-eye view of land few have seen. This is at the Sutter Buttes, about an hour north of Sacramento, one of California's last lands of mystery. Since it is surrounded by private property, few have trekked the Sutter Buttes and almost no one has seen Peace Valley, new state land that could become a park. To hike the Sutter Buttes, the access is with guided group walks with Middle Mountain Interpretive Hikes, sponsored by the Sutter Buttes Land Trust—great folks and well worth it.

The best trip is a three-mile round-trip hike to the North Butte. It starts as an easy walk, meandering up through a valley to a sub-ridge. A short way in, you will see an Indian grinding rock along a dry creekbed where ancient mortars have been hollowed out in the stone. From here, hike up the valley. It's common to spot red-tailed hawks, vultures, harriers, and deer. The lucky few see foxes, bobcats, owls, or golden eagles. You then break out above the valley. You face a 1,000-foot climb, something of an off-trail butt-kicker for the last half mile amid the volcanic crags, scree, and brush for the final push to the summit. You top out at 1,863-foot North Butte. From the summit, you can scan across multiple peaks, crowned by the South Butte at 2,117 feet. Despite some 40 million people living in California, only a scant few know this experience.

The Maidu called the Sutter Buttes "Esto Yamini," which means "Middle Mountain," and that's how the foundation got its name. Trips are best in fall, winter, and early spring. Some may also wonder how the Sutter Buttes qualifies as "The Smallest Mountain Range in the World." The answer is that land has to have an elevation of at least 2,000 feet to qualify as a mountain. At 2,117 feet, the Sutter Buttes just barely make the grade as a mountain range. The only trail access is through guided trips arranged with the Middle Mountain Foundation.

User Groups: Hikers only. No dogs, horses, or mountain bikes. No wheelchair facilities.

Permits: Advance reservations for guided group hikes are required at 530/671-6116. Most trips cost $35 (suggested donation). Roughly 10-20 participants are allowed on most hikes.

Maps: A brochure and map are available from trip leaders upon meeting at the Sutter County Museum.

Directions: Hiking groups meet at the Sutter County Museum in Yuba City. Directions are provided when the reservation is confirmed. After orientation, drivers will lead the route past several locked gates to the trailhead in Sutter Buttes.

Contact: Organized hike information, 530/671-6116, www.middlemountainhikes.org; Sutter Buttes Land Trust, Yuba City, 530/755-3568.

8 FAIRY FALLS LOOP

5.0 mi/2.5 hr

in Spenceville Wildlife Area near Smartville

Map 5.1, page 199

Fair Falls is a pretty spot of surprise in the foothills of the Sacramento Valley. The falls are called Shingle Falls, Fairy Falls, Dry Creek Falls, and Beale Falls. By any name, it is a striking destination in the oak woodlands east of Lincoln. From the parking area and trailhead, walk across a worn-out bridge to a fire road. Turn right on the fire road and walk a short distance to a fork. For the recommended five-mile loop, turn left. It's a steady climb to a ridge, and in hot weather, rates a 3, not a 2. You'll continue to a junction, where you turn right (there is a small sign) under a grove, through a gate, and you'll continue down toward the bottom of a gorge to a rock-edge view of the Upper Falls. Downstream, about 100 yards, you'll find a smaller waterfall. Rock trekkers can climb down to the plunge pool. There's also some swimming/wading holes along the stream.

To return, a road is routed right along the river, downstream, and reaches the fork/road junction. Turn left and it's a short distance back to the old bridge, which you cross again to reach parking. The best time to visit is from December through April, when the hills are saturated, the aquifer is flushed, and the waterfall is pumping. My dogs, from little Bart-Dog, as a puppy, to Buddy the golden, as a senior citizen, have always loved every trip here. Wild turkeys are common sightings. In turkey season, the Department of Fish and Wildlife conducts a permit system for turkey hunting, and hiking is not permitted. Seasonal hunting may be permitted for other species September-January.

User Groups: Hikers and dogs. Horses and mountain bikes not allowed on this trail. Horses allowed on marked trails and service roads elsewhere in the wildlife area. Mountain bikes are allowed only on service roads. No wheelchair facilities.

Permits: No permits are necessary. Parking and access are free. Organized groups must obtain a free permit.

Maps: Free maps of Spenceville Wildlife Area are available at information signposts in the refuge. For a topographic map, ask the USGS for Camp Far West.

Directions: From Marysville, take Highway

20 east for 15 miles to Smartville Road (just east and opposite a CDF fire station). Turn right (south) on Smartville Road and enter the wildlife area. At 0.9 mile, bear left at a fork (the road is signed Chuck Yeager) and continue about four miles to Waldo Road (gravel). Turn left on Waldo Road and drive 2.1 miles to Spenceville Road. Turn left and drive two miles to the end of the road, at a closed bridge. Park, walk across the bridge, and begin the hike.

Contact: Spenceville Wildlife Area, c/o Oroville Wildlife Area, Department of Fish and Wildlife, Oroville, 530/538-2236, www.wildlife.ca.gov.

9 HIDDEN FALLS LOOP

5.1 mi/2.25 hr

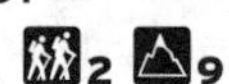

Hidden Falls Regional Park near Auburn

Map 5.2, page 200

This is a great hike for people who love canyons with rushing water. This loop includes a trail along two separate creeks, their confluences, two waterfalls, and several gorgeous pools. From the parking area, look for the picnic table near the trailhead. Turn right and take the Poppy Trail down into the ravine, following several switchbacks for one mile. After arriving at Deadman Creek, walk over a bridge that leads to a service road and continue a short distance to the Blue Oak Loop Trail on the right. The Blue Oak Loop Trail will route you 0.5-mile up canyon and then left up a short ridge, where you will cross a road. Continue straight for 0.7 mile on the Seven Pools Vista down to a lookout (the trail turns sharply left) over Coon Creek. Continue along Coon Creek, where junctions with the Seven Pools Loop and the Canyon View Trail appear in about one mile. Continue past Canyon View Falls, the Canyon View Bridge, and beyond to a spur on the right for Hidden Falls. Return by hiking up the Hidden Falls Access Trail and climbing out on Poppy Trail. This is one of the best trips in the Sierra foothills.

User Groups: Hikers, dogs, horses, and mountain bikes. A short trail near parking is partially wheelchair accessible.

Permits: Reservations for parking ($8 for full day, $4 for partial day) are required for all weekends, plus holidays and other high-volume use days. Reserve at www.placer.ca.gov. On weekdays, parking and access are free. A webcam showing parking lot and adjacent dirt parking area is available at https://www.placer.ca.gov/2623/Webcam

Maps: A trail map is posted at billboard near trailhead and is available online.

Directions: Take I-80 to Auburn and the exit for Highway 49 North. Turn north and drive 2.8 miles (get in left lane) to Atwood. Turn left at Atwood and drive 17 miles to Mount Vernon Road. Continue straight on Mount Vernon Road for 2.7 miles to Mears Drive. Turn right on Mears and drive one mile (turning left) to the park entrance.

Contact: Hidden Falls Regional Park, Placer County Parks and Recreation, 530/886-4901, www.placer.ca.gov.

10 CODFISH CREEK TRAIL

3.0 mi/1.5 hr

in Auburn State Recreation Area

Map 5.2, page 200

The Codfish Creek Trail follows an old mining route downstream along the North Fork American River, then cuts up the canyon of Codfish Creek. The highlight here is 60-foot Codfish Falls. The trail begins at the north side of the bridge, on Ponderosa Way, and heads downstream on sunny and exposed slopes. The path brings visitors to a series of cascades on Codfish Creek. At 1.2 miles, the trail turns right and leads upstream along Codfish Creek, heading away from the river, for canyon views. In March, April, and early May, you get the triple bonus of a full-flowing waterfall, lots of blooming wildflowers, and big canyon views.

User Groups: Hikers and dogs. No horses or mountain bikes. No wheelchair facilities.

Permits: No permits are necessary. Parking and access are free.

Maps: For a national forest map, which includes Auburn State Recreation Area lands, ask the U.S. Forest Service for Tahoe National Forest. For a topographic map, ask the USGS for Colfax.

Directions: From Sacramento, take I-80 east for 40 miles (past Auburn) to Weimar and the Weimar Crossroad exit. Take that exit, then a right at the fork off the off-ramp at Canyon Way (which becomes Ponderosa Way) and drive 5.5 miles (the road turns to dirt) to a bridge at the American River. Park near the bridge on the south side of the road (the side closest to the river) and look for the trailhead on the north side of the bridge; the trail heads downstream past the beach area. A high-clearance vehicle is recommended and four-wheel drive is helpful.

Contact: Auburn State Recreation Area, Auburn, 530/885-4527, www.parks.ca.gov.

11 RIVERBANK TRAIL

3.5 mi/2.0 hr 1 7

at Dry Creek Community Park near Roseville

Map 5.2, page 200

This local park provides a quick respite in Roseville. The trail runs along pretty Dry Creek, the centerpiece of Dry Creek Community Park. After significant rains in early spring, the riparian zone glows neon green as the creek forms a pretty stream. At the start, look for a paved bike trail and a dirt hiking trail. Turn right for the dirt trail routed toward Dry Creek. In the first stretch, you will walk near the river and past pools. You then get routed away from the creek, eventually arriving near a golf course on the right; continue a bit farther to a spur trail downstream. This park has a basketball court, tennis courts, and a pavilion. The Riverbank Trail is more of a walk than a hike.

User Groups: Hikers, dogs, and horses. A separate paved path is provided for bikes and wheelchairs.

Permits: Parking and access are free.

Maps: A trail map is posted at the park.

Directions: From Sacramento, take I-80 east to Exit 98 (near Citrus Heights) for Greenback Lane. Take that exit for 0.3 mile and get in one of the two left lanes to access Greenback Lane. Turn left and go 0.1 mile and then continue onto Elkhorn Boulevard for 1.7 miles to Walerga Road. Turn right and drive 2.8 miles to the park.

Contact: Dry Creek Community Park, Placer County Parks and Recreation, 530/886-4901, www.placer.ca.gov.

12 AMERICAN RIVER PARKWAY

0.25-32.0 mi one-way/0.5 hr-2 days

1 7

along the American River from Sacramento to Folsom

Map 5.2, page 200 BEST

The American River Parkway and Jedediah Smith Memorial Trail is the famous paved 32-mile path along the American River that links Folsom Lake on downstream past Fair Oaks, Rancho Cordova, and Sac State en route to Old Town Sacramento and Discovery Park. More than five million people use this trail every year. We admit this is the one trail we did not hike at all, but rather rode it out on a bike, a one-day trip with a shuttle car. There are 15 access points for short walks with river views. The prettiest stretch spans from Folsom Lake down past the dam into a riparian zone toward Nimbus.

Spring and fall are when the American River is prettiest. In spring, the trees and grass are green, the water is rolling fresh, and by May, schools of shad are swimming upstream. Come autumn, the leaves of the adjacent trees turn bright colors, lighting up the river. In the

American River

intervening summer months, 100-degree temperatures keep trail use low during the day, but when evening shade emerges, so do joggers and walkers. Walkers and joggers should stay off the paved portion, and should instead use the dirt trail or the shoulder of the bike trail.

Access: Inline skates or roller skates are allowed on the state park and county park portions of trail. The state park portion is two separate trails most of the route, but a 0.5-mile section is shared. All nine miles of state trail are paved, and wheelchairs are allowed. Elsewhere, wheelchairs are allowed on the actual trail, and wheelchair-accessible restrooms, fishing areas, and picnic grounds are available along the way. In addition, our experience was less than stellar on the lower portions of the parkway, downstream of the suspension bridge for the college, with a quite a few homeless, some of whom apparently felt that passing cyclists were an invasion force from another planet.

User Groups: Hikers, dogs, mountain bikes, inline skates, roller skates, and horses allowed, but horses are not advised. (See the note about restrictions for mountain bikes and hikers.)

Permits: No permits are required. Folsom Lake State Recreation Area at the head of the parkway charges a fee of $12 per vehicle at Beals Point; $10 at other state park access areas.

Maps: A trail map is available for a fee at the county parks department. For topographic maps, ask the USGS for Sacramento East, Carmichael, Citrus Heights, and Folsom.

Directions: The trail begins at Folsom Lake Recreation Area and ends at Discovery Park in Sacramento. From Sacramento, take U.S. 50 east for 18.4 miles to Exit 23 for Folsom Boulevard. Take that exit, go 0.2 mile, then bear left to take the ramp toward Folsom and Folsom Boulevard. Turn left on Folsom Boulevard and drive 3.6 miles, then continue straight (becomes Folsom-Auburn Boulevard) and go 2.0 miles to the park entrance. Park near the boat ramp.

Contact: American River Parkway Foundation, 916/486-2773, https://arpf.org; County of Sacramento, Parks and Recreation Division, Park Ranger Section, rangers, 916/875-7275, www.regionalparks.saccounty.net; Folsom Lake State Recreation Area, 916/988-0205, www.parks.ca.gov.

13 COSUMNES RIVER TRAIL

3.3 mi/2.0 hr 1 8

in Cosumnes River Preserve near Galt

Map 5.2, page 200

The marsh comes to life at dawn and dusk. The River Walk Trail is an easy 3.3-mile trip from start to finish to capture the best of it. The walk is nearly flat and routed amid the preserve's diversity of habitats: wetlands, cottonwood-willow riparian forests, grasslands, buttonbush thickets, valley oak savanna and the river corridor. Time it right and you have the chance to see birds and wildlife. The habitat changes quickly, so if you want to see wildlife, be ready. Bring binoculars and keep quiet; young adults who shout and hoot have about as much chance at sighting a sandhill crane as a polar bear in the desert. In winters with heavy rain, the trail can flood and become impassable. The Cosumnes River flows through one of the richest landscapes in the Delta, a mix of wetlands, riparian woodlands, river cuts, and sloughs that provides habitat for thousands of waterfowl, songbirds, hawks, and falcons. Coyotes, foxes, raccoons, otters, rabbits, and deer are common sightings. This is a great getaway for bird- and wildlife-watching, driving tours, easy walks, and hand-powered boating—either bring your own kayak or canoe or book a kayak trip with an outfitter. Free, guided walking tours are also available.

User Groups: Hikers only. No mountain bikes, dogs, or horses.

Permits: No permits are necessary. Parking and access are free; donations accepted.

Maps: A brochure and map are available at the visitors center.

Directions from Antioch: From Antioch, take Highway 160 (signed for Stockton/Rio Vista) and drive for 18.8 miles to Isleton (becomes Isleton Rd.) and continue eight miles to River Road (cross the bridge at Georgiana Slough). Turn right on River Road and drive (becomes Walnut Grove-Thornton Road) eight miles to Thornton (just after you cross I-5) and Thornton Road. Turn left on Thornton Road and drive 2.3 miles (you will cross a bridge over the Mokelumne River, becomes Franklin) and continue 0.7 mile to the preserve entrance on right (signed). Turn right and continue short distance to visitors center.

Directions from Sacramento: From Sacramento, take I-5 south to the Twin Cities Road exit (marked with a binoculars sign for wildlife viewing, about midway between Stockton and Sacramento). Take the Twin Cities Road exit and go east for exactly one mile, to the first stop sign at Franklin. Turn right on Franklin and drive 1.7 miles. Look for the visitors center on the left side of Franklin and park in the parking lot just past it.

Directions from Stockton: From Stockton, take I-5 north to the Thornton-Walnut Grove Road exit. Take that exit and go east to Thornton Road (just after a gas station). Turn left on Thornton and drive two miles (it becomes Franklin Blvd.) and continue over the Thornton-Franklin Bridge to parking and the visitors center.

Contact: Cosumnes River Preserve, Galt, 916/684-2816, www.cosumnes.org.

TAHOE AND NORTHERN SIERRA

Mount Tallac affords a view across Lake Tahoe like no other: a cobalt-blue expanse of water bordered by mountains that span miles of Sierra wildlands. The Tahoe area has a wide range of scenic hikes with access to hundreds of lakes. The best for scenic beauty are Echo Lakes, Donner, Fallen Leaf, Sardine, Caples, Loon, and Union Valley. The north end of the Northern Sierra starts near Bucks Lake and extends to Bear River Canyon. In between are the Lakes Basin Recreation Area in southern Plumas County, the Crystal Basin in the Sierra foothills west of Tahoe, Lake Davis near Portola, and the Carson River Canyon and Hope Valley south of Tahoe. It's true that people come here in droves, but if you're willing to hunt a bit, there are trails you can share with only chipmunks.

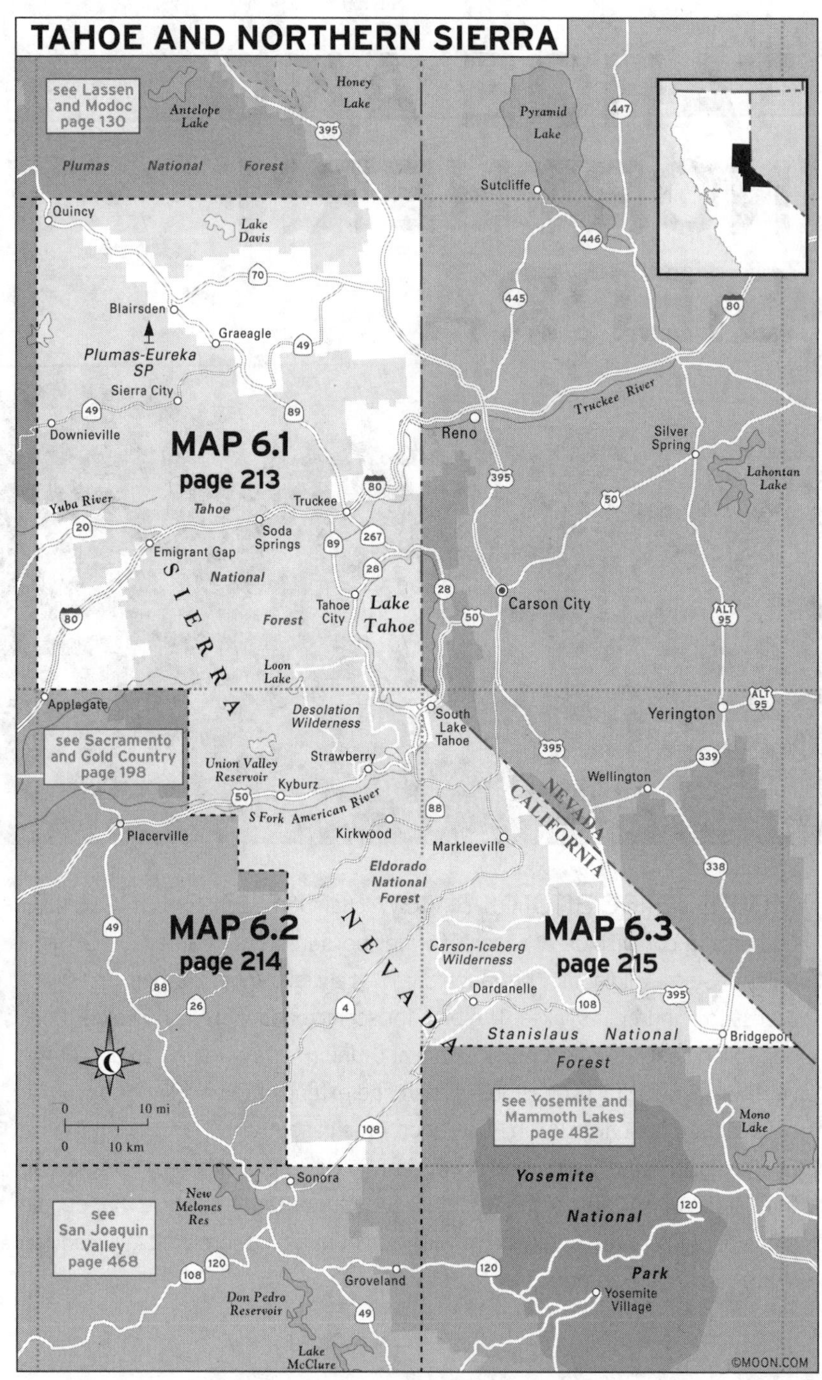
TAHOE AND NORTHERN SIERRA
see Lassen and Modoc page 130
Antelope Lake
Honey Lake
Pyramid Lake
Plumas National Forest
Sutcliffe
Quincy
Lake Davis
Blairsden
Graeagle
Plumas-Eureka SP
Sierra City
Downieville
MAP 6.1 page 213
Reno
Truckee River
Silver Spring
Lahontan Lake
Yuba River
Tahoe
Truckee
Soda Springs
Emigrant Gap
National
Carson City
Tahoe City
Lake Tahoe
Forest
SIERRA
Loon Lake
Applegate
Desolation Wilderness
South Lake Tahoe
Yerington
see Sacramento and Gold Country page 198
Union Valley Reservoir
Strawberry
Kyburz
Wellington
NEVADA
CALIFORNIA
S Fork American River
Placerville
Kirkwood
Markleeville
Eldorado National Forest
NEVADA
MAP 6.2 page 214
MAP 6.3 page 215
Carson-Iceberg Wilderness
Dardanelle
Stanislaus National Forest
Bridgeport
see Yosemite and Mammoth Lakes page 482
Mono Lake
0 10 mi
0 10 km
Sonora
New Melones Res
Yosemite National Park
see San Joaquin Valley page 468
Groveland
Yosemite Village
Don Pedro Reservoir
Lake McClure
©MOON.COM

Map 6.1

Sites 1-44
Pages 216-244

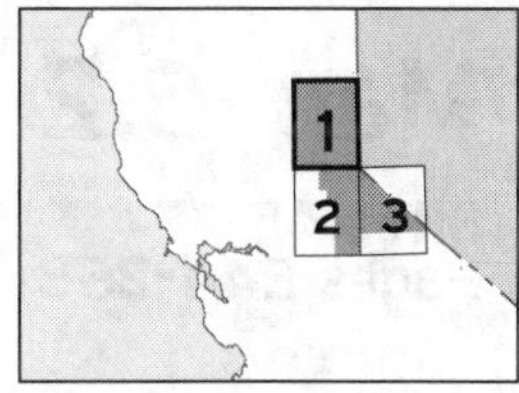

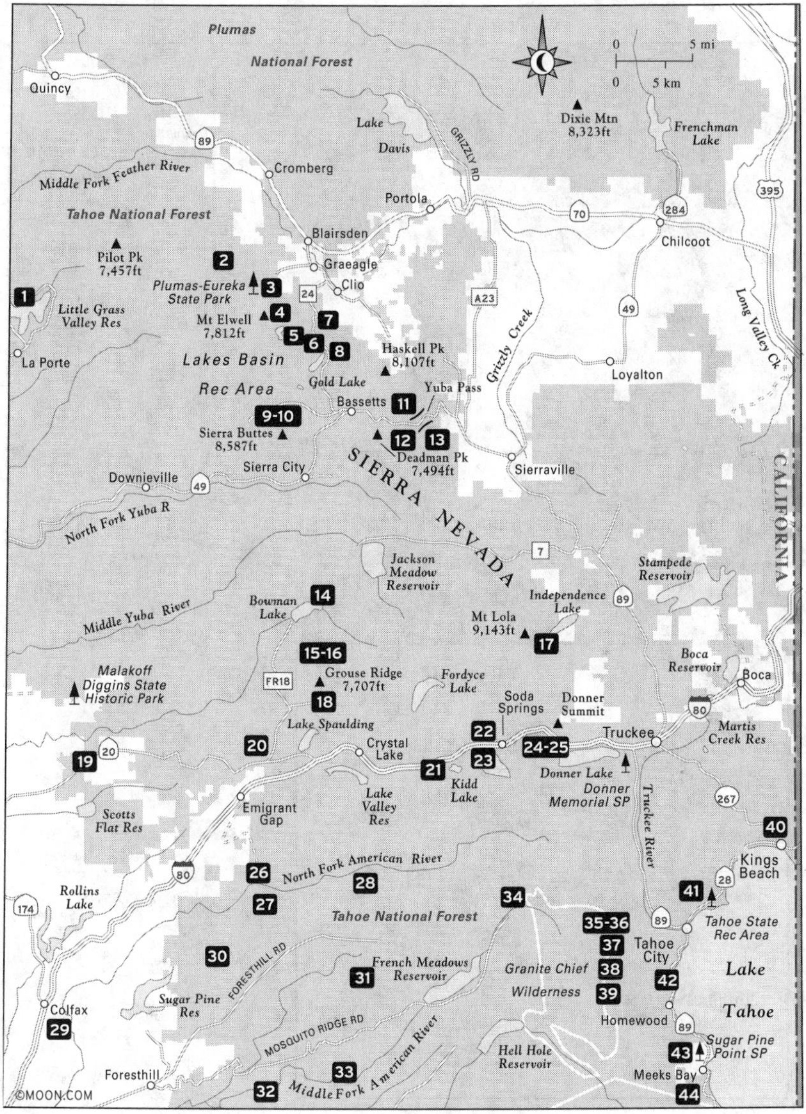

Plumas
National Forest
0 5 mi
0 5 km
Quincy
Lake
Davis
Grizzly Rd
Dixie Mtn
8,323ft
Frenchman
Lake
89
Middle Fork Feather River
Cromberg
Portola
395
Tahoe National Forest
70
284
Chilcoot
Blairsden
Pilot Pk
7,457ft
2
Graeagle
Plumas-Eureka State Park
3
Clio
24
A23
1
Little Grass Valley Res
Mt Elwell
7,812ft
4
7
Grizzly Creek
49
Long Valley Ck
5
6
8
La Porte
Lakes Basin
Rec Area
Haskell Pk
8,107ft
Loyalton
Gold Lake
Yuba Pass
Bassetts
11
9-10
Sierra Buttes
8,587ft
12
13
Deadman Pk
7,494ft
Sierra City
Sierraville
Downieville
49
Sierra Nevada
California
North Fork Yuba R
7
Jackson Meadow Reservoir
Stampede Reservoir
Bowman Lake
14
Independence Lake
89
Middle Yuba River
Mt Lola
9,143ft
17
15-16
Boca Reservoir
Malakoff Diggins State Historic Park
Grouse Ridge
7,707ft
Fordyce Lake
Boca
FR18
18
Soda Springs
Donner Summit
80
Lake Spaulding
Martis Creek Res
22
Truckee
20
Crystal Lake
24-25
19
20
23
21
Donner Lake
Kidd Lake
Donner Memorial SP
Lake Valley Res
267
Scotts Flat Res
Emigrant Gap
Truckee River
40
Kings Beach
26
North Fork American River
80
28
Rollins Lake
41
28
174
34
27
Tahoe National Forest
35-36
89
Tahoe State Rec Area
37
Tahoe City
30
Foresthill Rd
French Meadows Reservoir
Granite Chief
38
Lake
31
42
Wilderness
39
Tahoe
Sugar Pine Res
Colfax
Homewood
29
Mosquito Ridge Rd
89
Middle Fork American River
Hell Hole Reservoir
Sugar Pine Point SP
43
33
Foresthill
Meeks Bay
32
44

Map 6.2

Sites 45-77
Pages 244-268

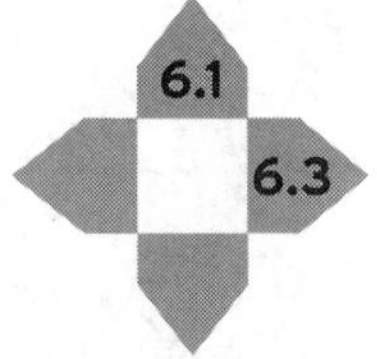

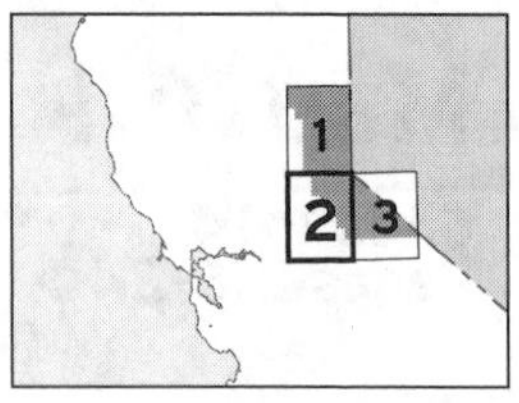

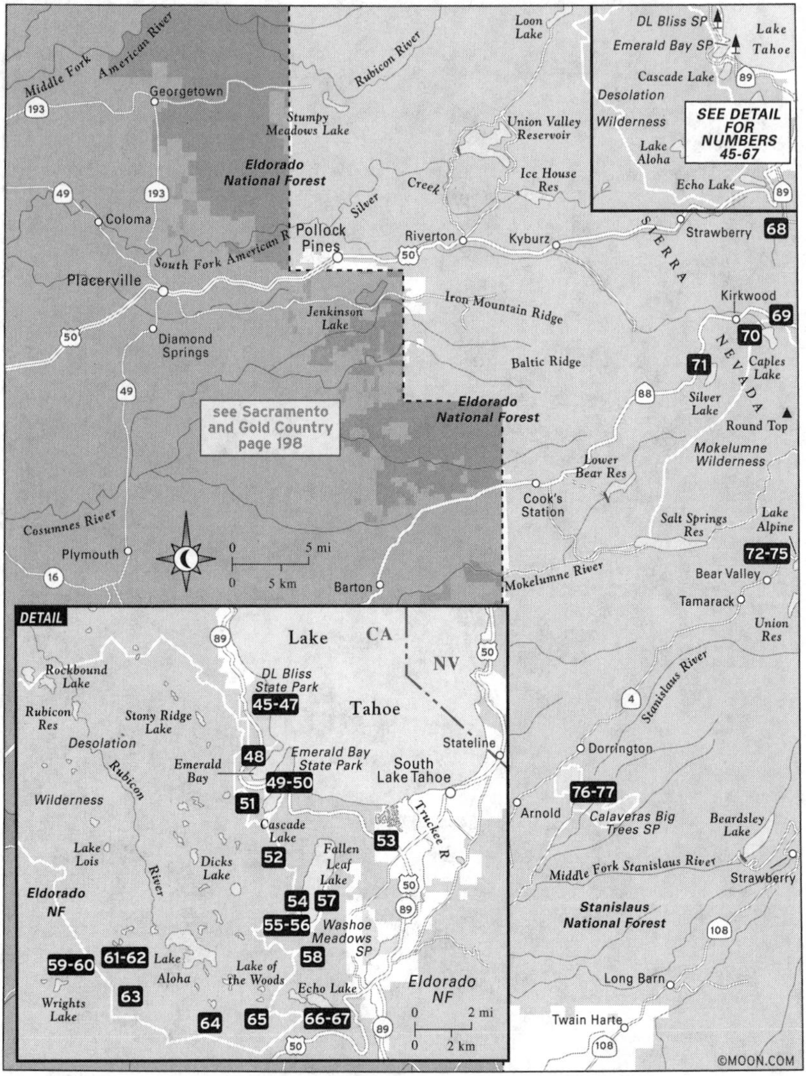

see Sacramento and Gold Country page 198

SEE DETAIL FOR NUMBERS 45-67

Map 6.3

Sites 78-103
Pages 268-285

6.2

1
2
3

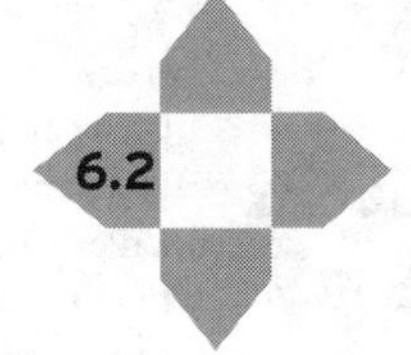

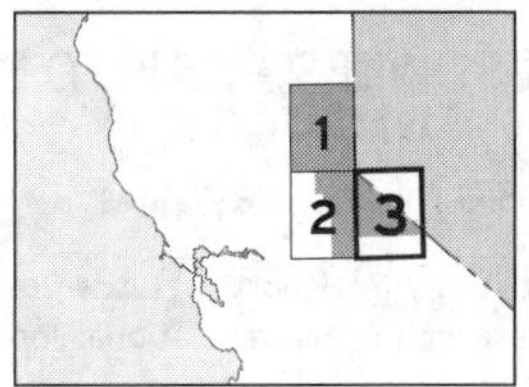

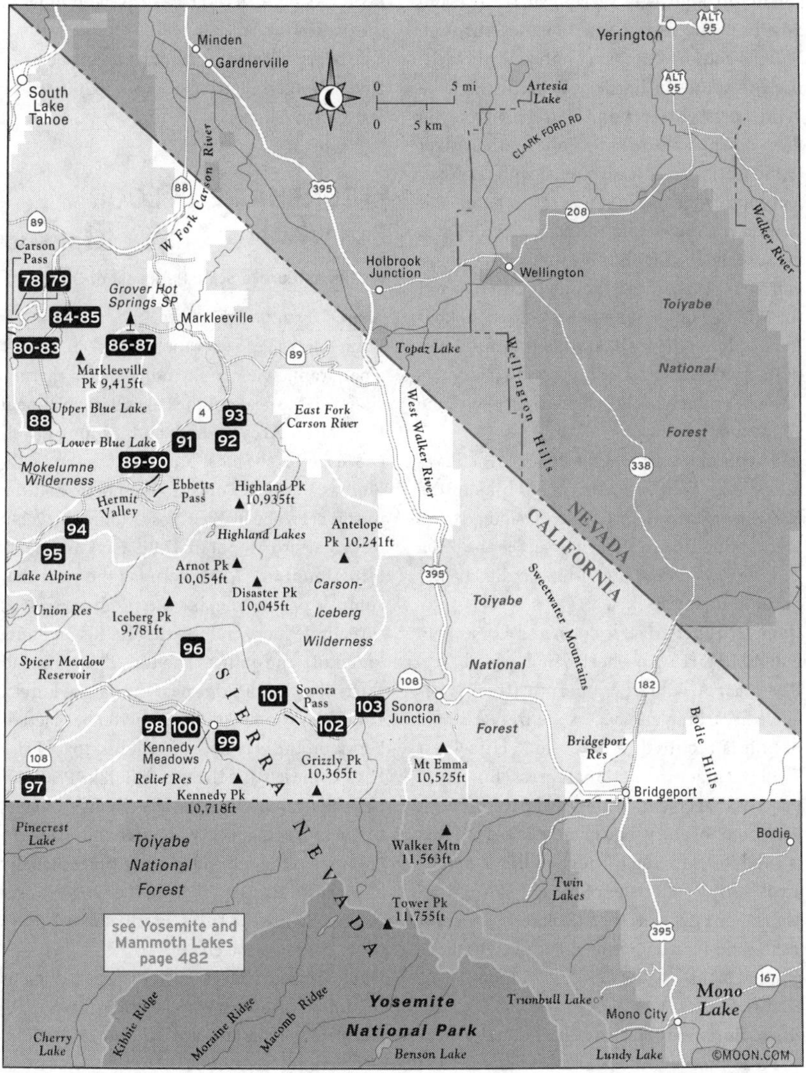

Minden
Gardnerville
Yerington
ALT 95
South Lake Tahoe
0 5 mi
0 5 km
Artesia Lake
CLARK FORD RD
W Fork Carson River
88
395
208
89
Carson Pass
78
79
Holbrook Junction
Wellington
Walker River
Grover Hot Springs SP
84-85
Markleeville
80-83
86-87
Topaz Lake
Wellington Hills
Toiyabe
National
Forest
Markleeville Pk 9,415ft
89
Upper Blue Lake
88
4
93
East Fork Carson River
West Walker River
Lower Blue Lake
91
92
89-90
Mokelumne Wilderness
Ebbetts Pass
Hermit Valley
Highland Pk 10,935ft
338
94
Highland Lakes
Antelope Pk 10,241ft
NEVADA
CALIFORNIA
95
Lake Alpine
Arnot Pk 10,054ft
Disaster Pk 10,045ft
Carson-Iceberg Wilderness
Sweetwater Mountains
Toiyabe
National
Forest
Union Res
Iceberg Pk 9,781ft
96
Spicer Meadow Reservoir
SIERRA
108
182
101
Sonora Pass
103
Sonora Junction
Bodie Hills
98
100
102
Kennedy Meadows
99
Bridgeport Res
108
Grizzly Pk 10,365ft
Mt Emma 10,525ft
Relief Res
Kennedy Pk 10,718ft
97
Bridgeport
Pinecrest Lake
Toiyabe
National
Forest
NEVADA
Walker Mtn 11,563ft
Bodie
Twin Lakes
Tower Pk 11,755ft
see Yosemite and Mammoth Lakes page 482
395
167
Kibbie Ridge
Moraine Ridge
Macomb Ridge
Yosemite
National Park
Trumbull Lake
Mono City
Mono Lake
Cherry Lake
Benson Lake
Lundy Lake
©MOON.COM

1 FOWLER PEAK TO BUCKS SUMMIT (PCT)

26.0 mi one-way/3 days 

at Fowler Peak north of Little Grass Valley Reservoir in Plumas National Forest

Map 6.1, page 213

Most Pacific Crest Trail (PCT) hikers will sprint through this section of trail. From Fowler Peak trailhead, it passes through Plumas National Forest country until reaching the southern border of the Bucks Lake Wilderness. It starts quite nicely, where you drop down to the Middle Fork Feather River (3,180 feet), a great trout stream with an excellent footbridge to get you across a gorge. We suggest you linger here and soak it in. Enjoy it, because the rest of this route won't exactly have you writing postcards home. It climbs from the Middle Fork Feather to 6,955-foot Lookout Rock, a long, dry pull, and then drops down to Bucks Creek. Most of this region is dry rattlesnake country, so watch your step, and time your water stops.

To continue north on the PCT, see the *Bucks Summit to Feather River (PCT)* hike in the *Sacramento and Gold Country* chapter. If you are walking this trail in reverse, see the *Yuba River to Fowler Peak (PCT)* hike in this chapter to continue south.

User Groups: Hikers, dogs, and horses. No mountain bikes. No wheelchair access.

Permits: A wilderness permit (free) is required. Parking and access are free. A single permit is required to hike the Pacific Crest Trail. Contact the national forest, Bureau of Land Management, or national park office at your point of entry for a combined permit that is good for traveling through multiple-permit areas during your dates of travel.

Maps: For a map, ask the U.S. Forest Service for Tahoe and Plumas National Forests. For topographic maps, ask the USGS for Onion Valley, Dogwood Peak, and Bucks Lake.

Directions: From Oroville, take Highway 162 east for eight miles to Highway 174 (Forbestown Road and the junction signed Challenge/LaPorte). Turn right on Forbestown Road and drive east to Highway 120/Quincy-LaPorte Road. Turn left and drive past LaPorte to Little Grass Valley Road. Turn left on Little Grass Valley Road and drive to Black Rock Campground and Forest Road 94. Bear left on Forest Road 94 and drive three miles to Forest Road 22N27. Turn right and drive four miles to the parking area.

Contact: Plumas National Forest, Feather River Ranger District, 530/534-6500, www.fs.usda.gov/plumas.

2 EUREKA PEAK LOOP

3.0 mi/2.0 hr 3 10

in Plumas-Eureka State Park east of Quincy

Map 6.1, page 213

From Eureka Peak (elevation 7,447 feet), you get a panoramic view of the north Sierra that includes all the peaks of the Lakes Basin National Recreation Area and beyond. Mount Elwell (7,818 feet) is the most prominent to the south, Plumas National Forest to the north, and the west is crowned by Blue Nose Mountain (7,290 feet), Stafford Mountain (7,019 feet), and Beartrap Mountain (7,232 feet). It's the vista that compels people to make the climb—a serious three-mile loop, and the first half is an hour-long huff-and-puff to the top. The trailhead starts at a parking area near the dam at Eureka Lake (elevation 6,300 feet). If you bear left at a fork on the way up, you will hike past False Peak to the left and then up to Eureka Peak and can turn it into a loop. It then climbs 1,150 feet to the top. Bring plenty of water and snacks to enjoy from the summit. At rare times (usually at night for illegal campers), the ranger closes the gate to Eureka Lake, which adds 1.2 miles to the hike on each end.

User Groups: Hikers only. No dogs, horses, or mountain bikes. No wheelchair facilities.

Permits: No permits are required, $8 day-use and parking fee.

Maps: A brochure and trail map is available for a fee from Plumas-Eureka State Park. For a topographic map, ask the USGS for Johnsville.
Directions: From Sacramento, take I-80 east for 97 miles to Truckee and the exit for Donner Pass Road/Highway 89 North. Follow that exit to the traffic circle, then take the second exit for 0.2 mile to another traffic circle. Take the third exit on that traffic circle to Highway 89 and drive 22.6 miles to Sierraville and a junction for Highway 49/Highway 89 (signed for Quincy/Downieville). Turn left (signed 49/89) and drive 4.9 miles to a turnoff for Highway 89. Turn right on Highway 89 and drive 17 miles to Johnsville Road. Turn left and drive 5.1 miles to Johnsville-McCrea Road. Turn left and drive 0.5 mile to the park entrance. From the kiosk, continue to the parking area; the trailhead is near the dam at Eureka Lake.
Contact: Plumas-Eureka State Park, 530/836-2380, www.parks.ca.gov.

3 GRASS LAKE TRAIL/ LITTLE JAMISON CREEK

3.8 mi/2.5 hr 2 8

in Plumas-Eureka State Park east of Quincy

Map 6.1, page 213

Your payoff destinations include pretty little Jamison Lake and several ghost town structures from the mining days.

From the trailhead at the Jamison Mine building, take the Grass Lake Trail. It follows along Little Jamison Creek. You'll find a short spur trail to Little Jamison Falls. That's a must-do, of course. Back on the trail, you will climb 1.75 miles to Grass Lake. The trail skirts the east side of the lake. For those on a day hike, this is far enough: a good trail from a historic site, a waterfall, a lake, and a picnic.

You can forge onward. It's another two miles to Jamison Lake, and with the trail climbing more steeply you can continue to spur trails for several lakes—Rock, Jamison, and Smith Lakes—and beyond to other nearby trails listed in the section. That includes Smith Lake and Mount Elwell. Note that the first half mile of trail is within the state park, and the remainder is in Plumas National Forest.
User Groups: Hikers, dogs, horses, and mountain bikes. No wheelchair facilities.
Permits: No permits are required; $8 day use and parking.
Maps: A brochure with trail map is available for a fee from Plumas-Eureka State Park. For a topographic map, ask the USGS for Johnsville.
Directions: From Sacramento, take I-80 east for 97 miles to Truckee and the exit for Donner Pass Road/Highway 89 North. Follow that exit to the traffic circle, then take the second exit for 0.2 mile to another traffic circle. Take the third exit on that traffic circle to Highway 89 and drive 22.6 miles to Sierraville and a junction for Highway 49/Highway 89 (signed for Quincy/Downieville). Turn left (signed 49/89) and drive 4.9 miles to a turnoff for Highway 89. Turn right on Highway 89 and drive 17 miles to Johnsonville Road. Turn left on Johnsonville Road and drive 4.6 miles to Jamison Mine Road. Turn left and drive 0.7 mile to the Jamison Mine Complex. The trailhead starts at the far end of the parking lot.
Contact: Plumas-Eureka State Park, 530/836-2380, www.parks.ca.gov.

4 MOUNT ELWELL TRAIL

10.4 mi/6 hr 4 10

at Smith Lake in Lakes Basin National Recreation Area south of Quincy

Map 6.1, page 213

This is one of the great off-the-radar hikes in the north Sierra. From atop Mount Elwell (7,818 feet), you're surrounded by the Lakes Basin National Recreation Area, a wildland filled with alpine lakes and granite peaks. You'll find yourself dreaming of the days when you might visit them. There are multiple ways to approach Mount Elwell. The Smith Lake trailhead is an excellent choice (many believe the best trailhead is at Lake Basin Campground near site 15, while others leave from Gray Eagle Lodge via Long Lake). Plan for a 5.2-mile trek one-way with a challenging 2,000-foot-plus elevation gain in two climbs; 5,720 feet to 7,818 feet. From the Smith Lake trailhead, head out for 0.8 mile to a junction with the Mount Elwell Trail on the left. The trail climbs through forest, passes Maiden Lake, and then gets even steeper as it rises up the flank of Elwell. The final ascent is a panorama you'll never forget. Long Lake sits at the foot of Mount Elwell and is one of the prettiest lakes in the region. You can return the way you came for a 10.4-mile day, or turn it into a 7.2-mile loop by instead steeply descending to the Long Lake Trail. Another route (see next listing) is available on the Long Lake Trail.

User Groups: Hikers, dogs, mountain bikes, and horses. No wheelchair facilities. No mountain bikes permitted on Pacific Crest Trail.

Permits: No permits are required. Parking and access are free.

Maps: A trail map is available for a fee at the Beckwourth Ranger District. For a map, ask the U.S. Forest Service for Plumas National Forest. For a topographic map, ask the USGS for Gold Lake.

Directions: From Sacramento, take I-80 east for 97 miles to Truckee and the exit for Donner Pass Road/Highway 89 North. Follow that exit to the traffic circle, then take the second exit for 0.2 mile to another traffic circle. Take the third exit on that traffic circle to Highway 89 and drive 22.6 miles to Sierraville and a junction for Highway 49/Highway 89 (signed for Quincy/Downieville). Turn left (signed 49/89) and drive 4.9 miles to a turnoff for Highway 89. Turn right on Highway 89 and drive 15.3 miles to the Gold Lake Highway. Turn left on the Gold Lake Highway and drive five miles to the sign for Gray Eagle Lodge. Turn right and drive 0.4 mile to a fork. Bear right a short distance to Smith Lake and the trailhead.

Contact: Plumas National Forest, Beckwourth Ranger District, 530/836-2575, www.fs.usda.gov/plumas.

5 LONG LAKE

2.5 mi/1.5 hr 

north of Sierra City

Map 6.1, page 213

Long Lake is a celestial-level setting in the heavenly Lakes Basin National Recreation Area. It's big, gorgeous, often cobalt blue, and nestled at the foot of Mount Elwell. The trailhead for this hike is at the Lakes Basin Campground (elevation 6,300 feet) near site 15. From here, the trail is clear and well maintained but requires a short huff-and-puff of a mile. Here you'll see the turnoff for a 0.25-mile spur trail to Long Lake. The trail skirts along the southeast shoreline. For an easy walk and a trail picnic at a gorgeous destination, this is it.

Most hikers will want to continue on to several other lakes and destinations nearby. It is one mile to little Silver Lake, 0.75 mile to Cub Lake, and another 0.5 mile to Little Bear and Big Bear Lakes. You can also connect to the Mount Elwell Trail.

Camping is permitted only at the Lakes Basin Campground. No camping is permitted at either Long or Silver Lakes.

User Groups: Hikers, dogs, mountain bikes, and horses. No wheelchair facilities. No mountain bikes permitted on Pacific Crest Trail.

Permits: No permits are required. Parking and access are free.

Maps: A trail map is available for a fee at the Beckwourth Ranger District. For a map, ask the U.S. Forest Service for Plumas National Forest. For a topographic map, ask the USGS for Gold Lake.

Directions: From Sacramento, take I-80 east for 97 miles to Truckee and the exit for Donner Pass Road/Highway 89 North. Follow that exit to the traffic circle, then take the second exit for 0.2 mile to another traffic circle. Take the third exit on that traffic circle to Highway 89 and drive 22.6 miles to Sierraville and a junction for Highway 49/Highway 89 (signed for Quincy/Downieville). Turn left (signed 49/89) and drive 4.9 miles to a turnoff for Highway 89. Turn right on Highway 89 and drive 15.3 miles to the Gold Lake Highway. Turn left on the Gold Lake Highway and drive about six miles until you see the sign for the Lakes Basin Campground. The trailhead is near site 15.

Contact: Plumas National Forest, Beckwourth Ranger District, 530/836-2575, www.fs.usda.gov/plumas.

6 BEAR LAKES LOOP

2.0 mi/1.0 hr 

on the southern boundary of Lakes Basin National Recreation Area north of Sierra City

Map 6.1, page 213

The one-mile hike to Big Bear Lake is an easy, popular, and pretty walk. For visitors who stay at Gold Lake Lodge, it's always a must-do. The trailhead is alongside the parking lot next to the road to the lodge; the trail is a closed road to Round Lake. It becomes a trail within a few hundred yards when routed west to Big Bear Lake, the first in a series of nearby beautiful alpine lakes in the Lakes Basin National Recreation Area. Although most day users return after a picnic at Big Bear Lake, the trip can easily be extended, either west to Round Lake or Silver Lake or north to Long Lake.

User Groups: Hikers, dogs, mountain bikes, and horses. No wheelchair facilities.

Permits: No permits are required. Parking and access are free.

Maps: A trail map is available for a fee from Beckwourth Ranger District. For a map, ask the U.S. Forest Service for Plumas National Forest. For a topographic map, ask the USGS for Gold Lake.

Directions: From Sacramento, take I-80 east for 97 miles to Truckee and the exit for Highway 89 North. Take that exit to the traffic circle, then take the third exit to Highway 89 and drive 22.6 miles to a junction for Highway 49/Highway 89 (signed for Quincy/Downieville). Turn left and drive 17.8 miles (stay on 49 at junctions) to Bassetts and the Gold Lake Highway. Turn right and drive 7.9 miles to the exit on left for Gold Lake Lodge and trailhead.

Contact: Plumas National Forest, Beckwourth Ranger District, 530/836-2575, www.fs.usda.gov/plumas.

7 FRAZIER FALLS TRAIL

1.0 mi/1.0 hr 

north of Sierra City

Map 6.1, page 213

Frazier Falls is a 178-foot, silver-tasseled waterfall that tumbles out of a chute into a rocky basin. It is like a miniature version of Feather Falls (near Lake Oroville). The trail is a 0.5-mile romp on a gentle paved route that leads to the scenic, fenced overlook of the falls. The best time to visit is early summer, when snowmelt from the high-country peaks fills Frazier Falls like a huge fountain. In addition, wildflowers along the trail in early summer add a splash of color, with violet lupine the most abundant. The road to the trailhead is paved all the way, the hike is easy, the falls are beautiful, and as you might expect, thousands of people make the trip every summer. Elevations span 6,200 to 6,240 feet; that's correct: it's flat.

User Groups: Hikers, wheelchairs, and dogs. No ATVs, mountain bikes, or horses. Wheelchair facilities are available.

Permits: No permits are required. Parking and access are free.

Maps: A trail map is available for a fee from Beckwourth Ranger District. For a map, ask the U.S. Forest Service for Plumas National Forest. For a topographic map, ask the USGS for Gold Lake.

Directions: From Sacramento, take I-80 east for 97 miles to Truckee and the exit for Donner Pass Road/Highway 89 North. Follow that exit to the traffic circle, then take the second exit for 0.2 mile to another traffic circle. Take the third exit on that traffic circle to Highway 89 and drive 22.6 miles to Sierraville and a junction for Highway 49/Highway 89 (signed for Quincy/Downieville). Turn left (signed 49/89) and drive 4.9 miles to a turnoff for Highway 89. Turn right on Highway 89 and drive 15.3 miles to the Gold Lake Highway. Turn left on the Gold Lake Highway and drive 1.7 miles to Frazier Creek Road. Turn left and drive 3.9 miles to the trailhead.

If you continue west on Gold Lake Highway for several miles, you will see another trailhead sign for Frazier Falls; it can also be reached on this route, but the road is unpaved.

Contact: Plumas National Forest, Beckwourth Ranger District, 530/836-2575, www.fs.usda.gov/plumas.

8 HASKELL PEAK TRAIL

4.2 mi/2.0 hr 3 10

north of Highway 49 in Tahoe National Forest

Map 6.1, page 213

Haskell Peak is one of the great but little-known lookouts. On clear days, visitors can see a series of mountain peaks both nearby and distant; on perfect days, they include a glimpse of Mount Shasta and Lassen Peak in Northern California, Mount Rose in Nevada, and the closer Sierra Buttes. To get this view requires a 1,100-foot climb over the course of 2.1 miles, where you top out at the 8,107-foot summit. The trail climbs at a decent, steady grade through heavy forest for the first mile. It then flattens and reaches an open area, where Haskell Peak comes into view. From here it's only a 0.25-mile (but very steep) climb to the top. You'll discover that Haskell Peak is the flume of an old volcano and has many unusual volcanic rock formations. A fire lookout was once perched here, but it's gone now. Elevations range from 7,000 to 8,107 feet.

User Groups: Hikers, dogs, horses, and mountain bikes. No wheelchair facilities.

Permits: No permits are required. Parking and access are free.

Maps: For a map, ask the U.S. Forest Service for Tahoe National Forest. For a topographic map, ask the USGS for Clio.

Directions: From Sacramento, take I-80 east for 97 miles to Truckee and the exit for Donner Pass Road/Highway 89 North. Follow that exit to the traffic circle, then take the second exit for 0.2 mile to another traffic circle. Take the third exit on that traffic circle to Highway 89 and drive 22.6 miles to Sierraville and a junction for Highway 49/Highway 89 (signed for Quincy/Downieville). Turn left and drive 17.8 miles (stay on 49 at junctions) to Bassetts and the Gold Lake Highway. Turn right and drive 3.7 miles to Forest Road 9 (Haskell Peak Road). Turn right and drive 8.4 miles. The trailhead is on the left; parking is available on either side of the road.

Contact: Tahoe National Forest, Yuba Ranger District, 530/478-6253, www.fs.usda.gov/tahoe.

9 DEER LAKE TRAIL

5.0 mi/3.5 hr 3 8

west of Packer Lake in Tahoe National Forest

Map 6.1, page 213

Most lakes are green, but Deer Lake is azure blue. With the spectacular Sierra Buttes in the background, this trip is popular. It gets some of the heaviest use of any trail in this section of Tahoe National Forest. It's a 2.5-mile hike to the lake where you climb 1,000 feet and top out at 7,110 feet.

From the trailhead, you'll climb through a basin and get a sweeping view of the massive Sierra Buttes and the surrounding forested slopes. As you head on, you'll cross a signed spur trail, a 0.25-mile route to Grass Lake. Most take the detour, and for some, this alone is enough of a trip. Deer sightings are common. Then, back on the trail to Deer Lake, it's onward, over the ridge and down to Deer Lake. On warm evenings, the brook trout can leave tiny circles while feeding on surface insects. This hike has it all, and that's why it often includes so many other people.

User Groups: Hikers, dogs, horses, and mountain bikes. No wheelchair facilities.

Permits: No permits are required. Parking and access are free.

Maps: A trail map is available for a fee at the Downieville Ranger District. For a map, ask the U.S. Forest Service for Tahoe National Forest. For a topographic map, ask the USGS for Sierra City.

Directions: From Sacramento, take I-80 east for 97 miles to Truckee and the exit for Donner Pass Road/Highway 89 North. Follow that exit to the traffic circle, then take the second exit for 0.2 mile to another traffic circle. Take the third exit on that traffic circle to Highway 89 and drive 22.6 miles to Sierraville and a junction for Highway 49/Highway 89 (signed for Quincy/Downieville). Turn left (signed 49/89) and drive 17.8 miles (stay on 49 at junctions) to Bassetts and the Gold Lake Highway. Turn right (north) on to Gold Lake Highway and drive 1.4 miles to Sardine Lake Road. Turn left on Sardine Lake Road and drive a short distance. Cross the Salmon Creek Bridge and continue 0.3 mile to Packer Lake Road. Turn right on Packer Lake Road and drive 2.5 miles to the trailhead. Parking is available in the Packsaddle camping area just opposite the trailhead.

Contact: Tahoe National Forest, Yuba Ranger District, 530/478-6253, www.fs.usda.gov/tahoe.

10 SIERRA BUTTES TRAIL

6.6 mi/3.5 hr 4 10

near Packer Lake in Tahoe National Forest

Map 6.1, page 213

The sensation can feel like you are walking on air. Many get dizzy. Some are afraid to look down. Most all feel a sense of rapture. This is your payoff at the 8,587-foot Sierra Buttes and its lookout station. A small grated walkway extends around the lookout, where you can look straight down, past your boots and into the open air below. You are atop a pinnacle that is roughly 5,000 feet over Sierra City on one side and 2,800 feet over Sardine Lakes on the other.

The 360-degree view is one of the best you can get with a short hike, but that's not what will stay with you for years. You will remember the act of faith required to traverse a set of metal stairways and grated deck that jut out over open space. Only the daring will look down to see the plummeting open space below. Put this one on your must-do list. The Sierra Buttes are a series of towering crags located in Tahoe National Forest that loom above the Yuba River Canyon, Sierra City and Highway 49.

It's a one-way hike of 3.3 miles, by my estimate, with a climb of about 2,400 feet. I did it in an hour, 10 minutes, with a steady, rhythmic pace that I estimated at a little less than my normal 2.5 mph.

The parking area and trailhead are at about 6,200 feet, where trail starts as an old jeep road (a designated OHV route is off to the right). You begin to climb right away. After making your way up to a ridge, it becomes a single-track hiking path, shaded below old-growth whitebark pine. At a few openings in the forest ahead of you, you can see how the route follows the ridge and rises to the southern spine of the buttes. In about a mile, look for a huge boulder field on your left. An unsigned cutoff spur leads about 30 yards to your first gorgeous lookout, of Young America Lake directly below and beyond to Upper and Lower Sardine Lake, backed by an overview of Mount Elwell and the Lakes Basin.

From here, the climb gets steeper. It's a short trip, so those not used to the grade or altitude can take plenty of time. Near tree line, the trail emerges and hits the old jeep road, the one used in the 1960s when the lookout was constructed, and you turn left, then know you are getting close. The trail bounds, rises, and carves its way through the lower buttes. To the distant north, 10,457-foot Lassen Peak comes into view. You continue up the trail, round a bend, and suddenly the lookout, top pinnacle, and the series of metal stairs are in front of you.

At the stairs, some people have no trouble bounding right up. Others need a steadying hand of comfort from behind. Some look down. Others? No way. The stairs jangle and rattle as you climb; you might hear a little voice in the back of your head daring you to look down. At one spot, where a set of stairs extends over open air, you realize why this hike is an act of faith. The final set of stairs gives you access to the grated catwalk deck around the lookout building, perched on the top of a crag. It can be eerie to peer down through the grate in some spots and see nothing but air so far below. Some get vertigo from the spatial disorientation and will suddenly grab on to the building or whoever is standing next to them. The view is fantastic. Directly below to the west, the Yuba River Canyon drops 5,000 feet in 10 miles and leads out toward the Sacramento Valley. To the south, you can scan across gorgeous French Meadows Reservoir, Grouse Ridge, and the Bowman Lakes and on to the distant snowy crest of the Crystal Basin on the edge of Tahoe. Below to the east is the showstopper, the Sardine Lakes.

As pretty as it is, what you will remember at the Sierra Buttes Lookout is not the view. It's the edge-of-the world, fear-tinged euphoria. The experience can open your pores and make every cell in your body feel alive.

User Groups: Hikers, dogs, and horses. No mountain bikes (except on jeep trail). No wheelchair access.

Permits: No permits are required. Parking and access are free.

Maps: A trail map is available for a fee from the Downieville Ranger District. For a map, ask the U.S. Forest Service for Tahoe National Forest. For a topographic map, ask the USGS for Sierra City.

Directions: From Sacramento, take I-80 east for 97 miles to Truckee and the exit for Highway 89 North. Follow that exit to the traffic circle, then take the third exit to Highway 89 and drive 22.6 miles to a junction for Highway 49/Highway 89 (signed for Quincy/Downieville). Turn left and drive 17.8 miles (stay on 49 at junctions) to Bassetts and the Gold Lake Highway. Turn right and drive 1.4 miles to Sardine Lake/Packer Lake Road. Turn left and drive a short distance to a junction signed Sardine Lakes ahead, Packer Lake to right. Turn right on Packer Lake Road. Continue past turnoff for Packer Lake and bear left at a fork (still paved), following the signs to a trailhead for the Pacific Crest Trail (do not bear right at a jeep road). Continue as road becomes dirt (OK for cars) to a parking area on left at trailhead. Parking and trailhead signed.

Contact: Tahoe National Forest, Yuba Ranger District, 530/478-6253, www.fs.usda.gov/tahoe.

11 CHAPMAN CREEK TRAIL

5.2 mi/1-3.0 hr — 2 — 7

east of Sierra City in Tahoe National Forest

Map 6.1, page 213

Chapman Creek is a babbling brook that you can walk alongside, or you can stop to picnic near it, fish a little in it, or do absolutely nothing. That's right, nothing. It's that kind of place. The trailhead, elevation 5,840 feet, is set at a campground, which provides easy access. Outside of campers, few others know of it. The trail winds easily along the contours of Chapman Creek under the canopy of a dense forest, rising gently along the way. It climbs to 6,400 feet, 560 feet in a span of 1.5 miles. The river is the lifeblood for a variety of birds and wildlife, but few visitors make the trip for that reason. Rather they come to stroll and let their minds wander and be free. Few do the entire trail, which official ends at Forest Road 09-13.

User Groups: Hikers, dogs, horses, and mountain bikes. No wheelchair facilities.

Permits: No permits are required. Parking and access are free.

Maps: For a map, ask the U.S. Forest Service for Tahoe National Forest. For a topographic map, ask the USGS for Sierra City.

Directions: From Sacramento, take I-80 east for 97 miles to Truckee and the exit for Donner Pass Road/Highway 89 North. Follow that exit to the traffic circle, then take the second exit for 0.2 mile to another traffic circle. Take the third exit on that traffic circle to Highway 89 and drive 22.6 miles to Sierraville and a junction for Highway 49/Highway 89 (signed for Quincy/Downieville). Turn left on Highway 49 and drive over Yuba Pass; continue for four miles to the Chapman Creek Campground on the right. The trailhead and a parking area are at the north end of the campground.

Contact: Tahoe National Forest, Yuba Ranger District, 530/478-6253, www.fs.usda.gov/tahoe.

12 WILD PLUM LOOP/ HAYPRESS CREEK

6.0 mi/1 day 3 8

east of Sierra City in Tahoe National Forest

Map 6.1, page 213

A canyon with a hidden stream and a waterfall surrounded by old-growth red fir make this a hike for the properly inspired. Why must you be properly inspired? The route to the trailhead causes it to get missed. The trail climbs from 4,400 feet up Haypress Creek to 5,840 feet, a 1,440-foot rise over just three miles. The trail starts out almost flat for the first 0.5 mile, and then it crosses over Haypress Creek on a footbridge. There's an excellent view of the Sierra Buttes in this area. Continue on Haypress Creek Trail, where you rise past a rocky area and into a once-logged forest. The trail soon enters an old-growth forest. It then contours along Haypress Canyon, and then passes by a pretty waterfall. This hike makes a great day trip with a picnic lunch, and trail use is typically quite light. Note that on the return trip, you turn right on the Pacific Crest Trail to complete the loop. Walk 0.5 mile and turn left at the Wild Plum Loop sign to return.

User Groups: Hikers, dogs, and horses. No mountain bikes. No wheelchair facilities.

Permits: No permits are required. Parking and access are free.

Maps: For a map, ask the U.S. Forest Service for Tahoe National Forest. For a topographic map, ask the USGS for Haypress Valley.

Directions: From Sacramento, take I-80 east for 97 miles to Truckee and the exit for Donner Pass Road/Highway 89 North. Follow that exit to the traffic circle, then take the second exit for 0.2 mile to another traffic circle. Take the third exit on that traffic circle to Highway 89 and drive 22.6 miles to Sierraville and a junction for Highway 49/Highway 89 (signed for Quincy/Downieville). Turn left on Highway 49 and drive 12 miles (past Bassetts) to Wild Plum Road (near the eastern end of Sierra City) at the sign for Wild Plum Campground. To then reach the trailhead, drive one mile on this road to the Wild Plum trailhead parking area. Walk through the campground to its upper loop, walk around a locked gate, and continue up the road 0.25 mile to the Wild Plum Loop Trail sign. Walk 0.25 mile to the intersection with the Pacific Crest Trail, turn left, and cross a bridge over Haypress Creek. Continue for 200 yards to the trailhead, on the right.

Contact: Tahoe National Forest, Yuba Ranger District, 530/478-6253, www.fs.usda.gov/tahoe.

13 YUBA RIVER TO FOWLER PEAK (PCT)

51.0 mi one-way/4 days 4 9

in Tahoe National Forest, off Highway 49 east of Sierra City

Map 6.1, page 213

Pristine alpine lakes and high mountain lookouts highlight this section of the Pacific Crest Trail. Although nearly as beautiful as the section of trail south near Tahoe, this stretch gets far less use. It starts at the Yuba River, and in the first two miles, it climbs an endless series of switchbacks up the back side of the Sierra Buttes. This is a long, grueling climb on exposed terrain with a great reward. Note that the spur trail up to the Sierra Buttes Fire Lookout is an additional 1,400-foot climb, but it furnishes one of the top lookouts in California. The trail then heads north. It skirts past the western border of the Gold Lakes Basin, where a dozen high alpine lakes make for easy side trips and camps. With some terrible switchbacks, the PCT passes Mount Gibraltar (7,343 feet), Stafford Mountain (7,019 feet), and Mount Etna (7,163 feet), and flanks below Pilot Peak (7,457 feet). It then heads along the western slope, eventually reaching the Fowler Peak trailhead.

To continue north on the PCT, see the *Fowler Peak to Bucks Summit (PCT)* hike in this chapter. If you are walking this trail in reverse, see the *Donner Pass to the Yuba River (PCT)* hike in this chapter.

User Groups: Hikers, dogs, and horses. No mountain bikes. No wheelchair access.

Permits: A wilderness permit (free) is required. Parking and access are free. A single permit is required to hike the Pacific Crest Trail. Contact the national forest, Bureau of Land Management, or national park office at your point of entry for a combined permit that is good for traveling through multiple-permit areas during your dates of travel.

Maps: For a map, ask the U.S. Forest Service for Tahoe National Forest. For topographic maps, ask the USGS for Haypress Valley, Sierra City, Mount Fillmore, and Onion Valley.

Directions: From Sacramento, take I-80 east for 97 miles to Truckee and the exit for Donner Pass Road/Highway 89 North. Follow that exit to the traffic circle, then take the second exit for 0.2 mile to another traffic circle. Take the third exit on that traffic circle to Highway 89 and drive 22.6 miles to Sierraville and a junction for Highway 49/Highway 89 (signed for Quincy/Downieville). Turn left on Highway 49 and drive 12 miles (past Bassetts) to near the eastern end of Sierra City. Look for the Pacific Crest Trail access sign and park on the right (north) side of the road.

Contact: Tahoe National Forest, Yuba Ranger District, 530/478-6253, www.fs.usda.gov/tahoe.

14 GROUSE RIDGE TO GLACIER LAKE

8.0 mi/4.0 hr

in Tahoe National Forest north of Emigrant Gap

Map 6.1, page 213

The prize destination is a hidden, pristine lake called Glacier Lake, set at the foot of a volcanic massif called Black Butte. Highlights include beautiful sweeping views of the Sierra and the opportunity for side trips to several other lakes. A round-trip from the trailhead to Glacier Lake and back is just under seven miles. It is one of the highlights of the Bowman Lakes Recreation Area, generally ranging 5,000-7,500 feet in elevation, featuring Sierra granite, pines, and dozens of alpine lakes.

It's a bumpy drive (four-wheel drive helps) up past a small campground to the Grouse Ridge trailhead and parking area. From the trailhead, the hike starts on an exposed ridge. Within just a few minutes, two gorgeous azure lakes come into view to your left, Milk Lake and Round Lake. Many creep over to the ridge to get a better look. Then, back on the trail, another pretty lake can be spotted off to your right, Sanford Lake. The trail then descends quickly into a forested valley, where you arrive at an unsigned trail junction (out of curiosity, we explored this and found it led down a canyon to pretty Downey Lake. This alone is a good trip, an easy 20-minute jaunt to get there). Continuing north, you pass a signed trail junction on your left (which is routed west down to Round Lake, Milk Lake, and then Carr and Feely Lakes), and then come to a trail cutoff on your right—this is your turn for Glacier Lake.

This cutoff trail passes through a series of meadows and stands of pines, rising steadily along the way, with exposed Sand Ridge (fantastic wildflowers in mid-June) directly off to your left. Eventually you will spot Black Butte, the craggy ridge set on the nearby horizon ahead, and realize that Glacier Lake, your destination, is set right at the foot of it. You will top a ridge and come across a series of small camping flats, popular in July and August, and descend to lake's edge, an elevation of 7,500 feet. This is a small and pristine setting, with the lake's clear, calm waters providing a sharp contrast to the high backdrop of the buttes, brown, black, and craggy, even crumbling in spots.

User Groups: Hikers, dogs, horses, and mountain bikes. No wheelchair facilities.

Permits: A campfire permit (free) is required for overnight use. Parking and access are free.

Maps: For a map, ask the U.S. Forest Service for Tahoe National Forest. For topographic maps, ask the USGS for Cisco Grove and English Mountain.

Directions: From Sacramento, take I-80 east past Emigrant Gap to the exit for Highway 20. Take that exit and go west four miles to Bowman Lake Road (Forest Road 18). Turn right on Bowman Lake Road and drive about five miles to Grouse Ridge Road. Turn right and go six miles (often rough) to a fork at Grouse Ridge. At the fork, bear right to the campground or bear left to the trailhead. A four-wheel-drive, high-clearance vehicle is recommended.

Contact: Tahoe National Forest, Nevada City Ranger District, 530/265-4531, www.fs.usda.gov/tahoe.

15 LINDSEY LAKES TRAIL

7.0 mi/3.0 hr

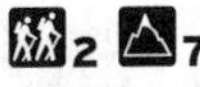

in Tahoe National Forest north of Emigrant Gap

Map 6.1, page 213

The highlight of Lindsey Lakes Trail is that it intersects with other trails, including the Grouse Ridge Trail, and is set in a gorgeous landscape that features Sierra alpine beauty. But the trail itself from Lindsey Lakes to Rock Lake is a service road closed to public vehicle traffic, so you're hiking up a road. This 3.5-mile trail dead-ends after climbing past the three Lindsey Lakes, and it offers a great optional side trip. From the trailhead at Lower Lindsey Lake (elevation 6,160 feet), hike up to the other lakes on a short trail (it's quite steep in several places) before you top out at 6,400 feet. The route gets medium use and accesses good swimming holes with cold water, but the fishing is poor. A side trip from the Lindsey Lakes Trail is Crooked Lakes Trail (excellent).

User Groups: Hikers, dogs, and horses. Mountain bikes not advised. No wheelchair facilities.

Permits: No permits are required. Parking and access are free.

Maps: For a map, ask the U.S. Forest Service for Tahoe National Forest. For topographic maps, ask the USGS for English Mountain and Graniteville.

Directions: From Sacramento, take I-80 east past Emigrant Gap to the exit for Highway 20. Take that exit and go west four miles to Bowman Lake Road (Forest Road 18). Turn right on Bowman Lake Road and drive 8.5 miles to a junction signed Lindsey Lake, Feely Lake, Carr Lake. Turn right (dirt, some rocks, passable for cars, SUV recommended) and drive four miles (at fork, turn left for Lindsey Lake, right for Carr and Feely Lake). Turn left and drive about a mile to Lindsey Lake and trailhead. The last half mile of road can be rough; high-clearance vehicles are advised.

Contact: Tahoe National Forest, Nevada City Ranger District, 530/265-4531, www.fs.usda.gov/tahoe.

16 CARR/FEELY TRAILHEAD TO PENNER LAKE

6.0 mi/3.0 hr 3 10

at Carr Lake in Tahoe National Forest north of Emigrant Gap

Map 6.1, page 213

This is the most popular trailhead in the Bowman Lakes Recreation Area. It's crowded all summer, and the parking lot fills early on summer weekends. The reason is because you get easy access to Carr Lake and Feeley Lake, and then launch into wildlands to gorgeous Island Lake and stunning Penner Lake, an easy six-mile round-trip. Dozens of small lakes are within reach on the Crooked Lakes Trail, Grouse Ridge Trail, and others. Milk Lake, for instance, is also gorgeous. The area feels like wilderness, but is not designated as wilderness. Mountain bikes are permitted on trails, though until all the snow melts off and surface dries out, conditions are poor for biking.

This is how you do it. From the parking area, walk back a short distance and turn right for a short climb past Carr Lake on the right. You emerge above Carr and Feely Lake (6,720 feet) coming into view on the left. The trail runs along the right side of Feely and then enters forest. It's a gentle climb then to Island Lake, named for the little rock "islands," as they call them, and the junction of the Crooked Lakes Trail (signed). Take the Crooked Lakes Trail through a fir forest for 1.5 miles, which includes a short climb, to Penner Lake. Penner Lake (along with Milk) is one of the prettiest lakes in the area. The ambitious can continue another mile to Upper Rock Lake.

User Groups: Hikers, dogs, mountain bikes, and horses. No wheelchair facilities.

Permits: No permits are required. Parking and access are free.

Maps: For a map, ask the U.S. Forest Service for Tahoe National Forest. For topographic maps, ask the USGS for English Mountain and Graniteville.

Directions: From Sacramento, take I-80 east past Emigrant Gap to the exit for Highway 20. Take that exit and go west four miles to Bowman Lake Road (Forest Road 18). Turn right on Bowman Lake Road and drive 8.5 miles to a junction signed Lindsey Lake, Feely Lake, Carr Lake. Turn right (dirt, some rocks, passable for cars, SUV recommended) and drive four miles (at fork, turn left for Lindsey Lake, right for Carr and Feely Lake). Turn right and drive about a mile to the parking area for Carr Lake and trailhead. The last half mile of road can be rough; high-clearance vehicles are advised, four-wheel drive is better.

Contact: Tahoe National Forest, Nevada City Ranger District, 530/265-4531, www.fs.usda.gov/tahoe.

17 DONNER PASS TO THE YUBA RIVER (PCT)

38.0 mi one-way/3 days 3 7

from Highway 80 to Highway 49 in Tahoe National Forest

Map 6.1, page 213

This is not one of the more glamorous sections of the Pacific Crest Trail. But it is still provides rewards. For the most part, the PCT here follows a crest that connects a series of small mountaintops before dropping down to Jackson Meadow Reservoir and Highway 49. Some good views are to be had on the first leg of the trail, so many that some PCT hikers begin to take them for granted after a while. The trail is routed past Castle Peak (elevation 9,103 feet), Basin Peak (9,015 feet), and Lacey Mountain (8,214 feet). Most can cover this much terrain for an ambitious first day, perhaps with stops at Paradise Lake or White Rock Lake. As the trail drops to Jackson Meadow Reservoir, the views end, but in time you'll catch sight of the lake; surrounded by firs, it is quite pretty. The PCT then skirts the east side of the reservoir, passes several drive-to campgrounds, heads through Bear Valley (not *the* Bear Valley), and drops

back side approach to Castle Peak

steeply to Milton Creek and four miles beyond that to Loves Falls at Highway 49.

To continue north on the PCT, see the *Yuba River to Fowler Peak (PCT)* hike in this chapter. If you are walking this trail in reverse, see the *Barker Pass to Donner Pass (PCT)* hike in this chapter.

User Groups: Hikers, dogs, and horses. No mountain bikes. No wheelchair facilities.

Permits: A campfire permit (free) is required for overnight use. Parking and access are free. A single permit is required to hike the Pacific Crest Trail. Contact the national forest, Bureau of Land Management, or national park office at your point of entry for a combined permit that is good for traveling through multiple-permit areas during your dates of travel.

Maps: For a map, ask the U.S. Forest Service for Tahoe National Forest. For topographic maps, ask the USGS for Norden, Soda Springs, Webber, Haypress Valley, Independence Lake, and English Mountain.

Directions: From Auburn, take I-80 east to the Boreal/Donner Summit and the signed exit for Pacific Crest trailhead parking area. Take that exit to parking. There is no hiker parking in the Donner Summit rest area.

Contact: Tahoe National Forest, Sierraville Ranger District, 530/994-3401, www.fs.usda.gov/tahoe.

18 CARR LAKE TO GLACIER LAKE

10.0 mi/1 day — 3 — 10

in Tahoe National Forest north of Emigrant Gap

Map 6.1, page 213

In just a few hours you can be transported to heaven. Some people, however, call it the Bowman Lakes Recreation Area. It is a five-mile hike with a 1,500-foot climb to reach Glacier Lake (7,000 feet). You pass lake after lake and then end up at a pristine setting with a high back wall. The small lake is set in a rock-bound bowl with the Black Buttes looming nearby. The tree cover is sparse, and the rock cover is abundant.

Start your hike from the trailhead at Carr

Lake. You then pass Carr Lake on the right, Feely Lake on the left, and then Island and Round Lakes. You'll drop down into forest and meadow landscape and reach a trail junction (right leads up to Grouse Ridge, another trailhead where you can start this trip). At the junction, continue east on Glacier Lake Trail. You will continue through a meadow and some forest. Here you start a gradual climb, passing a small lake before entering a rocky area and then dropping down to the pretty lake. Several backpacking campsites are available.

Some maps of Tahoe National Forest do not show the direct route to Glacier Lake. Our route climbs up through a beautiful canyon. One map I saw, on the other hand, shows the trail routed up a hot, exposed route on Sandy Ridge off to the left (no good). This trailhead is popular and the parking lot fills.

User Groups: Hikers, dogs, and horses. Mountain bikes not advised. No wheelchair facilities.

Permits: No permits are required. Parking and access are free.

Maps: For a map, ask the U.S. Forest Service for Tahoe National Forest. For topographic maps, ask the USGS for Cisco Grove and English Mountain.

Directions: From Sacramento, take I-80 east past Emigrant Gap to the exit for Highway 20. Take that exit and go west four miles to Bowman Lake Road (Forest Road 18). Turn right on Bowman Lake Road and drive 8.5 miles to a junction signed Lindsey Lake, Feely Lake, Carr Lake. Turn right (dirt, some rocks, passable for cars, SUV recommended) and drive four miles (at fork, turn left for Lindsey Lake, right for Carr and Feely Lake). Turn right and drive about a mile to the parking area for Carr Lake and trailhead. The last half mile of road can be rough; high-clearance vehicles are advised, four-wheel drive is better.

Contact: Tahoe National Forest, Nevada City Ranger District, 530/265-4531, www.fs.usda.gov/tahoe.

19 PIONEER TRAIL/ OMEGA OVERLOOK

1.0 mi/0.5 hr 1 8

east of Nevada City, off of Highway 20 in Tahoe National Forest

Map 6.1, page 213

The Caltrans Omega Overlook provides a view over the South Yuba River Canyon and beyond, as well as a historic site of a huge hydraulic gold-mining operation. There is a parking area, a restroom, and a viewing area. It is also a primary trailhead for the 25-mile Pioneer Trail. The Pioneer Trail is like taking a history lesson. You trace the route of the first wagon road, opened by emigrants and gold seekers in 1850. The trail is better suited for mountain biking. In fact, it has become almost exclusively a biking trip, but its historical significance still merits inclusion in this book. It provides a short out-and-back walk with a great view. Significant sites along the Pioneer Trail are Central House (once a stagecoach stop) and White Cloud and Skillman Flat (former millsites, one burned down).

A high percentage of mountain bikers seem to use the one-way trip downhill from Omega to Five Mile House, with a shuttle. When encountering other trail users, all need to remember to demonstrate the utmost courtesy; that means slow the heck down.

User Groups: Hikers, dogs, mountain bikes, and horses. No wheelchair facilities.

Permits: A campfire permit (free) is required for overnight use. Parking and access are free.

Maps: For a map, ask the U.S. Forest Service for Tahoe National Forest. For a topographic map, ask the USGS for Washington.

Directions: From Nevada City, take Highway 20 east and drive for 16.9 miles to Omega Overlook on the left. Turn left and drive a short distance to parking.

Contact: Tahoe National Forest, Nevada City Ranger District, 530/265-4531, www.fs.usda.gov/tahoe.

20 SIERRA DISCOVERY TRAIL

1.0 mi/0.5 hr 1 8

off Highway 20 near Lake Spaulding

Map 6.1, page 213 BEST

Many short interpretive trails are long on words in brochures and short on beauty. Not this one. From the parking area, the trail quickly leads into rich forest and to pretty Bear River. It provides glimpses of a series of gorgeous sites amid a forest of pines and cedars, with a payoff of a pretty stream and small waterfall. Much of the trail is soil cement or compressed gravel. It is designed as an interpretive loop walk, with information about ecosystems, wildlife, geology, and cultural history available. For Buddy, the family golden retriever, it's always a favorite.

User Groups: Hikers, dogs, and wheelchairs (with assistance). No horses or mountain bikes. Dogs permitted, but rangers strongly discourage bringing them on this trail.

Permits: No permits are necessary. Parking and access are free.

Maps: For a topographic map, ask the USGS for Blue Canyon.

Directions: From Sacramento, take I-80 east past Emigrant Gap to the exit for Highway 20. Take that exit and go west four miles to Bowman Lake Road (Forest Road 18). Turn right on Bowman Lake Road and drive 0.6 mile to the Sierra Discovery Trail parking lot on the left.

Contact: Pacific Gas & Electric, 916/386-5164, www.pge.com./recreation.

21 LOCH LEVEN LAKES

7.2 mi/4.0 hr 3 8

south of Cisco Grove in Tahoe National Forest

Map 6.1, page 213

Most people would like to know what heaven is like. This trip to Loch Leven Lakes is unlikely to be your final resting place, yet it provides a glimpse of what heaven might be. Although there is some road noise at the beginning of this trip, the end is well worth it. You get sweeping vistas of ridges and valleys, gorgeous high alpine meadows, and glaciated mountain terrain with a series of pretty lakes.

The trail starts at 5,680 feet, then works its way upward on a moderate grade to the southwest. Granite outcrops are numerous, and huge boulders (deposited by receding glaciers) lie sprinkled among Jeffrey pine and lodgepole pine. In the first 1.1 mile, the trail crosses a creek and railroad tracks. It then climbs through a forest. Here the trail becomes steeper, where you climb 800 feet in 1.25 miles. It then tops the summit and descends gently to Lower Loch Leven Lake (2.5 miles from the trailhead). Many people stop here, content to just take in the surroundings. But you can forge on for another mile, circling Middle Loch Leven Lake (2.8 miles from the trailhead) and heading east up to High Loch Leven Lake (3.6 miles from the trailhead), at 6,800 feet. At the south end of Lower Loch Leven Lake, turn left at the trail junction to see Middle and High Loch Leven Lakes (turning right at the junction will route you to Salmon Lake, a less-crowded alternative). Once you've come this far, beautiful High Loch Leven is an easy trip and a must-do.

But this hike is not without frustration: The first hour involves a continuous climb, with the echo of I-80 traffic in the background. You do not escape the noise until you top the ridge. Elevations range 5,680-6,850 feet at the ridge, a gain of 1,070 feet. With access so easy off I-80, the area can become inundated with people on summer weekends. With no trailhead quota, the numbers can affect the sense of a wild place.

User Groups: Hikers, dogs, and horses. Mountain bikes not advised. No wheelchair facilities.

Permits: No permits are required. Parking and access are free.

Maps: For a map, ask the U.S. Forest Service for Tahoe National Forest. For a topographic map, ask the USGS for Cisco Grove.

Directions: From Sacramento, take I-80 east

for 70 miles into the Sierra Nevada and to Exit 165 toward Cisco Grove. Take that exit a short distance to Hampshire Rocks Road. Turn left on Hampshire Rocks Road and drive (well signed) 0.4 miles (0.2 miles past the old Big Bend Visitor Center). The trailhead is on the opposite side of the road from the parking area.
Contact: Tahoe National Forest, Truckee Ranger District, 530/587-3558, www.fs.usda.gov/tahoe.

22 LOWER LOLA MONTEZ LAKE

6.0 mi/3.0 hr 2 8

in Tahoe National Forest near Soda Springs

Map 6.1, page 213

If timing is everything in love and the outdoors, then time this trip for the shoulder seasons, spring or fall. In summer, mountain bikers take over this trail. Traffic is high on weekends. Lower Lola Montez is a beautiful alpine lake set at 7,200 feet. Start at Toll Mountain Estates, a private community. The first 0.25 mile is on single-track. Then you reach a dirt road and turn right, cross Castle Creek, and continue until the road becomes single-track again. The route is marked all the way, and with all the people who ride this in summer, it's an easy track to follow.
User Groups: Hikers, dogs, horses, and mountain bikes. No wheelchair facilities.
Permits: No permits are required. Parking and access are free.
Maps: For a map, ask the U.S. Forest Service for Tahoe National Forest. For topographic maps, ask the USGS for Soda Springs and Norden.
Directions: From Auburn, take I-80 east for 55 miles to Soda Springs. Take the Soda Springs/Norden exit and cross the overpass to the north side of the freeway. Follow the paved road east, past the fire station, for 0.3 mile to the trailhead parking area.
Contact: Tahoe National Forest, Truckee Ranger District, 530/587-3558, www.fs.usda.gov/tahoe.

23 PALISADE CREEK TRAIL TO HEATH FALLS

10.0 mi/6.0 hr 3 10

in Tahoe National Forest near Soda Springs

Map 6.1, page 213

The hike to Heath Falls is like going on vacation on your credit card. You can have all the fun you want, but when you return home, you have to pay up. That's because the trip to the Heath Falls Overlook is downhill nearly all the way, where you descend 1,700 feet over five miles. Stunning alpine scenery will have you smiling the whole time. The return trip is a long and steady five-mile climb back uphill, so be sure you have plenty of trail snacks, water, and energy left for it.

The trail begins at the dam between the two Cascade Lakes, the first of many lakes you'll see on this trip. The big hunk of imposing rock you have to walk around is 7,704-foot Devils Peak. Take the right fork signed for the North Fork American River, and get ready for a steady diet of granite, lakes, and vistas. At 2.2 miles, the trail leaves the rocks behind and enters the forest, switchbacking downhill for two miles to the Palisade Creek Bridge. Look for an unsigned junction 300 yards beyond it, where Heath Falls Overlook Trail heads east. Follow it for 0.5 mile to the trail's end, at a vista of the American River's Heath Falls. After you enjoy the falls overlook, you've got to make the long climb home. Hope you have at least one Clif Bar left.

The Forest Service lists the Palisade Creek Trails as 11.1 miles long; their trail experts are referring to the entire length of that particular trail, end to end, one-way, rather than our preferred route to the waterfall and back.
User Groups: Hikers, dogs, and horses. No mountain bikes. No wheelchair facilities.

Permits: No permits are required. Parking and access are free.
Maps: For a map, ask the U.S. Forest Service for Tahoe National Forest. For topographic maps, ask the USGS for Soda Springs and Norden.
Directions: From Sacramento, take I-80 east for 79 miles to Exit 174 for Soda Springs/Norden. Take that exit for 0.2 mile to Donner Pass Road. Turn right on Donner Pass Road and drive 0.7 mile to Soda Springs Road. Turn right and drive 0.9 mile to Pahatsi Road. Turn right and drive 0.2 mile (turns to dirt, becomes Kidd Lakes Road) and continue straight for 3.8 miles (you pass Kidd Lake on your left and the Royal Gorge Devils Lookout Warming Hut on your right) to a fork. After the warming hut, take the left fork and drive 0.5 mile to the trailhead, signed as Palisade Creek Trail, on the north side of Cascade Lakes.
Contact: Tahoe National Forest, Truckee Ranger District, 530/587-3558, www.fs.usda.gov/tahoe.

24 WARREN LAKE

14.0 mi/2 days 

in Tahoe National Forest near Donner Summit

Map 6.1, page 213

The first 1.6 miles of this trail follow the same route as the Summit Lake Trail (see listing), along the PCT access trail and through the tunnel underneath I-80 to a fork. To reach Warren Lake, take the left fork (the right fork goes to Summit Lake). Summit Lake Trail is an easy stroll; the Warren Lake Trail climbs 1,500 feet and then drops 1,500 feet, which you must repeat on the return trip. The elevation change means you part company with most casual hikers.

From the fork, the route climbs through lodgepole pine and red fir forest to a saddle at three miles, where there are excellent views of much of the landscape you will hike through. The trail drops gently over the next 3.5 miles, into a wide valley basin that has a mix of volcanic and glaciated rocks. Wildflowers abound on the valley floor. After a brief climb to a ridge, the final mile is a steep descent, where you plummet 1,000 feet to Warren Lake. You'll find many campsites on the lake's west and south sides.

For Day 2, note that just before you reach the top of the ridge, about 1.3 miles from Warren Lake, there is a left spur trail that leads to Devils Oven Lake. It's a good day hike for Day 2.
User Groups: Hikers, dogs, horses, and mountain bikes. No wheelchair facilities. No mountain bikes on Pacific Crest Trail.
Permits: No permits are required. Parking and access are free.
Maps: For a map, ask the U.S. Forest Service for Tahoe National Forest. For a topographic map, ask the USGS for Norden.
Directions: From Sacramento, take I-80 east for 86 miles to Exit 176 for Castle Peak/Boreal Ridge Road exit (just west of Donner Summit). Take that exit and turn right, go a very short distance, and then immediately turn left, and drive 0.4 mile to the trailhead for Donner Summit and the Pacific Crest Trail.
Contact: Tahoe National Forest, Truckee Ranger District, 530/587-3558, www.fs.usda.gov/tahoe.

25 SUMMIT LAKE TRAIL

4.0 mi/2.0 hr 

in Tahoe National Forest near Donner Summit

Map 6.1, page 213

The Summit Lake Trail is a quick and easy leg-stretcher and a great hike for families. It leads two miles to a pretty alpine lake at 7,400 feet. It is crowded on weekends. You will find those who are not fit often complain that the short climb is harder than they expected. For those who live at sea level, it's rather the elevation that usually gets them. Start the trip at the PCT trailhead. Head east, where you roughly parallel the freeway. A half mile in, watch for an intersection. You must turn left and follow the PCT Access Trail north (signed for Castle Pass and Peter Grubb Hut) through a tunnel underneath I-80 (it's not as bad as it sounds). Once you're on the north side of the freeway, you'll reach a fork. Bear right for Summit Lake and Warren Lake, then start to climb a bit. The trail alternates through fir forest and occasional open ridges, with some excellent views to the south and east. At 1.6 miles, you'll see another trail fork: Warren Lake to the left and Summit Lake to the right. Bear right, and finish out your walk to the lake's edge.

User Groups: Hikers, dogs, horses. No mountain bikes. No wheelchair facilities.

Permits: No permits are required. Parking and access are free. No mountain bikes on Pacific Crest Trail.

Maps: For a map, ask the U.S. Forest Service for Tahoe National Forest. For a topographic map, ask the USGS for Norden.

Directions: From Sacramento, take I-80 east for 86 miles to Exit 176 for Castle Peak/Boreal Ridge Road exit (just west of Donner Summit). Take that exit and turn right, go a very short distance, and then immediately turn left, and drive 0.4 mile to the trailhead for Donner Summit and the Pacific Crest Trail.

Contact: Tahoe National Forest, Truckee Ranger District, 530/587-3558, www.fs.usda.gov/tahoe.

26 EUCHRE BAR TRAIL

10.5 mi/2 days

5 8

on the North Fork American River near Baxter in Tahoe National Forest

Map 6.1, page 213

This is an old mining trail built for a goatlike miner from the 1850s, steep on the way into the canyon with a 2,000-foot descent. For the trip back out of the canyon, it qualifies as a kill-me, eat-me hike. From the trailhead, the route winds steeply down to the river and Euchre Bar near Rawhide, where a suspension footbridge crosses the North Fork American River. The trail then leads upriver for 2.4 miles, along an excellent stretch of water for fishing, camping, panning for gold, and swimming (cold). The trail extends along the river for 5.3 miles. Sharp-eyed hikers will see rusted-out remnants from the gold rush era.

User Groups: Hikers, dogs, and horses. Mountain bikes not advised. No wheelchair facilities.

Permits: Campfire permits are required for overnight use. Parking and access are free.

Maps: For a map, ask the U.S. Forest Service for Tahoe National Forest. For topographic maps, ask the USGS for Dutch Flat and Westville.

Directions: From Sacramento, take I-80 east for 51 miles to Exit 146 for Alta. Take that exit 0.2 mile to Morton. Turn right on Morton, drive 100 feet to Casa Loma Road, then turn left on Casa Loma and drive three miles (requires several jogs, becomes rough, high-clearance recommended, four-wheel drive advised near end) to the trailhead.

Contact: Tahoe National Forest, Nevada City Ranger District, 530/265-4531, www.fs.usda.gov/tahoe.

27 ITALIAN BAR TRAIL

4.5 mi/3.5 hr

5 8

near the North Fork American River in Tahoe National Forest

Map 6.1, page 213

Miners in the 1850s were like mountain goats. Like any good goat, they knew the most direct route between two points was a straight line. As a result, this route—which miners once used to reach the North Fork American River—is almost straight down going in and straight up coming out, gaining 3,000 feet in elevation over the course of 2.25 miles. The grade was measured at 35 percent at its steepest slopes (from 4,834 to 2,447 feet). As you head down from the trailhead at 5,400 feet, you get little help from switchbacks. The trail ends at the river, and from there, you must scramble and hop from rock to rock along the riverbanks. Eventually you end up at a secluded spot where all seems perfect—until you start the hike back. When you face the 3,000-foot climb out, you will wonder how you ever talked yourself into doing this hike.

User Groups: Hikers, dogs, and horses. Mountain bikes not advised. No wheelchair facilities.

Permits: No permits are required. Parking and access are free.

Maps: For a map, ask the U.S. Forest Service for Tahoe National Forest. For a topographic map, ask the USGS for Westville.

Directions: Take I-80 to Auburn and the exit for Foresthill/Foresthill Road. Take that exit, turn east on Foresthill Road, and drive 15.5 miles to Foresthill (and the Forest Service district office). Continue on Foresthill Road for 14.5 miles to Humbug Ridge Road (Forest Road 66). Turn left and drive three miles north to the trailhead. Four-wheel-drive, high-clearance vehicles are advised.

Contact: American River Ranger District, 530/367-2224, www.fs.usda.gov/tahoe.

28 MUMFORD BAR TRAIL

7 mi/1 day

near the North Fork American River in Tahoe National Forest

Map 6.1, page 213

Get this in focus: This trail spans an elevation of 5,377 to 2,632 feet to the North Fork American, a descent of 2,745 feet in 3.5 miles. Of the steep trails that plummet into the canyon of the North Fork American, this seems to be the most popular. On the way down, you get pretty views of the river canyon, and then of Royal Gorge. It leads down to the Mumford Bar Cabin, restored for viewing. You can continue upstream from here on the American River Trail. Some areas here on the River Trail show damage from past forest fires.

User Groups: Hikers, dogs, and horses. Mountain bikes are not advised. No wheelchair facilities.

Permits: No permits are required. Parking and access are free.

Maps: For a map, ask the U.S. Forest Service for Tahoe National Forest. For topographic maps, ask the USGS for Duncan Peak and Westville.

Directions: Take I-80 to Auburn and the exit for Foresthill/Foresthill Road. Take that exit, turn east on Foresthill Road, and drive 15.5 miles to Foresthill (and the Forest Service district office). Continue another 17 miles northeast (the road becomes Foresthill Divide Road) to the Mumford Bar Campground. Turn left and drive through the campground and access a road (becomes passable only for four-wheel-drive vehicles; others should park in the developed area on top) and continue to the trailhead.

Contact: Tahoe National Forest, American River Ranger District, 530/367-2224, www.fs.usda.gov/tahoe.

29 STEVENS TRAIL

9.0 mi/5.0 hr

near Colfax

Map 6.1, page 213

The Stevens Trail is a surprise to many. The trailhead is right aside I-80 and the throngs drive right by without a clue. It takes a few short jogs to reach the trailhead, and then you're on your way. You leave the highway traffic behind in Colfax. The trail runs 4.5 miles down into the canyon of the North Fork American River, though many go out a ways, take in a canyon view, and then return. The features here are gentle terrain and long-distance canyon and stream views.

The parking area has a big trailhead sign, and this has become a popular trail for locals. You descend 1,200 feet over the course of 4.5 miles if you choose to head all the way to the river. From the ridge, continue on a gentle downhill path, where the return trip is up but well graded and not too difficult for most hikers. In wet years, there can be some small waterfalls. About two miles in, the trail splits; the upper trail (hikers only) leads to a creek crossing—little pool-and-drop cascades—and then rejoins with the main trail.

You can also see the railroad line that was built by Chinese laborers dangling in rope-strung baskets from the cliffs above. In the spring, you will also pass blooming wildflowers and buckeye trees. This trail is registered as a National Historic Trail. It was originally part of a livery trail from the town of Iowa Hill to Colfax. The entire historic route is no longer connected, with no bridge over the river, and the trail gone beyond that anyway. The biggest problem here is timing. This is no fun on a summer afternoon, with 90-degree temperatures and an afternoon climb out of a canyon.

Warning: Mountain lion encounters have occurred on this trail.

User Groups: Hikers, dogs, horses, and mountain bikes. No wheelchair facilities.

Permits: No permits are necessary. Parking and access are free.

Maps: For a topographic map, ask the USGS for Colfax.

Directions: From Sacramento, drive east on I-80 for four miles to Colfax and the exit signed Colfax-Grass Valley/Highway 174. Take that exit and drive a short distance (on the southeast side of I-80) to a stop sign at North Canyon (a frontage road). Turn left at North Canyon Way and drive one mile to the trailhead parking area. On weekends in spring, the parking lot can fill. Park on the road's shoulder and do not block the lanes.

Contact: Bureau of Land Management, Mother Lode Field Office, 916/941-3101, www.blm.gov/ca.

30 GREEN VALLEY TRAIL

5.2 mi/1 day

on the North Fork American River near Sugar Pine Reservoir

Map 6.1, page 213

The trip starts at a little-known trailhead near Sugar Pine Reservoir, beyond the Sugarpine Dam (elevation 4,080 feet). From there, Green Valley Trail is steep and often rocky. It descends 2,240 feet in 2.25 miles before reaching the river. We do not advise extending your trip from here.

The end point is a site along the North Fork American. Fishing is decent. At some point, you'll just want to watch the water go by, and try to forget what you have to do to return to your car. The price is steep. Run out of water on a hot day and the return trip will put you through more punishment than is typically handed out at Folsom Prison.

It is possible to continue downriver a short way or to cross the river (good luck) and hike upstream into Green Valley. However, these sections of the trail are in very poor condition, and the upstream route crosses private property owned by people who do not take kindly to visitors.

User Groups: Hikers, dogs, and horses. Mountain bikes are not advised. No wheelchair facilities.

Permits: No permits are required. Parking and access are free.

Maps: For a map, ask the U.S. Forest Service for Tahoe National Forest. For a topographic map, ask the USGS for Dutch Flat.

Directions: Take I-80 to Auburn and the exit for Foresthill/Foresthill Road. Take that exit, turn east on Foresthill Road, and drive 15.5 miles to Foresthill (and the Forest Service district office). Continue another 10 miles (it becomes Foresthill Divide Road, then Forest Road 10/Sugar Pine Road) and continue five miles (cross Sugar Pine Dam). From the dam, continue one mile to Elliot Ranch Road (just past the entrance to Sugar Pine Campground on the right). Turn north on Elliot Ranch Road and drive three miles to the trailhead on the left. High-clearance vehicles required, four-wheel drive advised.

Contact: Tahoe National Forest, American River Ranger District, 530/367-2224, www.fs.usda.gov/tahoe.

31 FOREST VIEW LOOP TRAIL

1.0 mi/0.5 hr 1 9

in Tahoe National Forest east of Foresthill

Map 6.1, page 213

This is an easy, short loop trail that is routed through California's northernmost grove of sequoias. It is set at 5,200 feet on Mosquito Ridge Road. The trail meanders through virgin old-growth forest, home to a half dozen monster-size trees. Along the 0.5-mile Big Trees Interpretive Trail are 16 stops marked with numbers that coincide with listings in a brochure that's available at the trailhead, allowing visitors to take an interesting and informative self-guided tour of the history of these massive trees. Linked with Forest View Trail, the entire loop can extend 1.5 miles. Despite the long drive to the trailhead on Mosquito Ridge, the trail gets quite a bit of use. The drive in provides views of an expansive foothill landscape before entering the conifers.

User Groups: Hikers and dogs. No horses or mountain bikes. No wheelchair facilities.

Permits: No permits are required. Parking and access are free.

Maps: Free interpretive brochures are available at the trailhead. For a map, ask the U.S. Forest Service for Tahoe National Forest. For a topographic map, ask the USGS for Greek Store.

Directions: Take I-80 to Auburn and the exit for Foresthill/Foresthill Road. Take that exit, turn east on Foresthill Road, and drive 15.5 miles to Foresthill (and the Forest Service district office), and then continue 1.2 miles to Mosquito Ridge Road. Turn right (east) on Mosquito Ridge Road and drive 24 miles to Forest Road 16. Turn right and drive 0.5 mile to parking and the trailhead.

Contact: Tahoe National Forest, American River Ranger District, 530/367-2224, www.fs.usda.gov/tahoe.

32 WESTERN STATES TRAIL: DEADWOOD TO ELDORADO CREEK

5.9 mi/3.0 hr 3 7

in Tahoe National Forest east of Foresthill

Map 6.1, page 213

The Western States Trail is best known for long-distance, competitive runs and equestrian rides. At times, mountain bikers take over the trail as well. This section captures one of the better stretches for hikers. From Deadwood (a historic cemetery), you drop about 2.5 miles down to Eldorado Creek and reach a bridge. This is a decent spot for swimming on a midsummer afternoon or fishing for trout on early summer evening. The trail continues over the bridge and climbs 1,600 feet to Michigan Bluff. Few do this. If you have to go up, most just want to do it once, and that's back to your car. The Michigan Bluff Trail is a section of the Western States Trail, which spans from Squaw Valley to Auburn.

User Groups: Hikers, dogs, horses, and mountain bikes. No wheelchair facilities.

Permits: No permits are required. Parking and access are free.

Maps: For a map, ask the U.S. Forest Service for Tahoe National Forest. For a topographic map, ask the USGS for Michigan Bluff.

Directions: Take I-80 to Auburn and the exit for Foresthill/Foresthill Road. Take that exit, turn east on Foresthill Road, and drive 15.5 miles to Foresthill (and the Forest Service district office). Continue northeast (it becomes Foresthill Divide Road) for 17 miles to Deadwood Ridge Road. Turn right (becomes dirt) and continue to the junction at

Deadwood Cemetery. Park in the pullout. The road degrades quickly. High-clearance vehicles recommended.

Contact: Tahoe National Forest, American River Ranger District, 530/367-2224, www.fs.usda.gov/tahoe.

33 GROUSE FALLS

1.0 mi/0.5 hr 1 10

in Tahoe National Forest near Foresthill

Map 6.1, page 213 BEST

Some waterfalls are simply mind-boggling in their beauty, and some provide the centerpiece of a beautiful setting. Grouse Falls is one of the latter. The hike is a 15-minute walk through old-growth forest to a viewing deck. From here you're looking out over a deep and wide canyon. The waterfall is about 0.5 mile away across the canyon. It's several hundred feet long, and when it's running full, it can seem like a scene out of Yosemite. The overlook is a wooden platform with benches where you can sit and admire the beauty. It just seems to be a little far away. You don't see or hear immense Grouse Falls until just before you come out to the overlook, and when you do, it can be a surprise. You need a tripod and long lens to best capture it in a photograph.

User Groups: Hikers, dogs, horses, and mountain bikes. No wheelchair facilities.

Permits: No permits are necessary. Parking and access are free.

Maps: For a map, ask the U.S. Forest Service for Tahoe National Forest. For a topographic map, ask the USGS for Michigan Bluff.

Directions: Take I-80 to Auburn and the exit for Foresthill/Foresthill Road. Take that exit, turn east on Foresthill Road, and drive 15.5 miles to Foresthill (and the Forest Service district office). Continue 1.2 miles to Mosquito Ridge Road. Turn right on Mosquito Ridge Road and drive 19.2 miles (the road becomes Foresthill Divide Road) to Peavine Ridge Road/Road 33. Turn left and drive 5.5 miles to a spur road for Grouse Falls. Turn left and go 0.5 mile to parking and the trailhead.

Contact: Tahoe National Forest, American River Ranger District, 530/367-2224, www.fs.usda.gov/tahoe.

34 MCGUIRE TRAIL/ WESTERN STATES TRAIL

7.4 mi/2.0 hr 2 8

at French Meadows Reservoir in Tahoe National Forest

Map 6.1, page 213

The McGuire Trail has become a favorite side trip for families visiting or camping at French Meadows Reservoir (elevation 5,290 feet). The highlights are sweeping views of the lake below. The trailhead is near the boat ramp, at the upper parking lot next to the restroom. From here, the trail traces the north shore of the lake, and in the process, is routed in and out of forest. It then rises up an easy grade to the top of Red Star Ridge (5,600 feet) and provides good views of the reservoir below. French Meadows is a beautiful and large lake, covering nearly 2,000 acres when full. It is stocked each year with trout that join a healthy population of resident brown trout and holdovers from stocks of rainbow trout from prior years.

User Groups: Hikers, dogs, horses, and mountain bikes. No wheelchair facilities.

Permits: No permits are required. Parking and access are free.

Maps: For a map, ask the U.S. Forest Service for Tahoe National Forest. For a topographic map, ask the USGS for Bunker Hill.

Directions: Take I-80 to Auburn and the exit for Foresthill/Foresthill Road. Take that exit, turn east on Foresthill Road, and drive 15.5 miles to Foresthill (and the Forest Service district office). Continue 1.2 miles to Mosquito Ridge Road. Turn right on Mosquito Ridge Road and drive 38 miles to the French Meadows Reservoir Dam. Cross the dam, turn left (still Mosquito Ridge Road), and drive 5.5 miles

(turn left at the intersection where the pavement ends, signed for boat ramp) to the trailhead, near McGuire Boat Ramp. The trailhead is at the upper parking lot next to the restroom.
Contact: Tahoe National Forest, American River Ranger District, 530/367-2224, www.fs.usda.gov/tahoe.

35 GRANITE CHIEF TRAIL TO TINKER KNOB

14.0 mi/2 days 4 10

in Tahoe National Forest near Squaw Valley

Map 6.1, page 213

Tinker Knob is not an easy summit to reach, but those who do always remember it. The hike starts at the Squaw Valley Fire Station, elevation 6,100 feet. That much is easy. The Granite Chief Trail climbs 2,000 feet over a span of 3.5 miles to the Pacific Crest Trail (at 8,400 feet). Most of the climb is forested, but there are occasional openings with views of Lake Tahoe and surrounding peaks. Many hikers choose to "cheat" and ride the tram at Squaw Valley to reach the PCT, then start hiking around from there.

When, at last, you gain the PCT, turn right (north) toward Tinker Knob. It's another 3.5 miles, most of it on an easier, winding grade along the top of a ridge. Yet there is a surprising, cruel stretch where you must drop downhill and then climb up again. The last section of trail is a series of switchbacks up to the Tinker Knob Saddle, then it's a brief 0.25-mile climb to the summit of Tinker Knob, at 8,950 feet. You like views? How about this one: a head-swiveling vista of Anderson Peak, Painted Rock, Silver Peak, the American River Canyon, Donner Lake, and Lake Tahoe.

One-way option with a shuttle: To make this a one-way trip of 11 miles, it can be done with a partner and a shuttle car. Leave one car at the Coldstream trailhead near Donner Memorial State Park. (It's at the horseshoe bend in the railroad tracks at the end of Coldstream Creek access road.) The Coldstream Trail meets the PCT just below the summit of Tinker Knob. After you gain the summit via the route described above, follow Coldstream Trail four miles down to its trailhead.

User Groups: Hikers, dogs, horses, and mountain bikes. No wheelchair facilities.
Permits: No permits are required. Parking and access are free.
Maps: For a map, ask the U.S. Forest Service for Tahoe National Forest. For topographic maps, ask the USGS for Tahoe City and Granite Chief.
Directions: From Truckee, take Highway 89 south and drive about eight miles to Squaw Valley Road. Turn right on Squaw Valley Road and drive 2.2 miles to the Squaw Valley Fire Station. The trail begins on its east side. You must leave your car in the large parking lot by the ski lift buildings, not by the fire station. Walk back across the bridge to the trailhead.
Contact: Tahoe National Forest, Truckee Ranger District, 530/587-3558, www.fs.usda.gov/tahoe.

36 GRANITE CHIEF TRAIL TO EMIGRANT PASS

12.0 mi/7.0 hr 4 9

in Tahoe National Forest near Squaw Valley

Map 6.1, page 213

The Granite Chief Trail begins at the Squaw Valley Fire Station (at 6,100 feet) and climbs, climbs, and climbs some more until it reaches the Pacific Crest Trail, some 2,300 feet (at 8,400 feet) and 3.5 miles later. This is why many hikers choose to ride the tram at Squaw Valley to reach the PCT, then start hiking around from there. But not you? You like a challenge, right? Well, in either case, see you at the top.

When you reach the PCT, turn left (south) toward Twin Peaks. The view of Lake Tahoe and its cobalt waters is stunning. Still ascending, hike for one mile on the PCT to the eastern flank of Granite Chief Peak (elevation 9,086 feet). Finally you begin to descend, and in one more mile you reach an intersection with Western States Trail. Turn left and take a 0.5-mile walk to visit the Watson Monument, a stone marker at Emigrant Pass. In early summer, you probably won't stay long if you arrive in the afternoon: Although the views are lovely, the wind is often fierce by mid- to late afternoon.

User Groups: Hikers, dogs, horses, and mountain bikes. No wheelchair facilities.

Permits: No permits are required. Parking and access are free.

Maps: For a map, ask the U.S. Forest Service for Tahoe National Forest. For topographic maps, ask the USGS for Tahoe City and Granite Chief.

Directions: From Truckee, take Highway 89 south and drive about eight miles to Squaw Valley Road. Turn right on Squaw Valley Road and drive 2.2 miles to the Squaw Valley Fire Station. The trail begins on its east side. You must leave your car in the large parking lot by the ski lift buildings, not by the fire station. Walk back across the bridge to the trailhead.

Contact: Tahoe National Forest, Truckee Ranger District, 530/587-3558, www.fs.usda.gov/tahoe.

37 FIVE LAKES

5.0 mi/2.0 hr 

in the Granite Chief Wilderness near Alpine Meadows

Map 6.1, page 213

In a hike of just an hour or so, there's a place at north Tahoe where you can reach a series of five wilderness lakes nestled in granite amid a pine forest. It's called the Five Lakes Trail, and it's one of the best short day hikes in California. It attracts a lot of folks in summer. Try it when the snow melts in spring and you can still have it to yourself. The trailhead is near Alpine Meadows Ski Area, with a sign, billboard, and map (on the right as you drive up). The hike is 2.5 miles one-way with a 1,000-foot climb into the Granite Chief Wilderness. At the trailhead, you park right on the road's shoulder, and you'll almost always see other cars marking the spot.

The first half mile of trail climbs right off, and if you are not acclimated to the elevation, it may take a while to catch your second wind. No problem. The trip is short, so if you need to, take your time. The climb eventually steadies out and most will find a nice rhythm as you rise up the flank of the canyon. At one point, you pass under a series of ski lift support structures for Alpine Meadows and can see up to the ridge to 8,637-foot Ward Peak. Much of the climb is amid exposed granite and manzanita, so you get big canyon views. At about two miles, you pop over the ridge and pass the boundary for the Granite Chief Wilderness. When you top the ridge at 7,400 feet, the trail then feeds you to a series of five pristine lakes linked by a mosaic of paths in forest. It's a short walk beyond to the first lake on the left. The fun is just beginning. A short strait connects two of the biggest lakes, my favorites. At the biggest of them, a granite slab on one side, boulders and forest on the other, edges clear blue water. The ambitious can hike on and link up with the Pacific Crest Trail. Most have a trail picnic aside their favorite lake, then return.

User Groups: Hikers, dogs, and horses. No mountain bikes. No wheelchair facilities.

Permits: No permits are required for day hiking. Parking and access are free.

Maps: For a map, ask the U.S. Forest Service for Tahoe National Forest. For topographic maps, ask the USGS for Tahoe City and Granite Chief.

Directions: From Sacramento, take I-80 east for 90 miles to Truckee and Exit 185 for Highway 89. Take that exit, turn right, arc slightly on the roundabout, then continue on 89 and drive 9.8 miles (past exit for Squaw Valley) to Alpine Meadows Road. Turn right and drive 2.5 miles to the trailhead on the right (look for parked cars along road; billboard and sign at trailhead).

Contact: Tahoe National Forest, Truckee Ranger District, 530/587-3558, www.fs.usda.gov/tahoe.

38 WARD CREEK TRAIL

6.0 mi/3.0 hr 1 9

in Tahoe National Forest near Tahoe City

Map 6.1, page 213

Ward Creek Trail is tame compared to some of the more famous hikes at Lake Tahoe. There's no stellar waterfall, no drop-dead gorgeous lake views, and no towering granite monoliths. But then again, there are no crowds either. For many, the trade-off is a good one. The route passes through fields of mule's ears and forests of sugar pines, with enough open sections to provide wide-open views of the surrounding mountain ridges.

The trail begins as an old dirt road, paralleling Ward Creek for 1.5 miles to a washed-out bridge and a Road Closed sign. Cross the creek on logs and continue hiking, now on a single-track. The trail climbs a little higher above Ward Creek, then enters a dense, lovely pine forest. You can go as far as you like (the trail continues to Twin Peaks, 5.3 miles from the trailhead). For the mileage suggested, turn around when you are about 0.5 mile into the trees and take an easy stroll home.

User Groups: Hikers, dogs, horses, and mountain bikes. No wheelchair facilities.

Permits: No permits are required. Parking and access are free.

Maps: For a map, ask the U.S. Forest Service for Lake Tahoe Basin Management Unit. For a topographic map, ask the USGS for Tahoe City.

Directions: From Truckee, take Highway 89 south and drive to Tahoe City. Turn right on Highway 89 and drive two miles to Pineland Drive (just north of Kilner Park). Turn right on Pineland Drive and go 0.5 mile to Twin Peaks Drive. Turn left and drive 1.7 miles. (Twin Peaks Drive becomes Ward Creek Boulevard.) At 1.7 miles, park in the pullout on the left side of the highway and begin hiking at the gated dirt road, Forest Service Road 15N62. If the gate is open, you can drive inside and park along the dirt road.

Contact: Lake Tahoe Basin Management Unit, South Lake Tahoe, 530/543-2600, www.fs.usda.gov/ltbmu; Taylor Creek Visitor Center, open mid-June through mid-September (closed Tues. and Wed.), weekends on shoulder season starting Memorial Day and after Labor Day weekends, 530/543-2674.

39 ELLIS PEAK TRAIL

6.0 mi/3.5 hr

in Tahoe National Forest near Tahoe City

Map 6.1, page 213

Some people will spend a week hiking 100 miles to get what is already available in three miles and a few hours at 8,740-foot Ellis Peak (there's one little trick and secret, and we'll get to that). Of the dozen or so landmark peaks that surround Lake Tahoe, Ellis Peak requires one of the shortest hikes, especially compared to renowned Tallac, Freel and Pyramid. Ellis sits on the threshold of world-class greatness; at the top, it can be difficult to decide which way to face. One side towers over north Lake Tahoe, while the other looks across a false summit and Desolation Wilderness. The Crystal Range and Loon Lake lie below to the southwest, the Granite Chief Wilderness to the northwest. Everywhere you look are miles of spectacular high Sierra grandeur.

This six-mile, round-trip hike has a total elevation gain of roughly 1,500 feet. If there's a catch, you'll find out right off. The trail is hardly grade and instead is steep in two spots. In the first mile, you'll climb about 800 feet through forest. As you emerge at a sub-ridge, notice a notch in the cliff on your left—you can peer down through a plummeting drop and see the parking area and your car below. That gives you a sense of how steep the trail is, and how high you are climbing so fast. As you continue ahead, you pass rafts of mule's ears at your feet, and off to the right is beautiful Loon Lake in the Crystal Basin. Once you top the first sub-ridge, the trail contours along the ridge, then sails down to a mountain saddle. It then climbs again and gains Knee Ridge. You will cross an OHV road, with oft-mosquito-y Ellis Lake a short distance to your left. The primary trail is straight ahead.

From the Ellis Lake junction, it's another 0.5-mile climb to the top. You emerge on an old dirt road for a bit to see a false summit directly ahead and to your left. Resist the urge to climb it. Instead, stay right and follow the trail as it arcs in a half circle, where it leads up another 0.25 mile to the top of Ellis Peak. After scrambling to the top of that pinnacle, it feels like you are on top of the world. Some of the rocks make perfect chairs. Sit and take in the views, expansive Tahoe blue on one side, an infinity of wilderness on the other.

User Groups: Hikers. Dogs and horses permitted, but not advised; only water at Ellis Lake. No mountain bikes (OHV route available 0.5 mile down road on left). No wheelchair facilities.

Permits: No permits are required. Parking and access are free.

Maps: For a map, ask the U.S. Forest Service for Lake Tahoe Basin Management Unit. For a topographic map, ask the USGS for Homewood.

Directions: Drive to Sacramento, then continue on I-80 east for 90 miles to Truckee and Exit 185 for Highway 89 South. Take that exit to a traffic circle, turn right, drive short distance to 89 South, and continue 13.5 miles to Tahoe City. Turn right (still 89) and drive 4.3 miles and look for sign on right for Kaspian Campground, and just beyond, Barker Pass Road/Forest Road 3 (unsigned). Turn right and drive seven miles (paved, watch for road bikes) into national forest. When road turns to dirt, drive short distance to Barker Pass, trailhead on left, and park along shoulder. Trailhead is signed.

Contact: Lake Tahoe Basin Management Unit, South Lake Tahoe, 530/543-2600, www.fs.usda.gov/ltbmu; Taylor Creek Visitor Center, open mid-June through mid-September (closed Tues. and Wed.), weekends on shoulder season starting Memorial Day and after Labor Day weekends, 530/543-2674.

40 STATELINE LOOKOUT

1.0 mi/0.5 hr 

off Highway 28 near Crystal Bay

Map 6.1, page 213

At this lookout above Tahoe at North Shore (elevation 7,014 feet), you can check out the views with telescopes. Or, hey, forget the telescopes and just look with your own eyes. Either way, the view is unforgettable. A short self-guided historical trail is also available. You can learn all about the cultural history of North Shore, which includes stories of timber, railroads, casinos, and resorts. But what you remember, of course, is the world-class view across Lake Tahoe and beyond to its mountain rim.

For years we avoided this trail because we thought it was just a tourist attraction, located at the lookout tower that straddles the Nevada and California state line. It turns out that *we* were the dumb tourists, because this little trail is great.

User Groups: Hikers, wheelchairs, and dogs. No horses or mountain bikes.

Permits: No permits are required. Parking and access are free.

Maps: For a map, ask the U.S. Forest Service for Lake Tahoe Basin Management Unit. For a topographic map, ask the USGS for Kings Beach.

Directions: From Truckee, take Highway 89 south and drive to Tahoe City and Highway 28. Turn left on Highway 28 and drive six miles to Reservoir Drive (just east of the old Tahoe Biltmore Casino). Turn left (north) and drive to Lake View Avenue. Turn right and drive through a residential area and continue to Forest Service Road 1601 (at an unmarked iron gate). Turn left on Forest Service Road 1601, park at the gate, and walk 0.5 mile to the lookout. Parking is limited. Do not look for a sign along Highway 28 that says "Stateline Lookout," because it doesn't exist.

Contact: Lake Tahoe Basin Management Unit, South Lake Tahoe, 530/543-2600, www.fs.usda.gov/ltbmu; Taylor Creek Visitor Center, open mid-June through mid-September (closed Tues. and Wed.), weekends on shoulder season starting Memorial Day and after Labor Day weekends, 530/543-2674.

41 BURTON CREEK LOOP

4.3 mi/2.5 hr 1 8

off Highway 28 near Tahoe City

Map 6.1, page 213

Burton Creek State Park has no visitors center, no campground, no entrance kiosk, and, unfortunately, no trail signs or official map. What really matters is that it has no crowds, a major bonus at Lake Tahoe. Yet the park spans more than 2,000 acres and is classified as an "undeveloped park," while, believe it or not, it is Lake Tahoe's second-largest state park.

A five-mile loop trip is possible. Start at the trailhead on the west side of North Tahoe High School. From there it's 0.4 mile to a trail junctions that rings the Burton Creek Natural Preserve. Burton Creek runs through its center. Turn right at that junction and complete the oblong loop along the riparian creek zone, a distance of 3.9 miles, to return to the junction. You will wander through a mix of fir and pine forest, open meadows, and creek-side riparian habitat. Although the trail is not signed, there are numbers painted at most intersections, which help you stay on track. There are a series of spur trails (with numbers) that lead to other trailheads.

User Groups: Hikers, leashed dogs, horses, and mountain bikes. No wheelchair facilities.

Permits: No permits are required. Parking and access are free.

Maps: PDF at website. For a topographic map, ask the USGS for Tahoe City.

Directions: From Truckee, take Highway 89 south and drive to Tahoe City and Highway 28. Turn left on Highway 28 and drive 2.3 miles to Old Mill Road. Turn left and drive 0.4 mile to Polaris Road. Turn left on Polaris Road and drive 0.5 mile to North Tahoe High School and the dirt road by the school parking lot. Park alongside the dirt road. Be careful not to block the gate.

Contact: Burton Creek State Park, 530/525-7232, www.parks.ca.gov.

42 BARKER PASS TO DONNER PASS (PCT)

31.4 mi one-way/3 days 3 9

from Barker Pass to Donner Pass

Map 6.1, page 213

The trailhead at Barker Pass (7,650 feet) is one of the best. It provides direct access to the Granite Chief Wilderness to the north or the Desolation Wilderness to the south. For PCT hikers who are heading north, the trip starts with a climb of 800 feet to enter Granite Chief. Once on the ridge, you're rewarded with 360-degree views of this high-mountain landscape, a mix of volcanic rock and granite ridges, much of it above tree line. Though hikers don't face the long, sustained climbs so common in the southern Sierra, it's enough of a roller-coaster ride to require hikers to be in excellent shape. The trail cuts the flank of Ward Peak, at 8,470 feet, then switchbacks steeply down to Five Lakes and Five Lakes Creek (where there's an opportunity to camp). The trail then continues up and down canyons all the way to Donner Pass. You can expect to see lots of hikers, because along the way, you'll pass near two ski resorts (Alpine Meadows and Squaw Valley), where hikers can use the ski lifts in the summer to gain easy elevation to the ridgeline, rather than having to grind out long, all-day climbs. Before making the final leg of this section to Donner Pass, a descent of more than 1,000 feet, hikers can enjoy breathtaking views of Donner Lake and the miles of surrounding high country.

To continue north on the PCT, see the

Donner Pass to the Yuba River (PCT) hike in this chapter. If you are walking this trail in reverse, see the *Echo Lakes Resort to Barker Pass (PCT)* hike in this chapter.

User Groups: Hikers, dogs, and horses. No mountain bikes. No wheelchair facilities.

Permits: A single permit is required to hike the Pacific Crest Trail. Contact the national forest, Bureau of Land Management, or national park office at your point of entry for a combined permit that is good for traveling through multiple-permit areas during your dates of travel.

Maps: For topographic maps, ask the USGS for Emerald Bay, Rockbound Valley, Homewood, Tahoe City, Granite Chief, and Norden.

Directions: To reach the Barker Pass trailhead: From Truckee, take Highway 89 south and drive to Tahoe City. Turn right on Highway 89 and drive south to Kaspian Picnic Grounds (0.5 mile north of Tahoe Pines) and Forest Road 15N03. Turn right (west) and drive seven miles to the trailhead.

For the Donner Pass trailhead: From Truckee, drive west on I-80 and exit at Castle Peak Area/Boreal Ridge, just west of the Donner Summit roadside rest area. The sign for the Pacific Crest trailhead is what you're looking for, and it's located on the south side of the highway.

Contact: Tahoe National Forest, Truckee Ranger District, 530/587-3558, www.fs.usda.gov/tahoe; Lake Tahoe Basin Management Unit, South Lake Tahoe, 530/543-2600, www.fs.usda.gov/ltbmu; Taylor Creek Visitor Center, open mid-June through mid-September (closed Tues. and Wed.), weekends on shoulder season starting Memorial Day and after Labor Day weekends, 530/543-2674.

43 GENERAL CREEK TO LILY POND

7.0 mi/3.5 hr

in Ed Z'berg Sugar Pine Point State Park near Lake Tahoe

Map 6.1, page 213

Lily Pond, a marshy, serene spot that is rare for the high Sierra provides serenity to go with its uniqueness. The only problem is the trail is a dirt road. This hike starts in Sugar Pine Point State Park. You begin by walking along a flat, open stretch of General Creek. You then hike gently uphill through the forest to the Lily Pond. At 2.5 miles from the campground, at the far end of the loop, you'll see the single-track turnoff signed for Lily Pond and Lost Lake. It's a one-mile hike through a rocky, dense forest to the pond, which is indeed covered with lilies. On your return, you can always take the south side of the loop for variety, then turn left on the bridge over General Creek to return to the start of the loop.

There are a several factors to enjoying this walk: If you're not staying in the General Creek Campground, the day-use parking area is more than 0.5 mile from site 149, where the trail begins. To make this walk to the trailhead more pleasant, be sure to take the single-track trail from the parking lot instead of walking along the paved camp road. The trail is somewhat hidden from view, so if you don't see it, ask the attendant in the entrance kiosk where it is. Next, when you finally meet up with the loop, be sure to take the north side of it, which is prettier than the south side, with lots of big sugar pines interspersed with Jeffreys and lodgepoles. The south side is mostly open meadows. A little history: This was the site of the 1960 Olympics biathlon. Nowadays in winter, the trail is part of a popular cross-country skiing loop. Finally, at the park's picnic sites and campsites, yellowjackets can be a pain in late summer.

User Groups: Hikers and mountain bikes. No dogs or horses. No wheelchair facilities.

Permits: No permits are required. A day-use fee of $8 is charged per vehicle.
Maps: A map of Sugar Pine Point State Park is available for a fee at the entrance station or as a PDF on the website. A Lake Tahoe map is available for a fee from Tom Harrison Maps. For a topographic map, ask the USGS for Homewood.
Directions: From Truckee, take Highway 89 south and drive to Tahoe City. Turn right on Highway 89 and drive south eight miles to the General Creek Campground entrance on the right. Turn right and park in one of the day-use areas by the entrance kiosk, then walk into the campground to site 149 and the start of the trail. You can walk into the camp on the park road or take the single-track trail that leads from the parking lot.
Contact: Ed Z'berg Sugar Pine Point State Park, Tahoma, 530/525-7982, www.parks.ca.gov.

44 MEEKS CREEK TRAIL TO RUBICON LAKE

15.0 mi/1-2 days 3 10

in the Desolation Wilderness

Map 6.1, page 213

This trek into the Desolation Wilderness is a moderate-level backpacking trip that's loaded with alpine lakes and classic Tahoe scenery. In summer, plan on sharing the trail with lots of other folks; in spring at ice-out at the lakes, you can have them to yourself. The trailhead doesn't look like much, a gate on a dirt road, with a billboard information sign nearby, but we know better. The trip starts as you hike on a closed dirt road that leads through a pretty valley, flat and easy, popular for locals with dogs in summer, for 1.3 miles. You then start to climb and, 2.5 miles in, arrive at the sign for entry to Desolation Wilderness. You hike parallel to Meeks Creek on a gently climbing trail. You're in forest most of the time, and in late spring and early summer, we've heard the mating calls of grouse here. You cross Meeks Creek, and during periods of high snowmelt, it can be impassable. You then continue straight to Lake Genevieve, at 4.5 miles. The lake is shallow but provides swimming. The trail then climbs up to larger Crag Lake, then continues to climb farther to small, lily-covered Shadow Lake. (A right fork beyond Crag Lake leads to small Hidden Lake, less than 0.25 mile off the main trail; it's a good side trip.) From Shadow Lake, it's a mile farther to Stony Ridge Lake, the largest of this series of lakes, and then yet another mile to gorgeous Rubicon Lake, 7.5 miles from the trailhead and with a total elevation gain of only 2,000 feet. The main steep stretch is right at the end, between Stony Ridge Lake and Rubicon Lake. Campsites can be found at most all of the lakes, but Rubicon Lake is the preferred site, since it's the most scenic of the group. There you have it, 7.5 miles on the way in and you get a lovely creek, six lakes, and a campsite at one of the prettiest lakes in the Tahoe Basin.
User Groups: Hikers, dogs, and horses. No mountain bikes. No wheelchair facilities.
Permits: Permits are required year-round for both day and overnight use. Day hikers may obtain a free permit from a ranger station or may self-issue at most major trailheads. Backpackers camping in Desolation Wilderness are subject to trailhead quotas. There is a $5 reservation fee, plus $5 per person for one night, $10 per person for two or more nights up to 14 days (nonrefundable), a $20 season pass for Desolation is available per person; reserve at www.recreation.gov. Children ages 12 and under are free. Golden Passes do not apply to personal-use permits. For groups, the cost of a single permit will not exceed $100.
Maps: For a map, ask the U.S. Forest Service for Desolation Wilderness or Lake Tahoe Basin Management Unit. A Lake Tahoe or Desolation Wilderness map is also available from Tom Harrison Maps. For topographic maps, ask the USGS for Homewood and Rockbound Valley.
Directions: From Truckee, take Highway 89

south and drive to Tahoe City. Turn right on Highway 89 and drive south for 10.5 miles to dirt access road and trailhead (look for historic cabin and gated dirt road next to parking).The trailhead is near the entrance of Meeks Bay Resort, on the opposite site of the road; if you drive south over the bridge at Meeks Creek, you have gone a short distance too far south.

Contact: Lake Tahoe Basin Management Unit, South Lake Tahoe, 530/543-2600, www.fs.usda.gov/ltbmu; Taylor Creek Visitor Center, open mid-June through mid-September (closed Tues. and Wed.), weekends on shoulder season starting Memorial Day and after Labor Day weekends, 530/543-2674.

45 RUBICON AND LIGHTHOUSE LOOP

2.0 mi/1.0 hr 1 10

in D. L. Bliss State Park on the west shore of Lake Tahoe

Map 6.2, page 214

When you visit South Lake Tahoe, this is one of the must-sees, must-dos. The trail edges along the steep cliffs on the west side of the lake and provides a panorama across Lake Tahoe. You can also turn it into an excellent short loop. The Rubicon Trail starts at Calawee Cove Beach. The trail is cut into a slope that faces the lake, at times with 100-foot drop-offs straight down to Lake Tahoe. Cable-type rails are in place in some sections for safety. Hike 0.25 mile to a spur trail that leads to the old lighthouse; there's no view, but check out the remains of a 1916 lighthouse. Then continue beyond it for another 0.5 mile. Every step of the way, the lake and mountain views are mind-boggling. You'll arrive at the trail junction. Bear right and walk to a parking lot, where you can pick up Lighthouse Trail and loop back to Calawee Cove Beach. If you want to see those lake vistas one more time, forget about the loop and just head back the way you came. Not everybody is up for hiking the entire length of the Rubicon Trail, but this hike provides a sample of the spectacular views.

User Groups: Hikers only. No dogs, horses, or mountain bikes. No wheelchair facilities.

Permits: No permits are required. A day-use fee of $10 is charged per vehicle.

Maps: A map of D. L. Bliss State Park is available for a fee at the entrance station. A Lake Tahoe map is available for a fee from Tom Harrison Maps. For a topographic map, ask the USGS for Emerald Bay.

Directions: From South Lake Tahoe, take Highway 89 north past Emerald Bay and continue a short distance to the entrance road for D. L. Bliss State Park. Turn right and drive 0.5 mile to the entrance station and continue for 0.7 mile to a fork. Turn right and drive another 0.7 mile to Calawee Cove Beach and the parking lot. The Rubicon Trail begins on the far side of the lot. If this lot is full, you will have to use one of the other day-use parking lots in the park.

Contact: D. L. Bliss State Park, 530/525-9529, www.parks.ca.gov.

46 RUBICON TRAIL

9.0 mi/5.0 hr 2 10

in D. L. Bliss State Park on the west shore of Lake Tahoe

Map 6.2, page 214 BEST

The Rubicon Trail is the premier easy day hike at Lake Tahoe. If you want the best scenery that Lake Tahoe offers, this is the trail. There is one little problem on pretty summer days. Right: It's you and often a zillion other hikers who want the same thing. If possible, walk this trail in the off-season; September, for instance, is great—and do it on a weekday. At dawn or dusk in summer, the trail, views, and experience can seem like a miracle. You get eye-popping scenery as you gaze out across the surface and deep into the depths of sparkling, clear, 12-mile-wide Lake Tahoe and beyond to the rim of mountains that surround it.

The trailhead is at the far side of the parking lot for Calawee Cove Beach. A short distance after you start, be sure to take the left fork, which will keep you on Rubicon Trail. The trail stays close to the lake edge and has very little elevation change, just some mild ups and downs, holding steady near 6,300 feet. The trail ventures south for several miles, with a series of spectacular lookouts across Lake Tahoe. Eventually it cuts inland at Emerald Point and then emerges along the shore of Emerald Bay. The ambitious can continue through forest, with the lake on your left, to the Emerald Bay Boat Camp and beyond to the foot of Emerald Bay. Highlights include Rubicon Point, Emerald Point, Emerald Bay, Fannette Island, Vikingsholm Castle, and Eagle Point. If you stop for a picnic, don't be surprised if several little chipmunk-like ground squirrels visit you, hoping for a handout.

An option is to hike the trip in the opposite direction. That, is, you can start and end your Rubicon hike at Vikingsholm. To do that, park at the Emerald Bay Overlook parking lot, hike down to Vikingsholm, and then head north to the boat-in campground and beyond. Finding a parking spot at the Overlook in summer, unless you arrive very early, can be like searching for a polar bear in the desert. You'll add on nearly two miles round-trip getting from the parking lot to Vikingsholm, during which there is a 600-foot elevation change. Regardless, some prefer this.

User Groups: Hikers only. No dogs, horses, or mountain bikes. No wheelchair facilities.

Permits: No permits are required. A day-use fee of $10 is charged per vehicle.

Maps: A map of D. L. Bliss State Park is available for a fee at the entrance station. A Lake Tahoe map is available for a fee from Tom Harrison Maps. For a topographic map, ask the USGS for Emerald Bay.

Directions: From South Lake Tahoe, take Highway 89 north past Emerald Bay and continue a short distance to the entrance road for D. L. Bliss State Park. Turn right and drive 0.5 mile to the entrance station, then continue for 0.7 mile to a fork. Turn right and drive another 0.7 mile to Calawee Cove Beach and the parking lot. The Rubicon Trail begins on the far side of the lot. If this lot is full, you will have to use one of the other day-use parking lots in the park.

Contact: D. L. Bliss State Park, 530/525-9529, www.parks.ca.gov.

47 BALANCING ROCK

1.0 mi/0.5 hr 1 8

in D. L. Bliss State Park on the west shore of Lake Tahoe

Map 6.2, page 214

The Balancing Rock is a big hunk of granite that has been a curiosity for eons at Lake Tahoe. It's a 130-ton rock that sits balanced on a small rock pedestal, like a giant golf ball on an itty-bitty golf tee. At one angle, it seems impossible. This is a short, easy interpretive trail that is routed to it. The trail's brochure explains that erosion will eventually wear away the pedestal and cause the Balancing Rock to lose its balance. Tahoe lovers have been awaiting this event forever, and it still hasn't happened. In addition to Balancing Rock, the trail shows off many of the plants and trees of the Tahoe area. It's a good learning experience for both kids and adults.

User Groups: Hikers only. No dogs, horses, or mountain bikes. No wheelchair facilities.

Permits: No permits are required. A day-use fee of $10 is charged per vehicle.

Maps: A map of D. L. Bliss State Park is available for a fee at the entrance station. A Lake Tahoe map is available for a fee from Tom Harrison Maps. For a topographic map, ask the USGS for Emerald Bay.

Directions: From South Lake Tahoe, take Highway 89 north past Emerald Bay and continue a short distance to the entrance road for D. L. Bliss State Park. Turn right and drive 0.5 mile to the entrance station, then continue for

Desolation Wilderness

0.7 mile to a fork. Turn left and drive 0.25 mile to the Balancing Rock parking lot, on the left.
Contact: D. L. Bliss State Park, 530/525-9529, www.parks.ca.gov.

48 VIKINGSHOLM

2.0 mi/1.0 hr 

in Emerald Bay State Park on the west shore of Lake Tahoe

Map 6.2, page 214

Start this trip at dawn and you'll have paradise in your grasp. Start it on a summer day, and grasping a parking spot at the Emerald Bay Overlook will seem like the impossible dream. This walk is a one-mile traipse on a service road with a 500-foot descent to Vikingsholm, a Viking castle built by an heiress in 1929. The beauty lies in the scenery spread out before you as you hike downhill. You'll see Fannette Island and the spectacular deep blue waters of Emerald Bay. The route also ventures through old-growth cedar and pine forest. You then arrive at Lake Tahoe's sandy shoreline. Although visitors have to pay a small entrance fee to tour the inside of the castle, you can hike to it for free and add on a side trip to the base of 150-foot Eagle Falls, located 0.25 mile from Vikingsholm. For many people, the surprise on this trail is that the return hike has a 500-foot elevation gain. What, you mean we have to breathe hard?

Arrive early. By midmorning on summer weekends, visitors can be forced to park up to two miles away.

User Groups: Hikers only. No dogs, horses, or mountain bikes. No wheelchair facilities.
Permits: No permits are required. A fee of $10 is charged per vehicle, $5 per person to tour the inside of the castle.
Maps: A map of Emerald Bay and D. L. Bliss State Parks is available for a fee at the visitors center at Vikingsholm. A Lake Tahoe map is available for a fee from Tom Harrison Maps. For a topographic map, ask the USGS for Emerald Bay.
Directions: From South Lake Tahoe, take Highway 89 north and drive nine miles to the Emerald Bay Overlook parking lot on the east

side of Highway 89. The trail begins from the lakeside of the parking lot.

Contact: Emerald Bay State Park, Eagle Point Kiosk, 530/541-3030, www.parks.ca.gov.

49 UPPER EAGLE FALLS AND EAGLE LAKE

2.0 mi/1.0 hr 2 9

off Highway 89 near South Lake Tahoe

Map 6.2, page 214

This is one of the three most popular walks in the Tahoe region, right there with the nearby walk down to Vikingsholm and the Rubicon Trail. The trailhead is at the Eagle Falls Picnic Area. Near the restroom, you'll see the sign that points the way to the Upper Eagle Falls Trail. It's a "designer" path, where natural granite is cut into flagstone-like stairs and an elaborate wooden bridge escorts visitors over the top of the falls. It's a beautiful walk, best taken early in the morning and during the week, when the masses aren't around. The waterfall pours right under the hikers' bridge. Just beyond the bridge, the designer aspect of the trail ends as you enter the Desolation Wilderness. From here, it's a 400-foot climb in less than a mile to reach pretty Eagle Lake, surrounded by granite cliffs. People fish and picnic here; some even try to swim in the icy water.

If you want to see the "other" Eagle Falls, the one that drops right along Highway 89, see the listing in this chapter.

User Groups: Hikers and dogs. No horses or mountain bikes. No wheelchair facilities.

Permits: Day hikers must fill out a free permit at the wilderness trailhead. A $5 parking fee is charged per vehicle.

Maps: For a map, ask the U.S. Forest Service for Desolation Wilderness or Lake Tahoe Basin Management Unit. A Lake Tahoe map is available for a fee from Tom Harrison Maps. For a topographic map, ask the USGS for Emerald Bay.

Directions: From South Lake Tahoe, take Highway 89 north and drive 8.5 miles to the Eagle Falls Picnic Area and trailhead. Turn left into the parking area or park in the roadside pullout just north of the picnic area on the west side of Highway 89.

Contact: Lake Tahoe Basin Management Unit, South Lake Tahoe, 530/543-2600, www.fs.usda.gov/ltbmu; Taylor Creek Visitor Center, open mid-June through mid-September (closed Tues. and Wed.), weekends on shoulder season starting Memorial Day and after Labor Day weekends, 530/543-2674.

50 VELMA LAKES

10.0 mi/5.0 hr 3 9

in the Desolation Wilderness

Map 6.2, page 214

The Velma Lakes are classic Desolation Wilderness: gorgeous, alpine jewels. This route follows the trail to Eagle Falls and Eagle Lake (see listing in this chapter) for the first mile, then climbs through a rugged, glaciated landscape, with only occasional hardy lodgepole pines and twisted junipers providing meager shade. The lack of trees and the abundance of rock mean wide-open views and plenty of granite drama: Welcome to the Sierra high country.

The trailhead is at the Eagle Falls Picnic Area. Near the restroom, you'll see the sign that points the way to the Upper Eagle Falls Trail. At three miles (you intersect the trail that heads left to Dicks Lake), stay right for Velma Lakes. In one mile, your trail heads directly to Middle Velma Lake, the most popular of the lakes. It has several granite islands sprinkled in cobalt blue water. It's popular for swimming, though often cold.

Just before Middle Velma Lake, you can take a left cutoff and head south to Upper Velma Lake in 0.5 mile. Another option is to take the trail, on your right, north along a creek, also 0.5 mile, to Lower Velma Lake. Remember to bring your sunscreen because the rocky trail to the Velma Lakes is exposed and open.

You can also begin the Velma Lakes hike from the trailhead at Bayview Campground. You will miss out on seeing Eagle Lake and a world-class view of Tahoe.

User Groups: Hikers and dogs. No horses or mountain bikes (the Bayview Trail provides access for horses; contact Tahoe Basin National Forest). No wheelchair facilities. To reach Velma Lakes, equestrians must access from another trailhead; Bayview trailhead is the best for this.

Permits: Permits are required year-round for both day and overnight use. Day hikers may obtain a free permit from a ranger station or may self-issue at most major trailheads. Backpackers camping in Desolation Wilderness are subject to trailhead quotas. There is a $5 reservation fee, plus $5 per person for one night, $10 per person for two or more nights up to 14 days (nonrefundable), a $20 season pass for Desolation is available per person; reserve at www.recreation.gov. Children ages 12 and under are free. For groups, the cost of a single permit will not exceed $100. A $5 parking fee is charged per vehicle.

Maps: For a map, ask the U.S. Forest Service for Desolation Wilderness or Lake Tahoe Basin Management Unit. A Lake Tahoe or Desolation Wilderness map is available from Tom Harrison Maps. For topographic maps, ask the USGS for Emerald Bay and Rockbound Valley.

Directions: From South Lake Tahoe, take Highway 89 north and drive 8.5 miles to the Eagle Falls Picnic Area and trailhead. Turn left into the parking area or park in the roadside pullout just north of the picnic area, on the west side of Highway 89.

Contact: Lake Tahoe Basin Management Unit, South Lake Tahoe, 530/543-2600, www.fs.usda.gov/ltbmu; Taylor Creek Visitor Center, open mid-June through mid-September (closed Tues. and Wed.), weekends on shoulder season starting Memorial Day and after Labor Day weekends, 530/543-2674.

51 CASCADE FALLS

2.0 mi/1.0 hr

off Highway 89 near South Lake Tahoe

Map 6.2, page 214

This trail is the best easy hike at Lake Tahoe. The one-mile trail leads to the brink of a stunning 200-foot cascade that drops into the southwest end of Cascade Lake. The trip is short and flat enough for almost anybody to make the trip, including young children, yet it still feels like wilderness.

From the trailhead at Bayview Campground, take the left fork signed for Cascade Falls. In five minutes, you get tremendous views of Cascade Lake (elevation 6,464 feet) below to your left. It isn't long and you start to hear and see the falls. The trail disintegrates as it nears the waterfall's edge, and hikers with children shouldn't get too close. Truth is, the best views are actually farther back on the trail. Upstream of the falls are some lovely pools surrounded by wide shelves of granite. Make sure you visit in spring or early summer, when the waterfall is flowing full and wide, because by August, it loses its drama.

User Groups: Hikers and dogs. No horses or mountain bikes. No wheelchair facilities.

Permits: No permits are required. Parking and access are free.

Maps: For a map, ask the U.S. Forest Service for Lake Tahoe Basin Management Unit. A Lake Tahoe map is available for a fee from Tom Harrison Maps. For a topographic map, ask the USGS for Emerald Bay.

Directions: From South Lake Tahoe, take Highway 89 north and drive 7.5 miles to the Bayview Campground. Turn left and drive to the far end of the campground to the trailhead parking area. If it's full, park on the shoulder of Highway 89 near the entrance to the campground.

Contact: Lake Tahoe Basin Management Unit, South Lake Tahoe, 530/543-2600, www.fs.usda.gov/ltbmu; Taylor Creek Visitor Center, open mid-June through mid-September (closed Tues.

and Wed.), weekends on shoulder season starting Memorial Day and after Labor Day weekends, 530/543-2674.

52 MOUNT TALLAC (TALLAC TRAILHEAD)

9.0 mi/6.0 hr  5 10

in the Desolation Wilderness near Fallen Leaf Lake

Map 6.2, page 214

There are two trailheads for Mount Tallac. Know the difference: If you are hiking Mount Tallac for the first time, start instead from the Glen Alpine trailhead. If you then want a steeper challenge, then the Mount Tallac trailhead is for you. Mount Tallac towers over Lake Tahoe and provides one of the most beautiful lookouts in North America. From the 9,735-foot summit, you look down on Fallen Leaf Lake, Cascade Lake, Emerald Bay, Lake Tahoe, and beyond to Mount Rose on the eastern Tahoe rim. To the west you can see across miles of Desolation Wilderness.

From this trailhead, you pay dearly for it: You climb 900 feet climb in the first 1.5 miles, and then 2,600 feet over the final three miles. From the trailhead, you make the first butt-kicker climb for 1.7 miles to Floating Island Lake. You get excellent views of Fallen Leaf Lake and Lake Tahoe along the way. Then it's another 0.7 mile to a trail junction just before Cathedral Lake, where a trail from Fallen Leaf Lake joins this one. Cathedral Lake is a good rest stop before making the final ascent to the top of Mount Tallac, a 2.4-mile butt-kicker of a climb on a rocky trail. It's made somewhat easier by a continuous and inspiring parade of vistas, including long-distance looks at Gilmore Lake, Susie Lake, and Lake Aloha. The trail ends 0.25 mile below the summit, where it meets the other Mount Tallac trail that emerges from Gilmore Lake. Bear right, and boulder hop your way to the top. The return trip down is terrible for many, a knee-screaming, toe-jamming affair that will have some questioning the purpose of life.

User Groups: Hikers and dogs. No horses or mountain bikes. No wheelchair facilities.

Permits: Permits are required year-round for both day and overnight use. Day hikers may obtain a free permit from a ranger station or may self-issue at most major trailheads. Backpackers camping in Desolation Wilderness are subject to trailhead quotas. There is a $5 reservation fee, plus $5 per person for one night, $10 per person for two or more nights up to 14 days (nonrefundable), a $20 season pass for Desolation is available per person; reserve at www.recreation.gov. Children ages 12 and under are free. Golden Passes do not apply to personal-use permits. For groups, the cost of a single permit will not exceed $100.

Maps: For a map, ask the U.S. Forest Service for Desolation Wilderness. A Lake Tahoe or Desolation Wilderness map is also available for a fee from Tom Harrison Maps. For a topographic map, ask the USGS for Emerald Bay.

Directions: From South Lake Tahoe, take Highway 89 north and drive 3.8 miles to the signed turnoff for Mount Tallac and Camp Concord (on the left, across the highway from the sign for Baldwin Beach). Drive 0.4 mile to the trailhead entrance road on the left. Turn left and drive 0.6 mile to the trailhead.

Contact: Lake Tahoe Basin Management Unit, South Lake Tahoe, 530/543-2600, www.fs.usda.gov/ltbmu; Taylor Creek Visitor Center, open mid-June through mid-September (closed Tues. and Wed.), weekends on shoulder season starting Memorial Day and after Labor Day weekends, 530/543-2674.

53 RAINBOW AND LAKE OF THE SKY TRAILS

0.5 mi/0.5 hr

in Tahoe National Forest near South Lake Tahoe

Map 6.2, page 214 **BEST**

At the Lake Tahoe Visitor Center, several short interpretive walks are available. The best are the Rainbow Trail and Lake of the Sky Trail. You can hike them both from the same starting point at the visitors center and combine an interesting nature lesson with a walk along Lake Tahoe's shoreline for exceptional scenery and views.

Start with Rainbow Trail, which leads from the visitors center's west side and takes you to Taylor Creek and its Stream Profile Chamber. The creek is where thousands of kokanee salmon come to spawn in the fall. You can view the fish through the glass walls of the profile chamber. You can also see them the ordinary way, just by peering into the creek as you walk. Then loop back to the visitors center and pick up Lake of the Sky Trail. You'll pass by Taylor Creek Marsh on your way to Tallac Point and Tahoe's shoreline. In summer, people go swimming at this sandy stretch of beach.

User Groups: Hikers and wheelchair users. No dogs, horses, or mountain bikes.

Permits: No permits are required. Parking and access are free.

Maps: For a map, ask the U.S. Forest Service for Lake Tahoe Basin Management Unit. A free forest recreation newspaper is also available. A Lake Tahoe map is available for a fee from Tom Harrison Maps. For a topographic map, ask the USGS for Emerald Bay.

Directions: From South Lake Tahoe, take Highway 89 north and drive three miles to the Lake Tahoe Visitor Center turnoff, on the right. Turn right and drive to the visitors center parking lot, where the trails begin.

Contact: Lake Tahoe Basin Management Unit, South Lake Tahoe, 530/543-2600, www.fs.usda.gov/ltbmu; Taylor Creek Visitor Center, open mid-June through mid-September (closed Tues. and Wed.), weekends on shoulder season starting Memorial Day and after Labor Day weekends, 530/543-2674.

54 MOUNT TALLAC LOOP (GLEN ALPINE TRAILHEAD)

11.8 mi/7.5 hr

in the Desolation Wilderness near Fallen Leaf Lake

Map 6.2, page 214

Your first steps on Mount Tallac are flamed by a craving for one of the greatest 360-degree views in North America. They are also tempered by the challenge of a 3,175-foot climb in 5.8 miles (one-way) to reach the summit. Tallac towers over Lake Tahoe, where the lake and sky seem to merge into a cobalt spectacle. Once at the top at 9,735 feet, you can then turn to the west and take in the granite, ice, and lakes of the vast Desolation Wilderness. In all, the scope covers more than 5,000 square miles of Tahoe paradise.

This preferred route (there are two routes up) starts from the Glen Alpine trailhead a short distance beyond the head of Fallen Leaf Lake. The trek comes in three stages. The trail starts easy and flat, and in the first mile, becomes a vintage road made of rocks that leads to a former historic camp and a few old cabins. On your left, you pass Glen Alpine Falls, best seen when flush with runoff from snowmelt. The air is scented with pine duff, and for those who are imprinted by Tahoe, the familiar tang in the air can make you feel like you are home again. You'll pass a sign that marks the entry point for Desolation Wilderness (a threshold moment) before climbing up Glen Alpine Canyon. Most make quick work of the first 1.7 miles to a trail junction, signed for Grass Lake on your left and Gilmore Lake on your right.

The second stage of the hike rises out of the canyon 2.6 miles to Gilmore Lake. It's a steady climb all the way, where trail builders installed enough switchbacks to keep the grade just right; we never went aerobic at any point, just walked right up. Even in early August, it is common to see tons of wildflowers, with lots of lupine, mule's ear, paintbrush, and rafts of corn lilies. Creeks are flush with clear, cold water, and miniature waterfalls. At times in late spring, if you stand too long to enjoy them, mosquitoes and biting flies will want to see how you taste, a small price to pay for beauty in the high country. Gilmore Lake, nestled in a basin at 8,290 feet at the foot of Tallac's back side, is a perfect stop for a rest or snack, with a confluence of trails to meet other hikers. Some will make camp here. It's one of the better lakes in Desolation to fish. At dusk, the trout rise to the surface to feed and can sound like little popguns going off.

The third stage is the last stretch to the summit, where you climb 1,445 feet in 1.6 miles. As you leave Gilmore, the climb is easy and the hillside is buried in greenery and tons of wildflowers. Soon enough, though, it gets steeper, and most will puff their way above tree line. The last 0.5 mile is the steepest as you approach the cragged rim. In the final steps, you reach the mountain crest and the Tahoe Basin is unveiled before you. The trail diminishes in the rock, but you can still make out a faint route that leads to the true summit. One of the most eye-popping views in North America is yours.

On top, there is a single rock perch that crowns Tallac's summit. Nearby, there are many slabs that seem built for you to take a seat, slow the world down, and take it all in. Pray for a clear day with no haze. Directly below you, the slope plummets 3,000 feet to Fallen Leaf Lake near your starting point. The view then extends across a sea of pines and aspens to Cascade Lake, Emerald Bay, and Lake Tahoe. The lake is so big and so deep blue that for many it evokes emotion that can last for years. The eastern horizon is topped by Monument Peak, Freel Peak, and Mount Rose in Nevada. The view to the west into Desolation is equally profound, across distant Aloha Lake to huge snow-packed slopes that reach up to Pyramid Peak, Mount Price, and the rim that crests the Crystal Basin.

If you have only one mountain to climb and one view to take in, this can often be the best choice.

User Groups: Hikers and dogs. No horses or mountain bikes. No wheelchair facilities.

Permits: Permits are required year-round for both day and overnight use. Day hikers may obtain a free permit from a ranger station or may self-issue at most major trailheads. Backpackers camping in Desolation Wilderness are subject to trailhead quotas. There is a $5 reservation fee, plus $5 per person for one night, $10 per person for two or more nights up to 14 days (nonrefundable), a $20 season pass for Desolation is available per person; reserve at www.recreation.gov. Children ages 12 and under are free. Golden Passes do not apply to personal-use permits. For groups, the cost of a single permit will not exceed $100.

Maps: For a map, ask the U.S. Forest Service for Desolation Wilderness. A Lake Tahoe or Desolation Wilderness map is also available for a fee from Tom Harrison Maps. For a topographic map, ask the USGS for Echo Lake.

Directions: From South Lake Tahoe, take Highway 89 north and drive 2.9 miles to Fallen Leaf Lake Road. Turn left and drive 4.8 miles on a narrow road (go slow, be ready for oncoming cars) past the Fallen Leaf Marina to a fork. Take the left fork on Road 1216, signed for Lily Lake and the Desolation Wilderness. Drive 0.7 mile to road's end, parking, and the trailhead.

Contact: Lake Tahoe Basin Management Unit, South Lake Tahoe, 530/543-2600, www.fs.usda.gov/ltbmu; Taylor Creek Visitor Center, open mid-June through mid-September (closed Tues. and Wed.), weekends on shoulder season starting Memorial Day and after Labor Day weekends, 530/543-2674.

55 GILMORE LAKE

7.6 mi/4.0 hr

in the Desolation Wilderness near Fallen Leaf Lake

Map 6.2, page 214

If you only have time to day-hike to one destination near South Lake Tahoe, Gilmore Lake is an excellent choice. Everything about this trek is classic Lake Tahoe and Desolation Wilderness. You get to visit a scenic alpine lake and, along the way, are treated to fields of wildflowers, mountain vistas, forests, and more. The only thing you don't get are views of Lake Tahoe. Of course, we're not the only ones who like this trail, so all the usual disclaimers are advised about timing your trip for the off-season or during the week.

With that said, take off from the Glen Alpine trailhead and hike up the road past the vintage cabin settlement on the right. The rocky road eventually becomes a rocky trail. This cobblestone-like stretch is by far the worst part of the hike; the rocks make it rough going for hikers' ankles and knees. At 1.5 miles in, you will reach a junction with the Grass Lake Trail. Bear right for Gilmore Lake. The trail surface improves dramatically. You then start a steady, rhythmic climb. In the next 1.5 miles, you'll pass a series of trail junctions (paths lead off to the left, to Susie and Heather Lakes). Bear right for Gilmore Lake, the largest lake in this area. You'll reach it at 3.5 miles, with a total 1,700-foot elevation gain. Despite the fact that many people cruise by Gilmore Lake each day on their way to climb Mount Tallac, few take the time to hang out for long by the lake's sapphire-blue waters. The lake, ringed by grassy, flower-filled meadows, manages to stay pristine.

User Groups: Hikers and dogs. No horses or mountain bikes. No wheelchair facilities.

Permits: Permits are required year-round for both day and overnight use. Day hikers may obtain a free permit from a ranger station or can self-issue at the Glen Alpine trailhead. Backpackers camping in Desolation Wilderness are subject to trailhead quotas. There is a $5 reservation fee, plus $5 per person for one night, $10 per person for two or more nights up to 14 days (nonrefundable), a $20 season pass for Desolation is available per person; reserve at www.recreation.gov. Children ages 12 and under are free. Golden Passes do not apply to personal-use permits. For groups, the cost of a single permit will not exceed $100.

Maps: For a map, ask the U.S. Forest Service for Desolation Wilderness. A Lake Tahoe or Desolation Wilderness map is also available for a fee from Tom Harrison Maps. For a topographic map, ask the USGS for Emerald Bay.

Directions: From South Lake Tahoe, take Highway 89 north and drive 2.9 miles to Fallen Leaf Lake Road. Turn left and drive 4.8 miles on a narrow road past the Fallen Leaf Marina to a fork. Take the left fork on Road 1216, signed for Lily Lake and the Desolation Wilderness. Drive 0.7 mile to the trailhead, at the road's end.

Contact: Lake Tahoe Basin Management Unit, South Lake Tahoe, 530/543-2600, www.fs.usda.gov/ltbmu; Taylor Creek Visitor Center, open mid-June through mid-September (closed Tues. and Wed.), weekends on shoulder season starting Memorial Day and after Labor Day weekends, 530/543-2674.

56 SUSIE AND HEATHER LAKES

10.0 mi/5.0 hr

3 9

in the Desolation Wilderness near Fallen Leaf Lake

Map 6.2, page 214

It doesn't take an expedition to see the alpine beauty of Desolation Wilderness. This trip, a day hike to Susie and Heather Lakes, is a perfect example. Start at the Glen Alpine trailhead. The trail to Susie and Heather Lakes begins as a rocky road. You will pass a waterfall on Glen Alpine Creek and a vintage resort, now something of a ghost town, on the right. At 1.2

miles, you'll see a sign for Gilmore, Susie, and Grass Lakes. Here you start to climb, steady and rhythmic (you'll pass a short cutoff on the left to little Grass Lake, which adds one mile to your trip each way). Continue straight, signed for Susie, Heather, and Aloha Lakes. At four miles, you'll reach the eastern shore of Susie Lake. The route runs along Susie Lake and continues to its southern edge, and then it is another mile to Heather Lake. The granite-lined lake is deep and wide and set in a landscape of classic high Sierra scenery. There you go. Everything you could ask for in just a day.

User Groups: Hikers, dogs, and horses. No mountain bikes. No wheelchair facilities.

Permits: Permits are required year-round for both day and overnight use. Day hikers may obtain a free permit from a ranger station or may self-issue at the Glen Alpine trailhead. Backpackers camping in Desolation Wilderness are subject to trailhead quotas. There is a $5 reservation fee, plus $5 per person for one night, $10 per person for two or more nights up to 14 days (nonrefundable), a $20 season pass for Desolation is available per person; reserve at www.recreation.gov. Children ages 12 and under are free. Golden Passes do not apply to personal-use permits. For groups, the cost of a single permit will not exceed $100.

Maps: For a map, ask the U.S. Forest Service for Desolation Wilderness. A Lake Tahoe or Desolation Wilderness map is also available for a fee from Tom Harrison Maps. For a topographic map, ask the USGS for Emerald Bay.

Directions: From South Lake Tahoe, take Highway 89 north and drive 2.9 miles to Fallen Leaf Lake Road. Turn left and drive 4.8 miles on a narrow road (go slow, watch for oncoming vehicles) past the Fallen Leaf Marina to a fork. Take the left fork on Road 1216, signed for Lily Lake and the Desolation Wilderness. Drive 0.7 mile to the trailhead, at the road's end.

Contact: Lake Tahoe Basin Management Unit, South Lake Tahoe, 530/543-2600, www.fs.usda.gov/ltbmu; Taylor Creek Visitor Center, open mid-June through mid-September (closed Tues. and Wed.), weekends on shoulder season starting Memorial Day and after Labor Day weekends, 530/543-2674.

57 FALLEN LEAF LAKE TRAIL

2.0 mi/1.0 hr 1 9

near South Lake Tahoe

Map 6.2, page 214 BEST

Fallen Leaf Lake, at 6,400 feet in elevation, is the second-largest lake in the Tahoe Basin. Many call it one of the prettiest. Most of its shorefront lands are privately owned. But this path allows you access to the area that is public. This is a short, mostly flat trail that leads to the lake and then along its northern edge to the dam, which you can walk across. Much of the trail hugs the lake's shoreline, so you can look out across the blue water and take in deep inside the feeling that comes with deep, sapphire waters. You also get excellent views of Glen Alpine Canyon and Mount Tallac. In the fall, the shoreline of Fallen Leaf Lake is one of the best spots near Tahoe to admire the quaking aspens as they turn from yellow to gold. Campers staying at Fallen Leaf Lake Campground can access this trail from their tents.

User Groups: Hikers, dogs, horses, and mountain bikes. No wheelchair facilities.

Permits: No permits are required. Parking and access are free.

Maps: For a map, ask the U.S. Forest Service for Lake Tahoe Basin Management Unit. A Lake Tahoe map is available for a fee from Tom Harrison Maps. For a topographic map, ask the USGS for Emerald Bay.

Directions: From South Lake Tahoe, take Highway 89 north and drive 2.9 miles to Fallen Leaf Lake Road. Turn left and drive 0.8 mile to the Fallen Leaf Lake dirt parking area on the right. It is not signed.

Contact: Lake Tahoe Basin Management Unit, South Lake Tahoe, 530/543-2600, www.fs.usda.gov/ltbmu; Taylor Creek Visitor Center, open mid-June through mid-September (closed Tues.

and Wed.), weekends on shoulder season starting Memorial Day and after Labor Day weekends, 530/543-2674.

58 ANGORA LAKES TRAIL

1.0 mi/0.5 hr 

at Angora Lake near South Lake Tahoe in Tahoe National Forest

Map 6.2, page 214 BEST

Upper Angora Lake is a pristine jewel backed by a high granite wall. From the parking lot, hike uphill on the signed dirt road, and in 15 minutes, you'll be looking at Lower Angora Lake off to the left, which has a few cabins on its far side. Continue beyond its edge another 0.25 mile and, voilà, you reach the upper lake and Angora Lakes Resort, built in 1917. Although the resort cabins are always rented far in advance, day users can buy lemonade and sit at a picnic table to watch the action, or take part in it at the small, picturesque lake. Action? What action? Rowboats can be rented for a few bucks for a romantic cruise about the little lake. In midsummer, toddlers wade around at the shallow beach area, and plenty of folks just plunk themselves down along the shoreline to stare at the bowl-shaped, glacial cirque lake. It has a high granite wall on its far side, where in early summer a waterfall of snowmelt flows down to the lake. The Angora Lakes are extremely popular with children's day camps and groups, and on some days, the little ones outnumber the old folks. If it feels like a day out of the 1920s, well it is; that's when the resort opened.

User Groups: Hikers, dogs, horses, and mountain bikes. No wheelchair facilities.

Permits: No permits are required. A parking fee of $7 is charged per vehicle.

Maps: For a map, ask the U.S. Forest Service for Lake Tahoe Basin Management Unit. A Lake Tahoe map is available for a fee from Tom Harrison Maps. For a topographic map, ask the USGS for Echo Lake.

Directions: From South Lake Tahoe, take Highway 89 north and drive 2.9 miles to Fallen Leaf Lake Road. Turn left and drive two miles to a fork. Turn left and drive 0.5 mile to Forest Road 12N14. Bear right on Forest Service Road 12N14 and drive 2.3 miles (great views to the right) to the road's end and the trailhead.

Contact: Lake Tahoe Basin Management Unit, South Lake Tahoe, 530/543-2600, www.fs.usda.gov/ltbmu; Taylor Creek Visitor Center, open mid-June through mid-September (closed Tues. and Wed.), weekends on shoulder season starting Memorial Day and after Labor Day weekends, 530/543-2674; Angora Lakes Resort, www.angoralakesresort.com.

59 GERTRUDE AND TYLER LAKES

9.0 mi/5.0 hr or 2 days 

in the Desolation Wilderness

Map 6.2, page 214

In the Wrights Lake area, there's many great trails and stellar hiking available. The trip to Gertrude and Tyler Lakes stands out as one of the best day hikes. It provides great scenery, a good workout, and a chance to practice your cross-country skills on the way to Tyler Lake (a defined trail leads to pretty Gertrude Lake; Tyler Lake, higher and lovelier, is found only by those who forge their own way). That can add an adventure if you desire.

Begin on Rockbound Pass Trail, where you pass Beauty Lake 0.5 mile out. You then continue on an easy path until 1.9 miles in, where you'll see a sign for Tyler Lake. Bear right and prepare to work a lot harder for the rest of the hike. One memorable 0.5-mile stretch goes straight uphill and will cause you to question your sanity; definitely a kill-me, eat-me kind of moment. The worst part doesn't last long, and the views of the spectacular peaks of the Crystal Range will reward you. At 3.5 miles, you'll reach a spur trail on the left that can be difficult to spot (a 100-yard walk leads to the grave of William Tyler, a rancher who died here in a blizzard in the 1920s). A half mile beyond this cutoff is Gertrude Lake, at 8,000 feet.

Note that just past the faint cutoff trail to the grave, there is a near-invisible fork on the right. That is the start of an unmaintained trail to Tyler Lake. Tyler is set 400 feet higher than Gertrude Lake. If you miss the trail turnoff, watch for occasional rock cairns and keep an eye on your trail map; Tyler Lake lies 0.5 mile southeast of Gertrude Lake.

Of the two lakes, Tyler is more beautiful, set in a granite basin with a few sparse pines on its shores. Because it's slightly difficult to locate, you have an excellent chance at solitude at Tyler Lake, even on summer weekends.

User Groups: Hikers, dogs, and horses. No mountain bikes. No wheelchair facilities.

Permits: Permits are required year-round for both day and overnight use. Day hikers may obtain a free permit from a ranger station or may self-issue at most major trailheads. Backpackers camping in Desolation Wilderness are subject to trailhead quotas. There is a $5 reservation fee, plus $5 per person for one night, $10 per person for two or more nights up to 14 days (nonrefundable), a $20 season pass for Desolation is available per person; reserve at www.recreation.gov. Children ages 12 and under are free. Golden Passes do not apply to personal-use permits. For groups, the cost of a single permit will not exceed $100.

Maps: For a map, ask the U.S. Forest Service for Desolation Wilderness or Eldorado National Forest. A Lake Tahoe or Desolation Wilderness map is also available from Tom Harrison Maps. For topographic maps, ask the USGS for Pyramid Peak and Rockbound Valley.

Directions: From Placerville, take Highway 50 east for 30 miles to Kyburz and continue five miles to the signed turnoff for Wrights Lake (about 21 miles west of South Lake Tahoe). Turn left (north) on Wrights Lake Road and drive eight miles to Wrights Lake Visitor Center. Continue straight past the visitors center for 0.5 mile to the Rockbound trailhead (on the way to Dark Lake).

Contact: Eldorado National Forest, Pacific Ranger District, 530/644-2349, www.fs.usda.gov/eldorado.

60 ROCKBOUND PASS AND LAKE DORIS

12.0 mi/6.0 hr-2 days 

in the Desolation Wilderness

Map 6.2, page 214

This is a trip to 8,650-foot Rockbound Pass for its epic views. Note that for the first 1.9 miles, follow the trail notes for the route to Gertrude and Tyler Lakes (see listing in this chapter). Then bear left to stay on the Rockbound Pass Trail. You then hike through mixed conifers to get your first glimpse of Rockbound Pass at 2.5 miles, a distant notch in the mountains to the north. To reach it, you then must descend a bit and cross the Jones Fork of Silver Creek, then parallel the stream on its course from Maud Lake. This becomes very rocky terrain. In some places, the trail is even blasted out of granite. At 4.5 miles, you'll reach the western shore of Maud Lake, elevation 7,700 feet. Many backpackers make camp here, while day hikers continue the ascent to the pass. It's not much farther; after a steady climb, you gain its wide summit at 5.9 miles. The views of Desolation Wilderness open wide, including views below on one side at Maud Lake and ahead to Lake Doris. Up on top at the pass, the winds can howl, especially in the spring. If that's the case, descend 0.5 mile to Lake Doris, just to the left of the trail, where you can make camp, or if you're day hiking, just hang out and rest. The total elevation gain on this trip is 1,700 feet, plus a short descent to Lake Doris.

User Groups: Hikers, dogs, and horses. No mountain bikes. No wheelchair facilities.

Permits: Permits are required year-round for both day and overnight use. Day hikers may obtain a free permit from a ranger station or may self-issue at most major trailheads. Backpackers camping in Desolation Wilderness are subject to trailhead quotas. There is a $5 reservation fee, plus $5 per person for one night, $10 per person for two or more nights up to 14 days (nonrefundable), a $20 season pass for Desolation is available per person; reserve at www.recreation.gov. Children ages 12 and under are free. Golden Passes do not apply to personal-use permits. For groups, the cost of a single permit will not exceed $100.

Directions: From Placerville, take Highway 50 east for 30 miles to Kyburz and continue five miles to the signed turnoff for Wrights Lake on the north side of the highway (about 21 miles west of South Lake Tahoe). Turn left (north) on Wrights Lake Road and drive eight miles to Wrights Lake Visitor Center. Continue straight for 0.5 mile to the Rockbound trailhead (on the way to Dark Lake).

Contact: Eldorado National Forest, Pacific Ranger District, 530/644-2349, www.fs.usda.gov/eldorado.

61 TWIN AND ISLAND LAKES

6.4 mi/4.0 hr or 2 days 3 10

in the Desolation Wilderness

Map 6.2, page 214

The hike to Twin and Island Lakes is hands down the most scenic in the gorgeous Wrights Lake area. In summer, you can expect plenty of company. Of the entire Desolation Wilderness, you get the most striking views on the hike. You'll have miles of solid granite under your feet. The trail is extremely well marked, and its moderate grade is suitable for all types of hikers. Start at the Twin Lakes trailhead. The first 1.2 miles features a gentle climb to the intersection with the trail to Grouse, Hemlock, and Smith Lakes. Bear left for Twin Lakes and climb up over the granite for 0.75 mile, when you crest a ridge and start to descend. The vistas of jagged Crystal Range peaks to the northeast make an awesome backdrop. At 2.5 miles, you'll reach the dam at Lower Twin Lake. Cross it and continue hiking along the lake's northwest shore to tiny Boomerang Lake, at three miles. The lake is shaped like its name and shallow enough to provide warm water for swimming. Another 0.25 mile on the trail brings you to the south end of Island Lake, where the vistas of the Crystal Range are the best of the trip. If you ever wanted to sell somebody on the beauty of the Northern Sierra, this trail would be the place to do it.

During the summer months, the only downer on the trip to Twin and Island Lakes is the high number of people who make this journey every day.

User Groups: Hikers, dogs, and horses. No mountain bikes. No wheelchair facilities.

Permits: Permits are required year-round for both day and overnight use. Day hikers may obtain a free permit from a ranger station or may self-issue at most major trailheads. Backpackers camping in Desolation Wilderness are subject to trailhead quotas. There is a $5 reservation fee, plus $5 per person for one night, $10 per person for two or more nights up to 14 days (nonrefundable), a $20 season pass for Desolation is available per person; reserve at www.recreation.gov. Children ages 12 and under are free. Golden Passes do not apply to personal-use permits. For groups, the cost of a single permit will not exceed $100.

Maps: For a map, ask the U.S. Forest Service for Eldorado National Forest or Desolation Wilderness. A Lake Tahoe or Desolation Wilderness map is also available for a fee from Tom Harrison Maps. For a topographic map, ask the USGS for Pyramid Peak.

Directions: From Placerville, take Highway 50 east for 30 miles to Kyburz and continue five miles to the signed turnoff for Wrights Lake (about 21 miles west of South Lake Tahoe). Turn left (north) on Wrights Lake Road and drive eight miles to Wrights Lake Visitor Center. Turn right and continue one mile beyond the campground to the end of the road and the Twin Lakes trailhead.

Contact: Eldorado National Forest, Pacific Ranger District, 530/644-2349, www.fs.usda.

gov/eldorado; Lake Tahoe Basin Management Unit, South Lake Tahoe, 530/543-2600, www.fs.usda.gov/ltbmu; Taylor Creek Visitor Center, open mid-June through mid-September (closed Tues. and Wed.), weekends on shoulder season starting Memorial Day and after Labor Day weekends, 530/543-2674.

62 GROUSE, HEMLOCK, AND SMITH LAKES

6.0 mi/3.0 hr or 2 days 4 10

in the Desolation Wilderness

Map 6.2, page 214

The Crystal Basin area is a magical place on the western edge of the Desolation Wilderness. The high peaks of the Crystal Range overlook the basin and its multitude of lakes. Several excellent day hikes and backpacking trips are possible in this area, most of which begin from popular Wrights Lake Campground. Of those, the trip to Grouse, Hemlock, and Smith Lakes is a favorite. That is despite a relentless climb required to reach all three lakes. From the parking area, start this trip on the Twin Lakes Trail. It arcs past a meadow and then enters a pine and fir forest that is interspersed with stretches of granite. At a trail junction 1.2 miles out, head right for Grouse, Hemlock, and Smith Lakes. Small and pretty Grouse Lake is a one-mile, heart-pumping climb away, with many fine glances back at Wrights Lake and Icehouse Reservoir as you ascend. Many backpackers camp at Grouse Lake (look for wood posts that indicate designated campsites; note that camping within 500 feet of Grouse Lake and its tributaries is prohibited). More hardy types and day hikers should head for Hemlock and Smith Lakes, farther uphill. The lakes get progressively prettier as you go, but the ascent gets steeper, too. Tiny Hemlock Lake is only 0.5 mile from Grouse Lake, and it features a spectacular rockslide on one shoreline and many scrawny hemlock trees on the other. Smith Lake lies another 0.5 mile beyond, way up high near tree line, at 8,700 feet, and it's a stunner.

User Groups: Hikers, dogs, and horses. No mountain bikes. No wheelchair facilities.

Permits: Permits are required year-round for both day and overnight use. Day hikers may obtain a free permit from a ranger station or may self-issue at most major trailheads. Backpackers camping in Desolation Wilderness are subject to trailhead quotas. There is a $5 reservation fee, plus $5 per person for one night, $10 per person for two or more nights up to 14 days (nonrefundable), a $20 season pass for Desolation is available per person; reserve at www.recreation.gov. Children ages 12 and under are free. Golden Passes do not apply to personal-use permits. For groups, the cost of a single permit will not exceed $100.

Maps: For a map, ask the U.S. Forest Service for Eldorado National Forest or Desolation Wilderness. A Lake Tahoe or Desolation Wilderness map is also available for a fee from Tom Harrison Maps. For a topographic map, ask the USGS for Pyramid Peak.

Directions: From Placerville, take Highway 50 east for 30 miles to Kyburz and continue five miles to the signed turnoff for Wrights Lake (about 21 miles west of South Lake Tahoe). Turn left (north) on Wrights Lake Road and drive eight miles to Wrights Lake Visitor Center. Turn right and continue one mile beyond the campground to the end of the road and the Twin Lakes trailhead.

Contact: Eldorado National Forest, Pacific Ranger District, 530/644-2349, www.fs.usda.gov/eldorado; Lake Tahoe Basin Management Unit, South Lake Tahoe, 530/543-2600, www.fs.usda.gov/ltbmu; Taylor Creek Visitor Center, open mid-June through mid-September (closed Tues. and Wed.), weekends on shoulder season starting Memorial Day and after Labor Day weekends, 530/543-2674.

63 LYONS CREEK TRAIL TO LAKE SYLVIA

9.0 mi/4.5 hr or 2 days 3 9

in the Desolation Wilderness

Map 6.2, page 214

There are no easy hikes in the Wrights Lake area, yet they are all beautiful. This trek to Lake Sylvia (and Lyons Lake for the ambitious), on the other hand, requires one of the lesser climbs: "only" a 1,700-foot elevation gain to visit two beautiful lakes. The trip's total mileage is long, but the grade is steady, that is, except for the final 0.5 mile to Lyons Lake.

From the trailhead, you start by hiking on the south side of Lyons Creek for four miles. You'll pass through woods and meadows, then cross the stream, and in 0.1 mile, reach a junction. Lake Sylvia is 0.5 mile to the right. Lyons Lake is to the left and steeply uphill. Take your pick, or better yet, go see both. Lake Sylvia is shadowed by Pyramid Peak and has good campsites along its shoreline. Lyons Lake requires a nasty 450-foot climb in 0.5 mile, but its superior scenery makes it well worth the effort.

If you're fond of walking along pretty streams, you know, where you are accompanied by the gurgle and babble of a creek as you hike, you'll love this hike. In addition, wildflowers are prolific in early summer. The views of Pyramid Peak, just shy of 10,000 feet in elevation, provide the backdrop.

Because this trailhead is a few miles distant from popular Wrights Lake Campground, it gets far fewer visitors than the trails that start right out of camp.

User Groups: Hikers, dogs, and horses. No mountain bikes. No wheelchair facilities.

Permits: Permits are required year-round for both day and overnight use. Day hikers may obtain a free permit from a ranger station or may self-issue at most major trailheads. Backpackers camping in Desolation Wilderness are subject to trailhead quotas. There is a $5 reservation fee, plus $5 per person for one night, $10 per person for two or more nights up to 14 days (nonrefundable), a $20 season pass for Desolation is available per person; reserve at www.recreation.gov. Children ages 12 and under are free. Golden Passes do not apply to personal-use permits. For groups, the cost of a single permit will not exceed $100.

Maps: For a map, ask the U.S. Forest Service for Eldorado National Forest or Desolation Wilderness. A Lake Tahoe or Desolation Wilderness map is also available for a fee from Tom Harrison Maps. For a topographic map, ask the USGS for Pyramid Peak.

Directions: From Placerville, take Highway 50 east for 30 miles to Kyburz and continue five miles to the signed turnoff for Wrights Lake (about 21 miles west of South Lake Tahoe). Turn left (north) on Wrights Lake Road and drive four miles to the signed spur for the Lyons Creek Trail. Turn right and drive a short distance to the trailhead.

Contact: Eldorado National Forest, Pacific Ranger District, 530/644-2349, www.fs.usda.gov/eldorado; Lake Tahoe Basin Management Unit, South Lake Tahoe, 530/543-2600, www.fs.usda.gov/ltbmu; Taylor Creek Visitor Center, open mid-June through mid-September (closed Tues. and Wed.), weekends on shoulder season starting Memorial Day and after Labor Day weekends, 530/543-2674.

64 HORSETAIL FALLS VISTA/ PYRAMID CREEK LOOP

2.0 mi/1.0 hr 1 9

in Eldorado National Forest near South Lake Tahoe

Map 6.2, page 214

This is the famous side trip for people driving to and from Tahoe on U.S. 50. It provides many pretty views of 90-foot Lower Horsetail Falls and Pyramid Creek's glacier-carved canyon. After a number of falls, injuries, and deaths when tourists slipped while climbing on wet rocks, rangers helped engineer and build the 1.5-mile Pyramid Creek Loop Trail. It is made for day users who just want to see Horsetail Falls and spectacular, granite-lined Pyramid Creek. About 0.5 mile on the main trail, the Pyramid Creek Loop takes off. About 15,000 people each summer glimpse the falls from their cars, then pull over at the giant parking lot by the trailhead and hike this trail to get closer to it. You are routed past a gorgeous stretch of Pyramid Creek called the Cascades. The trail stays outside of the wilderness boundary and provides a safe and easy alternative for casual visitors, points of conflict in the past.

User Groups: Hikers and dogs. No horses or mountain bikes. No wheelchair facilities.

Permits: No permits are required if you stay out of the wilderness boundary. Parking is $5 per vehicle.

Maps: For a map, ask the U.S. Forest Service for Eldorado National Forest. A Lake Tahoe map is available for a fee from Tom Harrison Maps. For a topographic map, ask the USGS for Echo Lake.

Directions: From Placerville, take Highway 50 east to Strawberry (about 20 miles from South Lake Tahoe) and continue about three miles to Twin Bridges and a large pullout on the north side of the highway (0.5 mile west of the turnoff for Camp Sacramento). Park in the designated parking lot for the signed trailhead.

Contact: Eldorado National Forest, Pacific Ranger District, 530/644-2349, www.fs.usda.gov/eldorado.

65 RALSTON PEAK

8.0 mi/5.0 hr 

in the Desolation Wilderness near South Lake Tahoe

Map 6.2, page 214

From Ralston Peak's 9,235-foot summit, you get an eye-popping view of Lake Tahoe, Fallen Leaf Lake, Carson Pass, Echo Lakes, and below you (to the north) Ralston Lake. This is simply a spectacular lookout. To get it, you may also find that your butt gets kicked. From trailhead to summit, you ascend from 6,400 to 9,240 feet over the course of four miles. The route has a little of everything: dense forest, open manzanita-covered slopes, meadows, and granite ridges. It also has lots of one thing: elevation gain.

To start, from the east side of the parking area, you walk north up the paved road for 200 yards and look for the trail that leads off on the left. This is your launch point. You then climb upward through nonstop trees and nonstop switchbacks for a mile, then enter a more open area as you pass the wilderness boundary sign at 1.5 miles. The views start to widen. Your lungs request a lunch break, but they don't get one until 2.5 miles up, when you finally gain the ridge. A half mile later, the break is over, and you climb again, this time to another ridge at 3.5 miles, covered in meadow grasses and wildflowers. You'll reach a trail on your right that leads to the summit. Part ways with the main trail, and in 0.5 mile, you scramble over jumbled rock to gain the 9,235-foot summit. Enjoy the panorama. You have earned it.

User Groups: Hikers and dogs. No horses or mountain bikes. No wheelchair facilities.

Permits: Permits are required year-round for both day and overnight use. Day hikers may obtain a free permit from a ranger station or may self-issue at most major trailheads. Backpackers camping in Desolation Wilderness are subject to trailhead quotas. There is a $5 reservation fee, plus $5 per person for one night, $10 per person for two or more nights up to 14 days (nonrefundable), a $20 season pass for Desolation is available per person; reserve at www.recreation.gov. Children ages 12 and under are free. Golden Passes do not apply to personal-use permits. For groups, the cost of a single permit will not exceed $100.

Maps: For a map, ask the U.S. Forest Service for Eldorado National Forest or Desolation Wilderness. A Lake Tahoe or Desolation Wilderness map is also available for a fee from Tom Harrison Maps. For a topographic map, ask the USGS for Echo Lake.

Directions: From Placerville, take Highway 50 east to Twin Bridges and then continue 1.5 miles to Camp Sacramento and the turnoff. There is a parking area off the north side of U.S. 50 and a sign for Ralston Trail to Lake of the Woods.

From South Lake Tahoe, take Highway 89 south for five miles to Highway 50. Turn right (west) on U.S. 50 and drive about 14 miles to the turnoff for Camp Sacramento (if you reach Twin Bridges, you've gone 1.5 miles too far west).

Contact: Eldorado National Forest, Pacific Ranger District, 530/644-2349, www.fs.usda.gov/eldorado; Lake Tahoe Basin Management Unit, South Lake Tahoe, 530/543-2600, www.fs.usda.gov/ltbmu; Taylor Creek Visitor Center, open mid-June through mid-September (closed Tues. and Wed.), weekends on shoulder season starting Memorial Day and after Labor Day weekends, 530/543-2674.

66 BOAT TAXI TO LAKE ALOHA

6.0-12.0 mi/3.5-6.0 hr 3 10

in the Desolation Wilderness

Map 6.2, page 214

This is a sensational trip, one of the great boat-and-hike adventures in California. You start with a boat taxi across the two Echo Lakes and get dropped off at the trailhead for the Pacific Crest Trail. Then it's an easy climb to great views with a series of spur trails to beautiful alpine lakes in Desolation Wilderness, crowned by Lake Aloha in Desolation Valley.

The hiker's parking lot is on a flat that overlooks Echo Chalet. Park and walk 0.25 mile downhill to the resort and the boat launch area, at the edge of Echo Lake. The boat taxi leaves at frequent intervals (or whenever more than two people show up) 8am to 6pm daily all summer. The trip costs $15 each way. The boat carries hikers two miles to the far end of Upper Echo Lake, and the boat ride is unique, too, where you pass many lovely lakeside cottages. You arrive at the border of the Desolation Wilderness, fresh, rested, and ready. If you instead hike the PCT both coming and going, it will add five miles to the trip.

From the boat taxi drop-off point, gain the main trail (Pacific Crest Trail) and head to your left. It's a 3.5-mile hike to the eastern edge of Lake Aloha. You start with a steady climb up to a ridge. Be sure to stop and turn around to enjoy the stunning lake view. After topping the ridge, the hike is an easy saunter. You'll pass several signed junctions with numerous trails along the way, all of which lead to various lakes in very short distances. Your best bet is to stay on the main path for Lake Aloha, then take some of the cutoffs to neighboring lakes on your way back. When you reach Lake Aloha's shore, hike along its beautiful north side for a distance, admiring the rocky coves and islands of the giant, shallow lake. At one time, Lake Aloha was several small lakes. They were dammed with a unique rock wall to create this huge body of water. The effect is a bit surreal, although beautiful. The lake's elevation is 8,116 feet.

On the trip back, take one or more of the signed trail junctions and visit Lake of the Woods, Lake Lucille, Lake Margery, Tamarack Lake, or Ralston Lake. All are less than one mile off the Lake Aloha Trail. Tamarack Lake is the best for scenery; Lake of the Woods is the best for fishing.

On the return trip, some bypass the boat taxi and continue on the Pacific Crest Trail back to the parking area. That will add 2.5 miles to your trip. The trail rises well above the lake, and eventually you will pass a series of vacation homes.

User Groups: Hikers and dogs (not advised because sharp rocks can bruise their foot pads). No horses or mountain bikes. No wheelchair facilities.

Permits: Boat taxi (not required) is $15 per hiker one-way, $8 for dogs. Permits are required year-round for both day and overnight use. Day hikers may obtain a free permit from a ranger station or may self-issue at most major trailheads. Backpackers camping in Desolation Wilderness are subject to trailhead quotas. There is a $5 reservation fee, plus $5 per person for one night, $10 per person for two or more nights up to 14 days (nonrefundable), a $20 season pass for Desolation is available per person; reserve at www.recreation.gov. Children ages 12 and under are free. Golden Passes do not apply to personal-use permits. For groups, the cost of a single permit will not exceed $100.

Maps: For a map, ask the U.S. Forest Service for Desolation Wilderness. A Lake Tahoe or Desolation Wilderness map is also available for a fee from Tom Harrison Maps. For a topographic map, ask the USGS for Echo Lake.

Directions: From Placerville, take Highway 50 east for 46 miles to Echo Summit (and Sierra at Tahoe Ski Resort) and then continue east on Highway 50 for 1.8 miles to Johnson Pass Road and a signed turnoff (brown sign) for Berkeley Camp/Echo Lake (one mile west of Echo Summit). Turn left and drive 0.5 mile to Echo Lakes Road. Turn left and drive one mile to a series of parking lots located 0.25 mile before the road ends at Echo Lakes Resort. Hikers not staying at the resort must park in one of the upper lots or alongside the road, not in the main lower lot by the resort, and walk down to the marina, boat taxi, or trailhead.

From South Lake Tahoe: Take Highway 89 south for five miles to U.S. 50. Turn right (west) on U.S. 50 and drive 5.5 miles to the signed turnoff for Echo Lakes on the right (one mile west of Echo Summit). Turn right and drive 0.5 mile to Echo Lakes Road. Turn left and drive one mile to a series of parking lots 0.25 mile before the road ends at Echo Lakes Resort.

Contact: Echo Lakes Chalet, 530/659-7207, www.echochalet.com; Eldorado National Forest, Pacific Ranger District, 530/644-2349, www.fs.usda.gov/eldorado; Lake Tahoe Basin Management Unit, South Lake Tahoe, 530/543-2600, www.fs.usda.gov/ltbmu; Taylor Creek Visitor Center, open mid-June through mid-September (closed Tues. and Wed.), weekends on shoulder season starting Memorial Day and after Labor Day weekends, 530/543-2674.

67 ECHO LAKES RESORT TO BARKER PASS (PCT)

32.3 mi one-way/3 days 

from Echo Lake to Forest Road 3 near Barker Pass

Map 6.2, page 214

The Desolation Wilderness and the neighboring Granite Chief Wilderness are filled with sculpted granite domes and hundreds of gemlike lakes. All is pristine, yet access is also quite easy, making this, along with the John Muir Trail, the most heavily used section of the PCT. The trip starts at Echo Lake (elevation 7,400 feet), climbs through pines past Upper Echo Lake, and then continues up and north toward Triangle Lake, one of dozens of lakes you pass on your northward route. They come and go in spectacular fashion: Lake Margery, Lake Aloha, and then Heather, Susie, and Gilmore Lakes, and finally Dicks Lake (at 9,380 feet). There are so many, in fact, that you can plan on a perfect campsite near a lake every night, providing you don't mind the company of other hikers drawn by classic beauty. The views are dramatic as well, across miles and miles of the glacial-carved granite, all of it marvelous high Sierra landscape. As you continue, you'll discover Upper and Middle Velma Lakes, both very pretty and with good fishing. The trail skirts the ridgeline, keeping the higher knobs to the east as it gradually descends toward Richardson Lake, just beyond the Desolation Wilderness boundary, ready now to enter the Granite Chief Wilderness to the north.

To continue north on the PCT, see the *Barker Pass to Donner Pass (PCT)* hike in this chapter. If you are walking this trail in reverse, see the *Carson Pass to Echo Lakes Resort (PCT)* hike in this chapter.

User Groups: Hikers, dogs, and horses. No

mountain bikes. No wheelchair facilities. No mountain bikes permitted on Pacific Crest Trail.

Permits: A single permit is required to hike the Pacific Crest Trail. Contact the national forest, Bureau of Land Management, or national park office at your point of entry for a combined permit that is good for traveling through multiple-permit areas during your dates of travel.

Maps: For topographic maps, ask the USGS for Echo Lake, Emerald Bay, and Rockbound Valley.

Directions: From Placerville, take Highway 50 east for 46 miles to Echo Summit (and Sierra at Tahoe Ski Resort) and then continue east on Highway 50 for 1.8 miles to Johnson Pass Road and a signed turnoff (brown sign) for Berkeley Camp/Echo Lake (one mile west of Echo Summit). Turn left and drive 0.5 mile to Echo Lakes Road. Turn left and drive one mile to a series of parking lots located 0.25 mile before the road ends at Echo Lakes Resort. Hikers not staying at the resort must park in one of the upper lots or alongside the road, not in the main lower lot by the resort, and walk down to the marina, boat taxi, or trailhead.

From South Lake Tahoe: Take Highway 89 south for five miles to U.S. 50. Turn right (west) on U.S. 50 and drive 5.5 miles to the signed turnoff for Echo Lakes on the right (one mile west of Echo Summit). Turn right and drive 0.5 mile to Echo Lakes Road. Turn left and drive one mile to parking 0.25 mile above Echo Lakes Resort.

To reach the Barker Pass trailhead from Tahoe Pines on Highway 89, head north for 0.5 mile to the Kaspian Picnic Grounds and then bear left (west) for seven miles on Forest Service Road 15N03.

Contact: Echo Lakes Chalet, 530/659-7207, www.echochalet.com; Lake Tahoe Basin Management Unit, South Lake Tahoe, 530/543-2600, www.fs.usda.gov/ltbmu; Taylor Creek Visitor Center, open mid-June through mid-September (closed Tues. and Wed.), weekends on shoulder season starting Memorial Day and after Labor Day weekends, 530/543-2674.

Echo Lakes

68 DARDANELLES LAKE AND ROUND LAKE

7.6 mi/4.5 hr 3 9

in Meiss Country south of Lake Tahoe

Map 6.2, page 214

Dardanelles Lake is nestled at an elevation of 7,740 feet, set in a pocket with a granite backdrop. It's striking and gorgeous. This trek provides a tour into "Meiss Country," that large and wonderful roadless area south of Lake Tahoe. The forces that shaped the land, ice (glaciers) and fire (volcanic action), have made their presence clearly visible.

The route to Dardanelles Lake and Round Lake, along the Tahoe Rim Trail, starts out steep but gets easier as it goes. From the parking lot, the trail heads south, and in about 100 yards crosses Highway 89, then makes an initial climb through fir and pine forest to Big Meadow. The meadow makes lovely, level walking for 0.25 mile; then it's back into the trees. Follow the trail signs for Round Lake until you complete a steep, short descent at two miles out. At the bottom of the hill, at Meiss Meadow Trail toward Christmas Valley, turn sharply right. Walk less than 0.25 mile, then turn left and cross a creek for the final 1.2 miles to Dardanelles Lake. It's good for swimming, fishing, and picnicking. If you time your trip for autumn, you'll be treated to a marvelous color display from the aspens and alders that grow along this trail's many streams.

On your return, retrace your steps to the junction at the bottom of the hill, then hike 0.75 mile in the opposite direction to visit Round Lake. Although not quite as scenic as Dardanelles Lake, Round Lake provides a stark, fascinating contrast to its neighbor: It is surrounded by volcanic rock formations, not granite cliffs.

Note that this trail is open to mountain bikers. On weekdays you might not see a single bike, but on weekends you'll see plenty.

User Groups: Hikers, dogs, horses, and mountain bikes. No wheelchair facilities.

Permits: No permits are required. Parking and access are free. A Forest Service permit (free) is required for overnight use.

Maps: For a map, ask the U.S. Forest Service for Lake Tahoe Basin Management Unit. A Lake Tahoe map is available for a fee from Tom Harrison Maps. For a topographic map, ask the USGS for Echo Lake.

Directions: From South Lake Tahoe, take Highway 89 south for five miles to Meyers and the junction with Highway 89, and then continue south on Highway 89 for five more miles to the Big Meadow trailhead parking area on the northwest side of the road. Turn left off the highway, then bear left and park near the restrooms. The trail begins from the south side of the parking lot loop and crosses Highway 89 in about 100 yards.

Contact: Lake Tahoe Basin Management Unit, South Lake Tahoe, 530/543-2600, www.fs.usda.gov/ltbmu; Taylor Creek Visitor Center, open mid-June through mid-September (closed Tues. and Wed.), weekends on shoulder season starting Memorial Day and after Labor Day weekends, 530/543-2674.

69 LAKE MARGARET

4.6 mi/3.0 hr 1 9

near Carson Pass and Kirkwood Lake

Map 6.2, page 214 BEST

Can you imagine a hike to an alpine lake with only a 500-foot elevation gain? It might seem too good to be true, but here you are. If you need an easy-hike fix, Lake Margaret can scratch the itch. The trail undulates gently, never gaining or losing more than a couple hundred feet. The first stretch is actually downhill. Then the path climbs gently over a small ridge and then descends again over granite slabs, where the route is marked with cairns. You'll cross branches of Caples Creek twice in the first mile. At 1.5 miles, the trail passes by a couple of tiny ponds. At two miles out, after crossing another creek, you'll find yourself in a lovely grove of aspens and knee-high wildflowers. At 2.3 miles, after about an hour of walking and only a minor expenditure of energy, you'll reach the granite shoreline of Lake Margaret. Swimming is excellent. A few tiny islands and many shoreline boulders make fine sunbathing spots. Figure on staying awhile. The lake's elevation is 7,500 feet. Note that although most of the trails in the Carson Pass area are famous for wildflowers, the proximity of several small streams makes the bloom especially showy on this path. The peak wildflower season is from mid-June to mid-August.

User Groups: Hikers, leashed dogs, horses, and mountain bikes. No wheelchair facilities.

Permits: No permits are required. Parking and access are free.

Maps: For a map, ask the U.S. Forest Service for Eldorado National Forest or Mokelumne Wilderness. For a topographic map, ask the USGS for Caples Lake.

Directions: From South Lake Tahoe, take Highway 89 south for five miles to Meyers and the junction with Highway 89, and then continue south on Highway 89 for 11 miles to Highway 88. Turn west on Highway 88 and drive 14.5 miles to the Lake Margaret sign, on the north side of the road (5.5 miles west of Carson Pass Summit, and 5.5 miles east of Silver Lake). Turn north and park at the trailhead parking area.

Contact: Eldorado National Forest, Amador Ranger District, 209/295-4251, www.fs.usda.gov/eldorado.

70 CAPLES LAKE TRAILHEAD TO EMIGRANT LAKE

8.0 mi/4.0 hr or 2 days 3 9

in the Mokelumne Wilderness near Caples Lake

Map 6.2, page 214

A climb of less than 1,000 feet leads to gorgeous Emigrant Lake at an elevation of 8,600 feet. The trail starts at the spillway at Caples Lake, along the lake's south side, and follows a historic emigrant route. The first two miles are right along the lake's edge, where you climb gently above the shoreline, always in the shade of big conifers. You continue along Emigrant Creek to a stream crossing at 3.5 miles, followed by another crossing. Most of the trail's ascent is packed into the last 1.8 miles. A few switchbacks ultimately carry you up to Emigrant Lake, a beautiful cirque lake. Covered Wagon Peak and Thimble Peak, at 9,500 feet, rise above the scene. The trail's total elevation gain is less than 1,000 feet, making this an easy day hike for most, even with its eight-mile distance.

The trailhead at Caples Lake is often jam-packed with backpackers, so do yourself a favor: visit here midweek or in the off-season, or make your trip a day hike instead of an overnighter. Why is this trail so popular? It's gorgeous and easy compared to other Sierra treks.

User Groups: Hikers, leashed dogs, and horses. No mountain bikes. No wheelchair facilities.

Permits: No day-hiking permits are required. A free wilderness permit is required for overnight stays; it is available from the Amador Ranger Station, the Carson Pass Information Station, or the Eldorado Information Center. Maximum group size for day use is 12. Maximum group size for overnight use is eight. No self-registration is available at the trailhead.

Maps: For a map, ask the U.S. Forest Service for Eldorado National Forest or Desolation Wilderness. For a topographic map, ask the USGS for Caples Lake.

Directions: From South Lake Tahoe, take Highway 50 south for roughly four miles to Meyers and the junction with Highway 89, and then continue south on Highway 89 for 11 miles to Highway 88. Turn right (west) on Highway 88 and drive 14 miles (five miles west of Carson Pass) to the west side of Caples Lake and the trailhead parking area.

Contact: Eldorado National Forest, Amador Ranger District, 209/295-4251, www.fs.usda.gov/eldorado.

71 MINKALO TRAIL

7.0 mi/3.5 hr 2 8

near Silver Lake

Map 6.2, page 214

For those hunkering down at Silver Lake, the best bet for a hike is the Minkalo Trail. The trail leads to Granite Lake in one mile and to Plasse's Resort, on the south side of the lake, in three miles. Why not hike to both, then buy a pizza or a Clif Bar at Plasse's Resort Trading Post to fuel up for the hike back to the Minkalo trailhead?

Silver Lake is located at an elevation of 7,300 feet along Highway 88. The trailhead is near the Kit Carson Lodge (see directions). The trail starts out rocky and stays that way for the first 0.25 mile. Cross a bridge over Squaw Creek to a right fork that leads to Plasse's Resort. Take the left fork first, which heads to Granite Lake. It takes about a 20-minute walk with a moderate climb. It's a pretty lake and good for swimming. After you've visited, return to the trail junction and hike south, soon coming close to the edge of Silver Lake. The trail then provides pretty lake views, including long looks at Treasure Island, Silver Lake's island. It takes about an hour to reach the campground at Plasse's, an excellent place for horse lovers (and pizza lovers).

User Groups: Hikers, leashed dogs, horses, and mountain bikes. No wheelchair facilities.

Permits: No permits are required. Parking and access are free.

Maps: For a map, ask the U.S. Forest Service for Eldorado National Forest or Desolation Wilderness. For a topographic map, ask the USGS for Caples Lake.

Directions: From South Lake Tahoe, take Highway 50 south for roughly four miles to Meyers and the junction with Highway 89, and then continue south on Highway 89 for 11 miles to Highway 88. Turn right (west) on Highway 88 and drive 15.5 miles (10.8 miles west of Carson Pass) to the turnoff for Kit Carson Lodge on the north side of the road. Turn north and drive past Kit Carson Lodge, go left at the first fork, and go right at the second fork, to the parking for Minkalo Trail. (It's a total of 1.4 miles from Highway 88.) Walk back down the road for about 40 yards to find the trailhead.

Contact: Eldorado National Forest, Amador Ranger District, 209/295-4251, www.fs.usda.gov/eldorado.

72 OSBORNE HILL

2.6 mi/1.5 hr

on Highway 4 near Lake Alpine

Map 6.2, page 214

We like the way Lake Alpine looks from close up on Lakeshore Trail, but then again, we like the way Lake Alpine looks from far up on Osborne Hill, also known as Osborne Point. A short, healthy climb brings you to the point, from which you can look down at the lake and beyond into the Carson-Iceberg Wilderness. The trail ends there but connects to Emigrant West Trail if you wish to hike farther. In spring, if you're itching for winter to be over so you can go hiking, Highway 4 is kept open as far as Silvertip Campground, but not always farther east. Thus if the snow is dwindling, you'll have access to this trailhead often long before you can access the others near Lake Alpine.

User Groups: Hikers, dogs, horses, and mountain bikes. No wheelchair facilities.

Permits: No permits are required. Parking and access are free.

Maps: For a map, ask the U.S. Forest Service for Stanislaus National Forest. For a topographic map, ask the USGS for Tamarack.

Directions: From Angels Camp, take Highway 4 east for 40 miles to Bear Valley. Set your odometer at Bear Valley and drive east on Highway 4 for three miles to the Osborne Ridge trailhead (just east of Silvertip Campground). Take the trail that leads from the south side of the road.

Contact: Stanislaus National Forest, Calaveras Ranger District, 209/813-6008, www.fs.usda.gov/stanislaus.

73 LAKESHORE TRAIL AND INSPIRATION POINT

4.0 mi/2.0 hr 2 8

on Highway 4 near Lake Alpine

Map 6.2, page 214

It's hard to say which trail is better, Lakeshore Trail or Inspiration Point Trail. To solve the dilemma, hike both of them together. The trip starts with a short walk down a dirt road, and then you turn right onto a single-track. After 10 minutes of hiking through a thick lodgepole pine forest peppered with tiny pine cones, you're at the edge of Lake Alpine, elevation 7,350 feet. Follow the trail to your left, and in another 10 minutes, you reach a left fork for Inspiration Point (Lakeshore Trail continues straight). You'll want to head out and back on both trails; it makes no difference which one you take first.

The Lakeshore Trail is flat and stays within 100 feet of the water's edge, offering many pretty lake views. Eventually the trail meets up with Slick Rock, a four-wheel-drive road, but there's no need to go that far. Just walk a mile or so to the dam, and then turn around and head back. The Inspiration Point Trail, on the other hand, is more of a workout: a steep one-mile climb to the summit at Inspiration Point, from which you can see for miles. Pick a clear day, and you'll be pointing out Lake Alpine, Elephant Rock, the Dardanelles, and Spicer Meadow Reservoir.

User Groups: Hikers, dogs, and horses. No mountain bikes. No wheelchair facilities.

Permits: No permits are required. Parking and access are free.

Maps: For a national forest map, ask for Stanislaus National Forest. For a topographic map, ask the USGS for Spicer Meadow Reservoir.

Directions: From Angels Camp, take Highway 4 east for 40 miles to Bear Valley. Set your odometer at Bear Valley and drive east on Highway 4 for 4.3 miles to the Lake Alpine East Shore trailhead turnoff, on the right. Turn right, drive 0.25 mile, and turn right again and drive 0.1 mile past Pine Marten Campground to the signed parking area and the trailhead.

Contact: Stanislaus National Forest, Calaveras Ranger District, 209/813-6008, www.fs.usda.gov/stanislaus.

74 DUCK LAKE

3.0 mi/1.5 hr  

in the Carson-Iceberg Wilderness off Highway 4 near Lake Alpine

Map 6.2, page 214

The trailhead at Silver Valley Campground is the start of the route to Duck Lake. It's also one of the busiest trailheads into the Carson-Iceberg Wilderness. The trip to Duck Lake is a great easy hike for families or people just in the mood for a stroll (the more ambitious can continue past the lake on an eight-mile round-trip to Rock Lake). It's only one mile to reach Duck Lake, but once you're there, you'll want to walk the loop trail around its perimeter, which adds another mile to your trip. The area is the site of a historic cow camp, where animals have grazed since the late 19th century. You can examine what's left of a few early-20th-century cowboy cabins.

User Groups: Hikers, dogs, and horses. No mountain bikes. No wheelchair facilities.

Permits: No day-use permits are required. Parking and access are free.

Maps: For a map, ask the U.S. Forest Service for Stanislaus National Forest or Carson-Iceberg Wilderness. For a topographic map, ask the USGS for Spicer Meadow Reservoir.

Directions: From Angels Camp, take Highway 4 east for 40 miles to Bear Valley. Set your odometer at Bear Valley and drive east on Highway 4 for 4.3 miles to the Lake Alpine East Shore trailhead turnoff on the right. Turn right and continue straight to Silver Valley Campground and the Silver Valley trailhead.

Contact: Stanislaus National Forest, Calaveras

Ranger District, 209/813-6008, www.fs.usda.gov/stanislaus.

75 WOODCHUCK BASIN TO WHEELER LAKE

6.4 mi/3.5 hr 3 8

in the Mokelumne Wilderness off Highway 4 near Lake Alpine

Map 6.2, page 214

Your goal is little Wheeler Lake, a fine overlooked lake (and we'll explain why). Start at the Woodchuck Basin trailhead, elevation 7,800 feet. The trail leads into the Mokelumne Wilderness, and after you climb uphill for 1.7 forested miles, you reach a junction where you can go left for Underwood Valley or right for tiny Wheeler Lake. Bear right, pass a Mokelumne Wilderness sign, and in moments, you plummet 1,000 feet in a 1.5-mile descent to Wheeler Lake. Think it over before you go, because you'll need to regain those 1,000 feet on the way home. That's why many choose not to do this hike, or make it an overnighter and camp. But if you're willing to take the plunge, you're treated to a picturesque, tree- and granite-lined lake, where you can pass the afternoon with little fear that you'll be bugged by a busload of other hikers.

User Groups: Hikers, leashed dogs, and horses. No mountain bikes. No wheelchair facilities.

Permits: No permits are required. Parking and access are free. A wilderness permit (free) is required for overnight use.

Maps: For a map, ask the U.S. Forest Service for Stanislaus National Forest or Mokelumne Wilderness. For a topographic map, ask the USGS for Spicer Meadow Reservoir.

Directions: From Angels Camp, take Highway 4 east for 40 miles to Bear Valley. Set your odometer at Bear Valley and drive east on Highway 4 for 5.5 miles to the Woodchuck Basin trailhead on the left. Turn left and drive 0.25 mile to the parking area.

Contact: Stanislaus National Forest, Calaveras Ranger District, 209/813-6008, www.fs.usda.gov/stanislaus.

76 DISCOVERY STUMP/ NORTH GROVE LOOP

1.0 mi/0.5 hr 1 7

in Calaveras Big Trees State Park

Map 6.2, page 214

The giant sequoia that nobody forgets is what is called the "Discovery Stump." Others just call it "The Big Stump." It's the most popular spot in the park. Start at the visitors center, then walk south a short distance past the campfire center to the stump. It is 24 feet in diameter. Everybody gets their picture taken on it. Here's the story: Back in the day, a gent wanted to prove how big the trees were to folks on the East Coast, so naturally, he cut the biggest one down, collected the bark and wasted the wood, then took it by railroad to the World's Fair and reassembled it to prove its size—except everybody thought it was a hoax. Then, shortly thereafter, the bark collection was burned in a fire. Surprised the guy didn't shoot a Bigfoot while he was at it? The giant stump has been used for just about everything, including a dance floor. According to projections, if it had been allowed to grow, it would be bigger than the General Sherman Tree in Sequoia National Park, the largest living thing by volume on the planet.

Once you have seen The Big Stump, which is what we call it, return to the North Grove Loop. It is routed in a loop in a grove of giant sequoias that include several mammoth-size trees. Note that the Pioneer Cabin Tree (actually an elongated stump), where the trail was once routed through a rectangular cutout in the high stump, went kerplunk and is a goner.

The easy trail is routed among the giant sequoias, near Big Tree Creek, and back, easy, short, and pretty. These trees, of course, are known for their tremendous diameter: It can take a few dozen people, linking hands, to

North Grove Loop

encircle one. This trip is actually best in winter after fresh snowfall, when your footsteps are the only signs of life and it feels like you are in a time machine. This trail gets very heavy use.

User Groups: Hikers and wheelchairs. No dogs, horses, or mountain bikes.

Permits: No permits are required. A state park entrance fee of $10 is charged each vehicle.

Maps: A brochure and trail map are available for a fee at Calaveras Big Trees State Park. For a topographic map, ask the USGS for Dorrington.

Directions: From Angels Camp, take Highway 4 east for 23 miles to Arnold, and then continue for four miles to the park entrance. The trailhead is adjacent to the park entrance.

Contact: Calaveras Big Trees State Park, 209/795-2334, www.parks.ca.gov.

77 SOUTH GROVE LOOP

5.0 mi/3.0 hr  2 8

northeast of Arnold on Highway 4

Map 6.2, page 214

The two largest sequoias in Calaveras Big Trees State Park are found on a spur trail of this hike, and that makes it a must-do for visitors. But so many tourists are content to just walk the little trail at the North Grove, look at "The Big Stump," and then hit the road. Why rush? As long as you're at the park, take the South Grove Loop. The loop itself is 3.5 miles long, but the highlight is a spur trail that branches off 0.75 mile to the Agassiz Tree and the Palace Hotel Tree, two monster-size specimens. For a great photograph, have someone take a picture of you standing at the base of one of these trees; you will look like a Lilliputian from *Gulliver's Travels.*

User Groups: Hikers only. No dogs, horses, or mountain bikes. No wheelchair facilities.

Permits: No permits are required. A state park entrance fee of $10 is charged each vehicle.

Maps: A brochure and trail map are available for a fee at Calaveras Big Trees State Park. For a topographic map, ask the USGS for Boards Crossing.

Directions: From Angels Camp, take Highway 4 east for 23 miles to Arnold, and then continue for four miles to the park entrance. Turn right into the park entrance, then drive down the parkway for nine miles to the trailhead, on the right. The road is closed in winter.

Contact: Calaveras Big Trees State Park, 209/795-2334, www.parks.ca.gov.

78 CARSON PASS TO ECHO LAKES RESORT (PCT)

15.8 mi one-way/1-2 days 4 10

from Carson Pass at Highway 88 north to Echo Lake near U.S. 50, just south of Lake Tahoe

Map 6.3, page 215 BEST

When you've hiked on the Pacific Crest Trail

for weeks, the first glimpse of Lake Tahoe in the distance can seem like a privileged view into heaven. I'll never forget it. That view is just a few miles from Ebbetts Pass. You start by hiking over a short mountain rim (nice view to the west of Caples Lake) and then you drop into the headwaters of the Truckee River. As you look northward after making the rim, Lake Tahoe suddenly comes into view. It's like having a divine vision. And finally there is water available from several small creeks as you walk into the Truckee headwaters. At the same time, you will be greeted by a high meadow surrounded by a light forest. All seems right with the world again. With Echo Lakes Resort within one day's hiking time, you will be amazed at how inspired (and fast) you can get on this section of trail. It's very pretty, weaving through lush canyons and along creeks, eventually reaching beautiful and tiny Showers Lake. Here the trail seems to drop off to never-never land; it descends quickly and steeply in the march toward Tahoe. Contentment reigns. When you reach Little Norway, however, reality sets in. Cars are everywhere. The trail suddenly grinds down amid cabins and vacation property. There's one last hill to climb, a real half hour of frustration—you're ready for your reward at the store—and then the PCT drops quickly to the parking lot for Echo Lakes.

To continue north on the PCT, see the *Echo Lakes Resort to Barker Pass (PCT)* hike in this chapter. If you are walking this trail in reverse, see the *Blue Lakes Road to Carson Pass (PCT)* hike in this chapter.

User Groups: Hikers, dogs, and horses. No mountain bikes. No wheelchair facilities.

Permits: A single permit is required to hike the Pacific Crest Trail. Contact the national forest, Bureau of Land Management, or national park office at your point of entry for a combined permit that is good for traveling through multiple-permit areas during your dates of travel.

Maps: For national forest maps, ask for Lake Tahoe Basin Management Unit, Tahoe National Forest, Eldorado National Forest, and Stanislaus National Forest. For topographic maps, ask the USGS for Carson Pass, Caples Lake, and Echo Lake.

Directions: From South Lake Tahoe, take Highway 50 south for roughly four miles to Meyers and the junction with Highway 89, and then continue south on Highway 89 for 11 miles to Highway 88. Turn right (west) on Highway 88 and drive 10 miles to Carson Pass.

For the Echo Lakes Resort trailhead: From South Lake Tahoe, take Highway 89 south for five miles to U.S. 50. Turn right (west) on U.S. 50 and drive 5.5 miles to the signed turnoff for Echo Lakes on the right (one mile west of Echo Summit). Turn right and drive 0.5 mile to Echo Lakes Road. Turn left and drive one mile to a series of parking lots located 0.25 mile before the road ends at Echo Lakes Resort. Hikers not staying at the resort must park in one of the upper lots or alongside the road, not in the main lower lot by the resort, and walk down to the marina, boat taxi, or trailhead.

Contact: Eldorado National Forest, Amador Ranger District, 209/295-4251, www.fs.usda.gov/eldorado; Lake Tahoe Basin Management Unit, South Lake Tahoe, 530/543-2600, www.fs.usda.gov/ltbmu; Taylor Creek Visitor Center, open mid-June through mid-September (closed Tues. and Wed.), weekends on shoulder season starting Memorial Day and after Labor Day weekends, 530/543-2674.

79 CARSON PASS TO SHOWERS LAKE

10.0 mi/6.0 hr

near Caples Lake in Meiss Country

Map 6.3, page 215

Here's a day hike on the Pacific Crest Trail into the land of Meiss Country, that is, the headwaters for the Upper Truckee River. Start this trip at the PCT trailhead on the north side of Carson Pass. You head uphill where you climb through Meiss Pass and then drop into a huge valley basin. Views along the way include

Mount Round Top, Elephant Back, and Red Lake Peak and expand to distant, far-off Lake Tahoe to the north. It's 2.9 miles to a fork with the Tahoe Rim Trail (TRT), just beyond a crossing of Upper Truckee River (little more than a creek here). While stopping to pump a canteen's worth of water here, we've had hummingbirds come up and eye us from a foot away.

At the fork, stay left on the PCT and TRT, and cross the river again on your way to Showers Lake, 2.1 miles farther. The last half mile of trail is a 350-foot descent to Showers Lake, with 9,590-foot Little Round Top poking up above it to the west. The trail leads along the east side of the lake, where campsites can be found. The lake is set at 8,790 feet and is the highest lake in the Upper Truckee River Basin. It's very pretty.

By the way, at that fork, the right fork leads 2.2 miles to Round Lake, Meiss Country's largest lake and a popular destination.

This trip is popular with the horsey set. A separate trail leads to Showers Lake from Schneider Camp, a large horse camp, so weekends bring a fair amount of horse traffic. Also note that the trip begins in Eldorado National Forest, but two-thirds of the trail is within jurisdiction of the Lake Tahoe Basin Management Unit. Note that no bikes are permitted on the PCT, but we've seen plenty of tire tread here on the trail.

User Groups: Hikers, leashed dogs, and horses. No mountain bikes. No wheelchair facilities.

Permits: No permits are required. A $5 parking fee is charged per vehicle. A wilderness permit (free) is required for overnight use. No mountain bikes permitted on Pacific Crest Trail.

Maps: For a map, ask the U.S. Forest Service for Eldorado National Forest or Mokelumne Wilderness. For topographic maps, ask the USGS for Caples Lake and Carson Pass.

Directions: From South Lake Tahoe, take Highway 50 south for roughly four miles to Meyers and the junction with Highway 89, and then continue south on Highway 89 for 11 miles to Highway 88. Turn right (west) on Highway 88 and drive 10 miles to Carson Pass Summit. The parking area and Meiss trailhead are on the right (north), across the highway from (and slightly west of) the Carson Pass Information Station.

Contact: Eldorado National Forest, Amador Ranger District, Pioneer, 209/295-4251 www.fs.usda.gov/eldorado.

80 WOODS LAKE TO WINNEMUCCA LAKE

3.0 mi/1.5 hr 2 10

in the Mokelumne Wilderness near Carson Pass

Map 6.3, page 215 **BEST**

Woods Lake is a little magical spot where you can drive right up, walk a few feet to the water's edge, and plunk in your fishing line. It's also the trailhead for numerous great hikes into the Mokelumne Wilderness, including this easy trip to deep blue Winnemucca Lake, set at the base of Mount Round Top (elevation 10,380 feet). From Woods Lake, the trip starts where you walk amid big conifers until you come out to a glacial moraine. A view emerges of Mount Round Top, a huge old volcanic vent. It's a stunning sight and, in an average winter, collects massive amounts of snow. In early summer, wildflowers bloom in profusion on the open slopes surrounding the path. From Woods Lake, it is only 1.5 miles of gentle to moderate climbing to reach the edge of Winnemucca Lake, nestled at the foot of Mount Round Top. The land here has been formed by volcanic action, so as you walk, wide-traveled hikers may have to remember that you aren't at Lassen Peak or Mount Shasta. The beauty attracts a ton of people, often 200 to 300 on summer weekends.

The peak season for wildflowers is mid-June to mid-August, at its very best in mid- to late July. If you hiked this trail in years past, you may remember that it once started by crossing a footbridge. That is no longer true.

User Groups: Hikers, leashed dogs, and horses. No mountain bikes. No wheelchair facilities.

Permits: A free wilderness permit is required for overnight stays; it is available from the Amador Ranger Station, the Carson Pass Information Station, or the Eldorado Information Center. A parking fee of $5 is charged, good for overnight use.

Maps: For a map, ask the U.S. Forest Service for Mokelumne Wilderness or Eldorado National Forest. For topographic maps, ask the USGS for Caples Lake and Carson Pass.

Directions: From South Lake Tahoe, take Highway 50 south for roughly four miles to Meyers and the junction with Highway 89, and then continue south on Highway 89 for 11 miles to Highway 88. Turn right (west) on Highway 88 and drive 12 miles to the Woods Lake Campground turnoff on the south side of the road (1.5 miles west of Carson Pass Summit). Turn left and drive one mile to the trailhead parking area (0.5 mile before reaching Woods Lake).

Contact: Eldorado National Forest, Amador Ranger District, 209/295-4251, www.fs.usda.gov/eldorado.

81 WOODS LAKE TRAILHEAD TO ROUND TOP LOOP

6.6 mi/4.0 hr

in the Mokelumne Wilderness near Carson Pass

Map 6.3, page 215

The mission on this hike is to connect the trailhead from Woods Lake to Winnemucca Lake and beyond to the top of 10,380-foot Mount Round Top. Your reward is a 10. You pay a bit for your pleasure. Start at the Woods Lake trailhead, and take the Winnemucca Lake Trail for the first 1.5 miles to Winnemucca's edge, as described in the previous hike. Then bear right and cross the stream on the west side of the lake. It's then one mile, uphill, to Round Top Lake, steep enough to get you puffing. The gorgeous volcanic scenery makes it all worthwhile. Round Top Lake is set below The Sisters, two peaks that are both over 10,000 feet high. You also have views of Mount Round Top and Fourth of July Peak. It's incredibly dramatic.

From the eastern edge of Round Top Lake, you'll see a path that is routed up the side of Mount Round Top. The grade is brutal, but when you reach the top after a final rocky scramble, you have a stunning view of the Dardanelles, Lake Tahoe, Caples Lake, Woods Lake, Round Top Lake, Winnemucca Lake, and Frog Lake. Summit City Canyon, 3,000 feet below the south side of Round Top, is stunning. At 10,380 feet, Mount Round Top is the highest peak in the Carson Pass area and the finest place for a bird's-eye view. The summit is more like a knife-thin, rocky ridge, so watch your footing. This is not a place for children or inexperienced hikers.

After your summit visit, return downhill to Round Top Lake to finish out your loop. Follow the lake's outlet creek on Lost Cabin Mine Trail for two miles back to Woods Lake Campground; then wind your way through the camp back to the Woods Lake Picnic Area, where you left your car.

User Groups: Hikers, leashed dogs, and horses. No mountain bikes. No wheelchair facilities.

Permits: A free wilderness permit is required for overnight stays; it is available from the Amador Ranger Station, the Carson Pass Information Station, or the Eldorado Information Center. A parking fee of $5 is charged, good for overnight use.

Maps: For a map, ask the U.S. Forest Service for Mokelumne Wilderness or Eldorado National Forest. For topographic maps, ask the USGS for Caples Lake and Carson Pass.

Directions: From South Lake Tahoe, take Highway 50 south for roughly four miles to Meyers and the junction with Highway 89, and then continue south on Highway 89 for 11 miles to Highway 88. Turn right (west) on Highway 88 and drive 12 miles to the Woods Lake Campground turnoff on the south side of the

road (1.5 miles west of Carson Pass Summit). Turn left and drive 1.5 miles to the trailhead parking area, by the picnic area at Woods Lake.
Contact: Eldorado National Forest, Amador Ranger District, 209/295-4251, www.fs.usda.gov/eldorado.

82 WOODS LAKE TRAILHEAD TO FOURTH OF JULY LAKE

8.8 mi/4.5 hr or 2 days 

in the Mokelumne Wilderness near Caples Lake

Map 6.3, page 215

In some parts of California, the idea of 200 to 300 hikers on a wilderness trail in a single day on a summer weekend is mind-boggling. Yet that is what you get here. Carson Pass and Woods Lake are stellar trailheads, and with several lakes and Mount Round Top so close, the crowds thus arrive. So timing becomes key, along with deciding which way to go. There are so many ways from so many trailheads, including ones at Carson Pass and Upper Blue Lake. If you pick early summer when the campground opens and the trail first clears of snow, you can still have it largely to yourself; same after mid-September, when the cold nights arrive.

The shortest and most direct route is from Woods Lake trailhead 0.5 mile before the Woods Lake Campground and picnic area. This includes a nice stopover at Round Top Lake, two miles in. You pass some old mining cabins before you enter the wilderness boundary. Pass the eastern flank of 9,000-foot Black Butte, an old volcanic vent that is similar in appearance to Mount Round Top a few miles to the east. In less than an hour, you arrive at Round Top Lake, a worthy destination in itself and a good spot for a snack break beneath the sturdy shoulders of the two peaks of The Sisters. It's only two more miles to Fourth of July Lake, but they are steep and downhill (which means you must climb back out on the way home). This is actually good news: It means you will leave the majority of the crowds behind. Most people give up at Fourth of July Saddle, a rocky overlook that sits 1,000 feet above the lake. In addition to the tough grade, the route is often dusty. At the lake, fishing is good for brook trout, and many campsites can be found near its edge. Late in the summer, a sandy beach gets exposed, good for swimmers.
User Groups: Hikers, leashed dogs, and horses. No mountain bikes. No wheelchair facilities.
Permits: A free wilderness permit is required for overnight stays; it is available from the Amador Ranger Station, the Carson Pass Information Station, or the Eldorado Information Center. A parking fee of $5 is charged, good for overnight use.
Maps: For a map, ask the U.S. Forest Service for Eldorado National Forest or Mokelumne Wilderness. For a topographic map, ask the USGS for Caples Lake.
Directions: From South Lake Tahoe, take Highway 50 south for roughly four miles to Meyers and the junction with Highway 89, and then continue south on Highway 89 for 11 miles to Highway 88. Turn right (west) on Highway 88 and drive 12 miles to the Woods Lake Campground turnoff on the south side of the road (1.5 miles west of Carson Pass Summit). Turn left and drive one mile to the trailhead (0.5 mile before the campground and picnic area).
Contact: Eldorado National Forest, Amador Ranger District, 209/295-4251, www.fs.usda.gov/eldorado.

83 FROG LAKE

1.8 mi/1.0 hr 

in the Mokelumne Wilderness near Carson Pass

Map 6.3, page 215

Any hiking trip from the Carson Pass trailhead in peak summer is going to be packed with people. So it is here, with 200-plus people out on weekends. That known, this trail is educational and beautiful. The short walk to Frog Lake is suitable even for small children (and if you're more ambitious, you can continue another 1.5 miles to beautiful Winnemucca Lake). At Frog Lake, you are provided with a fascinating view of Elephant Back (elevation 9,585 feet), which looks exactly like its name. It's a lava dome, a round mass of solid lava. The lake is a beautiful turquoise color, perfect for picnicking, although because the area is rather open and exposed, the wind sometimes blows with ferocity.

Plenty of people take this walk in early summer to see the wildflowers, especially lupine and Indian paintbrush, from mid-June to mid-August (best in late July). A huge patch of wild iris also blooms alongside Frog Lake. It's a sight to behold. There are many other species of wildflowers here. An identification sheet is posted at the billboard near the trailhead and at the visitors center.

At the visitors center, you can learn about Kit Carson, the great explorer for whom this pass was named, and you can learn about the geologic forces that shaped this region, which is called the Round Top Geologic Area. Evidence of both glacial and volcanic action can be seen with every step you take.

User Groups: Hikers, leashed dogs, and horses. No mountain bikes. No wheelchair facilities.

Permits: A free wilderness permit is required for overnight stays between April 1 and November 30; it is available from the Amador Ranger Station, the Carson Pass Information Station, or the Eldorado Information Center. A $5 parking fee is charged per vehicle.

Maps: For a map, ask the U.S. Forest Service for Eldorado National Forest or Mokelumne Wilderness. For a topographic map, ask the USGS for Carson Pass.

Directions: From South Lake Tahoe, take Highway 50 south for roughly four miles to Meyers and the junction with Highway 89, and then continue south on Highway 89 for 11 miles to Highway 88. Turn right (west) on Highway 88 and drive 10 miles to Carson Pass Summit. The parking area and trailhead are on the left, by the Carson Pass Information Station.

Contact: Eldorado National Forest, Amador Ranger District, 209/295-4251, www.fs.usda.gov/eldorado.

84 RAYMOND LAKE

11.0 mi/1-2 days 

in the Mokelumne Wilderness near Blue Lakes

Map 6.3, page 215

Despite a 3,000-foot climb, little Raymond Lake is a popular weekend trip. One reason is that it is a common stopover for PCT hikers, as well as weekenders who make this a two-day in-and-outer. That is, about five miles in and about five miles out, and that's why it works. The lake is about 10 acres in size and sits at 9,000 feet, with several small campsites sprinkled near the water. The trail starts near Wet Meadows Reservoir and heads east from the access road on the Pacific Crest Trail. It follows the PCT for 4.5 miles, a moderate ascent, to the junction with the Raymond Lake Trail. Turn right for the final mile. This final stretch is only a mile but a butt-kicker, mostly because you're already getting tired when you begin it. The lake is set below 10,000-foot Raymond Peak.

User Groups: Hikers, dogs, and horses. No mountain bikes. No wheelchair facilities.

Permits: A free wilderness permit is required for overnight stays; it is available on the wilderness bulletin board at the trailhead, from the ranger station in Markleeville, the Carson Pass Information Station, or the Carson Ranger district in Carson City. Groups are limited to 12, and no campfires are permitted above 8,000 feet.

Maps: For a map, ask the U.S. Forest Service for Humboldt-Toiyabe National Forest, Carson District. For topographic maps, ask the USGS for Pacific Valley and Ebbetts Pass.

Directions: From South Lake Tahoe, take Highway 50 south for roughly four miles to Meyers and the junction with Highway 89, and then continue south on Highway 89 for 11 miles to Highway 88. Turn right (west) on Highway 88 and drive 2.5 miles to the Blue Lakes turnoff on the south side of the road. Turn south and drive 11 miles to the left turnoff for Tamarack Lake and Wet Meadows. Bear left and drive three miles to the left turnoff for Lower Sunset Lake. Turn left and drive a short distance to the trailhead.

Contact: Humboldt-Toiyabe National Forest, Sparks, 775/331-6444, www.fs.usda.gov/htnf.

85 BLUE LAKE DAM TO GRANITE LAKE

4.0 mi/2.0 hr 1 9

in the Mokelumne Wilderness near Blue Lakes

Map 6.3, page 215

The trip starts at the dam at Upper Blue Lake. A well-signed and meandering route ventures one mile to enter the Mokelumne Wilderness. Another mile beyond the wilderness boundary is Granite Lake. To reach it requires a total 550-foot climb, but the trail is well graded and some will barely notice they are climbing. Note that a quarter mile past the boundary sign, you'll see a large pond, but don't mistake that for Granite Lake, which is another 20 minutes farther on the trail. When you arrive, you'll find this small lake set in a granite pocket. Don't be concerned if there are lots of cars in the dam parking lot. Most of them belong to anglers, not hikers. PG&E closed Blue Lakes in 2019 for renovation for recreation sites and reopened in early summer of 2020.

User Groups: Hikers, leashed dogs, and horses. No mountain bikes. No wheelchair facilities.

Permits: A free wilderness permit is required for overnight; it is available from the Amador Ranger Station, the Carson Pass Information Station, or the Eldorado Information Center.

Maps: For a map, ask the U.S. Forest Service for Eldorado National Forest. For a topographic map, ask the USGS for Pacific Valley.

Directions: From South Lake Tahoe, take Highway 50 south for roughly four miles to Meyers and the junction with Highway 89, and then continue south on Highway 89 for 11 miles to Highway 88. Turn right (west) on Highway 88 and drive 2.5 miles to the Blue Lakes turnoff on the south side of the road. Turn south and drive 12 miles to the fork at Lower Blue Lake. Turn right and drive 1.5 miles to the dam by Upper Blue Lake, shortly past Middle Creek Campground; turn left into the parking area. The Grouse Lake Trail leads to Granite Lake from the west side of the parking area.

Contact: Eldorado National Forest, Amador Ranger District, 209/295-4251, www.fs.usda.gov/eldorado.

86 HOT SPRINGS CREEK WATERFALL

3.0 mi/1.5 hr 2 8

in Grover Hot Springs State Park near Markleeville

Map 6.3, page 215

Your goal is a 50-foot waterfall, best in spring and early summer, of course. The route is a bit tricky, but even without a waterfall, this would be a great trail to walk. The route starts from just beyond the campgrounds in Grover Hot Springs State Park, an elevation of 5,900 feet. From here, you hike on the Burnside Lake and Charity Valley Trails for 0.5 mile, then reach a fork signed for the waterfall. Turn left at the fork, and in the process, some newcomers get confused where you reach a jumbled pile of boulders on the trail. Simply go up and over them. Hot Springs Canyon gradually narrows on its way to the falls, and when you near the creek's edge, you might see small trout swimming in its pools. You then arrive at the waterfall, perched at an elevation of 6,200 feet. Technically it is outside of state parkland and in Humboldt-Toiyabe National Forest, so you'll see backpackers' campfire rings on the cliff above the falls.

Highlights of the trail include the giant

Jeffrey pines of Hot Springs Valley, enclosed by rocky cliffs and 10,000-foot peaks.

User Groups: Hikers and leashed dogs (not recommended). No horses or mountain bikes. No wheelchair facilities.

Permits: No permits are required. A day-use fee is charged per vehicle; there is also a fee of $10 per person for use of the hot springs pool.

Maps: A map of Grover Hot Springs State Park is available for a fee at the entrance station. For a topographic map, ask the USGS for Markleeville.

Directions: From South Lake Tahoe, take Highway 50 south for roughly four miles to Meyers and the junction with Highway 89, and then continue south on Highway 89 for 11 miles to Highway 88. Turn right (east) on Highway 88 and drive 13 miles to Markleeville at Hot Springs Road. Turn right (west) on Hot Springs Road and drive 3.5 miles to the state park entrance. The signed trailhead is 0.25 mile beyond the entrance station and campground turnoffs, at a gated dirt road.

Contact: Grover Hot Springs State Park, 530/694-2248, pool information 530/694-2249, www.parks.ca.gov.

87 GROVER HOT SPRINGS TO BURNSIDE LAKE

8.4 mi/5.0 hr

in Humboldt-Toiyabe National Forest near Markleeville

Map 6.3, page 215

From Grover Hot Springs State Park, at 5,900 feet, the Burnside Lake Trail leaves in elevation and climbs west to Burnside Lake, at 8,160 feet, a gain of 2,260 feet. The climb is spaced out over four miles, so it's a steady workout to the lake. Along the way, you pass tall and majestic sugar pines and rocky outcrops, with 10,023-foot Hawkins Peak and 9,417-foot Markleeville Peak towering over the scene. The lake is about 10 surface acres and popular for trout fishing. Although you can start hiking on the trail from Hot Springs Road shortly before the state park entrance, it's best to begin from the trailhead at the park. That shaves one mile off your trip, but also when you return from your hike, you can take a dip in the 102- to 104-degree hot springs. At first you may encounter mountain bikers on the trail; they will soon branch off on their way to Charity Valley, a great mountain bike trek.

User Groups: Hikers, dogs, horses, and mountain bikes. No wheelchair facilities.

Permits: No permits are required. A day-use fee of $8 is charged per vehicle at Grover Hot Springs State Park; there is a fee of $7 per person for use of the hot springs pool.

Maps: For a map, ask the U.S. Forest Service for Humboldt-Toiyabe National Forest, Carson District. A map of Grover Hot Springs State Park is available for a fee at the entrance station. For a topographic map, ask the USGS for Markleeville.

Directions: From South Lake Tahoe, take Highway 89 south for five miles to Meyers and the junction with Highway 89, and then continue south on Highway 89 for 11 miles to Highway 88. Turn left on Highway 88/89 and drive 13 miles to Markleeville at Hot Springs Road. Turn right (west) on Hot Springs Road and drive 3.5 miles to the state park entrance. The signed trailhead is 0.25 mile beyond the entrance station and campground turnoffs at a gated dirt road. Another trailhead is outside the state park on Hot Springs Road, 0.75 mile before the state park entrance, and signed for Charity Valley and gets heavy mountain bike use.

Contact: Grover Hot Springs State Park, Markleeville, 530/694-2248, www.parks.ca.gov; Humboldt-Toiyabe National Forest, Sparks, 775/331-6444, www.fs.usda.gov/htnf.

88 BLUE LAKES ROAD TO CARSON PASS (PCT)

12.0 mi one-way/1 day 4 9

from Blue Lakes Road north to Carson Pass and Highway 88

Map 6.3, page 215

Many hikers underestimate the climb over Elephant Back to reach Carson Pass. After all, on a map, it doesn't look like much, and from a distance, as you size it up, it seems easy enough. Wrong. It's a long, grueling pull. The trip out of Blue Lakes starts easily, with a dirt road often in view and adding a bit of early angst to the affair. As you go, you keep wondering when the climb will begin. Well, eventually it does, and, alas, it takes a couple of hours, a long, steady march. After topping the Elephant Back, the route drops down to Carson Pass at a rest stop, where you'll likely meet humanity, but believe it or not, no water! When we hiked from Yosemite to Tahoe, this was the worst shock of the trip. Conserve yours if you plan to go onward, because it takes another hour of hiking before you'll reach the next trickle.

To continue north on the PCT, see the *Carson Pass to Echo Lakes Resort (PCT)* hike in this chapter. If you are walking this trail in reverse, see the *Ebbetts Pass to Blue Lakes Road (PCT)* hike in this chapter.

User Groups: Hikers, dogs, and horses. No mountain bikes. No wheelchair access.

Permits: A single permit is required to hike the Pacific Crest Trail. Contact the national forest, Bureau of Land Management, or national park office at your point of entry for a combined permit that is good for traveling through multiple-permit areas during your dates of travel.

Maps: For a map, ask the U.S. Forest Service for Lake Tahoe Basin Management Unit, Tahoe National Forest, Eldorado National Forest, and Stanislaus National Forest. For topographic maps, ask the USGS for Pacific Valley and Carson Pass.

Directions: To reach the Blue Lakes Road trailhead from the Highway 88/89 junction at Hope Valley, go west on Highway 88 to Blue Lakes Road and turn left. Stay on Blue Lakes Road for 11 miles to the trailhead parking, just before reaching Blue Lakes.

For the Carson Pass trailhead from the Highway 88/89 junction at Hope Valley, go west on Highway 88 to Carson Pass.

Contact: Eldorado National Forest, Amador Ranger District, 209/295-4251, www.fs.usda.gov/eldorado.

89 KINNEY LAKES

5.0 mi/2.5 hr

in Humboldt-Toiyabe National Forest near Ebbetts Pass

Map 6.3, page 215

From the Ebbetts Pass trailhead, Kinney Lakes is an easy tromp north on the Pacific Crest Trail. You pass little Sherrold Lake on the way to Upper Kinney Lake (which is actually a small reservoir). You start hiking at 8,700 feet at the pass, so even though this trail has an easy to moderate grade, your lungs are getting a workout. The trail leads through a landscape of big conifers with little undergrowth, typical of the high country. When the trees thin out, your views open wide. Raymond Peak and Reynolds Peak rule the skyline. At 1.6 miles, you reach a signed junction for Upper and Lower Kinney Lakes, and you can take your pick as to which one to visit first. The Pacific Crest Trail leads directly to the upper lake, while the lower lake must be visited by following an eastward fork from the PCT. The upper lake, though smaller, is the prettier of the two.

User Groups: Hikers, dogs, and horses. No mountain bikes. No wheelchair facilities.

Permits: Wilderness permits are required for overnight use. No campfires are allowed above 8,000 feet. Parking and access are free.

Maps: For a map, ask the U.S. Forest Service for Humboldt-Toiyabe National Forest, Carson District. For a topographic map, ask the USGS for Ebbetts Pass.

Directions: From Angels Camp, drive east on Highway 4 for about 40 miles to Bear Valley. Set your odometer at Bear Valley, and drive 15 miles farther east on Highway 4 to Ebbetts Pass and the trailhead parking area. The trail is on the north side of the road.

If you are coming from Markleeville, drive south on Highway 89/Highway 4 for 15 miles to Ebbetts Pass.

Contact: Humboldt-Toiyabe National Forest, Sparks, 775/331-6444, www.fs.usda.gov/htnf.

90 EBBETTS PASS TO BLUE LAKES ROAD (PCT)

17.7 mi one-way/1 day 3 8

from Highway 4 near Ebbetts Pass to Blue Lakes Road south of Carson Pass and Highway 88

Map 6.3, page 215

As you leave Ebbetts Pass and head north, you'll cross a series of fantastic volcanic formations in the Mokelumne Wilderness. The country here may look stark from a distance, but it is loaded with tiny wildflowers in every ravine. The trail is easy without a lot of climb and descent, then repeat; and a lot of hikers make great time in this area. The lack of available water can become a concern. Tank up whenever you get the chance, such as at Eagle Creek below Reynold Peak (9,690 feet). The Mokelumne Wilderness is a relative breeze, and you'll find yourself approaching civilization at a series of small lakes in Tahoe National Forest. The trail rises up a stark, windblown, sandy ridge, with excellent views of the Blue Lakes, but again, there is no water for several miles until you drop down near Lost Lake. You'll actually cross several roads on this stretch of trail, and maybe even see a car, a moment of irony for long-distance PCT hikers. But the going is easy; we think this is one of the fastest sections of the PCT in the central Sierra. To continue north on the PCT, see the *Blue Lakes Road to Carson Pass (PCT)* hike in this chapter.

User Groups: Hikers, dogs, and horses. No mountain bikes. No wheelchair facilities.

Permits: A single permit is required to hike the Pacific Crest Trail. Contact the national forest, Bureau of Land Management, or national park office at your point of entry for a combined permit that is good for traveling through multiple-permit areas during your dates of travel.

Maps: For a map, ask the U.S. Forest Service for Lake Tahoe Basin Management Unit, Tahoe National Forest, Eldorado National Forest, and Stanislaus National Forest. For topographic maps, ask the USGS for Ebbetts Pass, Pacific Valley, and Carson Pass.

Directions: To reach the Ebbetts Pass trailhead from Angels Camp, head east on Highway 4 to Ebbetts Pass.

To reach the Blue Lakes Road trailhead from the Highway 88/89 interchange at Hope Valley, head west on Highway 88 to Blue Lakes Road and turn left. Stay on Blue Lakes Road to the trailhead parking area, just before reaching Blue Lakes.

Contact: Eldorado National Forest, Amador Ranger District, 209/295-4251, www.fs.usda.gov/eldorado.

91 NOBLE LAKE

9.0 mi/4.5 hr 2 8

in Humboldt-Toiyabe National Forest near Ebbetts Pass

Map 6.3, page 215

Noble Lake lies just outside of the Carson-Iceberg Wilderness. You can best reach it with a gentle route from Ebbetts Pass. From Ebbetts Pass (elevation 8,700 feet), there's a 1,200-foot climb to the lake at 9,440 feet (which includes some easy ups and downs). The lake is a fine spot for camping or just spending an afternoon. It is not pristine gorgeous, but an 8, classic high Sierra, with big conifers, snowcapped peaks, hard granite, and lush meadows. From the trailhead parking area, the route follows a short 0.25-mile spur trail that climbs a short distance, then connects to the Pacific Crest Trail. You head south, of course, first climbing to a short ride, and then you make a long descent into Noble Canyon. At three miles, you will cross Noble Creek and then climb again to a high meadow. Soon you can see Noble Lake; the main lake is to the right of the trail, but a smaller, unnamed lake is to the left, about 650 feet off the trail. Both have decent campsites and many good rocks to sit on and relax. A boulder field above the campsites is loaded with ground squirrels, and if you hike overnight here with a dog, the squirrels will drive your dog crazy. I don't think Bart-Dog went to sleep the whole night. This lake is excellent for swimming but poor for fishing. For camping, group size is limited to 15 people, and a 100-foot setback from the lake is required.

User Groups: Hikers, dogs, and horses. No mountain bikes. No wheelchair facilities.

Permits: No day-hiking permits are required. A free wilderness permit is available at the trailhead (self-issue). Parking and access are free.

Maps: For a map, ask the U.S. Forest Service for Humboldt-Toiyabe National Forest, Carson District. For a topographic map, ask the USGS for Ebbetts Pass.

Directions: From Angels Camp at the intersection of Highways 4 and 49, go east on Highway 4 for 40 miles to Bear Valley. Set your odometer at Bear Valley, and drive 15 miles farther east on Highway 4 to Ebbetts Pass and the trailhead parking area (just east of Ebbetts Pass; do not park on Highway 4). The trailhead is on the south side of the road.

Contact: Humboldt-Toiyabe National Forest, Sparks, 775/331-6444, www.fs.usda.gov/htnf.

92 WOLF CREEK TRAIL TO WOLF CREEK FALLS

9.6 mi/5.0 hr 2 8

in the Carson-Iceberg Wilderness near Markleeville

Map 6.3, page 215

When fed by snowmelt on a warm early summer day, Wolf Creek Falls thunders over a volcanic cliff. That's your payoff, and amid the crowds in the Tahoe region, there's a good chance you'll have it to yourself. The trailhead is at an elevation of 6,480 feet. The trail is an old jeep road that is routed along Wolf Creek, uphill through forest, and in turn, provides shade most of the way. Wolf Creek is very pretty, especially when the sun catches it just right. Hike 4.3 miles out to a fork for the steep Bull Canyon Trail to Bull Lake. Bear left and continue 0.5 mile to Wolf Creek Falls. The waterfall is just off the trail to the left, about 50 yards beyond where the trail passes through a cattle fence. For waterfall lovers, this one is impressive early in the summer.

User Groups: Hikers, dogs, and horses. No mountain bikes. No wheelchair facilities.

Permits: A free wilderness permit is required for overnight stays; it is available at the trailhead. Parking and access are free.

Maps: For a map, ask the U.S. Forest Service for Humboldt-Toiyabe National Forest, Carson District, and Carson-Iceberg Wilderness. For a topographic map, ask the USGS for Wolf Creek.

Directions: From South Lake Tahoe, take Highway 50 south for roughly four miles to Meyers and the junction with Highway 89, and then continue south on Highway 89 for 11 miles to Highway 88. Turn left (east) on Highway 88 and drive 13 miles to Markleeville. From Markleeville, continue south on Highway 89 for four miles to Monitor Pass Junction and Highway 4. Bear right (south) on Highway 4 and drive 2.5 miles to the signed turnoff for Wolf Creek on the left. Turn left (south) and drive 4.9 miles to the trailhead, about 100 yards before the end of the road.

Contact: Humboldt-Toiyabe National Forest, Sparks, 775/331-6444, www.fs.usda.gov/htnf.

93 EAST CARSON RIVER TRAIL

4.0 mi/2.0 hr 

in the Carson-Iceberg Wilderness near Markleeville

Map 6.3, page 215

The East Carson River Trail can be your salvation in spring when there's still too much snow around Ebbetts Pass. Trailhead elevation is only 6,240 feet at the north side of Wolf Creek Meadows (private property), and this, along with its sun exposure, means it's snow-free before other nearby areas. At the start, you hike uphill a short distance to a trail junction and the boundary sign for the Carson-Iceberg Wilderness. Turn left (the right fork is the High Trail northern terminus). An interesting journey is 1.5 miles to Wolf Creek Lake (sometimes dry) and Railroad Canyon, the site of 19th-century logging operations.

User Groups: Hikers, dogs, and horses. No mountain bikes. No wheelchair facilities.

Permits: A free wilderness permit is required for overnight stays; it is available at the trailhead. Parking and access are free.

Maps: For a map, ask the U.S. Forest Service for Humboldt-Toiyabe National Forest, Carson District, and Carson-Iceberg Wilderness. For a topographic map, ask the USGS for Wolf Creek.

Directions: From South Lake Tahoe, take Highway 50 south for roughly four miles to Meyers and the junction with Highway 89, and then continue south on Highway 89 for 11 miles to Highway 88. Turn left (east) on Highway 88 and drive 13 miles to Markleeville. Continue south on Highway 89/Highway 4 for 7.5 miles to the signed turnoff for Wolf Creek on the left. Turn left (east) and drive 3.5 miles to the left turnoff signed for East Carson River Trail. Turn left and drive one mile to the road junction to Dixon Mine. Turn right and drive 0.25 mile to the trailhead.

Contact: Humboldt-Toiyabe National Forest, Sparks, 775/331-6444, www.fs.usda.gov/htnf.

94 MOSQUITO LAKES TO HEISER LAKE

4.8 mi/2.5 hr 

in the Carson-Iceberg Wilderness near Ebbetts Pass

Map 6.3, page 215

The trailhead is at Mosquito Lakes, a gorgeous little site perched at an elevation of 8,000 feet on Highway 4. You know you're in for a good trip when the trailhead is in such a pretty spot. And so it is here. The trail climbs and descends, then climbs and descends some more, mostly heading in a straight-line course due south to Heiser Lake. It's one of those rare trails where you've got to work equally hard whether on the way in or out. Two miles in, at a junction with the trail from Bull Run Lake, bear left and finish out the last 0.5 mile to Heiser Lake, set at 8,300 feet. The lake is granite bound, with a couple of tiny islands sticking out of its shallow waters. Quiet, pristine, gorgeous.

User Groups: Hikers, dogs, and horses. No mountain bikes. No wheelchair facilities.

Permits: No day-hiking permits are required. Parking and access are free. A wilderness permit (free) is required for overnight use.

Maps: For a map, ask the U.S. Forest Service for Stanislaus National Forest and Carson-Iceberg Wilderness. For topographic maps, ask the USGS for Pacific Valley and Spicer Meadow Reservoir.

Directions: From Angels Camp, take Highway 4 east for 40 miles to Bear Valley. Set your odometer at Bear Valley and drive 10 miles farther east on Highway 4 to the Mosquito Lakes trailhead and Heiser Lake Trail. Park on the right (south) side of the road, across from the campground; there is only enough space for a few cars.

Contact: Stanislaus National Forest, Calaveras Ranger District, 209/813-6008, www.fs.usda.gov/stanislaus.

95 BULL RUN LAKE

7.0 mi/4.0 hr

in the Carson-Iceberg Wilderness near Ebbetts Pass

Map 6.3, page 215

The hike to Bull Run Lake can be a side trip or an option to nearby Heiser Lake (see previous listing). The lake is set at 8,300 feet and a fine reward for your effort, nestled in a steep-walled granite bowl. Plus, most of the trail to Bull Run Lake is well graded, with one steep section in the last 0.5 mile. The trailhead is set at 7,800 feet. The first 1.3 miles are almost level, traveling slightly downhill through a grassy meadow that is filled with wildflowers in the early summer and turns golden by September. After that, you start to climb, mostly through pine forest and over stretches of granite with trail cairns. At 2.2 miles, watch for a trail junction. Turn right for Bull Run Lake (straight ahead, on the other hand, is Heiser Lake). After a brief flat stretch, prepare for a final mile of climbing, with the last part the steepest.

On summer weekends, you might have to share the trail to Bull Run Lake with some horses. After all, their owners like the big parking lot at the trailhead, large enough for horse trailers. Maybe you should pack along a few extra apples or carrots, eh? Rudd, my old companion was an apple horse, not a carrot horse.

User Groups: Hikers, dogs, and horses. No mountain bikes. No wheelchair facilities.

Permits: No day-hiking permits are required. Parking and access are free. A wilderness permit (free) is required for overnight use.

Maps: For a map, ask the U.S. Forest Service for Stanislaus National Forest or Carson-Iceberg Wilderness. For topographic maps, ask the USGS for Pacific Valley and Spicer Meadow Reservoir.

Directions: From Angels Camp, take Highway 4 east for 40 miles to Bear Valley. Set your odometer at Bear Valley and drive 8.5 miles farther east on Highway 4 to the Stanislaus Meadow turnoff on the right (Road 8N13). Turn right and drive a short distance to the trailhead parking area.

Contact: Stanislaus National Forest, Calaveras Ranger District, 209/813-6008, www.fs.usda.gov/stanislaus.

96 CLARK FORK TO BOULDER LAKE

8.0 mi/4.0 hr

in the Carson-Iceberg Wilderness on Clark Fork Stanislaus River

Map 6.3, page 215

This once beautiful trail now consists of a route through miles of blackened tree skeletons, burned in the 2018 Donnell Fire. In the years to come, you can watch the forest floor come back to life with greenery and wildflowers in the spring, but the stands of burned trees will provide a constant reminder of the inferno that swept through here. That aside, the river, the Clark Fork, is still pretty, and so is your destination at Boulder Lake, so it's still worth a visit. The trailhead is at Iceberg Meadow. You immediately enter the Carson-Iceberg Wilderness at the base of imposing Iceberg Peak. The trail starts where you hike upstream on the northern edge of the Clark Fork. This is a good trout stream, and through early summer, wildflowers are abundant amid the burned-out forest. At 2.5 miles you reach a junction near Boulder Creek. To reach Boulder Lake, turn left (straight takes you along the Clark Fork). The trail then climbs, steep at times, for 1.5 miles uphill to tiny Boulder Lake. It's a good workout to a pretty destination.

User Groups: Hikers, dogs, and horses. No mountain bikes. No wheelchair facilities.

Permits: A free wilderness permit is required for overnight stays and available from the

Summit Ranger Station. Parking and access are free.

Maps: For a map, ask the U.S. Forest Service for Stanislaus National Forest or Carson-Iceberg Wilderness. For a topographic map, ask the USGS for Donnell Lake.

Directions: From Sonora, take Highway 108 east for 46 miles to the left turnoff for Clark Fork Road (about 17 miles east of Strawberry). Turn left and follow Clark Fork Road for about seven miles to its end at the Clark Fork trailhead at Iceberg Meadow.

Contact: Stanislaus National Forest, Summit Ranger District, 209/965-3434, www.fs.usda.gov/stanislaus.

97 TRAIL OF THE GARGOYLES

3.0 mi/1.5 hr 1 8

near Strawberry and Pinecrest Lake in Stanislaus National Forest

Map 6.3, page 215 BEST

If this trail were named "Edge of the World," it would give you just what you might expect. The trailhead is in the middle of a 1.5-mile trail, which means you'll walk out and back in both directions. It starts out nondescript, but that quickly changes. The gargoyles—odd rock formations—soon line the trail, perched at the edge of a cliff at 7,400 feet in elevation. You walk just inches away from what appears to be the edge of the world, with only thin air between you and the densely forested basin several hundred feet below. It's an easy and nearly flat trail, but if you have kids, or adults that act like kids, keep an eye on them.

User Groups: Hikers and leashed dogs. No horses or mountain bikes. No wheelchair facilities.

Permits: No permits are required. Parking and access are free.

Maps: For a map, ask the U.S. Forest Service for Stanislaus National Forest. For a topographic map, ask the USGS for Pinecrest.

Directions: From Sonora, take Highway 108 east for 32 miles to Strawberry, and then continue east 2.4 miles to Herring Creek Road (Forest Road 4N12). Turn right on Herring Creek Road and drive 6.7 miles to an often-unsigned turnoff on the left. Turn left and drive 0.2 mile to the trailhead.

Contact: Stanislaus National Forest, Summit Ranger District, 209/965-3434, www.fs.usda.gov/stanislaus.

98 COLUMNS OF THE GIANTS

0.5 mi/0.5 hr 1 8

near Dardanelle

Map 6.3, page 215

The 2018 Donnell fire ravaged the forests near Dardanelle, but the 30-40 feet Columns of the Giants remain an awesome sight. Although many are still standing tall or at least at an angle, others have shattered into thousands of pieces, creating a giant pile of rubble, at times just a jumbled heap of rocks. An interpretive trail sign explains that underneath this rock pile is evidence of the last small ice age in the Sierra, frozen remnants of ice fields that are replenished each year by winter snow and cold. The rock formations at the end of the Columns of the Giants geological trail were formed 150,000 years ago, when a series of volcanic eruptions occurred. The lava flow cooled rapidly, probably during cold weather, and cracked into narrow, hexagonal, basalt columns. Make sure you bring your camera. This is the central Sierra's answer to Devils Postpile National Monument.

User Groups: Hikers and leashed dogs. No horses or mountain bikes. No wheelchair facilities.

Permits: No permits are required. Parking and access are free.

Maps: For a map, ask the U.S. Forest Service for Stanislaus National Forest. For a topographic map, ask the USGS for Dardanelle.

Directions: From Sonora, take Highway 108

east for 50 miles to Pigeon Flat Campground (two miles east of Dardanelle) on the south side of the highway. If you're traveling west on Highway 108, the campground is 12.6 miles west of Sonora Pass. Park in the day-use parking lot just outside the camp.

Contact: Stanislaus National Forest, Summit Ranger District, 209/965-3434, www.fs.usda.gov/stanislaus.

99 KENNEDY LAKE

14.8 mi/2 days — 3 — 8

in the Emigrant Wilderness near Dardanelle

Map 6.3, page 215

Follow the trail notes to Relief Reservoir (see listing in this chapter), but at 2.6 miles, take the left fork for Kennedy Lake. The trail climbs for another 1.6 miles, then goes flat for the final 3.2 miles to the lake. It's an easy two-day backpack trip, with low mileage and only a 1,200-foot elevation gain. Note that all the campsites are set downstream of the lake rather than along its shoreline.

This is a popular trailhead for people hiking and fishing Relief Reservoir and venturing into the Emigrant Wilderness, so expect at lot of cars in the Kennedy Meadows parking lot. If you have the time and inclination for a longer trip to Kennedy Lake, you will leave a lot of your fellow hikers behind. Even so, don't expect solitude. You'll likely share the lake with other backpackers, horse packers, and grazing cows.

User Groups: Hikers, leashed dogs, and horses. No mountain bikes. No wheelchair facilities.

Permits: A free wilderness permit is required for overnight stays and is available from the Summit Ranger Station. Parking and access are free.

Maps: For a map, ask the U.S. Forest Service for Stanislaus National Forest or Emigrant Wilderness. For a topographic map, ask the USGS for Sonora Pass.

Directions: From Sonora, take Highway 108 east for 55 miles to the turnoff for Kennedy Meadows (six miles east of Dardanelle) on the south side of the highway. Turn right and drive one mile to the large parking area. If you're traveling west on Highway 108, the Kennedy Meadows turnoff is 9.1 miles west of Sonora Pass.

Contact: Stanislaus National Forest, Summit Ranger District, 209/965-3434, www.fs.usda.gov/stanislaus.

100 HUCKLEBERRY TRAIL/ RELIEF RESERVOIR

6.7 mi/3.0 hr — 3 — 8

on the edge of the Emigrant Wilderness near Dardanelle

Map 6.3, page 215

At Kennedy Meadows along Highway 108, the trip starts from a mammoth trailhead and parking lot. At peak use, the number of vehicles might have you shaking your head. Many visitors take the three-mile trip to Relief Reservoir (elevation 7,200 feet), a PG&E lake, to do a little fishing, then hike back out. Others use this as a launch point into the Emigrant Wilderness. The Emigrant Wilderness is best known for its miles of high granite and small lakes in deep pockets. Relief Reservoir is the most popular.

The route is called the Huckleberry Trail and leads along the Stanislaus River. It passes the boundary for the Emigrant Wilderness at one mile, then skirts its edge. You will quickly understand why this trip is so popular. The river canyon gets more and more beautiful as you head deeper into it. The trail had to be blasted into the steep granite slopes. At 2.6 miles, you will pass a turnoff (on the left for Kennedy Creek and Kennedy Lake), and then proceed straight for another 0.5 mile to an overlook of Relief Reservoir. It's a steep drop down to the water's edge in the last 0.25 mile, which, of course, must be regained on the return trip.

At times, horses can chop up the trail, and the route is overused; a trail quota would help. Some weekends it seems you must pull off the path repeatedly to let horses pass.

User Groups: Hikers, leashed dogs, and horses. No mountain bikes. No wheelchair facilities.

Permits: No day-use permits are required. Parking and access are free. A Forest Service permit (free) is required for overnight use

Maps: For a map, ask the U.S. Forest Service for Stanislaus National Forest or Emigrant Wilderness. For a topographic map, ask the USGS for Sonora Pass.

Directions: From Sonora, take Highway 108 east for 55 miles to the Kennedy Meadows turnoff (six miles east of Dardanelle) on the south side of the highway. Turn right and go one mile to the well-signed parking area. Day hikers can park 0.5 mile farther down the road, near Kennedy Meadows Resort. If you're traveling west on Highway 108, the Kennedy Meadows turnoff is 9.1 miles west of Sonora Pass.

Contact: Stanislaus National Forest, Summit Ranger District, 209/965-3434, www.fs.usda.gov/stanislaus.

101 SARDINE FALLS

2.0 mi/1.0 hr 1 8

near Sonora Pass

Map 6.3, page 215

The goal is Sardine Falls, a gorgeous waterfall that cascades over a brink and sails down into a ravine and through forest. There is no formal trail along Highway 108 or sign that says "Sardine Falls." I always called it Sonora Pass Falls until I was told differently. You can glimpse the falls from Highway 108, and east of Sonora Pass, you'll see pullouts and what looks like old jeep roads. This is it. From parking, head across the northwest side of the meadow. Look for a route that is signed Route Closed to Motorized Vehicles; it's the most direct path. Cross Sardine Creek, which parallels Highway 108, and walk up the right side of larger McKay Creek. After climbing uphill over a rise, you'll hear and then see Sardine Falls, gracefully framed by a few sparse lodgepole pines. During peak snowmelt, a great find.

User Groups: Hikers, leashed dogs, and horses. No mountain bikes. No wheelchair facilities.

Permits: No permits are required. Parking and access are free.

Maps: For a map, ask the U.S. Forest Service for Humboldt-Toiyabe National Forest, Bridgeport District. For a topographic map, ask the USGS for Pickel Meadow.

Directions: From the junction of U.S. 395 and Highway 108, take Highway 108 west, drive 12.5 miles (2.5 miles east of Sonora Pass), and park along the road in the gravel pullouts near the overgrown jeep roads on the northwest side of the meadow.

Contact: Humboldt-Toiyabe National Forest, Bridgeport Ranger District, 760/932-7070, www.fs.usda.gov/htnf.

102 SONORA PASS TO EBBETTS PASS (PCT)

30.8 mi one-way/3 days 5 10

from Highway 108 at Sonora Pass north to Highway 4 near Ebbetts Pass

Map 6.3, page 215

This section of the Pacific Crest Trail does not have the glamorous reputation of the stretch of trail in the southern Sierra. For those of us who have hiked it, it's just as compelling. From Sonora Pass, you're forced to climb out for a good hour or two. Then you'll rise over Wolf Creek Gap (10,300 feet, the highest, most northern point on the PCT) and make the easy drop down along pretty Wolf Creek and to the Carson Canyon. Wolf Creek is gorgeous and can be good for fly-fishing. This is the start of the Carson-Iceberg Wilderness, a giant swath of land that is a rare, unpeopled paradise. The Sierra riparian zones here are lined with flowers, seemingly all kinds and all colors, often in luxuriant beds of greenness. The PCT climbs out of Carson Canyon around Boulder Peak, then down and up two more canyons. All the while, you keep crossing creeks filled with natural gardens. You wind your way across and through these areas and eventually climb a ridge, then head down, steeply at times, to Ebbetts Pass. There's no water here. No problem. A short half-hour climb and you can be pumping water, and maybe setting up camp too, at little Sherrold Lake, not far from the edge of the Mokelumne Wilderness.

To continue north on the PCT, see the *Ebbetts Pass to Blue Lakes Road (PCT)* hike in this chapter.

User Groups: Hikers, dogs, and horses. No mountain bikes. No wheelchair facilities.

Permits: A single permit is required to hike the Pacific Crest Trail. Contact the national forest, Bureau of Land Management, or national park office at your point of entry for a combined permit that is good for traveling through multiple-permit areas during your dates of travel.

Maps: For topographic maps, ask the USGS for Pickel Meadow, Disaster Peak, Dardanelles Cone, and Ebbetts Pass.

Directions: From Sonora, take Highway 108 east to Sonora Pass to the parking area and trailhead (south side of parking area).

Contact: Stanislaus National Forest, Summit Ranger District, 209/965-3434, www.fs.usda.gov/stanislaus.

103 SECRET AND POORE LAKES

6.5 mi/3.5 hr

near Sonora Pass

Map 6.3, page 215

This hike rates a solid 8, but we nudged it up to a 9 after discovering one of the most spectacular waterfalls in the Sierra above Poore Lake. This 6.5-mile loop trip begins at a footbridge over West Walker River at Leavitt Meadows Campground. After 0.25 mile, take the left fork for Secret Lake (this is no secret and you won't be alone here, most likely). Climb for nearly two miles through sage and Jeffrey pines, then descend 0.5 mile to Secret Lake. Much larger Poore Lake is visible over your left shoulder. Take a break at Secret Lake, then continue around the right side of the lake, hiking through sparse junipers and pines for 0.5 mile to the left turnoff for Poore Lake. Turn left for the final 0.75 mile to the large lake; this last section is the roughest. In spring, look for the waterfall above the lake.

When you are ready to return, retrace your steps to the junction. From the junction, you can loop back to the campground on a lower trail that follows closer to the West Walker River through Leavitt Meadow.

Notes: If Poore Lake turns out to be less than what you envisioned, you can always hike beyond the return loop junction to little Roosevelt Lake. No mountain bikes are permitted beyond Poore Lake, so that means Roosevelt Lake is free of them, at least in theory. In addition, there is no bridge available for off-road vehicles, so though this area was once an OHV spot, it is no longer. Finally, a nearby U.S. Marine training facility means it is possible you may see groups dressed in camo outfits running along the road. They do not fire their weapons here and they almost never enter the forest.

User Groups: Hikers, dogs, horses, and mountain bikes. No wheelchair facilities.

Permits: No day-use permits are required.

Campfire permits required for overnight use. Parking and access are free.

Maps: For a map, ask the U.S. Forest Service for Humboldt-Toiyabe National Forest, Bridgeport District. For a topographic map, ask the USGS for Pickel Meadow.

Directions: From the junction of U.S. 395 and Highway 108, take Highway 108 west for seven miles to Leavitt Meadows Campground, on the south side of the road. If you are coming from the west, the camp is eight miles east of Sonora Pass. Day hikers may park inside the campground; backpackers must park 0.25 mile west of the camp on Highway 108.

Contact: Humboldt-Toiyabe National Forest, Bridgeport Ranger District, 760/932-7070, www.fs.usda.gov/htnf.

SAN FRANCISCO BAY AREA

The Bay Area is home to 150 significant parks (including 12 with redwoods), 7,500 miles of hiking and biking trails, 45 lakes, 25 waterfalls, 100 miles of coast, mountains with incredible lookouts, bays with islands, and, in all, 1.2 million acres of greenbelt with hundreds of acres being added each year. Bay Area hikes cover Angel Island, Point Reyes National Seashore, the Marin Headlands, Sunol-Ohlone Wilderness, Butano Redwoods State Park, and Big Basin Redwoods State Park. These parks offer trails of all lengths—from weekend strolls to long-distance hikes with campgrounds like the Coast Trail and the Skyline-to-the-Sea. Demand at these parks is high, so plan ahead. But if you visit at nonpeak times (Mon.-Thurs.), it's like having the trail to yourself.

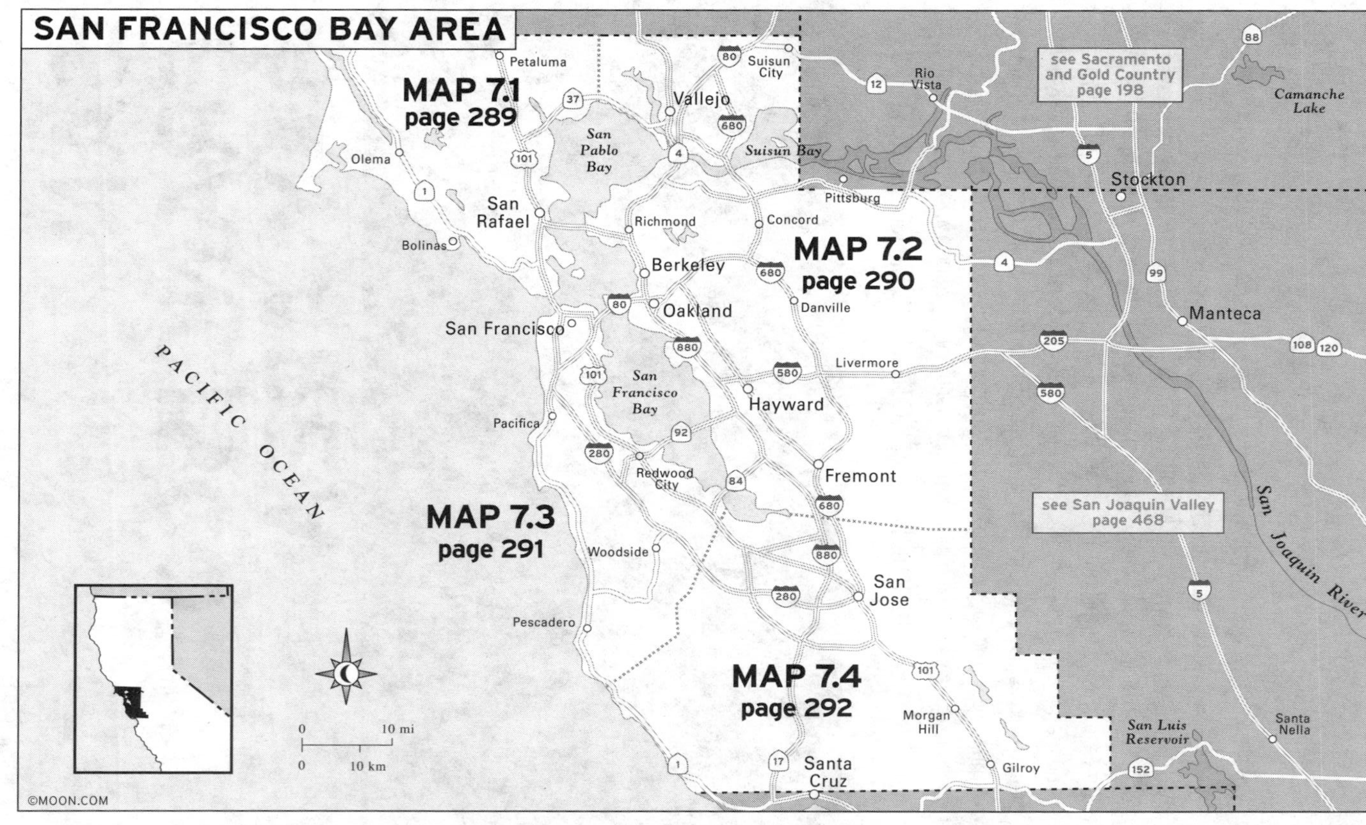

SAN FRANCISCO BAY AREA
MAP 7.1
page 289
MAP 7.2
page 290
MAP 7.3
page 291
MAP 7.4
page 292
see Sacramento and Gold Country page 198
see San Joaquin Valley page 468
PACIFIC OCEAN
San Pablo Bay
San Francisco Bay
Suisun Bay
San Joaquin River
San Luis Reservoir
Camanche Lake
Petaluma
Olema
Bolinas
San Rafael
San Francisco
Pacifica
Pescadero
Woodside
Redwood City
Richmond
Berkeley
Oakland
Vallejo
Suisun City
Concord
Danville
Pittsburg
Hayward
Fremont
Livermore
Rio Vista
San Jose
Santa Cruz
Morgan Hill
Gilroy
Stockton
Manteca
Santa Nella
0
10 mi
0
10 km
©MOON.COM

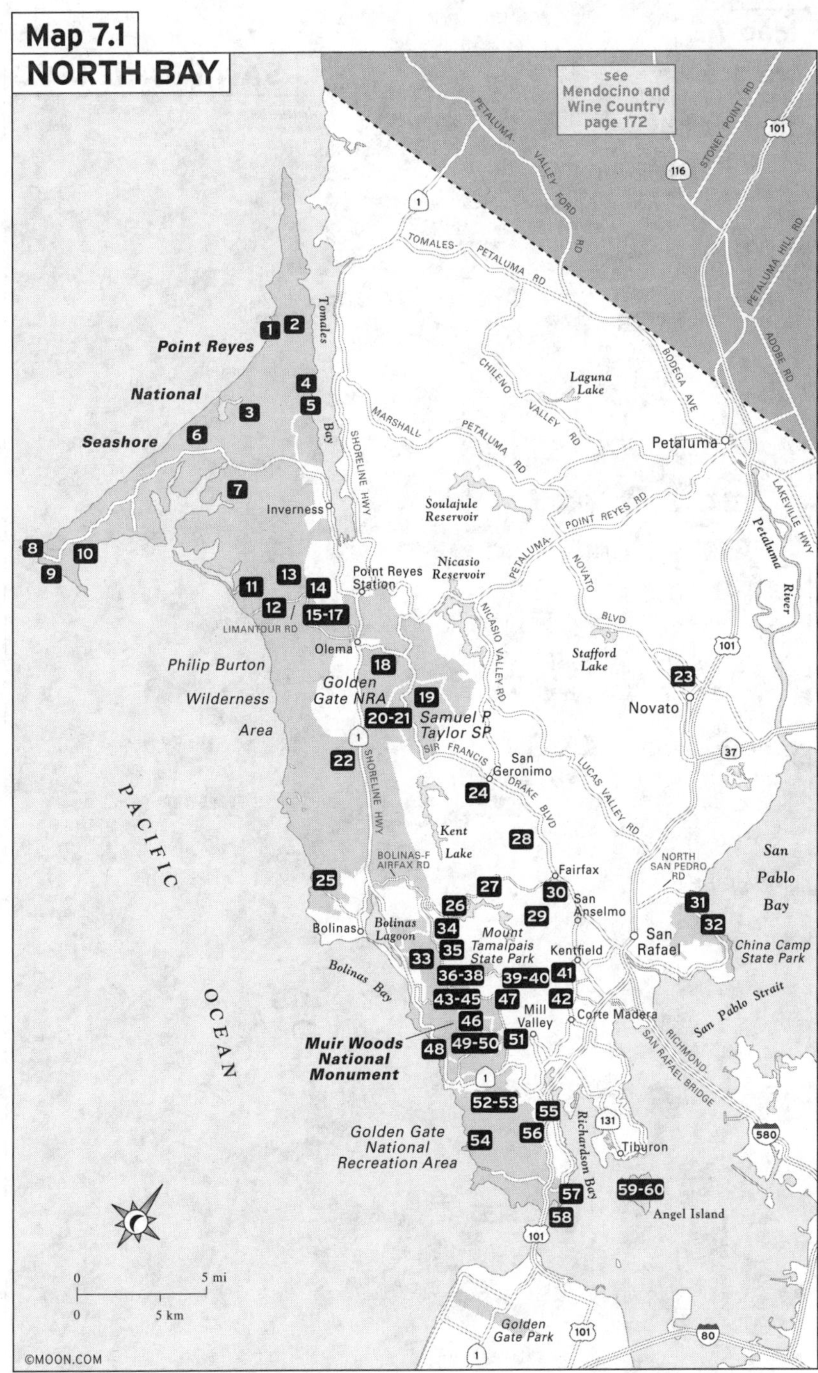

Map 7.1
NORTH BAY
see Mendocino and Wine Country page 172
Point Reyes National Seashore
Tomales Bay
Inverness
Point Reyes Station
Olema
LIMANTOUR RD
Philip Burton Wilderness Area
Golden Gate NRA
Samuel P Taylor SP
PACIFIC OCEAN
Bolinas
Bolinas Lagoon
Bolinas Bay
Mount Tamalpais State Park
Muir Woods National Monument
Golden Gate National Recreation Area
Golden Gate Park
Angel Island
Richardson Bay
Tiburon
Mill Valley
Corte Madera
Kentfield
San Anselmo
Fairfax
San Rafael
China Camp State Park
San Pablo Bay
San Pablo Strait
RICHMOND-SAN RAFAEL BRIDGE
NORTH SAN PEDRO RD
Novato
Stafford Lake
Petaluma
Petaluma River
Laguna Lake
Soulajule Reservoir
Nicasio Reservoir
Kent Lake
San Geronimo
SIR FRANCIS DRAKE BLVD
LUCAS VALLEY RD
NICASIO VALLEY RD
NOVATO BLVD
PETALUMA-POINT REYES RD
MARSHALL-PETALUMA RD
CHILENO VALLEY RD
TOMALES-PETALUMA RD
PETALUMA-VALLEY FORD RD
BODEGA AVE
STONEY POINT RD
PETALUMA HILL RD
ADOBE RD
LAKEVILLE HWY
SHORELINE HWY
BOLINAS-FAIRFAX RD
1
101
116
37
131
580
80
0 5 mi
0 5 km
©MOON.COM

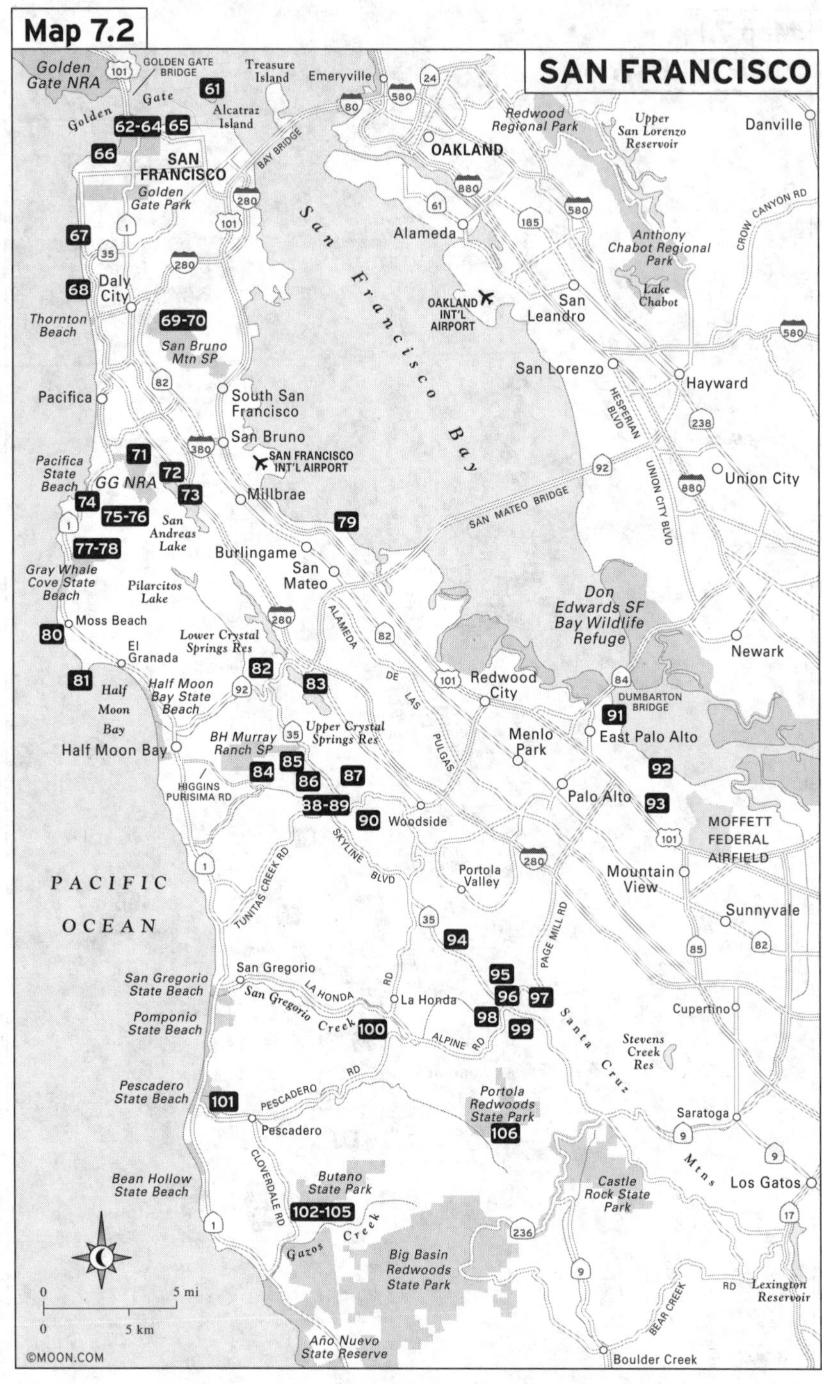
Map 7.2
SAN FRANCISCO
Golden Gate NRA
GOLDEN GATE BRIDGE
Golden Gate
Treasure Island
Alcatraz Island
Emeryville
SAN FRANCISCO
Golden Gate Park
BAY BRIDGE
OAKLAND
Redwood Regional Park
Upper San Lorenzo Reservoir
Danville
Alameda
San Francisco Bay
Anthony Chabot Regional Park
Lake Chabot
CROW CANYON RD
Daly City
Thornton Beach
San Bruno Mtn SP
OAKLAND INT'L AIRPORT
San Leandro
San Lorenzo
Hayward
HESPERIAN BLVD
Pacifica
South San Francisco
San Bruno
SAN FRANCISCO INT'L AIRPORT
Millbrae
Pacifica State Beach
GG NRA
San Andreas Lake
UNION CITY BLVD
Union City
SAN MATEO BRIDGE
Gray Whale Cove State Beach
Pilarcitos Lake
Burlingame
San Mateo
Don Edwards SF Bay Wildlife Refuge
Moss Beach
El Granada
Lower Crystal Springs Res
ALAMEDA DE LAS PULGAS
Newark
Half Moon Bay
Half Moon Bay State Beach
Redwood City
DUMBARTON BRIDGE
Upper Crystal Springs Res
BH Murray Ranch SP
Menlo Park
East Palo Alto
Half Moon Bay
HIGGINS PURISIMA RD
Palo Alto
Woodside
MOFFETT FEDERAL AIRFIELD
SKYLINE BLVD
TUNITAS CREEK RD
Portola Valley
Mountain View
PACIFIC OCEAN
Sunnyvale
PAGE MILL RD
San Gregorio
San Gregorio State Beach
LA HONDA RD
La Honda
San Gregorio Creek
Pomponio State Beach
ALPINE RD
Santa Cruz Mtns
Cupertino
Stevens Creek Res
Pescadero State Beach
PESCADERO RD
Portola Redwoods State Park
Pescadero
Saratoga
CLOVERDALE RD
Bean Hollow State Beach
Butano State Park
Castle Rock State Park
Los Gatos
Gazos Creek
Big Basin Redwoods State Park
Lexington Reservoir
BEAR CREEK RD
Año Nuevo State Reserve
Boulder Creek
0 5 mi
0 5 km
©MOON.COM
61
62-64
65
66
67
68
69-70
71
72
73
74
75-76
77-78
79
80
81
82
83
84
85
86
87
88-89
90
91
92
93
94
95
96
97
98
99
100
101
102-105
106

Map 7.3
EAST BAY

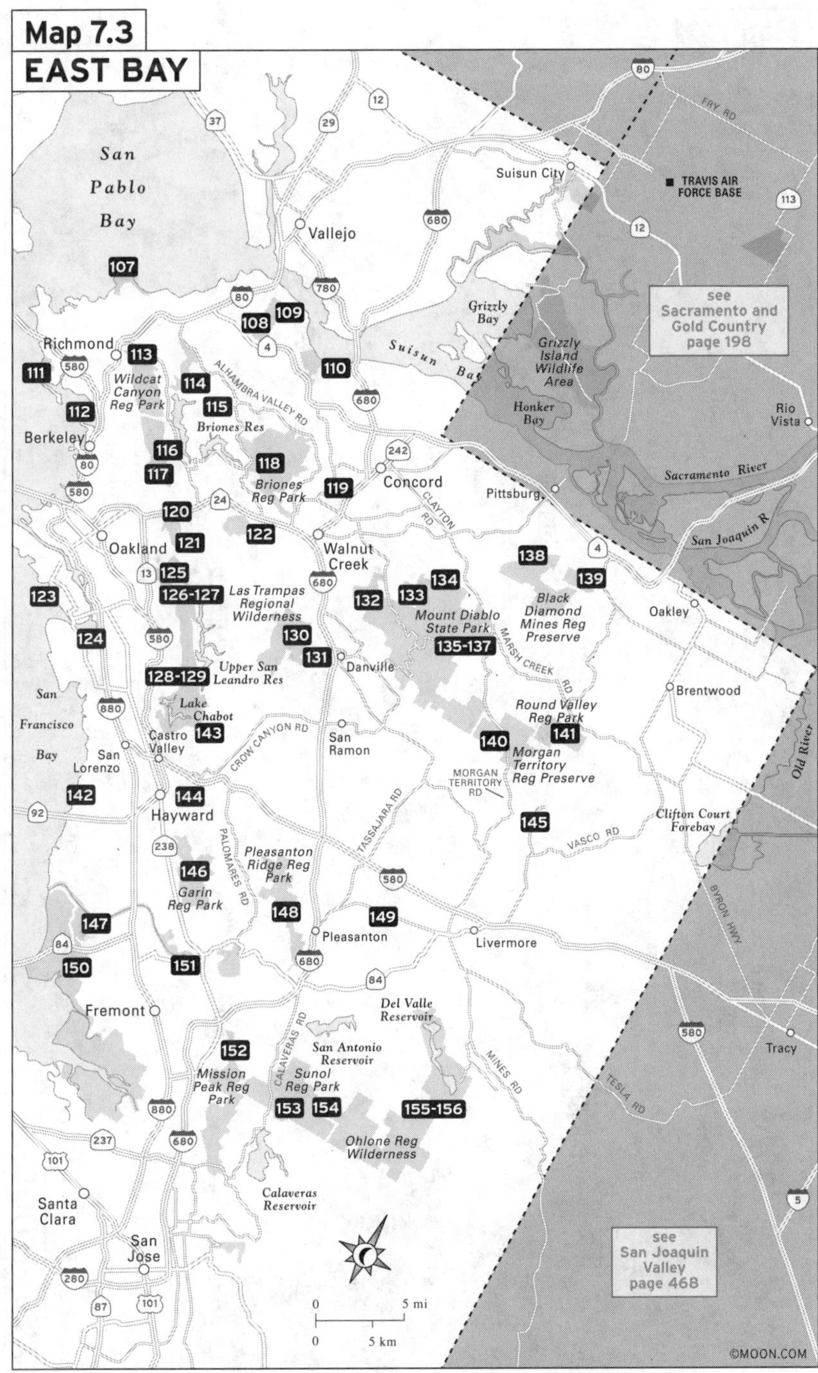

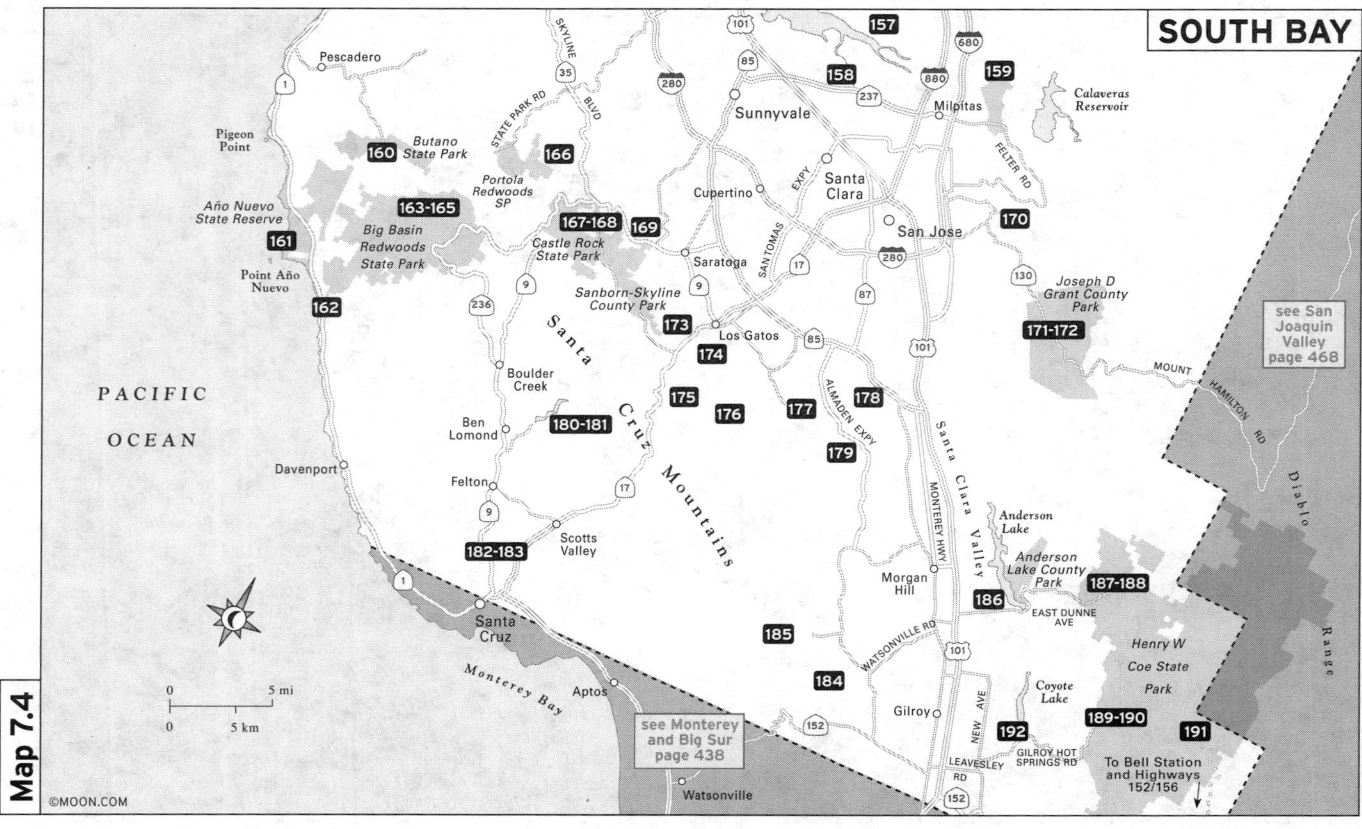
Map 7.4
SOUTH BAY
©MOON.COM
PACIFIC OCEAN
0 5 mi
0 5 km
Pescadero
Pigeon Point
Butano State Park
Año Nuevo State Reserve
Point Año Nuevo
Big Basin Redwoods State Park
Portola Redwoods SP
STATE PARK RD
SKYLINE BLVD
Castle Rock State Park
Sanborn-Skyline County Park
Davenport
Boulder Creek
Ben Lomond
Felton
Scotts Valley
Santa Cruz
Monterey Bay
Aptos
Santa Cruz Mountains
see Monterey and Big Sur page 438
Watsonville
Sunnyvale
Cupertino
Santa Clara
EXPY
SAN TOMAS
Saratoga
Los Gatos
San Jose
Milpitas
FELTER RD
Calaveras Reservoir
Joseph D Grant County Park
MOUNT HAMILTON RD
see San Joaquin Valley page 468
ALMADEN EXPY
MONTEREY HWY
Santa Clara Valley
Morgan Hill
WATSONVILLE RD
Gilroy
NEW AVE
LEAVESLEY RD
GILROY HOT SPRINGS RD
EAST DUNNE AVE
Anderson Lake
Anderson Lake County Park
Coyote Lake
Henry W Coe State Park
To Bell Station and Highways 152/156
Diablo Range
157
158
159
160
161
162
163-165
166
167-168
169
170
171-172
173
174
175
176
177
178
179
180-181
182-183
184
185
186
187-188
189-190
191
192

1 McCLURES BEACH TRAIL

1.0 mi/0.5 hr 1 7

in Point Reyes National Seashore

Map 7.1, page 289

Note: The McClures Beach Access Road closed in 2019 due to a road collapse and is scheduled to reopen in 2020.

Point Reyes National Seashore receives 2.5 million visitors per year; more than 70 percent of which arrive on the weekend. Plan you visit midweek and you may have places like McClures Beach to yourself.

An easy 0.5-mile downhill walk leads to McClures Beach with tidepools to the south and beachfront to the north. The best time to visit is during minus low tides, when the ocean rolls back and unveils acres of beach and a small collection of tidepools to the nearby south. Beachcombing along McClures Beach and Driftwood Beach (to the immediate north) during these low tides also can unveil unusual finds, although park rules prohibit you from taking anything. In fall and early winter, the sunsets here can be spectacular, especially when refracted light through layers of cirrus can make the sky look like a scene from *The Ten Commandments*. In summer, however, this is one of the foggiest places on the Pacific Coast. McClures Beach is an easy-to-reach spot that is often overlooked in the divine panorama of Point Reyes. It sits in the shadow of nearby Pierce Ranch, with its 500-strong elk herd. Many visitors never drive to the road's end to the trailhead to McClures Beach, except perhaps to use the restrooms, and can then find the trailhead by accident.

Note: During periods of big ocean swells, tidepooling at this beach can be dangerous, as incoming tides can cut you off, leaving no way to escape. Consult a tide table, and never turn your back on the waves.

User Groups: Hikers only. No dogs, horses, or mountain bikes. No wheelchair facilities.

Permits: No permits are required. Parking and access are free.

Maps: For a free map, write to Point Reyes National Seashore. For a topographic map, ask the USGS for Tomales.

Directions: From the Golden Gate Bridge, take U.S. 101 north for 7.5 miles to the exit for Sir Francis Drake Boulevard. Turn west and drive 20 miles to Olema and Highway 1. Turn right on Highway 1 and drive about 100 yards to Bear Valley Road. Turn left on Bear Valley Road and drive 2.4 miles to Sir Francis Drake. Turn left on Sir Francis Drake and drive 5.6 miles to Pierce Point Road. Bear right and drive nine miles to Pierce Ranch, then turn left and drive 0.5 mile to the parking area and the trailhead.

Contact: Point Reyes National Seashore, Bear Valley Visitors Center, 415/464-5100, www.nps.gov/pore.

2 TOMALES POINT TRAIL

6.0 mi/3.5 hr 2 10

in Point Reyes National Seashore

Map 7.1, page 289 **BEST**

This is the best hike in California for wildlife-watching. Imagine meeting up with an elk that stands five feet at the shoulders and has antlers that practically poke holes in the clouds. You have a better chance to see and photograph elk here than anyplace else in California. On one trip, we counted 13 elk, six deer, three rabbits, and a fox—all within a two-hour span. (I've even seen a bobcat and a mountain lion on this trail. The mountain lion sat up on its haunches about 25 feet away, stared at me point-blank for a minute, then turned and disappeared into the high grass.)

This hike starts on the main trail at the north end of the parking lot, just to the left of the ranch. The route has a flat walking surface and easy grades and is flanked much of the way to the west by the Pacific Ocean and to the east by Tomales Bay, both beautiful sights. About a mile in, elk paths cut into grass and low brush off to the right. The best suggestion is to trace out one or more of these elk trails. This provides numerous off-trail side trips where you can discover more beautiful views and elk. If you break off to the right and make the easy, short climb to a ridge, you can then turn left for a short walk to an overlook of a canyon that plunges down to Tomales Bay. This is not only gorgeous, but one of the better habitats for elk; you can often see harems with a bull anywhere from the rim on down to just above the beach and cove.

Most people make this a five-mile roundtrip. They hike north on the main trail to the top of a grade, a great lookout of Dillon Beach and Bodega Bay. The reason most people turn around here is that the trail descends several hundred feet, so if they continue north, it means an additional climb on the way back. It is six miles, but for most, it's an easy six. In summer, wind and fog occasionally take over.

In the evening (and in the fall, when the bulls collect harems), the herd will often congregate in a valley about three miles from the trailhead, and also in the deep valley that opens up to the east to Tomales Bay. For a spectacular bonus, continue hiking the extra 0.5 mile to Tomales Point.

In the future, the park plans to manage the herd to maintain an average of 125 elk. Note that it is a violation of federal law to herd, chase, or otherwise harass elk.

User Groups: Hikers and horses. Nearby Pierce Ranch (a former working ranch) is accessible to wheelchairs, but the Tomales Point Trail offers only marginal access. No dogs or mountain bikes.

Permits: No permits are required. Parking and access are free.

Maps: For a free map, write to Point Reyes National Seashore. For a topographic map, ask the USGS for Tomales.

Directions: From the Golden Gate Bridge, take U.S. 101 north for 7.5 miles to the exit for Sir Francis Drake Boulevard. Turn west and drive 20 miles to Olema and Highway 1. Turn right on Highway 1 and drive about 100 yards to Bear Valley Road. Turn left on Bear Valley Road and drive 2.4 miles to Sir Francis Drake. Turn left on Sir Francis Drake and drive 5.6 miles to Pierce Point Road. Bear right and drive nine miles to the Pierce Ranch parking area and the trailhead.

Contact: Point Reyes National Seashore, Bear Valley Visitors Center, 415/464-5100, www.nps.gov/pore.

3 ABBOTTS LAGOON TRAIL

3.2 mi/1.5 hr 1 9

in Point Reyes National Seashore

Map 7.1, page 289 **BEST**

Two hours at Abbotts Lagoon—a pretty coastal pond with adjacent grasslands on one side and wilderness-style beach on the other—can give you a glow that lasts for weeks. Yet many drive right past the trailhead while en route to Pierce Ranch to see the elk. You can do both. From the parking area it's a 1.6-mile walk, one-way, to the beach. It's gorgeous every step of the way, especially during a series of warm, clear days. The trail descends through coastal foothills, a working ranch to your left, grasslands and wetlands to your right. The walking is easy. About a mile in, you'll reach a bridge. The trail then skirts the shoreline of Abbotts Lagoon to your left as you emerge in sand dunes. The trail ends at a wilderness beach where you can stop and have a picnic, or continue for miles.

This is a diverse habitat matrix that can support waterfowl that require freshwater, migratory shorebirds, and songbirds that love the mix of coastal grasslands and a pond. If you see red-winged blackbirds, stop at the bench and listen to their call, one of the sweetest sound in nature.

User Groups: Hikers and mountain bikes (bikers on the first mile only; do not cross the bridge). The first portion of the trail is wheelchair accessible with assistance. No dogs or horses.

Permits: No permits are required. Parking and access are free.

Maps: For a free map, write to Point Reyes National Seashore. For a topographic map, ask the USGS for Drakes Bay.

Directions: From the Golden Gate Bridge, take U.S. 101 north for 7.5 miles to the exit for Sir Francis Drake Boulevard. Turn west and drive 20 miles to Olema and Highway 1. Turn right on Highway 1 and drive about 100 yards to Bear Valley Road. Turn left on Bear Valley Road and drive 2.4 miles to Sir Francis Drake. Turn left on Sir Francis Drake and drive 5.6 miles to Pierce Point Road. Bear right and drive 3.3 miles to a small parking area with restrooms. The trailhead is on the left side of the road.

Contact: Point Reyes National Seashore, Bear Valley Visitors Center, 415/464-5100, www.nps.gov/pore.

4 MARSHALL BEACH TRAIL

2.8 mi/1.5 hr 1 9

in Point Reyes National Seashore

Map 7.1, page 289

Marshall Beach is one of the more secluded beaches in Marin County. This pretty spot is set in a gorgeous cove along Tomales Bay. The water is often calm and pretty, sheltered from north winds by Inverness Ridge. The trailhead tends to be overlooked, because there are no signs directing hikers to it until you reach the trailhead itself. The hike is 1.4 miles one-way. You take an easy descent down into a gulch, and then to the cove that helps shelter the beach. It's the kind of place where you can just sit and watch the water lap gently at the shore. During the week, you can often have the spot all to yourself. In terms of the public's recognition, Marshall Beach is overshadowed by nearby Tomales Bay State Park.

User Groups: Hikers, horses, and mountain bikes. No dogs. No wheelchair facilities.

Permits: No permits are required. Parking and access are free.

Maps: For a free map, write to Point Reyes National Seashore. For a topographic map, ask the USGS for Tomales.

Directions: From the Golden Gate Bridge, take U.S. 101 north for 7.5 miles to the exit for Sir Francis Drake Boulevard. Turn west and drive 20 miles to Olema and Highway 1. Turn right on Highway 1 and drive about 100 yards to Bear Valley Road. Turn left on Bear Valley Road and drive 2.4 miles to Sir Francis Drake. Turn left on Sir Francis Drake and drive 5.6 miles to Pierce Point Road. Bear right and drive 1.3 miles (just past the entrance road for Tomales Bay State Park, on the right) to Duck Cove/Marshall Beach Road. Turn right and drive 2.6 miles (bear left at the fork) to the parking area for Marshall Beach Trail.

Contact: Point Reyes National Seashore, Bear Valley Visitors Center, 415/464-5100, www.nps.gov/pore.

5 JEPSON/JOHNSTONE TO PEBBLE BEACH

4.5 mi/2.5 hr 2 9

in Tomales Bay State Park

Map 7.1, page 289

This is an easy, pretty walk to a gorgeous picnic area and beach. The Jepson trailhead is in the upper Vista Point parking lot on the right side of the park road. The trail is routed into a lush coastal forest and out the other side (past a few trail junctions and a private road) for about a mile to the Johnstone Trail. At a junction with the trails to Pebble Beach and Shell Beach, turn left and descend another mile to the cutoff spur for Pebble Beach on the right. You can often have it to yourself.

If you fall in love with Tomales Bay State Park, there are several must-do trips. The highlights include: Heart's Desire Beach, Indian Beach, Shell Beach, beautiful water views, and the chance to hand-launch kayaks or canoes. The walk to Indian Beach is gorgeous. From the parking area for Heart's Desire Beach, the trail meanders along the pretty shore of Tomales Bay.

If you have a cartop boat that can be launched by hand, such as a canoe or kayak, then don't leave it behind. Tomales Bay often provides the best flat-water paddling in the Bay Area. If you paddle north along the western shore, you can often spot many elk in shoreline ravines.

Tomales Bay State Park is lost in the overwhelming shadow of the adjacent Point Reyes National Seashore. In addition, visiting Point Reyes is free, and this park costs $8 per vehicle, so many choose not to make the trip. Yet this is a great park with stellar destinations.

User Groups: Hikers only. The park headquarters is wheelchair accessible, but the trail is not. No dogs, horses, or mountain bikes.

Permits: A day-use fee of $8 is charged at the entrance station. An automated kiosk accepts credit cards.

Maps: A brochure and map are available for a fee at the entrance station to Tomales Bay State Park. For a topographic map, ask the USGS for Tomales.

Directions: From San Francisco, take U.S. 101 north over Golden Gate Bridge into Marin and continue 7.5 miles to Sir Francis Drake Boulevard. Take that exit west and drive 20 miles to Highway 1. Turn right on Highway 1 and drive 100 yards to Bear Valley Road. Turn left on Bear Valley Road and drive two miles to Sir Francis Drake Highway. Turn left on Sir Francis Drake Highway and drive 5.6 miles to Pierce Point Road. Bear right on Pierce Point Road and drive 1.2 miles to the entrance road on the right for Tomales Bay State Park (well signed). Turn right and drive 1.5 miles to the parking area. The trailhead is behind the restrooms at Heart's Desire Beach.

Contact: Tomales Bay State Park, Inverness, 415/669-1140 or 415/898-4362; Marin District Headquarters, 415/898-4362, www.parks.ca.gov.

6 SOUTH BEACH TRAIL

0.1-20.0 mi/0.25 hr-1 day 2 6

in Point Reyes National Seashore

Map 7.1, page 289

The stretch of beach at Point Reyes extends for nearly 10 miles, all of it pristine with white, foaming surf that rolls on endlessly. If you desire miles of untouched beachfront, you've come to the right place. An initial short trail leads from the parking area to South Beach, about three miles north of the Point Reyes Lighthouse. For the best stroll, walk south for about a mile to an expanse of sand dunes. Or walk as far as you'd like and turn around. It is wise to call ahead for weather conditions, as low fog is common, especially during the summer, and strong winds out of the northwest are typical on spring and early-summer afternoons. The beach makes a good picnic site and is one of the few places at Point Reyes where you can take a leashed dog.

A word of warning: Do not swim or bodysurf here. This stretch of coast is known for its treacherous undertow, the kind that can trap even the strongest swimmers, pulling people under and pushing them out to sea, despite their attempts to swim back to the beach.

User Groups: Hikers, dogs, and horses. No mountain bikes. No wheelchair facilities. Note that dogs may not be allowed if marine mammals are present.

Permits: No permits are required. Parking and access are free.

Maps: For a free map, write to Point Reyes National Seashore. For a topographic map, ask the USGS for Drakes Bay.

Directions: From the Golden Gate Bridge, take U.S. 101 north for 7.5 miles to the exit for Sir Francis Drake Boulevard. Turn west and drive 20 miles to Olema and Highway 1. Turn right on Highway 1 and drive about 100 yards to Bear Valley Road. Turn left on Bear Valley Road and drive 2.4 miles to Sir Francis Drake. Turn left on Sir Francis Drake and drive 11.6 miles to the access turnoff for the South Beach parking lot, on the right. Turn right and drive to the parking lot for South Beach.

Contact: Point Reyes National Seashore, Bear Valley Visitors Center, 415/464-5100, www.nps.gov/pore.

7 ESTERO TRAIL

7.8 mi/3.5 hr

in Point Reyes National Seashore

Map 7.1, page 289

The Estero Trail is one of the best hikes for most people at Point Reyes National Seashore. The Estero Trail crosses a valley, parallels a bay, ascends a ridge, and leads down to the waterfront, where a perfect, quiet picnic spot awaits. It's an ideal first hike for newcomers to Point Reyes. The 2,500-acre estuary has a series of five bays and inlets that are often drop-dead beautiful. The Estero Trail starts by dropping down into a small valley, where you walk across a bridge on the narrow inlet of Home Bay. Many go just to the bridge and back for a quick 2.5 miles round-trip. The surroundings include pretty, low-lying coastal foothills set at the threshold of Drakes Estero.

From here, the trail rises gently along the southeastern flank of the Estero with gorgeous water views along the way. At 2.4 miles in, you will reach a trail junction. Continue straight on Sunset Beach Trail, where it is an easy 1.5-mile glide down to Sunset Beach. This is a great picnic site for a trail lunch, set inside the mouth of the Estero, about a mile from the Pacific Ocean. This makes it a 7.8-mile round-trip.

There is an option to extend your trip. When you reach the trail junction with Sunset Beach Trail (straight), an option is to instead turn left (south). A 15-minute climb will take you to a short ridge and the junction of Drakes Head Trail. Here you get a sweeping view of Drakes Bay, Estero de Limantour, and more foothills.

User Groups: Hikers, horses, and mountain bikes. The first two miles are wheelchair-accessible, with assistance. No dogs.

Permits: No permits are required. Parking and access are free.

Maps: For a free map, write to Point Reyes National Seashore. For a topographic map, ask the USGS for Drakes Bay.

Directions: From the Golden Gate Bridge, take U.S. 101 north for 7.5 miles to the exit for Sir Francis Drake Boulevard. Turn west and drive 20 miles to Olema and Highway 1. Turn right on Highway 1 and drive about 100 yards to Bear Valley Road. Turn left on Bear Valley Road and drive 2.4 miles to Sir Francis Drake. Turn left on Sir Francis Drake and drive 7.5 miles to Estero Road, on the left. Turn left and drive one mile to the parking area.

Contact: Point Reyes National Seashore, Bear Valley Visitors Center, 415/464-5100, www.nps.gov/pore.

8 POINT REYES LIGHTHOUSE

0.8 mi/0.5 hr 1 8

in Point Reyes National Seashore

Map 7.1, page 289

In winter, there may be no better place on land from which to watch migrating whales (gray whales late Dec.-Apr., humpback whales and orcas May-Aug.). The point extends 10 miles west from the mainland coast, right in the path of whales, shorebirds, and sea creatures. Year-round, the lookout from Point Reyes Lighthouse can provide the kind of view to ignite the inspiration you may need to start a challenging project (like, say, writing a book). The half-mile walk is more rigorous than many expect. On the way in, you descend 308 steps to a bluff-top lookout where a front-of-the-rail view provides world-class moments. At the lighthouse, a railing at the point provides a perch for stunning ocean views. You can see for miles across the Pacific. On a good day, you might see 5 to 10 whale spouts, and if lucky, a breech or tail salute. On the way back, the climb up those 308 steps, equivalent to 30 stories on a high-rise, can catch some by surprise.

To see whales, scan the ocean for what looks like a little puff of smoke on the water's surface: a whale spout. When you find one, zoom in closer. The "Great Whale Highway" (as some call it) is just offshore of Point Reyes. On clear weekends, particularly in winter, the place can be crowded. A fence on the edge of the cliff keeps visitors from falling overboard from one of the most dramatic coastal lookouts anywhere. Sunsets here are unforgettable. In winter and early spring, a shuttle bus is required (see below).

User Groups: Hikers and mountain bikes (bikes are restricted from the stairs and not advised). No dogs or horses.

Permits: No permits are required. Parking and access are free.

Maps: For a free map, write to Point Reyes National Seashore. For a topographic map, ask the USGS for Drakes Bay.

Directions: From the Golden Gate Bridge, take U.S. 101 north for 7.5 miles to the exit for Sir Francis Drake Boulevard. Turn west and drive 20 miles to Olema and Highway 1. Turn right on Highway 1 and drive about 100 yards to Bear Valley Road. Turn left on Bear Valley Road and drive 2.4 miles to Sir Francis Drake. Turn left on Sir Francis Drake and drive 17.6 miles. At the T (left goes to Chimney Rock Headlands), continue straight ahead to the parking area for the Point Reyes Lighthouse.

Shuttle bus: On good weather weekends and holidays in winter (late Dec.-mid-Apr.) a shuttle bus is required. Tickets are at Drakes Beach Visitors Center (9:30am-3:30pm, $7). Drive to the South Beach Junction, where the road is blocked. Park and take shuttle bus. The shuttle buses run approximately every 20 minutes, 9:30am-3:30pm. The shuttle bus may not be required on weekdays or on stormy weekends.

Contact: Point Reyes National Seashore, Bear Valley Visitors Center, 415/464-5100, www.nps.gov/pore.

9 CHIMNEY ROCK TRAIL

2.8 mi/1.25 hr

in Point Reyes National Seashore

Map 7.1, page 289 BEST

This is one of the most eye-popping easy hikes in California. The trail starts at the south end of the parking lot, next to a park billboard, on a path that is largely sheltered by the towering headlands ridge to your right. In minutes, you will pass through a cypress forest and then emerge for pretty views of Drakes Bay off to your left. The trail then rises along an isthmus, with cliffs on each side. The ocean is on the right and Drakes Bay is on the left. The trail curves and rises up to the Chimney Rock Headlands, 0.5 mile in. Be sure to turn and look back for a fantastic 180-degree sweep, with the Pacific now on your left, Drakes Bay on your right. Often there are awesome winds that sweep up the cliffs here. The perch is sensational for views, with sightings of whale spouts in winter, the Farallon Islands, and then across the headlands to the north. Looking back to the east, you can take in the calm waters of Drakes Bay and beyond to Drakes Estero, Limantour, and Inverness Ridge. The main trail continues south to a lookout of a series of rock stacks that emerge from the ocean just beyond land's end. The biggest is Chimney Rock. One of the rock formations has a bridged archway where a surging ocean foams through the center, a natural phenomenon.

In peak spring season, you can often see unbelievable diversity of wildflowers on the lee side of the headlands on the Chimney Rock Trail, including rafts of Douglas iris and good numbers of checkerbloom. Because of exposure to wind, wildflowers tend to dry out sooner here than at more protected areas, but they are spectacular when you hit it right (hint: April).

User Groups: Hikers and mountain bikes. The first 0.25 mile of the trail is wheelchair-accessible. No dogs or horses.

Permits: No permits are required. Parking and access are free.

Maps: For a free map, write to Point Reyes National Seashore. For a topographic map, ask the USGS for Drakes Bay.

Directions: From the Golden Gate Bridge, take U.S. 101 north for 7.5 miles to the exit for Sir Francis Drake Boulevard. Turn west and drive 20 miles to Olema and Highway 1. Turn right on Highway 1 and drive about 100 yards to Bear Valley Road. Turn left on Bear Valley Road and drive 2.4 miles to Sir Francis Drake. Turn left on Sir Francis Drake and drive 17.4 miles toward the Point Reyes Lighthouse to a fork with Chimney Rock Road on the left. Turn left and drive one mile to the parking area and trailhead.

Shuttle bus: On good weather weekends and holidays in winter, usually late December to mid-April, a shuttle bus is required. Tickets are at Drakes Beach Visitors Center (9:30am-3:30pm, $7). Drive to the South Beach Junction, where the road is blocked. Park and take shuttle bus. The shuttle buses run approximately every 20 minutes, 9:30am-3:30pm The shuttle bus may not be required on weekdays or on stormy weekends.

Contact: Point Reyes National Seashore, Bear Valley Visitors Center, 415/464-5100, www.nps.gov/pore.

10 SIR FRANCIS DRAKE TRAIL

1.9 mi/1.0 hr

in Point Reyes National Seashore

Map 7.1, page 289

This spot is not exactly a secret. In fact, you might as well stand on the Golden Gate Bridge with a megaphone and announce its existence to the world. At the trailhead, for instance, you will discover a large parking lot and visitors center, complete with exhibits, maps, and books (maybe even this one, and if not, ask why; after all, we've hiked every trail in the park). The trail traces the back of the arcing beaches along Drakes Bay and provides scenic lookouts onto the bay's protected waters. The trail continues to the mouth of Drakes Estero, then returns via an inland loop that includes a short climb up, then down to a waterfront bluff. This is one of the more popular hikes at Point Reyes National Seashore, and why not? It is an easy walk, provides great scenic beauty, and traces three habitats: beach frontage, the mouth of a lagoon, and hillside bluffs. In some years, elephant seals are common sightings in winter.

User Groups: Hikers and mountain bikes. No dogs or horses. No wheelchair facilities.

Permits: No permits are required. Parking and access are free.

Maps: For a free map, write to Point Reyes National Seashore. For a topographic map, ask the USGS for Drakes Bay.

Directions: From the Golden Gate Bridge, take U.S. 101 north for 7.5 miles to the exit for Sir Francis Drake Boulevard. Turn west and drive 20 miles to Olema and Highway 1. Turn right on Highway 1 and drive about 100 yards to Bear Valley Road. Turn left on Bear Valley Road and drive 2.4 miles to Sir Francis Drake. Turn left on Sir Francis Drake, drive 11.1 miles, and look for the sign indicating a left turn to a visitors center. Turn left and drive 1.2 miles to the parking lot at the Kenneth Patrick Visitors Center and the trailhead.

Contact: Point Reyes National Seashore, Bear Valley Visitors Center, 415/464-5100, www.nps.gov/pore.

11 SKY TRAIL TO PALOMARIN

15.3 mi one-way/ 2 days

in Point Reyes National Seashore

Map 7.1, page 289

With a slight change of approach, one of the Bay Area's greatest overnight hikes can be made even greater. You do it by taking Sky Trail to Palomarin, with a shuttle car for a one-way hike. This trip starts on a Saturday at the Sky trailhead and parking lot, where you hike 7.1

miles to Glen Camp and spend the night. The next day, complete the route where you hike 8.2 miles out to Palomarin and your shuttle car. It splits the weekend into two even days, unlike the famed Coast Trail route. In addition, your best chance these days of getting a campsite on a Saturday night is at Glen Camp, with Wildcat sold out fast, spring through fall.

On Day 1, hike 7.1 miles to Glen Camp. Don't get disgruntled over the first 15 minutes, where the trail is routed up to the ridge on a service road, no views (but pretty bracken ferns and forget-me-nots). At 1.3 miles, you emerge at Sky Camp at 1,000 feet elevation, and with a short walk to the adjacent hill, the eye-popping views are revealed to the west. The expanse of Drakes Bay below is stunning, along with Arch Rock, Drakes Beach, Chimney Rock, and Point Reyes, from left to right. The views then sparkle for much of the hike, with the route occasionally passing through old-growth bishop pines. Over and over, you emerge for views below of Sculptured Beach, Point Resistance, and Arch Rock. Eventually you top out at Glen Camp. Be sure to bring a light tent. Morning fog can be wet.

On Day 2, hike 8.2 miles from Glen Camp to the end of the trail at Palomarin trailhead and your shuttle car. The day starts where you sail downhill and take in pretty views of Wildcat Valley, ocean breakers, and Wildcat Beach, and then connect with the Coast Trail. It is 0.8 mile to the Coast Trail, and then another 1.1 miles to Wildcat Camp.

To get a full front view of Alamere Falls, descend from Wildcat Camp to the beach and hike south one mile. The unsigned cutoff from the Coast Trail (on Alamere Creek) to the brink of the falls is closed to public access. Violators face tickets and expulsion.

From the bridge at Alamere Creek, it is 3.6 miles to the end of the trail and the parking lot at Palomarin. In the process, the route contours south in and out of coastal valleys, where you pass Wildcat Lake, Pelican Lake, and Bass Lake, all gorgeous en route to the trail's end. On a fresh, clear April weekend, this is one of the best ways to celebrate the coronation of spring.

User Groups: Hikers only. No wheelchair facilities.

Permits: Parking and access are free. Reservations and permit required for camping (www.recreation.gov).

Maps: For a free map, write to Point Reyes National Seashore. For a topographic map, ask the USGS for Drakes Bay.

Directions: To Bear Valley Visitors Center: From the Golden Gate Bridge, take U.S. 101 north for 7.5 miles to the exit for Sir Francis Drake Boulevard. Turn west and drive 20 miles to Olema and Highway 1. Turn right on Highway 1 and drive about 100 yards to Bear Valley Road. Turn left and drive 0.7 mile to the Seashore Information sign and access road for Bear Valley Visitors Center. Turn left and go a short distance to the visitors center (campers must pick up permits in person).

To Sky Trailhead: From Bear Valley Visitors Center, exit parking lot to Bear Valley Road. Turn left and drive a short distance to Sir Francis Drake Boulevard. Turn left on Bear Valley Road and drive two miles to Limantour Road. Turn left on Limantour and drive a little over three miles on access road to the Sky Trail parking and trailhead on the left.

Visitors center to Palomarin: From the visitors center, exit the parking lot to Bear Valley Road, turn right, and go 0.5 mile to Highway 1. Turn right and drive 9.3 miles to Olema-Bolinas Road on the right (the sign is always stolen; if you reach Bolinas Lagoon, turn around on Highway 1 and look for the road on left). Turn right and go 1.3 miles to the junction with Horseshoe Hill Road. Turn left (still Olema-Bolinas Road) and go 0.5 mile to Mesa Road. Turn right and go 4.8 miles (pass an antenna farm called The Towers) to the parking area.

Contact: Point Reyes National Seashore, Bear Valley Visitors Center, 415/464-5100, www.nps.gov/pore.

12 SKY TRAIL LOOP

9.6 mi/4.0 hr  3 10

in Point Reyes National Seashore

Map 7.1, page 289

Hit it right on a clear day and it can feel like you have a foothold in the heavens on the Point Reyes Sky Trail. From the trailhead at the parking area on Limantour Road, you pass around a gate to hike up a service road edged by cypress and, in the spring, occasional patches of forget-me-nots in the shade. The trail climbs, from gentle to moderate, to the south for 0.8 mile to a junction with the Fire Lane Trail (on the right). Ignore that and continue on the service road for another half mile to the Sky Camp. In the process, you will walk along the edge of the burn zone of the 1995 fire, with remnants of that event still visible. Notice the mix of fresh-sprouted grass, wildflowers, and young pines, and old cypress and pine that the fire missed, and the sprinkling of blackened tree skeletons that still stand. As you near Sky Camp, the views start to open up. When you reach the camp, look to your right for the nearby short hill to gain the best perch for the jaw-dropping view of Drakes Bay. This 1,000-foot ridgeline perch towers over Drakes Bay and the Pacific Ocean. Plunging below at your boot tips are miles of foothills reborn. Scan from right to left taking in Point Reyes, Chimney Rock, and the curving Limantour Beach to Arch Rock. You can simply turn back for a 2.6-mile romp (mostly downhill on the return).

Better yet, extend the trek to create a spectacular loop, down to the beach and then back up, for a 9.6-mile round-trip. From Sky Camp, stay on the Sky Trail along Inverness Ridge, sheltered by old-growth pines and firs, south to the Woodward Valley Trail. Turn right and sail down Woodward Valley Trail, with jaw-dropping views of the ocean, down to the Coast Trail. On the way down, you may experience the unbelievable feeling that you can sense the earth's curve on the distant horizon. Turn right on the Coast Trail, and in less than a mile, you'll pass Coast Camp, a good spot for your picnic for the day. Then continue ahead into a valley to the Laguna Trail/Fire Trail. Turn right. It's quite steep in a few spots back up to Sky Trail. Back on top, to complete the trip, turn left on Sky Trail and sail back to the parking area. This is one of the best coastal routes in California.

User Groups: Hikers only. Bikes and horses permitted to Sky Camp. No wheelchair facilities.

Permits: No permits are required. Parking and access are free. Permits are required to camp at Sky Camp. Reserve at www.recreation.gov; $20 per night for up to six per site; 11 campsites with picnic table, fire grills (charcoal only), drinking water, pit toilet. Garbage must be packed out.

Maps: For a free map, write to Point Reyes National Seashore. For a topographic map, ask the USGS for Drakes Bay.

Directions: From the Golden Gate Bridge, take U.S. 101 north for 7.5 miles to the exit for Sir Francis Drake Boulevard. Turn west

Sky Trail Loop

and drive 20 miles to Olema and Highway 1. Turn right and drive about 100 yards to Bear Valley Road. Turn left and drive 0.7 mile to the Seashore Information sign and access road for Bear Valley Visitors Center. Turn left and head a short distance to the visitors center (campers must pick up permits in person). From Bear Valley Visitors Center, return to Bear Valley Road. Turn left and drive 1.3 miles to Limantour Road (signed Hostel and Limantour Beach). Turn left and drive 3.4 miles to the access road on the left for Sky Trail. Turn left and drive a short distance to the parking area.

Contact: Point Reyes National Seashore, Bear Valley Visitors Center, 415/464-5100, www.nps.gov/pore.

13 COAST TRAIL

16.1 mi one-way/2-plus days 3 10

in Point Reyes National Seashore

Map 7.1, page 289 BEST

Of the handful of overnight hiking trips available in the Bay Area, Coast Trail provides the most extended tour into a land of charm. This continuous backcountry route is 16.1 miles long, one-way, enough to allow lingering hikers to spend a weekend at it, and short enough for the ambitious to tackle in a single day. The trail offers camps at ocean bluffs, a beach with sculptured rocks and tidepools, bluff-top lookouts with a chance to see passing whales, a rare waterfall from an ocean bluff that pours like a fountain to a beach and then runs into the ocean, and coastal freshwater lakes. There are only a few catches: You need a hiking partner who will double as a shuttle driver so you can leave a car at each end of the trail. You'll need to come prepared to cook your food using a small backpack stove, not a campfire. Tents are recommended, because the coastal weather is the most unpredictable in the Bay Area—clear, calm, and warm one day, then suddenly foggy, windy, moist, and clammy the next.

Day 1: The trailhead for Coast Trail is at the Point Reyes Hostel, from where you will hike north to south and keep the wind at your back and out of your face. The first camp, Coast Camp, is an easy 2.8 miles, ideal for those who head out on a Friday evening after work. As you hike in, you'll have a panoramic view of the coastal foothills. The sound of ocean waves will send you to sleep the first night, or, in some sensitive cases, might keep you awake.

If you try to hike the Coast Trail in two days, you will face a first-day tromp of 10.6 miles, direct to Wildcat Camp. Because of the additional time spent getting camping permits at the Bear Valley Visitors Center and setting up a shuttle car at the trail's end at Palomarin, most hikers get a late start, which means facing a late arrival at Wildcat. One option is to start instead at Sky Trail off Limantour Road and spend the night at Glen Camp (see the listing for *Sky Trail to Palomarin* in this chapter).

Day 2: From Coast Camp, the next day you will hike south, getting glimpses along the way of Sculptured Beach, with its magnificent rock stacks and tunnels. You'll see and pass Sculptured Beach, Kelham Beach, and Arch Rock. (The cutoff trail to Arch Rock is closed after a collapse in 2015.) The Coast Trail continues south to Wildcat Camp, set on a bluff above the beach. That makes a hike of 7.8 miles. It's an additional mile, one-way, to walk south on the beach for a view of Alamere Falls.

Day 3: Today, figure on a 5.5-mile closeout with plenty of great sideshows. You will hike past a series of coastal lakes, nearby Wildcat Lake and little Ocean Lake. After climbing to a short ridge, you will skirt above Pelican Lake and along the northern shore of Bass Lake. The trail then heads up a coastal hill, tops out at 563 feet, and then laterals down a canyon and back to ocean bluffs. Following the trail, you turn south and in a mile arrive at the Palomarin trailhead. You will be ready to reach your shuttle car and head for the barn. This is one of the Bay Area's greatest hikes. For many who want only the best, this is on their must-do list on a clear, warm coastal day at peak spring or fall.

User Groups: Hikers and horses. Mountain bikes permitted only from the Laguna trailhead to the Coast Campground and otherwise prohibited. Partially accessible to wheelchair users who have assistance. No dogs.

Permits: Parking and access are free. Reservations and a permit are required for camping (www.recreation.gov).

Maps: For a free map, write to Point Reyes National Seashore. For a topographic map, ask the USGS for Drakes Bay.

Directions: To Bear Valley Visitors Center: From the Golden Gate Bridge, take U.S. 101 north for 7.5 miles to the exit for Sir Francis Drake Boulevard. Turn west and drive 20 miles to Olema and Highway 1. Turn right and drive about 100 yards to Bear Valley Road. Turn left and drive 0.7 mile to the Seashore Information sign and access road for Bear Valley Visitors Center. Turn left and head a short distance to the visitors center (campers must pick up permits in person).

To Coast Trail trailhead: After getting a camping permit at Bear Valley Visitors Center, leave the parking lot and take the access road to Bear Valley Road. Turn left and drive to Limantour Road. Turn left and drive six miles, looking for the signed turn on the left for Point Reyes Hostel. Turn left on the access road for the Point Reyes Hostel and continue to where road ends at the parking lot. After parking, hike back to the hostel and look for the trailhead on the left (west, across the road from the hostel).

Visitors center to Palomarin: Exit the parking lot to Bear Valley Road, turn right and go 0.5 mile to Highway 1. Turn right and drive 9.3 miles to Olema-Bolinas Road on the right (the sign is always stolen; if you reach Bolinas Lagoon, turn around and look for the road on left). Turn right and go 1.3 miles to junction with Horseshoe Hill Road. Turn left (still Olema-Bolinas Road) and go 0.5 mile to Mesa Road. Turn right and go 4.8 miles (pass an antenna farm called The Towers) to the parking area.

Contact: Point Reyes National Seashore, Bear Valley Visitors Center, 415/464-5100, www.nps.gov/pore.

14 LAGUNA LOOP TRAIL

5.5 mi/2.5 hr 

in Point Reyes National Seashore

Map 7.1, page 289

The Laguna Loop Trail can make for a great Sunday morning walk. The trailhead is just 0.2 mile down the road from the Point Reyes Hostel, adjacent to the park's Environmental Education Center. From there, the trail continues 1.8 miles up to Inverness Ridge, with great views of Drakes Bay along the way. At the ridge, turn right and hike 0.7 mile toward Mount Wittenberg, which at 1,407 feet is the highest point at Point Reyes National Seashore. On the north flank of Mount Wittenberg, hikers should turn right on the Fire Lane Trail, which loops back around for three miles to the Laguna trailhead. This excellent loop hike entails a bit of a climb and offers Pacific lookouts, yet it is short enough to complete in a few hours.

User Groups: Hikers and horses. Mountain bikes are permitted only from the Laguna trailhead to the Coast Campground and are otherwise prohibited. No dogs. No wheelchair facilities.

Permits: No permits are required. Parking and access are free.

Maps: For a free map, write to Point Reyes National Seashore. For a topographic map, ask the USGS for Inverness.

Directions: From the Golden Gate Bridge, take U.S. 101 north for 7.5 miles to the exit for Sir Francis Drake Boulevard. Turn west and drive 20 miles to Olema and Highway 1. Turn right and drive about 100 yards to Bear Valley Road. Turn left at Bear Valley Road and drive two miles to Limantour Road. Turn left and drive six miles. Turn left on the access road for the Point Reyes Hostel and drive 0.2 mile past the hostel to the parking area and trailhead (on the right side of the road).

Contact: Point Reyes National Seashore, Bear Valley Visitors Center, 415/464-5100, www.nps.gov/pore.

15 MOUNT WITTENBERG LOOP

4.5 mi/2.5 hr 

in Point Reyes National Seashore near Olema

Map 7.1, page 289

One little turn off a major trail can lead to a landscape where hiking dreams come true. The Mount Wittenberg Loop is such a trek, one of the best short hikes in the Point Reyes National Seashore. The trail provides a route through deep forest, a climb with a steady grade, and then magnificent lookouts of Drakes Bay to the west and the Olema Valley to the east. The destination is the flank of Mount Wittenberg (at 1,407 feet, the highest in the park), but the best views are from the ridge just west of the rounded summit (not at the summit). After parking at the huge parking lot at Bear Valley Visitors Center, look for the trailhead for Bear Valley Trail at the south end of the parking area. This has long been one of the heaviest used trails in the Bay Area, and hence comes the trick: Hike on Bear Valley Trail for just 0.2 mile! On your right, look for the cutoff route for the Sky Trail. Bear right at the cutoff, and from here, it is a 1.4-mile hike with a climb of 1,200 feet. It's a steady grade and hikers in decent condition can easily handle it. You'll pass through old-growth forest and lush ravines, with occasional peephole-like lookouts to Olema Valley. It rises to the foot of Mount Wittenberg (and with another 100-foot climb, a cutoff trail takes hikers to the rounded summit). The views are not the greatest from the top, but instead from just nearby on Sky Trail. At Sky Trail, walk southwest 0.4 mile to the junction with Meadow Trail. In the process, there are dramatic views of Drakes Bay to the west and some hidden meadows to the east. You'll also have a panoramic shot of the coastal foothills. From Meadow Trail, turn left and you will glide downhill for 1.5 miles back down to Bear Valley Trail. The trail widens and flattens, and you'll see people again, then you walk out 0.8 mile to the parking lot. There you have it: To paradise and back in just a few hours.

Laguna Loop Trail, Inverness Ridge

User Groups: Hikers and horses. No dogs or mountain bikes. No wheelchair facilities.

Permits: No permits are required. Parking and access are free.

Maps: For a free map, write to Point Reyes National Seashore. For a topographic map, ask the USGS for Inverness.

Directions: From the Golden Gate Bridge, take U.S. 101 north for 7.5 miles to the exit for Sir Francis Drake Boulevard. Turn west and drive 20 miles to Olema and Highway 1. Turn right and drive about 100 yards to Bear Valley Road. Turn left and drive 0.7 mile to sign for Seashore Information and road on left. Turn left and drive to the parking lot for the Bear Valley Visitors Center. The trailhead is at the south end of the parking lot.

Contact: Point Reyes National Seashore, Bear

Valley Visitors Center, 415/464-5100, www.nps.gov/pore.

16 BEAR VALLEY TRAIL

8.2 mi/4.0 hr 1 7

in Point Reyes National Seashore near Olema

Map 7.1, page 289

This is one of the most popular trails in the park. It starts at the south end of the parking lot at the main visitors center and follows a heavily used service road through pretty forest. It leads past Divide Meadow to Bear Valley, then down along Coast Creek to the beach, a highlight.

User Groups: Hikers, mountain bikes (first three miles only), and horses (weekdays only). The 1.5-mile trail to Divide Meadow is wheelchair-accessible but requires a significant amount of assistance. No dogs.

Permits: No permits are required. Parking and access are free.

Maps: For a free map, write to Point Reyes National Seashore. For a topographic map, ask the USGS for Inverness.

Directions: From the Golden Gate Bridge, take U.S. 101 north for 7.5 miles to the exit for Sir Francis Drake Boulevard. Turn west and drive 20 miles to Olema and Highway 1. Turn right and drive about 100 yards to Bear Valley Road. Turn left and drive 0.7 mile to the sign for Seashore Information and a road on the left. Turn left and drive to the parking lot for the Bear Valley Visitors Center.

Contact: Point Reyes National Seashore, Bear Valley Visitors Center, 415/464-5100, www.nps.gov/pore.

17 EARTHQUAKE TRAIL

1.2 mi one-way/0.75 hr 1 7

in Point Reyes National Seashore near Olema

Map 7.1, page 289

The trailhead is right next to the picnic area at the Bear Valley Visitors Center. That makes this a popular easy walk. The geology also fascinates many. It is one of the world's classic examples of an earthquake fault line: the San Andreas Fault. Because we like big views, waterfalls, and wildflowers, it doesn't quite flip our pancake, but it does provide one of the best lessons you can get from the University of Nature.

The trail starts at the Bear Valley Picnic Area. It's a short, paved loop.

User Groups: Hikers and horses. No dogs or mountain bikes. No wheelchair facilities.

Permits: No permits are required. Parking and access are free.

Maps: For a free map, write to Point Reyes National Seashore. For a topographic map, ask the USGS for Inverness.

Directions: From the Golden Gate Bridge, take U.S. 101 north for 7.5 miles to the exit for Sir Francis Drake Boulevard. Turn west and drive 20 miles to Olema and Highway 1. Turn right and drive about 100 yards to Bear Valley Road. Turn left and drive 0.7 mile to the sign for Seashore Information and a road on the left. Turn left and drive to the parking lot for the Bear Valley Visitors Center.

Contact: Point Reyes National Seashore, Bear Valley Visitors Center, 415/464-5100, www.nps.gov/pore.

18 BOLINAS RIDGE

10.5 mi one-way/4.5 hr 3 9

in Marin County west of San Rafael

Map 7.1, page 289

The Bolinas Ridge Trail spans 10.5 miles (one-way) from Sir Francis Drake Boulevard south to Bolinas-Fairfax Road in west Marin County. From Bolinas Ridge, you start with hilltop views across the foothill grasslands and valleys and beyond to the Marin coast. It can be a good short walk, a better hike, and for ambitious mountain bikers, a sensational 20-mile loop with several cutoffs available for shorter options.

From the trailhead at Sir Francis Drake, the trail undulates up and down the foothills, with an overall climb of about 750 feet in six miles. You get views of Olema Valley, the San Andreas Rift Zone and beyond south to Bolinas Lagoon. Some just venture south for a few miles, then turn around when ready for a mostly downhill glide. If you continue south, the route descends, steeply at times, into redwoods. Most of the trail is an abandoned ranch road. The trail is routed for about five miles through open grasslands with lots of cows and several gates. Do not go off-trail, where ticks wait perched on the high grass to ambush you if you (or your dog) brush by.

Note: You can also start the trip from Samuel P. Taylor State Park, where secure parking is available. To do this, you connect out of Samuel P. Taylor on the Jewell Trail (the trail can wash out in winter).

User Groups: Hikers, dogs, horses, and mountain bikes. No wheelchair facilities.

Permits: No permits are required. Parking and access are free.

Maps: For a free map, write to Point Reyes National Seashore. For topographic maps, ask the USGS for Inverness, San Geronimo, and Bolinas.

Directions: From San Francisco, take U.S. 101 north over the Golden Gate Bridge and continue 8.7 miles to Larkspur and the exit for San Anselmo/Sir Francis Drake West. Take that exit, drive 0.4 mile, and merge onto Sir Francis Drake. Drive 19.4 miles, past Samuel P. Taylor State Park, to the trailhead on the left (if you reach Olema, you missed it: the trailhead is back one mile). Park on the shoulder.

Contact: Golden Gate National Recreation Area, Fort Mason, San Francisco, 415/561-4700, www.nps.gov/goga.

19 BARNABE PEAK LOOP

5.5 mi/3.5 hr  3  8

in Samuel P. Taylor State Park northwest of San Rafael

Map 7.1, page 289

From the summit of 1,466-foot Barnabe Peak, you get a sweeping lookout that spans from Mount Tamalpais to Point Reyes. The Barnabe Fire Road provides a 5.5-mile loop with a 1,300-foot climb to the top. An old lookout tower is positioned here, but there is no access. Most will plan a picnic at the base of the old tower.

A new trailhead starts from the Azalea Picnic Area, a day-use area inside the main entrance to Samuel P. Taylor State Park. Park, then walk toward the dump station. Before the bridge over Lagunitas Creek, take the North Creek Trail to cross Sir Francis Drake Boulevard. On the north side of Sir Francis Drake, you'll see the Madrone Group Campground, and from there, the Barnabe Fire Road. Now you're on your way.

Barnabe Peak is also accessible from Devil's Gulch via the Gravesite Road Trail. For that route, park in the Devil's Gulch parking area on the south shoulder of Sir Francis Drake. Walk across the road and up Devil's Gulch Road, then take the Devil's Gulch Trail to the trailhead for Gravesite Road. Follow Gravesite Road up to the junction with the Barnabe Peak Fire Road for the final leg to the top.

The route to Barnabe Peak via Bill's Trail out of Devil's Gulch (to Stairstep Falls) will reopen in 2020. Once winter sets in and the waterfall starts flowing, Bill's Trail will close to protect the endangered spotted owl and safeguard against possible impacts when the owls call for a mate, nest, or rear young.

Samuel P. Taylor State Park is located along Sir Francis Drake Boulevard in western Marin, best known for its stand of redwoods and the lush undergrowth in the canyon along the headwaters of Lagunitas Creek. The park covers 2,700 acres and features excellent hiking, biking, and camping.

User Groups: Hikers, dogs, and mountain bikes (bikes are not permitted on spur trails). No horses.

Permits: A state park day-use fee of $8 per vehicle is charged at the entrance station.

Maps: A brochure and map are available for a fee at the entrance station to Samuel P. Taylor State Park. For a topographic map, ask the USGS for San Geronimo.

Directions: To park headquarters: From the Golden Gate Bridge, take U.S. 101 north for 7.5 miles to the exit for Sir Francis Drake Boulevard. Take that exit west and drive 14.5 miles to the park entrance, on the left.

Contact: Samuel P. Taylor State Park, Lagunitas, 415/488-9897; Marin District Headquarters, 415/898-4362, www.parks.ca.gov.

20 PIONEER TREE TRAIL

1.6 mi/0.75 hr — 2, 7

in Samuel P. Taylor State Park northwest of San Rafael

Map 7.1, page 289

If you like big trees and a simple, short walk, the Pioneer Tree Trail in Samuel P. Taylor State Park will provide it. In just 0.5 mile, you will walk amid the park's prize grove of old-growth coastal redwoods, the species that produces the tallest trees in the world. Park at the Azalea Day Use Picnic Area then walk across the Salmon Crossing Bridge to the Cross Marin Trail. Turn left and walk a short distance on the Cross Marin Trail to the Pioneer Tree trailhead on the right. From here, it's 0.25-mile into the heart of the grove of old-growth redwoods. The trail then turns left sharply, and you walk another 0.25 mile. When you run out of big trees, most turn around and return at this point.

If you continue on, you will eventually reach a spur for the Pioneer Trail, less impressive than the behemoths in the Santa Cruz Mountains, and reach the Cross Marin Trail along Lagunitas Creek. Turn left and go 0.6 mile to reach your starting point, the picnic area. That is a 2.7-mile loop.

User Groups: Hikers only. No dogs, horses, or mountain bikes.

Permits: A state park day-use fee of $8 per vehicle is charged at the entrance station.

Maps: A brochure and map are available for a fee at the entrance station to Samuel P. Taylor State Park. For a topographic map, ask the USGS for San Geronimo.

Directions: From the Golden Gate Bridge, take U.S. 101 north for 7.5 miles to the exit for Sir Francis Drake Boulevard. Take that exit west and drive 14.5 miles to the park entrance, on the left. Park at the Azalea Day Use Picnic Area.

Contact: Samuel P. Taylor State Park, Lagunitas, 415/488-9897; Marin District Headquarters, 415/898-4362, www.parks.ca.gov.

21 KENT LAKE/PETERS DAM TRAIL

1.8 mi/1.0 hr — 1, 6

in northwest Marin County northwest of Fairfax

Map 7.1, page 289

The nearly four-mile-long Kent Lake is the largest reservoir for domestic water supply in Marin with an additional large arm extending east into Big Carson Creek. Only hikers and mountain bikers see it. Start by parking along Sir Francis Drake Boulevard at Shafter Bridge. Hike past the gate on Peters Dam Road (Lagunitas Creek to your right) to a junction (San Geronimo Ridge Road on your left, an excellent mountain bike ride), and continue ahead (at a spur, stay left on the main road). The road bends like a horseshoe, first to the left, then ahead, and then to the right as it rises up to Peters Dam. When the lake first emerges into view, it is an amazing sight, especially when the lake fills in late winter. Emerald water fills a long canyon, bordered on each side by rising slopes packed with conifers. Most people are astounded the first time they see Kent Lake, for they have no idea such a huge lake is tucked away in a Marin canyon. The road continues along the east side of the lake and then eventually rises up into forested slopes to a network of fire roads. No swimming or wading.

User Groups: Hikers, leashed dogs, and mountain bikes. No horses. No wheelchair facilities.

Permits: No permits are required. Groups are limited to 19 people. Parking and access are free.

Maps: For a free map, contact Point Reyes National Seashore, 415/464-5100, 1 Bear Valley Rd. Point Reyes Station, CA 94956, www.nps.gov/pore. For topographic maps, ask the USGS for San Geronimo and Bolinas.

Directions: From the Golden Gate Bridge, take U.S. 101 north for 7.5 miles to the exit for Sir Francis Drake Boulevard. Take that exit west and drive about 12 miles to Shafter Bridge and look for the signed turnoff for the Leo T. Cronin Fish Viewing Area/Peters Dam Road. Turn left and park at the Cronin lot.

Contact: Sky Oaks Ranger Station, 415/945-1180; Marin Municipal Water District, 415/945-1195, www.marinwater.org.

22 OLEMA VALLEY

3.0 mi/1.25 hr

in Point Reyes National Seashore south of Olema

Map 7.1, page 289

Olema Valley is a mix of lush meadows and forests that roughly traces the San Andreas Fault. The trailhead is at Five Brooks. Take the Stewart Trail, a road that runs past a duck pond, and then junctions quickly with the Olema Valley Trail. The meadow area attracts a lot of deer, morning and evening. It's 1.3 miles, which includes a short climb, to the headwaters of Pine Gulch Creek. From there, most continue a short distance, and then return when ready. An option is to continue southward for four miles or more to Olema Creek and along the San Andreas Fault. In wet weather, the creeks often flood the trail. If that is a concern, wear waterproof boots in winter. In summer, this has become a popular mountain bike route.

User Groups: Hikers, horses, and mountain bikes. No dogs. No wheelchair facilities.

Permits: No permits are required. Parking and access are free.

Maps: For a free map, contact Point Reyes National Seashore, 415/464-5100, 1 Bear Valley Rd. Point Reyes Station, CA 94956, www.nps.gov/pore. For a topographic map, ask the USGS for Bolinas.

Directions: From the Golden Gate Bridge, take U.S. 101 north for 7.5 miles to the exit for Sir Francis Drake Boulevard. Turn west and drive 20 miles to Olema and Highway 1. Turn left on Highway 1 and drive 3.6 miles to the access road for Five Brooks trailhead on the right (west). Turn right and drive to parking and continue to the Stewart Trail and the duck pond.

Contact: Point Reyes National Seashore, Bear Valley Visitors Center, 415/464-5100, www.nps.gov/pore.

23 MOUNT BURDELL

5.8 mi/3.0 hr 3 8

in Olompali State Historic Park near Novato

Map 7.1, page 289

The payoff at Olompali State Historic Park is the big view from the upper slopes and summit of 1,558-foot Mount Burdell as you tower over the expanse of San Pablo Bay. Below are the wetlands of Bahia Marsh and the Petaluma River near the Gnoss Field Airport. You can see the Sonoma Mountains to the north, across the bay to Carquinez Bridge to the east. It's a 5.8-mile round-trip to Burdell summit, a 1,500-foot climb. The hike is routed through pretty woodlands, up well-graded switchbacks, and emerges in grasslands with a picnic site on top. The habitat supports tons of deer and wild turkey.

Note: No mountain bikes or dogs are

permitted at Olompali State Historic Park, yet they are allowed at adjoining Mount Burdell Open Space Preserve. Near the summit, a trail connects the two parks, and if you see bikes or dogs, that is where they are coming from.

User Groups: Hikers. No dogs, horses, or mountain bikes. No wheelchair facilities on Mount Burdell Trail, but they are available near the parking area.

Permits: No permits are required. There is an $8 parking fee.

Maps: A trail map is posted at information billboard near the parking area. For a topographic map, ask the USGS for Burdell.

Directions: From San Francisco, take U.S. 101 north for about 25 miles (past Highway 37 on right) to Exit 463 for Atherton Avenue/San Marin Drive. Take that exit to Atherton. Turn left on Atherton and go 0.2 mile (cross the overpass over 101) to Redwood Boulevard. Turn right and drive 2.7 miles on Redwood (a frontage road, just west of 101) to the park entrance on the left.

Contact: Olompali State Historic Park, 415/892-3383, www.parks.ca.gov.

24 GREEN HILL/SAN GERONIMO RIDGE

4.0 mi one-way/ 2.5 hr 3 8

in Giacomini Open Space, Marin

Map 7.1, page 289

Giacomini Open Space is a hidden preserve that provides a gateway to 25,000 acres of wildlands. It is east of Fairfax on the flank of San Geronimo Ridge, at the foot of Marin's Mount Tamalpais. The drive in makes it off the radar for just about everybody but locals, and that makes it special, too. In two miles, you are transported from city driving (Sir Francis Drake) to the Willis Evans trailhead. This provides one of the fastest transformations from urban to wild in the Bay Area.

Most of this route is on land managed by the Marin Municipal Water District. From the gate (880 feet elevation), head up to Green Hill (1,418 feet, four miles round-trip) for big views. After hiking on fire roads, you emerge on top with a panorama across the wooded watershed lands. The ambitious few can continue on, but you pay a price coming back.

Giacomini Open Space encompasses 1,500 acres on the flanks of San Geronimo Ridge Fire Road. It adjoins Marin Watershed lands, and on the ridge, you get views of Kent Lake and across west Marin. A network of fire roads for mountain biking connects to the watershed lands and to other preserves.

User Groups: Hikers, mountain bikes, dogs and horses. Limited wheelchair facilities.

Permits: No permits are required. Parking and access are free.

Maps: A sheet map is available from Bay Ridge Trail Council. For topographic maps, ask the USGS for San Geronimo.

Directions: From San Francisco, take U.S. 101 north over the Golden Gate Bridge and continue 9.4 miles to Exit 450B (for San Anselmo and Sir Francis Drake Boulevard). Take that exit and drive 0.5 mile to the merge with Sir Francis Drake, then continue 9.5 miles (past Fairfax, near Woodacre) to Railroad Avenue. Turn left on Railroad and go 0.2 miles San Geronimo Valley Drive. Make a sharp right on San Geronimo Valley Drive and drive 0.5 miles to Redwood Canyon Drive. Turn left and drive 0.2 miles (the road jogs twice) to trailhead.

Contact: Marin County Open Space District, 415/ 499-6387, www.marincountyparks.org.

25 ALAMERE FALLS TRAIL

13.0 mi/1 day 2 10

in Point Reyes National Seashore northwest of Bolinas

Map 7.1, page 289

Alamere Falls tumbles over an ocean bluff, then cascades 40 feet to the beach below and into the Pacific Ocean. It is stunning, beautiful, and constantly changing as the rains come and go.

From the Palomarin trailhead, follow the southern end of the Coast Trail as it starts out on a service road that contours along the coastal foothills. At times you'll tower over the ocean and on clear days, the Farallon Islands look close enough to reach with a jump. The trail follows along the ocean for about a mile, then dips down into a ravine to climb out 500 feet to a sub-ridge and trail junction. Stay left on the Coast Trail for two miles, gently descending past pretty Bass Lake. A mile later, you'll hike along a sub-ridge that overlooks Pelican Lake, a bit bigger than Bass Lake and also gorgeous. This is an excellent area for wildflowers and for sighting deer and birds. After passing Pelican Lake, the route continues north and arrives at a small bridge at Alamere Creek.

You then continue another 1.3 miles to Wildcat Camp, where you drop down to the wilderness beach. It's one-mile walk south along the beach to the base of Alamere Falls for a full frontal, the best views and photo ops. Even with light flows in Alamere Creek, this is one of the Bay Area's most beautiful waterfalls. After toppling over a rocky brink to the beach 40 feet below, the water cuts an ever-changing mosaic in the sand before running into the ocean. At moderate or high flows, it charges over the cliff in a wide sheet of white water. At these times, it is one of the prettiest coastal waterfalls anywhere in the world.

Note: The unsigned cutoff from the Coast Trail (on Alamere Creek) to the brink of the falls is closed to public access. Violators face tickets and expulsion.

User Groups: Hikers and horses. No dogs or mountain bikes. No wheelchair facilities.

Permits: No permits are required. Parking and access are free.

Maps: For a free map, write to Point Reyes National Seashore. For topographic maps, ask the USGS for Bolinas and Double Point.

Directions: From San Francisco, take U.S. 101 north over the Golden Gate Bridge and continue nine miles to Exit 450B for Sir Francis Drake Boulevard/San Anselmo. Take that exit (stay in the second lane from the right), continue to Sir Francis Drake, and drive 21 miles to Highway 1. Turn left and drive nine miles to Olema-Bolinas Road on the right (the sign is always stolen; if you reach Bolinas Lagoon, turn around and look for a road on the left). Turn right and go 1.3 miles to the junction with Horseshoe Hill Road. Turn left (still Olema-Bolinas Road) and go 0.5 mile to Mesa Road. Turn right and go 4.8 miles (past an antenna farm called The Towers) to the parking area.

Contact: Point Reyes National Seashore, Bear Valley Visitors Center, 415/464-5100, www.nps.gov/pore.

26 KENT PUMP ROAD

2.0 mi/1.0 hr 

on Mount Tamalpais Watershed at Alpine Lake Dam

Map 7.1, page 289

Water-watching has become a spectator sport in Marin. You'll see why if you venture out pretty Bolinas-Fairfax Road. On the right of Alpine Dam, look for the gated service road. This is the Kent Pump Road. In winter and spring, walk down a short distance to get a view of the "waterfall," a 140-foot stepped cascade, as it flows across the back of the dam and into Lagunitas Creek. In summer months, this is the start of a great, easy walk to a picnic site. On the Kent Pump Road, walk down into the canyon and look for a cutoff route on your left that leads down to the creek. Stay alert for the second cutoff on your left, down to the creek. Your destination is a beautiful spot along the stream, sheltered beneath a hardwood canopy. Gorgeous. For most, this is the trip, a round-trip of about two miles.

The Kent Pump Road seems made to order for mountain biking. It descends into the canyon, with Lagunitas Creek on your left, and within two miles, you reach the headwaters of Kent Lake (full). The road is then routed along the lake and past two feeder creeks around a deep cove; a 9.6-mile round-trip, 250-foot descent on the way in. The trail gradient is generally good, from Alpine Dam (648 feet) to Kent Lake (403 feet).

Wildlife: In late March, April, and May, there is often an active osprey nest atop a dead snag near the end of the trail at Kent Lake. Bear scat has also been sighted and reported on the far reaches of Pump Road.

User Groups: Hikers, dogs, horses, and mountain bikes. No wheelchair facilities. No swimming or wading.

Permits: No permits are required. Groups are limited to 19 people. Parking and access are free. The watershed closes at sunset.

Maps: A hiking and biking map is available for a fee from the Marin Municipal Water District. For a topographic map, ask the USGS for Bolinas.

Directions: From San Francisco, take U.S. 101 over the Golden Gate Bridge and continue 7.5 miles to the exit for Sir Francis Drake Boulevard. Take that exit (toward San Anselmo) and continue 0.4 mile and merge with Sir Francis Drake Boulevard. Continue 3.5 miles (get in left lane) to Center Boulevard. Turn left on center and drive 1.7 miles into Fairfax (becomes Broadway Boulevard) to Bolinas Road. Turn left on Bolinas Road and drive 7.6 miles (becomes Bolinas-Fairfax Road, curvy) to Alpine Dam, where there is very limited parking on the shoulder on the right. Kent Pump Road (a gated service road) is on right.

Note: The parking area fills early on peak weekends in winter and spring.

Contact: Sky Oaks Ranger Station, 415/945-1180; Marin Municipal Water District, 415/945-1195, www.marinwater.org.

27 PINE MOUNTAIN/ CARSON FALLS

3.0 mi/1.5 hr 2 9

on Mount Tamalpais west of Fairfax

Map 7.1, page 289

Carson Falls has five decks and drops that span nearly 100 feet, from top to bottom. This hike is an easy three miles round-trip. The walk to this divine site is hidden in a deep valley on the north slopes of Mount Tamalpais. It's an easy stroll across hilly grasslands (often accompanied by a hawk or two floating overhead), followed by a short jog down a canyon into the Carson Creek drainage.

The trailhead (at 1,078 feet) is adjacent to one of the larger parking areas along Bolinas-Fairfax Road. After parking, cross Bolinas-Fairfax Road to reach the trailhead on Pine Mountain Road, a water district service road. The road climbs 400 feet over the course of a mile and merges into a junction with Oat Hill Road on the crest of a hill flanked on both sides by foothill grasslands. Turn left here and in 0.25 mile you'll reach a sign for the Carson Falls Trail on your right. Here you'll leave the fire roads and follow a trail for 0.5 mile to Little Carson Creek, a small bridge, and the series of waterfalls. You get a beautiful view upstream of four waterfalls, pool-and-drop, pouring over boulders. Just below you is the rim of a 35-foot free fall. The best view is near the brink of the last waterfall. Turn and look up. This is one of my favorite spots.

Plan to visit in late winter and early spring, when periods of heavy rainfall can saturate the ground and the falls are at their peak.

Note: The ravine is home to the threatened foothill yellow-legged frogs. Please stay out of the creek and pools to protect this population.

User Groups: Hikers, leashed dogs. Mountain bikes and horses are allowed on Pine Mountain and Oat Hill Roads, but not on the hiking trail down to Carson Falls. No wheelchair facilities. No swimming or wading.

Permits: No permits are required. Groups are

limited to 19 people. Parking and access are free. The watershed closes at sunset.

Maps: A hiking and biking map is available for a fee from the Marin Municipal Water District. For a topographic map, ask the USGS for Bolinas.

Directions: From San Francisco, take U.S. 101 over the Golden Gate Bridge and continue 7.5 miles to the exit for Sir Francis Drake Boulevard. Take that exit (toward San Anselmo) and continue 0.4 mile and merge with Sir Francis Drake Boulevard. Continue 3.5 miles (get in left lane) to Center Boulevard. Turn left on center and drive 1.7 miles into Fairfax (becomes Broadway Boulevard) to Bolinas Road. Turn left on Bolinas Road and drive for 3.8 miles (past the golf course) to the large dirt parking area on the left. The trailhead for Pine Mountain Road and an information billboard are across the road from the parking area.

Note: The parking area fills early on peak weekends in winter and spring.

Contact: Sky Oaks Ranger Station, 415/945-1180; Marin Municipal Water District, 415/945-1195, www.marinwater.org.

28 CARSON FALLS LOOP

7.4 mi/3.5 hr 

on Mount Tamalpais west of Fairfax

Map 7.1, page 289

How can you take a great hike and make it better? By hiking to Carson Falls and turning it into a stellar loop hike, sensational from late winter through spring. Start the trip by hiking up Pine Mountain Road for one mile (300 feet) to the junction with Oat Hill Road. The route up provides sweeping views of surrounding foothills and beyond, including an awesome look at the remote north flank of Mount Tamalpais, and glimpses of Alpine Lake. It's common to see red-tailed hawks hunting and hovering. At the ridge and road junction, turn left at Oat Hill Road and walk 0.25 mile, or about five minutes. At a large sign for the Carson Falls Trail, turn right and leave the fire roads behind. The trail is a series of switchbacks downhill for 0.5 mile. This fern-lined stretch of single-track deposits you on a narrow, artfully constructed footbridge above Little Carson Falls. Cross it and work your way down on the far side of the stream to the waterfalls. The best "ah" moment is just below the midway point, where you can look up and see three pool-and-drop waterfalls and a short cascade.

It's only a three-mile trip, out and back, to Carson Falls, but you can extend the trip into a great 7.4-mile loop hike. From the falls, continue down the Carson Falls Trail and into redwoods to the Kent Pump Road. Bear left and continue 1.4 miles above Kent Lake to Old Vee Road. Turn left and climb 1.2 miles up to Oat Hill Road. Turn left and hike 1.5 miles along the ridge to Pine Mountain Road. Turn right and return one mile downhill to the parking area. Rating: Fantastic.

User Groups: Hikers, leashed dogs. No wheelchair facilities. Mountain bikes and horses allowed on Pine Mountain and Oat Hill Roads, but not on the hiking trail down to Carson Falls. No swimming or wading.

Permits: No permits are required. Groups are limited to 19 people. Parking and access are free. Watershed closes at sunset.

Maps: A hiking and biking map is available for a fee from the Marin Municipal Water District. For a topographic map, ask the USGS for Bolinas.

Directions: From San Francisco, take U.S. 101 over the Golden Gate Bridge and continue 7.5 miles to the exit for Sir Francis Drake Boulevard. Take that exit (toward San Anselmo) and continue 0.4 mile and merge with Sir Francis Drake Boulevard. Continue 3.5 miles (get in left lane) to Center Boulevard. Turn left on center and drive 1.7 miles into Fairfax (becomes Broadway Boulevard) to Bolinas Road. Turn left on Bolinas Road and drive for 3.8 miles (past the golf course) to the large dirt parking area on the left. The trailhead for Pine Mountain Road and an information billboard are across the road from the parking area.

Note: The parking area fills early on peak weekends in winter and spring.

Contact: Sky Oaks Ranger Station, 415/945-1180; Marin Municipal Water District, 415/945-1195, www.marinwater.org.

29 LAGUNITAS-BON TEMPE LOOP

5.0 mi/2.5 hr

on Mount Tamalpais at Lake Lagunitas west of Fairfax

Map 7.1, page 289

This is our favorite hike at Bon Tempe and Lagunitas Lakes. As you clear the rise, Lake Lagunitas first comes into view and the beauty hits you all at once: A pristine little lake, backed by forest and the rising slopes of the northeast face of Mount Tamalpais. This walk is pretty, easy, featuring tons of birds and maybe a turtle or two sunning on a rock or log, and can be shorted to a really easy 40-minute loop around Lagunitas (easy enough for baby strollers).

The trailhead lies at an elevation of 740 feet at the Lagunitas Picnic Area, adjacent to Lake Lagunitas. Walk past the picnic area and then hike up to the earthen dam. You'll pop out with a pretty lake view and a sign warning visitors to watch out for migrating newts. Walk around Lake Lagunitas counterclockwise, where you eventually link up with Pilot Knob Trail. Turn left, hike past the parking area, and connect with Bon Tempe Shadyside Trail. This route circles the lake (with one short juncture on the Alex Forman/Sky Oaks Trail) and eventually leads all the way back to the parking area. As with any loop that links different trails, a map can be helpful, especially for newcomers. Pick one up at the entrance station.

User Groups: Hikers, leashed dogs and horses. Mountain bikes permitted on roads only. Limited wheelchair facilities. No swimming or wading.

Permits: A day-use fee of $8 is charged per vehicle. A self-pay station accepts credit cards, $1, $5, $10 and $20 bills, but cannot make change. Groups are limited to 19 people. Watershed closes at sunset and the gate is locked at Sky Oaks.

Maps: A hiking and biking map is available for a fee from the Marin Municipal Water District. For a topographic map, ask the USGS for Bolinas.

Directions: From San Francisco, take U.S. 101 over the Golden Gate Bridge and continue 7.5 miles to the exit for Sir Francis Drake Boulevard. Take that exit (toward San Anselmo) and continue 0.4 mile and merge with Sir Francis Drake Boulevard. Continue 3.5 miles (get in left lane) to Center Boulevard. Turn left on center and drive 1.7 miles into Fairfax (becomes Broadway Boulevard) to Bolinas Road. Turn left on Bolinas Road and drive 1.5 miles to Sky Oaks Road on left. Turn left and drive 0.5 mile to the entrance station. Then continue:

To Lagunitas Lake: From the entrance station, go 0.25 mile to a fork. Bear left and drive 1.25 miles to the parking and picnic area. Park and hike uphill on the service road to dam, lake, and trailhead.

To Bon Tempe Lake: From the entrance station, go 0.25 mile to a fork. Bear right on Bon Tempe Road and drive 0.2 mile to the parking area. Walk a short distance to the dam/spillway for lake access and the nearby trailhead.

Contact: Sky Oaks Ranger Station, 415/945-1180; Marin Municipal Water District, 415/945-1195, www.marinwater.org.

30 DEER PARK TRAIL/ BALD HILL

2.0 mi/1.25 hr 

on Mount Tamalpais near San Anselmo

Map 7.1, page 289

The trailhead at Deer Park is one of the most popular in the sphere of influence of Mount Tamalpais. The Deer Park Trail provides nature, peace, and a 350-foot climb in a mile. Pleasure you will get. The trail rises up the slopes of Bald Hill and the views open up around you. It is also common to see deer in this area, and wildflower blooms are quite good in the spring. This is also one of the areas where bear scat was sighted and verified. If you want even more, you'll have an opportunity to link up with a mosaic of other trails in the area. As you venture inland, the route enters land managed by the Marin Municipal Water District.

User Groups: Hikers only. No dogs, horses, or mountain bikes. No wheelchair facilities.

Permits: No permits are required. Groups are limited to 19 people. Parking and access are free.

Maps: A hiking and biking map is available for a fee from the Marin Municipal Water District. For a topographic map, ask the USGS for San Rafael.

Directions: From San Francisco, take U.S. 101 over the Golden Gate Bridge and continue 7.5 miles to the exit for Sir Francis Drake Boulevard. Take that exit (toward San Anselmo) and continue 0.4 mile and merge with Sir Francis Drake Boulevard. Continue 3.5 miles (get in left lane) to Center Boulevard. Turn left on center and drive 1.7 miles into Fairfax (becomes Broadway Boulevard) to Bolinas Road. Turn left on Bolinas Road and drive 0.5 mile to Porteous Avenue. Turn left on Porteous Avenue and continue to Deer County Park. If you walk behind the school on the left, and completely pass it, the trailhead will be on your left.

Contact: Marin County Parks, 415/473-6387, www.marincountyparks.org.

31 SHORELINE TRAIL

5.0 mi/2.5 hr 

in China Camp State Park east of San Rafael

Map 7.1, page 289

China Camp is on the shore of San Pablo Bay. The park provides sensational water views, picnic sites on bluffs overlooking the shore, great mountain biking, hikes through the woods to world-class lookouts, cultural history, camping, wetlands for birds, and a nearby fishing pier. The Shoreline Trail can provide an introduction. From the trailhead, the trail meanders along the shore of San Pablo Bay, bordered by undisturbed hills on one side and waterfront on the other. The first mile provides good lookouts across the bay; the last 0.5 mile crosses a meadow, then runs adjacent to tidal areas, marshes, and wetlands that are home to many species of waterfowl. The hike doesn't involve serious elevation gains or losses.

User Groups: Hikers, horses, and mountain bikes. No dogs. No wheelchair facilities.

Permits: No permits are required. A state park day-use fee of $5 per vehicle is charged at the entrance station. Get receipt to park at different sites.

Maps: A brochure and map are available for a fee at park headquarters or by contacting the state parks district office. For a topographic map, ask the USGS for San Quentin.

Directions: Take U.S. 101 to San Rafael and the exit for North San Pedro. Take that exit and drive east four miles to park. At the fork (with a kiosk and campground on right), stay left and drive one mile (past the picnic areas on the left) to the ranger station, on the right, and the trailheads.

Alternate directions if arriving from the south/San Francisco: From the Golden Gate Bridge, continue north on U.S. 101 for 11.5 miles and the exit for Central San Rafael. Take that exit for 0.2 mile to (second right) 2nd Street. Turn right at 2nd Street and drive (becomes 3rd Street) 0.7 mile (shopping center on right) and continue ahead 5.2 miles (slow down, speed trap at curves, then you'll pass Loch Lomond on right) to park entrance; trailheads, campground on left access roads, blufftop picnic sites on right.

Contact: China Camp State Park, 415/456-0766; California State Parks, Marin District, 415/898-4362, www.parks.ca.gov.

32 PATRICK'S POINT

5.0 mi/2.5 hr 

in China Camp State Park east of San Rafael

Map 7.1, page 289

A stroke of genius by a state park ranger has created the Bay Area's greatest new lookout. In this case, the strokes of genius were made by a chainsaw. Ranger Patrick Robards, a fire science specialist, ordered a hilltop grove of eucalyptus taken out at China Camp State Park. The result at this spot is a jaw-dropping, five-bridge view of the bay and the region's mountain peaks, as well as a Marin-360 that will have you wishing your neck could full-pivot swivel. So, we named the spot Patrick's Point, and the name has stuck.

This trip starts with the drive on North San Pedro Road from San Rafael out to the Marin shoreline along San Pablo Bay. When you reach a fork to a ranger kiosk, instead stay left on the main road (turning right to the kiosk will take you to the park's campground entrance). Continue on the main road past the sensational picnic areas (on the left, at water's edge) to the turnoff on the right to the ranger station. This is your starting point. From here, it is a 2.5-mile loop with a 500-foot climb to McNear's Ridge and Patrick's Point.

Near the ranger station, with the park map in hand, start at the Shoreline trailhead. Take the Shoreline Trail north (you'll have good views of the San Pablo Bay shore) to the Oak Ridge Trail. Turn left on the Oak Ridge Trail and climb steadily to a junction with the McNear's Fire Trail. Turn right and you pop out on top. Note that on the park map, the lookout is not marked.

What a view: On clear days, you can see the Bay Bridge, the Richmond-San Rafael Bridge, the Carquinez Bridge, the Benicia Bridge, and the tops of the Golden Gate Bridge. We've seen crystal clear days from this lookout where it seemed you could take a running start and then leap across the bay and land on Point Pinole.

User Groups: Hikers, horses, and mountain bikes. No dogs. No wheelchair facilities.

Permits: No permits are required. A fee of $5 per vehicle is charged at China Camp Village. Keep receipt to park at different sites.

Maps: A brochure and map are available for a fee at park headquarters or by contacting the state parks district office. For a topographic map, ask the USGS for San Quentin.

Directions: Take U.S. 101 to San Rafael and the exit for North San Pedro. Take that exit and drive east four miles to park. At the fork (with a kiosk and campground on right), stay left and drive one mile (past the picnic areas on the left) to the ranger station, on the right, and the trailheads.

Alternate directions if arriving from the south/San Francisco: From the Golden Gate Bridge, continue north on U.S. 101 for 11.5 miles and the exit for Central San Rafael. Take that exit for 0.2 mile to (second right) 2nd Street. Turn right at 2nd Street and drive (becomes 3rd Street) 0.7 mile (shopping center on right) and continue ahead 5.2 miles (slow down, speed trap at curves, then you'll pass Loch Lomond on right) to park entrance; trailheads, campground on left access roads, blufftop picnic sites on right.

Contact: China Camp State Park, 415/456-0766; California State Parks, Marin District, 415/898-4362, www.parks.ca.gov.

33 MARTIN GRIFFIN PRESERVE/AUDUBON CANYON RANCH TRAIL

0.4 mi/0.25 hr 2 8

in Martin Griffin Preserve near Bolinas Lagoon

Map 7.1, page 289 BEST

In most years, Audubon Canyon is a slice of paradise. This is the number one habitat on the Pacific Coast to view herons and egrets, those large, graceful seabirds, as they court, mate, nest, and rear their young. In some years, though (usually in drought), the birds have not shown up in significant enough numbers to make the trip, and worse, to open the property to the public. In some years, there have been no birds and the preserve remains closed.

From headquarters, the hike is short with a 200-foot climb that requires about 20 minutes to reach the canyon overlook. Benches are provided for rest stops. Scopes are installed at the top to peer across the valley and zero in on the giant nests in the redwoods. Bird-watchers might want to repeat this great trip again and again, tracking the mating process of the great birds. The ritual starts when the male offers the female a twig. If the offer is accepted, the two then build a nest together. If rebuffed, the male then seeks another mate. Not much different than humans, eh? May and June are usually the best times to come. In May, the eggs start hatching, and by June, there can be as many as 200 hatchlings in the different nests. They eagerly await breakfast, lunch, and dinner, which are provided when their huge parents return from Bolinas Lagoon and vomit the goodies all over the nest. Hey, what's for dessert? First flight is an amazing event, when the young birds are given the heave-ho and have about 100 feet to figure how this flying thing works.

Note: Martin Griffin Preserve was renamed to honor Marty Griffin and recognize his role in protecting the Marin coast. For 40 years, it was known as Bolinas Lagoon Preserve of Audubon Canyon Ranch. The preserve is open only on weekends and holidays (10am-4pm, mid-Mar.-mid-July).

User Groups: Hikers only. No dogs, horses, or mountain bikes. No wheelchair facilities.

Permits: Entrance to the ranch is free, but donations are requested; a $15 donation from families is suggested.

Maps: A small trail map and brochure are available at ranch headquarters. For a topographic map, ask the USGS for Bolinas.

Directions: From San Francisco, take U.S. 101 north over the Golden Gate Bridge and continue four miles to Marin and to Exit 445B for Highway 1/Stinson Beach. Take that exit and continue west for one mile to the stoplight at a T intersection (Tam Junction) for Shoreline Highway/Highway 1. Turn left on Shoreline Highway and drive 11 miles to Stinson Beach. Continue north on Highway 1 for 3.5 miles to the preserve entrance gate on the right.

Contact: Audubon Canyon Ranch, 415/868-9244, www.egret.org.

34 CATARACT FALLS

2.5 mi/1.5 hr 3 10

on Mount Tamalpais at Alpine Lake Dam

Map 7.1, page 289

Cataract Falls is not a single waterfall, but a series of cascades that rushes down a beautifully wooded canyon set in the northwest slopes of Mount Tamalpais. For those who search out the top-rated hikes, there's many a day when this trail is definitely a 10. At times, when the canyon is flush with water, it can rate as one of the best winter day hikes in California. In summer and fall, when the creek is rendered a trickle or even goes dry, it's more like a 7.

From the trailhead at the south end of Alpine Lake (elevation 644 feet), you face a 750-foot climb over the span of just a mile to reach the centerpiece falls at 1,400 feet. Some hikers take the route from the Laurel Dell trailhead, which has a 240-foot drop over 0.4 mile. The canyon's prettiest falls are at an elevation range of about 1,200 to 1,400 feet.

The trail starts by contouring along a cove of Alpine Lake. It then rises from the lake, climbing up into a lush canyon where there seems to be one small waterfall after another. These are not big free falls like in Yosemite, but rather small cascades, surrounded by luxuriant riparian beauty. Compared to almost anywhere in the Bay Area environs after such recent heavy rains, the collective beauty can seem nonpareil.

In late winter, especially when the skies have just cleared after heavy rains, the cascades in this canyon can look like something found in Hawaii. This is particularly true when rays of sunlight catch the droplets of water just right and the refracted light makes them sparkle. From top to bottom, there's one cascade after another, crowned by a silvery chute pouring into a plunge pool. After getting your fill of this sight, return the way you came.

The trailhead is a few hundred yards past the west side of the dam at Alpine Lake. This is the best-known fall in the region, and parking along the road is extremely limited, often making for a frustrating encounter on weekends, especially Sundays in winter after a Saturday rain.

User Groups: Hikers and dogs. No horses or mountain bikes. No wheelchair facilities. No swimming or wading.

Permits: No permits are required. Groups are limited to 19 people. Parking and access are free.

Maps: A hiking and biking map is available for a fee from the Marin Municipal Water District. For a topographic map, ask the USGS for Bolinas.

Directions: From San Francisco, take U.S. 101 over the Golden Gate Bridge and continue 7.5 miles to the exit for Sir Francis Drake Boulevard. Take that exit (toward San Anselmo) and continue 0.4 mile and merge with Sir Francis Drake Boulevard. Continue 3.5 miles (get in left lane) to Center Boulevard. Turn left on center and drive 1.7 miles into Fairfax (becomes Broadway Boulevard) to Bolinas Road. Turn left on Bolinas Road and drive eight miles, cross Alpine Dam, and continue a short distance to the trailhead on the left. Park on the road's shoulder (usually on the right). Leave at least six feet of clearance between your car and the center of the road.

Note: The parking area fills early on peak weekends in winter and spring.

Contact: Sky Oaks Ranger Station, 415/945-1180; Marin Municipal Water District, 415/945-1195, www.marinwater.org; Mount Tamalpais State Park, 415/388-2070; California State Parks, Marin District, 415/898-4362, www.parks.ca.gov.

35 LAUREL DELL LOOP

2.5 mi/1.5 hr 1 8

in Marin Water District on flank of Mount Tamalpais

Map 7.1, page 289

Laura Dell trailhead provides the easiest route to Cataract Falls. Instead of the climb from Bolinas-Fairfax Road and Alpine Lake (see the previous listing), here you start high and glide down to the upper set of falls, then return via a gentle loop. The trailhead is at 1,640 feet. Walk down fire road 0.7 mile to the Laurel Dell picnic site, then turn left on Cataract Trail for a one-mile descent into the steep canyon to see Cataract Falls. You'll descend past a series of tiny waterfalls in a lush setting. When running at full strength, the cascades are a precious sight. The canyon's prettiest falls are at an elevation range of about 1,200 feet. Many prefer first sight of the falls as a frontal, and that's when the trailhead at Bolinas-Fairfax Road/Alpine Lake is more popular.

To do this loop, continue along the Cataract Trail to the High Marsh Trail. Turn right on the High Marsh Trail, hike onward, and turn right at any of the next three trail intersections to return to the Laurel Dell trailhead. Of the three choices, the second makes the best return loop, as the short cutoff will put you within a few hundred yards of the trailhead.

User Groups: Hikers and dogs. No horses or mountain bikes. No wheelchair facilities.

Permits: No permits are required. Parking and access are free.

Maps: A brochure with map of Mount Tamalpais State Park is available for a small fee at the visitors center or by writing to the address below. For topographic maps, ask the USGS for Bolinas and San Rafael.

Directions: From San Francisco, take U.S. 101 north over the Golden Gate Bridge and continue four miles to Marin and the exit for Highway 1/Stinson Beach. Take that exit and continue west for one mile to the stoplight at T intersection for Shoreline Highway/Highway 1. Turn left on Shoreline Highway and drive 2.6 miles to the Panoramic Highway. Bear right on Panoramic Highway and drive (at junction for Muir Woods, continue straight) 5.2 miles to Pantoll Road. Bear right on Pantoll Road and go 1.4 miles to T intersection at Rock Spring and Ridgecrest Boulevard. Turn left and drive 1.4 miles to trailhead (look for fire road) on right.

Must-do summit: From Laurel Dell, turn left on Ridgecrest and drive 4.5 miles to East Peak.

Contact: Mount Tamalpais State Park, 415/388-2070; California State Parks, Marin District, 415/898-4362, www.parks.ca.gov.

36 O'ROURKE'S BENCH/ ROCK SPRINGS

0.6 mi/0.5 hr — 1 — 10

in Marin Water District on flank of Mount Tamalpais

Map 7.1, page 289

One of the best easy walks in the Bay Area with a world-class payoff is the stroll to O'Rourke's Bench. On a clear day, the view seems to span to infinity. From this perch at 2,040 feet, coastal hills and valley plunge at your feet to the Pacific Ocean. In one turn of the head, you can take in unbelievable miles of sunlit charm, up and down the coast, across to San Francisco, and on crystal days, to the Mount Diablo summit. No matter where you live, your age or level of outdoor orientation, O'Rourke's Bench is a must-do.

The walk: From Rock Spring Parking (1,972-foot elevation), cross Ridgecrest and look for the trail on the south side of the road (at a junction with Pantoll Road). From here, it's an easy 0.3-mile walk (about 15 minutes) to the stone bench; a gentle uphill climb of 70 feet, where you emerge from the woods to the bench and lookout. You'll find a treasured plaque that says: "Give me these hills and the friends I love. I ask no other heaven. To our Dad O'Rourke, in joyous celebration of his 76th birthday, Feb. 25th, 1927. From the friends to whom he showed this heaven."

It's always good: Even when the coast is buried in fog, the lookout perch is high enough to usually be above the stratus layer. It can be like peering across the top of a gorgeous sea of fog. On clear days, the ocean can sparkle in refracted silvers. Plus it can be one of the best places anywhere to see a sunset. In addition, a network of trails provides a mosaic of connected routes out of Rock Spring, Mountain Theater, Bootjack, and Pantoll trailheads on the west flank of Mount Tamalpais.

User Groups: Hikers only. No dogs, horses, or mountain bikes. No wheelchair facilities.

Permits: No permits are required. Parking and access are free.

Maps: A hiking and biking map is available for a fee from the Marin Municipal Water District. For a topographic map, ask the USGS for San Rafael.

Directions: From San Francisco, take U.S. 101 north over the Golden Gate Bridge and continue four miles to Marin and the exit for Highway 1/Stinson Beach. Take that exit and continue west for one mile to the stoplight at T intersection for Shoreline Highway/Highway 1. Turn left on Shoreline Highway and drive 2.6

miles to the Panoramic Highway. Bear right on Panoramic Highway and drive (at junction, continue straight) 5.2 miles to Pantoll Road. At Pantoll, bear right on Pantoll Road and go 1.4 miles to Rock Spring and a T intersection with Ridgecrest Boulevard. Continue straight ahead to parking for Rock Spring trailhead. If full, turn right on Ridgecrest and go 0.25 mile to Mountain Theater.

Contact: Mount Tamalpais State Park, 415/388-2070; California State Parks, Marin District, 415/898-4362, www.parks.ca.gov.

37 BARTH'S RETREAT

2.2 mi/1.0 hr 

in Marin Municipal Water District at Mount Tamalpais

Map 7.1, page 289

From Rock Spring (1,972 feet), you'll find a trailhead at the north end of the parking lot. From here, walk 0.1 mile (you'll pass a junction/trailhead for Cataract Trail on your left), then another 0.1 mile to a fork (1,965 feet) with the Simmons Trail and a cutoff on the right that goes to parking for Mountain Theater. Continue ahead on the Simmons Trail for 0.9 mile to Barth's Retreat (1,970 feet). Bring your trail lunch. This is one of Mount Tam's great walk-in picnic sites. Barth, by the way, was one Emil Barth, a prolific musician and hiker who constructed a camp here in the early 20th century. This route connects to an inland network of trails, from which you can explore for many treks, or simply return when ready.

User Groups: Hikers and leashed dogs. No horses or mountain bikes. No wheelchair facilities. Road is gated and locked at sunset.

Permits: No permits are required. Parking and access are free.

Maps: A hiking and biking map is available for a fee from the Marin Municipal Water District. For a topographic map, ask the USGS for San Rafael.

Directions: From San Francisco, take U.S. 101 north over the Golden Gate Bridge and continue four miles to Marin and the exit for Highway 1/Stinson Beach. Take that exit and continue west for one mile to the stoplight at T intersection for Shoreline Highway/Highway 1. Turn left on Shoreline Highway and drive 2.6 miles to the Panoramic Highway. Bear right on Panoramic Highway and drive (at junction, continue straight) 5.2 miles to Pantoll Road. At Pantoll, bear right on Pantoll Road and go 1.4 miles to Rock Spring and a T intersection with Ridgecrest Boulevard. Continue straight ahead to parking for Rock Spring trailhead. If full, turn right on Ridgecrest and go 0.25 mile to parking for Mountain Theater.

Contact: Sky Oaks Ranger Station, 415/945-1180; Marin Municipal Water District, 415/945-1195, www.marinwater.org.

38 MOUNTAIN THEATER/ WEST POINT INN

3.4 mi/1.5 hr 1 7

in Marin Municipal Water District on Mount Tamalpais

Map 7.1, page 289

High on the southern slope of Mount Tamalpais, West Point Inn has provided a destination with sensational views and a quiet refuge at night for more than 100 years. From parking at Mountain Theater (elevation 2,060 feet), take the Rock Spring Trail for 1.7 miles to West Point Inn (1,785 feet). The trail is an easy glide. Your destination is West Point Inn. At certain lookout points from the inn, the views are great. You tower over San Francisco Bay, the Marin Headlands and across the Pacific. On late nights with a full moon, a layer of fog below can shimmer in silvers. The view nearly equals that from 2,571-foot East Peak, but without the weekend crowd around the Gardner Lookout.

It was first built in 1904 for those who rode up from Mill Valley on the "Crookedest Railroad in the World." That old railroad line is now a great mountain bike trek, and several hiking trails lead to West Point Inn as well. The inn is run as a co-op and, like a step back in time, has no electricity.

User Groups: Hikers and leashed dogs. No horses or mountain bikes. No wheelchair facilities.

Permits: No permits are required. Parking and access are free. Road is gated and locked at sunset.

Maps: A brochure with map of Mount Tamalpais State Park is available for a small fee at the visitors center or by writing to the address below. For a topographic map, ask the USGS for San Rafael. Much of this trail is on Marin Municipal Water District land; contact that agency to obtain a detailed map for a fee.

Directions: From San Francisco, take U.S. 101 north over the Golden Gate Bridge and continue four miles to the exit for Highway 1/Stinson Beach. Take that exit and continue west for one mile to the stoplight at T intersection for Shoreline Highway/Highway 1. Turn left on Shoreline Highway and drive 2.6 miles to the Panoramic Highway. Bear right on Panoramic Highway and drive 5.3 miles to Pantoll. Bear right on Pantoll Road and drive 1.4 miles to a T with Ridgecrest Boulevard (Rock Spring parking and trailhead is directly ahead). Turn right on Ridgecrest and go 0.25 mile to the Mountain Theater trailhead.

Contact: Sky Oaks Ranger Station, 415/945-1180; Marin Municipal Water District, 415/945-1195, www.marinwater.org; Mount Tamalpais State Park, 415/388-2070; California State Parks, Marin District, 415/898-4362, www.parks.ca.gov; West Point Inn, 415/388-9955 (not for reservations), http://westpointinn.com.

39 EAST PEAK MOUNT TAMALPAIS

0.4 mi/0.5-1.0 hr

in Mount Tamalpais State Park

Map 7.1, page 289 BEST

Mount Tam is one of those rare spots that projects a feeling of power, and while standing on its highest point, you can sense that power flowing right through you. From Mount Tam's 2,571-foot East Peak there is no better place in the Bay Area to watch the sun set. How it makes you feel can stay with you for years. The hike is very short (after all, a parking lot is set right at the foot of the summit trail) but is quite steep. The trail rises about 330 feet to the top, at an elevation of 2,571 feet. An old lookout station is positioned at the summit, and hikers usually try to find a perch as close as possible to the top.

To the east, the bay resembles the Mediterranean Sea, like an azure pool sprinkled with islands. And at night, the lights of the bridges and the surrounding cities can give the Bay Area an almost surreal look. The true magic happens at sunset, particularly on foggy days. The peak stands well above the top of the fog layer, and when the fiery sun dips into that low stratus to the west, orange light can be refracted for hundreds of miles around. Witness this stunning sight even one time, and you will gain a new perspective about what might be possible in this world.

User Groups: Hikers only. Dogs are permitted on the paved trail but not on the mountaintop overlook. No horses or mountain bikes. No wheelchair access on the trail, but good views are available from the wheelchair-accessible parking lot. ADA access is available in the park.

Permits: No permits are required. A parking fee of $8 per vehicle is charged.

Maps: A brochure with map is available for a small fee from Mount Tamalpais State at the visitors center adjacent to the parking area. For a topographic map, ask the USGS for San Rafael.

Directions: From San Francisco, take U.S. 101 north over the Golden Gate Bridge and continue four miles to the exit for Highway 1/Stinson Beach. Take that exit and continue west for one mile to the stoplight at T intersection for Shoreline Highway/Highway 1. Turn left on Shoreline Highway and drive 2.6 miles to the Panoramic Highway. Bear right on Panoramic

Highway and drive 5.3 miles to Pantoll. Bear right on Pantoll Road and drive 1.4 miles to a T with Ridgecrest Boulevard. Turn right on Ridgecrest and go three miles to East Peak and parking. The road dead-ends at the parking area at the base of the summit and trailhead.

Contact: Mount Tamalpais State Park, 415/388-2070; California State Parks, Marin District, 415/898-4362, www.parks.ca.gov.

40 INSPIRATION POINT

2.6 mi/1.0 hr 2 10

in Mount Tamalpais State Park

Map 7.1, page 289

Inspiration Point provides an alternative to the East Peak of Mount Tamalpais. You can get a similar kind of magic without all the people. Park at the lot on the summit. Instead of heading up to the East Peak after parking, hike the fire road, Eldridge Grade. The trail wraps around the northern flank of the East Peak, then makes a hairpin turn to the left around North Knee, set at 2,000 feet. At this point, a view below of the bay comes into your scope. Inspiration Peak awaits just down the road. At the hairpin right turn, take the short cutoff trail on the left, and you will quickly reach the top at 2,040 feet. This is a vantage point for miles and miles of charmed views. All can seem enchanted. The elevation loss and gain is roughly 200 feet. Much of this trail is not on state park land but land managed by the Marin Municipal Water District.

User Groups: Hikers, dogs, and mountain bikes. No horses. No wheelchair access on the trail, but good views are available from the wheelchair-accessible parking lot.

Permits: No permits are required. A parking fee of $8 per vehicle is charged at the summit parking lot.

Maps: A brochure with map is available for a small fee from Mount Tamalpais State at the visitors center adjacent to the parking area. For a topographic map, ask the USGS for San Rafael.

Directions: From San Francisco, take U.S. 101 north over the Golden Gate Bridge and continue four miles to the exit for Highway 1/Stinson Beach. Take that exit and continue west for one mile to the stoplight at T intersection for Shoreline Highway/Highway 1. Turn left on Shoreline Highway and drive 2.6 miles to the Panoramic Highway. Bear right on Panoramic Highway and drive 5.3 miles to Pantoll. Bear right on Pantoll Road and drive 1.4 miles to a T with Ridgecrest Boulevard. Turn right on Ridgecrest and go three miles to East Peak and parking. The road dead-ends at the parking area at the base of the summit and trailhead.

Contact: Mount Tamalpais State Park, 415/388-2070; California State Parks, Marin District, 415/898-4362, www.parks.ca.gov.

41 PHOENIX LAKE LOOP

4.5 mi/1.5 hr 2 9

on Marin Municipal Watershed near Ross

Map 7.1, page 289

Trailhead parking is terrible, but the hike is great. The latter trumps the former as the Marin Municipal Water District told us this is one of the most popular hikes in the Mount Tamalpais Watershed. The little 25-acre jewel set in a pocket just west of the town of Ross is indeed well loved. If you get a parking spot, something of a miracle on weekends, you'll see the gate, and from there, it's an 0.3-mile walk on a fire road to the spillway (pretty in winter) and on to Phoenix Lake (174 feet elevation). The trail skirts above the lake to the right. Many just go to the lake, have a picnic, sit on one of the benches, fish a little, and then head back. For a loop around the lake, continue ahead to a major junction, the Phoenix Junction, one mile in (196 feet). Turn left on the Ord Trail, which skirts above the southern shore of the lake for 1.1 miles, then turns left (along the shoreline) for 0.7 mile and reaches the spur that takes you back to parking. The lake is pretty, the views of the watershed are great, and in spring, this one is spectacular.

Note: From Phoenix Junction, you can instead hike straight ahead to Lagunitas and Bon Tempe Lakes or turn right to the watershed interior and a junction called Six Points. Both are great hikes.

User Groups: Hikers and leashed dogs. Horses and mountain bikes restricted access to roads only. No wheelchair facilities. No swimming or wading.

Permits: No permits are required. Groups are limited to 19 people. Parking and access are free. Park closes at sunset and the parking lot is locked.

Maps: A hiking and biking map is available for a fee from the Marin Municipal Water District. For a topographic map, ask the USGS for San Rafael.

Directions: From San Francisco, take U.S. 101 over the Golden Gate Bridge and continue 7.5 miles to the exit for Sir Francis Drake Boulevard. Take that exit (toward San Anselmo) and continue 0.4 mile and merge with Sir Francis Drake Boulevard. Continue west for 2.5 miles to Lagunitas Road. Turn left on Lagunitas Road and drive 1.1 miles and park along the road. Parking is extremely limited, space for about 20 cars, and near a residential area with No Parking signs in front of homes. For the best approach, park outside the immediate area and walk in.

Contact: Sky Oaks Ranger Station, 415/945-1180; Marin Municipal Water District, 415/945-1195, www.marinwater.org.

42 DAWN FALLS

2.2 mi/1.0 hr

in Baltimore Canyon Open Space Preserve near Larkspur

Map 7.1, page 289

A pretty walk in the woods leads to one of Marin's romantic spots, Dawn Falls, your destination and reward in Baltimore Canyon Open Space. When refreshed by rain, Dawn Falls pours in a narrow stream over the brink and falls 25 feet in a silvery chute to the rocks below. It is named "Dawn Falls" because there are spring days when the early morning sunlight catches the water just right and refracts in color. Dry weather reduces the cascade to a trickle, and in drought, it goes dry.

From the parking area, it's a few minutes' walk down to Larkspur Creek, across the bridge to the junction with the Dawn Falls Trail. Turn right and you are on your way. The trail runs along the creek at the base of Baltimore Canyon (continue straight at a trail junction), then climbs 300 feet to the falls. You emerge on the left side, with a full-frontal view.

Note: There is no formal parking area, only limited street parking. In winter and early spring when the waterfall is flowing, the street parking can fill. Park in Larkspur instead and walk in.

User Groups: Hikers and dogs. No mountain bikes or horses. No wheelchair facilities.

Permits: No permits are required. Groups are limited to 19 people. Parking and access are free.

Maps: A hiking and biking map is available for a fee from the Marin Municipal Water District. For a topographic map, ask the USGS for San Rafael.

Directions: Take U.S. 101 in Marin to Corte Madera and the exit for Paradise/Tamalpais Drive. Take that exit to Tamalpais Drive, turn west and drive about a mile to Corte Madera Avenue. Turn right and drive (the road becomes Magnolia) about 0.6 mile to Madrone Avenue (the road narrows). Turn left on Madrone Avenue and drive 0.8 mile to the trailhead, at road's end.

Contact: Marin County Parks, 415/473-6387, www.marincountyparks.org.

43 BOOTJACK: MATT DAVIS TO WEST POINT INN

3.6 mi/2.0 hr 3 9

in Mount Tamalpais State Park

Map 7.1, page 289

With the campground at Bootjack, the Matt Davis Trail takes on new significance. The trailhead (1,400 feet) is on the north side of the Panoramic Highway. The trail is routed to a drainage for oft-dry Rattlesnake Creek. You then hike through hardwood forest to a trail junction (1,330 feet) near Laguna Creek, 1.3 miles in, with the Nora Trail. Turn left here and climb 455 feet over the course of 0.5 mile, through a series of switchbacks, to West Point Inn. The inn and its cabins were built at the turn of the 20th century and, like a trip in a time machine, have no electricity.

User Groups: Hikers only. No dogs, horses, or mountain bikes. No wheelchair facilities.

Permits: No permits are required. A parking fee of $8 per vehicle is charged.

Maps: A brochure with map is available for a small fee from Mount Tamalpais State at the visitors center adjacent to the parking area. For a topographic map, ask the USGS for San Rafael.

Directions: From San Francisco, take U.S. 101 north over the Golden Gate Bridge and continue four miles to Marin and the exit for Highway 1/Stinson Beach. Take that exit and continue west for 1 mile to the stoplight at T intersection for Shoreline Highway/Highway 1. Turn left on Shoreline Highway and drive 2.6 miles to the Panoramic Highway. At Panoramic Highway, bear right and drive (at junction for Muir Woods, continue straight) 4.7 miles to Bootjack on right.

Note: This parking area fills early on peak weekends in winter and spring.

Contact: Mount Tamalpais State Park, 415/388-2070; California State Parks, Marin District, 415/898-4362, www.parks.ca.gov; reserve cabins online at http://westpointinn.com.

44 PANTOLL: MATT DAVIS/ COAST TRAIL

6.4 mi/3.0 hr 2 10

on Mount Tamalpais

Map 7.1, page 289

We know people search through the book for hikes that are rated as 2s and 3s for difficulty, and 9s or 10s for scenic beauty. This is one of those hikes. Just pick a clear day. The reward is heart-touching views of the Pacific Ocean. There are places where you can stop, spread your arms wide toward the ocean, and feel as if the entire world is within your grasp. From Pantoll parking and staging area (1,500 feet), cross the road (careful on weekends) for the trailhead for the Matt Davis Trail. In turn, the Matt Davis Trail leads 1.6 miles into the woods, generally where you contour along the foothills to a trail junction (1,540 feet) with the Coast Trail. Here you turn right on the Coast Trail and climb 280 feet over the course of 1.6 miles to the Willow Camp Fire Road (1,820 feet). In the process, you will have a series of coastal lookouts to the west. The Coast Trail here generally parallels Ridgecrest Boulevard and passes just below Ballou Point. Return when ready.

User Groups: Hikers only. No dogs, horses, or mountain bikes. No wheelchair facilities.

Permits: No permits are required. A parking fee of $8 per vehicle is charged.

Maps: A brochure with map is available for a small fee from Mount Tamalpais State at the visitors center adjacent to the parking area. For a topographic map, ask the USGS for San Rafael.

Directions: From San Francisco, take U.S. 101 north over the Golden Gate Bridge and continue four miles to Marin and the exit for Highway 1/Stinson Beach. Take that exit and continue west for one mile to the stoplight at a T intersection for Shoreline Highway/Highway 1. Turn left on Shoreline Highway and drive 2.6 miles to the Panoramic Highway. Bear right on Panoramic Highway and drive 5.2 miles to Pantoll (at the four-way junction, continue straight). Turn left into the Pantoll parking area.

Note: The parking area fills early on peak weekends in winter and spring.

Contact: Mount Tamalpais State Park, 415/388-2070; California State Parks, Marin District, 415/898-4362, www.parks.ca.gov.

45 STEEP RAVINE TRAIL

3.4 mi/1.5 hr 2 10

on Mount Tamalpais

Map 7.1, page 289

Just add rain, and in a hike at Steep Ravine, the divine spirit of nature will baptize you. This is the prettiest canyon in Marin and one of the prettiest walks, when wet, that is, anywhere. From Pantoll, the trailhead is at the far west end of the parking area. From here, you descend quickly, including with steps, into the lush canyon. You'll arrive at the bottom of the ravine at pretty Webb Creek. Redwoods tower over you, and at times, the forest canopy closes off the sky. In some spots, ferns line the canyon walls. The trail follows Webb Creek, crossing the stream eight times in all. In less than a mile, you'll reach a drop-off with a ladder, and in high flows, this brink produces a small but pretty waterfall. The trail continues to a historic dam, 1.7 miles in, just downstream of the junction (and bridge) with the Dipsea Trail (580 feet elevation). It's a fine picnic site. Look close and you might see small fish in the pool. Head back when ready, a climb of 920 feet in 1.7 miles.

In the most violent rainstorms, this place is a refuge of peace. This is one of the few hikes best done during a rainstorm, and if that is not for you, try to time it just after heavy rain. In the canyon, the forest canopy protects you from a direct assault from the raindrops. Everything becomes vibrant with life as it drips with water.

User Groups: Hikers only. No dogs, horses, or mountain bikes. No wheelchair facilities.

Permits: No permits are required. A parking fee of $8 per vehicle is charged.

Maps: A brochure with map is available for a small fee from Mount Tamalpais State at the visitors center adjacent to the parking area. For a topographic map, ask the USGS for San Rafael.

Directions: From San Francisco, take U.S. 101 north over the Golden Gate Bridge and continue four miles to Marin and the exit for Highway 1/Stinson Beach. Take that exit and continue west for one mile to the stoplight at a T intersection for Shoreline Highway/Highway 1. Turn left on Shoreline Highway and drive 2.6 miles to the Panoramic Highway. Bear right on Panoramic Highway and drive 5.2 miles to Pantoll (at the four-way junction, continue straight). Turn left into the Pantoll parking area.

Note: The parking area fills early on peak weekends in winter and spring.

Contact: Mount Tamalpais State Park, 415/388-2070; California State Parks, Marin District, 415/898-4362, www.parks.ca.gov.

46 COAST VIEW TRAIL

5.2 mi/1.5 hr 

on Mount Tamalpais

Map 7.1, page 289

The Coast View Trail out of Pantoll has been a success in its test as a new multiuse trail at Mount Tamalpais State Park. Within five minutes, by bike or on foot, you will realize that state park rangers turned what was a good idea at headquarters into a stroke of genius in the field.

After parking, elevation 1,499 feet, face the ocean with the campground on your left and look for the service road ahead and to the left that heads west (it passes just above the Steep Ravine trailhead). This is how the trip starts, on a road. You will hike (or ride) on pavement a short distance to a ranger service area and then continue as the road turns into a dirt fire road. In another 30 seconds, you emerge at a clearing and with it, get the trail's first great lookout of the ocean and San Francisco. From here, continue straight on the fire road, heading southwest toward Muir Beach. The service road continues 0.6 mile, crosses the Dipsea Trail (1,200 feet), and then becomes the multiuse Coast View Trail. This trail is about half the width of a fire road, what mountain bikers would call a double-track. It is wide enough to pass on without those surprise "showdown" moments of truth with other trail users, yet narrow enough for an intimate feel. It is an easy downhill glide two miles to a foothill ridge (and gate) that overlooks Muir Beach (it's less than another mile to Highway 1). Return when ready, a climb of about 900 feet in 2.6 miles.

User Groups: Hikers and mountain bikes. No dogs or horses. No wheelchair facilities.

Permits: No permits are required. A parking fee of $8 per vehicle is charged.

Maps: A brochure with map is available for a small fee from Mount Tamalpais State at the visitors center adjacent to the parking area. For a topographic map, ask the USGS for San Rafael.

Directions: From San Francisco, take U.S. 101 north over the Golden Gate Bridge and continue four miles to Marin and the exit for Highway 1/Stinson Beach. Take that exit and continue west for one mile to the stoplight at a T intersection for Shoreline Highway/Highway 1. Turn left on Shoreline Highway and drive 2.6 miles to the Panoramic Highway. Bear right on Panoramic Highway and drive 5.2 miles to Pantoll (at the four-way junction, continue straight). Turn left into the Pantoll parking area.

The parking area fills early on peak weekends in winter and spring.

Contact: Mount Tamalpais State Park, 415/388-2070; California State Parks, Marin District, 415/898-4362, www.parks.ca.gov.

47 MOUNTAIN HOME

2.4 mi/1.0 hr

in Mount Tamalpais State Park

Map 7.1, page 289

This 1.2-mile hike at Mount Tamalpais ends at an inn, called the Tourist Club (private), perched on a mountainside. Park at the lot at Mountain Home, along Panoramic Highway. Take Panoramic Trail 0.4 mile (it parallels Panoramic Highway) to its junction with Redwood Trail. Turn right on the Redwood Trail and then descend mile to the Tourist Club. This route laterals across the mountain slope before it drops into a pocket.

User Groups: Hikers only. No dogs, horses, or mountain bikes. No wheelchair facilities.

Permits: No permits are required. Parking and access are free.

Maps: A brochure with map of Mount Tamalpais State Park is available for a small fee at the visitors center or by writing to the address below. For a topographic map, ask the USGS for San Rafael.

Directions: From San Francisco, take U.S. 101 north over the Golden Gate Bridge and continue four miles to Marin and the exit for Highway 1/Stinson Beach. Take that exit and continue west for one mile to the stoplight at a T intersection for Shoreline Highway/Highway 1. Turn left on Shoreline Highway and drive 2.6 miles to the Panoramic Highway. Bear right on Panoramic Highway and drive 2.6 miles to Mountain Home. The trailhead for Panoramic Trail is on the west side of the road.

Note: The parking area fills early on peak weekends in winter and spring.

Contact: Mount Tamalpais State Park, 415/388-2070; California State Parks, Marin District, 415/898-4362, www.parks.ca.gov; Tourist Club, 415/388-9987, www.touristclubsf.org.

48 MUIR BEACH OVERLOOK AND OWL TRAIL

3.5 mi/1.5 hr 1 10

on the Marin coast south of Stinson Beach

Map 7.1, page 289

The view from Muir Beach Overlook is drop-dead beautiful, the kind of place that will melt the steel around the most armored souls. A trip to the Overlook, a hike on the adjacent Owl Trail, and a visit to nearby Slide Ranch and the tidal reef below can be one of the best ways to capture the sparkling day on the Marin coast.

The Owl Trail starts at the north side of the parking lot (440 feet elevation) and extends past Slide Ranch to a beach with an extended tidepool reef; 3.5 miles round-trip. From the trailhead at 440 feet, you descend 240 feet in a mile through chaparral with ocean views. The trail is routed through low-lying brush, which makes wearing shorts a prickly proposition. You then arrive at Slide Ranch. Slide Ranch is a small working farm, with chickens, sheep, goats, and more (we've seen ducks here that think they are chickens), that is accessible to the public making for a great family trip. You then pass giant cypress trees (where great horned owls can nest, hence the name Owl Trail) and sail down to the beach. A rope is often available to descend a short slippery spot to the beach. At the beach during low tides, you'll find an extended tidal reef where you can rock hop, find lots of little crabs, and have a picnic.

User Groups: Hikers only. No dogs, horses, or mountain bikes. The Muir Beach Overlook is wheelchair accessible, but Owl Trail is not.

Permits: No permits are required. Parking and access are free.

Maps: A brochure and map are available at the Marin Headlands Visitors Center or by contacting the Golden Gate National Recreation Area, Marin Headlands. For a topographic map, ask the USGS for Point Bonita.

Directions: From San Francisco, take U.S. 101 north over the Golden Gate Bridge and continue four miles to Marin and the exit for Highway 1/Stinson Beach. Take that exit and continue west for one mile to the stoplight at a T intersection for Shoreline Highway/Highway 1. Turn left on Shoreline Highway and drive to a signed turn for Muir Beach Overlook. Turn left at the Muir Beach Overlook and drive a short distance to the parking area. The trailhead may at first seem hidden. It is often unsigned but located at the north side of the parking area.

Contact: Muir Woods National Monument, Mill Valley, 415/388-2595, www.nps.gov/muwo; Golden Gate National Recreation Area, visitors center, 415/561-4700.

49 REDWOOD CREEK TRAIL

1.5 mi/1.0 hr 1 10

in Muir Woods National Monument

Map 7.1, page 289 BEST

The renovated Redwood Creek Trail is now a thing of beauty. Thousands of people take this walk amid the giant redwoods, and yet with the boardwalks, some paved trail, there is no damage to this beautiful landscape. From the visitors center, take the Redwood Creek Trail out along Redwood Creek for 0.5 mile to a junction with the Fern Creek Trail (more on this to come) and then continue another 0.2 mile to a bridge (actually, it is Bridge 4). Cross the bridge to the Hillside Trail, turn left and return back to the bridge (actually, Bridge 1) and the visitors center. If you have physically challenged members of your group, the loop can be cut short at two other bridges.

The Fern Creek option: You can turn this trip into a gorgeous three-mile loop and escape the crowds. From the visitors center, follow the Redwood Creek Trail to a junction with Fern Creek Trail on the right. Turn right and hike Fern Creek Trail to the junction with the Lost Trail on the right. Turn right, then climb about 500 feet up to the junction with Canopy View Trail (it used to be called Ocean View Trail). Turn right again onto Canopy View Trail and follow the trail down to return to the valley floor.

User Groups: Hikers only. No dogs (except for seeing-eye dogs), horses, or mountain bikes. The first section of the trail is wheelchair-accessible.

Permits: Reservations for parking or shuttles are required (www.gomuirwoods.com, $8 per vehicle, $3 per shuttle). An entry fee of $15 per person is charged (free for those age 15 and younger).

Maps: A brochure and map are available for a fee at the visitors center or by contacting Muir Woods National Monument. For a topographic map, ask the USGS for San Rafael.

Directions: From San Francisco, take U.S. 101 north over the Golden Gate Bridge and continue four miles to Marin and to Exit 445B for Highway 1/Stinson Beach. Take that exit and continue west for one mile to the stoplight at a T intersection (Tam Junction) for Shoreline Highway/Highway 1. Turn left on Shoreline Highway and drive 2.6 miles to the Panoramic Highway. Bear right on Panoramic Highway and drive 0.8 mile to a junction with Muir Woods Road. Turn left and go 1.5 miles to the park entrance road (Camp Eastwood Road). Turn right and drive 0.2 mile to the parking lot. Note that a shuttle is available in summer and may be required during high-use periods.

Contact: Muir Woods National Monument, Mill Valley, 415/388-2595, www.nps.gov/muwo; Golden Gate National Recreation Area, visitors center, 415/561-4700.

50 CANOPY VIEW TRAIL

3.4 mi/1.5 hr — 2 — 8

in Muir Woods National Monument

Map 7.1, page 289

This trail is worth knowing. When you arrive at Muir Woods and see tour buses shooting out people like popcorn from a popping machine, you'll be glad you read this. That is because Canopy View Trail provides the best chance of getting away from the crowds. After passing the visitors center and starting down the paved path on the valley floor, turn right on Canopy View Trail. In under a minute you will enter a different world, a world of solitude, beautiful redwoods, and, alas, a steep ascent.

From the valley floor, the trail heads up the east side of the canyon on a steady grade, steep enough to get you puffing. It climbs 570 feet in 1.2 miles. You rise above the valley to where you can look down into a sea of redwoods. To complete the loop, turn left on Lost Trail, elevation 750 feet, which descends quite steeply over just 0.4 mile back to the valley floor, at 300 feet. There you turn left on Fern Creek Trail. Turn left onto the main trail to return to headquarters. It's a great escape.

Avid hikers who know the area will remember that this was once called the "Ocean View Trail," even though there was no ocean view. Some wanted the name changed to the Panoramic Trail. We like the new name, Canopy View Trail.

User Groups: Hikers only. No dogs (except for seeing-eye dogs), horses, or mountain bikes. The first section of the trail is wheelchair-accessible.

Permits: Reservations for parking or shuttles are required (www.gomuirwoods.com, $8 per vehicle, $3 per shuttle). An entry fee of $15 per person is charged (free for those age 15 and younger).

Maps: A brochure and map are available for a fee at the visitors center or by contacting Muir Woods National Monument. For a topographic map, ask the USGS for San Rafael.

Directions: From San Francisco, take U.S. 101 north over the Golden Gate Bridge and continue four miles to Marin and to Exit 445B for Highway 1/Stinson Beach. Take that exit and continue west for one mile to the stoplight at a T intersection (Tam Junction) for Shoreline Highway/Highway 1. Turn left on Shoreline Highway and drive 2.6 miles to the Panoramic Highway. Bear right on Panoramic Highway and drive 0.8 mile to a junction with Muir

Woods Road. Turn left and go 1.5 miles to the park entrance road (Camp Eastwood Road). Turn right and drive 0.2 mile to the parking lot. Note that a shuttle is available in summer and may be required during high-use periods. **Contact:** Muir Woods National Monument, Mill Valley, 415/388-2595, www.nps.gov/muwo; Golden Gate National Recreation Area, visitors center, 415/561-4700.

51 DIPSEA TRAIL

7.5 mi one-way/3.5 hr

on Mount Tamalpais from Mill Valley to Stinson Beach

Map 7.1, page 289

In your first steps on the Dipsea Trail, you walk—or run—in the strides of ghosts, shadows, and legends, just as thousands have done over the years. The cross-country Dipsea Trail race is world-renowned as the oldest and one of the most beautiful cross-country routes anywhere. The route spans 7.5 miles from Mill Valley to Stinson Beach, crossing the south flank of Mount Tamalpais, up and down from Old Mill Park through Muir Woods and Mount Tamalpais State Park and Steep Ravine en route to the coast. The origin of the name "Dipsea" has been argued about for years, but many figure it comes from the old days when some participants jumped into the ocean to cool off after completing the trek.

The route now has classy-looking mile markers along the way, and finally, after years, many junctions have trail signs. Regardless, the trip can turn into guesswork for newcomers. First-timers should go with a hiking partner who knows the way. With a shuttle car, you're looking at 7.5 miles one-way and with all the ridges and valleys, a cumulative climb of about 4,500 feet, and then a descent to Highway 1 at Stinson Beach.

The official starting point is the Mill Valley Depot, where you head a short distance down the street to Old Mill Park (elevation 120 feet). For hiking, instead park along the road at Old Mill Park (it has a restroom). At the far side of the park, you head uphill and reach the first of three sets of steps, 688 in all (formerly 671 before they were reworked). The steps are legendary among Dipsea runners. Jack Kirk, who ran the Dipsea for 67 straight years, is credited with the celebrated quote about the steps: "Old Dipsea runners never die. They just reach the 672nd step."

When the trail tops the stairs and reaches pavement, look for the arrows painted on the street to mark the way (at times, the arrows can be faint). They will route you along Sequoia Road, Walsh Drive, and then across the Panoramic Highway (elevation 560 feet) at Windy Gap. From here the trail continues across a hill peppered with expensive homes before plunging down a wooded canyon to the entrance of Muir Woods National Monument. Trail runners called this downhill plunge "Suicide."

Here, the trail signs improve. You emerge at the Muir Woods parking lot. At the bottom of the canyon, the trail crosses a temporary bridge (removed during high flows) at Redwood Creek (elevation 150 feet). You then grind out a climb in forest up past the Hogsback (elevation 730 feet), emerge past a grassland meadow, and then climb again into dense woodlands called The Rainforest. The climb gets steep as you rise through The Rainforest, up the 400-foot climb of Cardiac Hill, and then emerges at a clearing and trail junction (elevation 1,360 feet), the highest point on the route.

On clear days, this is where the ocean first comes into view. With portable restrooms, this site can provide the ideal lunch break. The major climbs are over, and the ocean is ahead. Unlike mono-landscapes in many areas, the Dipsea provides a mosaic of habitats, from oak woodlands, with bays, oaks, acacias and eucalyptus, into the conifers, with Douglas firs and redwoods, interspersed by meadows and riparian zones.

From that clearing with the view, you

descend 1.5 miles through cathedral redwoods into Steep Ravine. The trail crosses a bridge at Webb Creek (elevation 580 feet), where everybody stops to gaze upstream at the pretty brook, edged by sword ferns, bracken ferns, and redwoods, enclosed by a towering forest canopy. Newcomers to the Dipsea may think the climbs are all done, but Insult Hill waits ahead. After that short grind, your reward is that sensational ocean views are then revealed.

Much of the descent to Stinson Beach is breathtaking, where it feels like you can open your arms wide and take in the entire expanse of the Pacific. A panorama of the ocean, Stinson Beach, and beyond to Duxbury Point comes into view. Most seem to get a second wind and rocket out of the hardwood forest. You emerge along the Panoramic Highway (a short distance from Highway 1), where there is a large dirt area for parking on the north side. You have thus completed America's landmark cross-country route. There aren't many rites of passage and this is one of them.

The length of the Dipsea has been argued over time, but Darrell White, who runs the race and is on the Dipsea Board of Directors, walked the route with GPS and a mileage wheel and verified the exact distance at 7.51 miles. In the process, he installed the mileage markers, with classy brass plates embedded in small boulders.

User Groups: Hikers only. No dogs, horses, or mountain bikes. No wheelchair facilities.

Permits: No permits required. Parking and access are free at the primary trailhead, but the trail can be accessed from Muir Woods and Mount Tamalpais State Park, where there are fees. If you start at Mount Tamalpais State Park, an $8 fee is charged per vehicle.

Maps: The Dipsea Trail crosses several jurisdictions. A brochure with map of Mount Tamalpais State Park is available for a small fee at the visitors center or by contacting Mount Tamalpais State Park. For topographic maps, ask the USGS for San Rafael and Bolinas.

Logistics: Hikers should be partnered and work out a shuttle: Drive two cars to end of trail at Panoramic Highway at Stinson Beach and park one car at dirt area on wide shoulder on north side of Panoramic Highway across from trail end. Then drive other car to start of trail at Old Mill Park and park on street near park.

Directions: From San Francisco, take U.S. 101 north over the Golden Gate Bridge and continue four miles to Marin and to Exit 445B for Highway 1/Stinson Beach. Take that exit and continue west for one mile to the stoplight at a T intersection (Tam Junction) for Shoreline Highway/Highway 1. Continue straight onto Almonte Boulevard for 0.4 mile and then continue straight onto Miller Avenue for 1.8 miles (use the right lane to stay slightly left on Miller) to Throckmorton Avenue. Turn left on Throckmorton and drive 0.3 mile to the Old Mill Park on the left.

Contact: Old Mill Park, 415/388-4033, www.cityofmillvalley.org; Mount Tamalpais State Park, 415/388-2070; Muir Woods National Monument, 415/388-2595, www.nps.gov/muwo; Golden Gate National Recreation Area, 415/561-4700, www.nps.gov/goga.

52 TENNESSEE VALLEY

4.2 mi/2.0 hr 1 9

in the Marin Headlands near Sausalito

Map 7.1, page 289

Tennessee Cove is a drop-dead gorgeous cove that extends in a sculpted curve south to Tennessee Point, with many stacks and outcrops in the tidelands to the south that catch the brunt of waves. The hike travels through Tennessee Valley (flat, paved for 0.8 mile, and very popular) and continues at a fork (trail turns to gravel, both forks reconnect in 0.6 mile), then ventures past a small marsh en route to gorgeous Tennessee Cove on the Marin coast. On the way, you are flanked by hills glowing green and peppered with wildflowers. The views of the Pacific Ocean can be gorgeous and the sunsets memorable. This trail has become a favorite for family hiking or biking trips. It is often crowded on weekends, and even on weekday afternoons when the weather is clear. You can also break off this trail to hike up on the flank of the Marin Headlands for ocean views.

User Groups: Hikers, horses, and mountain bikes. (Horses and mountain bikes must take the forked fire road.) No dogs. No wheelchair facilities.

Permits: No permits are required. Parking and access are free.

Maps: A brochure and map are available at the Marin Headlands Visitors Center or by contacting the Golden Gate National Recreation Area. For a topographic map, ask the USGS for Point Bonita.

Directions: From San Francisco, take U.S. 101 over the Golden Gate Bridge and go four miles (through the Waldo Tunnel and into Marin City) to the exit for Highway 1/Stinson Beach. Take that exit and drive 0.6 mile to Tennessee Valley Road on the left. Turn left and go two miles to the road's end, parking, and trailheads.

Contact: Marin Headlands Visitors Center, 415/331-1540; Golden Gate National Recreation Area, visitors center, 415/561-4700, www.nps.gov/goga.

53 MIWOK LOOP

3.5 mi/2.0 hr

in the Marin Headlands near Sausalito

Map 7.1, page 289

You can get one of our favorite lookouts on this trail, where you scan west from high on the Marin Headlands and across the ocean. The hike starts at the Miwok Stables (elevation 200 feet). Take the Miwok Trail, where you hike north and rise into the hills. The trail turns left and heads west 0.6 mile, where you continue to climb to the junction of Miwok Trail and Coyote Ridge Road. At this point, to make the loop hike, turn left on Ridge Road, where the trail tops out at 1,000 feet. The next mile offers spectacular views of the ocean, and every step can be special. To return to the Miwok Stables, turn left at the Fox Trail, and hike 1.1 miles; go left again on the paved Tennessee Valley Trail, and hike out the last 0.4 mile to the stables. Get yourself a clear day for the ocean views and go for it.

If you are new to the Marin Headlands, you will often see the usual parade of people on the Tennessee Valley Trail, especially on warm days. While this is one of the best easy family walks with a payoff, there are other excellent choices available. This loop trail we created is one of them. The Miwok Loop is a nearly circular hike that traverses the pretty grasslands of the Marin Headlands. In the process, you connect a number of trails to provide for views and a workout.

Trail use is typically high on weekends, and that includes mountain bike traffic on Coyote Ridge Road. No problem. It works for everybody.

User Groups: Hikers, dogs, horses, and mountain bikes (partial access). No wheelchair facilities.

Permits: No permits are required. Parking and access are free.

Maps: A brochure and map are available at the Marin Headlands Visitors Center or by contacting the Golden Gate National Recreation Area. For a topographic map, ask the USGS for Point Bonita.

Directions: From San Francisco, take U.S. 101 over the Golden Gate Bridge and go four miles (through the Waldo Tunnel and into Marin City) to the exit for Highway 1/Stinson Beach. Take that exit and drive 0.6 mile to Tennessee Valley Road on the left. Turn left and go 1.7 miles to the road's end, parking, and trailheads.

Contact: Marin Headlands Visitors Center, 415/331-1540; Golden Gate National Recreation Area, visitors center, 415/561-4700, www.nps.gov/goga.

54 MARIN'S HILL 88

5.4 mi/2.0 hr

in the Marin Headlands near Sausalito

Map 7.1, page 289

Hill 88 is a 1,053-foot hilltop in the Marin Headlands. It towers over Rodeo Beach, with the Marin coast and ocean on one side, wilderness foothills on the other, and a pretty silhouette of Mount Tamalpais to the north, San Francisco to the south. The payoff views and natural beauty are a 10. Yet the trip requires a climb that makes you feel that you've earned something special. That makes the trip a perfect mesh of beauty and ambition.

To get to the top, the hike is 2.7 miles with a 1,000-foot climb, steep in one spot. The trip starts as an easy walk on a gated road, the Coastal Trail. It then climbs (with pretty coastal views), and in 1.5 miles, reaches Battery Townsley (a concrete bunker, largely buried). You then climb, steep at times, up to Wolf Ridge (steep enough for the route to be stepped in spots). A spur on the right leads 0.1 mile to Hill 88. This is like a military ghost town with old gun placements on a bunker and sensational views. When you head back, it can feel like the entire coast is at your feet. It's 5.4 miles round-trip.

An option is to turn it into a 5.5-mile loop. After your visit to Hill 88, to make the route a loop, instead turn right on Wolf Ridge. In 1.3 miles, turn right again on the Miwok Trail. It leads down to Gerbode Valley and back along Rodeo Lagoon (and the road) to parking. This is not featured because it means walking a bit along the road next to Rodeo Lagoon to get back to your parking spot.

User Groups: Hikers and horses. No mountain bikes permitted on this route at Wolf Ridge. Leashed dogs are permitted on this section of Coastal Trail and Wolf Ridge, but not on the spur to Hill 88. No wheelchair facilities.

Permits: No permits are required. Parking and access are free.

Maps: A brochure and map are available at the Marin Headlands Visitors Center or by contacting the Golden Gate National Recreation Area. For a topographic map, ask the USGS for Point Bonita.

Directions: From San Francisco, take U.S. 101 north over the Golden Gate Bridge to Marin and the exit for Alexander Avenue (just north of the bridge). Take that exit west and drive under the highway and curve south to Conzelman Road. Turn right on Conzelman and drive 1.1 miles to traffic circle at McCullough Road. Take first exit onto McCullough Road and continue 0.9 mile to Bunker Road. Turn left on Bunker Road and drive 1.8 miles (Rodeo Lagoon on left) to fork with Bunker Road on right. Continue straight ahead (becomes Mitchell Road, Fort Cronkhite on right, Rodeo Lagoon still on left) for 0.2 mile to end of road and turn right to parking lot for Rodeo Beach.

Trailhead: After parking, walk back to road. Turn right and walk short distance west to trailhead for Coastal Trail. It starts as a gated road.

Contact: Marin Headlands Visitors Center, 415/331-1540; Golden Gate National Recreation Area, visitors center, 415/561-4700, www.nps.gov/goga.

55 BOTHIN MARSH

1.0 mi/1.0 hr 1 9

in Mill Valley

Map 7.1, page 289

Bothin Marsh spans 106 acres with bridged inlets, sloughs, and tidal wetlands amid cordgrass and pickleweed that adjoin Richardson Bay. You can see shorebirds, both residents and migrants, here, and what you see often varies with tides and season; 125 bird species have been verified by photographs. From the trailhead adjacent to Almonte, the best walk is to turn left on the Mill Valley-Sausalito Path and go into the interior of the marsh and over a pretty bridge to Bay Front Park, with the option of continuing on the Bay Trail to Hauke Park.

This is a great site for bird-watching and easy walks with water views.

User Groups: Hikers, dogs, mountain bikes, and wheelchairs. No horses.

Permits: No permits are required. Parking and access are free.

Maps: For a topographic map, ask the USGS for San Francisco North.

Directions: From San Francisco, take U.S. 101 north over the Golden Gate Bridge and continue four miles to Marin and to Exit 445B for Highway 1/Stinson Beach. Take that exit and continue west for one mile to the stoplight at a T intersection (Tam Junction) for Shoreline Highway/Highway 1. Continue straight onto Almonte Boulevard (it becomes Miller) for one mile to trailhead/access on right (a T intersection for Almonte is adjacent to access gate).

Contact: Marin County Parks, 415/473-6387, www.marincountyparks.org.

56 MORNING SUN TRAIL

0.6-5.2 mi/0.5-3.0 hr 3 10

in the Marin Headlands near Sausalito

Map 7.1, page 289

You do this hike for one reason: the panoramic views of San Francisco Bay. There is a good parking area at the trailhead. You then climb about 400 feet and top out at 800 feet at the Alta Trail junction. The views are fantastic, where you can see across Richardson Bay to Angel Island and beyond across the bay to the East Bay skyline. This trail didn't get its name by accident: This is one of the best places in the Bay Area to catch a sunrise. After the short but steep climb to the junction with Alta Trail (a road), turn around and take in the dawn rush. The sunrise often casts yellows and oranges across San Francisco Bay. Want more? From the Alta Trail junction, you can easily extend your trip in either direction, then turn around when ready; or create a pretty 5.2-mile loop where you link the Rodeo Valley Trail and Bobcat Trail.

User Groups: Hikers only. No dogs, horses, or mountain bikes. No wheelchair facilities.

Permits: No permits are required. Parking and access are free.

Maps: A brochure and map are available at the Marin Headlands Visitors Center or by contacting the Golden Gate National Recreation Area. For a topographic map, ask the USGS for San Francisco North.

Directions: From San Francisco, drive north on U.S. 101 through the Waldo Tunnel. Take the Spencer Avenue exit, but keep straight on the frontage road on the east side of the freeway. (Do not turn right onto Spencer Avenue.) Drive about 0.5 mile, turn left, and drive under the freeway to the commuter parking area at the trailhead.

Contact: Marin Headlands Visitors Center, 415/331-1540; Golden Gate National Recreation Area, visitors center, 415/561-4700, www.nps.gov/goga.

57 YELLOW BLUFF TRAIL

1.5 mi/1.0 hr 1 10

in the Marin Headlands near the Golden Gate Bridge

Map 7.1, page 289

This is a little piece of heaven. From your vantage point on Yellow Bluff, San Francisco can look like the Land of Oz. Yellow Bluff is just east of the Golden Gate Bridge, the first major land point along the Marin shore at Fort Baker. You get a stunning lookout of the Golden Gate, across San Francisco Bay to the San Francisco waterfront and skyline, and the surrounding landmarks. The trail is flat, short, and unpublicized, and there are a few picnic tables nearby.

It's very easy to reach, yet missed by tourists. From East Fort Baker, walk on the trail that heads east near the shoreline of the bay. It leads along the shore to Yellow Bluff and a picnic site. You can turn the trip into a triangular loop hike where you continue along the shore, toward Sausalito, and turn left at the trail junction to return to Fort Baker. One of the great features of this area is that it is often sunny, even when the Marin Headlands to the nearby west lie buried in fog.

User Groups: Hikers, dogs, and mountain bikes. Fort Baker is wheelchair-accessible, but the trail is not. No horses.

Permits: No permits are required. Parking and access are free.

Maps: A brochure and map are available at the East Fort Baker Visitors Center or by contacting the Golden Gate National Recreation Area, Marin Headlands. For a topographic map, ask the USGS for San Francisco North.

Directions: From San Francisco, take U.S. 101 north over the Golden Gate Bridge to Marin and stay to the right at the split. Drive a very short distance, turn left, and drive a few hundred yards to a stop sign. Turn right and drive 0.5 mile to the parking area for Fort Baker.

Contact: Marin Headlands Visitors Center, 415/331-1540; Golden Gate National Recreation Area, visitors center, 415/561-4700, www.nps.gov/goga.

58 VISTA POINT/ BATTERY SPENCER

0.5 mi/0.5 hr 

in the Marin Headlands near the Golden Gate Bridge

Map 7.1, page 289

Play tourist and drive out to Battery Spencer. If the experience doesn't move you, head to the nearest emergency room and have your pulse checked. Battery Spencer is perched on a bluff top of the Marin Headlands, about eye-level with the top of the North Tower of the Golden Gate Bridge. The big payoff is the eye-popping panorama of San Francisco. A trip here can easily be extended with a hike or scenic drive.

If parking is full when you get there, pull over and wait a minute; a spot will open up. After parking, head right toward the old concrete outbuildings and foundations for Battery Spencer. Battery Spencer was a military outpost, best known for its coastal gun battery as part of the defense to the entrance to San Francisco Bay. It's a short walk on a wheelchair-accessible pathway to the bluff-top overlook of the Golden Gate. From the bluff, you get the classic towering view across the bridge to San Francisco. On the walk back, there's a picnic bench with a view below to Fort Baker and across the bay to Angel Island and Alcatraz.

You can go the extra mile, or in this case, 2.4 miles round-trip. Look for the gated service road on the west end of Battery Spencer. It leads down 1.2 miles, with a 475-foot descent, to a pretty valley, and then to Kirby Cove. This is a gorgeous beach with the water view of the Golden Gate Bridge. You'll also find a concrete battery, a few bluff-top tent sites, and in the valley, a campground for groups.

User Groups: Hikers and wheelchairs. No dogs, mountain bikes, or horses.

Permits: No permits are required. Parking and access are free.

Maps: A brochure and map are available at the East Fort Baker Visitors Center or by contacting the Golden Gate National Recreation Area. For a topographic map, ask the USGS for San Francisco North.

Directions: From San Francisco, take U.S. 101 north over the Golden Gate Bridge to Marin and continue 0.5 mile to the exit for Alexander Avenue. Take that exit west, keep left at the fork and drive 0.2 mile under the highway (signed for U.S. 101 South/San Francisco) and curve south to Conzelman Road, signed Marin Headlands Coastal Route. Turn right (west) on Conzelman and drive 0.3 mile to parking for Battery Spencer on left.

Contact: Marin Headlands Visitors Center, 415/331-1540; Golden Gate National Recreation Area, visitors center, 415/561-4700, www.nps.gov/goga.

59 PERIMETER TRAIL

5.0 mi/2.5 hr 2 10

on Angel Island State Park

Map 7.1, page 289 BEST

Pick a bright, blue-sky day at Angel Island and you get eye-popping views everywhere you turn. At the virtual center of San Francisco Bay, you are surrounded by dozens of world-renowned landmarks. If you hit it right, the view across the bay of the Golden Gate Bridge, San Francisco, and Marin Headlands can be magical. On the loop, you also see Raccoon Strait, Sausalito, the Bay Bridge, East Bay hills, and Alcatraz.

From the ferry dock at Ayala Cove, hike past the beach and visitors center and continue on a short spur that connects with Perimeter Road. Bear right and you'll then climb easily up through eucalyptus forest. The first highlight is Camp Reynolds, a Civil War-era barracks, with a great view of the Golden Gate Bridge. From here, the road points toward San Francisco, with a fantastic view of the San Francisco waterfront and high-rises as you pass above Point Blunt. The route bears left as you pass along Fort McDowell and the East Garrison. Little known is that a secluded and gorgeous beach is hidden in a cove below the garrison. The route continues in a loop past the North Garrison Immigration Station and China Cove with views of the East Bay waterfront and foothills, and then turns again to head back to Ayala Cove.

Always hike the loop in counterclockwise direction. The trail winds past old barracks and abandoned military buildings, climbs through lush eucalyptus forests and across high bluffs, and to lookouts. Every turn provides another awesome view.

User Groups: Hikers and mountain bikes (helmets are required for cyclists 17 years and under). The Perimeter Road is accessible to wheelchairs, but many portions are too steep for use. No dogs (except for seeing-eye dogs) or horses.

Permits: Ferry tickets include day-use fees and vary according to departure point and season; a fee is charged per bicycle. State Park annual day-use pass not accepted at Angel Island State Park.

Maps: You can purchase a brochure and topographic map for a fee at the park or by mail from the Angel Island Association. For a topographic map, ask the USGS for San Francisco North.

Directions: Ferry service to Angel Island is available from Tiburon, San Francisco, Vallejo, and Oakland/Alameda.

To the Tiburon ferry: Take U.S. 101 to Exit 447 for Highway 131 toward Tiburon Boulevard/E. Blithedale Avenue. Take that exit east for 0.3 mile to Tiburon Boulevard/Highway 131. Turn right on Tiburon Boulevard and drive 4.3 miles to entrance and parking for Tiburon Ferry.

To the San Francisco ferry: Take U.S. 101 to the exit for Marina Boulevard exit (near the southern foot of the Golden Gate Bridge). Take that exit and drive east on Marina Boulevard toward Fisherman's Wharf. Park at a parking garage or pay lot. The ferry departs from Pier 41.

To the Vallejo ferry: Take I-80 to I-780 and drive to Curtola Parkway. Take Curtola Parkway (which becomes Mare Island Way) and continue to 495 Mare Island Way; free parking is available. The docking area is directly across from the parking lot.

To the Oakland/Alameda ferry: In Oakland drive south on I-980 to the exit for Webster. Take that exit and drive west to the ferry dock at Jack London Square. The ferry goes to San Francisco at Pier 41.

Ferries: From San Francisco: Blue & Gold Fleet (415/705-8200, www.blueandgoldfleet.com, bicycles free); from Marin: Angel Island Tiburon Ferry (415/435-2131, www.angelislandferry.com).

Contact: Angel Island State Park, 415/435-1915 or 415/435-5390 (ranger's office); California

State Parks, Marin District, 415/898-4362, www.parks.ca.gov.

60 MOUNT LIVERMORE SUMMIT

4.5 mi/2.5 hr

on Angel Island State Park

Map 7.1, page 289

This is one of the most dramatic urban lookouts in the world. When standing atop Mount Livermore, you will be surrounded by landmarks in every direction. At 788 feet, this is the highest point on Angel Island. The views are spectacular at night, when the lights of the Golden Gate Bridge and the city glow with charm. From the visitors center, walk to the Perimeter Road and its junction with the Sunset Trail. The Sunset Trail starts where you hike west, just above the Perimeter Road (Perimeter Road is off to your right). The Sunset Trail instead bears left and climbs through a series of graded switchbacks, then turns left to rise up the south flank of the summit. After about two miles, you will reach a junction with the North Ridge Trail. Turn here and you will climb up for the final push to the top at 788 feet. The big views: Golden Gate Bridge, San Francisco waterfront, San Francisco Headlands, Marin Headlands, Raccoon Strait, Sausalito, Bay Bridge, East Bay hills, Alcatraz.

User Groups: Hikers only. No dogs (except for seeing-eye dogs), horses, or mountain bikes (they may not even be walked on this trail). No wheelchair facilities.

Permits: Ferry tickets include day-use fees and vary according to departure point and season; a fee is charged per bicycle. State Park annual day-use pass not accepted at Angel Island State Park.

Maps: You can purchase a brochure and topographic map for a fee at the park or by mail from the Angel Island Association. For a topographic map, ask the USGS for San Francisco North.

Directions: Ferry service to Angel Island is available from Tiburon, San Francisco, Vallejo, and Oakland/Alameda.

To the Tiburon ferry: Take U.S. 101 to Exit 447 for Highway 131 toward Tiburon Boulevard/E. Blithedale Avenue. Follow that exit east for 0.3 mile to Tiburon Boulevard/Highway 131. Turn right on Tiburon Boulevard and drive 4.3 miles to entrance and parking for Tiburon Ferry.

To the San Francisco ferry: Take U.S. 101 to the exit for Marina Boulevard (near the southern foot of the Golden Gate Bridge). Follow that exit and drive east on Marina Boulevard toward Fisherman's Wharf. Park at a parking garage or pay lot. The ferry departs from Pier 41.

To the Vallejo ferry: Take I-80 to I-780. Take I-780 and drive to Curtola Parkway. Take Curtola Parkway (which becomes Mare Island Way) and continue to 495 Mare Island Way, where free parking is available. The docking area is directly across from the parking lot.

To the Oakland/Alameda ferry: In Oakland drive south on I-980 to the exit for Webster. Take that exit and drive west to the ferry dock at Jack London Square. The ferry goes to San Francisco at Pier 41.

Ferries: From San Francisco: Blue & Gold Fleet (415/705-8200, www.blueandgoldfleet.com, bicycles free); from Marin: Angel Island Tiburon Ferry (415/435-2131, www.angelislandferry.com).

Contact: Angel Island State Park, 415/435-1915 or 415/435-5390 (ranger's office); California State Parks, Marin District, 415/898-4362, www.parks.ca.gov.

61 AGAVE TRAIL

1.5 mi/1.5 hr 1 8

on Alcatraz Island

Map 7.2, page 290

The Agave Trail at Alcatraz Island is only open from late September to February; the trail is closed from late winter into spring and summer to protect nesting birds. Named after the agave plant, which is common here, the trail provides some of the most breathtaking views found in the Bay Area.

Start at the ferry landing on the east side of Alcatraz and follow the trail as it traces the island rim to its southern tip. It's quite wide, with a few benches and cement picnic tables situated for sweeping views of both the East Bay and San Francisco. From its southern end, the trail is routed back to the historic parade ground atop the island, where you will find some sculptural masterpieces, including 110 stone steps. The parade ground is a haven for nesting birds (this area is closed to the public each spring). Birds are thriving in the restored wildlife habitat, especially at the southern end of the island. About 10,000 marine birds live here, mainly gulls, cormorants, and egrets. With about 5,000 visitors a day in summer, that's two birds for every person—wear a hat.

The old cell block is at the center of the island, with other buildings sprinkled along the eastern shore and on the northern tip. Ranger-led park tours are available, and visitors can rent audiotapes for a self-guided cell-house tour. Famous prisoners include The Birdman, Machine Gun Kelly, and Al Capone. The cells are only five feet by nine feet, yet because the warden ordered them painted two-tone, white over seafoam green, they give the illusion of a much larger space.

User Groups: Hikers only. No dogs, horses, or mountain bikes. No wheelchair facilities.

Permits: No permits are required. Entry tickets include the ferryboat trip to the island and audio tours are available from Alcatraz Cruises for an additional fee. Ferries depart from Pier 31/33 in San Francisco.

Maps: A map is available at the ferry landing for a fee. For a topographic map, ask the USGS for San Francisco North.

Directions: From the Peninsula: Take U.S. 101 north to San Francisco and continue to the split with I-280 (signed Downtown SF). At the split take I-280 for 0.5 mile, keep right at the fork (signed for I-280), then continue 3.3 miles to King Street. Continue on King Street for 0.7 mile to The Embarcadero and then continue 2.1 miles to Pier 33 and nearby parking.

From the East Bay: Take the Bay Bridge to San Francisco (stay in left lanes) and the exit on the left for Harrison Street (toward Embarcadero). Follow that exit for 0.4 mile (stay right) to Harrison Street. Turn right on Harrison and drive 0.3 mile to the Embarcadero. Turn left and drive 1.5 miles to Pier 33 and nearby parking.

From Marin: Take the Golden Gate Bridge to San Francisco and continue (stay left on the split for U.S. 101) about two miles to the exit for Marina Boulevard. Turn left on Marina and drive 1.1 miles to Laguna Street, and then continue on Laguna for 0.1 mile to Bay Street. Turn left on Bay Street and drive 1.4 miles to the Embarcadero and nearby parking.

Ferries: From San Francisco: Blue & Gold Fleet (415/705-8200, www.blueandgoldfleet.com).

Contact: Golden Gate National Recreation Area, 415/561-4900 or www.nps.gov/alcatraz; Alcatraz Cruises, 415/981-7625, www.alcatrazcruises.com.

62 COASTAL TRAIL/ BATTERY GODFREY

1.5 mi/1.0 hr 1 10

in the Presidio in San Francisco

Map 7.2, page 290

This one is a 10, worth the trip no matter where you live. It's often best when turbulent skies offer textures to the setting. To your right is a magazine-cover quality view of the Golden Gate Bridge. From the Coastal Trail, the cliffs plunge below to the waterfront and beyond to the entrance of the bay, with passing ships, fishing boats, and sailboats. Directly across is the Marin Headlands, topped by Hawk Hill and edged by Point Bonita and its lighthouse.

The trip starts at Battery Godfrey in the Presidio. It is perched on a bluff west of the

Golden Gate Bridge. You'll find the old concrete foundation for Battery Godfrey, fantastic views of the bridge, Marin Headlands and entrance to the bay, and a trailhead for the Coastal Trail.

From here, take the Coastal Trail toward the Golden Gate Bridge to a payoff spot called "Overlook." A bench is set perfectly for a view of the bridge and photographs. The trail extends north a short distance to the toll plaza, where you can walk under the road to the designated Overlook above Fort Point and the southern foot of the bridge. Return when ready.

Back at Battery Godfrey, if you want to extend your trip, you can venture south on the Coastal Trail. It is routed along Lincoln Boulevard to Battery Chamberlain and Baker Beach, and then beyond to China Beach.

Battery Godfrey was a turn-of-the-20th-century military site armed with three 12-inch guns that could fire 1,000-pound shells 10 miles. What's left is the concrete structure that supported the cannons.

User Groups: Hikers and wheelchairs. Dogs are not advised. No horses or mountain bikes.

Permits: No permits are required. Parking and access are free.

Maps: For a free map, contact the Presidio. For a topographic map, ask the USGS for San Francisco North.

Directions: From the Peninsula: Take I-280 north to Exit 47 signed for Highway 1/Pacifica. Drive 1.1 miles to the exit for Skyline Blvd./Highway 35N and merge onto Skyline Boulevard. Continue north 4.3 miles to a stop. Turn left on Great Highway and continue north 3.5 miles to the Cliff House; the road merges with Point Lobos Avenue. Bear right and drive 0.6 miles (becoming Geary St.) and continue 0.9 mile to 26th Avenue. Turn left on 26th and go 0.5 mile to El Camino Del Mar. Turn right and drive 0.2 mile (becoming Lincoln St.); continue 1.1 miles into the Presidio and Langdon Court (for lookout, Battery Godfrey). Turn left and drive to the parking lot.

From the East Bay: Take the Bay Bridge (I-80 West) to San Francisco and the Fremont Street exit. The off-ramp merges onto Fremont Street; stay left and then continue straight to Pine Street. Turn left on Pine and drive 1.3 miles to Van Ness Avenue. Turn right on Van Ness and go 0.8 mile to Lombard/U.S. 101. Turn left on Lombard and drive three miles to Exit 439 (for Presidio). Take that exit and continue a short distance to Lincoln Boulevard. Turn right on Lincoln and go 0.3 mile (under U.S. 101) to Langdon (for lookout, Battery Godfrey) on right. Turn right and drive a short distance to park.

From Marin: Take U.S. 101 south over the Golden Gate Bridge to Exit 439 toward 25th Avenue. Take that exit and continue 0.2 mile to Lincoln Boulevard. Turn right on Lincoln and go about 500 feet to Langdon (for lookout, Battery Godfrey) on right. Turn right and drive a short distance to the parking lot.

Contact: Presidio Visitors Center, 415/561-4323, www.nps.gov/prsf.

63 ECOLOGY TRAIL TO INSPIRATION POINT

2.5 mi/1.5 hr 1 10

in the Presidio in San Francisco

Map 7.2, page 290

The Presidio is best known for its shoreline lookouts of the Golden Gate. Instead, try this trip once and you will never forget it. The Ecology Trail is routed through Tennessee Hollow and a mixed forest, with occasional views that provide a hint to the payoff. In less than a mile you'll reach the turnoff on your right to Inspiration Point (it can also be reached by car). The view is fantastic: You get a panorama that spans below to the Palace of Fine Arts and beyond to the San Francisco waterfront, bay, and across to Angel Island and Alcatraz. World-class.

Then, at Inspiration Point, turn and look behind you. On the opposite side of Arguello Boulevard is a young cypress forest from which the 100-foot Goldsworthy's Spire pokes a hole in the sky. It is best accessed across the street from parking at the Presidio Café.

User Groups: Hikers and dogs. Bikes are not advised. Wheelchair access from parking at Inspiration Point.

Permits: No permits are required. Parking and access are free.

Maps: For a free map, contact the Presidio. For a topographic map, ask the USGS for San Francisco North.

Directions: From the parking lot, walk to the Inn at the Presidio on Moraga Avenue. At the corner with Hardie Avenue, turn right and walk a short distance to the trailhead.

From the Peninsula: Take U.S. 101 north to San Francisco and continue to the split with U.S. 101/Golden Gate Bridge-I-80/Bay Bridge. Stay left on U.S. 101 and follow Van Ness Avenue to Lombard Street; turn left on Lombard Street and continue to Letterman. Turn right on Letterman and drive 0.2 mile on Presidio to Funston. Turn left and drive 0.1 mile to Moraga Avenue and the trailhead adjacent to Inn at the Presidio.

From East Bay: Take the Bay Bridge to San Francisco and the exit for Fremont Street. Continue onto Front Street and follow the road a short distance to Pine Street. Turn left on Pine and drive 2.7 miles to Presidio Avenue. Turn left on Presidio and go 0.2 mile to Funston Avenue. Turn left on Funston and go 0.1 mile to Moraga Avenue. Turn right at Moraga and park in the lot on the right.

From Marin: Take the Golden Gate Bridge to San Francisco and continue to the split with U.S. 101/Marina. Stay left at the split for U.S. 101 and continue to Lombard Street. Turn right on Lombard and drive 0.3 mile to Letterman Drive. Turn right and drive 0.3 mile and continue ahead on Presidio Boulevard for 0.2 mile to Funston Avenue. Turn left on Funston and go 0.1 mile to Moraga. Turn right at Moraga (Inn at the Presidio is near the trailhead, on the left) and park in the lot on the right.

Contact: Presidio Visitors Center, 415/561-4323, www.nps.gov/prsf.

64 GOLDEN GATE BRIDGE

3.0 mi/1.25 hr 1 10

from San Francisco to Marin

Map 7.2, page 290

The top tourist walks in the world include the stroll to Yosemite Falls, the Redwood Creek Trail in Muir Woods, and this—the walk over the Golden Gate Bridge and back. And it makes sense: On a warm, clear day, the walk across the bridge feels like a surreal phenomenon and the view is incomparable. The bridge is 1.2 miles long, so most visitors walk halfway out, take in the view, then return to their cars (1.5-mile round-trip). If you walk from one end to the other and then return, it takes about an hour. The bridge deck is 220 feet above the water and the towers rise up 750 feet. Look up at the gated catwalk that rings the top of the South Tower. I was up there one spring day. As I looked straight down past my boots on the grated deck, I felt the tower waver slightly in the wind and an electric tremor course through my heart.

Parking is available at the north end of the bridge (at Vista Point) and at the south end, on each side of the toll plaza. On the San Francisco side, there is also some parking on the west side; you'll then walk through a short tunnel that runs under U.S. 101 and loops up to the pathway entrance.

From the walking lane at the center of the bridge, looking eastward, you can see Alcatraz, Angel Island and the bay framed by the San Francisco waterfront to your right and the East Bay hills on the horizon. From the bicycle lane, you get a near-equal panorama in the other direction: the Marin Headlands, mouth of the bay and beyond to the ocean, and the San Francisco Headlands, cliffs, and beaches to Point Lobos. Stash a windbreaker in a small pack. Even on clear days, a moist coastal breeze can cause a chill for some.

User Groups: Hikers, wheelchairs, dogs, and mountain bikes (on the west side of the bridge only). No horses.

Permits: No permits are required. Parking and access are free.

Maps: For a free map, contact the Golden Gate National Recreation Area. For a topographic map, ask the USGS for San Francisco North.

Directions: From the Peninsula: Take I-280 north to Daly City and the split with Highway 1. Stay left at the split and continue north on Highway 1 (19th Ave.) through Golden Gate Park. After passing through a tunnel, merge with U.S. 101 North (right lane). Continue 0.2 mile to the exit for Presidio/Golden Gate Bridge Vista Point. Parking and Vista Point are on the left.

From East Bay: Take the Bay Bridge to San Francisco and the exit for Fremont Street. Merge onto Fremont and go another 0.3 mile, continuing onto Front Street. Turn left on Pine Street and drive 1.4 miles to Franklin Street. Turn right on Franklin and drive 0.8 mile to Lombard/U.S. 101. Turn left on Lombard and drive three miles (U.S. 101) toward Golden Gate Bridge and the exit for Presidio/Golden Gate Bridge Vista Point. Parking and Vista Point are on the left.

Contact: Golden Gate National Recreation Area, Fort Mason, San Francisco, 415/561-4700, www.nps.gov/goga.

65 BAY TRAIL: MARINA GREEN TO FORT POINT

3.0 mi/1.25 hr — 1 — 10

on Crissy Field in San Francisco

Map 7.2, page 290

This is one of the most spectacular city walks in America. Marina Green is your launch point. From here along the Golden Gate Promenade, you get waterfront views that extend to the Golden Gate Bridge and across to Sausalito and Alcatraz. From parking, take the San Francisco Bay Trail west along Marina Green and work your way around the yacht harbors (you'll see lots of docked boats on your right) toward the St. Francis Yacht Club. Then continue toward the harbor entrance, past the Golden Gate Yacht Club, to the point at the end of the jetty and to the Wave Organ.

The Wave Organ is on the end of the point near the mouth of the harbor. It's a wave-activated acoustic sculpture that has 25 "organ pipes," actually made out of PVC and concrete. The movement of water into the pipes sets off tones that amplify water noises, best at high tides. The sound is subtle but San Francisco cool.

From the Wave Organ, head west past the yacht harbors and pick up the Golden Gate Promenade/Bay Trail. The route (paved) runs along the bay and beachfront and continues past Crissy Field and its marsh to the Presidio, Fort Point Pier, and beyond to Fort Point at the southern foot of the Golden Gate Bridge. Along the way, you get stunning views of the Golden Gate Bridge, the bay, and Alcatraz, along with access to the beach, restored ponds and marsh wetlands, and coastal sand dunes. For nonresidents, the trip to Crissy Field is a city adventure through San Francisco past many landmarks en route to the waterfront.

User Groups: Hikers, wheelchairs, dogs, and mountain bikes. No horses.

Permits: No permits are required. Parking and access are free.

Maps: For a free map, contact the Golden Gate National Recreation Area. For a topographic map, ask the USGS for San Francisco North.

Directions: From the Peninsula: Take U.S. 101 north to San Francisco and the exit for the Central Freeway. Continue onto Octavia Boulevard and turn right on Oak Street. Turn left on Franklin Street and drive two miles to Bay Street. Turn left on Bay and go 0.3 mile to Laguna Street. Turn right on Laguna and go 0.1 mile to Marina Boulevard (street turns left) and drive ahead short distance to entrance on right to Marina Green and parking.

From the East Bay: Take Bay Bridge to San

Francisco and, shortly after leaving bridge, to exit for Fremont Street. Follow that exit ramp for 0.8 mile, continue onto Front Street a short distance to Pine. Turn left on Pine and drive 1.4 miles to Franklin. Turn right on Franklin and drive one mile to Bay Street. Turn left on Bay and go 0.3 mile to Laguna Street. Turn right on Laguna and go 0.1 mile to Marina Boulevard (street turns left) and drive ahead a short distance to entrance on right to Marina Green and parking.

From Marin: Take Golden Gate Bridge to San Francisco and continue two miles (stay left at split on U.S. 101/Marina) onto Presidio Parkway and left turn for Marina Boulevard. Turn left on Marina and drive 0.8 mile to the entrance to Marina Green on the left and park.

Contact: Crissy Field Center, 415/561-7690; Golden Gate National Recreation Area, 415/561-4700, www.nps.gov/goga.

66 COASTAL TRAIL: LANDS END

3.0 mi/1.5 hr

in San Francisco

Map 7.2, page 290

San Francisco's Point Lobos and Lands End provide great views, easy adventures, and history. On any day, it is like walking across the grandest stage. The panorama starts right along the sidewalk. Along Point Lobos Avenue, toward the Cliff House uphill past Louis' restaurant, you get a lookout that spans across the mouth of the bay and out to sea to the Marin Headlands and Golden Gate Bridge. It's like a historic painting, with passing ships and fishing boats, pelicans, and cormorants. Continue uphill to Merrie Way, then turn left, that is, toward the Golden Gate.

From Merrie Way, stairs lead down to the historic Sutro Baths ruins. The foundation of the old structure and its seven swimming pools is about all that remains, and with historic photographs, you can reconstruct in your mind how it looked a century ago when thousands of people would visit on a Sunday afternoon. Along its leading edge, you get pretty ocean views where you can taste the salt air. Then return up the stairs to Merrie Way.

On the far side of Merrie Way, you'll see the trailhead for the Coastal Trail. From here, the Coastal Trail spans 1.25 miles, much of it along a former narrow-gauge rail line, on bluff tops amid cypress, out to Eagles Point next to Lincoln Park. From Eagles Point, the payoff is a view of China Beach, Baker Beach, and the coast that arcs in a curve out to the southern foot of the Golden Gate Bridge. During low tides on the Coastal Trail, look down along the cliffs and you can see relics of old shipwrecks that poke up through the sea's surface. A metal masthead and an engine block are the most easily identified.

User Groups: Hikers, wheelchairs, dogs, and mountain bikes (mountain bikes must be walked through narrow sections of the trail). No horses.

Permits: No permits are required. Parking and access are free.

Maps: For a free map, contact the Golden Gate National Recreation Area. For a topographic map, ask the USGS for San Francisco North.

Directions: In San Francisco, take Geary Boulevard west. As you approach the coast, it becomes Point Lobos Avenue; look for parking near the vicinity of GGNRA trailheads and Cliff House. The stairs down to the Sutro Baths ruins and water's edge are to the left of the parking lot; the trailhead for the Coastal Trail is at the end of Merrie Way.

From the Peninsula: Take I-280 north to Exit 47 signed for Highway 1/Pacifica. Take that exit and drive 1.1 miles up the hill to the exit for Skyline Blvd./Highway 35N. Take that exit, merge onto Skyline Boulevard and continue north 4.3 miles to a stop sign (Lake Merced on right, Fort Funston on left). Turn left on Great Highway and continue north 3.5 miles north to Cliff House and where it merges with Point

Lobos Avenue. Continue as road curves to right to parking areas.

From the East Bay: Take I-80E into San Francisco and to the merge for U.S. 101 North/ Central Freeway (also signed for Golden Gate Bridge). Take that merge to Central Freeway and go 1.1 miles (becomes Octavia Boulevard) to Fell Street. Turn left on Fell and go 1.2 miles to Masonic Avenue (just past Central). Turn right on Masonic and go 0.2 mile to Fulton Street (the third left). Turn left at Fulton and drive 3.6 miles to Great Highway. Turn right and go 0.3 mile to Point Lobos Avenue and continue short distance to parking and trailheads.

Contact: Golden Gate National Recreation Area, 415/561-4700, www.nps.gov/goga.

67 OCEAN BEACH ESPLANADE

3.0 mi/1.5 hr 1 8

on Ocean Beach along the Great Highway in San Francisco

Map 7.2, page 290

Ocean Beach spreads for miles along San Francisco's coastal Great Highway, from the Cliff House on south past Fort Funston to Mussel Rock. The Ocean Beach Esplanade is a paved route that borders the beach on one side and the Great Highway on the other. Here you can discover a long expanse of sand and a paved jogging trail. The nature of both the trail and the adjacent beach allows visitors to create trips of any length. The beach spans four miles, from Seal Rock (near the Cliff House) south to Fort Funston and beyond (see next hike). The huge swath of sand at Ocean Beach is popular with joggers, especially during low tides, when the hard-packed sand is uncovered. During minus low tides, this is the best area anywhere to find sand dollars; park rules prohibit picking them up. Never did understand the issue with this here; they just get ground up by the waves.

Warning: Do not swim here. There have been several drownings in this area due to riptides.

User Groups: Hikers, dogs, and horses. Partially wheelchair-accessible. No mountain bikes.

Permits: No permits are required. Parking and access are free.

Maps: For a free map, contact the Golden Gate National Recreation Area. For a topographic map, ask the USGS for San Francisco South.

Directions: In San Francisco, take Geary Boulevard west. As you approach the coast, it becomes Point Lobos Avenue. At the Cliff House, the road curves to the left and continues south as it becomes the Great Highway.

From the Peninsula: Take I-280 north to Exit 47 signed for Highway 1/Pacifica. Take that exit and drive 1.1 miles up the hill to the exit for Skyline Blvd./Highway 35N. Follow that exit, merge onto Skyline Boulevard and continue north 4.3 miles to a stop sign (Lake Merced on right, Fort Funston on left). Turn left on Great Highway and drive north. Parking is available along the road on the left.

From the East Bay: Take I-80 west into San Francisco. Use the right two lanes and follow the signs for U.S. 101 North/Central Freeway (also signed for Golden Gate Bridge), which will eventually lead you tp exit the freeway. Drive 1.1 miles onto Octavia Boulevard. Turn left on Fell Street and drive 1.2 miles to Masonic Avenue (just past Central). Turn right on Masonic and go 0.2 mile to Fulton Street (the third left). Turn left at Fulton and drive 3.6 miles to Great Highway. Turn left and look for parking along the right.

Contact: Golden Gate National Recreation Area, 415/561-4700, www.nps.gov/goga.

68 SUNSET TRAIL

1.5 mi/0.5 hr 1 8

at Fort Funston in San Francisco

Map 7.2, page 290

Fort Funston is perched on San Francisco's

coastal bluffs, with the Pacific on one side and Lake Merced on the other. This park is one of the most popular places in California to take dogs, and you can count on seeing plenty, up to dozens at a time. It is also the top hang-gliding spot in the Bay Area, and watching those daredevils soar is the main attraction. A viewing deck is adjacent to the parking area, where Sunset Trail begins.

Follow the wide Sunset Trail as it routes north through coastal bluffs and above sand dunes for 0.75 mile to the park's border. This is one of the most heavily used trails in the Bay Area. In fall and winter, the fog clears and the evening sunsets can make your spine tingle.

Down on the beach, you may see thick black sand unique to this part of the coast. It's not an oil spill; rather, the sand is an iron-ore derivative called magnetite. Magnetite lies in the sandstone cliff walls; as the sandstone erodes, it leaves the heavier iron-based magnetite on the beach. (If you bring a strong magnet to the beach, particles will stick to it.) Scan the cliff walls further and you might see a thick, chalky substance about a foot thick. These are veins of volcanic ash from an eruption of Mount Shasta 300 miles north; the ash made its way here via the Sacramento River and San Francisco Bay. (Former Funston ranger Steve Prokop said he once found a sabertooth tiger tooth here in a vein of volcanic ore.)

No beachcombing or collecting is permitted on Funston's beachfront. Beyond the park boundary, however, it is legal and you can often find sand dollars during low tides. From Center Hole to Mussel Rock, you can often have vast swaths of beach to yourself, especially on weekdays. Rating: Surprise discovery.

Restoration efforts here are ongoing. The Park Service replanted native flowers and plants to protect the bluffs. This has helped a colony of burrowing owls and bank swallows become reestablished. You may also see red-tailed hawks.

Hang gliding: Whether you watch or take part, this is a spectacular scene. Hang gliders launch from a designated area near the bluffs, then ride the updrafts from the cliffs. When the winds are right, you might see gliders flying nearly vertical—an amazing sight—then circle in a series of dipsy-doos. This is the one sport where gravity doesn't always win, especially in the spring, when the north winds come up every afternoon.

Fort Funston often gets more dogs in a week than many Bay Area parks get people in a month. If you have a dog, check posted rules before venturing out. (Dogs must be on leash in some areas of Ocean Beach to protect the endangered snowy plover.)

User Groups: Hikers, dogs, and horses. Partially wheelchair-accessible (on the paved jogging route). No mountain bikes.

Permits: No permits are required. Parking and access are free.

Maps: For a free map, contact the Golden Gate National Recreation Area. For a topographic map, ask the USGS for San Francisco South.

Directions: In San Francisco, drive west on Fell Street to Lincoln Avenue where it ends at the Great Highway. Turn left and drive south on Great Highway to the exit road on the right to the primary parking lot, or continue to Skyline Boulevard. Turn right (south) and drive a short distance to the secondary parking lot (unpaved at roadside) on the right, or a little less than a mile to the park entrance (also on the right). Both parking lots are accessible only on southbound Skyline Drive.

From the Peninsula: Take I-280 north to Highway 1 in Colma. Turn west on Highway 1 and drive one mile to Highway 35/Skyline Boulevard. Turn right (north) on Highway 35 and drive about five miles to a stop sign at John Muir Drive (adjacent to Lake Merced). Make a U-turn and drive a short way to parking on the right, or continue north to stop sign. Turn left on Great Highway and make a U-turn when able to exit for the main parking area.

Contact: Fort Funston, Golden Gate National Recreation Area, 415/561-4700, www.nps.gov/goga; dog information, 415/561-4728.

69 SUMMIT LOOP TRAIL

3.1 mi/1.5 hr 2 9

in San Bruno Mountain State and County Park

Map 7.2, page 290

San Bruno Mountain rises to an elevation of 1,314 feet (it's the big mountain on the north Peninsula near the Cow Palace, west of Monster Park). For unforgettable moments, take the Summit Loop Trail. On clear days, the views are incredible—the best are of South San Francisco Bay and across the East Bay foothills to Mount Diablo. Yet that's only a start. To the north, you can also see across San Francisco, from the downtown skyline to Twin Peaks. Scan to the west and past Sweeney Ridge to the slopes of Montara Mountain. On perfect days, you can even get a glimpse of Mount Tamalpais north in Marin.

The signed trailhead for the Summit Loop is at the south parking lot (not the main parking lot). From that lot, take the 100-yard connector spur that is routed to a three-way junction. Turn left for a short climb, and within a mile, you get sweeping views of South San Francisco Bay. Continue on the trail north (do not turn on the Dairy Ravine Trail) to the cutoff fork on the left for the lookout bench. Bring a friend, a picnic, and a camera. From your perch high atop San Bruno Mountain, you can look down on U.S. 101 in South San Francisco and easily imagine the temporary insanity that grips some drivers in their mission to reach San Francisco International Airport.

When you're ready, return to the main Summit Loop Trail. The trail climbs near the antenna-spiked mountaintop for 360-degree views. To complete the trip, head downhill on paved Radio Road, cross the road, and turn left at the signed trail to the right of the gated road. Follow the Summit Loop back to the parking lot. Various routes are also easy to follow with the park map.

User Groups: Hikers and horses. No dogs or mountain bikes. No wheelchair facilities.

Permits: No permits are required. An entrance fee of $6 per vehicle is charged (self-registration, cash only).

Maps: A brochure and map are available at the entrance kiosk. For a free trail map, contact San Bruno Mountain State and County Park. For a topographic map, ask the USGS for San Francisco South.

Directions: Takes U.S. 101 to Exit 429B for Brisbane/Cow Palace. Take that exit and merge to Bayshore Boulevard and drive two miles to Guadalupe Canyon Parkway. Turn west (right) and drive 2.2 miles to the park entrance. Turn right to entrance kiosk, then continue for 0.2 mile (loop under road to south side of Guadalupe Canyon Parkway) to parking area/trailhead and Radio Road. Continue straight on Radio Road and go two miles (uphill, paved) to summit parking and trailheads for Summit Loop and Ridge Trail.

Contact: San Bruno Mountain State and County Park, 650/589-5707, or 650/573-2592 (Coyote Point); San Mateo County Parks Department, 650/363-4020, http://parks.smcgov.org.

70 RIDGE TRAIL

4.4 mi/2.0 hr

in San Bruno Mountain State and County Park

Map 7.2, page 290

The Ridge Trail gets overlooked by newcomers to the park (because of the landmark qualities of the Summit Loop, the previous hike). From the south end of the parking area at the summit, the Ridge Trail extends along the Southeast Ridge for 2.2 miles to trail's end at a 1,000-foot perch overlooking the South Bay. On bright, crystal winter days, you can see the reflection of the domes at Lick Observatory on top of 4,209-foot Mount Hamilton east of San Jose. It's a sweeping view across the South Bay. You can often have it to yourself.

Near the parking area on top, you can see the remnants and foundation of one of the Bay Area's NIKE Missile radar sites. In addition, look for details along the trail. More than 100 million years ago, San Bruno Mountain was the bottom of the sea. Ancient marine deposits can be found throughout the park.

User Groups: Hikers and horses. No dogs or mountain bikes. No wheelchair facilities.

Permits: No permits are required. An entrance fee of $5 per vehicle is charged (self-registration, cash only).

Maps: For a free trail map, contact San Bruno Mountain State and County Park. For a topographic map, ask the USGS for San Francisco South.

Directions: From San Francisco, take U.S. 101 south for 3.3 miles to Exit 429B for Brisbane/Cow Palace. Take that exit and merge onto Bayshore Boulevard. Drive two miles to Guadalupe Canyon Parkway. Turn west (right) and drive 2.2 miles to the park entrance. Turn right through the entrance kiosk and park in the main lot.

Contact: San Bruno Mountain State and County Park, 650/589-5707 or 650/573-2592; San Mateo County Parks Department, 650/363-4020, http://parks.smcgov.org.

71 SWEENEY RIDGE

5.0 mi/3.0 hr

in San Bruno

Map 7.2, page 290

Sweeney Ridge can be an eye-popping getaway to take in a celebration of life. The drive up to it is within easy range of most Bay Area residents and the hits just keep on coming along the way, topped by gorgeous long-distance views.

Sweeney Ridge splits San Bruno to the east and Pacifica to the west. There are four trailheads, but the launch point with the best parking is at Skyline College at Parking Lot #2. From the trailhead to the locked gate, it is an estimated 700-foot climb (with a climb, drop, and climb again on the way in). On the ridge, you get sweeping views to your left of San Andreas Lake, the South Bay, and on the horizon, distant Mount Diablo. To your right, you can scan across the wilderness east flank of Montara Mountain, Pacifica, and the sea. You will pass a graffiti-smeared concrete shell of a building that was once a former NIKE radar station, the marker for the Portola Discovery Site, and then head beyond on the ridge to a cutoff trail on your right to South Meadow. Look for a cutoff trail to Cattle Hill on the right (it is unsigned and not on maps). Turn right, and in just five minutes, this small cutoff provides an overlook for what is known as South Meadow, an outstanding wildlife habitat with a stunning view of the ocean. On clear days, plan a picnic here, facing out to sea, and take in the view of Pacifica below, and on pristine days, across the ocean to the Farallon Islands. Wildlife includes lots of bush bunnies, decent numbers of small black-tailed deer, and if you're lucky, occasional fox or bobcat.

Sadly, access ends at the locked gate for the Crystal Springs Watershed (instead of allowing you to hike up a service road on the east flank of Montara Mountain, and then down the other side to Montara State Beach). A favorite approach is the South Meadow gate, where wildlife sightings (deer and bush bunnies) are best in the evening.

User Groups: Hikers, dogs, horses, and mountain bikes. No wheelchair facilities.

Permits: No permits are required. Parking and access are free.

Maps: For a free map, contact the Golden Gate National Recreation Area. For a topographic map, ask the USGS for San Francisco South.

Directions: From San Francisco, take I-280 south to Daly City and Exit 47B for Highway 1 south toward Pacifica. Take that exit and drive 1.1 miles up the hill to the exit for Skyline Boulevard/Highway 35. Take the exit for Highway 35 south and drive south on Skyline Boulevard for 3.5 miles (past Sharp Park Drive/Westborough) to College Drive. Turn right on College Drive and go 0.4 mile to College Loop Drive. Turn left and drive a short distance to Parking Lot #2 and the trailhead on south side.

From the Peninsula: Take I-280 north to Exit 41 for Skyline Boulevard/Highway 35. Take that exit and drive 2.8 miles north to College Drive. Turn left on College Drive and go 0.4 mile to College Loop Drive. Turn left and drive a short distance to Parking Lot #2 and the trailhead at south side.

Contact: Golden Gate National Recreation Area, 415/561-4700, www.nps.gov/goga.

72 SAN ANDREAS TRAIL

6.0 mi/3.0 hr 1 7

on Highway 35/Skyline Boulevard

Map 7.2, page 290

Of the county trails along the eastern border of Crystal Springs Watershed, this one provides the best views. The San Andreas Trail overlooks Upper San Andreas Lake, winding most of its way through wooded foothills. The only downer is that much of the route runs adjacent to Highway 35/Skyline Boulevard. Regardless, it is worth the trip, because to the west you can see the untouched slopes of Montara Mountain, a game preserve, and that sparkling lake—all off-limits to the public.

The trail starts near the northern end of the lake; a signed trailhead marker is posted on Skyline Boulevard. The route runs about three miles south to the next access point, at Hillcrest Boulevard, and from there, it connects to Sawyer Camp Trail. The view of Montara Mountain to the west is particularly enchanting during the summer, when rolling fogbanks crest the ridgeline: a spectacle.

User Groups: Hikers, horses, and mountain bikes. Note that the northern section is paved, but the southern section is not. There are some wheelchair-accessible facilities. No dogs.

Permits: No permits are required. Parking and access are free.

Maps: For a free trail map, contact San Mateo County Division of Parks. For a topographic map, ask the USGS for Montara Mountain.

Directions: To access the north gate: From I-280 in San Bruno, take the Westborough exit and drive west up the hill to the intersection with Highway 35/Skyline Boulevard. Turn left on Highway 35 and drive about 2.5 miles to the trailhead entrance on the right side of the road.

To access the south gate: On I-280, drive to the Millbrae Avenue exit. Take that exit and drive north on Skyline Boulevard, a frontage road on the west side of I-280, and continue to the parking area on the left.

Contact: San Mateo County Parks Department, 650/363-4020, http://parks.smcgov.org.

73 SAWYER CAMP RECREATION TRAIL

12.0 mi/5.0 hr 1 8

in San Mateo County southwest of San Bruno

Map 7.2, page 290

The six-mile Sawyer Camp Trail is the most popular segment of the 15.3-mile Crystal Springs Regional Trail. It is routed along a pretty lake and through a forest, so you get more nature. Most visitors access at the southern trailhead near Crystal Springs Dam. A trail over the dam opened in 2019, making for a great easy walk or a sensational 30-mile round-trip bike ride.

From the southern trailhead, you walk adjacent the northern end of Crystal Springs Reservoir. Views of the lake and beyond up Montara Mountain are beautiful. The trail runs adjacent to the lake for about three miles, then enters a gorgeous riparian area with a 600-year-old Jepson Laurel on the left. At 5.5 miles, you arrive at the dam for San Andreas Lake and, a half mile beyond, another access point and trailhead. The trail is paved and marked for two-way traffic, and even though park rangers occasionally use radar, high-end street bikes can easily cruise faster than the 15-mph speed limit. Watch out on blind turns. Portable restrooms are available at each trailhead and at two sites along the trail. From the trailhead at

Crystal Springs Dam, it is a 400-foot climb over six miles. On Saturday and Sunday mornings, it is crowded.

User Groups: Hikers, horses, and mountain bikes. There are some wheelchair-accessible facilities at the south end. No dogs.

Permits: No permits are required. Parking and access are free.

Maps: For a free trail map, contact San Mateo County Division of Parks. For a topographic map, ask the USGS for Montara Mountain.

Directions: Take I-280 to San Bruno and Exit 36 for Black Mountain Road. Take that exit a short distance to Highway 35 (frontage road west of I-280). Turn south on Highway 35 and drive 1.6 miles to parking and trailhead.

Contact: San Mateo County Parks Department, 650/363-4020, http://parks.smcgov.org.

74 MORI POINT TRAIL

2.5 mi/1.5 hr

in Pacifica near Pacifica State Beach/Linda Mar

Map 7.2, page 290

At Mori Point, all you need is a clear day. Your reward is big-time coastal views, a long expanse of beach, and a pretty walk. Mori Point is a dramatic coastal outcrop in Pacifica that is sometimes overlooked. On this route, you get access to extended beach frontage, a walk that starts out dead flat, with the option to climb to hilltop lookouts and bluff-top cliffs. Nearby is the best fishing pier on the Bay Area coast, Pacifica Pier, and adjacent is the Laguna Salada, a freshwater lagoon tucked on the edge of the Sharp Park Golf Course.

On the drive in, there isn't a sign on Highway 1 that says "Mori Point," so outside of locals and overnighters at the local hotels, it can get overlooked. From the trailhead at the corner of Beach Road and Clarendon, you walk south, with a dark-sand beach on your right, the golf course on your left, for about 0.7 mile. It's flat and pretty, with beach access all the way. For many, this is plenty. For others more ambitious, continue on.

The walk then turns into a short, steep hike that climbs to a coastal ridge. A matrix of trails from other trailheads converge on top. Most venture to the edge of the oceanfront cliffs; if you have young kids, keep them on a leash. You can explore to the top of the ridge for dramatic views. You can see north past Mussel Rock and along the San Francisco coast to the Cliff House, and beyond to the curving Point Reyes waterfront.

User Groups: Hikers and dogs. No horses or mountain bikes. No wheelchair facilities.

Permits: No permits are required. Parking and access are free.

Maps: For a topographic map, ask the USGS for Montara Mountain.

Directions: From San Francisco, take I-280 South to Daly City to the exit for Highway 1/Pacifica. Bear right at the exit from Highway 1 and drive 3.7 miles into Pacifica and to Exit 506 (toward Paloma Avenue/Francisco Boulevard). Take that exit and continue south 0.2 mile to Paloma Avenue. Turn right on Paloma and drive 0.2 mile to Beach Boulevard. Turn left on Beach and go 0.5 mile (you will pass Pacifica Pier on right) to parking on right and trailhead ahead at corner of Beach and Clarendon Road.

Access points and trailheads to the park are also available at Bradford Way, Mori Point Road, and the end of Fairway Drive.

Contact: Mori Point, Golden Gate National Recreation Area, Presidio Visitors Center, 415/561-4323, www.nps.gov/prsf; Pacifica Visitors Center, 650/355-4122, www.pacificachamber.com.

75 MONTARA MOUNTAIN TRAIL

7.0 mi/3.0 hr

in San Pedro Valley County Park in Pacifica

Map 7.2, page 290

Here's one of the best day hikes in the Bay Area. Just 20 minutes south of San Francisco is this sensational trail in San Pedro Valley County Park. The coastal beauty is divine, and hikers can carve out their own personal slice of heaven. The Montara Mountain Trail is the prize of the park, featuring the best viewing area for wispy Brooks Falls and great lookouts to the Pacific Coast.

From the west side of the parking lot, look for the signed trailhead for the Montara Mountain Trail. Take that uphill for 1.3 miles through the eucalyptus grove to the junction of the Brooks Creek Trail. Continue a short distance on the Montara Mountain Trail, where you will rise above tree line, to a spur that leads a short distance to a rock outcrop along San Pedro Ridge for a sensational coastal view to the north. The trail is routed uphill to a subridge to a junction, inside McNee Ranch/Montara Beach State Park, at a service road. Turn left for the final 1.1-mile push to reach the summit.

An array of antennas sit perched on top, so you'll have to shift your position to get views in every direction. On a clear spring day, the vistas are absolutely stunning in all directions—highlighted by the Pacific Ocean, the Farallon Islands, and miles of the adjacent off-limits Crystal Springs Watershed. If you look downslope to the southeast, you can glimpse a piece of gorgeous, off-limits Pilarcitos Lake. To the west, look for a separate sub-summit with a towering view of the coast.

On the way back, when you reach the fork with the Brooks Creek Trail, bear right and see if there is any water in Brooks Falls. There is a good lookout of the gorge across the canyon. Brooks Falls is connected in a series of narrow, silver-tasseled tiers in a chaparral-covered wilderness canyon. It falls 175 feet in all, from top to bottom, including breaks. At peak flow, there can be five strands. There never seems to be enough water in this waterfall, but it still is a very pretty gorge. It usually only runs in late winter and spring (best, of course, after several days of rain).

Though few take advantage of it, with a partner and a shuttle car, you could complete a great one-way hike. After you reach the top of Montara Mountain, hike 3.8 miles, where you sail down into McNee Ranch State Park above Montara and to Montara State Beach. You descend all the way, with glorious views for the entire route. So with cars parked at each end of the trail, you can hike 7.3 miles one-way from San Pedro Valley County Park, up Montara Mountain, and down to Montara State Beach.

User Groups: Hikers and horses (on designated trails only). Some trails and facilities are wheelchair-accessible. No dogs or mountain bikes.

Permits: No permits are required. An entrance fee of $6 per vehicle is charged.

Maps: For a free trail map, contact San Pedro Valley County Park. For a topographic map, ask the USGS for Montara Mountain.

Directions: From San Francisco, take Highway 1 south to Pacifica. Turn east on Linda Mar Boulevard and continue until it dead-ends, at Oddstad Boulevard. Turn right and drive to the park entrance, located about 50 yards on the left. The trailhead is on the southwest side of the parking lot.

Contact: San Pedro Valley County Park, 650/355-8289, http://parks.smcgov.org.

76 WEILER RANCH ROAD

1.5 mi/1.0 hr

in San Pedro Valley County Park in Pacifica

Map 7.2, page 290

From the north end of the parking area, take the service road to Weiler Ranch Road. Continue for a half mile to the end of the road at the headwaters of San Pedro Creek and the foot of the hills below Sweeney Ridge and San Francisco Fish and Wildlife Refuge. This is the best area in the park for wildlife sightings, with the best wildlife-watching opportunities at dusk. Weiler Ranch Road is a service road that is routed out through the heart of a valley nestled with meadows that attract wildlife at dawn and dusk. It's common to see deer and rabbits in the meadow, and red-tailed hawks and turkey vultures overhead. If you get real lucky, you might get a glimpse of a bobcat. In fact, we've had these wildlife sightings many times, but it's always best right at dusk. Turn back when ready.

The gate to the park is often closed at the best times to see wildlife, at dawn and dusk. One tip is to park outside the park entrance, so you have access even when gated.

User Groups: Hikers and horses (on designated trails only). Some trails and facilities are wheelchair-accessible. No dogs or mountain bikes.

Permits: No permits are required. An entrance fee of $6 per vehicle is charged.

Maps: A brochure and map are available at entrance kiosk and visitors center. For a free trail map, contact San Pedro Valley County Park. For a topographic map, ask the USGS for Montara Mountain.

Directions: From San Francisco, take Highway 1 south to Pacifica. Turn east on Linda Mar Boulevard and continue until it dead-ends at Oddstad Boulevard. Turn right and drive to the park entrance, located about 50 yards ahead on the left. The trailhead is on the southwest side of the parking lot.

Contact: San Pedro Valley County Park, 650/355-8289, http://parks.smcgov.org.

77 SAN PEDRO MOUNTAIN

6.0 mi/2.5 hr  

in McNee Ranch State Park in Montara

Map 7.2, page 290

On one side is an expanse of gorgeous beach, Montara State Beach. On the other is a 1,898-foot wilderness mountain, Montara Mountain, and McNee Ranch/Montara State Beach. Together they comprise a can't-miss get-out. If you can go early enough to beat the traffic, this one can be great, start to finish.

The park spans for miles from beachfront to mountaintop. You get access at the yellow pipe gate and service road (there is parking space for only a few cars; a better idea is to park down Highway 1 a short ways on the west side, then return on foot to the gate). At the gate, turn left and hike the trail that tracks along the coastal ridgelines, an easy to moderate climb that leads to an overlook of Gray Whale Cove and the ocean. From this viewpoint, you may feel an odd sense of irony: Below is Highway 1, typically filled with a stream of slow-moving cars driven by people who want to get somewhere else; meanwhile, you are in a place of peace and serenity, happy right where you are.

Montara State Beach is a long sandy beach with pretty waves, views of passing fishing boats and ships, and surf fishing for perch. The extreme north end has a feeling of seclusion, edged by a cliff, even with Highway 1 just above. This is one of the few state beaches in California to allow dogs.

User Groups: Hikers and dogs. No horses or mountain bikes. No wheelchair facilities.

Permits: No permits are required. Parking and access are free.

Maps: For a topographic map, ask the USGS for Montara Mountain.

Directions: Take I-280 to Daly City and the split for Highway 1/Pacifica. Follow Highway 1 south for 11 miles (through Pacifica and past Devil's Slide) and emerge at Montara State Beach on your right, McNee Ranch on your left.

From East Bay and Peninsula: Take U.S.

101 or I-280 to Highway 92 in San Mateo. Follow Highway 92 west to Half Moon Bay and Highway 1. Turn right on Highway 1 and drive six miles to Moss Beach, then continue two miles to Montara. Park on the beach side of highway at the north end of Montara State Beach or at southern end of beach adjacent to La Costanera Restaurant.

Contact: Half Moon Bay State Parks, 650/726-8820; Half Moon Bay State Beach Ranger Station, 650/726-8819, www.parks.ca.gov.

78 MONTARA MOUNTAIN/ MCNEE RANCH

7.6 mi/3.75 hr

in McNee Ranch State Park in Montara

Map 7.2, page 290

Of the two major routes to the top of Montara Mountain, this is the one with two butt-kicker sections. It is well worth it. On a clear day from the top of Montara Mountain, the Farallon Islands to the northwest appear so close you may think you could reach out and pluck them from the ocean. To the east, it looks as if you could take a giant leap across the bay and land atop Mount Diablo.

Some 10 miles to the north and south, there's nothing but mountain wilderness connecting Sweeney Ridge to the off-limits California State Fish and Game Reserve. By now you should be properly motivated for the climb. From the main access gate to the top, it's 3.8 miles, a rise of nearly 2,000 feet that includes two killer "ups."

From the pipe entrance gate, start the trip by hiking straight ahead, on the ranch-style service road. Follow this ranch road up the San Pedro Mountain ridgeline to the Montara Coastal Range. At the first fork, stay to the right on the dirt road as it climbs and turns.

Here's a secret: At the power lines, look for a deer trail on your left that is routed down through the chaparral to the west. This leads to an old concrete army bunker. Enjoy the history, then head back up to the main road/trail. (In my novel, *The Sweet Redemption*, I used this site as a key location for the story line.)

After a 20-minute wheezer of an ascent—yes, butt-kicker level—look for a cutoff spur trail at a flat spot on the left side of the trail. This 30-yard cutoff trail leads to a perch for a dazzling view of Pacifica and northward along the Pacific Coast. After catching your breath, return to the trail and continue on, heading up, up, and up, eventually topping out at the summit. An array of antennas are perched on top, so you'll have to shift your position to get views in each direction. All you need for this hike is a clear day, some water, and plenty of inspiration. If you need reason to stay fit, this hike is it.

User Groups: Hikers, dogs, and mountain bikes. No horses. No wheelchair facilities.

Permits: No permits are required. Parking and access are free.

Maps: For a topographic map, ask the USGS for Montara Mountain.

Directions: Take I-280 to Daly City and the split for Highway 1/Pacifica. Follow Highway 1 south for 11 miles (through Pacifica and past Devil's Slide) and emerge at Montara State Beach on your right, McNee Ranch on your left.

From East Bay and Peninsula: Take U.S. 101 or I-280 to Highway 92 in San Mateo. Follow Highway 92 west to Half Moon Bay and Highway 1. Turn right on Highway 1 and drive six miles to Moss Beach, then continue two miles to Montara. Park on the beach side of highway at the north end of Montara State Beach or at southern end of beach adjacent to La Costanera Restaurant.

Contact: Half Moon Bay State Parks, 650/726-8820; Half Moon Bay State Beach Ranger Station, 650/726-8819, www.parks.ca.gov.

79 COYOTE POINT/ SHORELINE TRAIL

1.0-10.0 mi/0.5-5.0 hr 1 7

in Coyote Point County Park in San Mateo

Map 7.2, page 290

Coyote Point is perched on the extended shore of the South Bay, an outstanding recreation site on the Peninsula. You get long-distance water views and a chance at many adventures. At the minimum, take the Marina Trail out to land's end at Coyote Point. You get a pretty view of the South Bay tidewaters, often with good numbers of shorebirds. It's just a start. Just east of the marina, take the gravel Shoreline Trail. These wetlands and adjacent flats attract resident ducks and geese, along with egrets, coots, sandpipers, and other migrants (avocets, for instance, arrive every March). You can take the Shoreline Trail along water's edge of the South Bay to where the trail turns north and then heads inland. In the process, you get a cool view of jets coming in for landings.

The Bay Trail can also be linked with the Promenade Trail and Bluff Trail (flat and easy) that roughly circles the recreation area.

User Groups: Hikers, wheelchairs, and mountain bikes. No dogs or horses.

Permits: No permits are required. An entrance fee of $6 per vehicle is charged.

Maps: For a free trail map, contact Coyote Point County Park. For a topographic map, ask the USGS for San Mateo.

Directions: Take U.S. 101 to San Mateo and Exit 417 (for Poplar Avenue). Take the exit and merge onto East Poplar; drive a short distance to North Humboldt Street. Turn right and go 0.4 mile to (third right) Peninsula Avenue. Turn right and go 0.2 mile to Coyote Point Drive. Continue on Coyote Point Drive for 0.5 mile to Coyote Point Marina.

From the south, take U.S. 101 north (eight miles north of Redwood City) to Exit 417B (for Peninsula Avenue). Take that exit, keep right at the fork, and continue a short distance to Airport Boulevard. Turn right on Airport Boulevard and drive to Coyote Point Drive. Turn left and drive 0.5 mile to Coyote Point Marina.

Contact: Coyote Point County Park, San Mateo, 650/573-2592; San Mateo County Division of Parks, 650/363-4020, http://parks.smcgov.org.

80 FITZGERALD MARINE RESERVE

1.0 mi/0.5 hr 1 9

in Moss Beach

Map 7.2, page 290 BEST

The Fitzgerald Marine Reserve provides the best tidepool hopping in California. After parking, it's a short walk down to the tidepools; from here, you walk on exposed rock, watching the wonders of the tidal waters. In the tidepools, you may see hermit crabs, rock crabs, sea anemones, sculpins, starfish, sea snails, and many other animals and plants in various colors. The best bet is to pick a minus low tide and explore the tidepool world. The closer you look, the better it gets. When you go tidepool hopping, there is nothing more fascinating than discovering a variety of tiny sea creatures. The reef spans 30 acres with hundreds and hundreds of pockets, crevices, and cuts every time a minus low tide rolls back to the ocean. Be sure to wear boots that grip well, and take care not to crush any fragile sea plants as you walk. An option during low tides is to continue walking south on the beach to a beautiful cove at the foot of the Moss Beach Distillery, a popular watering hole. No dogs, no beachcombing, no shell gathering. In other words, okay looky, but no touchy.

User Groups: Hikers only. No dogs, horses, or mountain bikes. No wheelchair facilities.

Permits: No permits are required. Parking and access are free.

Maps: For a topographic map, ask the USGS for Montara Mountain.

Directions: Take I-280 to Highway 1 in Daly

Pillar Point

City and drive through Pacifica, over Devil's Slide, and into Moss Beach. Turn right (west) at the signed turnoff at California Street and continue one mile to the parking area.

Contact: Fitzgerald Marine Reserve, Moss Beach, 650/728-3584; San Mateo County Parks Department, 650/363-4020 or 650/340-7598, http://parks.smcgov.org.

81 MAVERICKS BEACH

2.5 mi/1.5 hr 1 8

in Princeton at Half Moon Bay

Map 7.2, page 290

Mavericks is world famous for its big waves and surfing competition. But many people do not even know where it is. Even for those who know the place, it can be a stunner if you arrive at a nonpeak time: You will find a secluded stretch of beach at Pillar Point Head, hidden tidepools at low tides, and a pretty walk on a bluff that overlooks Pillar Point Harbor. When you drive Highway 1 along Half Moon Bay, you'll see a radar station that looks like a giant tennis ball at Pillar Point Head. Mavericks is located on the south side of Pillar Point Head. The parking lot is at the foot of the road that leads to the radar station.

From the parking lot, a trail extends along a bluff perched above a beach and waterfront of Pillar Point Harbor. You get views across the water, harbor, and beyond to the coastal hills. Birdlife is excellent, with grebes, gulls, and the usual suspects. I've seen otters on this side of the harbor, too. The walk leads out to the foot of the north rock jetty, which you can rock hop to fishing spots or continue to Mavericks Beach. From the foot of the jetty, you turn right and arrive at an extended sandy beach. When seas are calm, sea lions often play peekaboo amid nearby kelp beds. At the end of the beach at Pillar Point, minus low tides unveil expansive rocky tidepools and crevices. If you continue exploring, during low tides you can boulder hop your way around Pillar Point Head (a gap stops you from reaching a hidden beach).

The big waves for world-class surfing arrive just offshore during periods of huge ocean swells, often 15-foot swells or bigger, and often (but not always) timed at the top of the tide.

User Groups: Hikers, dogs, and horses (not advised). No mountain bikes. No wheelchair facilities.

Permits: No permits are required. Parking and access are free.

Maps: For a topographic map, ask the USGS for Half Moon Bay.

Directions: Take I-280 to Daly City and the exit for Highway 1/Pacifica. Take that exit and drive 15.2 miles to Princeton/El Granada and a lighted intersection with Capistrano Road. Turn right on Capistrano Road and drive 0.4 mile to Prospect Way. Turn left on Prospect and drive 350 feet to Broadway. Turn left on Broadway and go 150 feet to Princeton Avenue. Turn right on Princeton and drive 0.3 mile to West Point Avenue. Turn right on West Point and go 300 feet, then turn left and drive 0.5 mile to a short, signed cutoff on left to parking lot.

From East Bay and Peninsula: From San Mateo, take Highway 92 west for 12 miles to Half Moon Bay and the junction with Highway 1. Turn right on Highway 1 and drive 3.9 miles to Princeton/El Granada and a lighted intersection with Capistrano Road. Turn left and continue to Pillar Point as above.

Contact: Pillar Point Harbor, 650/726-5727, www.smharbor.com/pillarpoint; weather recording 650/726-6070.

82 FIFIELD-CAHILL TRAIL

10.0 mi one-way/ 5.0 hr 3 10

in Crystal Springs Watershed near Woodside

Map 7.2, page 290

The fight that took 70 years to win was resolved with one turn of a key. A locked gate at the Crystal Springs Watershed on the Peninsula was finally cracked open to the public. Access to the 23,000-acre watershed—which we once nicknamed the Forbidden Paradise—is finally possible, though by reservations only, where you join a group. Still, this is something special.

This trip is 10 miles one-way with a shuttle: from the Quarry Gate near Highway 92 and extending on the Bay Ridge Trail to Sweeney Ridge and then beyond to Sneath Lane Gate in San Bruno. The hike starts by passing through Quarry Gate. On a service road, climb 640 feet over the course of a mile to Cemetery Gate. This is the hardest part of the trip: a challenging climb on a bike, a steady rhythmic pull for hikers. You will pass through cypress forest and patches of chaparral, with views of Upper Crystal Springs.

Cemetery Gate to Five Points: After topping out at Cahill Ridge, enjoy an easy descent through old-growth cypress and Douglas fir and, farther north, redwoods. Keep an eye out on your left for a giant old-growth Douglas fir called "Big Doug." It's three miles to Five Points, a five-way road junction, and your link north to the Fifield Ridge Route.

Fifield Ridge to Portola Gate: This is the best part of the trip. From Five Points, you are routed up above hidden Pilarcitos Lake to Fifield Ridge, emerging in wilderness for stunning views of the wild east flank of Montara Mountain to your left. As you continue north, you then get sweeping views to your right of the South Bay. In spring, this area is loaded with wildflowers. Deer, bobcat, and fox provide occasional sightings.

Portola Gate to Sneath Lane: First pass a hidden meadow on your left with views of Pacifica and the ocean. Continue to the Bay Discovery Site, with a dramatic scope below of the Peninsula's wildlands, the lakes in the watershed, and the South Bay. The end of the trip is a downhill glide to the Sneath Lane Gate and your shuttle car.

As good as this is, it could get far better. For instance, another service road junctions with Fifield Ridge, providing a route up the little-seen eastern flank of Montara Mountain all the way to the 1,898-foot summit. Then the route goes over the top to McNee State Park and San Pedro Valley County Park. Opening that route would provide a sensational one-way hike, starting from the Sneath Lake access. You would climb to Sweeney Ridge, then into the watershed and to the summit of Montara Mountain, and then down the north side to McNee Ranch State Park in Montara.

User Groups: Hiking, biking, and horseback riding permitted, but not at the same time; volunteer trail leader required with all parties. No dogs. Limited wheelchair access from Skylawn trailhead.

Permits: Reservations are required. Reserve online at www.sfwater.org (click on Community, Explore). Public access is restricted to groups under the supervision of a trained leader on Wednesday, Saturday, and Sunday.

Maps: For a free trail map, contact San Francisco Public Utilities Commission. For a topographic map, ask the USGS for San Mateo.

Directions: To Quarry Gate: From the Peninsula, take I-280 to Highway 92. Turn west on Highway 92, drive over Crystal Springs Reservoir and continue 0.5 mile to Quarry Gate on right. Turn right and go short distance to parking and trailhead.

To Sneath Lane Trailhead: To drop off the shuttle car, take I-280 to San Bruno and the exit for Sneath Lane. Take that exit, and drive west on Sneath Lane to the road's end. Leave the car near the access point for Golden Gate National Recreation Area.

Contact: San Francisco Public Utilities Commission, 650/652-3203, www.sfwater.org.

83 CRYSTAL SPRINGS TRAIL

6.4 mi/3.0 hr 1 7

along Crystal Springs Reservoir near Woodside

Map 7.2, page 290

From the parking area, the Crystal Springs Trail runs along the border of San Francisco watershed land, adjacent to Canada Road. Your destination is 3.2 miles away at the Pulgas Water Temple, where waters from Hetch Hetchy in Yosemite arrive via pipe and thunder into this giant, sunken bathtub-like structure surrounded by Roman pillars and a canopy. It's quite a sight. Beautiful Crystal Springs Reservoir is off to the west for most of the hike, though it occasionally disappears from view behind a hill as you continue south. Deer are commonly seen in this area—a nice bonus. The adjacent road, Canada Road, is a famous family bike trip on Bicycle Sundays, when it is closed to all vehicles.

User Groups: Hikers and mountain bikes. No dogs or horses. No wheelchair facilities.

Permits: No permits are required. Parking and access are free.

Maps: For a free trail map, contact San Mateo County Division of Parks. For a topographic map, ask the USGS for San Mateo.

Directions: From I-280 in San Mateo, take the Highway 92 exit and drive west to Canada Road/Highway 95. Turn south on Canada Road and drive 0.2 mile to the parking area, on the right.

Contact: San Mateo County Parks Department, 650/363-4020, http://parks.smcgov.org.

84 HARKINS RIDGE LOOP FROM HALF MOON BAY

6.5 mi/3.5 hr 3 9

in Purisima Creek Redwoods Open Space Preserve

Map 7.2, page 290

One of our favorites. From the staging area on Higgins Canyon Road south of Half Moon Bay, take the trailhead for Harkins Ridge Trail. It is routed through a redwood canyon and then rises up a sub-ridge 1,600 feet, within earshot of Skyline. Turn left on the North Ridge Trail, then left again on Whittemore Gulch Trail and sail back down to the starting spot. For much of the route, deep valleys plunge on each side.

There's one steep spot, but it's shaded for the most part, with pretty valley views. The route then turns left and climbs out of the canyon to a ridge, where a few steep spots on the way up make for dramatic drops on each side into remote valleys. At three miles, just a short distance from Skyline (close enough that you might even hear people at the parking lot), you emerge at a junction with the North Ridge Trail. Turn left on the North Ridge Trail for 0.5 mile, then take another left on Whittemore Gulch Trail for the easy 2.8 mile downhill glide back to the trailhead.

This trip can also be started from Skyline as the Whittemore Gulch Loop, but the return trip will be up rather than down.

User Groups: The Purisima Creek Trail and Harkins Ridge Trail are open to hiking, biking, and horses. Bikes and horses often restricted on Whittemore Gulch Trail in wet weather. No dogs. No wheelchair facilities.

Permits: No permits are required. Parking and access are free.

Maps: For a free map, contact the Midpeninsula Regional Open Space District or pick one up at the trailhead. For a topographic map, ask the USGS for Woodside.

Directions: Take I-280 to Highway 92. Bear west on 92 and drive up to ridge and continue west to Half Moon Bay and lighted intersection at Main Street. Turn south (left) on Main Street and drive through town (about a mile) to Higgins-Purisima Road. Turn left on Higgins-Purisima and drive four miles (becomes curvy, watch out for bikes) to the staging area for Purisima Creek Redwoods Open Space Preserve on the left. If the small parking lot is full, park on the road's shoulder ahead, on the right. Do not block the road, which limits the ability of emergency vehicles to pass. Cars will be towed.

Contact: Midpeninsula Regional Open Space District, 650/691-1200, www.openspace.org.

85 WHITTEMORE GULCH LOOP FROM SKYLINE

6.5 mi/3.5 hr

in Purisima Creek Redwoods Open Space Preserve

Map 7.2, page 290

Purisima Creek Redwoods is a magnificent 4,752-acre preserve set on the western slopes of the Santa Cruz Mountains from Skyline Boulevard down to Half Moon Bay. One of the best ways to explore the area is on this great loop hike. You can make it a one-way trip by having a shuttle car waiting at the trail's end at the Higgins-Purisima parking access.

This trail starts at the Skyline Access on Skyline Boulevard, located at a parking area just south of a small building (it used to be a store). From the trailhead, descend a short distance to a junction with the North Ridge Trail. Turn right and descend a further 0.5 mile to a junction with the Whittemore Gulch Trail. The trail drops quickly at first, then more gradually to the rim of the canyon.

At the canyon rim, a series of switchbacks takes you down the hill about 1,000 feet into the redwood canyon. It is well graded (about 10 percent). In all, the descent is 1,600 feet. At the bottom of the forest floor, turn left on the Harkins Ridge Trail and climb 3.3 miles back to the top.

Timing: On weekday mornings, this place can be paradise—Purisima can feel like a vast uninhabited wilderness, complete with the long-distance coastal views and a hidden redwood canyon. On Sunday afternoons, however, it's often crowded. Mountain bikers can be an issue when they ride fast downhill on Harkins Ridge Trail.

User Groups: The Purisima Creek Trail and Harkins Ridge Trail are open to hiking, biking, and horses. Bikes and horses often restricted on Whittemore Gulch Trail in wet weather. No dogs. No wheelchair facilities.

Permits: No permits are required. Parking and access are free.

Maps: For a free map, contact the Midpeninsula Regional Open Space District or pick one up at the trailhead. For a topographic map, ask the USGS for Woodside.

Directions: Take I-280 to Highway 92. Bear west on 92 and drive past Crystal Springs and up to the ridge and the junction with Highway 35/Skyline. Turn left on Skyline and drive 4.5 miles to parking area on right, signed for preserve.

Contact: Midpeninsula Regional Open Space District, 650/691-1200, www.openspace.org.

86 REDWOOD TRAIL

0.5 mi/0.5 hr

in Purisima Creek Redwoods Open Space Preserve

Map 7.2, page 290

The 0.25-mile-long Redwood Trail allows just about anybody to experience the grandeur of a redwood forest. Anybody? People with baby strollers, wheelchairs, or walkers, as well as those recovering from poor health, will be able to do this trail. It starts at an elevation 2,000 feet on Skyline Boulevard and is routed north under a canopy of giant redwoods. At the end, there are picnic tables and restrooms. And the return trip is just as easy. Most people don't really hike the trail, they just kind of mosey along, seeing how it feels to wander freely among ancient trees.

User Groups: Hikers and wheelchairs. No dogs, horses, or mountain bikes.

Permits: No permits are required. Parking and access are free.

Maps: For a free map, contact the Midpeninsula Regional Open Space District or pick one up at the trailhead. For a topographic map, ask the USGS for Woodside.

Directions: Take I-280 to Highway 92. Bear west on 92 and drive past Crystal Springs and up to the ridge and the junction with Highway 35/Skyline. Turn left on Skyline and drive 4.5 miles (past parking area on right) and continue to mile marker 16.65 and parking area on right, signed for preserve and Redwood Trail.

Contact: Midpeninsula Regional Open Space District, 650/691-1200, www.openspace.org.

87 HUDDART PARK LOOP

7.5 mi/3.5 hr

in Woodside

Map 7.2, page 290

With two slight changes (and we'll get to that) this hike could be a 9. As it is, the Huddart Park Loop is still a treasure. Huddart Park covers 1,000 acres from the foothills near Woodside on up to Skyline Boulevard. Nestled in a grassy area surrounded by woods, you can picnic, play, or head off into the wild. The best hike is a 7.5-mile loop that provides a tour through deep woods and along hidden creeks. This trek includes a 1,400-foot climb, but because trail makers kept grades at 6 percent, it's a steady, rhythmic pull to the top for hikers or runners, with all junctions signed. The woods extend up the slopes of Kings Mountain, and a network of trails is routed through the redwoods, amid patches of hardwoods, and along small creeks.

Start the hike at the Zwierlein Picnic Area (set next to a small parking lot near a restroom). Be sure to grab a trail map first, though; there are dozens of loop options at virtually every junction. At the trailhead sign, start on the left by hiking 0.2 mile to the Dean Trail, and then continue down into the canyon to the bridge at McGarvey Gulch and the junction with the Crystal Springs Trail. Turn right, and from the start, the trail feels like a tunnel through vegetation. It then quickly drops into redwood forest and crosses two small wood bridges over a pretty creek. From here, the Crystal Springs Trail rises 3.4 miles and 1,400 feet to Skyline. The grade is perfect. From the bridge, it took us an hour and 15 minutes to reach the top (2,000 feet), always in rhythm.

Before reaching Skyline, turn left on Summit Springs Trail (a dirt road) and climb steeply for

0.4 mile to the top of the ridge and the Skyline Trail. Turn left on Skyline Trail and continue another 0.3 mile to the Chinquapin Trail on the left. The Chinquapin Trail is routed in and out of heavily wooded canyons near the headwaters of McGarvey Gulch creek, down all the way. It eventually links to the Dean Trail; turn left to be routed back to the Zwierlein trailhead and parking lot. Add variety to your hike, or make it shorter or longer, by carrying a map.

The park has applied crushed gravel on a good part of the route to stop erosion caused by horses; it looks almost paved. If some trees were cleared on the west-facing flank on the trail near Skyline, it could create a gorgeous sweeping view of the South Bay.

User Groups: Hikers and horses. Mountain bikes are permitted on paved roads only. Horses restricted when trails are wet. The Chickadee Trail at Huddart Park is wheelchair-accessible. No dogs.

Permits: No permits are required. An entrance fee of $6 per vehicle is charged.

Maps: A brochure and map are available in a box at the entrance. For a trail map, contact Huddart Park. For a topographic map, ask the USGS for Woodside.

Directions: From San Francisco, take I-280 south and drive 20 miles to Woodside and the exit for Highway 84/Woodside Road. Take that exit, turn west (right) on Woodside Road, and drive 2.8 miles to Woodside. Continue 1.7 miles to Kings Mountain Road. Turn right and drive 2.8 (curvy) miles to the park entrance on the right. Take the entrance road to the kiosk, then continue to the parking area at Zwierlein Picnic Area. The trailhead is on the far side of the parking lot (adjacent to a restroom).

Contact: Huddart Park, 650/851-0326; San Mateo County Parks Department, 650/363-4020 or 650/340-7598 (group tour reservations), http://parks.smcgov.org.

88 TAFONI MONOLITH TO VISTA POINT

6.5 mi/3.5 hr  

El Corte de Madera Creek Open Space Preserve

Map 7.2, page 290

This is a 6.5-mile walk with about everything you could ask for: a beautiful destination with big trees, epic views, parking, and nice folks on the trail. From the trailhead, the first leg is 0.5-mile through a mixed forest. The trail undulates up and down in short rises and falls north to another access point (Gate CM02) along Skyline Boulevard/Highway 35. To reach the Methuselah Tree, cross Skyline here and walk a short distance. The diameter of the base of the tree is 14 feet across, with a circumference of 44 feet—the biggest redwood on the north Peninsula. The park district estimates the tree is 1,800 years old.

From the Methuselah Tree, recross Skyline Boulevard and take the Sierra Morena Trail for 0.4 mile to the Fir Trail. Turn left and walk 0.6 mile to a major junction with the Tafoni Trail. From here, it's just 0.1 mile to the spur to the Tafoni, then another 0.1 mile with an easy descent to the Tafoni Monolith. The trail leads a short way into a canyon and to a viewing deck perched at the base of the Tafoni, a 50-foot sandstone monolith that juts up from the wooded slope. From the deck, you get a close-up view of what looks like etched fretwork in the rock. As you peer up, you can see a matrix of holes, hollows, and crevices. There's nothing else quite like it anywhere.

Return to the junction of the Tafoni Trail and Fir Trail and follow the Fir Trail to the DC-6 crash monument. A short cutoff then leads to Vista Point. You top out at a 2,200-foot sub-ridge, where a break in the forest provides a view to the west that extends to the coast and ocean.

El Corte de Madera preserve (ECDM for short) is big, covering a variety of landscapes with a matrix of trails and abandoned roads.

ECDM spans 2,906 acres with 36 miles of trails, with excellent easy hikes and outstanding mountain biking, including plenty of single-track. From what I've seen on the trail here, the people riding do everything they can to slow down, smile, greet, and pass hikers with care. Maybe there is hope for the human race after all.

User Groups: Hiking, mountain bikes, horses. No dogs. No bikes or horses on short spur to Tafoni Monolith. No wheelchair facilities.

Permits: Parking and access are free.

Maps: Obtain a free map at the trailhead or from the Midpeninsula Regional Open Space District. For a topographic map, ask the USGS for Woodside.

Directions: Take I-280 to the exit for Highway 35/Bunker Hill Road (also signed for Highway 92W). Follow that exit, continue 0.2 mile to frontage road, turn left and go 1.1 miles to Highway 92 (stoplight). Turn right on Highway 92 and drive two miles up the hill to a left turn lane for Highway 35/Skyline. Turn left and drive 9.6 miles to El Corte de Madera Open Space Preserve on the right. The Midpeninsula Open Space District has a large parking lot with a big sign off Highway 35, with a staging area with trail maps, trailhead, and portable restroom.

From the Peninsula: Take I-280 to Highway 84. Turn west on Highway 84 and drive about seven miles (curvy through Woodside) to Sky Londa and Highway 35 (Skyline Boulevard). Turn right (north) and go 2.8 miles to El Corte de Madera Open Space Preserve on the left.

From East Bay: Take Highway 92 west to Crystal Springs and continue to crest at Skyline. Turn left and drive 9.6 miles to parking on right.

Contact: Midpeninsula Regional Open Space District, 650/691-1200, www.openspace.org.

Tafoni Monolith

89 ALAMBIQUE TRAIL

4.5 mi/2.5 hr 2 7

in Wunderlich County Park near Woodside

Map 7.2, page 290

This trailhead features a 4.5-mile loop hike that drops into a remote redwood canyon with a creek, then rises back up, looping back through forest to the starting point. The only thing the trail lacks is a series of gorgeous lookouts. You want views? Not here.

The trip starts on the east side of Skyline Boulevard, where a large blue sign for the Bay Ridge Trail marks the trailhead. From Skyline, start the trip on the Alambique Trail (signed). Here you work your way down a canyon for two miles amid a second-growth redwood forest. On foggy mornings, moisture can be so heavy that it can drip from the branches of redwoods and Douglas firs like a sparse rain. Everything smells wet, dense, and old. Our personal preference is a fogbound morning, when the heavy air smothers distant sounds, creating perfect quiet.

It takes only about 40 minutes to reach a canyon bottom, where you cross a feeder stream to Alambique Creek. This watershed is home to many banana slugs and newts, and when the forest is dripping with moisture, they are often on the trail—so be careful not to accidentally squish the little fellers. Though the canyon is cool and moist, it is the kind of place you can sit for a while and enjoy a trail lunch in complete peace. For the moment, you can let the rest of the world worry about their latest problems. There's always something, right?

Shortly after a creek crossing, you will reach a four-way junction with the Skyline Trail in about two miles. To return to the starting point, take the sharpest right on the Skyline Trail and climb back out (with a few short drops) for 2.4 miles to a staging area.

If you want to extend your trip at the junction, instead turn left on the Alambique Trail. This is routed farther down into the park to an additional network of trails. The best offshoots are to The Meadows (turn left on Bear Gulch Trail for 0.3 mile) or to Alambique Flat (to the right for 0.2 mile). Amid the second-growth forest along the lower portion of the Alambique Trail, there is a single awesome redwood giant called the Methuselah Tree that still remains. Its trunk is roughly 45 feet around, with massive burls and a burned-out gap.

User Groups: Hikers and horses. No dogs or mountain bikes. No wheelchair facilities.

Permits: No permits are required. Parking and access are free.

Maps: For a trail map, contact Huddart Park. For a topographic map, ask the USGS for Woodside.

Directions: Take I-280 to Woodside and Highway 84. Turn east on Highway 84 and go to Sky Londa and Highway 35/Skyline Boulevard. Turn right (north) and go 2.5 miles to the trailhead, on the right (signed Bay Ridge Trail). Limited parking is available on the road's shoulder.

From the East Bay: Take Highway 92 west to the junction of I-280 and continue three miles to Highway 35/Skyline Boulevard. Turn left (south) and go 10 miles to the trailhead, on the left.

Contact: Wunderlich County Park, c/o Huddart Park, 650/851-1210 or 650/851-0326 (entry kiosk); San Mateo County Parks Department, 650/363-4020, http://parks.smcgov.org/.

90 MEADOW LOOP TRAIL

5.5 mi/3.0 hr 3 7

in Wunderlich County Park near Woodside

Map 7.2, page 290

Wunderlich County Park is one of the better spots on the Peninsula for clearing out the brain cobwebs. The network of trails here provides a variety of adventures, from short strolls to all-day treks. Take your pick. The Meadow Loop is the preferred route; it circles much of the park, first crossing through oak woodlands, then rising to open grasslands, and finally passing a second-growth redwood forest on the way back. The Alambique Trail spans from Wunderlich near Woodside (this hike) to Skyline and Highway 35 (the previous hike).

Make sure you have a trail map, then take this route: Near the park entrance off Woodside Road, look for the signed trailhead for Alambique Trail and hike for 0.7 mile. At the junction with Meadow Trail, turn right, hike for 0.4 mile, and then turn left on to Meadow Trail and climb up to The Meadows in 1.1 miles. This is a perfect picnic site, with rolling hills, grasslands, and great views. To complete the loop, forge onward, then turn right at Bear Gulch Trail and take it all the way back, including switchbacks, to the park entrance. This hike includes an elevation gain of nearly 1,000 feet, so come prepared for a workout.

User Groups: Hikers and horses. No dogs or mountain bikes. No wheelchair facilities.

Permits: No permits are required. A $6 fee is charged per vehicle.

Maps: For a free map, contact San Mateo County Division of Parks. For a topographic map, ask the USGS for Woodside.

Directions: From San Francisco, take I-280 south and drive 20 miles to the exit for Highway 84/Woodside Road. Take that exit to Woodside Road, turn right and drive 2.7 miles (through Woodside) to the park entrance on the right.

Contact: Wunderlich Park, c/o Huddart Park, 650/851-1210; San Mateo County Parks Department, 650/363-4020, http://parks.smcgov.org.

91 RAVENSWOOD OPEN SPACE PRESERVE

2.0 mi/0.75 hr 1 8

near East Palo Alto and Menlo Park

Map 7.2, page 290

The future is exciting at Ravenswood Open Space Preserve. A new segment of the Bay Trail will be constructed in the preserve and the preserve will be closed during this period (likely 2020). This new access will provide a great route with views of the South Bay and opportunities for bird-watching.

This 376-acre parcel of land is rich in marshland habitat and home to many types of birds. The highlights are two excellent observation decks. From the parking area at the end of Bay Road, backtrack by walking across a bridged slough to the trailhead on the north side of the road. You will immediately come to a fork in the road. You can turn right and walk 200 feet to an observation deck with great views of the South Bay. If you go left instead, you will find a hard-surface path that heads north and hooks out toward the bay to another wood observation deck. This is the primary destination for most visitors. There always seems to be egrets and herons, but sandpipers and dozens of other species will stop here on their migratory journeys.

User Groups: Hikers, wheelchairs, and mountain bikes. No dogs or horses.

Permits: No permits are required. Parking and access are free.

Maps: For a free map, contact the Midpeninsula Regional Open Space District. For a topographic map, ask the USGS for Mountain View.

Directions: Take U.S. 101 to Palo Alto and the exit for University Avenue. Take that exit and follow the signs a short distance to University Avenue/East Palo Alto, and continue three long blocks to Bay Road. Turn right on Bay Road and drive one mile (paved all the way) to the end of the road and the preserve entrance and parking on the left.

Contact: Midpeninsula Regional Open Space District, 650/691-1200, www.openspace.org.

92 SAN FRANSISQUITO TRAIL

4.0 mi/1.5 hr 1 7

at the Palo Alto Baylands Preserve

Map 7.2, page 290

Of the bay's 20 richest wetlands, the Palo Alto

Baylands Preserve offers some of the best access and sightings to take in the annual migrations in late fall, winter, and spring. You can sight residents year-round, as well as good opportunities for ground squirrels, rabbits, and foxes. From the Nature Center, take the trail that runs out along the slough and turns left to parallel the Palo Alto Municipal Airport. It's called the San Francisquito Trail. Many enjoy watching the small planes take off and land. The trail runs north to San Francisquito Creek. Here you turn right, and venture out to where the creek, which looks more like a tidal slough most of the year, enters the South Bay. Return when you're ready.

At peak migrations, you can see ducks, curlews, killdeers, willets, avocets, stilts, coots, herons, egrets, and other waterfowl making this stop on the Pacific Flyway. As they arrive to the bay's wetlands, they join resident marsh wrens, sandpipers, song sparrows, red-tailed hawks, and other wildlife including rabbits, ground squirrels, and foxes. Ground squirrels can provide a sideshow, along with surprise jackrabbits. The rabbits can pop up literally at your feet—and take your breath away by the shock—then sprint off at warp speed.

User Groups: Hikers, wheelchairs, and mountain bikes. No dogs or horses.

Permits: No permits are required. Parking and access are free.

Maps: For a topographic map, ask the USGS for Mountain View.

Directions: Take U.S. 101 to Palo Alto and the exit for Embarcadero East. Take that exit and drive east (past the golf course and airport on left) to a stop sign. Turn left and drive past the abandoned yacht harbor until you reach a sharp right turn. Park at the lot on the right (south). The nature preserve is on the left (north).

Contact: Palo Alto Baylands Nature Center, 650/617-3156, www.cityofpaloalto.org.

93 BAY TRAIL TO CHARLESTON SLOUGH

4.0 mi/1.5 hr 1 7

at Shoreline at Mountain View Park

Map 7.2, page 290

This 750-acre swath of wetlands, ponds, and levee trails is one of the Bay Area's great local parks. Plus it's free. It is located east of U.S. 101 in Mountain View near the Shoreline Amphitheater and spans to the shore of South San Francisco Bay. The park provides an array of recreation—bike, hike, and boat—plus on clear days, great long-distance views from the shore of the bay.

From the parking area at Shoreline Lake, walk north on the Bay Trail (a levee road) out past Charleston Slough (on your right). You then connect to the Adobe Creek Loop Trail (a right turn), which is routed out to the shore of the South Bay. Great views, bird-watching, and fresh air. A great easy walk, in other words. It's also a testament to the Bay Area's 10-mile "Bubble Rule." That's where residents rarely visit local destinations that are outside a 10-mile radius of their home and, in turn, miss out on many great parks.

This trail provides access to an expanse of wetlands and marsh habitat. Within minutes, with each step you will gain access to marshland that has been preserved in its natural state. From afar, the surroundings may appear to be nothing more than pickleweed and mud, but look closer, and you will begin to see the huge diversity of birds and wildlife that thrive in this very rich ecosystem. Egrets seem particularly plentiful.

User Groups: Hikers and mountain bikes. No dogs or horses. No wheelchair facilities.

Permits: No permits are required. Parking and access are free.

Maps: For a topographic map, ask the USGS for Mountain View.

Directions: From San Francisco, take U.S. 101 south for 34 miles to Mountain View and the exit for Rengstorff Avenue. Take that exit, keep right at the fork (signed for Amphitheatre Parkway) and merge onto Rengstorff Avenue. Then continue 0.3 mile to Amphitheatre Parkway. Continue onto Amphitheatre Parkway and drive 0.7 mile to North Shoreline Boulevard. Turn left and drive 1.4 miles (stay right at the island/golf course on left) to entrance for Shoreline Regional Park. Continue ahead and turn left to main parking area, boat ramp, aquatic center/boathouse, and trailheads.

Contact: Shoreline at Mountain View Park, 650/903-6392, www.mountainview.gov.

94 WINDY HILL LOOP

7.5 mi/3.5 hr 3 8

in Windy Hill Open Space Preserve

Map 7.2, page 290

For most, the big thing is the view from the top. The ridge rises up above oak woodlands, and from the grasslands across the hilltops on clear days you have unobstructed views to the east across the South Bay, East Bay hills, and to Mount Diablo on the horizon. In winter, an inversion layer like a lid at roughly 800-1,000 feet is common across the South Bay, and at other times, there is low-lying stratus. In each case, you can peer over the top like it's a foggy sea.

A 7.5-mile loop takes you around most of the preserve, a bottom-to-top-to-bottom route that connects several trails (be sure to have a trail map with you). From the Portola Gate, take the Spring Ridge Trail past Sausal Pond, and with a few cutoffs, to the Hamms Gulch Trail. That climbs to the top, with switchbacks to make the 600-foot climb (over 2.6 miles) less of a challenge. At the ridge, you turn right on the Lost Trail/Anniversary Trail and enjoy the views en route 1.1 mile to the Spring Ridge Trail. Turn right and sail back down.

From the 1,900-foot summit, a grass-covered hilltop, you can see San Francisco Bay on one side and the Pacific Ocean on the other. If views are all you want, just drive to the trailhead at Skyline and the 0.7-mile Anniversary Trail, which is routed from the parking area to the summit, provides them.

The park spans 1,335 acres from the foothills (elevation 600 feet) and up the slope to Skyline (1,200 feet), with staging areas both at the foot of the preserve near Portola Valley and on top of Skyline. Its location creates a microclimate and a procession of habitats across its landscape: oak woodlands, gulches with conifers and riparian zones, wetlands and a pond, and ridge-top grasslands.

User Groups: Hikers, horses, and dogs (allowed on Hamms Gulch Trail, Eagle Trail, and Anniversary Trail; prohibited on others). No mountain bikes (except on the preserve's Spring Ridge Trail). There are wheelchair facilities in the picnic area adjacent to the parking area.

Permits: No permits are required. Parking and access are free.

Maps: A brochure and map are available at the trailhead. For a free trail map and brochure, contact the Midpeninsula Regional Open Space District. For a topographic map, ask the USGS for Mindego Hill.

Directions: Take I-280 to the exit for Sand Hill Road near Menlo Park. Turn west on Sand Hill Road. Drive 2.1 miles (becomes Portola Rd.) and continue straight for 2.5 miles to signed parking on right.

Skyline Trailhead: Take I-280 to Woodside and the exit for Woodside Road/Highway 84. Turn west and drive 6.5 miles (curvy through Woodside) to Sky Londa and Skyline Boulevard/Highway 35. Turn left on Skyline and drive 2.3 miles to trailhead on left.

Contact: Midpeninsula Regional Open Space District, 650/691-1200, www.openspace.org.

95 NONETTE HANKO SAN ANDREAS FAULT TRAIL

0.6 mi/0.5 hr

in Los Trancos Open Space Preserve

Map 7.2, page 290

The Nonette Hanko San Andreas Fault Trail (named after Nonette Hanko, the founder of the Midpeninsula Open Space District) may not have heartbreaking beauty, but it is unique. This is a self-guided tour of an earthquake trail and includes several examples of fault movement. The 13 numbered signposts along the way correspond with numbered explanations in the park brochure. If you don't want a geology lesson, you may be content with the good views of the Peninsula from the 2,000-foot ridgeline. Most hikers connect San Andreas Fault Trail to Lost Creek Loop Trail, a pleasant and easy bonus leg that is routed into secluded spots along a pretty creek.

The Monte Bello Open Space Preserve is located on the other side of Page Mill Road and provides a more dynamic landscape. But if you want unique, you can get it on the Fault Trail.

User Groups: Hikers only. The trail is not wheelchair-accessible, but the parking lot is and offers a nice view. No dogs, horses, or mountain bikes.

Permits: No permits are required. Parking and access are free.

Maps: A brochure and map are available at the trailhead. For a free trail map, contact the Midpeninsula Regional Open Space District. For a topographic map, ask the USGS for Mindego Hill.

Directions: From I-280 in Palo Alto, turn west on Page Mill Road and drive seven twisty miles to the signed parking area, on the right. The Monte Bello Open Space Preserve is directly across the street, on the left (south).

Contact: Midpeninsula Regional Open Space District, 650/691-1200, www.openspace.org.

96 CLOUDS REST TRAIL

4.0 mi/2.0 hr

in Coal Creek Open Space Preserve

Map 7.2, page 290

The Clouds Rest Trail at Coal Creek Open Space Preserve is perched on the slopes from Skyline that face the South Bay. The trailhead is at Vista Point on Skyline, so the payoffs start before you take a step on the trail. From here, take Clouds Rest Trail to Alpine Road and back, an easy in-and-outer.

From the lookout, you tower over the South Bay. You get sweeping views across the foothills, the valley floor, and across the South Bay to the East Bay hills. You can point out Stanford Tower, the Dumbarton Bridge, Lick Observatory, and Mount Diablo.

The preserve spans from Skyline east across 508 acres. The preserve's trails, actually old ranch roads, cover only four miles as they traverse the grasslands past a classic-looking barn and down along a small creek. You can make a quick loop by following Clouds Rest Trail to Meadow Trail and returning back along Alpine Road or hiking farther north for an out-and-back trip. On a clear day, you'll never forget the view. Most Peninsula residents have never heard of the Coal Creek Open Space Preserve—it is one of the lesser-developed parklands in the Bay Area.

User Groups: Hikers, leashed dogs, horses, and mountain bikes. No wheelchair facilities.

Permits: No permits are required. Parking and access are free.

Maps: A brochure and map are available at the trailhead. For a free trail map, contact the Midpeninsula Regional Open Space District. For a topographic map, ask the USGS for Mindego Hill.

Directions: Take I-280 to Woodside and the exit for Woodside Road/Highway 84. Follow the exit to Woodside Road, turn west and drive 6.5 miles (through Woodside, enter redwoods, becomes curvy as you climb) to Sky Londa and Skyline Boulevard/Highway 35. Turn left on

Skyline and drive six miles to Caltrans Vista Point on left.

Alternate route from South Peninsula: Coal Creek Open Space Preserve and Vista Point are located 1.2 miles north of the junction of Page Mill Road and Skyline. Page Mill out of Palo Alto is narrow, twisty, with blind turns and dangerous for cars vs. bikes.

Contact: Midpeninsula Regional Open Space District, 650/691-1200, www.openspace.org.

97 BLACK MOUNTAIN

3.5 mi/2.0 hr 2 8

in Monte Bello Open Space Preserve

Map 7.2, page 290 BEST

The Monte Bello Open Space Preserve encompasses more than 3,537 acres of the most natural and scenic lands on the east-facing slopes of the Peninsula foothills. It includes 2,800-foot Black Mountain, the headwaters of Stevens Creek, and this pretty trail, which is crowned by great views and offers the opportunity to camp at a little-known backpack site. For most, a map is a must.

From the parking area, start the trip by taking the Stevens Creek Nature Trail for 0.3 mile (ignore the fork) to Canyon Trail. Turn right on Canyon Trail, and go 0.25 mile to the Bella Vista Trail. Turn left and climb a mile to the ridge and the Old Ranch Trail. Turn right on Old Ranch Trail and you will arrive at the Black Mountain Campground (permit only) in about 0.5 mile. In the process, you will pass the headwaters of Stevens Creek as well as the San Andreas Fault. You'll also get long-distance views of the valley and the ridge above San Jose and opportunities to see squirrels, hawks, rabbits, and deer. It's about a 500-foot climb from the parking area to the campground.

Then, from the campground, it's a 0.2 mile walk on Monte Bello Road to the summit of Black Mountain (some transmitters mar the perfection). On clear spring days, the views are eye-popping. For campers, bring flashlights with fresh batteries, and be sure to make the walk here in darkness for stargazing or time the trip for a meteor shower.

From the summit, another bonus is available by continuing on Monte Bello Road for a short distance to a picnic site on the right. It is set adjacent to a sprinkling of rock crags (Calera limestone) that look like a movie set simulating another planet (great for kids). There are more stellar views of the canyon and foothills below to the east.

User Groups: Hikers, horses, and mountain bikes (restricted from some trails). This trail is not open to wheelchairs, but the parking lot and a short side trail are wheelchair-accessible and offer a good view. No dogs.

Permits: No permits are required for day use. Campers must have reservation and permit for the backpack camp.

Maps: A brochure and map are available at the trailhead. For a free trail map, contact the Midpeninsula Regional Open Space District. For a topographic map, ask the USGS for Mindego Hill.

Directions: From I-280 in Palo Alto, turn west on Page Mill Road and drive seven twisty miles to the signed parking area for Monte Bello Open Space Preserve on the left (south). Los Trancos Open Space Preserve is directly across the street to the right (north).

Contact: Midpeninsula Regional Open Space District, 650/691-1200, www.openspace.org.

98 BOREL HILL TRAIL

1.4 mi/1.0 hr

in Russian Ridge Open Space Preserve

Map 7.2, page 290

Borel Hill is one of the great lookouts on the San Francisco Peninsula. The summit tops out at 2,572 feet and is surrounded by grasslands. Hikers get unobstructed, 360-degree views. Borel Hill is a favorite destination of hikers who visit the Russian Ridge Open Space Preserve.

From the parking area, hike north on the Bay

Area Ridge Trail over the course of 0.7 mile to Borel Hill. The hill is the highest spot around, bordered by grasslands and with no trees. You get gorgeous views west across coastal foothills to the azure-blue horizon of the sea. This trail connects to a network of routes that provide access to the interior of the preserve's 3,491 acres.

Russian Ridge is just across the road from Caltrans Vista Point on the Peninsula's Skyline. You get views across the South Bay there. Then cross the road and climb Borel Hill for the coastal panorama.

User Groups: Hikers, horses, and mountain bikes. A wheelchair-accessible trail starting at the parking area leads to Alpine Pond in the Skyline Ridge Open Space Preserve. No dogs.

Permits: No permits are required. Parking and access are free.

Maps: A brochure and map are available at the trailhead. For a free trail map, contact the Midpeninsula Regional Open Space District. For a topographic map, ask the USGS for Mindego Hill.

Directions: Take I-280 to Woodside and the exit for Woodside Road/Highway 84. Take the exit to Woodside Road, turn west and drive 6.5 miles (through Woodside, enter redwoods, becomes curvy as you climb) to Sky Londa and Skyline Boulevard/Highway 35. Turn left on Skyline and drive six miles to Caltrans Vista Point on left.

Alternate route from South Peninsula: Coal Creek Open Space Preserve and Vista Point are 1.2 miles north of the junction of Page Mill Road and Skyline. Page Mill out of Palo Alto is narrow, twisty, with blind turns and dangerous for cars vs. bikes.

Contact: Midpeninsula Regional Open Space District, 650/691-1200, www.openspace.org.

99 ALPINE POND/ SKYLINE RIDGE

3.0 mi/1.5 hr

in Skyline Ridge Open Space Preserve

Map 7.2, page 290

From the parking area, walk south through a tunnel and continue a short distance to Alpine Pond and the nature center. Gorgeous spot. Good bird-watching. A nature trail is available around the pond, but no fishing is permitted. Many folks can't believe how pretty little Alpine Pond is, the easiest payoff for visitors to Skyline Ridge Open Space. From this pond, the trail then pushes into the interior of the parkland, skirting the flank of the highest mountain in park boundaries (2,493 feet), and loops back to Skyline Boulevard. You play peekaboo here, heading in and out of woodlands and gaining occasional views of plunging canyons to the west. You can create a loop hike, but that requires going back on a fire road; most people return to the parking area via the same route they walked on the way in.

Note that another trailhead is located south from the junction of Skyline and Alpine Road. This leads a short distance down to pretty Horseshoe Lake.

User Groups: Hikers, horses, and mountain bikes. A wheelchair-accessible trail leads to Horseshoe Lake and around Alpine Pond. No dogs.

Permits: No permits are required. Parking and access are free.

Maps: A brochure and map are available at the trailhead. For a free trail map, contact the Midpeninsula Regional Open Space District. For a topographic map, ask the USGS for Mindego Hill.

Directions: Take I-280 to Woodside and the exit for Highway 84/Woodside Road. Take that exit, turn west on Woodside Road and drive 2.8 miles. Continue on Woodside Road/Highway 84 (becomes curvy) to Sky Londa and Highway 35/Skyline Boulevard. Turn left on Skyline and drive six miles to Vista Point parking on left or continue one mile to junction with Alpine Road. Turn right on Alpine Road and immediately look for exit on right to parking for Skyline Ridge Open Space. For trailhead to Horseshoe Lake, at junction of Skyline and Alpine Road, continue short distance south to parking and staging area on right.

Options from South Bay: From Palo Alto at I-280, take Page Mill Road west about 10 miles (narrow and curvy, watch for bikes) to Skyline/Highway 35. Continue straight on Alpine Road a short distance to exit for parking lot on right for Skyline Ridge.

The parking area is signed "Russian Ridge Open Space Preserve."

Contact: Midpeninsula Regional Open Space District, 650/691-1200, www.openspace.org.

100 RIDGE TRAIL LOOP

2.6 mi/1.25 hr — 2 — 8

in Sam McDonald County Park near La Honda

Map 7.2, page 290

This loop trail provides a stellar introduction to the area and makes an excellent hike year-round. It features about a 700-foot climb, a route through deep redwood canyons, and then ridge-top views across coastal foothills. Very enjoyable.

After a quick orientation with the park map (they're self-serve at the ranger station), choose the posted four-mile Ridge Trail Loop. As you enter the parking lot, the trailhead is on the right of the restroom. The hike starts on a narrow dirt path that is carved in the side of a steep redwood canyon, where you walk north. Even on hot Bay Area days, this forest is cool and refreshing, with occasional banana slugs on the trail. The trail contours up and down, then eventually rises into hardwood forest (mainly oaks, bays, and madrones) to a sub-ridge with a partial lookout to the north across miles of pretty foothills.

The trail then curves left (west) and climbs toward Towne Ridge. You emerge at a crossing of Pescadero Road (you're now heading south). You cross the road and the trail turns from single-track to a service road. The views to the west of the coastal foothills, into the Pescadero Creek Canyon, and across to Butano Rim start to open up. In March, April, and early May, there are also many blooming wildflowers, highlighted by occasional rafts of sprawling forget-me-nots. The trail/road contours up and down, generally climbing and you emerge in foothill grasslands (a ride-in horse camp is off to the left). Look to the left as well for the Towne Trail. Turn left on the Towne Trail and you descend into another deep redwood canyon. At a water tank, turn right on the Big Tree Loop, which is highlighted by a big redwood. The Big Tree Loop is routed to a crossing of Pescadero Road and the parking lot.

For a short side trip, visit the adjacent Heritage Grove. Across the road from the parking area, look for the trailhead for the Heritage Grove Trail. It's an easy walk to a small grove of old-growth redwoods. This is accessible along Alpine Road, with extremely limited parking along the road's shoulder.

User Groups: Hikers only. No dogs, horses, or mountain bikes. No wheelchair facilities.

Permits: No permits are required. A parking fee of $5 is charged per vehicle.

Maps: PDF at website. For a topographic map, ask the USGS for La Honda.

Directions: From San Francisco, take I-280 south and drive 20 miles to Woodside and the exit for Highway 84/Woodside Road. Take that exit, turn west (right) on Woodside Road, and drive 2.8 miles to Woodside. Continue straight on Woodside Road/Highway 84 for 10 miles (continue straight at Sky Londa at Skyline) to La Honda and continue a short distance to Pescadero Road on left. Turn left and drive 1.1 miles to Redwood Triangle and Pescadero Creek Road. Bear right and drive 0.7 mile to park entrance and parking on right.

Heritage Grove: At Redwood Triangle, turn southeast (right if emerging from San McDonald; left if approaching Sam McDonald from La Honda) on Alpine Road and drive short distance to Heritage Grove on right.

Coastal option: From Half Moon Bay, take Highway 1 south for 10 miles to San Gregorio and Highway 84. Turn left on 84 and drive 8.3 miles to Pescadero Road. Turn right and drive 1.1 miles to Redwood Triangle and Pescadero Creek Road. Bear right and drive 0.7 mile to park entrance on right.

Contact: Sam McDonald County Park, 650/879-0238; San Mateo County Parks Department, 650/363-4020, http://parks.smcgov.org.

101 PESCADERO MARSH

3.0 mi/1.5 hr 1 8

in Pescadero Marsh north of Pescadero

Map 7.2, page 290 BEST

On one side of the road is Pescadero Marsh Natural Preserve. On the other is Pescadero State Beach. Pescadero Marsh is a 600-acre wetland and lagoon fed by Pescadero Creek that is home for blue herons, egrets, and owls, and resting habitat for many migratory shorebirds. A dirt path, the North Pond Trail, ventures into the wetlands to Audubon Marsh and the edge of the lagoon and provides a three-mile hike. Roughly 200 migratory species of shorebirds, waterfowl, and raptors have been verified here. Deer and rabbits are common. Fox, skunk, and badger occasionally sighted.

A great easy trip is this three-mile loop through the marsh. From the parking area, take the North Pond Trail to the Sequoia Audubon Trail. The Sequoia Audubon Trail traces the edge of the marsh and then heads along Pescadero Creek. This dirt path ventures through the heart of the wetlands and provides a good chance to see many birds, as well as occasional deer.

Pescadero Marsh is just east of Highway 1 along Pescadero Creek, 15 miles south of Half Moon Bay. Just across the highway from Pescadero Marsh is the parking lot and access point for Pescadero State Beach.

User Groups: Hikers only. No dogs, horses, or mountain bikes. No wheelchair facilities.

Permits: No permits are required. Parking and access are free.

Maps: A map is available from Half Moon Bay State Parks. For a topographic map, ask the USGS for San Gregorio.

Directions: From the Peninsula in San Mateo, take Highway 92 west to Half Moon Bay. Turn south on Highway 1 and drive 17 miles to Pescadero Road. Turn left and drive about 0.25 mile to the parking area and trailhead on the left.

Contact: Pescadero State Beach, c/o Half Moon Bay State Parks, 650/726-8820; Half Moon Bay State Beach Ranger Station, 650/726-8819, www.parks.ca.gov.

102 MILL OX LOOP

5.0 mi/2.75 hr 3 8

in Butano State Park near Pescadero

Map 7.2, page 290

If you love redwoods and ferns but are also partial to sun and warm afternoons, the Mill Ox Loop at Butano State Park may be the ideal hike for you. Why? The Mill Ox Loop provides a tour through deep redwoods and amid open sun, both in good doses.

To find the Mill Ox trailhead, drive past the entry kiosk and continue ahead into the redwoods and look for the signed trailhead on your left. You park on the road's shoulder. The trail starts where you cross a small creek in a dense redwood forest, then heads up a very steep grade on switchbacks, emerging at the top of the canyon on Butano Fire Road. Some readers emailed that they were stunned at how steep this section is, but the climb is very short and the worst of it is over quickly.

At the Butano Fire Road, turn right. You will climb gradually as you head east toward the park's interior. The fire road gets plenty of sun, and plenty of shirts come off en route to 1,138 feet. At a few spots, if you turn and look back to the west, you have views of the Pacific Ocean. Continue to a junction with Jackson Flats Trail, turn right for the return loop. Here the trail descends quite steeply over a bare rock and sandstone facing for 0.25 mile, then links to a pretty dirt path. You then drop into Butano Canyon and the surrounding redwood forest. The forest is lush and beautiful as you return to the start point, where you walk past ferns, trillium, redwoods, and plenty of wild iris. This is one of our favorites.

User Groups: Hikers only. No dogs, horses, or mountain bikes. No wheelchair facilities.

Permits: No permits are required. A state park entrance fee of $10 is charged per vehicle.

Maps: A brochure and map are available at the entrance station. For a topographic map, ask the USGS for Franklin Point.

Directions: Take I-280 south to Daly City and the split for Highway 1/Pacifica. Follow Highway 1 south for 20 miles to Half Moon Bay. Continue south on Highway 1 for 15.2 miles to Pescadero Creek Road. Turn left and drive 2.5 miles (through Pescadero) to Cloverdale Road. Turn right and go 4.4 miles to park entrance road on left. Turn left and drive short distance to park entrance and kiosk.

From East Bay/Peninsula: From San Mateo, take Highway 92 west to Half Moon Bay and Highway 1. Turn left on Highway 1 and continue as above.

Contact: Butano State Park, 650/879-2040, www.parks.ca.gov.

103 TRAIL CAMP

10.0 mi/2 days 

in Butano State Park near Pescadero

Map 7.2, page 290

The Bay Area's most hidden and least known campground is Butano's (pronounced Butte-no) backpack campground, Trail Camp. Seven pretty sites are set in forest just below the west-facing Butano Rim at 1,550 feet. The prettiest site is No. 7, set amid towering Douglas firs. It takes a five-mile hike with a 1,500-foot climb to get here. Near the park entrance, take the Jackson Flats Trail. This is routed east uphill for 2.75 miles to the Canyon Trail. Take a right onto the Canyon Trail, which rises steeply at times, up to the camp.

Just above the Trail Camp, you will find a route that connects to the Butano Fire Road. If you head to the left (northwest), you can find an abandoned airstrip. At the end of the old strip, there are great views to the west of the Butano Canyon and beyond to the coast.

The heart of this park is a deep redwood canyon. From here, you can launch off on adventures that explore the slopes up to the horseshoe-shaped mountain rim. On the canyon floor, the place is cool, quiet, and lush. On the canyon rim, peer across a sea of conifers below to glimpses of the Pacific Ocean.

Note: You must pump-filter drinking water from a creek located 0.25 mile from camp. The creek can go dry. Absolutely no fires. Violators will be arrested and face expulsion.

User Groups: Hikers only. No dogs, horses, or mountain bikes. No wheelchair facilities.

Permits: A state park entrance fee of $10 is charged per vehicle. Camping permits to are by reservation only. Reservations, available dates, and more information are available at www.parks.ca.gov. Search "Butano" and click on link for "Backcountry Trail Camp," $15 per night per site. Permits include one vehicle, $10 per extra vehicle.

Maps: A brochure and map are available at the entrance station. For a topographic map, ask the USGS for Franklin Point.

Directions: Take I-280 south to Daly City and the split on right for Highway 1/Pacifica. Follow Highway 1 south for 20 miles to Half Moon Bay. Continue south on Highway 1 for 15.2 miles to Pescadero Creek Road. Turn left and drive 2.5 miles (through Pescadero) to Cloverdale Road. Turn right and go 4.4 miles to park entrance road on left. Turn left and drive short distance to park entrance and kiosk.

From East Bay and Peninsula: From San Mateo, take Highway 92 west to Half Moon Bay and Highway 1. Turn left on Highway 1 and continue as above.

Contact: Butano State Park, 650/879-2040; Half Moon Bay State Parks, 650/726-8820, www.parks.ca.gov.

104 BUTANO RIM LOOP

11.0 mi/1-2 days 

in Butano State Park near Pescadero

Map 7.2, page 290

This is one of the great rides on a mountain bike or on a horse, a 10. For hiking, the first half of the route on a fire road makes it a 9. Start at the Mill Ox trailhead, at an elevation of 200 feet. Hike up the steep grade (the steepest part of the trip) for a short distance to the Butano Fire Road (700 feet). Turn right and away you go. From here, trace the rim of Butano Canyon, and enjoy views of the redwood-filled valley (below) and the Pacific Ocean (behind you and off to the west). The trail climbs steadily before reaching 1,713 feet, where it crosses a short spur to an old, abandoned, overgrown airstrip on the ridgeline (at the west end of the airstrip, there's a great view to the west overlooking the Butano Canyon). Just past the airstrip, the trail enters forest. A signed cutoff on the right provides a short spur to the Trail Camp (at 1,550 feet). If you were to stay overnight, this would make a first-day total of 5.5 miles.

This is the halfway point and the rest of the trip is more sheltered. Turn right on the Olmo Fire Road and then hike out to the Doe Ridge/Goat Hill Trails, which drop back down into the Butano Canyon and the starting point. Much of this second half of the route is a soft dirt trail amid redwoods, and it laterals and descends into the south side of Butano Canyon.

User Groups: Hikers, bikes, horses to Trail Camp. No bikes on single-track after Trail Camp (bikes have access to China Grade and other routes). No wheelchair facilities.

Permits: A state park entrance fee of $10 is charged per vehicle. Camping permits are by reservation only. Reservations, available dates, and more information are available at www.parks.ca.gov. Search "Butano" and click on link for "Backcountry Trail Camp." Permits include one vehicle, $10 per extra vehicle.

Maps: A brochure and map are available at the entrance station. For a free trail map, contact Butano State Park. For a topographic map, ask the USGS for Franklin Point.

Directions: Take I-280 to Daly City and the split for Highway 1/Pacifica. Follow Highway 1 south for 20 miles to Half Moon Bay. Continue south on Highway 1 for 15.2 miles to Pescadero Creek Road. Turn left and drive 2.5 miles (through Pescadero) to Cloverdale Road. Turn right and go 4.4 miles to park entrance road on left. Turn left and drive short distance to park entrance and kiosk.

From East Bay/Peninsula: Drive to San Mateo and the junction with Highway 92. Take Highway 92 west over Crystal Springs Reservoir, and then continue eight miles to Half Moon Bay and Highway 1. Turn left on Highway 1 and continue as above.

Contact: Butano State Park, 650/879-2040; Half Moon Bay State Parks, 650/726-8820, www.parks.ca.gov.

105 AÑO NUEVO TRAIL

2.75 mi/1.5 hr 3 7

in Butano State Park near Pescadero

Map 7.2, page 290 

The Año Nuevo Trail climbs 730 feet in less than a mile to a lookout. It's one of the steepest stretches of trails on the coast. On the ridge, a park bench offers a place to sit and catch your breath, but it would take some tree trimming to regain that view. After catching your breath, continue on the Año Nuevo Trail and take a right on Olmo Fire Road for the junction with the Goat Hill Trail. Turn left and drop down steeply back into the canyon to complete the loop. Although short, this hike provides a good climb and a chance to walk through redwoods on the return descent. It's not unusual to see pileated woodpeckers on this loop.

It's called the Año Nuevo Trail because, at one time, you could get a view of Año Nuevo Island.

User Groups: Hikers only. No dogs, horses, or mountain bikes. No wheelchair facilities.

Permits: No permits are required. A day-use fee of $10 is charged per vehicle.

Maps: For a free trail map, contact Butano State Park. For a topographic map, ask the USGS for Franklin Point.

Directions: Take I-280 south to Daly City and the split on right for Highway 1/Pacifica. Follow Highway 1 south for 20 miles to Half Moon Bay. Continue south on Highway 1 for 15.2 miles to Pescadero Creek Road. Turn left and drive 2.5 miles (through Pescadero) to Cloverdale Road. Turn right and go 4.4 miles to park entrance road on left. Turn left and drive short distance to park entrance and kiosk. The trailhead is on the right (south).

From East Bay/Peninsula: Drive to San Mateo and the junction with Highway 92. Take Highway 92 west over Crystal Springs Reservoir, and then continue eight miles to Half Moon Bay and Highway 1. Turn left on Highway 1 and continue as above.

Contact: Butano State Park, 650/879-2040; Half Moon Bay State Parks, 650/726-8820, www.parks.ca.gov.

106 PETERS CREEK GROVE

12.5 mi/1 day 4 10

in Portola Redwoods State Park

Map 7.2, page 290

Portola Redwoods State Park is highlighted by a site we call "The Bay Area's Lost World," the remote Peters Creek Grove of old-growth redwoods. The grove is nestled in a distant canyon where the forest floor is covered with wall-to-wall sorrel. A few of the giants are 30-35 feet around; several are more than 200 feet tall.

The hike to the Peters Creek Grove is about a 12.5-mile round-trip with two grind-it-out climbs. From park headquarters it's a 5.5-mile trek up 1,000 feet to a ridge; you then plummet 600 feet into a deep canyon to connect to a one-mile loop trail that runs along each side of Peters Creek and amid the giant trees.

Since it is a long drive to reach Portola Redwoods, one option is to camp at a trail site (Slate Creek) 2.4 miles out from headquarters. It is on the route out to Peters Creek Grove.

Permits: A state park entrance fee of $10 is charged per vehicle; pay at the visitors center. Camping permits are by reservation only. Reservations, available dates, and more information available at www.parks.ca.gov. Search "Portola Redwoods" and click on link for "Backcountry Trail Camp," $15 per night per site. Permits include one vehicle, $10 per extra vehicle.

Maps: A map and brochure are available at the visitors center. For a topographic map, ask the USGS for Mindego Hill.

Directions: From San Francisco, take I-280 south and drive 20 miles to Woodside and the exit for Highway 84/Woodside Road. Take that exit, turn west (right) on Woodside Road, and drive 2.8 miles to Woodside. Continue straight on Woodside Road/Highway 84 for 5.8 miles to Sky Londa. Continue straight for 6.7 miles to La Honda, then a short distance to Pescadero Road on the left. Turn left and drive 1.1 miles to Redwood Triangle and Alpine Road. Turn left on Alpine Road and drive four miles (slow, narrow, twisty; 1.2 miles to Heritage Grove on right) to Portola State Park Road. Turn right (still twisty) and drive three miles to park entrance. Continue 0.5 mile to visitors center.

Contact: Portola Redwoods State Park, La Honda, 650/948-9098, www.parks.ca.gov.

107 BAY VIEW LOOP

3.0 mi/1.5 hr 1 8

in Point Pinole Regional Shoreline

Map 7.3, page 291

On the Bay View Loop, you can walk several miles along the shore of San Pablo Bay, or on a wooded bluff overlooking the shore, and take in a beautiful view of water, passing ships, and birds. The trip is unique from the start, where you park at the entrance station and catch a shuttle bus to the shoreline. There you will find a long, pretty, cobbled beach and beautiful views of San Pablo Bay, Marin, and Mount Tamalpais. An excellent fishing pier is also here. This is the launch point. Make sure you head out to the end of the pier to take in the water views and see if anybody has caught a sturgeon or striped bass.

Then take the Bay Trail. It is perched on a bluff above the cobbled beach. Along the way are beautiful glimpses of San Pablo Bay. The long-distance views across the bay of the Marin shoreline backed by Mount Tamalpais are exceptional. To turn this into a three-mile loop, turn back (left) on the Woods Trail. This trail is routed through a small eucalyptus forest, with occasional remnants of the dynamite era, a few small buildings, and pretty dirt roads. The trail eventually returns to the staging area.

A highlight of Point Pinole Regional Shoreline is a long, undisturbed stretch of shoreline on a cobbled beach along San Pablo Bay. The stone beach is unparalleled, as if this were the final resting place of every stone ever cast in the bay. It is a quiet place, where you can watch passing ships, go for an easy hike, take a dog for a walk, or fish from the pier. Yet the defining landscape feature of the park is the Hayward Fault—marked by the cliffs and Point Pinole itself as it goes out to sea.

In the World War II era, this was the site of the Giant Powder Company, that is, dynamite manufacturers. This was their fourth site in the Bay Area after factories blew up in San Francisco, South San Francisco, and Albany. So no one wanted to be anywhere near the place. The dynamite company built all the present trails and roads, planted eucalyptus trees, and is responsible for the basic layout of the park.

User Groups: Hikers, dogs, horses, and mountain bikes. The trail is partially wheelchair-accessible.

Permits: No permits are required. A $3 day-use fee is charged on weekends when the kiosk is attended. The shuttle costs $1 round-trip for people ages 12 through 61; it's free for seniors and $0.50 for youngsters 6 through 11. There is a fee for dogs ($2) on weekends.

Maps: A brochure and map are available at the trailhead. For a free trail map, phone the East Bay Regional Park District toll-free at 888/327-2757, option 5, ext. 2; follow directions, leave your name and address, and ask for the Point Pinole Regional Shoreline brochure. For a topographic map, ask the USGS for Richmond.

Directions: Take I-80 to Pinole and the exit for Fitzgerald Drive to Richmond Parkway. Follow that exit to Richmond Parkway and drive 1.3 miles to Atlas Road. Turn right on Atlas and drive 0.9 mile to Giant Road. Turn left on Giant and drive 0.5 mile to the park entrance on the right. Take the shuttle to the Point Pinole Pier and trailhead.

Contact: Point Pinole Regional Park, 888/327-2757; East Bay Regional Park District, www.ebparks.org.

108 SOARING EAGLE TRAIL

4.0 mi/2.0 hr 2 8

in Crockett Hills Regional Park near Crockett

Map 7.3, page 291

The highlights at Crockett Hills Regional Park are the ridge-top views, good prospects of seeing golden eagles, and well-hidden valley. There are five hilltops where you get sweeping views of San Pablo Bay. From the hilltops, you can see across Carquinez Strait, the Lower Delta, and to the west, a pretty silhouette of Mount Tamalpais. There is also a pretty valley from which you can often see golden eagles fly, hover, and search for ground squirrels.

From the staging area, take the Edwards Loop Trail for a one-mile climb to the tunnel at the Cummings Skyway. (Note that the signpost at the trailhead labels this the Edwards Loop Trail, while the shortest way up is marked on maps as the Crockett Hills Trail.) Walk through the tunnel and, on the other side, take the Soaring Eagle Trail (also signed as Bay Area Ridge Trail). This end of the Soaring Eagle Trail isn't marked on the signpost, which designates it as the junction of the Sky Trail and the Crockett Hills Trail, yet it is on the map. The trail contours the foothills and valleys to the Sky Trail. Turn left on Sky Trail and return to the tunnel to complete the loop.

For a bonus, at the junction of Soaring Eagle Trail and Sky Trail (this junction is properly marked), turn right and within 15 minutes, you'll reach the Big Valley Trail on the right. This is where we've seen a mated pair of golden eagles who often hunt and hover here at midmorning as the air temperature warms.

In the remote southern section of the park, you'll notice that birds flourish. A ravine with a small, unnamed pond edged by cattails is a sanctuary for red-winged blackbirds, many small songbirds, and kestrels, the smallest bird of prey in North America. It turns out that the wildlife habitat here supports all levels of the food chain.

User Groups: Hikers, mountain bikes, horses, and dogs. No wheelchair facilities.

Permits: No permits are required. Parking and access are free.

Maps: A brochure and map are available at the trailhead. For a free trail map, phone the East Bay Regional Park District toll-free at 888/327-2757, option 5, ext. 2; follow directions, leave your name and address, and ask for the Crockett Hills brochure.

Directions: From Concord: Take Highway 4 west to the exit for Cummings Skyway/Vallejo-Crockett. Follow that exit to Cummings Skyway and drive about 2.5 miles to Crockett Boulevard. Turn right and drive 0.7 mile to the staging area on the left.

From San Francisco: Take I-80 east to Crockett and Exit 26 for the Cummings Skyway. Follow that exit to Cummings Skyway and drive to Crockett Boulevard. Turn left and drive to staging area on the right.

Contact: Crockett Hills Regional Park, 925/228-0112 or 888/327-2757; East Bay Regional Park District, www.ebparks.org.

109 FRANKLIN RIDGE LOOP

2.0 mi/1.75 hr 3 9

at Carquinez Strait Regional Shoreline near Martinez

Map 7.3, page 291

It seems that everybody starts at the Nejedly Staging Area and its big parking lot and restroom. Instead, drive another 1.5 miles on Carquinez Scenic Drive. You'll see a gated trailhead/road on the left. Pullouts are available along the road to park (do not block the gated fire road). From here, you walk along a ranch road (a seasonal creek, often dry, is on your right) to a sharp left turn. You turn left and climb, steep but short on the Franklin Ridge Loop Trail. After about 10 minutes, you emerge in a valley over a sub-ridge. At one spot, you can see a silhouette of the lookout bench, under an oak, on a hilltop to your left. The trail then cuts off to your left and climbs a short distance to the hilltop vista point. If you have a dog, keep it on a leash here because the trail is edged by sharp star thistles. The bench is shaded on the ridge and a great site for a trail picnic.

As you gain the hill, the view over Martinez and Carquinez Strait is revealed all at once. On one side, you tower over Martinez and the Carquinez Strait, with long-distance views across Suisun Bay, the Mothball Fleet, and beyond to the Lower Delta. On another side, you see across to Benicia and west to San Pablo Bay and beyond to Mount Burdell. To the south are pretty rolling foothills, golden brown, where you can often sight black-tailed deer.

Sunsets can be absolutely spectacular here in winter, often with sunlight refracted through distant stratus and a dark silhouette of the horizon. Even after sunset, it remains pretty as the lights of the Benicia Bridge and nearby towns take hold.

The park covers 2,795 acres, most of it foothill country, with oaks, short ridges, and ravines. It is wild enough to provide habitat for wildlife; red-tailed hawks and deer are the most common. At dusk, it's possible to see great horned owls, kestrels, and occasionally even golden eagles.

As you the drive in, you will pass the historic Alhambra Cemetery on the right. A key to the locked access gate is available from the Martinez Police Department. At a site overlooking Carquinez Strait, you will find the headstone of one my heroes: Captain Joseph Walker, the greatest trailblazer of them all. It reads "Camped in Yosemite, Nov. 13, 1833."

User Groups: Hikers, dogs, horses, and mountain bikes. No wheelchair facilities.

Permits: No permits are required. Parking and access are free.

Maps: A brochure and map are available at the trailhead. For a free trail map, phone the East Bay Regional Park District toll-free at 888/327-2757, option 5, ext. 2; follow directions, leave your name and address, and ask for the Carquinez Strait Regional Shoreline brochure. For a topographic map, ask the USGS for Benicia.

Directions: From San Francisco, take I-80 East over Bay Bridge six miles (get in center/left lane) to split for 80-580/24. Stay left on I-80 East and drive about 15 miles to the exit for Highway 4 East. Take that exit, merge onto Highway 4 and drive 8.7 miles to the exit for Alhambra Avenue/Martinez. Follow that exit to Alhambra Avenue, turn left and go 2.1 miles to Buckley Street. Turn left on Buckley and continue 0.1 mile to Talbart Street. Turn right on Talbart and go three blocks to Carquinez Scenic Drive. Turn left and go 1.2 miles to Alhambra Cemetery on right, or continue short distance to Nejedly Staging Area (signed on left), and continue another 1.5 miles to gated trailhead on left (park at dirt pullouts).

Contact: Carquinez Strait Regional Shoreline, 925/228-0112 or 888/327-2757; East Bay Regional Park District, www.ebparks.org.

110 RADKE MARTINEZ SHORELINE

2.0 mi/1.0 hr 1 8

at Radke Martinez Regional Shoreline near Martinez

Map 7.3, page 291

You can change your world in just 2.5 miles of driving, from highway to park. Some might view Martinez Regional Shoreline and the nearby marina as a destination for locals only. Wrong. It provides a surprise escape hatch from the push-push-push on I-680 or Highway 4, only minutes away.

From the parking area off North Court Street, take the Killdeer Trail 0.25 mile to the Boardwalk Trail, turn left and walk a short distance to gorgeous Arch Bridge. It crosses Alhambra Creek and provides an elevated view of the wetlands. Then continue ahead, tidal wetlands to your left and Carquinez Strait to your right, and bear right on the Pickleweed Trail. The trail leads out to water's edge, 1.4 miles round-trip. You can extend another quarter mile on the Pickleweed Trail (it jogs left for a short distance) to a waterfront picnic site; two miles round-trip. The rewards are beautiful shoreline trails with water views, wildlife preserves for waterfowl, marine birds and songbirds, and a fishing pier set in the path of migratory striped bass and resident flounder. For those rushing to get in or out of the Bay Area, stop the clock and enjoy this trip.

Martinez Regional Shoreline and adjacent Waterfront Park are located on the banks of Carquinez Strait near downtown Martinez, just west of the Carquinez Bridge. While the parks are popular among locals for picnics, bocce ball, soccer, and softball, they shine best as a wetland preserve with several pretty trails with waterfront views.

Side trip: If you continue on North Court Street (past the entrance to Martinez Regional Shoreline), it leads to parking for the duck pond (on left) and the fishing pier (straight ahead). If you turn right on Tarantino Drive, it leads to access for the ball fields (on right) and dead-ends at a short trail to an observation platform for bird-watching. To reach the platform, take the path at the back right corner of the Martinez Yacht Club parking lot and walk past the two palm trees.

User Groups: Hikers and mountain bikes. No horses or dogs. The restrooms are wheelchair-accessible, but the trail is not.

Permits: No permits are required. Parking and access are free.

Maps: A brochure and map are available at the trailhead. For a free trail map, call the East Bay Regional Park District at 888/327-2757, option 5, ext. 2; follow directions, leave your name and address, and ask for the Martinez Regional Shoreline brochure. For a topographic map, ask the USGS for Benicia.

Directions: Take I-80 to Exit 23 for Highway 4. Follow that exit to Highway 4 and drive 8.7 miles to Exit 9 for Alhambra Avenue toward Martinez. Take that exit, turn left on Alhambra and go 2.1 miles to Marina Vista Avenue. Turn right on Marina Vista and go a short distance to Ferry Street. Turn left on Ferry Street and go a short distance to Joe DiMaggio Drive. Turn right and go a short distance to North Court Street. Turn left and drive to end: parking and Martinez Regional Shoreline are on left, fishing pier is ahead, marina is on right, Martinez Waterfront Park is on right.

Contact: Radke Martinez Regional Shoreline, 510/544-3122 or 888/327-2757; East Bay Regional Park District, www.ebparks.org.

111 FALSE GUN VISTA POINT

1.0 mi/0.75 hr

in Miller-Knox Regional Shoreline west of Richmond

Map 7.3, page 291

A little-known lookout over San Francisco Bay is the highlight of Miller-Knox Regional Shoreline, and getting to it requires only a short hike and climb. This parkland covers 307 acres of hill and shoreline property at Point Richmond, where strong afternoon winds in the summer create excellent conditions for kite flying. Whereas most people just make the short stroll along Keller Beach, this hike is preferred for the view. From the parking area, it leads about 0.5 mile up Old Country Road and Marine View Trail, making a right turn on Crest Trail to reach the False Gun Vista Point. In the process, the trail climbs 300 feet to the lookout at 322 feet. On clear days, you get picture-perfect views of San Francisco Bay and its many surrounding landmarks. Most people enjoy a landscaped picnic area with pretty views of the North Bay. Take it the extra mile, literally.

User Groups: Hikers and dogs. No horses or mountain bikes. No wheelchair facilities.

Permits: No permits are required. Parking and access are free.

Maps: A brochure and map are available at the trailhead. For a free trail map, phone the East Bay Regional Park District toll-free at 888/327-2757, option 5, ext. 2; follow directions, leave your name and address, and ask for the Miller-Knox Regional Shoreline brochure. For a topographic map, ask the USGS for San Quentin.

Directions: From Berkeley: Drive north on I-80 to the exit for I-580 west. Follow the exit for I-580 west to Canal Boulevard (lighted). Turn left on Canal Boulevard and drive 0.75 mile to Seacliff Drive. Turn right on Seacliff and drive 1.5 miles (Seacliff Drive becomes Brickyard Cove Road) to Dornan Drive. Turn right on Dornan and drive 0.5 mile to the parking entrance on the left.

Contact: Miller-Knox Regional Shoreline, 888/327-2757; East Bay Regional Park District, www.ebparks.org.

112 POINT ISABEL SHORELINE

1.0 mi/0.75 hr

at Point Isabel Regional Shoreline near Berkeley

Map 7.3, page 291

When it comes to California bests, Point Isabel ranks right at the top for best parks to bring a doggy. Half a million dogs a year visit Point Isabel Shoreline, the ultimate off-leash doggy destination in California, complete with showers, tennis balls, and treats. It's good for people, too. Beautiful bayfront views of San Francisco and the Golden Gate—plus the fact that it's a popular place to walk dogs—attract visitors to this stretch of shore. From the parking area, the trail extends northward along the shore of the bay, then east along Hoffman Channel, where it meets the Bay Trail, and offers great views of Hoffman Marsh. The best time to see birds here is in the fall, when year-round residents are joined by migratory species. Point Isabel extends into San Francisco Bay several miles north of Golden Gate Fields Racetrack, and the 21-acre park provides an easy shoreline walk, rich bird-watching opportunities, and those great views.

User Groups: Hikers and dogs, lots of dogs. Bicycles are permitted, but there is a high number of dog walkers. No horses. The restrooms and trail are wheelchair-accessible.

Permits: No permits are required. Parking and access are free.

Maps: A brochure and map are available at the trailhead. For a free trail map, phone the East Bay Regional Park District toll-free at 888/327-2757, option 5, ext. 2; follow directions, leave your name and address, and ask for the Point Isabel Regional Shoreline brochure. For a topographic map, ask the USGS for Richmond.

Directions: From I-80 in south Richmond, take the Central Avenue exit and drive west to Isabel Street. Turn right and drive to the parking area at the end of the road.

Contact: Point Isabel Regional Shoreline, 888/327-2757; East Bay Regional Park District, www.ebparks.org.

113 SAN PABLO RIDGE LOOP

6.2 mi/3.5 hr 3 10

in Wildcat Canyon Regional Park

Map 7.3, page 291

Of all the views of San Francisco Bay, this is certainly one of the best. From San Pablo Ridge, you get an eye-popping view of San Francisco Bay, Alcatraz, and across to the Golden Gate Bridge. Up on top, you can see south to Rocky Ridge and Las Trampas Regional Wilderness and northwest across San Pablo Bay to a silhouette of Mount Tamalpais. From the parking area, start the trip by heading south on the Wildcat Creek Trail to the junction with the Belgum Trail. Turn left on the Belgum Trail and connect to San Pablo Ridge. Turn right and climb about 750 feet over the course of 2.5 miles on San Pablo Ridge. Once on top, slow down and enjoy the cruise. You will find a series of hilltops to climb for 360-degreee panoramas. Make sure you do this. To loop around, head back on Mezue Trail, then right again on Wildcat Creek Trail, and walk back to the parking area.

It takes a short grunt of a hike to get to the top, but you'll find it well worth the grunting. These hilltops offer gorgeous views and can also be accessed out of Tilden Regional Park from Inspiration Point on Nimitz Way.

User Groups: Hikers, dogs, horses, and mountain bikes. No wheelchair facilities.

Permits: No permits are required. Parking and access are free.

Maps: A brochure and map are available at the trailhead. For a free trail map, phone the East Bay Regional Park District toll-free at

888/327-2757, option 5, ext. 2; follow directions, leave your name and address, and ask for the Wildcat Canyon Regional Park brochure. For a topographic map, ask the USGS for Richmond.
Directions: Take I-80 to Richmond and the exit to Solano Avenue. Take that exit a short distance to fork, keep left at fork (signed for Solano) and merge onto Amador Street. Continue on Amador for 0.4 mile (second stop sign) to McBryde Avenue. Turn right and drive 0.3 mile to parking (signed) on left.
Contact: Wildcat Canyon Regional Park, 510/544-3092 or 888/327-2757; East Bay Regional Park District, www.ebparks.org.

114 LAUREL LOOP TRAIL

0.7 mi/0.5 hr 1 8

in the Kennedy Grove Regional Recreation Area

Map 7.3, page 291

Kennedy Grove is set at the base of San Pablo Dam, where visitors will discover a rich grove of eucalyptus adjacent to a large lawn/meadow. This loop hike takes hikers through the eucalyptus and then back, skirting the lawn areas. It is best hiked in a clockwise direction, departing from the trailhead at the gate in the northeast corner of the parking area. This is the kind of park where people toss Frisbees, pass footballs, or play low-key games of softball.
User Groups: Hikers, dogs, and horses. No mountain bikes on the Seafoam Trail. Restrooms and a short walking path at park's main lawn area are wheelchair-accessible.
Permits: No permits are required. An entrance fee of $5 per vehicle is charged when the kiosk is attended; $2 for dogs.
Maps: A brochure and map are available at the trailhead. For a free trail map, phone the East Bay Regional Park District toll-free at 888/327-2757, option 5, ext. 2; follow directions, leave your name and address, and ask for the Kennedy Grove Regional Recreation Area brochure. For a topographic map, ask the USGS for Richmond.
Directions: From I-80 in Richmond, take the San Pablo Dam Road exit. Turn east and drive through El Sobrante for 3.5 miles to the park entrance (0.25 mile south of intersection of Castro Ranch Road), on the left. Follow the pavement to the northwestern parking lot.

From Highway 24 in Orinda, turn north on Camino Pablo and drive north along San Pablo Reservoir to the park entrance (one mile past main entrance to San Pablo Recreation Area) on the right.
Contact: Kennedy Grove Regional Park, 888/327-2757; East Bay Regional Park District, www.ebparks.org.

115 SOBRANTE RIDGE TRAIL

1.6 mi/1.0 hr 1 8

in the Sobrante Ridge Regional Preserve

Map 7.3, page 291

Sobrante Ridge Park covers 277 acres of a former ranch that spans across rolling hills, open ridgeline, and wooded ravines. This hike accesses the best of it. From the trailhead at Coach Drive, take Sobrante Ridge Trail, which rises in an elliptical half loop to the left. After 0.7 mile, you will come to the junction with Broken Oaks Trail. Turn left here and make the short loop (less than 0.25 mile long), and then retrace your steps on Sobrante Ridge Trail. The best of it is on top of the ridge. You get a pretty view of San Pablo Bay across to Mount Tamalpais. This walk provides an easy yet intimate look at one of the Bay Area's key parklands, a link to open space.
User Groups: Hikers, dogs, horses, and mountain bikes. No wheelchair facilities.
Permits: No permits are required. Parking and access are free.
Maps: A brochure and map are available at the trailhead. For a free trail map, phone the East Bay Regional Park District toll-free at 888/327-2757, option 5, ext. 2; follow directions,

leave your name and address, and ask for the Sobrante Ridge Regional Preserve brochure. For a topographic map, ask the USGS for Briones Valley.

Directions: Take I-80 to Richmond and the exit for San Pablo Dam Road. Follow that exit to San Pablo Dam and drive south for three miles (through El Sobrante) to Castro Ranch Road. Turn left on Castro Ranch Road and drive about two miles to Conestoga Way. Turn left on Conestoga and drive to Carriage Drive. Turn left on Carriage and go two blocks to Coach Drive. Turn right and proceed to the park entrance and parking area, at the end of the road.

Contact: Sobrante Ridge Regional Preserve, 888/327-2757; East Bay Regional Park District, www.ebparks.org.

116 BRIONES PEAK LOOP

5.6 mi/3.25 hr 3 8

in Briones Regional Park north of Lafayette

Map 7.3, page 291

Briones Regional Park is a vast wildland with a mosaic of trails for short walks, ambitious treks, mountain biking, and horseback riding. It is crowned by 1,483-foot Briones Peak, which offers great views. You get a panorama of miles of rolling foothills and beyond. In spring, the hills practically glow, alive with wildflowers, making this one of the best parks in Northern California.

From the parking area, start hiking on the Alhambra Creek Trail and Spengler Trail (turn right) to Old Briones Road Trail. Turn left and hike a half mile to Briones Crest Trail. Turn left again and you will rise to Briones Peak in less than a mile. To complete the loop, turn left on the Spengler Trail (it bends to the left), then right on Diablo View Trail, 1.1 miles back to parking. Though Briones Peak has a view west towards Mount Tamalpais, the views north and east are obscured by trees. A better panorama is available a 0.25-mile away at the junction of the Table Top and Spengler Trails, which has a bench near that junction.

At the end of the loop on the Diablo View Trail, you get a southeast-facing lookout that spans across the I-680 corridor, past Shell Ridge, and across the northwest slopes of Mount Diablo.

Briones is an island wilderness, bordered to the north by Martinez and the Highway 4 corridor, east by Walnut Creek and I-680, and south by Lafayette and Highway 24. The park spans 6,255 acres that stretch west past Briones Reservoir and beyond to San Pablo Reservoir.

User Groups: Hikers, dogs, and horses. Mountain bikes are allowed on all but the last mile of the loop. No wheelchair facilities.

Permits: No permits are required. An entrance fee of $3 per vehicle is charged when the kiosk is attended (there are five entrances at Briones, and only two have kiosks); $2 for dogs.

Maps: A brochure and map are available at the trailhead. For a free trail map, phone the East Bay Regional Park District toll-free at 888/327-2757, option 5, ext. 2; follow directions, leave your name and address, and ask for the Briones Regional Park brochure. For a topographic map, ask the USGS for Briones Valley.

Directions: From I-680 north of Pleasant Hill, take Highway 4 west for three miles to the Alhambra Avenue exit. Turn south on Alhambra Avenue, drive for 0.5 mile, and bear right onto Alhambra Valley Road. Drive another mile to Reliez Valley Road. Turn left and follow Reliez Valley Road 0.5 mile to the park entrance. Turn right and drive 0.5 mile to the parking area. Look for the trailhead indicating Alhambra Creek Trail.

From San Francisco, take the Bay Bridge east 6.4 miles (stay to the far right) to the split and I-580. Bear right on I-580 (stay to the far right) and go 1.6 miles to the exit for Highway 24. Take Highway 24 east, drive 0.9 mile to merge with Highway 24, and then continue 11.2 miles to the exit for Pleasant Hill Road. Take that exit 0.1 mile, keep left and continue 0.2 mile to fork, and then bear right, merge onto Pleasant Hill

Road and drive about a mile past Acalanes High School to Reliez Valley Road. Turn left and drive to the park entrance road.

Contact: Briones Regional Park, 888/327-2757 or 925/370-3020; East Bay Regional Park District, www.ebparks.org.

117 NIMITZ WAY

10.0 mi/4.0 hr 

in Tilden Regional Park in the Berkeley hills

Map 7.3, page 291

You are rewarded whether you walk (or ride) five minutes or five hours, or whether you are making your first visit or your 100th. In the first five minutes, you will reach a bench with a gorgeous view to the west over Meadows Canyon and beyond across the hills to the bay. The trail is paved for 4.1 miles and then turns to dirt and arrives at a gate. Continue through the gate; ahead of you, you'll see a towering hilltop. Walk to the top of that. You get a fantastic panorama of San Pablo Bay, San Francisco Bay, and silhouettes of distant peaks and landmarks across to San Francisco.

Nimitz Way is paved for the first two miles, with space on the shoulder, to accommodate all users. Mile markers are posted for joggers. What I do is ride a mountain bike past the gate and into Wildcat Regional Park (five miles), then drop the bike and hike to a hilltop for a view. This is one of the best bike-and-hikes in the Bay Area.

When you depart from Inspiration Point, look for the small grove of conifers on the left about two miles in. Then look closer. Yep, this is a grove of giant sequoias called the Rotary Peace Grove.

User Groups: Hikers, dogs, horses, and mountain bikes. The trail is partially wheelchair-accessible.

Permits: No permits are required. Parking and access are free.

Maps: A brochure and map are available at the trailhead. For a free trail map, phone the East Bay Regional Park District toll-free at 888/327-2757, option 5, ext. 2; follow directions, leave your name and address, and ask for the Tilden Regional Park brochure. For a topographic map, ask the USGS for Briones Valley.

Directions: From San Francisco, take the Bay Bridge east for 6.4 miles (stay far right) to the split and I-580. Bear right on 580 (stay far right) and go 1.5 miles to exit for Highway 24. Take Highway 24 and go seven miles (through tunnel) to Orinda and Exit 9/Moraga. Take that exit to stoplight at Camino Pablo. Turn left on Camino Pablo and go 2.3 miles to Wildcat Canyon Road. Turn left and go 2.4 miles to Inspiration Point and parking on the right. The parking lot often fills on weekends and afternoons, but turnover is high and spots often become quickly available.

From Walnut Creek, take Highway 24 east for 8.1 miles to Orinda and the exit for Camino Pablo. Take that exit, merge north on Camino Pablo and drive two miles to Wildcat Canyon Road. Turn left and drive 2.4 miles to Inspiration Point and parking on the right.

Contact: Tilden Regional Park, 888/327-2757; East Bay Regional Park District, www.ebparks.org.

118 BOTANIC GARDEN LOOP

0.4 mi/1.0 hr 1 9

in Tilden Regional Park in Berkeley hills

Map 7.3, page 291

If you have ever seen a flower, plant, or tree and wondered what the heck it was, you can get the answers on this walk. The Regional Parks District has carved out a 10-acre parcel at Tilden in the Berkeley hills, creating areas that represent 10 distinctive California landscapes and their respective flora. So what you get is a capsule look at the state's 160,000 square miles over the course of a walk that takes 1-2 hours—and the answer to your question.

Start at the visitors center, then plan a counterclockwise route. From the visitors center, turn left and then follow a right-bending horseshoe—you'll end up in a landscape that resembles the high Sierra. As you walk over a creek on a wood bridge, bear right through some hardwoods, emerging at what looks exactly like a Sierra meadow at 10,000 feet near Bishop Pass—complete with aspens, fir, meadow, and what could be an old miner's cabin. The adventure provides a series of such discoveries. The landscapes captured include Pacific Rain Forest, Southern California Desert, Sea Bluff, Shasta-Klamath, and Valley-Foothills.

The site has 1,500 plant, tree, and wildflower species, including 300 endangered species, with virtually all of the state's oaks, conifers, ceanothus, and manzanita species. One phenomenon of creating a mini-California is that, just like in the great outdoors across the state, there are blooming wildflowers over a seven-month period, depending on landscape. Typical blooms in April, for instance, are Douglas iris, ceanothus, monkey flower, poppies, and blue dicks. In May and June, mariposa tulips, western azalea, fireweed, and columbines, among many others, are at peak blooms.

User Groups: Hikers only. No dogs, horses, and mountain bikes. The trail is partially wheelchair-accessible.

Permits: No permits are required. Parking and access are free.

Maps: A brochure and map are available at the visitors center. For a free trail map, phone the East Bay Regional Park District toll-free at 888/327-2757, option 5, ext. 2; follow directions, leave your name and address, and ask for the Tilden Regional Park brochure.

Directions: Take Highway 24 to Orinda and the exit for Camino Pablo. Take that exit to Camino Pablo, turn north (left if coming from Berkeley, right if coming from Walnut Creek) and drive two miles to Wildcat Canyon Road. Turn left and go 3.7 miles to a junction with South Park Drive. Bear right for 20 yards to a parking lot across the road to the botanic gardens. Walk across the road to the signed entrance.

Contact: Regional Parks Botanic Garden, 510/544-3169 or 888/327-2757; East Bay Regional Park District, www.ebparks.org.

119 ABRIGO FALLS

2.7 mi/1.5 hr

in Briones Regional Park north of Orinda

Map 7.3, page 291

Little Abrigo Falls, the Bay Area's smallest waterfall (anything smaller is not a waterfall) and often one of the most elusive (and for some, most disappointing), can be the missing piece in a hiker's waterfall list. It goes dry in summer and fall, but it is a pretty little chute after heavy rains in winter. Start your hike at the Oak Grove picnic area at the Abrigo Valley trailhead. Continue past the Maud Whalen campsite 0.9 mile to the Wee-Ta-Chi campsite, and then continue 0.4 mile to the cutoff spur on the right to Abrigo Falls.

You'll hike amid grasslands, oaks, and bays and along canyons and creeks with riparian habitat. Watch for deer, red-tailed hawks, and golden eagles. Coyotes, foxes, bobcats, and mountain lions are seen occasionally, usually at dusk. A picnic area is available near the trailhead.

User Groups: Hikers, dogs, and horses. No wheelchair facilities.

Permits: No permits are required. An entrance fee of $3 per vehicle is charged when the kiosk is attended (there are five entrances at Briones, and only two have kiosks); there is a $2 fee for dogs.

Maps: A brochure and map are available at the trailhead. For a free trail map, phone the East Bay Regional Park District toll-free at 888/327-2757, option 5, ext. 2; follow directions, leave your name and address, and ask for the Briones Regional Park brochure. For a topographic map, ask the USGS for Briones Valley.

Directions: Take Highway 24 for 7.5 miles to Orinda and the exit for Camino Pablo North. Take Camino Pablo North for 2.2 miles to Bear

Creek Road on right. Turn right on Bear Creek Road and drive five miles to the signed turnoff on right for Bear Creek Staging Area (if you reach Alhambra Valley Road, you have gone too far). Turn right into the Bear Creek Staging Area to the Oak Grove picnic area and trailhead. The entrance to the parking lot and picnic area is on the left past the kiosk.

Contact: Briones Regional Park, 888/327-2757 or 925/370-3020; East Bay Regional Park District, 888/327-2757, www.ebparks.org.

120 ROUND TOP LOOP TRAIL

3.0 mi/1.5 hr 1 8

in Sibley Volcanic Regional Preserve

Map 7.3, page 291

A trek through a volcanic complex that dates 10.2 million years old is the payoff on this adventure. Your destination is Sibley Volcanic Regional Preserve, the Bay Area's best example of ancient volcanic geology. To see it, hike the Round Top Trail to the Volcanic Trail for a loop hike through the volcanic center of the park. For much of the trek, you walk amid prehistoric lava rock. Yet the park is easy to reach and within close range of many on both sides of the bay and along the Highway 24 corridor.

There are some side-trip options as well. Hike up the short, paved cutoff road to the water tank (signed on the map) for a sweeping view of a series of volcanic formations and your destinations on the Volcanic Trail. Few take advantage of this. You can also take a self-guided volcanic tour at the park, a 1.8-mile volcanic interpretive loop with numbered signposts, and many short cutoff trails. Mount Round Top, you can learn, was an infilling of a great crater and was tilted to the side by strains on the Hayward and Moraga fault systems.

In addition, the drive up features a series of pullouts along the west side of Grizzly Peak Boulevard for sensational lookouts below of the Bay Bridge, San Francisco Bay, and dozens of landmarks. These roadside vistas are among the best places in California to see a sunset.

The big dud is 1,763-foot Round Top Peak, the highest point in the park. It's a short, steep walk on a paved road to the top that ends at a series of transmitter stations and antennas. The views are completely blocked by trees and high vegetation.

User Groups: Hikers and dogs. Partially accessible for wheelchairs, horses, and mountain bikes. Mountain bikes OK on Skyline Trail between parking and Old Tunnel Road, paved roads, and fire trails. No bikes permitted on Round Top Road above cutoff on Skyline Trail, or Skyline Trail heading south, and Volcanic Loop (rules signed).

Permits: No permits are required. Parking and access are free.

Maps: A brochure and map are available at the trailhead. For a free trail map, phone the East Bay Regional Park District toll-free at 888/327-2757, option 5, ext. 2; follow directions, leave your name and address, and ask for the Sibley Volcanic Regional Preserve brochure. For a topographic map, ask the USGS for Briones Valley.

Directions: From the East Bay, take Highway 24 east for 5.3 miles (get in right lane) through tunnel to the exit for Fish Ranch Road. Take that exit, merge onto Old Tunnel Road and continue 0.2 mile to Fish Ranch Road. Turn right at Fish Ranch Road and go 0.8 mile to Grizzly Peak Boulevard. Turn left on Grizzly Peak Boulevard and drive 2.4 miles to Skyline Boulevard. Turn left on Skyline and drive short distance to park entrance and parking on left.

Contact: Robert Sibley Volcanic Regional Preserve, 888/327-2757; East Bay Regional Park District, www.ebparks.org.

121 HUCKLEBERRY LOOP PATH

1.7 mi/1.0 hr 2 7

in Huckleberry Botanic Regional Preserve

Map 7.3, page 291

If you know what you're looking for, this is a trip into an ecological wonderland. If you don't, well, it's still a rewarding, tranquil venture. That is because the Huckleberry Loop is routed through a remarkable variety of rare and beautiful plants. Pick up a brochure at the trailhead and follow the self-guided tour that points out the plants and points of interest specific to this area.

The Huckleberry Path starts at the staging area off of Skyline Boulevard. From the parking area, follow the path to the left fork. At the first junction in 0.5 mile, turn left and descend steeply through a mature bay forest. Follow the lower Huckleberry Path for 0.3 mile and experience the succession of forest, dense ferns, and huckleberries. At the junction with the Skyline National Trail and the Bay Area Ridge Trail, stay right. Continue on the Bay Area Ridge Trail for 0.5 mile until it again junctions with the Huckleberry Path on the right. After a steep stair climb, the Huckleberry Path resumes its loop back to the trailhead in a little over a mile. Along the way, explore the dead-end spur trails that branch off the upper Huckleberry Path on the right. The first trail spur shows off spectacular pallid manzanita specimens and provides a great viewpoint. The second spur provides another great view and several plants of interest including the western leatherwood.

User Groups: Hikers only on Huckleberry Path; no dogs, horses, or mountain bikes. Horses are allowed on the Skyline National Trail and the Bay Area Ridge Trail. No wheelchair facilities.

Permits: No permits are required. Parking and access are free.

Maps: A brochure and map are available at the trailhead. For a free trail map, phone the East Bay Regional Park District toll-free at 888/327-2757, option 5, ext. 2; follow directions, leave your name and address, and ask for the Huckleberry Botanic Regional Preserve brochure. For a topographic map, ask the USGS for Oakland East.

Directions: From the East Bay, take Highway 24 east for 5.3 miles (get in right lane) through tunnel to the exit for Fish Ranch Road. Take that exit, merge onto Old Tunnel Road and continue 0.2 mile to Fish Ranch Road. Turn right at Fish Ranch Road and go 0.8 mile to Grizzly Peak Boulevard. Turn left on Grizzly Peak Boulevard and drive 2.4 miles to Skyline Boulevard. Turn left on Skyline and drive a short distance past Robert Sibley Volcanic Regional Preserve to the park entrance and parking lot, on the left.

Contact: Huckleberry Botanic Regional Preserve, 888/327-2757; East Bay Regional Park District, www.ebparks.org.

122 LAFAYETTE-MORAGA TRAIL

7.75 mi one-way/4.0 hr 

north of the San Leandro Reservoir

Map 7.3, page 291

This trail is a hit with locals who use it for exercise, dog walks, jogs, even stroller walks. For nonlocals, not so much. The Lafayette-Moraga Trail is a 7.75-mile linear park. In other words, the trail is a park that forms a line from Lafayette to Moraga. All of it is paved. The trail starts at the Olympic Staging Area in Lafayette and curls to the left for the first 3.5 miles. It eventually heads south along Las Trampas Creek to Bollinger Canyon. It then passes through downtown Moraga to the Valle Vista Staging Area on Canyon Road.

User Groups: Hikers, wheelchairs, dogs, horses, and mountain bikes.

Permits: No permits are required except on EBMUD lands. Parking and access are free.

Maps: A brochure and map are available at the trailhead under the information panel. For a free trail map, phone the East Bay Regional Park District toll-free at 888/327-2757, option 5, ext. 2; follow directions, leave your name and address, and ask for the Lafayette-Moraga Regional Trail brochure. For topographic maps, ask the USGS for Walnut Creek and Las Trampas Ridge.

Directions: From Highway 24 near Lafayette, take the Pleasant Hill Road exit south. Drive one mile to Olympic Boulevard. Turn right and drive 0.1 mile to the Olympic Staging Area.

Contact: Contra Costa Trails Office, 510/544-3028; Lafayette-Moraga Linear Park, 888/327-2757; East Bay Regional Park District, www.ebparks.org.

123 SHORELINE TRAIL

5.0 mi/2.25 hr 1 8

at Crown Memorial State Beach in Alameda

Map 7.3, page 291

The revival of Crown Memorial State Beach is complete on the shore of San Francisco Bay in Alameda. A $5.7 million project restored the beach and dune system. The beach spans 2.5 miles and, on its north end, extends in a half-moon curve to Ballena Bay. The Shoreline Trail is paved and starts near the visitors center. Dunes adjoin the trail for a portion of the walk. You get sweeping views across South San Francisco Bay, best from the beach and bike trail along the southeast portions of the shoreline. There is also an overlook of the Elsie Roemer Bird Sanctuary. A series of eight picnic sites are located from the Crab Cove Visitors Center at the northwest end of the beach on past Freshwater Lagoon and the dunes. The best for a lookout of the bay is City View near the rental shop for windsurfing.

The tide book is your bible at Crown Memorial State Beach. High tide is the best time to observe seabirds such as loons, grebes, and ducks. Low tide, however, is the best time to watch shorebirds such as sandpipers poking around the exposed mudflats.

User Groups: Hikers, wheelchairs, dogs (on the paved trail only, not the beach), and mountain bikes. No horses.

Permits: No permits are required. An entrance fee of $5 per vehicle is charged when kiosk is attended; $2 for dogs.

Maps: A brochure and map are available at the trailhead. For a free trail map, phone the East Bay Regional Park District toll-free at 888/327-2757, option 5, ext. 2; follow directions, leave your name and address, and ask for the Crown Memorial State Beach brochure. For a topographic map, ask the USGS for Oakland West.

Directions: From San Francisco, take the Bay Bridge east for 5.2 miles (and stay to the right) to the split with I-80/580/880. Take the exit for I-880 South (signed for airport), go 1.6 miles and merge onto I-880 South and continue 1.2 miles to the exit for Broadway/Alameda. Take that exit and go 0.4 mile to 5th Street. Turn right on 5th Street, go 0.2 mile, stay right to stay on 5th Street and continue 0.7 mile (stay left) to merge with CA-260/Webster Street Tube. Turn left to merge with CA-260 and go one mile (when in the tube, get to the left) to Constitution Way (also signed by Marina Village Parkway) on left. Bear left toward Constitution Way for 0.3 mile, then continue on Constitution Way for 0.5 mile to 8th Street, and continue ahead on 8th Street for 0.6 mile to Otis Drive. Turn right on Otis Drive and go 0.1 mile to park entrance.

Contact: Crown Memorial State Beach, Crab Cove Visitors Center, 888/327-2757, ext. 3187; East Bay Regional Park District, www.ebparks.org.

124 ARROWHEAD MARSH

2.0 mi/1.0 hr 1 8

at Martin Luther King Regional Shoreline near Oakland

Map 7.3, page 291 **BEST**

Martin Luther King Jr. Regional Shoreline is on the southern edge of San Leandro Bay, just east of the Oakland International Airport. The access road and a nearby trail are routed between Arrowhead Marsh and New Marsh. The San Leandro Creek channel is on one side, and the airport channel is on the other, both of which feed into San Leandro Bay. From the main parking area, you can walk or ride a bike on the Arrowhead Marsh Trail along the airport channel for a mile to its back cove or along the San Leandro Creek channel for a mile to Hegenberger Road. Arrowhead Marsh is a 50-acre tidal marsh shaped like an arrowhead bordering San Leandro Bay a short walk from the primary parking area. Though this wetland is small, a huge variety of birds migrating on the Pacific Flyway use this marsh as a resting spot in winter. Bring your picnic, binoculars, bike, or kayak, and then get ready to launch, no matter what your preference. A series of four picnic areas with water views are located along the park entry road. A boardwalk extends over Arrowhead Marsh to a viewing platform on the edge of San Leandro Bay.

User Groups: Hikers, leashed dogs, wheelchairs, and mountain bikes. No horses.

Permits: No permits are required. Parking and access are free.

Maps: A brochure and map are available at the trailhead. For a free trail map, phone the East Bay Regional Park District toll-free at 888/327-2757, option 5, ext. 2; follow directions, leave your name and address, and ask for the Martin Luther King Regional Shoreline brochure. For a topographic map, ask the USGS for San Leandro.

Directions: From San Francisco, take Bay Bridge east for six miles (do not get in left lane) and continue to the split with I-80/880/580. At the split, take I-880 South for 0.5 mile, then bear left to continue on I-880 South and drive 8.3 miles to the exit for Hegenberger Road. Follow that exit for 0.3 mile to Hegenberger Road. Turn right on Hegenberger and drive 0.7 mile to Pardee Drive. Turn right and go 0.3 mile to Swan Way. Turn left and go 0.2 mile to park entrance road on right. Turn right and drive 0.8 mile to main parking area at end of road.

Contact: Martin Luther King Regional Shoreline, East Bay Regional Park District, 888/327-2757, www.ebparks.org.

125 GRAHAM TRAIL LOOP

0.75 mi/0.5 hr 1 6

in Roberts Regional Recreation Area

Map 7.3, page 291

A rare grove of redwoods lines the entrance of Roberts Regional Recreation Area. That makes it popular for short visits and picnics. If you want to enter a redwood forest in the East Bay without having to walk far, this is the best bet. From the entrance of the parking area, near the swimming pool, take the short trail that is linked to Graham Trail. Turn right, and you will be routed in a short circle past a restroom to Diablo Vista; then turn right and head back to the parking area. The walk is short and sweet, just right for those on a picnic who do not wish for a challenging encounter.

User Groups: Hikers and dogs. No horses or mountain bikes. The restroom is wheelchair-accessible, but the trail is not.

Permits: No permits are required. An entrance fee of $5 per vehicle is charged; $2 for dogs. A fee is charged for access to the swimming pool (wheelchair-accessible).

Maps: A brochure and map are available at the trailhead. For a free trail map, phone the East Bay Regional Park District toll-free at 888/327-2757, option 5, ext. 2; follow directions, leave your name and address, and ask for the Roberts Regional Recreation Area and Redwood Regional Park brochures. For a topographic map, ask the USGS for Oakland East.

Directions: From Highway 24 in the East Bay, drive to Highway 13 in Oakland. Turn south on Highway 13 and drive three miles to the exit for Joaquin Miller Road/Lincoln Avenue. Take that exit and continue to Monterey Boulevard. Turn on Monterey and go to Joaquin Miller

Road. Turn left and drive one mile (up the hill) to Skyline Boulevard. Turn left on Skyline Boulevard and drive about one mile (keep to the right) to the park entrance, on the right.

Contact: Roberts Regional Recreation Area, 888/327-2757; East Bay Regional Park District, www.ebparks.org.

126 STREAM TRAIL LOOP

4.5 mi/2.5 hr 

in Redwood Regional Park

Map 7.3, page 291

The surprise redwoods in the Oakland hills make Redwood Regional Park one of the Bay Area's better finds. Pretty Redwood Creek, recharged each winter by rain, runs down its center. When you drive in, from the main park entrance at Redwood Gate, take the park road to its end at the Canyon Meadow Staging Area. A trailhead here provides access to the Stream Trail. It is routed a quarter mile upstream to a bridge over the creek, then another 1.2 miles to another bridge crossing. The route goes another 0.8 mile up to a third bridge. Most turn around here. It's 4.5 miles round-trip, pretty and easy.

Just beyond the entry kiosk at Redwood Gate, a fish ladder is located a short distance ahead to your left. After February rains, a strain of wild trout found nowhere else swims up from Upper San Leandro Reservoir, jumps the ladder and spawns in the stream. A rarity to see. Fishing is not permitted in Redwood Creek, and no access is allowed downstream at Upper San Leandro Reservoir.

User Groups: Hikers, wheelchairs, dogs, and horses. No mountain bikes.

Permits: No permits are required. An entrance fee of $5 per vehicle is charged when the kiosk is attended; $2 for dogs.

Maps: A brochure and map are available at the trailhead. For a free trail map, phone the East Bay Regional Park District toll-free at 888/327-2757, option 5, ext. 2; follow directions, leave your name and address, and ask for the Redwood Regional Park brochure. For a topographic map, ask the USGS for Oakland East.

Directions: From San Francisco, take the Bay Bridge east for 6.4 miles (stay far right) to the split and I-580. Bear right on I-580 (stay far right) and go 6.2 miles to Exit 24 for 35th Avenue. Take that exit to the stop sign at 35th Avenue; turn left and drive 0.2 mile up hill (becomes Redwood Road) and continue straight for 2.3 miles to Redwood Regional Park on the left. Turn left and continue past the kiosk to the end of the road to parking for the Canyon Meadow Staging Area and trailheads for the Stream Trail (walks, hikes) and Canyon Trail (bikes).

From Highway 24: Take Highway 24 to the exit for Highway 13. Take that exit to Highway 13 South and drive to Redwood Road. Turn left on Redwood Road and drive two miles past Skyline Boulevard to the park entrance, on the left. Turn left and park at the Canyon Meadow Staging Area at the end of the road.

Contact: Redwood Regional Park, 888/327-2757; East Bay Regional Park District, www.ebparks.org.

127 EAST RIDGE LOOP

4.0 mi/2.5 hr 3 7

in Redwood Regional Park

Map 7.3, page 291

The number one hike at Redwood Regional Park, the Stream Trail, is pretty and easy. This trip is for hikers and mountain bikers with a little more ambition. From the parking area, turn right on Canyon Trail, climbing up to the East Ridge in 0.3 mile. Turn left onto the East Ridge Trail and make a loop by hiking out on the ridge, climbing much of the way. You climb roughly 900 feet. From atop the East Ridge, at 1,100 feet, you can look down into a canyon that appears to be a sea of redwoods. Another reward comes when you turn left and loop down into that canyon, where Redwood Creek awaits under the cool canopy of a lush forest. Follow Stream Trail back to the Canyon Meadow Staging Area.

User Groups: Hikers, dogs, and horses. No mountain bikes on Prince Trail or unpaved areas of Stream Trail. The paved areas are wheelchair-accessible.

Permits: No permits are required. An entrance fee of $5 per vehicle is charged when the kiosk is attended; $2 for dogs.

Maps: A brochure and map are available at the trailhead. For a free trail map, phone the East Bay Regional Park District toll-free at 888/327-2757, option 5, ext. 2; follow directions, leave your name and address, and ask for the Redwood Regional Park brochure. For a topographic map, ask the USGS for Oakland East.

Directions: From San Francisco, take the Bay Bridge east for 6.4 miles (stay far right) to the split and I-580. Bear right on I-580 (stay far right) and go 6.2 miles to Exit 24 for 35th Avenue. Take that exit to the stop sign at 35th Avenue, turn left, and drive 0.2 mile up hill (becomes Redwood Road). Continue straight for 2.3 miles to Redwood Regional Park on the left. Turn left, continue past the kiosk to the end of the road to parking for the Canyon Meadow Staging Area at the end of the road.

From Highway 24: Take Highway 24 to the exit for Highway 13. Take that exit to Highway 13 South and drive to Redwood Road. Turn left on Redwood Road and drive two miles past Skyline Boulevard to the park entrance, on the left. Turn left and park at the Canyon Meadow Staging Area at the end of the road.

Contact: Redwood Regional Park, 888/327-2757; East Bay Regional Park District, www.ebparks.org.

128 GRASS VALLEY LOOP

2.8 mi/1.5 hr 2 8

in Anthony Chabot Regional Park

Map 7.3, page 291 BEST

Grass Valley provides a simple paradise nestled in the East Bay hills. This meadow lines more than a mile of a valley floor that is framed on each side by the crowned rims of foothills. From late March through mid-April, you can find a quiet valley that glows in shades of greens from wild grass and sparkles with the blooms of golden poppies and tiny blue-eyed grass and wild radish. The scene is quiet and beautiful, and the Grass Valley Trail provides a route to this tranquility. Start at the Bort Meadow Staging Area (at the MacDonald trailhead for the East Bay Skyline National Trail) and hike downhill to the Bort Meadow Picnic Area. At the bottom of the valley, it feels secluded, quiet, and beautiful. Picnic tables are set in the shade of oaks at the head of Grass Valley. Near the picnic area, head south on Grass Valley Trail for 1.5 miles. Take your time and enjoy it. At Stonebridge and the junction with the Brandon Trail, turn right on the Brandon Trail, which runs north along the west side of Grass Valley, and return to the picnic area. To crown a perfect day, end the hike with lunch at Bort Meadow.

User Groups: Hikers, dogs, horses, and mountain bikes. No wheelchair facilities.

Permits: No permits are required. Parking and access are free.

Maps: A brochure and map are available at the trailhead. For a free trail map, phone the East Bay Regional Park District toll-free at 888/327-2757, option 5, ext. 2; follow directions, leave your name and address, and ask for the Anthony Chabot Regional Park brochure. For a topographic map, ask the USGS for Las Trampas Ridge.

Directions: From I-580 in Oakland, take the 35th Avenue exit and drive east (35th Avenue becomes Redwood Road). Follow Redwood Road past Skyline Boulevard and continue for 4.3 miles to the Bort Meadow Staging Area on the right.

Contact: Anthony Chabot Regional Park, 888/327-2757; East Bay Regional Park District, www.ebparks.org.

129 MACDONALD TRAIL

5.4 mi/3.25 hr  1 7

in Anthony Chabot Regional Park

Map 7.3, page 291

Start at the Bort Meadow Staging Area. From the north end of the parking lot, head north on the old ranch road, which is called the MacDonald Trail and is part of the East Bay National Skyline Trail. Head out north (to the right), where the trail meanders along an old ranch road, climbing only slightly above Bort Meadow and Grass Valley. At the ridge, turn and look south for a great view of Grass Valley—a divine sight in the springtime. From the ridge, the trail/road proceeds north, with valley and hilltop views along the way. Watch closely for the hidden bench on the right side of the trail. You can sit here and look out over the remote foothill country to the east. After enjoying the views, return the way you came. The trail eventually drops steeply and connects to Redwood Regional Park, but most people turn around and return when they reach the drop in the trail.

User Groups: Hikers, dogs, horses, and mountain bikes. No wheelchair facilities.

Permits: No permits are required. Parking and access are free.

Maps: A brochure and map are available at the trailhead. For a free trail map, phone the East Bay Regional Park District toll-free at 888/327-2757, option 5, ext. 2; follow directions, leave your name and address, and ask for the Anthony Chabot Regional Park brochure. For a topographic map, ask the USGS for Las Trampas Ridge.

Directions: From I-580 in Oakland, take the 35th Avenue exit and drive east (35th Avenue becomes Redwood Road). Follow Redwood Road past Skyline Boulevard and drive 4.3 miles to the Bort Meadow Staging Area on the right.

Contact: Anthony Chabot Regional Park, 888/327-2757; East Bay Regional Park District, www.ebparks.org.

130 ROCKY RIDGE LOOP

4.4 mi/2.5 hr  3 10

in Las Trampas Regional Wilderness south of Moraga

Map 7.3, page 291

Rocky Ridge provides the biggest bay view that is seen by the least. It's a ridge-top perch near San Ramon, just west of I-680. When you top the ridge, the view to the west emerges all at once, where you tower 2,000 feet over the South Bay. You can spot hundreds of landmarks in all directions. From the parking lot at 1,080 feet, the Rocky Ridge View Trail starts out as a service road and climbs 800 feet in 1.5 miles to a ridge trail. You continue—you can see the top all the way—and climb another 200 feet over the course of 0.7 mile as the views emerge over the bay. A spot called "Rock 2," at an elevation of 2,024 feet, is the prime payoff. With one sweep of the eye across the bay, you can scan from the high-rises of downtown San Francisco on south past the Bay Bridge, San Mateo Bridge, Dumbarton Bridge, and across to Skyline and Mount Umunhum on the far horizon. Mount Hamilton rises to the south. Then in a turn to the east, you can scan across Mount Rose and the Sunol-Ohlone Wilderness, Livermore Valley, and Mount Diablo.

On the west bay-facing flank of the ridge, those who love to find and explore unique geologic formations can have them in the hollowed-out sandstone at the wind caves and Devil's Hole. With map in hand, take a detour onto the Rocky Ridge View Trail to its junction with Sycamore Trail. Turn right on Sycamore Trail and tromp a little more than 0.25 mile down to the caves. This is a fairly steep, though short, descent. This area also has many raptors. In the spring, the wind out of the northwest will hit the ridge and get pushed straight up, which creates a lifting effect that the raptors can glide on and hunt for hours. Like many parks in the East Bay hills, the landscape is loaded with rabbits, and to a lesser extent, ground squirrels. With so much prey, many see bobcats on the hunt, as well as raptors, including golden eagles, several species of falcons, and red-tailed hawks.

User Groups: Hikers, dogs, and horses. No mountain bikes (but permitted on the park's service roads). No wheelchair facilities.

Permits: No permits are required. Parking and access are free. A permit is required to access and hike on adjoining EBMUD lands.

Maps: A brochure and map are available at the trailhead. For a free trail map, phone the East Bay Regional Park District toll-free at 888/327-2757, option 5, ext. 2; follow directions, leave your name and address, and ask for the Las Trampas Regional Wilderness brochure. For a topographic map, ask the USGS for Las Trampas Ridge.

Directions: From San Francisco, take I-80 East over the Bay Bridge for 5.8 miles (get in right lane) to the I-580 split. Bear right on I-580 East (get in right lane) and go 1.5 miles to exit for Highway 24. Take Highway 24 East (toward Walnut Creek) for 13.3 miles to the exit for I-680 South. Take that exit to I-680 South and drive 10.4 miles to Exit 36 for Crow Canyon Road. Take that exit and continue 0.4 mile to Crow Canyon Road. Turn right on Crow Canyon and go 1.1 miles to Bollinger Canyon Road. Turn right and drive four miles to end of road, parking, and trailheads. There is parking for about 45 vehicles.

Contact: Las Trampas Regional Wilderness, 888/327-2757 or 510/544-3276; East Bay Regional Park District, www.ebparks.org.

131 IRON HORSE REGIONAL TRAIL

1-28mi one-way/1-3 days 

in the San Ramon Valley

Map 7.3, page 291

The Iron Horse Regional Trail is a focal point of the national Rails to Trails program, which converts abandoned rail lines into hiking trails. The continuous trail runs 28 miles from Dublin north to Concord and Highway 4. The completed south portion starts at the Dublin-Pleasanton BART and goes north from there to Highway 4. This has become a prominent destination for locals out jogging, biking, and walking. The trail is a 10-foot wide asphalt strip, but the corridor ranges from 200 feet to as little as 12 feet in some areas of Walnut Creek. It is often hot and dry out here, with a few drinking fountains sprinkled along the way. Shade trees have been planted, affirmation of the sense of long-range vision.

The rail route that it follows was established in 1890 and abandoned officially in 1976. It took only two years to remove all the tracks, but the trail conversion is requiring quite a bit more time. The plan is to extend the Iron Horse Regional Trail into Livermore on the south end and to Carquinez Strait on the north.

User Groups: Hikers, wheelchairs, dogs, horses, and mountain bikes.

Permits: No permits are required. Parking and access are free.

Maps: A brochure and map are available at the trailheads. For a free trail map, phone the East Bay Regional Park District toll-free at 888/327-2757, option 5, ext. 2; follow directions, leave your name and address, and ask for the Iron Horse Regional Trail brochure. For a topographic map, ask the USGS for Las Trampas Ridge.

Directions: South trailhead: Take I-580 east to the Dublin-Pleasanton BART station and park. The trailhead begins on Santa Rita Road.

North trailhead: From I-680 in Walnut Creek, take the Rudgear Road exit. Turn east and park at either the park-and-ride lot (on the east side of the freeway) or the staging area (south side).

Contact: Iron Horse Regional Trail, 888/327-2757; East Bay Regional Park District, www.ebparks.org.

132 CASTLE ROCK TRAIL

3.9 mi/2.0 hr 2 7

in Diablo Foothills Regional Park on Mount Diablo

Map 7.3, page 291

The views of Castle Rock, towering Mount Diablo, and access to a shady ravine make a visit to Diablo Foothills Regional Park very special. The Castle Rocks are a series of sandstone crags that form pieces of wall in the foothills of Diablo. Thousands make the long drive to the top of Mount Diablo; this trip can be more memorable.

From the Orchard Staging Area, follow Castle Rock Trail south to Stage Road Trail. This pretty, shaded riparian zone runs along Pine Creek and the border of Mount Diablo State Park. To the east are Castle Rock's monolithic sandstone structures, gorgeous when the sun is low in the sky at dawn and dusk. At the junction with Buckeye Ravine Trail, turn right (west) to complete the loop along a short section of the Briones-to-Mount Diablo Regional Trail, with photo-quality views of Castle Rock and the silhouette of Mount Diablo. Buckeye Ravine Trail picks up again. After a short jaunt on Fairly Lantern Trail, the trail connects left with Shell Ridge Loop Trail for pretty, long-distance views. From there, you can decide which branch of the Shell Ridge Trail you wish to take back. The first branch (the Shell Ridge Loop Trail) is a bit mellow; the left branch is a bit longer and considerably more steep. Each branch will eventually drain into the same fairway on the Shell Ridge Trail, which quickly returns users to the Orchard Staging Area.

Diablo Foothills encompasses more than 1,000 acres and is linked to Shell Ridge Open Space on one side and Castle Rock Regional Recreation Area and Mount Diablo State Park on the other. There are several staging areas, and a network of trails links to the surrounding parks. The busy Walnut Creek/Concord corridor can cause many to overlook the nearby foothills of giant Diablo. Once you depart I-680, the procession to the park moves quickly from highway traffic, past city and suburbia, to rural landscapes and some of Diablo's wildest lands, prettiest trails, and striking geologic formations.

User Groups: Hikers, dogs, horses, and mountain bikes, partially wheelchair-accessible.

Permits: No permits are required. Parking and access are free.

Maps: A brochure and map are available at the trailhead. For a free trail map, phone the East Bay Regional Park District toll-free at 888/327-2757, option 5, ext. 2; follow directions, leave your name and address, and ask for the Diablo Foothills Regional Park brochure. For a topographic map, ask the USGS for Diablo.

Directions: From the Bay Bridge, bear right on I-580 (stay far right) and go 1.5 miles to exit for Highway 24. Take Highway 24 and drive 13.4 miles (through the tunnel) to Walnut Creek and I-680 (stay left). Continue on I-680 for 0.4 mile to exit for Ygnacio Valley Road. At bottom of the ramp, turn right on Ygnacio Valley Road and continue 2.2 miles to Walnut Avenue. Turn right onto Walnut Avenue and go 1.6 miles to a roundabout. Exit the roundabout to the right onto Castle Rock Road. Continue 1.5 miles to the Orchard Staging Area.

Contact: Diablo Foothills Regional Park, 888/327-2757; East Bay Regional Park District, www.ebparks.org.

133 MITCHELL CANYON LOOP

8.1 mi/4.5 hr 4 10

at Mitchell Canyon in Mount Diablo State Park

Map 7.3, page 291

High on the north flank of Mount Diablo, the world seems simple and clean, with a view that never ends. From Deer Flat and Meridian Ridge, you can peer down Mitchell Canyon, across the Carquinez Strait and San Joaquin Delta, and across miles of greenbelt to the silhouette of Mount St. Helena north of Calistoga.

Little Giant Loop on the flank of Mount Diablo

At Mount Diablo, the best way to commemorate the annual coronation of spring is from the Mitchell Canyon trailhead.

Our favorite trip here is an 8.1-mile loop, named the Mitchell Canyon Loop, and it takes most hikers about four hours to complete. It features an elevation gain of about 1,600 feet, a great picnic site with sensational views, and the option to fork off and create more ambitious trips.

The trip starts at the Mitchell Canyon Staging Area (elevation 600 feet) just outside of Clayton. This provides access to Mount Diablo's prettiest regions in spring.

In the first two miles, the climb is steady, and you can establish a good rhythm as you open the day and gain entry to Mitchell Canyon. You will pass amid grasslands, chaparral, and the first wildflowers of the year. In late March and April, this area features rafts of a purple bloom on a long stalk (linanthus), along with dozens of other species. In April and early May, there can also be hummingbirds, butterflies, and ladybugs galore (don't laugh—on one trip we saw maybe 50,000 ladybugs in a 100-yard radius).

Then it gets steep, climbing about 1,000 feet in a mile, but it's graded with switchbacks, making for a strong aerobic rhythm for hikers—but it's butt-kicker level for bikers. You will top out at Deer Flat and reach a fork in the trail. Everybody stops here, turns, and takes in the long-distance views, often enjoying a drink and maybe a trail snack at the picnic table. Deer Flat is primarily grasslands and chaparral, sprinkled with some small pines. The lookout points here tower over Mitchell Canyon and beyond to the valley flatlands to the north.

To complete the loop, turn left at Deer Flat to the Meridian Ridge Road (a dirt fire road with more great views) and continue to Murchio Gap at a major junction. The best route is to continue straight for a short distance to the Back Trail (no mountain bikes), turn left, and enjoy the saunter downhill into a canyon setting. At the Coulter Pine Trail (single-track, no bikes), turn left, which is routed back to the Mitchell Canyon trailhead and parking area.

Mount Diablo is beautiful in the spring. Sometimes we wish the experience could be captured in a bottle and then taken in little doses when needed for the rest of the year.

User Groups: Hikers and horses. Mountain bikes are allowed on a portion of this route. No dogs. No wheelchair facilities.

Permits: No permits are required. A state park entrance fee of $6 is charged for each vehicle at the Mitchell Canyon Staging Area.

Maps: A trail map is available from Mount Diablo State Park for a fee. For a topographic map, ask the USGS for Diablo.

Directions: From the Bay Bridge, bear right on I-580 and continue 1.6 miles (stay to the right) to Highway 24. Take Highway 24 east for 13.2 miles to Walnut Creek and I-680. Take I-680 north and go 0.4 mile to the exit for Ygnacio Valley Road. Take that exit, turn right, and drive 10 miles to Clayton and Clayton Road. Turn right on Clayton and drive one mile to Mitchell Canyon Road. Turn right and drive to the trailhead at the end of the road.

Contact: Mount Diablo State Park, 925/837-2525; Summit Visitors Center, 925/837-6119; www.parks.ca.gov or www.mdia.org.

134 FALLS TRAIL/ DONNER FALLS

7.6 mi/3.5 hr

in Mount Diablo State Park near Clayton

Map 7.3, page 291

In wet years, this hike is a 10. In dry years, a 6. In the spring, it's always at least an 8. Time it right and the world is yours. At Mount Diablo, the Bay Area's grand old mountain rising above the East Bay hills, there is a series of hidden waterfalls that can be as pretty as anything after a heavy rain. Reaching them requires a 7.6-mile hike, a good climb, and something of a fortune hunt.

From the Mitchell Canyon Staging Area, walk about 200 feet to Oak Road and turn left. This is a short but steep climb up to an oak woodland plateau. Continue on Oak Road until you meet the intersection of Murchio Road. Turn right and continue until you reach Donner Canyon Road, an old ranch road. Walk alongside a pretty creek set amid rolling hills peppered with oaks. At Cardinet Junction, turn left, and after a short time, cross the creek. Then it's a 600-foot climb in five switchbacks to reach the signed turnoff for the falls trail. As you go, enjoy views to the north of Clayton, Suisun Bay, and the Mothball Fleet. You also have a good chance of seeing rabbits, deer, and hawks.

From here, the trail turns to single-track and laterals the left side of a canyon. In wet years, the falls start to come in view one by one. The first is a 20-foot cascade across the other side of the canyon. Then moments later there's another fall, straight ahead, that's more of a chute. As you continue up the trail, two more come into view, including one short but pretty free fall. Continuing straight, the trail will guide you right across two streams, the source of the falls. Most stop to enjoy the treat. If you can time your trip for peak flow, it's a stunner.

When you're ready to head back: The trail loops back to Cardinet Junction, and from there it's an easy (but often muddy in winter) traipse downhill back to the trailhead. It's hard to imagine Diablo any prettier than on this hike.

User Groups: Hikers and horses. No dogs. Mountain bikes permitted on the service road, but not the single-track trail that provides access to the waterfalls. No wheelchair access.

Permits: No permits are required. Parking and access are free.

Maps: A trail map is available from Mount Diablo State Park for a fee. For a topographic map, ask the USGS for Diablo.

Directions: From the Bay Bridge, bear right on I-580 and continue 1.6 miles (stay to the right) to Highway 24. Take Highway 24 east for 13.2 miles to Walnut Creek and I-680. Take I-680 north and go 0.4 mile to the exit for Ygnacio Valley Road. Follow that exit, turn right, and drive 10 miles to Clayton and Clayton Road. Turn right on Clayton and drive one mile to

Mitchell Canyon Road. Turn right and drive to the trailhead at the end of the road.

Note: The City of Clayton implemented at Preferential Permit Parking Pilot Program near a trailhead on Regency Drive. It can only accommodate 20 vehicles. For this reason, you are likely to find no parking on Regency Drive. We now recommend starting your trip at the Mitchell Canyon Staging Area. This adds an hour to your trip, so you get a little more of exactly what you came for.

Contact: Mount Diablo State Park, 925/837-2525; Summit Visitors Center, 925/837-6119; www.parks.ca.gov or www.mdia.org.

135 DEVIL'S ELBOW/ NORTH PEAK

4.0 mi/2.5 hr 3 10

in Mount Diablo State Park near Walnut Creek

Map 7.3, page 291

According to Native American legend, at the dawn of time, Tuyshtak was the sacred birthplace of the world. Supernatural beings, the First People, lived here in the Bay Area. Tuyshtak, you see, is Mount Diablo, the old mountain that towers over the East Bay hills and San Joaquin Delta. It is still one of the best places anywhere in the spring to visit, explore, and take in the views.

The trail does not start at the summit. As you drive up and near the summit, look for the signed trailhead on the right. It is 0.7 mile from the overflow parking lot on top; you can usually park along the road's shoulder near the trailhead, signed Devil's Elbow/North Peak Trail. The hike starts easy, a downhill romp to Prospector's Gap. You then turn right toward the North Summit and start a rhythmic climb for about a mile, before facing a butt-kicker: a seemingly straight-up section of about 150 yards. This is one of the steepest sections of trail anywhere, but it's short. Once near the top, hike over to the crag to the east and scramble to the top. This is a sensational spot with a lookout view that towers over Brentwood and the Delta. This is a four-mile round-trip hike, but it feels longer and takes 2.5 hours.

Note: Mount Diablo is a "dry park." No beer, wine, or alcohol of any kind is permitted.

User Groups: Hikers only. Mountain bikes are permitted, but not recommended. No dogs or horses. No wheelchair access.

Permits: No permits are required. A state park entrance fee of $10 is charged for each vehicle.

Maps: A trail map is available from Mount Diablo State Park for a fee. For a topographic map, ask the USGS for Diablo.

Directions: North Gate: From San Francisco, take the Bay Bridge to the split and I-580. Bear right on I-580 and continue 1.6 miles (stay to the right) to Highway 24. Take 24 east for 13.2 miles to Walnut Creek. Take I-680 north and go 0.4 mile to the exit for Ygnacio Valley Road. Turn right on Ygnacio Valley Road and go 2.2 miles to Walnut Avenue. Bear right and go 1.5 miles to Oak Grove Road, then continue a short distance to North Gate Road. Turn left and go 1.4 miles to park entrance and kiosk. Continue 17 miles to the signed Devil's Elbow trailhead on the right. Parking is available on the shoulders of the road near the trailhead.

South Gate: Take Highway 24 to Walnut Creek (stay right) and I-680 south. Go south on I-680 and drive 7.2 miles to Danville and the exit for Diablo Road. Take Diablo Road east for 2.9 miles (at 0.7 mile, you jog right to stay on Diablo Road) to Mount Diablo Scenic Boulevard. Turn left and go 3.8 miles (becomes South Gate Road) to the kiosk at the park entrance. Continue on South Gate Road to Summit Road. Turn right and drive to the signed Devil's Elbow trailhead on the right. Parking is available on the shoulders of the road near the trailhead

Contact: Mount Diablo State Park, 925/837-2525; Summit Visitors Center, 925/837-6119; www.parks.ca.gov or www.mdia.org.

136 MARY BOWERMAN TRAIL

0.7 mi/0.5 hr 1 10

in Mount Diablo State Park near Walnut Creek

Map 7.3, page 291

From the parking lot, start your visit to the 3,819-foot summit of Mount Diablo by making the short walk to the old lookout station. Head up the stairs to the lookout perch that towers over the San Joaquin Delta and Sacramento Valley. From each side of the lookout, you get a chance to see long distances that encompass a vast, far-reaching landscape. On clear days in spring, the snow-covered Sierra Crest looks so close you feel like you could reach it in one giant leap.

As you drive in on the one-lane road, you'll see two lanes come together; once the two-lane road starts, you'll see the trailhead for the Mary Bowerman Trail. The trail runs on the shoulder of the summit in a clockwise route; the first half of the trail is wheelchair-accessible. It offers a variety of views every step of the way. You will see some fire damage, both on the south flank and into the valley below as well. It takes about a half hour.

The best time of year for this hike is in late March and April, when the hills glow neon green and the skies are often clear. Those familiar with the old mountain know this as the former Fire Interpretive Trail, a rim trail that rings the Diablo summit with fantastic views. In the first 0.25-mile, there's a viewpoint. On a clear day, you can make out the high-rises of downtown Sacramento. Farther along is another spot where you can see across the Devil's Pulpit and into Livermore Valley. Mary Bowerman, in case you don't recognize the name, was an esteemed Diablo botanist.

Note: Mount Diablo is a "dry park." No beer, wine, or alcohol of any kind is permitted.

User Groups: Hikers. The first half of the trail is wheelchair-accessible. No mountain bikes, dogs, or horses.

Permits: No permits are required. A state park entrance fee of $10 is charged for each vehicle.

Maps: A trail map is available from Mount Diablo State Park for a fee. For a topographic map, ask the USGS for Diablo.

Directions: North Gate: From San Francisco, take the Bay Bridge to the split and I-580. Bear right on I-580 and continue 1.6 miles (stay to the right) to Highway 24. Take 24 east for 13.2 miles to Walnut Creek. Take I-680 north and go 0.4 mile to the exit for Ygnacio Valley Road. Turn right on Ygnacio Valley and go 2.2 miles to Walnut Avenue. Bear right and go 1.5 miles to Oak Grove Road, then continue a short distance to North Gate Road. Turn left and go 1.4 miles to park entrance and kiosk. Continue 17 miles to upper summit parking lot.

South Gate: Take Highway 24 to Walnut Creek (stay right) and I-680 South. Go south on I-680 and drive 7.2 miles to Danville and the exit for Diablo Road. Take Diablo Road east for 2.9 miles (at 0.7 mile, you jog right to stay on Diablo Road) to Mount Diablo Scenic Boulevard. Turn left and go 3.8 miles (becomes South Gate Road) to the kiosk at the park entrance. Continue on South Gate Road to Summit Road. Turn right and drive to summit parking area, visitors center, and lookout.

Contact: Mount Diablo State Park, 925/837-2525; Summit Visitors Center, 925/837-6119; www.parks.ca.gov or www.mdia.org.

137 SENTINEL ROCK/ ROCK CITY

1.0 mi/2.0 hr 1 10

in Mount Diablo State Park near Danville

Map 7.3, page 291

Sentinel Rock at Mount Diablo's Rock City is a stunner. You will be forever imprinted by the sight of this series of sandstone monoliths and the adventures that await. You can explore for hours. The most popular trailhead starts at the Big Rock parking area at Rock City. From there, you can follow the Rock Trail to a series of sandstone rock formations, arriving at an overlook where Sentinel Rock is visible.

It's about 0.4 mile to Sentinel Rock, a massive crag of sandstone with hollows like swiss cheese. At the base of Sentinel Rock, on the east side, you'll find a carved staircase that signals the trek to the top (cables are set up for safety). There is a mosaic of unsigned trails in the area, and it can be confusing for first-timers. One suggestion is to follow Wall Point Road to a spur trail (CCC Trail) south to Sentinel Rock. Soak in the views, then return on the spur trail to Wall Point Road and continue following that northwest to other sandstone structures: the Wind Caves, Wall Point, and Lower Rock City. Below Lower Rock City, Boy Scout Rock is the big attraction. On its back side, it's an easy scramble to the top, and you can often see rock climbers rappelling down the face.

Note: Mount Diablo is a "dry park." No beer, wine, or alcohol of any kind is permitted.

User Groups: Hikers. No mountain bikes, dogs, horses, or wheelchair access on trail. Some wheelchair facilities at a picnic area.

Permits: No permits are required. A state park entrance fee of $10 is charged for each vehicle.

Maps: A trail map is available from Mount Diablo State Park for a fee. For a topographic map, ask the USGS for Diablo.

Directions: From San Francisco, take the Bay Bridge east for 6.4 miles (stay far right) to the split and I-580. Bear right on I-580 (stay far right) and go 1.5 miles to exit for Highway 24. Take Highway 24 and go 13.4 miles (through the tunnel) to Walnut Creek (stay right) and I-680 south. Take the exit to I-680 South and drive 7.2 miles to Danville and the exit for Diablo Road. Take Diablo Road east for 2.9 miles (at 0.7 mile, you jog right to stay on Diablo Road) to Mount Diablo Scenic Boulevard. Turn left and go 3.8 miles (becomes South Gate Road) to the kiosk at the park entrance. Continue 0.8 mile to Rock City and park at the Big Rock parking area.

Note: Avoid parking at the nearby campground for day use. Violators will be ticketed.

Contact: Mount Diablo State Park, 925/837-2525; Summit Visitors Center, 925/837-6119; www.parks.ca.gov or www.mdia.org.

138 HAZEL-ATLAS MINE

1.0-3.0 mi/1.5 hr

in Black Diamond Mines Regional Preserve near Antioch

Map 7.3, page 291

Here's a chance to combine a hike through pretty foothill country with an underground tour into the Bay Area's landmark coal and silica mines. Black Diamond Mines spans more than 7,500 acres, with 5,315 acres open to the public and a variety of routes amid 57 miles of trails for hiking (dogs permitted), biking, and horseback riding. The trails include valley walks and climbs to ridges for sweeping foothill views and a 3.2-mile hike with a moderate climb to a backpack-style primitive campground. Plan your trip for the Hazel-Atlas Mine Tour (noon and 3pm Sat.-Sun. Mar.-Nov.).

After passing the park's entrance kiosk (usually staffed only on weekends), drive straight past the first parking area on the left and continue about one mile to the end of the road. A parking area, picnic area, and several trailheads are located here. From this point, take the signed Hazel-Atlas Mine Trail for a short walk up the hill to the mine entrance on the left. (Remember: Access to the mines is permitted by guided tour only.) As you near the mine entrance, on hot days you can feel the rush of cool air emerging from deep below the surface. A few dozen hard hats are provided for public use (mandatory); choose from a wooden box set just inside the mine entrance. In the first 400 feet, you follow a rail line to the underground office of the sand mine boss on the left. Peering through the office door, you see an old desk, a variety of old glass bottles, and other vintage accessories. Outside is the switchback for the railcars.

The tunnel starts out small, and then opens with a series of cavernous chutes above and below you. Lighted stairways provide access to multiple chambers. Some spurs seem dark, deep, and endless, and are walled off by jail cell-like grates. There are multiple levels, and eventually they lead down into the coal mine chambers.

In the spring, this is one of the best of the 150 parks in the Bay Area for wildflower blooms. Deer, squirrels, foxes, hawks, and owls are common sightings.

Stewartville Backpack Camp: This public campground requires a 3.2-mile hike with a moderate climb. There is room for 20 people, with picnic tables and a pit toilet available. There is no drinking water (bring your own), and you must pack out all trash. Reservations required.

User Groups: Hikers, dogs, horses, and mountain bikes. The underground tours are accessible for hikers only. Limited wheelchair facilities.

Permits: No permits are required. A parking fee of $5 per vehicle is charged when the kiosk is attended; $2 per dog. Guided tours of the underground mining museum cost $5 per person; tickets can be purchased at the Sidney Flat Visitors Center. Reservations are required for Stewartville Backpack Camp (510/636-1684, $5 pp/night).

Maps: A brochure and map are available at the trailhead. For a free trail map, phone the East Bay Regional Park District toll-free at 888/327-2757, option 5, ext. 2; follow directions, leave your name and address, and ask for the Black Diamond Mines Regional Preserve brochure. For a topographic map, ask the USGS for Antioch South.

Directions: From the Bay Bridge, take I-80 northeast for 22 miles to the exit for Highway 4/Martinez. Take that exit and continue east on Highway 4 for 25 miles to Exit 26A for Somersville Road. Take that exit, turn right on Auto Center Road/Somersville Road, and continue three miles to the park entrance. Continue straight 0.7 mile to the parking lot and trailhead.

Contact: Black Diamond Mines Regional Preserve, 510/544-2750 or 888/327-2757; East Bay Regional Park District, www.ebparks.org.

139 CONTRA LOMA LOOP

1.6 mi/1.0 hr 

in Contra Loma Regional Park near Antioch

Map 7.3, page 291

Most people go to Contra Loma Regional Park to fish, swim, sunbathe, or picnic at Contra Loma Lake. This short loop trail provides an alternative to those activities, tracing along the northwest shore of the lake, then climbing up and over a short hill and looping back to the starting point. From the parking area, head out on the trail to the Cattail Cove Picnic Area. Just after that, the trail turns right, and you'll follow the shore of the lake, pass a fishing pier, and then start a 10-minute climb up a small hill. To close out the loop, glide down the hill. The trail turns left and a mile later returns to the Cattail Cove Picnic Area. A great, easy romp, this hike is best done in spring.

User Groups: Hikers, wheelchairs, dogs, horses, and mountain bikes.

Permits: No permits are required. A parking fee of $5 per vehicle is charged; $2 for dogs. An additional fee is charged for access to the swim lagoon.

Maps: A brochure and map are available at the trailhead. For a free trail map, phone the East Bay Regional Park District toll-free at 888/327-2757, option 5, ext. 2; follow directions, leave your name and address, and ask for the Contra Loma Regional Park brochure. For a topographic map, ask the USGS for Antioch South.

Directions: Take Highway 4 to Antioch and the exit for Lone Tree Way. Follow that exit to Lone Tree Way and drive south to Golf Course Road. Turn right on Golf Course Road and drive to Frederickson Lane. Bear right on Frederickson and drive to the entry gate. Pass the kiosk, bear left, and continue to the parking lot by the beach.

Contact: Contra Loma Regional Park, 888/327-2757; East Bay Regional Park District, www.ebparks.org.

140 VOLVON LOOP TRAIL/ BOB WALKER RIDGE

5.7 mi/3.0 hr

3 9

in Morgan Territory Regional Preserve north of Livermore

Map 7.3, page 291

Morgan Territory Regional Preserve is located within the traditional homeland of the Volvon, one of six tribes who spoke the Bay Miwok language. This trail, named after the first people to live here, is the preserve's feature hike. You can create an easy 5.7-mile loop where you trace along a ridge as it rises along sandstone hills. You reach a ridgeline with terrific views toward Los Vaqueros Reservoir below.

The staging area is set near the ridge at 1,900 feet. Start the trip by heading up the short hill (a 100-foot climb) on the Volvon Trail and then continue over the other side a short distance to the T (about 0.5 mile from the trailhead) at the intersection of the Blue Oak Trail. Then it's on to Bob Walker Ridge. Head north on the Blue Oak Trail and hike 1.3 miles to the Valley View Trail; a portable toilet is located here and you will pass a few other signed trail junctions. The trail meanders in and out of sub-ridge valleys, green and sprinkled with a few wildflowers in the spring, and is easy all the way. Continue right on the Valley View Trail and head to Bob Walker Ridge.

Here the trail is routed northward on a ranch road to a rounded mountain peak. There are beautiful views of Los Vaqueros Reservoir, as well as below to Round Valley, to the San Joaquin Valley to the east and Mount Diablo to the north.

The Loop Trail circles Bob Walker Ridge in a left-turning horseshoe and then links up again with the Volvon Trail. From here the Volvon Trail runs all the way back to the trailhead. As you near the parking lot, you can take a shortcut by turning right on the Concor Trail and then coasting downhill to the staging area. You can also extend the trip a mile by returning on the Corral Trail/Coyote Trail (hikers only, a good choice on weekends when the bikes are out).

The ridge was named in the 1990s for Bob Walker, a landscape photographer and open-space advocate who helped ensure that Morgan Territory was added to the East Bay Regional Park District. This parkland is most beautiful in the spring, and not just because the hills are greened up; one of the best wildflower displays in the Bay Area occurs here at that time. The one downer: too many cows.

User Groups: The first half of the loop is accessible to hikers, dogs, horses, and mountain bikes. The second half is for hikers and dogs only. No wheelchair facilities.

Permits: No permits are required. Parking and access are free.

Maps: A brochure and map are available at the trailhead. For a free trail map, phone the East Bay Regional Park District toll-free at 888/327-2757, option 5, ext. 2; follow directions, leave your name and address, and ask for the Morgan Territory Regional Preserve brochure. For a topographic map, ask the USGS for Tassajara.

Directions: From I-580 in Livermore, take the North Livermore Avenue exit and turn north. Drive to the junction of Morgan Territory Road and turn right. Drive 10.7 miles (narrow, drive slow) to the staging area on the right side of the road.

From I-680 in Concord, take the Clayton Road exit and head east. Clayton Road becomes Marsh Creek Road. Continue to Morgan Territory Road. Turn right and drive 9.4 miles (narrow, drive slow) to the staging area on the left side of the road.

Contact: Morgan Territory Regional Preserve, 510/544-3060 or 888/327-2757; East Bay Regional Park District, www.ebparks.org.

141 ROUND VALLEY LOOP

6.0 mi/3.0 hr 1 7

in Round Valley Regional Preserve

Map 7.3, page 291

Round Valley Regional Preserve sits in a beautiful pocket below the ridgeline that extends from the southeast flank of Mount Diablo, located off Marsh Creek Road. This park is a great back-road discovery. In the fall, it feels (and looks) like what field scout Ned MacKay calls "the East Bay's Serengeti Plain."

The trip starts with a pretty drive into the foothills of Contra Costa County. The park entrance is actually a staging area—a gravel parking lot with chemical toilets. This is the gateway to the 2,024-acre preserve. After parking, begin the trek by crossing the bridge at the staging area. The service road into Round Valley is called the Miwok Trail. Just over a mile in, there's a junction: You can continue into Round Valley on the Miwok Trail, go right and over a bridge onto the Murphy Meadow Trail, or go left and up a hill on the Hardy Canyon Trail. We've done them all and they are all good. From the ridge that overlooks Round Valley, you can get a spectacular photo of the valley with Mount Diablo in the background.

As you hike amid this riparian-oak woodland habitat, keep a lookout on the valley floor for wildlife and to the air for raptors. This area is loaded with ground squirrels, and they can pop up and down like a game of pop-goes-the-weasel. Because of the high squirrel population, there are an equally high numbers of raptors that feed on them, with lots of red-tailed hawks, but also golden eagles, prairie falcons, owls, and turkey vultures.

User Groups: Hikers, horses, and mountain bikes. No dogs, as dogs are not permitted in the adjoining Los Vaqueros Watershed to the south. No wheelchair facilities.

Permits: No permits are required. Parking and access are free.

Maps: A brochure and map are available at the trailhead. For a free trail map, phone the East Bay Regional Park District toll-free at 888/327-2757, option 5, ext. 2; follow directions, leave your name and address, and ask for the Round Valley Regional Park brochure. For a topographic map, ask the USGS for Diablo.

Directions: From San Francisco, take the Bay Bridge east for 6.4 miles (stay far right) to the split and I-580. Bear right on I-580 (stay far right) and go 1.5 miles to exit for Highway 24. Take Highway 24 and go 13.4 miles (through the tunnel) to Walnut Creek (stay left) and I-680 North. Continue on I-680 North for 0.4 mile to exit for Ygnacio Valley Road. At bottom of ramp turn right on Ygnacio Valley Road and drive 7.5 miles to Clayton Road. Turn right and go 2.5 miles (it becomes Marsh Creek Road) and then continue 12 miles (past Morgan Territory Road on right, Deer Valley Road on left) to entrance on right (signed) to Round Valley Regional Preserve (parking and trailhead visible from Marsh Creek Road).

Alternate route from Livermore: Take I-580 east to the exit for Vasco Avenue. Follow that exit, turn north on Vasco and go 12 miles to Camino Diablo Road. Turn left and go to junction with Marsh Creek Road and continue north 1.5 miles to the staging area on left.

Contact: Round Valley Regional Preserve, 888/327-2757; East Bay Regional Park District, www.ebparks.org.

142 COGSWELL MARSH LOOP

2.9 mi/1.5 hr 1 8

at Hayward Regional Shoreline in Hayward

Map 7.3, page 291

Cogswell Marsh, a 250-acre tidal wetland, is the heart of the 1,713-acre Hayward Regional Shoreline. It is located just north of Highway 92 and the San Mateo Bridge. It is so close to so many who drive right by, yet once afoot, has a feel of a world apart with big-time views and bird sightings. From the Peninsula, it's a quick shot over the bridge, yet few take that shot.

Cogswell Marsh Loop: From West Winton, hike south for 0.4 mile and then pick up the Bay Trail and continue south on the levee through Cogswell Marsh to Johnson's Landing. Turn right to route along the bay's shore and complete loop.

Longer trips can be crafted to the Oro Loma Marsh or beyond to the north on the Bay Trail. From West Winton, hike west for 0.3 mile to Hayward Landing. Turn right on the Bay Trail and head north, with the shore of the South Bay on your left, the 364-acre Oro Loma Marsh (constructed in 1997) on your right, to Bockman Channel, four miles round-trip. The ambitious can continue north, another half mile one-way over the San Lorenzo Creek and another 2.3 miles to San Leandro Marina.

User Groups: Hikers and mountain bikes. No dogs (south of flood control channel at West Winton Avenue) or horses. No wheelchair facilities.

Permits: No permits are required. Parking and access are free.

Maps: A brochure and map are available at the trailhead. For a free trail map, phone the East Bay Regional Park District toll-free at 888/327-2757, option 5, ext. 2; follow directions, leave your name and address, and ask for the Hayward Regional Shoreline brochure. For a topographic map, ask the USGS for San Leandro.

Directions: From San Francisco, take the Bay Bridge (get in right lane) to the split and Exit 8A and I-880. Merge right on I-880 south and drive 18 miles to Exit 28 for Winton Avenue. Take that exit, keep right at a fork, and merge onto West Winton Avenue. Drive 2.5 miles to the park office and continue a short distance to the parking area and trailhead.

From the Peninsula: Take U.S. 101 to exit for Highway 92 East. Take Highway 92 and drive 11 miles (over San Mateo Bridge) to Exit 24 for Clawiter Road/Eden Landing Road. Take that exit 0.2 mile to Clawiter Road, turn left, and go one mile to Depot Road. Turn left on Depot Road and go 0.7 mile to Cabot Boulevard. Turn right and go 1.1 miles to West Winton Avenue (second left). Turn left and drive 0.4 mile to park office; continue a short distance to the parking area and trailhead.

Contact: Hayward Regional Shoreline, 888/327-2757; East Bay Regional Park District, www.ebparks.org.

143 EAST BAY SKYLINE NATIONAL TRAIL

31.0 mi one-way/2-4 days 3 8

from Anthony Chabot to Wildcat Canyon Regional Park

Map 7.3, page 291

A 31-mile trail along the East Bay's skyline offers an opportunity for a long-distance hike that can be chopped into many short segments over the course of days or even weeks. The trail spans from the Castro Valley foothills northward to the ridgeline behind Richmond, crossing six regional parks for a view into the area's prettiest and wildest lands. The East Bay Skyline National Trail can be hiked from south to north in two days, but it can also be divided into seven sections from the different access points at the parking areas. Bicycles and horses are permitted on 65 percent of the trail, where it is wide enough to accommodate them.

It is a great trip, whether you do it all in one weekend or cover a bit at a time over several weeks. No permits are needed, leashed dogs are allowed in undeveloped areas or as posted, and access is free. There are no campgrounds directly along the way, but you can use a shuttle car and come back to do a different section each day. The marked absence of drinking water along much of the route is another drawback. Water is available at only four points over the 31 miles, at Lomas Cantadas, Sibley Preserve, Skyline Gate, and Bort Meadow. So come prepared with two full canteens per person, along with a hat and sunscreen. Following are detailed descriptions of the trail from south to north.

Bort Meadow

Proctor Gate to Bort Meadow, Lake Chabot, and Anthony Chabot Regional Park: The Brandon Trail starts adjacent to Willow Park Public Golf Course and is routed up a ridge. It then meanders on a ranch road in Anthony Chabot Regional Park. At Stonebridge (don't turn left at the trail junction!), the trail leads into Grass Valley and on to Bort Meadow. The trail climbs 600 feet, then drops 320 feet, all over 6.5 miles.

Directions: From I-580 in Oakland, take the 35th Avenue exit and drive east (35th Avenue becomes Redwood Road). Drive on Redwood Road to the Proctor Gate Staging Area on the east border of the park next to Willow Park Public Golf Course.

Bort Meadow to MacDonald Gate, Anthony Chabot Regional Park: If you are hiking the entire East Bay National Skyline Trail, the trail climbs steeply out of Bort Meadow. If you are starting at the parking area, however, no such climb is needed. The trail becomes a service road, from which you can turn and look south for the great view of Grass Valley. Hikers are completely exposed on the ascent; it's hot and dry in the afternoon, so it's best to go early in the morning. Once on top, it's an easy hike, with many wildflowers in spring. It then descends into a canyon, and drops you into MacDonald Staging Area. Continue on MacDonald Trail a very short distance to Big Bear Staging Area (hikers only, no bicycles). You will cross Redwood Road, putting you at the entrance to Redwood Regional Park. Bikers can exit on to Redwood Road, but should use caution. Distance: 2.7 miles; climbs 300 feet, then drops 500 feet.

Directions: From I-580 in Oakland, take the 35th Avenue exit and drive east (35th Avenue becomes Redwood Road). Drive on Redwood Road three miles past Skyline Boulevard to the Bort Meadow Staging Area on the right.

MacDonald Gate to Skyline Gate, Redwood Regional Park: Hikers have two options here, and the suggested route is to split off at French Trail to hike up the canyon bottom on Stream Trail, enveloped by redwoods. (Note that bikes are permitted on the section that overlaps with the Stream Trail, but only as far as Trail's End. Bikes are not permitted after that point.) The alternative, a must-do for bikers, is to take West Ridge Trail for a steep climb to the canyon rim, then drop to the junction at Skyline Gate. Distance: five miles; French Trail drops 200 feet, then climbs 400 feet; West Ridge Trail climbs 900 feet, then drops 200 feet.

Directions: From I-580 to the west or I-680 to the east, take Highway 24 to Highway 13 and go south to the exit for Redwood Road. Turn left at the traffic signal next to the shopping center, then bear left up the hill on Redwood Road. Continue driving east on Redwood Road for 1.7 miles from the intersection of Skyline Boulevard and turn right into the MacDonald Gate Staging Area.

Skyline Gate through Huckleberry Preserve to Sibley Preserve: This section of trail is a choice hike for nature lovers, who will see an abundance of birdlife and other animals, especially in the early morning and late evening. The trail passes through a deciduous woodland habitat, with a short but quite steep climb after entering Huckleberry Preserve. Distance: three miles; drops 200 feet, then climbs 480 feet.

Directions: From Highway 24 in Oakland, drive east to Highway 13. Go south and drive to Joaquin Miller Road, then head east until you hit Skyline Boulevard. Turn left on Skyline Boulevard and drive to the Skyline Gate Staging Area.

Sibley Preserve to Lomas Cantadas, Tilden Regional Park: A unique section of trail, this part crosses over the Caldecott Tunnel in a relatively unpeopled area. Many hawks are seen here, a nice bonus. Sibley is best known for its volcanic past, and hikers can take a side trip to Round Top Peak (see the *Round Top Loop Trail* listing in this chapter). This area was a volcanic region 10 million years ago, when the Hayward and Moraga fault systems greatly uplifted this land. Bicycles are permitted on the section of the Skyline Trail between Sibley Staging Area (6800 Skyline Blvd.) to Old Tunnel Staging Area. Distance: 3.4 miles; drops 300 feet, then climbs 600 feet.

Directions: From I-580 to the west or I-680 to the east, drive to Highway 24. Continue to just east of the Caldecott Tunnel and take the Fish Ranch Road exit northwest to Grizzly Peak Boulevard. Turn left and drive to Skyline Boulevard. The park entrance and parking area are on the left.

Lomas Cantadas to Inspiration Point, Tilden Regional Park: This section of trail starts at a major access area off Grizzly Peak Boulevard. Also possible is an adjacent side trip to Vollmer Peak, the highest point on East Bay Skyline National Trail. The trail is then routed north to Inspiration Point at Wildcat Canyon Road, another well-known access point, losing elevation most of the way. Many sweeping views of the East Bay's untouched foothills are found on this hike. Distance: three miles; drops 860 feet.

Directions: From I-580 to the west or I-680 to the east, drive to Highway 24. Continue to just east of the Caldecott Tunnel and take the Fish Ranch Road exit to Grizzly Peak Boulevard. At the stop sign, turn right and drive on Grizzly Peak Boulevard to Lomas Cantadas Road. Turn right, then immediately turn left, following the signs for the Steam Train to the parking area.

Inspiration Point (Tilden Regional Park) to Wildcat Canyon Regional Park: The last stretch starts at the most heavily used section of the entire route, then crosses its most dramatic and unpeopled terrain. From Inspiration Point, the trail is actually paved for four miles—ideal for bicycles and wheelchairs. Beyond that, the trail turns to dirt and traces San Pablo Ridge with inspiring views in all directions before dropping steeply into Wildcat Canyon Regional Park in the Richmond foothills. Distance: 7.2 miles; drops 800 feet.

Directions: From I-580 to the west or I-680 to the east, drive to Highway 24. Continue to just east of the Caldecott Tunnel and take the Fish Ranch Road exit northwest to Grizzly Peak Boulevard. Turn right, drive up the hill, and turn right on South Park Drive. Drive one mile to Wildcat Canyon Road, bear right, and drive to the parking area at Inspiration Point, on the left.

Alternate Route: To avoid South Park Drive, which is sometimes closed in the winter due to newt migrations, from Highway 24 go through the Caldecott Tunnel and exit at Orinda. Turn left on Camino Pablo. Drive north for about two miles, then turn left on Wildcat Canyon Road. Follow the road to Inspiration Point on the right.

User Groups: Hikers, dogs, horses, and mountain bikes. Horses and mountain bikes are restricted in some sections. Also see individual trailhead listings.

Permits: No permits are required. Access is free, but a parking fee may be charged at some trailheads.

Maps: For a map of the East Bay Skyline National Trail, contact the East Bay Regional Park District and request the individual regional parks map brochures.

Directions: See individual trailhead listings for specific directions.

Contact: East Bay Regional Park District, 888/327-2757, www.ebparks.org.

144 DON CASTRO LAKE LOOP

1.7 mi/1.0 hr 1 6

in Don Castro Regional Recreation Area

Map 7.3, page 291

Don Castro is a small (23 acres) but pretty lake that attracts swimmers to its lagoon and its clear, warm, blue waters. Take the Shoreline Trail along the north side of the lake. It leads to the upper end of the lake with a bridged crossing on your right and the Whispering Creek Trail. That runs the length of the remoter far side of the lake—easy, pretty, with good bird sightings. The trail (actually, it's a road) is routed around the lake for an easy walk or jog in a nice setting. The lake has a fishing pier, swimming lagoon, and is fed by San Lorenzo Creek.

User Groups: Hikers and dogs. Portions of the trail are paved for bicycle and wheelchair use. No horses.

Permits: No permits are required. An entrance fee of $5 per vehicle is charged when the kiosk is attended; $2 for dogs. A swimming fee is extra.

Maps: A brochure and map are available at the trailhead. For a free trail map, phone the East Bay Regional Park District toll-free at 888/327-2757, option 5, ext. 2; follow directions, leave your name and address, and ask for the Don Castro Regional Recreation Area brochure. For a topographic map, ask the USGS for Hayward.

Directions: Take I-580 east to Castro Valley and the exit for Grove Way. Take the exit for Grove Way (toward Crow Canyon Road) for 0.2 mile to Grove Way. Turn right and go 0.2 mile, bear slight left onto Center Street and continue 0.5 mile to Kelly Street. Turn left on Kelly and go 0.5 mile to Woodroe Avenue. Turn left on Woodroe and drive 0.5 mile to park entrance on the right.

From westbound I-580, take the exit for Castro Valley/E. Castro Valley Boulevard and drive west on E. Castro Valley Boulevard to Grove Way. Turn left on Grove and continue to Center Street. Bear slight left onto Center Street and continue 0.5 mile to Kelly Street. Turn left on Kelly and go 0.5 mile to Woodroe Avenue. Turn left on Woodroe and drive 0.5 mile to park entrance on the right.

Contact: Don Castro Regional Recreation Area, 510/544-3073 or 888/327-2757; East Bay Regional Park District, www.ebparks.org.

145 CREST TRAIL/ VISTA GRANDE

at North Gate, Los Vaqueros Reservoir near Brentwood

Map 7.3, page 291

From near the John Muir Interpretive Center, take the Crest Trail up to the ridge, where you emerge on the Vista Grande Trail. Turn left and walk toward the dam. You get sweeping views across Los Vaqueros Reservoir to the foothills of Morgan Territory and beyond to Mount Diablo. The trail then descends past the dam and back to the interpretive center.

The Los Vaqueros Watershed spans nearly 20,000 acres across deep valleys and foothills roughly between Livermore and Brentwood in remote Contra Costa County. It's the Bay Area's biggest lake. The adjoining foothills provide habitat for an abundance of ground squirrels. That furnishes a perpetual food source for the highest numbers of golden eagles (tops in winter when migrants arrive) and bobcats in the region. Other raptors are common.

User Groups: Hikers only; youth ages 12-17 must not hike alone; those under 12 years old must hike with an adult. No mountain bikes, dogs, or horses. Limited wheelchair facilities. Mountain bikes permitted on ranch-style roads elsewhere in watershed.

Permits: No permits are required. A fee of $6 per car is charged. No alcohol is allowed. Helmets are required for all bike riders. No privately owned boats permitted.

Maps: A brochure and map are available online and at the John Muir Interpretive Center.

Directions: In Contra Costa County, take Highway 4 east through Antioch past Hillcrest and merge left onto the Brentwood Bypass. Continue on the Bypass (past Oakley and Brentwood) to Walnut Boulevard. Turn right on Walnut and drive one mile to the entrance gate and parking at the John Muir Interpretive Center.

Contact: Los Vaqueros Marina, 925/371-2628, www.ccwater.com/losvaqueros.

146 VISTA LOOP

3.3 mi/2.0 hr

in Garin Regional Park in the Hayward foothills

Map 7.3, page 291

Garin spans a vast swath of greenbelt above Hayward, with foothills, canyons, creeks, and ponds. Garin Regional Park and adjoining Dry Creek Pioneer Regional Park encompass nearly 4,800 acres of wildlands. A 3.3-mile round-trip with a 550-foot climb tops out at 934-foot Vista Peak (and nearby 948-foot Garin Peak). From the parking area, walk 0.25 mile to Arroyo Flats and a trail junction. Turn left to connect with Vista Peak Loop Trail. On a clear day after a rain, you get a gorgeous view of the South Bay. Take your time and enjoy the views.

For family-style trips, a short walk leads to Jordan Pond and its ranch-style bass fishing, bird-watching, and picnic area. A trail circles the pond. A 20-mile network of ranch roads provides a matrix of routes for excellent mountain biking and horseback riding.

User Groups: Hikers, dogs, horses, and mountain bikes. No wheelchair facilities.

Permits: No permits are required. An entrance fee of $5 per vehicle is charged when the kiosk is attended; $2 for dogs.

Maps: A brochure and map are available at the trailhead. For a free trail map, phone the East Bay Regional Park District toll-free at 888/327-2757, option 5, ext. 2; follow directions, leave your name and address, and ask for the Garin and Dry Creek Pioneer Regional Parks brochure. For a topographic map, ask the USGS for Hayward.

Directions: From San Francisco, take I-80 east over the Bay Bridge (get in right lane) to the split with I-580/I-880. Take the fork for I-880 South, merge onto I-880 and drive 20 miles to Hayward and Exit 25 for Industrial Parkway. Take that exit to Industrial Parkway, turn left and drive to Mission Boulevard. Turn right and drive a short distance to Garin Avenue. Turn left on Garin and drive 0.8 mile to park entrance and parking.

Contact: Garin Regional Park, 888/327-2757; East Bay Regional Park District, www.ebparks.org.

147 BAYVIEW TRAIL

3.5 mi/1.5 hr 1 7

in Coyote Hills Regional Park near Fremont

Map 7.3, page 291

Coyote Hills is a special park with a rare blend of views, birds, walking trails, a bike route, and an Ohlone history that can make every trip special. Most first-time visitors take the paved Bayview Trail or climb to a hilltop for sweeping views across South San Francisco Bay and the East Bay foothills. But you'll likely return for a walk on the wood boardwalk amid a bird-filled marsh. Or take a guided tour of a Tuibun Ohlone village site (aka shell mound). With the support of the Ohlone, staff and volunteers have created structures that provide a window into what the early-day Ohlones structures may have been like. Interpretive walks are available most weekends.

The Bayview Trail is an easy, paved 3.5-mile walk that is routed around much of the park, including more than a mile of bay salt pond frontage. You can detour on a wood boardwalk through the Main Marsh.

Coyote Hills is located along the eastern shore of South San Francisco, bordered to the north by Alameda Creek and the Hayward Regional Shoreline. To the south is the Dumbarton Bridge and beyond that the Don Edwards San Francisco Bay National Wildlife Refuge.

User Groups: Hikers, dogs, horses, and mountain bikes. The trail is paved and technically wheelchair-accessible but quite steep in some sections.

Permits: The entrance fee is $5 per vehicle; $2 for dogs.

Maps: A brochure and map are available at the trailhead. For a free trail map, phone the East Bay Regional Park District toll-free at 888/327-2757, option 5, ext. 2; follow directions, leave your name and address, and ask for the Coyote Hills Regional Park brochure. For a topographic map, ask the USGS for Newark.

Directions: Take I-880 south from Oakland for 23.5 miles to the exit for Dumbarton Bridge/Highway 84. Take that exit, continue 0.4 mile, merge with Highway 84 West, and drive past Ardenwood Boulevard to the exit for Paseo Padre Parkway/Thornton Avenue. Turn right on Paseo Padre (the road becomes Patterson Ranch Road) and continue to the park entrance on the left.

From the Peninsula: Take U.S. 101 to the South Peninsula (south of Redwood City, 27 miles south of San Francisco) and the exit for Highway 84 East/Marsh Road. Follow that exit and go 0.2 mile to Highway 84/Marsh Road. Turn left and go 0.3 mile to Bayfront Expressway. Turn right and drive three miles (becomes Highway 84). Continue 4.6 miles (over Dumbarton Bridge) to the exit for Thornton Avenue (toward Paseo Padre Parkway). Take that exit for 0.2 mile and continue on Paseo Padre Parkway and drive one mile to Patterson Ranch Road. Turn left and drive 1.5 miles to park.

Contact: Coyote Hills Regional Park, visitors center, 510/544-3220; East Bay Regional Park District, www.ebparks.org.

148 RIDGELINE TRAIL

7.0 mi/4.0 hr 3 8

in Pleasanton Ridge Regional Park west of Pleasanton

Map 7.3, page 291

Pleasanton Ridge Regional Park is a huge swath of foothills and ridges that spans 5,271 acres. The Ridgeline Trail climbs to elevations of 1,600 feet, with the northern sections giving way to sweeping views featuring miles of rolling foothills and valleys at the threshold of Mount Diablo. From the parking area, elevation 300 feet, start hiking on Oak Tree Trail. The Oak Tree Trail is routed 1.4 miles up to Ridgeline Trail, and in the process, you climb 750 feet. Turn right on the Ridgeline Trail and hike two miles along the ridge. You can return on a loop route by the Thermalito Trail. You get excellent views across the Livermore Valley. Development in and around the park has been limited. The surroundings retain a wild feel.

User Groups: Hikers, dogs, horses, and mountain bikes. No wheelchair facilities.

Permits: No permits are required. Parking and access are free.

Maps: A brochure and map are available at the trailhead. For a free trail map, phone the East Bay Regional Park District toll-free at 888/327-2757, option 5, ext. 2; follow directions, leave your name and address, and ask for the Pleasanton Ridge Regional Park brochure. For a topographic map, ask the USGS for Dublin.

Directions: Take I-680 to Pleasanton and the exit for Castlewood Drive. Take that exit to Castlewood, turn west and drive to Foothill Road. Turn left (south) on Foothill and drive to the staging area (about two miles from Castlewood Drive).

Contact: Pleasanton Ridge Regional Park, 510/544-3030; East Bay Regional Park District, 888/327-2757, www.ebparks.org.

149 NORTH ARROYO TRAIL

1.3 mi/0.75 hr

in Shadow Cliffs Regional Recreation Area in Pleasanton

Map 7.3, page 291

The centerpiece at Shadow Cliffs is a pretty 80-acre lake on the outskirts of Pleasanton. It has one of the best swimming beaches at any lake in the Bay Area. It also provides fishing for trout and catfish and a spot for kayaking and other low-speed boating. Though you can't walk all the way around Shadow Cliffs Lake, you can explore a series of smaller ponds in the Arroyo area. From the back of the first parking area, take a trail over the top of a levee and down to the shore of the first pond. Then just follow North Arroyo Trail along the shores of several ponds for about 0.5 mile. For a view of the ponds, make the short climb up the adjacent levee. These ponds are water holes left over from a gravel quarry.

Shadow Cliffs Lake, the biggest pond covering some 80 acres, has been stocked with trout and catfish and can be one of the better fishing spots in the East Bay. It is also a good place to swim in season (it is not open to swimming year-round). In winter during heavy rains, the lake often has better clarity than any other lake in the Bay Area.

User Groups: Hikers and dogs. Portions of the trail are accessible to horses and mountain bikes, and wheelchair facilities are available.

Permits: No permits are required. A fee of $6 per vehicle is charged for parking; $2 for dogs.

Maps: A brochure and map are available at the trailhead. For a free trail map, phone the East Bay Regional Park District toll-free at 888/327-2757, option 5, ext. 2; follow directions, leave your name and address, and ask for the Shadow Cliffs Regional Recreation Area brochure. For a topographic map, ask the USGS for Livermore.

Directions: From San Francisco, take the Bay Bridge east 6.4 miles (stay to the far right) to the split and I-580. Bear right on I-580 (stay to the far right), merge with I-580 and drive 28 miles (continue east of I-580 at interchange with I-680) to Pleasanton and the exit for Santa Rita Road (toward Tassajara Road). Take that exit for 0.2 mile, keep right at fork (signed for downtown), merge with Santa Rita Road, and drive 1.7 miles to Valley Avenue. Turn left on Valley Avenue and drive 1.1 miles to Stanley Boulevard. Turn left on Stanley and go 0.7 mile to park entrance on the right.

Contact: Shadow Cliffs Regional Recreation Area, 510/544-3230 or 888/327-2757; East Bay Regional Park District, www.ebparks.org.

150 TIDELANDS TRAIL

2.5 mi/1.5 hr 1 7

in Don Edwards San Francisco Bay National Wildlife Refuge

Map 7.3, page 291

Roughly 1.5 million migratory waterfowl spend the winter on bay wetlands. Hundreds of thousands will arrive at the Don EdwardsSan Francisco Bay National Wildlife Refuge. As you too arrive, a 30,000-acre expanse of salt marshes, tidal flats, and beyond to the South Bay is unveiled to you. The visitors center at the refuge is perched on a hilltop with an observation deck for views of the marsh. Tidelands Trail and Newark Slough Trail provide easy walks with good bird-watching and bay views. This is actually a wide dirt pathway on a levee routed amid salt marsh and bay tidewaters. At first sight, it does not appear very pretty, but it gets better. The views of the South Bay and (on clear days) the surrounding foothills are a panoramic urban backdrop. More than 250 species in a given year use this habitat for food, resting space, and nesting sites. It is not unusual to see a half dozen species of ducks, an egret, a sandpiper, a willet, and herons in just 15 or 20 minutes.

This refuge not only has the longest name of any place around, but great views, bike rides, walks, fishing, and kayaking, and one of the better visitors centers available for free. Group nature tours on this trail are offered regularly on weekends.

User Groups: Hikers, dogs, and mountain bikes. There are no wheelchair facilities, but the trail can be navigated by most wheelchair users. No horses.

Permits: No permits are required. Parking and access are free.

Maps: For a free brochure, contact the refuge. For a topographic map, ask the USGS for Newark.

Directions: From San Francisco and the Peninsula: Take U.S. 101 to Menlo Park (27 miles south of San Francisco) and Exit 406 for Highway 84/East Marsh Road-Dumbarton Bridge. Take that exit and continue to Highway 84 East/Marsh Road and drive 7.6 miles (over Dumbarton Bridge) to Exit 36 for Thornton Avenue (toward Paseo Padre Parkway). Take Exit 36 to Thornton, turn right and go 0.6 mile to Marshlands Road. Turn right and go 0.5 mile to parking.

From East Bay counties: Take I-880 to Fremont (about 20 miles south of Oakland) and Exit 21 for Highway 84/Dumbarton Bridge. Follow that exit and continue 0.4 mile toward Dumbarton Bridge, merge with Highway 84 and drive 1.8 miles to Exit 36 for Paso Padre Parkway/Thornton Avenue. Take that exit to Thornton, turn left, and go 0.6 mile to Marshlands Road. Turn right and go 0.5 mile to parking.

Contact: Don Edwards San Francisco Bay National Wildlife Refuge, 510/792-0222, www.fws.gov/refuge/don_edwards_san_francisco_bay/.

151 ALAMEDA CREEK REGIONAL TRAIL

1-12.4 mi one-way/0.5 hr-1 day 1 8

on Alameda Creek from Niles to the South Bay

Map 7.3, page 291

By bike or on foot, the Alameda Creek Regional Trail provides a series of portals for entry to an extended tour of adventure. From Niles to San Francisco Bay at Coyote Hills, this trip is a can't-miss for fun, wildlife, and bay views. Unlike other regional trails, there are actually two routes; an unpaved route for walking, hiking, and horseback riding on the north side of Alameda Creek, and a paved pathway for biking and jogging on the south side of the creek.

The route, north side: Start to finish, the unpaved north side is 12.4 miles, one-way, and spans from Niles past Shinn Pond, Quarry Lakes, and extends the final four miles out to remote bay wetlands and where Alameda Creek enters the South Bay.

The route, south side: The paved route, a great bike trip, is 12 miles and passes the Kaiser water pits, has bridged access to Quarry Lakes, and extends west to Coyote Hills Regional Park and the shore of the South Bay.

Six parking areas are available with trailheads, with many other access points. If you do not want to do the entire round-trip (24-25 miles), enter the trail instead at Coyote Hills, Quarry Lakes, or Shinn Pond. North side/distances: Unpaved for walking, hiking, horseback riding. From Old Canyon Road/Niles Staging Area: Concrete Bridge/Thornton (2.3 miles one-way), Isherwood/Quarry Lakes (3.1), Alvarado Niles (5.3), Union City Blvd. (8.2), San Francisco Bay (12.4). South side/distances: Paved for bicycling, jogging. From Old Canyon Road/Niles Staging Area: Kaiser Ponds (1.4 miles one-way), Isherwood/Quarry Lakes (3.5), Alvarado (6.4), Coyote Hills (9.7), San Francisco Bay (12). As part of an Eagle Scout project, mileage markers are set along the routes.

At trail's end, on the paved southern trail, the official regional trail ends at the shore of the South Bay, directly adjacent to the Don Edwards San Francisco Bay National Wildlife Refuge to the south. It connects with the Shoreline Trail (dirt) on a land spit that extends south for bird-watching on tidal flats and bay views.

User Groups: South Trail: Hikers, dogs, and mountain bikes. North Trail: Hikers, dogs, and horses. No wheelchair facilities.

Permits: No permits are required. Parking and access are free.

Maps: A brochure and map are available at the trailhead. For a free trail map, phone the East Bay Regional Park District toll-free at 888/327-2757, option 5, ext. 2; follow directions, leave your name and address, and ask for the Alameda Creek Regional Trail brochure. For a topographic map, ask the USGS for Niles.

Directions: From San Francisco, take the Bay Bridge east for 6.4 miles to the split and I-880. Bear right, continue 1.6 miles to the merge with I-880, then drive 20.8 miles to the exit for Alvarado-Niles Road. Follow that exit 0.2 mile to Alvarado-Niles Road. Turn left and drive 3.5 miles, continue ahead on Niles Boulevard for 0.7 mile to Nursery Avenue. Turn left and drive 100 yards to Mission Boulevard. Turn right and go 1.1 miles to Niles Canyon Road. Turn left, go 0.1 mile (second right) to Old Canyon Road. Go a short distance, then turn left to stay on Old Canyon Road (drive over bridge at Alameda Creek; access to trailhead for unpaved Alameda Creek Trail on right near bridge before crossing), and continue to park entrance on left for Niles Staging Area (direct access to trailhead to paved trail on south side of Alameda Creek).

Contact: Alameda Creek Regional Trail, 510/544-3137 or 888/327-2757; East Bay Regional Park District, www.ebparks.org.

152 MISSION PEAK TRAIL

7.0 mi/5.0 hr 4 10

in Mission Peak Regional Preserve near Fremont

Map 7.3, page 291

Climbing 2,517-foot Mission Peak and touching the Summit Post has become a rite of passage. The mountain rises up above Fremont to tower over the South Bay and provides a panorama east over miles of East Bay hills topped by Mount Hamilton, Rose Peak, and Mount Diablo. The Summit Post is set in the summit crag, with pipes affixed to it you can peer through to ID sites around the Bay Area.

The best trailhead parking is at the Ohlone College trailhead. From there, take the Peak Trail (also signed Bay Area Ridge Trail) and hike about three miles up to the junction with the Peak Trail. Turn right for the final 0.5-mile to the summit for a seven-mile round-trip hike.

On weekday mornings, the number of hikers is fewer and you can take the historic trailhead at the end of Stanford Avenue for the Ohlone Wilderness Trail. From the Stanford Avenue trailhead, take the Hidden Valley Trail/Ohlone

Wilderness Trail for 2.6 miles, with a climb of about 1,500 feet, to the junction of the Peak Trail (elevation 2,000 feet). Turn right and it's another 0.5 mile with a 500-foot climb to the top for 6.2 miles round-trip.

Do not head up Mission Peak if you are out of shape. For some, it can turn into what we call a "kill-me, eat-me Donner Party hike." Plan about five hours for the round-trip, including time for lunch on top. The routes are former ranch roads; erosion is severe and cutting across switchbacks results in a loss of vegetation.

User Groups: Hikers, dogs, and horses. Mountain bikes are permitted on some trails on the flank of Mission Peak. No wheelchair facilities.

Permits: No permits are required. A parking fee may apply at the Ohlone College trailhead. Parking is free, but limited, at the Stanford Avenue trailhead.

Maps: A brochure and map are available at the trailhead. For a free trail map, phone the East Bay Regional Park District toll-free at 888/327-2757, option 5, ext. 2; follow directions, leave your name and address, and ask for the Mission Peak Regional Preserve brochure. For a topographic map, ask the USGS for Niles.

Directions: From San Francisco, take the Bay Bridge east for 6.4 miles to the split and I-880. Bear right, continue 1.6 miles to the merge with I-880, then drive 39 miles to Mission Boulevard in Fremont. Take that exit and continue 1.8 miles, merge with Mission Boulevard and continue 1.4 miles to Stanford Avenue. Turn right and drive to trailhead at end of road. Overflow parking is available at Ohlone College; from Stanford Avenue, continue north on Mission Boulevard.

Note: The Stanford Avenue trailhead parking area fills with cars on weekends. (A 9pm park curfew and $300 fine are often enforced.)

Contact: Mission Peak Regional Preserve, 510/544-3246 or 888/327-2757; East Bay Regional Park District, www.ebparks.org.

153 LITTLE YOSEMITE

1.8 mi/1.5 hr 

in Sunol Regional Wilderness near Sunol

Map 7.3, page 291

Little Yosemite is a miniature canyon with a pretty stream (Alameda Creek) with little pool-and-drop waterfalls at high flow in late winter. To see it, don't park near the visitors center, but instead drive a short distance east to the parking area past the corral. You'll find a gated ranch road, Camp Ohlone Road. That's where you start. It's less than a mile to Little Yosemite. The ranch road runs adjacent to Alameda Creek, over a bridge, easy and nearly flat, then over a short hill and down to the falls. At peak flow, it is always a surprise how beautiful the pool-and-drops can be. Bring a tripod for time-lapse photography to capture the flush of movement.

You can extend this trip by heading into the hills above the canyon. The Canyon View Trail, Cave Rock, and Cerro Este (1,720 feet) are all good treks.

User Groups: Hikers, dogs, horses, and mountain bikes. The Indian Joe Creek section of the loop is limited to hikers. Canyon View Trail is limited to hikers on the eastern half, and hikers and horses on the western half. The trail to Little Yosemite is wheelchair-accessible.

Permits: No permits are required for day use. A fee of $5 per vehicle is charged; $2 for dogs. A wilderness permit and a camping reservation are required for overnight backpackers.

Maps: A brochure and map are available at the trailhead. For a free trail map, phone the East Bay Regional Park District toll-free at 888/327-2757, option 5, ext. 2; follow directions, leave your name and address, and ask for the Sunol-Ohlone Regional Wilderness brochure. For a topographic map, ask the USGS for La Costa Valley.

Directions: From San Francisco, take the Bay Bridge east for 6.4 miles (stay far right) to the split and I-580. Bear right on I-580 east and drive 26 miles to I-680 south. Take exit to I-680 south and go 8.2 miles to exit for Calaveras Road/Highway 84. Take exit and go 0.4 mile to fork, stay left, and go short distance to Highway 84-Paloma Road. Turn left at Highway 84/ Paloma and drive under the freeway; continue 4.3 miles (becomes Calaveras Road) to Geary Road. Turn left at Geary and drive 2.3 miles to park entrance and continue to parking at corral at end of road.

Contact: Sunol Regional Wilderness, 510/544-3249 or 888/327-2757; East Bay Regional Park District, www.ebparks.org.

154 FLAG ROCK

4.2 mi/3.0 hr 

in Sunol Regional Wilderness near Sunol

Map 7.3, page 291

You get a perch that towers over the Alameda Creek Valley and beyond, with a bird's-eye view of hovering falcons, eagles, and hawks. This is a great tromp, but with a rough climb for those who are not fit. Flag Hill is a prominent rock outcropping that overlooks the valley floor in Sunol Regional Wilderness. The common route up is on Hayfield Road (2.13 miles one-way, with an 800-foot climb). This trail is actually a ranch-style road, which means you and your hiking buddy can walk side by side—a plus for some, but it can be steep, hot, and hard. Another route, the narrow Flag Hill Trail, is also quite steep (1.26 miles one-way, 800-foot climb).

But the views are gorgeous. At the top of Flag Hill, golden eagles, prairie falcons, turkey vultures, and red-tailed hawks take turns patrolling the skies along the canyon rim, you are often at eye level with hawks gliding in the rising thermals. Lots of ground squirrels for food mean lots of raptors. Directly below is Alameda Creek and valley. This region was once the bottom of an inland sea.

Sunol Regional Wilderness is a big park, spanning 6,859 acres. It is connected to the 9,736-acre Ohlone Wilderness, 4,395-acre Del Valle Regional Park, and the 20,000-acre Alameda Creek/San Antonio/Calaveras watersheds.

User Groups: Hikers, dogs, horses, and mountain bikes.

Permits: No permits are required for day use. A fee of $5 per vehicle is charged; $2 for dogs. A wilderness permit and a camping reservation are required for overnight backpackers.

Maps: A brochure and map are available at the trailhead. For a free trail map, phone the East Bay Regional Park District toll-free at 888/327-2757, option 5, ext. 2; follow directions, leave your name and address, and ask for the Sunol-Ohlone Regional Wilderness brochure. For a topographic map, ask the USGS for La Costa Valley. A topographic map/Wilderness Permit is also available for $2 from the Sunol Visitors Center.

Directions: From San Francisco, take the Bay Bridge east for 6.4 miles (stay far right) to the split and I-580. Bear right on I-580 east and drive 26 miles to I-680 south. Take exit to I-680 south and go 8.2 miles to exit for Calaveras Road/Highway 84. Take exit and go 0.4 mile to fork, stay left, and go short distance to Highway 84-Paloma Road. Turn left at 84/ Paloma and drive under freeway and continue 4.3 miles (becomes Calaveras Road) to Geary Road. Turn left at Geary and drive 2.3 miles to park entrance and continue to parking at corral at end of road.

Contact: Sunol Regional Wilderness, 510/544-3249 or 888/327-2757; East Bay Regional Park District, www.ebparks.org.

155 OHLONE WILDERNESS TRAIL

2.5-28.0 mi one-way/1-3 days 

in Sunol-Ohlone Regional Wilderness

Map 7.3, page 291

Hikers can traverse the East Bay's most unspoiled backcountry via the spectacular 28-mile Ohlone Wilderness Trail. The route crosses wildlands from start to finish. Always start south of Livermore at Del Valle Regional Park. The trail rises through fields of wildflowers, grasslands, and oaks. It also climbs three major summits, Rocky Ridge (elevation 2,426 feet), Rose Peak (elevation 3,817 feet), and Mission Peak (elevation 2,517 feet). It is best hiked as a three-day backpacking venture. You can set up trail camps at designated wilderness sites. You can also do the first section as a day hike.

The trailhead is on the southwest side of Del Valle Reservoir at the Lichen Bark Picnic Area. Shortly after you start the trek, you will reach a box on the right with a sign-in sheet. After the sign-in, the route starts to climb, easy at first, and then quickly rises more steeply. The trail weaves in a canyon and then up to a sub-ridge. In about 1.25 miles from the trailhead (quarter mile past the sign-in box), you will reach a clearing where you can turn and get a pretty view of Del Valle Reservoir.

On to Rocky Ridge: From the trailhead, it's 2.4 miles and a 1,700-foot climb to Rocky Ridge. The trail turns west and cuts up the far side of a deep canyon, and then rises very steeply to crest. Here's the catch: 1,600 feet of the climb is in 1.5 miles, one of the steepest sections of trail in the Bay Area. The payoff is a spectacular perch overlooking the Del Valle canyon to the east and beyond to 3,675-foot Cedar Mountain and the southern Diablo Range. Yet you can turn toward Rose Peak and take in a near-equal scope of wild landscape to the west. Wildflower blooms can be among the best in California near Rocky Ridge. An excellent side trip in late winter and early spring from here is to Murietta Falls; see next listed hike.

On to the trail camp: The trail drops 500 feet, then rises up 1,200 feet toward Wauhab Ridge. A short distance after a cow pond, you'll reach the signed Springboard Trail/Murietta Falls. Stewart's Camp, a wilderness-style camp for backpackers is about 0.5 mile from Murietta Falls. Drinking water and a restroom are available. Reservations required.

Trailhead to Rose Peak: From the trailhead, it's a round-trip of 19.5 miles to Rose Peak (which is why this is a favorite run of ambitious ultra runners). However, it can be a stunning disappointment. After all, at 3,817 feet, Rose Peak is the Bay Area's highest wilderness-style peak. But it is not a conical-shaped summit, so first-timers can get a letdown ("What, this is it?"). But since it is the heart of the Ohlone Wilderness, the 360-degree views from the top provide a fantastic panorama of oak/foothill wildlands, ridges, and canyons.

All the way: To complete the entire 28-mile trek, wilderness camps are set up at the 12- and 16-mile marks. Hiking the trail east to west is the only way to fly. This way you'll face the steepest ascent right at the beginning, when you are still fresh, and end with sweeping views of the South Bay. As you crest the final ridge, Mission Peak, you'll face a moment of truth: You can actually see your car waiting at the parking lot—even though it's still more than an hour away. This last stretch drops 2,100 feet in 3.5 miles, a terrible toe-jammer that will have your knees and thighs screaming for mercy. Weeks later, though, when you replay this adventure in your memory banks, the hike will suddenly seem like "fun."

Most backpackers will cover about 12 miles the first day, followed by two days at about eight miles each. Many even make it a weekend trip, camping 12 miles in on Saturday night, then completing the final 16 miles on Sunday. And it's not unusual for cross-country runners to run the entire route in a single day; an organized race is held here every year.

Note: It is essential to have your itinerary and water supply timed for the trail camps. This isn't difficult, but those who don't do this may have to be carried out by a camel. You might even encounter a moment of irony as you begin to feel a strange sense of solitude, yet know that just over the final ridge to the west is a pit with 6.8 million people.

User Groups: Hikers, dogs (daytime only, not permitted on overnight trips), and horses. No mountain bikes. No wheelchair facilities.

Permits: A trail permit/map for the Ohlone Wilderness Trail is required; $6 per vehicle at entrance station, $4 trail permit/map per person (includes mailing fee); $2 for dogs (no dogs permitted overnight); $5 per person, per night fee for wilderness camping.

Maps: You will receive a trail map when you purchase your permit. For a topographic map, ask the USGS for Mendenhall Springs.

Directions: From San Francisco, take I-80 east over the Bay Bridge (get in right lane) to the split with I-580. Bear right on I-580 east and drive 34 miles to Livermore and Exit 52A for Portola Avenue/North Livermore Avenue. Take that exit and go a short distance to Portola. Turn left and drive 0.8 mile to North Livermore Avenue. Turn right and drive 2.5 miles (through Livermore) and continue (the road becomes Tesla Avenue) 0.5 mile to Mines Road. Turn right and drive 3.5 miles to Del Valle Road. Continue straight (Mines Road turns left) on Del Valle Road and drive 3.1 miles to park entrance. Pay entrance fees and continue ahead to a fork. Turn left at the fork, drive less than a mile to the bridge at Del Valle Reservoir, cross it, then turn right and drive 0.5 mile to the Lichen Bark Picnic Area. Park and walk a short distance to the trailhead for the Ohlone Trail.

To reach the west trailhead/Mission Peak: From San Francisco, take the Bay Bridge east for 6.4 miles to the split and I-880. Bear right, continue 1.6 miles to the merge with I-880, then drive 39 miles to Mission Boulevard in Fremont. Take that exit and continue 1.8 miles, merge with Mission Boulevard, and continue 1.4 miles to Stanford Avenue. Turn right and drive to trailhead at end of road.

Contact: Del Valle Regional Park, 888/327-2757; Sunol Regional Wilderness, 510/544-3249; East Bay Regional Park District, www.ebparks.org.

156 MURIETTA FALLS TRAIL

12.25 mi/1 day 5 8

in Sunol-Ohlone Regional Wilderness

Map 7.3, page 291

The Bay Area's most mercurial destination is 100-foot Murietta Falls. It can feel like an endless trek to the mythical end of the rainbow; there is no guarantee of a pot of gold here either. The hike to Murietta Falls is a grueling round-trip hike of 12.25 miles, with a cumulative elevation gain of 4,000 feet. There's one steep spot up to Rocky Ridge that qualifies as a "kill-me, eat-me" kind of climb. When the hills are saturated and the aquifer is pumping, the gorge is transformed into this huge fountain of white water that pounds over the top and down the gorge in magical froth. This waterfall is a 100-foot cataract that tumbles down a rocky gorge, a beautiful mix of short free falls, horsetails, cascades, and chutes—not a free fall. In most years, it is only a trickle, and outside of winter, it goes dry. For those who want the big-time payoff to complete such a challenging trek, that is a colossal disappointment.

The trailhead for Murietta Falls is the Ohlone Wilderness Trail out of the southern end of Del Valle Regional Park.

You'll know within the first hour if you made a mistake. The hike starts with a 1,700-foot gain to Rocky Ridge (2.4 miles), with a pretty view to the north of Del Valle Reservoir and beyond, and then drops 500 feet in 0.5 mile to the bottom of a canyon. This is just the start. You then climb out of the canyon, gutting it out up 1,200 feet as you rise toward Wauhab Ridge, where you get more pretty long-distance foothill views. You will pass a series of impressive rock outcrops and then reach a little watering hole for cows (mapped as Johnny's Pond). From the pond, continue a short distance to the junction with the Springboard Trail, signed Murietta Falls, signpost 35.

Turn on this trail and walk about 0.25 mile (to a sharp turn in the trail)—then be sharp-eyed for the footpath on your left, along a small creek. Take this path to the brink of the falls. Alas, the view is lousy. No problem. From here, there is a well-worn route that everybody takes that leads down to the plunge pool of the falls. Here you get a picture-perfect view of the gorge and can enjoy a long picnic.

Some choose to extend the trip to two days by camping at a trail site called Stewart's Camp about 0.5 mile from the base of the falls. Although this splits the hiking distance into two days, it also means you must carry all your backpacking gear in and out, a heavy price.

Murietta Falls is named after Joaquin Murietta, of course, the legendary outlaw of the 1800s. If you hit it right, when the waterfall is gushing, you might wonder why such a beautiful place was named after a notorious killer. If you hit it wrong, however, you will understand. It is his final curse.

User Groups: Hikers, dogs (daytime only, not permitted on overnight trips), and horses. No mountain bikes. No wheelchair facilities.

Permits: A trail permit/map for the Ohlone Wilderness Trail is required; $6 per vehicle at entrance station, $4 trail permit/map per person (includes mailing fee); $2 for dogs (no dogs permitted overnight); $5 per person, per night fee for wilderness camping.

Maps: You will receive a trail map when you purchase your permit. For a topographic map, ask the USGS for Mendenhall Springs.

Directions: From San Francisco, take I-80 east over the Bay Bridge (get in right lane) to the split with I-580. Bear right on I-580 East and drive 34 miles to Livermore and Exit 52A for Portola Avenue/North Livermore Avenue. Take that exit and go a short distance to Portola. Turn left and drive 0.8 mile to North Livermore Avenue. Turn right and drive 2.5 miles (through Livermore) and continue (the road becomes Tesla Avenue) 0.5 mile to Mines Road. Turn right and drive 3.5 miles to Del Valle Road. Continue straight (Mines Road turns left) on Del Valle Road and drive 3.1 miles to park entrance. Pay entrance fees and continue ahead to a fork. Turn left at the fork, drive less than a mile to the bridge at Del Valle Reservoir, cross it, then turn right and drive 0.5 mile to the Lichen Bark Picnic Area. Park and walk a short distance to the trailhead for the Ohlone Trail.

Contact: Del Valle Regional Park, 888/327-2757; East Bay Regional Park District, www.ebparks.org.

157 SOUTH BAY NATURE TRAIL

2.0 mi/1.0 hr

in Don Edwards San Francisco Bay National Wildlife Refuge near Alviso

Map 7.4, page 292

This portion of the Don Edwards San Francisco Bay National Wildlife Refuge is set deep in the South Bay marsh near Alviso, where it receives scant attention compared to its big brother to the north at the Dumbarton Bridge.

The trailhead is at the Environmental Education Center. From here, you walk on a dirt path along a wild tidal marshland. You head north on a levee along Coyote Creek, which often looks more like a slough, in its course to entering the South Bay. As you stroll northward, you will delve into wilder and wilder habitat and in the process have a chance at seeing a dozen species of birds in a matter of minutes. The endangered salt marsh harvest mouse lives in this habitat. Guided nature walks are held regularly on weekend mornings. The sloughs and quiet waters here also make for a unique opportunity for saltwater canoeing and kayaking during high tides.

User Groups: Hikers and mountain bikes. No dogs or horses. No wheelchair facilities.

Permits: No permits are required. Parking and access are free.

Maps: A brochure and map are available at the trailhead. For a topographic map, ask the USGS for Mountain View.

Directions: Take U.S. 101 to Santa Clara and the exit for Montague Expressway. Follow the exit 0.4 mile for Montague Expressway (north) and drive 2.3 miles (get in left two lanes) to Zanker Road. Turn left on Zanker and drive 2.1 miles (toward Alicante Drive/De Soto) to Los Esteros Road, and continue on Los Esteroa Road for 1.4 miles to Grand Boulevard. Turn right on Grand Boulevard and drive 0.8 mile to parking and visitors center on the left.

Contact: Environmental Education Center, 408/262-5513; Don Edwards San Francisco Bay National Wildlife Refuge, 510/792-0222, www.fws.gov/refuge/don_edwards_san_francisco_bay/.

158 SUNNYVALE BAYLANDS

2.0 mi/1.0 hr — 1 — 6

in Sunnyvale

Map 7.4, page 292

Sunnyvale Baylands County Park really isn't much of a park at all, but rather a wildlife preserve surrounded by a levee that makes a trail for hiking and jogging. It covers 177 acres of South Bay marshland, home to blue herons, great egrets, avocets, black-necked stilts, mallards, pintails, and burrowing owls.

From the parking area adjacent to Highway 237, hike along the levee. You will turn left as it parallels Calabazas Creek. To your left is a seasonal wetlands preserve. The trail continues along the creek, then turns left again and runs alongside Guadalupe Slough. The open-water bird preserve will be just off to your left. One downer is the adjacent proximity of the highway, which is why it does not merit a higher rating, and yet it deserves entry as an urban wildlife area.

On nearly every trip, you will see a jackrabbit or two. In fact, these rabbits have a way of scaring the bejesus out of hikers. They hide in the weeds until you get close, then suddenly pop up and take off at warp speed, shocking you every time.

User Groups: Hikers only. No dogs, horses, or mountain bikes. No wheelchair facilities.

Permits: No permits are required. An entrance fee of $5 per vehicle is charged from May to October (season pass available), with no parking fee from November to April. No fees for walk-in or bike-in traffic.

Maps: For a free map, write to Sunnyvale Baylands County Park. For a topographic map, ask the USGS for Mountain View.

Directions: Take Highway 237 to the exit for Lawrence Expressway/Caribbean. Follow that exit and go 0.1 mile to Caribbean Drive North and drive 0.3 mile to park entrance on the right (if you arrive at the entrance for the Twin Creeks softball complex, you have gone a short distance too far).

Contact: Sunnyvale Baylands County Park, Sunnyvale, 408/730-7751, https://sunnyvale.ca.gov.

159 MONUMENT PEAK TRAIL

7.5 mi/4.0 hr — 3 — 8

in Ed R. Levin County Park

Map 7.4, page 292

The best view in the Bay Area that is missed the most is from 2,594-foot Monument Peak. It towers over the South Bay and Santa Clara Valley on one side, with miles of wilderness across remote Alameda and Santa Clara Counties on the other. You also get views of two hidden reservoirs, Calaveras and San Antonio.

The trailhead is at 300 feet at Sandy Wool Lake, which makes it a 2,300-foot climb over the course of about 3.75 miles. To start, take the Tularcitos Trail a short distance to the Agua Caliente Trail (you'll see the gate, signed). It starts out as an easy walk. After you pass Launch Site Road (hang gliding is popular in spring and early summer), the climb becomes steeper, and after a climb of 900 feet, you reach the junction of the Monument Peak Trail (actually an old road). Turn right, and it's about another hour to the top. Near the top, a jog on Monument Peak Road will get you near the summit, where a short cutoff will take you to the peak.

Monument Peak Road, a service road, and Monument Peak Trail, a dirt road, are two different routes.

User Groups: Hikers and horses. Leashed dogs permitted only on Calera Creek Trail and Agua Caliente Trail, a service road. No mountain bikes. No wheelchair facilities.

Permits: No permits are required. A day-use fee of $6 per vehicle is charged. Hikers are encouraged to wait two days after a rain before hiking in order to prevent trail damage.

Maps: For a free trail map, contact Ed R. Levin County Park. For topographic maps, ask the USGS for Milpitas and Calaveras Reservoir.

Directions: From the San Francisco: Take U.S 101 south for 35 miles to Mountain View and the exit for Highway 237. Follow that exit and merge onto Highway 237 east. Drive 6.5 miles on Highway 237, then exit (slight right) on Calaveras Boulevard and drive 3.5 miles. Turn left on Downing Road and drive a short distance to the park entrance. Proceed to the parking area near Sandy Wool Lake.

From the East Bay: At junction of I-580 and I-680 near Dublin, take I-680 south for 21 miles to the exit for East Calaveras Boulevard. Turn onto Downing Road and drive a short distance to the park entrance. Proceed to the parking area near Sandy Wool Lake.

Contact: Ed R. Levin County Park, 408/262-6980, www.sccgov.org/sites/parks.

160 OHLONE RIDGE TRAIL

1.5 mi/1.0 hr 

at Costanoa near Año Nuevo State Park Natural Preserve

Map 7.4, page 292

From Ohlone Ridge, you can face west and take in the scope of the Pacific Ocean, Año Nuevo, and miles of wild coast. Every care, stress, and worry will slip away like the outgoing tide. Ohlone Ridge is the easy must-do loop hike for every visitor to Costanoa, the coastal lodge, camp, and recreation getaway that provides a vacation destination. Day use is free.

Costanoa is set on hillside bluffs overlooking the ocean, just east of Highway 1 near Año Nuevo State Park Natural Preserve and the San Mateo and Santa Cruz County line. From the lodge headquarters, walk a short distance on the entrance road to the trail on the left. From here, the route passes Whitehouse Creek and rises through a meadow, then climbs into the foothill to a sub-ridge and lookout with a bench. The views of the local coast out toward Año Nuevo are sensational.

If you want more after this taste or are spending the night here: On the west side of the highway, the Atkinson Bluff Trail extends on the cliff edge overlooking the beach and is routed in a loop out to Franklin Point and past a secluded beach and tidepools.

What makes Costanoa work as a vacation getaway is the overnight accommodations. They feature 89 canvas bungalows with ocean views, deluxe-style lodge rooms and suites, and campsites for tents and RVs with hookups. Everything is deluxe, including the on-site store and restaurant.

User Groups: Hikers, mountain bikes, and horses. Mountain bike rentals and guided horseback riding trips are available. No dogs. Headquarters is wheelchair-accessible.

Permits: No permits are required. Day use and parking are free. Overnight camping and lodging are available.

Maps: A brochure and map are available at the check-in desk. For a topographic map, ask the USGS for Franklin Point.

Directions: From Half Moon Bay, take Highway 1 south and drive 26 miles (nine miles past the turnoff for Pescadero Road) to Rossi Road. Turn left and go 0.5 mile to parking.

Contact: Costanoa Lodge, 877/262-7848, www.costanoa.com.

161 AÑO NUEVO TRAIL

3.0 mi/2.0 hr 1 7

in Año Nuevo State Park Natural Preserve south of Pescadero

Map 7.4, page 292 BEST

Año Nuevo State Park Natural Preserve is home to one of the largest breeding colonies of northern elephant seals. Yep, this is the place where these giant creatures fight, mate, give birth, sunbathe, and make funny noises. So many people want to watch them that you must make reservations and join a tour group (Dec. 15-Mar. 31).

The rest of the year you are free to hike on your own with a free permit from the entrance station or visitors center. But note that the elephant seal population has increased to the point that there are now year-round residents on the beach here. This wildlife adventure has become one of the few sure things in the Bay Area.

After parking, start by hiking the well-signed trail through a series of sandy mounds and flats en route to the beach. The guided walk is along roped-off trails, where you wind your way a safe distance from the animals.

Elephant seals look like giant slugs and often weigh 3,000-5,000 pounds—even the newborns weigh 75 pounds. The old bulls reach nearly 20 feet in length and weigh as much as 5,000 pounds. With a 200mm camera lens, you can get excellent pictures. In mid-December, the males battle for harems. In February and March, hundreds of pups are born and weaned. The rest of the year, this is a nice place to enjoy a quiet beach walk, with decent numbers of the giant mammals available for photos.

User Groups: Hikers only. The first part of the trail is wheelchair-accessible; equal access tours can be arranged in advance online (www.parks.ca.gov/anonuevo). No dogs, horses, or mountain bikes.

Permits: A year-round parking fee of $10 is charged per vehicle. From December 15 through March, access to the preserve is available only by accompanying a ranger on a scheduled walk (800/444-4445, www.anonuevo.reservecalifornia.com, $7 pp).

April through September, access to the natural preserve is by permit (free) between 8:30am and 5pm (last permit issued at 3:30pm). There is no access to the natural preserve December 1-14, but the rest of the park remains open.

Maps: A map is available at the entrance station. For a topographic map, ask the USGS for Franklin Point.

Directions: From I-280 in San Mateo, turn west on Highway 92 and drive to Half Moon Bay and Highway 1. Turn left (south) on Highway 1 and drive 27 miles (6.5 miles south of turnoff for Pigeon Point Lighthouse) to the park entrance on the right (well signed).

Contact: Año Nuevo State Park Natural Preserve, Pescadero, 650/879-0227 or 650/879-2025, www.parks.ca.gov.

162 SKYLINE-TO-THE-SEA BYPASS TRAIL

3.0 mi/2.0 hr 3 9

at Rancho del Oso south of Año Nuevo

Map 7.4, page 292

Thousands walk by the cutoff to this trail every year. We tried it and found it an excellent route, best in spring when there are lots of forget-me-nots and many other wildflowers.

From the parking area, walk a short distance past the gate; at 0.2 mile, look for the cutoff on the left to the Skyline-to-the-Sea Bypass Trail. Turn left and you are on your way. (Mountain bike traffic is heavy at Rancho del Oso, but you'll find no bikes on this trail.) The trail climbs up a short ridge, then laterals along the mountain east about 1.5 miles and descends back down to the valley floor. In the process you get occasional peekaboo valley views off the Waddell Creek Valley. The trail junctions with the service road, the Skyline-to-the-Sea Trail. Turn right for the easy flat walk back to headquarters.

If you want more, visit the Nature and History Center on your way back and take the marsh trail to a pretty wetland and lagoon.

User Groups: Hikers only. No horses, mountain bikes, or dogs. No wheelchair facilities.

Permits: No permits are required. Free parking is available at nearby Waddell Beach. Permits required for overnight use.

Maps: A trail map is available on weekends at the ranger station for a fee. It can be also obtained by mail by calling Mountain Parks Foundation, 831/335-3174; credit cards accepted. For a topographic map, ask the USGS for Franklin Point.

Directions: From I-280 in San Mateo, turn west onto Highway 92 and drive to Half Moon Bay. Turn left (south) onto Highway 1 and drive 30.3 miles (past San Mateo/Santa Cruz county line) to park entrance on left (19 miles from Santa Cruz). Turn and park at Rancho del Oso.

Contact: Rancho del Oso Nature and History Center, 831/427-2288, http://ranchodeloso.org; Big Basin Redwoods State Park, 831/338-8860, www.parks.ca.gov.

163 REDWOOD LOOP NATURE TRAIL

0.6 mi/0.5 hr 1 9

in Big Basin Redwoods State Park

Map 7.4, page 292

At the foot of a giant redwood tree in Big Basin Redwoods State Park, it can feel like you are taking in immortality. Near park headquarters on the Redwood Trail, you'll find that tree, which is about 280 feet tall. It's still a behemoth even though the top 50 feet snapped off in a storm a few years ago (and a park sign credits it as 329 feet tall). For a first visit, walk the Redwood Loop Nature Trail just beyond the primary parking area. A flat, 0.6-mile loop meanders among groves of cathedral redwoods as well as the forest goliaths. Highlights include the base of a giant redwood with so many burls that it looks like a mutated, amorphous blob, the Mother of the Forest, Father of the Forest, and moments where cathedral-like filtered sunlight refracts through the high limbs of the forest canopy. The Mother of the Forest has a 70-foot circumference, Father of the Forest is 250 feet high, and the Santa Clara Tree is 17 feet in diameter.

User Groups: Hikers only. Wheelchair-accessible. No dogs, horses, or mountain bikes.

Permits: No permits are required. A state park entrance fee of $10 per vehicle is charged.

Maps: Detailed trail maps of Big Basin Redwoods State Park are available for a fee from Mountain Parks Foundation, 525 N. Big Trees Road, Felton, CA 95018, 831/335-3174. For topographic maps, ask the USGS for Castle Rock Ridge and Big Basin.

Directions: From San Francisco, take I-280 for 10 miles to Daly City and the exit for Highway 1. Bear right at that exit and take Highway 1 for 20 miles to Half Moon Bay and continue south for 50 miles into Santa Cruz and to a stoplight junction with Highway 9/River Street. Turn left on Highway 9 and drive 12 miles to Boulder Creek and lighted intersection with Highway 236/Big Basin Way. Turn left and go 6.4 miles to Little Basin Road (turn left for Little Basin) and continue 3.5 miles to Big Basin Redwoods (parking on left, pay fee, get brochure/map on right).

Alternate route: From San Francisco, take I-280 south to Cupertino and the exit for Highway 85. Take 85 South and drive to the exit for Sunnyvale-Saratoga Road. Take that exit, turn right (south) and drive into Saratoga to Big Basin Way/Highway 9. Turn right, drive short distance through town, and continue uphill (becomes curvy) to Skyline/Highway 35, and head straight 13 miles to Boulder Creek and Big Basin Way. Turn right and go 10 miles to park headquarters.

Contact: Big Basin Redwoods State Park, 831/338-8860, www.parks.ca.gov

164 BERRY CREEK FALLS

12.0 mi/6.0 hr 4 10

in Big Basin Redwoods State Park

Map 7.4, page 292

The Berry Creek Canyon and its succession of waterfalls are one of the prettiest spots in California. Our favorite spot here is just above the brink of Silver Falls, where you can reach out and touch the water, then take a few steps upstream and admire the lower chute of the Golden Cascade. Yet just above is a fall my brother Rambob named Aztec Falls, where clear water rushes over what looks like a golden sandstone temple. Downstream one mile is the famous Berry Creek Falls, a 70-foot waterfall framed by a canyon and complete with ferns, redwoods, and the sound of rushing water.

A section of trail has been rendered impassable by a massive slide and a quarter mile of downed redwoods. Until the trail is repaired, here's how to do this trek. From the main parking lot across from headquarters, walk past the amphitheater to the trail along Opal Creek. Turn right and walk a short distance to a bridge. Cross the bridge and walk upstream to the Sunset Trail. Turn left and follow the Sunset Trail as it climbs out of the basin floor amid big redwoods. After crossing the Middle Ridge Fire Road, cruise downhill a short distance to the Sunset Connector Trail. Turn left and follow it down past the headwaters of Kelly Creek, which feeds into the Skyline-to-the-Sea Trail. Then it's a nice, easy cruise down into Waddell Creek Canyon and on to Berry Creek. A signed right turn leads a short distance to Berry Creek Falls and its viewing platform.

You round a bend and suddenly, there it is, a divine waterfall. A small bench is perfectly situated for viewing the scene while eating a picnic lunch. At a steady pace, it takes one hour, 50 minutes. So despite the warning sign you will pass, it's a four-hour round-trip if you make it an in-and-outer. The best suggestion is to head beyond, up the canyon.

Go the long way—up the staircase, past the Cascade Falls (Silver Falls and Golden Falls), and return on Sunset Trail. At Silver Falls, it is possible to dunk your head into the streaming water without getting the rest of your body wet—a real thrill. At the brink, the trail is rock steps cut into the canyon, with a woven wire safety rail to keep you from falling off the cliff. Just upstream past the brink, Golden Falls is a beautiful cascade of water over golden sandstone, like a giant waterslide. One of the golden cascades looks like a miniature Aztec Temple.

Once you pass Golden Falls, the trail climbs out to a service road near Sunset Camp. Do not miss the right turn off the service road to Sunset Trail. From here, Sunset Trail meanders through the remotest sections of the park, in and out of chaparral and forest, then loops back into redwoods, and leads back to park headquarters. Though you can trim the hiking time down if you double back on the same trail you came in on, why cut the experience short? Getting an early start helps to ensure a carefree trip with no pressure to complete the loop by a certain time.

User Groups: Hikers only. No dogs, horses, or mountain bikes. No wheelchair facilities.

Permits: A state park entrance fee of $10 per vehicle is charged. Trail camp permits are by reservation only, $15 per night per site. Permits include one vehicle, $10 per extra vehicle.

Maps: Detailed trail maps of Big Basin Redwoods State Park are available for a fee from Mountain Parks Foundation in Felton (831/335-3174). For topographic maps, ask the USGS for Castle Rock Ridge and Big Basin.

Directions: From San Francisco, take I-280 for 10 miles to Daly City and the exit for Highway 1. Bear right at that exit and take Highway 1 for 20 miles to Half Moon Bay and continue south for 50 miles into Santa Cruz and to a stoplight junction with Highway 9/River Street. Turn left on Highway 9 and drive 12 miles to Boulder Creek and lighted intersection with Highway 236/Big Basin Way. Turn left and go 6.4 miles to Little Basin Road (turn left for Little Basin) and continue 3.5 miles to Big Basin Redwoods (parking on left, pay fee, get brochure/map on right).

Alternate route: From San Francisco, take I-280 south to Cupertino and the exit for Highway 85. Take 85 South and drive to the exit for Sunnyvale-Saratoga Road. Take that exit, turn right (south) and drive into Saratoga to Big Basin Way/Highway 9. Turn right, drive short distance through town, continue uphill (becomes curvy) to Skyline/Highway 35, and head straight 13 miles to Boulder Creek and Big Basin Way. Turn right and go 10 miles to park headquarters.

Contact: Big Basin Redwoods State Park, 831/338-8860, www.parks.ca.gov; Santa Cruz District, 831/429-2850; camping reservations, 800/444-7275; backpacking reservations, 831/338-8861; tent cabins, www.bigbasintentcabins.com, reserve at www.reserveamerica.com.

165 METEOR TRAIL

5.2 mi/2.5 hr

in Big Basin Redwoods State Park

Map 7.4, page 292

Under the heavy redwood canopy of Big Basin, most hikers don't worry about whether or not it's foggy on the coast. But with the park's best coastal lookout at trail's end, you don't want fog on this hike. The Meteor Trail starts at the parking area across the lot from park headquarters on the Skyline-to-the-Sea Trail. Walk over the wood bridge at Opal Creek and turn right. If you turn left and see a sign for Berry Creek Falls, you're going in the wrong direction.

For much of the route, you hike along Opal Creek, a pretty stream in the spring, surrounded by redwoods. Two miles out, you will arrive at the intersection with Meteor Trail. This is where you turn left and then climb 400 feet over the space of a mile to the Middle Ridge Fire Road. The Ocean View Summit (1,600 feet) is only a couple hundred yards off, featuring a glimpse to the west of the Waddell Creek watershed and the Pacific Coast. Return by doubling back the way you came. If you visit Big Basin and don't have time for the Berry Creek Falls hike, this is the next best option.

The view from the summit had been eclipsed by trees in recent years, but has broken spots now, thanks to a prescribed burn over a few hundred acres along the summit ridge.

The biggest of the park's redwoods is off the Meteor Trail, though not marked for easy sighting. Steve Sillett, a world-renowned scientist with a specialty in the ecology of tall trees, hiked out the Meteor Trail, and with Jim Speckler, verified its height of 328.12 feet by direct tape drop. According to the Native Tree Society, that could make it the tallest tree in the world south of 38 degrees latitude.

User Groups: Hikers only. No dogs, horses, or mountain bikes. No wheelchair facilities.

Permits: No permits are required. A state park entrance fee of $10 per vehicle is charged.

Maps: Detailed trail maps of Big Basin Redwoods State Park are available for a fee from Mountain Parks Foundation, Felton, 831/335-3174. For topographic maps, ask the USGS for Castle Rock Ridge and Big Basin.

Directions: From San Francisco, take I-280 for 10 miles to Daly City and the exit for Highway 1. Bear right at that exit and take Highway 1 for 20 miles to Half Moon Bay and continue south for 50 miles into Santa Cruz and to a stoplight junction with Highway 9/River Street. Turn left on Highway 9 and drive 12 miles to Boulder Creek and lighted intersection with Highway 236/Big Basin Way. Turn left and go 6.4 miles to Little Basin Road (turn left for Little Basin) and continue 3.5 miles to Big Basin Redwoods (parking on left, pay fee, get brochure/map on right).

Alternate route: From San Francisco, take I-280 south to Cupertino and the exit for Highway 85. Take 85 South and drive to the exit for Sunnyvale-Saratoga Road. Take that exit, turn right (south) and drive into Saratoga to Big Basin Way/Highway 9. Turn right, drive short distance through town, continue uphill (becomes curvy) to Skyline/Highway 35, and head straight 13 miles to Boulder Creek and Big Basin Way. Turn right and go 10 miles to park headquarters.

Contact: Big Basin Redwoods State Park, 831/338-8860, www.parks.ca.gov; Santa Cruz District, 831/429-2850; camping reservations, 800/444-7275; backpacking reservations, 831/338-8861; tent cabins, www.bigbasintentcabins.com, reserve at www.reserveamerica.com.

166 LONG RIDGE LOOP

4.6 mi/2.5 hr

in Long Ridge Open Space Preserve

Map 7.4, page 292

This is one of the best day hikes on the Peninsula, a place to recharge your senses in a few hours. After parking, get the brochure/trail map from the box near the trailhead and orient yourself. This adventure starts by heading west down into the adjacent valley and past the intersection with the Bay Ridge Trail at 0.4 mile, then reaches the junction with the Long Ridge Trail and Peters Creek Trail (at 0.5 mile). Here you turn right and make a climb through oak woodlands, including one short, steep spot, where the trail horseshoes its way eventually to the south up to Long Ridge Road (at 1.2 miles; a dirt service road). You then arrive at the Wallace Stegner Bench. This is a great coastal lookout, one of the best on the Peninsula. Everybody takes at least five minutes to enjoy it, and some even have a picnic.

From here, the going is easy to Four Corners, heading south on Long Ridge, with a slight elevation gain, rewarded by gorgeous views off to the west. On clear days, you get long-distance views of the ocean and, as you continue south, across miles of foothills and forested valleys. The highest point in San Mateo County, 2,600 feet, is just off the trail here, but it is hardly a prominent point in the landscape.

At Four Corners (2.5 miles), you turn left, encounter a series of switchbacks as you descend into a heavily wooded canyon, extremely lush in late winter and spring. The surprise of the trip is just ahead: You will pass a secret pond (3.0 miles), ringed by tules and quite pretty. To complete the loop hike, continue on the Peters Creek Trail, a rich riparian zone, back to the junction with Long Ridge Trail (4.1 miles). Turn right and hike back to the parking area (4.6 miles).

Trails are routed through a variety of beautiful landscapes, including sheltered canyons, creeks, meadows, and oak woodlands, past a beautiful hidden pond, and up on Long Ridge itself for great open views to the west of the Butano Rim and Pacific Ocean. And you can get this with one 4.6-mile loop trip, including only about a 400-foot climb. There is also a good chance of spotting wild turkeys, rabbits, deer, raptors, and songbirds.

User Groups: Hikers, horses, and mountain bikes (restricted from some trails, signed). No dogs. No wheelchair facilities.

Permits: No permits are required. Parking and access are free.

Maps: A brochure and map are available at the trailhead. For a free trail map, contact the Midpeninsula Regional Open Space District. For a topographic map, ask the USGS for Mindego Hill.

Directions: From San Francisco, take I-280 south and drive 20 miles to Woodside and the exit for Highway 84/Woodside Road. Follow that exit, turn west (right) on Woodside Road, and drive 2.8 miles to Woodside. Continue straight on Woodside Road/Highway 84 (becomes curvy) to Sky Londa and Highway 35/Skyline Boulevard. Turn left on Skyline and drive 7.2 miles to Page Mill Road, then continue straight on Skyline for 3.3 miles (a short distance past Portola Heights Road) to pullouts along Skyline for parking. The preserve entrance and trailhead are on the right.

From the South Bay: From Palo Alto at I-280, take Page Mill Road west about 10 miles (becomes curvy, watch out for bikes) to Skyline

Boulevard. Turn left and drive 3.3 miles to the preserve entrance on the right.

From Saratoga: Take Big Basin Way/ Highway 9 for about seven miles to Skyline Boulevard. Turn right and drive 3.6 miles to the preserve entrance on the left (parking is also available on the right shoulder).

Contact: Midpeninsula Regional Open Space District, 650/691-1200, www.openspace.org.

167 TRAIL CAMP LOOP

5.3 mi/2.5 hr 2 10

in Castle Rock State Park

Map 7.4, page 292

Here you can discover a great and easy 5.3-mile walk that takes about 2.5 hours. It is highlighted by a surprise waterfall with a viewing deck, honeycombed sandstone formations, sweeping views of the Santa Cruz Mountains and Monterey Bay to the west, and then a top-of-the-world perch atop Goat Rock.

From the parking area, take the short spur to the Saratoga Gap Trail. In the first few minutes, the trail descends into a lush riparian canyon. Within 0.5 mile, you arrive at the cutoff on your left for the viewing deck. This puts you at the brink of a canyon and adjacent to the waterfall, best after recent rainfall, of course. Back on the main trail, the route breaks out from forest and into the open along a rock facing. On stellar days, those with sharp vision can see the white foam of the breakers on the beaches of Monterey Bay to the west. As you head on, you will pass a series of sandstone formations to your right, where material has eroded over time to create a series of holes and cavities. The most dramatic of these is at Goat Rock, where the trail runs right past its base. At this spot there is a permanent climbing cable, and on weekends, climbers practice technical skills here.

The trail continues to a junction with Ridge Trail, a distance of 2.6 miles from the parking lot. At this junction, turn right and start the loop back to the parking area. The return loop features a gentle climb, primarily amid chaparral and woodlands. Watch for a cutoff trail on the right to Goat Rock Lookout. Don't miss this side trip; walk a short distance to the top of Goat Rock. You get sweeping, long-distance views across a sea of conifers and beyond to the ocean. Perches and scoops atop Goat Rock provide excellent picnic sites.

There are 32 miles of hiking trails in 3,600 acres of semi-wilderness land at this park, so you can extend your adventure.

User Groups: Hikers and horses. No dogs or mountain bikes. No wheelchair facilities.

Permits: No permits are required, but you must self-register at the park entrance. A day-use fee of $10 per vehicle is charged. Permits to camp are by reservation only. Reservations, available dates, and more information available at www.parks.ca.gov. Search "Castle Rock" and click on link for "Backcountry Trail Camp," $15 per night per site. Permits include one vehicle, $10 per extra vehicle.

Maps: A brochure and map are available at the trailhead. A trail map of Castle Rock State Park is available for a fee from Mountain Parks Foundation in Felton (831/335-3174). For a topographic map, ask the USGS for Castle Rock Ridge.

Directions: From San Francisco, take I-280 south and drive about 30 miles to Woodside and Exit 25 for Highway 84/Woodside Road. Take that exit, turn west (right) on Woodside Road, and drive one mile to Woodside. Continue straight on Woodside Road/Highway 84 and drive six miles (curvy) to Sky Londa and Highway 35/Skyline Boulevard. Turn left on Skyline and drive 14.3 miles. At a junction with Highway 9, continue straight ahead three miles to Castle Rock State Park on the right (the former entrance and parking area is now for campers only).

From South Bay: Take Highway 85 South toward Santa Cruz/Cupertino to Exit 14 for Saratoga Avenue. Take that exit to Saratoga Avenue. Turn right and drive 1.8 miles to Big Basin Way/Highway 9, and continue on

Highway 9 for 2.5 miles into Los Gatos. Turn right (still Big Basin Way/Highway 9, signed) and drive 4.8 miles up hill (becomes curvy) to junction and stop sign with Highway 35/Skyline. Turn left and drive 2.5 miles to park on right.

Contact: Castle Rock State Park, 408/867-2952; California State Parks, Santa Cruz District, 831/429-2850, www.parks.ca.gov.

168 SKYLINE-TO-THE-SEA TRAIL

34.0 mi one-way/2.5 days 3 10

in Castle Rock State Park

Map 7.4, page 292

This is one of the most worshipped trails in the Bay Area. The workings of this trail started with a vision to create a route that connected Castle Rock State Park on Skyline Ridge to Big Basin and then to Waddell Creek on the coast. The result, much of it built by volunteers, is this 34-mile backpack route, complete with primitive trail camps. It is ideal in many ways, including the fact that the hike is generally downhill, starting at 3,000 feet at Castle Rock and dropping all the way down to sea level. You get fantastic views, redwood forests, waterfalls, and backpack camps. Most hike the trail in three days, camping at Waterman Gap and at Big Basin headquarters, with a shuttle car waiting at the end of the trail at Waddell Creek on Highway 1.

From the trailhead at Castle Rock State Park, take the Saratoga Gap Trail, where your destination is Waterman Gap trail camp (water is available), for a first-day hike of 9.6 miles. In the first two miles, you will cross an open rock facing that leads past the foot of Goat Rock. As the landscape opens up, you get fantastic views of Big Basin and the Pacific Coast to the west. This will help you envision the upcoming route. You then drop down into the headwaters of the San Lorenzo River, pass an old homestead, and walk through mixed forest.

The logical plan for the second day is to hike from Waterman Gap 9.5 miles to Jay Camp at Big Basin headquarters. Once you cross Highway 9, you will enter the state park. For a few miles the route roughly parallels the park's access road. Then it breaks off, passes an open sandstone face with great westerly views, traces a narrow ridge, and drops down into a lush redwood canyon with a stream. Only Skyline-to-the-Sea hikers typically travel this area, so by seeing this landscape you join a select club. Eventually the trail emerges at the bottom of Big Basin, and you camp relatively near park headquarters. Although this camp is not a backcountry experience, the convenience of restrooms, coin showers, drinking water, and a small store are usually well received.

On the last day, from park headquarters, you face hiking 12.5 miles out to the finish. It starts by heading through giant redwoods, up and over the Big Basin rim, then down a wooded canyon. You will see beautiful 70-foot Berry Creek Falls, a free fall at high water and moss-lined water mosaic in low flows.

A section of trail has been rendered impassable by a massive slide and a quarter mile of downed redwoods. Until the trail is repaired, here's how to do this trek. From the main parking lot across from headquarters, walk past the amphitheater to the trail along Opal Creek. Turn right and walk a short distance to a bridge. Cross the bridge and walk upstream to the Sunset Trail. Turn left and follow the Sunset Trail as it climbs out of the basin floor amid big redwoods. After crossing the Middle Ridge Fire Road, cruise downhill a short distance to the Sunset Connector Trail. Turn left and follow it down past the headwaters of Kelly Creek, which feeds into the Skyline-to-the-Sea Trail. Then it's a nice, easy cruise down into Waddell Creek Canyon and to Berry Creek. A signed right turn leads a short distance to Berry Creek Falls and its viewing platform. At Berry Creek Falls, be sure to hike up the stairs to the brink of the waterfall, then head up the canyon to see Silver Falls (a gorgeous free fall, perfect for photographs), and then above that, Golden Falls, where clear water cascades over golden sandstone like a gigantic water slide. After that side-trip adventure, return to the main trail, turn west (right), and cross Waddell Creek.

From Berry Creek Falls to the coast is a breeze, crossing over the stream with a makeshift bridge, then making the sea-level walk to Rancho del Oso and the parking area. It's a shortcut to hike out on the service road and bike path, but in the spring, take the longer, official route that loops around the valley hills (to the north) and down to the parking area to see 20 or 30 species of wildflowers, including occasional rafts of forget-me-nots. Finish up at the coast, and experience a moment of exultation when you arrive at your vehicle.

User Groups: Hikers and horses. No dogs or mountain bikes. No wheelchair facilities.

Permits: Permits to camp are by reservation only. Reservations, available dates, and more information available at www.parks.ca.gov. Search "Big Basin Redwoods" and click on link for "Backcountry Trail Camp," $15 per night per site. Permits include one vehicle, $10 per extra vehicle.

Maps: Detailed trail maps of Castle Rock State Park and Big Basin Redwoods State Park are available for a fee from Mountain Parks Foundation in Felton (831/335-3174). A free information sheet and a mileage chart between trail camps are available from Big Basin Redwoods State Park (831/338-8861). For topographic maps, ask the USGS for Castle Rock Ridge and Big Basin.

Directions: From San Francisco, take I-280 south and drive about 30 miles (depending on starting point) to Woodside and Exit 25 for Highway 84/Woodside Road. Take that exit, turn west (right) on Woodside Road, and drive one mile to Woodside. Continue straight on Woodside Road/Highway 84 and drive six miles (becomes curvy) to Sky Londa and Highway 35/Skyline Boulevard. Turn left on Skyline and drive 14.3 miles. At a junction with Highway 9, continue straight ahead for three miles to Castle Rock State Park on the right (the old parking area is now reserved for campers).

From South Bay: Take Highway 85 South toward Santa Cruz/Cupertino to Exit 14 for Saratoga Avenue. Take that exit to Saratoga Avenue. Turn right and drive 1.8 miles to Big Basin Way/Highway 9, and continue on Highway 9 for 2.5 miles into Los Gatos. Turn right (still Big Basin Way/Highway 9, signed) and drive 4.8 miles up hill (becomes curvy) to junction and stop sign with Highway 35/Skyline. Turn left and drive 2.5 miles to park on right.

To Rancho del Oso: From I-280 in San Mateo, turn west onto Highway 92 and drive to Half Moon Bay. Turn left (south) onto Highway 1 and drive 30 miles (past San Mateo/Santa Cruz county line) to park entrance on left (19 miles from Santa Cruz). Turn left and park at Rancho del Oso. (Your vehicle must be registered in advance with park rangers.)

Contact: Big Basin Redwoods State Park, 831/338-8860; Castle Rock State Park, 408/867-2952; trail camp reservations, 831/338-8861, www.parks.ca.gov.

169 SUMMIT ROCK LOOP

2.0 mi/1.0 hr

in Sanborn County Park

Map 7.4, page 292

The lookout point at Summit Rock is perched just east of the Skyline Ridge. You tower over the Santa Clara Valley just below. From the trailhead across Highway 35 from Castle Rock State Park, hikers start on the Skyline Trail and head north, adjacent to the road. The Skyline Trail leads right into the Summit Rock Loop, providing easy access to this great lookout. For people who like their views to come even easier, a popular option at the Skyline trailhead is the 0.25-mile hike that leads to Indian Rock.

The park connects Sanborn Creek with the Skyline Ridge and covers some 2,850 acres of mountain terrain in between. Some people get thrown off because this park is technically in Sanborn County Park, yet the trailhead is nowhere near the park headquarters, but rather off Sanborn Road where full facilities, a campground, and other trails are available. So when you drive up Highway 9, ignore the signs for the park entrance.

User Groups: Hikers and horses. No dogs (otherwise permitted on most trails in Sanborn-Skyline; watch for signs at trailheads) or mountain bikes. No wheelchair facilities.

Permits: No permits are required. A day-use fee of $6 is charged per vehicle.

Maps: For a free trail map, contact Sanborn County Park. For a topographic map, ask the USGS for Castle Rock Ridge.

Directions: From San Francisco, take I-280 south and drive about 30 miles (depending on starting point) to Woodside and Exit 25 for Highway 84/Woodside Road. Take that exit, turn west (right) on Woodside Road, and drive one mile to Woodside. Continue straight on Woodside Road/Highway 84 and drive six miles (becomes curvy) to Sky Londa and Highway 35/Skyline Boulevard. Turn left on Skyline and drive 14.3 miles (at junction with Highway 9, continue straight ahead 2.5 miles) to Castle Rock State Park on left. The trailhead is roughly across from Castle Rock State Park.

From South Bay: Take Highway 85 South toward Santa Cruz/Cupertino to Exit 14 for Saratoga Avenue. Take that exit to Saratoga Avenue. Turn right and drive 1.8 miles to Big Basin Way/Highway 9, and continue on Highway 9 for 2.5 miles into Los Gatos. Turn right (still Big Basin Way/Highway 9, signed) and drive 4.8 miles up hill (becomes curvy) to junction and stop sign with Highway 35/ Skyline. Turn left and drive 2.5 miles to park on left. The trailhead is roughly across from Castle Rock State Park.

Contact: Sanborn County Park, Saratoga, 408/867-9959; Santa Clara County Parks and Recreation, 408/355-2201, www.sccgov.org/sites/parks.

170 EAGLE ROCK OVERLOOK LOOP

2.2 mi/1.0 hr 2 6

in Alum Rock City Park

Map 7.4, page 292

Eagle Rock is pretty short as far as mountains go, only 795 feet. But at Alum Rock City Park, it's the best perch in the vicinity for a picnic site and a view. When you drive into the park, after passing through the kiosk, continue to road's end at the east end of the park and the trailhead for the North Rim Trail near the bridge at Penitencia Creek. Take the North Rim Trail. It is routed on the north side of the valley for 0.9 mile and rises about 300 feet to a fork with the Eagle Rock Trail. Turn right and hike 0.2 mile to the Eagle Rock Lookout.

To turn this hike into a loop, from Eagle Rock, return to the North Rim. Turn right and descend 0.22 mile to a junction, and turn left to complete the descent to the Penitencia Creek Trail (more like a road). Turn left. It is routed back along the creek (with one bridge crossing) back past the playground and picnic area to the parking area. In the winter, after rain has cleared the air, it becomes a choice spot. Thirteen miles of trails provide access to the park's 700 acres, but this hike is our favorite.

Note: Some unsavory characters are known to occasionally frequent this park. Women are advised to avoid hiking solo.

User Groups: Hikers, horses, and mountain bikes. No dogs. No wheelchair facilities.

Permits: No permits are required. An entrance fee of $6 is charged on weekends and holidays; $10 per vehicle on high-use holidays.

Maps: A brochure and map are available at the trailhead. For a free trail map, contact Alum Rock City Park. For a topographic map, ask the USGS for Calaveras Reservoir.

Directions: From I-680 in San Jose, drive to the exit for McKee Road. Take that exit 0.1 mile, keep right at the fork, merge onto McKee Road and drive 0.8 mile to North White Road. Turn left on North White and drive 1.2 miles to Penitencia Creek Road. Turn right and drive 1.1 miles to the park entrance. From the park kiosk, continue east to the end of the road and trailhead.

Contact: Alum Rock City Park, San Jose, 408/277-4539 or 408/259-5477, www.sanjoseca.gov.

171 HALLS VALLEY LOOP

5.5 mi/3.0 hr 2 8

in Joseph D. Grant County Park

Map 7.4, page 292

Halls Valley Loop provides the best introduction to Grant County Park. As you drive in, park at the Grant Lake parking area along Mount Hamilton Road on the left as you come from San Jose (and not at the headquarters, for camping, on the right). Take the Bernal Trail along the east side of Grant Lake to a junction with the Halls Valley Trail. Bear left at the junction. This route skirts Halls Valley to the left, an open landscape of foothills and grasslands sprinkled with oaks, a quiet and pretty scene. The trail then heads out 2.5 miles, climbing east toward Mount Hamilton until it meets the Canada de Pala Trail. Turn right, hike up 0.4 mile, and turn right again on Los Huecos Trail to complete the loop. From here, it's a 1.8-mile trip back to the parking area. You will descend steeply on the way back to your car.

A great side trip is available for the ambitious. On the Pala Seca Trail, climb 2.2 miles and 500 feet up the ridge above Halls Valley to the park's highest point—Antler Point at 2,999 feet. From here, you can look out over the Santa Clara Valley.

This park covers 10,000 acres in the foothills of Mount Hamilton and can be the perfect setting for hiking and mountain biking. There is plenty of room for both endeavors, with 50 miles of trails, a combination of single-track and ranch roads.

User Groups: Hikers, leashed dogs, horses, and mountain bikes. No wheelchair facilities (wheelchair-accessible facilities available at headquarters).

Permits: No permits are required. An entrance fee of $6 per vehicle is charged (pay at the entrance across the street from the trailhead).

Maps: For a free trail map, contact Joseph D. Grant County Park. For a topographic map, ask the USGS for Lick Observatory.

Directions: Take U.S. 101 to San Jose and to Exit 382 for Capitol Expressway/Yerba Buena Road. Use one of the two right lanes for that exit and go 0.3 mile (then use one of left three lanes) to E. Capitol Expressway and continue 1.7 miles to Quimby Road. Turn right on Quimby Road and drive 6.8 miles to Highway 130/Mount Hamilton Road. Turn right and go 0.4 mile to the parking area near Grant Lake.

Contact: Joseph D. Grant County Park, San Jose, 408/274-6121; Santa Clara County Parks and Recreation, 408/355-2201, www.sccgov.org/sites/parks.

172 HOTEL TRAIL

7.0 mi/3.25 hr 2 8

in Joseph D. Grant County Park

Map 7.4, page 292

The landscape around Eagle Lake in Grant County Park provides visitors with precious tranquility as well as good chances of seeing wildlife. Eagle Lake, set in the southernmost reaches of the park's 10,000-plus acres, is the prime destination of the Hotel Trail. From the parking area, look for the trailhead for the Hotel Trail on the south side. Start the trek by hiking southeast on an old ranch road. Scan your surroundings for the wild turkeys that are commonly seen in this area. As you head deeper into the interior, you will be hiking through foothills country; cows are often encountered (keep your distance, of course). The route to Eagle Lake is a direct path of 3.5 miles where you climb a few hundred feet in the process. There are several options for side trips along the way: the best is to turn right on

Canada de Pala Trail and drop down about 0.5 mile to San Felipe Creek.

User Groups: Hikers, leashed dogs, horses, and mountain bikes. No wheelchair facilities.

Permits: No permits are required. An entrance fee of $6 per vehicle is charged.

Maps: For a free trail map, contact Joseph D. Grant County Park. For a topographic map, ask the USGS for Lick Observatory.

Directions: Take U.S. 101 to San Jose and to Exit 382 for Capitol Expressway/Yerba Buena Road. Use one of the two right lanes for that exit and go 0.3 mile (then use one of left three lanes) to E. Capitol Expressway and continue 1.7 miles to Quimby Road. Turn right on Quimby Road and drive 6.8 miles to Highway 130/Mount Hamilton Road. Turn right and go 0.4 mile. The Hotel Trail starts on the south side of the road, across the road from the Grant Lake parking lot.

Contact: Joseph D. Grant County Park, San Jose, 408/274-6121; Santa Clara County Parks and Recreation, 408/355-2201, www.sccgov.org/sites/parks.

173 AQUINAS/ SERENITY TRAIL

4.7 mi/2.75 hr

in El Sereno Open Space Preserve

Map 7.4, page 292

El Sereno Open Space is one of the lesser-used parklands in the Bay Area. Why? Not only is it remote, but there's room at the trailhead for only three to four vehicles to park. The spaces are free, but require a permit. What you have is a pullout along the end of Montevina Road, set near redwoods, and then a trailhead for what looks like a gated jeep trail. This is it, elevation 2,400 feet. Start by heading out 0.2 mile to a fork. Turn right on the Aquinas Trail. It bears east and contours in and out of the canyonlands for 2.7 miles to a junction on the left (with the Loma Vista Trail), 1,800 feet. Bear right (still Aquinas Trail) and walk 0.5 mile to the junction with the Serenity Trail. Turn right and walk out 1.3 miles, a gentle descent to the end of the trail at the preserve boundary, 1,400 feet. You have occasional views south of Lexington Reservoir and the Highway 17 corridor below.

User Groups: Hikers, leashed dogs, horses, and mountain bikes. No wheelchair facilities.

Permits: A free parking permit is required. Access is free.

Maps: A brochure and map are available at the trailhead. For a free trail map, contact the Midpeninsula Regional Open Space District. For a topographic map, ask the USGS for Castle Rock Ridge.

Directions: From the intersection of I-280 and Highway 17 in San Jose, turn south on Highway 17 and drive about eight miles to Los Gatos and continue to the exit for Bear Creek Road/Montevina Road. Take that exit to Montevina Road and continue three miles to the end of the road and trailhead. You must have a parking permit.

Contact: Midpeninsula Regional Open Space District, 650/691-1200, www.openspace.org.

174 MOUNT EL SOMBROSO

12.2 mi/1 day 5 9

in Sierra Azul Open Space Preserve

Map 7.4, page 292

You get a little bit of hell on this trail to gain entry to a whole lot of heaven. It's a 6.1-mile hike with a climb of 2,100 feet to the top of 2,999-foot Mount El Sombroso. You get a panoramic view of the Santa Clara Valley, and also to Mount Umunhum, which looks like a Borg spaceship out of Star Trek is perched atop it. Start at Lexington Reservoir County Park at the gated trailhead (SA22) for the Limekiln Trail. The trail rises up 5.1 miles to Woods Trail (no dogs past this junction), with Soda Springs Canyon falling off deep to your right. At times, it is a kill-me, eat-me hike, with no shade, very steep, and only the water you choose to bring.

The final mile skirts the summit of Mount El Sombroso. Up on top, you will get the sense of a paradox that landscape this wild could exist so close to so many people who will never set foot here.

User Groups: Hikers, horses, and mountain bikes. Leashed dogs are permitted on some. No wheelchair facilities.

Permits: No permits are required. A parking fee of $6 is charged at Lexington Reservoir County Park.

Maps: A brochure and map are available at the trailhead. For a free trail map, contact the Midpeninsula Regional Open Space District. For a topographic map, ask the USGS for Santa Teresa Hills.

Directions: From Los Gatos, drive south on Highway 17 for about four miles to the exit for Bear Creek Road. Take that exit, cross over the highway, enter Highway 17 north and drive 0.4 mile to Alma Bridge Road. Take Alma Bridge Road for 1.5 miles across the dam and park at Lexington Reservoir County Park. After parking, continue a short distance on Alma Bridge Road to the Limekiln trailhead at Gate SA22 on the left.

Contact: Midpeninsula Regional Open Space District, 650/691-1200, www.openspace.org; Lexington Reservoir County Park, 408/356-2729, www.sccgov.org/sites/parks.

175 LEXINGTON DAM TRAIL

1.0 mi/0.5 hr 1 6

in Lexington Reservoir County Park

Map 7.4, page 292

Lexington Reservoir can be one of the prettiest places in Santa Clara County. When the lake is full and spilling in late winter and early spring, some people show up just to stare at all the water. Take it the extra mile for a nice bonus. Park at the lot just east of the dam, then walk across the dam and turn right on the "Pedway." That's as far as many people get, as most come for the view of the lake from the dam. Keep walking, though, and you will be surprised, as the trail drops down along Los Gatos Creek. After 1.5 miles, it links up with Los Gatos Creek Trail. This trail is routed all the way into town and it's also a great bike route.

User Groups: Hikers and mountain bikes. No dogs or horses. No wheelchair facilities.

Permits: No permits are required. A day-use fee of $6 per vehicle is charged.

Maps: For a free trail map, contact Lexington Reservoir County Park. For a topographic map, ask the USGS for Los Gatos.

Directions: From Los Gatos, drive south on Highway 17 for about four miles to the exit for Bear Creek Road. Take that exit, cross over the highway, enter Highway 17 North and drive 0.4 mile to Alma Bridge Road. Take Alma Bridge Road for 1.5 miles across the dam and park at Lexington Reservoir County Park. After parking, continue a short distance on Alma Bridge Road to the Limekiln trailhead at Gate SA22 on the left.

Contact: Lexington Reservoir County Park, 408/356-2729, www.sccgov.org/sites/parks; Midpeninsula Regional Open Space District, 650/691-1200, www.openspace.org.

176 BALD MOUNTAIN/ MOUNT UMUNHUM TRAIL

1.0 mi/0.5 hr 1 9

in Sierra Azul Open Space Preserve south of Los Gatos

Map 7.4, page 292

The trailhead for Bald Mountain is along Mount Umunhum Road and leads 0.5 mile to 2,387-foot Bald Mountain and sweeping views across Santa Clara Valley and up to 3,486-foot Mount Umunhum. In an Ohlone language, Umunhum means "resting place of the hummingbird." It's the mountain that crowns the ridge to the west above Santa Clara Valley, of course. Nearby Bald Mountain and Mount El Sombroso both provide hiking access. From Blossom Hill near Los Gatos, the drive rises up from the valley floor, winds its way up through the pretty oak woodlands and foothills, and emerges high in the Sierra Azul Range. The views are sensational across the valley to Mount Hamilton and to the South Bay. On perfect fall days, you can see miles south to the ridge tops above the Hollister valley. This view is a highlight for the 18,670-acre Sierra Azul Open Space Preserve.

Note: The weird, square building on top of Mount Umunhum looks like a Borg spacecraft out of a Star Trek episode. It's a radar tower that was part of a former Air Force base from the Cold War era.

For the more ambitious, the Mount Umunhum Trail is available. The trail starts from the parking lot across Mount Umunhum Road and climbs 3.7 miles one-way to the Mount Umunhum summit, with a 1,187-foot elevation gain. It's 7.4 miles round-trip.

User Groups: Hikers only. No dogs, horses, or mountain bikes. No wheelchair facilities. Other multiuse trails are available.

Permits: No permits required. Parking and access are free.

Maps: A brochure and map are available at the trailhead. For a free trail map, contact the Midpeninsula Regional Open Space District. For a topographic map, ask the USGS for Santa Teresa Hills.

Directions: From the Peninsula, take U.S. 101 south to Highway 85. Merge right on 85 and drive 16 miles to the exit for Camden Avenue. Take that exit to Camden, turn left and drive 1.7 miles to Hicks Road. Turn right on Hicks, go 0.2 mile, turn left to stay on Hicks, and drive 6.1 miles (past Guadalupe Reservoir) up the mountain to Mount Umunhum Road. Turn right and drive up Mount Umunhum Road for 1.6 miles to the parking lot on the left. The trailhead is at the back of the parking lot.

Contact: Midpeninsula Regional Open Space District, 650/691-1200, www.openspace.org.

177 MINE HILL TRAIL LOOP

3.5 mi/2.0 hr 2 7

in Almaden Quicksilver County Park

Map 7.4, page 292

The Mine Hill Trail is the most unusual of the dozen trails that cover 34 miles across 4,152 acres at Almaden Quicksilver County Park. Almaden Quicksilver covers a vast terrain and has two reservoirs (Almaden and Guadalupe; don't eat the fish). It is the evidence of historical mining operations that makes it fascinating.

The Mine Hill Trail starts just inside the park entrance off of Almaden Road (Hacienda entrance). From here, Mine Hill Trail is routed out 1.1 miles to a junction (with the Randol Trail). Turn left (still on Mine Hill Trail) and go 0.7 mile (you will pass a cutoff for the Day Tunnel Trail) to another junction (still Day Tunnel Trail). Turn left and go 0.1 mile to English Camp and the junction with the English Camp Trail/Deep Gulch Trail. Turn left here and go 0.4 mile to a junction; stay right on the Deep Gulch for the final 1.2 miles back to parking.

In the spring, wildflower blooms are good. With a network of trails here, many routes and long trips are possible. Almaden was the site of the first "quicksilver" mine in North America. Mining began in 1845 and continued until 1975. There are still burnt ore dumps along the trail. Wallace Stegner set part of his novel *Angle of Repose* in the area now within the park.

User Groups: Hikers, mountain bikes (Hacienda/Wood/Mockingbird entrances only), and horses. Leashed dogs are permitted. No wheelchair trail access.

Permits: No permits are required. Park entrance is free.

Maps: A trail map is also available at the trailhead. For a topographic map, ask the USGS for Santa Teresa Hills.

Directions: Take Highway 82 to the exit for Almaden Expressway. Follow that exit and drive south on Almaden Expressway to Almaden Road. Turn right on Almaden Road and drive three miles through New Almaden to the Hacienda park entrance and unpaved staging area on the right. (Note that there are four major access points to the park.)

Contact: Almaden Quicksilver County Park, San Jose, 408/535-4070; Santa Clara County Parks and Recreation, 408/355-2201, www.sccgov.org/sites/parks.

178 COYOTE PEAK LOOP

2.9 mi/2.0 hr 2 7

in Santa Teresa County Park south of San Jose

Map 7.4, page 292

The most notable hike at Santa Teresa County Park is the tromp up to Coyote Peak. This feature destination provides a good loop hike and a lookout to the southern Santa Clara Valley. At the Pueblo day-use and picnic area, start the trip on Hidden Springs Trail (trailhead just east of the picnic area and parking), elevation 600 feet. Take the Hidden Springs Trail 0.6 mile to a junction with the Coyote Peak Trail. Turn right and climb 0.4 mile to the spur on the left that loops around Coyote Peak (1,155 feet). That is a climb of 555 feet in one mile. After you enjoy the summit, return a short distance to the main trail. Turn left at the junction, the Boundary Trail, and hike 0.8 feet in a half-moon arcing curve to the left around the flank of Coyote Peak to a junction with the Hidden Springs Trail. Turn left and sail 0.9 mile back to the trailhead.

User Groups: Hikers, mountain bikers, leashed dogs, and horses. Laurel Canyon Nature Trail is for hikers only. No wheelchair facilities.

Permits: No permits are required. A $6 park entrance fee is charged per vehicle.

Maps: A brochure and map are available at the trailhead. For a free trail map, contact Santa Teresa County Park. For a topographic map, ask the USGS for Santa Teresa Hills.

Directions: From San Jose, take U.S. 101 south to the exit for Bernal Road. Follow that exit to Bernal, turn west on Bernal Road and drive 1.3 miles (across Santa Teresa Boulevard, past the golf course) to the Pueblo day-use area.

Contact: Santa Teresa County Park, 408/225-0225; Santa Clara County Parks and Recreation, 408/355-2201, www.sccgov.org/sites/parks.

179 LOS CERRITOS TRAIL/ CALERO RESERVOIR

3.2 mi/2.0 hr 1 7

in Calero County Park southwest of San Jose

Map 7.4, page 292

The payoff for this hike is a view of Calero Reservoir to the north. Start near the entrance gate and take the Los Cerritos Trail to the right (west). The trail bears right, toward Calero Reservoir, and then runs along the southern shoreline of the reservoir before it makes a 180-degree looping left turn (if you don't want to climb, turn around and go back at this point). The trail climbs a few hundred feet to a sub-ridge. There it junctions with the Pena Trail. To complete the loop, turn left on the Pena Trail and make the descent back to the parking area.

At the junction with the Pena Trail, an option is to instead turn right on the Los Vallecitos Trail, and then turn left on Figueroa Trail. It is prettiest and add adds two miles to the trip.

User Groups: Hikers and horses. No dogs or mountain bikes. No wheelchair facilities.

Permits: No permits are required. Park entrance is free at this access point for hiking, but a fee is charged at the boat ramp at Calero.

Maps: A brochure and map are available at the trailhead. For a topographic map, ask the USGS for Santa Teresa Hills.

Directions: From San Jose, take U.S. 101 south to the exit for Bailey Avenue. Take that exit, turn right onto Bailey Avenue and drive three miles to McKean Road. Turn left on McKean Road for 0.5 mile to the park entrance on the right. Drive to the sign for the park office and park adjacent to the ranger office.

Contact: Calero County Park, 408/535-4070; Santa Clara County Parks and Recreation, 408/355-2201, www.sccgov.org/sites/parks.

180 LOCH LOMOND LOOP

5.0 mi/3.25 hr 

in Loch Lomond Recreation Area near Ben Lomond

Map 7.4, page 292

Loch Lomond Reservoir is a jewel set in the Santa Cruz Mountains. There is no prettier lake in the greater Bay Area than this, complete with an island and with shores lined by conifers. Of the 12 miles of trails here, the best hike is the Loch Lomond Loop. From the parking area, take the Loch Trail, a level path that extends northward along the lakeshore for 1.5 miles out to Deer Flat. There you turn uphill on Highland Trail, where you climb, at a moderate ascent, and work your way to the east up the ridge. It peaks out at a weather station where you get a sweeping view of the lake below and the surrounding forested mountains.

To complete the loop, continue southward along the ridge down to the Glen Corrie Picnic Area (or you can take the paved road back to the starting point). Great lake, great views, great hike.

This park closes from mid-September through February.

User Groups: Hikers and dogs. No horses or mountain bikes. No wheelchair facilities.

Permits: No permits are required. A day-use fee of $4 per vehicle is charged; $1 for dogs. The Loch Lomond Recreation Area is open only from March 1 through September 15. Rangers are on duty during the winter and will cite trespassers.

Maps: For a free trail map, contact Loch Lomond Recreation Area. For a topographic map, ask the USGS for Felton.

Directions: From San Francisco, take I-280 to Daly City and the exit for Highway 1. Bear right at that exit and take Highway 1 to Half Moon Bay and continue south into Santa Cruz and Exit 442 for Ocean Street. Turn left on Ocean Street and drive 0.3 mile to Graham Hill Road. Continue on Graham Hill Road for 5.3 miles to East Zayante Road. Turn right on East Zayante Road and go 2.6 miles to Lompico Road. Turn left and go 1.7 miles to West Drive. Turn left and drive 0.5 mile (it jogs twice on Trinkling Creek Lane) to Sequoia Drive. Turn right on Sequoia and go 0.2 mile (it jogs left); it then becomes Loch Lomond Way. Continue to the entrance station.

Alternate route: From San Francisco, take I-280 south to Cupertino and the exit for Highway 82. Take Highway 82 south to the exit for Sunnyvale-Saratoga Road. Take that exit, turn right (south), and drive into Saratoga to Big Basin Way/Highway 9. Turn right, drive a short distance through town, and continue up the hill (curvy) to Skyline/Highway 35. Drive straight through the intersection and continue (curvy and fun) to Felton and Graham Hill Road. Turn left on Graham Hill Road and after two stoplights reach East Zayante Road. Turn left on East Zayante and continue as above. The trailhead is adjacent to the boat ramp.

Contact: Loch Lomond Recreation Area, Felton, 831/420-5320; marina 831/335-7424, www.cityofsantacruz.com.

181 BIG TREES NATURE TRAIL

1.0 mi/0.5 hr 

in Loch Lomond Recreation Area near Ben Lomond

Map 7.4, page 292

This short trail starts at the Glen Corrie Picnic Area and provides a reminder of the power of nature. First, pick up a free trail guide at the park store. As the trail ascends, numbered signs note many natural features and plants of the redwood forest. The only remaining old-growth redwoods in this watershed are located near the ridge. These massive, 500- to 1,000-year-old trees offer a glimpse into the area's old-growth magnificence before it was logged. Just around the bend from the giant trees is a highly disturbed area that suffered major storm damage during the 1970s and '80s from high winds, snowfall, and heavy rainfall. The biggest hit came from a January 1982 storm in which 15 inches of rain fell in a 24-hour period, causing major debris flows (mudslides). As the trail descends through this still-recovering area, you'll notice many trees that had their tops knocked off. The debris flows clogged existing drainage channels and created several massive logjams. Remnants of early-20th-century logging activities can also be seen along this short, fascinating trail.

This park closes from mid-September through February.

User Groups: Hikers and dogs. No horses or mountain bikes. No wheelchair facilities.

Permits: No permits are required. A day-use fee of $4 per vehicle is charged; there is also a fee for dogs. The Loch Lomond Recreation Area is open only March 1-September 15. Rangers are on duty during the winter and will cite trespassers.

Maps: For a free trail map, contact Loch Lomond Recreation Area. For a topographic map, ask the USGS for Felton.

Directions: From San Francisco, take I-280 to Daly City and the exit for Highway 1. Bear right at that exit and take Highway 1 to Half Moon Bay. Continue south into Santa Cruz and Exit 442 for Ocean Street. Turn left on Ocean Street and go 0.3 mile to Graham Hill Road. Continue on Graham Hill Road for 5.3 miles to East Zayante Road. Turn right on East Zayante Road and go 2.6 miles to Lompico Road. Turn left and drive 1.7 miles to West Drive. Turn left and go 0.5 mile (it jogs twice on Trinkling Creek Lane) to Sequoia Drive. Turn right on Sequoia and drive 0.2 mile (it jogs left); it then becomes Loch Lomond Way. Continue to entrance station.

Alternate route: From San Francisco, take I-280 south to Cupertino and the exit for Highway 82. Take Highway 82 south and the exit for Sunnyvale-Saratoga Road. Take that exit, turn right (south), and drive into Saratoga to Big Basin Way/Highway 9. Turn right, drive a short distance through town, and continue up the hill (curvy) to Skyline/Highway 35. Continue straight through the intersection and on to Felton and Graham Hill Road (curvy and fun). Turn left on Graham Hill Road and drive past stoplights to East Zayante Road. Turn left on East Zayante and continue as above.

Contact: Loch Lomond Recreation Area, Felton, 831/420-5320, www.cityofsantacruz.com.

182 REDWOOD GROVE LOOP TRAIL

0.8 mi/0.5 hr — 1 — 9

in Henry Cowell Redwoods State Park near Santa Cruz

Map 7.4, page 292

A 40-acre grove of old-growth redwoods is the crown jewel of Henry Cowell Redwoods. This is a short, flat (and wide) trail that loops through the best of it. The trailhead is at a parking area just south of the park office and entrance. The trail ventures a short distance to a junction. Either way you turn, it meanders through the old growth for about a 10-minute walk and returns in the loop back to this junction. In addition to the old-growth redwoods, there are also some large Douglas firs and California bays. What is most striking is the burl on some of the old-growth giants, where they look like something out of a science fiction film. There are numbered sites along the trail that correspond to a brochure interpretive guide. Only one problem, or for some, maybe not: You can occasionally hear the Roaring Camp Railroad rumbling past nearby, with occasional blasts of its whistle.

User Groups: Hikers and horses. No dogs or mountain bikes. No wheelchair facilities.
Permits: No permits are required. A fee of $10 is charged per vehicle.
Maps: Park maps are available at the visitors center at the main unit of Henry Cowell State Park on Highway 9. For a topographic map, ask the USGS for Felton.
Directions: Take I-280 to Cupertino and the junction with Highway 85. Bear south on Highway 85 and drive seven miles to the exit for Highway 17 south. Take that exit (signed toward Santa Cruz) and drive 18.7 miles to the exit for Mount Hermon Road (signed for Felton/Big Basin). Take that exit to Mount Hermon Road. Turn right and drive 3.5 miles to Graham Hill Road. Turn right and go 0.2 mile to Highway 9. Turn left on Highway 9 and go 0.6 mile to N. Big Trees Park Road. Turn left and drive 0.5 mile to the park entrance and continue a short distance to parking on right (directly across from Roaring Camp Big Trees Railroad).

Alternate route: From Half Moon Bay, take Highway 1 south for 48 miles into Santa Cruz and the signed turnoff for Highway 1 (get in left lane). Turn left on Highway 1 and drive 11.7 miles to signed turn for Highway 9 (get in left lane). Turn left and drive 5.8 miles to N. Big Trees Park Road (signed for park). Turn right and drive 0.5 mile to park entrance and continue short distance to parking on right (directly across from Roaring Camp Big Trees Railroad).
Contact: Henry Cowell Redwoods State Park, 831/335-4598; nature center, 831/335-7077, www.parks.ca.gov.

183 EAGLE CREEK TRAIL

3.0 mi/1.5 hr 1 8

in Henry Cowell Redwoods State Park near Santa Cruz

Map 7.4, page 292

There are three places you don't want to miss on a visit to Henry Cowell Redwoods State Park. The first one is Eagle Creek Trail, the most direct hiking route to River Trail and the San Lorenzo River. Another is the park's observation deck, offering first-class views on clear days. And, of course, the 40-acre old-growth grove of redwoods, detailed in the previous hike.

The Eagle Creek Trail starts between campsite Nos. 82 and 84, crosses Eagle Creek, and continues adjacent to the stream as it heads out toward the San Lorenzo River. As you hike this portion of the trail, you are surrounded by redwoods. The trail then crosses Pipeline Road and junctions with the River Trail. Many people turn around and head back at this point. A great way to extend your hike is to go north on the River Trail alongside the river and add an extra three miles to the trip.

A good side trip at Henry Cowell is the observation deck, the highest point in the park. It's only a 0.3-mile hike from the campground via Pine Trail, which starts near site 49. Right alongside the observation deck are a few ponderosa pines, growing far from their normal range in the Sierra Nevada. You'll recognize them by their distinctive jigsaw-puzzle bark. Except on foggy days, you get a panorama of the local coast.
User Groups: Hikers and horses. No dogs or mountain bikes. No wheelchair facilities.
Permits: No permits are required. A day-use fee of $10 is charged per vehicle.
Maps: Park maps are available at the campground entrance station or at the park visitors center off Highway 9. For a topographic map, ask the USGS for Felton.
Directions: From San Jose, drive south on Highway 17 for 24 miles to Scotts Valley. Take the Mount Hermon Road exit, turn right, and drive toward Felton for about one mile to Lockewood Lane. Turn left on Lockewood Lane and drive one mile to Graham Hill Road. Turn left on Graham Hill Road and drive 0.5 mile to the campground entrance on the right. The trailhead is between campsite Nos. 82 and 84.

Contact: Henry Cowell Redwoods State Park, 831/335-4598; nature center, 831/335-7077, www.parks.ca.gov.

184 BAYVIEW LOOP

1.0 mi/0.5 hr 1 8

in Mount Madonna County Park west of Gilroy

Map 7.4, page 292

On perfect days, you get views of Monterey Bay. The trailhead for the Bayview Trail is located near the park entrance station (and nearby campground, restrooms, and yurts), at 1,270 feet. A short ways past the entrance station, look for the trail on the left (west side of the road). Turn left and walk 0.3 mile to a junction. Turn right on a nice footpath (still Bayview Trail) and hike 0.5 mile to the Sprig Trail. Turn right, then return 0.2 mile to the starting point. An easy walk with a payoff and a pretty introduction to a great park.

Mount Madonna County Park provides great scenic beauty, good hiking, camping, and horseback riding. The park is set around the highest peak, Mount Madonna, in the southern range of the Santa Cruz Mountains. With a network of 18 miles of hiking trails, the best routes are combinations of different trails. By linking them, you can make your adventure as short or as long as desired.

User Groups: Hikers, horses, and dogs. No mountain bikes. No wheelchair facilities.

Permits: No permits are required. A day-use fee of $6 is charged per vehicle.

Maps: A free trail map is available at the park entrance station. For a topographic map, ask the USGS for Mount Madonna.

Directions: From San Jose, drive south on U.S. 101 to Morgan Hill and Exit 365 for Tennant Avenue. Take that exit and drive 0.4 mile to Tennant Avenue. Turn right on Tennant Avenue and go 0.9 mile to Monterey Avenue. Turn left on Monterey and go a short distance to Watsonville Road/County Road G8. Turn right and drive 7.4 miles to Highway 152. Turn right and drive 5.1 miles to Pole Line Road. Turn right and drive 1.5 miles to park entrance.

Contact: Mount Madonna County Park, 408/842-2341; Santa Clara County Parks and Recreation, 408/355-2201, www.sccgov.org/sites/parks.

185 UVAS PARK WATERFALL LOOP

3.0 mi/2.0 hr 2 9

in Uvas Canyon County Park near Morgan Hill

Map 7.4, page 292

Uvas Canyon County Park is a little slice of waterfall heaven on the east side of the Santa Cruz Mountains. The best advice is to visit during the rainy season, preferably just after a good downpour when the waterfalls are at peak flows. In late winter and spring, it is so pretty and so popular on weekends that parking reservations are required from January-July 4 on weekends and holidays.

The trailhead is at the Black Rock Picnic Area and is routed up Swanson Creek. You'll pass Black Rock Falls (a 30-foot cascade, clear water over black rock), then Basin Falls (where a 20-foot stream flows into a hollowed-out rock that looks like a big tub if you get the right angle), and then a short ways beyond to Upper Falls. That's just 0.7 mile, or a 1.5-mile round-trip. Note there is also a service road that is routed up the canyon that some take by accident as the hike. At high flows, Black Rock Falls is often the prettiest. At low flows, Upper Falls is still very pretty.

From Upper Falls, continue to hike up Swanson Creek, a bit of a climb. You will then cross Swanson Creek to the left (do not take what looks like a faint trail farther up the canyon). Take the Contour Trail, which is routed in and out of several ravines, to the Alec Canyon Trail (a service road). Turn left and sail downhill. A pretty lookout east over the canyon toward the Santa Clara Valley is available here. It's a final 0.5 mile back to the starting point.

Ambitious side trip: At the junction of the Contour Trail and the Alec Canyon Trail, instead of turning left and heading back to the trailhead, you can instead go the extra mile. Turn right and hike up a half mile, the steepest trail section in the park, past Manzanita Point to a spur (0.2 mile) on the right to 40-foot Triple Falls. That adds 1.4 miles to the trip and makes it a 4.5-mile hike. In rainy season, the climb is well worth it. In summer, well, it's not.

User Groups: Hikers and dogs. No horses or mountain bikes. No wheelchair facilities.

Permits: A parking permit is required (www.sccgov.org) on weekends and holidays January-July 4. No permits are required weekdays or July 5-December. A day-use fee of $6 is charged per vehicle.

Maps: A brochure and map are available at the trailhead. For a topographic map, ask the USGS for Loma Prieta.

Directions: Take U.S. 101 south of San Jose to Coyote and the exit for Bailey Avenue. Take that exit, turn right on Bailey Avenue and drive 3.2 miles to McKean Road. Turn left on McKean Road and drive 6.1 miles (at 2.4 miles, it becomes Uvas Road) to Croy Road. Turn right on Croy Road and drive 4.4 miles (go slow, passes through Sveadal) to park entrance.

Contact: Uvas Canyon County Park, 408/779-9232; Santa Clara County Parks and Recreation, 408/355-2201, www.sccgov.org/sites/parks.

186 SYCAMORE NATURE TRAIL

1.2 mi/0.5 hr

along Coyote Creek south of San Jose

Map 7.4, page 292

From the Walnut Rest Area, this is a pretty, easy nature walk along Coyote Creek. The setting is nice and peaceful, the kind of place you enjoy in the moment, not a trek with a distant payoff. The trail starts where you walk on a path with Coyote Creek on your right. You head downstream for a short stretch, then cross a bridge and walk along the far side of the creek to a picnic site. Easy, simple, with a nice payoff.

User Groups: Hikers only. An equestrian trail is available nearby for horses. The Coyote Creek Parkway is available nearby for mountain bikes, leashed dogs, wheelchairs.

Permits: No permits are required. Parking and access are free. A day-use fee of $6 is charged per vehicle if parking at nearby Anderson Lake County Park or Hellyer County Park.

Maps: A brochure and map are available at the trailhead. For a free map, contact Coyote County Park. For a topographic map, ask the USGS for Morgan Hill.

Directions: From San Jose, take U.S. 101 south for six miles to Coyote and the exit for Cochran Road. Take that exit to Cochran Road, turn east and drive (toward the base of Anderson Dam) to the parking area for Walnut Rest Area on the left (right is signed for Anderson Lake).

Contact: Coyote Creek Parkway, 408/779-3634; Santa Clara County Parks and Recreation, 408/355-2201, www.sccgov.org/sites/parks.

187 FROG POND LOOP

4.7 mi/3.0 hr 2 7

in Henry W. Coe State Park east of Morgan Hill

Map 7.4, page 292

From headquarters, the Frog Pond Loop is a day hike that provides a glimpse of the park's primitive charms, along with a sampling of a few of the ups and downs. Think of it as a test case: If you like this, then load your backpack for an overnighter and launch off on one of the butt-kickers from here or the Hunting Hollow trailhead.

Start this trip from park headquarters at Monument Trail (elevation 2,500 feet), located about 100 yards from the visitors center. The trip starts by hiking 0.5 mile to Hobbs Road, climbing to nearly 3,000 feet. At Hobbs Road, turn left and tromp down for 0.8 mile into Little Fork Coyote Creek (2,400 feet). This stream is very pretty in the spring, and though you must then walk out of the canyon, it is a tranquil and memorable setting. Then make the short 0.25-mile rise from the creek up to Frog Pond. This first leg is about 1.6 miles. Frog Pond is a pretty little spot, complete with fishing line hanging from tree limbs (this lake is fished often and the catch rates are low). The trail continues, but many people then simply return the way they came.

Henry W. Coe State Park is the Bay Area's backyard wilderness. This wildland is south of Mount Hamilton and covers 87,000 acres and 134 square miles, the largest state park in Northern California. A trip to headquarters provides a visitors center and access to a drive-in campground with excellent stargazing. The best trailheads are not at headquarters, but at Hunting Hollow. From headquarters, the trips into the park's interior are very long and difficult.

User Groups: Hikers, horses, and mountain bikes. No dogs. No wheelchair facilities. After 0.5 inch of rain or more, bikes are prohibited from single-track trails for 48 hours.

Permits: A state park day-use fee of $8 per vehicle is charged. No permits are required unless you plan to camp in the backcountry.

Maps: A brochure and map are available at the visitors center. For a detailed topographic map, contact Pine Ridge Association (Morgan Hill, 408/779-2728, www.coepark.org). For a topographic map, ask the USGS for Mount Sizer.

Directions: Take U.S. 101 south of San Jose to Morgan Hill and the exit for East Dunne Avenue. Take that exit, turn east on East Dunne Avenue and drive (over the bridge at the head of Lake Anderson) for 13 miles (slow and twisty) to the park headquarters and visitors center.

Contact: Henry W. Coe State Park, 408/779-2728, www.parks.ca.gov.

188 MISSISSIPPI LAKE TRAIL

27.0 mi/3 days 5 8

in Henry W. Coe State Park east of Morgan Hill

Map 7.4, page 292

Mississippi Lake is the marquee destination at Henry W. Coe State Park, a small lake edged by tules that provides a wilderness-style pond for bass fishing and nearby trail campsites. It is set in the virtual center of this huge park, and reaching Mississippi Lake requires an extended endurance test.

An early start is paramount. From park headquarters, begin this expedition by hiking out on Corral Trail for 1.9 miles to its junction with Manzanita Point Road. Turn right and hike 1.5 miles, past the group campgrounds, to China Hole Trail on the left. This can seem like a launch point off the edge of the earth: The China Hole Trail drops from 2,320 feet elevation to 1,150 feet in the course of 2.6 miles. Switchbacks have improved the trail gradient to about 10 percent.

At China Hole, you'll reach the East Fork of Coyote Creek, a beautiful stream that is cool, fresh, and full of water in late winter and early spring. Then you'll hike through The Narrows en route to Los Cruzeros, and in the process, add 1.1 miles to the day. Los Cruzeros is one of the park's prettiest spots, a junction of canyons and streams. A trail camp is available at Los Cruzeros. Before you leave the stream, make sure you pump two canteens full of water.

From here, you start to climb. You hike out on Willow Ridge Trail for 1.6 miles with an elevation gain of 1,350 feet to Willow Ridge Road. Turn left on Willow Ridge Road for a series of foothill-like climbs and drops as the trip extends 3.8 miles to the southern edge (and earth dam) at Mississippi Lake. The nearest trail camp, Mississippi Creek Horse Camp, is one mile south of the lake. That makes the trip a one-way excursion of 13.5 miles. It's a long and challenging day, especially if temperatures are hot.

This is a grueling hike from headquarters.

Many unprepared hikers have suffered from dehydration and had to be rescued by park staff. Some hikers will try to shortcut the trip by bringing a mountain bike, but find themselves pushing the bike uphill, then speeding fast on downhill portions. Many can accomplish the hike in two days, but after the workout, you'll most likely want to relax on day two and head back to your car on day three.

It is Coe's preeminent destination. The lake borders the 23,000-acre Orestimba Wilderness to the east; fishing for bass, swimming in cool waters in early summer, and viewing wildflower blooms in spring are exceptional. If you catch it just right, the color of the lake seems almost tourmaline, a beautiful sight in this foothill wildland.

Even though Henry W. Coe State Park has been open to the public only since 1981, a few legends have already developed, and the most mysterious involves Mississippi Lake. The lake once had a one-of-a-kind ability to create huge trout. The first time I visited, scientists had documented 26-inch wild trout that were only 18 months old. The trout are long gone now, as low water in the feeder creek prevented spawning in droughts; any trout you catch should be released immediately. Still, the legendary huge trout of Mississippi Lake have inspired many to make the trip out, often out of curiosity, to see such a unique habitat. Bass were planted in 1991 and have taken over the lake and provide good fishing.

User Groups: Hikers, horses, and mountain bikes. No dogs. No wheelchair facilities. After 0.5 inch of rain, bikes are prohibited from single-track trails for 48 hours.

Permits: A trail map and camp permit are required. A state park day-use fee of $8 per vehicle is charged.

Maps: A brochure and map are available at park headquarters. For a detailed topographic map, contact Pine Ridge Association (Morgan Hill, 408/779-2728, www.coepark.org). For topographic maps, ask the USGS for Mount Sizer and Mississippi Creek.

Directions: Take U.S. 101 south of San Jose to Morgan Hill and the exit for East Dunne Avenue. Take that exit, turn east on East Dunne Avenue and drive (over the bridge at the head of Lake Anderson) for 13 miles (slow and twisty) to the park headquarters and visitors center.

Contact: Henry W. Coe State Park, 408/779-2728, www.parks.ca.gov.

189 COIT LAKE

11.8 mi/2 days

in Henry W. Coe State Park east of Morgan Hill

Map 7.4, page 292

The Hunting Hollow trailhead near Coyote Lake east of Gilroy is a great launch point for Kelly Lake and Coit Lake. Start by parking at Hunting Hollow or along the shoulder of the road at the Coyote Creek Gate. From the Coyote Creek Gate, walk a short distance (about 0.1 mile) and look for Grizzly Gulch Trail off to the right. Take Grizzly Gulch Trail. After just five minutes (0.2 mile) you will reach a fork. Take the left fork to stay on Grizzly Gulch Trail, where you will start a climb through oak woodlands, ridges, and canyons. This extends for 1.2 miles to another fork, with the elevation nearly 1,900 feet. Bear right, staying on Grizzly Gulch Trail, and head out for one mile on the road to a fork with Dexter Trail (2,000 feet). Bear to the left on Dexter Trail, and continue the climb for another 0.6 mile (topping out at 2,400 feet) before finally reaching Wasano Ridge and Wasano Ridge Road. Turn left and hike 0.2 mile on the road to Kelly Lake Trail. Turn right and enjoy the one-mile descent to Kelly Lake. So far you have invested 3.3 miles with a 1,500-foot climb and 300-foot descent. Much of the route feels like foothill wilderness, and with mountain bikers on ambitious treks on the park's ranch-style roads, you'll have it to yourself.

After enjoying pretty Kelly Lake, you are ready to top off the trip by heading 1.5 miles to Coit Lake and the campground that is available there. Most of this is a climb. From below the earth dam at Kelly Lake, take the right fork on Coit Road and climb out 0.8 mile to the junction with Willow Road (2,386 feet). Simply continue straight for 0.3 mile and you will reach the inlet to Coit Lake. A well-worn trail circles the lake. From the Coyote Creek Gate trailhead to Coit Lake with this route will make for a 5.8-mile hike for the day, one-way.

This is a great trip at the peak of spring, with 400 species of wildflowers documented, as well as deer, coyote, bobcat, fox, wild turkey, hawks, owls, eagles, and, of course, pigs.

Overnight users are required to obtain a camping/wilderness permit. Hikers who choose to enter by the Coyote Creek access point must have a trail map. And if the limited parking along the road's shoulder at the Coyote Creek Gate is full, you must instead park at the Hunting Hollow parking area (along Gilroy Springs Road, the access road you drove in on), which will add two miles to this route.

User Groups: Hikers, horses, and mountain bikes. No dogs. No wheelchair facilities.

Permits: A trail map and camp permit are required. A self-registration area is available at the Hunting Hollow parking area, located just off the trailhead access road. A state park day-use fee of $8 per vehicle is charged. After 0.5 inch of rain or more, bikes are prohibited from single-track trails for 48 hours.

Maps: A brochure and map are available at the trailhead. For a detailed topographic map, contact Pine Ridge Association (Morgan Hill, 408/779-2728, www.coepark.org). For topographic maps, ask the USGS for Gilroy Hot Springs and Mississippi Creek.

Directions: Take U.S. 101 south (30 miles south of San Jose) to Gilroy and Exit 357 for Leavesley Road/Highway 152. Take that exit to Leavesley, turn left and go 1.8 miles to New Avenue. Turn left and go 0.6 mile to Roop Road. Turn right and go 1.9 miles, turn left to stay on Roop (well signed) and continue 3.3 miles (becomes Gilroy Hot Springs Road) to Hunting Hollow parking on right (nine miles from U.S. 101) or continue 1.8 miles to Coyote Gate.

Contact: Henry W. Coe State Park, 408/779-2728, www.parks.ca.gov.

190 ROOSTER COMB LOOP (LONG VERSION)

60.0 mi/6 days 5 7

in Henry W. Coe State Park southeast of San Jose

Map 7.4, page 292 **BEST**

No trail on public land in the Bay Area provides access to remoter wildlands. A series of short cutoff trips can take you to the park's best fishing spots and little-seen gems: Mississippi Lake, Mustang Pond, Jackrabbit Lake, Paradise Lake, and all the way out to Orestimba Creek. You also climb the Rooster Comb, a rock formation that looks something like a miniature stegosaurus-back rim.

There is no metropolitan area in the world with such a remote area, but you have to pay dearly for your pleasures. Either that or border on insanity. To some, Paradise Lake will seem like a mirage after you've walked 33 miles.

For this 60-mile loop, start at the Coyote Creek entrance gate or the nearby (two miles) Hunting Hollow parking area. From the gate, it's a 5.8-mile trip to Coit Lake (see listing in this chapter).

From Coit Lake, take Coit Road out 4.2 miles to Pacheco Junction, then continue on Coit Road another 1.8 miles to a major fork. This fork marks the beginning and the end of the Rooster Comb Loop. At this point, you have traveled 11.8 miles.

Turn left at this fork, taking County Line Road, to start the Rooster Comb Loop and a route, in a clockwise manner, through the Orestimba Wilderness Zone. From the fork, it is 2.7 miles to the short cutoff to Mississippi Lake. Stop, rest up, tank up, fuel up, and get your thoughts straight before heading out. That is because from Mississippi Lake, the trip heads off into a land that seems to have no end. Take County Line Road to a short cutoff, Chaparral

Trail, and then link that to Red Creek Road. Turn right, and it is 6.1 miles to Robinson Creek Trail. Turn left and hike along Robinson Creek, a remote canyon with a sliver of water, for 5.6 miles to Orestimba Creek Road.

Turn right on Orestimba Creek Road and you start your return, though it won't seem like it, from the depths of the wilderness. The route heads 3.2 miles to a cutoff trail on the right for Rooster Comb Summit Trail. This is a must-do, if you've come this far, a 1.4-mile hike with a 600-foot climb (2.8 miles round-trip) up the north flank of the Rooster Comb, where you top out at 1,836 feet.

From here you head back, going south on Orestimba Creek Road. You'll pass short cutoff trails for Paradise Lake, Mustang Pond, and Kingbird Pond, a distance of 8.7 miles back to the fork with Coit Road. This area is so far away from anything that it can feel unbelievable to be here. It is also typically dry and hot most of the year, and in 2015, drought hit the ponds hard. I have flown it, driven it with rangers, and hiked it, and the remoteness you will feel at one of the ponds, where you camp, swim, or fish, is amazing for a destination in the greater Bay Area.

When you reach the junction with Coit Road, you have completed the loop, a distance of 36.9 miles (including the Rooster Comb Summit trail). Turn left and return the final 11.6 miles back to the Coyote Creek entrance station. This route does not including side-trip cutoff trails to several lakes, which can typically add another 10 miles to the trip.

So there you have it: 60 miles, best done in five or six days, exploring a land that few have seen and fewer yet have experienced.

Several trail camps are situated along the way, and camping is permitted throughout the wilderness area. If the weather turns hot, physically unprepared hikers can find themselves in real danger. Let me say that again before you head off full of excitement and a limited amount of logic: unprepared hikers can find themselves in real danger. OK? Got it? Very few do this trip. Be sure to purchase added life insurance before embarking. Not only is it just plain long, but it includes seven climbs that'll have you cussing, and yet explores the park's remotest wildlands. It's like nothing else.

User Groups: Hikers, horses, and mountain bikes. No dogs. No wheelchair facilities. After 0.5 inch of rain, bikes are prohibited from single-track trails for 48 hours.

Permits: A trail map and camp permit are required. A self-registration area is available at the Hunting Hollow parking area just off the trailhead access road. A state park day-use fee of $8 per vehicle is charged.

Maps: A brochure and map are available at park headquarters. For a detailed topographic map for a fee, contact Pine Ridge Association (Morgan Hill, 408/779-2728, www.coepark.org). For topographic maps, ask the USGS for Gilroy Hot Springs and Mississippi Creek.

Directions: Take U.S. 101 south (30 miles south of San Jose) to Gilroy and Exit 357 for Leavesley Road/Highway 152. Take that exit to Leavesley, turn left and go 1.8 miles to New Avenue. Turn left and go 0.6 mile to Roop Road. Turn right and go 1.9 miles, turn left to stay on Roop (well signed) and continue 3.3 miles (becomes Gilroy Hot Springs Road) to Hunting Hollow Parking on right (nine miles from U.S. 101) or continue 1.8 miles to Coyote Gate.

Contact: Henry W. Coe State Park, 408/779-2728, www.parks.ca.gov.

191 DOWDY RANCH/ ROOSTER COMB LOOP

27.5 mi/3 days 4 9

in Orestimba Wilderness at Henry W. Coe State Park

Map 7.4, page 292

The Dowdy Ranch trailhead, out of Bell Station on Highway 152, usually opens in early May and stays open weekends through Labor Day. It is closed the rest of the year. Few seem to realize the opportunity at hand. The trailhead provides nearby access to the Orestima

Wilderness, including bass fishing at Jackrabbit Lake and a great campsite at the foot of the Rooster Comb. This is how it works from the Dowdy Ranch trailhead:

Hole in the Rock, 1.9 miles: Your destination is a fantastic swimming hole on Pacheco Creek. To get there from the new trailhead, take the main Kaiser-Etna Road (1.9 miles) or the North Fork Trail (2.7 miles). When you reach the creek, walk upstream a few hundred yards to find Hole in the Rock. Another decent swimming hole is located if you head downstream instead.

Kingbird Pond, 7.9 miles: Little Kingbird Pond provides bass fishing and is the first fishing spot out of Bell Station. To reach it, take Kaiser-Etna Road five miles to a four-way junction. Go straight (north) on Orestimba Creek Road for 2.4 miles to the Kingbird Pond Trail. Turn right and go 0.5 mile to the pond. Once you get to Orestimba Corral, about six miles in, the route is pretty flat, with just gentle hills.

Mustang Pond, 11.1 miles: This little lake is only 3.2 miles from Kingbird Pond, but there are several creek crossings on this route. At high water you might get wet, but it's a lot of fun. From Kingbird Pond, head 0.5 mile back to the Orestimba Creek Road. Turn right (so you're going north) and head 2.2 miles to the Mustang Pond Trail on the right. It's 0.5 mile to this pond.

Jackrabbit Lake, 13.9 miles: This lake is about twice the size of Kingbird and Mustang, and provides what is probably the best bass fishing in the park. It is only 2.8 miles from Mustang Pond. To get there, from Mustang Pond continue on the Mustang Pond Trail (it horseshoes) northwest to Orestimba Creek Road. Turn right, heading north again, and go 0.75 mile to a spur junction with Long Ridge Road. Turn right and go 1.2 miles, a bit of a climb, to an unsigned spur junction on the left that we call Jackrabbit Lake Road. Turn left and push out a short climb and drop of 0.4 mile to the lake.

Base of Rooster Comb, 16.5 miles: The Rooster Comb is a large, rocky exposed ridge formation that rises up 500 feet from the valley floor to an elevation of 1,836 feet. Below, Orestimba Creek Flat is a good area to camp. To get here from Jackrabbit Lake, it's a 2.6-mile ride: Backtrack on Jackrabbit Lake Trail to Long Ridge Road. Turn right and return to Orestimba Creek Road. Turn north (right) and go one mile to the base of the Rooster Comb.

Return to park entrance: From the Rooster Comb, it's 11 miles back to the park access at Dowdy Ranch. This makes for a fantastic 27.5-mile loop, with three lakes and plenty of places to camp.

With April showers and a warm May, the valley flats below Rooster Comb can yield tremendous wildflower blooms: owl clover, California poppy, shooting stars, butter and eggs, and rafts of smooth layia. The layia is found almost only in undeveloped grasslands and an awesome bloom—kind of like a daisy, yet with yellow petals tipped in white, in spectacular clusters.

Since Henry W. Coe State Park opened in 1959, this area has been out of reach for almost all that time. It took a 56-mile round-trip with about a 15,000-foot aggregate vertical climb to reach Jackrabbit Lake. You can add a lot of miles if you visit the Rooster Comb and the best small lakes for fishing—Jackrabbit Lake, Mustang Pond, Kingbird Pond, and several others. In the process, you will explore the matrixes of valleys, creeks, and foothill grasslands for wildflowers and wildlife. From park headquarters or Hunting Hollow, the route is so long and grueling that almost nobody tries it. We've been back in this wild country on perfect spring days and the fishing, wildlife, wildflowers, and campsites can be spectacular.

User Groups: Hikers, horses, and mountain bikes. No dogs. No wheelchair facilities.

Permits: A trail map and camp permit are required. A state park day-use fee of $8 per vehicle is charged. After 0.5 inch of rain or more, bikes are prohibited from single-track trails for 48 hours.

Maps: A brochure and map are available at Dowdy Visitors Center. For a detailed topographic map, contact Pine Ridge Association (Morgan Hill, 408/779-2728, www.coepark.org).

Directions: Take U.S. 101 south (30 miles south of San Jose) to Gilroy and Exit 357 for Leavesley Road/Highway 152. Take that exit to Leavesley, turn left and go 1.8 miles to New Avenue. Turn left and go 0.6 mile to Roop Road. Turn right and go 1.9 miles, turn left to stay on Roop (well signed) and continue 3.3 miles (becomes Gilroy Hot Springs Road) to Hunting Hollow Parking on right (nine miles from U.S. 101) or continue 1.8 miles to Coyote Gate.

Contact: Henry W. Coe State Park, 408/779-2728, www.parks.ca.gov.

192 HARVEY BEAR/ COYOTE RIDGE TRAIL

6.0 mi/3.0 hr

in Coyote Lake Harvey Bear County Park near Coyote Reservoir

Map 7.4, page 292

You get spectacular views on this, where you scan across southern Santa Clara Valley and beyond across the Santa Cruz Mountains. To the east, you take in gorgeous Coyote Lake backed by a wilderness ridge to the east. Yet with Coyote Reservoir and Henry W. Coe State Park so nearby, many still overlook this trip.

Start at the Mendoza Staging Area for Harvey Bear, named after the landowner whose family made the park possible. From there, you venture off on the 4.5-mile Coyote Ridge Trail, where most hike out for the views and then return. It is dedicated as a section of the perpetual work-in-progress, the 500-mile Bay Ridge Trail. The landscape consists of rolling hills with oaks and buckeyes and lots of wild turkey, deer, squirrels, red-tailed hawks, and turkey vultures. On summer mornings, it seems spotting wild turkey is a sure thing. You can get in a nice rhythm for easy climbs that average only 200 feet, and then take in the dramatic views of the lower Santa Clara Valley off to the west and gorgeous Coyote Lake backed by a wilderness ridge to the east. Return when ready. The parkland adjoins Coyote Lake, creating a continuous swath of 4,595 acres of public land. An option is a fairly new loop route, Rancho La Polka.

User Groups: Hikers, mountain bikes, horses, and dogs on leash. No wheelchair facilities.

Permits: A fee of $6 per vehicle is charged. No permit required.

Maps: A brochure and map are available at the trailhead.

Directions: Take U.S. 101 south to Gilroy and the exit for Leavesley Road. Follow that exit, turn east, and drive two miles to New Avenue. Turn left and go 0.5 mile to Roop Road. Turn right and go three miles (it becomes Gilroy Hot Springs Road) to the park entrance and staging area on the left.

Contact: Coyote Lake Harvey Bear County Park, 408/842-7800; Santa Clara County Parks and Recreation, 408/355-2201, www.sccgov.org/sites/parks.

MONTEREY AND BIG SUR

This visually stunning coast contains 130 miles of oceanfront drama that runs from Davenport to San Simeon. Largely undeveloped, this region offers rugged cliffs, redwood forests, rock-strewn beaches, and waterfalls.

South of Carmel, services are clustered in Big Sur, Lucia, and Gorda. In between, a string of state parks provide a bounty of trails: Point Lobos State Reserve, Garrapata State Park, Andrew Molera State Park, Julia Pfeiffer Burns State Park, Pfeiffer Big Sur State Park, and Limekiln State Park. As you walk these parks' trails, you have a near guarantee of spotting migrating gray whales or fuzzy sea otters. For a more remote adventure, head to the Ventana Wilderness or Silver Peak Wilderness. Or head inland to Pinnacles National Park, where trails tunnel through volcanic caves and ascend over and around craggy rock formations.

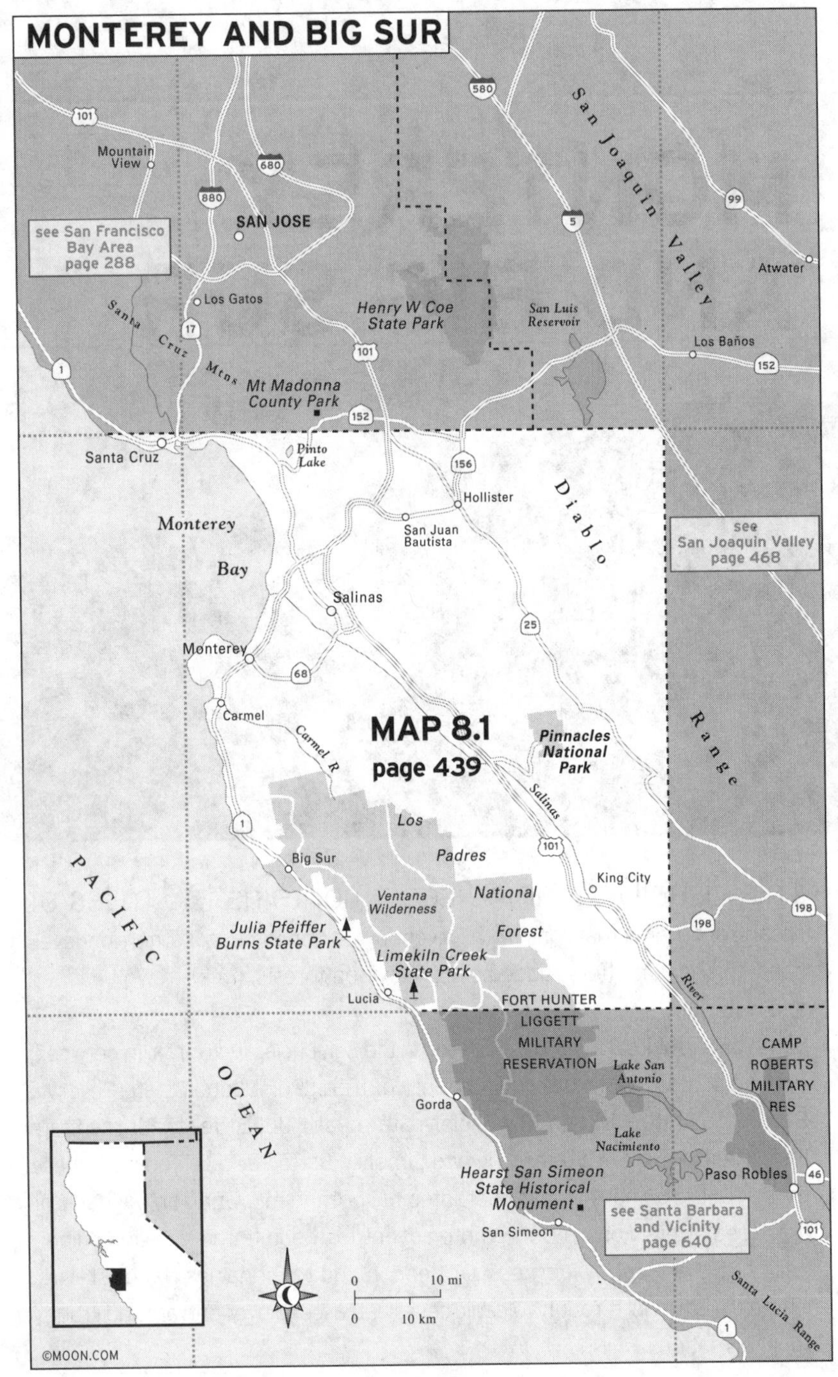
MONTEREY AND BIG SUR
Mountain View
SAN JOSE
see San Francisco Bay Area page 288
Los Gatos
Santa Cruz Mtns
Henry W Coe State Park
San Luis Reservoir
San Joaquin Valley
Atwater
Los Baños
Mt Madonna County Park
Santa Cruz
Pinto Lake
Hollister
San Juan Bautista
Diablo
see San Joaquin Valley page 468
Monterey
Bay
Salinas
Monterey
Carmel
Carmel R
MAP 8.1
page 439
Pinnacles National Park
Range
Salinas
Los
Padres
National
Forest
Big Sur
Ventana Wilderness
King City
PACIFIC
Julia Pfeiffer Burns State Park
Limekiln Creek State Park
River
Lucia
FORT HUNTER LIGGETT MILITARY RESERVATION
CAMP ROBERTS MILITARY RES
Lake San Antonio
OCEAN
Gorda
Lake Nacimiento
Hearst San Simeon State Historical Monument
Paso Robles
see Santa Barbara and Vicinity page 640
San Simeon
Santa Lucia Range
0 10 mi
0 10 km
©MOON.COM

Map 8.1

Sites 1-36
Pages 440-465

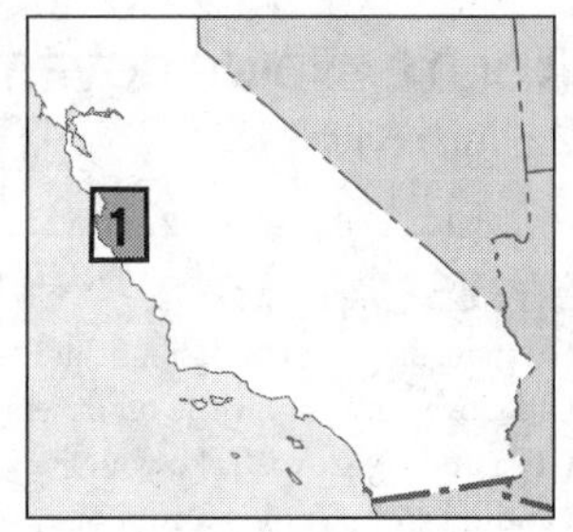

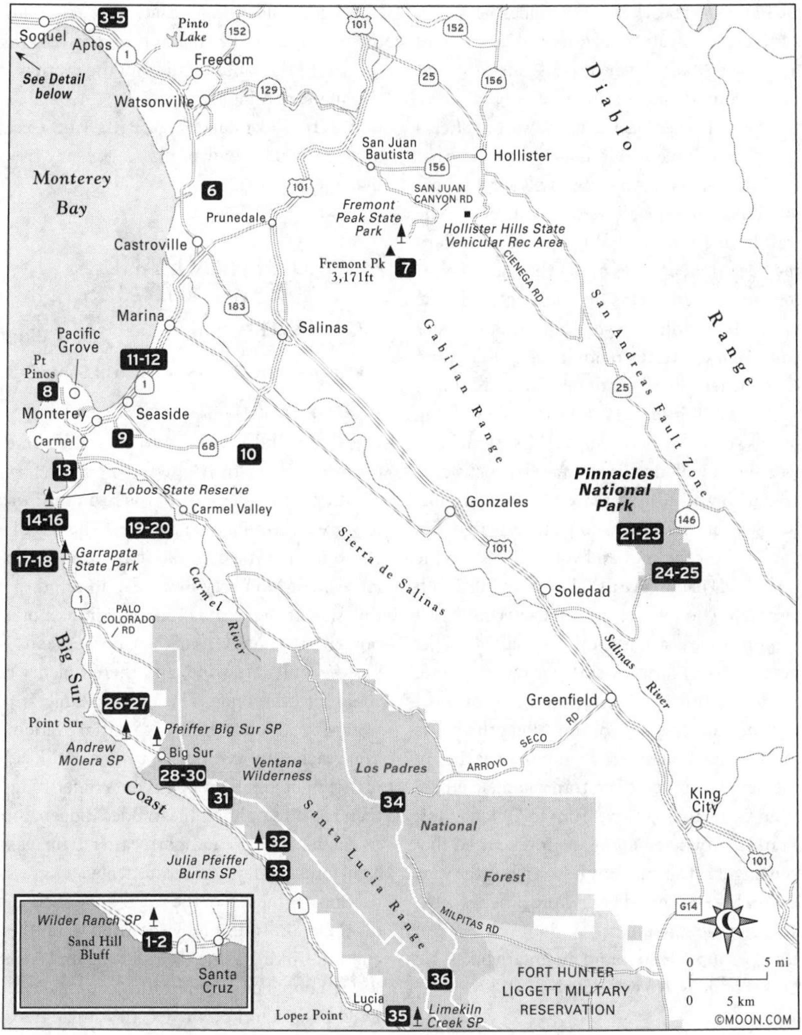

Soquel
Aptos
3-5
Pinto Lake
Freedom
Watsonville
See Detail below
Monterey Bay
6
Prunedale
Castroville
San Juan Bautista
Hollister
Diablo Range
SAN JUAN CANYON RD
Fremont Peak State Park
Hollister Hills State Vehicular Rec Area
Fremont Pk 3,171ft
7
CIENEGA RD
Marina
Salinas
Pacific Grove
Pt Pinos
8
11-12
Monterey
Seaside
Carmel
9
10
13
Pt Lobos State Reserve
14-16
Carmel Valley
19-20
17-18
Garrapata State Park
Gabilan Range
San Andreas Fault Zone
Gonzales
Pinnacles National Park
21-23
24-25
Sierra de Salinas
Soledad
Carmel River
PALO COLORADO RD
Big Sur
26-27
Point Sur
Pfeiffer Big Sur SP
Andrew Molera SP
Big Sur
28-30
Ventana Wilderness
Los Padres National Forest
31
34
Coast
Salinas River
Greenfield
ARROYO SECO RD
King City
Santa Lucia Range
32
33
Julia Pfeiffer Burns SP
MILPITAS RD
Wilder Ranch SP
Sand Hill Bluff
1-2
Santa Cruz
36
FORT HUNTER LIGGETT MILITARY RESERVATION
Lucia
Lopez Point
35
Limekiln Creek SP
0 5 mi
0 5 km
©MOON.COM

1 OLD LANDING COVE TRAIL

2.5 mi/1.5 hr

1 10

in Wilder Ranch State Park north of Santa Cruz

Map 8.1, page 439 BEST

On some maps and park signs this trail is called Old Cove Landing, while on others it's called Old Landing Cove. Take your pick. The Old Landing Cove Trail is a gem of a coastal hike that offers a look at a seal rookery, some spectacular pocket beaches, and a hidden fern cave. Although the trail is open to both hikers and mountain bikers, everybody seems to mind their manners and get along fine.

The trail leads past Brussels sprouts fields to the coast. An odd but interesting fact is that 12 percent of our nation's Brussels sprouts production happens right here in this park. The trail leads from the main parking lot toward the ocean, then traces along the coastal bluff tops, with farm fields on your right and the dramatic coastline on your left. In short order you reach the trail's namesake, Old Landing Cove, where small schooners loaded lumber in the late 19th century. A little more walking brings you to the bluffs above the seal rookery, where you look down on huge flat rocks covered with wall-to-wall seals. Finally, near post No. 8, a spur trail leads down to a small beach cove. Follow the spur and you will find on the inland side of the cove a shallow cave filled with ferns from floor to ceiling. A quarter-mile past the fern-cave beach is another excellent pocket beach, perfect for picnicking or lying around. Although this is a fine destination for most visitors, you can keep hiking along the bluffs beyond this beach to several more beaches in the next few miles. (The trail's name changes from Old Landing Cove Trail to Ohlone Bluff Trail.) If you keep going, be forewarned that you might get an anatomy lesson along the way: Both Three-Mile and Four-Mile Beaches often attract nude sunbathers.

User Groups: Hikers and mountain bikes. No horses or dogs. No wheelchair facilities.

Permits: No permits are required. A $10 day-use fee is charged per vehicle.

Maps: A free map of Wilder Ranch is available at the entrance station or by free download at www.parks.ca.gov. A more detailed map is available from Pease Press (www.peasepress.com). For a topographic map, go to the USGS website to download Santa Cruz.

Directions: From Santa Cruz, drive north on Highway 1 for four miles. Turn left into the entrance for Wilder Ranch State Park and follow the park road to its end, at the main parking area. Take the signed trail from the southwest side of the parking lot.

Contact: Wilder Ranch State Park, Santa Cruz, 831/423-9703, www.parks.ca.gov or www.thatsmypark.org.

2 WILDER RIDGE AND ZANE GREY TRAILS

6.0 mi/3.0 hr

in Wilder Ranch State Park north of Santa Cruz

Map 8.1, page 439

Once you find your way to the hiker/biker tunnel underneath Highway 1 near the farm buildings at Wilder Ranch, you're on your way to a great six-mile hike with just enough of a climb to give you a workout and a spectacular vista of Monterey Bay. Keep in mind that this side of the park is the domain of mountain bikers—hundreds of them on weekends—but the trails are wide, and there's plenty of room for everybody. The Wilder Ridge Trail features a 500-foot climb to a coastal overlook. You reach it by exiting the tunnel and heading straight and then uphill on Wilder Ridge, then bearing right on the Wilder Ridge Loop. At about 2.5 miles out, shortly after Twin Oaks Trail forks right, you come to an obvious grassy overlook at the top of the ridge—about 40 feet off the main trail. Enjoy the wide vista, then continue hiking along the ridge top on Wilder Ridge Loop. For an interesting loop, take the Zane Grey cutoff on the left (it's single track) and then go left again on the other side of the Wilder Ridge Loop.

User Groups: Hikers, horses, and mountain bikes. No dogs. No wheelchair facilities.

Permits: No permits are required. A $10 day-use fee is charged per vehicle.

Maps: A free map of Wilder Ranch State Park is available at the entrance station or by free download at www.parks.ca.gov. A more detailed map is available from Pease Press (www.peasepress.com). For a topographic map, go to the USGS website to download Santa Cruz.

Directions: From Santa Cruz, drive north on Highway 1 for four miles. Turn left into the entrance for Wilder Ranch State Park and follow the park road to its end, at the main parking area. Take the trail signed "Nature Trail" from the southwest side of the parking lot. Walk down the park road to the Wilder Ranch and Cultural Preserve, then through the cultural preserve to the picnic area and chicken coops, to reach the tunnel that leads underneath Highway 1.

Contact: Wilder Ranch State Park, Santa Cruz, 831/423-9703, www.parks.ca.gov or www.thatsmypark.org.

3 MAPLE FALLS

7.0-9.0 mi/4.5 hr 3 9

in The Forest of Nisene Marks State Park near Aptos

Map 8.1, page 439

It's either a seven- or nine-mile round-trip hike to Maple Falls, and it all depends on whether the park road is gated at Porter Picnic Area, the main trailhead. In winter and spring, the road is usually closed, which means you need to walk an extra mile in each direction in order to see the falls. Winter and spring are the best seasons to go, of course, because that's when Maple Falls is flowing at its fullest. The trip starts out with an easy walk on Aptos Creek Fire Road, which you'll share with mountain bikers. Follow it 0.25 mile past Porter Picnic Area, where you turn left on Loma Prieta Grade Trail. The second-growth redwood and Douglas fir forest just keeps getting thicker, greener, and prettier, and the trail turns to sweet single track. Where Loma Prieta Grade splits, stay to the right, heading toward Bridge Creek Historic Site, for the shortest route to the falls. You can take the other side of the Loma Prieta Grade Loop on your way back if you still have the energy. When you reach Bridge Creek Historic Site, the site of a former logging camp, the maintained trail ends, and you begin a fun 0.5-mile stream scramble to Maple Falls, following the course of Bridge Creek. The canyon narrows as you travel through a dense green world of ferns, moss, foliage, and water, and at last you reach the back of the canyon, where 30-foot Maple Falls spills over the wall.

User Groups: Hikers only. No dogs or horses. Mountain bikes allowed only on fire roads. No wheelchair facilities.

Permits: No permits are required. An $8 day-use fee is charged per vehicle.

Maps: A free map of The Forest of Nisene Marks is available at the entrance kiosk or by free download at www.parks.ca.gov. A more detailed map is available from Pease Press (www.peasepress.com). For topographic maps, go to the USGS website to download Laurel, Soquel, and Loma Prieta.

Directions: From Santa Cruz, drive south on Highway 1 for six miles to the Aptos/State Park Drive exit. Bear left at the exit, cross over the highway, then turn right on Soquel Drive and drive 0.5 mile. Turn left on Aptos Creek Road. Stop at the entrance kiosk, then continue up the park road and park at Porter Picnic Area. In the winter months, you must park at George's Picnic Area, a mile before Porter Picnic Area, because the park road is gated off at that point.

Contact: The Forest of Nisene Marks State Park, Aptos, 831/763-7063 or 831/429-2850, www.parks.ca.gov or www.thatsmypark.org.

4 LOMA PRIETA EARTHQUAKE EPICENTER

4.0 mi/2.0 hr  2 8

in The Forest of Nisene Marks State Park near Aptos

Map 8.1, page 439

The destination on this trail is the epicenter of the 1989 Loma Prieta earthquake, but the pleasure of the trip has little to do with its interesting geological history. Instead, the joy is in the scenery, a lush second-growth redwood forest that regenerated after a clear-cut operation at the end of the 19th century. The hike follows Aptos Creek Fire Road, which leads gently uphill (expect plenty of mountain bikers and joggers on the weekends). At 1.5 miles from the Porter Picnic Area, cross a footbridge and descend a bit on the trail until you come to the spot where a large sign proclaims the proximity of the earthquake epicenter. There's a small bike rack. Cross the creek and continue up the single-track Aptos Creek Trail for 0.5 mile to the actual epicenter, where you will see surprisingly little evidence of anything earth-shaking, but rather a lovely and peaceful redwood forest. Turn around here for a four-mile round-trip (or six miles if you had to start from George's Picnic Area instead of Porter Picnic Area).

It's possible, although quite challenging, to hike Five Finger Falls from the epicenter by following Aptos Creek Trail for 4.5 additional miles. This epic hike has long been a favorite of intrepid waterfall lovers, who revel in the chance to see one of the least visited waterfalls in the Santa Cruz mountains. However, almost every winter, this trail is subject to weather-related damage, including landslides and flood-level waters in Aptos Creek. During the rainy months, plan on getting wet feet, as you must walk in the creek where the trail peters out. There is never any guarantee that you will reach your destination when you set out for Five Finger Falls, but nonetheless, this hike remains a beloved challenge for waterfall aficionados.

User Groups: Hikers and mountain bikes

Forest of Nisene Marks State Park

(bikers must stay on the fire roads). No dogs or horses. No wheelchair facilities.
Permits: No permits are required. An $8 day-use fee is charged per vehicle.
Maps: A free map of the The Forest of Nisene Marks State Park is available at the entrance kiosk or by free download at www.parks.ca.gov. A more detailed map is available from Pease Press (www.peasepress.com). For topographic maps, go to the USGS website to download Laurel, Soquel, and Loma Prieta.
Directions: From Santa Cruz, drive south on Highway 1 for six miles to the Aptos/State Park Drive exit. Bear left at the exit, cross over the highway, then turn right on Soquel Drive and drive 0.5 mile. Turn left on Aptos Creek Road. Stop at the entrance kiosk, then continue up the park road and park at Porter Picnic Area. In the winter months, you must park at George's Picnic Area, a mile before Porter Picnic Area, because the park road is gated off at that point.
Contact: The Forest of Nisene Marks State Park, Aptos, 831/763-7063 or 831/429-2850, www.parks.ca.gov or www.thatsmypark.org.

5 WEST RIDGE AND APTOS CREEK LOOP

12.5 mi/7.0 hr or 2 days 4 9

in The Forest of Nisene Marks State Park near Aptos

Map 8.1, page 439

The West Ridge and Aptos Creek Loop is the grand tour of the Forest of Nisene Marks State Park, suitable only for hikers in good condition and with a lot of time on their hands. An option is to get reservations for West Ridge Trail Camp and turn this into an overnight trip; the camp is situated conveniently near Sand Point Overlook—a great spot for sunsets. (Backpacking stoves are necessary; no campfires are allowed.) From George's Picnic Area, walk up Aptos Creek Road for 0.25 mile to the left cutoff for West Ridge Trail, and start climbing uphill along the west ridge of Aptos Canyon. (You can also take Loma Prieta Grade Trail if you prefer. Follow the left side of its loop, then take the connector trail to West Ridge Trail.) Finally you ascend all the way to Hinckley Ridge (at 1,300 feet) and meet up with the fire road that leads to West Ridge Trail Camp and Sand Point Overlook. From the overlook at 1,500 feet, you can see down into the densely forested Bridge Creek drainage and far off across sky-blue Monterey Bay. Finish out the loop with a long downhill walk on Aptos Creek Fire Road, a wide path through dense redwoods and Douglas firs.
User Groups: Hikers and mountain bikes. No dogs or horses. No wheelchair facilities.
Permits: No permits are required. An $8 day-use fee is charged per vehicle. An advance reservation is necessary to stay overnight at West Ridge Trail Camp; call the park for reservations.
Maps: A free map of The Forest of Nisene Marks State Park is available at the entrance kiosk or by free download at www.parks.ca.gov. A more detailed map is available from Pease Press (www.peasepress.com). For topographic maps, go to the USGS website to download Laurel, Soquel, and Loma Prieta.
Directions: From Santa Cruz, drive south on Highway 1 for six miles to the Aptos/State Park Drive exit. Bear left at the exit, cross over the highway, then turn right on Soquel Drive and drive 0.5 mile. Turn left on Aptos Creek Road. Stop at the entrance kiosk, then continue up the park road and park at George's Picnic Area.
Contact: The Forest of Nisene Marks State Park, Aptos, 831/763-7063 or 831/429-2850, www.parks.ca.gov or www.thatsmypark.org.

6 ELKHORN SLOUGH SOUTH MARSH LOOP

2.5 mi/1.5 hr 1 8

near Moss Landing

Map 8.1, page 439 BEST

Elkhorn Slough's 1,700 acres of marsh and tidal

flats comprise the precious borderline between sea and land, home to thousands of species of birds, fish, and invertebrates. It's California's second-largest salt marsh, where birds numbering in the thousands can be seen. Hikers with binoculars (and sometimes with just their own eyes) may spot a long list of species that includes peregrine falcons, American white pelicans, and thousands of shore birds. The South Marsh Loop Trail is a 2.5-mile walking tour of this salty, marshy, bird-filled land, crossing footbridges over the slough and staying close to mudflats and the water's edge. Make sure you take all the spurs off the loop, including the short walk to Hummingbird Island, which sits right on the edge of the main channel of the Slough.

Note: The reserve is open Wednesday through Sunday from 9am-5pm. Guided tours are available on Saturday and Sunday.

User Groups: Hikers only. No dogs, horses, or mountain bikes. Several boardwalks and overlook areas are wheelchair accessible.

Permits: No permits are required. A $4 entrance fee is charged per adult. Children under 16 and anyone in possession of a California fishing or hunting license may enter free.

Maps: A map of Elkhorn Slough is available at the visitors center and online. For a topographic map, go to the USGS website to download Moss Landing.

Directions: From Highway 1 at Moss Landing, turn east on Dolan Road by the PG&E power station. Drive three miles to Elkhorn Road, turn left (north), and drive two miles to the reserve entrance. The trail begins by the visitors center.

Contact: Elkhorn Slough National Estuarine Research Reserve, Moss Landing, 831/728-2822, www.elkhornslough.org.

7 FREMONT PEAK TRAIL

0.6 mi/0.5 hr

in Fremont Peak State Park near San Juan Bautista

Map 8.1, page 439

Fremont Peak State Park is a small park with a big view. There are only five miles of hiking trails here, including the most popular 0.6-mile trail to the summit of Fremont Peak (elevation 3,169 feet). But that one little trip packs one heck of a punch. Pick a clear day in winter or spring (summer gets brutally hot, and the visibility can be worse) to make the narrow and winding drive from San Juan Bautista, and prepare to witness a panorama of Monterey Bay, Santa Cruz, Salinas, Watsonville, Hollister, and the Santa Lucia Mountains. From the southwest parking area, walk up the gated, paved service road for several yards, and then cut off to the right on the signed Peak Trail, which winds its way up the mountain. The last 50 yards is very rocky, and the final summit climb is a bit of a scramble. Ignore the close-by radio transmitters, and check out the far-off views.

Another popular activity at the park is stargazing. Fremont Peak Observatory is open to the public on Saturday nights from April to October when there is no moon, and observatory members hold astronomy programs here. Visit the FPOA website for a program schedule, www.fpoa.net.

User Groups: Hikers only. No dogs, horses, or mountain bikes. No wheelchair facilities.

Permits: No permits are required. A $6 day-use fee is charged per vehicle.

Maps: A map of Fremont Peak State Park is available at the entrance kiosk. For a topographic map, go to the USGS website to download San Juan Bautista.

Directions: From Gilroy, drive south on U.S. 101 for 11 miles to the Highway 156 East/San Juan Bautista exit. Turn east on Highway 156 and drive three miles to San Juan Bautista. Then turn right (south) on the Alameda and then right on San Juan Canyon Road. (It's signed for the state park.) Follow it 11 miles to its end in Fremont Peak State Park. Park in the southwest parking area.

Contact: Fremont Peak State Park, San Juan Bautista, 831/623-4255, www.parks.ca.gov; Fremont Peak Observatory, 831/623-2465, www.fpoa.net.

8 ASILOMAR COAST TRAIL

2.4 mi/1.5 hr 1 9

in Pacific Grove

Map 8.1, page 439 BEST

Even if you aren't lucky enough to attend a conference at the historic Asilomar Conference Center, you can still walk its adjoining Asilomar Coast Trail, a spectacular 1.2-mile trail along coastal bluffs above rugged, windswept Asilomar Beach. There's no fee to park here, and you'll find plenty of coastal beauty and many side trails to explore. You'll see waves crashing against jagged rocks, plentiful tidepools, tiny pocket beaches, wide sandy stretches with big white dunes, and much sea life. Be sure to take the separate boardwalk trail (on the west side of the conference center) that leads across the dunes. Kite-flying is a popular activity on this windswept beach. While you're here, make sure to visit the Asilomar Dunes Preserve's 25 acres of restored dune habitat. A quarter-mile boardwalk trail begins just north of the Grace Dodge Chapel.

User Groups: Hikers and dogs. No horses or mountain bikes. Portions of the trail are wheelchair-accessible.

Permits: No permits are required. Parking and access are free.

Maps: For a topographic map, go to the USGS website to download Monterey.

Directions: From Salinas on U.S. 101, take the Highway 68/Monterey exit and drive 15 miles into Monterey. Continue into Pacific Grove, where Highway 68 becomes Sunset Drive. Continue to Asilomar State Beach. Park alongside Sunset Drive; the trail begins opposite the conference center.

Contact: Asilomar State Beach, Pacific Grove, 831/646-6440, www.parks.ca.gov.

9 SKYLINE NATURE AND JACKS PEAK TRAILS

1.2 mi/0.5 hr 1 9

in Jacks Peak County Park near Monterey

Map 8.1, page 439

At 1,068 feet, Jacks Peak is the highest point on the Monterey Peninsula. Hey, it's not the High Sierra, but this summit is still worthy of a hike. The peak and its surrounding park are named after David Jacks, the guy who got his name on Monterey Jack cheese. The Skyline Nature Trail is an easy loop walk around the summit of Jacks Peak, set amid a dense forest of Monterey pines. The Jacks Peak Trail is a smaller loop inside Skyline Nature Trail loop, and you can easily branch off the latter to join the former for a half-hour walk that provides unparalleled views of Carmel Valley, the Monterey Peninsula, Point Lobos, the Santa Lucia Mountains, and the Pacific Ocean. That's on a clear day, of course, which is not every day in Monterey. Even though the view is about the same on both trail loops, make sure you walk a leg of Jacks Peak Trail to the top of Jacks Peak, where you can sit on a bench and pull out a picnic of Jack cheese sandwiches. Don't plan on watching the sun set from here, though; unfortunately the park closes before then.

User Groups: Hikers and dogs. No horses or mountain bikes. No wheelchair facilities.

Permits: No permits are required. A $2 per person entrance fee is charged (plus $2 per dog).

Maps: A free map of Jacks Peak County Park is available at the entrance station or by download at www.co.monterey.ca.us/parks. For a topographic map, go to the USGS website to download Seaside.

Directions: From Monterey, take Highway 68

east from Highway 1 for 1.7 miles to Olmsted Road. Turn right on Olmsted Road and drive 1.5 miles to Jacks Peak Drive, then follow Jacks Peak Drive to the park entrance. After passing through the entrance kiosk, turn right and drive to the parking area for Jacks Peak.

Contact: Jacks Peak County Park, Monterey, 888/588-2267, www.co.monterey.ca.us/parks.

10 OLLASON PEAK

7.6 mi/3.5 hr 3 7

in Toro County Park near Monterey

Map 8.1, page 439

Pick a cool day in spring to take this inspiring jaunt to the top of Ollason Peak, elevation 1,800 feet, high up and far away from the madding crowds of popular Toro County Park. Even with a cool breeze, Ollason Trail can be a butt-kicker, with many steep sections over a less-than-smooth route. It leads from the Quail Meadow Group Picnic Area and climbs through wide grasslands and occasional oak groves, most of the time on a wide double-track trail. Increasingly wide views and an excellent variety of grassland wildflowers are your reward for the work. After a long stint heading southwest, the trail suddenly veers east, then resumes its southern course for the final climb to Ollason Peak, nearly four miles from the trailhead. You get lovely views toward Monterey Bay and the Central Valley from the summit, plus a set of rugged-looking peaks to the east. Retrace your steps from there or continue a little farther to Coyote Spring Trail, bearing left for a 7.6-mile loop. If you're making the loop, be sure to watch for the left turnoff on Cougar Ridge from Coyote Spring, which returns you to a connector trail back to Quail Meadow.

User Groups: Hikers and dogs. Mountain bikes and horses allowed on only a portion of the trail. No wheelchair facilities.

Permits: No permits are required. A $2 per person entrance fee is charged (plus $2 per dog).

Maps: A free map of Toro County Park is available at the entrance station or by download at www.co.monterey.ca.us/parks. For a topographic map, go to the USGS website to download Spreckels.

Directions: From Monterey, take Highway 68 east from Highway 1 for 13 miles to the Portola Drive exit. Turn right into the Toro County Park entrance road. Drive 0.5 mile past the entrance kiosk to the parking area by Quail Meadow Group Picnic Area.

Contact: Toro County Park, Salinas, 831/484-1108, www.co.monterey.ca.us/parks.

11 FORT ORD DUNES STATE PARK

1.0-8.0 mi/1-5 hr 1 9

in Fort Ord Dunes State Park near Marina

Map 8.1, page 439

One of the newest parks in the California State Park system, Fort Ord Dunes State Park opened in 2009 and provides access to a four-mile-long stretch of beach that was once the "backyard" of an old military training base. Plans are in the works to open a campground near the Fort Ord's ammunitions storage bunkers, but for now, the park consists of a brand new boardwalk trail that leads to a blufftop viewing platform at Lookout Point, placards and exhibits on this region's military history, and a quarter-mile path leading to a seemingly endless stretch of sand, where you can wander as far as you wish. There's so much walkable coastline here, you'll want at least a half a day to explore, and you won't have to deal with the crowds that flock to the beaches farther south. Forget the hectic world as you gaze at your solitary footprints in the sand, and marvel at the fact that this gorgeous beach was once used for artillery target practice and maneuver training. Steep dunes are carpeted in colorful nonnative ice plants as well as native dune plants like dune gilia and Monterey spineflower. The park also has a five-mile paved road that parallels

Highway 1 (dogs are allowed on this road) and access to the paved Monterey Recreation Trail.

User Groups: Hikers only. No dogs, horses, or mountain bikes permitted on the beach. Part of the trail is wheelchair-accessible.

Permits: No permits are required.

Maps: For a topographic map, go to the USGS website to download Monterey.

Directions: From Monterey and points south, take Highway 1 north to the Lightfighter Drive exit and turn left on Second Avenue, left on Ninth Street, then follow the overpass into the park. From Marina and points north, take Highway 1 south to the Imjin Parkway exit. Turn on Second Avenue and follow signs to Fort Ord Dunes State Park.

Contact: Fort Ord Dunes State Park, Marina, 831/649-2836, www.parks.ca.gov.

12 EOLIAN DUNES PRESERVE

1.0-3.0 mi/2.0 hr — 1 — 9

in Eolian Dunes Preserve near Seaside

Map 8.1, page 439

Most people are in such a big rush to get to their weekend destination in Carmel or Big Sur that they blow by Seaside and Sand City at 60 miles per hour. But as you zoom along Highway 1, you can't help but notice the giant sand dunes that rise alongside the highway, and the colorful paragliders that often soar above them. Why not pull over and stop for a walk? The dunes were formed during the Pleistocene era near the end of the last ice age, about 10,000 years ago. These massive mounds of sand are protected as Eolian Dunes Preserve, and the only way to access them is to take a walk (or bike ride) on the paved Monterey Bay Coastal Trail. The dunes have been restored with native plants, which create a colorful flower show during the early spring months, and there's no better spot to get a wide perspective on Monterey Bay than from the top of the one of these silky soft dunes. If it's windy here, which it often is, you can always find a hollowed-out valley between the dunes' peaks to hunker down in and watch the gliders flying above you. During the 20th century, the dunes bore the inglorious name of Landfill Dunes Preserve—the area was a garbage damp in the 1940s—but mercifully, in 2007 the name was changed to "eolian," which means deposited or produced by wind.

User Groups: Hikers and dogs. No horses or mountain bikes. Part of the trail is wheelchair-accessible.

Permits: No permits are required.

Maps: For a topographic map, go to the USGS website to download Monterey.

Directions: From Marina, take Highway 1 south to Seaside. Exit at California Avenue and drive south to Playa Avenue in Sand City. Follow the Playa Avenue overpass across Highway 1 to the Coastal Trail and the preserve.

Contact: Monterey Peninsula Regional Park District, Seaside, 831/372-3196, www.mprpd.org.

13 CARMEL MEADOWS TRAIL

3.0/1.5 hr — 1 — 9

in Carmel River State Beach near Carmel

Map 8.1, page 439

Carmel is famous for its stunning white sand, so it's no surprise that the in-town Carmel City Beach is always packed with sun-worshipers, dog walkers, families with kids, and lovers holding hands. That's all well and good, but if you'd like a lot less people and a little more zen with your scenic Carmel coastline stroll, head to Carmel Meadows. Two trailheads are located a couple blocks from each other, and parking is fairly limited, but you can park at either one to start your trip (the trails connect). From the trailhead at the end of Calla La Cruz, a paved trail leads to the Portola Crespi Cross, perched on a high hill with a fine view of the sea. This cross commemorates the spot (not the exact spot, but close enough) where intrepid explorers Captain Gaspar de Portola and Father Carlo Crespi placed a signal cross in 1769. Portola eventually became the founder of Monterey. From the Ribera Road trailhead, a path leads across a grassy seaside terrace and down a set of stairs to mile-long Carmel River State Beach on Carmel Bay. As postcard-perfect as it looks, the beach isn't safe for swimming—it's notorious for rip currents and a heavy undertow—but it's ideal for birdwatching at the lagoon just before the Carmel River empties into the sea. Walk both trails for a total three miles and an incredible dose of coastal eye-candy.

User Groups: Hikers and dogs. No horses or mountain bikes. Part of the trail is wheelchair-accessible.

Permits: No permits are required.

Maps: For a topographic map, go to the USGS website to download Monterey.

Directions: From Highway 1 in Carmel, turn west on Ribera Road. Follow Ribera Road for a half-mile, then turn right onto Calla La Cruz. Park where the road ends. (You can also start this hike by following Ribera Road to its end.)

Contact: Carmel River State Beach, Carmel, 831/649-2836, www.parks.ca.gov.

14 LACE LICHEN TRAIL TO SEA LION POINT

2.0 mi/1.0 hr

in Point Lobos State Reserve near Carmel

Map 8.1, page 439

On summer weekends, the cars are parked in a long line along the road outside Point Lobos State Reserve, one of the crown jewels of the state park system, which sees more than 600,000 visitors each year. (Phone or check the park website before you go: In 2020, the park may institute a reservation system for weekend visits.) Even on weekdays, the parking lots are often full—your best bet is to arrive at 8am when the gates open—but the reserve's stunning coastal beauty and plentiful wildlife explain why. Point Lobos also holds a claim to literary fame—Robert Louis Stevenson used this rocky coast as the inspiration for his novel *Treasure Island*.

One of the best destinations at Point Lobos is Sea Lion Point, where you can look for cute little sea otters floating on their backs in the kelp beds and chubby harbor seals and sea lions hauling out on the rocks. The best way to reach the point is by hiking the Lace Lichen Trail from the park entrance kiosk, which roughly parallels the park road. Extended and improved in 2015, this wheelchair-accessible trail saves you the hassle of driving through the reserve and fighting for a parking spot. The trail is named for the gray-green lichen that many call "old man's beard," which hangs from the branches of Monterey pines and coast live oaks. The lace lichen is not a parasite and does not harm the trees; in fact, it helps the trees to retain moisture. You'll see plenty of it as you head toward Sea Lion Point. Once you arrive, you'll be caught up in the spectacle of hundreds of blubbery pinnipeds hauled out on the rocks and on the beaches. In the last few years, the stairs to the lower point have been closed because the seals and sea lions have been coming to shore in such large numbers that they are now using every inch of available real estate. Some biologists believe that the pinnipeds are establishing a permanent colony here, much like they have at Año Nuevo and San Simeon.

User Groups: Hikers only. No dogs, horses, or mountain bikes. Part of the trail is wheelchair-accessible.

Permits: No permits are required. A $10 day-use fee is charged per vehicle.

Maps: A map of Point Lobos State Reserve is available at the entrance station or by download at www.parks.ca.gov. For a topographic map, go to the USGS website to download Monterey.

Directions: From Carmel at Rio Road, drive south on Highway 1 for three miles to the entrance to Point Lobos State Reserve, on the right. Turn right and drive through the entrance kiosk, and continue straight to the

Sea lions bask in the Carmel sunshine.

information station and Sea Lion Point parking area.

Contact: Point Lobos State Reserve, Carmel, 831/624-4909, www.pointlobos.org.

15 WHALER'S KNOLL AND CYPRESS GROVE

3.0 mi/2.0 hr

in Point Lobos State Reserve near Carmel

Map 8.1, page 439

Two excellent trails lead from the north side of the Sea Lion Point parking area near the information station at Point Lobos, and you can connect them to make a stellar three-mile round-trip. Start by hiking on Cypress Grove Trail, which shows off the park's Monterey cypress trees, one of only two remaining native Monterey cypress groves on earth. (The other grove is across Carmel Bay at Cypress Point.) These gnarled, old-growth trees have been windsculpted into surreal shapes, their limbs decorated with a velvety orange algae called trentepohlia. In between the trees' branches are picture-perfect ocean views. The trail loops around and heads back toward the parking area, but just before you reach it, turn left on North Shore Trail and climb a bit to the right turnoff for Whaler's Knoll Trail. Follow the loose switchbacks uphill to the top of Whaler's Knoll, a bluff top that provides the best view in the park. Early twentieth-century whale spotters used this high knoll to scan the seas for the spouts of whales. When they spotted them, they would hang a signal flag, alerting the whaling boats to head out to sea. From Whaler's Knoll, head downhill and make a loop along the coast on North Shore Trail. (Phone or check the park website before you go: In 2020, the park may institute a reservation system for weekend visits.)

User Groups: Hikers only. No dogs, horses, or mountain bikes. No wheelchair facilities.

Permits: No permits are required. A $10 day-use fee is charged per vehicle.

Maps: A map of Point Lobos State Reserve is available at the entrance station or by free download at www.parks.ca.gov. For a topographic map, go to the USGS website to download Monterey.

Directions: From Carmel at Rio Road, drive south on Highway 1 for three miles to the entrance to Point Lobos State Reserve on the right. Turn right and drive through the entrance kiosk and continue straight to the information station and Sea Lion Point parking area.
Contact: Point Lobos State Reserve, Carmel, 831/624-4909, www.pointlobos.org.

16 POINT LOBOS PERIMETER

6.0 mi/3.0 hr 2 10

in Point Lobos State Reserve near Carmel

Map 8.1, page 439 BEST

The perimeter hike at Point Lobos connects a number of trails to view some of the park's best highlights. Make sure you get a map at the entrance station so you can scope out the many side-trip options that are possible (and the many shortcuts if you're getting tired). Starting from the Sea Lion Point parking area, make your first destination Sea Lion Point. Then bear left on Sand Hill Trail and connect to South Shore Trail. The latter leads along the quieter, south part of the park, past numerous spectacular beaches and coves, to the wheelchair-accessible Bird Island Trail. The stark cliffs of Bird Island become a massive Brandt's cormorant colony in spring and summer. Take the staircase down to Gibson Beach, a glorious stretch of white sand. (You may be tempted to visit emerald-green China Cove, which is arguably one of California's most alluring beach coves, but it has been closed to the public since 2015. If it's still closed when you visit, obey the posted signs.) From Bird Island Trail, connect with South Plateau Trail, follow it northward, cross the park road to follow Carmelo Meadow Trail, and bear right for a side-trip to Granite Point. Don't miss this; it's a rocky outcrop on a short loop trail with great views toward Carmel to the north. Then, retrace your steps along Granite Point Trail and finish out your loop by walking along the park's northern shoreline, following Granite Point Trail to Cabin Trail to North Shore Trail. Other possible side-trips include the Whaler's Cabin cultural history museum (the cabin was built by Chinese fishermen and its foundation is made of whale bones), a lookout of Guillemot Island and its millions of birds (from a spur trail), or Whaler's Knoll and Cypress Grove. If you take all of the possible side-trips along the route, this hike will take you almost all day—and what a fine day it will be. (Phone or check the park website before you go: In 2020, the park may institute a reservation system for weekend visits.)
User Groups: Hikers only. No dogs, horses, or mountain bikes. Wheelchair users can travel on the Bird Island Trail.
Permits: No permits are required. A $10 day-use fee is charged per vehicle.
Maps: A map of Point Lobos State Reserve is available at the entrance station or by free download at www.parks.ca.gov. For a topographic map, go to the USGS website to download Monterey.
Directions: From Carmel at Rio Road, drive south on Highway 1 for three miles to the entrance to Point Lobos State Reserve on the right. Turn right and drive through the entrance kiosk; continue straight to the information station and Sea Lion Point parking area.
Contact: Point Lobos State Reserve, Carmel, 831/624-4909, www.pointlobos.org.

17 ROCKY RIDGE AND SOBERANES CANYON LOOP

7.0 mi/3.5 hr 3 10

in Garrapata State Park south of Carmel

Map 8.1, page 439 BEST

Garrapata State Park is situated on both sides of Highway 1, with its western trails skirting the ocean blufftops and eastern trails heading up inland canyons. The park's inland side was badly burned in the 2016 Soberanes Fire, and as of September 2019, the Soberanes Canyon section of this loop trail has been reopened, and the Rocky Ridge section is expected to reopen in 2020. When it does, hikers will be able to once again enjoy this long, heart-pumping loop trip, which travels through a remarkable variety of terrain. In spring, the wildflower display along these coastal hills will blow you away. Both the number and variety of species is truly remarkable.

Begin hiking on Soberanes Canyon Trail. What starts out as a ranch road through cactus- and chaparral-covered hillsides quickly becomes single-track trail through an increasingly narrow and wet canyon. The big surprise is a gorgeous stand of redwoods along Soberanes Creek, an extreme contrast to the chaparral and cacti at the start of the trail. The grove is a good turnaround spot for those looking for a short, easy trip. If you continue on, the trail begins a substantial ascent with not nearly enough switchbacks; after the initial easy grade of this trail, this stretch comes as a major surprise for many hikers. The trail then travels north to meet up with Peak Trail heading right, which leads to 1,977-foot Doud Peak, and Rocky Ridge Trail heading left. In case you are wondering why you are so out of breath, you've just climbed 1,850 feet in just under three miles. Unless you are feeling an irresistible urge to bag Doud Peak, turn left and finish out your loop on Rocky Ridge Trail, where on a clear day you can look out over the ocean for miles. The trail then winds back down the hillsides and deposits you back at your car on Highway 1.

User Groups: Hikers only. No dogs, horses, or mountain bikes. No wheelchair facilities.

Permits: No permits are required. Parking and access are free.

Maps: A map of Garrapata State Park is available for free download at www.parks.ca.gov. For a topographic map, go to the USGS website to download Soberanes Point.

Directions: From Carmel at Rio Road, drive south on Highway 1 for seven miles to mile marker 13 and the dirt pullouts along the highway at Garrapata State Park. It's four miles south of Point Lobos State Park and easy to miss; go slowly and watch for cars parked alongside the road. The Soberanes Canyon Trail begins on the east side of the road.

Contact: Garrapata State Park, Big Sur, 831/667-2315 or 831/649-2836, www.parks.ca.gov.

18 SOBERANES POINT TRAIL

2.0 mi/1.0 hr 2 9

in Garrapata State Park south of Carmel

Map 8.1, page 439

You can access Soberanes Point Trail from three different gates along Highway 1, so if you miss mile marker 13, you can always stop at markers 15 or 16. Wherever you begin, you'll end up on a spectacular and easy set of trails that joins in a series of loops around Soberanes Point, all basically around Whale Peak. If you time your trip at low tide, you'll have access to some excellent tidepools, and even if not, you have views of rocky shoreline bluffs and plenty of birdlife and other animals. Many anglers try their luck rock fishing here at the point, and it's also a popular spot for whale-watching from November to January. Note that if you start from mile marker 13, you can hike a short loop to your right and then a much larger loop to your left. If you start from mile marker 15, you're at the middle of the larger loop, so you can start hiking either right or left. Just wander as you please; the coastline and the perimeter of the point make it impossible to get lost.

User Groups: Hikers only. No dogs, horses, or mountain bikes. No wheelchair facilities.

Permits: A map of Garrapata State Park is available for free download at www.parks.ca.gov. No permits are required. Parking and access are free.

Maps: For a topographic map, go to the USGS website to download Soberanes Point.

Directions: From Carmel at Rio Road, drive south on Highway 1 for seven miles to mile marker 13 and the dirt pullouts along the highway at Garrapata State Park. It's four miles south of Point Lobos State Park and easy to miss; go slowly and watch for cars parked alongside the road. The Soberanes Point Trail begins on the east side of the road.

Contact: Garrapata State Park, Big Sur, 831/667-2315 or 831/649-2836, www.parks.ca.gov.

19 LUPINE, WATERFALL, AND MESA LOOP

3.2 mi/1.5 hr 2 8

in Garland Ranch Regional Park near Carmel

Map 8.1, page 439

Garland Ranch's excellent visitors center is the perfect place to begin your trip to this 4,500-acre park. Take a look inside, get a trail map, and learn a few things about the area's animals, trees, and wildflowers. The center is also the trailhead for this combined loop on Lupine, Waterfall, and Mesa Trails. Although the park's waterfall flows only during the wettest of rainy seasons, its well maintained trails are good to walk year-round. Begin by heading to the left (southeast) from the visitors center on Lupine Loop, which travels along the open, flat floodplains of the Carmel River. In 0.5 mile, leave the loop and continue straight on the Waterfall Trail, then climb through a more shady area to the rocky cliff where the waterfall sometimes falls. Beyond it, you'll ascend more seriously to the mesa, a large high meadow with views of Carmel Valley and beyond. Continuing uphill, 300 feet to the south lies Mesa Pond, which offers year-round fishing for smallmouth bass and bluegill (catch and release only, no fishing license required). Two benches are situated at the pond's eastern edge. Follow Mesa Trail back downhill to the other side of Lupine Loop and follow Lupine Loop back to the visitors center. In springtime, expect to be wowed by the wildflower show. They don't call this "Lupine Loop" for nothing.

User Groups: Hikers, dogs, and horses. No mountain bikes. No wheelchair facilities.

Permits: No permits are required. Parking and access are free.

Maps: A free map of Garland Ranch Regional Park is available by download at www.mprpd.org. For topographic maps, go to the USGS website to download Mount Carmel and Carmel Valley.

Directions: From Highway 1 at Carmel, turn east on Carmel Valley Road. Drive 8.6 miles on Carmel Valley Road to the Garland Ranch parking area, on the right side of the road. From late spring to fall, you can walk across the river bridge from the parking lot to access the trails. In the winter months when the bridge is removed, walk 300 feet west of the parking lot and cross the vehicle bridge.

Contact: Garland Ranch Regional Park Visitor Center, 831/659-6065; Monterey Peninsula Regional Park District, Monterey, 831/659-4488 (ranger station) or 831/372-3196 (administrative office), www.mprpd.org.

20 SNIVLEY'S RIDGE TRAIL

5.6 mi/3.0 hr 3 8

in Garland Ranch Regional Park near Carmel

Map 8.1, page 439

If it's winter or spring, a trip to the top of Snivley's Ridge could be just what you need to keep your hiking legs in shape. It's a healthy, 1,600-foot climb up to the ridge, plus a 250-foot climb to get to the ridge's highest point, so be prepared to pant a little. Much of the walk is exposed; be sure to bring water, and pick a cool day to hike the trail. From the visitors center, set out on either side of Lupine Loop (heading left is a little shorter), and continue uphill on Mesa Trail to its junction with Fern Trail. This stretch is moist and shady, so enjoy it while you can. Follow Fern Trail as it steeply ascends, turn left on Sage Trail and then right on Sky Trail, and continue to climb. Well-graded switchbacks make it easier. Many people stop where Sky Trail meets Snivley's Ridge Trail, at a bench with a panoramic view of Carmel Valley, the forested Santa Lucia Mountains, and the ocean. But those determined to go as high as possible should turn right on Snivley's Ridge Trail and walk another 0.75 mile west to the ridge with its spectacular views of Carmel Bay and the Monterey Peninsula. Turn left on the trail that leads to the park's highest point at 2,038 feet. Note: If you want to get to this high point via a slightly longer but less steep route, you can follow Mesa Trail all the way to Sky Trail and bypass the steep Fern Trail.

User Groups: Hikers, dogs, and horses. No mountain bikes. No wheelchair facilities.

Permits: No permits are required. Parking and access are free.

Maps: A free map of Garland Ranch Regional Park is available by download at www.mprpd.org. For topographic maps, go to the USGS website to download Mount Carmel and Carmel Valley.

Directions: From Highway 1 at Carmel, turn east on Carmel Valley Road. Drive 8.6 miles on Carmel Valley Road to the Garland Ranch parking area, on the right side of the road. From late spring to fall, you can walk across the river bridge from the parking lot to access the trails. In the winter months, when the bridge is removed, walk 300 feet west of the parking lot and cross the vehicle bridge.

Contact: Garland Ranch Regional Park Visitor Center, 831/659-6065; Monterey Peninsula Regional Park District, Monterey, 831/659-4488 (ranger station) or 831/372-3196 (administrative office), www.mprpd.org.

21 CONDOR GULCH AND HIGH PEAKS LOOP

5.3 mi/3.0-5.0 hr

in Pinnacles National Park near Soledad

Map 8.1, page 439

The Condor Gulch Trail begins across the road from the Bear Gulch Nature Center, and it's a good 30-minute climb up the hill on a smooth, winding trail to an overlook of High Peaks. Starting early is recommended, especially in warmer temperatures, since this trail is exposed and can get extremely hot in the afternoons. The scent of wild black sage is enticingly aromatic along the route, and your eyes are continually drawn to the colorful lichens growing on equally colorful rocks. The overlook is a piped railing on a high ledge, and it's a good spot to look out over the canyon you just climbed. It's also a good turnaround spot if you don't want to go farther. If you do, continue uphill for 0.7 mile to a junction with High Peaks Trail and turn left. In just over a half-mile, you'll reach a split in the trail. One path heads toward the steep and narrow section of the High Peaks Trail; the other toward the Tunnel Trail. Here, people who are afraid of heights should consider taking Tunnel Trail downhill. They can then turn left on the Juniper Canyon Trail to meet up with their fellow hikers at a bench and an overlook area at the junction of Juniper Canyon Trail and High Peaks Trail. This adds about one mile to the total mileage of this hike. Those willing to have an adventure should continue on the High Peaks Trail through narrow passageways and over and under the steep rock formations of the High Peaks.

In many places, the trail is a series of steps and handrails that have been carved into the rock. The near-vertical drop-offs appear daunting, but this trail gives an amazing up-close view of the rock formations in addition to the chance to see falcons or California condors. After 0.7 mile, you'll reach Scout Peak, where there is a bench, a fine view to the west, and a restroom. Take advantage of any or all of these, then turn left to stay on the High Peaks Trail and head back to Bear Gulch. You'll have to walk down Moses Spring Trail a short distance to get back to your car. There is an option to add about a mile to this hike by visiting the reservoir and Bear Gulch Cave. That detour takes a right turn at the Rim Trail about 1.5 miles below Scout Peak.

User Groups: Hikers only. No dogs, horses, or mountain bikes. No wheelchair facilities.

Permits: No permits are required. There is a $30 per vehicle entrance fee, good for seven days, at Pinnacles National Park.

Maps: A free map of Pinnacles National Park is available at the visitors center or by download at www.nps.gov/pinn. For topographic maps, go to the USGS website to download Bickmore Canyon and North Chalone Peak.

Directions: From King City on U.S. 101, take the First Street exit and head east. First Street turns into Highway G13/Bitterwater Road. Follow it for 15 miles to Highway 25, where you turn left (north). Follow Highway 25 for 14 miles to Highway 146. Turn left on Highway 146 and drive 1.9 miles to Pinnacles Visitors Center, then continue another 3.5 miles to Bear Gulch Nature Center. The trailhead for the Condor Gulch Trail is across the road from Bear Gulch Nature Center.

Alternatively, from Gilroy, drive south on U.S. 101 for two miles and take the Highway 25 exit. Drive south on Highway 25 for 43 miles to Highway 146. Turn right on Highway 146 and drive 1.9 miles to Pinnacles Visitors Center, then continue another 3.5 miles to Bear Gulch Nature Center. The trailhead for the Condor Gulch Trail is across the road from Bear Gulch Nature Center.

Contact: Pinnacles National Park, Paicines, 831/389-4485, www.nps.gov/pinn.

22 BEAR GULCH CAVE

2.2 mi/1.5 hr

in Pinnacles National Park near Soledad

Map 8.1, page 439

Pinnacles National Park is well loved for its craggy volcanic formations, abundant hiking trails, and challenging rock climbing. But what many visitors come to see is Bear Gulch Cave, a tunnel-like jumble of boulders formed by thousands of years of water erosion. But Bear Gulch Cave has some very special residents, a colony of Townsend's big-eared bats, and they need peace and quiet. So the Park Service has installed a system of gates to protect the roosting bats and allow visitors access to the lower part of the cave for 10 months of the year (mid-July-mid-May). During short periods in October and March when the bats leave their home, the entire cave is open to visitors, and this is the best time to visit. (Phone the park before making the long drive to confirm the current status of Bear Gulch Cave; the bats don't conform to an exact timetable, and occasionally the entire cave is closed for safety due to flooding.) Be sure to come prepared for this adventure. Bring a flashlight (or cell phone with a light) and good walking shoes, and be mentally prepared to wedge through clefts in the rock, duck your head under ledges, and squint in the darkness to locate painted arrows pointing the way through the maze. The adventure is easy enough for children to accomplish, and fun for all ages.

User Groups: Hikers only. No dogs, horses, or mountain bikes. No wheelchair facilities.

Permits: No permits are required. There is a $30 per vehicle entrance fee, good for seven days, at Pinnacles National Park.

Maps: A free map of Pinnacles National Park is available at the visitors center or by download at www.nps.gov/pinn. For topographic maps, go to the USGS website to download Bickmore Canyon and North Chalone Peak.

Directions: From King City on U.S. 101, take the First Street exit and head east. First Street turns into Highway G13/Bitterwater Road. Follow it for 15 miles to Highway 25, where you turn left (north). Follow Highway 25 for 14 miles to Highway 146. Turn left on Highway 146 and drive 1.9 miles to Pinnacles Visitors Center, then continue another three miles to Bear Gulch Nature Center and the Bear Gulch Cave trailhead.

Alternatively, from Gilroy, drive south on U.S. 101 for two miles and take the Highway 25 exit. Drive south on Highway 25 for 43 miles to Highway 146. Turn right on Highway

146 and drive 1.9 miles to Pinnacles Visitors Center, then continue another 3.5 miles to Bear Gulch Nature Center and the Bear Gulch Cave trailhead.

Contact: Pinnacles National Park, Paicines, 831/389-4485, www.nps.gov/pinn.

23 NORTH CHALONE PEAK

9.0 mi/3.0-5.0 hr 4 9

in Pinnacles National Park near Soledad

Map 8.1, page 439

Sure, the High Peaks at Pinnacles National Park are high—about 2,700 feet. But if you want to go higher and get a better look around, take this hike to North Chalone Peak. Located in the western area of the park at 3,304 feet in elevation, North Chalone Peak has a decommissioned fire lookout tower on its summit. It's a great place to take in the view and enjoy some peace and quiet. This trail is much less traveled than the popular High Peaks Loop.

Take Moses Spring Trail from the Bear Gulch Nature Center parking lot, and then climb the stairs up to Bear Gulch Reservoir. Continue over the dam and along the left side of the reservoir until you meet the signed trail for North Chalone Peak. You are likely to see a posse of rock climbers who are busy doing their thing on the cliff faces around the reservoir. As you start along the North Chalone Peak Trail, you are only one mile from the nature center, but you've left the vast majority of people behind. Enjoy the fascinating volcanic rock formations and spring wildflowers on the next stretch of trail. At 3.5 miles, you'll climb a stile to cross the park's pig-proof fence, then follow the trail until it meets up with a fire road. This road will lead you to another stile over the pig fence. After crossing this fence, the summit is a short distance ahead. The final 0.75 mile is the steepest stretch of the whole trip, but the reward at the top is a fine view of the Salinas River curving through its valley, the Santa Lucia Mountains, and all of Pinnacles. During winter the Santa Lucias may be snow dusted, and on very rare, crystal-clear days, you can see all the way to the Pacific Ocean.

Pinnacles National Park

User Groups: Hikers only. No dogs, horses, or mountain bikes. No wheelchair facilities.

Permits: No permits are required. There is a $30 per vehicle entrance fee at Pinnacles National Park, good for seven days.

Maps: A free map of Pinnacles National Park is available at the visitors center or by download at www.nps.gov/pinn. For topographic maps, go to the USGS website to download Bickmore Canyon and North Chalone Peak.

Directions: From King City on U.S. 101, take the First Street exit and head east. First Street turns into Highway G13/Bitterwater Road. Follow it for 15 miles to Highway 25, where you turn left (north). Follow Highway 25 for 14 miles to Highway 146. Turn left on Highway 146 and drive 1.9 miles to Pinnacles Visitors Center, then continue another 3.5 miles to Bear Gulch Nature Center and the trailhead.

Alternatively, from Gilroy, drive south on U.S. 101 for two miles and take the Highway 25 exit. Drive south on Highway 25 for 43

miles to Highway 146. Turn right on Highway 146 and drive 1.9 miles to Pinnacles Visitors Center, then continue another three miles to Bear Gulch Nature Center and the trailhead.
Contact: Pinnacles National Park, Paicines, 831/389-4485, www.nps.gov/pinn.

24 BALCONIES CAVE

2.4 mi/1.5 hr 2 10

in Pinnacles National Park near Soledad

Map 8.1, page 439

Pinnacles National Park has two famous sets of caves: Bear Gulch Cave, on the east side of the park; and Balconies Cave, on the west. Access to Bear Gulch Cave is often partially restricted in order to protect the resident bats, but Balconies Cave is open almost year-round (except immediately after the heaviest rains when the water can be dangerously high). Got your flashlight (or cell phone light) and sturdy footwear? Then get ready for tons of fun. Set off on the Balconies Trail, following the often dry west fork of Chalone Creek toward the narrow canyon between Machete Ridge and the Balconies. A mere 0.6 mile brings you to some huge, colorful, lichen-covered volcanic rocks. The sounds of the wind in the gray pines and the scurrying of squirrels keep you company. At the junction with the Balconies Cliffs Trail, you have a choice: go left over the cliffs and then loop back through the cave, or go right to enter the cave immediately. If you go right, you face a steep downhill scramble that some less agile hikers find difficult. (It's much easier to climb up this than down it.) Either way, you'll eventually find yourself in the cave. Flip on your light and proceed through a narrow slotlike canyon, squeezing through clefts in the rock, ducking under boulders, and climbing down rocky staircases. Note: If you drove all the way to the east side of the park but you want to visit Balconies Cave, you don't have to drive 1.5 hours around the park's perimeter to get to this trailhead. Balconies Cave can also be reached from the east side via a much longer hike on the Old Pinnacles Trail.
User Groups: Hikers only. No dogs, horses, or mountain bikes. No wheelchair facilities.
Permits: No permits are required. There is a $30 per vehicle entrance fee at Pinnacles National Park, good for seven days.
Maps: A free map of Pinnacles National Park is available at the ranger station or by download at www.nps.gov/pinn. For topographic maps, go to the USGS website to download Bickmore Canyon and North Chalone Peak.
Directions: From Salinas, drive south on U.S. 101 for 22 miles to Soledad, and take the Soledad/Highway 146 exit. Drive east on Highway 146 for 10 miles to the West Side Visitors Contact Station. (The road is signed for West Pinnacles.) Then continue another two miles to the road's end at the trailhead parking lot. (Note: You can also hike to Balconies Cave from the east side of the park via the Old Pinnacles Trail.)
Contact: Pinnacles National Park, Paicines, 831/389-4485, www.nps.gov/pinn.

25 JUNIPER CANYON AND HIGH PEAKS LOOP

8.4 mi/5.0 hr

in Pinnacles National Park near Soledad

Map 8.1, page 439

Pinnacles National Park is a hiker's park. The first clue you get is that no road connects the east and west sides of the park, so the only way to get from one side to the other is to walk. And that's just fine, especially since the park's first-rate trail system makes it possible to string together a loop tour around the park on the Juniper Canyon Trail, High Peaks Trail (the part known as the Steep and Narrow Section), Old Pinnacles Trail, and Balconies Trail. If you follow the trails in this order, you get almost all your climbing done in the first half of the trip and then have a fairly easy and flat home stretch.

Begin hiking from the right side of the large parking lot at the end of Highway 146, following Juniper Canyon Trail from grasslands into the rocky hills. The trail gets steeper as you go, but it's well built and has many switchbacks. Ignore the Tunnel Trail turnoff at 1.2 miles, and keep climbing to the junction with High Peaks Trail, at 1.8 miles. Here, at a saddle, are fine views to the west and east, as well as a bench and restroom. The High Peaks Trail goes both north and southeast. Turn north (left) and prepare yourself for the most thrilling part of the trip: a narrow and exciting stretch of trail with many handrails and footholds carved into the rock. Continue on the High Peaks Trail for 3.3 miles until it ends at the Bench Trail. Make a left onto the Bench Trail and soon it becomes the Old Pinnacles Trail, a pleasant route that meanders along the west fork of Chalone Creek. In winter, the creek runs with water, and spring wildflowers are tremendous. In 2.3 miles, you'll go through six unbridged creek crossings and reach a fork for the Balconies Trail. If you've never been to Balconies Cave, take the left fork, which leads you through it. (The right fork climbs above the cave and offers some excellent views.) After ducking your head and bending your knees a lot as you wander through the cave, you'll come out to an easy and flat section of the Balconies Trail, which brings you back to the trailhead parking lot. If you pick a cool day and carry plenty of water, this is a stellar half-day hike at Pinnacles.

User Groups: Hikers only. No dogs, horses, or mountain bikes. No wheelchair facilities.

Permits: No permits are required. There is a $30 per vehicle entrance fee at Pinnacles National Park, good for seven days.

Maps: A free map of Pinnacles National Park is available at the ranger station or by download at www.nps.gov/pinn. For topographic maps, go to the USGS website to download Bickmore Canyon and North Chalone Peak.

Directions: From Salinas, drive south on U.S. 101 for 22 miles to Soledad, and take the Soledad/Highway 146 exit. Drive east on Highway 146 for 10 miles to the West Side Visitors Contact Station. (The road is signed for West Pinnacles.) Then continue another two miles to the road's end at the trailhead parking lot.

Contact: Pinnacles National Park, Paicines, 831/389-4485, www.nps.gov/pinn.

26 MOLERA POINT TRAIL

2.5 mi/1.5 hr 1 9

in Andrew Molera State Park north of Big Sur

Map 8.1, page 439

Andrew Molera is a low-key state park without all the development and fanfare that often comes with state park status. But the park has plenty to offer for hikers and coast lovers. An easy trail leads from the park's main parking lot to Molera Point, where you can look down on spectacular Molera Beach and count the sea lions lying on the rocks. To reach the point, take the trail from the right side of the main parking lot, signed for the campground (not the main trail to the beach, which starts with a bridge crossing). The Molera Point Trail stays on the north side of the Big Sur River and winds past the park's walk-in camp, set in a wide meadow, and historic Cooper Cabin, which was built in 1861 and is the oldest structure on the Big Sur coast. At the river's mouth, the trail forks to the right, heading out to Molera Point. Check out the view from this often windswept promontory; then if the tide is low, go play on the beach at the river's edge before heading back.

User Groups: Hikers and horses. No dogs or mountain bikes. No wheelchair facilities.

Permits: No permits are required. A $10 day-use fee is charged per vehicle.

Maps: A map of Andrew Molera State Park is available at the entrance station or by free download at www.parks.ca.gov. For a topographic map, go to the USGS website to download Big Sur.

Directions: From Carmel, drive 22 miles south on Highway 1 to Andrew Molera State Park's main entrance, on the west side of the highway. Trails begin at the parking lot. The park is two miles north of Big Sur.

Contact: Andrew Molera State Park, Big Sur, 831/667-2315 or 831/649-2836, www.parks.ca.gov.

27 MOLERA STATE PARK LOOP

8.0 mi/4.0 hr 3 10

in Andrew Molera State Park north of Big Sur

Map 8.1, page 439

This big loop around the western side of Andrew Molera State Park is easiest in summer, when the footbridge is in place over the Big Sur River. If the bridge isn't there, you must take off your shoes and socks and suffer through a very cold ford over smooth, rounded rocks. But this trail is worth the effort. It offers several miles of lovely ocean vistas, plus a visit to a remote beach. Start by taking the path from the west side of the parking lot, and immediately cross the river. In a few minutes of walking, you'll leave the crowds behind as you turn left (south) on the River Trail, then in less than a mile, turn right on the single-track Hidden Trail. Enjoy a heart-pumping climb through forest and meadows up to the Ridge Trail, where you turn left and hike southward, paralleling the ocean. The Ridge Trail is a wide fire road and rolls gently, still heading generally uphill. In addition to the ocean vistas to the west, you also have fine views inland of Big Sur's rugged peaks, and you pass through a small, surprising grove of redwood trees.

At 3.5 miles, the Ridge Trail meets the Panorama Trail at a bench and overlook point. Turn right and start to switchback steeply downhill toward the ocean, enjoying more wide views all the way. Spring wildflowers are lovely along the open hillsides. As you near the coast, you'll reach a junction with the Spring Trail. Turn left for a few hundred feet to a lovely, driftwood-laden beach. This makes a perfect lunch stop, provided the wind isn't howling. A fascinating log jam at the beach's entrance

Andrew Molera State Park

makes for great photographs. For your return, follow the Bluffs Trail 2.5 miles back to Molera Beach. This is the loveliest stretch of the entire loop, offering long and beautiful looks at Molera Point and beach and Point Sur Light Station. Finally, take the trail from Molera Beach back to the parking lot. Wow, what a perfect Big Sur day.

User Groups: Hikers and horses. No dogs. Mountain bikes are allowed on Ridge Trail and part of Bluffs Trail only. No wheelchair facilities.

Permits: No permits are required. A $10 day-use fee is charged per vehicle.

Maps: A map of Andrew Molera State Park is available at the entrance station or by free download at www.parks.ca.gov. For a topographic map, go to the USGS website to download Big Sur.

Directions: From Carmel, drive 22 miles south on Highway 1 to Andrew Molera State Park's main entrance, on the west side of the highway. Trails begin at the parking lot. (The park is two miles north of Big Sur.)

Contact: Andrew Molera State Park, Big Sur, 831/667-2315 or 831/649-2836, www.parks.ca.gov.

28 VALLEY VIEW AND PFEIFFER FALLS

3.0 mi/1.0 hr 2 8

in Pfeiffer Big Sur State Park near Big Sur

Map 8.1, page 439

The Pfeiffer Falls Trail section of this popular hiking loop suffered serious damage in Big Sur's recent wildfires, but you can still hike the Valley View Trail to glimpse Pfeiffer Falls, a 60-foot waterfall that streams down a vertical rock face. By sticking with Valley View Trail, you'll also gain a great view of the Big Sur Valley. Start at the Ernst Ewoldsen Memorial Nature Center at Pfeiffer Big Sur State Park. Follow Valley View Trail uphill through the redwoods for about a mile to a trail fork. If the right-hand trail to Pfeiffer Falls is open, switchback downhill for 0.2 mile to a bridge over Pfeiffer Creek located near the base of the falls. Enjoy the watery splendor, then backtrack and continue uphill beyond the junction to the high point of Valley View Trail, where the shady redwoods are replaced by sun-loving oaks. Brilliant blooms of Douglas iris color the ground in the spring. The path tops out at an overlook of the Big Sur River Valley looking northwest to Point Sur. The sight of tiny cars on Highway 1 somewhat diminishes the effect, but it's still a worthy view. Until the Pfeiffer Falls Trail reopens, your return trip is a simple backtrack on Valley View Trail back to the nature center.

User Groups: Hikers only. No dogs, horses, or mountain bikes. No wheelchair facilities.

Permits: No permits are required. A $10 day-use fee is charged per vehicle.

Maps: A map of Pfeiffer Big Sur State Park is available at the entrance station or by free download at www.parks.ca.gov. For a topographic map, go to the USGS website to download Big Sur.

Directions: From Carmel, drive 26 miles south on Highway 1 to Pfeiffer Big Sur State Park, on the east side of the highway. It's two miles south of Big Sur. Drive through the entrance kiosk, turn left at the lodge, and then turn right, following the signs to the Pfeiffer Falls trailhead and the nature center. Park just beyond the nature center. The trail is on the left side of the lot, signed as Oak Grove Trail, Valley View Trail, and Pfeiffer Falls Trail. If the small parking lot is full, you may have to park by the lodge and walk to the trailhead.

Contact: Pfeiffer Big Sur State Park, Big Sur, 831/667-2315 or 831/649-2836, www.parks.ca.gov.

29 MOUNT MANUEL

9.0 mi/5.0 hr 4 9

on the southern edge of the Ventana Wilderness near Big Sur

Map 8.1, page 439

This trail leads to one of the best vantage points in the Ventana Wilderness, the summit of Mount Manuel, where all of Big Sur, the Santa Lucia Mountains, and the Pacific Ocean are spread out before you. Odd as it seems, the trail starts out by the softball fields and picnic areas at Pfeiffer Big Sur State Park. Over the course of the trail's 4.5-mile length, you'll climb 3,100 feet to Mount Manuel's summit at 3,379 feet in elevation, so make sure you have fresh soles on your boots and plenty of water. Pick a cool day to make the climb, because although the trail starts in the trees, the vast majority of the route is completely exposed. Winter and spring are usually the best seasons to head for the summit, both for the clarity of the view (less chance of fog) and for cool temperatures.

Negotiate your way through a half-mile series of signed, state park trails to access the official start of the Mount Manuel Trail. You'll enter Los Padres National Forest and begin a long series of switchbacks over chaparral-covered slopes. As you climb, you gain views of the Big Sur River canyon and the coast. About three miles from the start, the trail enters a forest of tanoaks, bay laurels, and redwoods, then exits it again, returning to the chaparral. Finally you arrive near the summit, or rather, a series of summits. Head for the highest point, where the view of the vast Pacific Ocean and the beauty of the Santa Lucia Mountains will blow you away.

User Groups: Hikers only. No dogs, horses, or mountain bikes. No wheelchair facilities.

Permits: No day hiking permits are required. A $10 day-use fee is charged per vehicle.

Maps: A Ventana Wilderness or Los Padres National Forest map is available from the U.S. Forest Service. For topographic maps, go to the USGS website to download Pfeiffer Point and Big Sur.

Directions: From Carmel, drive 26 miles south on Highway 1 to Pfeiffer Big Sur State Park, on the east side of the highway. It's two miles south of Big Sur. Drive through the entrance kiosk and continue straight past the campfire center to the parking lot near the picnic areas and softball field. The trailhead is signed for Oak Grove Trail and Mount Manuel.

Contact: Big Sur Station, Highway 1, Big Sur, 831/667-2315 or 831/649-2836, www.parks.ca.gov; Los Padres National Forest, Monterey Ranger District, King City, 831/385-5434, www.fs.usda.gov/lpnf.

30 BUZZARDS ROOST OVERLOOK

4.0 mi/2.0 hr 3 9

in Pfeiffer Big Sur State Park near Big Sur

Map 8.1, page 439

Hikers looking for a bit of a challenge in Pfeiffer Big Sur State Park will want to try out this trail to the Buzzards Roost Overlook. Compared to other trails in the park, this trail gets surprisingly little traffic unless there are large groups camping at the nearby group campground. The trail leads along the Big Sur River through a forest of many splendid redwoods, switches back uphill onto slopes filled with oaks and bays, and finally climbs into chaparral country. You get to walk in every kind of Big Sur terrain. High up on Pfeiffer Ridge, there's a 360-degree view of the Pacific Ocean, the Big Sur River gorge, and the Santa Lucia Mountains, providing a fine reward for your effort in climbing here. The trailhead is at 200 feet in elevation, and the overlook is at nearly 1,000 feet.

User Groups: Hikers only. No dogs, horses, or mountain bikes. No wheelchair facilities.

Permits: No permits are required. A $10 day-use fee is charged per vehicle.

Maps: A map of Pfeiffer Big Sur State Park is available at the entrance station or by free download at www.parks.ca.gov. For topographic maps, go to the USGS website to download Big Sur and Pfeiffer Point.

Directions: From Carmel, drive 26 miles south on Highway 1 to Pfeiffer Big Sur State Park, on the east side of the highway. It's two miles south of Big Sur. Drive through the entrance kiosk, go past the lodge, and turn right to cross the bridge over the Big Sur River. A parking area is on the left side of the road. The Buzzards Roost trailhead is signed.

Contact: Pfeiffer Big Sur State Park, Big Sur, 831/667-2315 or 831/649-2836, www.parks.ca.gov.

31 SYKES HOT SPRINGS

20.0 mi/2 days 

in the Ventana Wilderness near Big Sur

Map 8.1, page 439

Note: As of late 2019, the Pine Ridge Trail and Sykes Hot Springs are closed due to 2016 wildfire damage and subsequent 2017 winter storm damage. The Forest Service plans to reopen the trail by 2020 or 2021; check with the Big Sur Ranger Station for updates.

The trip to Sykes Hot Springs is one that just about every California backpacker takes at one time or another. This is a quintessential Big Sur/Ventana Wilderness trip, with deep swimming holes, three hot springs pools, and plenty of coastal mountain scenery. Fall and winter are the best times to visit, and if you go on a weekday, you might just get the hot springs all to yourself. The first four miles of Pine Ridge Trail will have you huffing and puffing through shadeless switchbacks, with only occasional breaks as the path travels through small redwood groves. The route eventually levels and gets much easier. At a junction just past the four-mile mark, the left trail leads to Ventana Camp, one mile farther. This camp near Ventana Creek makes a great overnight for people who have gotten a late start; it even has a "wilderness toilet." At 5.4 miles, the trail reaches Terrace Creek Camp, another option for spending the night. At 7.0 miles, you reach the Big Sur River for the first time, and another camp at Barlow Flat. You'll cross the river at 9.7 miles and head for Sykes Camp and the hot springs. Note that after a period of rain, this can be a difficult or even impossible ford, so if you plan to hike in the wet season, check on conditions before setting out. The hot springs are less than a quarter mile from the camp. Depending on current conditions, two or three pools are terraced along the Big Sur River. The largest of the group is 10 feet long and gracefully sheltered by a large boulder. It averages 100 degrees; the other pools are slightly cooler.

User Groups: Hikers, dogs, and horses. No mountain bikes. No wheelchair facilities.

Permits: A California campfire permit is required year-round for overnight stays whether you are using a camp stove or building a fire; permits are free and available online at www.fs.usda.gov/lpnf or in person at the Big Sur Visitors Center. An $8 parking fee is charged per vehicle.

Maps: A Ventana Wilderness or Los Padres National Forest map is available from the U.S. Forest Service. For topographic maps, go to the USGS website to download Pfeiffer Point, Partington Ridge, and Ventana Cones.

Directions: From Carmel, drive 30 miles south on Highway 1 to Big Sur Station, on the east side of the highway. It's three miles south of Big Sur. The Pine Ridge Trail begins behind the ranger station at the backpacker's parking lot.

Contact: Big Sur Station, Highway 1, Big Sur, 831/667-2315 or 831/649-2836; Los Padres National Forest, Monterey Ranger District, King City, 831/385-5434, www.fs.usda.gov/lpnf.

32 PARTINGTON POINT AND TANBARK TRAILS

4.0 mi/2.0 hr 2 9

in Julia Pfeiffer Burns State Park south of Big Sur

Map 8.1, page 439

If you want to hike at Julia Pfeiffer Burns State Park without the crowds, a combined out-and-back trip on Partington Point and Tanbark Trails could be just your cup of tea. The two trails are about as different as any trails could be, except that they both start from the same point along Highway 1. The Partington Point Trail is a dirt road that leads westward and steeply downhill to an obvious fork at 0.5 mile. The right fork leads a few hundred feet to a tiny rock-strewn beach at Partington Creek's mouth. The left fork leads into the redwoods, across a wooden footbridge, and through a rock tunnel built in the 1880s by pioneer John Partington. On the tunnel's far side is the remains of a narrow dog-hole port at Partington Cove, where lumber was loaded onto seagoing freighters. Partington Point is home to the park's underwater playground of caves and natural bridges, but unless you're a scuba diver, they'll be hidden from your sight. But there's still plenty to enjoy here. Have a seat on a rock and look for sea otters, sea lions, and pelicans. Also keep your eyes peeled for spouting whales.

After visiting Partington Cove, hike back uphill and cross the highway to the start of Tanbark Trail, which leads along Partington Creek, heading inland. You can walk a short half-mile loop on the trail (a bridge carries you across Partington Creek and then back down the other side), or you can continue farther, climbing steeply uphill for 1.5 miles to a confluence of streams at a spot known as Swiss Camp. A half-mile beyond Swiss Camp, your trail junctions with a fire road, which leads to the historic Tin House (it was constructed by Lathrop Brown in 1944 out of tin from two old gas stations), 3.2 miles from the trailhead. Follow the fire road steeply downhill, enjoying fantastic coastal views all the way (hiking poles are handy for this steep descent). The dirt road ends at Highway 1, and you'll need to walk alongside the highway for a mile to get back to your car (head north, or to your right).

User Groups: Hikers only. No dogs, horses, or mountain bikes. No wheelchair facilities.

Permits: No permits are required. Parking and access are free.

Maps: A map of Julia Pfeiffer Burns State Park is available at the entrance kiosk (2.2 miles south of this trailhead) or by free download at www.parks.ca.gov. For a topographic map, go to the USGS website to download Partington Ridge.

Directions: From Carmel, drive 34 miles south on Highway 1 to a dirt pullout along the highway and the trailheads for the Partington Point and Tanbark Trails. The trailheads are 10.5 miles south of Big Sur and 2.2 miles north of the main entrance to Julia Pfeiffer Burns State Park. Partington Point Trail is on the west side of the highway; Tanbark Trail is on the east side.

Contact: Julia Pfeiffer Burns State Park, Big Sur, 831/667-2315 or 831/649-2836, www.parks.ca.gov.

33 MCWAY FALLS OVERLOOK

0.5 mi/0.5 hr 1 9

in Julia Pfeiffer Burns State Park south of Big Sur

Map 8.1, page 439 BEST

After Yosemite Falls and Bridalveil Fall, McWay Falls is probably the waterfall that appears most often on family snapshots of California vacations. Although few know its name, its image is unforgettable: an 80-foot waterfall leaping off a rugged ocean bluff and pouring gracefully into the Pacific. The walk to the waterfall's overlook is on a paved trail that leads through a tunnel underneath Highway 1 and comes out to a spectacular overlook of McWay Cove. A bench is placed along the trail, and you can sit

McWay Falls

there and admire the action—and maybe even catch sight of a passing gray whale. A few hundred feet beyond the bench, the trail ends at the ruins of Waterfall House, the home of Lathrop and Helen Hooper Brown in the 1940s. There's not much left of it now, but at one time, it was quite a place.

User Groups: Hikers only. No dogs, horses, or mountain bikes. The McWay Falls Overlook Trail is wheelchair-accessible via a special bridge that bypasses the stairs from the parking lot.

Permits: No permits are required. A $10 day-use fee is charged per vehicle.

Maps: A map of Julia Pfeiffer Burns State Park is available at the entrance kiosk or by free download at www.parks.ca.gov. For a topographic map, go to the USGS website to download Partington Ridge.

Directions: From Carmel, drive 37 miles south on Highway 1 to Julia Pfeiffer Burns State Park, located on the east side of the highway, 13 miles south of Big Sur. Drive through the entrance kiosk and park near the restrooms. The Overlook Trail starts on a series of wooden stairs across the pavement from the restrooms.

Contact: Julia Pfeiffer Burns State Park, Big Sur, 831/667-2315 or 831/649-2836, www.parks.ca.gov.

34 PINE VALLEY

10.6-13.0 mi/6.0 hr or 2 days 3 10

in the Ventana Wilderness near Carmel Valley

Map 8.1, page 439

The Pine Valley hike is a great one-night backpacking trip or long day hike into the Ventana Wilderness and can easily be extended into a 13-mile loop. The hike begins on the northern end of Pine Ridge Trail at China Campground, following an up-and-down course that soon becomes more down than up. At 3.5 miles, you turn right on Carmel River Trail and descend some more to the headwaters of the Carmel River and the beginning of a fir and ponderosa pine forest. Pine Valley Camp is 5.3 miles from the trailhead, set in lush Pine Valley, a spacious high meadow lined with ferns, ponderosa pines, and rocky sandstone formations. A short side-trip to Pine Falls is possible from the camp; follow a well-worn route downstream along the river for 0.5 mile to the waterfall. From there, you can retrace your steps to the trailhead for a 10.6-mile round-trip, or make camp at Pine Valley, or take the trail from the upper end of camp, which meets up with Pine Ridge Trail. Turn left on Pine Ridge Trail and hike back to the trailhead to complete a 13-mile loop.

User Groups: Hikers, dogs, and horses. No mountain bikes. No wheelchair facilities.

Permits: A California campfire permit is required year-round for overnight stays whether you are using a camp stove or building a fire; permits are free and available online at www.fs.usda.gov/lpnf or in person at the King City Forest Service office or the Big Sur Visitors Center.

Maps: A Ventana Wilderness or Los Padres National Forest map is available from the U.S. Forest Service. For a topographic map, go to the USGS website to download Chews Ridge.

Directions: From Greenfield on U.S. 101, take the G-16/Monterey County Road exit and drive west for 29 miles. Turn south on Tassajara Road and drive 1.3 miles to Cachagua Road. Turn left and drive nine miles to the trailhead, located just past the turnoff for China Campground. High-clearance vehicles are recommended. The county sometimes closes the road during bad weather; call the Monterey Ranger District before traveling.

Contact: Los Padres National Forest, Monterey Ranger District, King City, 831/385-5434, www.fs.usda.gov/lpnf.

35 LIMEKILN TRAIL AND LIMEKILN FALLS

1.8 mi/1.0 hr 2 10

in Limekiln State Park south of Big Sur

Map 8.1, page 439

Limekiln State Park is so far south of Big Sur that it doesn't get inundated by as many visitors as Pfeiffer Big Sur and Julia Pfeiffer Burns State Parks do. The Limekiln Trail leads from the inland campground into Hare Canyon's gorgeous redwood forest. It follows Limekiln Creek for a half-mile to the park's namesake limekilns, which were used to make limestone bricks and cement in the 1880s. The four kilns look like giant smokestacks with mossy, brick bottoms; they're interesting to see and photograph, but in the wet season, they are not the biggest attraction on this trail. What is? A fork off the main trail leads to Limekiln Falls, a spectacular 100-foot waterfall that drops over a limestone face. When the water is running with vigor, you'll probably end up with wet feet as you boulder-hop your way to its base—but it's worth it. This waterfall is a beauty.

If you find yourself enchanted by the lands of this state park and want to hike farther, consider following the Alvin Trail to Twitchell Flats, a fork off the Limekiln Trail. This trail quickly leaves the redwoods behind and travels uphill through coastal grasslands, finally reaching the Twitchell Jeep Trail and an 1880s homestead site where you can see the remains of a foundation, hearth, and cistern. The ocean views on this trail make all the climbing worth it. Some hikers use this trail to access Stony Ridge and the summit of Cone Peak—an arduous trek but worth it for the views.

User Groups: Hikers only. No dogs, horses, or mountain bikes. No wheelchair facilities.

Permits: No permits are required. An $8 day-use fee is charged per vehicle.

Maps: A map of Limekiln State Park is available at the entrance kiosk or by free download at www.parks.ca.gov. For a topographic map, go to the USGS website to download Lopez Point.

Directions: From Carmel, drive 52 miles south on Highway 1 to Limekiln State Park, on the east side of the highway. It's 2.5 miles south of Lucia and 14.8 miles south of Julia Pfeiffer Burns State Park. The trailhead is at the far side of the inland campground.

Contact: Limekiln State Park, Big Sur, 831/667-2315 or 831/667-2403, www.parks.ca.gov.

36 CONE PEAK LOOKOUT TRAIL

4.8 mi/2.5 hr 3 10

in the Ventana Wilderness north of Lucia

Map 8.1, page 439

The 2.4-mile climb to Cone Peak is a classic Ventana Wilderness adventure, and the fun begins with the drive to the trailhead. But check your calendar before you go: Cone Peak Road is often closed during the rainy season (Nov.-Mar.), so time your trip for late spring to early fall. As your car chugs its way uphill from the coast, first you gain wide Pacific views, then views of the inland mountain ranges. But those are nothing compared to the views you get at the fire lookout on Cone Peak's summit, at 5,155 feet above sea level. This is the second highest mountain in the Santa Lucia Range (after 5,862-foot Junipero Serra Peak, also known as "Pinkolam" and much harder to hike), but what makes this summit really special is the fact that it is only three miles from the ocean. The average gradient from sea level to the summit is about 30 percent, which creates an extremely dramatic, high-contrast view. The short hike from the trailhead to the summit is a steep climb, and the last mile feels like it goes straight up (total elevation gain is 1,400 feet). Make sure you have plenty of water with you, and in the spring months, bring along a wildflower identification book. These slopes are littered with penstemon, poppies, sticky monkeyflower, paintbrush, and many other colorful blooms. After zig-zagging upward through a mix of low chapparal, hardwoods, and then conifers (mostly Coulter pines), you reach a trail junction at 1.9 miles. Go east (right) and walk the final half-mile to the fire lookout. In this last stretch, the trail is literally cut into the rock. At the top you'll find the historic lookout tower, built in 1923, as well as an eye-popping vista. You can see as far as 100 miles on clear days, and if the fog has burned off, you can look down the west side of Cone Peak for almost a vertical mile to the ocean. Be sure to pack along a good map, so you can name all the peaks and valleys in the 360-degree panorama that surrounds you.

User Groups: Hikers, dogs, and horses. No mountain bikes. No wheelchair facilities.

Permits: No permits are required. Parking and access are free.

Maps: A Ventana Wilderness or Los Padres National Forest map is available from the U.S. Forest Service. For a topographic map, go to the USGS website to download Cone Peak.

Directions: From Big Sur, drive 27 miles south on Highway 1 to Kirk Creek Campground, on the west side of the highway, and the left turnoff for Nacimiento-Fergusson Road, on the east side of the highway. Turn left and drive 7.2 miles, then turn left on the dirt Coast Ridge Road (sometimes called Cone Peak Road) and drive 5.5 miles to the trailhead on the left (do not follow the road to its end). Park off the road; there is space for about six cars. A high-clearance vehicle is recommended, although not always necessary. Note: Coast Ridge Road/Cone Peak Road is often closed during the rainy season (Nov.-Mar.).

Contact: Los Padres National Forest, Monterey Ranger District, King City, 831/385-5434, www.fs.usda.gov/lpnf.

SAN JOAQUIN VALLEY

The San Joaquin Valley is best known for its agricultural bounty, not its wilderness. But the region's few untouched natural areas offer a unique look into the Golden State's past, when vast open plains and untamed waterways comprised a huge part of central California. An extensive wetland ecosystem is preserved at Los Banos Wildlife Area and the San Luis National Wildlife Refuge complex, creating a paradise for birdwatchers. Carrizo Plain National Monument is considered California's largest nature preserve, containing thousands of acres of grassland prairie. Wildflowers carpet the grasslands in early spring, sandhill cranes visit in winter, and pronghorn and tule elk roam year-round. In the San Joaquin Valley, a pair of binoculars and a sense of wonder are as necessary as hiking boots.

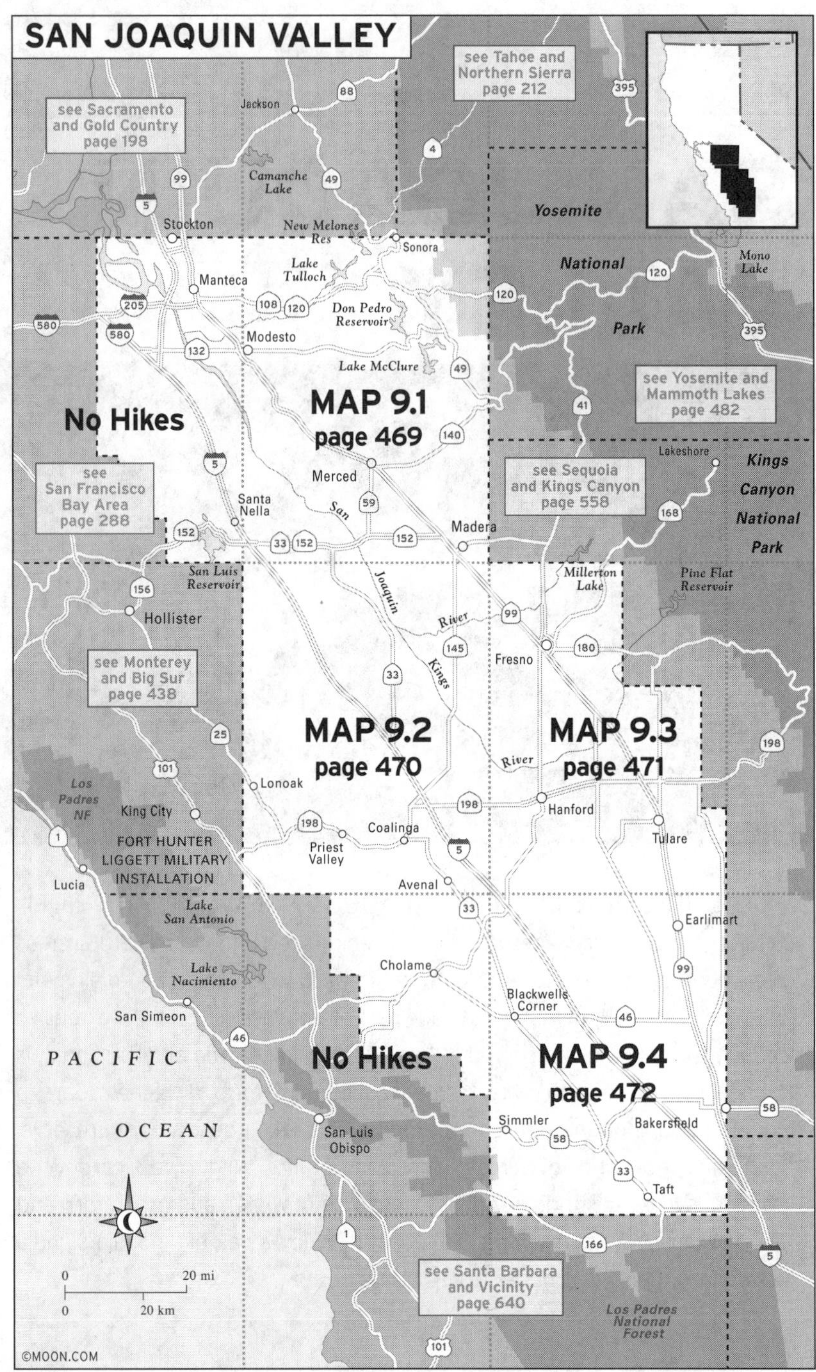
SAN JOAQUIN VALLEY
see Tahoe and Northern Sierra page 212
see Sacramento and Gold Country page 198
Jackson
Camanche Lake
Stockton
New Melones Res
Sonora
Yosemite
National
Park
Mono Lake
Lake Tulloch
Manteca
Don Pedro Reservoir
Modesto
Lake McClure
MAP 9.1
page 469
No Hikes
see Yosemite and Mammoth Lakes page 482
see San Francisco Bay Area page 288
Merced
Santa Nella
San
Madera
see Sequoia and Kings Canyon page 558
Lakeshore
Kings
Canyon
National
Park
San Luis Reservoir
Millerton Lake
Pine Flat Reservoir
Hollister
Joaquin
River
Fresno
see Monterey and Big Sur page 438
Kings
MAP 9.2
page 470
MAP 9.3
page 471
River
Los Padres NF
Lonoak
King City
Hanford
FORT HUNTER LIGGETT MILITARY INSTALLATION
Coalinga
Priest Valley
Tulare
Lucia
Avenal
Lake San Antonio
Earlimart
Lake Nacimiento
Cholame
Blackwells Corner
San Simeon
PACIFIC
OCEAN
No Hikes
MAP 9.4
page 472
San Luis Obispo
Simmler
Bakersfield
Taft
see Santa Barbara and Vicinity page 640
Los Padres National Forest
0 20 mi
0 20 km
©MOON.COM

Map 9.1

Sites 1-7
Pages 473-477

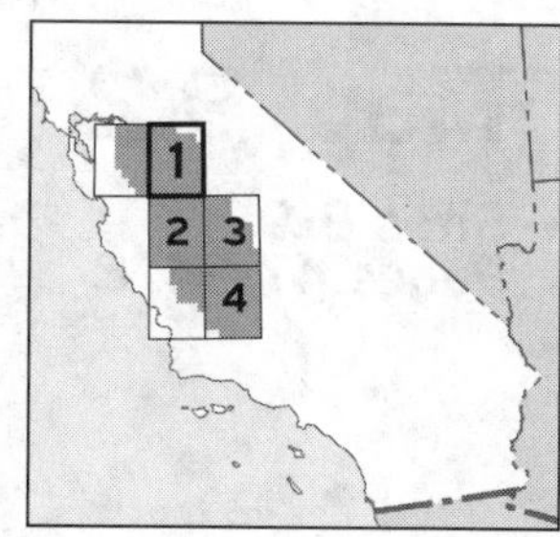

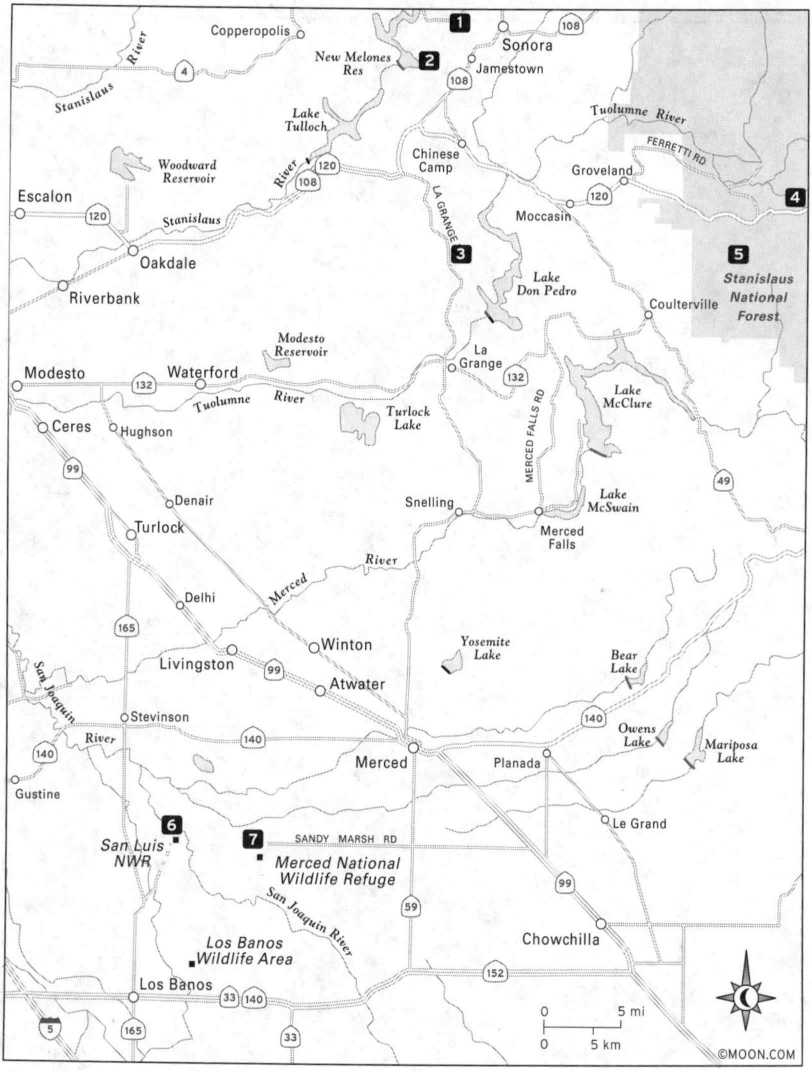

Copperopolis
New Melones Res
Sonora
Jamestown
Stanislaus River
Lake Tulloch
Tuolumne River
Woodward Reservoir
Chinese Camp
Ferretti Rd
Groveland
Escalon
La Grange
Moccasin
Oakdale
Riverbank
Lake Don Pedro
Coulterville
Stanislaus National Forest
Modesto Reservoir
Modesto
Waterford
Tuolumne River
Turlock Lake
Lake McClure
Ceres
Hughson
Merced Falls Rd
Denair
Turlock
Snelling
Lake McSwain
Merced Falls
Merced River
Delhi
Yosemite Lake
Winton
Livingston
Atwater
Bear Lake
San Joaquin River
Stevinson
Owens Lake
Mariposa Lake
Merced
Planada
Gustine
Le Grand
San Luis NWR
Sandy Marsh Rd
Merced National Wildlife Refuge
San Joaquin River
Chowchilla
Los Banos Wildlife Area
Los Banos
0 5 mi
0 5 km

Map 9.2

Sites 8-9
Pages 477-478

9.1
9.3

1
2
3
4

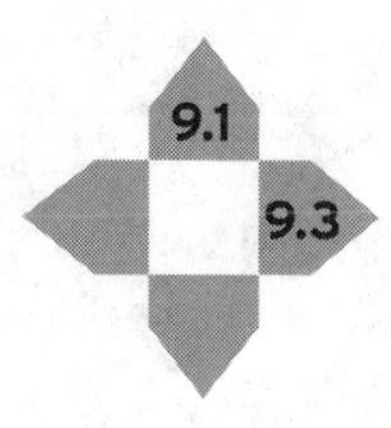

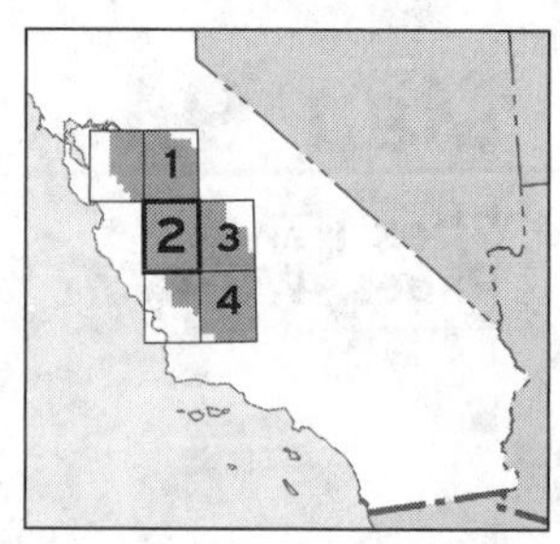

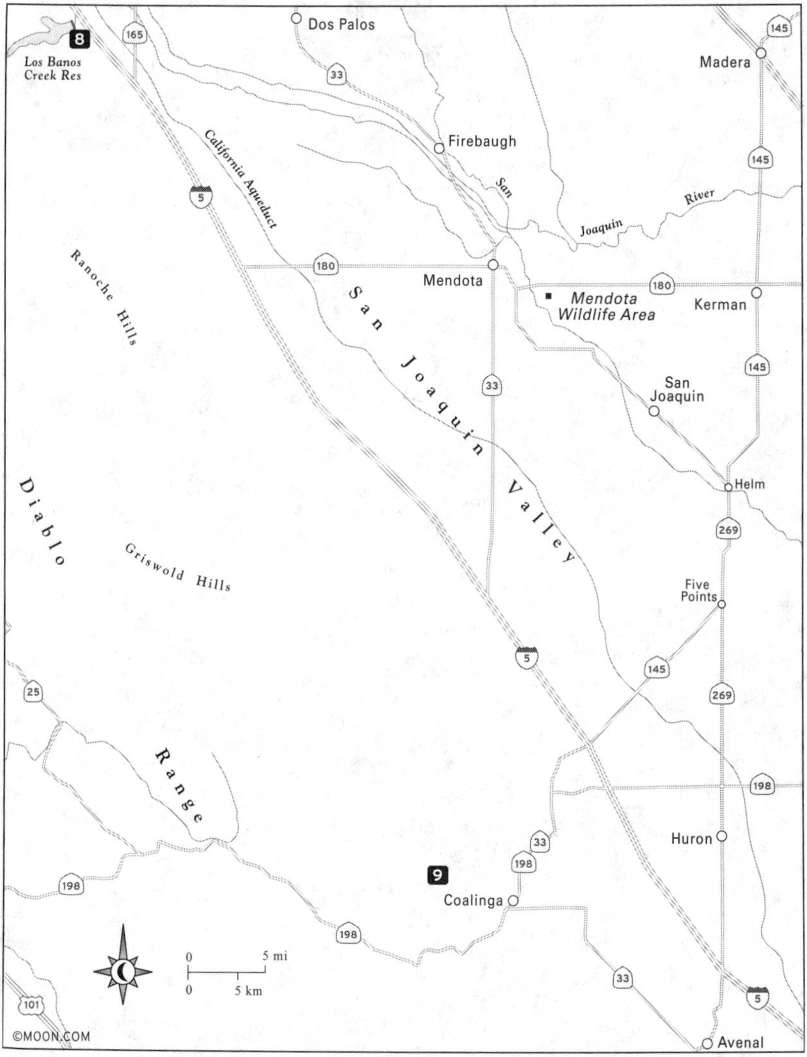

8
Los Banos Creek Res
165
Dos Palos
33
145
Madera
Firebaugh
California Aqueduct
5
San
Joaquin
River
145
Ranoche Hills
180
Mendota
180
Mendota Wildlife Area
Kerman
San Joaquin Valley
145
33
San Joaquin
Helm
Diablo
269
Griswold Hills
Five Points
5
145
25
269
Range
198
33
Huron
198
9
198
Coalinga
198
0
5 mi
0
5 km
33
101
5
Avenal
©MOON.COM

Map 9.3

Sites 10-11
Pages 478-479

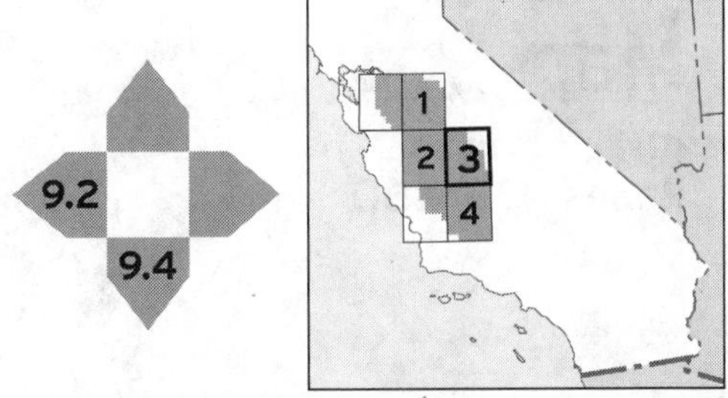

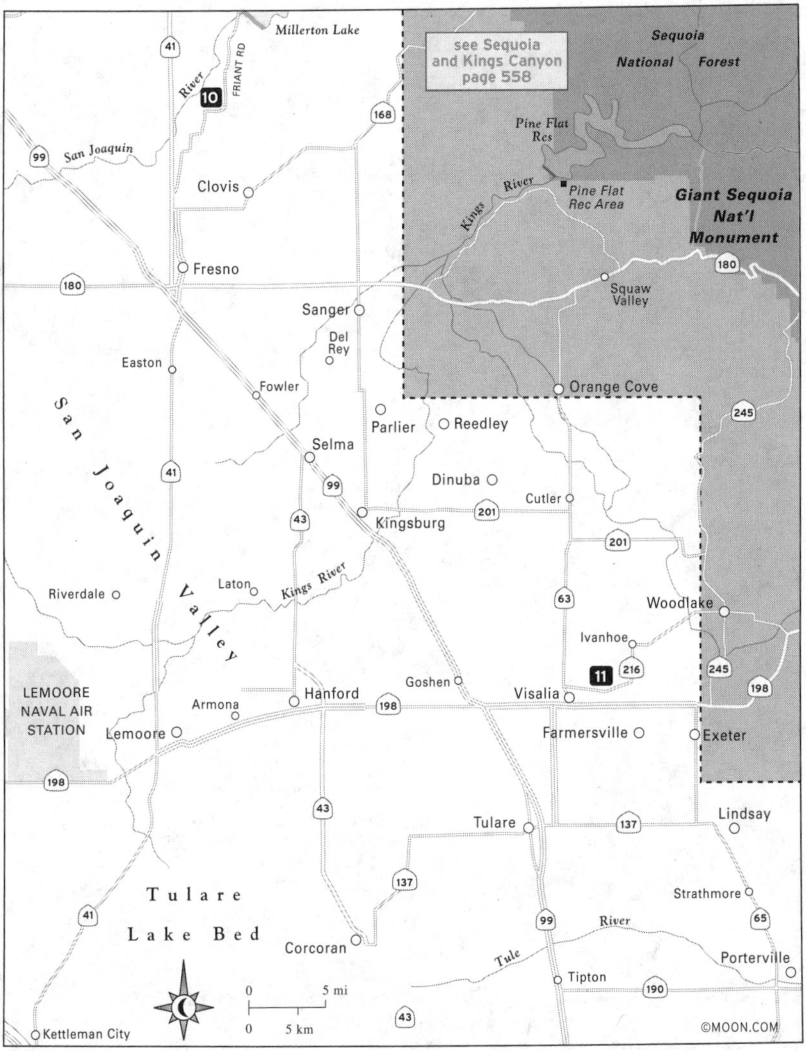

Millerton Lake
FRIANT RD
River
10
41
168
99
San Joaquin
Clovis
Fresno
180
see Sequoia and Kings Canyon page 558
Sequoia National Forest
Pine Flat Res
Kings River
Pine Flat Rec Area
Giant Sequoia Nat'l Monument
180
Squaw Valley
Sanger
Del Rey
Easton
Fowler
Orange Cove
San Joaquin Valley
Parlier
Reedley
245
Selma
41
99
Dinuba
Cutler
201
43
Kingsburg
201
Laton
Kings River
Riverdale
63
Woodlake
Ivanhoe
216
11
245
198
LEMOORE NAVAL AIR STATION
Goshen
Hanford
Armona
198
Visalia
Lemoore
Farmersville
Exeter
198
43
Tulare
137
Lindsay
137
Tulare Lake Bed
Strathmore
41
99
River
65
Corcoran
Tule
Porterville
Tipton
190
0 5 mi
0 5 km
43
Kettleman City
©MOON.COM

Map 9.4

Sites 12-13
Pages 479-480

9.3

1
2
3
4

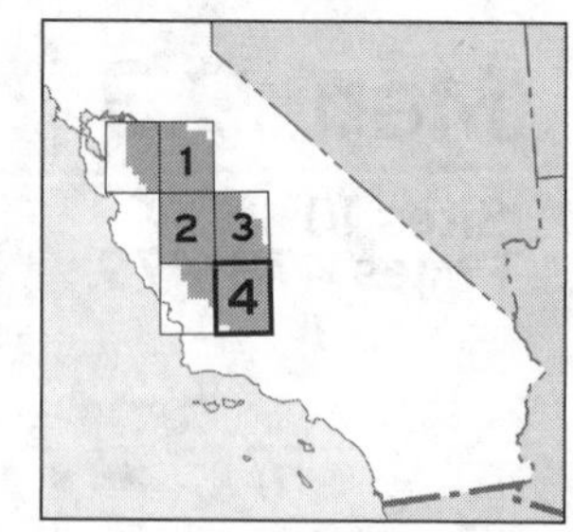

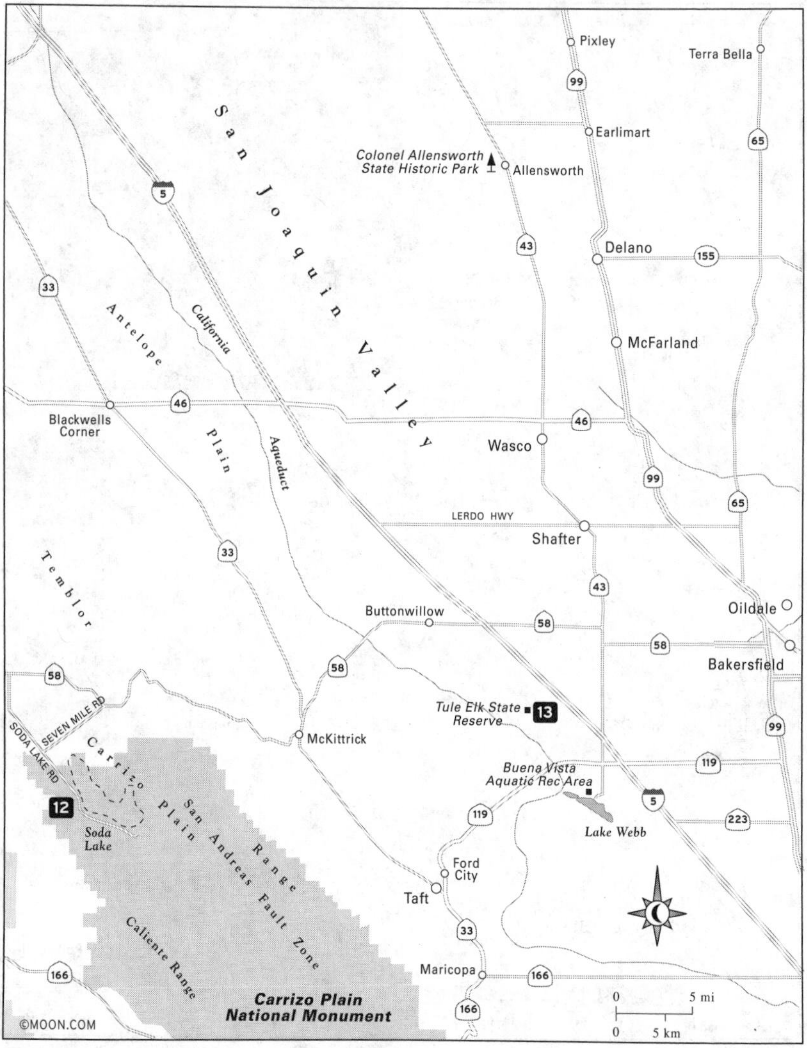

Pixley
Terra Bella
99
Earlimart
65
San Joaquin Valley
Colonel Allensworth State Historic Park
Allensworth
5
43
Delano
155
33
Antelope Plain
California Aqueduct
McFarland
Blackwells Corner
46
46
Wasco
99
65
LERDO HWY
Shafter
33
Temblor
43
Buttonwillow
58
Oildale
58
Bakersfield
58
58
Tule Elk State Reserve
13
SEVEN MILE RD
SODA LAKE RD
McKittrick
99
Carrizo Plain
Buena Vista Aquatic Rec Area
119
12
119
5
223
Soda Lake
San Andreas Fault Zone
Range
Lake Webb
Ford City
Taft
Caliente Range
33
Maricopa
166
166
166
Carrizo Plain National Monument
©MOON.COM
0
5 mi
0
5 km

1 NATURAL BRIDGES

1.4 mi/1.0 hr 

at New Melones Reservoir near Sonora

Map 9.1, page 469

This short, easy trail leads from Parrotts Ferry Road to Natural Bridges, a unique series of limestone caves with Coyote Creek running through them. This geologic wonder is only a short drive from downtown Sonora, but it's like nothing else around this Gold Rush town. The upper Natural Bridge is 270 feet high, and the clear water underneath it creates a popular locals' swimming hole. Because Coyote Creek is spring-fed, the water is cool year-round. Most swimmers bring inner tubes with them so they can float through the cave. The rocky trail that accesses the upper bridge has a 300-foot elevation gain, but is easily accomplished by children and adults alike. Because it takes thousands of years to create the cave's fragile formations, visitors are asked not to touch them. The oil on human hands can stop the formations from growing. A second bridge lies downstream from the upper bridge, accessible by a rough, unmaintained trail. If you are willing to walk the extra 0.5 mile to the lower bridge, you have a greater chance of solitude.

User Groups: Hikers only. No dogs, horses, or mountain bikes. No wheelchair facilities.

Permits: No permits are required. Parking and access are free.

Maps: A free map is available at the New Melones Visitors Center or by download at www.usbr.gov. For a topographic map, go to the USGS website to download Sonora.

Directions: From Highway 49 in Sonora, take the turnoff for Parrotts Ferry Road (signed for Columbia State Historic Park). Drive north on Parrotts Ferry Road for about seven miles, crossing the bridge over New Melones Reservoir, to the trailhead on the left side of the road (1.2 miles north of the highway bridge and four miles south of the Hwy. 4 junction).

Contact: New Melones Reservoir Visitors Center, Sonora, 209/536-9543 or 209/536-9094, www.usbr.gov.

2 TABLE MOUNTAIN

3.0 mi/1.5 hr 

at New Melones Reservoir near Jamestown

Map 9.1, page 469

Wildflower lovers, this is your trail. The only trick is timing your visit for the exact period when Table Mountain is at its most colorful splendor. Of course, the timing of the bloom varies from year to year, so your best bet is to call the New Melones Visitors Center starting in late February to see how the flowers are coming along. When they say "go time," don't wait too long. Some years the bloom is over by late April, although Table Mountain's high vistas are there for the taking at any time of year. From the pavement's end at the yellow gate, the trail crosses through a grassy oak woodland dotted with basalt (volcanic) rocks. Straight ahead is Table Mountain, a 2,200-foot-high, 1,200-foot-wide, flat-topped plateau that juts upward from the surrounding lowlands. The plateau was formed by a lava flow about 10 million years ago, when a volcano erupted east of Sonora Pass. Its volcanic soil creates ideal conditions for vernal pools in February and March (look for fairy shrimp in the pools) and a colorful array of grassland wildflowers in April and May, including lupine, Indian paintbrush, blue dicks, and goldfields. Although this trail's distance is short, the last 0.5 mile is slow-going because it requires a modicum of scrambling over rough volcanic rock. Be sure to wear sturdy boots or shoes.

User Groups: Hikers, dogs, horses, and mountain bikes. No wheelchair facilities.

Permits: No permits are required. Parking and access are free.

Maps: A free map is available at the New Melones Visitors Center or by download at www.usbr.gov. For a topographic map, go to the USGS website to download Sonora.

Directions: From Highway 49 in Sonora, drive south for three miles to Jamestown, then turn right (north) on Rawhide Road. Drive two miles and turn left on Shell Road; follow Shell Road 1.8 miles (take the left fork) to the pavement's end at a yellow gate across the road. The trail begins to the right of the gate. (You can choose to continue driving past the yellow gate for another mile on a dirt road, but a high-clearance vehicle may be necessary. This will shorten your hike considerably.)

Contact: New Melones Reservoir Visitors Center, Sonora, 209/536-9543 or 209/536-9094, www.usbr.gov.

3 RED HILLS

5.0 mi/2.5 hr

near Chinese Camp and La Grange

Map 9.1, page 469

Flower aficionados, check your calendar. Is it late March to early May? Then head for the Red Hills Area of Critical Environmental Concern, the very long name for 11 square miles of gray-pine-studded Bureau of Land Management (BLM) land in the Sierra foothills. This is not a place you would ever want to visit in the heat of summer, but in early spring, the rocky landscape comes alive with color from coreopsis, five-spots, bird's-eye gilia, fiddlenecks, goldfields, poppies, and other native wildflowers. The serpentine soil here supports a wide variety of plants, including seven that are rare and/or endangered. Keep an eye out for California verbena, which grows here and nowhere else in the world. It can be found near the stream that parallels Red Hills Road. Numerous loop hikes are possible in the preserve; a good starter hike is to set off on Soaproot Ridge Trail, then bear left and walk Overlook Loop to Verbena Loop. From there you can walk back to your car on Red Hills Road, or cross the road and walk back most of the way on Red Hills Trail, which parallels the road. As you hike, keep scanning the sky for bald eagles, which are fond of this area because of its proximity to huge Don Pedro Reservoir.

User Groups: Hikers, dogs, horses, and mountain bikes. No wheelchair facilities.

Permits: No permits are required. Parking and access are free.

Maps: A free trail map can be downloaded at www.blm.gov/ca. For a topographic map, go to the USGS website to download Chinese Camp.

Directions: From Sonora, take Highway 49 south for 15 miles to Chinese Camp. Turn right (south) on Red Hills Road and drive one mile to the trailhead parking on the left.

Or, from Oakdale, drive east on Highway 108/120 for about 20 miles. Turn right on La Grange Road. Drive 1.5 miles and turn left on Red Hills Road. Drive 0.75 mile to the trailhead parking lot on the right side of the road.

Contact: Bureau of Land Management Mother Lode Field Office, El Dorado Hills, 916/941-3101, www.blm.gov/ca.

4 RAINBOW POOL AND CONFLUENCE TRAIL

2.5 mi/1.5 hr

in Stanislaus National Forest near Groveland

Map 9.1, page 469

While everybody else is hanging out at Rainbow Pool, a popular swimming hole and waterfall right off Highway 120, you can leave the thronging crowds behind by taking this short but steep hike to the confluence of the South Fork and Middle Fork of the Tuolumne River. Rainbow Pool is located on the south side of Highway 120, but you'll park your car and start hiking on the north side, heading steeply downhill on an old dirt road known as the Confluence Trail, which parallels the cascading South Fork as it tumbles down a dramatic, rocky gorge. In the springtime, when the powerful Tuolumne is frothing with excess snowmelt, this canyon can really roar with noise. The watery extravaganza reaches a deafening crescendo at the canyon bottom, where the two forks of the river merge. This was once the site of the South Fork Tunnel Camp, one of the major construction sites for the Hetch Hetchy Reservoir system. The old road you are walking on was used to haul men and building materials back and forth to the camp. Where the road ends at a particularly scenic point in the narrow gorge, just retrace your steps back uphill. After a hot, sweaty ascent back to your car, you might just want to walk (or drive) over to Rainbow Pool and take a dip in its always refreshing waters.

User Groups: Hikers, dogs, horses, and mountain bikes. No wheelchair facilities.

Permits: No permits are required. Parking and access are free.

Maps: A Stanislaus National Forest map is available from the U.S. Forest Service. For a topographic map, go to the USGS website to download Jawbone Ridge.

Directions: From Groveland, drive east on Highway 120 for 14 miles to the left turnoff for Cherry Lake Road. Turn left and then left again immediately. Drive about 100 yards and park in the dirt pullout just before the gate across the road. Walk past the gate and then turn right and follow the unsigned dirt road heading downhill.

Contact: Groveland Ranger District, Stanislaus National Forest, Groveland, 209/962-7825, www.fs.usda.gov/stanislaus.

5 DIANA FALLS AND POOLS

1.5 mi/0.5 hr 1 8

in Stanislaus National Forest near Greeley Hill

Map 9.1, page 469

You could think of it as a neighborhood backyard swimming hole, except there's no neighborhood anywhere nearby. Diana Falls is located not far from the towns of Groveland and Coulterville and within an hour's drive of Yosemite National Park. But it's not on the road to any of those places, so you won't come across it by accident. It's an out-of-the-way waterfall on Bean Creek, near its confluence with the North Fork Merced River. From the trailhead, hike along the west side of the river, following an old dirt road for 0.5 mile. Here the Merced River is a small, tame stream, with bunches of Indian rhubarb growing along its banks. The dirt road gets narrower as you walk. At a fork in the trail, bear right. You'll leave the river and hike along the Bean Creek canyon. In just a few minutes, or about 250 yards, you'll reach the brink of 20-foot-tall Diana Falls. Several spurs descend the slope to its base and to the many cool swimming holes that locals call Diana Pools. There may be no better place to spend a hot summer afternoon.

User Groups: Hikers, dogs, horses, and mountain bikes. No wheelchair facilities.

Permits: No permits are required. Parking and access are free.

Maps: A Stanislaus National Forest map is available from the U.S. Forest Service. For a topographic map, go to the USGS website to download Groveland.

Directions: From Groveland, drive east on Highway 120 for seven miles to the right turnoff for Smith Station Road (also signed as County Road J132 to Coulterville). Turn right and drive 5.7 miles, then turn sharply left on Greeley Hill Road. Drive 4.2 miles to the trailhead, just before a one-lane bridge. The trail begins on the right at the gated dirt road signed as "Road Closed."

Contact: Groveland Ranger District, Stanislaus National Forest, Groveland, 209/962-7825, www.fs.usda.gov/stanislaus.

6 CHESTER, SOUSA, AND WINTON MARSH TRAILS

4.0 mi/2.0 hr 1 8

in the San Luis National Wildlife Refuge north of Los Banos

Map 9.1, page 469 BEST

The San Luis National Wildlife Refuge offers two main driving tours: the Tule Elk Auto Tour

Loop and the Waterfowl Auto Tour Loop, and both are great opportunities for visitors to see wildlife. But if you want to get out of your car and on to your feet for a while, check out the three short hiking trails located off the 8.5-mile Waterfowl Auto Tour Loop. Walk all three, and you can easily chalk up about four miles of exercise. The trails lead to three different marsh areas, each with its own character.

As you drive the auto route, the first trailhead you reach is for the Chester Marsh Trail. It's open for hiking only from February to September; from October to January, it is part of the refuge's hunting area. It's a one-mile loop, and you can pick up an interpretive brochure at the trailhead. After your walk, get back in your car and continue driving along the Waterfowl Auto Tour Route until you reach the trailhead for the Sousa Marsh. This area consists of an inner and outer loop trail through a canopy of riparian trees. The longest trail (1.2 miles) goes to the Sousa observation platform, with its telescope and benches. The 0.7-mile Winton Marsh Trail, located just beyond the Sousa Marsh parking lot, also leads to an observation platform and several benches situated slightly above the marsh, so you can pull out your binoculars and peer at the feathered fowl below. What will you see? The usual cabal: ducks, geese, moorhens, coots, pheasants, snipe, hawks, owls, egrets, herons, and even some rare types, like the endangered tricolored blackbird. In case you haven't gotten the idea yet, this place is crawling with wildlife. Even while just driving around, we saw a coyote and about a zillion bunnies, in addition to numerous Swainson's hawks.

User Groups: Hikers and dogs. No horses or mountain bikes. No wheelchair facilities.

Permits: No permits are required. Parking and access are free.

Maps: A free map is available at the refuge visitors center. For a topographic map, go to the USGS website to download Los Banos.

Directions: From Los Banos on Highway 152/33, drive north on Highway 165 (Mercey Springs Road) for 6.4 miles to Wolfsen Road. Bear right and follow Wolfsen Road for 2.5 miles into the National Wildlife Refuge. Follow the signs for the Waterfowl Auto Tour Loop.

Contact: San Luis National Wildlife Refuge, Los Banos, 209/826-3508, www.fws.gov/refuge/san_luis.

7 MEADOWLARK TRAIL

1.5 mi/1.0 hr

in the Merced National Wildlife Refuge southwest of Merced

Map 9.1, page 469

It doesn't seem like a 1.5-mile loop trail could offer much in the way of a pay-off, but you may be surprised by the rewards on the Meadowlark Trail. First off, it's one of only two places in the Merced National Wildlife Refuge where you're allowed to get out of your car and walk. Walking is prohibited in most of the preserve in order to reduce the disturbance to the thousands of geese and cranes that winter here. Driving your car along the Auto Tour Route is okay, though; it turns out that birds aren't bothered much by cars. The Meadowlark Trail gives you a chance to stretch your legs within the wildlife refuge, which serves as a precious island of wildlife habitat in the midst of Merced's vast agricultural fields. A thicket of tules, cattails, and willows in the refuge provides heavy cover for birds—particularly raptors, wintering shorebirds, and waterfowl. Because morning fog is common here in the winter months, bird-watching is often better at midday, when you may see concentrations of snow geese and Ross's geese. Magnificent sandhill cranes also make an appearance in winter. The rest of the year, you're more likely to see a variety of raptors. Barn owls are particularly common—one visitor saw 14 of them while walking this short loop. Great horned owls and a variety of hawks are also frequently sighted.

User Groups: Hikers and dogs. No horses or mountain bikes. No wheelchair facilities.

Permits: No permits are required. Parking and access are free.
Maps: A free map is available at the San Luis National Wildlife Refuge headquarters. For a topographic map, go to the USGS website to download Los Banos.
Directions: From Merced, take Highway 59 south for eight miles. Turn west on Sandy Mush Road and drive eight miles to the refuge entrance.
Contact: San Luis National Wildlife Refuge, Los Banos, 209/826-3508, www.fws.gov/refuge/merced.

8 PATH OF THE PADRES

5.0 mi/8.0 hr 2 8

on Los Banos Creek, in San Luis Reservoir State Recreation Area

Map 9.2, page 470 BEST

You have to plan way in advance to take this unusual hike at Los Banos Creek Reservoir. That's because the only way to go is in the company of a guide and via boat to the trailhead, and guided trips are offered only on weekends in March and early April. The trip has become so popular that it usually sells out as soon as reservations are available, which is typically February 1 each year. Although the hike itself is only five miles, the trip is an all-day affair, so don't forget to bring plenty of water, snacks, and lunch. It begins at 8am with a boat ride down the long and narrow reservoir, which is set in a steep-walled canyon and is popular for fishing. At the reservoir's far end, everyone gets off the boat and hikes 2.5 miles up the narrow canyon of Los Banos Creek, where old-growth sycamore groves and a cornucopia of spring wildflowers may be seen. Sturdy shoes are a must as the trail is rocky in places. As you walk, your guide will teach you about how the native Yokut Indians used the plants in this area, and you'll see bedrock mortars that they used for pounding acorns and natural medicines. Bird-watchers may thrill to see a peregrine falcon or other cliff-dwelling species. If the conditions are right, the hike may include an optional climb to the top of a knoll that offers panoramic views of the surrounding valleys and the Coast Range. So why is this trail called the Path of the Padres? Because the fathers at Mission San Juan Bautista traveled along the creek in the early 19th century to evangelize the Yokut Indians of the Central Valley. Along the way, they often bathed in the creek, which is why the town nearby is named "Los Banos."
User Groups: Hikers only. No dogs, horses, or mountain bikes. No wheelchair facilities.
Permits: Reservations are required; phone 209/826-1197 to reserve a space starting February 1. A $20 fee is charged for the reservation and guided tour (children must be at least 6 years old); the fee also covers your $8 per vehicle park entrance fee.
Maps: For a topographic map, go to the USGS website to download Los Banos Valley.
Directions: From I-5 at the junction with Highway 152 (south of Santa Nella), turn east on Highway 152 and drive 2.5 miles. Turn right (south) on Volta Road and drive one mile. Turn left (east) on Pioneer Road and drive 0.8 mile, then turn right on Canyon Road. Drive south on Canyon Road for five miles to Los Banos Creek Reservoir. (You will cross back to the west side of I-5.) Park near the boat ramp.
Contact: San Luis Reservoir State Recreation Area, Four Rivers Sector, Gustine, 209/826-1197, www.parks.ca.gov.

9 COALINGA MINERAL SPRINGS NATIONAL RECREATION TRAIL

4.8 mi/2.5 hr 2 8

northwest of Coalinga

Map 9.2, page 470

Most people don't realize that there's a National Recreation Trail out here near Coalinga, the town that was made famous by an earthquake, but it's true. In winter and spring, this is a first-class hike to the summit of Kreyenhagen Peak (elevation 3,558 feet), climbing through chaparral-covered hillsides. The trail begins at the far end of the picnic area and crosses a dry streambed, then begins to ascend. It's well graded all the way, with the second mile slightly steeper than the first. Plenty of switchbacks ease you through it. Views are good all the way up this 2.4-mile trail, but the impressive vista from the summit ridge includes the Diablo Range, the San Joaquin Valley, and miles of surrounding Bureau of Land Management (BLM) land. Considering how little effort is required to get here, it's quite a view. Have a seat on one of the rock outcrops and take it all in.

User Groups: Hikers, dogs, horses, and mountain bikes. No wheelchair facilities.

Permits: No permits are required. A $3 day-use fee is charged per vehicle.

Maps: Free trail maps are available at the trailhead. For a topographic map, go to the USGS website to download Curry Mountain.

Directions: From Coalinga, drive 20 miles west on Highway 198 to the Coalinga Mineral Springs County Park exit. Turn right (north) and drive four miles to Coalinga Mineral Springs County Park. Park in the main lot and walk to the far end of the park. The trail begins across the creek bed.

Contact: Bureau of Land Management, Hollister Field Office, Hollister, 831/630-5000, www.ca.blm.gov/hollister.

10 LEWIS S. EATON TRAIL

1.0-12.0 mi/0.5-5.5 hr 1 7

on the San Joaquin River near Fresno

Map 9.3, page 471

Woodward Park is the kind of city park that has a disc golf course, children's playgrounds, a dog park, and barbecue areas. But the park covers 300 acres, so there's more to explore. Check out the beautiful Japanese gardens, or bring your binoculars and look for interesting avian species by the lake in the park's southeast corner. If you want to get some exercise, the park is a convenient access point for the San Joaquin River Parkway, also called the Lewis S. Eaton Trail. When completed, the multiuse parkway will cover a 22-mile distance between Highway 99 and Friant Dam in Millerton Lake State Park. Currently six miles are finished, which means you can walk, jog, rollerblade, bike, or cruise in a wheelchair up to 12 miles round-trip on a paved trail that parallels the river and Friant Road for its entire distance. The good folks at the San Joaquin River Parkway and Conservation Trust are working hard to add to the current trail system; various loops and extensions from the paved trail are in the works. If you want to explore some of them, start with the River Access Trail, which branches off the Lewis S. Eaton Trail on the north side of Woodward Park. The trail meanders down to the riverbanks at the Jensen River Ranch.

User Groups: Hikers, dogs, horses, mountain bikes, and wheelchairs.

Permits: No permits are required. A $5 fee is charged per vehicle ($7 on holidays).

Maps: A park map is available at the entrance kiosk. For a topographic map, go to the USGS website to download Fresno North.

Directions: From Highway 41 heading north in Fresno, take the Friant Road exit. Turn left on Audubon Avenue and then turn right into Woodward Park.

Contact: Woodward Regional Park, Fresno, 559/621-2900, www.fresno.gov.

11 KAWEAH OAKS PRESERVE

2.0 mi/1.0 hr 1 7

east of Visalia

Map 9.3, page 471

The Kaweah Oaks Preserve is Tulare County's premier private nature preserve, a small remnant of what was once a vast valley oak forest. Groves of majestic oaks still stand, as well as wild grapevines growing as high as 30 feet.

Four easy hiking trails take you through a vast alkali meadow, valley oak riparian forests, sycamore woodlands, wild roses, valley elderberries, and swamp habitat. From the parking area, enter through the obvious gateway, which features maps and interpretive signage, and pick up a trail guide. Head west down the old ranch road to the picnic area on the left (less than a quarter-mile). Follow the ranch road west or north to hike the self-guided interpretive trails. Because this is a grazing area, leave all cattle gates the way you found them, whether open or closed, and keep Fido on his leash. As you stroll, listen for sounds of birdlife, and watch for herons, hawks, and owls, as well as the preserve's five species of woodpeckers. In addition to the diverse birdlife, you'll enjoy abundant native flora, including valley oak, California sycamores, cottonwoods, and willows growing near the streams. This is a good walk for late winter, spring, or fall. In the heat of summer, confine your visits to the early morning, when the valley is at its coolest. The preserve closes at dusk, so evening walks are not an option.

User Groups: Hikers and dogs. No horses or mountain bikes. No wheelchair facilities.

Permits: No permits are required. Parking and access are free.

Maps: For a topographic map, go to the USGS website to download Visalia. Trail guides are available at the trailhead for a $3 donation.

Directions: From Tulare on Highway 99, drive north for 10 miles and turn east on Highway 198. Drive 13 miles on Highway 198, passing through Visalia, and take the left turnoff for Road 182. Drive 0.5 mile north on Road 182 to the trailhead parking area on the left.

Contact: Sequoia Riverlands Trust, Visalia, 559/738-0211, www.sequoiariverlands.org.

12 CARRIZO PLAIN AND PAINTED ROCK

1.4 mi/1.0 hr 1 9

in Carrizo Plains National Monument, eastern San Luis Obispo County

Map 9.4, page 472 **BEST**

Carrizo Plain is California's largest remaining grassland ecosystem, a huge tract of wild land that is synonymous with abundant wildlife, spring wildflowers, and peace and quiet. It's often called "America's Serengeti." This national monument's far-flung location, a long drive from almost everywhere, keeps it uncrowded almost all year long, except for early spring, when conditions are right. For a few weeks every March and April, wildflowers fill the valley and cover the mountain slopes, attracting photographers and visitors from all over the country. These few weeks of spring are the only time you'll have much human company at Carrizo Plain.

Most visitors drive to the north end of the monument to see Soda Lake, a 3,000-acre expanse that comprises one of the largest remaining alkaline wetlands left in California. It's dry for most of the year, but during the wet season, it attracts migrating birds. Tule elk, pronghorn, coyotes, and other wildlife can also be seen in various areas of the monument.

Soda Lake and the surrounding grasslands are spectacular enough, but if you've driven all the way out here, you don't want to miss a visit to Painted Rock. The interior of this rounded sandstone amphitheater has some of the most significant Native American pictographs in the country. Although many have been vandalized, Painted Rock is still considered a very sacred place by Native Americans. You must obtain a permit in advance for either a self-guided or docent-led hike to the 55-foot-high rock formation, a 1.4-mile round-trip. While visiting, please respect the site by not touching the paintings or rock.

User Groups: Hikers only. No dogs, horses, or mountain bikes. No wheelchair facilities.

Permits: The monument is open year-round, but you must have a permit to visit Painted Rock. From July 16 to the end of February, you must obtain a self-guided hike permit and a gate access code. From mid-March to May 31, you can visit Painted Rock only on a guided tour. (From June 1 to July 15, Painted Rock is closed to visitors to protect nesting birds.) Permits and tour reservations can be obtained at www.recreation.gov or by phoning 877/444-6777. Parking and access are free.

Maps: Download a map and brochure of Carrizo Plain National Monument from the Bureau of Land Management (BLM). For a topographic map, go to the USGS website to download Painted Rock.

Directions: From San Luis Obispo on U.S. 101, drive north for 10 miles and take the Santa Margarita/Highway 58 exit. Drive east on Highway 58 for 50 miles to the Soda Lake Road turnoff. Turn right (south) and drive 13.5 miles to the Painted Rock Trail and Goodwin Education Center turnoff. Turn right and drive to the visitors center, then turn left and drive two miles to the Painted Rock trailhead.

Contact: Bureau of Land Management, Bakersfield Field Office, Bakersfield, 661/391-6000; Goodwin Education Center at Carrizo Plain (open Thurs.-Sun. Dec.-May, 9am-4pm), 805/475-2131, wwww.blm.gov.

13 TULE ELK STATE NATURAL RESERVE

0.25 mi/0.25 hr 1 8

off I-5 west of Bakersfield

Map 9.4, page 472 BEST

Most people just don't know that there's a herd of magnificent tule elk wandering around a few miles from I-5. If you didn't know, better pull off the highway and get yourself to the Tule Elk State Natural Reserve near Tupman. There aren't a lot of trails to choose from, and you won't do any extreme physical exertion here, but if you've been driving on I-5 long enough, just getting out of the car and stretching your legs is a big deal. The animals are most active in the late summer, when their rutting season begins. Bring binoculars for your best chance at a good view, or take a stroll to the walk-up platform, where you can look through a spotting scope at the elk. Make sure you stop in at the visitors center and check out the interesting displays on the elk and the history of the Central Valley. And if you happen to be in the area on the fourth Saturday of the month, show up at 11am for a ranger-led "auto safari" tour of the reserve. This is a great way for photographers to get awesome shots of tule elk.

User Groups: Hikers and dogs. No horses or mountain bikes. Some facilities are wheelchair-accessible.

Permits: No permits are required. An $8 day-use fee is charged per vehicle.

Maps: For a topographic map, go to the USGS website to download Tupman.

Directions: From the junction of I-5 and Highway 99 north of the Grapevine, drive north on I-5 for 33 miles to the Stockdale Highway exit. Drive west for 1.2 miles and turn left (south) on Morris Road. Drive 1.6 miles on Morris Road. The road turns right at Station Road. After 0.25 mile, turn left into the Tule Elk State Natural Reserve. The route is well signed.

Contact: Tule Elk State Natural Reserve, Buttonwillow, 661/764-6881, www.parks.ca.gov.

YOSEMITE AND MAMMOTH LAKES

Plunging waterfalls, stark granite, alpine lakes, pristine meadows, giant sequoias, and raging rivers—you'll find them all in this region, which encompasses not only Yosemite National Park but also Mammoth Lakes and the Eastern Sierra.

The centerpiece is Yosemite National Park, a must-see on every hiker's itinerary. Just beyond the park boundaries lie the Hoover, Ansel Adams, and John Muir wilderness areas. To the east of Yosemite, Mammoth Lakes and June Lake offer unusual diversity—volcanic craters, hot springs, lava flows, the saline waters of Mono Lake, and the geologic wonders of Devils Postpile National Monument. The prime season here is April through October, but the higher elevations are often accessible only from June to September. To avoid the crowds in hot spots like Yosemite Valley, travel in the offseason or on weekdays.

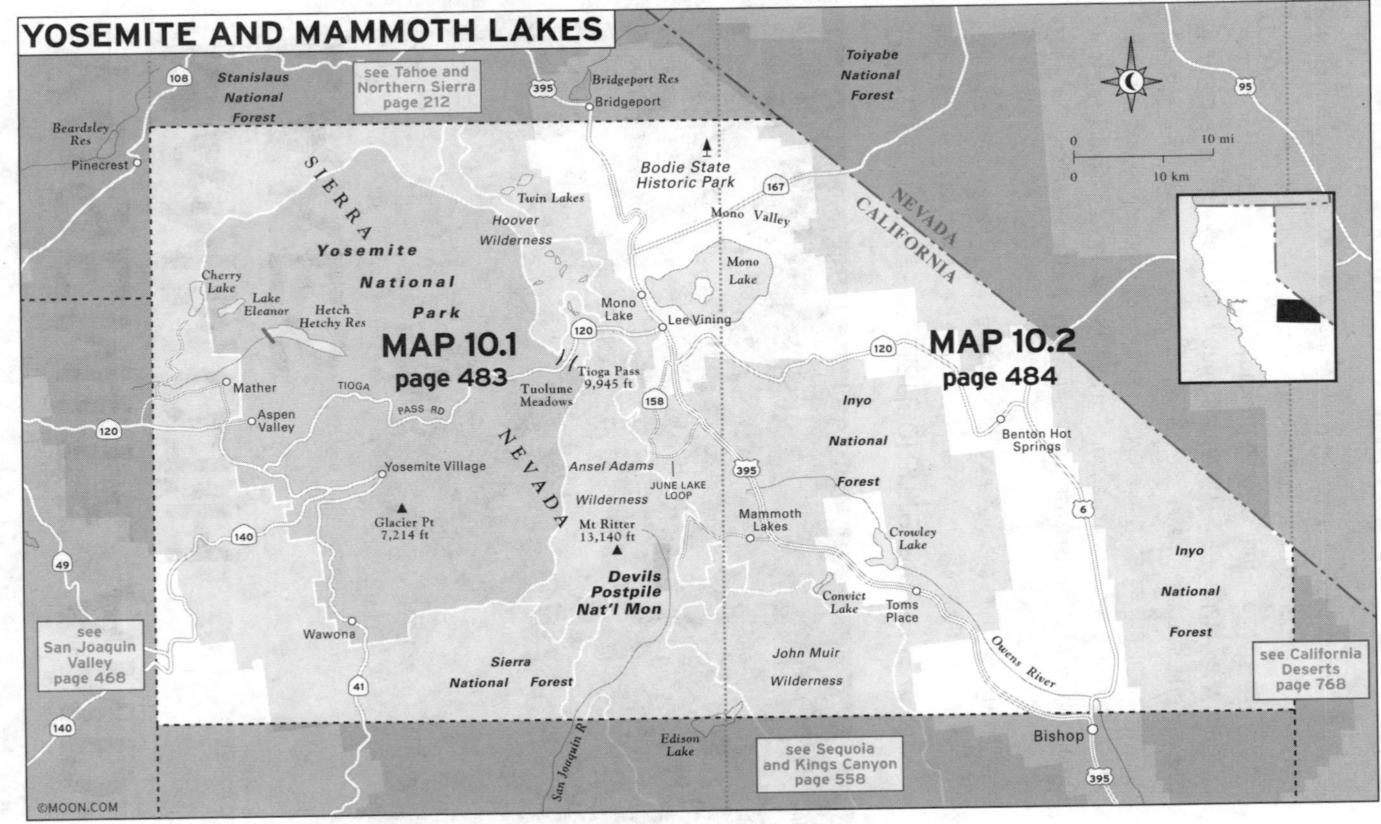

YOSEMITE AND MAMMOTH LAKES
Stanislaus National Forest
see Tahoe and Northern Sierra page 212
Bridgeport Res
Bridgeport
Toiyabe National Forest
Beardsley Res
Pinecrest
Bodie State Historic Park
SIERRA
NEVADA
Twin Lakes
Hoover Wilderness
Yosemite National Park
Mono Valley
Mono Lake
NEVADA
CALIFORNIA
Cherry Lake
Lake Eleanor
Hetch Hetchy Res
Mono Lake
Lee Vining
MAP 10.1 page 483
MAP 10.2 page 484
Mather
TIOGA PASS RD
Tioga Pass 9,945 ft
Tuolumne Meadows
Aspen Valley
Inyo National Forest
Benton Hot Springs
Yosemite Village
Ansel Adams Wilderness
JUNE LAKE LOOP
Glacier Pt 7,214 ft
Mt Ritter 13,140 ft
Mammoth Lakes
Crowley Lake
Devils Postpile Nat'l Mon
Convict Lake
Toms Place
Wawona
see San Joaquin Valley page 468
Sierra National Forest
John Muir Wilderness
Owens River
Inyo National Forest
see California Deserts page 768
Bishop
Edison Lake
San Joaquin R
see Sequoia and Kings Canyon page 558
0 10 mi
0 10 km
108
395
95
167
120
158
6
140
49
41
©MOON.COM

Map 10.1

Sites 1-92
Pages 485-551

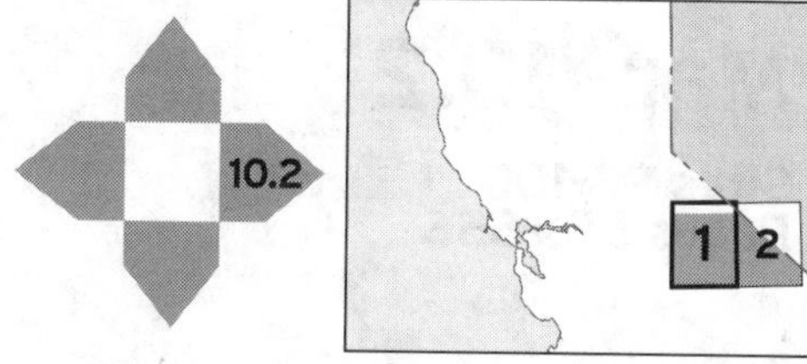

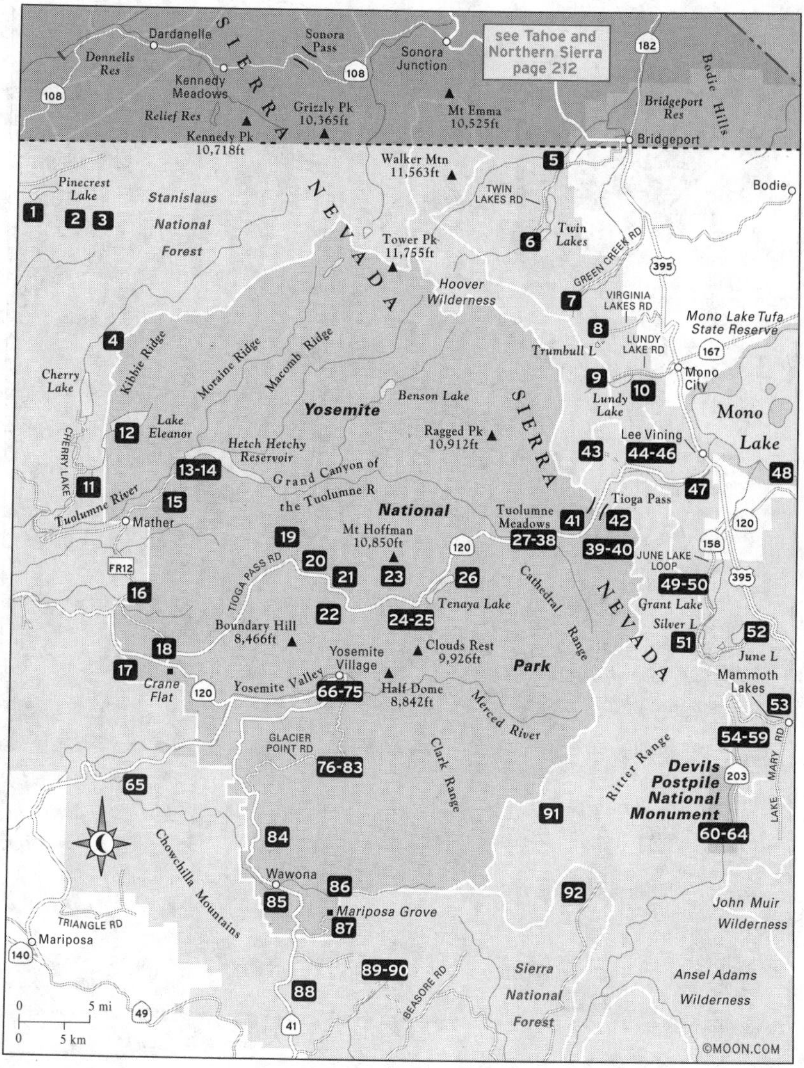

see Tahoe and Northern Sierra page 212

Dardanelle
Donnells Res
Sonora Pass
Sonora Junction
Kennedy Meadows
Relief Res
Grizzly Pk 10,365ft
Mt Emma 10,525ft
Kennedy Pk 10,718ft
Bridgeport Res
Bridgeport
Bodie Hills
Bodie
Walker Mtn 11,563ft
TWIN LAKES RD
Twin Lakes
Tower Pk 11,755ft
Pinecrest Lake
Stanislaus National Forest
SIERRA NEVADA
GREEN CREEK RD
Hoover Wilderness
VIRGINIA LAKES RD
Mono Lake Tufa State Reserve
LUNDY LAKE RD
Trumbull L
Mono City
Kibbie Ridge
Moraine Ridge
Macomb Ridge
Cherry Lake
Benson Lake
Lundy Lake
Mono Lake
Yosemite National Park
Lake Eleanor
Ragged Pk 10,912ft
Lee Vining
CHERRY LAKE
Hetch Hetchy Reservoir
Grand Canyon of the Tuolumne R
Tioga Pass
Tuolumne River
Tuolumne Meadows
Mather
Mt Hoffman 10,850ft
JUNE LAKE LOOP
FR12
TIOGA PASS RD
Cathedral Range
Tenaya Lake
Grant Lake
Silver L
Boundary Hill 8,466ft
Clouds Rest 9,926ft
June L
Yosemite Village
Mammoth Lakes
Crane Flat
Yosemite Valley
Half Dome 8,842ft
Merced River
GLACIER POINT RD
Clark Range
Ritter Range
Devils Postpile National Monument
MARY RD
LAKE
Chowchilla Mountains
Wawona
Mariposa Grove
John Muir Wilderness
TRIANGLE RD
Mariposa
BEASORE RD
Sierra National Forest
Ansel Adams Wilderness
0 5 mi
0 5 km

1, 2, 3, 4, 5, 6, 7, 8, 9, 10, 11, 12, 13-14, 15, 16, 17, 18, 19, 20, 21, 22, 23, 24-25, 26, 27-38, 39-40, 41, 42, 43, 44-46, 47, 48, 49-50, 51, 52, 53, 54-59, 60-64, 65, 66-75, 76-83, 84, 85, 86, 87, 88, 89-90, 91, 92

108, 182, 395, 167, 120, 158, 203, 140, 49, 41

Map 10.2

Sites 93-100
Pages 551-556

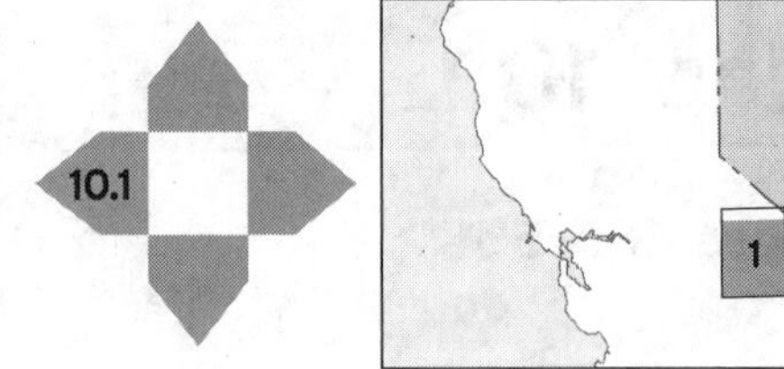

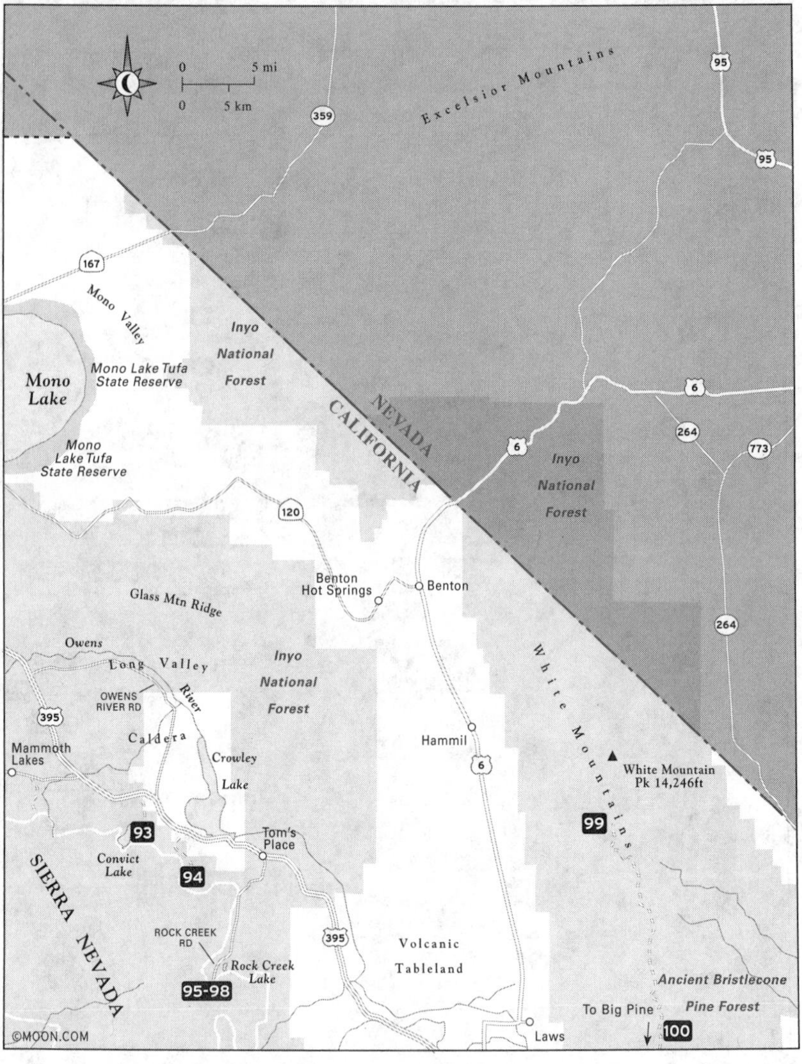

0 5 mi
0 5 km
Excelsior Mountains
95
359
95
167
Mono Valley
Mono Lake
Mono Lake Tufa State Reserve
Inyo National Forest
Mono Lake Tufa State Reserve
NEVADA
CALIFORNIA
6
264
773
6
Inyo National Forest
120
Benton Hot Springs
Benton
Glass Mtn Ridge
264
White Mountains
Owens
Long Valley
Inyo National Forest
OWENS RIVER RD
River
395
Caldera
Hammil
Mammoth Lakes
Crowley Lake
6
White Mountain Pk 14,246ft
99
93
Tom's Place
Convict Lake
94
SIERRA NEVADA
ROCK CREEK RD
395
Volcanic Tableland
Rock Creek Lake
95-98
Ancient Bristlecone Pine Forest
To Big Pine
100
Laws

1 PINECREST LAKE NATIONAL RECREATION TRAIL

4.2 mi / 2.0 hr

1 7

on Pinecrest Lake near Strawberry in Stanislaus National Forest

Map 10.1, page 483 BEST

Pinecrest Lake is a tremendously popular family vacation resort just off Highway 108, the kind of place that people go year after year for a week of boating, camping, and fishing. Many own or rent cabins and stay all summer. The trail that circles its shoreline is a lot like the lake itself—it's pretty and extremely popular. The four-mile loop makes a pleasant early morning walk or run, provided you're up and at it before the crowds get out of bed. In the afternoons, you can hike to the east side of the lake and follow a spur trail along the South Fork Stanislaus River to some excellent swimming holes known as Cleo's Bath. This trail is by no means a wilderness experience, but it's a pleasant walk. If you're looking for solitude, try it on an autumn weekday.

User Groups: Hikers and dogs. No horses or mountain bikes. Part of this trail is wheelchair-accessible.

Permits: No permits are required. Parking and access are free.

Maps: An Emigrant Wilderness map is available from Tom Harrison Maps or Stanislaus National Forest. For a topographic map, go to the USGS website to download Pinecrest.

Directions: From Sonora, drive east on Highway 108 for 31 miles to the Pinecrest turnoff. Turn right on Pinecrest Lake Road and continue for another mile to the day-use parking area, on the south side of the lake. Park as close to the end of the road as possible.

Contact: Stanislaus National Forest, Summit Ranger District, Pinecrest, 209/965-3434, www.fs.usda.gov/stanislaus.

2 CAMP AND BEAR LAKES

8.0 mi / 4.0 hr

2 9

in the Emigrant Wilderness near Pinecrest Lake

Map 10.1, page 483

The Crabtree trailhead, at elevation 7,180 feet, is the trailhead of choice for most casual hikers and backpackers entering the Emigrant Wilderness. It's easy to reach and allows access to many excellent destinations with a relatively short walk. From Crabtree, it's a moderate 2.6-mile hike to Camp Lake, which is just inside the Emigrant Wilderness boundary. This lake is best as a day-hiking destination, but some backpackers opt to spend the night here (there is a one-night limit). A better choice is to continue another 1.5 miles to Bear Lake, accessible via a one-mile left spur trail. Both lakes offer stellar granite-country scenery, good (but icy) swimming, decent rainbow trout fishing, and the chance to see plenty of early summer wildflowers. You, too, can be wowed by the wandering daisies and blue lupine. You'll face only one sustained hill climb along the route; most of the trail gently undulates. Watch for beaver evidence at Bear Lake.

User Groups: Hikers, dogs, and horses. No mountain bikes. No wheelchair facilities.

Permits: A free wilderness permit is required for overnight stays and is available from the Summit Ranger Station. There is a one-night stay limit at Camp Lake. Parking and access are free.

Maps: An Emigrant Wilderness map is available from Tom Harrison Maps or Stanislaus National Forest. For a topographic map, go to the USGS website to download Pinecrest.

Directions: From Sonora, drive east on Highway 108 for 31 miles to the Pinecrest turnoff. Turn right on Pinecrest Lake Road and continue 0.5 mile to the right fork for Dodge Ridge Ski Area. Bear right and drive 2.9 miles, then turn right at the sign for Aspen Meadow and Gianelli trailhead. Drive 0.5 mile, turn left, and drive four miles to the turnoff for the Crabtree trailhead (follow the signs). Turn right and drive 0.25 mile.

Contact: Stanislaus National Forest, Summit Ranger District, Pinecrest, 209/965-3434, www.fs.usda.gov/stanislaus.

3 BURST ROCK/ POWELL LAKE

4.6 mi / 2.5 hr 

in the Emigrant Wilderness near Pinecrest Lake

Map 10.1, page 483

Both Burst Rock and Powell Lake are supreme day-hike destinations, but they present a problem for first-time visitors: Neither one is located right along the trail and neither one is signed. This results in a lot of people wandering around asking, "So which rock is Burst Rock?" The answer: it's the entire plateau above the plaque commemorating the Clark-Skidmore Emigrant Party of 1852. You'll see it after hiking gently but steadily uphill for 1.3 miles. At the wilderness boundary sign, cut off to your left for about 50 yards and you'll witness an incredible vista looking out over the valley below. Retrace your steps and continue another mile until you reach a fork. Go left for less than 0.25 mile to Powell Lake, a favorite spot of young anglers. If you miss the fork, shortly you'll catch sight of the lake, off to your left. The peninsula of rocks that juts out into the water is the perfect place for afternoon sunning and swimming. If you fall in love with this beautiful area and want to return for a longer hike or a backpack trip, the Gianelli Trail leads to beautiful Chewing Gum Lake in a little over four miles one-way.

User Groups: Hikers, dogs, and horses. No mountain bikes. No wheelchair facilities.

Permits: A free wilderness permit is required for overnight stays and is available from the Summit Ranger Station. There is a one-night stay limit at Powell Lake. Parking and access are free.

Maps: An Emigrant Wilderness map is available from Tom Harrison Maps or Stanislaus National Forest. For a topographic map, go to the USGS website to download Pinecrest.

Directions: From Sonora, drive east on Highway 108 for 31 miles to the Pinecrest turnoff. Turn right on Pinecrest Lake Road and continue for 0.5 mile to the right fork for Dodge Ridge Ski Area. Bear right, drive 2.9 miles, and turn right at the sign for Aspen Meadow and Gianelli Cabin trailhead. Drive 0.5 mile, turn left, and drive 8.3 miles to the trailhead parking area. The route is well signed.

Contact: Stanislaus National Forest, Summit Ranger District, Pinecrest, 209/965-3434, www.fs.usda.gov/stanislaus.

4 KIBBIE LAKE

8.4 mi / 1-2 days 

in northwest Yosemite National Park

Map 10.1, page 483

This day hike or easy backpacking trip starts near Cherry Lake in Stanislaus National Forest and heads into the Hetch Hetchy region of Yosemite. Much of this area was severely burned in the massive Rim Fire of 2013, but that just makes this trip all the more interesting—especially the long drive to Cherry Lake, which offers many views of the fire's aftermath. In the spring, you can see thousands of colorful lupines blooming along the roadsides. Kibbie Lake is a rewarding weekend trip for all levels of backpackers since the one-way distance is only 4.2 miles. From the trailhead, follow the Kibbie Ridge Trail 1.2 miles to the Kibbie Lake Trail, then go right and head for the lake in another three miles. Near this main junction you leave Stanislaus National Forest and enter Yosemite National Park, so dogs are not allowed past this point. The trail deposits you at the southern tip of the granite-bound lake, elevation 6,513 feet. Although quite large (more than 100 surface acres), Kibbie Lake is fairly shallow and supports a good population of rainbow trout. The long and narrow body of water has high rocky cliffs on some of its shoreline, so not all of it is easily accessible. On summer weekends, the lake gets visited fairly heavily, but on weekdays, you are likely to be the only soul around.

Note: Check your calendar before you go. The gate at Cherry Lake is closed in the winter months and open from April 1 to December 15.

User Groups: Hikers and horses. No dogs or mountain bikes. No wheelchair facilities.

Permits: Parking and access are free (the trailhead is outside the main Yosemite entrance stations). Wilderness permits are required for overnight stays; call the Groveland Ranger District no more than 24 hours in advance of your trip to obtain a permit.

Maps: A Hetch Hetchy map is available from Tom Harrison Maps. For topographic maps, go to the USGS website to download Kibbie Lake and Hetch Hetchy Reservoir.

Directions: From Groveland, drive east on Highway 120 for 14 miles toward Yosemite National Park. Turn left on Cherry Lake Road and drive 24 miles to Cherry Lake's dam, then cross it. On the far side of the dam, bear right and drive 0.4 mile, then turn left on Road 1N45Y and follow it for 4.5 miles to its end at the Kibbie Ridge trailhead.

Contact: Stanislaus National Forest, Groveland Ranger District, Groveland, 209/962-7825, www.fs.usda.gov/stanislaus.

5 BUCKEYE CREEK TRAIL

5.0 mi / 2.5 hr

in Humboldt-Toiyabe National Forest west of Bridgeport and Highway 395

Map 10.1, page 483

You can hike up to eight miles one-way along Buckeye Creek to the Hoover Wilderness boundary below the Buckeye Roughs. But most hikers do less than that; they just take off from Buckeye Campground (7,000 feet), maybe pack along their fishing rods, and walk a couple of miles each way up and down the stream. Brook trout are planted close to the campground all summer. It's rare to hike far in the Eastern Sierra without having to climb, but that's what you get here at the base of Buckeye Canyon. If you don't like to fish, there's plenty of other stuff to do, like admire the wildflowers in the meadows or gape at the impressive walls of glacial summits and ridges that surround you. A popular hot spring is found in Buckeye Creek less than a mile from the campground, but be forewarned: You may get an anatomy lesson there. Occasional Buckeye Creek bathers have been spotted wearing only birthday suits. Note: The lower portions of the Buckeye Creek Trail can be difficult to follow. Cattle graze this area in the summer and create their own trail system.

User Groups: Hikers, dogs, and horses. No mountain bikes. No wheelchair facilities.

Permits: No day-hiking permits are required. Parking and access are free.

Maps: A Hoover Wilderness map is available from Tom Harrison Maps or the U.S. Forest Service. For a topographic map, go to the USGS website to download Twin Lakes.

Directions: From Bridgeport on U.S. 395, drive west on Twin Lakes Road for seven miles to the Buckeye Road turnoff. Turn right on Buckeye Road and drive 3.5 miles to the Buckeye Campground and trailhead. (Buckeye Road turns to dirt at Doc and Al's Resort.)

Contact: Humboldt-Toiyabe National Forest, Bridgeport Ranger District, HC Bridgeport, 760/932-7070, www.fs.usada.gov/htnf.

6 BARNEY LAKE TRAIL

7.8 mi / 5.0 hr

in the Hoover Wilderness west of Bridgeport

Map 10.1, page 483

Some call it Barney Lake Trail and others call it Robinson Creek Trail. Whatever you call it, you should know that this is the busiest trail into the Hoover Wilderness. Why? It's downright easy, gaining only 1,000 feet along its four-mile length. The remedy for the crowds? Start hiking very early in the day, before the hundreds of campers in the Twin Lakes area have risen from their sleeping bags. You must park outside Mono Village Campground and then walk due east through it to reach the trailhead, which is signed for Barney Lake. (The attendant in the camp entrance kiosk can point you to the trailhead. Day hikers can park for free but backpackers must pay a parking fee.) The trail roughly parallels Robinson Creek, first in a pine forest and then skirting big meadows highlighted by vast stands of aspen trees. While in the wide open meadows, you are rewarded with impressive views of the jagged Sawtooth Range. The path passes a Hoover Wilderness sign at 1.5 miles, then climbs a bit more steeply and reaches the lake at 3.9 miles. If you get there before everyone else, you are one lucky hiker. Ambitious day hikers and backpackers can continue another 3.5 miles to larger Peeler Lake. Because of the amount of aspens seen along this trail, it's a real treat to hike here from late September to mid-October when the color show happens.

User Groups: Hikers, dogs, and horses. No mountain bikes. No wheelchair facilities.

Permits: A free wilderness permit is required for overnight stays and is available from the Bridgeport Ranger Station. Quotas are in effect from the end of June to mid-September; permits are available in advance by mail for this period for a $3 fee per person.

Maps: A Hoover Wilderness map is available from Tom Harrison Maps or the U.S. Forest Service. For a topographic map, go to the USGS website to download Twin Lakes.

Directions: From Bridgeport on U.S. 395, drive west on Twin Lakes Road for 13.2 miles to the signed parking area, on the west end of the lakes, near Mono Village Campground.

Contact: Humboldt-Toiyabe National Forest, Bridgeport Ranger District, Bridgeport, 760/932-7070, www.fs.usada.gov/htnf.

7 GREEN, EAST, AND WEST LAKES

8.6-11.6 mi / 5.0 hr 3 9

in the Hoover Wilderness west of Bridgeport

Map 10.1, page 483

Three beautiful lakes—Green, East, and West—are situated right around 9,000 feet in elevation in the spectacular Hoover Wilderness. They offer fair trout fishing and are accessible via Green Creek Trail (sometimes called Green Lake Trail). It's only 4.6 miles round-trip to Green Lake, but you can go two miles farther for an 8.6-mile round-trip that includes East Lake as well. Or, you can take a 1.5-mile spur off the main trail for a much steeper (but well worth it) jaunt to stark, rockbound West Lake. Some people make a short backpacking trip out of it and see all three lakes. If you do, note that Green Lake is the only one of the three that is just below 9,000 feet in elevation, which means it is the only one where campfires are permitted. (You must use the established campfire rings.) At the other, higher lakes, only backpacking stoves are allowed. The fishing is generally better at East and West Lakes than at Green Lake, although it's nothing to write home about. The high mountain scenery, on the other hand, will knock your socks off.

The Green Creek Trail climbs, of course—but not so much that you'll be worn out when you reach Green Lake; just enough to provide you with expansive valley views most of the way. The path closely parallels the tumbling cascades of the main fork of Green Creek, and the July wildflower show is outstanding here. (The autumn aspen show is also noteworthy.) The turnoff for West Lake is on the right at 2.2 miles. This trail makes a memorably steep 1,000-foot ascent over 1.5 miles, climbing high above Green Lake. After the easy grade of the first two miles of trail, this last stretch can really take you by surprise. For solitude lovers, West Lake is your best bet. The main trail reaches the shore of Green Lake 200 yards past the West Lake turnoff. East Lake can be reached by following the main trail (go left at the fork) and gaining another 500 feet in elevation over two miles. All three lakes are sparkling, rock-bound gems, so you can't go wrong here no matter which one you choose to visit.

User Groups: Hikers, dogs, and horses. No mountain bikes. No wheelchair facilities.

Permits: A free wilderness permit is required for overnight stays and is available from the Bridgeport Ranger Station. Quotas are in effect from the end of June to mid-September; permits are available in advance by mail for this period for a $3 fee per person.

Maps: A Hoover Wilderness map is available from Tom Harrison Maps or the U.S. Forest Service. For a topographic map, go to the USGS website to download Twin Lakes.

Directions: From Bridgeport, drive south on U.S. 395 for 4.5 miles to Green Creek Road (dirt). Turn west and drive 8.2 miles to the signed trailhead parking area, shortly before Green Creek Campground.

Contact: Humboldt-Toiyabe National Forest, Bridgeport Ranger District, Bridgeport, 760/932-7070, www.fs.usada.gov/htnf.

8 VIRGINIA LAKES TRAIL

6.2-10.2 mi / 3.0 hr-2 days 3 9

in the Hoover Wilderness south of Bridgeport

Map 10.1, page 483

Virginia Lakes form the gateway to a beautiful high-mountain basin that contains eight small alpine lakes within a two-mile radius. The trailhead is at the Big Virginia Lake day-use area, set at 9,500 feet between mountain peaks that jut 12,000 feet into the sky. From here, you hike west past Blue Lake to Cooney Lake and on to Frog Lakes (a very easy 1.4 miles), then start climbing seriously, continuing 1.8 more miles to 11,100-foot Summit Pass. The landscape here is windswept, barren, and beautiful—a mix of rock, occasional whitebark pines, and high alpine wildflowers. Many hikers take a look at the scene from the pass, then retreat to one of the aforementioned lakes to spend the afternoon, making a 6.2-mile day. If you continue beyond the pass, you curve downhill through dozens of switchbacks for 1.4 miles, then climb gently 0.5 mile west to Summit Lake (at 10,203 feet), on the northeast boundary of Yosemite National Park. Summit Lake is set between Camiaca Peak (11,739 feet) to the north and Excelsior Mountain (12,446 feet) to the south. This is the logical place for backpackers to make camp, and for day-trippers to turn around for a 10.2-mile day. If you want to take a longer trip into even wilder country, you can do so from this point. The trail skirts Summit Lake's north side, then enters Yosemite National Park in Virginia Canyon, one of the least-visited areas of the park. Another option is to take the fork right before Summit Lake that leads east (right) to the double Hoover Lakes, connecting with the Green Creek Trail. Some backpackers and day hikers make a one-way hike of about 11 miles out of this trip by arranging to have a shuttle car waiting for them at the Green Creek trailhead (see listing in this chapter).

User Groups: Hikers, dogs, and horses. No dogs on trail in the Yosemite National Park portion. No mountain bikes. No wheelchair facilities.

Permits: A free wilderness permit is required for overnight stays and is available from the Bridgeport Ranger Station. Quotas are in effect from the end of June to mid-September; permits are available in advance by mail for this period for a $3 fee per person.

Maps: A Hoover Wilderness map is available from Tom Harrison Maps or the U.S. Forest Service. For a topographic map, go to the USGS website to download Dunderberg Peak.

Directions: From Bridgeport, drive 13.5 miles south on U.S. 395 (or from Lee Vining, drive 12 miles north on U.S. 395) to Conway Summit. Turn west on Virginia Lakes Road and drive 6.5 miles to the trailhead, at the Big Virginia Lake day-use area.

Contact: Humboldt-Toiyabe National Forest,

Bridgeport Ranger District, Bridgeport, 760/932-7070, www.fs.usada.gov/htnf.

9 LUNDY CANYON TRAIL

4.4-10.0 mi / 2.0 hr-2 days 3 9

north of Lee Vining in the Hoover Wilderness

Map 10.1, page 483 BEST

The Lundy Canyon Trail is the back door into the 20 Lakes Basin, a well-traveled area of the Hoover Wilderness that is most commonly accessed from Saddlebag Lake off Highway 120. The trailhead lies about two miles past Lundy Lake, a long, narrow pool set at 7,800 feet. From here, the trail rises along Mill Creek, passing several beaver ponds, a dilapidated trapper's cabin, and two small but boisterous waterfalls (Lower and Upper Lundy Falls, also called Mill Creek Falls) as it heads into the Hoover Wilderness. Most visitors hike to the first or second falls, enjoying the gorgeous Eastern Sierra scenery with a relatively mellow walk, then hike back out. Those who continue discover that the trail, which climbed gently but steadily for the first 2.2 miles, suddenly reaches what appears to be the back of the canyon. But look straight up the canyon wall to your left—that's where the path continues, although it isn't much of a path, and after a heavy snow year, small avalanches often bury it with rocks. This unmaintained "route" leads 0.8 mile upward on a perilous wall of loose shale, and the difficulty rating for this trail changes abruptly from a 3 to a 5. Proceed at your own risk. If you make it to the top of the canyon wall, you come out to a beautiful high mountain meadow and a junction near the austere shores of Lake Helen, elevation 10,100 feet (3.3 miles from your start). By going right, you can follow the trail to Shamrock and Steelhead Lakes. Shamrock is 0.3 mile farther and dotted with many islands; Steelhead is another 0.5 mile beyond and is framed by 12,242-foot North Peak, towering above. The opposite trail goes left to Odell Lake (3.6 miles from your start). From Odell Lake, you could continue on to Hummingbird Lake, then to the north shore of Saddlebag Lake. If you can arrange a car shuttle at Saddlebag Lake, you can extend your trip into a one-way hike of seven miles, and that would save you the harrowing trip back down that shale-covered slope.

Note: One of the best times to visit here is in October, when Lundy Canyon's stands of quaking aspen turn bright gold and seem to dance in the breeze. This is one of the best places to admire fall colors in the Eastern Sierra. July is another first-rate time to visit; the canyon's wildflower displays are remarkable.

User Groups: Hikers, horses, and dogs. No mountain bikes. No wheelchair facilities.

Permits: A free wilderness permit is required for overnight stays and is available from the Mono Basin Scenic Area Visitors Center. There are no quotas on this trail, so advance reservations are not required.

Maps: A Hoover Wilderness map is available from Tom Harrison Maps or the U.S. Forest Service. For topographic maps, go to the USGS website to download Lundy and Dunderberg Peak.

Directions: From Lee Vining, drive north on U.S. 395 for seven miles to Lundy Lake Road. Turn west on Lundy Lake Road and drive five miles to Lundy Lake. Continue beyond the lake and Lundy Lake Resort, driving two miles farther on a dirt road that ends at the trailhead.

Contact: Inyo National Forest, Mono Basin Scenic Area Visitors Center, Lee Vining, 760/647-3044, www.fs.usda.gov/inyo.

10 LAKE CANYON AND MAY LUNDY MINE

7.0 mi / 3.5 hr or 2 days

north of Lee Vining in the Hoover Wilderness

Map 10.1, page 483

The Lundy Lake area is blessed with two first-rate day-hiking trails that lead into two separate and distinct canyons: Lundy Canyon (see listing in this chapter) and Lake Canyon. Both paths offer so many rewards that when you drive up to Lundy Lake, it's hard to decide which one to take. History buffs and fishing-minded hikers would do well to take this trip from Lundy's dam into Lake Canyon, where they can see the remains of the May Lundy Mine. The mine was worked continuously for two decades starting in 1878, producing a total of about $2 million in gold. As a result, the surrounding community of Lundy grew to support 500 people, despite severe winters and deadly avalanches. Besides mining, a primary activity here was the operation of three sawmills along Lundy Creek, used to supply timber to the nearby bustling gold rush town of Bodie.

The hike to the May Lundy Mine is a fairly steep 3.5 miles one-way, climbing above Lundy Lake on the old mine road that was built in 1881. You can see the trail plain as day from the trailhead on the east side of Lundy Lake. The road/trail passes Blue Lake and Crystal Lake, where mining relics can be found. Crystal Lake's waters are poisoned from mining activity, so don't filter water or camp here. Continue on the main trail, and you'll see the mine remains—old railcar tracks, tailings, and a closed-off mine shaft. Just beyond is Oneida Lake, which has waters that were used to run the stamp mill for the mine. Even without the fascinating traces of history, this is an extraordinarily beautiful place. You'll want to linger awhile at sparkling Oneida Lake. Both the scenery and the fishing are quite rewarding.

User Groups: Hikers, horses, and dogs. No mountain bikes. No wheelchair facilities.

Permits: A free wilderness permit is required for overnight stays and is available from the Mono Basin Scenic Area Visitors Center. There are no quotas on this trail, so advance reservations are not required.

Maps: A Mono Lake map is available from Tom Harrison Maps. An Inyo National Forest map is available from the U.S. Forest Service. For a topographic map, go to the USGS website to download Lundy.

Directions: From Lee Vining, drive north on U.S. 395 for seven miles to Lundy Lake Road. Turn west on Lundy Lake Road and drive five miles to Lundy Lake's dam, on the east side of the lake. Turn left and drive 0.25 mile to a locked gate and trailhead.

Contact: Inyo National Forest, Mono Basin Scenic Area Visitors Center, Lee Vining, 760/647-3044, www.fs.usda.gov/inyo.

11 PRESTON FLAT TRAIL

8.8 mi / 4.0 hr or 2 days 2 8

in Stanislaus National Forest

Map 10.1, page 483

Although some day hikers choose to suffer through the nearly intolerable grade of the Poopenaut Valley Trail to reach the swimming holes and fishing spots on the Tuolumne River's free-flowing stretch west of Hetch Hetchy Dam, a much more pleasant approach is on the Preston Flat Trail. The trailhead is off Cherry Lake Road in Stanislaus National Forest, near the epicenter of the 2013 Rim Fire, the third largest wildfire in California's history. But this foothill ecosystem is well adapted to fire, and the Preston Flat Trail shows plenty of regrowth already. A walk here is a fascinating study in wildfire ecology and recovery.

The path travels 4.4 miles up the north side of the Tuolumne River Canyon on a gently undulating grade. Shortly before the trail's end is a rock chimney and a few other remains of an old cabin that was built here by a homesteader named Preston. A few hundred yards farther is a photogenic vista of Preston Falls, a cascade formed where the Tuolumne River drops 15 feet over a granite ledge into a wide, clear pool. The cataract is just a half-mile downstream of Yosemite's boundary line. If you want to stay overnight, you can. Several good campsites are found along the trail, which sticks closely to the river for most of its length.

Compared to the Poopenaut Valley Trail, the Preston Flat Trail is by far the better choice for hikers who wish to reach the river. Hike it in early spring, when the raging Tuolumne River provides the most exciting viewing. Those who wish to fish or swim should wait to visit until late spring or early summer, when the river quiets down. Winter is also a great option; the elevation is low enough that the trail is always snow-free.

User Groups: Hikers, horses, dogs, and mountain bikes. No wheelchair facilities.

Permits: A free campfire permit is required for overnight stays and is available from the Groveland Ranger Station. Parking and access are free.

Maps: A Stanislaus National Forest map is available from the U.S. Forest Service. For a topographic map, go to the USGS website to download Cherry Lake South.

Directions: From Groveland drive east on Highway 120 for 14 miles toward Yosemite. Turn left on Cherry Lake Road and drive 8.5 miles to Early Intake, where you cross a bridge over the Tuolumne River. Turn right on the far side of the bridge and drive 0.8 mile to the trailhead parking area at the end of the road, just beyond Kirkwood Powerhouse.

Contact: Stanislaus National Forest, Groveland Ranger District, Groveland, 209/962-7825, www.fs.usda.gov/stanislaus.

12 LAKE ELEANOR

3.0 mi / 1.5 hr 1 8

in northwest Yosemite National Park

Map 10.1, page 483

Lake Eleanor is a reservoir in the Hetch Hetchy region of Yosemite—not as famous or as large as Hetch Hetchy itself, but still having an important role in the San Francisco water storage system. The forest surrounding the lake was obliterated in the 2013 Rim Fire, and the Forest Service closed off access to Lake Eleanor and nearby Cherry Lake for nearly two years. It's open now, and it's incredible to see how much foliage is regenerating in this scorched landscape. Eleanor is no longer the beautiful Sierra gem that it once was, but it's still worth a visit and a short walk, if only to witness the fascinating process of fire regrowth.

Originally a naturally shallow glacial lake, Lake Eleanor was "improved" by the city of San Francisco by damming Eleanor Creek in 1928, five years before O'Shaughnessy Dam at Hetch Hetchy was completed. The dam raised the lake's water level 40 feet. Today it is the second largest lake in Yosemite after Hetch Hetchy. Its waters are not used by San Francisco as a drinking supply but rather to generate power. Set at an elevation of 4,657 feet, Lake Eleanor is popular with anglers who tote along a fishing rod while traversing the trail around the three-mile-long lake's edge. The access road to Lake Eleanor ends at a gate 0.25 mile before the lake, so start your hike there, then take a mellow walk along the lake's south and west shores. Much of Lake Eleanor's western side is dotted with islands.

It takes more than an hour's drive from Highway 120 to access Lake Eleanor, so people who come here to hike or fish often plan on spending the night. A first-come, first-served campground is located at nearby Cherry Lake, and several backpacking campsites are located on the northwest edge of Lake Eleanor (a wilderness permit is required). Note: Check your calendar before you go. The gate at Cherry Lake is closed in the winter months, so you can access Lake Eleanor only from April 1 to December 15.

User Groups: Hikers and horses. No dogs or mountain bikes. No wheelchair facilities.

Permits: No permits are required for day hiking. Parking and access are free (the trailhead is outside the main Yosemite entrance stations).

Maps: A Hetch Hetchy map is available from Tom Harrison Maps. For a topographic map, go to the USGS website to download Lake Eleanor.

Directions: From Groveland, drive east on Highway 120 for 14 miles toward Yosemite National Park. Turn left on Cherry Lake Road and drive 24 miles to Cherry Lake's dam, then across it. On the far side of the dam, bear right and drive 0.4 mile, then turn right on the dirt road that is signed for Lake Eleanor. Follow this road four miles to its end, at the gated Yosemite National Park boundary, 0.25 mile south of the lake.

Contact: Stanislaus National Forest, Groveland Ranger District, Groveland, 209/962-7825, www.fs.usda.gov/stanislaus.

13 WAPAMA FALL

4.8 mi / 2.5 hr 

in northwest Yosemite National Park

Map 10.1, page 483

The trail to this spectacular early-season waterfall starts by crossing the giant O'Shaughnessy Dam, where you may pause to curse (or admire, depending on your sensibilities) the San Francisco politicians who, in 1908, believed that flooding Hetch Hetchy Valley was a good idea. In terms of geology and natural features, Hetch Hetchy is a near twin to Yosemite Valley, although somewhat smaller in scale. The valley today is filled by an immense reservoir that supplies water and power to the city of San Francisco and environs. After walking across its impressive dam and passing through a dimly lit, 500-foot-long tunnel, the trail opens out to a mixed forest along the edge of the deep blue lake. Here you will start to see some burned trees and other evidence of the 2013 Rim Fire. In 1.5 miles you reach Tueeulala Fall, a delicate wisp of a freefall that only runs during peak snowmelt, and is often dry by late May. Less than a mile farther you reach powerful Wapama Fall on Falls Creek, a Bridalveil-like plume of white water that makes a dramatic plunge into the reservoir. Depending on how early in the year you visit, you may get soaking wet standing on the sturdy steel bridges that cross over Wapama Fall's coursing flow. In early spring, Wapama Falls sometimes flows so furiously that the park rangers have to close this trail. In late spring and early summer, the temperature can get hot out at Hetch Hetchy, so this spray of water can be very refreshing. If this is your first trip to this part of Yosemite, be sure to stop and read the interpretive plaques at the dam that explain about the building of Hetch Hetchy Reservoir and its service to the city of San Francisco. Whatever else you may think about it, it's a fascinating story.

User Groups: Hikers only. No dogs, horses, or mountain bikes. No wheelchair facilities.

Permits: No permits are required. There is a $35 entrance fee per vehicle at Yosemite National Park, good for seven days.

Maps: A Hetch Hetchy map is available from Tom Harrison Maps. For topographic maps, go to the USGS website to download Lake Eleanor and Hetch Hetchy Reservoir.

Directions: From Groveland, drive east on Highway 120 for 22.5 miles to the Evergreen Road turnoff signed for Hetch Hetchy Reservoir on the left, a mile west of the Big Oak Flat entrance to Yosemite. Drive north on Evergreen Road for 7.4 miles and turn right on Hetch Hetchy Road. Drive nine miles to the dam and trailhead.

Contact: Yosemite National Park, Yosemite, 209/372-0200 or 209/372-0740 (permit reservations), www.nps.gov/yose or www.nps.gov/yose/wilderness (permit reservations).

14 RANCHERIA FALLS

13.0 mi / 1 or 2 days 3 9

in northwest Yosemite National Park

Map 10.1, page 483

It's spring and you are hungering for a Yosemite backpacking trip, but Tuolumne Meadows is knee-deep in melting snow. This is a good time to hike the northern edge of Hetch Hetchy Reservoir (elevation 3,796 feet), admiring three stunning waterfalls along the way: Tueeulala, Wapama, and Rancheria. This easy backpacking trip (or long day hike, if you prefer) travels along the length of the reservoir to its far eastern edge, where the bears are some of the boldest in all of Yosemite. (Bear canisters are required for backpackers.) Whereas Tueeulala and Wapama Falls are both freefalling cataracts, Rancheria Falls is a series of rolling cascades pouring over polished granite.

To make the trip, follow the trail notes for Wapama Falls (see listing in this chapter), then continue onward, following the trail as it contours along the reservoir's edge. You'll see some burn evidence from the 2013 Rim Fire, and it's fascinating to notice how some trees were scorched while their neighbors were not. For much of the walk you are high above the water, which allows fine views of Kolana Rock and its neighboring granite formations across the reservoir. The trail follows a gentle grade with many small ups and downs, gaining only 1,300 feet along its entire length. This trip is manageable even for beginning backpackers. Shoreline trout fishing in the reservoir can be good in spring and fall. And remember: Swimming in Hetch Hetchy is not allowed.

User Groups: Hikers and horses. No dogs or mountain bikes. No wheelchair facilities.

Permits: There is a $35 entrance fee per vehicle at Yosemite National Park, good for seven days. Wilderness permits are required for overnight stays. They are available on a first-come, first-served basis up to two days in advance at the Yosemite Wilderness kiosk near your chosen trailhead, or up to 24 weeks in advance through Yosemite's online wilderness reservation system at www.yosemiteconservancy.org for a $5 reservation fee per person.

Maps: A Hetch Hetchy map is available from Tom Harrison Maps. For topographic maps, go to the USGS website to download Lake Eleanor and Hetch Hetchy Reservoir.

Directions: From Groveland, drive east on Highway 120 for 22.5 miles to the Evergreen Road turnoff signed for Hetch Hetchy Reservoir on the left, a mile west of the Big Oak Flat entrance to Yosemite. Drive north on Evergreen Road for 7.4 miles and turn right on Hetch Hetchy Road. Drive nine miles to the dam and trailhead.

Contact: Yosemite National Park, Yosemite, 209/372-0200 or 209/372-0740 (permit reservations), www.nps.gov/yose or www.nps.gov/yose/wilderness (permit reservations).

15 SMITH PEAK

15.0 mi / 1 or 2 days

in northwest Yosemite National Park

Map 10.1, page 483

Smith Peak and its environs were severely burned in the 2013 Rim Fire, but the Park Service reopened the trail to the peak quickly. This is a different hike than it used to be (there are a lot less trees!), but the view from the top (7,751 feet) is still worth the effort. The route begins by the Mather Ranger Station. Follow the Lookout Point Trail for 1.2 miles, then turn right on the trail signed for Smith Meadow. You'll travel through a fire-scarred forest, then climb up a ridge to meet up with Cottonwood Creek at Lower Cottonwood Meadow, shortly followed by Upper Cottonwood Meadow. Smith Meadow lies another two miles farther, and just beyond it you'll find a junction of trails. The path on the right is another popular route to Smith Peak leading from White Wolf Campground off Tioga Road. Campsites are found a short distance to the west at this junction. Get a good night's rest before bagging Smith Peak the next morning. (You've hiked six miles thus far; it's only 1.5 more to the summit.) The peak, like the nearby meadows, was named after a 1920s sheep rancher. Many people day hike this trail, but it's possible to camp very near the summit, and if you do, you'll be treated to a memorable sunset and sunrise, plus a panoramic view of the Grand Canyon of the Tuolumne River, situated 4,000 dramatic feet below you. To the east, Yosemite's high country peaks are prominent, among them distinctive Mount Conness, Matterhorn Peak, and Mount Hoffman. Total elevation gain on this trip is 2,900 feet.

User Groups: Hikers only. No dogs, horses, or mountain bikes. No wheelchair facilities.
Permits: There is a $35 entrance fee per vehicle at Yosemite National Park, good for seven days. Wilderness permits are required for overnight stays. They are available on a first-come, first-served basis up to two days in advance at the Yosemite Wilderness kiosk near your chosen trailhead, or up to 24 weeks in advance through Yosemite's online wilderness reservation system at www.yosemiteconservancy.org for a $5 reservation fee per person.
Maps: A Hetch Hetchy map is available from Tom Harrison Maps. For topographic maps, go to the USGS website to download Hetch Hetchy Reservoir.
Directions: From Groveland, drive east on Highway 120 for 22.5 miles to the Evergreen Road turnoff (on the left), signed for Hetch Hetchy Reservoir (it's a mile west of the Big Oak Flat entrance to Yosemite). Drive north on Evergreen Road for 7.4 miles, then turn right on Hetch Hetchy Road. Drive 1.6 miles to the entrance kiosk by the Mather Ranger Station; the trail begins 100 yards past the entrance kiosk, just beyond the ranger station, on the right.
Contact: Yosemite National Park, Yosemite, 209/372-0200 or 209/372-0740 (permit reservations), www.nps.gov/yose or www.nps.gov/yose/wilderness (permit reservations).

16 CARLON FALLS

3.8 mi / 2.5 hr

on the border of Stanislaus National Forest and northwest Yosemite National Park

Map 10.1, page 483

Carlon Falls is a pretty cascade on the South Fork Tuolumne River in the far western region of Yosemite. It is so far west that the trailhead is actually in Stanislaus National Forest, outside the park border, in a forested area that was hard hit by the 2013 Rim Fire. But the trail to Carlon Falls was spared, and this short, easy hike remains one of the most popular on the west side of the park. The trailhead is across the river from Carlon Day-Use Area, a popular picnicking and fishing spot on the Tuolumne River. Follow the trail for a mere 50 feet and you enter Yosemite National Park, but with no park entrance fee and no waiting in line at the entrance kiosk. The path skirts along the river's northern bank to reach the falls in just under two miles. It's almost completely shaded, mostly level (except for one brief steep climb that skirts a landslide area), and fairly easy to follow, although it does require clambering over a few fallen trees. The waterfall drops in two tiers over wide granite ledges, and the riverbanks surrounding it are covered with big conifers and dense foliage. A bonus is that unlike most Yosemite waterfalls, Carlon Falls runs year-round. The waterfall's namesakes are Dan and Donna Carlon, who operated the popular Carl Inn from 1916 to 1930 near what is now the Carlon Day-Use Area. This trail is popular with swimmers and anglers in summer, but mostly deserted the rest of the year.
User Groups: Hikers only. No dogs, horses, or mountain bikes. No wheelchair facilities.
Permits: No permits are required. Parking and access are free.
Maps: For a topographic map, go to the USGS website to download Ackerson Mountain.
Directions: From Groveland, drive east on Highway 120 for 22.5 miles to the Evergreen Road turnoff, signed for Hetch Hetchy Reservoir, one mile west of the Big Oak Flat entrance to Yosemite. Follow Evergreen Road north for one mile to the far side of the bridge just past Carlon Day-Use Area. Park on the right at the closed-off dirt road on the north side of the bridge, signed only as No Camping. There is room for about five cars. Begin hiking on the closed road, heading upstream. The road narrows to a single track after about 100 yards.
Contact: Yosemite National Park, Yosemite, 209/372-0200, www.nps.gov/yose.

17 MERCED GROVE

3.0 mi / 1.5 hr 2 8

in western Yosemite National Park

Map 10.1, page 483

There are three giant sequoia groves in Yosemite National Park—Merced, Tuolumne, and Mariposa. Because the Merced Grove is the smallest of the three groves and requires the longest walk to reach it, it is the least visited. Generally it only gets traffic from people who enter Yosemite at the Big Oak Flat entrance and drive by it on their way to Yosemite Valley. The hiking is on a closed-off dirt road that is ideal for snowshoeing in winter. The trail cuts a level course through a mixed conifer forest for the first 0.5 mile. Bear left at the only junction and head downhill through a canopy of white firs, incense cedars, ponderosa pines, and sugar pines. You reach the small sequoia grove at 1.5 miles; the first group of six trees will take your breath away. Continue another 100 yards past these beauties; the two largest sequoias of the Merced Grove are directly across from a handsome old log cabin. It was originally built as a retreat for the park superintendent but is no longer used. Retrace your steps from the cabin, hiking uphill for your return.

User Groups: Hikers only. No dogs, horses, or mountain bikes. No wheelchair facilities.

Permits: No permits are required. There is a $35 entrance fee per vehicle at Yosemite National Park, good for seven days.

Maps: A Yosemite National Park map is available from Tom Harrison Maps. For a topographic map, go to the USGS website to download Ackerson Mountain.

Directions: From Merced, drive 70 miles northeast on Highway 140 to Yosemite National Park. Follow the signs toward Yosemite Valley, entering through the Arch Rock entrance station. Continue 4.5 miles to the left turnoff for Highway 120, looping back out of the valley on Big Oak Flat Road. Continue straight on Big Oak Flat Road for 13.5 miles (past the Tioga Pass Road turnoff) to the Merced Grove parking area, on the left. If you enter Yosemite at the Big Oak Flat entrance station on Highway 120, drive 4.3 miles southeast to reach the trailhead, on your right.

Contact: Yosemite National Park, Yosemite, 209/372-0200, www.nps.gov/yose.

18 TUOLUMNE GROVE

2.5 mi / 1.5 hr 2 8

in western Yosemite National Park

Map 10.1, page 483

Up until 1993 you could drive right in to the Tuolumne Grove of Giant Sequoias, but now the road is closed off and visitors have to hike in. The grove is found on the old Big Oak Flat Road, a paved, six-mile historic road/trail that is open to bikes and hikers (although bikes are a rarity here). This is a popular destination, so arrive early in the morning to have the best chance at solitude. Leave your car at the parking lot near Crane Flat and hike downhill into the big trees. It's one mile to the first sequoias. The Tuolumne Grove's claim to fame is that it has one of the two remaining walk-through trees in Yosemite; this one is called the Dead Giant. It's a tall stump that was tunneled in 1878. Go ahead, walk through it—everybody does. At a small picnic area, a half-mile trail loops around the forest. Make sure you save some energy for the trip back uphill to the parking lot; the moderate grade ascends 550 feet. The old paved road continues downhill beyond the grove all the way to Hodgdon Meadow Campground. Some people hike the entire six-mile distance, then have someone pick them up at Hodgdon Meadow.

User Groups: Hikers and mountain bikes. No dogs or horses. No wheelchair facilities.

Permits: No permits are required. There is a $35 entrance fee per vehicle at Yosemite National Park, good for seven days.

Maps: A Yosemite National Park map is available from Tom Harrison Maps. For a topographic map, go to the USGS website to download Ackerson Mountain.

Directions: From Merced, drive 70 miles northeast on Highway 140 to Yosemite National Park. Follow the signs toward Yosemite Valley, entering through the Arch Rock entrance station. Continue 4.5 miles to the left turnoff for Highway 120, looping back out of the valley on Big Oak Flat Road. In 9.3 miles at Crane Flat, turn right on Tioga Pass Road, then drive 0.5 mile to the Tuolumne Grove parking lot, on the left, near Crane Flat. If you enter Yosemite at the Big Oak Flat entrance station on Highway 120, drive 7.7 miles southeast to the Crane Flat/Highway 120 East turnoff. Turn left and drive 0.5 mile to the Tuolumne Grove trailhead.

Contact: Yosemite National Park, Yosemite, 209/372-0200, www.nps.gov/yose.

19 HARDEN LAKE

5.6 mi / 3.0 hr 2 8

off Tioga Pass Road in Yosemite National Park

Map 10.1, page 483

Harden Lake itself isn't a scene stealer—by late summer, it's not much more than a large pond, framed by a few stands of aspen trees on its northeast shore. But many people come here for another reason, and that's to see the wildflowers that bloom in a region known informally as Harden's Gardens, about a quarter-mile beyond the lake. July is the most dependable month for the wildflower bloom. Plus there are other rewards, including fine views of the Grand Canyon of the Tuolumne River just a half-mile north of the lake. Also, because of the small size of Harden Lake, it is dependably warm for swimming by midsummer. The hike is simple enough. The trail follows White Wolf's gravel service road (a stretch of the original Tioga Road) past the campground entrance and across the Tuolumne River. Follow the obvious signs that point you through a few junctions to a blossom-filled marshy area. A few more steps and you're at the lake. If you haven't yet gotten your fill of the flower show, proceed a short distance farther and feast your eyes on Harden's Gardens.

User Groups: Hikers only. No dogs, horses, or mountain bikes. No wheelchair facilities.

Permits: No permits are required. There is a $35 entrance fee per vehicle at Yosemite National Park, good for seven days.

Maps: A Yosemite National Park map is available from Tom Harrison Maps. For a topographic map, go to the USGS website to download Tamarack Flat.

Directions: From Merced, drive 70 miles northeast on Highway 140 to Yosemite National Park. Follow the signs to Yosemite Valley, entering through the Arch Rock entrance station. Continue 4.5 miles to the left turnoff for Highway 120, looping back out of the valley on Big Oak Flat Road. In 9.3 miles at Crane Flat, turn right on Tioga Pass Road and drive 14 miles to the left turnoff for White Wolf. Turn left and drive one mile to the lodge and trailhead.

Contact: Yosemite National Park, Yosemite, 209/372-0200, www.nps.gov/yose.

20 LUKENS LAKE

1.5-4.6 mi / 1.0-2.0 hr 1 8

off Tioga Pass Road in Yosemite National Park

Map 10.1, page 483

The Lukens Lake Trail is the perfect introductory lake hike for families in Yosemite National Park. A six-year-old could make the trip easily. A bonus is that the trailhead is on the western end of Tioga Road, so it's quickly reached from points in Yosemite Valley. The trail is 0.75 mile long and leads from Tioga Road up to a saddle, then drops down to a meadow on the lake's eastern edge. The path winds through a dense red fir forest, filled with mammoth trees, then skirts alongside a corn lily-filled meadow to the southern edge of the shallow, spring-fed lake (the trail used to travel on the lake's north side, but it was rerouted). If you time it right—usually late July—you may see a spectacular wildflower show featuring thousands of pink shooting stars. Swimming in Lukens Lake is highly recommended; by midsummer, this is one of the warmest lakes in the park. If you want to take a longer trail to Lukens Lake, you can start from the trailhead at White Wolf Lodge and make a 4.6-mile round-trip.

User Groups: Hikers only. No dogs, horses, or mountain bikes. No wheelchair facilities.

Permits: No permits are required. There is a $35 entrance fee per vehicle at Yosemite National Park, good for seven days.

Maps: A Yosemite National Park map is available from Tom Harrison Maps. For a topographic map, go to the USGS website to download Tamarack Flat.

Directions: From Merced, drive 70 miles northeast on Highway 140 to Yosemite National Park. Follow the signs to Yosemite Valley, entering through the Arch Rock entrance station. Continue 4.5 miles to the left turnoff for Highway 120, looping back out of the valley on Big Oak Flat Road. In 9.3 miles at Crane Flat, turn right on Tioga Pass Road and drive 16.2 miles to the Lukens Lake trailhead parking area, on the south side of the road. The trail begins across the road.

Contact: Yosemite National Park, Yosemite, 209/372-0200, www.nps.gov/yose.

21 TEN LAKES / GRANT LAKES

12.8 mi / 1 or 2 days 

off Tioga Pass Road in Yosemite National Park

Map 10.1, page 483

The Ten Lakes area is incredibly popular with backpackers, so get your wilderness permit early. Or get an early-morning start and make this trip as a day hike; just be prepared for some serious climbing and long miles. From the Ten Lakes trailhead at Tioga Pass Road (elevation 7,500 feet), the path climbs steadily for the first four miles. There's only one brutally steep stretch, which comes between miles four and five, after a pretty stroll around Half Moon Meadow. A series of tight switchbacks pulls you through a nasty 800-foot elevation gain to the top of a ridge and the Ten Lakes/Grant Lakes junction. From there, you make a choice. Turn right to reach Grant Lakes and head mostly downhill for a mile; or, to reach Ten Lakes, continue straight, soon heading steeply downhill for 1.4 miles. The Grant Lakes offer a little more solitude (good for day hikers), while the two larger of the Ten Lakes have the best campsites, with many trees along their shorelines offering protection from the wind. All of the lakes are sparkling, rockbound beauties. Whether you go to Ten Lakes or Grant Lakes, don't miss taking a side-trip to the rocky overlook above the Ten Lakes Basin. It's only 0.5 mile from the Ten Lakes/Grant Lakes junction (continue straight for Ten Lakes, then take the unsigned trail to the left of the main trail and head for the highest point). Four of the Ten Lakes are visible from this promontory, as well as a section of the Grand Canyon of the Tuolumne.

User Groups: Hikers only. No dogs, horses, or mountain bikes. No wheelchair facilities.

Permits: There is a $35 entrance fee per vehicle at Yosemite National Park, good for seven days. Wilderness permits are required for overnight stays. They are available on a first-come, first-served basis up to two days in advance at the Yosemite Wilderness kiosk near your chosen trailhead, or up to 24 weeks in advance through Yosemite's online wilderness reservation system at www.yosemiteconservancy.org for a $5 reservation fee per person.

Maps: A Yosemite National Park map is available from Tom Harrison Maps. For topographic maps, go to the USGS website to download Yosemite Falls and Ten Lakes.

Directions: From Merced, drive 70 miles northeast on Highway 140 to Yosemite National Park. Follow the signs toward Yosemite Valley, entering through the Arch Rock entrance station. Continue 4.5 miles to the left turnoff for Highway 120, looping back out of the valley on

Big Oak Flat Road. In 9.3 miles at Crane Flat, turn right on Tioga Pass Road and drive 19.4 miles to the Yosemite Creek and Ten Lakes trailhead parking area, which is on the south side of the road. The trail begins on the north side of the road.

Contact: Yosemite National Park, Yosemite, 209/372-0200 or 209/372-0740 (permit reservations), www.nps.gov/yose or www.nps.gov/yose/wilderness (permit reservations).

22 NORTH DOME

9.0 mi / 5.0 hr 

off Tioga Pass Road in Yosemite National Park

Map 10.1, page 483

There are those who say that climbing Half Dome is a bit of a disappointment, and not just because of the crowds. When you reach the top and check out the commanding view, the panorama of granite is not quite as awesome as you may expect, and that's because you can't see Half Dome—you're standing on it.

That's a dilemma that's easy to fix. If Half Dome is an absolute necessity in your view of Yosemite, climb North Dome instead, which offers a heart-stopping view of that big piece of granite. The route is not for the faint of heart, but when you are way up high looking down at Tenaya Canyon and across at Half Dome and Clouds Rest—well, you'll know why you came here. The preferred route to North Dome begins at the Porcupine Creek trailhead on Tioga Pass Road, and has only a 1,500-foot gain to the summit. A dirt access road quickly brings you to a proper trail, signed as Porcupine Creek. Continue straight at two possible junctions near the 2.5-mile mark, heading due south for North Dome. After the third mile, your views begin to open up, providing fine vistas of North Dome and Half Dome and increasing your anticipation. At the trail junction at 4.5 miles, take the left spur for the final hike to North Dome's summit. Surprise—it's a downhill grade to reach it. Hope you brought a full supply of film or memory cards with you; the view from the top is sublime. Half Dome, just across the canyon, appears close enough to touch. Clouds Rest is a dramatic sight to the northeast. To the southwest, you can see cars crawling along the Yosemite Valley floor. On your return trip, consider taking the unsigned spur trail two miles from North Dome, at an obvious saddle. The spur leads a steep 0.25 mile to Indian Rock, the only natural arch on land in Yosemite. It's great fun to climb around on.

User Groups: Hikers only. No dogs, horses, or mountain bikes. No wheelchair facilities.

Permits: There is a $35 entrance fee per vehicle at Yosemite National Park, good for seven days. Wilderness permits are required for overnight stays. They are available on a first-come, first-served basis up to two days in advance at the Yosemite Wilderness kiosk near your chosen trailhead, or up to 24 weeks in advance through Yosemite's online wilderness reservation system at www.yosemiteconservancy.org for a $5 reservation fee per person.

Maps: A Half Dome or Yosemite National Park map is available from Tom Harrison Maps. For a topographic map, go to the USGS website to download Yosemite Falls.

Directions: From Merced, drive 70 miles northeast on Highway 140 to Yosemite National Park. Follow the signs toward Yosemite Valley, entering through the Arch Rock entrance station. Continue 4.5 miles to the left turnoff for Highway 120, looping back out of the valley on Big Oak Flat Road. In 9.3 miles at Crane Flat, turn right on Tioga Pass Road and drive 24.5 miles to the Porcupine Creek trailhead parking area, on the right, a mile past Porcupine Flat Campground.

Contact: Yosemite National Park, Yosemite, 209/372-0200 or 209/372-0740 (permit reservations), www.nps.gov/yose or www.nps.gov/yose/wilderness (permit reservations).

23 MAY LAKE AND MOUNT HOFFMAN

2.4-6.0 mi / 2.0-4.0 hr 1 9

off Tioga Pass Road in Yosemite National Park

Map 10.1, page 483 BEST

Here's a hike that you can take the kids on—well, the first part, anyway. It's an easy 1.2 miles to May Lake, tucked in below 10,850-foot Mount Hoffman. The trail to the lake has a total elevation gain of only 400 feet, and better yet, it's downhill all the way home. Attaining the summit of Mount Hoffman, on the other hand, requires a challenging ascent, and is best left to more seasoned hikers. (Leave the kids at home if you are going to continue from the shores of May Lake to the top of Mount Hoffman.) The trail to both destinations begins at the Snow Flat trailhead (two miles off Tioga Pass Road), passes through a lodgepole pine forest, climbs up a granite-lined slope, then drops down to May Lake's southern shore. A High Sierra Camp is located here. Wandering along the scenic, granite-ringed shoreline is a pleasant way to spend the afternoon.

To turn this easy walk into a moderate butt-kicker, follow the obvious use trail to the west, which leads around to the north side of May Lake. From the northwest shore, a fairly distinct use trail leads to Hoffman's summit. This is not an official park trail, and it requires scrambling skills and sure footing, especially as you near the top. It also requires good lungs and legs: You have to gain another 1,500 feet in about two miles. So why do it? The view from Mount Hoffman's ridgeline is first-class, with Half Dome, Clouds Rest, Tenaya Lake, and May Lake all in sight. Mount Hoffman is the exact geographical center of Yosemite National Park. The peak has two main summits; the one with the weather station on top is the highest. Explore the entire ridgeline, and visit both summits if you have the time; the view is surprisingly different.

User Groups: Hikers and horses. No dogs or mountain bikes. No wheelchair facilities.

Permits: No permits are required. There is a $35 entrance fee per vehicle at Yosemite National Park, good for seven days.

Maps: A Tuolumne Meadows or Yosemite National Park map is available from Tom Harrison Maps. For a topographic map, go to the USGS website to download Tenaya Lake.

Directions: From Merced, drive 70 miles northeast on Highway 140 to Yosemite National Park. Follow the signs toward Yosemite Valley, entering through the Arch Rock entrance station. Continue 4.5 miles to the left turnoff for Highway 120, looping back out of the valley on Big Oak Flat Road. In 9.3 miles at Crane Flat, turn right on Tioga Pass Road and drive 26.6 miles to the May Lake Road turnoff, on the left (near road marker T-21). Drive two miles to the trailhead parking lot.

Contact: Yosemite National Park, Yosemite, 209/372-0200, www.nps.gov/yose.

24 CLOUDS REST

14.0 mi / 8.0 hr 3 10

off Tioga Pass Road in Yosemite National Park

Map 10.1, page 483 BEST

Hiking to Clouds Rest is a trip that's as epic as climbing Half Dome, but with far fewer people elbowing you along the way. With a 2,300-foot climb and 14 miles to cover, it's not for those who are out of shape. The trail ascends steadily for the first four miles, descends steeply for 0.5 mile, then climbs again more moderately. Keep the faith—the first 2.5 miles from the trailhead are the toughest. The final summit ascent is a little dicey because of the terrifying dropoffs, but as with other Yosemite peaks, watch your footing on the granite slabs, and you'll be fine. Overall, the route is much safer than climbing Half Dome, because the final ascent is far more gradual, and there are no cables to maneuver. The view from the top of Clouds Rest—of Tenaya Canyon, Half Dome, Yosemite Valley, Tenaya Lake, the Clark Range, and various peaks and ridges—will knock your socks off (hope you brought along an extra pair). Note: If this long hike has made you hot and sweaty, you can stop at the Sunrise Lakes for a swim on the way back—the first lake is only 0.25 mile from the Clouds Rest/Sunrise Trail junction.

User Groups: Hikers only. No dogs, horses, or mountain bikes. No wheelchair facilities.

Permits: No permits are required. There is a $35 entrance fee per vehicle at Yosemite National Park, good for seven days.

Maps: A Tuolumne Meadows or Yosemite National Park map is available from Tom Harrison Maps. For a topographic map, go to the USGS website to download Tenaya Lake.

Directions: From Merced, drive 70 miles northeast on Highway 140 to Yosemite National Park. Follow the signs toward Yosemite Valley, entering through the Arch Rock entrance station. Continue 4.5 miles to the left turnoff for Highway 120, looping back out of the valley on Big Oak Flat Road. In 9.3 miles at Crane Flat, turn right on Tioga Pass Road and drive 30.3 miles to the Sunrise Lakes trailhead, on the south side of the highway just west of Tenaya Lake.

Contact: Yosemite National Park, Yosemite, 209/372-0200, www.nps.gov/yose.

25 SUNRISE LAKES

7.5 mi / 4.5 hr or 2 days 

off Tioga Pass Road in Yosemite National Park

Map 10.1, page 483

With all the people hiking to Clouds Rest, combined with all the people hiking to the Sunrise Lakes, the Sunrise trailhead can look like a mall parking lot on a Saturday. But don't be scared off; the hike to Sunrise Lakes is a great day hike or easy backpacking trip, especially during the week or off-season, with only a 1,000-foot elevation gain and a ton of stellar scenery, including great views of Clouds Rest at your back as you hike the final stretch to the lakes. You follow the trail as it climbs steeply above the edge of Tenaya Canyon. At 2.5 miles, turn left at the sign for the Sunrise High Sierra Camp. In about 10 minutes of easy walking, Lower Sunrise Lake shows up on the right, and the other lakes are shortly after it, on the left. The upper lake is the largest and by far the most popular; lots of folks like to swim and picnic there on warm summer days. Backpackers can pick a site here or continue onward for two more miles to the backpackers' camp or the High Sierra Camp, depending on where they've made their plans.

User Groups: Hikers only. No dogs, horses, or mountain bikes. No wheelchair facilities.

Permits: There is a $35 entrance fee per vehicle at Yosemite National Park, good for seven days. Wilderness permits are required for overnight stays. They are available on a first-come, first-served basis up to two days in advance at the Yosemite Wilderness kiosk near your chosen trailhead, or up to 24 weeks in advance through Yosemite's online wilderness reservation system at www.yosemiteconservancy.org for a $5 reservation fee per person.

Maps: A Tuolumne Meadows or Yosemite National Park map is available from Tom Harrison Maps. For a topographic map, go to the USGS website to download Tenaya Lake.

Directions: From Merced, drive 70 miles northeast on Highway 140 to Yosemite National Park. Follow the signs toward Yosemite Valley, entering through the Arch Rock entrance station. Continue 4.5 miles to the left turnoff for Highway 120, looping back out of the valley on Big Oak Flat Road. In 9.3 miles at Crane Flat, turn right on Tioga Pass Road and drive 30.3 miles to the Sunrise Lakes trailhead, on the south side of the highway just west of Tenaya Lake.

Contact: Yosemite National Park, Yosemite, 209/372-0200 or 209/372-0740 (permit reservations), www.nps.gov/yose or www.nps.gov/yose/wilderness (permit reservations).

26 TENAYA LAKE

2.0 mi / 1.0 hr

off Tioga Pass Road in Yosemite National Park

Map 10.1, page 483

Lots of people drive east down Tioga Pass Road in a big rush to get to Tuolumne Meadows, but when they see giant Tenaya Lake right along the road, they stop short in their tire tracks. Luckily the 150-acre, sapphire-blue lake has a parking lot and picnic area at its east end, where you can leave your car and take a stroll down to the lake's edge. Although most people stop at the white-sand beach and picnic tables to watch the rock climbers on nearby Polly Dome, you can leave the crowds behind by strolling to the south side of the beach and joining the trail built by the Yosemite Conservancy. The path leads along the back side of Tenaya Lake, far from the road on the north side. When you get to the lake's west end, where the trail continues but the water views end, just turn around and walk back. It's a perfect, easy hike alongside one of the most beautiful lakes in Yosemite.

User Groups: Hikers only. No dogs, horses, or mountain bikes. No wheelchair facilities.

Permits: No permits are required. There is a $35 entrance fee per vehicle at Yosemite National Park, good for seven days.

Maps: A Tuolumne Meadows or Yosemite National Park map is available from Tom Harrison Maps. For a topographic map, go to the USGS website to download Tenaya Lake.

Directions: From Merced, drive 70 miles northeast on Highway 140 to Yosemite National Park. Follow the signs toward Yosemite Valley, entering through the Arch Rock entrance station. Continue 4.5 miles to the left turnoff for Highway 120, looping back out of the valley on Big Oak Flat Road. In 9.3 miles at Crane Flat, turn right on Tioga Pass Road and drive 31.7 miles to the eastern Tenaya Lake Picnic Area (another Tenaya Lake picnic area lies 0.5 mile west). The trail leads from the parking lot.

Contact: Yosemite National Park, Yosemite, 209/372-0200, www.nps.gov/yose.

27 CATHEDRAL LAKES

7.4 mi / 4.0 hr or 2 days 3 10

near Tuolumne Meadows in Yosemite National Park

Map 10.1, page 483

The Cathedral Lakes are a tremendously popular easy backpacking destination in Yosemite, but it's such a short hike to reach them that they also make a great day trip. Located on a 0.5-mile spur off John Muir Trail, the lakes are within a classic glacial cirque, tucked in below 10,840-foot Cathedral Peak. It's as scenic a spot as you'll find anywhere in Yosemite. Campsites are found close to the lakes, but you will need to secure your wilderness permit way in advance in order to spend the night. From the trail's start at Tioga Pass Road, you hike 3.2 miles on the John Muir Trail, with a 1,000-foot elevation gain. Much of the trail is shaded by lodgepole pines, but when the path breaks out of the trees, views of surrounding peaks (especially distinctive Cathedral Peak, which looks remarkably different from every angle) keep you oohing and ahhing the whole way. At 3.2 miles, turn right on the Cathedral Lake spur to reach the lower, larger lake in 0.5 mile. You'll follow the lake's inlet stream through a gorgeous meadow to the water's edge—then start snapping photographs like crazy. Many hikers stop here and go no farther, but it's a pity not to see Upper Cathedral Lake as well. To reach the upper lake, retrace your steps to John Muir Trail and continue another 0.5 mile. Fishing is often better in the upper lake, and the scenery is even more sublime.

User Groups: Hikers and horses. No dogs or mountain bikes. No wheelchair facilities.

Permits: There is a $35 entrance fee per vehicle at Yosemite National Park, good for seven days. Wilderness permits are required for overnight stays. They are available on a first-come, first-served basis up to two days in advance at the Yosemite Wilderness kiosk near your chosen trailhead, or up to 24 weeks in advance through Yosemite's online wilderness reservation system at www.yosemiteconservancy.org for a $5 reservation fee per person.

Maps: A Tuolumne Meadows or Yosemite National Park map is available from Tom Harrison Maps. For a topographic map, go to the USGS website to download Tenaya Lake.

Directions: From Merced, drive 70 miles northeast on Highway 140 to Yosemite National Park. Follow the signs toward Yosemite Valley, entering through the Arch Rock entrance station. Continue 4.5 miles to the left turnoff for Highway 120, looping back out of the valley on Big Oak Flat Road. In 9.3 miles at Crane Flat, turn right on Tioga Pass Road and drive 37.4 miles to the Cathedral Lakes trailhead, on the right, by Tuolumne Meadows. Park your car in the pullouts on either side of Tioga Pass Road near the trailhead; there is no formal parking lot.

Contact: Yosemite National Park, Yosemite, 209/372-0200 or 209/372-0740 (permit reservations), www.nps.gov/yose or www.nps.gov/yose/wilderness (permit reservations).

28 VOGELSANG LOOP

19.0 mi / 3 or 4 days

near Tuolumne Meadows in Yosemite National Park

Map 10.1, page 483

Although this loop is popular with hikers staying at the Vogelsang High Sierra Camp, backpackers who plan early can get a wilderness permit for their own self-designed trip. The traditional route is to head out on the western side of the loop along Rafferty Creek, then take a short spur and spend the night at Vogelsang Lake, which is without question the most visually dramatic spot seen on this trip. It's flanked by Fletcher Peak, a steep and rugged wall of glacier-carved granite. Few trees can grow in this sparse, high-alpine environment. The next day, you rejoin the loop and continue eastward to Evelyn Lake, another favorite camping spot. When it's time to return, you hike down to Lyell Fork, a 2,000-foot descent that takes a few hours, then meet up with John Muir Trail and follow it north through lush green and

Cathedral Peak towers over Cathedral Lakes

gorgeous Lyell Canyon, back to the trailhead at Tuolumne Meadows. The trailhead is at 8,600 feet—plenty high to start—and for the most part, the trail undulates along, never gaining or losing more than 2,000 feet.

User Groups: Hikers and horses. No dogs or mountain bikes. No wheelchair facilities.

Permits: There is a $35 entrance fee per vehicle at Yosemite National Park, good for seven days. Wilderness permits are required for overnight stays. They are available on a first-come, first-served basis up to two days in advance at the Yosemite Wilderness kiosk near your chosen trailhead, or up to 24 weeks in advance through Yosemite's online wilderness reservation system at www.yosemiteconservancy.org for a $5 reservation fee per person.

Maps: A Tuolumne Meadows or Yosemite National Park map is available from Tom Harrison Maps. For a topographic map, go to the USGS website to download Vogelsang Peak.

Directions: From Merced, drive 70 miles northeast on Highway 140 to Yosemite National Park. Follow the signs toward Yosemite Valley, entering through the Arch Rock entrance station. Continue 4.5 miles to the left turnoff for Highway 120, looping back out of the valley on Big Oak Flat Road. In 9.3 miles at Crane Flat, turn right on Tioga Pass Road and drive 39.5 miles to the Tuolumne Lodge and Wilderness Permits turnoff, on the right. Turn right and drive 0.4 mile toward Tuolumne Lodge. Park in the lot on the left signed for Dog Lake and John Muir Trail. The trail begins across the road from the parking lot. Additional parking is available in the Wilderness Permit parking lot, at the turnoff from Tioga Pass Road.

Contact: Yosemite National Park, Yosemite, 209/372-0200 or 209/372-0740 (permit reservations), www.nps.gov/yose or www.nps.gov/yose/wilderness (permit reservations).

29 LOWER GAYLOR LAKE

8.0 mi / 4.0 hr

near Tioga Pass in Yosemite National Park

Map 10.1, page 483

This mellow, pretty hike starts on John Muir Trail near Tuolumne Lodge, then heads east along the south side of the Dana Fork of the Tuolumne River. After two miles, the trail crosses the river and Tioga Pass Road, and heads uphill through a dense lodgepole pine forest to Lower Gaylor Lake, elevation 10,049 feet. The shallow lake is a deep turquoise color and is surrounded by a grassy alpine meadow. From its edge, you gain wide vistas of the peaks in the Tuolumne Meadows area. This is classic high-country beauty at its finest. Note: If you wish to get to the Middle and Upper Gaylor Lakes from the lower lake, you have to go cross-country. An easier way is to drive to the Tioga Pass trailhead and follow the trail notes in this chapter for the *Middle and Upper Gaylor Lakes* hike. Elevation at this trailhead is 9,250 feet; the total gain is about 800 feet to Lower Gaylor Lake, a gentle climb the whole way.

User Groups: Hikers only. No dogs, horses, or mountain bikes. No wheelchair facilities.

Permits: No permits are required. There is a $35 entrance fee per vehicle at Yosemite National Park, good for seven days.

Maps: A Tuolumne Meadows or Yosemite National Park map is available from Tom Harrison Maps. For topographic maps, go to the USGS website to download Vogelsang Peak and Tioga Pass.

Directions: From Merced, drive 70 miles northeast on Highway 140 to Yosemite National Park. Follow the signs toward Yosemite Valley, entering through the Arch Rock entrance station. Continue 4.5 miles to the left turnoff for Highway 120, looping back out of the valley on Big Oak Flat Road. In 9.3 miles at Crane Flat, turn right on Tioga Pass Road and drive 39.5 miles to the Tuolumne Lodge and Wilderness Permits turnoff, on the right. Turn right and drive 0.4 mile toward Tuolumne Lodge, then park in the lot on the left signed for Dog Lake and John Muir Trail. The trail begins across the road from the parking lot. Additional parking is available in the Wilderness Permit parking lot, at the turnoff from Tioga Pass Road.

Contact: Yosemite National Park, Yosemite, 209/372-0200, www.nps.gov/yose.

30 ELIZABETH LAKE

4.5 mi / 2.5 hr

near Tuolumne Meadows in Yosemite National Park

Map 10.1, page 483

Starting at the trailhead elevation of 8,600 feet, you have a mere 850-foot elevation gain over 2.25 miles to get to lovely Elizabeth Lake, set in a basin at the foot of distinctive Unicorn Peak. It's a day hike that is attainable for almost anybody, and you can bet that every camper at Tuolumne Meadows Campground makes the trip at some point during their vacation. For noncampers, the trailhead is a bit tricky to find—it's tucked into the back of Tuolumne Meadows Campground, across from the group camp restrooms. Once you locate it, be prepared to climb steeply for the first mile, then breathe easier when the trail levels out. Fortunately the route is mostly shaded by a dense grove of lodgepole pines. Upon reaching its shore, you'll see that Elizabeth Lake is a gorgeous body of alpine water. Some visitors swim or fish here; others try to climb Unicorn Peak (10,900 feet); most are happy to sit near the lake's edge and admire the views of the sculpted peak and its neighbors in the Cathedral Range.

User Groups: Hikers only. No dogs, horses, or mountain bikes. No wheelchair facilities.

Permits: No permits are required. There is a $35 entrance fee per vehicle at Yosemite National Park, good for seven days.

Maps: A Tuolumne Meadows or Yosemite National Park map is available from Tom Harrison Maps. For a topographic map, go to the USGS website to download Vogelsang Peak.

Directions: From Merced, drive 70 miles northeast on Highway 140 to Yosemite National Park. Follow the signs toward Yosemite Valley, entering through the Arch Rock entrance station. Continue 4.5 miles to the left turnoff for Highway 120, looping back out of the valley on Big Oak Flat Road. In 9.3 miles at Crane Flat, turn right on Tioga Pass Road and drive 39 miles to the Tuolumne Meadows Campground. Turn right and follow the signs through the main camp to the group camp. The trail begins across from the group camp restrooms, near group site No. B49.

Contact: Yosemite National Park, Yosemite, 209/372-0200, www.nps.gov/yose.

31 LYELL CANYON

6.0 mi / 3.0 hr

near Tuolumne Meadows in Yosemite National Park

Map 10.1, page 483

This hike is one of the easiest in the Yosemite high country, and since it starts out beautiful and stays that way, you can hike it as long or as short as you like. The total trail length is six miles one-way, paralleling the Lyell Fork of the Tuolumne River on the Pacific Crest Trail/John Muir Trail. But most people just head out for two or three miles, carrying their fishing rods, and then turn back. To reach the Lyell Fork, you must first cross the Dana Fork on a footbridge less than 0.5 mile from the parking lot. Then after 0.5 mile, you cross the Lyell Fork on a second footbridge, and head left along the river's south side. A third bridge takes you across Rafferty Creek and into Lyell Canyon. If you like looking at gorgeous meadows and a meandering river, this is your hike. Small trout are plentiful. A bonus is that backpacking sites are located three to four miles out on the trail, so if you get a wilderness permit, you can linger for a few days in paradise.

User Groups: Hikers and horses. No dogs or mountain bikes. No wheelchair facilities.

Permits: No permits are required. There is a $35 entrance fee per vehicle at Yosemite National Park, good for seven days.
Maps: A Tuolumne Meadows or Yosemite National Park map is available from Tom Harrison Maps. For a topographic map, go to the USGS website to download Vogelsang Peak.
Directions: From Merced, drive 70 miles northeast on Highway 140 to Yosemite National Park. Follow the signs toward Yosemite Valley, entering through the Arch Rock entrance station. Continue 4.5 miles to the left turnoff for Highway 120, looping back out of the valley on Big Oak Flat Road. In 9.3 miles at Crane Flat, turn right on Tioga Pass Road and drive 39.5 miles to the Tuolumne Lodge and Wilderness Permits turnoff, on the right. Turn right and drive 0.4 mile toward Tuolumne Lodge; park in the lot on the left signed for Dog Lake and John Muir Trail. The John Muir Trail begins across the road from the parking lot. Additional parking is available in the Wilderness Permit parking lot, at the turnoff from Tioga Pass Road.
Contact: Yosemite National Park, Yosemite, 209/372-0200, www.nps.gov/yose.

32 YOUNG LAKES LOOP

14.6 mi / 1 or 2 days 

near Tuolumne Meadows in Yosemite National Park

Map 10.1, page 483

Starting from the Lembert Dome parking lot at 8,600 feet in elevation, the Young Lakes Loop is a classic Yosemite trip that works equally well as a short backpacking trip or a long day hike. The destination is a series of lakes set in a deep and wide glacial cirque—the kind of awesome scenery that sticks in your mind months later, when you're sitting at a desk somewhere staring at your computer screen. The trip starts with a walk down the wide dirt road that leads to Soda Spring. Pick up the trail near Parson's Lodge that leads to Glen Aulin, and follow it through lodgepole pines for 1.8 miles until you see the right turnoff for Young Lakes. Follow Young Lakes Trail for 3.5 more miles, climbing steadily. At 5.5 miles out, you'll see the return leg of your loop leading off to the right (signed for Dog Lake). You'll continue straight for another 1.5 miles to Lower Young Lake and a stunning view of Ragged Peak, Mount Conness, and White Mountain. Two more lakes are accessible within a mile to the east. If you have the energy, don't miss the third, upper lake, the most visually stunning of them all, perched in a high meadow at 10,218 feet in elevation. When you're ready to head home, retrace your steps to the junction, and take the eastern (left) fork, returning via Dog Lake and Lembert Dome. Be forewarned: If you loop back this way, it won't be an all-downhill cruise, but the scenery makes the additional climbing worthwhile. If you're exhausted from your trip to the lakes, skip the loop and return the way you came—it's downhill all the way.
User Groups: Hikers and horses. No dogs or mountain bikes. No wheelchair facilities.
Permits: There is a $35 entrance fee per vehicle at Yosemite National Park, good for seven days. Wilderness permits are required for overnight stays. They are available on a first-come, first-served basis up to two days in advance at the Yosemite Wilderness kiosk near your chosen trailhead, or up to 24 weeks in advance through Yosemite's online wilderness reservation system at www.yosemiteconservancy.org for a $5 reservation fee per person.
Maps: A Yosemite National Park map is available from Tom Harrison Maps. For topographic maps, go to the USGS website to download Tioga Pass and Falls Ridge.
Directions: From Merced, drive 70 miles northeast on Highway 140 to Yosemite National Park. Follow the signs toward Yosemite Valley, entering through the Arch Rock entrance station. Continue 4.5 miles to the left turnoff for Highway 120, looping back out of the valley on Big Oak Flat Road. In 9.3 miles at Crane Flat, turn right on Tioga Pass Road and drive 39 miles to the Lembert Dome/Soda Spring/Dog

Lake/Glen Aulin trailhead parking, on the left. Begin hiking on the western edge of the parking lot, where there is a gated dirt road signed for Soda Spring.

Contact: Yosemite National Park, Yosemite, 209/372-0200 or 209/372-0740 (permit reservations), www.nps.gov/yose or www.nps.gov/yose/wilderness (permit reservations).

33 WATERWHEEL FALLS

16.0 mi / 1 or 2 days 3 10

near Tuolumne Meadows in Yosemite National Park

Map 10.1, page 483 BEST

This hike could be called the Epic Waterfall Trip. If you hike the entire route, you'll see so many waterfalls and so much water along the way that you'll have enough memories to get you through a 10-year drought. Arrange for a wilderness permit in advance, or reserve a stay at the Glen Aulin High Sierra Camp, so that you can divide the 16 miles over two or more days. If you're in good enough shape, you can do the trip in one day, because the trail is nearly level for the first four miles (a 400-foot elevation loss), then descends more steeply over the next four miles (a 1,500-foot elevation loss). Unfortunately, all the climbing must be done on the way home, so you must reserve your energy and have plenty of food and water (or at least a purifying device so you can filter water from the river).

Follow the trail notes for Glen Aulin and Tuolumne Falls (see listing in this chapter) for the first four miles of trail; then continue downstream past Glen Aulin Camp, alternating between stretches of stunning flower- and aspen-lined meadows and stark granite slabs. Waterwheel Falls is only three miles from the camp, and two other major cascades, California and LeConte, are along the way. To see all three falls, make sure you take each spur trail you see that leads to the river; none of the waterfalls is apparent from the main trail. Other hikers will stop you on the trail to ask if you know where the waterfalls are. Whereas all three falls are long white-water cascades, Waterwheel is considered Yosemite's most unusual-looking waterfall because it has sections of churning water that dip into deep holes in the granite, then shoot out with such velocity that they double back on themselves. When the river level is high, they actually appear to circle around like waterwheels.

User Groups: Hikers and horses. No dogs or mountain bikes. No wheelchair facilities.

Permits: There is a $35 entrance fee per vehicle at Yosemite National Park, good for seven days. Wilderness permits are required for overnight stays. They are available on a first-come, first-served basis up to two days in advance at the Yosemite Wilderness kiosk near your chosen trailhead, or up to 24 weeks in advance through Yosemite's online wilderness reservation system at www.yosemiteconservancy.org for a $5 reservation fee per person.

Maps: A Tuolumne Meadows or Yosemite National Park map is available from Tom Harrison Maps. For topographic maps, go to the USGS website to download Tioga Pass and Falls Ridge.

Directions: From Merced, drive 70 miles northeast on Highway 140 to Yosemite National Park. Follow the signs toward Yosemite Valley, entering through the Arch Rock entrance station. Continue 4.5 miles to the left turnoff for Highway 120, looping back out of the valley on Big Oak Flat Road. In 9.3 miles at Crane Flat, turn right on Tioga Pass Road and drive 39 miles to the Lembert Dome/Soda Spring/Dog Lake/Glen Aulin trailhead parking, on the left. Begin hiking on the western edge of the parking lot, where there is a gated dirt road signed for Soda Spring.

Contact: Yosemite National Park, Yosemite, 209/372-0200 or 209/372-0740 (permit reservations), www.nps.gov/yose or www.nps.gov/yose/wilderness (permit reservations).

34 GLEN AULIN AND TUOLUMNE FALLS

9.0 mi / 5.0 hr 2 9

near Tuolumne Meadows in Yosemite National Park

Map 10.1, page 483 BEST

Those who aren't up for the Epic Waterfall Trip to Waterwheel Falls (see listing in this chapter) can take this trip instead and maybe even sneak in a good meal at the Glen Aulin High Sierra Camp. To stay in the camp, you must reserve a spot far in advance, but you can often purchase a hot meal just by showing up. Tuolumne Falls drop right by the High Sierra Camp, and reaching the waterfall requires only a 4.5-mile walk with a 400-foot elevation loss. The return climb is easy, with most of the ascent being in the first mile as you head up and over the various cascades of Tuolumne Falls on granite stairs. Follow the dirt road from the Lembert Dome parking lot toward Soda Spring. When you near Parson's Lodge, veer right on the signed trail to Glen Aulin. You'll walk through lodgepole pine forest, then move closer to the Tuolumne River and get incredible views of Cathedral and Unicorn Peaks, as well as Fairview Dome. After three miles, you'll cross the Tuolumne on a footbridge, and in another 0.25 mile, you'll reach the first stunning drop of Tuolumne Falls, a 100-foot, churning freefall. Keep descending past more cascades to the base of the falls, where another footbridge leads back across the river and to Glen Aulin. Pick a spot downstream beside a river pool or near the bridge at the base of the waterfall, have a seat, and ponder the exquisite beauty of this place.

User Groups: Hikers and horses. No dogs or mountain bikes. No wheelchair facilities.

Permits: No permits are required. There is a $35 entrance fee per vehicle at Yosemite National Park, good for seven days.

Maps: A Tuolumne Meadows or Yosemite National Park map is available from Tom Harrison Maps. For topographic maps, go to the USGS website to download Tioga Pass and Falls Ridge.

Directions: From Merced, drive 70 miles northeast on Highway 140 to Yosemite National Park. Follow the signs toward Yosemite Valley, entering through the Arch Rock entrance station. Continue 4.5 miles to the left turnoff for Highway 120, looping back out of the valley on Big Oak Flat Road. In 9.3 miles at Crane Flat, turn right on Tioga Pass Road and drive 39 miles to the Lembert Dome/Soda Spring/Dog Lake/Glen Aulin trailhead parking, on the left. Begin hiking on the western edge of the parking lot, where there is a gated dirt road signed for Soda Spring.

Contact: Yosemite National Park, Yosemite, 209/372-0200, www.nps.gov/yose.

35 LEMBERT DOME

2.8 mi / 1.5 hr 3 10

near Tuolumne Meadows in Yosemite National Park

Map 10.1, page 483

Lembert Dome is a *roche moutonné* (a French geologic term that means it looks something like a sheep). We never see the resemblance, but we did feel like a couple of mountain goats when we climbed Lembert Dome, elevation 9,450 feet. From the parking area at the base, you can see rock climbers practicing their stuff on the steep side of the dome, but luckily the hiker's trail heads around to the more-sloped back side. You can walk right up the granite—no ropes necessary. The Dog Lake and Lembert Dome Trail winds its way steeply around to the dome's north side (see listing in this chapter); from there, pick any route along the granite that looks manageable. When you reach the top of the dome, you know that you've accomplished something. The view from its highest point—of Tuolumne Meadows and surrounding peaks and domes—is more than worth the effort.

User Groups: Hikers only. No dogs, horses, or mountain bikes. No wheelchair facilities.

Permits: No permits are required. There is a $35 entrance fee per vehicle at Yosemite National Park, good for seven days.

Maps: A Tuolumne Meadows or Yosemite National Park map is available from Tom Harrison Maps. For a topographic map, go to the USGS website to download Tioga Pass.

Directions: From Merced, drive 70 miles northeast on Highway 140 to Yosemite National Park. Follow the signs toward Yosemite Valley, entering through the Arch Rock entrance station. Continue 4.5 miles to the left turnoff for Highway 120, looping back out of the valley on Big Oak Flat Road. In 9.3 miles at Crane Flat, turn right on Tioga Pass Road and drive 39 miles to the Lembert Dome/Soda Spring/Dog Lake/Glen Aulin trailhead parking, on the left. Begin hiking on the trail near the restrooms.

Contact: Yosemite National Park, Yosemite, 209/372-0200, www.nps.gov/yose.

36 DOG LAKE

3.4 mi / 2.0 hr

near Tuolumne Meadows in Yosemite National Park

Map 10.1, page 483

Dog Lake is an easy-to-reach destination from Tuolumne Meadows, a perfect place for a family to spend an afternoon in the high country. The hike begins near the base of Lembert Dome, then heads through a gorgeous meadow that offers views of snowy Cathedral and Unicorn Peaks. The trail traverses a granite slab, then splits off from the path to Lembert Dome and starts to climb quite steeply through a lodgepole pine and fir forest. When you reach an intersection with Young Lakes Trail, you're only 0.25 mile from Dog Lake. The lake is a delight, although with its grassy shoreline, it is often plagued with mosquitoes (don't forget the bug spray). Set at 9,170 feet in elevation, it is wide, shallow, and deep blue. The colorful peaks to the east are Mount Dana and Mount Gibbs. You can hike around Dog Lake's perimeter if you please, take a swim in late summer, or just sit by the peaceful shoreline and relax.

User Groups: Hikers and horses. No dogs or mountain bikes. No wheelchair facilities.

Permits: No permits are required. There is a $35 entrance fee per vehicle at Yosemite National Park, good for seven days.

Maps: A Tuolumne Meadows or Yosemite National Park map is available from Tom Harrison Maps. For a topographic map, go to the USGS website to download Tioga Pass.

Directions: From Merced, drive 70 miles northeast on Highway 140 to Yosemite National Park. Follow the signs toward Yosemite Valley, entering through the Arch Rock entrance station. Continue 4.5 miles to the left turnoff for Highway 120, looping back out of the valley on Big Oak Flat Road. In 9.3 miles at Crane Flat, turn right on Tioga Pass Road and drive 39 miles to the Lembert Dome/Soda Spring/Dog Lake/Glen Aulin trailhead parking, on the left. Begin hiking on the trail near the restrooms.

Contact: Yosemite National Park, Yosemite, 209/372-0200, www.nps.gov/yose.

37 TUOLUMNE MEADOWS TO SONORA PASS (PCT)

77.0 mi one-way / 8 days 5 10

from Tuolumne Meadows on Highway 120 north to Sonora Pass on Highway 108

Map 10.1, page 483

This is a spectacular week-plus backpack trip that follows a section of the Pacific Crest Trail (PCT). The beauty of this region's deep canyons, glacial-cut peaks, verdant meadows, and abundant wildlife makes it a hiker's paradise.

From Tuolumne Meadows, the trail starts out deceptively easy as it follows the Tuolumne River toward the Grand Canyon of the Tuolumne River. It heads gently downhill to Glen Aulin, where you get a great view of Tuolumne Falls. When you cross the bridge at the base of the falls and head up-canyon, you'll leave the day hikers behind. In the next three days, you'll go up one canyon and down the next, one after another, with breathtaking views and long, demanding climbs. Highlights include Matterhorn Canyon (many deer, trout, and views), Benson Lake (the largest white-sand beach in the Sierra Nevada), Dorothy Lake (panoramic views to the north), and many pristine, high-country meadows. The incredible clouds of mosquitoes at the Wilmer Lake area during early summer can be a major annoyance.

When you leave Yosemite and enter Humboldt-Toiyabe National Forest, the landscape changes quickly from glacial-cut granite to volcanic rock. The trail drops past several pretty lakes and into a river drainage, and at points can be difficult to follow. In a few areas, you may be surprised to meet up with grazing cows, especially from midsummer onward. You'll make a long, slow, climb up toward Leavitt Pass, set just below 10,800-foot Leavitt Peak. This landscape is entirely above tree line, in gray, stark country. At Leavitt Pass, the wind whistles by at high speed almost year-round. The final drop down to Sonora Pass is a one-hour descent that seems to wind all over the mountain. When you reach Highway 108, cross the road and walk about 100 yards west to a large day-use parking area. That's where your car shuttle should be waiting for you.

User Groups: Hikers and horses. No dogs or mountain bikes. No wheelchair facilities.

Permits: A wilderness permit is required for traveling through various wilderness and special-use areas the trail traverses. Contact either the Wilderness Office of the National Park Service or the Stanislaus National Forest for a permit that is good for the length of your trip. There is a $35 entrance fee per vehicle at Yosemite National Park, good for seven days.

Maps: For topographic maps, go to the USGS website to download Pickel Meadow, Tower Peak, Piute Mountain, Matterhorn Peak, Dunderberg Peak, Vogelsang Peak, Tioga Pass, Falls Ridge, Buckeye Ridge, and Sonora Pass.

Directions: From Merced, drive 70 miles northeast on Highway 140 to Yosemite National Park. Follow the signs toward Yosemite Valley, entering through the Arch Rock entrance station. Continue 4.5 miles to the left turnoff for Highway 120, looping back out of the valley on Big Oak Flat Road. In 9.3 miles at Crane Flat, turn right on Tioga Pass Road and drive 39 miles to the Lembert Dome/Soda Spring/Dog Lake/Glen Aulin trailhead parking, on the left. Begin hiking on the western edge of the parking lot, where there is a gated dirt road signed for Soda Spring.

Contact: Yosemite National Park, Yosemite, 209/372-0200, www.nps.gov/yose; Stanislaus National Forest, Calaveras Ranger Station, Hathaway Pines, 209/795-1381, www.fs.usda.gov/stanislaus.

38 TUOLUMNE MEADOWS TO YOSEMITE VALLEY (JMT)

22.0 mi one-way / 2 days 5 10

near Tuolumne Meadows in Yosemite National Park

Map 10.1, page 483

The first glimpses of Yosemite Valley will seem like a privileged view into heaven after having hiked the entire John Muir Trail (JMT) from Mount Whitney. For hikers making only this 22-mile section, the rewards can seem just as profound. The trip starts at Tuolumne Meadows, where backpackers can buy a good cheap breakfast, obtain wilderness permits, and camp in a special area set aside for JMT hikers. When you take your first steps away from Tuolumne Meadows, resist the urge to rush to the finish line in order to close out a historic expedition. Instead, relax and enjoy the downhill glide, always remembering that you are in sacred land. Compared to the rest of the JMT, this leg will come with far less strain, starting with a 3.1-mile tromp past Cathedral Lakes and requiring a 0.5-mile walk on a signed cutoff trail. If you can time it right, this area can make a great layover camp, with deep, emerald-green water and Cathedral Peak in the background. Beyond Cathedral Lakes, the trail makes a relatively short 500-foot climb over Cathedral Pass, skirts Tresidder Peak, and then descends through pristine Long Meadow. After passing Sunrise Trail Camp, a decent layover, the trail picks up little Sunrise Creek and follows it all the way down to Little Yosemite Valley, a popular trail camp. From Cathedral Lakes, it's 14.5 miles to the junction of Half Dome Trail, and another 2.2 miles to Little Yosemite.

For JMT hikers, making the climb to the top of Half Dome is a must, even though it often means putting up with a parade of people and even delays waiting for the line to move at the climbing cable. The Half Dome climb starts with a steep hike for the first mile, followed by steep switchbacks across granite on good trail to the foot of Half Dome's back wall. Here you'll find climbing cables to aid your final 300-foot ascent, and as you go, you'll discover breathtaking views of Tenaya Canyon. This is considered one of the world's glamour hikes, and while it turns hiking into an act of faith, we have seen eight-year-olds and 70-year-olds make the cable climb. By the way, if you take on Half Dome, be certain to have two canteens of water per person. Adding the Half Dome side-trip to the rest of the JMT leg will add a round-trip of 5.2 miles to your hike. Because of its proximity to Half Dome, the Little Yosemite Valley Trail Camp is often crowded. From here, though, it's an easy five-mile hike downhill to Yosemite Valley. Again, try not to speed through to the end, even though it's an easy tromp downhill all the way. The magic is in the moment.

From Little Yosemite, the JMT is routed along the Merced River. In a mile, you'll reach Liberty Cap, and shortly later, Nevada Fall. Then down, down you go, with the trail often turning to giant granite steps, down past Emerald Pool and then to Vernal Fall, another spectacular waterfall. Since Vernal Fall is just 1.7 miles from the end of the trail, you'll start meeting lots of day hikers coming from the other direction, many gasping for breath as they make the uphill climb out of Yosemite Valley. Many will ask how far you've hiked; some may even want to take your photograph. It may feel a bit inane, but, hey, enjoy it. After all, you just finished John Muir Trail, the greatest hiking trail in the world.

User Groups: Hikers and horses. No dogs or mountain bikes. No wheelchair facilities.

Permits: A wilderness permit is required for traveling through various wilderness and special-use areas that the trail traverses. Contact the Wilderness Office of the National Park Service for a permit that is good for the length of your trip. There is a $35 entrance fee per vehicle at Yosemite National Park, good for seven days.

Maps: A John Muir Trail Map Pack is available from Tom Harrison Maps. For topographic maps, go to the USGS website to download Vogelsang Peak, Half Dome, Yosemite Falls, and Tenaya Peak.

Directions: From Merced, drive 70 miles northeast on Highway 140 to Yosemite National Park. Follow the signs toward Yosemite Valley, entering through the Arch Rock entrance station. Continue 4.5 miles to the left turnoff for Highway 120, looping back out of the valley on Big Oak Flat Road. In 9.3 miles at Crane Flat, turn right on Tioga Pass Road and drive 39.5 miles to the Tuolumne Lodge and Wilderness Permits turnoff, on the right. Turn right and drive 0.4 mile toward Tuolumne Lodge; park in the lot on the left signed for Dog Lake and John Muir Trail. The John Muir Trail begins across the road from the parking lot. Additional parking is available in the Wilderness Permit parking lot, at the turnoff from Tioga Road.

Contact: Yosemite National Park, Yosemite, 209/372-0200 or 209/372-0740 (permit reservations), www.nps.gov/yose or www.nps.gov/yose/wilderness (permit reservations).

39 MONO PASS

8.4 mi / 4.5 hr 2 9

near Tioga Pass in Yosemite National Park

Map 10.1, page 483

With an elevation gain of only 900 feet spread out over four miles, you'll hardly even notice you're climbing on the route to Mono Pass. That's if you're acclimated, of course, because you start out at 9,700 feet, where the air is mighty thin. The Mono Pass Trail begins in a mix of lodgepole pines and grassy meadows, then crosses the Dana Fork of the Tuolumne River, which is an easy boulder-hop by midsummer. (Earlier in the season you may need to find a log to cross.) The trail soon meets up with Parker Pass Creek and parallels it for most of the trip. As you proceed, you'll gain great views of Mount Gibbs, Mount Dana, and the Kuna Crest. At a trail junction at 2.0 miles, bear left and start to climb more noticeably. When you reach the Mono Pass sign at 3.8 miles, take the right spur trail (unsigned). It leads 0.3 mile to a cluster of four 19th-century mining cabins, which have been beautifully restored. It's fascinating to explore the small cabins and surrounding mine ruins and consider the hard life of those who lived and worked here. Then, heading back to the main trail, continue another 0.5 mile beyond the sign marking Mono Pass for the best views of the trip. From a granite promontory above a water-filled tarn, you can see far down Bloody Canyon to Mono Lake and the surrounding desert.

User Groups: Hikers and horses. No dogs or mountain bikes. No wheelchair facilities.

Permits: No permits are required. There is a $35 entrance fee per vehicle at Yosemite National Park, good for seven days.

Maps: A Yosemite High Country map is available from Tom Harrison Maps. For a topographic map, go to the USGS website to download Tioga Pass.

Directions: From Merced, drive 70 miles northeast on Highway 140 to Yosemite National Park. Follow the signs toward Yosemite Valley, entering through the Arch Rock entrance station. Continue 4.5 miles to the left turnoff for Highway 120, looping back out of the valley on Big Oak Flat Road. In 9.3 miles at Crane Flat, turn right on Tioga Pass Road and drive 44.5 miles to the Mono Pass trailhead on the right, 1.5 miles west of Tioga Pass.

Contact: Yosemite National Park, Yosemite, 209/372-0200, www.nps.gov/yose.

40 SPILLWAY AND HELEN LAKES

9.0 mi / 5.0 hr 3 9

near Tioga Pass in Yosemite National Park

Map 10.1, page 483

Another option on the Mono Pass Trail (see trail notes for previous hike) is to take the right fork at 2.0 miles and head for Spillway Lake, a wide, shallow lake that is only 1.6 miles from this junction, and then large Helen Lake, which is reached by some easy cross-country travel. It seems like a completely different trip than the aforementioned hike to Mono Pass. The highlights here are two high alpine lakes that epitomize the beauty of the Yosemite high country. Backpackers rarely travel to these lakes, so day hikers are likely to have more solitude here. The views of the Kuna Crest and the high alpine meadow surrounding the upper reaches of Parker Pass Creek will take your breath away. A maintained trail travels to Spillway Lake, and from its southeast edge you simply follow Helen Lake's outlet creek uphill to the shores of Helen Lake. Helen Lake is set at 11,000 feet in elevation, and it's as lovely as any high mountain lake can be. Total elevation gain to see both lakes is only 1,300 feet.

User Groups: Hikers only. No dogs, horses, or mountain bikes. No wheelchair facilities.

Permits: No permits are required. There is a $35 entrance fee per vehicle at Yosemite National Park, good for seven days.

Maps: A Yosemite High Country map is available from Tom Harrison Maps. For a topographic map, go to the USGS website to download Tioga Pass.

Directions: From Merced, drive 70 miles northeast on Highway 140 to Yosemite National Park. Follow the signs toward Yosemite Valley, entering through the Arch Rock entrance station. Continue 4.5 miles to the left turnoff for Highway 120, looping back out of the valley on Big Oak Flat Road. In 9.3 miles at Crane Flat, turn right on Tioga Pass Road and drive 44.5 miles to the Mono Pass trailhead on the right, 1.5 miles west of Tioga Pass.

Contact: Yosemite National Park, Yosemite, 209/372-0200, www.nps.gov/yose.

41 MIDDLE AND UPPER GAYLOR LAKES

4.0 mi / 2.5 hr — 3 — 9

near Tioga Pass in Yosemite National Park

Map 10.1, page 483

Middle and Upper Gaylor Lakes are deservedly popular destinations, because of the short distance required to reach them and their great opportunities for trout fishing. Oh yeah, and then there is the amazing high-alpine scenery. Starting near Tioga Pass (at nearly 10,000 feet), the trail climbs a steep ridge and then drops down to Middle Gaylor Lake. Although it's only one mile of ascent, it's a high-elevation butt-kicker that causes many to beg for mercy. From the middle lake, you can follow the creek gently uphill to the east for another mile to reach smaller Upper Gaylor Lake. Be sure to take the trail around its north side and uphill for a few hundred yards to the site of the Great Sierra Mine and the remains of an old stone cabin. The Great Sierra Mine turned out to be not so great—no silver ore was ever refined, and the mine was eventually abandoned. The hauntingly beautiful glacial scenery is what remains. Total elevation gain on the hike to Upper Gaylor Lake is about 1,000 feet, and it's worth every step. If you want to see more of this sublime lake basin, the twin Granite Lakes lie about 0.75 mile northwest of Middle Gaylor Lake. Although there is no formal trail, it's an easy cross-country ramble to see the Granite Lakes as well, which are tucked in below a massive granite cirque.

User Groups: Hikers only. No dogs, horses, or mountain bikes. No wheelchair facilities.

Permits: No permits are required. There is a $35 entrance fee per vehicle at Yosemite National Park, good for seven days.

Maps: A Yosemite High Country map is available from Tom Harrison Maps. For a topographic map, go to the USGS website to download Tioga Pass.

Directions: From Merced, drive 70 miles northeast on Highway 140 to Yosemite National Park. Follow the signs toward Yosemite Valley, entering through the Arch Rock entrance station. Continue 4.5 miles to the left turnoff for Highway 120, looping back out of the valley on Big Oak Flat Road. In 9.3 miles at Crane Flat, turn right on Tioga Pass Road and drive 46 miles to the parking lot just west of the Tioga Pass entrance station, on the north side of Tioga Pass Road.

Contact: Yosemite National Park, Yosemite, 209/372-0200, www.nps.gov/yose.

42 MOUNT DANA

6.0 mi / 4.0 hr — 4 — 9

near Tioga Pass in Yosemite National Park

Map 10.1, page 483 BEST

Mount Dana is a grueling hike. Yet many hikers make the trip every summer, perhaps as some sort of rite of passage to affirm that the long winter has truly ended in the high country. The path to the 13,053-foot summit requires a 3,100-foot elevation gain condensed into a mere three miles. To make matters more difficult, there is no maintained trail, only a series of informal "use" trails created by generations of hearty Yosemite hikers who have traveled the route. To join their ranks, leave your car at the Gaylor Lakes trailhead by the Tioga Pass entrance station, then cross the road and hike southeast on the unsigned but obvious trail that begins just a few feet from the park entrance kiosk. The path starts with a pleasant ramble through Dana Meadows, then enters a dense lodgepole pine forest. Soon the grade becomes more intense, but this first stretch of climbing is highlighted by a spectacular wildflower show that usually peaks in late July. Lupine, larkspur, Indian paintbrush, senecia—they're all here, in all their glory. The climbing gets tougher on the second mile of the hike, but stick with it and soon you've climbed above 11,000 feet, and now you're above tree line. The path keeps ascending to the 11,600-foot mark, where a giant trail cairn marks a large, rock-covered plateau. This is a good place to rest and do a check on your physical and mental state. Although the summit may look close from here, you still have a long, hard way to go. Two fairly obvious paths head uphill from this point; if you're feeling comfortable with the altitude, pick either one and continue onward, zigzagging your way up the shale-covered slope. In the final mile you must gain 1,500 feet, and to say it is slow going would be a major understatement. There's no shade, often a fierce wind, plenty of loose rock underfoot, and the breathtakingly thin air of high altitude. With what may seem like your last breath, you finally reach the summit, where you are witness to one of the finest views in the Sierra. Your field of vision encompasses Mono Lake, Ellery and Saddlebag Lakes, Glacier Canyon, Tuolumne Meadows, Lembert Dome, and an untold wealth of high peaks. Bring a map and identify all you can survey, or forget the map and just take in the majesty of it all.

A few tips for making the ascent safely: First, wait until mid-July or later to make the trip, as Mount Dana can be snow-covered long into the summer. Second, get an early start in the morning so you have no chance of encountering afternoon thunderstorms. Third, carry (and drink) as much water as you can. Fourth, wear good sunglasses and sun protection at this high elevation. And lastly, pace yourself to give your body a chance to adjust to the 13,000-foot altitude.

User Groups: Hikers only. No dogs, horses, or mountain bikes. No wheelchair facilities.

Permits: No permits are required. There is a $35 entrance fee per vehicle at Yosemite National Park, good for seven days.

Maps: A Yosemite High Country map is available from Tom Harrison Maps. For a topographic map, go to the USGS website to download Tioga Pass.

Directions: From Merced, drive 70 miles northeast on Highway 140 to Yosemite National Park. Follow the signs toward Yosemite Valley, entering through the Arch Rock entrance station. Continue 4.5 miles to the left turnoff for Highway 120, looping back out of the valley on Big Oak Flat Road. In 9.3 miles at Crane Flat, turn right on Tioga Pass Road and drive 46 miles to the parking lot just west of the Tioga Pass entrance station, on the north side of Tioga Pass Road. The trail begins on the south side of Tioga Pass Road; begin hiking on the unsigned trail across from the park entrance kiosk.

Contact: Yosemite National Park, Yosemite, 209/372-0200, www.nps.gov/yose.

43 BENNETTVILLE

2.6 mi / 2.0 hr

in Inyo National Forest just east of Tioga Pass

Map 10.1, page 483

This first-class high-country hike is suitable for even the most novice hikers, and is sure to spark your imagination. The remote high-country region of Bennettville was the site of a 19th-century silver mining community. Although the town thrived only from 1882 to 1884, it was the primary reason for the construction of the Tioga Pass Road from the west. The original road, called the Great Sierra Wagon Road, was built by the Great Sierra Consolidated Silver Company in anticipation of the riches they would make from the mines at Bennettville and nearby. Ultimately, no valuable minerals were ever extracted, and the company went broke in record time. A mostly level trail leads to the two buildings that remain from Bennettville's heyday: the assay office and barn/bunkhouse. An open mine tunnel lined with railcar tracks can also be seen, as well as some rusting mining equipment. Much of the machinery and supplies for this mine was hauled here from the May Lundy Mine over Dore Pass. Men and animals carried several tons of equipment on their backs and on sleds, sometimes through driving snowstorms in the middle of winter at this 10,000-foot elevation.

You can extend this hike by following the trail alongside Mine Creek 0.5 mile uphill from the mine buildings to small Shell Lake, followed by three more shallow lakes in the next mile or so: Mine, Fantail, and finally Spuller. More mine sites can be seen along the way. The high-country landscape here is a mix of open meadows, delicate high-alpine wildflowers, and wind-sculpted whitebark pines. The scenery is as good as you'll find anywhere, and you'll want to return to this area again and again.

User Groups: Hikers, horses, and dogs. No mountain bikes past Shell Lake (wilderness boundary). No wheelchair facilities.

Permits: No permits are required. Parking and access are free.

Maps: A Yosemite High Country map is available from Tom Harrison Maps. An Inyo National Forest map is available from the U.S. Forest Service. For a topographic map, go to the USGS website to download Tioga Pass.

Directions: From Merced, drive 70 miles northeast on Highway 140 to Yosemite National Park. Follow the signs toward Yosemite Valley, entering through the Arch Rock entrance station. Continue 4.5 miles to the left turnoff for Highway 120, looping back out of the valley on Big Oak Flat Road. In 9.3 miles at Crane Flat, turn right on Tioga Pass Road and drive 48 miles (you'll exit the park) to the Saddlebag Lake turnoff, on the left, two miles east of Tioga Pass. Turn left, and then left again immediately, to enter Junction Campground. The trail begins at the campground entrance.

Contact: Inyo National Forest, Mono Basin Scenic Area Visitors Center, Lee Vining, 760/647-3044, www.fs.usda.gov/inyo.

44 GARDISKY LAKE

2.0 mi / 2.0 hr

in Hoover Wilderness just east of Tioga Pass

Map 10.1, page 483

How can a two-mile round-trip hike be rated a 3 for difficulty? It can because it goes straight up, gaining 700 feet in just one mile, with not nearly enough switchbacks. Although the trail distance is short, the trailhead is set at 9,800 feet, which means you need to be well acclimated to pant your way through that steep of a grade. The trip offers many rewards, though, including many fewer people than at nearby Saddlebag Lake and a stellar high-alpine setting. Once you huff and puff your way to the ridge top, you have a nearly level 0.25-mile stroll through a fragile alpine meadow to reach the lake, a shallow body of water surrounded by high-alpine meadows. That 11,513-foot mountain you see as you climb (ahead and to your right) is Tioga Peak; from the southwest edge of Gardisky Lake it's a short but steep tromp to its windy summit (this will add a couple extra miles and 1,000 feet of extra elevation gain to your day). White Mountain and Mount Conness are also prominent, both over 12,000 feet.

User Groups: Hikers, horses, and dogs. No mountain bikes. No wheelchair facilities.

Permits: No permits are required for day-use; an overnight permit is required for backpacking. Parking and access are free.

Maps: A Yosemite High Country map is available from Tom Harrison Maps. An Inyo National Forest map is available from the U.S. Forest Service. For a topographic map, go to the USGS website to download Tioga Pass.

Directions: From Merced, drive 70 miles

northeast on Highway 140 to Yosemite National Park. Follow the signs toward Yosemite Valley, entering through the Arch Rock entrance station. Continue 4.5 miles to the left turnoff for Highway 120, looping back out of the valley on Big Oak Flat Road. In 9.3 miles at Crane Flat, turn right on Tioga Pass Road and drive 48 miles (you'll exit the park) to the Saddlebag Lake turnoff, on the left, two miles east of Tioga Pass. Turn left and go 1.3 miles to the trailhead parking area, on the west side of the road before you reach Saddlebag Lake. The trail begins across the road.

Contact: Inyo National Forest, Mono Basin Scenic Area Visitors Center, Lee Vining, 760/647-3044, www.fs.usda.gov/inyo.

45 SLATE CREEK TRAIL TO GREEN TREBLE LAKE

4.5 mi / 2.0 hr 2 9

in Hoover Wilderness just east of Tioga Pass

Map 10.1, page 483

One of the most beautiful and serene campgrounds in the High Sierra, Sawmill Walk-In Camp is accessed by a quarter-mile walk from its parking area. A wide trail continues through and past the campsites into Hall Research Natural Area, a specially protected region of Inyo National Forest that is open to day hikers only (no backpacking). The trail leads one mile to Timberline Station, an old research station built in 1929. From here you can cross Slate Creek and hike another mile to Green Treble Lake at the headwaters of Slate Creek. Where two forks of the creek join, about 0.5 mile beyond Timberline Station, follow the south fork (left) another 0.5 mile to Green Treble Lake. This is a remarkably level hike at 10,000-plus feet in elevation—pristine high country that is only accessible a few months each year. You know you are in a special place when you are here.

User Groups: Hikers, horses, and dogs. No mountain bikes. No wheelchair facilities.

Permits: No permits are required. Parking and access are free.

Maps: A Yosemite High Country map is available from Tom Harrison Maps. An Inyo National Forest map is available from the U.S. Forest Service. For a topographic map, go to the USGS website to download Tioga Pass.

Directions: From Merced, drive 70 miles northeast on Highway 140 to Yosemite National Park. Follow the signs toward Yosemite Valley, entering through the Arch Rock entrance station. Continue 4.5 miles to the left turnoff for Highway 120, looping back out of the valley on Big Oak Flat Road. In 9.3 miles at Crane Flat, turn right on Tioga Pass Road and drive 48 miles (you'll exit the park) to the Saddlebag Lake turnoff, on the left, two miles east of Tioga Pass. Turn left and drive 1.5 miles north on Saddlebag Lake Road to Sawmill Campground's parking area on the left.

Contact: Inyo National Forest, Mono Basin Scenic Area Visitors Center, Lee Vining, 760/647-3044, www.fs.usda.gov/inyo.

46 SADDLEBAG LAKE LOOP

8.4 mi / 4.0 hr 2 9

in Inyo National Forest just east of Tioga Pass

Map 10.1, page 483

Starting from the resort buildings at the south end of 10,087-foot Saddlebag Lake, you can design a wonderfully scenic hiking trip into the 20 Lakes Basin of any length that suits your time and energy. For many years, the Saddlebag Lake Resort ran a boat taxi across the lake, which gave hikers the option to cut several miles off this trip, but the resort has been closed since 2016. The good news is that means there are a lot less people hiking this gorgeous loop. To do it, start on the trail on either the lake's east or west side. The east side trail is more scenic; the west side trail is shorter (for the west-side trail, start by crossing the dam). If you just want to make a short 3.6-mile loop, hike out on one trail and back on the other, but be sure to take the short left spur at Saddlebag's northwest edge to Greenstone Lake, which is backed by photogenic North Peak. If you want to hike farther, you can continue past Greenstone Lake to Wasco Lake and then on to deep, stark Steelhead Lake (three miles out if you start on the west side trail). Several more lakes lie beyond, including Shamrock, Helen, and Odell. If you hike the entire loop and visit all six lakes that lie immediately beyond Saddlebag, you'll have an 8.4-mile day. No matter how far you go, you'll be awed by the incredible high-country scenery—a blend of blue sky, granite, water, and hardy whitebark pines.

User Groups: Hikers and dogs. No horses or mountain bikes. No wheelchair facilities.

Permits: No permits are required. Parking and access are free.

Maps: A Yosemite High Country map is available from Tom Harrison Maps. An Inyo National Forest map is available from the U.S. Forest Service. For a topographic map, go to the USGS website to download Tioga Pass.

Directions: From Merced, drive 70 miles northeast on Highway 140 to Yosemite National Park. Follow the signs toward Yosemite Valley, entering through the Arch Rock entrance station. Continue 4.5 miles to the left turnoff for Highway 120, looping back out of the valley on Big Oak Flat Road. In 9.3 miles at Crane Flat, turn right on Tioga Pass Road and drive 48 miles (you'll exit the park) to the Saddlebag Lake turnoff, on the left, two miles east of Tioga Pass. Turn left and drive another 2.7 miles to the trailhead parking area.

Contact: Inyo National Forest, Mono Basin Scenic Area Visitors Center, Lee Vining, 760/647-3044, www.fs.usda.gov/inyo.

47 GIBBS LAKE

5.4 mi / 2.5 hr or 2 days

west of Lee Vining on the northern boundary of the Ansel Adams Wilderness

Map 10.1, page 483

The 2.7-mile hike from Upper Horse Meadow to Gibbs Lake is a great day hike that sees surprisingly few people. Since the trailhead isn't located at a lake or some other attractive setting, nobody gets here by accident. The trail starts at Upper Horse Meadow (elevation 8,000 feet), and climbs up Gibbs Canyon to Gibbs Lake, at 9,530 feet. That's about a 1,500-foot climb, but unfortunately the first stretch goes straight uphill on an old dirt road with nary a switchback. Once you get through that grunt of an ascent, the rest of the route is on a much mellower grade as it travels alongside Gibbs Creek. The trail ends at Gibbs Lake, a lovely glacial cirque that is backed by bare granite and fronted by conifers. Are you feeling ambitious? If you study the lake's back wall for a few minutes, it will soon become obvious that there is another, higher lake in this drainage. If you are sure-footed and have plenty of energy, you can pick out your route and go take a look at that lake. Although Gibbs Lake is pretty, the higher Kidney Lake (10,388 feet) is a stunner. It will take you about 40 minutes of challenging cross-country scrambling to get from Gibbs to Kidney; you'll gain almost 900 feet in less than a mile. Just pick your route carefully and go slow. Kidney Lake is indeed kidney-shaped, and it is flanked by the Dana Plateau on one side and Mount Gibbs (12,773 feet) on the other.

Note: While not required, high-clearance vehicles are a good idea on Forest Road 1N16.

User Groups: Hikers, horses, and dogs. No mountain bikes beyond the wilderness boundary. No wheelchair facilities.

Permits: A free wilderness permit is required for overnight stays and is available from the Mono Basin Scenic Area Visitors Center. Quotas are in effect from May 1 to November

1; for this period, permits are available in advance for a $5 reservation fee per person.

Maps: Mono Lake and Mammoth High Country maps are available from Tom Harrison Maps. An Inyo National Forest or Ansel Adams Wilderness map is available from the U.S. Forest Service. For a topographic map, go to the USGS website to download Lee Vining.

Directions: From Lee Vining, drive 1.3 miles south on U.S. 395 and turn west on unsigned Forest Road 1N16 (look for the sign indicating Horse Meadow). Drive 3.4 miles past Upper Horse Meadow to the trailhead at the end of the road.

Contact: Inyo National Forest, Mono Basin Scenic Area Visitors Center, Lee Vining, 760/647-3044, www.fs.usda.gov/inyo.

48 MONO LAKE SOUTH TUFA TRAIL

1.0 mi / 0.5 hr — 1 9

at the southern end of Mono Lake in Mono Lake Tufa State Reserve

Map 10.1, page 483 BEST

The strange and remarkable tufa towers at Mono Lake create one of the most extraordinary landscapes in California. The terrain resembles a moonscape, but a strangely beautiful one. The area is extremely popular with photographers, especially at sunset. This short loop trail is the best way to get a good look at the tufa formations, which are formed when calcium-rich underwater springs are released from the lake bottom and then combine with Mono Lake's saline water, forming calcium carbonate. The trail leads through sagebrush plains to the southern shore of the lake, where the tufas rest like old, untouched earth castles. Some of them poke out of the lake surface; others are high and dry on land. Mono Lake itself is vast (covering 60 square miles) and is estimated to be more than 700,000 years old, making it one of the oldest lakes in North America. The lake's basin has become one of the world's most prolific stopover points for gulls, grebes, plovers, and phalaropes during their annual southbound flights. That's because the alkaline properties of the water create prime habitat for brine shrimp (an ideal food for these birds), and the lake's two large islands provide isolation from predators. Eighty-five percent of the California gull population was born at Mono Lake.

User Groups: Hikers, horses, dogs, and wheelchairs. No mountain bikes.

Permits: No permits are required. A $3 entrance fee is charged per adult. Children under 16 are free.

Maps: A Mono Lake map is available from Tom Harrison Maps. For topographic maps, go to the USGS website to download Lee Vining and Mono Mills.

Directions: From Lee Vining, drive five miles south on U.S. 395 and turn east on Highway 120 (signed for Mono Lake South Tufa). Drive 4.7 miles, then turn left and drive one mile on a dirt road to the parking area.

Contact: Mono Lake Tufa State Natural Reserve, 760/647-6331, www.parks.ca.gov; Inyo National Forest, Mono Basin Scenic Area Visitors Center, Lee Vining, 760/647-3044, www.fs.usda.gov/inyo.

49 BLOODY CANYON TRAIL

8.2 mi / 5.0 hr — 4 9

southwest of Lee Vining at the northeastern boundary of the Ansel Adams Wilderness

Map 10.1, page 483

Lower Sardine Lake is a jewel cradled in a high glacial cirque at 9,888 feet, the kind of lake that makes the Ansel Adams Wilderness one of the most treasured places in the world. Beyond the first easy mile, this hike is tough and steep. Much of the trail is a historic Native American trading route, used by the Indians of the Mono Basin to visit the Indians of the Yosemite high country. The first mile to Walker Lake is an easy downhill cruise, dropping 600 feet in elevation. Walker Lake is a popular destination for anglers and has a small private resort on its eastern shore. From the aspen-lined western edge of the lake, you head up Bloody Canyon, climbing nearly 2,000 feet in about three miles. The hike parallels Walker Creek, requiring two stream crossings on the way up to Lower Sardine Lake. For anyone who is either out of shape or not acclimated to the altitude, the climb can be rough going. As you near Lower Sardine Lake, the sight of a beautiful waterfall (the lake's outlet stream) will help to spur you on. When you reach the lake at elevation 9,888 feet, you'll find it is surrounded by rocky cliffs on three sides and provides great views of the Mono Basin to the east. Backpackers can continue hiking up and over Mono Pass and into Yosemite National Park's backcountry, but to do so, they face still more of a climb. Remember that if you are entering the national park, dogs are not allowed.

User Groups: Hikers, horses, and dogs. No mountain bikes beyond the wilderness boundary. No wheelchair facilities.

Permits: A free wilderness permit is required for overnight stays and is available from the Mono Basin Scenic Area Visitors Center. Quotas are in effect from May 1 to November 1; for this period, permits are available in advance for a $5 reservation fee per person.

Maps: Yosemite High Country and Mammoth High Country maps are available from Tom Harrison Maps. An Inyo National Forest or Ansel Adams Wilderness map is available from the U.S. Forest Service. For topographic maps, go to the USGS website to download Mount Dana and Koip Peak.

Directions: From Lee Vining, drive five miles south on U.S. 395 to the north end of the June Lake Loop (Highway 158). Turn right and drive 1.3 miles on Highway 158, then turn right on a dirt road signed for Parker and Walker Lakes. Drive 0.5 mile to a junction, turn right, then drive 0.3 mile and turn right again, following the signs for Walker Lake. Drive 0.5 mile and turn left on Forest Road 1S23. Drive 2.7 miles to the Walker Lake trailhead.

Contact: Inyo National Forest, Mono Basin

Mono Lake South Tufa Trail

Scenic Area Visitors Center, Lee Vining, 760/647-3044, www.fs.usda.gov/inyo.

50 PARKER LAKE TRAIL

3.8 mi / 2.0 hr 2 8

in the Ansel Adams Wilderness west of Grant Lake

Map 10.1, page 483 **BEST**

This short trail has a whole lot going for it. The beauty of Parker Lake and towering Parker Peak could knock your boots right off—or at least your socks. Although the nearby June Lake Loop gets a lot of vacation traffic, this trailhead is obscure enough that most visitors pass it by. And get this: The 1.9-mile-long trail has an elevation gain of only a little more than 300 feet. Beginning at an elevation of 8,000 feet above Parker Creek, the trail follows the creek upstream on a fairly mellow grade before arriving at Parker Lake, at 8,318 feet. As you ascend, the landscape transitions from sagebrush plains into a mixed forest alongside Parker Creek, complete with quaking aspens and mammoth-sized Jeffrey pines. Look behind you once in a while, and you'll catch great views of Mono Lake. In short order, you will suddenly emerge from the forest onto the lake's shore. Parker Lake is a deep blue beauty backed by 12,861-foot Parker Peak—a great place to have a picnic or just sit and enjoy the scenery. The only downer on this trip is that many of the largest aspen trees have had their trunks carved with initials by idiots. Let's hope they didn't know any better. Please teach your children never, ever to carve into trees.

User Groups: Hikers, dogs, and horses. No mountain bikes. No wheelchair facilities.

Permits: A free wilderness permit is required for overnight stays and is available from the Mono Basin Scenic Area Visitors Center. Quotas are in effect from May 1 to November 1; for this period, permits are available in advance for a $5 reservation fee per person.

Maps: A Mammoth High Country map is available from Tom Harrison Maps. An Inyo National Forest or Ansel Adams Wilderness map is available from the U.S. Forest Service. For topographic maps, go to the USGS website to download Mount Dana and Koip Peak.

Directions: From Lee Vining, drive five miles south on U.S. 395 to the north end of the June Lake Loop (Highway 158). Turn right and drive 1.3 miles on Highway 158, then turn right on a dirt road signed for Parker and Walker Lakes. Drive 2.4 miles to the Parker Lake trailhead, at the end of the road.

Contact: Inyo National Forest, Mono Basin Scenic Area Visitors Center, Lee Vining, 760/647-3044, www.fs.usda.gov/inyo.

51 RUSH CREEK TRAIL

19.2 mi / 3 days 4 10

on the eastern boundary of the Ansel Adams Wilderness west of June Lake

Map 10.1, page 483

Some places will never change, and people are drawn to them because they provide a sense of permanence that can't be found anywhere else. That is how it is at the Rush Creek headwaters. Created from drops of melting snow near the Sierra crest (at 10,500 feet), this stream runs downhill for miles, rolling into the forest like a swirling, emerald-green fountain. Even a short visit requires a long drive to the trailhead, followed by a demanding backpacking trek. In the process, hikers contend with a 10-mile climb out, ice-cold stream crossings, and the possibility of afternoon thunderstorms, in which lightning bolts and thunderclaps rattle off the canyon rims.

The trailhead lies near the pack station at Silver Lake (elevation 7,215 feet). After departing Silver Lake, follow the trail as it climbs above the June Lake Loop and soon starts to parallel Lower Rush Creek. You'll cross over an old tramway system that was used for the hydroelectric projects found in this watershed. Near the dam at Agnew Lake, you reach a trail junction, 2.2 miles from your start. The left fork heads up to Agnew Pass, but continue straight and in one more mile you arrive at beautiful Gem Lake (9,058 feet) and then Waugh Lake (9,442 feet), at the seven-mile point. Many visitors never venture farther than these lakes, simply stopping to camp, swim, or fish. But upstream of Waugh Lake is where you find the Rush Creek headwaters, along with the flawless symmetry of the untouched high country. Getting there requires a total climb of 3,300 feet over the course of 9.6 miles, but it is one of the prettiest streams anywhere and is well worth the effort.

Note: Because this trail begins near the Silver Lake pack station, it is heavily used by horses. On some days, the amount of horse "evidence" on this trail can be a real downer, especially in the first few miles.

User Groups: Hikers, dogs, and horses. No mountain bikes. No wheelchair facilities.

Permits: A free wilderness permit is required for overnight stays and is available from the Mono Basin Scenic Area Visitors Center. Quotas are in effect from May 1 to November 1; for this period, permits are available in advance for a $5 reservation fee per person.

Maps: A Mammoth High Country map is available from Tom Harrison Maps. An Inyo National Forest or Ansel Adams Wilderness map is available from the U.S. Forest Service. For topographic maps, go to the USGS website to download June Lake and Koip Peak.

Directions: From Lee Vining, drive about 11 miles south on U.S. 395 to June Lake Junction. Turn right on Highway 158/June Lake Road and drive 7.2 miles to the Rush Creek trailhead, between Silver Lake Resort and the pack station.

Contact: Inyo National Forest, Mono Basin Scenic Area Visitors Center, Lee Vining, 760/647-3044, www.fs.usda.gov/inyo.

52 YOST LAKE

4.8-9.4 mi / 2.5 hr-1 day

in Hoover Wilderness near June Lake

Map 10.1, page 483

Yost Lake is a small glacial lake hidden at 9,000 feet on the June Mountain slopes. Many people visit the June Lake area for years without even knowing Yost exists. But it is up here, tucked away and accessible only to those willing to hike. From the trailhead (7,800 feet) at June Lake, Yost Meadows Trail rises very steeply in the first mile, climbing 800 feet—a real butt-kicker for many. That discourages many from going farther—after all, it is 4.7 miles to the lake. But after that first grunt of a climb, the trail gets much easier, contouring across the mountain slopes. It rises gradually to the headwaters of Yost Creek and then drops into the small basin that guards the lake.

A shorter option is to begin at the Yost Creek/Fern Lake trailhead, making it a much shorter, 4.8-mile round-trip. It is just as pretty, but it has a more difficult grade and can be slippery for those not wearing heavy, firm-gripping hiking boots. The trailhead is located three miles west of the town of June Lake, on the west (left) side of June Lake Road, past the ski resort.

User Groups: Hikers, horses, and dogs. No mountain bikes. No wheelchair facilities.

Permits: No permits are required for day-use; an overnight permit is required for backpacking. Parking and access are free.

Maps: A Mammoth High Country map is available from Tom Harrison Maps. An Inyo National Forest or Ansel Adams Wilderness map is available from the U.S. Forest Service. For topographic maps, go to the USGS website to download June Lake and Mammoth Mountain.

Directions: From Lee Vining, drive about 11 miles south on U.S. 395 to June Lake Junction. Go right on Highway 158/June Lake Road and drive two miles to the town of June Lake. The trailhead is on the west (left), across the road from the fire station.

Contact: Inyo National Forest, Mono Basin Scenic Area Visitors Center, Lee Vining, 760/647-3044, www.fs.usda.gov/inyo.

53 INYO CRATERS

0.5 mi / 0.5 hr

in Inyo National Forest north of Mammoth Lakes

Map 10.1, page 483

A geologic phenomenon, the Inyo Craters make a great destination for an easy day hike in the Mammoth Lakes area. They are part of a chain of craters and other volcanic formations that reaches from Mammoth Lake to Mono Lake. The craters—evidence of Mammoth's fiery past—are the remains of a volcanic explosion of steam that occurred a mere 600 years ago. At that time, the mountain was a smoldering volcano. Magma pushed up into the water table, heated the water, and kaboom! The result was a phreatic blast that created these craters. The hike to see them is a short, gentle climb, but the elevation sucks the air out of many visitors who have just arrived in Mammoth. The trail leads through a lovely open forest of red fir and Jeffrey pine. In each of the two Inyo Craters a small pond fills with melted snow each spring, and at least some water remains throughout the summer.

User Groups: Hikers, horses, and dogs. No mountain bikes. No wheelchair facilities.

Permits: No permits are required. Parking and access are free.

Maps: A Mammoth High Country map is available from Tom Harrison Maps. An Inyo National Forest map is available from the U.S. Forest Service. For a topographic map, go to the USGS website to download Mammoth Mountain.

Directions: From the Mammoth Lakes junction on U.S. 395, turn west on Highway 203 and drive four miles through the town of Mammoth Lakes to the junction of Minaret Road/Highway 203 and Lake Mary Road. Turn right on Minaret Road and drive one mile. At the sign for Mammoth Lakes Scenic Loop, turn right and drive 2.7 miles. Turn left at the sign for Inyo Craters (the road turns to dirt) and drive 1.3 more miles to the Inyo Craters parking lot.

Contact: Inyo National Forest, Mammoth Lakes Welcome Center, Mammoth Lakes, 760/924-5500, www.fs.usda.gov/inyo.

54 BARRETT AND TJ LAKES

1.0 mi / 0.5 hr

1 8

at Lake George in Mammoth Lakes

Map 10.1, page 483

Campers at Lake George and Mammoth Lakes visitors who just want a short and easy day hike will be pleased to find that this no-sweat trail provides access to hidden Barrett and TJ Lakes. The trail starts on the northeast shore of Lake George (which in itself is a gorgeous spot), follows the lakeshore for about 100 yards, then climbs alongside a small stream to little Barrett Lake. The tiny lake is framed by Red Mountain in the background. Hey, this was so easy, you might as well continue another 0.25 mile to TJ Lake, the more scenic of the two lakes. The distinctive granite fin of Crystal Crag (10,377 feet) towers above TJ Lake's basin, adding drama to the scene. In addition to the pretty but popular lakes, this trail shows off some lovely mountain meadows, gilded with colorful penstemon, shooting stars, and paintbrush in midsummer.

User Groups: Hikers and horses. No mountain bikes. No wheelchair facilities.

Permits: No permits are required. Parking and access are free.

Maps: A Mammoth High Country map is available from Tom Harrison Maps. An Inyo National Forest map is available from the U.S. Forest Service. For a topographic map, go to the USGS website to download Crystal Crag.

Directions: From the Mammoth Lakes junction on U.S. 395, turn west on Highway 203 and drive four miles through the town of

Mammoth Lakes to the junction of Minaret Road/Highway 203 and Lake Mary Road. Continue straight on Lake Mary Road and drive four miles to a junction for Lake George. Turn left here, drive 0.3 mile, then turn right and drive another 0.4 mile to Lake George. The trailhead is located near the campground.

Contact: Inyo National Forest, Mammoth Lakes Welcome Center, Mammoth Lakes, 760/924-5500, www.fs.usda.gov/inyo.

55 CRYSTAL LAKE

3.2 mi / 2.0 hr 2 9

at Lake George in Mammoth Lakes

Map 10.1, page 483

If you think Lake George is gorgeous, wait until you see Crystal Lake, located southwest of Lake George in a bowl scoured by glaciers and tucked into a hollow below 10,377-foot Crystal Crag. The trail to reach it has a 700-foot elevation gain and is pleasantly shaded by a hearty hemlock, pine, and fir forest. The path begins near the cabins at Woods Lodge but rises quickly above them. Many hikers huff and puff as they climb this ridge, but the view of the Mammoth Lakes Basin makes it all worthwhile. This high ridge gives you a bird's-eye look at the basin's four major lakes: George, Mary, Mamie, and Twin. At a junction at 1.3 miles, go left and you'll descend 0.3 mile to the outlet of Crystal Lake. The lake is a true jewel, highlighted by permanent snowfields that line its granite backdrop. You aren't likely to find much solitude here, since the lake is so easy to reach, but the scenery more than makes up for it.

If you want to turn this into a longer hike, you can take the other trail at the fork and head for Mammoth Crest, two miles farther and at 10,400 feet. The trail gains another 700 feet as it leaves the forest and enters a stark, volcanic landscape peppered with whitebark pines. The expansive view from the high point on the crest includes the Mammoth Lakes Basin, the San Joaquin River, the Minarets and the Ritter Range, and Mammoth Mountain. If this hike hasn't taken your breath away, the vista will.

User Groups: Hikers, horses, and dogs. Mountain bikes are not advised. No wheelchair facilities.

Permits: No permits are required. Parking and access are free.

Maps: A Mammoth High Country map is available from Tom Harrison Maps. An Inyo National Forest map is available from the U.S. Forest Service. For a topographic map, go to the USGS website to download Crystal Crag.

Directions: From the Mammoth Lakes junction on U.S. 395, turn west on Highway 203 and drive four miles through the town of Mammoth Lakes to the junction of Minaret Road/Highway 203 and Lake Mary Road. Continue straight on Lake Mary Road and drive four miles to a junction for Lake George. Turn left, drive 0.3 mile, then turn right and drive another 0.4 mile to Lake George. The trailhead is on the right, near some cabins.

Contact: Inyo National Forest, Mammoth Lakes Welcome Center, Mammoth Lakes, 760/924-5500, www.fs.usda.gov/inyo.

56 EMERALD LAKE AND SKY MEADOWS

4.0 mi / 2.0 hr 2 9

at Lake Mary in Mammoth Lakes

Map 10.1, page 483

This is one of the Eastern Sierra's premier wildflower trails, and it's easy enough for children to hike. The trail starts just south of Lake Mary, at the end of the Coldwater Campground road. The hike is short and direct, climbing straight to Emerald Lake on a wide, well-used path. A trail branches off to the right to Barrett and TJ Lakes, but just keep heading straight uphill to reach Emerald Lake. Picnickers are often found seated among the rocks by the water's edge, although by midsummer, the lake dwindles to something that more closely resembles a pond. No matter, the lake is just one small part of this trail's beauty. The trail skirts the east shore of Emerald Lake and continues along its inlet stream, where wildflowers grow in profusion. Among the wide variety of species to be seen and admired, one standout is the tall orange tiger lilies, a flower that is showy enough to be in a florist's shop. It has a scent that will knock your socks off. From here, the trail climbs more gradually as it leads you past Gentian Meadow (you may hear the voices of rock climbers as they climb the cliffs beyond the meadow) to the southeast edge of Sky Meadows. Beyond the meadows, permanent snowfields decorate the granite cliffs of Mammoth Crest.

User Groups: Hikers, dogs, and horses. No mountain bikes allowed past the wilderness boundary. No wheelchair facilities.

Permits: No day permits are required. Parking and access are free.

Maps: A Mammoth High Country map is available from Tom Harrison Maps. An Inyo National Forest map is available from the U.S. Forest Service. For a topographic map, go to the USGS website to download Crystal Crag.

Directions: From the Mammoth Lakes junction on U.S. 395, turn west on Highway 203 and drive four miles through the town of Mammoth Lakes to the junction of Minaret Road/Highway 203 and Lake Mary Road. Continue straight on Lake Mary Road and drive 3.5 miles to a fork just before Lake Mary; turn left and drive 0.6 mile to the Coldwater Campground turnoff, on the left. Turn left and drive 0.5 mile through the camp to the trailhead, at the first parking lot.

Contact: Inyo National Forest, Mammoth Lakes Welcome Center, Mammoth Lakes, 760/924-5500, www.fs.usda.gov/inyo.

57 DUCK LAKE

10.0 mi / 6.0 hr or 2 days 

in the John Muir Wilderness near Mammoth Lakes

Map 10.1, page 483

How far you hike on Duck Pass Trail is up to you, but if it were up to us, we'd hike at least as far as five miles to Duck Lake, elevation 10,450 feet. Sure, lots of people stop at the other lakes this trail passes along the way—Arrowhead Lake at 1.3 miles out, Skelton Lake at two miles, or Barney Lake at three miles—and these make fine destinations. But you might as well see them all and then keep climbing through Duck Pass to much larger Duck Lake, at five miles. The pass is only a 1,600-foot climb from the trailhead at Coldwater Campground, with plenty of well-graded switchbacks. Just beyond the pass, the trail drops 300 feet to reach Duck Lake, one of the largest natural lakes in the Eastern Sierra. Your first glimpse of its size will blow your mind. Most of the climbing is in the stretch from Barney Lake to the pass, as the trail switchbacks up a talus-covered slope. Day hikers can make their way from Duck Lake on a faint path to Pika Lake, which is visible in the distance about a half-mile away. Backpackers can continue on to Purple Lake (at 7.5 miles) and Lake Virginia (at nine miles). There are usually tons of people on this trail, but with this kind of scenery, everybody is in a good mood.

User Groups: Hikers, dogs, and horses. No mountain bikes allowed past the wilderness boundary. No wheelchair facilities.

Permits: A free wilderness permit is required for overnight stays and is available from the Mammoth Lakes Welcome Center. Quotas are in effect from May 1 to November 1; for this period, permits are available in advance for a $5 reservation fee per person.

Maps: A Mammoth High Country map is available from Tom Harrison Maps. An Inyo National Forest or John Muir Wilderness map is available from the U.S. Forest Service. For a topographic map, go to the USGS website to download Crystal Crag.

Directions: From the Mammoth Lakes junction on U.S. 395, turn west on Highway 203 and drive four miles, through the town of Mammoth Lakes, to the junction of Minaret Road/Highway 203 and Lake Mary Road. Continue straight on Lake Mary Road and drive 3.5 miles to a fork just before Lake Mary; turn left and drive 0.6 mile to the Coldwater Campground turnoff, on the left. Turn left and drive 0.8 mile through the camp to the Duck Pass trailhead at the farthest parking lot.

Contact: Inyo National Forest, Mammoth Lakes Welcome Center, Mammoth Lakes, 760/924-5500, www.fs.usda.gov/inyo.

58 VALENTINE LAKE TRAIL

11.2 mi / 6.0 hr or 2 days 3 9

in the John Muir Wilderness south of Mammoth Lakes

Map 10.1, page 483

The Mammoth Lakes area is one of the Eastern Sierra's star attractions, yet nearby Valentine Lake is perhaps overlooked because the trailhead (at 7,600 feet) is not found at one of the lakes in the Mammoth Lakes Basin. Or perhaps it's because the climb required to get there is so steep. Regardless of the reason, a morning's hike—rising some 1,900 feet over 5.6 miles, but with most of the climb compressed in the first two miles to Sherwin Lake—gets you to Valentine Lake, which sits at 9,698 feet.

Some say the lake is shaped like a teardrop, but we think it looks more like a drop of sweat. The hike starts out with a very steep climb (including 0.5 mile of sandy switchbacks in a dry pine forest) and doesn't level out for the first two miles. You'll pass a side trail to the Sherwin Lakes at 2.9 miles (a fine destination for those who have had enough, or those who just want to catch fish). From the Sherwin Lakes junction, the grade lessens dramatically, gently climbing and finally meeting up with Valentine Lake's outlet stream. Valentine Lake has rocky cliffs ringing its edges, making it difficult to explore its shoreline. Pick a spot and toss in a line; the lake has plentiful brook trout.

User Groups: Hikers, dogs, and horses. No mountain bikes. No wheelchair facilities.

Permits: A free wilderness permit is required for overnight stays and is available from the Mammoth Lakes Welcome Center. Quotas are in effect from May 1 to November 1; for this period, permits are available in advance for a $5 reservation fee per person.

Maps: A Mammoth High Country map is available from Tom Harrison Maps. An Inyo National Forest or John Muir Wilderness map is available from the U.S. Forest Service. For a topographic map, go to the USGS website to download Crystal Crag.

Directions: From the Mammoth Lakes junction on U.S. 395, turn west on Highway 203 and drive 2.6 miles to Old Mammoth Road. Turn left and drive 0.8 mile to Sherwin Creek Road. Turn left and drive 2.9 miles to the signed trailhead on the right for Valentine Lake (past the Sherwin Creek Campground and YMCA camp).

Contact: Inyo National Forest, Mammoth Lakes Welcome Center, Mammoth Lakes, 760/924-5500, www.fs.usda.gov/inyo.

59 RED CONES LOOP

6.7 mi / 4.0 hr

in Horseshoe Lake in Mammoth Lakes

Map 10.1, page 483

Horseshoe Lake, elevation 8,900 feet, lies at the end of the Mammoth Lakes road and has an excellent trailhead that makes for a great day hike. Don't be put off by the dead trees and the barren look of the place. A relatively small area by the lake has been affected by carbon-dioxide gas venting up through the soil—the result of seismic activity. You get away from this strange-looking forest quickly. Set out from the northwest side of the lake, ascend the slope,

Vernal Fall, a Yosemite highlight

and take the left fork for McLeod Lake. In just under two miles, you'll reach the start of the loop. Go right to reach Crater Meadow, a beautiful little spot set just below Red Cones, and then circle around to Upper Crater Meadow. Either meadow is a fine destination for a picnic lunch in peace. The contrast is striking: Just a short distance below, there are typically many people at Twin Lakes, Lake Mary, Lake Mamie, and Lake George, yet you are separated from them by Mammoth Pass. You will be surprised at how relatively few people take this loop hike, and glad that you made the choice to do so.

User Groups: Hikers, dogs, and horses. No mountain bikes. No wheelchair facilities.

Permits: No permits are required. Parking and access are free.

Maps: A Mammoth High Country map is available from Tom Harrison Maps. An Inyo National Forest map is available from the U.S. Forest Service. For a topographic map, go to the USGS website to download Crystal Crag.

Directions: From the Mammoth Lakes junction on U.S. 395, turn west on Highway 203 and drive four miles through the town of Mammoth Lakes to the junction of Minaret Road/Highway 203 and Lake Mary Road. Continue straight on Lake Mary Road and drive 4.8 miles to the road's end, at Horseshoe Lake. The trailhead is on the northwest side of the lake, signed for Mammoth Pass.

Contact: Inyo National Forest, Mammoth Lakes Welcome Center, Mammoth Lakes, 760/924-5500, www.fs.usda.gov/inyo.

60 DEVILS POSTPILE AND RAINBOW FALLS

2.0-5.0 mi / 1.0-2.0 hr 2 10

in Devils Postpile National Monument west of Mammoth Lakes

Map 10.1, page 483 BEST

The first time you lay eyes on 101-foot Rainbow Falls, the tall, wide, and forceful waterfall comes as an awesome surprise. Most first-time visitors see it before or after a trip to the Devils Postpile, a fascinating collection of volcanic rock columns and rubble left from a lava flow nearly 100,000 years ago. It's like nothing you've seen anywhere else. You can hike to Rainbow Falls two ways, either from the ranger station at Devils Postpile National Monument or from the Rainbow Falls trailhead, near Reds Meadow Resort. Either way, this is one of the best short hikes in California.

Your best bet is to start at the ranger station, then pass by the Devils Postpile lava columns in only 0.5 mile. Stop and gape at this geologic wonder, and perhaps take the short but steep side-trip to the top of the columns, then continue downhill to Rainbow Falls, at 2.5 miles. (If you start at the trailhead by Reds Meadow, your trip to Rainbow Falls is only one mile, but you'll miss out on the Postpile.)

In order to see the rainbow that gives the waterfall its name, you must show up in late morning or at midday. The rainbow is the result of a prism effect from sun's rays refracting through the falling water. Two overlook areas across from the waterfall's brink give you an excellent view, but you can hike down a series of stairs to the falls' base for an even better vantage point. If you're inspired, you can travel another 0.5 mile on the trail to find a smaller waterfall on the San Joaquin River, called Lower Falls.

User Groups: Hikers and horses. No mountain bikes. Dogs must be leashed in the national monument. No wheelchair facilities.

Permits: Each person entering the Devils Postpile/Reds Meadow area must purchase an access pass. (See *Access Note,* below.) The fee is $8 per adult and $4 for children ages 3-15. Children ages 2 and under are free. Passes may be purchased at the Mammoth Mountain Adventure Center at Mammoth Ski Area.

Maps: A Devils Postpile map is available from Tom Harrison Maps. An Inyo National Forest map is available from the U.S. Forest Service. For a topographic map, go to the USGS website to download Mammoth Mountain.

Directions: From the Mammoth Lakes junction on U.S. 395, turn west on Highway 203 and drive four miles through the town of Mammoth Lakes to Minaret Road (still Highway 203). Turn right and drive 4.5 miles to the shuttle bus terminal (adjacent to the Mammoth Mountain Ski Area). Purchase an access pass and board a shuttle bus here. Disembark at the Devils Postpile Ranger Station or Rainbow Falls trailhead, which is just before Reds Meadow Resort.

Access Note: Visitors arriving between 7am and 7pm are required to ride a shuttle bus (free with purchase of an access pass) from Mammoth Mountain Ski Area. If you are camping in the Devils Postpile area, or if you arrive before 7am, you are permitted to drive your own car instead of taking the shuttle, but you must pay an entrance fee of $10 per vehicle.

Contact: Inyo National Forest, Mammoth Lakes Welcome Center, Mammoth Lakes, 760/924-5500, www.fs.usda.gov/inyo; Devils Postpile National Monument, Mammoth Lakes, 760/934-2289 (summer only), www.nps.gov/depo.

61 MINARET LAKE

16.0 mi / 2 days 3 10

in the Ansel Adams Wilderness west of Mammoth Lakes

Map 10.1, page 483

Minaret Lake is a real prize, set just below the awesome glacial-carved Ritter Range, at 9,793 feet. Reaching it requires an eight-mile hike with a 2,400-foot elevation gain, and every step is completely worth it. From the trailhead at Devils Postpile Ranger Station, you hike south to access a bridge across the San Joaquin River, then head northward two miles on John Muir Trail. (You can also start from Upper Soda Spring Campground and hike south on the Pacific Crest Trail, then turn north on the John Muir Trail. The distance is about the same.) After passing tiny Johnston Lake, you reach the junction with Minaret Lake Trail. Turn left and follow Minaret Creek. The trail rises with the creek and in the last mile climbs steeply above tree line before skirting the Minaret Lake outlet and tracing the line of the north shore. The granite peaks that form the lake's backdrop are

Clyde and Ken Minaret. Good campsites are found around Minaret Lake's rocky shore, but the choicest site is on the small peninsula that juts out into the lake. If you want to do some exploring, Cecile Lake (at 10,239 feet) can be reached via a cross-country route to the northwest of the lake.

User Groups: Hikers, dogs, and horses. Dogs must be leashed in national monument. No mountain bikes. No wheelchair facilities.

Permits: Each person entering the Devils Postpile/Reds Meadow area must purchase an access pass. (See *Access Note,* below.) The fee is $8 per adult and $4 for children ages 3-15. Children ages 2 and under are free. Passes may be purchased at the Mammoth Mountain Adventure Center at Mammoth Ski Area.

A free wilderness permit is required for overnight stays and is available from the Mammoth Lakes Welcome Center. Quotas are in effect from May 1 to November 1; for this period, permits are available in advance for a $5 reservation fee per person.

Maps: A Devils Postpile map is available from Tom Harrison Maps. An Inyo National Forest or Ansel Adams Wilderness map is available from the U.S. Forest Service. For topographic maps, go to the USGS website to download Mammoth Mountain and Mount Ritter.

Directions: From the Mammoth Lakes junction on U.S. 395, turn west on Highway 203 and drive four miles through the town of Mammoth Lakes to Minaret Road (still Highway 203). Turn right and drive 4.5 miles to the shuttle bus terminal (adjacent to the Mammoth Mountain Ski Area). Purchase an access pass and board a shuttle bus here. Disembark at the Devils Postpile Ranger Station.

Note: Visitors arriving between 7am and 7pm are required to ride a shuttle bus (free with purchase of an access pass) from Mammoth Mountain Ski Area. If you are camping in the Devils Postpile area, or if you arrive before 7am, you are permitted to drive your own car instead of taking the shuttle, but you must pay an entrance fee of $10 per vehicle.

Contact: Inyo National Forest, Mammoth Lakes Welcome Center, Mammoth Lakes, 760/924-5500, www.fs.usda.gov/inyo; Devils Postpile National Monument, Mammoth Lakes, 760/934-2289 (summer only), www.nps.gov/depo.

62 FERN LAKE LOOP

10.0-16.0 mi / 1-2 days

in the Ansel Adams Wilderness west of Mammoth Lakes

Map 10.1, page 483

Fern Lake can be the destination on an ambitious day hike from Devils Postpile, or the start of a great 15-mile backpacking loop. Either way, this is an excellent hike that has become very popular. Starting from the ranger station at Devils Postpile, you head south to access the bridge across the San Joaquin River, then follow the King Creek Trail. About two miles in, you face a crossing of King Creek that can be tricky early in the summer. Exercise some caution. Then climb through the pine forest to reach a junction, at 4.9 miles. Follow the spur to Fern Lake, elevation 8,800 feet, where many good campsites are found. The lake is set in a small rock bowl at tree line, below Iron Mountain, in the Minarets. Day hikers will often while away a few hours here and then retrace their steps for a 10-mile round-trip.

Those continuing onward will find the trail pokes in and out of sparse forest for the next two miles to Becks Cabin. From here, a one-mile side-trip leads to Superior Lake (7.5 miles from your start, and at 9,400 feet), another excellent spot for an overnight. A faint path leads 0.7 mile from Superior Lake to the two Beck Lakes (at 9,800 feet), which are surrounded by high granite ridges. A visit to Beck Lakes—set in a glacial-formed pocket below the Minarets and amid celestial mountain scenery—is highly recommended. When you return to the loop at Becks Cabin, you have a 4.8-mile descent to reach John Muir Trail, where you turn right and head back to the bridge and the ranger station.

User Groups: Hikers, dogs, and horses. Dogs must be leashed in national monument. No mountain bikes. No wheelchair facilities.

Permits: Each person entering the Devils Postpile/Reds Meadow area must purchase an access pass. (See *Access Note,* below.) The fee is $8 per adult and $4 for children ages 3-15. Children ages 2 and under are free. Passes may be purchased at the Mammoth Mountain Adventure Center at Mammoth Ski Area.

A free wilderness permit is required for overnight stays and is available from the Mammoth Lakes Welcome Center. Quotas are in effect from May 1 to November 1; for this period, permits are available in advance for a $5 reservation fee per person.

Maps: A Devils Postpile map is available from Tom Harrison Maps. An Inyo National Forest or Ansel Adams Wilderness map is available from the U.S. Forest Service. For topographic maps, go to the USGS website to download Mammoth Mountain and Mount Ritter.

Directions: From the Mammoth Lakes junction on U.S. 395, turn west on Highway 203 and drive four miles through the town of Mammoth Lakes to Minaret Road (still Highway 203). Turn right and drive 4.5 miles to the shuttle bus terminal (adjacent to the Mammoth Mountain Ski Area). Purchase an access pass and board a shuttle bus here. Disembark at the Devils Postpile Ranger Station.

Note: Visitors arriving between 7am and 7pm are required to ride a shuttle bus (free with purchase of an access pass) from Mammoth Mountain Ski Area. If you are camping in the Devils Postpile area, or if you arrive before 7am, you are permitted to drive your own car instead of taking the shuttle, but you must pay an entrance fee of $10 per vehicle.

Contact: Inyo National Forest, Mammoth Lakes Welcome Center, Mammoth Lakes, 760/924-5500, www.fs.usda.gov/inyo; Devils Postpile National Monument, Mammoth Lakes, 760/934-2289 (summer only), www.nps.gov/depo.

63 SHADOW LAKE

7.6 mi / 4.0 hr or 2 days

in the Ansel Adams Wilderness west of Mammoth Lakes

Map 10.1, page 483

Shadow Lake is one of the most popular destinations in the Devils Postpile region simply because of its sheer beauty. The only unpleasant part of this hike is making your way through the busy trailhead parking lots at Agnew Meadows. Once that's accomplished and you're on the trail, all is bliss, as long as you're in good condition and ready for a sustained climb. (Campers at Agnew Meadows can cut a half-mile off this trip each way by starting from the trail at camp, not from the trailhead parking lot.) The route starts out quite mellow as it wanders through the wildflowers at Agnew Meadows. It then follows the River Trail along the middle fork of the San Joaquin River. Just beyond shallow Olaine Lake (at two miles) lies a junction, where you go left for Shadow Lake. Cross a bridge and prepare to climb. A long series of steep, shadeless switchbacks ensues as you climb alongside a narrow creek gorge. Fortunately the view looking down the San Joaquin River Canyon becomes ever more grand as you rise upward. At last you reach the waterfall on Shadow Lake's outlet stream and then climb the final stretch to the lake. Its backdrop is like something you've seen on a million Sierra postcards, with the Minarets and Mounts Ritter and Banner towering above the lake. Day hikers have the best deal here; they can just pick a spot along the 8,737-foot lakeshore and drink in the view. Camping is not permitted at Shadow Lake, so backpackers must continue on to smaller Rosalie Lake (much more climbing over the next two miles). Ediza Lake is also a popular overnight option, 2.5 miles from Shadow Lake.

User Groups: Hikers, dogs, and horses. No mountain bikes. No wheelchair facilities.

Permits: Each person entering the Devils Postpile/Reds Meadow area must purchase an access pass. (See *Access Note,* below.) The fee is $8 per adult and $4 for children ages 3-15. Children ages 2 and under are free. Passes may be purchased at the Mammoth Mountain Adventure Center at Mammoth Ski Area.

A free wilderness permit is required for overnight stays and is available from the Mammoth Lakes Welcome Center. Quotas are in effect from May 1 to November 1; for this period, permits are available in advance for a $5 reservation fee per person.

Maps: A Devils Postpile map is available from Tom Harrison Maps. An Inyo National Forest or Ansel Adams Wilderness map is available from the U.S. Forest Service. For topographic maps, go to the USGS website to download Crystal Crag and Cattle Mountain.

Directions: From the Mammoth Lakes junction on U.S. 395, turn west on Highway 203 and drive four miles through the town of Mammoth Lakes to Minaret Road (still Highway 203). Turn right and drive 4.5 miles to the shuttle bus terminal (adjacent to the Mammoth Mountain Ski Area). Purchase an access pass and board a shuttle bus here. Disembark at the Agnew Meadows Campground. Walk through the trailhead parking lots to the Shadow Lake trailhead.

Note: Visitors arriving between 7am and 7pm are required to ride a shuttle bus (free with purchase of an access pass) from Mammoth Mountain Ski Area. If you are camping in the Devils Postpile area, or if you arrive before 7am, you are permitted to drive your own car instead of taking the shuttle, but you must pay an entrance fee of $10 per vehicle.

Contact: Inyo National Forest, Mammoth Lakes Welcome Center, Mammoth Lakes, 760/924-5500, www.fs.usda.gov/inyo; Devils Postpile National Monument, Mammoth Lakes, 760/934-2289 (summer only), www.nps.gov/depo.

64 AGNEW MEADOWS TO TUOLUMNE MEADOWS (JMT/PCT)

28.0 mi one-way / 3 days 5 10

from the Agnew Meadows trailhead north to the trailhead parking area at Tuolumne Meadows on Highway 120

Map 10.1, page 483

This section of the JMT/PCT features breathtaking views of the Minarets, many glacial-cut lakes, and the wondrous descent into Yosemite. The PCT starts here by leaving Reds Meadow, an excellent place to arrange a food drop and a chance to eat your first cheeseburger in weeks. The trail heads out into the most beautiful section of Inyo National Forest and the Ansel Adams Wilderness. All in a row, the PCT passes Rosalie, Shadow, Garnet, and Thousand Island Lakes. If they look like Ansel Adams's pictures in real life, it's because they are. The background setting of Banner and Ritter Peaks is among the most spectacular anywhere. From Thousand Island Lake, the PCT makes a fair climb over Island Pass (10,200 feet), then drops down into the headwaters of Rush Creek, where emerald green flows swirl over boulders, pouring like a wilderness fountain. From here, it's a decent, steady ascent back above tree line to Donohue Pass (11,056 feet), the southern wilderness border of Yosemite National Park. It was here, while munching a trail lunch, that we saw a huge landslide on the westward canyon wall. A massive amount of rock material fell in just a few seconds—an unforgettable show of natural forces. The trail becomes quite blocky at Donohue Pass, and you rock hop your way down to the headwaters of Lyell Fork, a pretzel-like stream that meanders through the meadows. It pours all the way to Tuolumne Meadows, and following it, the trail is nearly flat for more than four miles. At Tuolumne Meadows you can resupply—and get another cheeseburger.

To continue north on the JMT, see the *Tuolumne Meadows to Yosemite Valley (JMT)* hike in this chapter. If you are walking this trail in reverse, see the *Lake Thomas Edison to Agnew Meadows (JMT/PCT)* hike in the *Sequoia and Kings Canyon* chapter.

User Groups: Hikers and horses. No dogs or mountain bikes. No wheelchair facilities.

Permits: A wilderness permit is required for traveling through various wilderness and special-use areas the trail traverses. Contact either the Inyo National Forest or Yosemite National Park for a permit that is good for the length of your trip.

Maps: A John Muir Trail Map Pack is available from Tom Harrison Maps. An Inyo National Forest map is available from the U.S. Forest Service. For topographic maps, go to the USGS website to download Vogelsang Peak, Mount Ritter, Koip Peak, and Mammoth Mountain.

Directions: From Lee Vining, drive 26 miles south on Highway 395 to Mammoth Junction. Turn west on Highway 203/Minaret Summit Road to the town of Mammoth Lakes and drive 14 miles to the Agnew Meadows Campground and the trailhead parking area.

Contact: Yosemite National Park, Yosemite, 209/372-0200, www.nps.gov/yose; Inyo National Forest, Mono Basin Scenic Area Visitors Center, Lee Vining, 760/647-3044, www.fs.usda.gov/inyo.

65 HITE COVE TRAIL

9.0 mi / 5.0 hr

on the South Fork Merced River in Sierra National Forest

Map 10.1, page 483 BEST

Considered by many to be the premier Sierra spring wildflower trail, Hite Cove Trail offers hikers a look at 60 flower varieties, including goldfields, lupine, poppies, brodaiea, monkeyflower, shooting stars, fiesta flowers, fairy lanterns, baby blue eyes, and Indian pinks. To see them, visit from late February to early May, before the show is over. Conveniently, this is usually the only time of the year when the trail is open, because the first 0.75 mile of trail is on private property, and access is restricted during fire season.

You start hiking on a paved driveway, but the asphalt only lasts for a few yards, then the trail transitions to a narrow single track that hugs the side of the steep canyon wall, high above the South Fork Merced River. Even if you aren't terribly interested in wildflowers, the river and canyon views are tremendous. About one mile out is an obvious rock outcrop, a few feet off the trail, where you can sit and enjoy the rushing river below. Another 0.5 mile farther, the trail drops down right alongside the river, and where the current mellows out, there are many tempting swimming holes. Those wishing to turn this hike into an overnight trip can camp at Hite Cove, the site of the 1879 Hite Cove Hotel. A campfire permit is required for overnight stays. From there, you can continue hiking to Devils Gulch, 2.5 miles farther. To do so, however, requires crossing the South Fork Merced River at Hite Cove, a difficult feat early in the year.

Note: As of September 2019, the Hite Cove Trail is closed due to damage from the 2018 Ferguson Fire, but the Forest Service plans to reopen it by March 2020. Call the Bass Lake Ranger Station or visit the Sierra National Forest website to make sure this trail is open before planning your trip. Access to the trail is restricted during fire season.

User Groups: Hikers, dogs, and horses. No mountain bikes. No wheelchair facilities.

Permits: No permits are required. Parking and access are free.

Maps: A Sierra National Forest map is available from the U.S. Forest Service. For a topographic map, go to the USGS website to download El Portal.

Directions: From Mariposa, drive 22 miles east on Highway 140 to Savage's Trading Post. The parking area is on the north side of the road, but the trail begins on the south side, near Savage's Trading Post.

Contact: Sierra National Forest, Bass Lake

Ranger Station, North Fork, 559/877-2218, www.fs.usda.gov/sierra.

66 UPPER YOSEMITE FALL

7.4 mi / 5.0 hr 4 10

in Yosemite Valley

Map 10.1, page 483 BEST

At 2,425 feet, Yosemite Falls is the highest waterfall in North America. That's why hundreds of park visitors hike this strenuous trail every day in the spring and summer. There's no feeling quite like standing at the waterfall's brink and realizing you've conquered a landmark of this magnitude.

Still, if you tucker out on this demanding climb to Upper Yosemite Fall, just remember that you always have a fallback position: you can hike only 1.2 miles one-way to the Columbia Point overlook, which is reached via more than 100 switchbacks and a total gain of 1,200 feet, then call it a day. The view of Yosemite Valley from Columbia Point is a stunner, and plenty of people who planned on hiking to Upper Yosemite Fall turn around here and still leave satisfied.

Those who push on are also rewarded. After a level section and then a short, surprising descent, you get your first full-impact view of horsetail-shaped Upper Yosemite Fall. In the spring and early summer months, this view will blow you away. The trail then switchbacks upward, more steeply now, through a canyon to the west of the fall, which allows passage to the top of the north rim of Yosemite Valley. At this point, you've gained 2,700 feet and hiked 3.5 miles; it's only another 0.2 mile to the brink of Upper Yosemite Fall. (Make sure you take the spur trail signed as Overlook.) From the metal fence above the fall's lip, you gain an incredible perspective on the waterfall's drop and the valley floor far below.

If this trip hasn't provided you with enough exertion, continue another 0.75 mile, crossing the bridge above the falls, to Yosemite Point at 6,936 feet in elevation, where you get a stunning view of the south rim of the Valley, Half Dome, and North Dome, and a look at the top of Lost Arrow Spire, a single shaft of granite jutting into the sky.

User Groups: Hikers only. No dogs, horses, or mountain bikes. No wheelchair facilities.

Permits: No permits are required. There is a $35 entrance fee per vehicle at Yosemite National Park, good for seven days.

Maps: A Half Dome or Yosemite National Park map is available from Tom Harrison Maps. For a topographic map, go to the USGS website to download Yosemite Falls.

Directions: From Merced, drive 70 miles northeast on Highway 140 to Yosemite National Park. Follow the signs toward Yosemite Valley, entering through the Arch Rock entrance station. Continue on Highway 140/El Portal Road, which becomes Southside Drive, for 10.5 miles. Just beyond the Yosemite Chapel, bear left at the fork and head toward Yosemite Village and the visitors center, then turn left and drive west on Northside Drive 0.75 mile to the parking lot. Park in the lot (do not park in the spaces marked Permit Parking Only), then walk to Camp 4, which is across Northside Drive and 0.25 mile west of Yosemite Lodge. You may not park in the Camp 4 lot unless you are camping there. If you are riding the free Yosemite Valley shuttle bus, disembark at Camp 4 or Yosemite Lodge.

Contact: Yosemite National Park, Yosemite, 209/372-0200, www.nps.gov/yose.

67 EAGLE PEAK

13.5 mi / 1 or 2 days

in Yosemite Valley

Map 10.1, page 483

If you seek more of a challenge than the day hike to Upper Yosemite Fall, the trail to Eagle Peak delivers the stunning destinations of the shorter trip (Columbia Point and Upper Yosemite Fall) plus an additional three miles one-way to a lookout atop the highest rock of the Three Brothers formation. Here, the vista is sublime. All of Yosemite Valley comes into view from the top of Eagle Peak, including an interesting perspective on North Dome, Clouds Rest, and Half Dome. On rare, extremely clear days you can also see the mountains and foothills of the Coast Range, 100 miles to the west.

Follow the trail notes for the hike to Upper Yosemite Fall (see listing in this chapter), then after taking the spur trail to the fall's brink, backtrack 0.25 mile to the trail junction for Eagle Peak Trail. Follow Eagle Peak Trail northwest for 1.5 miles, enjoying plentiful shade from Jeffrey pines and white firs, then hike south for one mile through Eagle Peak Meadows (prepare to get your feet wet here unless it is very late in summer). At a trail junction with El Capitan Trail, bear left for a 0.6-mile ascent to your final destination—the summit of Eagle Peak, elevation 7,779 feet. After completing this trip, you'll never view the Three Brothers from the valley floor the same way again.

User Groups: Hikers only. No dogs, horses, or mountain bikes. No wheelchair facilities.

Permits: There is a $35 entrance fee per vehicle at Yosemite National Park, good for seven days. Wilderness permits are required for overnight stays. They are available on a first-come, first-served basis up to two days in advance at the Yosemite Wilderness kiosk near your chosen trailhead, or up to 24 weeks in advance through Yosemite's online wilderness reservation system at www.yosemiteconservancy.org for a $5 reservation fee per person.

Maps: A Half Dome or Yosemite National Park map is available from Tom Harrison Maps. For a topographic map, go to the USGS website to download Yosemite Falls.

Directions: From Merced, drive 70 miles northeast on Highway 140 to Yosemite National Park. Follow the signs toward Yosemite Valley and enter through the Arch Rock entrance station. Continue on Highway 140/El Portal Road, which becomes Southside Drive, for 10.5 miles. Just beyond the Yosemite Chapel, bear left at the fork and head toward Yosemite Village and the visitors center, then turn left and drive west on Northside Drive 0.75 mile to the parking lot. Park in the lot (do not park in the spaces marked Permit Parking Only), then walk to Camp 4, which is across Northside Drive and 0.25 mile west of Yosemite Lodge. You may not park in the Camp 4 lot unless you are camping there. If you are riding the free Yosemite Valley shuttle bus, disembark at Camp 4 or Yosemite Lodge.

Contact: Yosemite National Park, Yosemite, 209/372-0200 or 209/372-0740 (permit reservations), www.nps.gov/yose or www.nps.gov/yose/wilderness (permit reservations).

68 LOWER YOSEMITE FALL

1.1 mi / 0.5 hr 1 9

in Yosemite Valley

Map 10.1, page 483 **BEST**

It's so short you can hardly call it a hike, and the route is perpetually crawling with people. Still, the trail to Lower Yosemite Fall is an absolute must for visitors to Yosemite Valley. When the falls are roaring with snowmelt in the spring and early summer, they never disappoint even the most seasoned hiker.

The only problem is that many visitors can't figure out where to leave their car and start the hike. Your best bet is to ride the shuttle bus from other points in the Valley, which deposits you at the "new" Yosemite Fall Trailhead, an attractive log structure positioned alongside Northside Drive. You can also park your car alongside the road near the shuttle bus stop, but good luck finding a space in the summer months. Either way, once you get started, the trail is simple enough to follow. Within about 10 minutes of walking, you are standing at the footbridge below the falls, and in the spring you can get soaking wet from the incredible mist and spray. By late summer, on the other hand, the fall often dries up completely. Be sure to walk the entire loop instead of just heading out-and-back to the falls; there is much to see along the way. And most important of all: if you really want to see the waterfall at its most magnificent, plan your trip for some time between April and June, during peak snowmelt. Seasoned waterfall lovers should also plan to visit on full moon nights in spring; if conditions are just right, a "moonbow" will appear surrounding the lower fall.

User Groups: Hikers and wheelchairs. No dogs, horses, or mountain bikes.

Permits: No permits are required. There is a $35 entrance fee per vehicle at Yosemite National Park, good for seven days.

Maps: A Half Dome or Yosemite National Park map is available from Tom Harrison Maps. For a topographic map, go to the USGS website to download Half Dome.

Directions: From Merced, drive 70 miles northeast on Highway 140 to Yosemite National Park. Follow the signs to Yosemite Valley, entering through the Arch Rock entrance station. Continue on Highway 140/El Portal Road, which becomes Southside Drive, for 10.5 miles. Just beyond the Yosemite Chapel, bear left at the fork and head toward Yosemite Village and the visitors center, then turn left and drive west on Northside Drive 0.75 mile to the parking lot. Park in the lot (do not park in the spaces marked Permit Parking Only). The trail begins across Northside Drive from Yosemite Lodge. You can also park on either side of Northside Drive near the Lower Yosemite Fall bus shuttle stop and walk from there.

Contact: Yosemite National Park, Yosemite, 209/372-0200, www.nps.gov/yose.

69 MIST TRAIL TO VERNAL FALL

3.0 mi / 2.0 hr

in Yosemite Valley

Map 10.1, page 483

This is a hike that every visitor to the Valley should take, even if it's the only trail they walk all year. Despite how crowded the trail inevitably is, this is a world-class hike to one of the most photographed waterfalls in the world. Make your trip more enjoyable by starting as early in the morning as possible, before the hordes are out in full force.

Start by taking the free Yosemite shuttle bus to the trailhead at Happy Isles. (Or you can add on an extra mile each way by hiking from the day-use parking area in Curry Village to Happy Isles.) The partially paved route is a moderate 500-foot climb to the Vernal Fall footbridge, then a very steep tromp up the seemingly endless granite staircase to the top of the fall. Although many people hike only to the footbridge, 0.8 mile from Happy Isles, it's definitely worth the extra effort to push on another 0.5 mile to reach the top of Vernal Fall.

Doing so means ascending another 500 feet on the Mist Trail's famous granite stairway, which frames the edge of Vernal Fall. You will come so close to the plunging spray that you may feel as if you are part of it. Sometimes you are—during peak snowmelt in spring, hikers are frequently drenched in spray and mist. Remember to bring a rain poncho if you don't like getting wet.

When you reach the 317-foot-high fall's brink, you can stand at the railing and watch the dizzying flow of rushing whitewater as it tumbles downward. This is a trip you have to do at least once in your life.

Warning: Do not cross or wade the Merced River at the top of Vernal Falls, and do not under any circumstances climb over the railing, especially during peak flows. Fatalities do occur here; don't be one of them.

User Groups: Hikers only. No dogs, horses, or mountain bikes. No wheelchair facilities.

Permits: No permits are required. There is a $35 entrance fee per vehicle at Yosemite National Park, good for seven days.

Maps: A Half Dome or Yosemite National Park map is available from Tom Harrison Maps. For a topographic map, go to the USGS website to download Half Dome.

Directions: From Merced, drive 70 miles northeast on Highway 140 to Yosemite National Park. Follow the signs toward Yosemite Valley, entering through the Arch Rock entrance station. Continue on Highway 140/El Portal Road, which becomes Southside Drive, for 11.6 miles to the day-use parking lot at Curry Village. Then ride the free Yosemite Valley shuttle bus to Happy Isles. In winter, when the shuttle does not run, you must hike from the day-use parking lot in Curry Village, adding two miles to your round-trip. The Mist Trail may be closed in winter; call to check on weather conditions.

Contact: Yosemite National Park, Yosemite, 209/372-0200, www.nps.gov/yose.

70 MIST TRAIL AND JOHN MUIR LOOP TO NEVADA FALL

6.8 mi / 4.0 hr 3 10

in Yosemite Valley

Map 10.1, page 483 BEST

You can hike either the John Muir Trail or Mist Trail to reach Yosemite's classic Nevada Fall, but the best choice is to make a loop out of it by hiking up on the Mist Trail, then down partway or all the way on the John Muir Trail. Both trails join above and below Nevada Fall, so you have some options. By hiking uphill rather than downhill on the Mist Trail's treacherous granite staircase, you can look around at the gorgeous scenery every time you stop to catch your breath. The John Muir Trail is somewhat less scenic, especially in its lower reaches, so save it for the way back downhill.

Start at Happy Isles and follow the signed trail to the footbridge over the Merced River, below Vernal Fall. After crossing the bridge, stay close along the river's edge on the Mist

Mist Trail and John Muir Loop to Nevada Fall

Trail for 1.2 miles to the top of Vernal Fall. If it's springtime, make sure you bring your rain gear for this stretch, or you will be drenched in spray. After a brief rest at the waterfall overlook, continue along the river's edge, passing a gorgeous stretch of stream known as the Emerald Pool, still following the Mist Trail. In 0.5 mile, the path crosses the river again, then climbs another mile to the brink of Nevada Fall. Total elevation gain to the top of the 594-foot falls is 2,600 feet, a healthy ascent. But when you get to walk this close to two world-class waterfalls, who's complaining? For your return trip, cross the footbridge above Nevada Fall and follow John Muir Trail to loop back. As you descend, check out the great view of Nevada Fall with Liberty Cap in the background. This is one of the most memorable scenes in Yosemite Valley.

Note: You can cut back over to the Mist Trail at Clark Point, just above Vernal Fall, if you so desire. That way, you get a second chance to see Vernal Fall and hike the Mist Trail's granite staircase. But let your knees decide—plenty of hikers don't want to face those stairs a second time, especially in the downhill direction.

User Groups: Hikers only. No dogs or mountain bikes. Horses are allowed only on John Muir Trail. No wheelchair facilities.

Permits: No permits are required. There is a $35 entrance fee per vehicle at Yosemite National Park, good for seven days.

Maps: A Half Dome or Yosemite National Park map is available from Tom Harrison Maps. For a topographic map, go to the USGS website to download Half Dome.

Directions: From Merced, drive 70 miles northeast on Highway 140 to Yosemite National Park. Follow the signs toward Yosemite Valley, entering through the Arch Rock entrance station. Continue on Highway 140/El Portal Road, which becomes Southside Drive, for 11.6 miles to the day-use parking lot at Curry Village. Then ride the free Yosemite Valley shuttle bus to Happy Isles, stop No. 16. In winter, when the shuttle does not run, you must hike from the day-use parking lot in Curry Village, adding two miles to your round-trip. Trails may be closed in winter; call to check on weather conditions.

Contact: Yosemite National Park, Yosemite, 209/372-0200, www.nps.gov/yose.

71 MIRROR LAKE LOOP

4.6 mi / 2.0 hr 1 7

in Yosemite Valley

Map 10.1, page 483

Thousands of Yosemite visitors walk to Mirror Lake every day in summer, but the vast majority of them miss the best part of this hike. The first thing you need to know: Mirror Lake is not really a lake; it's a large, shallow pool in Tenaya Creek. The pool is undergoing the process of sedimentation (filling with sand and gravel from Tenaya Creek), so every year it shrinks a little more. Many visitors walk up and down this canyon, shake their heads, and ask each other "Where's Mirror Lake?" If you know what you are looking for, the shallow pool is interesting to see, especially when its still waters produce a lovely reflective image of the granite domes above. But if you leave Mirror Lake behind and head back a mile or more into Tenaya Canyon, you will get the most out of this hike, and perhaps find the kind of quiet nature experience that most visitors seek in Yosemite.

Start by riding the free shuttle from Curry Village parking lot to Mirror Lake Junction. (Or walk there, if you wish, adding 1.5 miles round-trip to your hike.) From the bus stop, walk 0.5 mile on pavement to Mirror Lake and check out the interpretive signs at its edges. Then follow the foot trail up Tenaya Creek for 1.5 miles, passing the left turnoff for Snow Creek Trail. When you reach a footbridge across Tenaya Creek, cross it and loop back on the other side. Views of Half Dome, Mount Watkins, and neighboring granite walls are spectacular, and the forested creek canyon presents an intimate amphitheater in which to view them. Find a boulder somewhere, have a seat, and take in the show. This loop trail is nearly level the whole way, and once you go beyond Mirror Lake and into the lower Tenaya Creek Canyon, you are likely to find a little solitude.

User Groups: Hikers only. No dogs, horses, or mountain bikes. No wheelchair facilities.

Permits: No permits are required. There is a $35 entrance fee per vehicle at Yosemite National Park, good for seven days.

Maps: A Half Dome or Yosemite National Park map is available from Tom Harrison Maps. For a topographic map, go to the USGS website to download Half Dome.

Directions: From Merced, drive 70 miles northeast on Highway 140 to Yosemite National Park. Follow the signs toward Yosemite Valley, entering through the Arch Rock entrance station. Continue on Highway 140/El Portal Road, which becomes Southside Drive, for 11.6 miles to the day-use parking lot at Curry Village. Then ride the free Yosemite Valley shuttle bus to Mirror Lake Junction.

Contact: Yosemite National Park, Yosemite, 209/372-0200, www.nps.gov/yose.

72 HALF DOME

17.0 mi / 1 or 2 days 

in Yosemite Valley

Map 10.1, page 483 **BEST**

No argument about it, Half Dome is one of those once-in-your-life-you-gotta-do-it hikes. Just be sure you know what you're in for before you set out on this epic trail. For starters, you need to get a permit whether you plan to day-hike or backpack to the summit. Next, you need to know that the season is fairly short: if the weather cooperates, the Half Dome cables are usually in place from the weekend before Memorial Day in May through Columbus Day in early October. Attempting to climb the dome when the cables are not in place is extremely dangerous, so don't even consider it. The trail itself is 17 miles round-trip with a 4,800-foot elevation gain, a demanding hike by any standards. You need to be in solid physical shape. The vast majority of hikers make the trek in a single long day, and that's why a permit system was put in place to manage traffic and help keep hikers safe. A maximum of 300 people per day are granted permits to ascend Half Dome. Of those 300 hikers, approximately 225 are day hikers and 75 are backpackers. Day-hiking permits are distributed by preseason lottery via the website www.recreation.gov. Lottery applications are taken **online March 1-31** at www.recreation.gov. Hikers who didn't enter or succeed in the preseason lottery can try their luck at the daily lottery. Approximately **50 day-hiking permits** are available each day during the hiking season. To apply for a daily lottery permit, go to www.recreation.gov or call 877/444-6777. For the daily lottery you must **apply online two days prior** to your desired hiking date, and you are notified of the lottery results late the same night. Hikers who want to climb Half Dome as part of an overnight trip need to follow a completely different process; they must obtain a **wilderness permit** for backpacking and request a **Half Dome permit** for hiking to the summit.

Got your permit? Okay, now check the contents of your backpack. All day hikers should be sure to bring a load of water and food with them. You'll be handing it out to others who are not so well prepared, as well as gulping it down yourself. To begin the trip, follow either the John Muir Trail or the Mist Trail from Happy Isles to the top of Nevada Fall (the Mist Trail is 0.6 mile shorter), then go left and enter Little Yosemite Valley, where backpackers make camp. At 6.2 miles the John Muir Trail splits off from the Half Dome Trail and you head left for Half Dome. Just under two miles later you approach Half Dome's shoulder, which is a massive hump that is informally called Sub Dome. This is where a ranger is usually stationed to check to make sure that you have a permit (people without permits will not be allowed beyond the base of Sub Dome). A granite stairway, consisting of about 600 steps, leads

Half Dome

you up the dauntingly steep face of Sub Dome. Then the trail descends a bit, and you reach the steel cables that run 200 yards up the back of Half Dome. Here, many people start praying a lot and wishing there weren't so many other hikers on the cables at the same time. Pick up a pair of old work gloves from the pile at the base of the cable route; you'll need them to protect your hands as you pull yourself up the cables. It takes both hands and feet to haul yourself up 440 feet of nearly vertical granite. Many hikers are surprised by how much arm strength this requires. But when you reach the top, the views are so incredible that you forget all about your tired arms and feet. There's plenty of room for everyone on top of Half Dome; its vast, mostly flat surface covers about 13 acres.

To make the trip easier, you can choose to split the hike into two days by camping at Little Yosemite Valley, 4.7 miles in (a wilderness permit is required; see notes above). This lets you save the final ascent for the next day. If you're backpacking, you may also choose to hike to Little Yosemite Valley Camp from Glacier Point, spend the night, summit Half Dome first thing in the morning, then hike back out via Happy Isles and Yosemite Valley. You'll need to arrange a car shuttle or ride the Glacier Point bus from Yosemite Lodge, but this is a great way to see an incredible amount of scenery in two days and avoid the climb up the Mist Trail to Little Yosemite Valley Camp.

User Groups: Hikers only. No dogs, horses, or mountain bikes. No wheelchair facilities.

Permits: There is a $35 entrance fee per vehicle at Yosemite National Park, good for seven days. Permits are required for anyone day-hiking or backpacking to Half Dome's summit (see notes above for instructions on how to apply for a permit).

Maps: A Half Dome or Yosemite National Park map is available from Tom Harrison Maps. For a topographic map, go to the USGS website to download Half Dome.

Directions: From Merced, drive 70 miles northeast on Highway 140 to Yosemite National Park. Follow the signs toward Yosemite Valley, entering through the Arch Rock entrance station. Continue on Highway 140/El Portal Road, which becomes Southside Drive, for 11.6 miles to the day-use parking lot at Curry Village. Then ride the free Yosemite Valley shuttle bus to Happy Isles.

Contact: Yosemite National Park, Yosemite, 209/372-0200 or 209/372-0740 (permit reservations), www.nps.gov/yose or www.nps.gov/yose/wilderness (permit reservations).

73 INSPIRATION AND STANFORD POINTS

7.6 mi / 4.0 hr 3 9

in Yosemite Valley near the Wawona Tunnel

Map 10.1, page 483

Many consider the view from Inspiration Point at the entrance to the Wawona Tunnel to be one of the finest scenes in Yosemite—a wide panorama of Yosemite Valley, El Capitan, Half Dome, and Bridalveil Fall. If you like this view, you may want to see more of it by taking this hike from the trailhead at the vista point parking lot. The Pohono Trail leads uphill on a moderately steep grade until at 1.3 miles it reaches the "old" Inspiration Point. This is where the road to Yosemite Valley went through in the days before the Wawona Tunnel, and the view is now largely obscured by trees. Keep climbing, however, because with another 1,000 feet of elevation gain, you will cross Meadow Brook and reach the left cutoff trail for Stanford Point. You're 3.8 miles from the trailhead and you've climbed 2,200 feet, but your reward is an eagle's-eye view of the valley floor, 3,000 feet below, and a vista to the east of Half Dome and all its granite cousins. This stretch of the Pohono Trail is a dependable workout and the trail is never crowded with hikers.

User Groups: Hikers only. No dogs, horses, or mountain bikes. No wheelchair facilities.

Permits: No permits are required. There is a $35 entrance fee per vehicle at Yosemite National Park, good for seven days.

Maps: A Yosemite National Park map is available from Tom Harrison Maps. For a topographic map, go to the USGS website to download El Capitan.

Directions: From Merced, drive 70 miles northeast on Highway 140 to Yosemite National Park. Follow the signs to Yosemite Valley, entering through the Arch Rock entrance station. Continue 6.3 miles on Highway 140/El Portal Road, which becomes Southside Drive, and turn right at the fork for Highway 41/Wawona/Fresno. Continue 1.5 miles to the parking lots on either side of the road just before you enter the Wawona Tunnel. The trailhead is at the parking lot on the left (south) side of the road.

Contact: Yosemite National Park, Yosemite, 209/372-0200, www.nps.gov/yose.

74 BRIDALVEIL FALL

0.5 mi / 0.5 hr — 1 / 9

in Yosemite Valley

Map 10.1, page 483 BEST

Bridalveil Fall is right up there with Lower Yosemite Fall as a must-do walk for visitors (including nonhikers) to Yosemite Valley. Like that other famous waterfall walk, the path to Bridalveil Fall is paved with people. But the best thing about this waterfall is that unlike other falls in Yosemite Valley, Bridalveil runs year-round. It never dries up and disappoints visitors. The walk to its overlook is short and nearly level; the trail delivers you to a small viewing area about 70 yards from the fall. You can look straight up and see Bridalveil Creek plunging 620 feet off the edge of the south canyon wall. In high wind the fall billows and sways; if you are lucky you might see rainbows dancing in its mist. Another bonus is that your position at the Bridalveil overlook is such that if you do an about-face, you have an excellent view of Ribbon Fall flowing off the northern Yosemite Valley rim. Ribbon Fall is the highest single drop in the park at 1,612 feet, but it only flows in the earliest months of spring.

User Groups: Hikers and wheelchairs. No dogs, horses, or mountain bikes.

Permits: No permits are required. There is a $35 entrance fee per vehicle at Yosemite National Park, good for seven days.

Maps: A Yosemite National Park map is available from Tom Harrison Maps. For a topographic map, go to the USGS website to download El Capitan.

Directions: From Merced, drive 70 miles northeast on Highway 140 to Yosemite National Park. Follow the signs toward Yosemite Valley, entering through the Arch Rock entrance station. Continue for 6.3 miles on Highway 140/El Portal Road, which becomes Southside Drive, and turn right at the fork for Highway 41/Wawona/Fresno. Turn left almost immediately into the Bridalveil Fall parking lot. The trail begins at the far end of the parking lot. If you are driving into Yosemite Valley on Highway 41 from the south, watch for the Bridalveil Fall turnoff on your right about one mile after you exit the Wawona Tunnel.

Contact: Yosemite National Park, Yosemite, 209/372-0200, www.nps.gov/yose.

75 FOUR-MILE TRAIL

9.6 mi / 6.0 hr 3 8

in Yosemite Valley

Map 10.1, page 483

Many years ago, we hiked this trail on our first-ever visit to Yosemite and were shocked when we got to the top and found a giant parking lot and refreshment stand located there. What, you mean we could have driven to the high point on this trail? It's true, but your arrival at dramatic Glacier Point is somehow made all the more meaningful if you get there the hard way, which means hiking Four-Mile Trail all the way up from the valley floor, gaining 3,220 feet in 4.8 miles (not 4.0 miles, as the name implies). The trail is partially shaded and makes for a terrific day hike with an early morning start. Then you can have a leisurely brunch or lunch from your bird's-eye perch on Glacier Point. Don't like what you brought in your daypack? No problem. A snack shop sells hot dogs and the like all summer. From Glacier Point, you have unobstructed views of just about every major landmark in Yosemite Valley—most notably Half Dome, Basket Dome, Yosemite Falls, Vernal and Nevada Falls, and the valley floor far, far below you.

User Groups: Hikers only. No dogs, horses, or mountain bikes. No wheelchair facilities.

Permits: No permits are required. There is a $35 entrance fee per vehicle at Yosemite National Park, good for seven days.

Maps: A Half Dome or Yosemite National Park map is available from Tom Harrison Maps. For a topographic map, go to the USGS website to download Half Dome.

Directions: From Merced, drive 70 miles northeast on Highway 140 to Yosemite National Park. Follow the signs to Yosemite Valley, entering through the Arch Rock entrance station. Continue on Highway 140/El Portal Road, which becomes Southside Drive, for 9.5 miles. The trailhead is located next to mile marker V18 on the right side of Southside Drive. Park in the pullouts along the road.

Contact: Yosemite National Park, Yosemite, 209/372-0200, www.nps.gov/yose.

76 MCGURK MEADOW AND DEWEY POINT

2.0-7.0 mi / 1.0-4.0 hr 2 8

off Glacier Point Road in Yosemite National Park

Map 10.1, page 483 BEST

Some trails seem to capture the essence of Yosemite, and the McGurk Meadow Trail is one of those. The trailhead is the first one you reach as you wind along Glacier Point Road to spectacular Glacier Point. It's worth a stop to take the short walk through a fir and pine forest to pristine McGurk Meadow, a mile-long meadow crossed by a footbridge over a small feeder creek. A quarter-mile before the meadow the trail passes an old pioneer cabin, still standing in half-decent repair.

You can turn around at the meadow for a short and easy trip, or you can follow the trail until it connects to the Pohono Trail, which traverses Yosemite's south rim. An ideal destination is Dewey Point, a spectacular promontory with an unforgettable view of Yosemite Valley, located just off the Pohono Trail. That option turns this hike into a seven-mile round-trip.

User Groups: Hikers only. No dogs, horses, or mountain bikes. No wheelchair facilities.

Permits: No permits are required. There is a $35 entrance fee per vehicle at Yosemite National Park, good for seven days.

Maps: A Yosemite National Park map is available from Tom Harrison Maps. For a topographic map, go to the USGS website to download El Capitan.

Directions: From Merced, drive 70 miles northeast on Highway 140 to Yosemite National Park. Follow the signs toward Yosemite Valley, entering through the Arch Rock entrance station. Continue 6.3 miles on Highway 140/El Portal Road, which becomes Southside Drive, and turn right at the fork for Highway 41/Wawona/Fresno. Continue for 9.2 miles, turn left on Glacier Point Road, and drive 7.5 miles to the McGurk Meadow trailhead, on the left. Park in the pullout about 75 yards farther up the road.

Contact: Yosemite National Park, Yosemite, 209/372-0200, www.nps.gov/yose.

77 BRIDALVEIL CREEK

3.2 mi / 1.5 hr — 1 / 7

off Glacier Point Road in Yosemite National Park

Map 10.1, page 483

Perhaps the best time to take this hike to Bridalveil Creek is immediately after visiting Bridalveil Fall. After a short walk from Glacier Point Road through a forested area, you wind up at the edge of Bridalveil Creek, a babbling brook that seems far too tame to produce the giant waterfall downstream. To make the trip, follow Ostrander Lake Trail from Glacier Point Road for 1.4 miles. This stretch is almost completely level and is framed by colorful bunches of lupine in midsummer. When the trail splits, take the right fork toward Bridalveil Creek. The stream is so tame here that there is no bridge to cross—it's an easy rock hop by midsummer, although it can be a dangerous crossing in late spring. Pick a spot along its banks, and spend some time counting the wildflowers or the small, darting trout. If you are camping at Bridalveil Creek Campground or just heading up the road to visit Glacier Point, this easy walk is a pleasant leg-stretcher that will take you away from the crowds that throng so many of Yosemite's famous destinations.

User Groups: Hikers only. No dogs, horses, or mountain bikes. No wheelchair facilities.

Permits: No permits are required. There is a $35 entrance fee per vehicle at Yosemite National Park, good for seven days.

Maps: A Yosemite National Park map is available from Tom Harrison Maps. For a topographic map, go to the USGS website to download Half Dome.

Directions: From Merced, drive 70 miles northeast on Highway 140 to Yosemite National Park. Follow the signs toward Yosemite Valley, entering through the Arch Rock entrance station. Continue for 6.3 miles on Highway 140/El Portal Road, which becomes Southside Drive, and turn right at the fork for Highway 41/Wawona/Fresno. Continue for 9.2 miles, turn left on Glacier Point Road, and drive another 8.9 miles to the Ostrander Lake trailhead, on the right.

Contact: Yosemite National Park, Yosemite, 209/372-0200, www.nps.gov/yose.

78 OSTRANDER LAKE

12.5 mi / 1 or 2 days — 2 / 8

off Glacier Point Road in Yosemite National Park

Map 10.1, page 483

While many people take short day hikes from Glacier Point Road, a longer 12.5-mile trip to Ostrander Lake may better suit your taste. The trail is surprisingly easy, considering the long miles, and the first half is quite level. You can hike out and back in a day, or get a wilderness permit and camp near the lake's shores. The wide blue lake, set at 8,580 feet, is a popular destination for cross-country skiers in the winter, as is evidenced by the stone Ostrander Ski Hut and the ski markers tacked high up on trees along the route. Although the trail (really an old road) begins in a regenerated forest fire area, it traverses a typical high-country landscape of firs, pines, and, as you ascend, granite. You have to gain 1,600 feet along the way, most of it in the final three miles to the lake. The culmination of the climb occurs at nearly six miles out, as you reach the trail's highest point, a saddle on top of 8,700-foot Horizon Ridge. Here you are rewarded with excellent views of Half Dome, North Dome, Basket Dome, and Liberty Cap. This is a fine place to catch your breath. From here, the lake is less than 0.5 mile farther. On summer days, bring your swimsuit and a book, and plan to spend a few hours on Ostrander's sand- and boulder-lined shoreline.

User Groups: Hikers only. No dogs, horses, or mountain bikes. No wheelchair facilities.

Permits: There is a $35 entrance fee per vehicle at Yosemite National Park, good for seven days. Wilderness permits are required for overnight stays. They are available on a first-come, first-served basis up to two days in advance at the Yosemite Wilderness kiosk near your chosen trailhead, or up to 24 weeks in advance through Yosemite's online wilderness reservation system at www.yosemiteconservancy.org for a $5 reservation fee per person.

Maps: A Yosemite National Park map is available from Tom Harrison Maps. For topographic maps, go to the USGS website to download Half Dome and Mariposa Grove.

Directions: From Merced, drive 70 miles northeast on Highway 140 to Yosemite National Park. Follow the signs toward Yosemite Valley, entering through the Arch Rock entrance station. Continue for 6.3 miles on Highway 140/El Portal Road, which becomes Southside Drive, and turn right at the fork for Highway 41/Wawona/Fresno. Continue for 9.2 miles, turn left on Glacier Point Road, and drive 8.9 miles to the Ostrander Lake trailhead, on the right.

Contact: Yosemite National Park, Yosemite, 209/372-0200 or 209/372-0740 (permit reservations), www.nps.gov/yose or www.nps.gov/yose/wilderness (permit reservations).

79 SENTINEL DOME

2.2 mi / 1.0 hr

off Glacier Point Road in Yosemite National Park

Map 10.1, page 483 **BEST**

It's hard to believe you can get so much for so little, but on Sentinel Dome Trail, you can. The granite dome is located about a mile before Glacier Point on Glacier Point Road, and its elevation is 1,000 feet higher than the point's. Views from the dome's summit extend a full 360 degrees. A short and nearly level walk leads you to the base of the dome, and a 100-yard climb up its smooth granite back side brings you to its summit. There you are greeted by stunning vistas in all directions, including an unusual perspective on Upper and Lower Yosemite Falls. This is one of the best places in Yosemite to watch the sun set. To make a longer excursion, you can easily combine this hike with the hike to Taft Point and the Fissures (see listing in this chapter), which starts from the same trailhead but heads in the opposite direction.

User Groups: Hikers only. No dogs, horses, or mountain bikes. No wheelchair facilities.

Permits: No permits are required. There is a $35 entrance fee per vehicle at Yosemite National Park, good for seven days.

Maps: A Half Dome or Yosemite National Park map is available from Tom Harrison Maps. For a topographic map, go to the USGS website to download Half Dome.

Directions: From Merced, drive 70 miles northeast on Highway 140 to Yosemite National Park. Follow the signs to Yosemite Valley, entering through the Arch Rock entrance station. Continue 6.3 miles on Highway 140/El Portal Road, which becomes Southside Drive, and turn right at the fork for Highway 41/Wawona/Fresno. Continue for 9.2 miles, turn left on Glacier Point Road, and drive 13.2 miles to the Taft Point/Sentinel Dome trailhead parking lot, on the left side of the road.

Contact: Yosemite National Park, Yosemite, 209/372-0200, www.nps.gov/yose.

80 TAFT POINT AND THE FISSURES

2.2 mi / 1.0 hr 1 8

off Glacier Point Road in Yosemite National Park

Map 10.1, page 483

It's not so much the sweeping vista from Taft Point that you remember (although certainly you could say that the views of Yosemite's north rim and the valley floor are stunning). What you remember is the incredible sense of awe that you feel, perhaps mixed with a little fear and a lot of respect, as you peer down into the fissures in Taft Point's granite—huge cracks in the rock that plunge hundreds of feet down toward the valley. One of the fissures has a couple of large boulders captured in its jaws; they're stuck there, waiting for the next big earthquake or ice age to set them free. Be sure to walk to the metal railing along the edge of Taft Point's cliff, where you can hold on tight and peer down at the valley far, far below. If you have kids with you or anyone who is afraid of heights, be sure to keep a tight handhold on them.

User Groups: Hikers only. No dogs, horses, or mountain bikes. No wheelchair facilities.

Permits: No permits are required. There is a $35 entrance fee per vehicle at Yosemite National Park, good for seven days.

Maps: A Half Dome or Yosemite National Park map is available from Tom Harrison Maps. For a topographic map, go to the USGS website to download Half Dome.

Directions: From Merced, drive 70 miles northeast on Highway 140 to Yosemite National Park. Follow the signs to Yosemite Valley, entering through the Arch Rock entrance station. Continue for 6.3 miles on Highway 140/El Portal Road, which becomes Southside Drive, and turn right at the fork for Highway 41/Wawona/Fresno. Continue for 9.2 miles, turn left on Glacier Point Road, and drive 13.2 miles to the Taft Point/Sentinel Dome trailhead parking lot, on the left side of the road.

Contact: Yosemite National Park, Yosemite, 209/372-0200, www.nps.gov/yose.

81 POHONO TRAIL

13.0 mi one-way / 7.0 hr 

off Glacier Point Road in Yosemite National Park

Map 10.1, page 483

If you can arrange a shuttle trip, Pohono Trail from Glacier Point downhill to its end at Wawona Tunnel is worth every step of its 13 miles. The two ends of the trail have the best drive-to viewpoints in all of Yosemite, and in between, you are treated to dozens of other scenic spots (including Sentinel Dome, at 1.5 miles, and Taft Point, at 3.8 miles), as well as four bird's-eye lookouts over the valley floor: Inspiration, Stanford, Dewey, and Crocker Points. Starting at Glacier Point and ending at Wawona Tunnel, you'll cover a 2,800-foot descent, but there are some "ups" along the way, too—like at the very beginning (from Glacier Point to Sentinel Dome), and between Bridalveil Creek and Dewey Point. The trail stays on or near Yosemite Valley's southern rim the entire way except for one major detour into the woods to access the bridge crossing of Bridalveil Creek. Remember to bring along a good map, because many of the trail's best offerings are just off the main path. If you don't take the short spur routes to reach them, you'll miss out on some spectacular scenery.

The view of Yosemite Falls from Pohono Trail in front of Sentinel Dome is the best in all of Yosemite. For the best overall vista along the trail, it's a toss-up between Glacier Point, Taft Point, and Dewey Point.

User Groups: Hikers only. No dogs, horses, or mountain bikes. No wheelchair facilities.

Permits: There is a $35 entrance fee per vehicle at Yosemite National Park, good for seven days.

Wilderness permits are required for overnight stays. They are available on a first-come, first-served basis up to two days in advance at the Yosemite Wilderness kiosk near your chosen trailhead, or up to 24 weeks in advance through Yosemite's online wilderness reservation system at www.yosemiteconservancy.org for a $5 reservation fee per person.

Maps: A Yosemite National Park map is available from Tom Harrison Maps. For topographic maps, go to the USGS website to download Half Dome and El Capitan.

Directions: From Merced, drive 70 miles northeast on Highway 140 to Yosemite National Park. Follow the signs to Yosemite Valley, entering through the Arch Rock entrance station. Continue for 6.3 miles on Highway 140/El Portal Road, which becomes Southside Drive, and turn right at the fork for Highway 41/Wawona/Fresno. Continue for 9.2 miles, turn left on Glacier Point Road, and drive 15.7 miles to Glacier Point. Park and walk toward the main viewing area across from the café and gift shop. Look for the Pohono Trail sign about 150 feet southeast of the café building, on your right.

Contact: Yosemite National Park, Yosemite, 209/372-0200 or 209/372-0740 (permit reservations), www.nps.gov/yose or www.nps.gov/yose/wilderness (permit reservations).

82 PANORAMA TRAIL

8.5 mi one-way / 5.0 hr 

off Glacier Point Road in Yosemite National Park

Map 10.1, page 483 **BEST**

The Panorama Trail follows a spectacular route from Glacier Point to Yosemite Valley, heading downhill most of the way, but you must have a shuttle car waiting at the end or it's one heck of a long climb back up. A great option is to take the Yosemite Lodge tour bus for one leg of the trip; call 209/372-1240 to reserve a seat (fee required).

The aptly named Panorama Trail begins at Glacier Point, elevation 7,214 feet. You switchback downhill, accompanied by ever-changing perspectives on Half Dome, Basket Dome, North Dome, Liberty Cap, and, in the distance, Vernal and Nevada Falls. You will gape a lot. After passing Illilouette Fall and ascending a bit for the first time on the trip, continue eastward to the Panorama Trail's end near the top of Nevada Fall. Turn right to reach the top of the fall and have a rest at the overlook, then continue downhill on the Mist Trail on the north side of the river. After a view-filled descent along the north side of Nevada Fall, you'll cross the river in 1.4 miles and walk alongside lovely Emerald Pool on your way to the top of Vernal Fall. Enjoy the show here, then tromp down the granite staircase on the busy trail back to Happy Isles. From there you can take the free valley shuttle bus back to your car, parked somewhere in Yosemite Valley.

Note: The route has a 3,200-foot elevation loss over its course, but there is also a 760-foot climb after you cross Illilouette Creek. Also be forewarned that while the starting miles of the trip are quite tranquil, the final two miles by Vernal Fall are usually a parade of people.

User Groups: Hikers only. No dogs, horses, or mountain bikes. No wheelchair facilities.

Permits: No permits are required. There is a $35 entrance fee per vehicle at Yosemite National Park, good for seven days.

Maps: A Half Dome or Yosemite National Park map is available from Tom Harrison Maps. For a topographic map, go to the USGS website to download Half Dome.

Directions: From Merced, drive 70 miles northeast on Highway 140 to Yosemite National Park. Follow the signs to Yosemite Valley, entering through the Arch Rock entrance station. Continue for 6.3 miles on Highway 140/El Portal Road, which becomes Southside Drive, and turn right at the fork for Highway 41/Wawona/Fresno. Continue for 9.2 miles, turn left on Glacier Point Road, and drive 15.7 miles to Glacier Point. Park and walk toward the main viewing area, across from the café and gift shop. Look for the Panorama Trail sign about 150 feet southeast of the café building, on your right.

Contact: Yosemite National Park, Yosemite, 209/372-0200, www.nps.gov/yose; lodge tour buses, 209/372-1240.

83 ILLILOUETTE FALL

4.0 mi / 2.5 hr 2 10

off Glacier Point Road in Yosemite National Park

Map 10.1, page 483

Those who can't afford the time or make the car shuttle arrangements necessary to hike the entire Panorama Trail should at least take this incredible out-and-back trip on the top portion of the route. Glacier Point is your starting point, and the bridge above Illilouette Fall becomes your destination, but what happens in between is sheer magic. Some say that hiking Panorama Trail is like staring at a life-size Yosemite postcard, but we say it's more like being in the postcard. As you walk, you feel as if you've become one with the magnificent panorama of Half Dome, Basket Dome, North Dome, Liberty Cap, and far-off Vernal and Nevada Falls. The trail is downhill all the way to Illilouette Fall in two miles, which means you have a 1,200-foot elevation gain on the return trip. The path is extremely well graded, so even children can make the climb. After viewing the waterfall from a trailside overlook, walk another 0.25 mile and stand on the bridge that is perched just above the 370-foot drop. For obvious reasons, don't think about swimming here.

User Groups: Hikers only. No dogs, horses, or mountain bikes. No wheelchair facilities.

Permits: No permits are required. There is a $35 entrance fee per vehicle at Yosemite National Park, good for seven days.

Maps: A Half Dome or Yosemite National Park map is available from Tom Harrison Maps. For a topographic map, go to the USGS website to download Half Dome.

Directions: From Merced, drive 70 miles northeast on Highway 140 to Yosemite National Park. Follow the signs to Yosemite Valley, entering through the Arch Rock entrance station. Continue for 6.3 miles on Highway 140/El Portal Road, which becomes Southside Drive, and turn right at the fork for Highway 41/Wawona/Fresno. Continue for 9.2 miles, turn left on Glacier Point Road, and drive 15.7 miles to Glacier Point. Park and walk toward the main viewing area, across from the café and gift shop. Look for the Panorama Trail sign on your right, about 150 feet southeast of the café building.

Contact: Yosemite National Park, Yosemite, 209/372-0200, www.nps.gov/yose.

84 ALDER CREEK FALLS

8.2 mi / 5.0 hr 3 9

off Highway 41 near Wawona in Yosemite National Park

Map 10.1, page 483

Maybe the best thing about Alder Creek Falls is that with all the world-famous waterfalls in Yosemite, this one just plain gets overlooked. Or maybe the best thing is the fun hike to reach it, starting with the challenge of locating the hidden trailhead along Highway 41. After you accomplish this feat, you begin with a one-mile beeline hike straight uphill through the forest, which will surely get your heart pumping. At the top of the ridge and a trail junction, turn left and hike through the trees for two more miles, still heading uphill but now more gently. Three miles from the trailhead, the route suddenly goes level as it joins an old railroad grade, and then it's a one-mile easy stroll to the spot where Alder Creek takes the plunge off a granite lip. The waterfall is about 250 feet tall, and the best view of it is from the trail, about 100 yards away from it. If you choose to keep hiking beyond the falls, you'll find many fine picnic spots among meadows filled with wildflowers.

User Groups: Hikers and horses. No dogs or mountain bikes. No wheelchair facilities.

Permits: There is a $35 entrance fee per vehicle at Yosemite National Park, good for seven days. Wilderness permits are required for overnight stays. They are available on a first-come, first-served basis up to two days in advance at the Yosemite Wilderness kiosk near your chosen trailhead, or up to 24 weeks in advance through Yosemite's online wilderness reservation system at www.yosemiteconservancy.org for a $5 reservation fee per person.

Maps: A Yosemite National Park map is available from Tom Harrison Maps. For a topographic map, go to the USGS website to download Wawona.

Directions: From Merced, drive 55 miles northeast on Highway 140 to Yosemite National Park. Follow the signs to Yosemite Valley, entering through the Arch Rock entrance station. Continue for 6.3 miles on Highway 140/El Portal Road, which becomes Southside Drive, and turn right at the fork for Highway 41/Wawona/Fresno. Drive south on Highway 41 for 21 miles to a hairpin turn in the road (if you are coming from the south, it is exactly 4.2 miles north of Chilnualna Falls Road in Wawona). Park in the large dirt pullout on the west side of the road; the trailhead is on the east side of Highway 41. There is no marker except for a Yosemite Wilderness sign.

Contact: Yosemite National Park, Yosemite, 209/372-0200 or 209/372-0740 (permit reservations), www.nps.gov/yose or www.nps.gov/yose/wilderness (permit reservations).

85 WAWONA MEADOW LOOP

3.2 mi / 1.25 hr 1 7

off Highway 41 near Wawona in Yosemite National Park

Map 10.1, page 483

Sometimes you just want to take a stroll in the park, and the Wawona Meadow Loop is exactly that. Many hikers ignore this trail because of its proximity to the Wawona Golf Course, but they are missing out on an easy, pleasant meander. On this level trail (a former stage road), you can see terrific wildflowers in early summer and enjoy the good company of butterflies as you take a lazy stroll. From the signed trailhead across the road from the Wawona Hotel, hike to your left on the dirt road, following the split rail fence. At the end of the meadow the old road crosses the stream and returns to the hotel on the north side of the golf course. If you wish, you can even bring your dog or ride your bike on this trail. If you're staying at the Wawona Hotel, you can hike from there, crossing the Wawona Road on your way out and back.

User Groups: Hikers, dogs, and mountain bikes. No horses. No wheelchair facilities.

Permits: No permits are required. There is a $35 entrance fee per vehicle at Yosemite National Park, good for seven days.

Maps: A Yosemite National Park map is available from Tom Harrison Maps. For a topographic map, go to the USGS website to download Wawona.

Directions: From Merced, drive 70 miles northeast on Highway 140 to Yosemite National Park. Follow the signs toward Yosemite Valley, entering through the Arch Rock entrance station. Continue for 6.3 miles on Highway 140/El Portal Road, which becomes Southside Drive, and turn right at the fork for Highway 41/Wawona/Fresno. Drive 27 miles to the trailhead, which is just south of the golf course and across the road from the Wawona Hotel.

Contact: Yosemite National Park, Yosemite, 209/372-0200, www.nps.gov/yose.

86 CHILNUALNA FALL

8.2 mi / 5.0 hr 3 9

off Highway 41 near Wawona in Yosemite National Park

Map 10.1, page 483

Are you ready to climb? It's good to be mentally prepared for this hike, which includes a steady four-mile uphill, gaining 2,400 feet to reach the top of Chilnualna Fall. Pick a nice, cool day because this trail is in the lower-elevation part of Yosemite. Your nose will be continually assaulted with the intoxicating smell of bear clover, which together with manzanita and oaks makes up the majority of the vegetation along the route. Halfway up you get a great view of Wawona Dome (elevation 6,897 feet) from a granite overlook. This is a great place to take a break and stretch your hamstrings. Shortly thereafter you glimpse a section of Chilnualna Falls high up on a cliff wall, still far ahead. The trail leads above the brink of the fall's lower drop to a series of higher cascades. Keep hiking until you reach the uppermost cascade, which consists of five pool-and-drop tiers just 100 yards off the granite-lined trail. You'll want to spread out a picnic here before you begin the long descent back to the trailhead.

User Groups: Hikers and horses. No dogs or mountain bikes. No wheelchair facilities.

Permits: There is a $35 entrance fee per vehicle at Yosemite National Park, good for seven days. Wilderness permits are required for overnight stays. They are available on a first-come, first-served basis up to two days in advance at the Yosemite Wilderness kiosk near your chosen trailhead, or up to 24 weeks in advance through Yosemite's online wilderness reservation system at www.yosemiteconservancy.org for a $5 reservation fee per person.

Maps: A Yosemite National Park map is available from Tom Harrison Maps. For topographic maps, go to the USGS website to download Wawona and Mariposa Grove.

Directions: From Merced, drive 55 miles northeast on Highway 140 to Yosemite National Park. Follow the signs to Yosemite Valley, entering through the Arch Rock entrance station. Continue for 6.3 miles on Highway 140/El Portal Road, which becomes Southside Drive, and turn right at the fork for Highway 41/Wawona/Fresno. Drive south on Highway 41 for 25 miles to Wawona, and turn left on Chilnualna Falls Road. Drive 1.7 miles east and park in the lot on the right side of the road. Walk back to Chilnualna Falls Road and pick up the single-track trail across the pavement.

Contact: Yosemite National Park, Yosemite, 209/372-0200 or 209/372-0740 (permit reservations), www.nps.gov/yose or www.nps.gov/yose/wilderness (permit reservations).

87 MARIPOSA GROVE

2.0-6.4 mi / 1.0-3.0 hr 2 8

off Highway 41 near Wawona in Yosemite National Park

Map 10.1, page 483

After a two-year closure and a major facelift,

Chilnualna Falls

Yosemite's Mariposa Grove reopened in fall 2018. Its larger-than-life giant sequoia trees offer an even bigger wow factor than before. Gone are the exhaust-emitting tram rides, tacky gift shop, and paved roads between the lower and upper groves. In their place are improved parking and access (leave your car at Yosemite's South Entrance and ride a free shuttle to the lower grove) and wheelchair-accessible trails and boardwalks. The awe-inspiring experience of seeing the gargantuan Grizzly Giant tree—and approximately 500 more mature sequoias—is now better than ever. At more than 100 feet in circumference, the Grizzly Giant's girth is mind-boggling. It's one of the oldest known giant sequoias, still standing tall after more than 2,700 years. If you want to see only the most famous trees in the grove, including the Grizzly Giant, take the well-signed two-mile hike through the lower grove and turn around at the signs pointing to the upper grove. If you hike the entire lower and upper grove, you will cover 6.4 miles of trail. For the best chance of avoiding the summer crowds, time your visit for early in the morning or just before sunset.

User Groups: Hikers only. No dogs, horses, or mountain bikes. No wheelchair facilities.

Permits: No permits are required. There is a $35 entrance fee per vehicle at Yosemite National Park, good for seven days.

Maps: A brochure and trail map are available at the trailhead. A Yosemite National Park map is available from Tom Harrison Maps. For a topographic map, go to the USGS website to download Mariposa Grove.

Directions: From Merced, drive 70 miles northeast on Highway 140 to Yosemite National Park. Follow the signs toward Yosemite Valley, entering through the Arch Rock entrance station. Continue for 6.3 miles on Highway 140/El Portal Road, which becomes Southside Drive, and turn right at the fork for Highway 41/Wawona/Fresno. Drive 32 miles to the Mariposa Grove parking area by Yosemite's south entrance, then ride the shuttle bus to the grove's trailhead. (If you enter the park on Highway 41 from the south, the parking area will be just after you pass through the entrance station.)

Contact: Yosemite National Park, Yosemite, 209/372-0200, www.nps.gov/yose.

88 LEWIS CREEK NATIONAL RECREATION TRAIL

4.0 mi / 2.0 hr 1 8

off Highway 41 north of Oakhurst

Map 10.1, page 483

Three separate trailheads access the Lewis Creek National Recreation Trail, but unless you want to hike its entire 3.7-mile one-way distance, the best place to start is at the trail's midpoint, just off Highway 41. From this roadside trailhead, you can take a 10-minute walk south to Corlieu Falls and/or walk 1.8 miles north to see Red Rock Falls. Neither waterfall is a showstopper, although both are pretty. Instead, the highlight of the trip is the hike itself, a gorgeous walk along flower-lined Lewis Creek, following the route of the historic Madera Sugar Pine lumber flume. Sugar Pine Lumber Company used the flume (an artificial river in a huge wooden trough) to float lumber over 50 miles to the town of Madera. You'll pass many anglers along the hike; Lewis Creek is stocked with catchable trout. Fishing is best below Corlieu Falls. In addition, the white western azaleas along the stream bloom in profusion in early summer, shaded by a thick canopy of dogwoods, oaks, ponderosa pines, and incense cedars.

User Groups: Hikers and dogs. No horses or mountain bikes. No wheelchair facilities.

Permits: No permits are required. Parking and access are free.

Maps: A Sierra National Forest map is available from the U.S. Forest Service. For a topographic map, go to the USGS website to download Ahwahnee.

Directions: From Oakhurst, drive north on

Highway 41 for eight miles to the signed trailhead for Lewis Creek Trail, on the east side of the highway. The trailhead is four miles south of Westfall Picnic Area.

Contact: Sierra National Forest, Bass Lake Ranger Station, North Fork, 559/877-2218, www.fs.usda.gov/sierra.

89 SHADOW OF THE GIANTS

1.2 mi / 0.5 hr 1 9

off Highway 41 south of Yosemite National Park and north of Oakhurst in Sierra National Forest

Map 10.1, page 483 BEST

Shadow of the Giants is a National Recreation Trail that is located within the Nelder Grove of Giant Sequoias. For the sheer numbers of sequoias and the blissful peace and quiet, it beats the heck out of the sequoia groves a few miles north, in Yosemite National Park. On a Saturday afternoon in June, it's not impossible to walk the one-mile interpretive trail all by yourself. The self-guided signs along the trail are interesting and informative, and the babble of Nelder Creek is a perfect accompaniment to the huge, majestic trees. In addition to the sequoias, the forest is filled with western azaleas, dogwoods, incense cedars, wild rose, sugar pines, and white firs. What's the best thing we learned on the trail? The bark of mature sequoias is so soft that squirrels use it to line their nests. The trail makes an easy loop and is set at 5,000 feet in elevation. The best sequoias are at the far end of the loop, so make sure you walk all the way.

User Groups: Hikers and dogs. No horses or mountain bikes. No wheelchair facilities.

Permits: No permits are required. Parking and access are free.

Maps: A Sierra National Forest map is available from the U.S. Forest Service. For a topographic map, go to the USGS website to download Bass Lake.

Directions: From Oakhurst, drive north on Highway 41 for five miles to Sky Ranch Road/Road 632. Turn east on Sky Ranch Road and drive six miles to the turnoff for Nelder Grove. Turn left, drive 1.5 miles, and take the left fork, signed for Shadow of the Giants. (The right fork takes you to an interpretive site and additional trails). Drive 0.5 mile to the trailhead.

Contact: Sierra National Forest, Bass Lake Ranger Station, North Fork, 559/877-2218, www.fs.usda.gov/sierra.

90 FRESNO DOME

2.0 mi / 1.0 hr

off Highway 41 south of Yosemite National Park and north of Oakhurst

Map 10.1, page 483

It's best to plan one hour of time for this trip, but you may want to leave room for more, because once you reach the top of Fresno Dome, you won't want to leave. The trailhead elevation is 8,000 feet, and the trail is beautiful right from the start. It traverses a verdant meadow filled with corn lilies, quaking aspens, and lavender shooting stars. The first 0.5 mile is completely flat; in the second 0.5 mile, you climb up the sloped back side of Fresno Dome. After a moderate ascent (manageable by almost anybody), you're rewarded with 360-degree views, mostly of conifer-filled valleys. You can just make out a corner of Bass Lake, the town of Oakhurst, and the far-off snowy peaks of the Ansel Adams Wilderness. From up on top of Fresno Dome, it all looks like heaven.

User Groups: Hikers and dogs. No horses or mountain bikes. No wheelchair facilities.

Permits: No permits are required. Parking and access are free.

Maps: A Sierra National Forest map is available from the U.S. Forest Service. For a topographic map, go to the USGS website to download Bass Lake.

Directions: From Oakhurst, drive north on Highway 41 for five miles to Sky Ranch Road/Road 632. Turn east on Sky Ranch Road, drive approximately 12 miles, and bear left at the sign for Fresno Dome Campground. Drive 4.8 miles to the trailhead (two miles past the camp).

Contact: Sierra National Forest, Bass Lake Ranger Station, North Fork, 559/877-2218, www.fs.usda.gov/sierra/.

91 THE NICHE AND CORA LAKES

8.6 mi / 4.0 hr-2 days 

in the Ansel Adams Wilderness southeast of Yosemite National Park

Map 10.1, page 483

Reaching the trailhead for The Niche and Cora Lakes requires a long drive on the Sierra Vista National Scenic Byway, the showpiece road of the North Fork area. If you have the time for it, it's a great trip. The best approach is to drive out and spend the night at Granite Creek Campground or nearby Clover Meadow Campground, then start hiking the next day. The trip starts with a 3.1-mile gentle ascent through red firs and lodgepole pines to The Niche (at 8,000 feet), where you enter the Ansel Adams Wilderness boundary. Bear left and follow the signs to Cora Lakes, at 4.3 miles. Only one of the Cora Lakes is of substantial size; that's the lower lake, the first one you come to, on the left. The lake is partly forested and has dependable trout fishing. Because the total ascent to Cora Lakes is only 1,200 feet, you may have some energy left to burn. Backpackers should consider adding on a jaunt to Joe Crane Lake, another four miles to the north. The lake has a long and lovely sandy beach, good fishing, and even better swimming than at Cora Lakes.

User Groups: Hikers, dogs, and horses. No mountain bikes. No wheelchair facilities.

Permits: A free wilderness permit is required for overnight stays and is available from the Bass Lake Ranger Station. Quotas are in effect year-round; permits can be reserved in advance for a $5 reservation fee per person.

Maps: A Sierra National Forest or Ansel Adams Wilderness map is available from the U.S. Forest Service. For a topographic map, go to the USGS website to download Timber Knob.

Directions: From the town of North Fork south of Bass Lake, drive southeast on Road 225 to Minarets Road. Turn left (north) on Minarets Road/Road 81 and follow it for approximately 50 winding miles to the Clover Meadow Ranger Station/Granite Creek turnoff, on the right. Drive 4.5 miles to the Isberg trailhead, just beyond Granite Creek Campground.

Contact: Sierra National Forest, Bass Lake Ranger Station, North Fork, 559/877-2218, www.fs.usda.gov/sierra.

92 JACKASS LAKES

7.2 mi / 4.0 hr or 2 days 

in the Ansel Adams Wilderness southeast of Yosemite National Park

Map 10.1, page 483

Campers in the Clover Meadow and Upper Chiquito campground areas have this pleasant day hike to enjoy. The trailhead is an easy reach (right off of Beasore Road), and in about two hours of hiking, you can be cooling your toes in the crystal-blue waters of Lower Jackass Lake. The trail climbs immediately from the road, then enters the Ansel Adams Wilderness boundary in one mile. This first mile can be hot and steep, but it's over with quickly. At the boundary, the grade mellows out, and you reach a junction just before the lakes, at 3.4 miles. The right fork goes to Lower Jackass Lake (the largest of three choices) in 0.2 mile, and the left fork goes to the tiny upper lake. A third lake lies in the basin above the upper lake. Many people just bear right at the junction and visit Lower Jackass Lake, which at 8,600 feet is backed by granite cliffs and offers good swimming and fishing prospects. No, this isn't the most beautiful lake in the Sierra, but if you just want to visit a pretty spot without a whole lot of effort, this trip fits the bill.

User Groups: Hikers, dogs, and horses. No mountain bikes. No wheelchair facilities.

Permits: A free wilderness permit is required for overnight stays and is available from the Bass Lake Ranger Station. Quotas are in effect year-round; permits can be reserved in advance for a $5 reservation fee per person.

Maps: A Sierra National Forest or Ansel Adams Wilderness map is available from the U.S. Forest Service. For a topographic map, go to the USGS website to download Timber Knob.

Directions: From Oakhurst, drive north on Highway 41 for four miles, then turn right on Road 222 toward Bass Lake. In four miles, bear left on Road 274. Drive two miles and turn left on Beasore Road (gravel). Drive 29 miles to a turnoff for the Norris Trailhead. Bear left and drive two miles to the trailhead parking area.

Contact: Sierra National Forest, Bass Lake Ranger Station, North Fork, 559/877-2218, www.fs.usda.gov/sierra.

93 CONVICT CANYON TO LAKE DOROTHY

15.0 mi / 2 days 3 10

in the John Muir Wilderness south of Mammoth Lakes

Map 10.2, page 484 BEST

Framed by a back wall of bare granite peaks, Convict Lake is a mountain shrine, and the trail that leads from here into the backcountry wilderness makes hikers feel as if they're ascending into heaven. But this is no easy trip. Not only is there a 2,700-foot climb, but a tricky and sometimes dangerous stream crossing is involved. To complicate matters, much of the trail into Convict Canyon has been washed out by frequent landslides, and the Forest Service has given up on trail maintenance. Still, this canyon is worth seeing—just be prepared for a serious hike.

Begin your trek at Convict Lake (7,621 feet). A trail circles the lake, and it doesn't matter whether you follow the north shore trail or the south shore trail. Either way you'll have plenty of company until you reach the far (west) side of the lake, where the Convict Canyon Trail takes off. You'll start to climb right away, and this section can be steep and hot, but it's fairly easy to follow except for a few washed-out sections. Occasional stands of aspen provide welcome shade. At about three miles, you must ford Convict Creek, which can be dangerous in the early summer because of high snowmelt. (By autumn, it may be a simple rock-hop.) Several attempts to bridge this crossing have failed, as the bridge always gets washed out by high flows in early summer.

Beyond the crossing, the trail gets sketchier, and the drop-offs get steeper. You'll climb high above the creek, becoming more intimate with the magnificent, colorful walls of Convict Canyon. This place is a geologist's dream. Finally you'll climb high enough to enter the high country above tree line at 10,000 feet. Only scattered stands of whitebark pines grow on the edge of Mildred Lake (4.9 miles out), a great place for day hikers to call it a day. A sketchy use trail switchbacks from the back side of Mildred up to Lake Dorothy at 6.2 miles (10,275 feet), Lake Genevieve at 7.2 miles (10,000 feet), and beyond them, Bighorn, Edith, and Cloverleaf Lakes. Backpackers can take their pick. Lake Dorothy is by far the largest of the lot and is well known for its white sand beaches. You can spend days exploring this high-mountain paradise—but it comes with a price.

Note: The crossing of Convict Creek is considered to be one of the most treacherous in the Sierra Nevada. This trail should only be hiked late in the season, when the stream flow has dropped. Check with the Mammoth Lakes Welcome Center for current conditions before planning a trip.

User Groups: Hikers, dogs, and horses. No mountain bikes. No wheelchair facilities.

Permits: A free wilderness permit is required for overnight stays and is available from the Mammoth Lakes Welcome Center. Quotas are in effect from May 1 to November 1; for this period, permits are available in advance for a $5 reservation fee per person.

Maps: A Mammoth High Country map is available from Tom Harrison Maps. An Inyo National Forest or John Muir Wilderness map is available from the U.S. Forest Service. For a topographic map, go to the USGS website to download Bloody Mountain.

Directions: From U.S. 395 at the Mammoth Lakes junction, drive south for six miles to Convict Lake Road. Turn west and drive 1.8 miles to a spur road on the right as you near the lake. Turn right and drive 0.25 mile to the parking area for the trailhead.

Contact: Inyo National Forest, Mammoth Lakes Welcome Center, Mammoth Lakes, 760/924-5500, www.fs.usda.gov/inyo.

94 MCGEE CREEK TO STEELHEAD LAKE

11.4 mi / 6.0 hr or 2 days 3 9

in the John Muir Wilderness

Map 10.2, page 484 BEST

Unlike many trails leading into the John Muir Wilderness, the McGee Creek Trail has the benefit of starting out with a fairly gentle grade. It follows the remains of an old mining road (now just a narrow trail), and it gives your legs and lungs the opportunity to warm up before climbing more seriously. Get an early start, though, because in the first two miles, you pass through sun-baked plains of sage and rabbit brush. There is very little shade, but you are heading toward a colorful and dramatic mountain backdrop: Mount Baldwin on the right, Mount Crocker on the left, and Red and White Mountain straight ahead—all at over 12,000 feet in elevation. To your left, along McGee Creek, grows a lush garden of aspens and cottonwoods. You'll pass Horsetail Falls on the right at two miles out, and soon the trail enters a lodgepole pine forest. The climb steepens, and at 4.5 miles, you reach a junction with Steelhead Lake Trail heading left (east). Switchbacks carry you to a short spur to tiny Grass Lake, then to much larger Steelhead Lake (10,350 feet). The total climb is 2,300 feet over 5.7 miles, but most of the work is in the last 1.2 miles.

User Groups: Hikers, dogs, and horses. No mountain bikes. No wheelchair facilities.

Permits: A free wilderness permit is required for overnight stays and is available from the Bishop/White Mountain Ranger Station. Quotas are in effect from May 1 to November 1; for this period, permits are available in advance for a $5 reservation fee per person.

Maps: A Mammoth High Country map is available from Tom Harrison Maps. An Inyo National Forest or John Muir Wilderness map is available from the U.S. Forest Service. For a topographic map, go to the USGS website to download Convict Lake.

Directions: From U.S. 395 at the Mammoth Lakes junction, drive south eight miles to the McGee Creek Road turnoff on the right (30 miles north of Bishop). Drive three miles southwest on McGee Creek Road (past the pack station) to the trailhead.

Contact: Inyo National Forest, White Mountain Ranger District, Bishop, 760/873-2500, www.fs.usda.gov/inyo.

95 MONO PASS

7.4 mi / 4.0 hr 4 10

in the John Muir Wilderness

Map 10.2, page 484

Since wilderness permits are hard to come by for this trail, your best bet is a day hike up to scenic, austere Mono Pass, where William Brewer and his party crossed the Sierra in 1864. Trailhead elevation is 10,300 feet, and the pass is at 12,600 feet, so get ready to climb in thin air (gasp). Also, expect it to be cold and windy at the pass, no matter how warm it is at the trailhead. Start your trip by following the trail alongside Rock Creek, with a wall of mammoth mountain peaks surrounding you. A half-mile in, leave most of the crowds behind as you bear right for Mono Pass, switchbacking uphill. As you climb, you gain a view of Little Lakes Valley below, as well as continual eyefuls of classic Sierra scenery—clear blue sky, jagged mountain backdrops, and plenty of rock. Pass the side trail to Ruby Lake at two miles out (save this 0.25-mile spur for your return trip). Continue on the rocky, treeless trail until at last you reach the summit, where you get a full panoramic view, which is probably hardly different from when Brewer saw it more than a century ago. That peak just to the east of you is Mount Starr, elevation 12,835 feet. To the south, the 13,000-foot-plus peaks reign: Mount Abbot and Mount Mills. Mono Rock and the Mono Recesses lie to the west, and the blue lakes of the Pioneer Basin are to the north.

User Groups: Hikers, dogs, and horses. No mountain bikes. No wheelchair facilities.

Permits: No permits are required for day-use. A free wilderness permit is required for overnight stays and is available from the Bishop/White Mountain Ranger Station. Quotas are in effect from May 1 to November 1; permits are available in advance for a $5 reservation fee per person. Parking and access are free.

Maps: A Mono Divide High Country map is available from Tom Harrison Maps. A John Muir Wilderness map is available from the U.S. Forest Service. For topographic maps, go to the USGS website to download Mount Morgan and Mount Abbot.

Directions: From U.S. 395 at the Mammoth Lakes junction, drive south 15 miles to Tom's Place and the Rock Creek Road turnoff, on the right (24 miles north of Bishop). Follow Rock Creek Road southwest for 10.5 miles to its end, at the Mosquito Flat parking area.

Contact: Inyo National Forest, White Mountain Ranger District, Bishop, 760/873-2500, www.fs.usda.gov/inyo.

96 LITTLE LAKES VALLEY

3.0-9.0 mi / 2.0-5.0 hr 2 10

in the John Muir Wilderness

Map 10.2, page 484

If the mileage shown above reflects some indecision, that's because the Little Lakes Valley makes it hard to decide which lake to visit or how far to hike. It's best to decide as you go, depending on how busy the trail is and how your energy is holding up. The Little Lakes Valley is a spectacularly beautiful, glacially carved area that is littered with lakes both large and small, and is surrounded by 13,000-foot peaks. What makes it even more special is that its trailhead is at 10,300 feet, so your car does most of the climbing, instead of your feet. For this reason, the trail is extremely popular, especially with beginning backpackers, day hikers, and dog walkers.

The trail leads past Mack Lake and shallow Marsh Lake to Heart Lake, 1.5 miles in. Box Lake is 0.25 mile farther, and then another 0.25 mile farther is the still larger Long Lake, both popular destinations right along the trail. Those with more stamina can continue to Chickenfoot Lake, at 3.0 miles out, or the Gem Lakes, at 3.5 miles. Most people consider the Gem Lakes to be the most gorgeous of the lot, but frankly, it's pretty hard to choose. Those who are willing and able continue upward through 11,100-foot Morgan Pass and descend a couple hundred feet to Upper and Lower Morgan Lakes, at 4 and 4.5 miles out, respectively. There are enough hiking options along this one trail to keep most lake-lovers busy for a week.

User Groups: Hikers, dogs, and horses. No mountain bikes. No wheelchair facilities.

Permits: A free wilderness permit is required for overnight stays and is available from the Bishop/White Mountain Ranger Station. Quotas are in effect from May 1 to November 1; for this period, permits are available in advance for a $5 reservation fee per person.

Maps: A Mono Divide High Country map is

available from Tom Harrison Maps. A John Muir Wilderness map is available from the U.S. Forest Service. For topographic maps, go to the USGS website to download Mount Morgan and Mount Abbot.

Directions: From U.S. 395 at the Mammoth Lakes junction, drive south 15 miles to Tom's Place and the Rock Creek Road turnoff, on the right (24 miles north of Bishop). Follow Rock Creek Road southwest for 10.5 miles to its end, at the Mosquito Flat parking area.

Contact: Inyo National Forest, White Mountain Ranger District, Bishop, 760/873-2500, www.fs.usda.gov/inyo.

97 TAMARACK LAKES

9.4 mi / 6.0 hr or 2 days  3 10

in the John Muir Wilderness

Map 10.2, page 484

This fantastic Eastern Sierra hike offers a great deal of variety in terrain, a couple of gorgeous lakes with good fishing prospects, and the chance of seeing bighorn sheep. Perhaps best of all, this trail sees a lot less foot traffic than the other pathways in the popular Rock Creek area. The trailhead elevation at Rock Creek Lake is 9,700 feet, so the first stretch of this trail can be a bit breathtaking as you climb steadily for a mile on a brushy slope. Soon the trail levels out and follows an old dirt road for a while, which connects to a mountain-biking route in Sand Canyon. The terrain you are walking through is dry and sandy, with only a few pines to create some sparse shade, and it gives little indication of the dramatic high-country scenery that lies ahead. You'll pass a turnoff for Francis Lake on the right (0.7 mile distant), and shortly thereafter, Kenneth Lake on the left (0.1 mile distant). Kenneth Lake is really just a muddy pond, which usually dries up by late summer, but its surrounding meadow is filled with blooming gentian in late summer. Stay on the path to Tamarack Lakes, and you'll find that the climbing you will face will result in a dramatic change of landscape. The trail ascends over a series of glacial moraines, and you soon find yourself in a high-alpine area, where Bighorn sheep are sometimes seen grazing on the fragile grasses. You'll pass the left turnoff for Dorothy Lake (there are good camping spots here, but fishing is usually poor), but stay right, and in another mile, you will begin to follow the outlet stream from the Tamarack Lakes. Now the real work begins, as you must gain 800 more feet to climb into the high basin to the Tamarack Lakes. The trail ends at a small tarn just before the largest Tamarack Lake. Just beyond the big Tamarack Lake is Buck Lake, which most people assume is just another of the Tamarack Lakes. The lakes are set in a steeply sloped rocky bowl and have that barren, austere look that is common to lakes above 11,000 feet. You won't find much in the way of flat, soft spots to put your tent, but the scenery more than makes up for it. The largest Tamarack Lake has good fishing for golden trout. The total elevation gain on this hike is 2,000 feet, and it is worth every bit of it.

User Groups: Hikers, dogs, and horses. No mountain bikes. No wheelchair facilities.

Permits: A free wilderness permit is required for overnight stays and is available from the Bishop/White Mountain Ranger Station. Quotas are in effect from May 1 to November 1; for this period, permits are available in advance for a $5 reservation fee per person.

Maps: A Mono Divide High Country map is available from Tom Harrison Maps. A John Muir Wilderness map is available from the U.S. Forest Service. For a topographic map, go to the USGS website to download Mount Morgan.

Directions: From U.S. 395 at the Mammoth Lakes junction, drive south 15 miles to Tom's Place and the Rock Creek Road turnoff, on the right (24 miles north of Bishop). Follow Rock Creek Road southwest for 8.5 miles to the left turnoff for Rock Creek Lakes campground. Turn left and drive 0.4 mile to the trailhead.

Contact: Inyo National Forest, White

Mountain Ranger District, Bishop, 760/873-2500, www.fs.usda.gov/inyo.

98 RUBY LAKE

4.5 mi / 2.5 hr

in the John Muir Wilderness

Map 10.2, page 484

For both day hikers and backpackers, the Little Lakes Valley is the premier destination from the Rock Creek Canyon trailhead. The only problem is the crowds, especially on the weekends, which can turn a supposedly peaceful wilderness experience into a large group encounter. A visit to Ruby Lake is a possible solution, because it's off the main trail that leads into the Little Lakes Valley, situated instead on the right fork that leads to Mono Pass. Since most trail users on this fork are backpackers heading to Mono Pass and the Pioneer Basin beyond, few take the time to stop at Ruby Lake, 0.25 mile off the main trail. From the trailhead, hike 0.5 mile, and bear right at the junction for Mono Pass. Grunt it out through the switchbacks as you enjoy a series of stunning vistas of the Little Lakes Valley. You'll reach the Ruby Lake spur trail at two miles out, on the left. A 0.25-mile walk brings you to cliffbound Ruby Lake, which is much larger than you'd expect and perfectly ringed by granite. The fishing is not great, but the picnicking is highly recommended. The lake's elevation is 11,121 feet.

User Groups: Hikers, dogs, and horses. No mountain bikes. No wheelchair facilities.

Permits: No permits are required for day-use. A free wilderness permit is required for overnight stays and is available from the Bishop/White Mountain Ranger Station. Quotas are in effect from May 1 to November 1; permits are available in advance for a $5 reservation fee per person. Parking and access are free.

Maps: A Mono Divide High Country map is available from Tom Harrison Maps. A John Muir Wilderness map is available from the U.S. Forest Service. For topographic maps, go to the USGS website to download Mount Abbot and Mount Morgan.

Directions: From U.S. 395 at the Mammoth Lakes junction, drive south 15 miles to Tom's Place and the Rock Creek Road turnoff, on the right (24 miles north of Bishop). Follow Rock Creek Road southwest for 10.5 miles to its end, at the Mosquito Flat parking area.

Contact: Inyo National Forest, White Mountain Ranger District, Bishop, 760/873-2500, www.fs.usda.gov/inyo.

99 WHITE MOUNTAIN PEAK TRAIL

14.4 mi / 8.0 hr

in Inyo National Forest northeast of Bishop

Map 10.2, page 484 BEST

White Mountain Peak is the third-tallest peak in California, only 259 feet lower than the highest, Mount Whitney (Mount Williamson is second in line), yet it is little known to hikers outside of the area. In contrast to Whitney, this 14,246-foot summit is not reached by a narrow foot trail, but instead via an old Navy-built road that climbs 2,600 feet in 7.2 miles. The trail starts at a locked gate at 11,630 feet in elevation and then leads past Mount Barcroft (13,040 feet) on a long grind. The road/trail is completely above tree line, so it's exposed and often windswept. Sunscreen alone won't suffice here; wear a hat to give yourself a break from the sun. If you aren't acclimated, the high altitude will make the trip very difficult. The summit constitutes an impressive granite massif with grand views. To the east, you can see 200 miles into Nevada; to the west, the Owens Valley and Volcanic Tableland, plus a wide panorama of the Sierra Nevada. Some hikers choose to pack along their headlamps and do all or part of the trip by moonlight. The road/trail is simple to navigate, so this is easily accomplished. Forget turning this into a backpack trip: The area is so exposed that you won't find a suitable place to camp. Also, if you are planning an early summer visit, call the White Mountain Ranger Station to be sure the dirt road to the trailhead is open. The road is frequently snowed in at the higher elevations until mid-June or later.

User Groups: Hikers only. Dogs, horses, and mountain bikes permitted, but not advised due to extremely high altitudes. No wheelchair facilities.

Permits: No permits are required. Parking and access are free.

Maps: An Inyo National Forest map is available from the U.S. Forest Service. For a topographic map, go to the USGS website to download White Mountain Peak.

Directions: From U.S. 395 at Big Pine, take Highway 168 east for 13 miles to White Mountain Road. Turn left on White Mountain Road and drive north for 10.5 miles to Schulman Grove. Continue on White Mountain Road (it becomes unpaved just past the Schulman Grove turnoff) for 16 miles to the locked gate and trailhead, at the road's end.

Contact: Inyo National Forest, White Mountain Ranger Station, Bishop, 760/873-2500, www.fs.usda.gov/inyo.

100 METHUSELAH TRAIL

4.2 mi / 2.5 hr 2 8

in Inyo National Forest northeast of Bishop

Map 10.2, page 484 BEST

The Methuselah Tree is the prize of the Ancient Bristlecone Pine Forest. Here for more than 4,000 years, it's the oldest documented living tree in the world. But forest rangers won't tell you which one it is, out of fear that some dimwit will cut it down. So you have to be satisfied just knowing you have walked among the ancients, rather than actually seeing the grandfather of all trees. No matter; each one of the thousands of trees here will impress you with its beautifully sculpted form. Amateur photographers have a field day along this trail. The path starts at the patio of the Schulman Grove Visitors Center (elevation 10,000 feet) and follows a meandering route through a forest of ancient and younger bristlecone pines, plus a few limber pines and pinyon pines. The first half of the loop drops 800 feet, which of course must be regained on your return, but the climb is nicely spread out. Still, if you're not acclimated, the high elevation will leave you huffing and puffing. Plan on bringing a picnic with you (you're a long way from the nearest convenience store), and make sure you spend some time at the excellent visitors center, which is open daily. If you want to hike a bit more, try the one-mile Discovery Trail loop (more bristlecone pines) or the one-mile Bristlecone Cabin Trail, which leads to an old Mexican mine site. If you're accustomed to modern conveniences, it's worth noting that cell phone service is limited in the area and water is not available at the trailhead or visitors center. Make sure your vehicle is well stocked for the trip.

User Groups: Hikers and leashed dogs. No horses or mountain bikes. No wheelchair facilities.

Permits: No permits are required. There is a $3 fee per adult with a maximum of $6 per vehicle.

Maps: Brochures and trail maps are available at the trailhead. An Inyo National Forest map is available from the U.S. Forest Service. For a topographic map, go to the USGS website to download Westgard Pass.

Directions: From U.S. 395 at Big Pine, take Highway 168 east for 13 miles to White Mountain Road. Turn left on White Mountain Road and drive north for 10.5 miles to Schulman Grove, on the right.

Contact: Inyo National Forest, White Mountain Ranger Station, Bishop, 760/873-2500, www.fs.usda.gov/inyo.

SEQUOIA AND KINGS CANYON

Sequoia and Kings Canyon National Parks are famous for their giant sequoia groves, tall mountains, deep canyons, roaring rivers, and spectacular hiking trails with views of the Great Western Divide's jagged peaks. These two side-by-side national parks offer classic Sierra scenery without the infamous overcrowding that plagues Yosemite, their neighbor to the north. Tacked on to the border of Sequoia and Kings Canyon is Giant Sequoia National Monument, designated to increase protection for the last remaining giant sequoia groves in the world. On the east side of these parks, a bounty of trailheads lie at the end of almost every road leading west off U.S. 395. From Bishop to Big Pine to Independence to Lone Pine, each canyon road leads to a wilderness trailhead and a wealth of hiking opportunities.

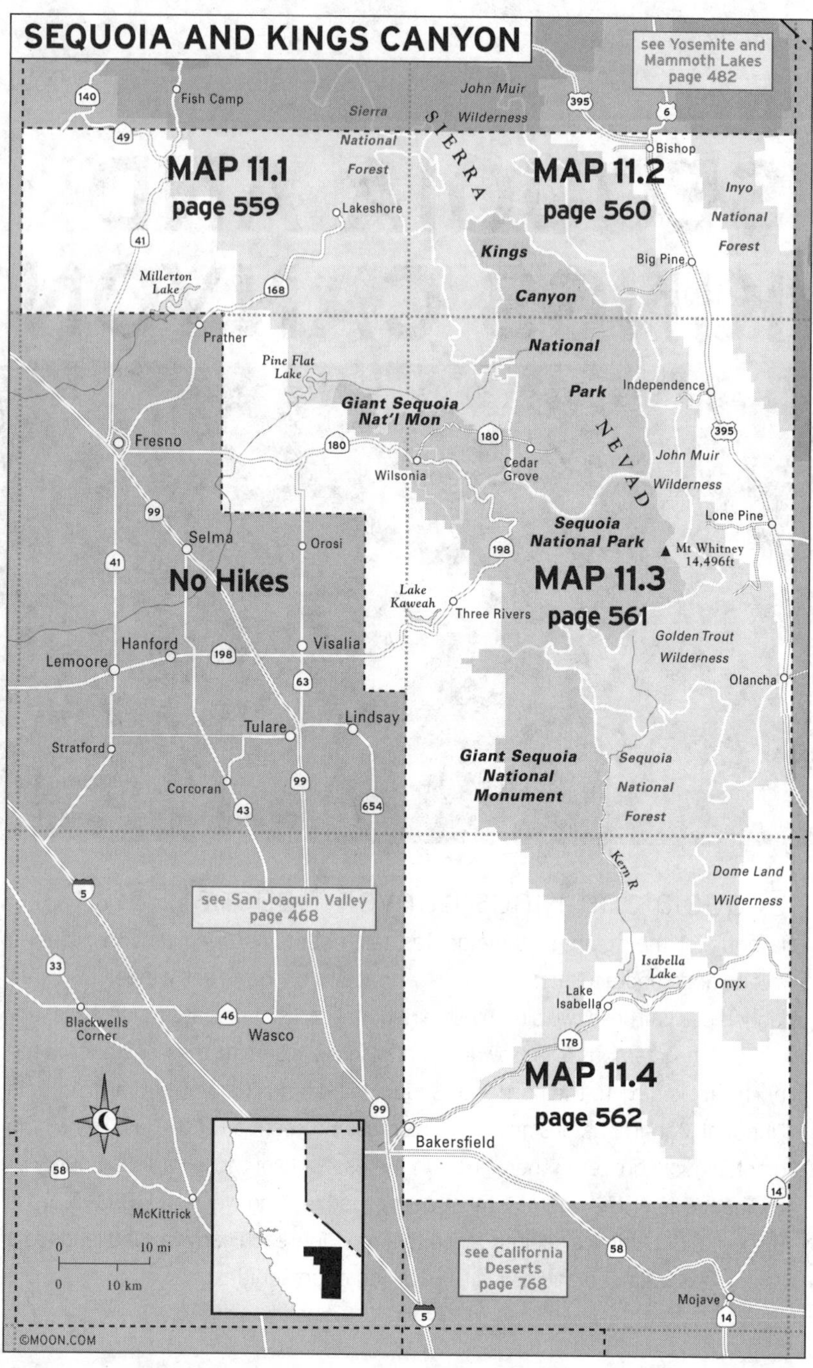
SEQUOIA AND KINGS CANYON
see Yosemite and Mammoth Lakes page 482
Fish Camp
John Muir Wilderness
Sierra National Forest
SIERRA
Bishop
MAP 11.1 page 559
MAP 11.2 page 560
Inyo National Forest
Lakeshore
Kings Canyon National Park
Big Pine
Millerton Lake
Prather
Pine Flat Lake
Independence
Giant Sequoia Nat'l Mon
Fresno
NEVADA
John Muir Wilderness
Cedar Grove
Wilsonia
Sequoia National Park
Lone Pine
Selma
Orosi
Mt Whitney 14,496ft
No Hikes
MAP 11.3 page 561
Lake Kaweah
Three Rivers
Hanford
Visalia
Golden Trout Wilderness
Lemoore
Olancha
Tulare
Lindsay
Stratford
Giant Sequoia National Monument
Sequoia National Forest
Corcoran
Kern R
Dome Land Wilderness
see San Joaquin Valley page 468
Isabella Lake
Onyx
Lake Isabella
Blackwells Corner
Wasco
MAP 11.4 page 562
Bakersfield
McKittrick
0 10 mi
0 10 km
see California Deserts page 768
Mojave
©MOON.COM

Map 11.1

Sites 1-10
Pages 563-568

11.2

1
2
3
4

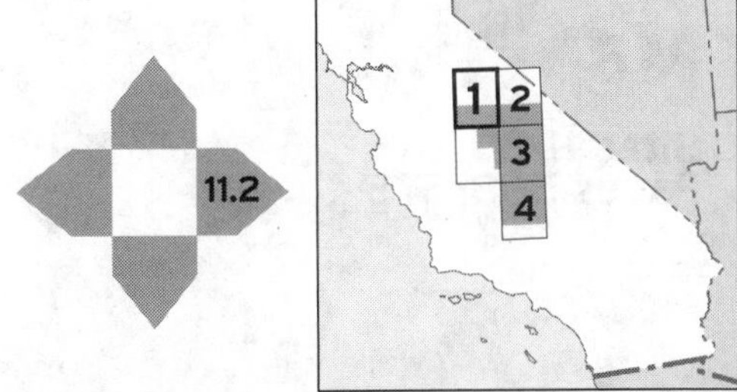

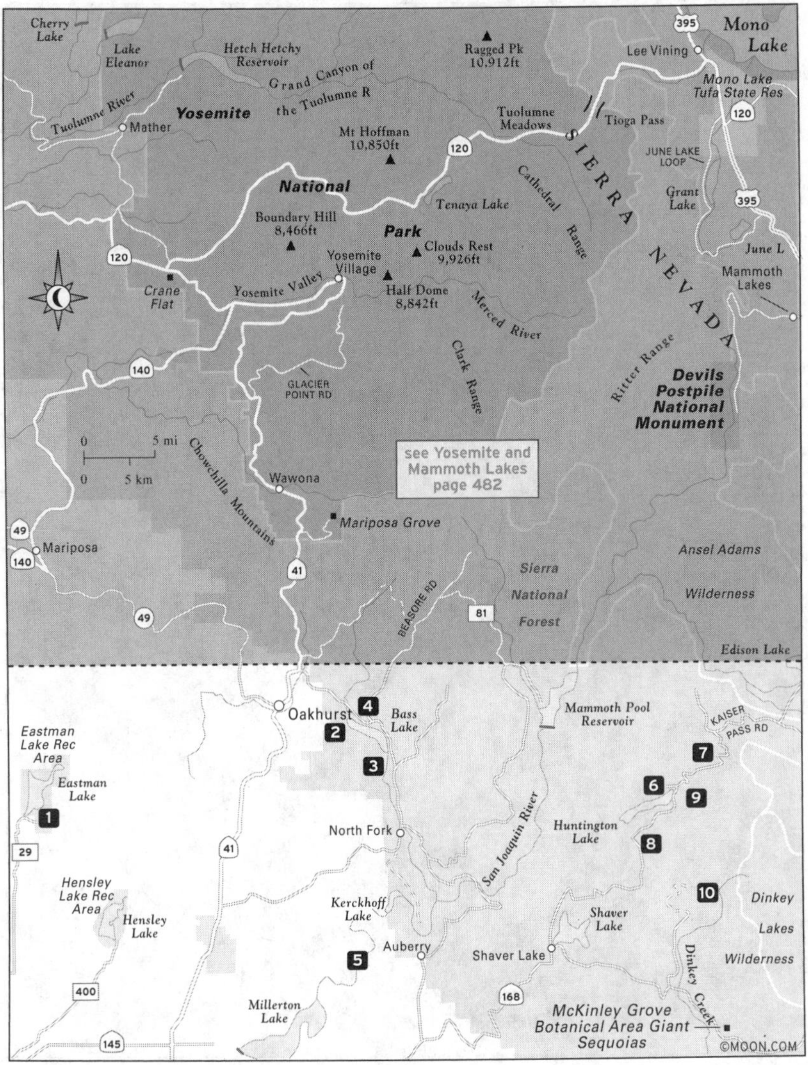

Cherry Lake
Lake Eleanor
Hetch Hetchy Reservoir
Grand Canyon of the Tuolumne R
Ragged Pk 10,912ft
395
Mono Lake
Lee Vining
Mono Lake Tufa State Res
Tuolumne River
Mather
Yosemite
Tuolumne Meadows
Tioga Pass
120
Mt Hoffman 10,850ft
120
SIERRA NEVADA
JUNE LAKE LOOP
Cathedral Range
National
Tenaya Lake
Grant Lake
395
Boundary Hill 8,466ft
Park
Clouds Rest 9,926ft
June L
120
Yosemite Village
Mammoth Lakes
Crane Flat
Yosemite Valley
Half Dome 8,842ft
Merced River
Clark Range
Ritter Range
140
GLACIER POINT RD
Devils Postpile National Monument
0 5 mi
0 5 km
Chowchilla Mountains
see Yosemite and Mammoth Lakes page 482
Wawona
49
Mariposa
140
Mariposa Grove
Ansel Adams Wilderness
41
Sierra National Forest
BEASORE RD
81
49
Edison Lake
Oakhurst
4
Bass Lake
Mammoth Pool Reservoir
KAISER PASS RD
Eastman Lake Rec Area
2
7
3
6
Eastman Lake
9
1
North Fork
San Joaquin River
Huntington Lake
8
29
41
Hensley Lake Rec Area
10
Dinkey Lakes Wilderness
Hensley Lake
Kerckhoff Lake
Shaver Lake
5
Auberry
Shaver Lake
Dinkey Creek
400
168
Millerton Lake
McKinley Grove Botanical Area Giant Sequoias
145
©MOON.COM

Map 11.2

Sites 11-20
Pages 568-575

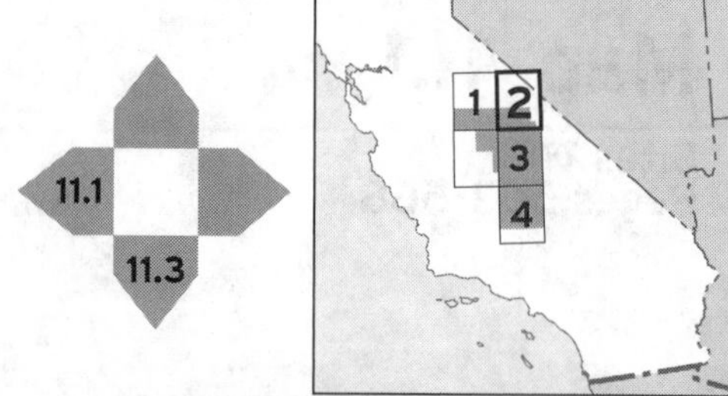

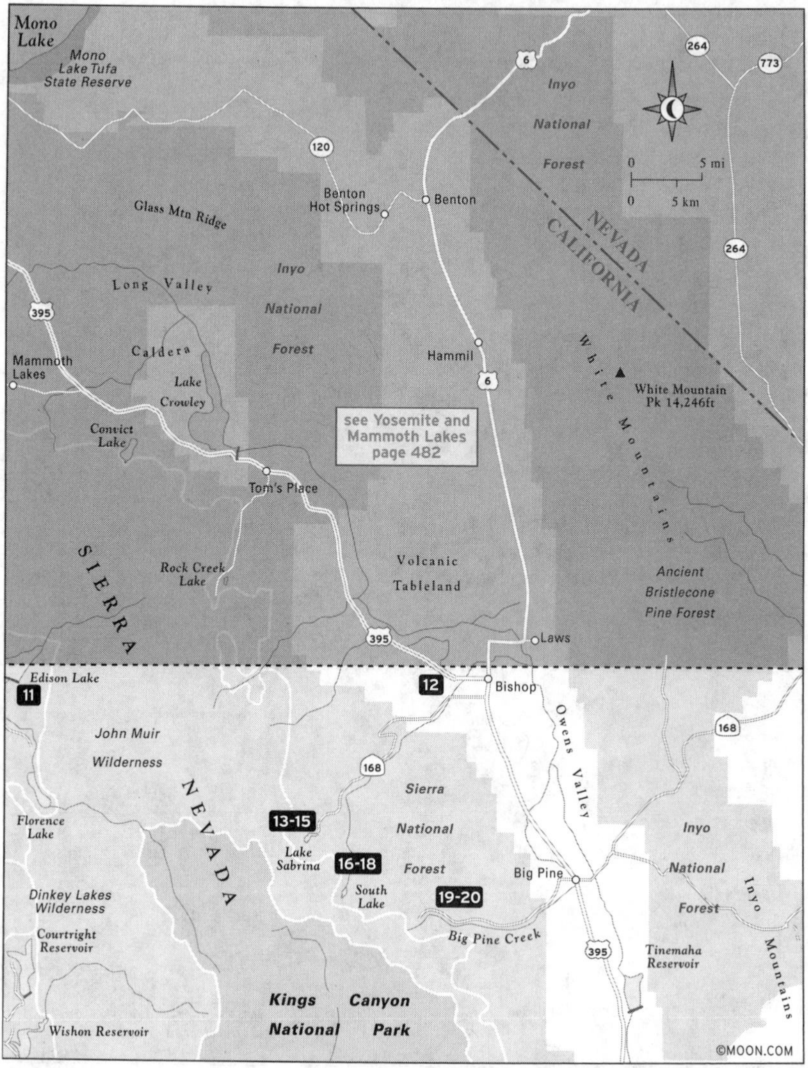

Mono Lake
Mono Lake Tufa State Reserve
Glass Mtn Ridge
Benton Hot Springs
Benton
120
6
264
773
Inyo National Forest
0 5 mi
0 5 km
NEVADA
CALIFORNIA
264
Long Valley Caldera
395
Mammoth Lakes
Lake Crowley
Convict Lake
Inyo National Forest
Hammil
6
White Mountains
White Mountain Pk 14,246ft
see Yosemite and Mammoth Lakes page 482
Tom's Place
SIERRA
Rock Creek Lake
Volcanic Tableland
Ancient Bristlecone Pine Forest
395
Laws
Edison Lake
11
12
Bishop
John Muir Wilderness
NEVADA
Owens Valley
168
168
Sierra National Forest
13-15
Florence Lake
Lake Sabrina
16-18
South Lake
19-20
Big Pine
Inyo National Forest
Inyo Mountains
Dinkey Lakes Wilderness
Courtright Reservoir
Big Pine Creek
395
Tinemaha Reservoir
Kings Canyon National Park
Wishon Reservoir

Map 11.3

Sites 21-105
Pages 575-631

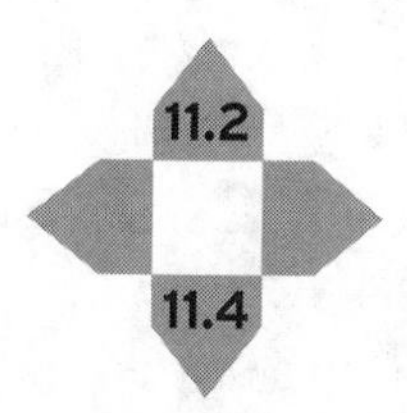

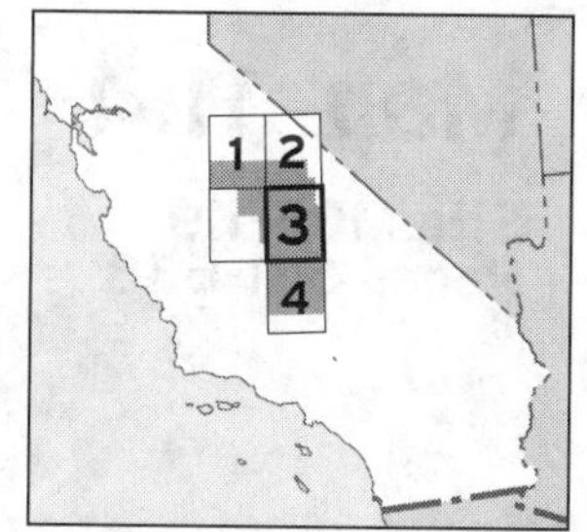

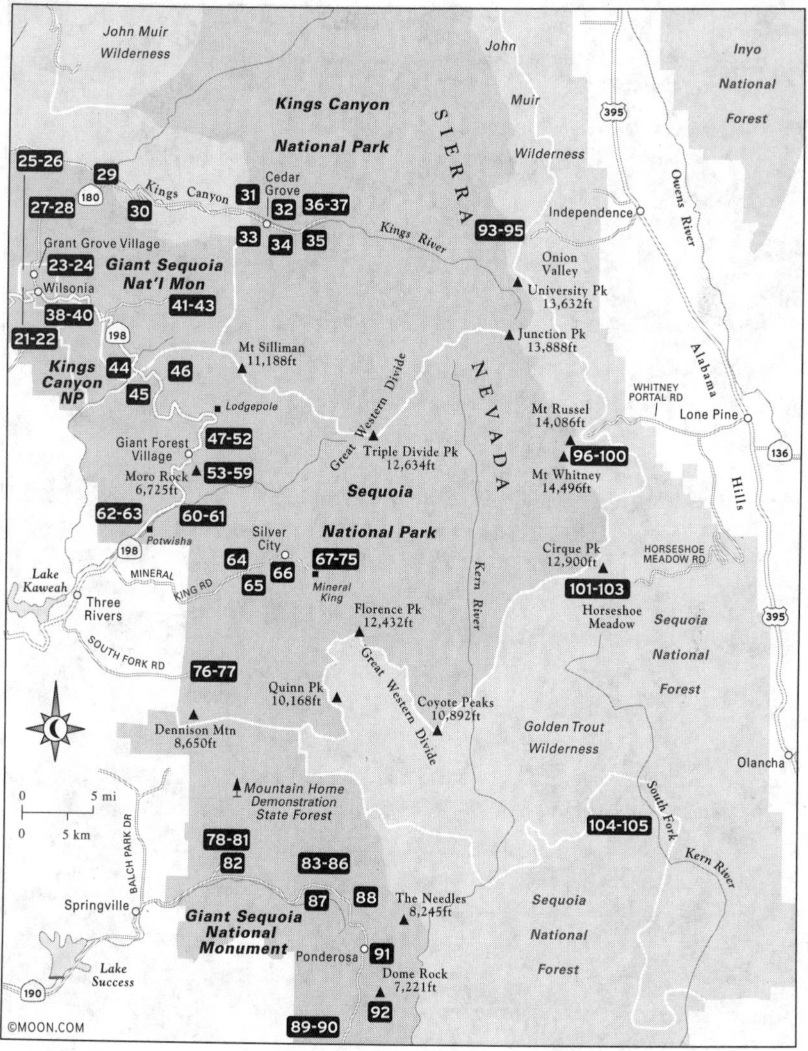

John Muir Wilderness
Kings Canyon National Park
John Muir Wilderness
Inyo National Forest
SIERRA NEVADA
395
25-26
29
180
Kings Canyon
27-28
30
31
Cedar Grove
32
36-37
Independence
Owens River
Kings River
93-95
33
34
35
Grant Grove Village
23-24
Giant Sequoia Nat'l Mon
Onion Valley
Wilsonia
University Pk 13,632ft
41-43
38-40
198
21-22
Junction Pk 13,888ft
Mt Silliman 11,188ft
Alabama Hills
Kings Canyon NP
44
46
45
Great Western Divide
Lodgepole
WHITNEY PORTAL RD
Mt Russel 14,086ft
Lone Pine
Giant Forest Village
47-52
Triple Divide Pk 12,634ft
136
96-100
Moro Rock 6,725ft
53-59
Mt Whitney 14,496ft
Sequoia National Park
62-63
60-61
Silver City
Potwisha
198
Cirque Pk 12,900ft
HORSESHOE MEADOW RD
64
67-75
Lake Kaweah
MINERAL KING RD
66
65
Mineral King
101-103
Three Rivers
Kern River
Horseshoe Meadow
Sequoia National Forest
Florence Pk 12,432ft
395
SOUTH FORK RD
76-77
Great Western Divide
Quinn Pk 10,168ft
Coyote Peaks 10,892ft
Dennison Mtn 8,650ft
Golden Trout Wilderness
Olancha
0 5 mi
0 5 km
Mountain Home Demonstration State Forest
South Fork Kern River
104-105
BALCH PARK DR
78-81
82
83-86
Springville
87
88
The Needles 8,245ft
Sequoia National Forest
Giant Sequoia National Monument
Ponderosa
91
Lake Success
Dome Rock 7,221ft
190
92
©MOON.COM
89-90

Map 11.4

Sites 106-119
Pages 631-638

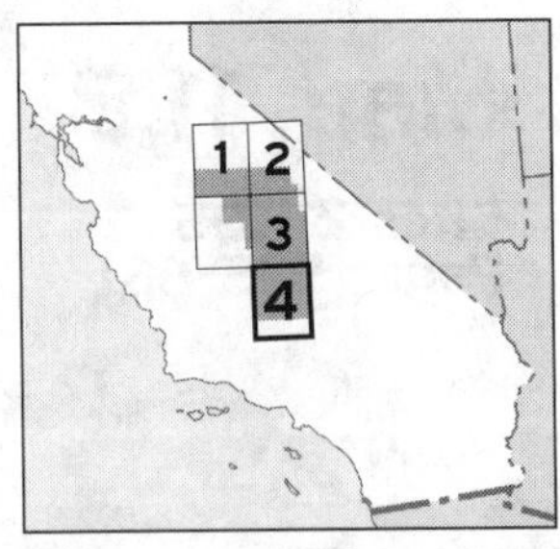

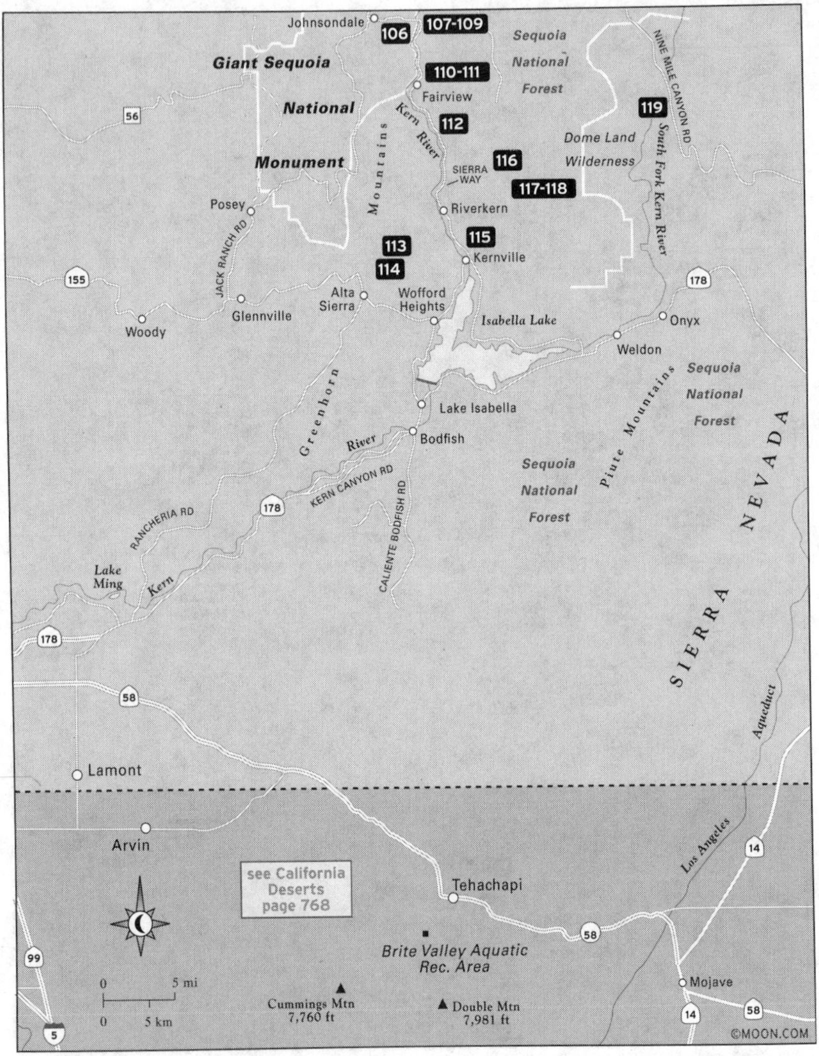

Johnsondale
106
107-109
Giant Sequoia National Monument
Sequoia National Forest
110-111
Fairview
Kern River
112
Mountains
NINE MILE CANYON RD
119
South Fork Kern River
Dome Land Wilderness
56
116
SIERRA WAY
117-118
Posey
Riverkern
JACK RANCH RD
115
113
114
Kernville
155
178
Alta Sierra
Wofford Heights
Glennville
Woody
Isabella Lake
Onyx
Weldon
Greenhorn
Lake Isabella
Sequoia National Forest
Piute Mountains
Bodfish
River
KERN CANYON RD
Sequoia National Forest
SIERRA NEVADA
RANCHERIA RD
178
CALIENTE BODFISH RD
Lake Ming
Kern
178
58
Aqueduct
Lamont
Arvin
Los Angeles
14
see California Deserts page 768
Tehachapi
58
Brite Valley Aquatic Rec. Area
99
Mojave
0 5 mi
0 5 km
Cummings Mtn 7,760 ft
Double Mtn 7,981 ft
14
58
5

1 LAKEVIEW TRAIL

4.2 mi one-way/2.0 hr 

on the southeast shore of Eastman Lake east of Chowchilla

Map 11.1, page 559

Let's get one thing straight: You don't want to hike here at midday in July. Got it? Good. But if it's spring and the wildflowers are in bloom, you'd be wise to head out here to Eastman Lake, then hike the Lakeview Trail that leads along its south and east sides. Sure, a reservoir is a reservoir, but when the water level is high, the grasslands are green, and the flowers are blooming, this reservoir can seem like a little slice of paradise in the Central Valley. The Lakeview Trail leads a total of 4.2 miles one-way from the trailhead at the group campground to Raymond Bridge. Hike as little or as much of it as you please, watching for birds and identifying the wildflowers as you go. Bald eagle sightings are not uncommon. You probably won't have a lot of human company on this trail; after all, most people come to Eastman Lake to fish, not hike. In addition to its trophy bass fishery, the lake also boasts populations of crappie, bluegill, and catfish. They even stock rainbow trout here in the winter when the temperature cools down.

User Groups: Hikers, dogs, horses, and mountain bikes. No wheelchair facilities.

Permits: No permits are required. A $5 day-use fee is charged.

Maps: A free map of Eastman Lake is available at the visitors center. For a topographic map, go to the USGS website to download Raymond.

Directions: From Merced, drive south on Highway 99 for 20 miles to Chowchilla. Take the Avenue 26 exit and head east for 17 miles. Turn north on County Road 29 and drive eight miles to the lake entrance. Turn right and drive to the parking area by Cordorniz Group Campground.

Contact: U.S. Army Corps of Engineers, Eastman Lake, Raymond, 559/689-3255.

2 WAY OF THE MONO

0.5 mi/0.5 hr 

on the northwest end of Bass Lake near Oakhurst

Map 11.1, page 559

The Way of the Mono is an educational trail that teaches about the Mono Indians, who were the first people to live in the Bass Lake area. They inhabited the area for more than 1,000 years. The interpretive displays along the trail point out grinding holes in the rocks, where the Mono people pounded acorns into meal, and describe different methods they used to live through the area's seasonal changes. In addition to a cultural history lesson, the trail also offers beautiful vistas of Bass Lake and its surroundings. Check out the view from the large granite outcrop of Bass Lake and surrounding peaks. This great loop hike takes only about 20 minutes to walk, but leaves you with a much greater understanding of the Bass Lake area.

User Groups: Hikers and dogs. No horses or mountain bikes. No wheelchair facilities.

Permits: No permits are required. Parking and access are free at the trailhead; parking in the day-use area is $3.

Maps: A Sierra National Forest map is available from the U.S. Forest Service. For a topographic map, go to the USGS website to download Bass Lake.

Directions: From Oakhurst, drive north on Highway 41 for four miles and then turn right on Road 222. Drive four miles and bear right to stay on Road 222. The signed trailhead parking area is across from Little Denver Church Day Use Area, between the Forks Resort and the California Land Management Office.

Contact: Sierra National Forest, Bass Lake Ranger District, North Fork, 559/877-2218, www.fs.usda.gov/sierra.

3 GOAT MOUNTAIN FIRE LOOKOUT

8.0 mi/4.0 hr 3 8

on the south end of Bass Lake near Oakhurst

Map 11.1, page 559

The route to Goat Mountain Fire Lookout can be hiked from trailheads at either Forks Campground or Spring Cove Campground. This is a must-do hike for the legions of campers who spend their summer vacations at Bass Lake. Both trails intersect in about two miles, then join and form one path for the last two miles to the lookout. No matter how you do it, the grade is memorably steep, but also rewarding. As you climb up the trail, you have nearly nonstop views of Bass Lake and the forested valleys surrounding it. You'll also be breathing hard. If you can talk someone into driving a second car to the other trailhead and campground, you can turn this into a pleasant semi-loop trip by hiking up one trail and down the other. Note: This trail has become increasingly popular with mountain bikers in the last few years. If you don't like sharing the trail with them, plan your hike for a weekday, when you're more likely to be out here by yourself. The fire lookout is perched at 4,675 feet in elevation, set on top of a 20-foot steel tower, and offers a 360-degree view.

User Groups: Hikers, dogs, horses, and mountain bikes. No wheelchair facilities.

Permits: No permits are required. Parking and access are free in the campgrounds, but $3 if you park in the day-use area.

Maps: A Sierra National Forest map is available from the U.S. Forest Service. For a topographic map, go to the USGS website to download Bass Lake.

Directions: From Oakhurst, drive north on Highway 41 for four miles and turn right on Road 222. Drive four miles and bear right to stay on Road 222. Continue along the western shore of Bass Lake for about five miles to Spring Cove Campground. The Spring Cove Trail begins on the east side of the campground entrance. If there is no parking there, you can park at Rocky Point Picnic Area ($3 fee). You can also hike to Goat Mountain Fire Lookout from Forks Campground, three miles north on Road 222.

Contact: Sierra National Forest, Bass Lake Ranger District, North Fork, 559/877-2218, www.fs.usda.gov/sierra.

4 WILLOW CREEK

4.8 mi/2.5 hr

on the northeast end of Bass Lake near Oakhurst

Map 11.1, page 559

Most people hike Willow Creek Trail with one of two things in mind: fishing or swimming. You can't blame them, since the moderately steep trail runs alongside Willow Creek and offers myriad quiet pools and fast, granite-lined cascades. The Forest Service requests that visitors don't swim upstream of Angel Falls, a wide cascade that looks like angel wings, because the creek is used as a domestic water supply. Downstream swimming is allowed, but be wary of the slippery granite. At 2.4 miles from the trailhead, be sure to take the left spur for Devils Slide, at a junction where the main trail continues to its end (0.4 mile farther) at McLeod Flat Road. Devils Slide is a remarkable granite water slide, with large rounded indentations in the rock. A chain-link fence keeps hikers off the dangerously slick granite. From Devils Slide, head back to the main trail and retrace your steps downhill. Expect to see some great views of bright-blue Bass Lake on the return trip.

User Groups: Hikers and dogs. No horses or mountain bikes. No wheelchair facilities.

Permits: No permits are required. Parking and access are free.

Maps: A Sierra National Forest map is available from the U.S. Forest Service. For a topographic map, go to the USGS website to download Bass Lake.

Directions: From Oakhurst, drive north on

Highway 41 for four miles and turn right on Road 222. Drive four miles and bear left on Road 274. Drive one mile to the trailhead parking area, on the left side of the road, on the west side of the highway bridge over Willow Creek. Alternatively, you can park near Falls Beach Picnic Area on Road 222 by Bass Lake's dam and access the trail via a connector route alongside Willow Creek.

Contact: Sierra National Forest, Bass Lake Ranger District, North Fork, 559/877-2218, www.fs.usda.gov/sierra.

5 SQUAW LEAP LOOP

7.8 mi/4.0 hr 2 8

near Millerton Lake

Map 11.1, page 559

The Squaw Leap area, managed by the Bureau of Land Management, straddles the San Joaquin River upstream of Millerton Lake State Park. This pretty foothill country is best visited in winter or spring, primarily due to the cooler temperatures but also for a chance to see wildflowers. The well-built Six-Mile Loop Trail, which is actually 7.8 miles as described here, rolls through chaparral country. Ceanothus and manzanita line the hillsides; gray pines and blue oaks dot the landscape. The trail begins with a one-mile stretch that leads you down to the river and the start of the loop. A surprisingly well-built footbridge takes you across the river canyon, where you have fine views of whitewater cascades, both upstream and down. On the far side of the bridge, go left on River Trail for 0.7 mile, then bear right on Ridge Trail. At mileage marker 3, you have a fine view of the river canyon; this is the best place to stop for a snack. Ridge Trail brings you right back downhill to the bridge you crossed earlier; cross it again and head back to your car to finish out the trip.

User Groups: Hikers, dogs, horses, and mountain bikes. No wheelchair facilities.

Permits: No permits are required. Parking and access are free.

Maps: For a topographic map, go to the USGS website to download Millerton Lake East.

Directions: From Fresno, drive 37 miles east on Highway 168 and turn left on Auberry Road. Drive through Auberry and turn left on Powerhouse Road. Drive 1.9 miles and turn left on Smalley Road at the sign for Squaw Leap Management Area. Park by the campground and signed trailhead.

Contact: Bureau of Land Management, Bakersfield Field Office, Bakersfield, 661/391-6000, www.ca.blm.gov/bakersfield.

6 KAISER PEAK

10.6 mi/6.0 hr or 2 days 4 9

in the Kaiser Wilderness north of Huntington Lake near Lakeshore

Map 11.1, page 559

While many visitors to Huntington Lake take the short strolls to Rancheria Falls or the Indian Pools on Big Creek, far fewer attempt the ascent of Kaiser Peak. Why? Because it's a butt-kicking, 5.3-mile climb to the top, gaining 3,000 feet of elevation on the way to the 10,320-foot peak. Luckily, you get many excellent views of Huntington Lake on the way up, and at the halfway point, you can scramble up for a view and a rest on huge College Rock. Then it's up, up, and up some more, for what seems like an eternity. Finally, you gain the rocky summit, and at last you know why you came. You're wowed by incredible 360-degree views, which take in Mammoth Pool Reservoir, Huntington Lake, Shaver Lake, Mount Ritter, and Mount Goddard. Wow. Backpackers looking for more mileage can turn the hike into a 14-mile loop trip.

User Groups: Hikers, dogs, and horses. No mountain bikes. No wheelchair facilities.

Permits: A free wilderness permit is required for overnight stays and is available from the High Sierra/Prather Ranger Station. Quotas are in effect year-round; permits are available in advance for a $5 reservation fee per person.

Maps: A Sierra National Forest or Kaiser Wilderness map is available from the U.S. Forest Service. For a topographic map, go to the USGS website to download Kaiser Peak.

Directions: From Fresno, drive northeast on Highway 168 through Clovis for 70 miles to Huntington Lake, turn left on Huntington Lake Road, and drive one mile. Look for the large sign for the horse stables and pack station, and turn right. Follow the pack station road (Deer Creek Road) for 0.5 mile to the hikers' parking area. The trailhead is signed Kaiser Loop Trail.

Contact: Sierra National Forest, High Sierra Ranger District, Prather, 559/855-5360, www.fs.usda.gov/sierra.

7 TWIN LAKES AND GEORGE LAKE

8.0-9.8 mi/6.0-7.0 hr or 2 days 

in the Kaiser Wilderness north of Huntington Lake near Lakeshore

Map 11.1, page 559

Trails into the Kaiser Wilderness always seem to come with a climb, and the route to Twin Lakes and George Lake is no exception. But if you're willing to work your heart and lungs, your reward is a spectacular day hike or backpacking trip to three scenic alpine lakes. Along the way, you must ascend to Kaiser Ridge and cross over it through Potter Pass. You're witness to wildflower-filled meadows, dense conifer forests, and a classic Sierra view from the pass. You can easily make out the jagged outline of the Minarets. It's a great spot to stop and catch your breath. Then it's downhill from the pass to the granite-lined Twin Lakes, at three miles out. Many people make this their destination, then turn around for a six-mile round-trip. If you do, make sure you visit the second Twin Lake, which is much prettier than the first. For those continuing onward, it's uphill again to George Lake, 1.3 miles from Upper Twin Lake. The final push is definitely worth it. Trailhead elevation is 8,200 feet, Twin Lakes are at 8,800 feet, and George Lake is at 9,300 feet. Another good route to these lakes is from the trailhead near Sample Meadow Campground, farther north on Kaiser Pass Road. If you're willing to drive farther, this trail has less of a climb.

User Groups: Hikers, dogs, and horses. No mountain bikes. No wheelchair facilities.

Permits: A free wilderness permit is required for overnight stays and is available from the High Sierra/Prather Ranger Station. Quotas are in effect year-round; permits are available in advance for a $5 reservation fee per person.

Maps: A Sierra National Forest or Kaiser Wilderness map is available from the U.S. Forest Service. For a topographic map, go to the USGS website to download Kaiser Peak.

Directions: From Fresno, drive northeast on Highway 168 through Clovis for 70 miles to Huntington Lake; turn right on Kaiser Pass Road and drive 4.8 miles to a large parking area on the south side of the road. The trail begins across the road from the parking area. Look for a trail sign for Trail 24E03, Twin Lakes and Potter Pass. Park on the south side of the road; the trail begins on the north side of the road.

Contact: Sierra National Forest, High Sierra Ranger District, Prather, 559/855-5360, www.fs.usda.gov/sierra.

8 INDIAN POOLS

1.5 mi/1.0 hr 1 8

off Highway 168 near Huntington Lake

Map 11.1, page 559

When campers at Huntington Lake's many campgrounds are looking for a place to cool off in the afternoon, Indian Pools is where they go. The hike is really a walk, suitable for all ages and abilities. You can stop almost anywhere you like along Big Creek, pick a pool, and wade in. The trailhead is a bit tricky to find; it's all the way at the far end of the Sierra

Summit Ski Area parking lot, near some mobile homes and trailers. Ignore the wide dirt road and instead look for the single-track trail signed for Indian Pools. It's a smooth, dirt path that quickly meets up with Big Creek. Flowers bloom in profusion along the stream and the rocky areas of the trail. The official path ends 0.7 mile east of the trailhead, at a huge, clear pool that is big enough to jump into and swim across. A use trail continues farther upstream, marked by trail cairns. If you follow it, you can reach quieter, more private pools.

User Groups: Hikers and dogs. No horses or mountain bikes. No wheelchair facilities.

Permits: No permits are required. Parking and access are free.

Maps: A Sierra National Forest map is available from the U.S. Forest Service. For a topographic map, go to the USGS website to download Huntington Lake.

Directions: From Fresno, drive northeast on Highway 168 through Clovis for 70 miles, past Shaver Lake. One mile before reaching Huntington Lake, turn right at the signed Sierra Summit Ski Area. Drive 0.5 mile to the far end of the ski area parking lot and look for the signed trailhead for Indian Pools. Occasionally the Sierra Summit parking lot is closed, and you must park on Highway 168 and walk the short distance into the ski area.

Contact: Sierra National Forest, High Sierra Ranger District, Prather, 559/855-5360, www.fs.usda.gov/sierra.

9 RANCHERIA FALLS

2.0 mi/1.0 hr — 1 — 9

off Highway 168 near Huntington Lake

Map 11.1, page 559

At 7,760 feet in elevation in Sierra National Forest, the air is clean and fresh, butterflies flutter amid the wildflowers, and a 150-foot waterfall sparkles in the sunlight. Wanna go? It's an easy trip, with the trailhead located close to popular Huntington Lake. The hike to Rancheria Falls is a well-graded one mile on a National Recreation Trail, suitable for hikers of all levels. The route leads through a fir forest with an understory of wildflowers and gooseberry, and it delivers you at Rancheria Falls' base, where you watch the creek tumble over a 50-foot-wide rock ledge. On weekends the destination can be a little crowded, but you can pick a boulder downstream from the falls and call it your own. Then have a seat and watch the watery spectacle unfold.

User Groups: Hikers, dogs, horses, and mountain bikes. No wheelchair facilities.

Permits: No permits are required. Parking and access are free.

Maps: A Sierra National Forest map is available from the U.S. Forest Service. For a topographic map, go to the USGS website to download Huntington Lake.

Directions: From Fresno, drive northeast on Highway 168 through Clovis for 70 miles, past Shaver Lake. A half-mile before reaching Huntington Lake, take the right turnoff signed for Rancheria Falls (Road 8S31). Follow the dirt road for 1.3 miles to the signed trailhead, at a sharp curve in the road. Park off the road.

Contact: Sierra National Forest, High Sierra Ranger District, Prather, 559/855-5360, www.fs.usda.gov/sierra.

10 DINKEY LAKES

7.0 mi/4.0 hr or 2 days — 2 — 9

in Dinkey Lakes Wilderness off Highway 168 near Shaver Lake

Map 11.1, page 559

We've never met anybody who doesn't love the Dinkey Lakes. What's not to love? The small wilderness area has dozens of lakes, and most are so easily accessible that you can see them in a day hike rather than packing along all your gear for an overnight stay. The trip begins with a stream crossing over Dinkey Creek, where you are immediately awed by the incredible array of colors in the rock streambed.

Walk on level trail through a flower-filled forest, recross the creek, and start to climb. At 1.3 miles, you reach the junction for the start of the loop. Go right and meet Mystery Lake at 1.6 miles, Swede Lake at 2.3 miles, South Lake at 3.2 miles, and finally First Dinkey Lake at 3.8 miles. First Dinkey Lake is the most beautiful of them all. After taking in the scenery, continue on the loop, now heading westward back to the parking lot. One caveat: Don't expect much solitude. The easy hiking here makes this area extremely popular. Note: The loop described here works as either a day hike or backpacking trip, but if you choose to backpack, you can explore much farther, taking the spurs off the end of the main loop, between South Lake and First Dinkey Lake, to Second Dinkey Lake, Island Lake, Rock Lake, and so on.

User Groups: Hikers, dogs, and horses. No mountain bikes. No wheelchair facilities.

Permits: A wilderness permit is required for overnight stays and is available from the High Sierra/Prather Ranger Station. Quotas are in effect year-round; permits are available in advance for a $5 reservation fee per person.

Maps: A Dinkey Lakes Wilderness map is available from Tom Harrison Maps or the U.S. Forest Service. For topographic maps, go to the USGS website to download Huntington Lake and Dogtooth Peak.

Directions: From Fresno, drive northeast on Highway 168 through Clovis for 50 miles to the town of Shaver Lake. Turn right on Dinkey Creek Road and drive nine miles. Turn left on Rock Creek Road/9S09, drive six miles, turn right on 9S10, and drive 4.7 miles. Turn right at the sign for Dinkey Lakes, on Road 9S62, and drive 2.2 miles to the trailhead. These last two miles are very rough road. Stay left at the fork to bypass the four-wheel-drive area and go straight to the trailhead.

Contact: Sierra National Forest, High Sierra Ranger District, Prather, 559/855-5360, www.fs.usda.gov/sierra.

11 LAKE THOMAS EDISON TO AGNEW MEADOWS (JMT /PCT)

38.0 mi one-way/3 days 4 10

from Lake Thomas Edison north to Agnew Meadows

Map 11.2, page 560

The world is not perfect, but the scene from Silver Pass comes close. At 10,900 feet, you scan a bare, high-granite landscape sprinkled with alpine lakes. Just north of the pass are five small lakes: Chief, Papoose, Warrior, Squaw, and Lake of the Lone Indian. This is the highlight on this 38-mile section of the Pacific Crest Trail. The trip starts at Mono Creek, with a good resupply point at Edison Lake (7,650 feet), just two miles away. From the Mono Creek junction, you head north toward Silver Pass, climbing along Silver Pass Creek much of the way. Before you get to Silver Pass, there's a stream crossing that can be dangerous in high-runoff conditions. Top Silver Pass at 10,900 feet, and enjoy a five-mile descent and then a quick ascent to Tully Hole (9,250 feet). Climbing north, you pass Deer Creek, Purple Lake, and Lake Virginia. You head up to Red Cones and then make a steady descent toward Devils Postpile National Monument. A good resupply point is at nearby Reds Meadows Pack Station.

To continue north on the John Muir Trail/Pacific Crest Trail (JMT/PCT), see the *Agnew Meadows to Tuolumne Meadows (JMT/PCT)* hike in the *Yosemite and Mammoth Lakes* chapter. If you are walking this trail in reverse, see the *Whitney Portal to Lake Thomas Edison (JMT/PCT)* hike in this chapter.

Note: For food drop information, call the Vermillion Valley Resort. It is open only in summer and fall.

User Groups: Hikers, dogs, and horses. No mountain bikes. No wheelchair facilities.

Permits: A wilderness permit is required for traveling through various wilderness and special-use areas the trail traverses. Contact the

Inyo National Forest or Sierra National Forest at the addresses below.

Maps: A John Muir Trail Map Pack is available from Tom Harrison Maps. For topographic maps, go to the USGS website to download Mammoth Mountain, Crystal Crag, Bloody Mountain, Graveyard Peak, Mount Ritter, and Coip Peak.

Directions: From Fresno, drive northeast on Highway 168 for about 68 miles to the Lakeshore Resort Area, at Huntington Lake. Turn northeast onto Kaiser Pass Road/Forest Service 4S01. Kaiser Pass Road becomes Edison Lake Road at Mono Hot Springs. Drive another five miles north, past the Vermillion Resort and Campground, and beyond to the parking area for backcountry hikers. The trail begins near the west end of the lake.

Contact: Inyo National Forest, Mammoth Ranger Station, Mammoth Lakes, 760/924-5500 or 760/873-2400 (permits), www.fs.usda.gov/inyo; Sierra National Forest, High Sierra Ranger District, Prather, 559/855-5360, www.fs.usda.gov/sierra; Vermillion Valley Resort, 559/855-6558 (food drop).

12 HONEYMOON LAKE

12.4 mi/1-2 days 3 8

in the John Muir Wilderness

Map 11.2, page 560

Since the trailhead elevation in Pine Creek Canyon is only 7,400 feet, the best destinations must be gained with a serious climb. That includes Honeymoon Lake, 6.2 miles and a 3,200-foot ascent away. Luckily, you pass Upper and Lower Pine Lake along the route, and there's enough spectacular scenery to keep you motivated as you huff and puff. An early morning start is highly recommended; this trail is exposed and usually very hot, especially in its lower reaches. The route begins by the pack station in the trees along Pine Creek, then joins a mining road that leads to the Brownstone Mine. The huge tungsten mine at 8,000 feet was active from 1918 until 1999, and many of the buildings remain. As you switchback up and out of the trees, you gain views of the Owens River Valley and the desertlike White Mountains. Above the mine, the road becomes an extremely rocky trail as it ascends more switchbacks to meet first Lower and then Upper Pine Lake, at 4.0 and 5.0 miles. The upper lake at 10,400 feet is reached by following the trail along the lower lake's northwest shore. Less than a mile past the upper lake, leave the main trail that continues to Pine Creek Pass and take the right fork toward Granite Park and Italy Pass. Granite-bound Honeymoon Lake lies about 200 yards from the junction, set at 10,600 feet. This spot makes a great base camp for exploring the rocky wonderland of Granite Park.

User Groups: Hikers, dogs, and horses. No mountain bikes. No wheelchair facilities.

Permits: A free wilderness permit is required year-round for overnight stays and is available from the Bishop/White Mountain Ranger Station. Quotas are in effect from May 1 to November 1; permits are available in advance for a $5 reservation fee per person.

Maps: A John Muir Wilderness map is available from the U.S. Forest Service. A map of the Mono Divide High County is available from Tom Harrison Maps. For topographic maps, go to the USGS website to download Bishop and Tungsten Hills.

Directions: From Bishop, drive north on U.S. 395 for seven miles and turn left (west) on Pine Creek Road. Drive 9.5 miles to the trailhead parking area, near the pack station, on the left side of the road.

Contact: Inyo National Forest, White Mountain Ranger Station, Bishop, 760/873-2500, www.fs.usda.gov/inyo.

13 BLUE LAKE

6.0 mi/3.0 hr or 2 days 3 10

in the John Muir Wilderness

Map 11.2, page 560 BEST

The Sabrina Basin Trail leads to a series of gorgeous alpine lakes set below lofty, 13,000-foot granite peaks. Of these, one of the most popular and easiest to reach is scenic Blue Lake, a popular spot for photographers, trout anglers, and cold-water swimmers. If you catch the light just right, you can take pictures of Blue Lake with towering Mount Thompson and the Thompson Ridge mirrored on its surface. It's a 1,250-foot climb to the lake (at 10,400 feet), but it's spread out moderately over three miles. Mule packers frequently utilize this trail; if you see them, be sure to get out of their way. Start by hiking along the shore of Lake Sabrina, heading in and out of the shade of aspen trees, then switchback your way uphill to Blue Lake. You'll want solid shoes for this rock-lined trail. If you get inspired to see more of this high-alpine scenery, you can bear left from Blue Lake to Donkey Lake and the Baboon Lakes (1.5 miles farther), both much smaller and more intimate than Blue Lake, or bear right and hike eastward to the Emerald Lakes and Dingleberry Lake (1.8 miles farther). Any of these are likely to have fewer visitors than Blue Lake.

User Groups: Hikers, dogs, and horses. No mountain bikes. No wheelchair facilities.

Permits: A free wilderness permit is required year-round for overnight stays and is available from the Bishop/White Mountain Ranger Station. Quotas are in effect from May 1 to November 1; permits are available in advance for a $5 reservation fee per person.

Maps: A John Muir Wilderness map is available from the U.S. Forest Service. A Bishop Pass map is available from Tom Harrison Maps. For topographic maps, go to the USGS website to download Mount Thompson and Mount Darwin.

Directions: From Bishop on U.S. 395, turn west on Line Street/Highway 168 and drive 18.5 miles to Lake Sabrina. Day-use parking is located near the end of the road, just before the boat launch area. Backpackers' parking is located at a turnout near the road to North Lake, 0.5 mile before the end of the road.

Contact: Inyo National Forest, White Mountain Ranger Station, Bishop, 760/873-2500, www.fs.usda.gov/inyo.

14 LAMARCK LAKES

6.0 mi/3.0 hr or 2 days 4 9

in the John Muir Wilderness

Map 11.2, page 560

The only downer on the Lamarck Lakes Trail is that from the trailhead parking lot, you must walk 0.5 mile down a dirt road to get to the actual trailhead, which is located in North Lake Campground. Skirt the problem by camping at this pretty little campground, one of the best in the Bishop Creek canyon, then start walking right from your tent. The trailhead is found at the signboard near the walk-in campsites, and the path heads through the aspens and crosses Bishop Creek on a footbridge. You'll climb steadily for one mile through a lodgepole pine forest, gaining 600 feet to the left fork for Grass Lake, a small and shallow lake in a wide meadow. Grass Lake is worth a brief glance, but it doesn't hold a candle to the Lamarck Lakes, so you may want to save your energy. Staying on the main trail, you leave the trees behind and begin a much more brutal ascent, marked by very short switchbacks and thigh-pumping stair-steps. In another mile and 700 feet of gain, you'll reach the Lower Lamarck Lake, set in a rock-lined granite basin. Look for Mount Emerson, Mount Lamarck, and the red-colored Piute Crags in the background. Many people make this lake their destination for the day, but it's worth the extra effort to hike the final mile to Upper Lamarck Lake, which is more than double the size of the lower lake and a deep cobalt blue. (Follow the trail alongside the creek to get there.) Upper Lamarck Lake is known for its large trout, so pack along a rod and a fishing license. Those looking for an adventure can make their way from the Lower Lamarck Lake to the Wonder Lakes, set in the basin northwest of Lower Lamarck. Trailhead elevation for this hike is 9,300 feet, the lower lake is at 10,662 feet, and the upper lake is at 10,918 feet.

User Groups: Hikers, dogs, and horses. No mountain bikes. No wheelchair facilities.

Permits: A free wilderness permit is required year-round for overnight stays and is available from the Bishop/White Mountain Ranger Station. Quotas are in effect from May 1 to November 1; permits are available in advance for a $5 reservation fee per person.

Maps: A John Muir Wilderness map is available from the U.S. Forest Service. A Bishop Pass map is available from Tom Harrison Maps. For topographic maps, go to the USGS website to download Mount Thompson and Mount Darwin.

Directions: From Bishop on U.S. 395, turn west on Line Street/Highway 168 and drive 18 miles toward Lake Sabrina. Just before reaching the lake, turn right at the turnoff for North Lake. Drive 1.5 miles and turn right to park in the hiker parking lot by North Lake, near the pack station. Then walk 0.5 mile down the road to the trailhead, at the edge of North Lake Campground.

Contact: Inyo National Forest, White Mountain Ranger Station, Bishop, 760/873-2500, www.fs.usda.gov/inyo.

15 PIUTE LAKE & PIUTE PASS

10.4 mi/5.0 hr 3 9

in the John Muir Wilderness

Map 11.2, page 560

The well graded trail to Piute Pass offers hikers and backpackers relatively easy access to the high country, plus the chance to stop at several lakes along the way to the 11,423-foot pass. Start by walking 0.5 mile from the trailhead parking area to North Lake Campground, then follow the trail by the walk-in sites marked for Piute Pass. A steep climb in the first mile will leave you panting. Fortunately, the route is shaded by lodgepole pines, and at the point where you leave the forest, the grade lessens. As you curve your way up the ridge, be sure to stop occasionally and look back at the incredibly deep valley below and the rust-colored Piute Crags towering above. You're likely to say "wow" a bunch of times. A series of switchbacks take you to the spot where Loch Leven Lake is nestled in a rocky glacial bowl at 10,743 feet, set right alongside the trail. The trail continues another 1.2 miles to Piute Lake, now on an even easier grade. Anglers fish for brown and rainbow trout in the deep blue lake, set in grassy green tundra and surrounded by lingering patches of snow. The elevation is just shy of 11,000 feet, and on the far side of the lake you'll notice a sturdy stone cabin, which is used for snow surveys in the winter. You now have only one mile and a couple hundred feet to go to reach the top of Piute Pass, so you might as well continue. At the top, look down on Summit Lake and start daydreaming about a future backpacking trip: The trail continues downhill into Humphreys Basin. Total elevation gain to the pass is 2,100 feet.

User Groups: Hikers, dogs, and horses. No mountain bikes. No wheelchair facilities.

Permits: No permits are required for day use. A free wilderness permit is required for overnight stays and is available from the Bishop/White Mountain Ranger Station. Quotas are in effect from May 1 to November 1; permits are available in advance for a $5 reservation fee per person. Parking and access are free.

Maps: A John Muir Wilderness map is available from the U.S. Forest Service. A Bishop Pass map is available from Tom Harrison Maps. For topographic maps, go to the USGS website to download Mount Thompson and Mount Darwin.

Directions: From Bishop on U.S. 395, turn west on Line Street/Highway 168 and drive 18 miles toward Lake Sabrina. Just before reaching the lake, turn right at the turnoff for North Lake. Drive 1.5 miles and turn right to park in the hiker parking lot by North Lake, near the pack station. Walk 0.5 mile down the road to the trailhead, at the edge of North Lake Campground.

Contact: Inyo National Forest, White Mountain Ranger Station, Bishop, 760/873-2500, www.fs.usda.gov/inyo.

16 TYEE LAKES

7.0 mi/4.0 hr or 2 days 3 9

in the John Muir Wilderness

Map 11.2, page 560 BEST

There's so much excellent hiking in the South Fork Bishop Creek Canyon, it's hard to choose where to go. Since so many backpackers opt for Bishop Pass Trail and its many lakes (see listing in this chapter), day hikers would do well to choose this trail to the Tyee Lakes instead. Just make sure that you are in the mood for hiking up, because you'll do plenty of that, with a total 2,000-foot elevation gain to the highest lakes. From the bridge over Bishop Creek, your climb begins immediately as you tromp up a hillside covered with sagebrush and aspens, gradually making your way through a few dozen switchbacks. You get great views of the Bishop Creek Canyon as you climb, which is an especially beautiful sight when the aspens are putting on their autumn color show. The trail enters a lodgepole pine forest, and after two miles of climbing, the grade eases up, and you reach one of the smaller, lower Tyee Lakes at 2.3 miles. Another 0.5 mile of climbing brings you to the next small lake (called Tyee Lake number two). These first two lakes are small and pondlike, edged with grass, and not worth much more than a quick glance. But keep pushing onward, and in another 0.5 mile, you reach one of the larger Tyee Lakes (number three). The fourth and fifth lakes are only 0.25 mile farther and are separated by a small boulder field. The fifth lake is very small, but the fourth lake (elevation 11,015 feet) is large and beautiful. Backpackers usually set up their tent at the third lake and then day hike to the fourth and fifth lakes. Named for a brand of salmon eggs, the Tyee Lakes offer dependably good trout fishing and the chance to enjoy plenty of classic high Sierra scenery. Backpackers looking to make a semi-loop can arrange to have a car waiting at Lake Sabrina in Bishop Creek Canyon, then continue from the Tyee Lakes to George Lake and then Lake Sabrina.

User Groups: Hikers, dogs, and horses. No mountain bikes. No wheelchair facilities.

Permits: A free wilderness permit is required year-round for overnight stays and is available from the Bishop/White Mountain Ranger Station. Quotas are in effect from May 1 to November 1; permits are available in advance for a $5 reservation fee per person.

Maps: A John Muir Wilderness map is available from the U.S. Forest Service. A Bishop Pass map is available from Tom Harrison Maps. For a topographic map, go to the USGS website to download Mount Thompson.

Directions: From Bishop on U.S. 395, turn west on Line Street/Highway 168 and drive 14 miles to the junction for South Lake. Go left and drive 4.5 miles on South Lake Road to the footbridge that crosses Bishop Creek. It is on the right, just before Willow Campground, and it is signed as Tyee Lakes and George Lake trailhead. Park alongside the road.

Contact: Inyo National Forest, White Mountain Ranger Station, Bishop, 760/873-2500, www.fs.usda.gov/inyo.

17 GREEN AND BROWN LAKES

6.6 mi/3.0 hr 3 9

in the John Muir Wilderness

Map 11.2, page 560

Brown Lake and Green Lake are two excellent day-hiking destinations from the South

Lake trailhead in Bishop Creek's South Fork Canyon. With only a 1,500-foot climb, you can visit both lakes, maybe do a little fishing for rainbow trout, and be home in time for supper. Access the trail from the pack station trailhead, and follow a stock trail as it climbs along Bishop Creek through a conifer forest and joins the main Green Lake Trail at one mile. Bear left and level out to an alpine meadow at two miles, where you have a spectacular view of Mount Tom behind you. Soon you'll meet Brown Lake's outlet stream and the little lake itself (really a pond), at 2.5 miles and 10,750 feet. Pay a brief visit, then continue another 0.5 mile to much larger and prettier Green Lake, at 11,050 feet, surrounded by wildflowers and ancient-looking whitebark pines. Both lakes host an abundance of rainbow trout, who might just invite themselves to dinner.

User Groups: Hikers, dogs, and horses. No mountain bikes. No wheelchair facilities.

Permits: No permits are required. Parking and access are free.

Maps: A John Muir Wilderness map is available from the U.S. Forest Service. A Bishop Pass map is available from Tom Harrison Maps. For a topographic map, go to the USGS website to download Mount Thompson.

Directions: From Bishop on U.S. 395, turn west on Line Street/Highway 168 and drive 14 miles to the junction for South Lake. Go left and drive six miles on South Lake Road to Parchers Resort and pack station, on the left side of the road, just beyond Willow Campground.

Contact: Inyo National Forest, White Mountain Ranger Station, Bishop, 760/873-2500, www.fs.usda.gov/inyo.

18 RUWAU AND CHOCOLATE LAKES LOOP

6.6 mi/3.5 hr or 2 days 3 10

in the John Muir Wilderness

Map 11.2, page 560

Lakes, lakes, lakes everywhere. That's how it is on Bishop Pass Trail, where in the space of only five miles you can access Long Lake, Spearhead Lake, Saddlerock Lake, Bishop Lake, and so on. But if you prefer a loop trip to an out-and-back hike, Bishop Pass Trail provides another lake-filled option: a two-mile hike to Long Lake, then a circular route to Ruwau Lake, the Chocolate Lakes, and Bull Lake. It's the kind of trip that fills your mind with precious memories of blue-sky Sierra scenery and gemlike, rock-lined lakes. Still, the trip is not for everyone; some of the trail is an indistinct route with steep, rocky sections that are not an official trail. Bring a good map with you.

The trail begins on the south side of the parking lot, and you head uphill along the eastern shore of South Lake. The views begin almost immediately, particularly of South Lake, Mount Thompson, and Mount Goode. Take the left fork at 0.75 mile, heading for Long Lake and Bishop Pass. Continue straight, ignoring all turnoffs as you hike up around the spectacular western shore of Long Lake, popular with anglers and backpackers. At 2.5 miles (before you reach the lake's far end), instead of continuing straight to Saddlerock Lake and Bishop Pass, take the left fork for Ruwau Lake, a steep but short 0.5 mile away. Skirt the edge of Ruwau Lake for about 75 yards, then look for a use trail leading uphill to your left. Make a steep uphill climb for 0.5 mile to the ridgetop, where you'll look down and see the Chocolate Lakes, set below Chocolate Peak. Make the steep descent to the lakes, picking your way along the rocky slope. Once you're there, the hard part is over. You'll find an easy-to-follow trail at the Chocolate Lakes, and then you'll walk downhill for 0.5 mile to Bull Lake, which is big, round, and beautiful. From Bull Lake, you keep on hiking, and in less than 0.25 mile, you rejoin Bishop Pass Trail. Turn right and walk just under two miles back to the parking lot. Wow, what a day.

User Groups: Hikers, dogs, and horses. No mountain bikes. No wheelchair facilities.

Permits: A free wilderness permit is required

year-round for overnight stays and is available from the Bishop/White Mountain Ranger Station. Quotas are in effect from May 1 to November 1; permits are available in advance for a $5 reservation fee per person.

Maps: A John Muir Wilderness map is available from the U.S. Forest Service. A Bishop Pass map is available from Tom Harrison Maps. For a topographic map, go to the USGS website to download Mount Thompson.

Directions: From Bishop on U.S. 395, turn west on Line Street/Highway 168 and drive 14 miles to the junction for South Lake. Go left and drive 7.5 miles on South Lake Road to the end of the road and the trailhead parking area. This parking is for day-use only. If you are backpacking, you must park 1.5 miles from the trailhead, east of Parchers Resort.

Contact: Inyo National Forest, White Mountain Ranger Station, Bishop, 760/873-2500, www.fs.usda.gov/inyo.

19 FIRST AND SECOND FALLS

3.0 mi/1.5 hr

in the John Muir Wilderness

Map 11.2, page 560

If you're camping or fishing in Big Pine Canyon, or maybe just wandering around exploring the area, there's a great walk to take starting from the end of the road near Glacier Lodge. Since it's just a day hike, you can park in the parking area right by the lodge and save yourself the long walk from the backpackers' parking lot.

Head west from the trailhead on the wide road, passing some private cabins, and in seconds you cross a bridge over First Falls, a noisy, 200-foot-long whitewater cascade. Bear right onto a narrower trail and start switchbacking uphill, paralleling the cascade. As you climb, you get awesome views into Big Pine Canyon's South Fork. At the top of the falls, cross another bridge over the creek and take a hard left onto a dirt road, staying along the creek. Now it's a flat stroll into the north fork of Big Pine Canyon. Your goal is Second Falls, a larger, more impressive cascade than First Falls; it's less than a mile away and clearly visible from the trail. Since the route is set along the canyon bottom, you get many interesting vistas along the way, from the tall surrounding canyon walls to occasional lodgepole pines and many mountain wildflowers. When the trail starts to climb out of the canyon, take the left spur cutoff to head closer to the waterfall, or just pick a big rock to sit on and admire the scenery.

User Groups: Hikers, dogs, and horses. No mountain bikes. No wheelchair facilities.

Permits: No permits are required for day use. Parking and access are free.

Maps: A John Muir Wilderness map is available from the U.S. Forest Service. A Palisades map is available from Tom Harrison Maps. For a topographic map, go to the USGS website to download Coyote Flat.

Directions: From Bishop, drive 15 miles south on U.S. 395 to Big Pine. Turn right (west) on Crocker Street, which becomes Glacier Lodge Road, and drive 10.5 miles to Glacier Lodge and the Big Pine Canyon trailhead, at the end of the road. Day hikers may park in the day-use area near the lodge, but backpackers must park 0.5 mile east, on Glacier Lodge Road, in the backpackers' parking lot.

Contact: Inyo National Forest, White Mountain Ranger Station, Bishop, 760/873-2500, www.fs.usda.gov/inyo.

20 FIRST AND SECOND LAKES

9.6 mi/6.0 hr or 2 days 3 9

in the John Muir Wilderness

Map 11.2, page 560

The trail to First and Second Lakes in Big Pine Canyon follows the same route as the trail to First and Second Falls, above, but then continues onward, climbing up and over Second Falls on the well-graded trail to Cienaga Mirth, at three miles out. Off to the left of the trail you'll see a magnificent stone cabin (now sometimes used as a backcountry ranger residence) built by movie star Lon Chaney. Wildflowers are excellent at the swampy, spring-fed mirth. You reach First Lake at 4.5 miles, and Second Lake is just a few hundred yards farther. By Second Lake, you've climbed to over 10,000 feet, and the lake water is a stunning glacial blue-green. Those who wish to see more lakes can continue on a loop past Second Lake to Third, Fourth, Fifth, and Black Lakes, making a long, 14-mile day. Fifth Lake, just off the loop by a third of a mile, is the most scenic. You'll see hardy mountaineer-types with climbing equipment turning left beyond Third Lake. They're hiking a full nine miles one-way to the edge of Palisade Glacier, the southernmost glacier in the Sierra. Considering it has a 5,000-foot elevation gain, the route to the glacier is not for everybody.

User Groups: Hikers, dogs, and horses. No mountain bikes. No wheelchair facilities.

Permits: A free wilderness permit is required year-round for overnight stays and is available from the Bishop/White Mountain Ranger Station. Quotas are in effect from May 1 to November 1; permits are available in advance for a $5 reservation fee per person.

Maps: A John Muir Wilderness map is available from the U.S. Forest Service. A Palisades map is available from Tom Harrison Maps. For topographic maps, go to the USGS website to download Coyote Flat and Split Mountain.

Directions: From Bishop, drive 15 miles south on U.S. 395 to Big Pine. Turn right (west) on Crocker Street, which becomes Glacier Lodge Road, and drive 10.5 miles to Glacier Lodge and the Big Pine Canyon trailhead, at the end of the road. Day hikers may park in the day-use area near the lodge, but backpackers must park 0.5 mile east, on Glacier Lodge Road, in the backpackers' parking lot.

Contact: Inyo National Forest, White Mountain Ranger Station, Bishop, 760/873-2500, www.fs.usda.gov/inyo.

21 BIG STUMP TRAIL

1.0 mi/0.5 hr

in the Grant Grove area of Kings Canyon National Park

Map 11.3, page 561

Normally it would be hard for us to get excited about a trail called the Big Stump Trail. In fact, this sort of thing could be quite depressing. But Big Stump Trail, at the entrance to Kings Canyon National Park, is a pleasant nature walk and provides an excellent history lesson as well. The size of the mammoth trees—oops, make that stumps—just blows you away. Most of the big trees were cut for timber in the 1880s, and you'll see the remains of logging activities. Be sure to pick up an interpretive brochure at the Kings Canyon Visitors Center or at the trailhead. The trail is a short loop that circles a meadow. A few mature sequoias still thrive along the route, including one in the first 50 feet from the parking lot. The path's highlights include the Burnt Monarch, a shell of a giant sequoia that has been ravaged by fire but still stands, and the Mark Twain Stump. The latter belonged to a 26-foot-wide tree that took two men 13 days to cut down.

User Groups: Hikers only. No dogs, horses, or mountain bikes. No wheelchair facilities.

Permits: No permits are required. There is a $35 entrance fee per vehicle at Sequoia and Kings Canyon National Parks, good for seven days.

Maps: A Sequoia and Kings Canyon map is available from Tom Harrison Maps. For a topographic map, go to the USGS website to download Hume.

Directions: From Fresno, drive east on Highway 180 for 55 miles to the Big Stump Entrance at Kings Canyon National Park. The trail begins 0.5 mile past the entrance station, at the Big Stump Picnic Area.

Contact: Sequoia and Kings Canyon National Parks, Three Rivers, 559/565-3341 or 559/565-4307, www.nps.gov/seki.

22 SUNSET TRAIL

5.0 mi/2.5 hr 2 8

in the Grant Grove area of Kings Canyon National Park

Map 11.3, page 561

The Sunset Trail leaves Sunset Campground (elevation 6,590 feet) and heads gently downhill for 2.25 miles to Ella Falls, a pretty 40-foot cascade on Sequoia Creek. At 1.5 miles down the trail, you reach a junction with South Boundary Trail and can take a short side-trip to the left to Viola Falls, which isn't much of a waterfall but is a memorably scenic spot on granite-sculpted Sequoia Creek. Most people just mosey down the trail, enjoying the big pines and firs and the flowering western azaleas, and maybe stealing a kiss on one of the wooden footbridges. If you like, you can follow the trail for its entire 2.5-mile length to Sequoia Lake. Although the lake is privately owned, hikers are allowed to walk along its edge. While you're enjoying the lake, don't forget that the return trip is all uphill with a 1,300-foot elevation gain, so save some water and energy.

User Groups: Hikers only. No dogs, horses, or mountain bikes. No wheelchair facilities.

Permits: No permits are required. There is a $35 entrance fee per vehicle at Sequoia and Kings Canyon National Parks, good for seven days.

Maps: A Sequoia and Kings Canyon map is available from Tom Harrison Maps. For topographic maps, go to the USGS website to download Hume and General Grant Grove.

Directions: From Fresno, drive east on Highway 180 for 55 miles to the Big Stump Entrance at Kings Canyon National Park. Continue 1.5 miles and turn left, following signs for Kings Canyon. Drive 1.5 miles to Grant Grove Village, and park in the large parking lot near the visitors center. Cross the road and walk on the paved trail toward Sunset Campground's amphitheater. Continue heading left through the camp to site No. 118, where the trail begins.

Contact: Sequoia and Kings Canyon National Parks, Three Rivers, 559/565-3341 or 559/565-4307, www.nps.gov/seki.

23 MANZANITA AND AZALEA TRAILS

3.3 mi/2.0 hr 2 7

in the Grant Grove area of Kings Canyon National Park

Map 11.3, page 561

This hike is a good exercise route for vacationers staying in Grant Grove Village or in the nearby campgrounds. It climbs 800 feet, which gives your heart and lungs a workout, and it's pretty every step of the way. From the edge of the dirt service road by the tent cabins, Manzanita Trail climbs a dry slope uphill to Park Ridge. Near the top, you'll parallel the dirt road that leads to the Park Ridge Fire Lookout. Then Manzanita Trail meets up with Azalea Trail, and you'll descend on a much shadier, moister slope. The azaleas bloom bright white with prolific, showy blossoms in June and July. Azalea Trail ends at Wilsonia, a private community within the national park, so just retrace your steps to return back to your car.

User Groups: Hikers only. No dogs, horses, or mountain bikes. No wheelchair facilities.

Permits: No permits are required. There is a $35 entrance fee per vehicle at Sequoia and Kings Canyon National Parks, good for seven days.

Maps: A Sequoia and Kings Canyon map is available from Tom Harrison Maps. For a topographic map, go to the USGS website to download Hume.

Directions: From Fresno, drive east on Highway 180 for 55 miles to the Big Stump Entrance at Kings Canyon National Park. Continue 1.5 miles and turn left, following signs for Kings Canyon. Drive 1.5 miles to Grant Grove Village and park in the large parking lot near the visitors center. Walk on the service road near the tent cabins to reach the start of the Manzanita Trail.

Contact: Sequoia and Kings Canyon National Parks, Three Rivers, 559/565-3341 or 559/565-4307, www.nps.gov/seki.

24 PANORAMIC POINT AND PARK RIDGE LOOKOUT

4.7 mi/3.0 hr 

in the Grant Grove area of Kings Canyon National Park

Map 11.3, page 561

Start your trip by taking the 300-yard paved walk from the parking area to Panoramic Point, which delivers what its name implies. An interpretive display names the many peaks and valleys you can see, including the big pointy one, which is Mount Goddard at 13,560 feet. From Panoramic Point, take the dirt Park Ridge Trail that leads to the right along the ridge. Your views continue as you contour along the ridgeline, climbing gently uphill. The trail intersects a dirt road, which you follow for about 50 yards; then bear left onto the trail again. You'll intersect this dirt road once more about 100 yards before the Park Ridge Fire Lookout. Follow the road to the lookout tower, and check out the nifty outdoor shower at its base. If someone is stationed in the tower and gives you permission to come up, do so and sign the visitors register. (The lookout person rarely gets visitors on cloudy days, but he or she gets a lot of company when it's sunny and you can see for miles around.) The lookout is operated by volunteers during the fire season, which is usually May to October. For your return trip, you can walk down the trail back to Panoramic Point or take the shorter fire road, which also leads back to the parking lot. Views are far better along the trail than on the fire road.

User Groups: Hikers only. No dogs, horses, or mountain bikes. No wheelchair facilities.

Permits: No permits are required. There is a $35 entrance fee per vehicle at Sequoia and Kings Canyon National Parks, good for seven days.

Maps: A Sequoia and Kings Canyon map is available from Tom Harrison Maps. For a topographic map, go to the USGS website to download Hume.

Directions: From Fresno, drive east on Highway 180 for 55 miles to the Big Stump Entrance at Kings Canyon National Park. Continue 1.5 miles and turn left, following signs for Kings Canyon. Drive 1.5 miles to Grant Grove Village and turn right by the visitors center and store. Follow the road past the cabins, and just before the John Muir Lodge, turn right on the road signed for Panoramic Point. It's 2.3 miles from the visitors center to Panoramic Point.

Contact: Sequoia and Kings Canyon National Parks, Three Rivers, 559/565-3341 or 559/565-4307, www.nps.gov/seki.

25 GENERAL GRANT TREE TRAIL

0.6 mi/0.5 hr 1 8

in the Grant Grove area of Kings Canyon National Park

Map 11.3, page 561 BEST

This paved loop through a giant sequoia grove allows visitors a look at the General Grant Tree, the second-largest tree in the world. Estimated to be 1,800 to 2,000 years old, the General Grant is 267 feet tall and 107 feet in circumference at its base. Every year since 1926, the City of Sanger has held a Christmas celebration around its base, and so the tree is known as "the Nation's Christmas Tree." Its neighbors include the Fallen Monarch, a hollow downed tree that is so wide, it was once used as a park employee camp. Also nearby is a group of big sequoias named after various U.S. states. It may seem a little campy, but there are many excellent photo opportunities in the grove. A bonus: Most, but not all, of this trail is accessible to wheelchair users.

General Grant Tree Trail

User Groups: Hikers. No dogs, horses, or mountain bikes. Partial wheelchair accessibility.

Permits: No permits are required. There is a $35 entrance fee per vehicle at Sequoia and Kings Canyon National Parks, good for seven days.

Maps: A Sequoia and Kings Canyon map is available from Tom Harrison Maps. For topographic maps, go to the USGS website to download Hume and General Grant Grove.

Directions: From Fresno, drive east on Highway 180 for 55 miles to the Big Stump Entrance at Kings Canyon National Park. Continue 1.5 miles and turn left, following signs for Kings Canyon. Drive one mile, passing Grant Grove Village, to the left turnoff for General Grant Tree. Turn left and follow the access road for 0.75 mile to the parking lot.

Contact: Sequoia and Kings Canyon National Parks, Three Rivers, 559/565-3341 or 559/565-4307, www.nps.gov/seki.

26 NORTH GROVE AND DEAD GIANT LOOP

3.0 mi/1.5 hr 2 7

in the Grant Grove area of Kings Canyon National Park

Map 11.3, page 561

For people who want a little more hiking than what the General Grant Tree Trail (see listing in this chapter) provides, the combined North Grove and Dead Giant Loop Trails are the answer. The walk begins at the oversized vehicle parking at the General Grant Tree parking lot. Past the gate, follow an old dirt road that leads downhill through a mixed forest of sequoia, sugar pine, white fir, and dogwood. Don't expect to see dense groves of sequoias here; the big trees are few and far between. However, the forest is pleasant, quiet, and shady.

Stay to the right at the first junction to follow the posted North Grove Loop Trail. At the bottom of the hill, you'll pass an obscure junction with an old wagon road that was used to take logged sequoias to the mill. Continue to a more obvious junction at one mile out. Turn right and walk 0.25 mile downhill to Lion Meadow. Turn right on a single-track trail and circle around the meadow, heading for the Dead Giant. This sequoia, like some others in the park, is a nearly hollow, dead tree that somehow keeps standing. From the Dead Giant, it's a short tromp to the Sequoia Lake Overlook, a tranquil high point where you can have a snack and enjoy the view of the large, private lake in Sequoia National Forest. From the overlook, backtrack a few yards and turn right to finish out the loop, returning uphill on the wide dirt road. There is a 400-foot gain on the return.

User Groups: Hikers only. No dogs, horses, or mountain bikes. No wheelchair facilities.

Permits: No permits are required. There is a $35 entrance fee per vehicle at Sequoia and Kings Canyon National Parks, good for seven days.

Maps: A Sequoia and Kings Canyon map is available from Tom Harrison Maps. For topographic maps, go to the USGS website to download Hume and General Grant Grove.

Directions: From Fresno, drive east on Highway 180 for 55 miles to the Big Stump Entrance at Kings Canyon National Park. Continue 1.5 miles and turn left, following signs for Kings Canyon. Drive two miles, passing Grant Grove Village, to the left turnoff for General Grant Tree. Turn left and follow the access road for one mile to the parking lot. The North Grove Loop starts from the far end of the lower parking lot.

Contact: Sequoia and Kings Canyon National Parks, Three Rivers, 559/565-3341 or 559/565-4307, www.nps.gov/seki.

27 CHICAGO STUMP TRAIL

0.5 mi/0.5 hr — 1 — 7

in Giant Sequoia National Monument north of the Grant Grove area of Kings Canyon National Park

Map 11.3, page 561

Before the loggers extracted their toll, the Converse Basin once sheltered one of the largest and finest groves of giant sequoias in the world. Where the giants once stood, second-growth sequoias have now taken hold. This short and easy stroll takes you through a regenerated mixed forest to the Chicago Stump, a massive stump that belonged to one of the largest trees in the area. The General Noble tree was cut down in 1893, and the lower portion of the tree was reassembled and exhibited at the Chicago World's Fair. People couldn't believe the tree's massive size—they called it the "California Hoax." The stump remaining in this meadow is at least 10 feet high and over 25 feet wide. In addition to its historical interest, this easy trail provides a pleasant, peaceful change from the hustle and bustle of the neighboring national parks.

User Groups: Hikers, horses, and dogs. No mountain bikes. No wheelchair facilities.

Permits: No permits are required. There is a $35 entrance fee per vehicle at Sequoia and Kings Canyon National Parks, good for seven days.

Maps: A Sequoia National Forest map is available from the U.S. Forest Service. A map of Sequoia and Kings Canyon is available from Tom Harrison Maps. For a topographic map, go to the USGS website to download Hume.

Directions: From Fresno, drive east on Highway 180 for 55 miles to the Big Stump Entrance at Kings Canyon National Park. Continue 1.5 miles and turn left, following signs for Kings Canyon. Drive approximately 4.5 miles, passing Grant Grove Village, and turn left at the sign for Forest Road 13S03. Drive two miles, turn right on Road 13S65, and continue 0.1 mile to the Chicago Stump trailhead.

Contact: Giant Sequoia National Monument/Sequoia National Forest, Hume Lake Ranger District, Dunlap, 559/338-2251, www.fs.usda.gov/sequoia.

28 BOOLE TREE LOOP

2.5 mi/1.0 hr 2 9

in Giant Sequoia National Monument north of the Grant Grove area of Kings Canyon National Park

Map 11.3, page 561

The drive in to the Boole Tree trailhead is worth the trip by itself. You pass through a beautiful, ghostly meadow filled with giant sequoia stumps. It's an otherworldly sight that may stay engrained in your memory for a long time. The Boole Tree hike is a loop, and it's a good idea to take the right side of the loop first, making the ascent more gradual. You climb 500 feet to the top of a ridge, then descend the other side, reaching the Boole Tree in one mile. (It's just off the main loop, accessible via a short, obvious spur.) At 269 feet tall and with a diameter of 35 feet, the Boole Tree is the largest tree in any of the national forests, and it's the sixth largest tree in the world. It is one of a very few giant sequoias left standing in the Converse Basin grove, as the rest were clear-cut in the late 1800s. Although some people go see the Boole Tree and then turn around, it's better to finish out the loop. You'll be rewarded with a stellar view of Spanish Mountain and the Kings River Canyon.

User Groups: Hikers, horses, and dogs. No mountain bikes. No wheelchair facilities.

Permits: No permits are required. There is a $35 entrance fee per vehicle at Sequoia and Kings Canyon National Parks, good for seven days.

Maps: A Sequoia National Forest map is available from the U.S. Forest Service. A map of Sequoia and Kings Canyon is available from Tom Harrison Maps. For a topographic map, go to the USGS website to download Hume.

Directions: From Fresno, drive east on Highway 180 for 55 miles to the Big Stump Entrance at Kings Canyon National Park. Continue 1.5 miles and turn left, following signs for Kings Canyon. Drive approximately six miles, passing Grant Grove Village. Turn left at the sign for Forest Road 13S55, Boole Tree, Converse Basin, and Stump Meadow. Drive 2.6 miles, and park in the wide parking pullout.

Contact: Giant Sequoia National Monument/Sequoia National Forest, Hume Lake Ranger District, Dunlap, 559/338-2251, www.fs.usda.gov/sequoia.

29 YUCCA POINT

4.0 mi/2.25 hr

in Giant Sequoia National Monument west of the Cedar Grove area of Kings Canyon National Park

Map 11.3, page 561

The Yucca Point Trail is an upside-down hike—the kind where you go down on the way in (so easy) and up on the way back (not so easy). The path descends from Highway 180 to the Kings River, dropping 1,200 feet along the way. As long as you don't climb uphill at high noon, the hike back is not as bad as it looks from the top. The trail is well graded; the only hardship is that the terrain is all chaparral, so there's almost no shade, just the occasional tall yucca plant. The path is mostly used by anglers heading down to the wild trout section of the Kings River, but hikers enjoy the excellent views it provides. In spring, Tenmile Creek's waterfall is a rushing torrent, and wildflower fans will find dozens of interesting species growing alongside this trail. In summer, the trail is hot and dry, but the payoff is the river's cool, emerald green pools.

User Groups: Hikers only. No dogs, horses, or mountain bikes. No wheelchair facilities.

Permits: No permits are required. There is a $35 entrance fee per vehicle for access to this section of Sequoia National Forest, payable at any of the entrance stations to Kings Canyon and Sequoia National Parks. The fee is good for seven days in both the national forest and the national parks.

Maps: A Sequoia National Forest map is available from the U.S. Forest Service. A map of Sequoia and Kings Canyon is available from

Tom Harrison Maps. For a topographic map, go to the USGS website to download Wren Peak.

Directions: From Fresno, drive east on Highway 180 for 55 miles to the Big Stump Entrance at Kings Canyon National Park. Continue 1.5 miles and turn left, following signs for Kings Canyon. Drive another 16 miles on Highway 180, past Grant Grove and Kings Canyon Lodge, to the Yucca Point trailhead, on the left. Park in the pullouts alongside Highway 180.

Contact: Giant Sequoia National Monument/Sequoia National Forest, Hume Lake Ranger District, Dunlap, 559/338-2251, www.fs.usda.gov/sequoia.

30 WINDY CLIFFS

3.0 mi/1.5 hr

in Giant Sequoia National Monument west of the Cedar Grove area of Kings Canyon National Park

Map 11.3, page 561

You have to pay a fee to tour Boyden Cave, one of many limestone caverns in the vicinity of Kings Canyon and Sequoia National Parks, and the parking lot is always busy with carloads and busloads of people waiting to take the tour. (The cave was closed for four years after the 2015 Rough Fire, but it's been reopened.) Filled with stalagmites, stalactites, and beautiful flowstone formations, the cave is a showstopper and definitely worth a visit. But while you're there, you can also take this stellar hike instead and get million-dollar views of Kings Canyon for free. From the cave gift shop, walk up the paved path and take the left fork near the entrance to the cave (you'll need to go under the rope that borders the trail to the cave). The trail has a metal bar across it, but the Forest Service says it's perfectly legal to hike it; they just don't want to encourage casual looky-loos because the trail is unmaintained with very steep drop-offs. Once on the trail, in no time you'll climb a little higher and see a sweeping panorama of Highway 180 and the fast-flowing Kings River below. In one mile, Boulder Creek cascades down the hillside. The path ends when it reaches creekside at 1.5 miles. (A faint path continues, but it's badly overgrown.) Note: Poison oak is prolific along this trail, so it might be a good idea to wear long pants and long sleeves.

User Groups: Hikers only. No dogs, horses, or mountain bikes. No wheelchair facilities.

Permits: No permits are required. There is a $35 per vehicle entrance fee for access to this section of Sequoia National Forest, payable at any of the entrance stations to Kings Canyon and Sequoia National Parks. The fee is good for seven days in both the national forest and the national parks.

Maps: A Sequoia National Forest map is available from the U.S. Forest Service. A map of Sequoia and Kings Canyon is available from Tom Harrison Maps. For a topographic map, go to the USGS website to download Wren Peak.

Directions: From Fresno, drive east on Highway 180 for 55 miles to the Big Stump Entrance at Kings Canyon National Park. Continue 1.5 miles and turn left, following signs for Kings Canyon. Drive 22 miles on Highway 180, passing Grant Grove and Kings Canyon Lodge, to the parking area for Boyden Cave, on the right side of the road.

Contact: Giant Sequoia National Monument/Sequoia National Forest, Hume Lake Ranger District, Dunlap, 559/338-2251, www.fs.usda.gov/sequoia.

31 LEWIS CREEK TRAIL

11.6 mi/6.0 hr or 2 days

4 9

off Highway 180 in the Cedar Grove area of Kings Canyon National Park

Map 11.3, page 561

Up, up, and up. If you're willing to climb 3,200 feet over the course of 5.5 miles, your reward is pristine Frypan Meadow, at 7,800 feet in elevation. In early summer, the meadow is green and littered with wildflowers, creating a glorious vision after the hot, sunny climb. But there's no way to see it without first putting in some effort on the Lewis Creek Trail. The good news is that if the first mile or so proves to be too demanding, or too hot if you don't start first thing in the morning, you can always take the right fork at 1.6 miles and head back downhill on Hotel Creek Trail, making a seven-mile loop out of the trip. If you push onward on Lewis Creek Trail, you cross lovely Comb Creek (at 3.2 miles), then Lewis Creek one mile farther. Many day hikers make the Lewis Creek crossing their destination; its pools make fine swimming holes. Backpackers continue another 1.5 miles to Frypan Meadow. If you have your wilderness permit, campsites are available there.

User Groups: Hikers and horses. No dogs or mountain bikes. No wheelchair facilities.

Permits: There is a $35 entrance fee per vehicle at Sequoia and Kings Canyon National Parks, good for seven days. Wilderness permits are required for overnight stays. They are available on a first-come, first-served basis at the wilderness permit station at Roads End or the Kings Canyon Visitors Center. For advanced wilderness permits or information on trail conditions, go to www.nps.gov/seki. Trailhead quotas are in effect from May to September.

Maps: A Sequoia and Kings Canyon map is available from Tom Harrison Maps. For a topographic map, go to the USGS website to download Cedar Grove.

Directions: From Fresno, drive east on Highway 180 for 55 miles to the Big Stump Entrance at Kings Canyon National Park. Continue 1.5 miles and turn left, following signs for Kings Canyon and Cedar Grove. Drive 31 miles on Highway 180 to the Lewis Creek Trail parking area, on the north side of the road, before you reach Cedar Grove Village.

Contact: Sequoia and Kings Canyon National Parks, Three Rivers, 559/565-3341 or 559/565-4307, www.nps.gov/seki.

32 HOTEL CREEK TRAIL TO CEDAR GROVE OVERLOOK

5.0 mi/2.5 hr 3 9

off Highway 180 in the Cedar Grove area of Kings Canyon National Park

Map 11.3, page 561

The destination on this trip is a stunning overlook of Kings Canyon, the deepest canyon in the continental United States with a plunge of 8,200 feet at its deepest point. In truth, the canyon vistas are continual for most of the hike, so if you don't make it to the overlook, you'll still get an eyeful. The Hotel Creek Trail consists of dozens of switchbacks over open, sunny slopes, climbing 1,200 feet over two miles to a trail junction with Overlook Trail. Turn left to head to the overlook, which peers down on Cedar Grove and the length of Kings Canyon. Some of the best views are of Monarch Divide's high peaks to the north. We hope you came with picnic supplies. For a five-mile round-trip, retrace your steps back to Cedar Grove. If you want to walk farther, you can continue from the overlook junction for another 1.5 miles and turn left, hiking downhill on Lewis Creek Trail and making a seven-mile loop out of the trip. This stretch of Lewis Creek Trail is lined with sweet-smelling ceanothus. Unfortunately, the final 1.2 miles of the loop parallels a park road. Along the way, the trail overlooks a level area next to the South Fork Kings River where wildlife can often be spotted among the meadows and shrubs.

User Groups: Hikers and horses. No dogs or mountain bikes. No wheelchair facilities.

Permits: No permits are required. There is a $35 entrance fee per vehicle at Sequoia and Kings Canyon National Parks, good for seven days.

Maps: A Sequoia and Kings Canyon map is available from Tom Harrison Maps. For a topographic map, go to the USGS website to download Cedar Grove.

Directions: From Fresno, drive east on Highway 180 for 55 miles to the Big Stump

Entrance at Kings Canyon National Park. Continue 1.5 miles and turn left, following signs for Kings Canyon and Cedar Grove. Drive 31.5 miles on Highway 180 to Cedar Grove Village. Turn left at the sign for the visitors center and Cedar Grove Lodge. Continue on the main road past the lodge for 0.25 mile and turn right. The Hotel Creek trailhead is on the left after a few hundred feet.

Contact: Sequoia and Kings Canyon National Parks, Three Rivers, 559/565-3341 or 559/565-4307, www.nps.gov/seki.

33 DON CECIL TRAIL TO LOOKOUT PEAK

12.0 mi/7.0 hr 5 10

off Highway 180 in the Cedar Grove area of Kings Canyon National Park

Map 11.3, page 561 BEST

Lookout Peak, at 8,531 feet in elevation, is a summit worth ascending, even though it's an all-day trip with a 3,900-foot elevation gain. From the top, you get an unforgettable Sierra view, with Cedar Grove far below you and peaks and ridges all around. In addition, just a few hundred yards from the summit is Summit Meadow, filled with summer wildflowers. The key is to carry plenty of water and plan on an early-morning start to beat the heat. You can filter water from Sheep Creek, one mile in. Luckily, there's a decent amount of shade in the first few miles. Even though this trailhead is located right by the Cedar Grove campgrounds, few people hike all the way to the peak, so you have a chance at peace and quiet along the trail. The only downer on this hike is that when you near the summit, you see that other people have driven their cars on an alternate route to Lookout Peak (from the Big Meadows area of Giant Sequoia National Monument), and they are gaining the summit after only a 0.25-mile hike. Hey, at least you earned it.

User Groups: Hikers and horses. No dogs or mountain bikes. No wheelchair facilities.

Permits: No permits are required. There is a $35 entrance fee per vehicle at Sequoia and Kings Canyon National Parks, good for seven days.

Maps: A Sequoia and Kings Canyon map is available from Tom Harrison Maps. For a topographic map, go to the USGS website to download Cedar Grove.

Directions: From Fresno, drive east on Highway 180 for 55 miles to the Big Stump Entrance at Kings Canyon National Park. Continue 1.5 miles and turn left, following signs for Kings Canyon and Cedar Grove. Drive 31.5 miles on Highway 180 and take the right fork for Cedar Grove. The Don Cecil trailhead is on the right side of the road, just beyond the turnoff for Cedar Grove Village and the visitors center. If you reach Canyon View and Moraine Campgrounds, you've gone too far.

Contact: Sequoia and Kings Canyon National Parks, Three Rivers, 559/565-3341 or 559/565-4307, www.nps.gov/seki.

34 ROARING RIVER FALLS

0.4 mi/0.25 hr 1 8

off Highway 180 in the Cedar Grove area of Kings Canyon National Park

Map 11.3, page 561 BEST

It's an easy stroll to Roaring River Falls, a pretty waterfall that drops through a narrow gorge into the South Fork Kings River. It's the only waterfall in Sequoia and Kings Canyon National Parks that is partially accessible via wheelchair. (The trail is paved and accessible for most of its length, but one section may be too steep for some wheelchair users.) If hikers want a longer walk, they can continue downstream on the River Trail to Zumwalt Meadow in 1.6 miles or Road's End in 2.7 miles. What's extraordinary about the waterfall is not the cascade itself, but the giant rocky pool into which it falls; it's at least 50 feet wide. From where the paved trail ends, at the edge of the pool, the waterfall is perfectly framed by two big conifers. Many beautiful photos have been snapped here.

User Groups: Hikers and wheelchairs. No dogs, horses, or mountain bikes.

Permits: No permits are required. There is a $35 entrance fee per vehicle at Sequoia and Kings Canyon National Parks, good for seven days.

Maps: A Sequoia and Kings Canyon map is available from Tom Harrison Maps. For a topographic map, go to the USGS website to download Sphinx.

Directions: From Fresno, drive east on Highway 180 for 55 miles to the Big Stump Entrance at Kings Canyon National Park. Continue 1.5 miles and turn left, following signs for Kings Canyon and Cedar Grove. Continue 35 miles on Highway 180 to the sign for Roaring River Falls and the River Trail, three miles past Cedar Grove Village. The trailhead is on the right side of the road.

Contact: Sequoia and Kings Canyon National Parks, Three Rivers, 559/565-3341 or 559/565-4307, www.nps.gov/seki.

35 ZUMWALT MEADOW LOOP

2.0 mi/1.0 hr 1 9

off Highway 180 in the Cedar Grove area of Kings Canyon National Park

Map 11.3, page 561 BEST

What's the prettiest easy hike in Kings Canyon National Park? The Zumwalt Meadow Loop Trail wins hands down. A scenic two-mile walk along the South Fork Kings River, the Zumwalt Meadow Loop is a delight for hikers of all abilities. Many people bring their fishing rods along to try their luck in the river, but for most, the hiking is better than the fishing. From the parking area, walk downstream along the river to an old suspension footbridge, cross it, and walk back upstream. The loop begins at an obvious fork, and you can hike it in either direction. The south side traverses a boulder field of jumbled rocks that have tumbled down from the Grand Sentinel (elevation 8,504 feet). The north side cuts through a thick, waist-high fern forest and follows a wooden walkway over a marsh. Views of 8,717-foot North Dome are awe inspiring. Trees, meadow, rock, stream, river, canyon walls—Zumwalt Meadow Trail has it all.

User Groups: Hikers only. No dogs, horses, or mountain bikes. No wheelchair facilities.

Permits: No permits are required. There is a $35 entrance fee per vehicle at Sequoia and Kings Canyon National Parks, good for seven days.

Maps: A Sequoia and Kings Canyon map is available from Tom Harrison Maps. For a topographic map, go to the USGS website to download Cedar Grove.

Directions: From Fresno, drive east on Highway 180 for 55 miles to the Big Stump Entrance at Kings Canyon National Park. Continue 1.5 miles and turn left, following signs for Kings Canyon and Cedar Grove. Continue 36 miles on Highway 180 to the parking area for Zumwalt Meadow, on the right side of the road.

Contact: Sequoia and Kings Canyon National Parks, Three Rivers, 559/565-3341 or 559/565-4307, www.nps.gov/seki.

36 MIST FALLS

9.2 mi/5.0 hr 2 9

off Highway 180 in the Cedar Grove area of Kings Canyon National Park

Map 11.3, page 561

The Mist Falls Trail is probably the most well-used pathway in Kings Canyon National Park, with good reason. It's a stellar 4.6-mile walk to an impressive cascade on the South Fork Kings River, with only a 650-foot gain in elevation along the way. Many backpackers use this trail to access Paradise Valley and points beyond, while most day hikers turn around at Mist Falls. The first two miles are a flat walk up the Kings River Valley, with canyon walls towering above you on both sides. You spend a lot of time craning your neck, looking up at the high canyon rims, from which springtime waterfalls cascade down. You're in a dry, open forest much of the time.

At two miles, you'll reach a trail junction. Bear left, then start to climb over granite. The farther you go, the more expansive the views become; make sure you keep turning around so you can take in the whole panorama. At four miles, the river starts to look more waterfall-like, with crashing pools and rocky granite slides becoming increasingly vertical. A quarter-mile later you reach Mist Falls, which fans out over a 45-foot wide granite ledge and crashes into a boulder-lined pool. It creates a tremendous spray and mist in early summer, and mellows out as the season progresses. Take a look at the falls, then walk back down the trail 0.2 mile to the obvious, immense slab of granite you just passed. This is a favorite spot to have lunch, with its wide-open view of 10,007-foot Avalanche Peak. Look carefully and you can pick out the stone face of The Sphinx.

There are two ways to beat the crowds on this path. First, start early in the morning. Second, hike part of the route on an alternate trail on the river's south side. This trail travels from the Road's End parking lot to the Bailey Bridge at the trail intersection mentioned above. If you get an early start, save this alternate route for the return trip. By then, the day hikers will be out in full force.

User Groups: Hikers and horses. No dogs or mountain bikes. No wheelchair facilities.

Permits: No permits are required. There is a $35 entrance fee per vehicle at Sequoia and Kings Canyon National Parks, good for seven days.

Maps: A Sequoia and Kings Canyon map is available from Tom Harrison Maps. For a topographic map, go to the USGS website to download Sphinx.

Directions: From Fresno, drive east on Highway 180 for 55 miles to the Big Stump Entrance at Kings Canyon National Park. Continue 1.5 miles and turn left, following signs for Kings Canyon and Cedar Grove. Continue 38 miles on Highway 180 to Road's End, six miles past Cedar Grove Village. The trailhead is at the east end of the parking lot, near the wilderness ranger station.

Contact: Sequoia and Kings Canyon National Parks, Three Rivers, 559/565-3341 or 559/565-4307, www.nps.gov/seki.

37 COPPER CREEK TRAIL

21.0 mi/3-4 days 5 9

off Highway 180 in the Cedar Grove area of Kings Canyon National Park

Map 11.3, page 561

The Copper Creek trailhead is at 5,000 feet, and Granite Lake is at 9,972 feet, so it's not hard to do the math. If you're up for a backpacking trip with a 5,000-foot elevation gain over 10 miles, the Granite Lake Basin is your ticket to happiness. But keep in mind that the route can be hot and dry as it switchbacks up manzanita-covered slopes; this trail is considered one of the most strenuous in the Cedar Grove area. Your first night's camp is at Lower Tent Meadow, four miles in and at 7,800 feet. After that, things start to get really good. With Mount Hutchings looming over your left shoulder, the second day's six miles will go easier, bringing you to rocky, jewel-like Granite Lake in only a few hours. You must have a backpacking stove for camping by the lake or anywhere above 10,000 feet.

User Groups: Hikers and horses. No dogs or mountain bikes. No wheelchair facilities.

Permits: There is a $35 entrance fee per vehicle at Sequoia and Kings Canyon National Parks, good for seven days. Wilderness permits are required for overnight stays. They are available on a first-come, first-served basis at the wilderness permit station at Roads End or the Kings Canyon Visitors Center. For advanced wilderness permits or information on trail conditions, go to www.nps.gov/seki. Trailhead quotas are in effect from May to September.

Maps: A Sequoia and Kings Canyon map is available from Tom Harrison Maps. For a topographic map, go to the USGS website to download Sphinx.

Directions: From Fresno, drive east on Highway 180 for 55 miles to the Big Stump Entrance at Kings Canyon National Park. Continue 1.5 miles and turn left, following signs for Kings Canyon and Cedar Grove. Continue 38 miles on Highway 180 to Road's End, six miles past Cedar Grove Village. The trail begins at the long-term parking area.

Contact: Sequoia and Kings Canyon National Parks, Three Rivers, 559/565-3341 or 559/565-4307, www.nps.gov/seki.

38 REDWOOD CANYON

4.0 mi/2.0 hr 2 10

southeast of the Grant Grove area of Kings Canyon National Park

Map 11.3, page 561 BEST

Several loop trips are possible in the Redwood Mountain area of Kings Canyon National Park, but one of the prettiest and simplest trips is just an out-and-back walk on Redwood Canyon Trail, paralleling Redwood Creek. The beauty begins before you even start walking; on the last mile of the drive to the trailhead, the dirt access road winds through giant sequoias that are so close, you can reach out your car window and touch them. The trail leads downhill from the parking area, and in just over 0.3 mile, you reach a junction and follow Redwood Creek Trail to the right. You'll find that this sequoia grove is far denser than many. Because they are situated by Redwood Creek, the sequoias grow amid a thriving background of dogwoods, firs, ceanothus, and mountain misery. Though the standing sequoias are impressive, some of the fallen ones are really amazing, because you get a close-up look at their immense size. Make sure you hike the full two miles to the stream crossing of Redwood Creek. Some of the best tree specimens are found there, near the junction with Sugar Bowl Loop Trail. The return trip is all uphill but easier than you'd expect.

User Groups: Hikers only. No dogs, horses, or mountain bikes. No wheelchair facilities.

Permits: No permits are required. There is a $35 entrance fee per vehicle at Sequoia and Kings Canyon National Parks, good for seven days.

Maps: A Sequoia and Kings Canyon map is available from Tom Harrison Maps. For a topographic map, go to the USGS website to download General Grant Grove.

Directions: From Fresno, drive east on Highway 180 for 55 miles to the Big Stump Entrance at Kings Canyon National Park. Continue 1.5 miles and turn right on the Generals Highway, heading for Sequoia National Park. Drive approximately three miles on the Generals Highway to Quail Flat, signed for Hume Lake to the left, and turn right on the dirt road to Redwood Saddle. Drive 1.5 miles and park in the parking lot. Take the trail signed for the Hart Tree and Redwood Canyon.

Contact: Sequoia and Kings Canyon National Parks, Three Rivers, 559/565-3341 or 559/565-4307, www.nps.gov/seki.

39 REDWOOD MOUNTAIN LOOP

10.0 mi/5.0 hr 3 10

southeast of the Grant Grove area of Kings Canyon National Park

Map 11.3, page 561

If you have most of a day to hike in the Redwood Mountain area of Kings Canyon National Park, you're in luck. This is one of the best day hikes in all of Kings Canyon. The Redwood Mountain Loop combines the best highlights of the area into one long trail, on which you'll wander in near solitude among the giant sequoias. If the paved, crowded trails to the General Grant Tree and the General

Sherman Tree turn you off, this trail will turn you on. Start by hiking on the signed Burnt Grove/Sugar Bowl Loop Trail, which leads uphill from the parking lot. It's one mile to Burnt Grove and 2.5 miles to Sugar Bowl Grove; both are very dense stands of sequoias. Beyond the groves you descend for two miles to intersect with Redwood Canyon Trail. Head downhill and cross Redwood Creek, then proceed to the Fallen Goliath, a mammoth downed tree. One mile farther, you reach the Hart Tree, the largest tree in this area and a real show-stopper. In the final three miles, you get to walk through the Tunnel Log, a hollowed sequoia, and pass by pretty Hart Meadow. Note: If you tire out halfway through this loop, you can always follow the Redwood Canyon Trail uphill back to the start, cutting three miles off your round-trip.

User Groups: Hikers only. No dogs, horses, or mountain bikes. No wheelchair facilities.

Permits: No permits are required. There is a $35 entrance fee per vehicle at Sequoia and Kings Canyon National Parks, good for seven days.

Maps: A Sequoia and Kings Canyon map is available from Tom Harrison Maps. For a topographic map, go to the USGS website to download General Grant Grove.

Directions: From Fresno, drive east on Highway 180 for 55 miles to the Big Stump Entrance at Kings Canyon National Park. Continue 1.5 miles and turn right on the Generals Highway, heading for Sequoia National Park. Drive approximately three miles on the Generals Highway to Quail Flat, signed for Hume Lake to the left, and turn right on the dirt road to Redwood Saddle. Drive 1.5 miles and park in the parking lot. Take the trail signed as Burnt Grove/Sugar Bowl Loop.

Contact: Sequoia and Kings Canyon National Parks, Three Rivers, 559/565-3341 or 559/565-4307, www.nps.gov/seki.

40 BUENA VISTA PEAK

2.0 mi/1.0 hr

southeast of the Grant Grove area of Kings Canyon National Park

Map 11.3, page 561

Forget driving to the Kings Canyon Overlook, because just across the road is a trailhead with an easy walk and even better views, plus a chance at a private picnic spot. Buena Vista Peak is not a summit but a rocky dome, peaking at 7,603 feet, and it is one of the highest points west of Generals Highway. It offers far-reaching views of what looks like a million conifers at your feet and the hazy foothills to the southwest. But the best vistas are to the east of the snowcapped peaks of the John Muir and Monarch Wildernesses. An easy half-hour walk takes you up the back side of the dome, passing through pine and fir forest, manzanita, and sage, and walking by some interesting rock formations. Don't miss the giant boulder sculptures in the trail's first 0.25 mile. At the top of Buena Vista Peak, you can wander all around the spacious granite summit, enjoying different perspectives on the vista, before heading back to the parking lot. It's downhill all the way.

User Groups: Hikers only. No dogs, horses, or mountain bikes. No wheelchair facilities.

Permits: No permits are required. There is a $35 entrance fee per vehicle at Sequoia and Kings Canyon National Parks, good for seven days.

Maps: A Sequoia and Kings Canyon map is available from Tom Harrison Maps. For a topographic map, go to the USGS website to download General Grant Grove.

Directions: From Fresno, drive east on Highway 180 for 55 miles to the Big Stump Entrance at Kings Canyon National Park. Continue 1.5 miles and turn right on the Generals Highway, heading for Sequoia National Park. Drive approximately five miles on the Generals Highway to the Buena Vista trailhead on the right, just across the road and slightly beyond the large pullout for the Kings Canyon Overlook, on the left.

Contact: Sequoia and Kings Canyon National Parks, Three Rivers, 559/565-3341 or 559/565-4307, www.nps.gov/seki.

41 WEAVER LAKE

6.2 mi/3.0 hr or 2 days 2 9

in the Jennie Lakes Wilderness

Map 11.3, page 561

Tucked into a corner just outside the border of Kings Canyon and Sequoia National Parks, the Jennie Lakes Wilderness is a 10,500-acre wilderness area that is often overlooked by park visitors. It offers much of the same scenery as the national parks, with beautiful lakes, meadows, forests, and streams, but without all the fanfare and crowds. Weaver Lake is the easiest-to-reach destination in the wilderness, and it makes a perfect family backpacking trip or an equally nice day hike. The trail is well signed and passes through a mix of fir forest and meadows. At 1.7 miles, take the left fork for Weaver Lake, climbing uphill to the lake's basin. You'll spy the shelflike slabs of Shell Mountain peeking out above the trees. At 8,700 feet in elevation, shallow but pretty Weaver Lake is set at the base of Shell Mountain's high, rounded ridge. You can try your luck fishing, or just find a lakeside seat and gaze at the view. On warm days, the brave go swimming.

Note: The road to Big Meadows is usually the last road to open in the area after snowmelt. If you're planning an early season trip, call to check on road and trail conditions.

User Groups: Hikers, dogs, and horses. No mountain bikes. No wheelchair facilities.

Permits: A free campfire permit is required for overnight stays and is available from the Hume Lake Ranger Station. There is a $35 entrance fee per vehicle at Sequoia and Kings Canyon National Parks, good for seven days in both the National Forest and the National Parks.

Maps: A Jennie Lakes Wilderness map is available from the U.S. Forest Service. A map of Sequoia and Kings Canyon is available from

Buena Vista Peak

Tom Harrison Maps. For a topographic map, go to the USGS website to download Muir Grove.
Directions: From Fresno, drive east on Highway 180 for 55 miles to the Big Stump Entrance at Kings Canyon National Park. Continue 1.5 miles and turn right on the Generals Highway, heading for Sequoia National Park. Drive seven miles and turn left on Forest Road 14S11, at the sign for Big Meadows and Horse Corral. Drive three miles to the Big Meadows trailhead.
Contact: Giant Sequoia National Monument/Sequoia National Forest, Hume Lake Ranger District, Dunlap, 559/338-2251, www.fs.usda.gov/sequoia.

42 JENNIE ELLIS LAKE

12.0 mi/6.0 hr or 2 days 3 10

in the Jennie Lakes Wilderness

Map 11.3, page 561

This trail into the Jennie Lakes Wilderness offers more of a challenge than the route to Weaver Lake, climbing 1,500 feet over six miles with some short, steep pitches. The rewards are also greater, because Jennie Ellis Lake is a beauty and receives fewer visitors than Weaver Lake. The trail is the same as the Weaver Lake Trail for 1.7 miles, but at the fork, you bear right for Jennie Ellis Lake. The trail climbs and dips through fir, pine, and manzanita forest, then crosses Poop Out Pass at 4.7 miles, the highest point on this trip. At nearly six miles, you reach the outlet stream for Jennie Ellis Lake. Follow the short spur trail to the lake, set at 9,000 feet. With a white granite backdrop and some sparse trees, the shoreline looks austere and barren, but beautiful just the same. Campsites are found around the lake, and catching fish for dinner is a fair possibility. If you only came for the day, find a comfortable spot to sit and admire the scenery before you head back.

Note: There is a somewhat shorter trail to reach Jennie Ellis Lake from Stony Creek Campground (10 miles round-trip instead of 12), but shorter doesn't necessarily mean easier. The shorter trail requires a 2,500-foot climb over the first 3.5 miles to Poop Out Pass, with several noticeably steep pitches along the way. At the pass, the two trails join and are one and the same on the final stretch to the lake.
User Groups: Hikers, dogs, and horses. No mountain bikes. No wheelchair facilities.
Permits: A free campfire permit is required for overnight stays and is available from the Hume Lake Ranger Station. There is a $35 entrance fee per vehicle at Sequoia and Kings Canyon National Parks, good for seven days in both the National Forest and the National Parks.
Maps: A Jennie Lakes Wilderness map is available from the U.S. Forest Service. A map of Sequoia and Kings Canyon is available from Tom Harrison Maps. For a topographic map, go to the USGS website to download Muir Grove.
Directions: From Fresno, drive east on Highway 180 for 55 miles to the Big Stump Entrance at Kings Canyon National Park. Continue 1.5 miles and turn right on the Generals Highway, heading for Sequoia National Park. Drive seven miles and turn left on Forest Road 14S11, at the sign for Big Meadows and Horse Corral. Drive three miles to the Big Meadows trailhead.
Contact: Giant Sequoia National Monument/Sequoia National Forest, Hume Lake Ranger District, Dunlap, 559/338-2251, www.fs.usda.gov/sequoia.

43 MITCHELL PEAK

5.2 mi/3.0 hr 4 9

in the Jennie Lakes Wilderness

Map 11.3, page 561

If you have the legs for a 2,000-foot climb over 2.6 miles, you can stand atop the summit of Mitchell Peak, the highest point in the Jennie Lakes Wilderness, at 10,365 feet in elevation. The peak used to have a fire lookout tower on top of it, but the Forest Service stopped using it and burned it down. What remains is the fabulous view, one of the best in this area. It's a one-mile climb from the trailhead to Marvin Pass and the boundary of the Jennie Lakes Wilderness. Bear left (east) and climb some more. At 1.6 miles, you reach the next junction, signed for Mitchell Peak. Head left (north), and in one more mile, you'll make the brief climb to Mitchell's summit, which straddles the border of Kings Canyon National Park. From your rocky perch, you can look out on the Great Western Divide and the Silliman Crest. It's an exemplary spot to catch your breath.

User Groups: Hikers, dogs, and horses. No mountain bikes. No wheelchair facilities.

Permits: A free campfire permit is required for overnight stays and is available from the Hume Lake Ranger Station. There is a $35 entrance fee per vehicle at Sequoia and Kings Canyon National Parks, good for seven days in both the National Forest and the National Parks.

Maps: A Jennie Lakes Wilderness map is available from the U.S. Forest Service. A map of Sequoia and Kings Canyon is available from Tom Harrison Maps. For a topographic map, go to the USGS website to download Muir Grove.

Directions: From Fresno, drive east on Highway 180 for 55 miles to the Big Stump Entrance at Kings Canyon National Park. Continue 1.5 miles and turn right on the Generals Highway, heading for Sequoia National Park. Drive seven miles and turn left on Forest Road 14S11, at the sign for Big Meadow and Horse Corral. Drive four miles to the Big Meadow Campground and continue six more miles to Horse Corral Meadow. Turn right on Forest Road 13S12 and drive 2.8 miles to the Marvin Pass trailhead.

Contact: Giant Sequoia National Monument/Sequoia National Forest, Hume Lake Ranger District, Dunlap, 559/338-2251, www.fs.usda.gov/sequoia.

44 BIG BALDY

4.6 mi/2.5 hr

southeast of the Grant Grove area of Kings Canyon National Park

Map 11.3, page 561

The trip to Big Baldy comes with a million views and a little workout besides. Views? We're talking Redwood Canyon, Redwood Mountain, Buena Vista Peak, Little Baldy, Buck Rock, and the Great Western Divide. A little workout? You've got to climb 1,000 feet, but it's nicely spread out over two miles. The trail alternates between thick forest cover and open granite areas as it winds along the rim of Redwood Canyon. In the forested stretches, we were amazed at how many birds were singing in the tall firs and cedars. The trail's initial vistas are to the west, but they keep changing and getting more interesting all the way to Big Baldy's 8,209-foot summit, where your view opens up to 360 degrees. Here you get your first wide-open views of the high Sierra peaks and the Great Western Divide to the east. This trail is so fun and rewarding, with so little suffering involved, that you may feel like you're getting away with something. A bonus: Because the first mile of trail faces to the west, this is a great area for watching the sunset. Big Baldy Trail is also ideal for snowshoeing in the winter.

User Groups: Hikers only. No dogs, horses, or mountain bikes. No wheelchair facilities.

Permits: No permits are required. There is a $35 entrance fee per vehicle at Sequoia and Kings Canyon National Parks, good for seven days.

Maps: A Sequoia and Kings Canyon map is available from Tom Harrison Maps. For a topographic map, go to the USGS website to download Muir Grove.

Directions: From Fresno, drive east on Highway 180 for 55 miles to the Big Stump Entrance at Kings Canyon National Park. Continue 1.5 miles and turn right on the Generals Highway, heading for Sequoia National Park. Drive approximately 6.5 miles on the Generals Highway to the Big Baldy trailhead, on the right, shortly before the turnoff for Big Meadows, on the left.

Contact: Sequoia and Kings Canyon National Parks, Three Rivers, 559/565-3341 or 559/565-4307, www.nps.gov/seki.

45 MUIR GROVE

4.0 mi/2.0 hr

northwest of the Lodgepole area of Sequoia National Park

Map 11.3, page 561

Few people hike this trail unless they are staying at Dorst Campground, so you have a lot better chance of seeing giant sequoias in solitude in the Muir Grove than at many places in the park. After crossing a wooden footbridge, the trail enters a mixed forest of red fir, white fir, sugar pines, and incense cedars. In early summer, you can count the many varieties of wildflowers along the trail, especially where you cross tiny streams. The trail heads west and curves around a deeply carved canyon at one mile out. Just off the trail to your right is a bare granite slab with an inspiring westward view. The trail undulates, never climbing or dropping much, making this an easy and pleasant stroll. At 1.9 miles, you reach the Muir Grove, a small, pristine grove of huge sequoias. The first one you come to on your left is a doozy. The grove is made even more enchanting by the thick undergrowth of blue and purple lupine blooming amid the trees in early summer.

User Groups: Hikers only. No dogs, horses, or mountain bikes. No wheelchair facilities.

Permits: No permits are required. There is a $35 entrance fee per vehicle at Sequoia and Kings Canyon National Parks, good for seven days.

Maps: A Sequoia and Kings Canyon map is available from Tom Harrison Maps. For a topographic map, go to the USGS website to download Muir Grove.

Directions: From Fresno, drive east on Highway 180 for 55 miles to the Big Stump Entrance at Kings Canyon National Park. Continue 1.5 miles and turn right on the Generals Highway, heading for Sequoia National Park. Drive approximately 17 miles on the Generals Highway to the right turnoff for Dorst Campground. Turn right and drive through the campground to the amphitheater parking lot. Park there; the trail begins at a footbridge between the amphitheater parking lot and the group campground.

Contact: Sequoia and Kings Canyon National Parks, Three Rivers, 559/565-3341 or 559/565-4307, www.nps.gov/seki.

46 LITTLE BALDY

3.5 mi/2.0 hr

2 9

northwest of the Lodgepole area of Sequoia National Park

Map 11.3, page 561

Little Baldy, Big Baldy, Buena Vista Peak. Along this stretch of the Generals Highway, there are so many peak trails that offer far-reaching views, it's hard to choose where to start. Little Baldy Trail is a great choice. It's a little more challenging than the Buena Vista Peak Trail, but it's shorter than Big Baldy Trail, and it offers eye-popping drama for remarkably little effort. Some claim that Little Baldy's view of the Silliman Crest, the Great Western Divide, Castle Rocks, Moro Rock, the Kaweah River Canyon, and the San Joaquin foothills is the best panorama in the park.

To see for yourself, set out from the trailhead, climbing through long, tree-shaded switchbacks, heading first north, then south. Check out the unusual view of Big Baldy off to your left (far across the highway) as you climb. After 1.2 miles, the trail leaves the forest and its many wildflowers, and your views start to open up. Hike along Little Baldy's ridgeline and make the final steep summit ascent. The trail gets a little hard to discern as you near Little Baldy's wide, bare summit, but just wander around until you find the highest spot with the best view. Take a seat—you'll want to stay a while.

Note: Be sure to pick a clear day for this hike. In summer, your best bet is to hike the trail early in the morning, before the Central Valley haze rises to the mountains.

User Groups: Hikers only. No dogs, horses, or mountain bikes. No wheelchair facilities.

Permits: No permits are required. There is a $35 entrance fee per vehicle at Sequoia and Kings Canyon National Parks, good for seven days.

Maps: A Sequoia and Kings Canyon map is available from Tom Harrison Maps. For topographic maps, go to the USGS website to download Muir Grove and Giant Forest.

Directions: From Fresno, drive east on Highway 180 for 55 miles to the Big Stump Entrance at Kings Canyon National Park. Continue 1.5 miles and turn right on the Generals Highway, heading for Sequoia National Park. Drive approximately 18 miles on the Generals Highway to the Little Baldy trailhead, on the left, a mile beyond the turnoff for Dorst Campground.

Contact: Sequoia and Kings Canyon National Parks, Three Rivers, 559/565-3341 or 559/565-4307, www.nps.gov/seki.

47 THE LAKES TRAIL

13.0 mi/2-3 days

off the Generals Highway in the Wolverton area of Sequoia National Park

Map 11.3, page 561

The Wolverton trailhead is at 7,200 feet, which gives you a boost at the start for this trip into the high country. The Lakes Trail is the most popular backpacking trip in Sequoia National Park, and it's easy to see why. Wide-open views and dramatic granite walls are standard fare as you hike. Part of the route is on a loop, with one side of the loop traveling to the Watchtower—a 1,600-foot-tall granite cliff that offers incredible vistas of Tokopah Valley and beyond. The trailside scenery begins in red fir forest, then enters polished granite country, and culminates in a rocky basin with three gemlike lakes—Heather, Emerald, and Pear—as well as many sparkling creeks. The total climb to Pear Lake is a mere 2,300 feet, spread out over 6.5 miles. Backpackers take note: You may camp only at Emerald and Pear Lakes, and no campfires are allowed.

Note: The Watchtower Trail usually isn't open until midsummer. When it is closed, you must take the alternate Hump Trail, which is not as scenic. If you're planning a trip for early in the year, check with the park to be sure Watchtower Trail is open.

User Groups: Hikers only. No dogs, horses, or mountain bikes. No wheelchair facilities.

Permits: There is a $35 entrance fee per vehicle at Sequoia and Kings Canyon National Parks, good for seven days. Wilderness permits are required for overnight stays. They are available on a first-come, first-served basis at the Lodgepole Visitors Center. For advanced wilderness permits or information on trail conditions, go to www.nps.gov/seki. Trailhead quotas are in effect from May to September.

Maps: A Sequoia and Kings Canyon map is available from Tom Harrison Maps. For a topographic map, go to the USGS website to download Lodgepole.

Directions: From Fresno, drive east on Highway 180 for 55 miles to the Big Stump Entrance at Kings Canyon National Park. Continue 1.5 miles and turn right on the Generals Highway, heading for Sequoia National Park. Drive approximately 27 miles on the Generals Highway, past the Lodgepole Village turnoff, to the Wolverton turnoff, on the left (east) side of the road. Turn left and drive to the parking area and trailhead.

Contact: Sequoia and Kings Canyon National Parks, Three Rivers, 559/565-3341 or 559/565-4307, www.nps.gov/seki.

48 HEATHER LAKE AND THE WATCHTOWER

9.0 mi/5.0 hr 3 10

off the Generals Highway in the Wolverton area of Sequoia National Park

Map 11.3, page 561

There's no reason that day hikers should be denied the incredible joys of hiking Lakes Trail from the Wolverton area of Sequoia National Park. You don't have to carry a backpack, get a wilderness permit, or have two or more free days to hike the first part of Lakes Trail, which ascends to the top of the 1,600-foot Watchtower (a big chunk of granite) and then continues to rocky Heather Lake. If you're hiking in spring or early summer, call the park first to make sure Watchtower Trail is open. Otherwise you'll have to take the alternate Hump Trail, which is steeper and nowhere near as scenic. The route to the Watchtower is a ledge trail, blasted into hard granite, which creeps along the high rim of Tokopah Valley. Your view is 1,500 feet straight down. You can even see tiny people walking on the path to Tokopah Falls. It's incredible, although perhaps not a good idea for people who are afraid of heights. Walking up to the Watchtower is plenty exciting, but it's even more so when you reach the other side, where you can look back and see what you were walking on. Just 0.75 mile farther and you're at Heather Lake, which is designated for day use only, so it has no campsites. It has a steep granite backdrop and a few rocky ledges to sit on. Too many people here when you arrive? No big deal. It's only another 0.5 mile to even prettier Emerald Lake, and the trail is nearly level. After a rest, you get to head back and hike the Watchtower route all over again.

User Groups: Hikers only. No dogs, horses, or mountain bikes. No wheelchair facilities.

Permits: No permits are required. There is a $35 entrance fee per vehicle at Sequoia and Kings Canyon National Parks, good for seven days.

Maps: A Sequoia and Kings Canyon map is available from Tom Harrison Maps. For a topographic map, go to the USGS website to download Lodgepole.

Directions: From Fresno, drive east on Highway 180 for 55 miles to the Big Stump Entrance at Kings Canyon National Park. Continue 1.5 miles and turn right on the Generals Highway, heading for Sequoia National Park. Drive approximately 27 miles on the Generals Highway, past the Lodgepole Village turnoff, to the Wolverton turnoff on the left (east) side of the road. Turn left and drive to the parking area and trailhead.

Contact: Sequoia and Kings Canyon National Parks, Three Rivers, 559/565-3341 or 559/565-4307, www.nps.gov/seki.

49 ALTA PEAK

13.0 mi/1-2 days 5 10

off the Generals Highway in the Wolverton area of Sequoia National Park

Map 11.3, page 561 **BEST**

You say you like heights? You like vistas? Here's your trail, a 4,000-foot climb to the top of Alta Peak, an 11,204-foot summit in the Alta Country. Alta Peak and Mount Whitney are the only major summits in Sequoia National Park that have established trails, but both of them are still butt-kickers to reach. The trail to Alta Peak and Alta Meadow starts out the same as the Lakes Trail (from the Wolverton parking area), then it heads south (right) to Panther Gap, at 1.8 miles. After climbing through the forest to Panther Gap (at 8,450 feet), you get your first set of eye-popping views—of the Middle Fork Kaweah River and the Great Western Divide. Continue on the Alta Trail to Mehrten Meadow (at 3.9 miles), a popular camping spot, then reach a junction where you can go left for Alta Peak or right to Alta Meadow. You'll want to take both spurs if you have the time and energy. If you're exhausted, just walk to Alta Meadow, with its flower-filled grasses and exquisite mountain views, a flat one mile away. Alta Peak is two miles away via the left fork, with a 2,000-foot climb. These two miles are considered one of the toughest stretches of trail in Sequoia National Park due to the brutal grade and the 10,000-plus foot elevation here above tree line. The summit is at 11,204 feet, and, of course, it offers a complete panorama. Even Mount Whitney and the Coast Range are visible on a clear day.

User Groups: Hikers only. No dogs, horses, or mountain bikes. No wheelchair facilities.

Permits: There is a $35 entrance fee per vehicle at Sequoia and Kings Canyon National Parks, good for seven days. Wilderness permits are required for overnight stays. They are available on a first-come, first-served basis at the Lodgepole Visitors Center. For advanced wilderness permits or information on trail conditions, go to www.nps.gov/seki. Trailhead quotas are in effect from May to September.

Maps: A Sequoia and Kings Canyon map is available from Tom Harrison Maps. For a topographic map, go to the USGS website to download Lodgepole.

Directions: From Fresno, drive east on Highway 180 for 55 miles to the Big Stump Entrance at Kings Canyon National Park. Continue 1.5 miles and turn right on the Generals Highway, heading for Sequoia National Park. Drive approximately 27 miles on the Generals Highway, past the Lodgepole Village turnoff, to the Wolverton turnoff, on the left (east) side of the road. Turn left and drive to the parking area and trailhead.

Contact: Sequoia and Kings Canyon National Parks, Three Rivers, 559/565-3341 or 559/565-4307, www.nps.gov/seki.

50 PANTHER GAP LOOP

6.0 mi/3.5 hr 3 8

off the Generals Highway in the Wolverton area of Sequoia National Park

Map 11.3, page 561

If you're not up for the marathon trip to Alta Peak, you can still get a taste of the high country on this loop from the Wolverton trailhead. Start hiking on the Lakes Trail from the east end of the Wolverton parking lot, and at 1.8 miles, bear right on the Alta Trail to parallel Wolverton Creek, following it to Panther Gap. Here, at 8,450 feet, you get an inspiring vista of the Middle Fork Kaweah River and the Great Western Divide. Check out 9,081-foot Castle Rocks, an obvious landmark. From the gap, turn right (west) and follow the Alta Trail to Panther Peak and Panther Meadow, then on to Red Fir Meadow. Finally, at 4.6 miles, bear right and complete the loop by descending to Long Meadow and then edging along its east side to return to the parking lot. By the way, don't get any smart ideas about hiking this loop in the opposite direction—it's a much steeper climb.

User Groups: Hikers and horses. No dogs or mountain bikes. No wheelchair facilities.

Permits: No permits are required. There is a $35 entrance fee per vehicle at Sequoia and Kings Canyon National Parks, good for seven days.

Maps: A Sequoia and Kings Canyon map is available from Tom Harrison Maps. For a topographic map, go to the USGS website to download Lodgepole.

Directions: From Fresno, drive east on Highway 180 for 55 miles to the Big Stump Entrance at Kings Canyon National Park. Continue 1.5 miles and turn right on the Generals Highway, heading for Sequoia National Park. Drive approximately 27 miles on the Generals Highway, past the Lodgepole Village turnoff, to the Wolverton turnoff, on the left (east) side of the road. Turn left and drive to the parking area and trailhead.

Contact: Sequoia and Kings Canyon National Parks, Three Rivers, 559/565-3341 or 559/565-4307, www.nps.gov/seki.

51 TOKOPAH FALLS

3.6 mi/2.0 hr 1 10

off the Generals Highway in the Giant Forest area of Sequoia National Park

Map 11.3, page 561 BEST

This is unquestionably the best waterfall day hike in Sequoia and Kings Canyon National Parks, leading to 1,200-foot-high Tokopah Falls. It's also a perfect family hike, easy on the feet and even easier on the eyes. The scenery is spectacular the whole way, from the up-close looks at wildflowers and granite boulders to the more distant views of the Watchtower, a 1,600-foot glacially carved cliff on the south side of Tokopah Valley. Then there's the valley itself, with Tokopah Falls pouring down the smooth back curve of its U shape. Because the trail begins by the three huge Lodgepole Campgrounds, it sees a lot of foot traffic. Your best bet is to start early in the morning. Another unusual feature of the trail? Hikers see more yellow-bellied marmots on the Tokopah Falls route than anywhere else in the two parks. We saw at least 40 of the cute little blond guys sunning themselves on rocks. If you're lucky, one of them will whistle at you as you walk by.

User Groups: Hikers and horses. No dogs or mountain bikes. No wheelchair facilities.

Permits: No permits are required. There is a $35 entrance fee per vehicle at Sequoia and Kings Canyon National Parks, good for seven days.

Maps: A Sequoia and Kings Canyon map is available from Tom Harrison Maps. For a topographic map, go to the USGS website to download Lodgepole.

Directions: From Fresno, drive east on Highway 180 for 55 miles to the Big Stump Entrance at Kings Canyon National Park. Continue 1.5 miles and turn right on the Generals Highway, heading for Sequoia National Park. Drive approximately 25 miles on the Generals Highway to the Lodgepole Campground turnoff, then drive 0.75 mile to the Log Bridge area of Lodgepole Camp. Park in the large lot just before the bridge over the Marble Fork Kaweah River, and walk 150 yards to the trailhead, which is just after you cross the bridge.

Contact: Sequoia and Kings Canyon National Parks, Three Rivers, 559/565-3341 or 559/565-4307, www.nps.gov/seki.

52 TWIN LAKES

13.6 mi/1-2 days 3 9

off the Generals Highway in the Giant Forest area of Sequoia National Park

Map 11.3, page 561

From the Lodgepole Campground trailhead (at 6,740 feet), the Twin Lakes are a 2,800-foot elevation gain and 6.8 miles away, making this a moderate backpacking trip or a long, strenuous day hike. It's a classic Sequoia National Park trip; one that is heavily traveled each summer. The terrain is an interesting mix of dense conifer forests, glacial moraine, and open meadows. From the trailhead, you climb past Wolverton's

Tokopah Falls

Rock to Cahoon Meadow at three miles, 0.5 mile beyond a crossing of Silliman Creek. You then continue to Cahoon Gap at 4.2 miles, cross over Clover Creek at five miles (campsites are found along the creek), bear right at the J. O. Pass Trail junction at 5.5 miles, and reach the Twin Lakes at 6.8 miles. The trail leads you directly to the larger Twin Lake; the smaller one is reached by following a spur. Both are shallow and have forested banks; some hikers try their luck fishing in the larger lake. Backpackers spending the night at Twin Lakes can hike farther the next day—over rocky Silliman Pass (at 10,100 feet) to the less-visited Ranger Lakes, three miles farther. Note: Campfires are not allowed at Twin Lakes.

User Groups: Hikers and horses. No dogs or mountain bikes. No wheelchair facilities.

Permits: There is a $35 entrance fee per vehicle at Sequoia and Kings Canyon National Parks, good for seven days. Wilderness permits are required for overnight stays. They are available on a first-come, first-served basis at the Lodgepole Visitors Center. For advanced wilderness permits or information on trail conditions, go to www.nps.gov/seki. Trailhead quotas are in effect from May to September.

Maps: A Sequoia and Kings Canyon map is available from Tom Harrison Maps. For a topographic map, go to the USGS website to download Lodgepole.

Directions: From Fresno, drive east on Highway 180 for 55 miles to the Big Stump Entrance at Kings Canyon National Park. Continue 1.5 miles and turn right on the Generals Highway, heading for Sequoia National Park. Drive approximately 25 miles on the Generals Highway to the Lodgepole Campground turnoff, and then drive 0.75 mile to the Log Bridge area of Lodgepole Camp. The Twin Lakes trailhead is just beyond the Tokopah Falls trailhead and the bridge over the Marble Fork Kaweah River.

Contact: Sequoia and Kings Canyon National Parks, Three Rivers, 559/565-3341 or 559/565-4307, www.nps.gov/seki.

53 CONGRESS TRAIL LOOP

2.9 mi/1.5 hr 1 9

off the Generals Highway in the Giant Forest area of Sequoia National Park

Map 11.3, page 561 **BEST**

The Congress Trail, a two-mile loop that starts (and ends) at the General Sherman Tree, is a much-traveled route through the Giant Forest's prize grove of sequoias. The General Sherman sees the greatest number of visitors, because it is recognized as the largest living thing in the world (not by height, but by volume). After you leave its side and start on the Congress Trail, the crowds lessen substantially. You'll pass by many huge trees with placards displaying their very patriotic names, like the House and Senate clusters, the McKinley Tree, the Lincoln Tree, and... well, you get the idea. Every single giant sequoia is worth stopping to gape at the wonder of these trees. We rate the Congress Trail as the best level, easy trail for sequoia viewing in the park. Plus, the farther you walk, the more solitude you get. Make sure you pick up an interpretive brochure at the trailhead or at the Lodgepole Visitors Center.

The parking area for the Sherman Tree and the Congress Trail is 0.4 mile from the Sherman Tree for a total mileage of 2.9 miles—two miles for the loop plus the out-and-back to the parking area. (You can't park on the Generals Highway by the Sherman Tree unless your vehicle has a disability license plate. This parking area is now reserved for the Giant Forest shuttle bus and wheelchair users only).

User Groups: Hikers only. No dogs, horses, or mountain bikes. Wheelchair users can access this trail; in some areas they may need assistance.

Permits: No permits are required. There is a $35 entrance fee per vehicle at Sequoia and Kings Canyon National Parks, good for seven days.

Maps: A Sequoia and Kings Canyon map is available from Tom Harrison Maps. For a topographic map, go to the USGS website to download Giant Forest.

Directions: From Fresno, drive east on Highway 180 for 55 miles to the Big Stump Entrance at Kings Canyon National Park. Continue 1.5 miles and turn right on the Generals Highway, heading for Sequoia National Park. Drive approximately 27 miles on the Generals Highway, past Lodgepole Village, to the Wolverton turnoff on the left (east) side of the road. Turn left and drive to the General Sherman Tree parking area. (If you are riding the free Giant Forest shuttle bus, you can disembark right at the Sherman Tree. For details see www.sequoiashuttle.com.)

Contact: Sequoia and Kings Canyon National Parks, Three Rivers, 559/565-3341 or 559/565-4307, www.nps.gov/seki.

54 HAZELWOOD AND HUCKLEBERRY LOOP

4.5 mi/2.0 hr 2 8

off the Generals Highway in the Giant Forest area of Sequoia National Park

Map 11.3, page 561

This hike combines two loop trails in the Giant Forest area for an easy but excellent day hike, passing by many giant sequoias and peaceful grassy meadows. A bonus: These trails are generally less crowded than the other day hikes in the Giant Forest area.

From the Generals Highway, pick up the Hazelwood Nature Trail and take the right side of the loop to join Alta Trail and Huckleberry Meadow Trail Loop. Take Alta Trail for 0.25 mile and bear right on Huckleberry Meadow Trail, climbing a bit for one mile to the site of Squatter's Cabin, one of the oldest structures in Sequoia National Park, dating back to the 1880s. To stay on the loop, turn left by the cabin (don't take the trail signed for The Dead Giant). The trail skirts the edge of Huckleberry Meadow and heads north to Circle Meadow, where giant sequoias line the meadow's edges. There are several junctions, but stay on Huckleberry Meadow Trail. A half-mile farther is a short spur trail on the left heading to the Washington Tree. Follow the spur to see the second-largest tree in the world (after General Sherman)—it's 30 feet in diameter and 246.1 feet tall. The trip finishes out on Alta Trail, where you return to Hazelwood Nature Trail and walk the opposite side of its short loop back to the Generals Highway.

User Groups: Hikers only. No dogs, horses, or mountain bikes. No wheelchair facilities.

Permits: No permits are required. There is a $35 entrance fee per vehicle at Sequoia and Kings Canyon National Parks, good for seven days.

Maps: A Sequoia and Kings Canyon map is available from Tom Harrison Maps. For topographic maps, go to the USGS website to download Giant Forest and Lodgepole.

Directions: From Fresno, drive east on Highway 180 for 55 miles to the Big Stump Entrance at Kings Canyon National Park. Continue 1.5 miles and turn right on the Generals Highway, heading for Sequoia National Park. Drive approximately 30 miles on the Generals Highway, past Lodgepole and Wolverton, to the Giant Forest area of Sequoia National Park. The Hazelwood trailhead is on the south side of the highway, 0.25 mile before you reach the Giant Forest Museum.

Contact: Sequoia and Kings Canyon National Parks, Three Rivers, 559/565-3341 or 559/565-4307, www.nps.gov/seki.

55 HIGH SIERRA TRAIL TO HAMILTON LAKE

30.0 mi/3 days 3 10

off the Generals Highway in the Giant Forest area of Sequoia National Park

Map 11.3, page 561

This is a classic, easy-to-moderate, three-day backpacking trip in the High Sierra, with a two-night stay at Bearpaw Meadow Camp, a shady campground that clings to the edge of a granite gorge. The route follows High Sierra Trail from Crescent Meadow to Eagle View, then continues for 10 nearly level miles along the north rim of the Middle Fork Kaweah River Canyon. It's views, views, views all the way.

After a good night's sleep at Bearpaw Meadow, elevation 7,700 feet (reservations for a wilderness permit are definitely necessary in the summer months), you start out on an eight-mile round-trip day hike to Upper and Lower Hamilton Lake (at 8,300 feet), set in a glacially carved basin at the base of the peaks of the Great Western Divide. On the final day, you hike 11 miles back to Crescent Meadow, once again witnessing 180-degree views from the sunny High Sierra Trail. By the time it's all over and you're back home, your mind is completely blown by all the high-country beauty, and you've shot about a million pictures, none of which can compare to the experience of actually being there.

User Groups: Hikers only. No dogs, horses, or mountain bikes. No wheelchair facilities.

Permits: There is a $35 entrance fee per vehicle at Sequoia and Kings Canyon National Parks, good for seven days. Wilderness permits are required for overnight stays. They are available on a first-come, first-served basis at the Lodgepole Visitors Center. For advanced wilderness permits or information on trail conditions, go to www.nps.gov/seki. Trailhead quotas are in effect from May to September.

Maps: A Sequoia and Kings Canyon map is available from Tom Harrison Maps. For topographic maps, go to the USGS website to download Giant Forest and Lodgepole.

Directions: From Fresno, drive east on Highway 180 for 55 miles to the Big Stump Entrance at Kings Canyon National Park. Continue 1.5 miles and turn right on the Generals Highway, heading for Sequoia National Park. Drive approximately 30 miles on the Generals Highway, past Lodgepole and Wolverton, to the Giant Forest area of Sequoia National Park. Just beyond the museum, turn left on Crescent Meadow Road and drive 3.5 miles to the Crescent Meadow parking area.

Contact: Sequoia and Kings Canyon National Parks, Three Rivers, 559/565-3341 or 559/565-4307, www.nps.gov/seki.

56 HIGH SIERRA TRAIL AND EAGLE VIEW

1.5 mi/1.0 hr 1 10

off the Generals Highway in the Giant Forest area of Sequoia National Park

Map 11.3, page 561

Are you ready to be wowed? From the lower parking lot at Crescent Meadow, follow the trail that leads to the southern edge of Crescent Meadow, and at 0.1 mile, take the right fork that leads up the ridge on High Sierra Trail toward Eagle View. The High Sierra Trail is a popular trans-Sierra route that eventually leads to Mount Whitney, the highest peak in the contiguous United States. On this trip you won't go quite that far, but you will get a taste of the visual delights of this extraordinary trail. In less than 0.5 mile, you'll gain the ridge and start getting wondrous, edge-of-the-world views. Numerous wildflowers line the path, which hugs the edge of this high ridge. At 0.7 mile, you'll reach Eagle View, an unsigned but obvious lookout from which you get a fascinating look at Moro Rock to your right, Castle Rocks straight ahead, and dozens of peaks and ridges of the Western Divide far across the canyon. The vistas are so fine and the trail is so good that you may just want to keep walking all the way to Mount Whitney.

User Groups: Hikers only. No dogs, horses, or mountain bikes. No wheelchair facilities.

Permits: No permits are required. There is a $35 entrance fee per vehicle at Sequoia and Kings Canyon National Parks, good for seven days.

Maps: A Sequoia and Kings Canyon map is available from Tom Harrison Maps. For

High Sierra Trail and Eagle View

topographic maps, go to the USGS website to download Giant Forest and Lodgepole.

Directions: From Fresno, drive east on Highway 180 for 55 miles to the Big Stump Entrance at Kings Canyon National Park. Continue 1.5 miles and turn right on the Generals Highway, heading for Sequoia National Park. Drive approximately 30 miles on the Generals Highway, past Lodgepole and Wolverton, to the Giant Forest area of Sequoia National Park. Just beyond the museum, turn left on Crescent Meadow Road and drive 3.5 miles to the Crescent Meadow parking area.

Contact: Sequoia and Kings Canyon National Parks, Three Rivers, 559/565-3341 or 559/565-4307, www.nps.gov/seki.

57 CRESCENT MEADOW AND THARP'S LOG

1.6 mi/1.0 hr 1 8

off the Generals Highway in the Giant Forest area of Sequoia National Park

Map 11.3, page 561

Crescent Meadow is more than 1.5 miles long and is surrounded by giant sequoias. John Muir called it "the gem of the Sierras." We don't know how Muir would feel about the pavement that lines the trail around this precious meadow, but we hope he'd like this loop hike anyhow. Follow the pavement for 200 yards from the eastern side of the parking lot, and just like that, you're at the southern edge of beautiful Crescent Meadow. Take the right fork and head for Log Meadow and Tharp's Log. Log Meadow is as large and beautiful as Crescent Meadow, and Tharp's Log was the homestead of Hale Tharp, the first white man to enter this forest. He grazed cattle and horses here, and built a modest home inside a fallen, fire-hollowed sequoia. You can look inside Tharp's Log and see his bed, fireplace, dining room table, and the door and windows he fashioned into the log. (Children find this incredibly thrilling.) From Tharp's Log, continue your loop back to Crescent Meadow and around its west side, where you return to the north edge of the parking lot.

User Groups: Hikers and wheelchairs (with assistance). No dogs, horses, or mountain bikes.

Permits: No permits are required. There is a $35 entrance fee per vehicle at Sequoia and Kings Canyon National Parks, good for seven days.

Maps: A Sequoia and Kings Canyon map is available from Tom Harrison Maps. For topographic maps, go to the USGS website to download Giant Forest and Lodgepole.

Directions: From Fresno, drive east on Highway 180 for 55 miles to the Big Stump Entrance at Kings Canyon National Park. Continue 1.5 miles and turn right on the Generals Highway, heading for Sequoia National Park. Drive approximately 30 miles on the Generals Highway, past Lodgepole and Wolverton, to the Giant Forest area of Sequoia National Park. Just beyond the museum, turn left on Crescent Meadow Road and drive 3.5 miles to the Crescent Meadow parking area.

Contact: Sequoia and Kings Canyon National Parks, Three Rivers, 559/565-3341 or 559/565-4307, www.nps.gov/seki.

58 MORO ROCK

0.6 mi/0.5 hr 2 10

off the Generals Highway in the Giant Forest area of Sequoia National Park

Map 11.3, page 561 **BEST**

Just about everybody has heard of Moro Rock, the prominent, pointy granite dome with the top-of-the-world sunset vistas, and if you're visiting the Giant Forest area of Sequoia National Park, well, you just have to hike to the top of it. When you climb those 380 stairs to the dome's summit and check out the view, you realize that unlike many famous attractions, Moro Rock is not overrated. It's as great as everybody says, and maybe even better. If you start your trip from the Moro Rock parking area, it's only 0.3 mile to the top, climbing switchbacks, ramps, and granite stairs the whole way. Railings line the rock-blasted trail to keep you from dropping off the 6,725-foot granite dome. What's the view like? Well, on a clear day, you can see all the way to the Coast Range, 100 miles away. In closer focus is the Middle Fork Kaweah River, the Great Western Divide, Castle Rocks (at 9,180 feet), Triple Divide Peak (at 12,634 feet), Mount Stewart (at 12,205 feet), and on and on. In a word, it's awesome. And even better, you don't get this view just from the top of Moro Rock—you get it all the way up, at every turn in the trail.

If you want the absolute best visibility, show up early in the morning, before the afternoon haze from the Central Valley obscures the view. On the other hand, that same haze creates amazingly colorful sunsets, so early evening is another fine time to be on top of Moro Rock.

User Groups: Hikers only. No dogs, horses, or mountain bikes. No wheelchair facilities.

Permits: No permits are required. There is a $35 entrance fee per vehicle at Sequoia and Kings Canyon National Parks, good for seven days.

Maps: A Sequoia and Kings Canyon map is available from Tom Harrison Maps. For a topographic map, go to the USGS website to download Giant Forest.

Directions: From Fresno, drive east on Highway 180 for 55 miles to the Big Stump Entrance at Kings Canyon National Park. Continue 1.5 miles and turn right on the Generals Highway, heading for Sequoia National Park. Drive approximately 30 miles on the Generals Highway, past Lodgepole and Wolverton, to the Giant Forest area of Sequoia National Park. Just beyond the museum, turn left on Crescent Meadow Road, drive 1.5 miles, and take the right fork to the Moro Rock parking area.

Contact: Sequoia and Kings Canyon National

Parks, Three Rivers, 559/565-3341 or 559/565-4307, www.nps.gov/seki.

59 SUNSET ROCK

2.0 mi/1.0 hr 1 9

off the Generals Highway in the Giant Forest area of Sequoia National Park

Map 11.3, page 561

The trail to Sunset Rock is a first-rate easy hike, perfect at sunset or any time. It gets much less traffic than you might expect, considering its proximity to Giant Forest. Leave your car in the lot across from the Giant Forest museum (make sure you stop in before or after your trip), then pick up the trail on the west side of the lot. The level path leads through a mixed forest (with a handful of giant sequoias) and crosses Little Deer Creek on its way to Sunset Rock. The rock is a gargantuan, flat piece of granite—about the size of a football field—set at 6,412 feet in elevation. Standing on it, you get a terrific overlook of Little Baldy to your right and a sea of conifers below, in the Marble Fork Kaweah River Canyon.

User Groups: Hikers only. No dogs, horses, or mountain bikes. No wheelchair facilities.

Permits: No permits are required. There is a $35 entrance fee per vehicle at Sequoia and Kings Canyon National Parks, good for seven days.

Maps: A Sequoia and Kings Canyon map is available from Tom Harrison Maps. For a topographic map, go to the USGS website to download Giant Forest.

Directions: From Fresno, drive east on Highway 180 for 55 miles to the Big Stump Entrance at Kings Canyon National Park. Continue 1.5 miles and turn right on the Generals Highway, heading for Sequoia National Park. Drive approximately 30 miles on the Generals Highway, past Lodgepole and Wolverton, to the Giant Forest area of Sequoia National Park. Park in the lot across from the Giant Forest museum, then pick up the signed trail on the west side of the lot.

Contact: Sequoia and Kings Canyon National Parks, Three Rivers, 559/565-3341 or 559/565-4307, www.nps.gov/seki.

60 PARADISE CREEK TRAIL

1.2 mi/0.75 hr 1 8

off Highway 198 in the Foothills region of Sequoia National Park

Map 11.3, page 561 BEST

From Buckeye Flat Campground, Paradise Creek Trail meanders through oaks and buckeyes, and crosses a long, picturesque footbridge over the Middle Fork Kaweah River. An inviting, Olympic-sized pool is on the right side of the bridge, where campers often go swimming on summer afternoons. Save the pool for after your hike; for now, take the signed Paradise Creek Trail, at the far side of the bridge. You'll briefly visit the creek and then leave it, climbing into oak and grassland terrain. There are some high views of Moro Rock and Hanging Rock, but most of the beauty is right at your feet, in the springtime flowers that grow in the grasses and in the leafy blue oaks that shade them. The maintained trail ends when it reaches Paradise Creek again, although a faint route continues along its banks.

User Groups: Hikers only. No dogs, horses, or mountain bikes. No wheelchair facilities.

Permits: No permits are required. There is a $35 entrance fee per vehicle at Sequoia and Kings Canyon National Parks, good for seven days.

Maps: A Sequoia and Kings Canyon map is available from Tom Harrison Maps. For a topographic map, go to the USGS website to download Giant Forest.

Directions: From Visalia, drive east on Highway 198 for 47 miles to the turnoff, on the right, for Buckeye Flat Campground, across from Hospital Rock. Turn right and drive 0.6 mile to the campground. Park in any of the dirt pullouts outside of the camp entrance; no day-use parking is allowed in the camp. You can also park at Hospital Rock and walk to the campground. The trailhead is near campsite No. 28.

Contact: Sequoia and Kings Canyon National Parks, Three Rivers, 559/565-3341 or 559/565-3135, www.nps.gov/seki.

61 MIDDLE FORK TRAIL TO PANTHER CREEK

6.0 mi/3.0 hr  2 8

off Highway 198 in the Foothills region of Sequoia National Park

Map 11.3, page 561

You want to be alone? You don't want to see anybody else on the trail? Just sign up for this trip any time between June and September, when the foothills have warmed up to their summer extremes. Don't be fooled by this path's name: The Middle Fork Trail is no streamside meander. Rather, it's a shadeless, exposed trail that leads high along the canyon of the Middle Fork Kaweah River—always at least 250 feet above it. In summer, it's hot as Hades, but this trail is perfect in winter and spring. Whereas most other trails in Sequoia and Kings Canyon are still snowed under, you can take an early-season day hike or backpacking trip along Middle Fork Trail. The main destination is Panther Creek (at three miles), where the trail leads across the brink of Panther Creek's 100-foot dive into the Kaweah River. But you can hike farther if you wish. Although Middle Fork Trail is set in grasslands and chaparral, it offers some stunning views of the area's geology, including Moro Rock, Castle Rocks, and the Great Western Divide. We hiked this trail in August, and despite the fact that we were wilting from the heat, the expansive views kept our spirits up.

User Groups: Hikers only. No dogs, horses, or mountain bikes. No wheelchair facilities.

Permits: No permits are required. There is a $35 entrance fee per vehicle at Sequoia and Kings Canyon National Parks, good for seven days.

Maps: A Sequoia and Kings Canyon map is available from Tom Harrison Maps. For a topographic map, go to the USGS website to download Giant Forest.

Directions: From Visalia, drive east on Highway 198 for 47 miles to the turnoff, on the right, for Buckeye Flat Campground, across from Hospital Rock. Turn right and drive 0.5 mile to a left fork just before the campground. Bear left on the dirt road and drive 1.3 miles to the trailhead and parking area. In the winter, you must park at Hospital Rock and walk in to the trailhead, adding 3.6 miles to your round-trip.

Contact: Sequoia and Kings Canyon National Parks, Three Rivers, 559/565-3341 or 559/565-3135, www.nps.gov/seki.

62 POTWISHA TO HOSPITAL ROCK

5.0 mi/2.5 hr  

off Highway 198 in the Foothills region of Sequoia National Park

Map 11.3, page 561

First, some advice: Don't hike this trail on a hot day. If it's summertime and you want to see the Monache Indian historical sites at Potwisha and Hospital Rock, drive to each of them and see them separately. In winter or spring, however, it's far more fun to take this five-mile hike through chaparral and oak woodlands, especially in March, when the wildflowers bloom. In the first 100 yards from the trailhead, you'll see Native American grinding holes and pictographs that look roughly like people and animals. You'll also pass many tempting pools in the Middle Fork Kaweah, which are frequented by swimmers and bathers in the summer. The trail climbs a gradual 2.5 miles from Potwisha to Hospital Rock, crossing the highway after the first mile. When you reach Hospital Rock, which is just a few feet off the road to Buckeye Flat Campground, you see a huge display of pictographs on its side. Across the campground road are more grinding holes in the boulders, and near them, a short paved path leads to deep pools and sandy beaches on the Middle Fork. Another path leads from the camp road to the underside of Hospital Rock, where there's a large, cavelike shelter. This is where a Native American medicine man healed the sick and injured, resulting in a white man naming this place Hospital Rock.

User Groups: Hikers only. No dogs, horses, or mountain bikes. No wheelchair facilities.

Permits: No permits are required. There is a $35 entrance fee per vehicle at Sequoia and Kings Canyon National Parks, good for seven days.

Maps: A Sequoia and Kings Canyon map is available from Tom Harrison Maps. For a topographic map, go to the USGS website to download Giant Forest.

Directions: From Visalia, drive east on Highway 198 for 44 miles to the turnoff, on the left, for Potwisha Campground, 3.8 miles east of the Ash Mountain entrance station to Sequoia National Park. Don't turn left into Potwisha campground; instead, turn right on the paved road opposite the campground. Drive past the RV dumping station to the signed trailhead and parking area.

Contact: Sequoia and Kings Canyon National Parks, Three Rivers, 559/565-3341 or 559/565-3135, www.nps.gov/seki.

63 MARBLE FALLS

7.0 mi/4.0 hr 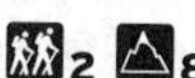

off Highway 198 in the Foothills region of Sequoia National Park

Map 11.3, page 561

This is the waterfall to see in Sequoia National Park in late winter and spring. March and April are particularly good months to visit because of high flows in the Marble Fork Kaweah River and blooming wildflowers in the grasslands and chaparral that line the trail. From its rather banal start as a dirt road, this trail just keeps getting better as it follows the Marble Fork Kaweah River. There are no trail junctions to worry about; at 3.5 miles, the path simply dead-ends near the lower cascades of Marble Falls. Although much of the falls are hidden in the narrow, rocky river gorge, tucked out of sight, what is visible is an impressive billowing cascade of whitewater. Be very careful on the slippery granite near the river's edges; the current and the cold water are even more dangerous than they look. Aside from the waterfalls and the wildflowers, the other highlights on this trail are the colorful outcroppings of marble, particularly in the last mile as you near the falls. Remember, though, that in summer this area of the park can bake like an oven. If you make the trip to the falls from late May to September, get an early morning start.

User Groups: Hikers only. No dogs, horses, or mountain bikes. No wheelchair facilities.

Permits: No permits are required. There is a $35 entrance fee per vehicle at Sequoia and Kings Canyon National Parks, good for seven days.

Maps: A Sequoia and Kings Canyon map is available from Tom Harrison Maps. For a topographic map, go to the USGS website to download Giant Forest.

Directions: From Visalia, drive east on Highway 198 for 44 miles to the turnoff, on the left, for Potwisha Campground, 3.8 miles east of the Ash Mountain entrance station to Sequoia National Park. The trail begins across from campsite No. 15 in Potwisha Campground; park in the trailhead parking area in the camp.

Contact: Sequoia and Kings Canyon National Parks, Three Rivers, 559/565-3341 or 559/565-3135, www.nps.gov/seki.

64 PARADISE RIDGE

3.2 mi/1.5 hr 3 9

off Highway 198 in the Mineral King region of Sequoia National Park

Map 11.3, page 561

OK, you've just driven the 20 twisting miles into Mineral King from Three Rivers. You're tired, dusty, and itching to get out of the car and move your legs. What's the first trail you can reach in Mineral King? The Paradise Ridge Trail, and it climbs right away, getting you huffing and puffing and clearing out the road dust from your lungs. After the initial steepness of the trail, the grade becomes easier as it moves into switchbacks ascending the hill. Although much of this forest has been burned in recent years, the giant sequoia trees are thriving, some in clusters as large as 10 or more. At your feet are tons of ferns. As you climb, the views just keep improving—you see the East Fork Kaweah River Canyon below you, and far off, the Great Western Divide. You can hike all the way to the top of the ridge at three miles, but the views aren't any better there than they are on the way up. Most people just cruise uphill a way, and turn around when they've had enough. Besides the big trees and the big views, our favorite thing about this trail was that we saw more bears than people.

User Groups: Hikers and horses. No dogs or mountain bikes. No wheelchair facilities.

Permits: No permits are required. There is a $35 entrance fee per vehicle at Sequoia and Kings Canyon National Parks, good for seven days.

Maps: A Mineral King map is available from Tom Harrison Maps. For a topographic map, go to the USGS website to download Silver City.

Directions: From Visalia, drive east on Highway 198 for 38 miles to Mineral King Road, 2.5 miles east of Three Rivers. If you reach the Ash Mountain entrance station, you've gone too far. Turn right on Mineral King Road and drive 20 miles to the Hockett Trail parking area, on the right, 0.25 mile past Atwell Mill Camp. Park there and walk back west on Mineral King Road about 0.3 mile to the trailhead for Paradise Ridge, on the north side of the road.

Contact: Sequoia and Kings Canyon National Parks, Three Rivers, 559/565-3341 or 559/565-3135, www.nps.gov/seki.

65 HOCKETT TRAIL TO EAST FORK BRIDGE

4.0 mi/2.0 hr 1 8

off Highway 198 in the Mineral King region of Sequoia National Park

Map 11.3, page 561

The Hockett Trail makes a fine day-hiking path in Mineral King. It's suitable for all kinds of hikers. Families with small children can just walk a mile downhill to the footbridge over the East Fork Kaweah River, where there is a small waterfall and many sculptured granite pools, and then turn around and head back. People looking for a longer trip can continue another mile to the East Fork Grove of sequoias and Deer Creek. Although some of this forest has been burned in recent years, most of the big conifers were spared, and the area is still quite beautiful. The trail starts in an area of sequoia stumps, near where the Atwell Mill cut lumber in the 1880s. Live sequoias still flourish farther down the path, near the river's edge; apparently they were spared because of their distance from the mill. The trail is well graded, and even the uphill return is only a moderate climb.

User Groups: Hikers and horses. No dogs or mountain bikes. No wheelchair facilities.

Permits: No permits are required. There is a $35 entrance fee per vehicle at Sequoia and Kings Canyon National Parks, good for seven days.

Maps: A Mineral King map is available from Tom Harrison Maps. For a topographic map, go to the USGS website to download Mineral King.

Directions: From Visalia, drive east on

Highway 198 for 38 miles to Mineral King Road, 2.5 miles east of Three Rivers. If you reach the Ash Mountain entrance station, you've gone too far. Turn right on Mineral King Road and drive 20 miles to the Hockett Trail parking area, on the right, 0.25 mile past Atwell Mill Camp. Park there and walk into the campground to campsite No. 16, where the trail begins.

Contact: Sequoia and Kings Canyon National Parks, Three Rivers, 559/565-3341 or 559/565-3135, www.nps.gov/seki.

66 COLD SPRINGS NATURE TRAIL

2.0 mi/1.0 hr 

off Highway 198 in the Mineral King region of Sequoia National Park

Map 11.3, page 561

You may not expect much from a campground nature trail, but Cold Springs Nature Trail is guaranteed to exceed your expectations. Not only is it lined with wildflowers along the East Fork Kaweah River and informative signposts that teach you to identify junipers, red and white firs, cottonwoods, and aspens, but the views of the Sawtooth Ridge are glorious. The loop is less than 0.5 mile, but from the far end of it, the trail continues along the East Fork Kaweah River, heading another mile into Mineral King Valley. Walk to the loop's far end, and then continue at least another 0.25 mile along the trail. It just gets prettier as it goes. You're in for a real treat if you take this walk right before sunset, when the valley's surrounding mountain peaks turn every imaginable shade of pink, orange, and coral, reflecting the sun setting in the west. The vistas are so beautiful that they can practically make you weep.

User Groups: Hikers and horses. No dogs or mountain bikes. No wheelchair facilities.

Permits: No permits are required. There is a $35 entrance fee per vehicle at Sequoia and Kings Canyon National Parks, good for seven days.

Maps: A Mineral King map is available from Tom Harrison Maps. For a topographic map, go to the USGS website to download Mineral King.

Directions: From Visalia, drive east on Highway 198 for 38 miles to Mineral King Road, 2.5 miles east of Three Rivers. If you reach the Ash Mountain entrance station, you've gone too far. Turn right on Mineral King Road and drive 23.5 miles to Cold Springs Campground on the right. The trail begins near site six. If you aren't staying in the camp, you can park by the Mineral King Ranger Station and walk into the campground.

Contact: Sequoia and Kings Canyon National Parks, Three Rivers, 559/565-3341 or 559/565-3135, www.nps.gov/seki.

67 FAREWELL GAP TRAIL TO ASPEN FLAT

2.0 mi/1.0 hr 1 9

off Highway 198 in the Mineral King region of Sequoia National Park

Map 11.3, page 561 **BEST**

If ever there was a perfect family hike, this would have to be it. Actually, if ever there was a perfect hike for every two-legged person on the planet, this would have to be it. The glacial-cut Mineral King Valley—a peaceful paradise of meadows, streams, and 100-year-old cabins—has to be one of the most scenic places in the West, and possibly in the world. An easy stroll along the canyon floor leads you past waterfalls and along the headwaters of the East Fork Kaweah River, in the awesome shelter of thousand-foot cliffs. After walking to the trailhead near the horse corral, you follow Farewell Gap Trail (an old dirt road) for a mile, then cross Crystal Creek and take the right fork off the main trail. This brings you closer to the river, where you follow a narrow use trail to Aspen Flat (a lovely grove of trees), or to Soda Springs, situated right along the river's edge. There you can see mineral springs bubbling up from the ground, turning the earth around them a bright orange color. Bring a fishing rod on this trail if you like, but be absolutely certain to bring your camera.

User Groups: Hikers and horses. No dogs or mountain bikes. No wheelchair facilities.

Permits: No permits are required. There is a $35 entrance fee per vehicle at Sequoia and Kings Canyon National Parks, good for seven days.

Maps: A Mineral King map is available from Tom Harrison Maps. For a topographic map, go to the USGS website to download Mineral King.

Directions: From Visalia, drive east on Highway 198 for 38 miles to Mineral King Road, 2.5 miles east of Three Rivers. If you reach the Ash Mountain entrance station, you've gone too far. Turn right on Mineral King Road and drive 25 miles to the end of the road and the Eagle/Mosquito trailhead. Take the right fork at the end of the road to reach the parking area. Walk back out of the parking lot and follow the road to the horse corral; the Farewell Gap Trail begins just beyond it.

Contact: Sequoia and Kings Canyon National Parks, Three Rivers, 559/565-3341 or 559/565-3135, www.nps.gov/seki.

68 MOSQUITO LAKES

8.0 mi/4.0 hr or 2 days

off Highway 198 in the Mineral King region of Sequoia National Park

Map 11.3, page 561

Ah, paradise. You know you're in it as soon as you park your car at the end of Mineral King Road. The Eagle/Mosquito trailhead is at 7,830 feet, and you set out from the parking lot near one of Mineral King's adorable cabins, left from the early 20th century and privately owned. Feel jealous? Keep walking; you'll get over it. In minutes you cross a footbridge over Spring Creek's cascade, called Tufa Falls because of the calcium carbonate in Spring Creek's water. Don't expect to see much of a waterfall—most of it is hidden by brush. At one mile, you reach the junction for Eagle Lake, the Mosquito Lakes, and White Chief Trails. Take the right fork, climbing steadily. At two miles, you reach the Mosquito Lakes junction and go right, leaving Eagle Lake Trail for another day. Climb up and then down the other side of Miner's Ridge, at 9,300 feet. The final descent covers 0.5 mile; you reach Mosquito Lake number one at 9,040 feet and 3.6 miles. It's considered to be the easiest lake to reach in Mineral King, with a mostly shaded trail and only a 1,500-foot gain on the way in, plus a 250-foot gain on the way out. Still, if you've visited any of the other spectacular Mineral King lakes, this lake will look a little disappointing. It's small, shallow, and greenish. But fear not: This is the first of several Mosquito Lakes, all of which are linked by Mosquito Creek. Hikers with excess energy can follow the stream uphill to four more lakes. There is no maintained trail to the upper lakes, but if you follow the use trail near the stream, the going is easier. The use trail begins on the west side of the stream at the first lake, navigates around the rocky slope behind the lake, and then crosses the stream above it. The climb from lake number one to lake number two is steep, with a 600-foot elevation gain in 0.5 mile, but it's worth it. Lake number two is the usual destination for day hikers; it's a blue, deep, granite-bound beauty and makes for an eight-mile round-trip. Backpackers will find the first campsites at Mosquito Lake number two (no camping is allowed at the first lake). Mosquito Lake number five is five miles from the Eagle/Mosquito trailhead.

User Groups: Hikers and horses. No dogs or mountain bikes. No wheelchair facilities.

Permits: There is a $35 entrance fee per vehicle at Sequoia and Kings Canyon National Parks, good for seven days. Wilderness permits are required for overnight stays. They are available on a first-come, first-served basis at the

Mineral King Ranger Station. For advanced wilderness permits or information on trail conditions, go to www.nps.gov/seki. Trailhead quotas are in effect from May to September.

Maps: A Mineral King map is available from Tom Harrison Maps. For a topographic map, go to the USGS website to download Mineral King.

Directions: From Visalia, drive east on Highway 198 for 38 miles to Mineral King Road, 2.5 miles east of Three Rivers. If you reach the Ash Mountain entrance station, you've gone too far. Turn right on Mineral King Road and drive 25 miles to the end of the road and the Eagle/Mosquito trailhead. Take the right fork at the end of the road to reach the parking area. The trail begins at the far end of the parking lot.

Contact: Sequoia and Kings Canyon National Parks, Three Rivers, 559/565-3341 or 559/565-3135, www.nps.gov/seki.

69 EAGLE LAKE TRAIL

6.8 mi/4.0 hr

3 10

off Highway 198 in the Mineral King region of Sequoia National Park

Map 11.3, page 561

Eagle Lake has always been the glamour destination in Mineral King; the trail to hike if you can hike only one trail in the area. Why? The blue-green lake is drop-dead gorgeous, that's why, and the trail to reach it is challenging but manageable for most day hikers, with a 2,200-foot elevation gain spread out over 3.4 miles. The Eagle Lake Trail follows the same route as the Mosquito Lakes Trail (see listing in this chapter) until the two-mile point, near the Eagle Sink Holes. These geological oddities are small craters in the ground where Eagle Creek suddenly disappears underground. At the trail junction by the sink holes, go left for Eagle Lake. Enjoy the brief flat stretch here, because shortly, you'll gain another 1,000 feet over 1.4 miles. Much of the climb is in an exposed, rocky area—a large boulder field that gets baked by the sun on warm days. Well-graded switchbacks and beautiful scenery make it easier. Soon you arrive at Eagle Lake's dam, at 10,000 feet. The big lake is surrounded by glacially carved rock and has a few rocky islands. Brook trout swim in its clear waters. The trail continues along the lake's west side to many good picnicking spots and photo opportunities. Campsites are found near the lake; no camping is allowed between the trail and the lake.

User Groups: Hikers and horses. No dogs or mountain bikes. No wheelchair facilities.

Permits: There is a $35 entrance fee per vehicle at Sequoia and Kings Canyon National Parks, good for seven days. Wilderness permits are required for overnight stays. They are available on a first-come, first-served basis at the Mineral King Ranger Station. For advanced wilderness permits or information on trail conditions, go to www.nps.gov/seki. Trailhead quotas are in effect from May to September.

Maps: A Mineral King map is available from Tom Harrison Maps. For a topographic map, go to the USGS website to download Mineral King.

Directions: From Visalia, drive east on Highway 198 for 38 miles to Mineral King Road, 2.5 miles east of Three Rivers. If you reach the Ash Mountain entrance station, you've gone too far. Turn right on Mineral King Road and drive 25 miles to the end of the road and the Eagle/Mosquito trailhead. Take the right fork at the end of the road to reach the parking area. The trail begins at the far end of the parking lot.

Contact: Sequoia and Kings Canyon National Parks, Three Rivers, 559/565-3341 or 559/565-3135, www.nps.gov/seki.

70 FRANKLIN LAKES

10.8 mi/6.0 hr or 2 days 3 10

off Highway 198 in the Mineral King region of Sequoia National Park

Map 11.3, page 561

Maybe the best thing about hiking to Franklin Lakes is the waterfalls you get to pass along the way—especially our favorite cascades, on Franklin Creek. Or maybe it's the prolific wildflowers along the trail, or the spectacular views over Mineral King Valley that you gain as you climb. Maybe it's the big lake itself, set below Tulare and Florence Peaks, or the fact that the trail to reach it is so well graded, with a 2,500-foot elevation gain spread out over 5.4 miles. What the heck—this trail is about as close to hiking perfection as you get.

The first two miles are nearly flat; the route winds along the bottom of Mineral King's canyon, following Farewell Gap Trail alongside the East Fork Kaweah River. You'll pass Tufa Falls, across the canyon, at 0.25 mile and Crystal Creek's cascades, on your side of the canyon, at one mile. The trail leaves the valley floor and starts to climb moderately, reaching the bottom of Franklin Creek's cascades at 1.7 miles. After crossing Franklin Creek, you continue south along Farewell Canyon, negotiating some switchbacks as you gain elevation. The views get better and better. One mile farther, Franklin Lakes Trail forks left off Farewell Gap Trail and starts climbing in earnest up the Franklin Creek Valley. At nearly 10,000 feet, the trail crosses Franklin Creek again, then parallels the creek for another mile to the largest Franklin Lake. Note that when you see the lake's dam straight ahead and an obvious campsite about 150 yards below it to the right of the trail, you should cut off the main trail. Walk to the camp and follow its use trail to the dam and the lake. The main trail switchbacks up and above the lake but doesn't go directly to its shoreline. Franklin Lake is a dramatic sight, surrounded by steep, snow-covered slopes and a few pines and junipers. Rainbow Mountain is on its northeast side; Tulare Peak is to the southwest.

User Groups: Hikers and horses. No dogs or mountain bikes. No wheelchair facilities.

Permits: There is a $35 entrance fee per vehicle at Sequoia and Kings Canyon National Parks, good for seven days. Wilderness permits are required for overnight stays. They are available on a first-come, first-served basis at the Mineral King Ranger Station. For advanced wilderness permits or information on trail conditions, go to www.nps.gov/seki. Trailhead quotas are in effect from May to September.

Maps: A Mineral King map is available from Tom Harrison Maps. For a topographic map, go to the USGS website to download Mineral King.

Directions: From Visalia, drive east on Highway 198 for 38 miles to Mineral King Road, 2.5 miles east of Three Rivers. If you reach the Ash Mountain entrance station, you've gone too far. Turn right on Mineral King Road and drive 25 miles to the end of the road and the Eagle/Mosquito trailhead. Take the right fork at the end of the road to reach the parking area. Walk back out of the parking lot, and follow the road to the horse corral; Farewell Gap Trail begins just beyond it.

Contact: Sequoia and Kings Canyon National Parks, Three Rivers, 559/565-3341 or 559/565-3135, www.nps.gov/seki.

71 WHITE CHIEF MINE TRAIL

5.8 mi/3.0 hr 3 10

off Highway 198 in the Mineral King region of Sequoia National Park

Map 11.3, page 561

If you're one of those liberated hikers who doesn't need to have an alpine lake in your itinerary to be happy, the trail to White Chief Bowl is a scenic route with much to offer, including an exploration of the White Chief Mine tunnel. Until the Park Service purchased it in 1998, the mine was private property within the national park and off-limits to hikers.

The first mile of the trail is the same as the route to Eagle and Mosquito Lakes, but you'll leave nearly everyone behind when you continue straight at the one-mile junction, while others bear right for Eagle Lake and the Mosquito Lakes. The White Chief Trail continues with a hefty grade—this second mile is the toughest part of the whole trip—until it tops out at the edge of a gorgeous meadow. Just after you cross a seasonal stream (often a dry ravine by late summer), look for the ruins of Crabtree Cabin, to the right of the trail. The cabin ruins are what is left of the oldest remaining structure in Mineral King. It was built by the discoverer of the White Chief Mine in the 1870s. Next comes White Chief Meadows, surrounded by high granite walls and filled with dozens of downed trees, evidence of harsh winter avalanches.

Beyond the meadow, the trail ascends slightly until it nears a waterfall on White Chief Creek. Shortly before the falls, the trail crosses the creek and heads uphill. Look for the opening to White Chief Mine in a layer of white rock just above the trail. Scramble off the trail a few yards to reach it. The mine tunnel is tall enough to walk into and dead-ends in about 150 feet. Beyond the mine, the trail continues to Upper White Chief Bowl and passes dozens of limestone caverns along the way. Although tempting, these caverns should only be explored by those who are experienced and well equipped.

User Groups: Hikers and horses. No dogs or mountain bikes. No wheelchair facilities.

Permits: No permits are required. There is a $35 entrance fee per vehicle at Sequoia and Kings Canyon National Parks, good for seven days.

Maps: A Mineral King map is available from Tom Harrison Maps. For a topographic map, go to the USGS website to download Mineral King.

Directions: From Visalia, drive east on Highway 198 for 38 miles to Mineral King Road, 2.5 miles east of Three Rivers. If you reach the Ash Mountain entrance station, you've gone too far. Turn right on Mineral King Road and drive 25 miles to the end of the road and the Eagle/Mosquito trailhead. Take the right fork at the end of the road to reach the parking area. The trail begins from the far end of the parking lot.

Contact: Sequoia and Kings Canyon National Parks, Three Rivers, 559/565-3341 or 559/565-3135, www.nps.gov/seki.

72 TIMBER GAP TRAIL

4.0 mi/2.0 hr

off Highway 198 in the Mineral King region of Sequoia National Park

Map 11.3, page 561

On this short but steep trail, you'll stand witness to the mining history of Mineral King. The trail climbs abruptly from the Sawtooth trailhead on an old mining path along Monarch Creek, and forks in 0.25 mile. Take the left fork for Timber Gap, which climbs through a dense fir forest and then opens out to switchbacks in a wide and treeless slope—the result of continual winter avalanches. The exposed slope is home to many mountain wildflowers. The climb ends in two miles at Timber Gap, elevation 9,450 feet, a forested pass. The stumps you see among the red firs remain from early miners who cut down the trees to fuel their fires and support their mining tunnels. A faint path heads east from the pass and leads to the remains of the Empire Mine and its buildings in just over one mile.

User Groups: Hikers and horses. No dogs or mountain bikes. No wheelchair facilities.

Permits: No permits are required. There is a $35 entrance fee per vehicle at Sequoia and Kings Canyon National Parks, good for seven days.

Maps: A Mineral King map is available from Tom Harrison Maps. For a topographic map, go to the USGS website to download Mineral King.

Directions: From Visalia, drive east on Highway 198 for 38 miles to Mineral King Road, 2.5 miles east of Three Rivers. If you reach the Ash Mountain entrance station, you've gone too far. Turn right on Mineral King Road and drive 24.5 miles to the Sawtooth parking area, 0.5 mile before the end of the road.

Contact: Sequoia and Kings Canyon National Parks, Three Rivers, 559/565-3341 or 559/565-3135, www.nps.gov/seki.

73 MONARCH LAKES

8.4 mi/5.0 hr or 2 days  3 10

off Highway 198 in the Mineral King region of Sequoia National Park

Map 11.3, page 561

The Monarch Lakes Trail leads from the Sawtooth trailhead at 8,000 feet in elevation and climbs 2,500 feet to the rocky, gemlike Monarch Lakes. The first lake is good, but the second lake is simply awesome, and the scenery along the trail is unforgettable. Walk 0.25 mile from the trailhead and take the right fork for Monarch and Crystal Lakes. After one steep mile, you'll reach Groundhog Meadow, named for the adorable yellow-bellied marmots that inhabit the area. (We like their blond coats and shrill whistles.) Beyond the meadow, the trail starts seriously switchbacking in and out of red fir forest, making a gut-thumping climb to the Crystal Lake trail junction. The trail forks sharply right for Crystal Lake, but you head left for one more mile—a relatively smooth mile, with the easiest grade of the whole route—to Lower Monarch Lake. (This section crosses an incredible talus slope.) Snow can often be found near the lake even in late summer, and the vista is dramatic, with Sawtooth Peak dominating the skyline. If you have a wilderness permit, you can find a campsite near the lake.

While the main trail continues north to Sawtooth Pass, a use trail leads southeast from the lower lake for 0.5 mile to Upper Monarch

Monarch Lakes

Lake. Basically you head directly up the cliff that forms the back wall of the lower lake. It's worth the climb. The upper lake is wide, deep blue, and dramatic, set at the base of barren, pointy Monarch Peak. The view from the upper lake's basin, looking back down at the lower lake and various Mineral King peaks, is breathtaking. A big surprise is that the upper lake has been dammed, like many of the high lakes in Mineral King, and is operated by Southern California Edison. Note: If you're backpacking and want to take a first-rate side-trip, the trail to Sawtooth Pass is a 1.3-mile, 1,200-foot climb that's not easy, but Sawtooth Pass offers one of the best views in the Southern Sierra.

User Groups: Hikers and horses. No dogs or mountain bikes. No wheelchair facilities.

Permits: There is a $35 entrance fee per vehicle at Sequoia and Kings Canyon National Parks, good for seven days. Wilderness permits are required for overnight stays. They are available on a first-come, first-served basis at the Mineral King Ranger Station. For advanced wilderness permits or information on trail conditions, go to www.nps.gov/seki. Trailhead quotas are in effect from May to September.

Maps: A Mineral King map is available from Tom Harrison Maps. For a topographic map, go to the USGS website to download Mineral King.

Directions: From Visalia, drive east on Highway 198 for 38 miles to Mineral King Road, 2.5 miles east of Three Rivers. If you reach the Ash Mountain entrance station, you've gone too far. Turn right on Mineral King Road and drive 24.5 miles to the Sawtooth parking area, 0.5 mile before the end of the road.

Contact: Sequoia and Kings Canyon National Parks, Three Rivers, 559/565-3341 or 559/565-3135, www.nps.gov/seki.

74 CRYSTAL LAKE TRAIL

9.8 mi/6.0 hr or 2 days

off Highway 198 in the Mineral King region of Sequoia National Park

Map 11.3, page 561

The long and arduous path to Crystal Lake follows the same route as the trail to Monarch Lakes (see listing in this chapter) for the first 3.2 miles. In Chihuahua Bowl, a sharp right-hand turn puts you on the trail to Crystal Lake. In 0.5 mile, the trail leads past the ruins of the Chihuahua Mine (on the right), one of Mineral King's last hopes for silver riches. Like the other mines in the area, it never produced ore to equal the miners' dreams. The trail climbs abruptly over a rocky slope to a ridge of reddish foxtail pines, where your vista opens wide. Far off you can see the Farewell Gap peaks, and down below you see the Cobalt Lakes and Crystal Creek, pouring down to the Mineral King Valley and the East Fork Kaweah River. The trail continues, following more switchbacks, to upper Crystal Creek and Crystal Lake, which has been dammed. Off to the left (north), Mineral Peak stands out at 11,500 feet, and to the right (south), Rainbow Mountain shows off its colorful rock. Views are spectacular in every direction. If you scramble 0.25 mile off-trail toward Mineral Peak, you will reach Little Crystal Lake, where you have a near guarantee of solitude and a vista you won't forget.

User Groups: Hikers and horses. No dogs or mountain bikes. No wheelchair facilities.

Permits: There is a $35 entrance fee per vehicle at Sequoia and Kings Canyon National Parks, good for seven days. Wilderness permits are required for overnight stays. They are available on a first-come, first-served basis at the Mineral King Ranger Station. For advanced wilderness permits or information on trail conditions, go to www.nps.gov/seki. Trailhead quotas are in effect from May to September.

Maps: A Mineral King map is available from Tom Harrison Maps. For a topographic map, go to the USGS website to download Mineral King.

Directions: From Visalia, drive east on Highway 198 for 38 miles to Mineral King Road, 2.5 miles east of Three Rivers. If you reach the Ash Mountain entrance station, you've gone too far. Turn right on Mineral King Road and drive 24.5 miles to the Sawtooth parking area, 0.5 mile before the end of the road.

Contact: Sequoia and Kings Canyon National Parks, Three Rivers, 559/565-3341 or 559/565-3135, www.nps.gov/seki.

75 BLACK WOLF FALLS

0.5 mi/0.5 hr 1 8

off Highway 198 in the Mineral King region of Sequoia National Park

Map 11.3, page 561

This hike is really just a stroll, and the destination is readily apparent from the Sawtooth trailhead: Black Wolf Falls, tumbling down the canyon wall in Mineral King Valley. But aside from the chance to get close to a pretty waterfall, the hike is interesting because of its historical significance. Black Wolf's name is actually an alteration of its original moniker, which was Black Wall Falls, named for the Black Wall copper mine that was located at the waterfall's base. Back in the 1870s, when miners believed that Mineral King was rich in more than just scenery, they mined the base of Monarch Creek with a modicum of success. Today you can walk right up to the falls and see the mine tunnel on its right side (it looks like a cave, but don't go inside; it's unstable). In summer, rangers lead group hikes to the waterfall and talk about Mineral King's mining history. Although the route to Black Wolf Falls isn't an official trail, the path is well used and clearly visible. If you can find its beginning across the road from the No Parking Any Time sign, the rest of the hike is easy.

User Groups: Hikers only. No dogs, horses, or mountain bikes. No wheelchair facilities.

Permits: No permits are required. There is a $35 entrance fee per vehicle at Sequoia and Kings Canyon National Parks, good for seven days.

Maps: A Mineral King map is available from Tom Harrison Maps. For a topographic map, go to the USGS website to download Mineral King.

Directions: From Visalia, drive east on Highway 198 for 38 miles to Mineral King Road, 2.5 miles east of Three Rivers. If you reach the Ash Mountain entrance station, you've gone too far. Turn right on Mineral King Road and drive 24.5 miles to the Sawtooth parking area, 0.5 mile before the end of the road. Walk up the road toward Black Wolf Falls, then look for a use trail across the road from the No Parking Any Time sign, just beyond where Monarch Creek flows under the road.

Contact: Sequoia and Kings Canyon National Parks, Three Rivers, 559/565-3341 or 559/565-3135, www.nps.gov/seki.

76 LADYBUG TRAIL

3.8 mi/2.0 hr 2 8

off Highway 198 in the South Fork region of Sequoia National Park

Map 11.3, page 561 BEST

The South Fork area is the forgotten region of Sequoia National Park. Accessible only by a 13-mile dead-end road out of Three Rivers, South Fork is the place to go when you just want to get away from it all. Solitude in a national park? You can find it here (mostly because it takes about 40 minutes just to drive from Highway 198 in Three Rivers to the trailhead). The elevation is low (only 3,600 feet), so the area is accessible year-round, and there may be no finer winter walk than a hike on Ladybug Trail out of South Fork. The trail leaves the far end of South Fork Campground and heads through an oak and bay forest along the South Fork Kaweah

River. At 1.7 miles, you reach Ladybug Camp, a primitive camping area along the river's edge, in the shade of pines and firs. A short scramble downstream of the camp gives you a look at Ladybug Falls, a 25-foot waterfall set in a rocky grotto. If you continue upstream, the trail leads another few hundred yards and then switchbacks uphill, heading for Whiskey Log Camp. A use trail leaves the main trail and continues a short distance upriver, where there are many beautiful rocky pools. And in case you haven't guessed, the trail, camp, and falls are named for the millions of ladybugs that winter near the river, then take flight in the spring to head back to the Central Valley to feed.

User Groups: Hikers and horses. No dogs or mountain bikes. No wheelchair facilities.

Permits: No permits are required. There is a $35 entrance fee per vehicle at Sequoia and Kings Canyon National Parks, good for seven days.

Maps: A Sequoia and Kings Canyon map is available from Tom Harrison Maps. For a topographic map, go to the USGS website to download Dennison Peak.

Directions: From Visalia, drive east on Highway 198 for 35 miles to one mile west of Three Rivers. Turn right on South Fork Drive and drive 12.8 miles to South Fork Campground. (Nine miles out, the road turns to dirt.) Park at the Ladybug trailhead parking area.

Contact: Sequoia and Kings Canyon National Parks, Three Rivers, 559/565-3341 or 559/565-3135, www.nps.gov/seki.

77 GARFIELD-HOCKETT TRAIL

5.8 mi/3.0 hr — 3 / 9

off Highway 198 in the South Fork region of Sequoia National Park

Map 11.3, page 561

The trip to the magnificent Garfield Grove is only 2.9 miles from South Fork Campground, and if you don't mind a steep climb and possibly sharing the trail with horse packers, you should be sure to take this hike. The trail climbs immediately and keeps climbing, but fortunately, it is shaded by oaks most of the way. The ascent rewards you with a continual view of distant Homer's Nose, a granite landmark that, although prominent, looks a little like anybody's nose. In just under three miles of nonstop climbing, you reach the first of many sequoias in the Garfield Grove, reported to be one of the largest groves in the national parks. By the time you reach it, you've gained 2,000 feet in elevation, so pick a big tree to lean against, pull out a snack, and take a breather.

User Groups: Hikers and horses. No dogs or mountain bikes. No wheelchair facilities.

Permits: No permits are required. There is a $35 entrance fee per vehicle at Sequoia and Kings Canyon National Parks, good for seven days.

Maps: A Sequoia and Kings Canyon map is available from Tom Harrison Maps. For topographic maps, go to the USGS website to download Dennison Peak.

Directions: From Visalia, drive east on Highway 198 for 35 miles to one mile west of Three Rivers. Turn right on South Fork Drive and drive 12.8 miles to South Fork Campground. (Nine miles out, the road turns to dirt.) Park at the trailhead at the far end of the campground loop, just before the parking lot for the Ladybug Trailhead.

Contact: Sequoia and Kings Canyon National Parks, Three Rivers, 559/565-3341 or 559/565-3135, www.nps.gov/seki.

78 FORESTRY INFORMATION TRAIL

1.0 mi/0.5 hr — 1 / 7

in Mountain Home Demonstration State Forest off Highway 190 near Springville

Map 11.3, page 561

Balch Park is the small county-run park within

the borders of Mountain Home Demonstration State Forest, and its easy, one-mile nature trail is a great place to take your kids for the afternoon. The trail begins next to the main entrance to Balch Park Camp, across from the kiosk, and your first stop is a visit to the Hollow Log, which was used as a dwelling by various pioneers, Indians, and prospectors. You also get to see the Lady Alice Tree, which in the early 20th century was incorrectly billed as the largest tree in the world. Nonetheless, it's no slacker in the size department. Continuing along the route, you'll see and learn all about the trees and plants that thrive here, plus interesting stuff about forestry management practices.

User Groups: Hikers, dogs, and horses. No mountain bikes. No wheelchair facilities.

Permits: No permits are required. Balch Park charges a $1 per person day-use fee.

Maps: A free brochure and map of Mountain Home Demonstration State Forest, which includes Balch Park, are available from state forest headquarters. For a topographic map, go to the USGS website to download Camp Wishon.

Directions: From Porterville, drive east on Highway 190 for 18 miles to Springville. At Springville, turn left (north) on Balch Park Road/Road 239, drive 3.5 miles, and turn right on Bear Creek Road/Road 220. Drive 14 miles to Mountain Home Demonstration State Forest Headquarters, pick up a free forest map, and then continue 1.5 miles farther to the entrance to Balch Park.

Contact: Balch Park, 559/539-3896; Mountain Home Demonstration State Forest, Springville, 559/539-2321 (summer) or 559/539-2855 (winter).

79 ADAM AND EVE LOOP TRAIL

2.0 mi/1.0 hr

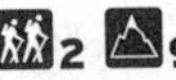

in Mountain Home Demonstration State Forest off Highway 190 near Springville

Map 11.3, page 561

On the Adam and Eve Loop Trail you can see the Adam Tree standing tall and proud, but its companion, the Eve Tree, is no longer thriving. It (she?) was axed during the infamous sequoia logging years, but the tree kept up the good fight until 2001, when a forest fire ended its life. The burnt snag remains. This trail is best accessed at the public corrals, one-quarter mile north of the pack station on Summit Road. Park at the corrals and begin your trip by taking the left side of the loop, heading uphill to the Adam Tree, the second-largest tree in this state forest, at 240 feet tall and 27 feet in diameter. You'll see the Eve Tree snag shortly thereafter. The big draw on the trail is visiting the "Indian bathtubs" at Tub Flat, halfway around the loop; these are basins, formed in solid granite, that were probably used by Native Americans. No one is sure whether they are natural or handmade. The basins are much larger than the traditional Indian grinding holes that are found elsewhere in the Sierra. True to their name, they are large enough to bathe in.

User Groups: Hikers, dogs, and horses. No mountain bikes. No wheelchair facilities.

Permits: No permits are required. Parking and access are free.

Maps: A free brochure and map of Mountain Home Demonstration State Forest are available from forest headquarters. For a topographic map, go to the USGS website to download Camp Wishon.

Directions: From Porterville, drive east on Highway 190 for 18 miles to Springville. At Springville, turn left (north) on Balch Park Road/Road 239 and drive 3.5 miles; then turn right on Bear Creek Road/Road 220. Drive 14 miles to Mountain Home Demonstration State Forest Headquarters, pick up a free forest map, and then continue one mile farther, turning right at the sign for Hidden Falls Recreation Area. Drive 3.5 miles to the public corrals, which are located one-quarter mile north of the pack station (before Shake Camp Campground). Park at the corrals.

Contact: Mountain Home Demonstration State Forest, Springville, 559/539-2321 (summer) or 559/539-2855 (winter).

80 REDWOOD CROSSING

4.0 mi/2.0 hr 1 9

in Mountain Home Demonstration State Forest off Highway 190 near Springville

Map 11.3, page 561

An excellent easy hike for campers and day visitors at Mountain Home Demonstration State Forest is on Long Meadow Trail, from Shake Camp Campground to Redwood Crossing, on the Tule River. The trail starts by the public corral (elevation 6,800 feet) and leads through logged sequoia stumps to a thick mixed forest on the slopes high above the Wishon Fork Tule River. When the trail reaches clearings in the trees, the views of the Great Western Divide are excellent. At two miles out, you reach Redwood Crossing, a boulder-lined stretch of the river. Those willing to ford can cross to the other side and head into the Golden Trout Wilderness, but day hikers should pull out a picnic at the river's edge and make an afternoon of it. Backpackers heading for the wilderness need to secure a wilderness permit from the Western Divide Ranger District office.

User Groups: Hikers, dogs, and horses. No mountain bikes. No wheelchair facilities.

Permits: No permits are required. Parking and access are free.

Maps: A free brochure and map of Mountain Home Demonstration State Forest are available from forest headquarters. For a topographic map, go to the USGS website to download Camp Wishon.

Directions: From Porterville, drive east on Highway 190 for 18 miles to Springville. At Springville, turn left (north) on Balch Park Road/Road 239, drive 3.5 miles, and turn right on Bear Creek Road/Road 220. Drive 14 miles to Mountain Home Demonstration State Forest Headquarters, pick up a free forest map, and then continue one mile farther. Turn right at the sign for Hidden Falls Recreation Area. Drive 3.5 miles to Shake Camp Campground. The Long Meadow trailhead is located by the public corral.

Contact: Mountain Home Demonstration State Forest, Springville, 559/539-2321 (summer) or 559/539-2855 (winter); Western Divide Ranger District, Springville, 559/539-2607, www.fs.usda.gov/sequoia.

81 MOSES GULCH TRAIL

4.0 mi/2.0 hr 2 9

in Mountain Home Demonstration State Forest off Highway 190 near Springville

Map 11.3, page 561

For a less-crowded alternative to the popular Redwood Crossing (see listing in this chapter), you can take the other trail from the public corral at Shake Camp Campground and wind your way through stands of beautiful virgin sequoias to the Wishon Fork Tule River at Moses Gulch Campground. The Moses Gulch Trail crosses forest roads twice—the only downer—but it's an easy walk for families, and it's peaceful besides. Once you reach the river (at two miles), you have the option of hiking alongside it to the north or south, adding some distance to your trip. The northern stretch leads to Hidden Falls Campground (the home of many small falls and pools), and the southern stretch crosses pretty Galena and Silver Creeks, leading past a mining cabin and an old copper mine.

User Groups: Hikers, dogs, and horses. No mountain bikes. No wheelchair facilities.

Permits: No permits are required. Parking and access are free.

Maps: A free brochure and map of Mountain

Home Demonstration State Forest are available from forest headquarters. For a topographic map, go to the USGS website to download Camp Wishon.

Directions: From Porterville, drive east on Highway 190 for 18 miles to Springville. At Springville, turn left (north) on Balch Park Road/Road 239, drive 3.5 miles, and then turn right on Bear Creek Road/Road 220. Drive 14 miles to Mountain Home Demonstration State Forest Headquarters and pick up a free forest map, then continue one mile farther and turn right at the sign for Hidden Falls Recreation Area. Drive 3.5 miles to Shake Camp Campground. The Moses Gulch trailhead is behind (south of) the public corral.

Contact: Mountain Home Demonstration State Forest, Springville, 559/539-2321 (summer) or 559/539-2855 (winter).

82 DOYLE TRAIL

6.0 mi/3.0 hr

in Giant Sequoia National Monument near Springville

Map 11.3, page 561

The Doyle Trail is a great alternative to the heat of the San Joaquin Valley. It's in the transition zone between foothills and conifers, with plenty of shade from tall manzanita, oaks, madrones, and pines. Squirrels and lizards are your primary companions on the trail, which laterals along the slopes above the Wishon fork of the Tule River. From the gated trailhead, hike up the paved road and bear left to bypass Doyle Springs, a community of private cabins. Follow the trail that is signed Trail to Upstream Fishing. The route climbs gently through the forest for 2.5 miles and then suddenly descends to the same level as the river, where there are some primitive campsites available. Then the trail rises again, climbing for another 0.5 mile to a clearing on the right, where there is an outcrop of jagged green rock alongside the river. Leave the trail and cross over the rock, where you'll find a few picture-perfect swimming holes and small waterfalls.

User Groups: Hikers, dogs, and horses. No mountain bikes. No wheelchair facilities.

Permits: A free wilderness permit is required for overnight stays and is available from the Springville or Kernville Ranger Stations at the addresses below. Parking and access are free.

Maps: A Sequoia National Forest map is available from the U.S. Forest Service. For a topographic map, go to the USGS website to download Camp Wishon.

Directions: From Porterville, drive east on Highway 190 for 18 miles to Springville. From Springville, continue east on Highway 190 for 7.5 miles to Wishon Drive/Road 208, a left fork. Turn left and drive four miles on Wishon Drive, then take the left fork, which is signed for day-use parking (above the campground). Drive 0.25 mile and park off the road, near the gate.

Contact: Giant Sequoia National Monument/Sequoia National Forest, Western Divide Ranger District, Springville, 559/539-2607, www.fs.usda.gov/sequoia.

83 JORDAN PEAK LOOKOUT

1.8 mi/1.0 hr 1 9

in Giant Sequoia National Monument near Quaking Aspen

Map 11.3, page 561

You'll see some logging activity out here by Jordan Peak, but if you can put up with it, you can climb a mere 600 feet over less than a mile to reach the summit of this 9,100-foot mountain. Few summits are so easily attained (it's a well-graded and well-maintained trail), and this one is not lacking in dramatic vistas. You can see the Wishon Fork Canyon of the Tule River, Camp Nelson, the Sequoia Crest, Slate Mountain, Maggie Mountain, and Moses Mountain close up, and the Tehachapis and the Coast Range far, far away. The peak is covered with microwave equipment, but it doesn't mar the stupendous view. Head west from the trailhead on Jordan Lookout Trail, switchbacking up until you reach the catwalked stairs to the lookout, which was built in 1934. All the materials to construct the lookout were hauled in by mules.

User Groups: Hikers, dogs, horses, and mountain bikes. No wheelchair facilities.

Permits: No permits are required. Parking and access are free.

Maps: A Sequoia National Forest map is available from the U.S. Forest Service. For a topographic map, go to the USGS website to download Sentinel Peak.

Directions: From Porterville, drive 45 miles east on Highway 190 to Forest Service Road 21S50, near Quaking Aspen Campground. Turn left on Road 21S50 and drive five miles. Bear left and continue on Road 21S50 for 2.8 miles, bearing left on Road 20S71, signed for Jordan Peak Lookout, and following it one mile to its end, at the trailhead.

Contact: Giant Sequoia National Monument/Sequoia National Forest, Western Divide Ranger District, Springville, 559/539-2607, www.fs.usda.gov/sequoia.

84 CLICKS CREEK TRAIL

14.0 mi/2 days

in the Golden Trout Wilderness near Quaking Aspen

Map 11.3, page 561

If you like peace and quiet on your backpacking trips, Clicks Creek Trail, in the Golden Trout Wilderness, may suit you just fine. The trail leads northeast from Log Cabin Meadow (elevation 7,800 feet), heading steadily downhill along Clicks Creek to the Little Kern River. The route crosses the creek several times. Shade lovers will thrill at the conifer forests that line the route, interspersed by large and grassy meadows, and anglers can bring along their gear to try their luck with the golden trout in the river. There are many possible campsites along the Little Kern, where the elevation is 6,200 feet.

User Groups: Hikers, dogs, and horses. No mountain bikes. No wheelchair facilities.

Permits: A free wilderness permit is required for overnight stays and is available from the Springville or Kernville Ranger Stations at the addresses below. Parking and access are free.

Maps: A Golden Trout Wilderness map is available from the U.S. Forest Service or Tom Harrison Maps. For a topographic map, go to the USGS website to download Sentinel Peak.

Directions: From Porterville, drive 45 miles east on Highway 190 to Forest Service Road 21S50 near Quaking Aspen Campground. Turn left on Road 21S50 and drive five miles; bear left and continue on Road 21S50 for 1.5 miles to the Clicks Creek trailhead, at Log Cabin Meadow.

Contact: Sequoia National Forest, Western Divide Ranger District, Springville, 559/539-2607, www.fs.usda.gov/sequoia; Sequoia National Forest, Kern River Ranger District, Kernville, 760/376-3781, www.fs.usda.gov/sequoia.

85 JOHN JORDAN/HOSSACK MEADOW TRAIL

5.0-6.0 mi/2.5-3.0 hr

in Giant Sequoia National Monument near Quaking Aspen

Map 11.3, page 561

Your route on the John Jordan Trail begins with a crossing of McIntyre Creek, then traverses a level mile to an old fence, gate, and McIntyre Rock—a huge pile of granite boulders with an excellent view. Climb on top of the rock's well-graded, cracking-granite back side and peer over its startlingly steep front side. Surprise! It's straight down, about 600 feet. The trail heads downhill through a red fir forest to Nelson Creek, the site of some logging work. Although you can walk another 0.5 mile to the trail's end (at Hossack Meadow), most people turn around at the sight of logged trees, making for a five-mile round-trip with a 1,000-foot elevation gain on the return. So who was John Jordan, anyway? He was a trailblazer in the 1870s who unfortunately was most famous for drowning in the Kern River on his way back to the Central Valley to tell everybody he had completed this trail, a proposed toll road.

User Groups: Hikers, dogs, horses, and mountain bikes. No wheelchair facilities.

Permits: No permits are required. Parking and access are free.

Maps: A Sequoia National Forest map is available from the U.S. Forest Service. For a topographic map, go to the USGS website to download Sentinel Peak.

Directions: From Porterville, drive 45 miles east on Highway 190 to Forest Service Road 21S50, near Quaking Aspen Campground. Turn left on Road 21S50 and drive 6.6 miles, then bear left on Road 20S81. Follow Road 20S81 for 1.4 miles to the signed trailhead.

Contact: Giant Sequoia National Monument/ Sequoia National Forest, Western Divide Ranger District, Springville, 559/539-2607, www.fs.usda.gov/sequoia.

86 FREEMAN CREEK TRAIL

4.0 mi/2.0 hr

in Giant Sequoia National Monument near Quaking Aspen

Map 11.3, page 561

The easternmost grove of sequoias in the world is your destination on Freeman Creek Trail. Compared to most sequoia groves in the Sierra, the trees of the 1,700-acre Freeman Creek Grove are mere adolescents—probably not more than 1,000 years old. Among them is a tree named for former President George Bush Sr., who visited the grove in 1992. The trail is a pleasant downhill stroll along Freeman Creek, reaching the first sequoias in about one mile, after crossing the creek. In between the big trees are large meadow areas (many of which bloom with spring and summer wildflowers) and forests of red firs. Many campsites are found along the creek. The path finally ends at Lloyd Meadows, three miles from the trailhead, but most people don't travel that far, since it requires too much climbing on the way back. Two miles out and back is just about the perfect trail length.

User Groups: Hikers, dogs, horses, and mountain bikes. No wheelchair facilities.

Permits: No permits are required. Parking and access are free.

Maps: A Sequoia National Forest map is available from the U.S. Forest Service. For topographic maps, go to the USGS website to download Sentinel Peak.

Directions: From Porterville, drive 45 miles east on Highway 190 to Forest Service Road 21S50, near Quaking Aspen Campground. Turn left on Road 21S50 and drive 0.5 mile, then turn right at the sign for the Freeman Creek Grove.

Contact: Giant Sequoia National Monument/ Sequoia National Forest, Western Divide Ranger District, Springville, 559/539-2607, www.fs.usda.gov/sequoia.

87 SUMMIT TRAIL TO SLATE MOUNTAIN

8.0 mi/4.0 hr 3 9

in Giant Sequoia National Monument near Quaking Aspen

Map 11.3, page 561

If you're staying at Quaking Aspen Campground, you can set out on Summit National Recreation Trail from outside your tent door, but if you're not, drive to the trailhead just south of the camp off Road 21S78. Few people hike all 12 miles of the trail, but many take this four-mile jaunt to the summit of 9,302-foot Slate Mountain, the highest peak in the area. The first two miles of trail are easy, climbing gently through meadows and forest (some logging activity can be seen); then the route climbs more steeply, ascending first the east side and then the north side of

Slate Mountain. Views of the granite spires of The Needles and Olancha Peak can be seen. At 3.8 miles you reach a junction with Bear Creek Trail, and from there, it's a short scramble to your left to the top of Slate Mountain, which is a big pile of rocks with a tremendous 360-degree view. There's no trail, but a couple well-worn routes are visible.

User Groups: Hikers, dogs, horses, and mountain bikes. No wheelchair facilities.

Permits: No permits are required. Parking and access are free.

Maps: A Sequoia National Forest map is available from the U.S. Forest Service. For a topographic map, go to the USGS website to download Sentinel Peak.

Directions: From Porterville, drive 46 miles east on Highway 190 to Forest Service Road 21S78, which is 0.5 mile south of Quaking Aspen Campground. Turn right on Road 21S78 and drive 0.5 mile to the Summit trailhead.

Contact: Giant Sequoia National Monument/ Sequoia National Forest, Western Divide Ranger District, Springville, 559/539-2607, www.fs.usda.gov/sequoia.

88 THE NEEDLES SPIRES

5.0 mi/2.5 hr

in Giant Sequoia National Monument near Quaking Aspen

Map 11.3, page 561 **BEST**

It's tragic but true—the historic and precariously perched Needles Fire Lookout burned down in 2011 after an ember escaped from its chimney. But you can still take this wonderful easy day-hike in Giant Sequoia National Monument to the site where the lookout once stood and enjoy almost nonstop views of the Sequoia backcountry. At the trail's start is a placard with an old black-and-white photo that shows what the Needles fire lookout looked like early in the 20th century. Five minutes down the trail, you leave the forest and come out to two wooden benches. This is a great spot to stare out at the magnificent view of the Kern River Basin before you. Look ahead and you'll see The Needles' tall granite spires; the highest spire is at elevation 8,245 feet. The trail goes up, then down, then up again, through firs, ponderosas, sugar pines, granite, and sand. The only steep section is the final set of switchbacks up The Needles. The fire lookout tower is sadly missing from its perch on top of the high spire that local rock climbers call The Magician, but hopefully it will be rebuilt one day. For now, you can ascend the wood and metal staircase that once led to the structure—now a stairway to nowhere—then admire the breathtaking view of Lloyd Meadow, the Kern River drainage, Mount Whitney, Olancha Peak, Farewell Gap, and Dome Rock. This is one of the most inspiring views in the southern Sierra.

User Groups: Hikers, dogs, horses, and mountain bikes. No wheelchair facilities.

Permits: No permits are required. Parking and access are free.

Maps: A Sequoia National Forest map is available from the U.S. Forest Service. For topographic maps, go to the USGS website to download Sentinel Peak and Durrwood Creek.

Directions: From Porterville, drive 46 miles east on Highway 190 to Forest Service Road 21S05, which is 0.5 mile south of Quaking Aspen Campground. Turn left (east) on Road 21S05 and drive 2.8 miles to the trailhead.

Contact: Giant Sequoia National Monument/ Sequoia National Forest, Western Divide Ranger District, Springville, 559/539-2607, www.fs.usda.gov/sequoia.

89 TRAIL OF 100 GIANTS

0.5 mi/0.5 hr

in Giant Sequoia National Monument near Johnsondale

Map 11.3, page 561 **BEST**

The Trail of 100 Giants is as good as many of the giant sequoia trails in Sequoia and Kings Canyon National Parks. Trailhead elevation is

6,400 feet, and the trail is an easy and nearly flat loop that is paved and suitable for wheelchairs and baby strollers. Located within the Long Meadow Giant Sequoia Grove, the second-most southern grove where sequoias are found, the big trees on the Trail of 100 Giants are situated amid a mixed forest of cedars and pines. A dozen interpretive signs along the path unlock the secrets of this forest. As you walk in from the parking lot across the road, the first sequoia tree on your right is a doozy—probably the best one on the loop. Of all the sequoia groves we've seen and admired, the Trail of 100 Giants grove stands out because it has an unusual amount of twins—two sequoias growing tightly side by side in order to share resources. In fact, this grove even has one twin that rangers call a "sequedar," a sequoia and a cedar that have grown together. If you're staying at Redwood Meadow Campground, you have your own entrance to this loop, so you don't have to drive down the road to the main trailhead and parking lot.

User Groups: Hikers, wheelchairs, dogs, and horses. No mountain bikes.

Permits: No permits are required. A $5 parking fee is charged per vehicle.

Maps: A Sequoia National Forest map is available from the U.S. Forest Service. For a topographic map, go to the USGS website to download Johnsondale.

Directions: From Kernville on the north end of Isabella Lake, drive north on Sierra Way/Road 99 for 27 miles to Johnsondale R-Ranch. Continue west (the road becomes Road 50) for 5.5 miles, turn right on the Western Divide Highway, and drive 2.4 miles to the trailhead parking area, on the right, just before Redwood Meadow Campground. Cross the road to begin the trail.

Contact: Giant Sequoia National Monument/Sequoia National Forest, Western Divide Ranger District, Springville, 559/539-2607, www.fs.usda.gov/sequoia.

90 MULE PEAK LOOKOUT

1.2 mi/1.0 hr  

in Giant Sequoia National Monument near Johnsondale

Map 11.3, page 561

While rock climbers come to Mule Peak to do their daring work, hikers can take a not-so-daring walk up the back side of Mule Peak; it's attainable for all ages and levels of hikers. The area around the peak has been logged, but much of the forest has grown back. The trail follows a series of easy switchbacks up the hillside, gaining 600 feet to the summit of Mule Peak (elevation 8,142 feet). A lookout tower is positioned there, built in 1936 and still in operation by Sequoia National Forest. The summit view includes Onion Meadow Peak, Table Mountain, the Tule River Valley, and the Tule River Indian Reservation to the west.

User Groups: Hikers, dogs, horses, and mountain bikes. No wheelchair facilities.

Permits: No permits are required. Parking and access are free.

Maps: A Sequoia National Forest map is available from the U.S. Forest Service. For a topographic map, go to the USGS website to download Sentinel Peak.

Directions: From Kernville on the north end of Isabella Lake, drive north on Sierra Way/Road 99 for 27 miles to Johnsondale R-Ranch. Continue west (the road becomes Road 50), then in 5.5 miles, turn right on the Western Divide Highway. Drive five miles to the left turnoff signed for Mule Peak/Road 22S03. Turn left and follow Road 22S03 for five miles to the Mule Peak trailhead.

Contact: Giant Sequoia National Monument/Sequoia National Forest, Western Divide Ranger District, Springville, 559/539-2607, www.fs.usda.gov/sequoia.

91 DOME ROCK

0.25 mi/0.5 hr 1 9

in Giant Sequoia National Monument near Quaking Aspen

Map 11.3, page 561

Dome Rock wins the prize for "Granite Dome with the Most Pedestrian Name." But never mind. It also wins the prize for "Shortest Walk to an Incredible View." Trailhead elevation is 7,200 feet, and the trail is really just a route leading from the left side of the parking lot. Signs at the parking lot warn you not to drop or throw anything off the top of the dome, because there are rock climbers down below on the dome's steep side. It's a mere five-minute walk to the top of Dome Rock—a huge cap of bare granite—where the views are incredible of Slate Mountain, Isabella Lake, and The Needles. You'll want to hang around here for a while to ooh and aah. If your scrambling skills are good, consider checking out another stunning destination just a few miles from here. Jump back in your car and drive back to the Western Divide Highway, then head south for four miles to an unmarked pullout on the east side of the road, 0.25 mile south of the Crawford Road turnoff. Start hiking on the dirt road that begins at the turnout; bear right where it forks. The path draws near to Nobe Young Creek, and soon you will hear a noisy waterfall. Take one of several spur trails on your left leading down to the base of the 125-foot fall, which drops over three granite ledges. The entire hike is only one mile round-trip, but because there is no formal trail, it's not for novices. Wear good boots and use caution on the steep and slippery slope.

User Groups: Hikers, dogs, horses, and mountain bikes. No wheelchair facilities.

Permits: No permits are required. Parking and access are free.

Maps: A Sequoia National Forest map is available from the U.S. Forest Service. For a topographic map go to the USGS website to download Sentinel Peak.

Directions: From Kernville on the north end of Isabella Lake, drive north on Sierra Way/ Road 99 for 27 miles to Johnsondale R-Ranch. Continue west (the road becomes Road 50) for 5.5 miles, and turn right on the Western Divide Highway. Drive 12 miles to the Dome Rock/Road 21S69 turnoff, on the right, across from Peppermint Work Center. Turn right and follow the dirt road for a few hundred yards; where it forks, bear left and continue to the trailhead, 0.5 mile from the Western Divide Highway. If you're traveling from the north, the turnoff is two miles south of Ponderosa Lodge.

Contact: Giant Sequoia National Monument/ Sequoia National Forest, Western Divide Ranger District, Springville, 559/539-2607, www.fs.usda.gov/sequoia.

92 ALDER CREEK TRAIL

1.8 mi/1.0 hr 1 8

in Giant Sequoia National Monument near Johnsondale

Map 11.3, page 561 BEST

The granite slabs and pools on Alder Creek have gotten so popular with hikers, swimmers, and picnickers that the Forest Service has installed No Parking Any Time signs all over the road near the trailhead. But as long as you park where you're supposed to (off the road, in the day-use parking area), you can still pay a visit to the tons-of-fun pools and slides along Alder Creek. To reach them, walk up the gated dirt road (Road 22S83) and turn right on the single-track trail. The path descends to the confluence of Alder Creek and Dry Meadow Creek, where there is a long length of swimming holes and rocky slides that pour into them. Make sure you wear denim or some other heavy material on your backside so you can while away many happy hours pretending you are a river otter. It's exhilarating, but please use caution as you slip and slide. Slick granite can be very unforgiving.

User Groups: Hikers and dogs. No horses or mountain bikes. No wheelchair facilities.

Permits: No permits are required. Parking and access are free.

Maps: A Sequoia National Forest map is available from the U.S. Forest Service. For a topographic map, go to the USGS website to download Sentinel Peak.

Directions: From Kernville on the north end of Lake Isabella, drive north on Sierra Way/Road 99 for 27 miles to 0.5 mile north of Johnsondale R-Ranch. Turn right on Road 22S82 and drive 5.7 miles to the day-use parking area, on the right side of the road. Walk across Road 22S82 to the gated dirt road and the trailhead.

Contact: Giant Sequoia National Monument/Sequoia National Forest, Western Divide Ranger District, Springville, 559/539-2607, www.fs.usda.gov/sequoia.

93 KEARSARGE PASS

10.0 mi/6.0 hr or 2 days 

in the John Muir Wilderness in Inyo National Forest

Map 11.3, page 561

The trailhead elevation for Kearsarge Pass Trail is 9,200 feet, and the elevation at Kearsarge Pass is 11,823 feet. Five miles and a good amount of climbing lie in between, but the route is well graded, and the scenery is spectacular. The trail, which was once an Indian trading route, leads to the backcountry of Kings Canyon National Park, but most day hikers just make the trip to the pass. Along the way, you are witness to several sparkling lakes and whitewater cascades, and a wealth of high-country wildflowers. Not surprisingly, this is a very popular trail. Remember to bring sunglasses, sunscreen, and a jacket for the summit, which is windy and exposed.

The trail climbs gradually from the trailhead, often nearing Independence Creek then veering away again as it winds through a multitude of switchbacks. You pass Little Pothole Lake at 1.5 miles, Gilbert Lake at 2.2 miles, and Flower Lake at 2.6 miles. Continue climbing high above tree line to Kearsarge Pass. You'll get a long-distance view of Heart Lake and pass the left spur trail leading to Big Pothole Lake along the way. Finally, just when you think you can climb no farther, you reach the pass, at five miles. A sign announces your arrival in Kings Canyon Park, and extraordinary Sierra views surround you. You'll gaze at Bullfrog and Kearsarge Lakes, University Peak, and Mount Gould.

Note: If you decide to turn this into an overnight trip, food storage regulations are in effect. Bear-resistant canisters are required for all backpackers, and no wood fires are permitted. Good camping and fishing is located 3.5 miles beyond the pass, at Charlotte Lake, but a one-night stay limit is in effect.

User Groups: Hikers, dogs, and horses. Dogs are allowed to Kearsarge Pass, but not beyond it. No mountain bikes. No wheelchair facilities.

Permits: A free wilderness permit is required year-round for overnight stays and is available from the Eastern Sierra Interagency Visitor Center, 1.5 miles south of Lone Pine. Quotas are in effect from May 1 to November 1; permits are available in advance for a $5 reservation fee per person.

Maps: A John Muir Wilderness map is available from the U.S. Forest Service. A Kearsarge Pass map is available from Tom Harrison Maps. For a topographic map, go to the USGS website to download Kearsarge Peak.

Directions: From Lone Pine, drive 15 miles north on U.S. 395 to Independence. Turn west on Market Street, which becomes Onion Valley Road. Drive 14 miles to the end of the road and the trailhead parking area.

Contact: Inyo National Forest, Mount Whitney Ranger Station, Lone Pine, 760/876-6200, www.fs.usda.gov/inyo; Eastern Sierra Interagency Visitor Center, 760/876-6222.

94 FLOWER AND MATLOCK LAKES

6.4 mi/3.5 hr 2 8

in the John Muir Wilderness in Inyo National Forest

Map 11.3, page 561

If you don't have the time or the energy for Kearsarge Pass (see listing in this chapter), the route to Flower Lake and Matlock Lake is a good second choice. Although it doesn't offer the astounding views that the pass has, it is still a stellar trip into dramatic granite country. Both lakes are deep blue waterways that draw in all the color of the Sierra sky. The trail climbs gradually from the trailhead, switchbacking along Independence Creek. You pass Little Pothole Lake at 1.5 miles and Gilbert Lake at 2.2 miles, reaching a junction for Matlock Lake at 2.5 miles. Continue straight for 0.1 mile to Flower Lake, then retrace your steps to the junction and head south for 0.7 mile to larger Matlock Lake. Pull out your camera and a picnic, and while away some time before returning to the trailhead.

User Groups: Hikers, dogs, and horses. No mountain bikes. No wheelchair facilities.

Permits: No day-hiking permits are required. Parking and access are free.

Maps: A John Muir Wilderness map is available from the U.S. Forest Service. A Kearsarge Pass map is available from Tom Harrison Maps. For a topographic map, go to the USGS website to download Kearsarge Peak.

Directions: From Lone Pine, drive 15 miles north on U.S. 395 to Independence. Turn west on Market Street, which becomes Onion Valley Road. Drive 14 miles to the end of the road and the trailhead parking area.

Contact: Inyo National Forest, Mount Whitney Ranger Station, Lone Pine, 760/876-6200, www.fs.usda.gov/inyo; Eastern Sierra Interagency Visitor Center, 760/876-6222.

95 ROBINSON LAKE

3.0 mi/2.0 hr 4 9

in the John Muir Wilderness in Inyo National Forest

Map 11.3, page 561

The Robinson Lake Trail is best described as relentlessly steep but mercifully short. The hike is challenging in places due to the grade, loose surface, and relative obscurity of the trail, but the destination is superlative. In addition to beautiful Robinson Lake (at 10,500 feet), you get a close and personal view of 11,744-foot Independence Peak and an excellent wildflower display along Robinson Creek. Start at the trailhead by campsite No. 7 in Onion Valley Campground. Watch out for the overgrown vegetation that can sometimes hide the trail. Just climb, catch your breath, and climb some more. After a fairly punishing ascent, you'll reach the small, shallow lake in less than an hour. Campsites and picnicking sites are found in the sand on the lake's east side, or in the pine forest on the northwest side. Equally as pretty as the lake are the views from its shores of the valley below. Plan your trip for July to September; the trail is usually free of snow by midsummer. But whenever you go, watch your footing carefully. This trail is not maintained very often.

User Groups: Hikers, dogs, and horses. No mountain bikes. No wheelchair facilities.

Permits: No day-hiking permits are required. Parking and access are free.

Maps: A John Muir Wilderness map is available from the U.S. Forest Service. A Kearsarge Pass map is available from Tom Harrison Maps. For a topographic map, go to the USGS website to download Kearsarge Peak.

Directions: From Lone Pine, drive 15 miles north on U.S. 395 to Independence. Turn west on Market Street, which becomes Onion Valley Road. Drive 14 miles to the end of the road and the hikers' parking area. Walk into Onion Valley Campground to find the trailhead, by site No. 7.

Contact: Inyo National Forest, Mount Whitney Ranger Station, Lone Pine, 760/876-6200, www.fs.usda.gov/inyo; Eastern Sierra Interagency Visitor Center, 760/876-6222.

96 MOUNT WHITNEY TRAIL

22.0 mi/15.0 hr or 2-3 days 5 10

in the John Muir Wilderness

Map 11.3, page 561 BEST

Mount Whitney, at 14,505 feet in elevation, is the highest peak in the contiguous United States and also one of the most popular "fourteeners" to climb. The peak has become so well traveled that not only are quotas enforced for backpackers, but even day hikers must obtain a wilderness permit to hike the trail. About 100 day-hikers and 60 backpackers are granted a Mount Whitney permit each day during the quota period, May 1 to November 1. Reserve your spot through the Mount Whitney preseason lottery at www.recreation.gov. The lottery is held February 1 to March 15 each year. After the lottery, any day-hiking spaces remaining can be reserved up to two days before your hike. And, yes, many people do hike the entire 22-mile round-trip trail in one single day, ascending and descending more than a vertical mile along the way (6,131 feet in all), but it means a predawn start and a grueling march. Many people who try this suffer from a variety of ailments, including dehydration, hypoglycemia, and even altitude sickness, and never make it to the top. Others make it, but realize they would have had a lot more fun if they had divided the trip into two or even three days. So here's the smart way to hike Mount Whitney: Get your wilderness permit way in advance (see the permit information below), and plan your trip for a weekday, not a weekend. If possible, wait to make the climb until September or early October, when the crowds have thinned considerably; August sees the highest trail usage. Spend a couple days at high elevation (10,000 or higher) before you set out on the Mount Whitney Trail. Come prepared with sunglasses, sunscreen, good boots, and warm clothes for the summit. And since all solid human waste must be packed out (not buried, as is permitted in other areas of the Sierra), it's a good idea to obtain a free "human waste pack-out kit" from the Eastern Sierra Interagency Visitor Center before leaving on your trip. Consider this: In a typical summer, visitors to Mount Whitney pack out more than 7,000 pounds of human waste. For more information on the Mount Whitney Trail, see the trail notes for the *Whitney Portal to Lake Thomas Edison (JMT/PCT)* hike in this chapter.

User Groups: Hikers only. No dogs, horses, or mountain bikes. (Dogs are allowed on the first 6.2 miles of trail, but not beyond.) No wheelchair facilities.

Permits: A wilderness permit is required year-round for both day hikers and backpackers and is available from the Eastern Sierra Interagency Visitor Center, 1.5 mile south of Lone Pine at the junction of U.S. 396 and Hwy. 136. Quotas are in effect from May 1 to November 1 for both day hikers and backpackers. Permit application forms are entered into a lottery from Feb. 1 to March 15 each year for all dates in the quota period (May 1 to November 1). Submit a permit application form online at www.recreation.gov, or phone 760/873-2483 for more information. There is a $15 reservation fee per person. Bear canisters are required for overnight stays and no wood fires are permitted.

Maps: A Mount Whitney Zone map is available from Tom Harrison Maps. For topographic maps, go to the USGS website to download Mount Whitney and Mount Langley.

Directions: From Lone Pine on U.S. 395, drive west on Whitney Portal Road for 13 miles to the end of the road and the trailhead.

Contact: Inyo National Forest, Mount Whitney Ranger Station, Lone Pine, 760/876-6200, www.fs.usda.gov/inyo; Eastern Sierra Interagency Visitor Center, 760/876-6222.

97 WHITNEY PORTAL NATIONAL RECREATION TRAIL

4.0 mi one-way/2.0 hr 1 9

in Inyo National Forest near Whitney Portal

Map 11.3, page 561

Don't confuse this trail with the Mount Whitney Trail, because except for their nearby trailheads, they have zero in common. Although if you try to hike the Whitney Portal National Recreation Trail in both directions, instead of as a one-way downhill hike, you may find it feels darn near as demanding as the Mount Whitney Trail, which climbs nearly 6,000 feet to the top of Mount Whitney. (Okay, maybe not quite that demanding.) The recreation trail begins at Whitney Portal (elevation 8,360 feet) and heads downhill through conifers and granite to Lone Pine Campground (elevation 5,640). The best thing about the route is that no matter how crowded it is at Whitney Portal, this trail gets surprisingly few hikers, especially after the first 0.5 mile, which skirts Whitney Portal Campground. You get to leave the multitudes behind as you walk downhill along Lone Pine Creek, among the good company of granite formations and big pines. Vistas are excellent along the way, including Mount Whitney to the west and the Alabama Hills and White Mountains to the east.

User Groups: Hikers, dogs, and horses. No mountain bikes. No wheelchair facilities.

Permits: No permits are required. Parking and access are free.

Maps: A Mount Whitney High Country map is available from Tom Harrison Maps. For a topographic map, go to the USGS website to download Mount Langley.

Directions: From Lone Pine on U.S. 395, drive west on Whitney Portal Road for 13 miles to the end of the road and the trailhead, located across from the fishing pond. You will need to leave a shuttle car or arrange a pickup at Lone Pine Campground, four miles downhill on Whitney Portal Road.

Contact: Inyo National Forest, Mount Whitney Ranger Station, Lone Pine, 760/876-6200, www.fs.usda.gov/inyo; Eastern Sierra Interagency Visitor Center, 760/876-6222.

98 MEYSAN LAKE

11.0 mi/6.0 hr or 2 days  5 9

in the John Muir Wilderness near Mount Whitney

Map 11.3, page 561

The Meysan Lake Trail is less popular than the neighboring trail to the top of Mount Whitney, but still, you should get your wilderness permit in advance or plan on day hiking. Better yet, plan your trip for late September and during the week. The trail to Meysan Lake is long, steep, hot, and dry—let's just say it's grueling—but it leads to a beautiful alpine lake basin and provides spectacular views of granite walls. It also gives climbers access to climbing routes on Mount Mallory and Lone Pine Peak. The trail is parallel to Meysan Creek and is not well maintained, which makes it even more demanding. You reach a left fork for Grass Lake at 4.5 miles, where the first water is available. The right fork continues to Camp Lake and its beautiful meadow (at five miles). The elevation here is 11,200 feet. The trail from Camp Lake to Meysan Lake is rather sketchy. Head to the right of Camp Lake, cross the inlet stream, and watch for rock cairns marking the way up the steep, rocky slope. Meysan Lake is often still frozen as late as June, even though the trail can be as hot as an oven. The trailhead elevation is 7,900 feet; Meysan Lake is at 11,460 feet.

User Groups: Hikers and dogs. No horses or mountain bikes. No wheelchair facilities.

Permits: A free wilderness permit is required year-round for overnight stays and is available from the Eastern Sierra Interagency Visitor Center, 1.5 miles south of Lone Pine. Quotas are in effect from May 1 to November 1; permits are available in advance for a $5 reservation fee per person.

Maps: A John Muir Wilderness map is available from the U.S. Forest Service. A Mount Whitney Zone map is available from Tom Harrison Maps. For topographic maps, go to the USGS website to download Mount Whitney and Mount Langley.

Directions: From Lone Pine on U.S. 395, drive west on Whitney Portal Road for 12 miles to Whitney Portal Campground and the Meysan Lake trailhead. Park on the side of Whitney Portal Road by the camp and walk through the camp to reach the trailhead.

Contact: Inyo National Forest, Mount Whitney Ranger Station, Lone Pine, 760/876-6200, www.fs.usda.gov/inyo; Eastern Sierra Interagency Visitor Center, 760/876-6222.

99 LONE PINE LAKE

5.8 mi/3.0 hr 

in the John Muir Wilderness near Whitney Portal

Map 11.3, page 561

The route to the top of Mount Whitney is so popular and so overcrowded that it has permits and quotas and regulations up the wazoo, but guess what? Sweet little Lone Pine Lake is just outside of the regulated Mount Whitney Zone, so you can hike to it anytime without dealing with any bureaucracy. However, you will have to deal with extremely limited parking at the trailhead during the summer months, so plan your trip for September or later if at all possible. Hiking to Lone Pine Lake is a fun trip for people who have always daydreamed of climbing Mount Whitney, because it follows the first three miles of the summit trail. While other people are trudging along carrying heavy backpacks, you're stepping lightly, with only a sandwich and a bottle of water in your day pack. The trail leads through Jeffrey pines and manzanita to the John Muir Wilderness border at one mile, then switchbacks uphill and opens up to views of the Alabama Hills far below. You'll cross Lone Pine Creek at 2.8 miles, then bear left at a junction to leave the main Mount Whitney Trail and head a few hundred yards to Lone Pine Lake. It's a sweet spot, and although privacy is rare, you have a greater chance of it after Labor Day and on a weekday. Who knows, you may just get so inspired that next time you'll come back and hike all the way to the summit.

User Groups: Hikers and dogs. No horses or mountain bikes. No wheelchair facilities.

Permits: No day-hiking permits are required. A Mount Whitney wilderness permit is required for overnight stays. Parking and access are free.

Maps: A John Muir Wilderness map is available from the U.S. Forest Service. A Mount Whitney Zone map is available from Tom Harrison Maps. For topographic maps, go to the USGS website to download Mount Whitney and Mount Langley.

Directions: From Lone Pine on U.S. 395, drive west on Whitney Portal Road for 13 miles to the end of the road and the Mount Whitney trailhead.

Contact: Inyo National Forest, Mount Whitney Ranger Station, Lone Pine, 760/876-6200, www.fs.usda.gov/inyo; Eastern Sierra Interagency Visitor Center, 760/876-6222.

100 WHITNEY PORTAL TO LAKE THOMAS EDISON (JMT/PCT)

112.0 mi one-way/11 days 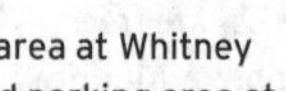

from the trailhead parking area at Whitney Portal north to the trailhead parking area at Lake Thomas Edison

Map 11.3, page 561 BEST

You can have a foothold in the sky with every step on the John Muir Trail (JMT). This part of the trail is shared with the Pacific Crest Trail (PCT) and starts at practically the tip-top of North America—Mount Whitney—and takes you northward across a land of 12,000-foot passes and Ansel Adams-style panoramas.

From the trailhead at Whitney Portal, the hike climbs more than 6,100 feet over the course of 11 miles to reach Whitney's summit at 14,505 feet. That includes an ascent of more than 100 switchbacks, which are often snow covered even late in summer, to reach Trail Crest (13,560 feet). Here you turn right and take Summit Trail. In the final stretch to the top, the ridge is cut by huge notch windows in the rock; you look through, and the bottom drops out more than 10,000 feet to the town of Lone Pine below, at an elevation of 3,800 feet. Finally you make it to the top and notice how the surrounding giant blocks of rock look as if they were sculpted with a giant hammer and chisel. From here, the entire Western Divide is visible, and to the north, rows of mountain peaks are lined up for miles to the horizon. Be sure to sign your name in the register, kept in a lightning-proof metal box. You may feel a bit dizzy from the altitude, but you'll know you're someplace very special.

The journey farther north is just as captivating. The route drops into Sequoia National Park, then climbs above timberline for almost a day's worth of hiking as it nears Forester Pass (13,180 feet). It's not only the highest point on the PCT; it's the most dangerous section of trail on the entire route as well. The trail is narrow and steep, cut into a high vertical slab of rock, and is typically icy, with an iced-over snowfield near the top that's particularly treacherous. An ice ax is an absolute must. If you slip here, you could fall thousands of feet.

Once through Forester, the trail heads onward into the John Muir Wilderness along Bubbs Creek, with great wildflowers at nearby Vidette Meadow. Then it's up and over Kearsarge Pass (10,710 feet), and after a short drop, you're back climbing again, this time over Glen Pass (11,978 feet)—a spectacular, boulder-strewn ridge with great views to the north looking into Kings Canyon National Park. Just two miles from Glen Pass is Rae Lakes, a fantasy spot for camping (one-night limit), with pristine meadows, shoreline campsites, and lots of eager brook trout.

The JMT then heads through Kings Canyon National Park by following sparkling streams much of the way, finally climbing up and over Pinchot Pass (12,130 feet), then back down along the upper Kings River for a long, steady ascent over Mather Pass (12,100 feet). The wonders continue as you hike along Palisade Lakes, then down into LeConte Canyon, followed by an endless climb up to Muir Pass (11,965 feet). In early summer, snowfields are common here, and this can be difficult and trying, especially if your boots keep post-holing through the snow. The country near Muir Pass is extremely stark—nothing but sculpted granite, ice, and a few small turquoise lakes—crowned by the stone Muir Hut at the pass, where hikers can duck in and hide for safety from sudden afternoon thunderstorms and lightning bolts.

The views astound many visitors as the trail drops into Evolution Valley. It's like a trip back to the beginning of time, where all is pure and primary, yet incredibly lush and beautiful. You finally leave Kings Canyon National Park, following the headwaters of the San Joaquin River into Sierra National Forest. After bottoming out at 7,890 feet, the trail rises steeply in switchback after switchback as it enters the John Muir Wilderness. Finally you top Selden Pass (10,900 feet), take in an incredible view (where the rows of surrounding mountaintops look like the Great Pyramids), then make the easy one-mile descent to Marie Lakes, a pretty campsite with excellent trout fishing near the lake's outlet.

The final push on this section of the JMT is climbing up Bear Mountain, then down a terrible, toe-jamming stretch to Mono Creek. Here you make a left turn and continue for two more miles until you come to Edison Lake, an excellent place to have a food stash waiting. (To continue north on the JMT/PCT, see the *Lake Thomas Edison to Agnew Meadows* hike in this chapter.)

Note: Crossing Mono Creek at the North

Fork can be dangerous during high-runoff conditions.

User Groups: Hikers and horses. No dogs or mountain bikes. No wheelchair facilities.

Permits: A wilderness permit is required for traveling through various wilderness and special-use areas the trail traverses. Contact the Eastern Sierra Interagency Visitor Center for more information.

Maps: A John Muir Trail Map Pack is available from Tom Harrison Maps. For topographic maps, go to the USGS website to download Mount Whitney, Mount Williamson, Kearsarge Peak, Mount Clarence King, Mount Pinchot, North Palisade, Mount Goddard, Mount Darwin, Mount Henry, Ward Mountain, Florence Lake, and Graveyard Peak.

Directions: To reach the Mount Whitney trailhead from Lone Pine and U.S. 395, head west on Whitney Portal Road for approximately 13 miles to Whitney Portal and the trailhead for the Mount Whitney Trail. To reach the Lake Thomas Edison trailhead from the town of Shaver Lake, drive north on Highway 168 for approximately 21 miles to the town of Lakeshore. Turn northeast onto Kaiser Pass Road/Forest Service 4S01. Kaiser Pass Road becomes Edison Lake Road at Mono Hot Springs. Drive another five miles north past town to the Vermillion Campground and parking area for backcountry hikers. The PCT begins near the east end of the lake.

Contact: Inyo National Forest, Mount Whitney Ranger Station, Lone Pine, 760/876-6200 or 760/873-2400, www.fs.usda.gov/inyo; Sierra National Forest, High Sierra Ranger District, Prather, 559/855-5360, www.fs.usda.gov/sequoia; Sequoia National Forest, Sequoia National Forest, Kern River Ranger District, Kernville, 760/376-3781, www.fs.usda.gov/sequoia; Eastern Sierra Interagency Visitor Center, 760/876-6222.

101 COTTONWOOD LAKES

10.0-12.5 mi/6.0 hr or 2 days 2 10

in the John Muir Wilderness south of Mount Whitney

Map 11.3, page 561

The trailhead elevation is just over 10,000 feet here at Horseshoe Meadow, which makes this a wildly popular trailhead for climbing deeper into the backcountry. With the trailhead situated so high, you get a jump on the ascent; your four wheels do the work, instead of your two feet. An unusual feature of this hike is that it passes through two wilderness areas—first a small portion of the Golden Trout Wilderness and then the John Muir Wilderness. Cottonwood Creek accompanies you for much of the trip. The trail starts out in a sandy pine forest with a mellow grade. At 3.7 miles you reach a junction. Most hikers go left; the trail forms a loop around Cottonwood Lakes numbers one, two, and three. If you just want to see the closest lake and head back without making a loop, Cottonwood Lake number one is to the left, 1.5 miles from the junction. Your round-trip will be an even 10 miles. If you complete the whole loop, passing all three lakes, you'll travel 11.5 miles. But the most beautiful lakes by far are numbers four and five, worth an extra 0.5 mile of hiking beyond the far end of the loop. Total elevation gain is only 1,000 feet. Once at the lakes, remember two points: 1) Because the Cottonwood Lakes are home to golden trout, special fishing regulations are in effect, so get updated on the latest rules. 2) No wood fires are allowed, so bring your backpacking stove.

User Groups: Hikers, dogs, and horses. No mountain bikes. No wheelchair facilities.

Permits: A free wilderness permit is required year-round for overnight stays and is available from the Eastern Sierra Interagency Visitor Center, 1.5 miles south of Lone Pine. Quotas are in effect from May 1 to November 1; permits are available in advance for a $5 reservation fee per person. Bear canisters are required.

Maps: A John Muir Wilderness map is available from the U.S. Forest Service. A Mount Whitney High Country map is available from Tom Harrison Maps. For a topographic map, go to the USGS website to download Cirque Peak.
Directions: From Lone Pine on U.S. 395, drive west on Whitney Portal Road for 3.3 miles and turn left (south) on Horseshoe Meadow Road. Continue 19.5 miles and bear right for the Cottonwood Lakes trailhead parking area, near the end of Horseshoe Meadow Road.
Contact: Inyo National Forest, Mount Whitney Ranger Station, Lone Pine, 760/876-6200, www.fs.usda.gov/inyo; Eastern Sierra Interagency Visitor Center, 760/876-6222.

102 COTTONWOOD PASS

8.0 mi/5.0 hr or 2 days 

in the Golden Trout Wilderness

Map 11.3, page 561

The Cottonwood Pass Trail provides access to the Pacific Crest Trail and the Kern Plateau, a land of stark, sub-alpine meadows. You're entering the Golden Trout Wilderness, home of California's state fish and located at the very south end of the Sierra Nevada. This is where the steep, nearly perpendicular mountains start to mellow out into more gentle terrain—mostly in the form of rolling high-country hills and meadows. Start from wide Horseshoe Meadow and climb gently through forest for the first two miles of trail. Shortly, the switchbacks begin and the ascent becomes serious. After a 1,100-foot climb, you reach the pass (at four miles), where you can gaze out at the Great Western Divide, Big Whitney Meadows, and the Inyo Mountains. Bring a jacket with you for the windy, 11,250-foot summit. Ambitious hikers can continue beyond the pass and take the right fork for Chicken Spring Lake, one mile away on the Pacific Crest Trail (no campfires allowed).
User Groups: Hikers, dogs, and horses. No mountain bikes. No wheelchair facilities.
Permits: A free wilderness permit is required year-round for overnight stays and is available from the Eastern Sierra Interagency Visitor Center, 1.5 miles south of Lone Pine. Quotas are in effect from the last Friday in June to September 15; permits are available in advance for a $5 reservation fee per person.
Maps: A Golden Trout Wilderness map is available from the U.S. Forest Service or Tom Harrison Maps. For a topographic map, go to the USGS website to download Cirque Peak.
Directions: From Lone Pine on U.S. 395, drive west on Whitney Portal Road for 3.3 miles and turn left (south) on Horseshoe Meadow Road. Continue 19.5 miles to the Horseshoe Meadow trailhead, on the left, at the end of Horseshoe Meadow Road.
Contact: Inyo National Forest, Mount Whitney Ranger Station, Lone Pine, 760/876-6200, www.fs.usda.gov/inyo; Eastern Sierra Interagency Visitor Center, 760/876-6222.

103 TRAIL PASS

5.0 mi/3.0 hr 1 7

in the Golden Trout Wilderness

Map 11.3, page 561

Trail Pass may not be as spectacular as the other trails at Horseshoe Meadow, but it has two things going for it—far fewer people and an easier grade. It's only five miles round-trip from the trailhead to the pass, with a mere 500-foot elevation gain—unheard of in these parts. The main folks using the trail are backpackers accessing the Pacific Crest Trail and Golden Trout Wilderness, so, a lot of the time, you can have this gently rolling, high-country terrain all to yourself. Follow the trail from the parking area to a junction 0.25 mile in, and bear left. In another 0.5 mile, the trail forks, and you bear right for Trail Pass. You'll hike past Horseshoe Meadow and Round Valley, where you'll have the company of many packhorses. Views of Mount Langley and Cirque Peak are sure to inspire you. The pass is situated at 10,500 feet, just below Trail Peak (at 11,600 feet).

User Groups: Hikers, dogs, and horses. No mountain bikes. No wheelchair facilities.
Permits: No day-hiking permits are required. Parking and access are free. A free wilderness permit is required year-round for overnight stays and is available from the Eastern Sierra Interagency Visitor Center, 1.5 miles south of Lone Pine.
Maps: A Golden Trout Wilderness map is available from the U.S. Forest Service or Tom Harrison Maps. For a topographic map, go to the USGS website to download Cirque Peak.
Directions: From Lone Pine on U.S. 395, drive west on Whitney Portal Road for 3.3 miles and turn left (south) on Horseshoe Meadow Road. Continue 19.5 miles to the Horseshoe Meadow trailhead, on the right, at the end of Horseshoe Meadow Road.
Contact: Inyo National Forest, Mount Whitney Ranger Station, Lone Pine, 760/876-6200, www.fs.usda.gov/inyo; Eastern Sierra Interagency Visitor Center, 760/876-6222.

104 CASA VIEJA MEADOW

4.0 mi/2.0 hr 2 9

in the Golden Trout Wilderness

Map 11.3, page 561 BEST

The Blackrock Mountain trailhead, at 8,800 feet, is the jump-off point for a variety of backpacking trips into the Golden Trout Wilderness. But day hikers can also sample the delights of this large, waterway-filled land, the home of California's state fish, the golden trout. From the end of Blackrock Road, walk for less than 0.25 mile to the wilderness boundary, then head gently downhill through a red fir forest to the western edge of Casa Vieja Meadow. There you'll find a snow survey cabin and a wide expanse of grass and wildflowers. Hope your day pack is full of picnic supplies. At the far end of the meadow, you must ford Ninemile Creek to continue hiking farther, so make this your turnaround point. Some people try their luck fishing here. You'll have a gradual 800-foot elevation gain on your return trip.
User Groups: Hikers, dogs, and horses. No mountain bikes. No wheelchair facilities.
Permits: No permits are required. Parking and access are free.
Maps: A Golden Trout Wilderness map is available from the U.S. Forest Service or Tom Harrison Maps. For a topographic map, go to the USGS website to download Casa Vieja Meadows.
Directions: From Kernville on the north end of Isabella Lake, drive north on Sierra Way/Road 99 for 22 miles to the turnoff for Sherman Pass Road/22S05. Turn right and drive approximately 35 miles on Sherman Pass Road to the Blackrock Information Station; continue straight on Road 21S03/Blackrock Road. Follow Road 21S03 north for eight miles to the end of the road and the Blackrock Mountain trailhead.
Contact: Sequoia National Forest, Kern River Ranger District, Kernville, 760/376-3781, www.fs.usda.gov/sequoia; Inyo National Forest, Mount Whitney Ranger Station, Lone Pine, 760/876-6200, www.fs.usda.gov/inyo.

105 JORDAN HOT SPRINGS

12.0 mi/7.0 hr or 2 days 4 9

in the Golden Trout Wilderness

Map 11.3, page 561

You can do it in a day if you're ambitious, or you can take a more leisurely two-day trip to Jordan Hot Springs. But however you do it, it's critical to remember that almost all the work is on the way home. The trail is a descent (sometimes knee-jarring) to the grounds of an old hot springs resort, which was closed when this area became part of the Golden Trout Wilderness. The original buildings still stand, and the hot springs are still hot, which is the reason that this is one of the most popular trips in the wilderness. From the trailhead, take Blackrock Trail for two miles to Casa Vieja

Meadow (see listing in this chapter), then cross Ninemile Creek and turn left (west) on Jordan Hot Springs Trail. Hike another three miles downhill along Ninemile Creek, crossing it a few more times. Once you reach the old resort, have a good soak and pull your energy together, because you've got a 2,600-foot gain on the return trip.

User Groups: Hikers, dogs, and horses. No mountain bikes. No wheelchair facilities.

Permits: A free wilderness permit is required year-round for overnight stays and is available from the Kern River Ranger Station. Parking and access are free.

Maps: A Golden Trout Wilderness map is available from the U.S. Forest Service or Tom Harrison Maps. For a topographic map, go to the USGS website to download Casa Vieja Meadows.

Directions: From Kernville on the north end of Isabella Lake, drive north on Sierra Way/Road 99 for 22 miles to the right turnoff for Sherman Pass Road/22S05. Turn right and drive approximately 35 miles on Sherman Pass Road to the Blackrock Information Station; continue straight on Road 21S03/Blackrock Road. Follow Road 21S03 north for eight miles to the end of the road and the Blackrock Mountain trailhead.

Contact: Sequoia National Forest, Kern River Ranger District, Kernville, 760/376-3781, www.fs.usda.gov/sequoia.

106 NORTH FORK KERN RIVER TRAIL

10.4 mi/5.0 hr or 2 days 2 8

in Sequoia National Forest north of Kernville

Map 11.4, page 562

Sometimes you just want to walk alongside a beautiful river, and if that's what you're in the mood for, the Wild and Scenic North Fork Kern is a first-rate choice. From the giant parking lot, walk across the hikers' bridge (separate from but next to the highway bridge) to reach the far side of the river, and then descend on stairs to reach the trail. The North Fork Kern River Trail winds along gently, heading deep into the dramatic Kern Canyon, sometimes under the shade of digger pines, live oaks, and incense cedars, and sometimes out in the bright sunshine. Spring wildflowers are stunning, especially in March and April. Spring river rafters are also entertaining to watch. Most people who walk this trail bring a fishing rod with them, and if you do, make sure you're up-to-date on the special fishing regulations. They're in effect for the first four miles of river, which is a wild trout area. Backpackers will find many campsites along the trail, including some that are under the cavelike canopy of big boulders. This easy, mellow trail offers something for everyone. Note: If you venture out here at the height of spring runoff, parts of the trail may be submerged.

User Groups: Hikers and dogs. No mountain bikes or horses. No wheelchair facilities.

Permits: A free campfire permit is required for overnight stays and is available from the Springville or Kernville Ranger Stations at the addresses below. Parking and access are free.

Maps: A Sequoia National Forest map is available from the U.S. Forest Service. For a topographic map, go to the USGS website to download Fairview.

Directions: From Kernville on the north end of Lake Isabella, drive north on Sierra Way/Road 99 for 22 miles to the Johnsondale highway bridge over the Kern River. Turn right and park in the large paved parking lot by the signboard at the bridge.

Contact: Sequoia National Forest, Kern River Ranger District, Kernville, 760/376-3781, www.fs.usda.gov/sequoia; Western Divide Ranger District, Springville, 559/539-2607, www.fs.usda.gov/sequoia.

107 SHERMAN PEAK TRAIL

4.0 mi/2.0 hr 1 9

in Sequoia National Forest near Sherman Pass

Map 11.4, page 562

From the Sherman Pass Vista along the highway, you can look to the north to Mount Whitney and the Great Western Divide. After crossing the highway and hiking Sherman Peak Trail to the top of Sherman Peak (at 9,909 feet), you can pivot around and have a panoramic look at an even bigger chunk of the world. The trail is mostly forested with red firs and pines, and is gradual enough for children to climb. If you read the interpretive display at the vista, you'll be able to identify the myriad of the mountains you're looking at from the peak, including Split Rock and Dome Rock. It's only a 700-foot climb to the summit, mostly through a series of easy switchbacks. At one time, a fire lookout tower was positioned up here, but modern technology made it obsolete and it was taken down.

User Groups: Hikers, dogs, horses, and mountain bikes. No wheelchair facilities.

Permits: No permits are required. Parking and access are free.

Maps: A Sequoia National Forest map is available from the U.S. Forest Service. For topographic maps, go to the USGS website to download Durrwood Creek and Sirretta Peak.

Directions: From Kernville on the north end of Lake Isabella, drive north on Sierra Way/Road 99 for 22 miles to the right turnoff for Sherman Pass Road/22S05. Turn right and drive approximately 15 miles on Sherman Pass Road to the Sherman Pass Vista. The trailhead is across the road.

Contact: Sequoia National Forest, Kern River Ranger District, Kernville, 760/376-3781, www.fs.usda.gov/sequoia.

108 BALD MOUNTAIN LOOKOUT

0.25 mi/0.25 hr 1 9

in Sequoia National Forest on the north edge of the Dome Land Wilderness

Map 11.4, page 562

This short hike to the summit of 9,430-foot Bald Mountain is the easiest possible introduction to the Dome Land Wilderness. It's a brief stroll to the lookout, which is perched on the very northern edge of the wilderness. This region is famous for its many granite domes and monolithic rocks, the happy hunting ground of rock climbers from all over Southern California. Of the many big hunks of rock, Church Dome is perhaps the most outstanding, and it can be seen from here directly to the south. White Dome and Black Mountain are also visible (east of Church Dome), as well as a sweeping vista of the Kern Plateau, the Whitney Range, and the Great Western Divide. Bald Mountain Lookout has the distinction of being the highest fire lookout tower in the southern Sierra Nevada.

User Groups: Hikers, dogs, horses, and mountain bikes. No wheelchair facilities.

Permits: No permits are required. Parking and access are free.

Maps: A Sequoia National Forest or Dome Land Wilderness map is available from the U.S. Forest Service. For a topographic map, go to the USGS website to download Crag Peak.

Directions: From Kernville on the north end of Lake Isabella, drive north on Sierra Way/Road 99 for 22 miles to the right turnoff for Sherman Pass Road/22S05. Turn right and drive approximately 25 miles on Sherman Pass Road to Forest Service Road 22S77, signed for Bald Mountain Lookout. Turn east (right) on Road 22S77 and follow it for one mile to its end.

Contact: Sequoia National Forest, Kern River Ranger District, Kernville, 760/376-3781, www.fs.usda.gov/sequoia.

109 JACKASS CREEK NATIONAL RECREATION TRAIL

5.0 mi/2.5 hr 2 9

in Sequoia National Forest near the South Sierra Wilderness

Map 11.4, page 562

The Jackass Creek Trail is way out there on the Kern Plateau, at a trailhead elevation of 8,000 feet. The trail climbs 5.5 miles to Jackass Peak (elevation 9,245 feet) on the border of the South Sierra Wilderness. Most people don't bother traveling that far; instead, they follow the trail along Jackass Creek for a couple of miles through red fir forest to the western edge of Jackass Meadow. In addition to the beautiful meadow, the trail offers a look at many handsome old-growth aspens. The trail is an old dirt road, wide enough for holding hands with your hiking partner. Unfortunately, it's also wide enough for motorcycles, which are allowed here. Our recommendation? Hike this trail in late September or early October for the best show of autumn colors, and for the best chance at having the trail to yourself. If you drive all the way out here and see a parking lot full of motorcycle trailers, try hiking the nearby Hooker Meadow Trail instead (the trailhead is at the end of Road 21S29, just east of Fish Creek Campground). The machines aren't allowed there, and this trail also leads to an outstanding grove of quaking aspens.

User Groups: Hikers, dogs, horses, and mountain bikes. No wheelchair facilities.

Permits: No permits are required. Parking and access are free.

Maps: A Sequoia National Forest map is available from the U.S. Forest Service. For a topographic map, go to the USGS website to download Crag Peak.

Directions: From Kernville on the north end of Lake Isabella, drive north on Sierra Way/Road 99 for 22 miles to the right turnoff for Sherman Pass Road/22S05. Turn right and drive approximately 35 miles on Sherman Pass Road to the four-way intersection with Road 21S03, near Blackrock Information Station. Turn right to continue on Road 22S05, and drive five miles to Fish Creek Campground and Road 21S01, where the trail begins.

Contact: Sequoia National Forest, Kern River Ranger District, Kernville, 760/376-3781, www.fs.usda.gov/sequoia.

110 WHISKEY FLAT TRAIL

5.0 mi/2.5 hr 2 8

in Sequoia National Forest near Fairview

Map 11.4, page 562

The Whiskey Flat Trail is a 14.5-mile trail that parallels the Kern River from Fairview Lodge all the way south to Burlando Road in Kernville. Primarily used by anglers working the Kern River, it's also a good springtime stroll for river lovers. If you walk out and back for a few miles on the northern end of the trail by Fairview, you can end the day with a meal at Fairview Lodge's restaurant, where you can brag about the fish you did or didn't catch, like everybody else there. The Whiskey Flat Trail can be somewhat difficult to follow, especially in springtime, when the numerous creeks you must cross are running full. Early in the year, the creeks can sometimes be impassable. The path begins on a suspension bridge, which is reminiscent of Huck Finn and his friends. You can hike as far as you please; a good distance is 2.5 miles out, or about an hour's walk each way. The terrain is grasslands and chaparral, with occasional digger pines, which means no shade but plenty of spring wildflowers. Although the route is basically level, there are numerous steep stretches where you climb in and out of stream drainages running into the Kern. The trailhead elevation is 2,800 feet.

User Groups: Hikers, dogs, horses, and mountain bikes. No wheelchair facilities.

Permits: No permits are required. Parking and access are free.

Maps: A Sequoia National Forest map is

available from the U.S. Forest Service. For a topographic map, go to the USGS website to download Fairview.

Directions: From Kernville on the north end of Lake Isabella, drive north on Sierra Way/Road 99 for 17 miles to Fairview and the Fairview Lodge, on the left side of the road. A large parking area and a trailhead for the Whiskey Flat Trail are to the right of the lodge.

Contact: Sequoia National Forest, Kern River Ranger District, Kernville, 760/376-3781, www.fs.usda.gov/sequoia.

111 PACKSADDLE CAVE TRAIL

4.6 mi/2.3 hr 2 8

in Sequoia National Forest near Fairview

Map 11.4, page 562

Everybody enjoys the trip to Packsaddle Cave, even though the cave was long ago vandalized of its jewel-like stalactites and stalagmites. Nonetheless, the appeal of visiting the limestone cave keeps this trail well used and fairly well maintained. From the parking lot on Sierra Way, cross the highway and hike uphill on the path, huffing and puffing through some steep pitches. This is not a trail for summertime, because there is little shade among the manzanita, sagebrush, and deer brush, and the total climb is about 1,200 feet. At 1.8 miles, you cross Packsaddle Creek and see several campsites near it. Continue a short distance farther; the cave is off to the left, 0.25 mile before this trail's junction with Rincon Trail. Don't forget your flashlight so you can take a peek inside.

User Groups: Hikers, dogs, horses, and mountain bikes. No wheelchair facilities.

Permits: No permits are required. Parking and access are free.

Maps: A Sequoia National Forest map is available from the U.S. Forest Service. For a topographic map, go to the USGS website to download Fairview.

Directions: From Kernville on the north end of Lake Isabella, drive north on Sierra Way/Road 99 for 18 miles to the Packsaddle Cave trailhead, on the right, 0.25 mile beyond Fairview Campground. The parking area is across the road.

Contact: Sequoia National Forest, Kern River Ranger District, Kernville, 760/376-3781, www.fs.usda.gov/sequoia.

112 RINCON TRAIL

4.0 mi/2.0 hr 2 7

in Sequoia National Forest near Fairview

Map 11.4, page 562

Let's say right away that this Rincon has absolutely nothing in common with the other Rincon, the classic surfing break on the Ventura coast. For one, there's no water here, and two, there's no cool ocean breeze. That means you should plan your hike for winter or spring, before the Kern Valley heats up. The trail leads first east and then steadily north along the Rincon Fault, heading for Forks of the Kern. It undulates, following the drainages of Salmon and other creeks. The destination on this trail is the long-distance view of Salmon Creek Falls, about two miles in, and the good fishing and camping prospects on the way along Salmon Creek. The trail crosses Salmon Creek on a bridge 1.7 miles in, but the waterfall view is about 0.25 mile farther. You may want to bring your binoculars to get a good look. If you wish to hike farther on Rincon Trail, it intersects the route to Packsaddle Cave in another two miles, then crosses Sherman Pass Road in another 2.5 miles, and keeps going straight north all the way to Forks of the Kern. The total one-way trail length is a whopping 19.5 miles. Be forewarned that the Rincon Trail is popular with motorcycle enthusiasts, so your peaceful nature experience may be shattered by their noise.

User Groups: Hikers, dogs, and mountain bikes. No horses. No wheelchair facilities.

Permits: No permits are required. Parking and access are free.

Maps: A Sequoia National Forest map is available from the U.S. Forest Service. For a topographic map, go to the USGS website to download Kernville.

Directions: From Kernville on the north end of Isabella Lake, drive north on Sierra Way/Road 99 for 13 miles to the Rincon trailhead, on the right, across from the Ant Canyon dispersed camping area.

Contact: Sequoia National Forest, Kern River Ranger District, Kernville, 760/376-3781, www.fs.usda.gov/sequoia.

113 SUNDAY PEAK TRAIL

3.4 mi/2.0 hr

in Sequoia National Forest near Wofford Heights

Map 11.4, page 562

From the Sunday Peak trailhead, at 7,200 feet in the Greenhorn Mountains, it's a 1,000-foot climb to the top of Sunday Peak, an excellent day hike for families. The grade is moderate and shaded by big conifers, and the destination is perfect on a day when the heat is sweltering down near Isabella Lake. From the top, you can look down at the Kern River Valley and feel sorry for all those people sweating it out down there. The peak's fire lookout tower was abandoned and then destroyed by the Forest Service in the 1950s when it was determined that nearby Tobias Peak was a better spot to have a lookout. However, the wide-angle views of the Kern Valley, Kern Plateau, and far-off high Sierra peaks are still here for the taking. There are many good picnicking spots on the summit.

User Groups: Hikers, dogs, horses, and mountain bikes. No wheelchair facilities.

Permits: No permits are required. Parking and access are free.

Maps: A Sequoia National Forest map is available from the U.S. Forest Service. For a topographic map, go to the USGS website to download Posey.

Directions: From Wofford Heights on the west side of Isabella Lake, turn west on Highway 155 and drive eight miles to Greenhorn Summit. Turn right on Road 24S15/Forest Highway 90, signed for Portuguese Pass, and drive 6.5 miles north to the parking area for Sunday Peak Trail, near the Girl Scout Camp.

Contact: Sequoia National Forest, Kern River Ranger District, Kernville, 760/376-3781, www.fs.usda.gov/sequoia.

114 UNAL TRAIL

3.0 mi/1.5 hr 1 8

in Sequoia National Forest near Wofford Heights

Map 11.4, page 562 BEST

This is a first-rate trail for families or for anybody who wants a good leg-stretching walk or run around a beautiful mountain. The Unal Trail is a three-mile loop that climbs gently for two miles to Unal Peak, and then descends in one mile of switchbacks back to the trailhead. (After the first 100 yards, where the trail forks, be sure you take the left fork and hike the trail clockwise.) The trail passes a Native American cultural site on the return of the loop, the homestead of the Tubatulabal Indians. With only a 700-foot climb and an excellent grade, even mountain bikers can manage this trail, although few bother with it. You'll likely see some deer on the hillsides, and the view from the top of Unal Peak makes the whole world seem peaceful and serene. Although most of the trail is lined with conifers, the top of the loop is a little exposed and catches a strong breeze.

User Groups: Hikers, dogs, horses, and mountain bikes. No wheelchair facilities.

Permits: No permits are required. Parking and access are free.

Maps: A Sequoia National Forest map is available from the U.S. Forest Service. For a topographic map, go to the USGS website to download Posey.

Directions: From Wofford Heights on the west

side of Lake Isabella, turn west on Highway 155 and drive eight miles to Greenhorn Summit. Turn left at the sign for Shirley Ski Meadows and drive 100 yards to the Greenhorn Fire Station and Unal trailhead, on the right side of the road.

Contact: Sequoia National Forest, Kern River Ranger District, Kernville, 760/376-3781, www.fs.usda.gov/sequoia.

115 CANNELL MEADOW NATIONAL RECREATION TRAIL

24.0 mi/3 days 4 8

in Sequoia National Forest north of Kernville

Map 11.4, page 562

The Cannell Meadow National Recreation Trail is the first trailhead you reach out of Kernville, and if it's summertime, you should start at the other end of this 12-mile trail. That's because the Kernville end is at 2,800 feet, set in rocky chaparral and digger pine country, and, goodness, it's hot out here. Still, if you can time your trip for late winter or spring, hiking this end of Cannell Trail is a great adventure, watching the terrain and environment change as the elevation rises. The shadeless trail climbs right away, through sage and occasional live oaks, affording views of the Kern River Valley. The trail gets steeper and steeper as you near conifer country at Pine Flat, but then you also get some blessed shade. It crosses Cannell Creek twice and reaches the Cannell Meadow Forest Service Cabin, a log cabin that was built in 1904. Cannell Meadow is a beautiful spot on the western edge of the Kern Plateau, edged by Jeffrey and lodgepole pines. Elevation is 7,500 feet, which means a total climb of 4,700 feet. Spread it out over a few days.

User Groups: Hikers, dogs, horses, and mountain bikes. No wheelchair facilities.

Permits: A free campfire permit is required for overnight stays and is available from the Kernville Ranger Station. Parking and access are free.

Maps: A Sequoia National Forest map is available from the U.S. Forest Service. For a topographic map, go to the USGS website to download Kernville.

Directions: From Kernville on the north end of Isabella Lake, drive north on Sierra Way/Road 99 for 1.4 miles to the Cannell Meadow trailhead, on the right. Parking is available near the horse corrals.

Contact: Sequoia National Forest, Kern River Ranger District, Kernville, 760/376-3781, www.fs.usda.gov/sequoia.

116 SALMON CREEK FALLS

8.0 mi/4.0 hr or 2 days 2 9

in Sequoia National Forest near Big Meadow

Map 11.4, page 562

The eight-mile round-trip to the brink of Salmon Creek Falls is a stellar walk through lodgepole pines and white fir, with a chance for fishing, skinny-dipping, and admiring a lot of beautiful scenery at 7,600 feet in elevation. Since there are campsites located along the trail, it's easy enough to turn the trip into an overnight excursion, but the trail also makes a good, long, day hike. The trail is downhill all the way, dropping 600 feet over 0.5 mile, and follows granite-lined Salmon Creek. After skirting the edge of Horse Meadow, you simply follow the creek's meander. Trails run on both sides of the stream for the first two miles, so you can walk either side, but then they join as one. The path comes to an end above Salmon Creek Falls, where you can swim, fish, and camp, but don't expect to gaze out at the big waterfall. There's no way to get a good look at it from here, since you're perched on top of it.

User Groups: Hikers, dogs, horses, and mountain bikes. No wheelchair facilities.

Permits: A free campfire permit is required for overnight stays and is available from the

Springville or Kernville Ranger Stations at the addresses below. Parking and access are free.

Maps: A Sequoia National Forest map is available from the U.S. Forest Service. For topographic maps, go to the USGS website to download Sirretta Peak and Fairview.

Directions: From Kernville on the north end of Isabella Lake, drive north on Sierra Way/Road 99 for 22 miles to the right turnoff for Sherman Pass Road/22S05. Turn right and drive 6.1 miles on Sherman Pass Road, then turn right on Road 22S12, signed for Horse Meadow Campground. Drive 6.3 miles on Road 22S12 until you reach a fork. Stay straight. At eight miles, bear left. At 9.3 miles, turn right at the Horse Meadow Campground sign (Road 23S10). You'll reach the camp at 10.7 miles, but take the right turnoff just before the camp to reach the trailhead.

Contact: Sequoia National Forest, Kern River Ranger District, Kernville, 760/376-3781, www.fs.usda.gov/sequoia; Western Divide Ranger District, Springville, 559/539-2607, www.fs.usda.gov/sequoia.

117 SIRRETTA PEAK

8.0 mi/5.0 hr 4 10

near the Dome Land Wilderness

Map 11.4, page 562

Hey, what's that big meadow down there? It's Big Meadow, of course, that huge expanse of green you see from the top of Sirretta Peak. From Sirretta's summit, you get an eyeful of it, as well as long, lingering glances at the many granite domes of the Dome Land Wilderness Area, Sirretta and Deadwood Meadows, and the peaks of the High Sierra. The route to the peak starts at Big Meadow's northern edge, then travels north on Cannell Trail for 0.5 mile. Bear right (northeast) at the fork with Sirretta Peak Trail and climb 2.5 miles to a spur trail that leads to the summit. There are many switchbacks and plenty of fine views along the way. Take the left spur (it's obvious) for 0.5 mile to the rocky summit, and congratulate yourself on your fine mountaineering skills. The trail has an elevation gain of 1,200 feet, and if you decide to make the final summit climb, you'll add on another 700 feet. Sirretta Peak is just shy of 10,000 feet in elevation.

User Groups: Hikers and dogs. No horses or mountain bikes. No wheelchair facilities.

Permits: No day-hiking permits are required. Parking and access are free.

Maps: A Sequoia National Forest map is available from the U.S. Forest Service. For a topographic map, go to the USGS website to download Sirretta Peak.

Directions: From Kernville on the north end of Isabella Lake, drive north on Sierra Way/Road 99 for 22 miles to the right turnoff for Sherman Pass Road/22S05. Turn right and drive 6.1 miles on Sherman Pass Road. Turn right on Road 22S12, signed for Horse Meadow Campground, and drive 6.3 miles on Road 22S12 until you reach a fork. Stay straight. At eight miles, bear left, staying on Road 22S12. Continue four more miles, passing the Horse Meadow Campground turnoff, to Road 23S07, at the northern edge of Big Meadow. Turn left on Road 23S07 and drive 0.5 mile to the Cannell trailhead.

Contact: Sequoia National Forest, Kern River Ranger District, Kernville, 760/376-3781, www.fs.usda.gov/sequoia.

118 MANTER MEADOW LOOP

10.0 mi/6.0 hr 2 9

in the Dome Land Wilderness

Map 11.4, page 562 BEST

For people who love meadows, granite, and solitude, this loop trip is just about perfect. From the South Manter trailhead at 7,800 feet, the trail goes uphill for four miles to Manter Meadow, so bring your wildflower identification book and a map to identify surrounding peaks and domes. Along the way, several side trails branch off the main trail, leading to some of the granite domes of the Dome Land Wilderness, including spectacular Taylor

Dome and Church Dome. A two-mile loop trail encircles the entire perimeter of the meadow, which you can add on to your trip if you wish. At the meadow's western edge, South Manter Trail meets North Manter Trail, and you follow the latter back to Forest Service Road 23S07 (the road you drove in on). Then it's a 1.5-mile walk on the dirt road back to your car. If you want to avoid the road, hike South Manter Trail both ways, and take the loop walk around the meadow. The mileage is about equal to the other trip.

User Groups: Hikers, dogs, and horses. No mountain bikes. No wheelchair facilities.

Permits: No permits are required. Parking and access are free.

Maps: A Sequoia National Forest or Dome Land Wilderness map is available from the U.S. Forest Service. For a topographic map, go to the USGS website to download Sirretta Peak.

Directions: From Kernville on the north end of Isabella Lake, drive north on Sierra Way/Road 99 for 22 miles to the right turnoff for Sherman Pass Road/22S05. Turn right and drive 6.1 miles on Sherman Pass Road. Turn right on Road 22S12, signed for Horse Meadow Campground, and drive 6.3 miles on Road 22S12 until you reach a fork. Stay straight. At eight miles, bear left, staying on Road 22S12. Continue four more miles, passing the Horse Meadow Campground turnoff, to Road 23S07 at the northern edge of Big Meadow. Turn left on Road 23S07 and drive three miles to the southeast edge of Big Meadow and the South Manter trailhead.

Contact: Sequoia National Forest, Kern River Ranger District, Kernville, 760/376-3781, www.fs.usda.gov/sequoia.

119 ROCKHOUSE BASIN

8.6 mi/4.0 hr

on the eastern side of the Dome Land Wilderness

Map 11.4, page 562

You're driving along in no-man's-land on Highway 178 between U.S. 395 and Lake Isabella, staring at thousands of those odd-looking piñon pines. This is the transition zone between the Mojave Desert to the east and the Sierra Nevada to the west, and it doesn't look quite like either one of them. Want to see this strange land up close? This hike to Rockhouse Basin can take you there, and since it requires a long drive on dirt roads to reach the trailhead, you're likely to be free of the Eastern Sierra's hiking masses. The trail heads downhill through a burned area, losing about 1,500 feet in elevation on its way to the Kern River and Rockhouse Basin. A half-mile from the trailhead, turn right and head north to Rockhouse Basin, where the noise of cicadas serenades you almost as loudly as the river. Explore the rocks and cool off in the river. It can be as hot as Hades out here, so plan your trip for early in the year, when you can hike along the Kern River in relative comfort.

User Groups: Hikers, dogs, and horses. No mountain bikes. No wheelchair facilities.

Permits: No permits are required. Parking and access are free.

Maps: A Sequoia National Forest or Dome Land Wilderness map is available from the U.S. Forest Service. For a topographic map, go to the USGS website to download Rockhouse Basin.

Directions: From the junction of Highway 14 and Highway 178 north of Mojave, drive west on Highway 178 for 18 miles to the right turnoff for Chimney Peak National Backcountry Byway, or Canebrake Road. Turn right and drive approximately nine miles. Turn left (west) on Long Valley Loop Road and drive 13 miles to the gate at the start of Rockhouse Basin Trail.

Contact: Bureau of Land Management, Ridgecrest Field Office, Ridgecrest, 760/384-5400, www.ca.blm.gov/ridgecrest; Sequoia National Forest, Kern River Ranger District, Kernville, 760/376-3781, www.fs.usda.gov/sequoia.

SANTA BARBARA AND VICINITY

The Santa Barbara region extends 200 miles from the artsy town of Cambria and terraced vineyards of Paso Robles to the white sands of Ventura. Many would argue that this is Southern California's finest stretch of coast. Paths wind along the tops of oceanside bluffs and traverse coastal grasslands. Inland mountain trails lead to waterfalls, coastal viewpoints, and sculpted sandstone formations. Perhaps the most remarkable land in this region is a parcel surrounded entirely by water—the five rugged and remote islands of Channel Islands National Park, which lie 25 miles off Santa Barbara's coast. Each island is unique, offering a wealth of wildlife viewing opportunities and hiking trails. Pack along your tent, binoculars, and a cooler, and plan to stay for a few days.

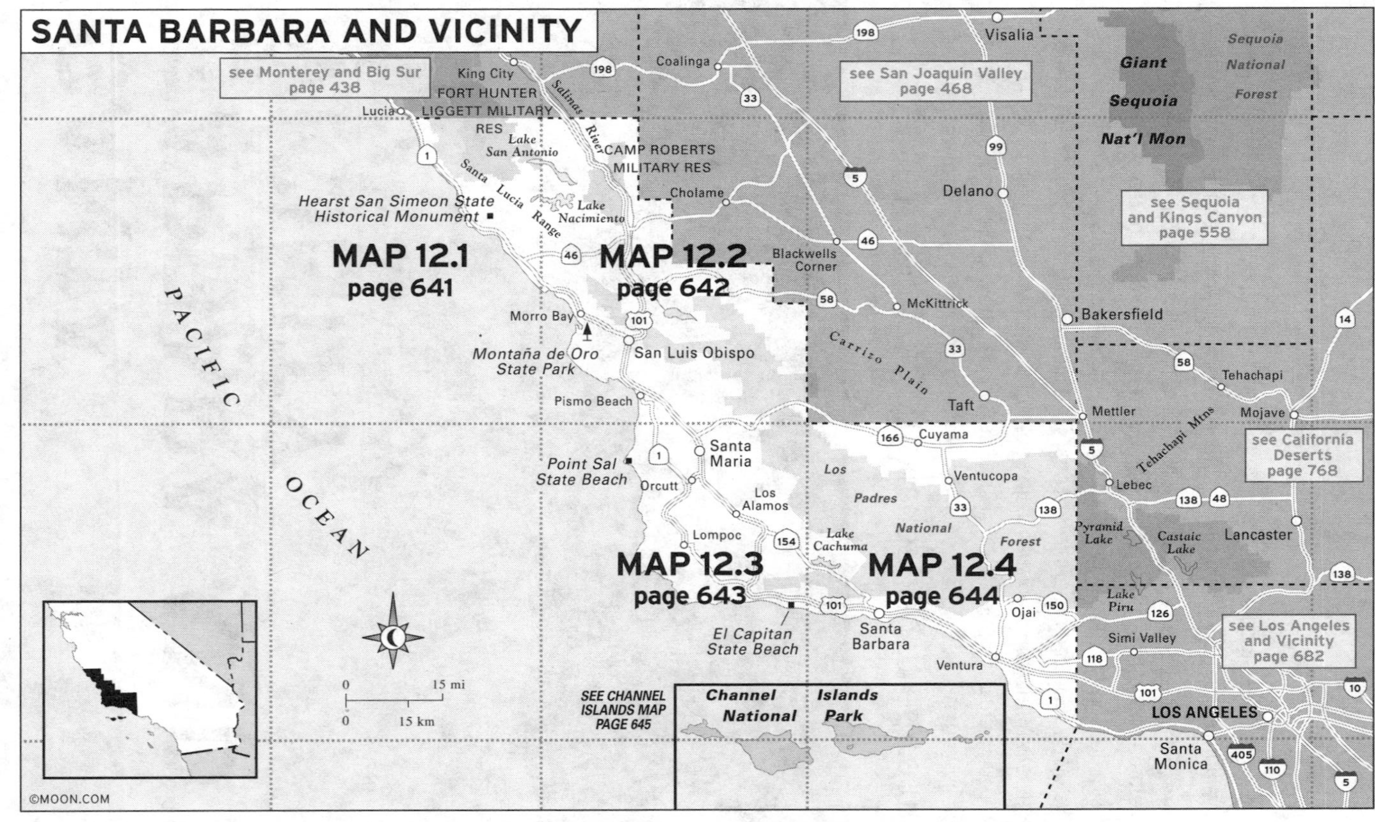

SANTA BARBARA AND VICINITY
see Monterey and Big Sur page 438
see San Joaquin Valley page 468
see Sequoia and Kings Canyon page 558
see California Deserts page 768
see Los Angeles and Vicinity page 682
MAP 12.1 page 641
MAP 12.2 page 642
MAP 12.3 page 643
MAP 12.4 page 644
SEE CHANNEL ISLANDS MAP PAGE 645
Channel Islands National Park
PACIFIC OCEAN
Lucia
King City
FORT HUNTER LIGGETT MILITARY RES
Lake San Antonio
Lake Nacimiento
Salinas River
Santa Lucia Range
CAMP ROBERTS MILITARY RES
Hearst San Simeon State Historical Monument
Morro Bay
Montaña de Oro State Park
Pismo Beach
San Luis Obispo
Point Sal State Beach
Orcutt
Santa Maria
Lompoc
Los Alamos
El Capitan State Beach
Lake Cachuma
Los Padres National Forest
Santa Barbara
Ventura
Ojai
Cuyama
Ventucopa
Coalinga
Cholame
Blackwells Corner
Carrizo Plain
McKittrick
Taft
Delano
Visalia
Bakersfield
Mettler
Lebec
Tehachapi Mtns
Tehachapi
Mojave
Lancaster
Pyramid Lake
Lake Piru
Castaic Lake
Simi Valley
Santa Monica
LOS ANGELES
Giant Sequoia Nat'l Mon
Sequoia National Forest
0 15 mi
0 15 km
©MOON.COM

Map 12.1

Sites 1-3
Pages 646-647

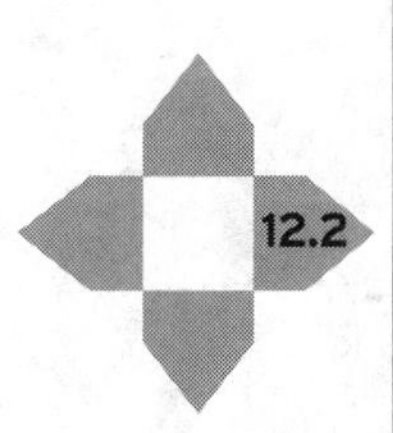

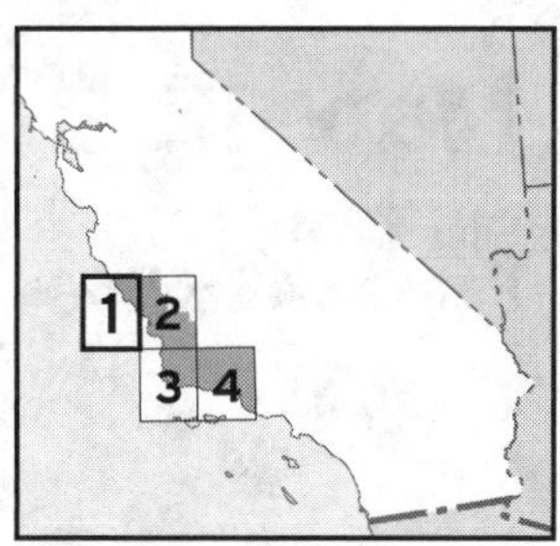

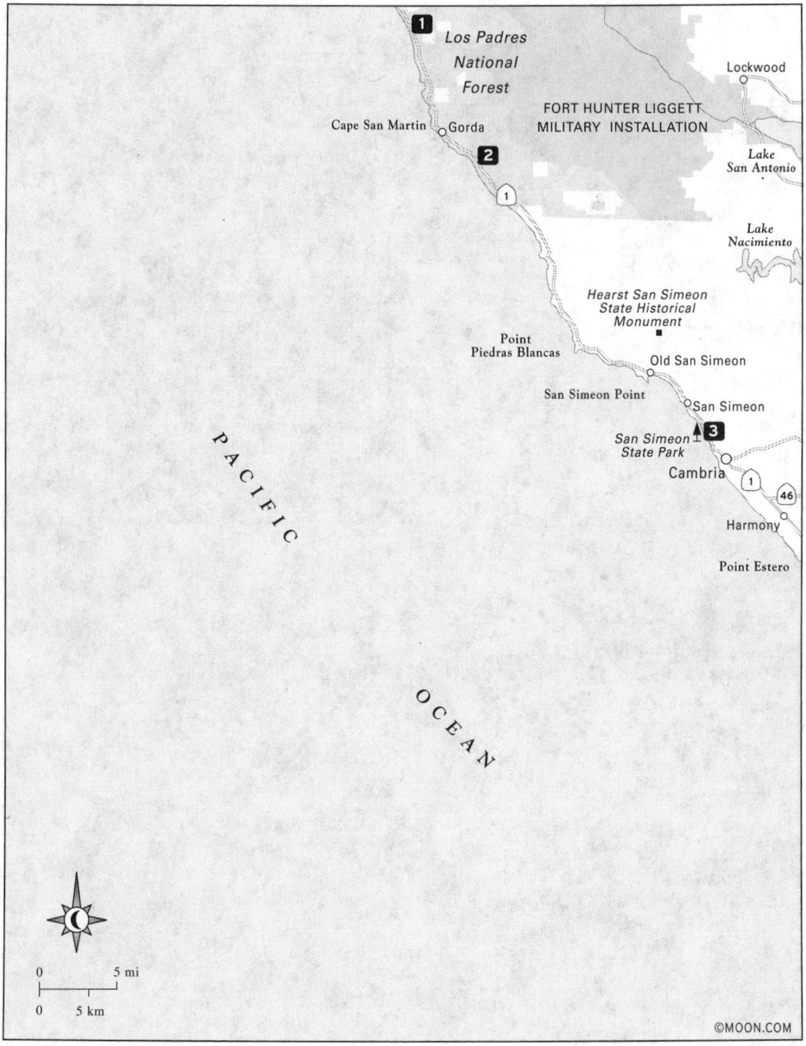

12.2

1
2
3
4

1
Los Padres
National
Forest
Lockwood
FORT HUNTER LIGGETT
MILITARY INSTALLATION
Cape San Martin
Gorda
2
1
Lake
San Antonio
Lake
Nacimiento
Hearst San Simeon
State Historical
Monument
Point
Piedras Blancas
Old San Simeon
San Simeon Point
San Simeon
San Simeon
State Park
3
Cambria
1
46
Harmony
Point Estero
PACIFIC
OCEAN
0
5 mi
0
5 km
©MOON.COM

Map 12.2

Sites 4-16
Pages 648-656

12.1
12.3

1
2
3
4

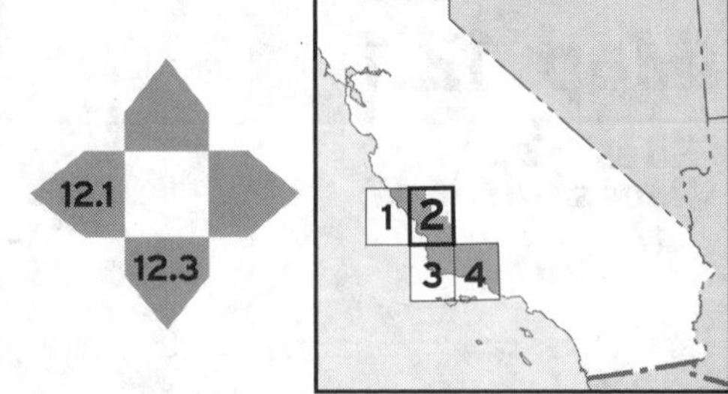

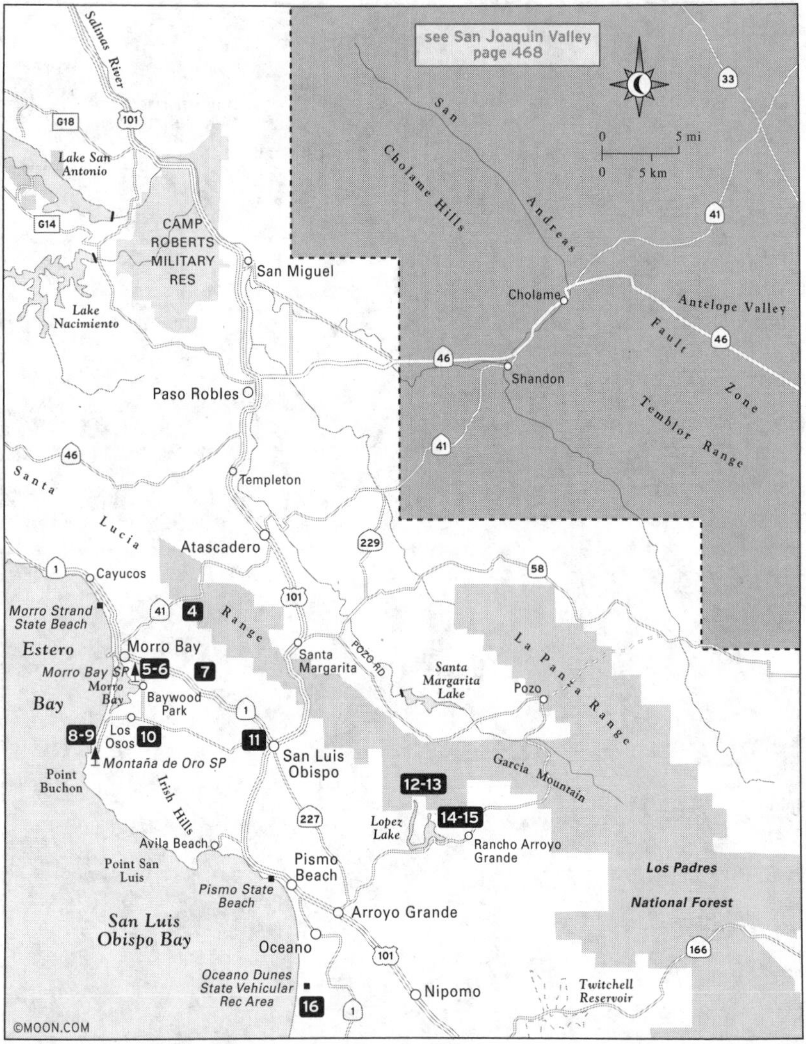

see San Joaquin Valley
page 468
Salinas River
101
G18
Lake San Antonio
G14
CAMP ROBERTS MILITARY RES
San Miguel
Lake Nacimiento
San Andreas
Cholame Hills
33
0 5 mi
0 5 km
41
Cholame
Antelope Valley
Fault Zone
46
Shandon
Paso Robles
Temblor Range
41
46
Santa Lucia Range
Templeton
Atascadero
229
1
Cayucos
58
Morro Strand State Beach
41
4
101
Estero Bay
Morro Bay
Morro Bay SP
5-6
7
Morro Bay
Santa Margarita
POZO RD
Santa Margarita Lake
La Panza Range
Pozo
Baywood Park
1
8-9
Los Osos
10
11
San Luis Obispo
Montaña de Oro SP
Garcia Mountain
Point Buchon
Irish Hills
12-13
227
Lopez Lake
14-15
Avila Beach
Rancho Arroyo Grande
Point San Luis
Pismo Beach
Los Padres National Forest
Pismo State Beach
Arroyo Grande
San Luis Obispo Bay
Oceano
101
166
Oceano Dunes State Vehicular Rec Area
Nipomo
Twitchell Reservoir
16
1
©MOON.COM

Map 12.3

Sites 17-21
Pages 656-658

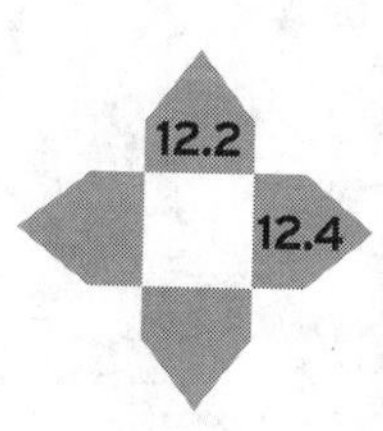

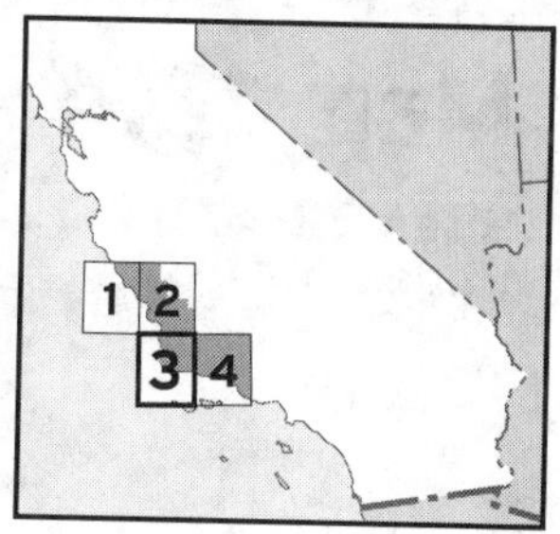

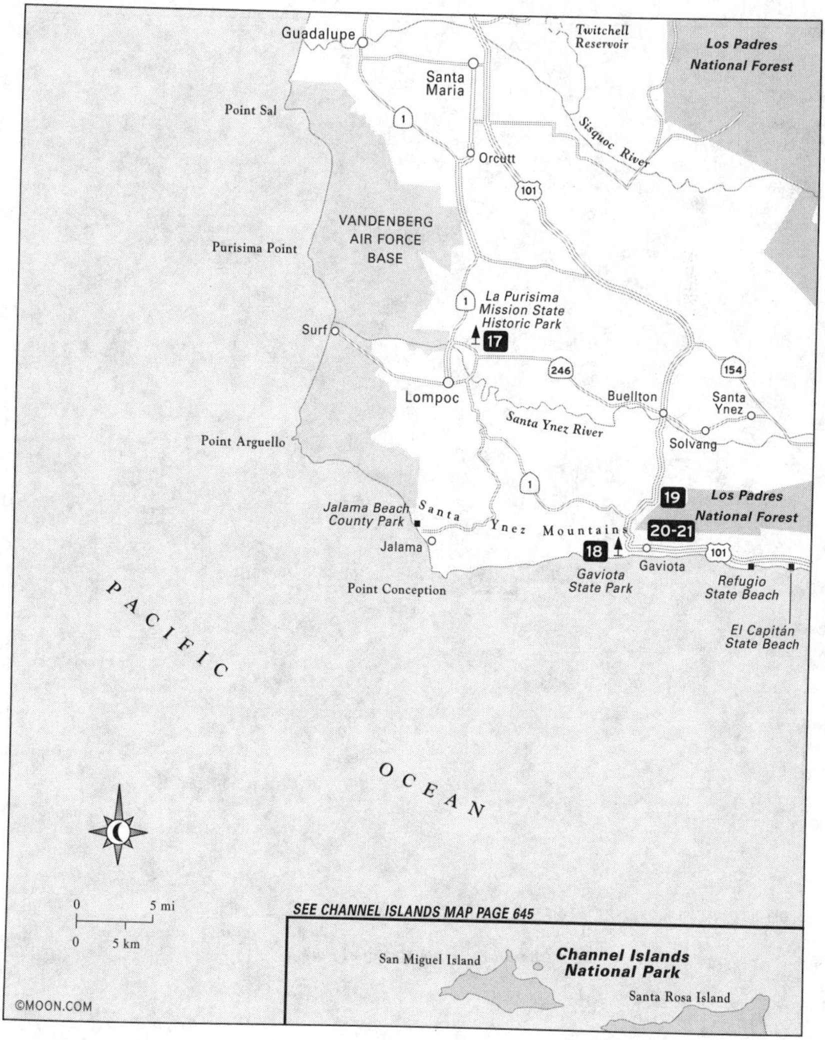

Guadalupe
Twitchell Reservoir
Los Padres National Forest
Santa Maria
Point Sal
1
Sisquoc River
Orcutt
101
VANDENBERG AIR FORCE BASE
Purisima Point
1
La Purisima Mission State Historic Park
17
Surf
246
154
Lompoc
Buellton
Santa Ynez
Santa Ynez River
Solvang
Point Arguello
1
19
Los Padres National Forest
Jalama Beach County Park
Santa Ynez Mountains
20-21
Jalama
18
Gaviota
101
Gaviota State Park
Refugio State Beach
Point Conception
El Capitán State Beach
PACIFIC OCEAN
0 5 mi
0 5 km

SEE CHANNEL ISLANDS MAP PAGE 645

San Miguel Island
Channel Islands National Park
Santa Rosa Island

Map 12.4

Sites 22-47
Pages 659-675

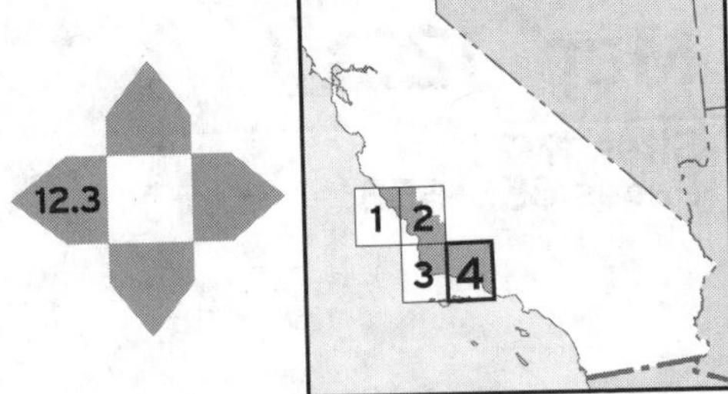

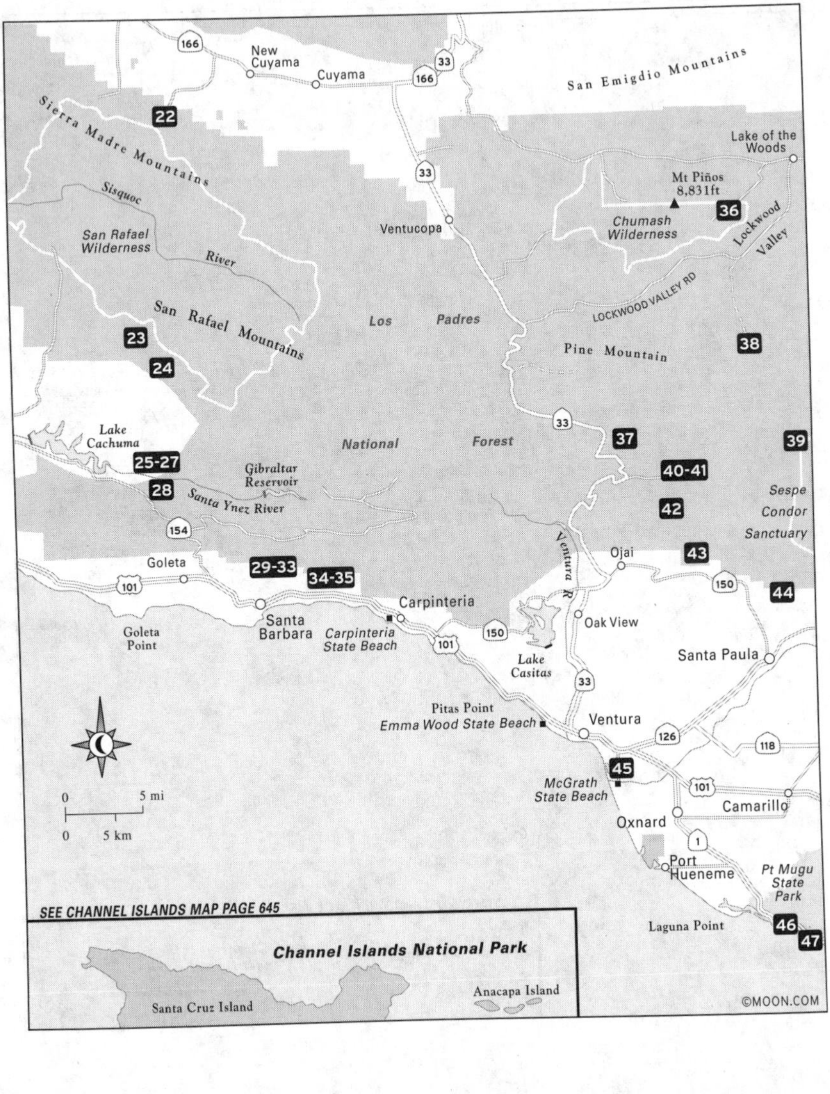

166
New Cuyama
Cuyama
33
166
San Emigdio Mountains
22
Sierra Madre Mountains
Sisquoc
San Rafael Wilderness
River
33
Ventucopa
Lake of the Woods
Mt Piños 8,831ft
36
Chumash Wilderness
Lockwood Valley
LOCKWOOD VALLEY RD
San Rafael Mountains
23
24
Los Padres
Pine Mountain
38
Lake Cachuma
25-27
National
Forest
33
37
39
Gibraltar Reservoir
28
Santa Ynez River
40-41
42
Sespe Condor Sanctuary
154
Ventura R
Goleta
29-33
34-35
Ojai
43
150
44
101
Santa Barbara
Carpinteria
Oak View
Goleta Point
Carpinteria State Beach
150
101
Lake Casitas
Santa Paula
33
Pitas Point
Emma Wood State Beach
Ventura
126
118
45
McGrath State Beach
101
Camarillo
Oxnard
1
Port Hueneme
Pt Mugu State Park
0 5 mi
0 5 km

SEE CHANNEL ISLANDS MAP PAGE 645

Channel Islands National Park
Santa Cruz Island
Anacapa Island
Laguna Point
46
47

Channel Islands Detail Map

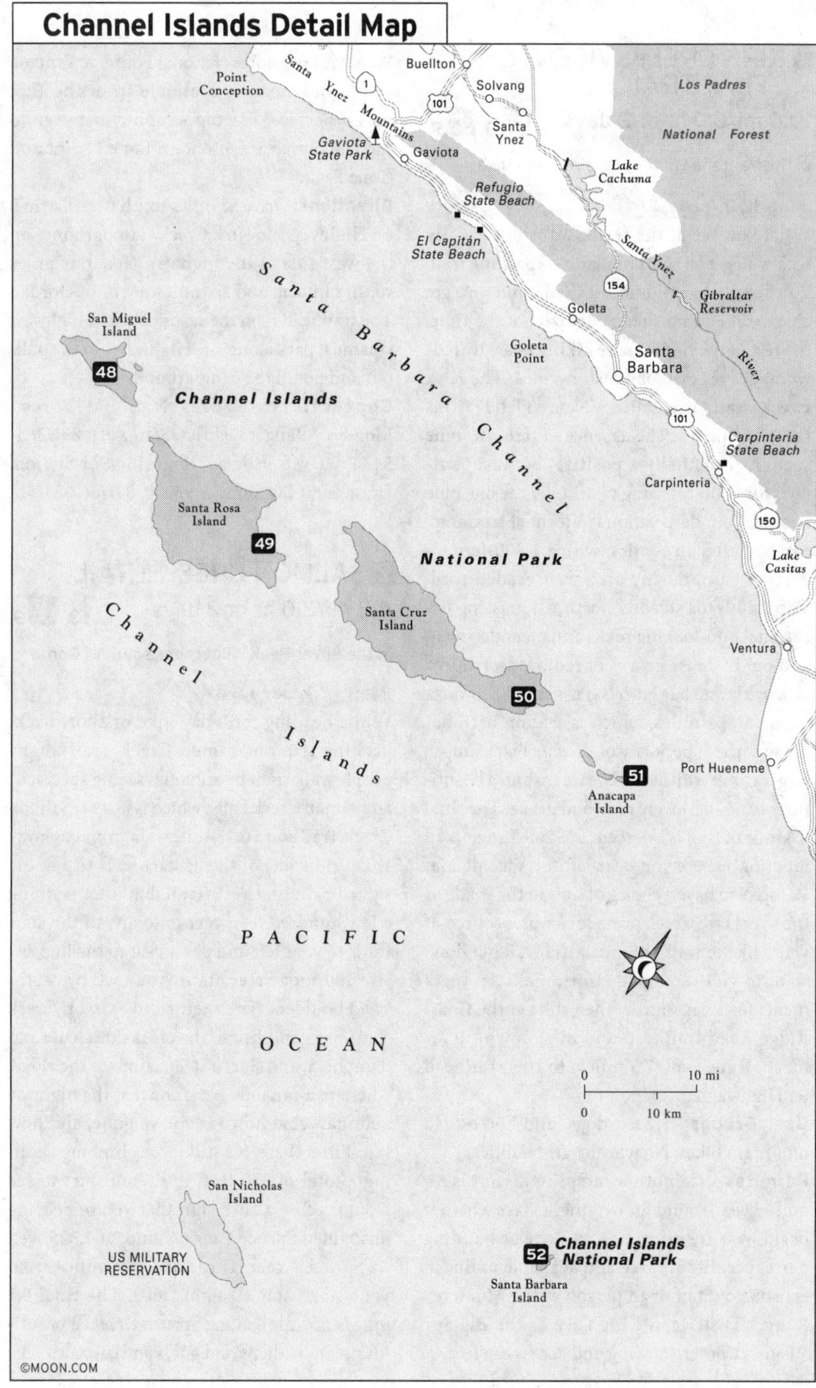

1 KIRK CREEK/VICENTE FLAT TRAIL

10.0 mi/6.0 hr or 2 days 3 9

in the Ventana Wilderness south of Lucia

Map 12.1, page 641

What you see at the trailhead is not exactly what you get on this popular backpacking trail. You see chaparral and no shade, but you get chaparral and no shade only part of the time; the rest of the time, you're hiking in shady redwood groves or along lush ravines. The Kirk Creek Trail (also called Vicente Flat Trail) is full of surprises. The absence of trees in some sections is actually a positive, because it allows for wide-reaching views over the big, blue Pacific. Your destination is Vicente Flat Camp, reached after five miles, with a 1,800-foot elevation gain, mostly on a well-graded trail. The trail leads steadily northeast, passing occasional odd-looking rocks and meandering in and out of dense groves of redwoods, madrones, oaks, and bay laurels. Pass small Espinoza Camp at 3.2 miles, which is seldom used because of the superiority of Vicente Flat Camp, a larger camp with a nearby stream and a beautiful setting in a lovely redwood grove. The final 0.5 mile of trail is a descent to Stone Ridge Trail junction, where you bear left for Vicente Flat Camp. You have a choice of sites in the shade or the sun; Hare Creek provides a water source. If you'd like to walk this beautiful trail but don't want to go to so much effort, make arrangements for a car shuttle, then start at the Coast Ridge Road trailhead and hike downhill almost all the way (7.5 miles) to this trailhead on Highway 1.

User Groups: Hikers, dogs, and horses. No mountain bikes. No wheelchair facilities.

Permits: A California campfire permit is required year-round for overnight stays whether or not you are using a camp stove or building a fire; permits are free and available online at fs.usda.gov/lpnf or in person at the Monterey Ranger District in King City or the Big Sur Visitors Center. Parking and access are free.

Maps: A Los Padres National Forest or Ventana Wilderness map is available from the U.S. Forest Service. For topographic maps, go to the USGS website to obtain Lopez Point and Cone Peak.

Directions: Drive 55 miles south from Carmel on Highway 1 to Kirk Creek Campground, on the west side of the highway. (It's four miles south of Lucia and six miles north of Gorda.) The trailhead is on the east side of the highway; you must park alongside Highway 1 in the pullout and not in the campground.

Contact: Los Padres National Forest, Monterey Ranger District, King City, 831/385-5434, www.fs.usda.gov/lpnf; Big Sur Station, Highway 1, Big Sur, CA 93920, 831/667-2315.

2 SALMON CREEK TRAIL

4.2 mi/2.0 hr or 2 days 3 9

in the Silver Peak Wilderness south of Gorda

Map 12.1, page 641

While heading for a day hike or short backpacking trip on Salmon Creek Trail, many people walk right by and miss seeing spectacular Salmon Creek Falls, which is just off Salmon Creek Trail and a 0.25-mile walk from Highway 1. Don't be one of them; start your trip at the signed Salmon Creek Trail, but after walking a few hundred feet, veer onto any of the spur trails to your left and pay a visit to the impressive 100-foot waterfall, surrounded by cabin-sized boulders. Then return to Salmon Creek Trail, say good-bye to the creekside shade and dampness, and start a steep climb to the ridge, where you can look back down at the highway and marvel at how far you've gone, and how fast. From there, it's still more climbing, gaining a total of 800 feet, until you start to see Douglas firs, a sure sign that you're nearing misnamed Spruce Creek Camp, at 1,325 feet. At Spruce Creek Trail fork, two miles from your start, stay straight (left). The final 0.1 mile is downhill along Spruce Creek, a beautiful stream with myriad pools and cascades. The camp here is blissfully shaded by Douglas firs, and there are many good spots to stick your feet (or other body parts) into the stream. If you want to spend the night but somebody already has this spot (which happens often due to its proximity to the highway), you can continue another mile to Estrella Camp. If you want to explore more of this beautiful area, follow the right fork instead of the left fork at 2.0 miles out, and you'll climb higher up over a ridge to a beautiful meadow known as Dutra Flats.

User Groups: Hikers, dogs, and horses. No mountain bikes. No wheelchair facilities.

Permits: A California campfire permit is required for overnight stays year-round whether or not you are using a camp stove or building a fire; permits are free and available online at fs.usda.gov/lpnf or in person at the Monterey Ranger District in King City or the Big Sur Visitors Center. Parking and access are free.

Maps: A Los Padres National Forest or Ventana Wilderness map is available from the U.S. Forest Service. For a topographic map, go to the USGS website to download Villa Creek.

Directions: From Big Sur, drive 33 miles south on Highway 1 to Gorda; continue 7.6 miles south of Gorda to the trailhead for Salmon Creek Trail, on the east side of the highway at a hairpin turn. Park in the large parking pullout along the road. The Salmon Creek Trail leads from the south end of the guardrail.

Contact: Los Padres National Forest, Monterey Ranger District, King City, 831/385-5434, www.fs.usda.gov/lpnf; Big Sur Station, Highway 1, Big Sur, 831/667-2315.

3 LEFFINGWELL LANDING AND MOONSTONE BEACH

4.0 mi/2.0 hr

2 8

near Cambria

Map 12.1, page 641

What's the best time to make the trip to Cambria? That's easy—in the spring, when the rolling hills along Highway 46 on the drive to the coast are lush and green. Of course, any time of year is a good time to walk the trail that leads from Leffingwell Landing along the bluffs above Moonstone Beach. Although Moonstone Beach Drive parallels the trail all the way, the road isn't much of a bother, because the vistas out to sea hold all of your attention. The parking lot at Leffingwell Landing is in the middle of this trail, which means you can walk out and back in both directions. To the south you may have a wet creek crossing at Leffingwell Creek, but you can go around it via the golf course. The bluff trail's southern terminus is at the intersection of Moonstone Beach Drive and Weymouth Street, but you can descend to the beach there and keep walking. If you go the other direction, about 0.25 mile north of Leffingwell Landing, the trail again descends on a wooden staircase to the beach, and you continue your walk there. In addition to the coastal vistas from the bluffs, there are many colorful patches of ice plant and cypress trees, as well as several benches and overlooks (accessible via short spurs off the main trail)—places where you can find a spot to call your own. We watched a winter squall come in from one of these overlooks; it was sudden, dramatic, and beautiful. Right below Leffingwell Landing are fine tidepools to be explored. Keep on the lookout for passing whales in the winter.

User Groups: Hikers and dogs. No horses or mountain bikes. No wheelchair facilities.

Permits: No permits are required. Parking and access are free.

Maps: A park map is available by free download at www.parks.ca.gov. For a topographic map, go to the USGS website to download Cambria.

Directions: From north of Templeton on U.S. 101, take the Highway 46 West/Cambria/Hearst Castle exit. Drive west on Highway 46 for 22 miles to Highway 1; continue three miles north on Highway 1, past Cambria, to Moonstone Beach Drive. Turn left on Moonstone Beach Drive and park at Leffingwell Landing.

Contact: San Simeon State Beach, San Simeon

District, San Simeon, 805/927-2020 or 805/927-2068, www.parks.ca.gov.

4 CERRO ALTO SUMMIT

7.0 mi/3.5 hr 3 9

off Highway 41, east of Morro Bay

Map 12.2, page 642

We hope you like to climb, because that's what you do on Cerro Alto Trail to the summit of Cerro Alto, elevation 2,620 feet. The 1,600-foot ascent is divided over 3.5 miles of mostly steep terrain, but the reward for your exertion is one of the finest views of the Central Coast—a panoramic vista of the Pacific Ocean, Whale Rock Reservoir, Morro Bay, Piedras Blancas Lighthouse, and the Santa Lucia Mountains. In recent years, the trails to Cerro Alto have become extremely popular with mountain bikers. If you don't like sharing the trail with bikes, visit on a weekday. From the trailhead at the far end of the Cerro Alto Campground road, follow a pleasant trail alongside Morro Creek in a bay and live oak forest, then leave the shady stream behind (too soon) and head for chaparral country. After 0.75 mile, bear left, and shortly thereafter bear right. After a series of switchbacks and some rocky sections of trail, you reach the road to the peak, at 1.7 miles. Turn left and circle the peak as you climb another 0.25 mile to the summit. The view is divine even before you get to the top, for one simple reason: Located on West Cuesta Ridge, Cerro Alto is one of the highest points in this coastal region.

Note: If you want to semi-loop back from the summit, you can take a shorter trail on the way back. Retrace your steps downhill for 1.2 miles, then turn left and prepare for an incredibly steep descent of only one mile back to the campground. Your knees may not be very happy with you when this is over.

User Groups: Hikers, dogs, horses, and mountain bikes. No wheelchair facilities.

Permits: No permits are required. A national forest Adventure Pass is required for each vehicle; fees are $5 for one day or $30 for a year. Interagency access passes are also accepted. If you don't have a pass, you can pay $5 at the trailhead parking lot.

Maps: A Los Padres National Forest map is available from the U.S. Forest Service. For a topographic map, go to the USGS website to download Atascadero.

Directions: From Atascadero on U.S. 101, take the Highway 41 West/Morro Bay exit. Drive eight miles west on Highway 41 to Cerro Alto Campground, on the left. (Or, from Morro Bay on Highway 1, exit on Highway 41 and drive eight miles east to Cerro Alto Campground, on the right.) Turn in to the campground entrance and follow the road all the way to its end, at the hikers' parking lot near the camp host's residence. Start hiking on the signed Cerro Alto Trail from there.

Contact: Los Padres National Forest, Santa Lucia Ranger District, Santa Maria, 805/925-9538, www.fs.usda.gov/lpnf.

5 BLACK HILL

0.5 mi/0.5 hr

in Morro Bay State Park near Morro Bay

Map 12.2, page 642

The Black Hill Trail in Morro Bay State Park is no wilderness trek, but it does provide a wonderful view with an amazingly short walk—one that thousands of Central Coast visitors take every summer. Black Hill is an ancient 597-foot volcanic plug, the most accessible of the "Nine Sisters" or nine *morros* in the San Luis Obispo/Morro Bay area. The short trail offers a big payoff; Black Hill's summit overlooks Morro Bay and its estuary, Estero Point, Cayucos, Chorro Valley, and the nearby *morros* of Cerro Cabrillo and Hollister Peak. From the parking lot at the end of Black Hill Road, it's just a quarter-mile walk to the rocky summit. The only tricky part is finding the trailhead, which is at the top of a maze of roads at the Morro Bay Golf Course. If you want to take a longer walk to reach Black Hill, you can start at a separate trailhead on Park View Road and hike for about a mile to reach the top. And, if you are visiting Morro Bay State Park between February and June, don't miss a short side-trip to the park's Heron Rookery Natural Preserve, across State Park Road from the golf course and just north of the natural history museum. Here you can walk near a grove of eucalyptus and cypress trees where double-breasted cormorants, great egrets, and great blue herons nest in the trees.

User Groups: Hikers and horses. No dogs or mountain bikes. No wheelchair facilities.

Permits: No permits are required. Parking and access are free.

Maps: A map of Morro Bay State Park is available at the natural history museum on State Park Road, or by free download at www.parks.ca.gov. For a topographic map, go to the USGS website to download Morro Bay South.

Directions: From San Luis Obispo, take Highway 1 north to the Los Osos/Baywood Park exit. Turn left, drive one mile and turn right on State Park Road. Drive a short distance and then turn right on Park View Road and follow it up the hill to the golf course. Turn right on Black Hill Road and follow it to its end.

Contact: Morro Bay State Park, Morro Bay, 805/772-7434; San Luis Obispo Coast State Parks, 805/927-2065, www.parks.ca.gov.

6 CERRO CABRILLO

3.0 mi/1.5 hr 

in Morro Bay State Park near Morro Bay

Map 12.2, page 642

You hardly realize you're in a state park when you reach the trailhead for Cerro Cabrillo, which is just a small dirt parking lot alongside a busy road. Where's the entrance kiosk? What about the state park entrance fee? Where are all the campgrounds and restrooms? None of that applies here at Morro Bay State Park's Cerro Cabrillo Trail, which is a quiet refuge from the hustle and bustle of Morro Bay tourism. Cerro Cabrillo, also known as Cabrillo Peak, is one of nine *morros*—small volcanic plugs that lie in a loose chain along the central coast. (Morro Rock is the most famous of the group.) Although no trail goes to the top of Cerro Cabrillo, you can hike on the peak's lower reaches on Quarry Trail and Park Ridge Trail. Both are accessible from two small parking areas off South Bay Boulevard; if you miss the first one, just take the second. The Park Ridge Trail goes straight up, then veers left and joins Quarry Trail. The Cerro Cabrillo area contains a variety of native plants and grasslands, including these spring bloomers: bird's eye gilia, brodiea, and mariposa lilies. On the sunniest slopes, coastal sage scrub grows, including black sage and bush monkeyflower. Translation? No shade. That makes the views of Morro Bay and Morro Rock first class, but it also means you'd better carry water.

User Groups: Hikers, horses, and mountain bikes. No dogs. No wheelchair facilities.

Permits: No permits are required. Parking and access are free.

Maps: A map of Morro Bay State Park is available at the natural history museum on State Park Road, or by free download at www.parks.ca.gov. For a topographic map, go to the USGS website to download Morro Bay South.

Directions: From San Luis Obispo, take Highway 1 northwest for 11 miles to Morro Bay. Take the Morro Bay State Park exit and continue on South Bay Boulevard. In 0.75 mile, continue straight ahead over the bridge and drive another 0.5 mile to the Cerro Cabrillo dirt parking lot, on the left side of the road. The first parking lot is for the Quarry Trail; another parking lot shortly following it is for the Park Ridge Trail. Park at either; the two trails join.

Contact: Morro Bay State Park, Morro Bay, 805/772-7434; San Luis Obispo Coast State Parks, 805/927-2065, www.parks.ca.gov.

7 EAGLE ROCK

2.2 mi/1.0 hr 2 8

in El Chorro Regional Park in San Luis Obispo

Map 12.2, page 642

El Chorro Regional Park is better known for its popular off-leash dog park and golf course than it is for its hiking trails, but the park's Eagle Rock Trail is a little gem that deserves some recognition. The well-maintained trail starts from the gate just past the dog park. Be sure to pick up an interpretive brochure at the trailhead, which will help you spot Native American grinding holes, pack rat nests, and other interesting features along the path. Follow Dairy Creek Trail, a paved road, for about 100 yards to the start of the Eagle Rock Trail. The path climbs up into the coastal hills, gaining just enough elevation to bring you to Eagle Rock Vista, where you can enjoy big views of Morro Rock and the coastline. The trail eventually loops back downhill on the paved Dairy Creek Trail, traveling past coast live oaks and spring wildflowers. Most of the time you're likely to have this trail all to yourself, and that's just fine, because there's nothing to distract you from the fine vistas. And one more thing—don't be surprised if you hear the occasional sound of gunfire in the distance. It's coming from nearby Camp San Luis Obispo, a military base.

User Groups: Hikers, dogs, horses, and mountain bikes. No wheelchair facilities.

Permits: No permits are required. A $3 entrance fee is charged per vehicle.

Maps: Free brochures and trail maps are available at the park entrance station and trailhead. For a topographic map, go to the USGS website to download San Luis Obispo.

Directions: From San Luis Obispo, drive six miles north on Highway 1 to El Chorro Regional Park (across from Cuesta College). Turn right and drive past the baseball fields to the end of the day-use area, by the dog park. Park your car and walk through the gate for about 100 yards to the trail's start.

Contact: El Chorro Regional Park, San Luis Obispo County Parks, San Luis Obispo, 805/781-5930, www.slocountyparks.org.

8 MONTAÑA DE ORO BLUFFS TRAIL

3.0 mi/1.5 hr 1 10

in Montaña de Oro State Park west of San Luis Obispo

Map 12.2, page 642 

How can a park this good be free of charge? We can't figure it out, but we're glad it is. The Bluffs Trail at Montaña de Oro State Park is one of the finest coast walks in Central California, blissfully free of the blight of human development and loaded with classic oceanside beauty. This wheelchair-accessible trail winds along the top of Montaña de Oro's shale and sediment bluffs, with nonstop views of rocky offshore outcrops, colorful rock cliffs and arches, and the big blue Pacific. In addition to all the coastal vistas, the grasses alongside the trail explode in a display of orange poppies and other wildflowers in February, March, and April. The trail ends at the Coon Creek parking lot and trailhead. A good side-trip is to explore the Spooner's Cove beach right across from the historic Spooner Ranch house visitors center turnoff, near where you left your car.

User Groups: Hikers and mountain bikes. No dogs or horses. The trail is wheelchair-accessible.

Permits: No permits are required. Parking and access are free.

Maps: A map of Montaña de Oro State Park is available at the park entrance, the visitors center, or by free download at www.parks.ca.gov. For a topographic map, go to the USGS website to download Morro Bay South.

Directions: From U.S. 101 in San Luis Obispo, take the Los Osos exit and head west on Los Osos Valley Road. Drive 12 miles on Los Osos Valley Road to the Montaña de Oro entrance. Continue 2.5 miles to the small parking area on the right side of the road, 100 yards beyond the left turnoff for the visitors center. The signed Bluffs Trail begins there.

Contact: Montaña de Oro State Park, Los Osos, 805/528-0513; Morro Bay State Park, 805/772-7434; San Luis Obispo Coast State Parks, 805/927-2065, www.parks.ca.gov.

9 VALENCIA AND OATS PEAKS

7.0 mi/3.5 hr 

in Montaña de Oro State Park west of San Luis Obispo

Map 12.2, page 642

With a cool ocean breeze keeping you comfortable, this seven-mile round-trip hike to two coastal peaks is a spectacular day trip. If you forget to carry water and/or hike in the heat of high noon, it can be a nightmare, so come prepared. The Valencia and Oats Peak Trails begin on Los Osos Valley Road, 0.25 mile south of the Spooner Ranch house visitors center. The wide route heads inland for a steady ascent of 500 feet per mile through grasslands, wildflowers, chaparral, and coastal scrub. There are several junctions; all are well marked.

In two miles, and with an elevation gain of 1,100 feet, you arrive at the top of Valencia Peak, elevation 1,347 feet. On a clear day you can see all the way from Point Buchon (south) to Piedras Blancas (north). No map is needed to pick out Rocky Butte, Morro Rock (that's an easy one), and the Morro Bay estuary.

From this high point, you descend for a mile, losing nearly 500 feet, to join a road that connects to Oats Peak Trail, then hike upward once again on Oats Peak Trail. The summit is reached in 1.2 miles, and a survey marker proclaims its 1,373-foot elevation. From Oats Peak, you can walk along the ridge for a while to enjoy more of the spectacular views of the ocean, Morro Rock, and the inland mountains, or you can head back downhill. Follow Oats Peak, Beebee, and Valencia Trails for a 2.9-mile descent (via Beebe Trail) to the Valencia Peak Trailhead. If you take Oats Peak Trail all the way back, you'll follow a rerouted and much longer (5.4 miles instead of 2.9 miles) path and have a 10-minute walk on the park road to get back to your car. One more thing to think about: If you can possibly visit between February and April, you get a good chance at crystal-clear vistas and the best chance of seeing Montaña de Oro's signature wildflower display. These hills are "mountains of gold" in season; hence the park's name.

User Groups: Hikers and horses. No dogs or mountain bikes. No wheelchair facilities.

Permits: No permits are required. Parking and access are free.

Maps: A map of Montaña de Oro State Park is available at the park entrance, the visitors center, or by free download at www.parks.ca.gov. For a topographic map, go to the USGS website to download Morro Bay South.

Directions: From U.S. 101 in San Luis Obispo, take the Los Osos exit and head west on Los Osos Valley Road. Drive 12 miles on Los Osos Valley Road to the Montaña de Oro entrance. Continue 2.5 miles to the small parking area on both sides of the road, 100 yards beyond the left turnoff for the visitors center. The Valencia Peak Trail begins on the left side of the road.

Contact: Montaña de Oro State Park, Los Osos, 805/528-0513; Morro Bay State Park, 805/772-7434; San Luis Obispo Coast State Parks, 805/927-2065, www.parks.ca.gov.

10 LOS OSOS OAKS RESERVE

2.0 mi/1.0 hr  

west of San Luis Obispo in Los Osos

Map 12.2, page 642

It's hard to believe that a bunch of old oak trees right alongside a busy road could make for such great walking, but they do. The hike is an odd mix of elements, since you hear road noise much of the time, but the forest still seems peaceful. The venerable old oaks in Los Osos

Oaks Reserve are as old as 800 years, and they can be visited by wandering on any of three short, flat trails. It's easy to walk a brief stretch on all of them. The Chumash Loop, Oak View Trail, and Los Osos Creek Trail all lead from the parking lot and split off from each other. Oak View is just a short out-and-back trip through the trees and provides the best look at the reserve's highlights; Chumash Loop is a little longer and loops around the reserve. The Los Osos Creek Trail is the least impressive of the three, showing off the fewest fine tree specimens and following a marshy stretch of creek. The oak forest is a mix of very large, old trees with moss hanging from their branches, and tiny, dwarfed ones. Some of the oaks' trunks and branches are so twisted, gnarled, and wrinkled that they look like a tangled web of elephants' trunks. If you're into photography, this is the kind of place that is best captured in black and white. And, if the coast is foggy, this hike is ideal, because all the beauty of the forest is close enough to touch.

User Groups: Hikers only. No dogs, horses, or mountain bikes. No wheelchair facilities.

Permits: No permits are required. Parking and access are free.

Maps: For a topographic map, go to the USGS website to download Morro Bay South.

Directions: From U.S. 101 in San Luis Obispo, take the Los Osos exit and head west on Los Osos Valley Road. Drive 8.5 miles on Los Osos Valley Road to the Los Osos Oaks Reserve, on the left side of the road, which is marked by a small sign. The reserve is exactly one mile east of 10th Street, in Los Osos, and just west of the bear statue on the road. There is a small parking area by the trailhead, just off Los Osos Valley Road.

Contact: Los Osos Oaks Reserve, Morro Bay State Park, Morro Bay, 805/772-7434; San Luis Obispo Coast State Parks, 805/927-2065, www.parks.ca.gov.

11 BISHOP PEAK

4.4 mi/2.0 hr

in Bishop Peak Natural Reserve in San Luis Obispo

Map 12.2, page 642

People have been hiking to Bishop Peak for centuries, but it wasn't until 1998 that this trail from the end of Patricia Drive was completed through a joint effort by government agencies and volunteers. Constructed by the Sierra Club, California Conservation Corps, and California Department of Forestry, this well-built pathway allows easy neighborhood access to one of the most prominent of the nine San Luis Obispo-area *morros*. It's the kind of trail that local people flock to for an early morning or after-work walk, often in the company of their canine companions (leashes are required). The trail leads from the west side of Patricia Drive and travels uphill, gaining a total of 1,200 feet in elevation. Go left at the first junction, heading around a cattle pond. You'll soon leave the open grasslands behind and enter a dense oak and bay laurel forest, where several short spur trails lead to rock-climbing sites. At a signed junction, head left to follow the summit trail to Bishop Peak. The last mile is a dramatic climb through well-graded switchbacks to the peak's rocky summit at elevation 1,559 feet. Once on top, enjoy the fine vista of all of San Luis Obispo, but watch your footing. It's easy to get inspired by the views and be tempted to climb to the top of the highest rock, but this has resulted in a few tragic accidents. Note: If you don't have the time or energy to summit Bishop Peak, you can always hike the Felsman Loop instead, which travels along the peak's lower slopes. Access the Felsman Loop by turning right at this trail's first junction instead of left.

User Groups: Hikers and dogs. No horses or mountain bikes. No wheelchair facilities.

Permits: No permits are required. Parking and access are free.

Maps: A map of Bishop Peak Natural Reserve is available for free download at www.slocity.org.

For a topographic map, go to the USGS website to download San Luis Obispo.

Directions: From San Luis Obispo, head west on Foothill Boulevard. Turn right on Patricia Drive and drive about one mile. Continue past the stop sign at Highland Drive for 0.25 mile to the trailhead on the left, just past Patricia Court. Park on the left (west) side of Patricia Drive, away from the private driveways.

Contact: City of San Luis Obispo Parks and Recreation, San Luis Obispo, 805/781-7300, www.slocity.org.

12 BIG FALLS

3.0 mi/1.5 hr

in the Santa Lucia Wilderness near Arroyo Grande

Map 12.2, page 642 BEST

The journey to Big Falls in the Santa Lucia Wilderness is a wacky, water-filled adventure. Even as late as June, the drive to the trailhead can require dozens of crossings of Lopez Creek. In some places, the stream simply becomes the road. Compared to the drive, the hike is surprisingly easy and fast. You walk through a fern- and flower-filled sycamore and oak forest to the first waterfall, only 0.5 mile in. This is not actually Big Falls; it's a smaller waterfall, although plenty of people mistake it for Big Falls. This waterfall is only about 30 feet high, with many small trout swimming in its lower pool and a much deeper pool just above its lip. Sunbathers enjoy the rocky pools upstream. You can continue hiking beyond this cataract to the real Big Falls, another mile farther. Spring wildflowers are excellent along the route. The terrain gets drier and rockier as you climb up out of the canyon to Big Falls, and you'll find different types of flowers and foliage on this upper part of the trail. Big Falls is about 80 feet tall, but it's only impressive early in the year. By June it has much less flow than the smaller waterfall downstream. If you want to hike more, the trail continues beyond Big Falls for another mile, making an exposed and steep ascent to Hi Mountain Road.

User Groups: Hikers, dogs, and horses. No mountain bikes. No wheelchair facilities.

Permits: No day-use permits are required. Parking and access are free.

Maps: A Los Padres National Forest map is available from the U.S. Forest Service. For a topographic map, go to the USGS website to download Tar Spring Ridge.

Directions: From San Luis Obispo, drive 15 miles south on U.S. 101 to Arroyo Grande and the Highway 227/Lopez Lake exit. Head east on Highway 227 and turn right on Lopez Drive, following the signs toward Lopez Lake for 10.3 miles. Turn right on Hi Mountain Road (before Lopez Lake's entrance station). Drive 0.8 mile, turn left on Upper Lopez Canyon Road, and drive 6.3 miles, passing a Scout Camp, and turn right. In 0.1 mile, the pavement ends. Continue for 3.5 miles on the dirt road, crossing Lopez Creek numerous times in the wet season, to the Big Falls trailhead. The trail leads from the right side of the road. Note: Four-wheel-drive vehicles are recommended.

Contact: Los Padres National Forest, Santa Lucia Ranger District, Santa Maria, 805/925-9538, www.fs.usda.gov/lpnf.

13 LITTLE FALLS

1.0 mi/0.5 hr

in the Santa Lucia Wilderness near Arroyo Grande

Map 12.2, page 642 BEST

Little Falls is just as pretty as its neighbor Big Falls (see listing in this chapter), and getting to it requires the same wet and rugged drive, but a lot less of it. If your car isn't up to the 3.5 miles of rocky road and stream crossings that it takes to get to Big Falls, maybe you can convince it to go only 1.6 miles to Little Falls. If even that's too much, you can always park where the pavement ends and walk to Little Falls, adding 3.2 miles round-trip to the mileage shown above.

It's still a fairly easy hike, offering plenty of lovely scenery. You hike from the trailhead along Little Falls Creek—a cool, shady stream that is teeming with small trout and lined with oaks, sycamores, bays, and maples. Maidenhair and giant woodwardia ferns line its rocky pools. After only 15 minutes of hiking (less than 0.5 mile), you'll see a spur trail heading off to the left, which you can follow upstream for a few hundred feet to Little Falls, a 50-foot limestone waterfall. The main trail continues beyond this spur to many fine, water-carved pools—perfect for wading. The trail eventually climbs out of the canyon to Hi Mountain Road.

User Groups: Hikers, dogs, and horses. No mountain bikes. No wheelchair facilities.

Permits: No day-use permits are required. Parking and access are free.

Maps: A Los Padres National Forest map is available from the U.S. Forest Service. For a topographic map, go to the USGS website to download Tar Spring Ridge.

Directions: From San Luis Obispo, drive 15 miles south on U.S. 101 to Arroyo Grande and the Highway 227/Lopez Lake exit. Head east on Highway 227; turn right on Lopez Drive, and follow the signs toward Lopez Lake for 10.3 miles. Turn right on Hi Mountain Road (before Lopez Lake's entrance station). Drive 0.8 mile and turn left on Upper Lopez Canyon Road. Drive 6.3 miles, passing a Scout Camp, and then turn right. The pavement ends 0.1 mile farther ahead. Continue for 1.6 miles on the dirt road, crossing Lopez Creek numerous times in the wet season, to the Little Falls trailhead (the sign can be hard to spot; check your odometer carefully). The trail leads from the right side of the road. Note: Four-wheel-drive vehicles are recommended.

Contact: Los Padres National Forest, Santa Lucia Ranger District, Santa Maria, 805/925-9538, www.fs.usda.gov/lpnf.

14 DUNA VISTA LOOP AND ENCINAL TRAILS

2.2-7.2 mi/1.0-3.0 hr 2 9

at Lopez Lake northeast of Arroyo Grande

Map 12.2, page 642

Most people on the Central Coast know that Lopez Lake is ideal for water recreation—boating, waterskiing, windsurfing, fishing, you name it—but not everyone knows that the park is also great for hiking, especially in springtime. The best path in the park, Duna Vista Loop, is accessible via either a long hike or a short hike and a boat ride. The latter option works great for people who want to go hiking while their loved ones go fishing; they can be dropped off and picked up later. If you're going by boat, there are two ways to access the Duna Vista Loop Trail. From the Encinal Boat Camp dock on the Lopez arm of the lake, follow the Encinal Trail about 0.6 mile to the Duna Vista Loop Trail junction. Or, from the Wittenburg arm at Miller Cove, follow the Duna Vista Loop Trail up to the Encinal Trail junction. You can start from either trailhead, or arrange a shuttle pickup with a friend so that you can start at one end and finish at the other. California fuchsias bloom along the trail, mixed in among the sage and chaparral. After a 600-foot-climb, you're rewarded with views of the Santa Lucia Wilderness, the Pacific Ocean, and Pismo Dunes. If you can't arrange a boat ride, you can start your trip from the Duna Vista Loop Trailhead on the far side of the park. Start walking from the end of Lopez Drive along the Wittenburg arm. You will pass through Camp French (a Scout camp), and then skirt along the Wittenburg arm on the opposite side of the lake from where you started. The trail will start to climb and then loop back on itself at Millers Cove. Keep in mind that this extends a 2.2-mile round-trip to 7.2-miles round-trip.

User Groups: Hikers, horses, dogs, and mountain bikes. No wheelchair facilities.

Permits: No permits are required. A $10 day-use fee is charged per vehicle.

Maps: A map of Lopez Lake Recreation Area is available at the ranger station. For a topographic map, go to the USGS website to download Tar Spring Ridge.

Directions: From San Luis Obispo, drive 15 miles south on U.S. 101 to Arroyo Grande and the Highway 227/Lopez Lake exit. Head east on Highway 227 and turn right on Lopez Drive, following the signs to Lopez Lake for 10.4 miles. To reach the Duna Vista Loop Trail, you can take a boat ride up the Wittenburg or Lopez arms of the lake, or add four miles to your trip by hiking from the Wittenburg trailhead. To reach the latter, drive 1.5 miles past the park entrance station to the parking area near where the park road is gated.

Contact: Lopez Lake Recreation Area, Arroyo Grande, 805/788-2381, www.slocountyparks.org.

15 BLACKBERRY SPRINGS AND HIGH RIDGE LOOP

2.0 mi/1.0 hr 2 9

at Lopez Lake northeast of Arroyo Grande

Map 12.2, page 642

Great views of the grassy hills and blue water of Lopez Lake are yours for the taking on High Ridge Trail. Start from the Blackberry Springs trailhead at Squirrel Campground. As you hike uphill through a foliage-rich creek canyon, watch for fruit-covered blackberry bushes in early summer. Many other plants along the trail are also edible and were used by the Chumash. The trail steepens as it climbs to connect with High Ridge Trail at 0.75 mile, where you turn left and wander along a firebreak, which offers wide-open views. It's hot and sunny up here, so that may dictate how far you wander, but the trail travels 2.2 miles before it drops down to the Wittenburg arm of the lake. You may as well just head out for 0.5 mile or so, enjoy the views of the Santa Lucia Wilderness and the coast, and then turn around and head back. Another option is to turn right instead of left on the High Ridge Trail, walk 0.5 mile, and connect with the Turkey Ridge Trail. Take the Turkey Ridge Trail back to the parking lot by Squirrel Campground for a nice two-mile loop trip.

User Groups: Hikers and dogs. No horses or mountain bikes. No wheelchair facilities.

Permits: No permits are required. A $10 day-use fee is charged per vehicle.

Maps: A map of Lopez Lake Recreation Area is available at the ranger station. For a topographic map, go to the USGS website to download Tar Spring Ridge.

Directions: From San Luis Obispo, drive 15 miles south on U.S. 101 to Arroyo Grande and the Highway 227/Lopez Lake exit. Head east on Highway 227 and turn right on Lopez Drive, following the signs to Lopez Lake for 10.4 miles. Continue past the entrance station to Squirrel Campground and the trailhead for the Blackberry Springs Trail.

Contact: Lopez Lake Recreation Area, Arroyo Grande, 805/788-2381, www.slocountyparks.org.

16 OSO FLACO LAKE

3.0 mi/1.5 hr 1 9

southwest of Arroyo Grande

Map 12.2, page 642

Oso Flaco Lake and its environs were the site of an extensive dune restoration and native plant revegetation project in the 1980s. The result is an 800-acre natural area that is the perfect place to view coastal wildflowers and wildlife. The trail to Oso Flaco Lake starts out on a gravel causeway for 0.3 mile, then cuts off to the left on a wooden boardwalk and footbridge that bisects the small lake, one of the few remaining freshwater dune lakes. Immediately you are in the good company of shorebirds and waterfowl, including ducks that play hide-and-seek in the islands of reeds. The boardwalk extends beyond the lake's border and over a series of sand dunes. It serves the dual purpose of making the trail suitable for wheelchairs and protecting the dunes' fragile plant life, which includes several threatened species. (Wheelchair users: After heavy rains, the boardwalk may be partially submerged under a few inches of water. Call the park to check trail conditions before planning a visit in winter or spring.) Where the boardwalk ends, you can continue walking on the dunes or head to the beach on your right. By the way, what does Oso Flaco mean? Skinny bear. But it's been a long time since they've seen one of those around here.

User Groups: Hikers and wheelchairs. No dogs, horses, or mountain bikes.

Permits: No permits are required. A $5 day-use fee is charged per vehicle.

Maps: For a topographic map, go to the USGS website to download Oceano.

Directions: From Santa Maria on U.S. 101, take the Highway 166/Guadalupe exit, drive nine miles west, and then turn north on Highway 1 at Guadalupe. Drive 3.6 miles to Oso Flaco Lake Road, turn left, and drive three miles to the trailhead, at the end of the road.

Contact: Oceano Dunes State Vehicular Recreation Area, Oceano, 805/473-7230 or 805/473-7223, www.parks.ca.gov.

17 LAS ZANJAS AND EL CAMINO REAL LOOP

2.5 mi/1.25 hr

at La Purisima Mission north of Lompoc

Map 12.3, page 643

If you came to La Purisima Mission seeking heavenly sanctuary but instead found a bunch of screaming school kids, you can still find your heaven in the hills surrounding the mission. There's a surprising number of good hiking trails here, considering this is a state historic park and not a recreation park. The best place to start is on a level loop trail around the mission. Set out on Las Zanjas Trail (also spelled Las Zonas on some signs), a wide service road that leads behind the mission buildings and follows the park's aqueduct. If you like, take the short cutoff on the right to the large cross on the hill (the trail is signed as Vista de la Cruz). A steep climb of 0.3 mile gives you wide views of the mission area and the Pacific Coast. Then continue on Las Zanjas to the park boundary, where you can loop back on El Camino Real, an old paved park road. Along the way, you'll be accompanied by cool ocean breezes, blooming buckeye trees and bush monkeyflower, and green grasslands in springtime. Be sure to take a tour of the mission before or after your hike.

User Groups: Hikers, dogs, horses, and mountain bikes. No wheelchair facilities.

Permits: No permits are required. A $6 day-use fee is charged per vehicle.

Maps: A map of La Purisima Mission State Historic Park is available at the entrance station or visitors center. For a topographic map, go to the USGS website to download Los Alamos.

Directions: From Buellton on U.S. 101, take the Solvang/Lompoc/Highway 246 exit, drive west 13.2 miles, and turn right on Purisima Road. The park entrance is one mile down the road, on the right. The trailhead is at the far end of the parking lot, near the visitors center.

Contact: La Purisima Mission State Historic Park, Lompoc, 805/733-3713, www.lapurisimamission.org.

18 GAVIOTA OVERLOOK

3.0 mi/1.5 hr

in Gaviota State Park near Gaviota

Map 12.3, page 643

If you don't mind a little climbing to get a great coastal view, Gaviota Overlook Trail will suit you just fine. The trail (really a ranch road) is completely out in the open as it climbs from U.S. 101 to the top of the ridge above Gaviota Beach, but as long as the weather is cool, it's an easy ascent. There are two main trail forks; bear left at both. Since this is coastal grasslands territory, wildflowers are prolific in springtime, but the area appears arid-looking by late summer. No matter; the view from the top is priceless—miles of open ocean on the one side (including the Channel Islands), and miles of grasslands and chaparral on the other side. Hey, where are all the condominiums? Just kidding. The trail ends at some microwave towers below the highest point on the ridge, but the views are just fine from where you are. The only catch on this trail is that the trailhead is darn near impossible to find, so follow directions precisely.

User Groups: Hikers, horses, and mountain bikes. No dogs. No wheelchair facilities.

Permits: No permits are required. Parking and access are free.

Maps: A map of Gaviota State Park is available for free download at www.parks.ca.gov. For topographic maps, go to the USGS website to download Solvang and Gaviota.

Directions: Drive south from Buellton on U.S. 101 for 10 miles to just north of Gaviota Pass, to the blue sign that reads Rest Area 1 Mile, Tourist Information. Immediately beyond it you'll drive over a concrete bridge and must quickly turn right into the very small parking area just beyond the bridge. It's easy to miss. If you reach the rest area, you've gone past it. (Coming from Santa Barbara and points south on U.S. 101, you must exit at Highway 1/Lompoc, then get back on the freeway heading south.)

Contact: Gaviota State Park, Refugio State Beach, Goleta, 805/968-1033, www.parks.ca.gov.

19 NOJOQUI FALLS

0.5 mi/0.5 hr 1 8

Nojoqui Falls County Park near Gaviota

Map 12.3, page 643

A favorite spot for road-trippers cruising up-coast on U.S. 101, Nojoqui Falls County Park has only one short hiking trail, but it comes with a huge payoff. An easy stroll from the parking area leads to impressive Nojoqui Falls, which drops 80 feet over a sandstone cliff that is almost completely covered with delicate Venus maidenhair ferns. The trail is rewarding no

At low tide, sandstone formations are revealed at Gaviota State Beach

matter how much or how little the waterfall is flowing; it passes through a cooling canopy of oaks and laurels, with Nojoqui Creek babbling alongside. Check out the interesting rocks along the route. They're made of shale, while the waterfall cliff is made of sandstone. You'll see the difference. There's a stair-stepped rock perch right by the waterfall's pool, where you can sit in the shade of big-leaf maples and admire the scene. By the way, how do you pronounce the name of this waterfall and park? It's "no-HO-wee." Not "no-HO-kee" or, heaven forbid, "no-JOKE-ee."

User Groups: Hikers and dogs. No horses or mountain bikes. No wheelchair facilities.

Permits: No permits are required. Parking and access are free.

Maps: For a topographic map, go to the USGS website to download Solvang.

Directions: From Santa Barbara, drive 40 miles north on U.S. 101 to the signed turnoff for Nojoqui Park, north of Gaviota State Beach. Drive one mile on the Old Coast Highway and turn east on Alisal Road. Drive 0.8 mile to the park entrance on your right. Drive 0.25 mile down the park access road to the parking lot and trailhead. The trail starts from the far end of the parking lot loop.

Contact: Nojoqui Falls County Park, 805/688-4217; Santa Barbara County Parks and Recreation, Santa Maria, 805/934-6123 or 805/568-2461, www.sbparks.com.

20 GAVIOTA HOT SPRINGS

1.0 mi/0.5 hr 2 6

in Gaviota State Park near Gaviota

Map 12.3, page 643

Gaviota State Park got smart and started charging people to park at this trailhead since hot springs always draw a crowd. Still, if you show up first thing in the morning or anytime during the week, you can most likely soak all by yourself in one of the two small pools here. They're not very big, very deep, or especially hot, but they're easy to reach and great for a soak. Getting there requires a short but steep climb from the trailhead, mostly on a fire road. The smell of sulfur and the sway of the palm tree above the upper pool will lull you into believing you're at your own private spa. The upper pool is the hotter of the two, nearly at bathtub temperature. If you look closely, you can see little bubbles coming up from the ground under the pool—that's geology in action. If you want to hike more, you can combine this trip with the trek to Gaviota Peak (see listing in this chapter), or take a separate short hike to see Gaviota's sandstone wind caves.

User Groups: Hikers, horses, and mountain bikes. No dogs. No wheelchair facilities.

Permits: No permits are required. A $10 day-use fee is charged per vehicle.

Maps: A map of Gaviota State Park is available for free download at www.parks.ca.gov. For a topographic map, go to the USGS website to download Gaviota.

Directions: From Santa Barbara, drive north on U.S. 101 for 35 miles, pass through the tunnel at Gaviota Pass, and take the first exit after the tunnel, which is signed as Highway 1/Lompoc/Vandenburg Air Force Base. At the stop sign, turn right and head south on the frontage road that parallels the freeway. (Don't bear left on Highway 1.) The frontage road ends in 0.25 mile at the trailhead parking area.

Contact: Gaviota State Park, Refugio State Beach, Goleta, 805/968-1033, www.parks.ca.gov.

21 GAVIOTA PEAK

6.2 mi/3.5 hr 

in Gaviota State Park near Gaviota

Map 12.3, page 643

Gaviota State Park's best hike for a solid workout and glorious ocean views is this trail to Gaviota Peak. Start from the Gaviota Hot Springs trailhead, but instead of taking the short spur trail to Gaviota Hot Springs, head left on Gaviota Peak Trail and begin your assault on Gaviota Hill—oops, that's Gaviota Peak, elevation 2,450 feet. The climb isn't too bad (2,100 feet in 3.1 miles), but geez, it can get hot here since there's almost no shade. The trail is a dirt road with a few single-track sections that climbs a series of knolls on its way to Gaviota Peak. Technically the peak is actually in Los Padres National Forest, not in the state park. Once you're there, you'll find the views are downright awesome. What can you see? Point Conception, the Pacific, the Channel Islands, Lompoc Valley, and Gaviota Pass at your feet. Hopefully you picked a day when the fog wasn't visiting. Lots of hikers choose to make a loop out of this hike by going uphill on Gaviota Peak Trail and returning downhill via Trespass Trail (the mileage is about the same).

User Groups: Hikers, horses, and mountain bikes. No dogs. No wheelchair facilities.

Permits: No permits are required. A $10 day-use fee is charged per vehicle.

Maps: A map of Gaviota State Park is available for free download at www.parks.ca.gov. For a topographic map, go to the USGS website to download Gaviota.

Directions: Drive north from Santa Barbara on U.S. 101 for 35 miles, pass through the tunnel at Gaviota Pass, and take the first exit after the tunnel, which is signed as Highway 1/Lompoc/Vandenburg Air Force Base. Turn right at the stop sign and head south on the frontage road that parallels the freeway. (Don't bear left onto Highway 1.) The frontage road ends in 0.25 mile at the trailhead parking area.

Contact: Gaviota State Park, Refugio State Beach, Goleta, 805/968-1033, www.parks.ca.gov.

22 MCPHERSON PEAK TRAIL

10.0 mi/2 days 4 8

in San Rafael Wilderness

Map 12.4, page 644

McPherson Peak, elevation 5,747 feet, is just on the edge of the spectacular San Rafael Wilderness, a land of condors and steep canyons. Although the trail is steep and can be hot in summer, it gives hikers outstanding views of the wilderness and the desertlike lands of Cuyama to the northeast. From Aliso Park Campground, you start hiking on the dirt road that is signed for Hog Pen Spring Campground, quickly saying good-bye to the shady canyon. Reach the camp in 1.5 miles (there's a spring nearby if you need water); then pick up a trail that continues climbing, now more steeply, to Sierra Madre Road, on the wilderness boundary. Turn right on the dirt road and hike another 2.5 miles through chaparral to McPherson Peak, passing McPherson Camp along the way. The camp has a spring and is an excellent place to spend the night. You can watch the sunset from McPherson Peak and then crawl into your sleeping bag and watch the stars.

User Groups: Hikers, dogs, horses, and mountain bikes (mountain bikes may not go past the wilderness boundary). No wheelchair facilities.

Permits: A free California campfire permit is required year-round for building a fire or using a backpacking stove; permits are available at the Santa Maria Ranger Station. Parking and access are free if you park outside the campground.

Maps: A Los Padres National Forest map is available from the U.S. Forest Service. For a topographic map, go to the USGS website to download Peak Mountain.

Directions: From Santa Maria on U.S. 101, take Highway 166 east for 48 miles to just west of New Cuyama. Turn right (south) on Aliso Canyon Road and follow it for six miles to Aliso Park Campground. Park outside the campground. The dirt road can be very rough; high-clearance vehicles are recommended. If you are coming from Ventura or Ojai, take Highway 33 north to Highway 166, then go west past New Cuyama.

Contact: Los Padres National Forest, Santa Lucia Ranger District, Santa Maria, 805/925-9538, www.fs.usda.gov/lpnf.

23 UPPER MANZANA CREEK TRAIL

14.0 mi/1-2 days 3 8

in San Rafael Wilderness

Map 12.4, page 644

From Nira Campground, a major entry point into the San Rafael Wilderness, you can hike east or west along Manzana Creek. Hikers and backpackers can take Upper Manzana Creek Trail to the east and stop at any one of several excellent campsites, including Manzana (six miles out) and Manzana Narrows (seven miles out). Both are set near inviting swimming holes. The trail climbs gently from the campground, sometimes switchbacking away from the creek but always returning. A modicum of shade is provided by blue oaks and gray pines, mixed in among the low-lying chaparral and manzanita. Note: The creek gets low and is less attractive by midsummer, but that winter hiking can be dangerous if the water level is too high. March through May is the best time to visit.

User Groups: Hikers, dogs, and horses. No mountain bikes. No wheelchair facilities.

Permits: A free California campfire permit is required year-round for building a fire or using a backpacking stove; permits are available at the Santa Maria Ranger Station. A National Forest Adventure Pass is required for each vehicle; fees are $5 for one day or $30 for a year. Interagency access passes are also accepted.

Maps: A Los Padres National Forest map is available from the U.S. Forest Service. For a topographic map, go to the USGS website to download Bald Mountain.

Directions: From Santa Barbara on U.S. 101, take Highway 154 north and drive 23 miles, past Lake Cachuma, to Armour Ranch Road. Turn right and drive 1.5 miles to Happy Canyon Road (not suitable for trailers). Turn right and drive 14 miles to Cachuma Saddle and a junction with Figueroa Mountain Road; then continue straight on Sunset Valley Road and follow it for 5.6 miles to its end at Nira Campground. Park in the hikers' parking lot.

Contact: Los Padres National Forest, Santa Lucia Ranger District, Santa Maria, 805/925-9538, www.fs.usda.gov/lpnf.

24 PIÑO ALTO TRAIL

0.5 mi/0.5 hr 1 8

on Figueroa Mountain in Los Padres National Forest

Map 12.4, page 644 BEST

Figueroa Mountain is one of the most popular wildflower-viewing spots in all of the Central Coast, with a spectacular springtime bloom cloaking its slopes from February through April. But a trip to the mountain is a great escape at any time of year, and a good way to appreciate the uniqueness of this area is to hike the short Piño Alto Interpretive Trail. Whether or not the flower show is happening, the high views will knock your socks off. From one point on the trail, the Santa Ynez Valley is visible for some 20 miles from the northwest to the southeast. You can see Cuyama, Lake Cachuma, the Santa Ynez Mountains, and sometimes even the Channel Islands far off to sea. The trail is located at 4,600 feet in elevation, situated among ponderosa and Jeffrey pines and big cone spruce. Conifers? In Santa Barbara? That's right. The paved trail surface makes it suitable for wheelchairs. If you want wider vistas, make sure that you drive 0.5 mile uphill from the trailhead parking lot to the Figueroa lookout tower site. From there you can survey all the mountains of the San Rafael Wilderness. Note: If you like what you see on Figueroa Mountain, many longer day hikes are possible on the nearby Davy Brown/Fir Canyon Trail, starting at either Davy Brown Campground or at the trailhead on Figueroa Mountain Road.

User Groups: Hikers, wheelchairs, and dogs. No horses or mountain bikes.

Permits: No permits are required. A National Forest Adventure Pass is required for each vehicle; fees are $5 for one day or $30 for a year. Interagency access passes are also accepted.

Maps: A Los Padres National Forest map is available from the U.S. Forest Service. For a topographic map, go to the USGS website to download Figueroa Mountain.

Directions: From Santa Barbara, drive north on U.S. 101, through Buellton, for 45 miles to the Highway 154 East turnoff. Turn east onto Highway 154 and drive three miles to Los Olivos, then turn north (left) on Figueroa Mountain Road. Drive 13 miles to the fork for Figueroa Mountain Lookout Road (dirt). Bear left and drive two miles to the Piño Alto Picnic Area.

Contact: Los Padres National Forest, Santa Lucia Ranger District, Santa Maria, 805/925-9538, www.fs.usda.gov/lpnf.

25 SNYDER TRAIL

12.0 mi/7.0 hr 3 9

near the Santa Ynez Recreation Area

Map 12.4, page 644

While Snyder Trail may start out looking like a plain old fire road at its lower end at Paradise Road, by the time it climbs six miles to East Camino Cielo, it becomes a lovely single-track trail that is bordered by more wildflowers than you can count and has more wide-reaching vistas than you can imagine. Don't bother twisting your neck to catch the views on your way up, because on your return trip downhill, they will be laid out in front of you. The nice thing about the trail is that you start gaining vistas fairly quickly, so if you're tiring of the climb, you can simply find a knoll somewhere, have a seat, and pull out your sandwiches. If you decide to go all the way up, a popular side-trip to the ruins of Knapp's Castle (see listing in this chapter) is just before the top. Take the gated dirt road on the left, 5.5 miles up. If you hike the Snyder Trail's entire length, you'll be tired by the end of the day, but you'll have a whole storehouse of fine memories. One caveat: This trail is also popular with mountain bikers, usually heading in the downhill direction. Watch out for them.

User Groups: Hikers, dogs, horses, and mountain bikes. No wheelchair facilities.

Permits: No permits are required. Parking and access are free.

Maps: A Los Padres National Forest map is available from the U.S. Forest Service. For a topographic map, go to the USGS website to download San Marcos Pass.

Directions: From U.S. 101 in Santa Barbara, take the Highway 154/State Street exit and drive north for 11.5 miles. Turn right on Paradise Road and drive 4.2 miles to the trailhead for the Snyder Trail, which is at a locked gate on the right side of the road 0.25 mile west of the Los Prietos Ranger Station.

Contact: Los Padres National Forest, Santa Barbara Ranger District, Santa Barbara, 805/967-3481, www.fs.usda.gov/lpnf.

26 ALISO CANYON LOOP TRAIL

3.5 mi/2.0 hr 3 8

in the Santa Ynez Recreation Area

Map 12.4, page 644

From the east end of Sage Hill Campground, you can set off on Aliso Canyon Trail and choose between a one-mile interpretive walk or a 3.5-mile loop trail. The former is the first mile of the latter and follows Aliso Creek. Be sure to bring along a trail brochure so you can learn all about how the Chumash Indians lived in this area and what plants they used and ate. In the spring, a wildflower-identification book also may be a good idea, as the variety of flowers along this short route is surprising. At the end of the interpretive trail, you can either turn around and hike back, or continue on the longer loop trip. To do so, walk back a few feet to a trail junction and ascend for 0.5 mile to a meadow on a grassy plateau. From there, you climb rather steeply to the top of the ridge that divides Aliso and Oso Canyons, where there are excellent views of the Santa Ynez Canyon and distant mountains. At the ridge top, turn right (often there is no trail sign), following the ridge's backbone. You'll loop around and soon head back downhill. Note: After winter rains, the sloping trails beyond the interpretive trail are often badly eroded. If you're walking the entire loop, wear some good boots.

User Groups: Hikers, dogs, horses, and mountain bikes. No wheelchair facilities.

Permits: No permits are required. A National Forest Adventure Pass is required for each vehicle; fees are $5 for one day or $30 for a year. Interagency access passes are also accepted.

Maps: A Los Padres National Forest map is available from the U.S. Forest Service. For a topographic map, go to the USGS website to download San Marcos Pass.

Directions: From U.S. 101 in Santa Barbara, take the Highway 154/State Street exit and drive north for about 11.5 miles. Turn right on Paradise Road and drive 4.5 miles to the ranger station. Turn left at the ranger station and drive one mile to Sage Hill Campground. Proceed to the day-use area at the east end of the camp and the trailhead for the Aliso Canyon Trail.

Contact: Los Padres National Forest, Santa Barbara Ranger District, Santa Barbara, 805/967-3481, www.fs.usda.gov/lpnf.

27 SANTA CRUZ TRAIL

4.0 mi/2.0 hr 1 8

in the Santa Ynez Recreation Area

Map 12.4, page 644

The Santa Cruz Trail is one of the most popular in the Santa Ynez Recreation Area, and it's no wonder. The hiking is easy and the swimming holes along Oso Creek are plentiful. Cooling off in the water is the number-one reason that people pay a visit to the Santa Ynez Recreation Area in summertime. The destination on this trip is Nineteen Oaks Camp, a popular picnicking spot near the base of Little Pine Mountain. The trail follows an unattractive dirt road out of Upper Oso Campground, but it becomes a lovely single-track trail as it continues into the shady canyon. The sandstone-carved creek pools are lovely to see even when the water level is low, and as you climb a bit, you get views of Little Pine Mountain. A spur trail on the right, at 1.9 miles, leads a few hundred yards to Nineteen Oaks Camp, with shady oaks and a few campsites and picnic tables. Most day hikers end their trip there before the trail begins its hot, exposed switchbacks to the top of Little Pine Mountain, elevation 4,506 feet. Be forewarned: You may see off-road motorcyclists at the trailhead, but don't let them scare you. They'll be exiting your trail in the first mile.

User Groups: Hikers, dogs, horses, and mountain bikes. No wheelchair facilities.

Permits: No permits are required. A National Forest Adventure Pass is required for each vehicle; fees are $5 for one day or $30 for a year. Interagency access passes are also accepted.

Maps: A Los Padres National Forest map is available from the U.S. Forest Service. For a topographic map, go to the USGS website to download San Marcos Pass.

Directions: From U.S. 101 in Santa Barbara, take the Highway 154/State Street exit and drive north for 11.5 miles. Turn right on Paradise Road and drive 5.5 miles, past the ranger station, to the left turnoff for Upper Oso Campground. Turn left and drive one mile to the campground.

Contact: Los Padres National Forest, Santa Barbara Ranger District, Santa Barbara, 805/967-3481, www.fs.usda.gov/lpnf.

28 KNAPP'S CASTLE

0.8 mi/0.5 hr 1 9

north of Santa Barbara

Map 12.4, page 644

Some trails are just right for all kinds of hikers, no matter their fitness level, and the trail to Knapp's Castle is one of those. The tricky part is that Knapp's Castle, or technically just the scattering of chimneys, stonework, and archways that are the remains of Knapp's Castle, is on a chunk of private property within Los Padres National Forest, and it's only by the good graces of the landowner that the public is allowed to hike there. There's construction going on at the castle ruins—and lots of rumors that the structure will be completely rebuilt—but As of October 2019, the owner still allows hikers to visit the land, and if we all mind our manners, hopefully this beautiful spot with its impressive view of the Santa Ynez Mountains will remain open to the public for many years to come. So who was the Knapp of Knapp's Castle? George Owen Knapp was the former chairman of the board of Union Carbide, and in 1916 he built a five-bedroom sandstone mansion on this site. His mountain lodge hosted many of Knapp's rich and important friends, who were treated to after-dinner concerts by the resident organist playing the lodge's massive pipe organ. Although the building burned down in a canyon fire in 1940, its foundation still stands, and the site offers a fine spot to sit and look out over the Santa Ynez River Canyon and distant mountains. You can even see far-off Lake Cachuma. The trail to reach Knapp's Castle is a well-graded dirt road. You hike past the gate signed as Private Property Ahead, pass through another gate, stay on the dirt road, and reach the castle remains and its amazing vista in less than 0.5 mile of walking. If you want to get more exercise than just this short stroll, you can always explore the adjacent Snyder Trail.

Note: Because Knapp's Castle is on private property, its accessibility to the public is subject to change at any time. Call the Santa Barbara Ranger District office for an update before visiting.

User Groups: Hikers and dogs. No horses or mountain bikes. No wheelchair facilities.

Permits: No permits are required. Parking and access are free.

Maps: A Los Padres National Forest map is available from the U.S. Forest Service. For a topographic map, go to the USGS website to download San Marcos Pass.

Directions: From U.S. 101 in Santa Barbara, take the Highway 154/State Street exit and drive north for eight miles. Turn right on East Camino Cielo and drive 2.9 miles to the parking pullout on the right, across from a locked gate and dirt road on the left. The gate is signed Private Property Ahead.

Contact: Los Padres National Forest, Santa Barbara Ranger District, Santa Barbara, 805/967-3481, www.fs.usda.gov/lpnf.

29 SEVEN FALLS

3.0 mi/1.5 hr

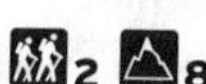

north of Santa Barbara

Map 12.4, page 644

Seven Falls is a perfect springtime day trip in Santa Barbara, best visited between February and April. It has a little bit of everything: waterfalls, swimming holes, vistas, wildflowers, and a good trail. The trail has a lot of unsigned junctions, however, so remember to stay left at all of them until after you cross Mission Creek for the second time. From the end of Tunnel Road, start hiking on the gated continuation of the road, passing a water tank and heading uphill on pavement for 0.75 mile. After a few minutes of climbing, you'll be able to see all the way out to the ocean. Cross a bridge over Mission Creek and continue hiking straight ahead on the road, which turns to dirt. In a few hundred feet you come to a junction; a sign on your left directs you to Jesusita Trail. Follow it to the left and bear left again as the path cuts down on single-track to Mission Creek, where you'll find many good swimming holes. Cross the creek, but instead of following the continuation of the Jesusita Trail, head to your right, upstream, on a use trail. (Remember, this is the only right turn on the route.) After 0.25 mile of combined hiking and scrambling, you'll reach the first of the sandstone-carved cascades of Seven Falls. These falls flow with force only immediately after a period of rain, but the sandstone pools and canyon walls are pretty to look at even when the creek is nearly dry.

User Groups: Hikers, dogs, horses, and mountain bikes. No wheelchair facilities.

Permits: No permits are required. Parking and access are free.

Maps: A Los Padres National Forest map is available from the U.S. Forest Service. For a topographic map, go to the USGS website to download Santa Barbara.

Directions: From U.S. 101 in Santa Barbara, take the Mission Street exit and follow it east for just over a mile, crossing State Street. When Mission Street ends, turn left on Laguna Street and drive past the Santa Barbara Mission, turning right on Los Olivos, directly in front of the mission. Passing the mission, bear left on Mission Canyon Road for 0.8 mile. Turn right on Foothill Boulevard. In 0.1 mile, turn left onto the continuation of Mission Canyon Road. Then bear left on Tunnel Road and follow it for 1.1 miles until it ends. Park alongside the road on the right.

Contact: Los Padres National Forest, Santa Barbara Ranger District, Santa Barbara, 805/967-3481, www.fs.usda.gov/lpnf.

30 INSPIRATION POINT

5.0 mi/2.5 hr

3 9

north of Santa Barbara

Map 12.4, page 644

The trail to Inspiration Point is sure to get you inspired if only because it's a great path for year-round exercise in Santa Barbara. Follow the Tunnel Road Trail to Jesusita Trail, as if you were going to Seven Falls (see listing in this chapter), but after crossing Mission Creek, keep following the main Jesusita Trail instead. Get ready for a switchbacking climb up to Inspiration Point, which is only one mile away. The tan-colored rock outcrops you see everywhere are coldwater sandstone; often you'll see hang gliders taking off from some of the highest rocks and gliding, seemingly effortlessly, overhead. When you reach Inspiration Point at 1,750 feet, you are rewarded with sweeping views of the Pacific Coast, Santa Barbara and Goleta, and the Channel Islands.

User Groups: Hikers, dogs, horses, and mountain bikes. No wheelchair facilities.

Permits: No permits are required. Parking and access are free.

Maps: A Los Padres National Forest map is available from the U.S. Forest Service. For a topographic map, go to the USGS website to download Santa Barbara.

Directions: From U.S. 101 in Santa Barbara, take the Mission Street exit and follow it east for just over a mile, crossing State Street. When Mission Street ends, turn left on Laguna Street and drive past the Santa Barbara Mission, turning right on Los Olivos, directly in front of the mission. Passing the mission, bear left on Mission Canyon Road for 0.8 mile. Turn right on Foothill Boulevard. In 0.1 mile, turn left onto the continuation of Mission Canyon Road. Then bear left on Tunnel Road and follow it for 1.1 miles until it ends. Park alongside the road on the right.

Contact: Los Padres National Forest, Santa Barbara Ranger District, Santa Barbara, 805/967-3481, www.fs.usda.gov/lpnf.

31 RATTLESNAKE CANYON

5.0 mi/2.5 hr

3 8

north of Santa Barbara

Map 12.4, page 644

Rattlesnake Canyon Trail is probably the most popular canyon trail in Santa Barbara and also one of the prettiest, despite its menacing name. The lower reaches of the trail can look like a parade, especially on weekends, but the higher you go, the fewer folks you see. The path is especially popular with people walking their dogs. Rattlesnake Canyon is a lush riparian environment around a year-round creek; a place where the plant life is so lavish that you may think you're in Mendocino or the northern coast. The trail starts out as a wide dirt path (an old carriage road) but soon narrows to single track. It crosses rocky Rattlesnake Creek many times, tunneling through a forest of oak, bay, and sycamore trees on the lower stretch of the trail. In the spring and summer months, the wildflowers here are as good as you'll find anywhere in Santa Barbara. As you climb out of the canyon, you'll gain increasingly broad views of the Pacific Coast and Channel Islands. Watch for hang gliders soaring overhead. At an intersection with a connector trail to Tunnel Trail at 1.7 miles, bear right to finish the steep climb to Gibraltar Road. Suddenly your surroundings aren't quite so lush anymore, but the coastal views—well, on a clear day, they don't get much better than this.

User Groups: Hikers, dogs, and horses. No mountain bikes. No wheelchair facilities.

Permits: No permits are required. Parking and access are free.

Maps: A Los Padres National Forest map is available from the U.S. Forest Service. For a topographic map, go to the USGS website to download Santa Barbara.

Directions: From U.S. 101 in Santa Barbara, take the Mission Street exit and follow it east for just over a mile, crossing State Street. When Mission Street ends, turn left on Laguna Street and drive past the Santa Barbara Mission, turning right on Los Olivos, directly in front of the mission. Passing the mission, bear left on Mission Canyon Road for 0.8 mile. Turn right on Foothill Boulevard. In 0.1 mile, turn left onto the continuation of Mission Canyon Road. Drive 0.4 mile and turn right on Las Conoas Road. Drive 1.2 miles and park on the right side of the road, across from the sign for Skofield Park and Rattlesnake Canyon Wilderness Area.

Contact: Los Padres National Forest, Santa Barbara Ranger District, Santa Barbara, 805/967-3481, www.fs.usda.gov/lpnf.

32 MONTECITO OVERLOOK

3.0 mi/1.5 hr 3 9

in Montecito

Map 12.4, page 644

Note: This trail was badly damaged in Montecito's tragic January 2018 mudslide. As of October 2019, the trail is officially open, but check with the Santa Barbara Ranger District for a conditions update.

For people who think the mountains in Santa Barbara are all chaparral-covered slopes, this trail is an eye-opener to the lush beauty of the mountain canyons. The climb to Montecito Overlook is a good aerobic workout, but not extremely hard, and affords great views of the Santa Barbara coast and Channel Islands. Many people don't go all the way to the overlook; they just hike through the shady forest to the confluence of the east and middle forks of Cold Springs Creek and find themselves a cool pool to soak their feet. From the roadside pullout, follow the path through the alders alongside Cold Springs Creek, staying on the creek's right (east) side. After the first mile, you leave the creek and begin to switchback uphill to the overlook—really just a flat semi-clearing where the trail intersects a dirt road. Pick any spot amid the invading brush where the views are clear and wide. The best spot is a few hundred feet down the road to your right. Hikers looking for more trail to cover can continue another two miles to Montecito Peak, elevation 3,214 feet. The climb is steep and hot (no shade), but for many it's worth it. In addition to the views of the Santa Barbara coast, you can see all the way to the Santa Monica Mountains.

User Groups: Hikers, dogs, horses, and mountain bikes. No wheelchair facilities.

Permits: No permits are required. Parking and access are free.

Maps: A Los Padres National Forest map is available from the U.S. Forest Service. For a topographic map, go to the USGS website to download Santa Barbara.

Directions: From Santa Barbara, drive south

on U.S. 101 for four miles and exit on Hot Springs Road. Turn left on Hot Springs Road and drive 2.5 miles to Mountain Drive. Turn left and continue 1.2 miles to the Cold Springs trailhead. Park off the road, near the sharp curve where the creek runs across the road. The trail is marked by a rusty Forest Service sign.

Contact: Los Padres National Forest, Santa Barbara Ranger District, Santa Barbara, 805/967-3481, www.fs.usda.gov/lpnf.

33 WEST FORK COLD SPRINGS

4.0 mi/2.0 hr 3 9

in Montecito

Map 12.4, page 644

Note: This trail was badly damaged in Montecito's tragic January 2018 mudslide. As of October 2019, the trail is officially open, but check with the Santa Barbara Ranger District for a conditions update.

The West Fork Cold Springs Trail covers some diverse terrain, showing off the wide variety of landscapes that the Santa Barbara region has to offer. Start hiking on East Fork Cold Springs Trail from the trailhead near Mountain Drive. After a 0.5-mile stretch through a shady forest canopy alongside the creek, you'll reach the confluence of the east and middle forks of Cold Springs Creek. Cross the creek here and watch carefully for the West Fork trail sign. Soon you leave the dense, shady, fern-laden area surrounding Cold Springs Creek and climb out of the canyon into a drier and more exposed landscape. In the rainy season, look for spectacular Tangerine Falls up ahead, in the Middle Fork Canyon; the waterfall is clearly visible, although distant, from the West Fork Trail. (There used to be an unmaintained path that led to Tangerine Falls, but since the 2018 mudslide, the easiest way to get to the waterfall is by scrambling up the creekbed.) Whether you remain on the West Fork Trail or take the cutoff for Tangerine Falls, you'll climb high enough to gain great views of the valley below and the Montecito coast. On your return trip, exercise some caution—the West Fork Trail is steep and eroded in places, especially when wet. But that's a small price to pay for beauty along this trail and the relative solitude available here, compared to the more popular East Fork Trail.

User Groups: Hikers, dogs, horses, and mountain bikes. No wheelchair facilities.

Permits: No permits are required. Parking and access are free.

Maps: A Los Padres National Forest map is available from the U.S. Forest Service. For a topographic map, go to the USGS website to download Santa Barbara.

Directions: From Santa Barbara, drive south on U.S. 101 for four miles and exit on Hot Springs Road. Turn left on Hot Springs Road and drive 2.5 miles to Mountain Drive. Turn left and continue 1.2 miles to the Cold Springs trailhead. Park off the road, near the sharp curve where the creek crosses the road.

Contact: Los Padres National Forest, Santa Barbara Ranger District, Santa Barbara, 805/967-3481, www.fs.usda.gov/lpnf.

34 SAN YSIDRO TRAIL

8.0 mi/4.5 hr 3 9

in Montecito

Map 12.4, page 644

If you like running water, San Ysidro Canyon is your chance at seeing some, even long after the last rain. Other streams in the Santa Barbara area are often nearly dry by May, but San Ysidro keeps on flowing year-round. The trail up its canyon offers many possible destinations and stopping points; few hike all the way to its terminus, at East Camino Cielo—it's four miles one-way with a 3,000-foot elevation gain. The rewards are great no matter how far you go, beginning with swimming holes and waterfalls in the first two miles of trail, mostly under the shade of oaks and sycamores. After a rocky section, you climb out of the canyon into chaparral country, entering into a series of steep, exposed switchbacks. Most people give up somewhere along this stretch, but those who continue come out near Cold Spring Saddle on East Camino Cielo, elevation 3,480 feet. From there, you'll feel on top of the world.

Note: This trail was badly damaged in Montecito's tragic January 2018 mudslide. As of October 2019, the first two miles of trail are in good repair, but the upper section of trail is difficult to negotiate. Most hikers choose to turn around after the waterfalls.

User Groups: Hikers, dogs, horses, and mountain bikes. No wheelchair facilities.

Permits: No permits are required. Parking and access are free.

Maps: A Los Padres National Forest map is available from the U.S. Forest Service. For a topographic map, go to the USGS website to download Carpinteria.

Directions: From U.S. 101 in Montecito, take the San Ysidro Road exit and head east for one mile to East Valley Road/Highway 192. Turn right on East Valley Road/Highway 192 and travel 0.9 mile. Turn left on Park Lane and drive 0.4 mile; then bear left on East Mountain Drive and drive 0.25 mile to the end of the road. Park alongside the road and walk to the trailhead, on the right.

Contact: Los Padres National Forest, Santa Barbara Ranger District, Santa Barbara, 805/967-3481, www.fs.usda.gov/lpnf.

35 MCMENEMY TRAIL

2.5 mi/1.0 hr 2 8

in Montecito

Map 12.4, page 644

If you only have time for a short hike, this lovely trip in San Ysidro Canyon includes a stint on McMenemy Trail, an old favorite of many Santa Barbara hikers. It has just enough of a climb to make you feel that you did your workout for the day but enough lovely views to make you forget that hiking is technically "exercise." Begin your trip on the San Ysidro Trail (see listing in this chapter), but bear left at the sign for McMenemy Trail, 0.5 mile in. You'll pass the San Ysidro Ranch, then tackle a series of switchbacks that bring you to the Colonel's stone bench—Colonel McMenemy, that is—where you have a fine view down into Montecito and out to the coast. It's a good place to catch your breath, read a book, or have a picnic. A horse hitch is available, just in case you came on the back of Trigger, Old Paint, or Mr. Ed. If you want to keep hiking, you can make a five-mile loop by continuing on the McMenemy Trail; turn right at the Saddle Rock Trail. Then turn right again on the Edison Catwalk to return to the San Ysidro Trail.

User Groups: Hikers, dogs, horses, and mountain bikes. No wheelchair facilities.

Permits: No permits are required. Parking and access are free.

Maps: A Los Padres National Forest map is available from the U.S. Forest Service. For a topographic map, go to the USGS website to download Carpinteria.

Directions: From U.S. 101 in Montecito, take the San Ysidro Road exit and head east for one mile to East Valley Road/Highway 192. Turn right on East Valley Road/Highway 192 and travel 0.9 mile. Turn left on Park Lane and drive 0.4 mile; then bear left on East Mountain Drive and drive 0.25 mile to the end of the road. Park alongside the road and walk to the trailhead, on the right.

Contact: Los Padres National Forest, Santa Barbara Ranger District, Santa Barbara, 805/967-3481, www.fs.usda.gov/lpnf.

36 VINCENT TUMAMAIT TRAIL

8.6 mi/4.0 hr 3 9

in the Chumash Wilderness west of Frazier Park

Map 12.4, page 644

A day hike in the Chumash Wilderness means

the possibility of seeing a magnificent condor fly overhead, as well as a visit to Mount Pinos (8,831 feet), the highest point in Los Padres National Forest. This is conifer country, with the peak covered in snow a good part of the year, to the great delight of Southern California cross-country skiers. The Vincent Tumamait Trail begins on the summit of Mount Pinos and runs five miles to Mount Abel, elevation 8,286 feet (also called Mount Cerro Noroeste). If you wish, you can leave a car at Mount Abel and take a one-way shuttle trip between the two impressive peaks. The closest you can park to the summit of Mount Pinos is 1.8 miles away at the Chula Vista parking area; the summit road has been closed for several years to protect sacred Chumash Indian sites. Instead, you hike 1.8 miles to the summit, gaining only about 600 feet, check out the far-reaching views, then set off on Vincent Tumamait Trail. Head out two miles, downhill at first and then up Sawmill Mountain to the North Fork Trail junction. Bear left at the junction and walk 0.5 mile to primitive Sheep Camp, a sweet spot in the shade of fir and pine trees, where you can open up your day pack and have lunch. After a rest, you'll be all fueled up for the uphill return trip to the summit, and then the final 1.8-mile descent to your car. As you hike, keep scanning the skies for those giant condors, many of which nest in the nearby condor sanctuary. So who was Vincent Tumamait? He was a Chumash elder and a beloved storyteller who lived from 1919 to 1992.

User Groups: Hikers, dogs, and horses. No mountain bikes. No wheelchair facilities.

Permits: No permits are required for day-hiking. A California campfire permit is required for overnight stays year-round whether you are using a camp stove or building a fire; permits are free and available online at www.fs.usda.gov/lpnf or in person at any Southern California National Forest ranger station. Parking and access are free.

Maps: A Los Padres National Forest map is available from the U.S. Forest Service. For a topographic map, go to the USGS website to download Sawmill Mountain.

Directions: From I-5 near Lebec, take the Frazier Park/Mount Pinos exit and turn west. Drive 12 miles on Frazier Mountain Park Road, which will become Cuddy Valley Road. At 12 miles, bear left on Mount Pinos Highway and drive 10 miles to the Chula Vista parking lot (Mount Pinos Winter Recreation Area). Begin hiking on the dirt road to Mount Pinos Summit (the gated dirt road on the west side).

Contact: Los Padres National Forest, Mount Pinos Ranger District, Frazier Park, 661/245-3731, www.fs.usda.gov/lpnf.

37 POTRERO JOHN

3.2 mi or 5.4 mi/1.5 hr or 3.0 hr 

in the Sespe Wilderness north of Ojai

Map 12.4, page 644

There's nothing nicer than a trail that follows a stream, especially in a place as notoriously dry as Ojai. The Potrero John Trail follows Potrero John Creek to Potrero John Camp, set at 4,140 feet in elevation. The creek has water most of the year but frequently dries up in the summer, so visit here in winter or spring if possible. From the roadside trailhead, the trail starts out with a brief steep pitch, but it quickly levels off. The trail travels along the bottom of a narrow canyon, with conifers growing precariously on the steep canyon walls. It follows the canyon floor for 1.5 miles, then crosses the creek on a bridge and enters primitive Potrero John Camp, which consists of a rock-lined fire pit and rusty metal barbecue, plus some stone and log benches. You have a fair chance of having this spot all to yourself because the maintained trail ends just beyond the camp. In the wet season, though, intrepid visitors keep on hiking in the drainage beyond the camp because they want to see Potrero John Falls, 1.2 miles farther upstream. Depending on how much it has rained in the weeks before your visit, the going can be very difficult or very easy, and your feet can get completely soaked or not wet at all. There's no real trail, but just stay along the creek and you'll get there eventually. Plan at least an hour to traverse the 1.2 miles from the campground to the falls—maybe double that if the water is high and the rocks slippery. When you reach the waterfall, you'll know why you went to the effort: Potrero John's 70-foot-high drop is a stunner. This sparkling freefall is one of the best waterfalls in Los Padres National Forest.

User Groups: Hikers, dogs, and horses. No mountain bikes. No wheelchair facilities.

Permits: No day-hiking permits are required. Parking and access are free.

Maps: A Los Padres National Forest map is available from the U.S. Forest Service. A map of the Sespe Wilderness is available from Tom Harrison Maps. For a topographic map, go to the USGS website to download Lion Canyon.

Directions: From Ojai, drive north on Highway 33 for 21 miles to where Potrero John Creek crosses the highway, by mile marker 32.10. The trailhead is signed on the right (north) side of the road.

Contact: Los Padres National Forest, Ojai Ranger District, Ojai, 805/646-4348, www.fs.usda.gov/lpnf.

38 CEDAR CREEK AND THE FISHBOWLS

11.8 mi/6.0 hr or 2 days 3 9

in the Sespe Wilderness northeast of Ojai

Map 12.4, page 644 BEST

Despite the length of this trail and the fact that the area has been badly burned by wildfires in recent years, the Fishbowls along Piru Creek remain a popular spot, mostly because there is little that is finer in life than a creek with good swimming holes. That and the fact that the trail has a moderate elevation gain, so even with the nearly 12-mile round-trip, it is a manageable day hike for most people. Note that the Thorn Meadows Campground, a mile from the trailhead, is no longer open due to fire and storm damage. Start hiking at the Cedar Creek trailhead and follow the south fork of Piru Creek. What starts out as a wide dirt road eventually narrows to a single-track trail. At 3.5 miles, bear right on the Fishbowls Trail, hike along a ridgeline that offers big views of the partly burned forest below, then descend to Fishbowls Camp. Walk upstream from the camp for about 300 yards to reach the Fishbowls, a series of rounded sandstone pools on Piru Creek. Note: In late summer, gnats can be an annoyance along this trail, so consider bringing a mosquito/gnat head net.

User Groups: Hikers, dogs, and horses. No mountain bikes. No wheelchair facilities.

Permits: A California campfire permit is required for overnight stays year-round whether or not you are using a camp stove or building a fire; permits are free and available online at fs.usda.gov/lpnf or in person at any Southern California National Forest ranger station. Parking and access are free.

Maps: A Los Padres National Forest map is available from the U.S. Forest Service. A map of the Sespe Wilderness is available from Tom Harrison Maps. For a topographic map, go to the USGS website to download Lockwood Valley.

Directions: From Ojai, drive 40 miles north on Highway 33 and turn right on Lockwood Valley Road. Drive approximately 15 miles and turn right on Mutau Road. Drive 7.5 miles and turn right on Thorn Meadows Road. Drive 0.5 mile to the Cedar Creek trailhead.

Contact: Los Padres National Forest, Mount Pinos Ranger District, Frazier Park, 661/245-3731, www.fs.usda.gov/lpnf.

39 SESPE HOT SPRINGS

17.0 mi/8.0 hr or 2 days 

in the Sespe Wilderness northeast of Ojai

Map 12.4, page 644

Sespe Hot Springs have the hottest natural mineral water in Southern California, reaching temperatures as hot as 210°F. This year-round spring heats several pools downstream on Sespe Creek to a temperature warm enough for bathing. While this sounds like an ideal year-round destination, don't even think about making a summer trip. The air temperature here is often close to 100°F, and there is no vegetation around the springs. In fact, it looks something like the surface of the moon. Still, in fall, winter, or spring, the hot springs are a wonderful spot. Hike in 1.5 miles on the main wilderness trail to a fork where Little Mutau Creek Trail goes left and Johnson Ridge Trail goes right. Bear right and follow Johnson Ridge Trail, which years ago was open to motorcycle use but is now part of the Sespe Wilderness. It drops steeply to Sespe Creek over the next 6.2 miles, with almost no shade along the route. You'll lose 2,500 feet along the way. A final left spur leads you a half-mile to the hot springs; you'll probably smell the sulfur before you see the pools. You've now hiked just over eight miles, so if you head back out you'll have a 17-mile day. To spend the night, you must hike another mile south from the springs to Sespe Camp. The nearest water is another half-mile away in Sespe Creek; carry plenty with you as a backup.

Note: There are two other routes to Sespe Hot Springs, one via the Alder Creek Trail in Fillmore and the other on the Sespe River Trail in Ojai's Rose Valley Recreation Area.

User Groups: Hikers, dogs, and horses. No mountain bikes. No wheelchair facilities.

Permits: A California campfire permit is required for overnight stays year-round whether or not you are using a camp stove or building a fire; permits are free and available online at fs.usda.gov/lpnf or in person at any Southern California National Forest ranger station. Parking and access are free.

Maps: A Los Padres National Forest map is available from the U.S. Forest Service. A map of the Sespe Wilderness is available from Tom Harrison Maps. For a topographic map, go to the USGS website to download Lockwood Valley.

Directions: From Ojai, drive 40 miles north on Highway 33 and turn right on Lockwood Valley Road. Drive approximately 15 miles and turn right on Mutau Road. Follow Mutau Road to its end (about 10 miles), at the Mutau Flat trailhead.

Or, from I-5, take the Frazier Mountain Road exit. Drive six miles and turn left on Lockwood Valley Road. Drive approximately 10 miles and turn right on Mutau Road. Follow Mutau Road to its end (about 10 miles), at the Mutau Flat trailhead.

Contact: Los Padres National Forest, Mount Pinos Ranger District, Frazier Park, 661/245-3731, www.fs.usda.gov/lpnf.

40 PIEDRA BLANCA

3.0 mi/2.0 hr 2 9

in the Rose Valley Recreation Area north of Ojai

Map 12.4, page 644

Sandstone lovers, this is your spot. Piedra Blanca is a series of huge, rounded sandstone boulders that are somewhat otherworldly looking. If rocks can look sensual, these do. They're set in the Rose Valley Recreation Area, just a short stretch away from Sespe Creek, in what looks a lot like the desert—plenty of sand, desert scrub, and rocks. Start from the Piedra Blanca Trailhead. In the first 0.5 mile you will cross Lion Creek and two branches of the Sespe River. At the junction, turn left and follow the signs. The rocks of Piedra Blanca are clearly visible, so it's easy to see where you're going. Although the trail continues down the back side of the boulders and beyond, most people just climb to the top of the rocks, then spend some time wandering around and exploring. As you might guess, this is a first-class spot for watching sunsets.

User Groups: Hikers, dogs, and horses. No mountain bikes. No wheelchair facilities.

Permits: No permits are required. Parking and access are free.

Maps: A Los Padres National Forest map is available from the U.S. Forest Service. For a topographic map, go to the USGS website to download Lion Canyon.

Directions: From Ojai, drive north on Highway 33 for 15 miles to Sespe River Road/Rose Valley Road and the sign for Rose Valley Recreation Area. Turn right and drive 6.5 miles to the Piedra Blanca Trailhead.

Contact: Los Padres National Forest, Ojai Ranger District, Ojai, 805/646-4348, www.fs.usda.gov/lpnf.

41 SESPE RIVER TRAIL TO BEAR CREEK CAMP

9.0 mi/1-2 days 3 9

in the Sespe Wilderness north of Ojai

Map 12.4, page 644

The Sespe River Trail is an easy way to access the Sespe Wilderness, on a mostly level trail that follows the river—but keep in mind that it's hot as Hades out here in the summertime, and plan your trip for the cooler months. A typical destination on this trail is Bear Creek Camp, 4.5 miles out, but you could hike another 5 miles to Willett Hot Springs (or sleep at Bear Creek and then go soak at the hot springs the next day). Start your trip at the Piedra Blanca Trailhead. In the first half-mile, you will cross Lion Creek and two branches of the Sespe River. At a junction, turn right and follow the riverbed, hiking downstream on another old road, which was once a four-wheel-drive route to the Sespe Hot Springs. If you're lucky, you'll visit when the creek level is high enough so that there are plenty of deep pools accessible for swimming. In good years, almost every bend in the river offers a tempting pool, but by late summer, the stream can drop to a trickle. Dispersed camping spots are plentiful along this trail. By the way, this is called the Sespe River Trail, but on maps, the "river" is called "creek." Generally it looks much more like the latter than the former.

User Groups: Hikers, dogs, and horses. No mountain bikes. No wheelchair facilities.

Permits: A free California campfire permit is required year-round for building a fire or using a backpacking stove; permits are available at any California Forest Service ranger station. Parking and access are free.

Maps: A Los Padres National Forest map is available from the U.S. Forest Service. A map of the Sespe Wilderness is available from Tom Harrison Maps. For a topographic map, go to the USGS website to download Lion Canyon.

Directions: From Ojai, drive north on Highway 33 for 15 miles to Sespe River Road/Rose Valley Road and the sign for Rose Valley Recreation Area. Turn right and drive 6.5 miles to the Piedra Blanca Trailhead by Lion Campground.

Contact: Los Padres National Forest, Ojai Ranger District, Ojai, 805/646-4348, www.fs.usda.gov/lpnf.

42 ROSE VALLEY FALLS

0.8 mi/0.5 hr 1 9

in the Rose Valley Recreation Area north of Ojai

Map 12.4, page 644

The trip to Rose Valley Falls is an easy walk in the woods to the base of a stunning and unusual sandstone waterfall. If you're making the drive to Rose Valley Recreation Area to camp, fish, or hike, a side-trip to Rose Valley Falls is just about mandatory. Start hiking on the signed trail in Rose Valley Campground. The path is bordered on both sides by oaks and fragrant bays, and it parallels Rose Creek. Cross the creek a few times, and as you walk into the canyon, keep looking ahead (up high) for your first glimpse of the 300-foot waterfall. If it has rained lately, you'll see it for sure. In 15 minutes you reach the base of the waterfall, which is glaringly different in appearance from the falls you just saw. That's because this is the bottom tier of huge Rose Valley Falls, and you were seeing the upper tier. The lower tier is layered with limestone and sandstone slabs and oozing with wet moss. You can't resist touching it. Some daredevils attempt to climb up and over this lower tier to see more of the upper part of the waterfall, but this should only be attempted by experts with proper climbing equipment.

User Groups: Hikers, dogs, horses, and mountain bikes. No wheelchair facilities.

Permits: No permits are required. A National Forest Adventure Pass is required for each vehicle; fees are $5 for one day or $30 for a year. Interagency access passes are also accepted.

Maps: A Los Padres National Forest map is available from the U.S. Forest Service. For a topographic map, go to the USGS website to download Lion Canyon.

Directions: From Ojai, drive north on Highway 33 for 15 miles to Sespe River Road/Rose Valley Road and the sign for Rose Valley Recreation Area. Turn right, drive three miles, then turn right again on Chief Peak Road, at the sign for Rose Valley Camp. Drive 0.6 mile to the campground. The trail leads from the far end of the camp.

Contact: Los Padres National Forest, Ojai Ranger District, Ojai, 805/646-4348, www.fs.usda.gov/lpnf.

43 NORDHOFF PEAK

12 mi/6.0 hr 4 9

east of Ojai

Map 12.4, page 644

The hike to Nordhoff Peak is a rite of passage for Ojai hikers. After all, journalist Charles Nordhoff was the guy who made Ojai famous. In the late 19th century, he wrote various magazine articles about Ojai Valley's many charms, which encouraged people to move here, with the dream of a new life. Nordhoff's summit is at 4,425 feet—high enough to get an occasional few inches of snow—and a hike to the top is a fine way to spend an early spring day in Ojai. That's if you're up to the challenge of the six-mile, 2,800-foot climb, of course. Forget hiking in the heat of summer; much of the trail is on dusty, open fire roads, without shade. From the Gridley trailhead, hike up to Gridley Fire Road and turn right, passing by seemingly endless avocado groves. Continuing straight ahead, you'll enter a shadier canyon and pass the primitive camp at Gridley Spring. This is almost the halfway point (2.7 miles); take a breather. The next three miles are steeper, so drink lots of water before you start switchbacking your way up to Nordhoff Fire Road, where you turn left and hike one more mile to the peak. If you think that after all this climbing you ought to get some good views, you won't be disappointed. The last mile of trail offers awesome vistas. When you reach the skeleton of the old Nordhoff Fire Lookout Tower, you can see all the way to the Pacific Ocean and Channel Islands, Ojai Valley and Lake Casitas closer in, and miles of Los Padres National Forest and its wilderness areas.

User Groups: Hikers, dogs, horses, and mountain bikes. No wheelchair facilities.

Permits: No permits are required. Parking and access are free.

Maps: A Los Padres National Forest map is available from the U.S. Forest Service. For a topographic map, go to the USGS website to download Ojai.

Directions: From Ojai at the intersection of Highways 150 and 33, drive east on Highway 150 for two miles and turn left on Gridley Road, 0.25 mile past the ranger station. Drive 1.5 miles north on Gridley Road until it dead-ends. The trailhead is on the north side of the road.

Contact: Los Padres National Forest, Ojai Ranger District, Ojai, 805/646-4348, www.fs.usda.gov/lpnf.

44 SANTA PAULA CANYON TO BIG CONE CAMP

6.8 mi/3.5 hr or 2 days 2 8

east of Ojai in Los Padres National Forest

Map 12.4, page 644 **BEST**

What starts out rather pedestrian soon gets much more interesting on the Santa Paula Canyon Trail. The canyon's main attractions are a narrow gorge and beautiful waterfalls that cascade into deep pools of water, but the first 1.3 miles of the route are mostly on pavement, meandering around the grounds of Thomas Aquinas College and a private ranch and oil-drilling operation. It's hard to believe that this was ground zero for the December 2017 Thomas wildfire; there's been a tremendous amount of new growth since the burn. The college's grounds are green and pastoral, and this hike remains one of the most popular in Ventura County. (Hike it on a weekday, not a weekend, for the best experience.) At 3.4 miles, the route passes Big Cone Camp, which has a few campsites set in a shady grove of big-cone Douglas firs. The trail leads a short distance from the camp steeply down to the main and east forks of Santa Paula Creek, where waterfalls and swimming holes await. Since this camp is heavily used, if you want to spend the night in peace, consider traveling less than a mile farther up the trail to Cross Camp. Just beyond the camp, the stream enters a canyon highlighted by a waterfall called the Punchbowl. The only disappointment in this lovely canyon is that many of its rocks and boulders have been defiled with ugly graffiti. The Forest Service has made efforts to remove the tagging, but the ugly damage is there.

User Groups: Hikers and dogs. No horses or mountain bikes. No wheelchair facilities.

Permits: A free California campfire permit is required year-round for building a fire or using a backpacking stove; permits are available at the Ojai Ranger Station. Parking and access are free.

Maps: A Los Padres National Forest map is available from the U.S. Forest Service. For a topographic map, go to the USGS website to download Santa Paula Peak.

Directions: From Ojai at the junction of Highways 33 and 150, drive east on Highway 150 for 11.5 miles to Thomas Aquinas College on the left (look for iron gates and stone buildings). Drive 100 yards farther to the parking pullout on the right side of the road, just beyond the highway bridge over Santa Paula Creek. Park there and walk back across the bridge to the paved road on the right side of the college.

Contact: Los Padres National Forest, Ojai Ranger District, Ojai, 805/646-4348, www.fs.usda.gov/lpnf.

45 MCGRATH STATE BEACH NATURE TRAIL

0.5 mi/0.5 hr 1 7

in McGrath State Beach in Oxnard

Map 12.4, page 644 **BEST**

There's a great little nature trail at McGrath State Beach that offers a far different hike from a walk along the sandy public beach. The trail runs along the Santa Clara Estuary, which is designated as a natural preserve. It's the place where the Santa Clara River joins the Pacific Ocean. In that meeting place, freshwater and saltwater plants and animals intermingle, which means you have the chance to see migrating birds, resident shorebirds, and fish swimming in the estuary. The problem is that this meeting place is in constant flux, especially during the stormy months of winter. Some years this trail gets completely washed out, or buried in driftwood, or overgrown. As a general rule, you can count on more of the trail existing in the summer months. The path starts out in a shaded willow thicket, a secluded and peaceful change from the hustle and bustle of the beach campground. Watch for the endangered California least tern or Belding's savannah sparrow. When you reach the beach, you can continue hiking along the shoreline, or turn around and head back.

User Groups: Hikers only. No dogs, horses, or mountain bikes. A short stretch of this trail is wheelchair-accessible.

Permits: No permits are required. A $10 day-use fee is charged per vehicle.

Maps: For a topographic map, go to the USGS website to download Ventura.

Directions: From U.S. 101 in Ventura, take the Seaward Avenue exit to Harbor Boulevard. Turn south on Harbor Boulevard and drive four miles to the park entrance. The nature trail begins at the day-use parking lot, a quick right turn after the entrance kiosk. (If you are traveling north on U.S. 101, you must take the Victoria Avenue exit to reach Harbor Boulevard.)

Contact: McGrath State Beach, Ventura, 805/654-4744, www.parks.ca.gov.

46 LA JOLLA VALLEY LOOP

5.5 mi/3.0 hr or 2 days 2 9

in Point Mugu State Park south of Oxnard

Map 12.4, page 644

We rate Point Mugu State Park as the best of all the parks in the Santa Monica Mountains, partly because of its more remote northern location, partly because of its proximity to the ocean, and partly because of its fine hiking trails. One of the best of the latter is this loop trip starting in La Jolla Canyon, which can be an excellent day hike or an easy two-day backpacking trip with an overnight at La Jolla Valley walk-in camp. Follow the La Jolla Canyon Trail from the Ray Miller trailhead (that's the wide dirt trail on the left, not the single-track trail on the right) gently uphill. You hike through an open valley that is continually freshened by ocean breezes blowing through the canyon. Pass a small seasonal waterfall that is bracketed on both sides by canyon walls covered in bright yellow coreopsis, then climb into a rocky area, where hidden among the chaparral are rock caves that were once used by Native Americans. Go right at the first fork 1.2 miles in (going left will be the return of your loop), and left at a second fork signed for La Jolla Valley walk-in camp. Situated in a high meadow of native grasses, the camp is 0.4 mile beyond a cattail-bordered pond. From the camp, bear left on the dirt road that runs just north of it, which soon narrows to double track. Continue on La Jolla Valley Loop Trail and circle around, through more native grasses, back to La Jolla Canyon Trail. Turn right on La Jolla Canyon Trail to head down the canyon to your car. This trip is outstanding in winter or spring, when the hillside grasses are green and the wildflowers bloom. If you like, you can make this loop longer by detouring around Mugu Peak on Chumash Trail and Mugu Peak Trail, which will add 1.5 more miles to your round-trip.

User Groups: Hikers and horses. No dogs or mountain bikes. No wheelchair facilities.

Permits: No day-hiking permits are necessary. Backpacking campsites are available on a first-come, first-served basis; backpackers must register at Thornhill-Broome Campground ($7 fee per person per night). An $8 day-use fee is charged per vehicle at the Ray Miller trailhead.

Maps: A trail map is available from any park ranger station, or by free download at www.parks.ca.gov. A map of Point Mugu State Park is available from Tom Harrison Maps. For a topographic map, go to the USGS website to download Point Mugu.

Directions: From U.S. 101 in Agoura Hills, exit at Kanan Road and drive 12.5 miles to Highway 1/Pacific Coast Highway on the Malibu coast. Turn west (right) and drive 14.8 miles to the La Jolla Canyon trailhead parking area on the right, one mile west of Big Sycamore Canyon Campground.

Alternatively, from Highway 1/Pacific Coast Highway in Malibu, drive west on Highway 1 for 22 miles to the La Jolla Canyon trailhead parking area, on the right.

Contact: Point Mugu State Park, Malibu, 805/488-5223 or 805/488-1827; California State

Parks, Angeles District, Calabasas, 818/880-0363, www.parks.ca.gov.

47 BIG SYCAMORE CANYON LOOP

9.2 mi/5.5 hr 2 9

in Point Mugu State Park south of Oxnard

Map 12.4, page 644

If you don't mind hiking on fire roads and maybe sharing the trail with mountain bikers and horses, this loop trip in Point Mugu State Park offers a shady stroll in a sycamore-lined canyon, followed by miles and miles of unforgettable coastal views. Start from the gate at the far end of the campground and follow the Big Sycamore Canyon Trail as it climbs very gently uphill, paralleling the creek. The sycamore trees here are large and old, and from October to February, you may spot monarch butterflies that cluster among them for the winter. You'll cross Big Sycamore Creek a half-dozen times before the 2.9-mile mark, where you'll turn left on the Wood Canyon Vista Trail (also signed as the Backbone Trail). This trail gently ascends about 750 feet over its 1.8-mile distance, topping out at Overlook Fire Road. Turn left here for a long, rambling walk back to the trailhead. Overlook Fire Road divides Point Mugu's two canyons, Big Sycamore and La Jolla, and is a ridge-top route that offers nonstop views of the coastline to the west and the canyons on either side of you. On a clear day, it's glorious.

Note: When you near the end of the trail, you can take the single-track Scenic Trail to return to the trailhead. It shaves off a little distance, and it's more interesting than the final stretch of the fire road.

User Groups: Hikers and mountain bikes. No dogs or horses. No wheelchair facilities.

Permits: No permits are required. A $12 day-use fee is charged per vehicle.

Maps: A trail map is available from any park ranger station, or by free download at www.parks.ca.gov. A map of Point Mugu State Park is available from Tom Harrison Maps. For a topographic map, go to the USGS website to download Point Mugu.

Directions: From U.S. 101 in Agoura Hills, exit at Kanan Road and drive 12.5 miles to Highway 1/Pacific Coast Highway on the Malibu coast. Turn west (right) and drive 13.8 miles to Big Sycamore Canyon Campground at Point Mugu State Park. Park to the left of the entrance kiosk in the day-use lot, then walk to the far end of the campground to access the trailhead.

Alternatively, from Highway 1 in Malibu, drive west on Highway 1 for 21 miles to Sycamore Canyon Campground, on the right.

Contact: Point Mugu State Park, Malibu, 805/488-5223 or 805/488-1827; California State Parks, Angeles District, Calabasas, 818/880-0363, www.parks.ca.gov.

48 CALICHE FOREST AND POINT BENNETT

15.0 mi/2 days 3 10

on San Miguel Island in Channel Islands National Park

Channel Islands Detail Map, page 645 BEST

San Miguel Island is 58 miles from Ventura Harbor and getting there requires a boat ride nearly four hours long: very, very long. Adding to the challenge, strong winds and fog are nearly constant on the island, so you must plan accordingly for both hiking and camping. Of course, if you're willing, the reward is having a spectacular island practically all to yourself. No more than 30 campers are allowed on San Miguel Island at one time, and only rarely do that many people show up at once.

From Cuyler Harbor, where a skiff drops you off, you hike eastward along the beach for 0.5 mile, then follow the path another 0.5 mile over a large sand dune, then up Nidever Canyon. It's a steep stretch, especially if you're carrying a lot of camping gear. When you reach the ridge at the top, you can take a short spur to see a stone monument to Juan Rodriguez Cabrillo, who claimed this island for the Spaniards in 1542, and who may or may not be buried here—nobody's sure. The trail continues to the campground, and then to the remains of the Lester Ranch. The Lester family lived on the island for 12 years and grazed sheep here. Outside of the ranger station area, which includes Cuyler Harbor and its beach, Nidever Canyon, the Cabrillo Monument, and Lester Ranch, you may hike only in the company of a ranger—and you should definitely do that. In the right season, you'll be able to witness an incredible wildlife show. Up to five different species of pinnipeds—seals and sea lions—comprising more than 30,000 individuals can be seen at certain times of the year at Point Bennett, a 14-mile round-trip hike from the campground. Plan for a long, day hike with variable weather, and bring lots of water with you. Another interesting feature along the way is the Caliche Forest, where the calcium-carbonate sand castings of dead plant roots and trunks stand like frozen statues. They're a bit like the tufa spires at Mono Lake. It's a seven-mile round-trip to the Caliche Forest.

Note: For those who do not wish to camp, the boat concessionaire offers one-day trips to San Miguel Island. Such trips typically include a guided day hike to the Caliche Forest with a naturalist or ranger.

User Groups: Hikers only. No dogs, horses, or mountain bikes. No wheelchair facilities.

Permits: If you choose to stay overnight, a camping permit is required (877/444-6777 or www.recreation.gov). The camping fee is $15 per night. A fee is charged for boat transportation to the island. As of October 2019, the boat fare is $147 per adult for an overnight camping trip or $105 per adult for a day trip.

Maps: A free map of Channel Islands National Park is available by download at www.nps.gov/chis. A more detailed map is available for a fee from Trails Illustrated. For topographic maps, go to the USGS website to download San Miguel Island East and San Miguel Island West.

Directions: Island Packers provides boat transportation to San Miguel Island from Ventura

Ventura harbor

Harbor. Reservations are required and should be downloaded before you get your camping permit; 805/642-7688 or 805/642-1393, www.islandpackers.com.

Contact: Channel Islands National Park, Ventura, 805/658-5700 or 805/658-5730, www.nps.gov/chis.

49 TORREY PINES TRAIL

5.0 mi/2.5 hr 2 8

on Santa Rosa Island in Channel Islands National Park

Channel Islands Detail Map, page 645

One of the many charms of Santa Rosa Island is that you can fly there in about 20 minutes in a small plane instead of taking a three-hour boat ride from Ventura or Santa Barbara harbors, both of which are about 40 miles away. The National Park Service has one air concessionaire, Channel Islands Aviation, that takes passengers to the island (in addition to the boat concessionaire, Island Packers). For people prone to seasickness, this makes Santa Rosa Island the Channel Island of choice, as long as they have the kind of bank account that can support this kind of trip. Another of the island's charms is its stand of Torrey pines—yes, the same conifers you see at Torrey Pines State Reserve, in San Diego. These are the only two places in the world where those slow-growing, windswept pines are found, and no one knows why. To see them from the boat pier or the landing strip, follow the main dirt road to the southeast, paralleling the coast. Near the far (southeast) end of the landing strip on the inland side, you'll see a gate and a road that leads uphill to Water Canyon Campground. Pass this gate and continue to the next junction of roads, where you can choose to hike up above the Torrey pines or down below. You can make a loop and circle around the grove if you like, or just take the lower road to stay along the coast and avoid any further climbing. The higher you go, of course, the more outstanding the coastal views.

Another great hiking option for visitors to Santa Rosa Island is the Cherry Canyon Trail, which leads to scenic views of Bechers Bay, the historic Vail Vickers Ranch, and a large sandy stretch known as Skunk Point.

User Groups: Hikers only. No dogs, horses, or mountain bikes. No wheelchair facilities.

Permits: If you choose to stay overnight, you must get a camping permit (877/444-6777 or www.recreation.gov). The camping fee is $15 per night. A fee is charged for transportation to the island. As of October 2019, the boat fare is $82 per adult for a day trip or $114 per adult for an overnight camping trip. Air travel is by charter flight only; fares start at $1,200 per trip.

Maps: A free map of Channel Islands National Park is available by download at www.nps.gov/chis. A more detailed map is available from Trails Illustrated. For topographic maps, go to the USGS website to download Santa Rosa Island North and East.

Directions: Island Packers provides boat transportation to Santa Rosa Island from Ventura Harbor. Reservations are required and should be downloaded before you get your camping permit; 805/642-7688 or 805/642-1393, www.islandpackers.com. Channel Islands Aviation provides air transportation to Santa Rosa Island from Camarillo Airport; 805/987-1301, www.flycia.com.

Contact: Channel Islands National Park, Ventura, 805/658-5700 or 805/658-5730, www.nps.gov/chis.

50 POTATO HARBOR TRAIL

5.0 mi/2.5 hr 3 8

on east Santa Cruz Island in Channel Islands National Park

Channel Islands Detail Map, page 645

Only the eastern quarter of huge Santa Cruz Island belongs to the National Park Service; the other 76 percent of the island is managed by the Nature Conservancy. Although it's possible to hike on the Nature Conservancy's land, you may do so only with a special landing permit and in the company of an Island Packers guide. If you prefer to wander on your own or if you want to camp overnight on the island, you need to visit the eastern, national park side of Santa Cruz Island. The boat ride is short enough (it takes a little over an hour to cover about 20 miles) to make this a day trip. If you want to stay overnight, the National Park Service runs a campground in Scorpion Canyon, and a backcountry camp called Del Norte, 10 miles to the west. You'll have the luxury of water faucets at Scorpion but not at Del Norte.

The trail to Potato Harbor begins at Scorpion campground, which is 0.5 mile beyond Scorpion Anchorage, where the boat drops you off. Head back into the upper end of the campground (passing the ranch and the first set of campsites) until you see a road veering off to the right, climbing above the canyon. Like almost all of the trails on eastern Santa Cruz Island, this trail is a wide dirt road, best hiked before the end of summer, when it can be dry and dusty. The road climbs steeply for 0.5 mile, then goes mostly flat, continuing along the bluff tops almost straight west, paralleling the mainland coast. Far ahead you can see a long series of hills and canyons that eventually fade out of view in the haze, and it's easy to assume that these belong to one of the neighboring Channel Islands. Wrong. They are more of the immense bulk of this island—the largest in the chain, at 96 square miles. At two miles out, the trail curves to the southwest, following the line of a fence at the bluff's edge. Look for a spur trail that leads to the edge, and follow it to the obvious view of Potato Harbor—a potato-shaped cove lined with rugged cliffs and filled with deep, clear water.

If you're camping on the island and have more time than the day-trippers, make sure you take the seven-mile round-trip hike to Smuggler's Cove and its lovely cobble beach. A stand of eucalyptus provides a shady picnic area at the Pacific's edge.

User Groups: Hikers only. No dogs, horses, or mountain bikes. No wheelchair facilities.

Permits: If you choose to stay overnight, you must get a camping permit (877/444-6777 or www.recreation.gov). The camping fee is $15 per night. A fee is charged for boat transportation to the island. As of October 2019, the boat fare is $59 per adult for a day trip, or $79 per adult for an overnight trip.

Maps: A free map of Channel Islands National Park is available by download at www.nps.gov/chis. A more detailed map is available from Trails Illustrated. For topographic maps, go to the USGS website to download Santa Cruz Island C and D.

Directions: Island Packers provides boat transportation to Santa Cruz Island from Ventura Harbor. Reservations are required; 805/642-7688 or 805/642-1393, www.islandpackers.com.

Contact: Channel Islands National Park, Ventura, 805/658-5700 or 805/658-5730, www.nps.gov/chis.

51 EAST ANACAPA ISLAND LOOP TRAIL

2.0 mi/1.0 hr 2 10

on Anacapa Island in Channel Islands National Park

Channel Islands Detail Map, page 645

Of all the Channel Islands to choose from, why do so many people choose Anacapa? Because it's easy. At only 12 miles from Port Hueneme, it's the closest island to the mainland. The boat ride takes less than an hour. As you cruise, you're likely to be entertained by dolphins, sea lions, and sometimes even flying fish. The island is actually three tiny islets; the boat drops you off on the easternmost of the three. If you're feeling the slightest bit seasick, you'll quickly get over it when the boat pulls away and your first task is to climb up the

154 metal steps that cling to the island's cliffs. You'll get plenty of fresh air as you make your way to the island's visitors center, pick up some interpretive information, and set out on this trail, which tours this entire 0.3-square-mile islet. The trail's main highlights are two overlooks at Inspiration Point and Cathedral Cove, where you can look down on seals and sea lions on the rocks below. From Inspiration Point, you can also gaze at the other two Anacapa islets and huge Santa Cruz Island beyond them. Bring your binoculars: There are millions of opportunities for bird-watching, particularly when thousands of western gulls nest in spring and summer. Where you can see over the edge of the rocky cliffs, you'll spot some of the island's 130 sea caves, which attract kayakers all summer long.

Spring wildflowers are superb on Anacapa, including the giant coreopsis, which blooms so brilliantly that its yellow glow can sometimes be seen from the mainland. The bloom period varies from year to year, but generally occurs from late February to mid-April. The beaches on East Anacapa are not accessible because the sea cliffs are hundreds of feet high, but on calm days, you can swim at the landing cove. Bring your snorkeling gear so you can look eye-to-eye with the garibaldis and giant sea kelp.

Even though the island is small and its one hiking trail is short, this rates as one of the greatest day trips possible in California. Don't miss it.

User Groups: Hikers only. No dogs, horses, or mountain bikes. No wheelchair facilities.

Permits: If you choose to stay overnight, you must get a camping permit (877/444-6777 or www.recreation.gov). The camping fee is $15 per night. A fee is charged for boat transportation to the island. As of October 2019, the boat fare is $59 per adult for a day trip, or $79 per adult for an overnight trip.

Maps: A free map of Channel Islands National Park is available by download at www.nps.gov/chis. A more detailed map is available from Trails Illustrated. For a topographic map, go to the USGS website to download Anacapa Island.

Directions: Island Packers provides boat transportation to Anacapa Island from Ventura Harbor and Oxnard (Channel Island Harbor). Reservations are required; 805/642-7688 or 805/642-1393, www.islandpackers.com.

Contact: Channel Islands National Park, Ventura, 805/658-5700 or 805/658-5730, www.nps.gov/chis.

52 SIGNAL PEAK LOOP TRAIL

2.5 mi/1.5 hr 2 9

on Santa Barbara Island in Channel Islands National Park

Channel Islands Detail Map, page 645

Santa Barbara Island is the loneliest island in Channel Islands National Park. Located about 50 miles south of Ventura, it is geographically isolated from the other four islands that make up the national park, being closer in latitude to San Pedro than to Santa Barbara or Ventura. (Yet it's much farther out to sea than developed Catalina Island, which is its closest neighbor.) Getting to Santa Barbara Island requires a 2.5-3-hour boat ride from Ventura, and the boat concessionaire runs less than a dozen trips to the island each year—much less frequently than to the other islands. The island's land mass is only one square mile; it's the smallest of the Channel Islands. Similar to Anacapa Island in its bald, grassy landscape, Santa Barbara Island has 5.5 miles of hiking trails, all of which are worth exploring. One of the best is Signal Peak Trail, which makes a loop over much of the south half of the island, from the landing cove to Signal Peak, which at 634 feet is the highest point on the island. A great feature of this trail is its fine views of Sutil Island, an even smaller island that lies 0.25 mile southwest of Santa Barbara Island. (Sutil Island is an important seabird rookery; bird-watching is first rate all over Santa Barbara Island.) The trail begins by heading inland from the landing cove. Take the left fork 0.5 mile out to head south, and curve around the southern end of the island to Signal Peak, on the southwest edge. From the peak, you loop back through the center of the island over gently rolling grasslands.

If you're wondering what season to visit Santa Barbara Island, keep this in mind: As on Anacapa Island, the giant coreopsis produces its huge yellow flowers here in May, when you could almost consider swimming in the landing cove.

User Groups: Hikers only. No dogs, horses, or mountain bikes. No wheelchair facilities.

Permits: If you choose to stay overnight, you must get a camping permit (877/444-6777 or www.recreation.gov). The camping reservation fee is $15 per night. A fee is charged for boat transportation to the island. As of October 2019, the fare is $82 per adult for a day trip or $114 per adult for an overnight trip.

Maps: A free map of Channel Islands National Park is available by download at www.nps.gov/chis. A more detailed map is available from Trails Illustrated. For a topographic map, go to the USGS website to download Santa Barbara Island.

Directions: Island Packers provides boat transportation to Santa Barbara Island from Ventura Harbor; reservations are required.

Contact: Channel Islands National Park, Ventura, 805/658-5700 or 805/658-5730, www.nps.gov/chis; boat trips: Island Packers, 805/642-7688 or 805/642-1393, www.islandpackers.com.

LOS ANGELES AND VICINITY

Islands, mountains, beaches, and lakes–the Los Angeles region offers huge diversity. A wealth of sizeable peaks are contained within its mountain ranges, including the Southern California hiker's "big three": Mount San Jacinto at 10,834 feet, Mount Baldy at 10,064 feet, and Mount San Gorgonio at 11,503 feet. But you don't have to be a peak-bagger to hike here. The San Gabriel Mountains sustain a network of 500 miles of trails. The San Bernardino Mountains, one of the highest mountain ranges in California, contain three major recreation lakes: Big Bear, Arrowhead, and Silverwood. The Santa Monica Mountains are laced with gentler trails in the coastal hills. And if you'd rather see Los Angeles from a more distant perspective, hop on the Catalina ferry and hike on an island 12 miles out at sea.

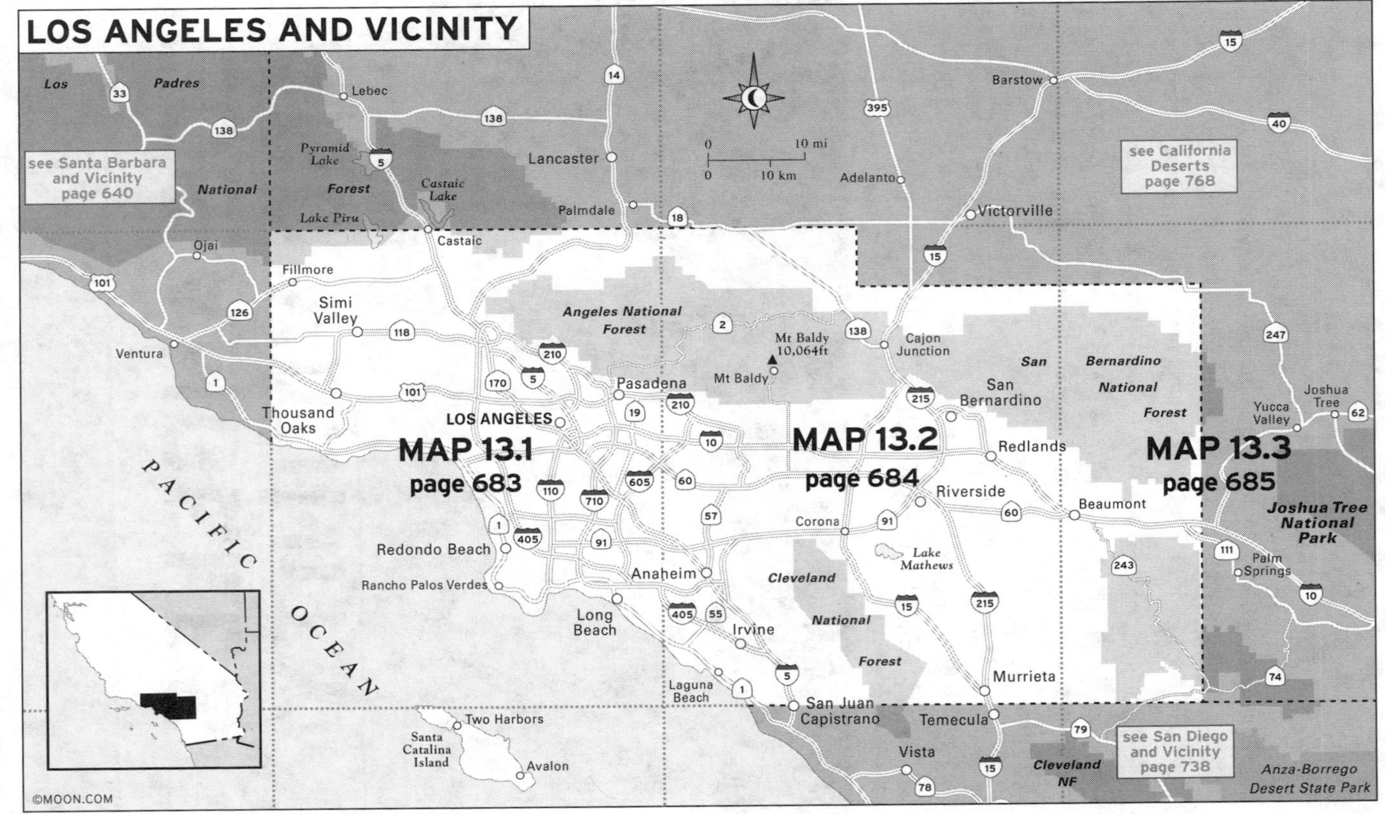

LOS ANGELES AND VICINITY
see Santa Barbara and Vicinity page 640
see California Deserts page 768
see San Diego and Vicinity page 738
MAP 13.1 page 683
MAP 13.2 page 684
MAP 13.3 page 685
PACIFIC OCEAN
Los Padres National Forest
Angeles National Forest
San Bernardino National Forest
Cleveland National Forest
Cleveland NF
Joshua Tree National Park
Anza-Borrego Desert State Park
Lebec
Pyramid Lake
Castaic Lake
Lake Piru
Lancaster
Palmdale
Barstow
Adelanto
Victorville
Castaic
Ojai
Fillmore
Simi Valley
Ventura
Thousand Oaks
LOS ANGELES
Pasadena
Mt Baldy
Mt Baldy 10,064ft
Cajon Junction
San Bernardino
Redlands
Riverside
Corona
Lake Mathews
Beaumont
Redondo Beach
Rancho Palos Verdes
Anaheim
Long Beach
Irvine
Laguna Beach
San Juan Capistrano
Temecula
Murrieta
Vista
Yucca Valley
Joshua Tree
Palm Springs
Two Harbors
Santa Catalina Island
Avalon
0 10 mi
0 10 km
©MOON.COM

Map 13.1

Sites 1-33
Pages 686-709

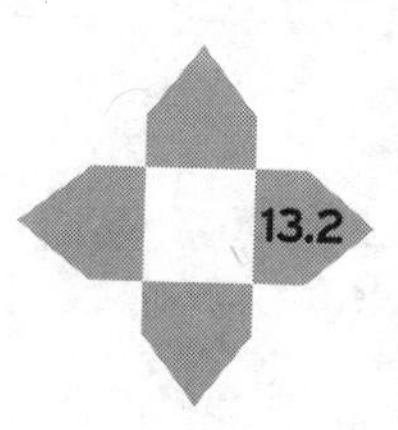

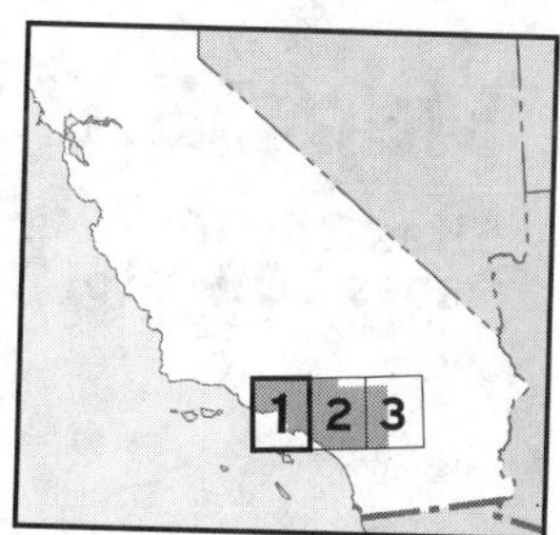

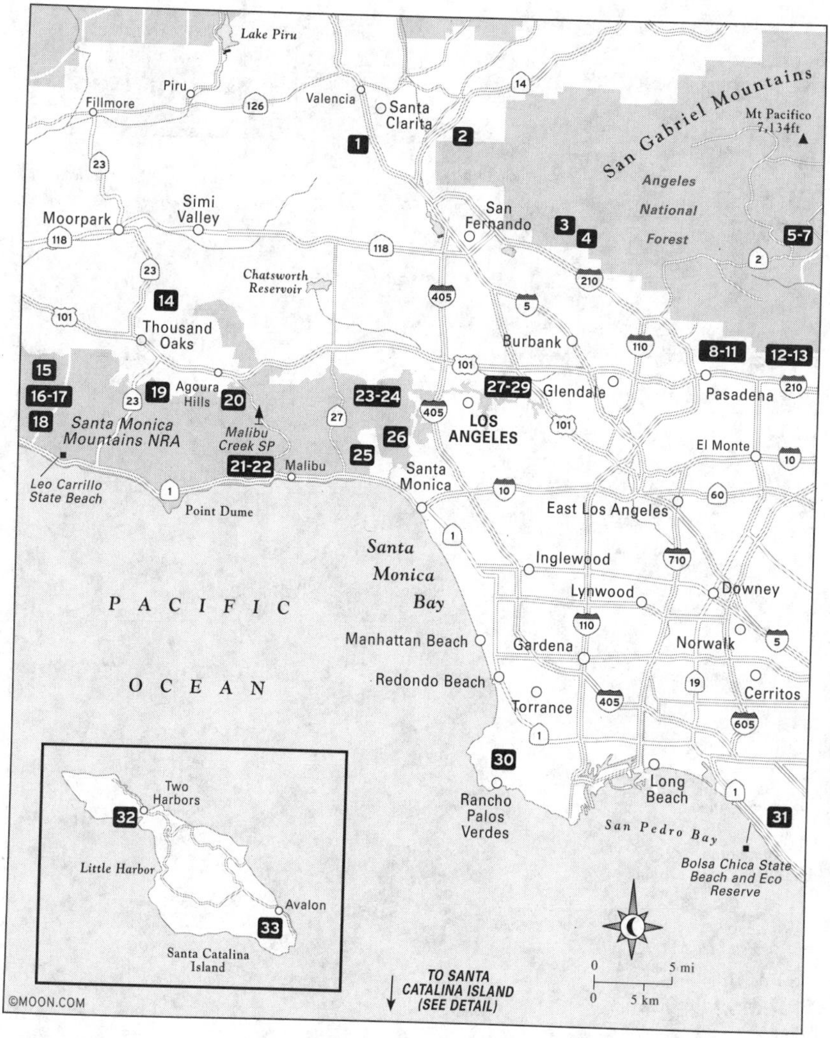

Lake Piru
Piru
Fillmore
126
Valencia
Santa Clarita
14
1
2
San Gabriel Mountains
Mt Pacifico 7,134ft
23
Angeles National Forest
Moorpark
Simi Valley
118
San Fernando
3
4
5-7
118
2
23
Chatsworth Reservoir
405
210
5
14
101
Thousand Oaks
Burbank
110
8-11
12-13
15
16-17
19
Agoura Hills
20
23-24
101
27-29
Glendale
Pasadena
210
23
27
405
LOS ANGELES
101
18
Santa Monica Mountains NRA
Malibu Creek SP
26
25
El Monte
10
21-22
Malibu
Santa Monica
Leo Carrillo State Beach
1
10
60
Point Dume
East Los Angeles
1
Santa Monica Bay
Inglewood
710
PACIFIC
Lynwood
Downey
110
Manhattan Beach
Gardena
Norwalk
5
OCEAN
Redondo Beach
19
Cerritos
Torrance
405
605
1
30
Two Harbors
32
Rancho Palos Verdes
Long Beach
1
31
San Pedro Bay
Little Harbor
Bolsa Chica State Beach and Eco Reserve
Avalon
33
Santa Catalina Island
TO SANTA CATALINA ISLAND (SEE DETAIL)
0 5 mi
0 5 km

Map 13.2

Sites 34-56
Pages 709-726

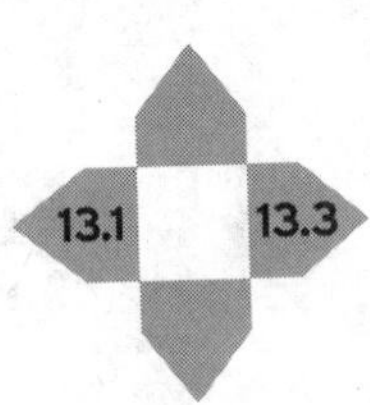

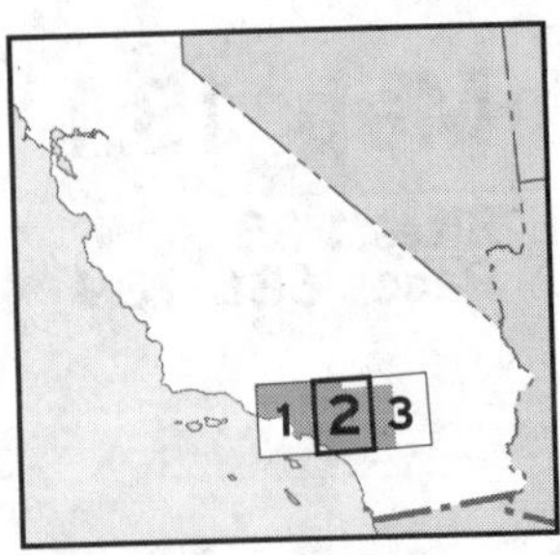

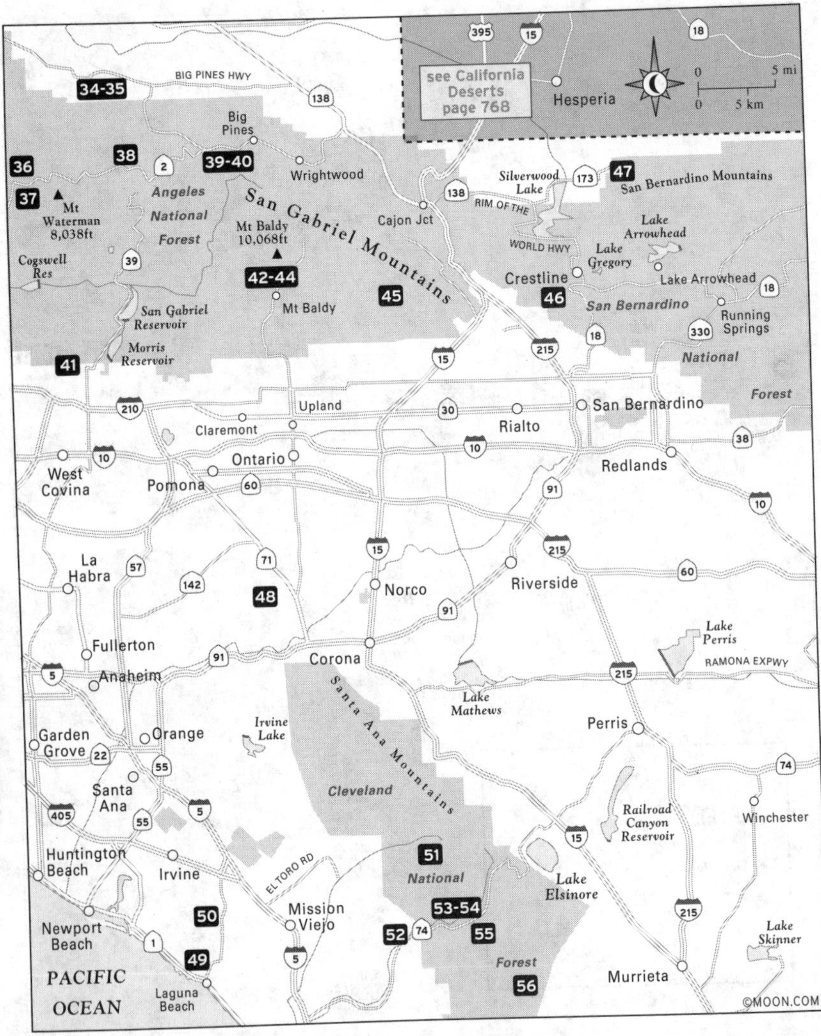

see California Deserts page 768

395
15
18
Hesperia
0 5 mi
0 5 km
BIG PINES HWY
34-35
138
Big Pines
36
38
2
39-40
Wrightwood
37
Mt Waterman 8,038ft
Angeles National Forest
San Gabriel Mountains
Mt Baldy 10,068ft
Cajon Jct
Silverwood Lake
173
47
San Bernardino Mountains
RIM OF THE WORLD HWY
Lake Arrowhead
Lake Gregory
Cogswell Res
39
42-44
45
Crestline
46
Lake Arrowhead
Mt Baldy
San Bernardino
Running Springs
330
San Gabriel Reservoir
Morris Reservoir
41
15
215
18
National
Forest
210
Upland
30
Rialto
San Bernardino
Claremont
10
38
Ontario
West Covina
Pomona
60
Redlands
91
10
La Habra
57
142
71
48
15
Norco
215
Riverside
60
91
Fullerton
91
Corona
Lake Perris
RAMONA EXPWY
5
Anaheim
215
Santa Ana Mountains
Lake Mathews
Irvine Lake
Perris
Garden Grove
22
Orange
55
74
Santa Ana
Cleveland
405
55
5
Railroad Canyon Reservoir
Winchester
15
Huntington Beach
Irvine
51
EL TORO RD
National
Lake Elsinore
50
Mission Viejo
53-54
215
Newport Beach
52
74
55
Lake Skinner
1
49
5
Forest
PACIFIC OCEAN
Laguna Beach
56
Murrieta

Map 13.3

Sites 57-72
Pages 726-736

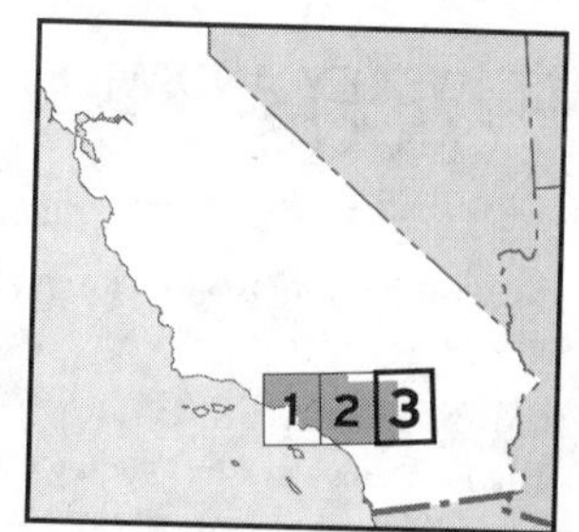

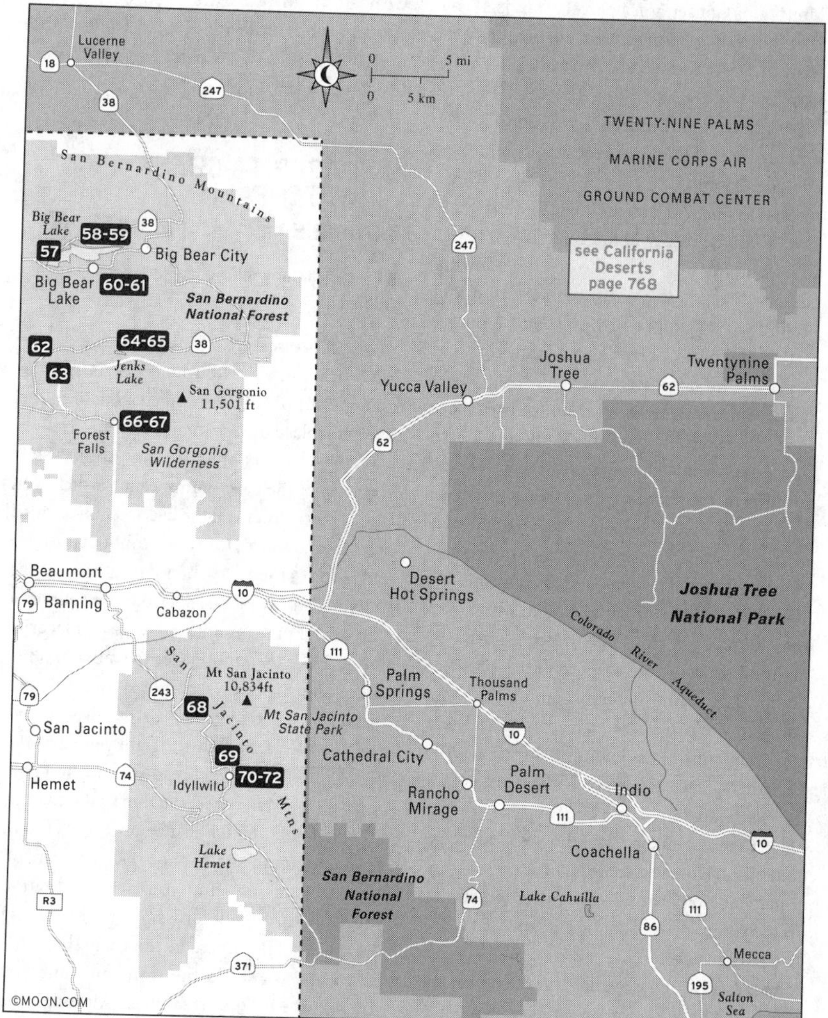

Lucerne Valley
18
247
38
0 5 mi
0 5 km
TWENTY-NINE PALMS
MARINE CORPS AIR
GROUND COMBAT CENTER
San Bernardino Mountains
Big Bear Lake
58-59
38
57
Big Bear City
Big Bear Lake
60-61
San Bernardino National Forest
247
see California Deserts page 768
62
64-65
38
Jenks Lake
63
San Gorgonio 11,501 ft
66-67
Forest Falls
San Gorgonio Wilderness
Joshua Tree
Twentynine Palms
Yucca Valley
62
62
Beaumont
79
Banning
Cabazon
10
Desert Hot Springs
Joshua Tree National Park
Colorado River Aqueduct
111
San Jacinto Mtns
Mt San Jacinto 10,834ft
243
79
68
Palm Springs
Thousand Palms
Mt San Jacinto State Park
San Jacinto
10
69
Cathedral City
70-72
74
Hemet
Idyllwild
Palm Desert
Rancho Mirage
Indio
111
10
Coachella
Lake Hemet
San Bernardino National Forest
R3
74
Lake Cahuilla
111
86
Mecca
371
195
Salton Sea

1 TOWSLEY AND WILEY CANYONS

5.0 mi/2.5 hr 3 8

in Ed Davis Park in Towsley Canyon south of Valencia

Map 13.1, page 683

Little Ed Davis Park in Towsley Canyon is a part of the larger Santa Clarita Woodlands Park, which is a part of the giant Santa Monica Mountains Conservancy parcel of lands. If you visit the park any time except during the sweltering heat of summer, you can walk a five-mile loop and pay a visit to all of Towsley Canyon's major plant communities—grasslands, sage and scrub, riparian, oak woodlands, and just about everything except old-growth redwood forest—in one short trip. How can a park this close to I-5 be this wild looking? We can't figure it out, but it is. Start the trip by following the park entrance road through the first and second parking lots, heading past the ranger station and picnic area. The road quickly turns to gravel and becomes more trail-like. Only a mile from your car the canyon walls squeeze in as you enter a remarkable section of Death Valley-style sandstone narrows. If there is water running in Towsley Canyon's stream, you'll get your feet wet here. Too soon, the narrows come to an end, and you begin a surprisingly steep climb to one of the park's highest points. As you ascend, watch for tar seeps coming up from the ground right alongside the trail. At the top of the climb, you gain big views of the sprawling Santa Clara Valley, which is enough to make you glad you're up here instead of down there. The loop continues downhill through Wiley Canyon, which is much greener and lusher than Towsley Canyon.

User Groups: Hikers, dogs, horses, and mountain bikes. No wheelchair facilities.

Permits: No permits are required. Parking is free if you park outside the entrance gate; $7 if you park inside.

Maps: A trail map is available at the ranger station and nature center, or can be downloaded at www.mrca.ca.gov. For topographic maps, go to the USGS website to download Newhall and Oat Mountain.

Directions: From the San Fernando Valley, drive north on I-5 to Santa Clarita (five miles north of the I-5 and Highway 14 junction). Take the Calgrove exit, turn left (west), drive 0.4 mile, and turn right into the park entrance. You can park outside the gate for free, or inside the gate for a $7 fee.

Contact: Mountains Recreation and Conservation Authority, Malibu, 310/589-3200 or 310/858-7272, www.mrca.ca.gov; Towsley Canyon rangers, 661/255-2974.

2 PLACERITA CREEK WATERFALL

5.5 mi/2.5 hr

in Placerita Canyon County Park southeast of Valencia

Map 13.1, page 683

Placerita Canyon County Park is just far enough out of the Los Angeles Basin to feel like someplace different, and its trails are easy enough for hikers of almost any ability. Start your trip at the park nature center, where you should pay a visit to all the live and taxidermied animals and learn a thing or two about the flora and fauna of the area. Then start hiking on the Canyon Trail, which leads from the southeast side of the parking lot and crosses Placerita Creek. Hike through Placerita Canyon, often under the shade of sycamores and oaks, to Walker Ranch Group Campground. At its far side, look for a trail on the right signed as the Waterfall Trail, and get ready for the best part of the trip. (Make sure you don't take the Los Piñetos Trail, which is just before the Waterfall Trail and doesn't go to the falls.) The canyon begins to narrow, and you twist and curve your way through it, crossing and recrossing the creek a few times. In the final 100 yards before the waterfall, the trail ends, and you simply hike up the streambed. Although the waterfall is only 25 feet high, it forms a lovely little grotto—a perfect place for a snack before heading back. Note: This waterfall is seasonal, so if you show up in August, you're unlikely to find any falling water.

User Groups: Hikers and dogs. No horses or mountain bikes. No wheelchair facilities.

Permits: No permits are required. Parking and access are free.

Maps: Free maps of Placerita Canyon County Park are available at the park nature center. For topographic maps, go to the USGS website to download San Fernando and Mint Canyon.

Directions: From the San Fernando Valley, drive north on I-5 to Highway 14. Follow Highway 14 northeast for four miles to Newhall; exit on Placerita Canyon Road. Turn right (east) and drive 1.5 miles to the park entrance, on the right. Park in the nature center parking lot.

Contact: Placerita Canyon County Park, Newhall, 661/259-7721, www.placerita.org.

3 TRAIL CANYON

4.0 mi/2.0 hr

in Angeles National Forest near Sunland

Map 13.1, page 683

Trail Canyon is located on the western side of the San Gabriel Mountains in an area that was nearly obliterated in the Station Fire of 2009. After the fire, the canyon was closed to the public for almost three years, but for the most part, the leafy forests that grace this canyon survived the flames, and Gold Creek still flows with cheerful abandon. Trail Canyon Falls, a 40-foot-high waterfall, makes a fine destination for a day-hike, especially during the wet spring months. Getting to the falls during the rainy season has always been a bit of an adventure, with several stream crossings along the way. After about a mile of wet walking, the trail climbs out of the canyon and rises high above the creek. At 2.0 miles out, a sharp left curve suddenly reveals the waterfall a short distance

Trail Canyon

ahead. The trail leads to the top of the falls, where the creek spills over a smooth granite precipice. Even if you visit in late summer and the falls are not running with much enthusiasm, you'll still enjoy this woodsy hike, but for the best experience, go soon after a rain.

User Groups: Hikers, dogs, horses, and mountain bikes. No wheelchair facilities.

Permits: No permits are required. A National Forest Adventure Pass is required for each vehicle; fees are $5 for one day or $30 for a year. Interagency access passes are also accepted.

Maps: An Angeles National Forest map is available from the U.S. Forest Service. A map of the Angeles Front Country is available from Tom Harrison Maps. For a topographic map, go to the USGS website to download Sunland.

Directions: From I-210 in Sunland, take the Sunland Boulevard exit. Cross Sunland Boulevard and head east on Foothill Boulevard for 0.75 mile. Turn left (north) on Oro Vista Avenue. In 0.8 mile, Oro Vista Avenue turns into Big Tujunga Canyon Road. Drive four miles on Big Tujunga Canyon Road to a sign for Trail Canyon on the left. Bear left on a dirt road (Road 3N29), drive 0.25 mile to a fork, then bear right and drive 0.25 mile to a large parking lot. The trailhead is on the left side of the lot.

Contact: Angeles National Forest, Los Angeles River Ranger District, San Fernando, 818/899-1900, www.fs.usda.gov/angeles.

4 MOUNT LUKENS

7.6 mi/4.0 hr

in Angeles National Forest near Sunland

Map 13.1, page 683

Mount Lukens, also known as Sister Elsie Peak, has always been a favorite butt-kicker hike for fit L.A. hikers. It was badly burned in the Station Fire of 2009, but today the mountain offers an excellent lesson in fire ecology. The big-cone Douglas firs that once graced the peak's upper slopes were badly burned, but the 5,074-foot summit still offers an inspiring view. Although there are several ways to hike to the top, the Stone Canyon Trail has always been a popular choice, despite the fact that the trail gains 3,300 feet in less than four miles. The trail starts out fairly mellow but once it starts to climb, there is no rest for the weary. Stone Canyon Trail leads for 3.4 seemingly relentless miles to a fire road. Turn left (east) to walk the final quarter-mile to the top. The summit view is rewarding: the Verdugo Mountains are spread out before you, with downtown L.A. beyond. On clear days, the Pacific Ocean and Catalina Island round out the scene. Before you make the trip, keep in mind that this trail is mostly without shade and can really bake in summer, so confine your hiking to the cooler months. However, one factor can stop you in your tracks in the winter. The Stone Canyon Trail requires a crossing of Big Tujunga Creek in the first 100 yards, and after big rains, the stream can be impassable. Most of the year, it's a fairly easy boulder-hop.

User Groups: Hikers, dogs, horses, and mountain bikes. No wheelchair facilities.

Permits: No permits are required. A National Forest Adventure Pass is required for each vehicle; fees are $5 for one day or $30 for a year. Interagency access passes are also accepted.

Maps: An Angeles National Forest map is available from the U.S. Forest Service. A map of the Angeles Front Country is available from Tom Harrison Maps. For a topographic map, go to the USGS website to download Sunland.

Directions: From I-210 in Sunland, take the Sunland Boulevard exit. Cross Sunland Boulevard and head east on Foothill Boulevard for 0.75 mile. Turn left (north) on Oro Vista Avenue. In 0.8 mile, Oro Vista Avenue turns into Big Tujunga Canyon Road. Drive 5.5 miles on Big Tujunga Canyon Road to Doske Road. Turn right on Doske Road and park at Wildwood Picnic Area. This lot is usually closed from November to March; if so you must park in pullouts alongside the road. The trail begins at the far eastern end of the picnic area parking lot.

Contact: Angeles National Forest, Los Angeles River Ranger District, San Fernando, 818/899-1900, www.fs.usda.gov/angeles.

5 MOUNT HILLYER

6.0 mi/3.0 hr

in Angeles National Forest near the Chilao Visitors Center

Map 13.1, page 683

What, you say you have never heard of Mount Hillyer? Well, it doesn't have the clout or the elevation of Mount Baden-Powell or Mount Baldy, but it is one of the nicest places to seek out a little solitude in a wooded, rocky wonderland. The route to Mount Hillyer is a 1,100-foot climb spread out over three miles, following a short stretch of the 14-mile Silver Moccasin National Recreation Trail. The trail starts in chaparral and occasional gray pines, interspersed with many tall, blooming yucca plants in the spring. After a moderate one-mile climb, you near the edge of Horse Flats Campground and turn left to pick up the Mount Hillyer Trail. The path climbs through a steep, rocky area and delivers you to Hillyer's summit, which some hikers describe as "just a bump on a hill." On our first trip here, we walked right past the summit without even noticing it. It's the pile of boulders just off the trail to your left. If you find yourself hiking downhill for a while, heading toward looming Mount Pacifico, you've missed the summit. Views of the surrounding mountains are only fair from the summit, but the air is clean and sweet, and the crowds are nonexistent. Mount Hillyer is surrounded by beautiful stands of Jeffrey pines and incense cedars. The sound of the wind in the pines is divine.

User Groups: Hikers, dogs, horses, and mountain bikes. No wheelchair facilities.

Permits: No permits are required. A National Forest Adventure Pass is required for each vehicle; fees are $5 for one day or $30 for a year. Interagency access passes are also accepted.

Maps: An Angeles National Forest map is available from the U.S. Forest Service. A map of the Angeles Front Country is available from Tom Harrison Maps. For a topographic map, go to the USGS website to download Chilao Flat.

Directions: From I-210 in La Cañada, take Highway 2/Angeles Crest Highway northeast for 26.5 miles to the Chilao Visitors Center turnoff on the left (not the turnoff for Chilao Campgrounds). Drive 0.7 mile on the Chilao Visitors Center road to a small parking pullout where the Silver Moccasin Trail crosses the road. Park here and follow the trail that is signed for Horse Flats Campground.

Contact: Angeles National Forest, Los Angeles River Ranger District, San Fernando, 818/899-1900, www.fs.usda.gov/angeles.

6 DEVIL'S CANYON TRAIL

7.0 mi/4.0 hr or 2 days 4 8

in San Gabriel Mountains National Monument near Chilao

Map 13.1, page 683

This is an upside-down hike—down on the way in and up, up, up on the way out. Trailhead elevation is 5,200 feet, and it is a trail of extremes. There's chaparral on some slopes and tall pines and big-cone Douglas fir on others (although many trees were burned in the last decade's wildfires). There's a bit of sun, then shade. It's dry for the first two miles, but then you reach a tributary creek and follow its meander. The trip down to Devil's Canyon is usually pretty quick—about an hour-and-a-half for most people—and considering that, you'd think this trail would see more use. But instead this is one spot in the San Gabriels where you often have a chance at solitude. When you reach the edge of Devil's Creek, you'll find plenty of flat spots for a picnic and a few primitive campsites. Some intrepid hikers choose to continue down the canyon beyond the trail's end to search for the Devil's Canyon waterfalls, but prolific poison oak and slippery rocks will stop most sane people from doing so. Remember to save plenty of energy and water for the 3.5-mile trip from the canyon back to the trailhead, which has a 2,000-foot elevation gain. It's easy to convince yourself that the miles on the way up are twice as long as they were on the trip down.

User Groups: Hikers and horses. No dogs or mountain bikes. No wheelchair facilities.

Permits: No permits are required for day hiking. A free campfire permit is required for hikers using a backpacking stove (no campfires permitted). A National Forest Adventure Pass is required for each vehicle; fees are $5 for one day or $30 for a year. Interagency access passes are also accepted.

Maps: An Angeles National Forest map is available from the U.S. Forest Service. A map of the Angeles High Country is available from Tom Harrison Maps. For topographic maps, go to the USGS website to download Chilao Flat and Waterman Mountain.

Directions: From I-210 in La Cañada, take Highway 2/Angeles Crest Highway northeast for 25.5 miles to the Chilao Campground turnoff on the left, then continue past it for 0.75 mile to a parking lot on the left side of the highway. (It is 0.25 mile west of the Chilao Visitors Center turnoff.) The signed Devil's Canyon trailhead is located across the road.

Contact: Angeles National Forest, Los Angeles River Ranger District, San Fernando, 818/899-1900, www.fs.usda.gov/angeles.

7 GABRIELINO NATIONAL RECREATION TRAIL TO BEAR CANYON

8.0 mi/4.0 hr or 2 days 3 8

in San Gabriel Mountains National Monument near La Cañada

Map 13.1, page 683 BEST

The area surrounding Switzer Picnic Area, Switzer Falls, and Bear Canyon was badly burned in 2009 wildfires, and the water slides, mini cascades, and pools of spectacular Arroyo Seco and Bear Canyon were silted in by runoff. But a decade later, the creeks are clear, and the area is extremely popular with Los Angeles hikers. Gabrielino National Recreation Trail is your ticket to visiting this area. Begin hiking from the Switzer Picnic Area, heading downstream on the smooth dirt trail. A few creek crossings and one mile of trail will bring you to the site of the old Commodore Switzer Trail Camp. Cross the stream once more and head uphill, still on the Gabrielino National Recreation Trail. The trail passes 50-foot Switzer Falls, affording a decent view of it from across the canyon. A stone foundation is the remains of the Switzer Chapel, where visitors at Switzer's Camp, a popular trail resort in the early 20th century, attended Sunday services above the falls. A few steps farther brings you to a junction where the Gabrielino National Recreation Trail heads right and uphill, and the Bear Canyon Trail heads left and

Gabrielino National Recreation Trail to Bear Canyon

downhill. Enjoy the lofty view of Arroyo Seco Canyon from this point, then bear left and descend steeply for 0.25 mile, being cautious of the steep dropoffs. At the canyon bottom, take a quick detour to the left to see the lower cascades of Switzer Falls, then retrace your steps to this junction and follow the Bear Canyon Trail downstream. The canyon becomes increasingly wild here and you may have this special place all to yourself. One mile from the junction below Switzer Falls you reach a fork in the creek. Head upstream for another 1.2 miles to Bear Canyon Trail Camp. (This last stretch of trail was in poor repair; the path crosses and recrosses the creek dozens of times and can be difficult to discern.)

User Groups: Hikers, dogs, horses, and mountain bikes. No wheelchair facilities.

Permits: No permits are required for day hiking. A free campfire permit is required for hikers using a backpacking stove (no campfires permitted). A National Forest Adventure Pass is required for each vehicle; fees are $5 for one day or $30 for a year. Interagency access passes are also accepted.

Maps: An Angeles National Forest map is available from the U.S. Forest Service. A map of the Mount Wilson area is available from Tom Harrison Maps. For topographic maps, go to the USGS website to download Condor Peak and Pasadena.

Directions: From I-210 in La Cañada, take Highway 2/Angeles Crest Highway northeast for 9.8 miles to Switzer Picnic Area. It is on the south side of the road, 0.5 mile past Clear Creek Information Station. Turn right, drive down the access road 0.3 mile, and park in the main lot.

Contact: Angeles National Forest, Los Angeles River Ranger District, San Fernando, 818/899-1900, www.fs.usda.gov/angeles.

8 MILLARD FALLS

1.0 mi/0.5 hr

in Angeles National Forest near Pasadena

Map 13.1, page 683

If you want to guarantee your kids (or adult friends) a good time, take them to Millard Campground for the short hike and scramble to Millard Falls. In springtime, make sure you're dressed to get wet, because you may have to spend more time in the stream than on a dry trail, especially if it has rained lately. There is no official trail to the falls; it's just a well-used route that follows the stream, making an easy adventure that is suitable for hikers of all abilities. The only minus is the abundance of carvings found on the smooth-barked alder trees; the carvings desecrate almost every tree, as high as human hands can reach. (Take this opportunity to teach your children never, ever to carve anything on trees.) The route to the falls is a 0.5-mile walk up the stream canyon, partly in the creek and partly on trail. Start walking at the edge of the campground just beyond the camp host's site, where the trail leads to the right and passes a couple of cabins. Simply head upstream, rock hopping where necessary, until the canyon walls come together at 60-foot Millard Falls. The stream splits in two at the fall's lip, forced to detour around two boulders that are stuck in the waterfall's notch. The two streams rejoin about two-thirds of the way down, creating a tremendous rush of water in springtime. Trailhead elevation is 1,900 feet.

User Groups: Hikers and dogs. No horses or mountain bikes. No wheelchair facilities.

Permits: No permits are required. A National Forest Adventure Pass is required for each vehicle; fees are $5 for one day or $30 for a year. Interagency access passes are also accepted.

Maps: An Angeles National Forest map is available from the U.S. Forest Service. Maps of the Angeles Front Country and High Country are available from Tom Harrison Maps. For a topographic map, go to the USGS website to download Pasadena.

Directions: From I-210 in Pasadena, exit on Lake Avenue and drive north for 3.5 miles to Loma Alta Drive. Turn west (left) on Loma Alta Drive and drive one mile to Chaney Trail at the flashing yellow light. Turn right and drive 1.5 miles on Chaney Trail, keeping left at the fork, to Millard Campground. Park in the parking lot and follow the fire road on the right (as you drove in) that leads into the campground.
Contact: Angeles National Forest, Los Angeles River Ranger District, San Fernando, 818/899-1900, www.fs.usda.gov/angeles.

9 EATON CANYON

3.0 mi/1.5 hr

in Eaton Canyon Natural Area

Map 13.1, page 683

Eaton Canyon Natural Area is the kind of place where elementary school groups come in the spring. The buses unload their cargoes of children, who then set off (on what may be their first real hike) through Eaton Canyon's wash. And what a fine introduction to the outdoors—a hike along Eaton Canyon in the good company of cacti, chaparral plants, willows, oaks, and occasionally bunnies, lizards, and red-tailed hawks. This park's trails connect to trails in Angeles National Forest, including the trail to one of its most popular features, Eaton Canyon Falls. Start at the Eaton Canyon Nature Center, where you can pick up a free map of the area, then walk to the far north end of the parking lot and take the dirt road straight past the picnic shelter. Cross the wash and hike along the wide canyon trail, with the wash on your left. The stream attracts a large variety of wildlife, especially birds that sing all day in this canyon. Just before a bridge where your trail intersects with the Mount Wilson Toll Road, cut down to the wash and pass under the bridge. From there, hike upstream, crossing the creek several times as the canyon narrows on its way to Eaton Canyon Falls. Sadly, the waterfall's cliffs are often found desecrated by graffiti, but the falls remain a well-loved destination.

One odd side note: If you hear the sound of gunfire at the trailhead, don't panic—the local police have a shooting range nearby. As you walk into the canyon, you'll quickly get away from the noise.
User Groups: Hikers, dogs, and horses. No mountain bikes. No wheelchair facilities.
Permits: No permits are required. Parking and access are free.
Maps: A free map of Eaton Canyon Natural Area is available at the nature center. For topographic maps, go to the USGS website to download Pasadena and Mount Wilson.
Directions: Heading east from I-210 in Pasadena, take the Sierra Madre Boulevard/Altadena Drive exit and go north on Altadena Drive for 1.6 miles. Turn right into the entrance for Eaton Canyon Natural Area, which is one block north of New York Drive. If you are heading west on I-210, take the San Gabriel Boulevard/San Marino exit. Turn right (north) at the second light, which is Altadena Drive, and drive 1.5 miles to the park entrance.
Contact: Eaton Canyon Natural Area, Pasadena, 626/398-5420, www.ecnca.org.

10 BIG SANTA ANITA CANYON LOOP

8.9 mi/5.0 hr

in Angeles National Forest near Arcadia

Map 13.1, page 683

Big Santa Anita Canyon is probably the top easy day-hike destination in all of the Los Angeles River District of Angeles National Forest. The shady, overgrown, magical gulch is just a handful of miles from the Pasadena freeway. Its easy-to-moderate trails provide a short, simple, and sweet escape from urban life. The problem is that the access road to the trailhead at Chantry Flat is subject to washouts and landslides almost every winter, so the trails here are often inaccessible for more months of the year than they are accessible. Check for current status of the Chantry Flat Road before making the drive. The other problem is that when the road is open and the weather is good, this place is incredibly popular. The parking lots sometimes fill up by 8am on sunny weekend days, so get an early start.

Assuming you can get in, start hiking on the Gabrielino National Recreation Trail downhill. It's paved for the first 0.7 mile heading down into the canyon. When you reach the bottom, cross the Roberts Footbridge and stay to the right on the dirt pathway. Day hikers can't help but covet the adorable summer cabins in the canyon, which are privately owned on land leased from the Forest Service. The artificial waterfalls you see are small check dams, designed (poorly) to keep the creek from flooding. Walking under the shade of oaks and alders, and along Big Santa Anita Creek for one mile upstream, leads you to 60-foot-high Sturtevant Falls. Where the Gabrielino Trail forks left and heads uphill, continue straight along the creek, admiring ferns and vines as you walk another 0.25 mile to the waterfall. It drops 60 feet over a granite cliff into a perfectly-shaped rock bowl. After a visit, retrace your steps to the junction and follow the Gabrielino Trail uphill. Take the lower trail (the upper trail is safer for horses), which clings to the steep hillsides as it climbs above Sturtevant Falls to Cascade Picnic Area, a shady spot alongside the fern-lined creek. Take a break here before continuing uphill for another mile to Spruce Grove Trail Camp. A quarter-mile beyond the camp, you'll bear left on the Mount Zion Trail to begin the return leg of the loop. The trail drops very steeply down to Hoegee's Camp, where you connect with the Lower Winter Creek Trail, which travels 1.5 back to the Roberts Footbridge and the start of your loop. It's a quick 0.6-mile hike back uphill on the paved road to your car.

User Groups: Hikers, dogs, horses, and mountain bikes. No wheelchair facilities.

Permits: No permits are required. A National Forest Adventure Pass is required for each vehicle; fees are $5 for one day or $30 for a year. Interagency access passes are also accepted.

Maps: An Angeles National Forest map is available from the U.S. Forest Service. A map of the Mount Wilson area is available from Tom Harrison Maps. For a topographic map, go to the USGS website to download Mount Wilson.

Directions: From I-210 in Pasadena, drive seven miles east to Arcadia. Exit on Santa Anita Avenue and drive six miles north to the road's end, at Chantry Flat. The trail begins across the road from the first parking area.

Contact: Angeles National Forest, Los Angeles River Ranger District, San Fernando, 818/899-1900, www.fs.usda.gov/angeles.

11 FIRST WATER TRAIL TO HERMIT FALLS

3.0 mi/1.5 hr 2 9

in Angeles National Forest near Arcadia

Map 13.1, page 683

You say you flat out refuse to hike on pavement? Then the trip on the Gabrielino Trail to Sturtevant Falls may not be right for you, but don't bypass beautiful Big Santa Anita Canyon because of it. An alternate trail drops down into the canyon, but this one is on gorgeous single-track trail all the way, lined with tall oaks and alders, huge chain ferns, slender sword ferns, and a half-dozen other fern varieties. You begin at the same trailhead, and the first few hundred yards of the walk are the same, but then you veer off the Gabrielino Trail at the sign for the First Water Trail and Hermit Falls (on your right). The trail switchbacks gently down into the canyon and then heads south (downstream) along the north fork of Big Santa Anita Creek. The near-constant shade of the canyon, combined with the presence of a year-round stream, makes it possible for every inch of ground to spring forth plant life. As on the Gabrielino Trail, you pass many artificial waterfalls (made by check dams on Santa Anita Creek) that are surprisingly beautiful. The First

Water Trail crosses the creek a few times, which can be a little tricky early in the year, and follows the stream on its downstream course. The trail ends at the last cabin in the canyon, just above Hermit Falls. Pick a granite boulder, have a seat, and watch the water flow by. In the winter months, this is a very peaceful spot, perfect for nature-lovers, but in the late spring and summer, Hermit Falls has become a raucous hangout spot, complete with coolers of beer. As you can imagine, the cabin owners aren't very happy about that.

User Groups: Hikers, dogs, horses, and mountain bikes. No wheelchair facilities.

Permits: No permits are required. A National Forest Adventure Pass is required for each vehicle; fees are $5 for one day or $30 for a year. Interagency access passes are also accepted.

Maps: An Angeles National Forest map is available from the U.S. Forest Service. A map of the Mount Wilson area is available from Tom Harrison Maps. For a topographic map, go to the USGS website to download Mount Wilson.

Directions: From I-210 in Pasadena, drive seven miles east to Arcadia. Exit on Santa Anita Avenue and drive six miles north to the road's end, at Chantry Flat. The trail begins across the road from the first parking area.

Contact: Angeles National Forest, Los Angeles River Ranger District, San Fernando, 818/899-1900, www.fs.usda.gov/angeles.

12 MONROVIA CANYON FALLS

1.4-3.4 mi/1.0-2.0 hr 1 9

in Monrovia Canyon Park

Map 13.1, page 683

Everything about Monrovia Canyon Park is a great experience, including the hike to the park's showpiece: Monrovia Canyon Falls. Three different trailheads allow you to select the distance you wish to hike: Starting at the Bill Cull trailhead by the entrance station, the hike is 3.4 miles round-trip. Starting at the middle parking lot makes a 2.0-mile round-trip. Starting from the trailhead behind the nature center is the easiest, shortest round-trip of 1.4 miles—perfect for families with small children. No matter how you do it, you'll hike through a lush and lovely stream canyon, passing several check dams along the creek. The dense woodland is crowded with oaks, alders, and ferns, creating cool and pleasant shade. When you reach the base of the 40-foot waterfall, you'll find many big rocks that are perfectly situated for gazing in admiration.

Note: Check your calendar before you go. Monrovia Canyon Park is closed on Tuesdays. The rest of the week, the park is open only from 8am to 5pm.

User Groups: Hikers and dogs. No horses or mountain bikes. No wheelchair facilities.

Permits: No permits are required. A $6 per vehicle fee is charged on weekends, $5 on weekdays.

Maps: A free park map is available at the nature center or entrance station. For a topographic map, go to the USGS website to download Azusa.

Directions: From I-210 in Monrovia, take the Myrtle Avenue exit and drive north for one mile through Old Town Monrovia to Foothill Boulevard. Turn right and drive 0.2 mile to Canyon Boulevard. Turn left and drive 1.6 miles to the park (bear right where the road forks). Drive past the entrance kiosk for 0.5 mile and park near the picnic area and nature center, for the shortest hike to the falls.

Contact: Monrovia Canyon Park, Monrovia, 626/256-8282 or 626/256-8246, www.cityofmonrovia.org.

13 BEN OVERTURFF TRAIL

6.4 mi/3.0 hr 3 7

in Monrovia Canyon Park

Map 13.1, page 683

Ben Overturff was the man who made Monrovia Canyon a popular recreation area in the early 20th century. He ran Deer Park Lodge, a wilderness getaway for city dwellers, from 1910 to 1945. This trail to the site of Deer Park Lodge was reconstructed in the 1990s and named in his honor. From the lower parking lot by the entrance station, walk up the park road about 50 yards to the right turnoff for the Trask Boy Scout Camp. Turn right and ascend 1.25 miles along this mostly paved access road. You'll pass the massive, 157-foot-high Sawpit Dam, which was built for flood control in 1927. It's the only interesting sight on this rather unpleasant stint of pavement. Sawpit Canyon Road soon turns to dirt and continues its monotonous climb. At 1.3 miles, you leave the dull fire road behind and join the single-track Ben Overturff Trail. Follow the trail as it winds its way up Sawpit and Sycamore Canyons, mostly in the shade of a bay laurel and oak forest. One memorable stretch skirts across a narrow, backbone ridge separating the two canyons. At 2.5 miles from the start, you reach the Twin Springs Junction and bear left. A few minutes later is a second junction, where you bear left again and soon reach the Deer Park Lodge site, comprised of a few crumbling foundations, rusted pipes and mattress springs, and bits and pieces of stone walls and steps. This is the turnaround point for this hike; if you want to loop back instead of retracing your steps, connect to Sawpit Canyon Road at either of the two junctions you passed, then follow the road back down to the trailhead.

Note: Check your calendar before you go. Although the entire park is closed on Tuesdays, the Ben Overturff Trail is closed on Tuesdays and Wednesdays. Otherwise, the park is open from 8am to 5pm.

User Groups: Hikers and dogs. Horses, mountain bikes, and wheelchairs can use only the fire road portion of the trail.

Permits: No permits are required. A $6 per vehicle fee is charged on weekends, $5 on weekdays.

Maps: A free brochure and trail map of the Ben Overturff Trail is available at the nature center. For a topographic map, go to the USGS website to download Azusa.

Directions: From I-210 in Monrovia, take the Myrtle Avenue exit and drive north for one mile through Old Town Monrovia to Foothill Boulevard. Turn right and drive 0.2 mile to Canyon Boulevard. Turn left and drive 1.6 miles to the park (veer right where the road forks). Park at the first available parking lot just before the entrance station.

Contact: Monrovia Canyon Park, Monrovia, 626/256-8282 or 626/256-8246, www.cityofmonrovia.org.

14 WILDWOOD PARK LOOP

4.0 mi/2.0 hr 2 8

in Wildwood Park in Thousand Oaks

Map 13.1, page 683

Wildwood Park is one of the best-kept park secrets in Los Angeles, known mostly to the school kids who come here for outdoor field trips in the spring. From the Arboles trailhead in Thousand Oaks, you can hike downhill into Wildwood Canyon and then stroll along its year-round stream, which produces a stunningly beautiful waterfall when the stream flow is strong. Numerous trails cross and interconnect throughout the park, so you can put together a different loop trip or out-and-back hike every time you visit.

For first timers, a good tour is to hike due west on the Mesa Trail for 0.5 mile to the North Tepee Trail and turn left, dropping down into the canyon. Once there, walk to your right, and then bear left at the next fork, which puts you right at the base of the 70-foot waterfall. Hey, isn't Los Angeles supposed to be a semi-arid desert? Yes, but it's full of surprises. (It's also full of rules; don't even think about swimming here.) From the falls, you can continue walking downstream and then pick up the Lizard Rock Trail to loop back to the Mesa Trail. The presence of year-round water makes this canyon a haven for wildlife; look for mule deer, rabbits, coyotes, and numerous songbirds and raptors. Interpretive signs teach you to identify various plants and trees along the stream.

User Groups: Hikers, dogs, horses, and mountain bikes. No wheelchair facilities.

Permits: No permits are required. Parking and access are free.

Maps: Park maps are available at the park visitors center. For a topographic map, go to the USGS website to download Thousand Oaks.

Directions: From U.S. 101 in Thousand Oaks, take the Lynn Road exit and head north. Drive 2.5 miles to Avenida de los Arboles, then turn left. Drive 0.9 mile and make a U-turn into the Arboles parking lot, on the left side of the road.

Contact: Conejo Recreation and Park District, Thousand Oaks, 805/381-2741 or 805/495-6471, www.crpd.org.

15 SATWIWA LOOP TRAIL AND WATERFALL

3.0 mi/1.5 hr 2 9

in Santa Monica Mountains National Recreation Area near Newbury Park

Map 13.1, page 683

You know the hike will be good when, at the trailhead parking lot, you're greeted by two friendly roadrunners and a half-dozen bunnies. That's how it is at Rancho Sierra Vista/Satwiwa, a part of Santa Monica Mountains National Recreation Area, just a couple miles off U.S. 101. The park's proximity to millions of L.A. commuters makes it a perfect place to show up after work and hike or jog on Satwiwa Loop Trail, and in the rainy season, you can take a side-trip to see the waterfall just inside the border of Point Mugu State Park. From the parking lot, walk up the paved Sycamore Canyon Trail for a few hundred yards, then bear left on the Satwiwa Loop Trail by the Satwiwa Native American Indian Culture Center. Be sure to take a peek at the dome-shaped stick dwelling, known to the Chumash as an "ap," which was reconstructed to show traditional Native American life. Follow the Satwiwa Loop for just under a mile, passing a small pond, a windmill, and grassy hillsides, then connect to the Old Boney Trail, on the south side of the loop. The Old Boney Trail leads downhill, and where the Upper Sycamore Canyon Trail comes in sharply from the right; stay left on the Old Boney Trail and cross the creek (an easy rockhop even in winter and spring). Walk about 100 yards and then make one final left. In about 50 yards of easy stream scrambling, you're at Sycamore Canyon Falls. The waterfall is a pretty, multitiered cascade over sandstone, with a surprising amount of foliage growing around it (including some nasty poison oak). Even when the fall is only a trickle, the big-leaf maples and woodwardia ferns are a delight to visit.

User Groups: Hikers and dogs. (Dogs are not allowed past the border of Point Mugu State Park or at the waterfall, only on the Satwiwa Loop.) No horses or mountain bikes. No wheelchair facilities.

Permits: No permits are required. Parking and access are free.

Maps: Free trail maps are available at the trailhead or by download at www.nps.gov/samo. A map of Point Mugu State Park is available from Tom Harrison Maps. For a topographic map, go to the USGS website to download Newbury Park.

Directions: From U.S. 101 in Thousand Oaks, exit at Lynn Road and head south for 5.5 miles. Turn left at Via Goleta and drive 0.75 mile to the last parking area. Walk up the trail leading toward the Satwiwa Native American Culture Center.

Contact: Santa Monica Mountains National Recreation Area, Calabasas, 805/370-2301, www.nps.gov/samo.

16 GROTTO TRAIL

3.4 mi/2.0 hr 

in Santa Monica Mountains National Recreation Area at Circle X Ranch

Map 13.1, page 683

If you don't mind hiking downhill to your destination and then uphill on your return, the Grotto Trail is a fine route for a little excursion in the Santa Monica Mountains. The trail roughly follows the west fork of the Arroyo Sequit on its downhill course to the Grotto, an area of jumbled volcanic boulders, many that are bigger than your average Volkswagen. Hidden among the giant rocks are small caves, pools, and waterfalls. After a brief walk downhill from the Circle X Ranch Ranger Station parking lot, you access the Grotto by following the Grotto Trail from the ranch's group campground. The 1.3-mile trail makes a moderate descent on a pleasant grade. The 500-foot elevation loss must be gained back on the return trip, but fortunately there is a good amount of shade along the route. Only 0.3 mile beyond the campground you meet up with the Canyon View Trail coming in from the left. A few footsteps farther, you cross over the brink of 35-foot-high Botsford Falls, named by the legions of Boy Scouts who frequented the Circle X Campground. After a stint through a lovely grassland meadow, the trail moves close to the water again. Keep traveling gently downhill on this charming pathway and soon you emerge just above the sycamore-shaded Grotto. When the water is high, the trail disappears and you must boulder hop. Just keep heading downstream as far as it is safe to travel, then stand back and listen to the water roar. The Grotto's boulders are tempting to climb on and explore, but be extra careful. Many people have slipped and fallen here. And although dogs are allowed on the main trail, they aren't allowed past the streambed before the boulders.

User Groups: Hikers and dogs (main trail only). No horses or mountain bikes. No wheelchair facilities.

Permits: No permits are required. Parking and access are free.

Maps: Maps are available by free download at www.nps.gov/samo. A map of Point Mugu State Park, which includes Circle X Ranch, is available from Tom Harrison Maps. For a topographic map, go to the USGS website to download Triunfo Pass.

Directions: From Highway 1/Pacific Coast Highway in Malibu, drive northwest for 10 miles to Yerba Buena Road, 1.5 miles past Leo Carrillo State Park. Turn right and drive 5.3 miles up Yerba Buena Road to the entrance to Circle X Ranch on the right. Park by the ranger station, then follow the trail to the group campground. The Grotto Trail begins at the group camp.

Contact: Santa Monica Mountains National Recreation Area, Calabasas, 805/370-2301, www.nps.gov/samo; Circle X Ranger Station, 310/457-6408.

17 MISHE MOKWA AND SANDSTONE PEAK LOOP

6.0 mi/3.0 hr 3 9

in Santa Monica Mountains National Recreation Area near Circle X Ranch

Map 13.1, page 683

A great six-mile loop in the Santa Monica Mountains begins a short distance from Circle X Ranch, on Yerba Buena Road. See all those wild-looking volcanic outcrops on the hillsides? That's where you're going. You can hike the loop in either direction, but most people start on the Mishe Mokwa Trail. From the trailhead, hike uphill for 0.25 mile and take the right fork to access Mishe Mokwa's single track. It's 1.9 gentle miles on trail bordered by chaparral and spring wildflowers to a stream crossing and Split Rock, a big boulder with a cleft in the middle. It's an unspoken requirement to walk through the cleft. A picnic area at Split Rock is set among the oaks and sycamores, ideally situated for catching some shade.

From there, continue on the well-signed loop, now in more exposed terrain. At 3.2 miles from the start, turn left to join the Backbone Trail, a wide road. A half-mile farther, be sure to take the short right spur to Inspiration Point for inspiring views of the coast, and shortly beyond that, take the next right spur to 3,111-foot Sandstone Peak, the highest point in the Santa Monica Mountains. Despite its name, the peak is not made of sandstone; it's volcanic rock. The views are outstanding. On the clearest days, you can pick out six of the Channel Islands, plus far inland, the high peaks of the San Gabriel Mountains. Sandstone Peak actually has another name, Mount Allen, so when you climb to the top and see the Mount Allen plaque, don't think you're in the wrong place.

User Groups: Hikers and dogs. No horses or mountain bikes. No wheelchair facilities.

Permits: No permits are required. Parking and access are free.

Maps: Maps are available by free download at www.nps.gov/samo. A map of Point Mugu State Park, which includes Sandstone Peak, is available from Tom Harrison Maps. For a topographic map, go to the USGS website to download Triunfo Pass.

Directions: From Highway 1/Pacific Coast Highway in Malibu, drive northwest for 10 miles to Yerba Buena Road, 1.5 miles past Leo Carrillo State Park. Turn right and drive 7.2 miles up Yerba Buena Road to the Mishe Mokwa trailhead on the left (not the Sandstone Peak trailhead, which is 0.7 mile before the Mishe Mokwa trailhead).

Contact: Santa Monica Mountains National Recreation Area, Calabasas, 805/370-2301, www.nps.gov/samo.

18 NICHOLAS FLAT TRAIL

7.0 mi/3.5 hr 3 9

in Leo Carrillo State Park near Malibu

Map 13.1, page 683

Most Southern California state beaches are long stretches of sand with big campgrounds and lots of happy beachgoers, but few have any hiking trails worth writing home about. Leo Carrillo State Park is the exception to the rule, with a couple excellent trails that are far more than just a stroll along the sand. The Nicholas Flat Trail is the park's best path, a fairly steep trail that climbs from the coast to a pond at Nicholas Flat, where redwing blackbirds and other songbirds are easily seen. Start hiking from the Willow Creek/Nicholas Flat trailhead, and at the first junction, take either path. The Nicholas Flat Trail on the left is shorter but steeper; Willow Creek is longer, gentler, and more scenic. Both trails connect in less than a mile, where a spur trail heads off to a spot signed as Ocean Vista. This is a fine viewpoint and an excellent spot to look for passing whales in winter. From the spur trail, backtrack a few feet and then continue uphill on the Nicholas Flat Trail. The climb gets steeper from here, and you'll gain 1,200 feet more as you climb along an extended ridgeline, but you are rewarded with many more spectacular vistas along the way (just turn around and take a look), plus in spring, a bonanza of wildflowers—mariposa lilies, poppies, golden yarrow, and popcorn flower among them. At 2.7 miles from the start, after the trail has attained its highest point, you reach a junction of trails, shortly followed by another junction. Follow the signs and you'll come out at the artificial pond at Nicholas Flat after a total 3.5 miles of hiking. Originally used for cattle ranching, the huge pond is mostly tule-lined except for its southwest edge. Sit still for a moment and you'll notice that the pond is a very birdy place. Red-winged blackbirds, starlings, mallards, coots, and myriad other species can be seen by those willing to wait and watch. A small, lightweight pair of binoculars would come in handy here.

If the best spots around the pond are already taken, you can follow a half-mile loop around the grasslands at Nicholas Flat and pick another spot for a rest and a picnic lunch. When it's time to start heading back, the best part of the trip is about to start. Not only is the route entirely downhill except for a brief initial climb, but you can look forward to nearly nonstop ocean views all the way. When you're finished hiking this trail, make sure to check out the beach across the road (take the pedestrian tunnel under the highway), where you'll find a sea-carved tunnel and many small caves and pocket beaches.

User Groups: Hikers only. No horses, dogs, or mountain bikes. Wheelchair users have access to the park's "sand wheelchairs" to explore the beach area.

Permits: No permits are required. A $12 day-use fee is charged per vehicle (the fee is reduced if you are staying three hours or less).

Maps: A map of Leo Carrillo State Park is available at the park entrance station or visitors center, or by free download at www.parks.ca.gov. A map of Point Mugu State Park, which includes Leo Carrillo State Park, is available from Tom Harrison Maps. For a topographic map, go to the USGS website to download Triunfo Pass.

Directions: From U.S. 101 in Agoura Hills, exit at Kanan Road and drive 12.5 miles to Highway 1/Pacific Coast Highway on the Malibu coast. Turn west (right) and drive eight miles to Leo Carrillo State Park. Turn right into the park entrance and park in the day-use lot (fee charged), or park for free on Pacific Coast Highway just outside the park entrance. The Nicholas Flat Trail begins by the entrance kiosk on the inland side of the highway.

Contact: Leo Carrillo State Park, Malibu, 805/488-5223, 805/488-1827, or 818/880-0363, www.parks.ca.gov.

19 MEADOW TRAIL AND OCEAN OVERLOOK LOOP

3.0 mi/1.5 hr 2 9

in Charmlee Wilderness Park near Zuma Beach

Map 13.1, page 683

Charmlee Wilderness Park was hit hard by the November 2018 Woolsey fire, and as of September 2019, it still has not officially reopened. However, hikers haven't stopped visiting; they simply park outside the gates and walk into the park. The Mountains Recreation and Conservation Authority hopes to re-open the gates by spring 2020. There's no question that this spot's incredible Pacific views will be as awesome as ever—maybe even more so because so many of the park's trees have burned. Charmlee is four miles up the hill from Zuma Beach, high enough so that you don't have to climb anywhere to gain a view. The park's hiking trails are all fire roads and fairly flat, so this is a good place to bring your friends who aren't serious hikers. From the park's picnic area, follow Old Ranch Road for 0.25 mile to the old ranch foundation, surrounded by a meadow filled with wildflower blooms in spring. Here, at a T-junction, go left, and walk 0.5 mile to the old ranch reservoir. From the reservoir, you can loop back by heading left or right; all trails eventually connect back with the Old Ranch Road. From several points, you have vistas in almost every direction, not just to the coast but also up and down the Boney Mountain Ridge of the Santa Monica Mountains. On clear days, it's easy to discern a couple of the Channel Islands.

User Groups: Hikers, dogs, horses, and mountain bikes. No wheelchair facilities.

Permits: No permits are required. A $7 day-use fee is charged per vehicle.

Maps: A map of the Santa Monica Mountains is available from Tom Harrison Maps. For topographic maps, go to the USGS website to download Triunfo and Point Dume.

Directions: From Highway 1 in Zuma Beach, drive north on Encinal Canyon Road for four miles to the park entrance on the left. Turn left and drive 0.4 mile to the parking area near the park office and restrooms.

Contact: Charmlee Wilderness Park, Mountains Recreation and Conservation Authority, Malibu, 310/589-3200, www.mrca.ca.gov.

20 ROCK POOL AND CENTURY LAKE

4.4 mi/2.0 hr 2 8

in Malibu Creek State Park

Map 13.1, page 683

The first time you lay eyes on the Rock Pool at Malibu Creek State Park or cross the wide bridge over Malibu Creek or visit pretty blue Century Lake, you may have to ask yourself the question: Where am I? Suddenly it's hard to believe you're in Los Angeles, and just a few miles off the freeway—but you are. Malibu Creek State Park sustained some fire damage from the November 2018 Woolsey fire, but the worst damage occurred at Paramount Ranch and Western Town, not here. By the Rock Pool and Century Lake, the landscape is somewhat charred but still beautifully wild. Start hiking from the large main parking area on the flat fire road, called Crags Road, that heads for the visitors center. Continue past the visitors center on a wide bridge, and take the left spur to the Rock Pool, a startlingly beautiful pool in Malibu Creek that is dammed by huge volcanic boulders. Although the pool can nearly dry up in late summer, during the rainy season and shortly thereafter, it's quite dramatic. Retrace your steps to Crags Road (you'll probably pass some rock climbers practicing their craft on an outcrop along the spur trail), turn left, and continue your park tour by visiting Century Lake, which was dammed in 1901; it's now silting up and slowly becoming a marsh. Walk another 0.5 mile along Crags Road. From there, retrace your steps through the park to the trailhead.

User Groups: Hikers, horses, and mountain bikes. No dogs. No wheelchair facilities.

Permits: No permits are required. A $12 day-use fee is charged per vehicle (the fee is reduced if you are staying three hours or less).

Maps: A map of Malibu Creek State Park is available at the park entrance station or by free download at www.parks.ca.gov, or from Tom Harrison Maps. For a topographic map, go to the USGS website to download Point Dume.

Directions: From Agoura Hills on U.S. 101, take the Las Virgenes exit and drive 3.5 miles south to the entrance to Malibu Creek State Park, on the right. Continue past the entrance kiosk to the day-use parking area.

From Malibu on Highway 1, drive north on Malibu Canyon Road/Las Virgenes Road for six miles to the park entrance, on the left.

Contact: Malibu Creek State Park, Calabasas, 818/880-0367 or 818/880-0363, www.parks.ca.gov or www.malibucreekstatepark.org.

21 ESCONDIDO FALLS

4.2 mi/2.0 hr

in Escondido Canyon near Malibu

Map 13.1, page 683

This beautiful parkland was closed to the public for several months after the November 2018 Woolsey fire, but hikers rejoiced when it reopened in 2019. That said, this trail's first mile is still a bit odd due to an access problem. Hikers have to park in the lot at the start of Winding Way and then walk up the paved road for a mile, past some gargantuan Malibu homes, to the actual beginning of the Escondido Canyon Trail. It's weird, but worth it. (Try not to gawk too much at all the affluence.) When you reach the trail sign for the Edward Albert Escondido Canyon Trailhead, veer off to the left, heading down into the canyon. You'll walk upstream, crossing the creek numerous times. The nearly level path tunnels through the shade of sycamore trees and opens out to grassy flats; it's a lovely sylvan setting all the way. About 0.5 mile from the start of the "real" trail, you'll glimpse a big waterfall up ahead, and in 0.5 mile more, you're at its base. This is the lower tier of the huge, 150-foot-tall limestone waterfall, the tallest in the Santa Monica Mountains. You may be tempted to climb above this cascade to reach the falls' much larger upper tier, but don't do it. The public property (and the official trail) ends at the lower falls.

User Groups: Hikers, dogs, horses, and mountain bikes. No wheelchair facilities.
Permits: No permits are required. Parking and access are free.
Maps: A map of Malibu Creek State Park, which includes Escondido Canyon, is available from Tom Harrison Maps. For a topographic map, go to the USGS website to download Point Dume.
Directions: From Malibu, drive west on Highway 1 for 5.5 miles to Winding Way East, on the right, and the large sign for Winding Way Trail. If you reach Kanan Dume Road, you've gone 1.5 miles too far. Turn right, then left immediately into the well-signed parking lot.
Contact: Mountains Recreation and Conservation Authority, Malibu, 310/589-3200, www.mrca.ca.gov.

22 SOLSTICE CANYON TRAIL AND RISING SUN LOOP

2.8 mi/1.2 hr 2 8

in Santa Monica Mountains National Recreation Area near Malibu

Map 13.1, page 683

Solstice Canyon has long been a favorite hiking spot for Malibu-area locals, because it's easy to reach and dependably serene. This easy loop travels along the Solstice Canyon Trail to the Roberts Ranch site and returns via the winding Rising Sun Trail. Although the first mile on the Solstice Canyon Trail is on pavement, it parallels Solstice Creek and is a pleasant stroll.

Hike past the restrooms at the parking lot, then turn right at the T-junction and hike up the canyon, enjoying an array of wildflowers in spring. The old stone Keller House that once stood here, one of the oldest houses in Malibu, was destroyed in the 2007 Corral Canyon fire. Continue to the ruins of Tropical Terrace, at the Roberts Ranch. This once-beautiful home burned down in a fire in 1982 (and many more fires have burned through here since), but its stone terraces and foundation remain. If you walk around to the far side of the foundation, you'll discover a 30-foot waterfall that drops on Solstice Creek. Enjoy its sweet music and maybe a sandwich from your pack. Head back to the Roberts Ranch ruins, then cross the creek and pick up the Rising Sun Trail, which undulates over the hillsides for 1.7 miles. From there you can take the left side of the TRW Loop Trail back to the parking lot.
User Groups: Hikers, dogs, and horses. Mountain bikes are allowed only on the Solstice Canyon Trail. No wheelchair facilities.
Permits: No permits are required. Parking and access are free.
Maps: A free trail map is available at the parking area or by download at www.nps.gov/samo. A map of Malibu Creek State Park, which includes Solstice Canyon, is available from Tom Harrison Maps. For a topographic map, go to the USGS website to download Malibu Beach.
Directions: From Malibu, drive west on Highway 1 for 3.5 miles and turn right on Corral Canyon Road. Drive 0.2 mile to the

Escondido Falls

park entrance, on the left. Turn left and drive 0.3 mile to the parking area. Start hiking on the paved road.
Contact: Santa Monica Mountains National Recreation Area, Calabasas, 805/370-2301, www.nps.gov/samo.

23 EAGLE ROCK LOOP

4.5 mi/2.5 hr 

at Trippet Ranch in Topanga State Park

Map 13.1, page 683

Topanga State Park's most notable feature is sandstone Eagle Rock, and a loop hike from Trippet Ranch takes you to see it. One half of this loop travels on Musch Trail, a hikers-only path, while the other half travels on fire roads. If you are a single-track lover, or if you don't like sharing the trail with bikes, simply take Musch Trail out and back to Eagle Rock. From the trailhead, the Musch Trail travels through a mix of oak and bay forest, grassy meadows, and chaparral. In one mile you reach Musch Camp, a pleasant hike-in camp that is surrounded by meadows. A restroom and horse corral are located here. From the camp, the trail gets even better—flower-filled grasslands and oak groves await. Look for mariposa lilies, blue-eyed grass, and owl's clover in bloom in springtime. Two miles from the start you reach Eagle Junction, where your trail meets up with a passel of fire roads. Take a hard left on Eagle Rock Fire Road, and climb steeply for 0.5 mile to Eagle Rock. After just a few minutes of walking, you come around a curve and get your first big-impact view of it. The rock is so large and prominent that it may remind you of the big granite domes of the Sierra, but Eagle Rock is made of sandstone. Your trail runs right alongside the rock; leave the trail so you can explore its many caves, hollows, nooks, and crannies. Perhaps best of all are the views of the Santa Ynez Canyon below and the ocean beyond. When you've had enough, retrace your steps to the Eagle Junction, then choose between a return trip on the Musch Trail (making this a five-mile round-trip) or a loop back on the fire road. To make the loop, bear left on Eagle Springs Fire Road for a 4.5-mile round-trip.
User Groups: Hikers, horses, and mountain bikes. No dogs. No wheelchair facilities.
Permits: No permits are required. A $10 day-use fee is charged per vehicle.
Maps: A map of Topanga State Park is available at the Trippet Ranch ranger station or by free download at www.parks.ca.gov, or from Tom Harrison Maps. For a topographic map, go to the USGS website to download Topanga.
Directions: From Santa Monica, drive north on Highway 1 and turn right on Topanga Canyon Boulevard. Drive 4.7 miles to Entrada Road, then turn right and drive one mile to the park entrance at Trippet Ranch. The trailhead is at the far side of the parking lot.
Contact: Topanga State Park, Topanga, 310/455-2465, www.parks.ca.gov.

24 SANTA YNEZ CANYON

2.4 mi/1.2 hr 2 8

in Topanga State Park in Pacific Palisades

Map 13.1, page 683

Topanga State Park is a park with nebulous borders, a patchwork of wilderness interspersed between continually growing housing developments. The park's Santa Ynez Canyon Trail, for instance, begins in a residential neighborhood where you park your car right along the street. The surprising thing is that once you walk about 50 yards on the trail, you feel as if you've gotten away from it all, especially the sights and sounds of urban living. The canyon bottom makes for level walking and is pleasantly shaded by oaks, willows, and sycamores. Five-foot-tall tiger lilies grow alongside the trail.

At 0.5 mile in, cross the creek (don't take the spur trail up its right side), and you'll shortly reach a trail junction, where you should go right. The left fork continues for several miles, all the way to Trippet Ranch and the main section of Topanga State Park. A short walk and stream scramble brings you to the base of Santa Ynez Canyon's 15-foot limestone waterfall, a lovely spot that unfortunately has been defiled by graffiti. Even so, it's worth a look, and the canyon walk is pleasant whether or not the stream is flowing strong.

User Groups: Hikers only. No dogs, horses, or mountain bikes. No wheelchair facilities.

Permits: No permits are required. Parking and access are free.

Maps: A map of Topanga State Park is available at the Trippet Ranch ranger station or by free download at www.parks.ca.gov, or from Tom Harrison Maps. For a topographic map, go to the USGS website to download Topanga.

Directions: From Santa Monica, drive north on Highway 1 and turn right on Sunset Boulevard in Pacific Palisades. Drive 0.5 mile and turn left on Palisades Drive. Drive 2.4 miles, and then turn left onto Vereda de la Montura. The trailhead is at the intersection of Camino de Yatasto (a private road) and Vereda de la Montura. Park alongside the road.

Contact: Topanga State Park, Topanga, 310/455-2465, www.parks.ca.gov.

25 TEMESCAL CANYON AND RIDGE LOOP

3.8 mi/2.0 hr

in Temescal Gateway Park in Pacific Palisades

Map 13.1, page 683

Here's an urban-edge hike—smack in the middle of Pacific Palisades—that will make you forget all about the proximity of the urban edge. Sure, it can be crowded here, but deservedly so. For its scenic beauty alone, this loop hike is one of the best treks in the Santa Monica Mountains. The signed trail leads from beyond the camp store, heading up and around the park's youth camp. In about 100 feet you'll come to a junction and the start of your loop: the Temescal Canyon Trail on the right and the Temescal Ridge Trail on the left. Go right on the Temescal Canyon Trail and climb very gradually uphill. In 0.5 mile, at a boardwalk over the wide wash of Temescal Creek, you pass a Topanga State Park boundary sign. The trail then climbs again, now more earnestly. The path is lined with small rounded pebbles embedded in conglomerate rock. Bunnies and lizards scurry by as you parallel the stream, hiking underneath a canopy of big-leaf maples and sycamores. At 1.1 miles, you cross a footbridge over a small, seasonal waterfall, then you'll cross over to the west side of the canyon to ascend to an intersection with the Temescal Ridge Trail. Follow the Temescal Ridge Trail as it ascends for another 0.25 mile and then levels out, offering stupendous views of the coast and Santa Monica Bay. In spring, this high ridge is lined with wildflowers—mariposa lilies, purple nightshade, California poppies, and monkeyflower, to name a few. A few steps farther and you're at Skull Rock, a somewhat spooky-looking sandstone formation, with what looks like eyeholes and a large forehead. After a thorough examination of the rock and its neighboring sandstone outcrops, return to the junction and finish out the loop by heading downhill on the Temescal Ridge Trail, with fine views of the coast entertaining you as you walk.

User Groups: Hikers only. No dogs, horses, or mountain bikes. No wheelchair facilities.

Permits: No permits are required. A $7 day-use fee is charged per vehicle. Annual passes are available.

Maps: A free trail map is available at the Temescal Gateway Park kiosk. A map of the Topanga State Park, which includes Temescal Gateway Park, is available from Tom Harrison Maps. For a topographic map, go to the USGS website to download Topanga.

Directions: From Santa Monica, drive north on Highway 1 to Temescal Canyon Road in Pacific Palisades. Turn right and drive one mile to Sunset Boulevard, then cross it to enter Temescal Gateway Park. Continue up the park road for 0.5 mile to the parking lot just before the camp store.

Contact: Temescal Gateway Park, Pacific Palisades, 310/454-1395, www.mrca.ca.gov.

26 INSPIRATION POINT TRAIL

3.8 mi/2.0 hr 

in Will Rogers State Historic Park

Map 13.1, page 683

Most folks come to Will Rogers State Historic Park to visit the home of the late "cowboy philosopher" and humorist Will Rogers. His humble abode was a gigantic 31-room ranch/mansion. But even if you never heard of the guy and have no interest in cowboy decorating style, this short hike to Inspiration Point and beyond makes a visit to the park worthwhile. Finding the trailhead is a bit tricky; it's behind the Rogerses' mansion, at the far edge of the grassy lawn. Cross a tiny footbridge, and you'll see the trailhead sign. The wide dirt road is dually signed as Rogers Road Trail and Inspiration Point Trail. A very easy climb of 0.9 mile brings you to a junction of trails and the Inspiration Point turnoff on your left. Go left and walk 100 yards to the summit of Inspiration Point, where the view includes the Pacific Ocean, the rugged Santa Monica Mountains, and downtown Los Angeles to the southeast. Considering the visual expanse, it's hard to believe you're at only 750 feet in elevation. On the clearest of days, you can see all the way to Catalina Island, 20-plus miles away. There's a horse-hitching post on the summit (this being a cowboy's park, of course), and a few picnic tables and benches. After enjoying the vista, head back down to the junction, then go left at the sign that marks the Backbone Trail and the entrance to Topanga State Park. Continue uphill on the Backbone Trail, climbing for another 0.9 mile. The trail crosses over a bridge that spans Chicken Ridge, a remarkably narrow sandstone ridge that gives much deeper meaning to the moniker "Backbone Trail." A high overlook with an even more commanding view than Inspiration Point is situated just above the bridged section of trail. Make this your turnaround for the hike and enjoy more views as you make your way back downhill.

User Groups: Hikers and horses. No dogs or mountain bikes. No wheelchair facilities.

Permits: No permits are required. A $12 day-use fee is charged per vehicle.

Maps: A map of Will Rogers State Historic Park is available at the park entrance station or by free download at www.parks.ca.gov. For a topographic map, go to the USGS website to download Topanga.

Directions: From Highway 1/Pacific Coast Highway in Pacific Palisades, turn north on Temescal Canyon Road. Drive one mile to Sunset Boulevard. Turn right and drive 1.4 miles to Will Rogers State Park Road, then turn left and drive one mile to the park entrance. The trail begins behind, and just east of, the Rogerses' ranch house, near the nature center and horse arena.

Contact: Will Rogers State Historic Park, Pacific Palisades, 310/454-8212 or 818/880-0363, www.parks.ca.gov.

27 RUNYON CANYON

3.4 mi/1.5 hr  

in Runyon Canyon Park near Hollywood

Map 13.1, page 683

Runyon Canyon Park is Hollywood's favorite neighborhood escape, where the young and hip socialize while getting a little nature time and staying in shape. The park isn't exactly wilderness, but it's a good example of how necessary city parks are for the people who live and work near them. It's a great place to take your dog for a walk, too; there are always tons of pooches here. Once you find street parking around the Fuller Avenue entrance—not an easy task on weekends—enter the park and take the main trail to the right. Walking this loop counterclockwise provides a steep climb in the beginning, then a longer, gradual descent. The trail ascends about 0.5 mile to the first overlook, dubbed Inspiration Point (like so many other high points in the Los Angeles area). The point offers good views of Hollywood, but it gets even better. The dirt trail narrows and ascends steeply up some steps to Cloud's Rest, the second and main overlook. Here you can catch your breath and take in the views near and far. The people-watching here is almost as good as the view, which takes in the famous Hollywood sign, Griffith Observatory, and, on exceptionally clear days, the distant ocean and even Catalina Island.

After quenching your visual appetite, continue on the trail, which now heads downhill. Almost immediately there's a turnoff to the right, which will lead to a third overlook in about 0.75 mile, at Mulholland Drive. Or, finish the loop by skipping the third overlook and continuing on the main trail downhill.

User Groups: Hikers, horses, and dogs. No mountain bikes. No wheelchair facilities.

Permits: No permits are required. Parking and access are free.

Maps: For a topographic map, go to the USGS website to download Beverly Hills.

Directions: From U.S. 101 in Hollywood, exit at Highland Avenue and head south 0.5 mile to Franklin Avenue. Turn right (west) on Franklin. Drive 0.6 mile and turn right (north) on Fuller Avenue. Runyon Canyon Park is in 0.25 mile at the end of Fuller Avenue. Street parking fills up quickly on weekends; beware of permit parking zones on surrounding streets.

Contact: Runyon Canyon Park, Los Angeles, 323/644-6661, www.laparks.org.

28 HASTAIN TRAIL

2.3 mi/1.5 hr

in Franklin Canyon Recreation Area near Beverly Hills

Map 13.1, page 683

Despite being just a few miles from Hollywood and Studio City, Franklin Canyon always seems remarkably peaceful. Once in the canyon, you can't even hear the ever-present hum of the L.A. freeways. A hike on the park's Hastain Trail is a moderate climb on a fire road to an overlook with views of Franklin Canyon, its reservoir, west Los Angeles, and all the way out to the ocean on clear days. The fire road ascends along chaparral-covered slopes. Along the way, you'll enjoy a quintessential L.A. view. If you know what you are looking for, you can pick out the Beverly Hills estate of your favorite celebrity. Beyond the mansions are the Wilshire high-rises, and farther beyond is the serene Pacific Ocean. After nearly a mile, you'll depart the fire road and veer right on a single-track trail that descends to the Doheny ranch house and grassy picnic area below. The ranch served as a weekend retreat for Edward Doheny, who discovered oil in Los Angeles in 1892. Walk back to your car on a trail that parallels the park road. As you hike, be sure to obey all posted trail signs; this trail borders private property and some sections are closed off. Before or after your hike, be sure to stop in at the park's Sooky Goldman Nature Center, where you can learn all about the natural history of the Santa Monica Mountains.

User Groups: Hikers, dogs, and horses. No mountain bikes. No wheelchair facilities.

Permits: No permits are required. Parking and access are free.

Maps: A trail map is available at the Sooky Goldman Nature Center or can be downloaded at www.mrca.ca.gov. For a topographic map, go to the USGS website to download Beverly Hills.

Directions: From U.S. 101 in Studio City, take the Coldwater Canyon exit and drive south for 2.3 miles to the intersection of Mulholland Drive and Franklin Canyon Drive. Turn right on Franklin Canyon Drive. Drive 1.5 miles to the fork with Lake Drive, and bear left on Lake Drive. Just beyond the park entrance, look for a parking area and trailhead at a fire road, on the left.

Contact: Mountains Recreation and

Conservation Authority, Malibu, 310/589-3200 or 310/858-7272, www.mrca.ca.gov.

29 MOUNT HOLLYWOOD

3.0 mi/1.5 hr 2 8

in Griffith Park

Map 13.1, page 683

No trail in Griffith Park is more popular than this one to the top of Mount Hollywood. Why? Because the view from the top is unforgettable. Out-of-towners need to be told that this is not the peak that bears the famous Hollywood sign—that's Mount Lee—although you can see that sign from this peak. Start hiking across the street from the Griffith Observatory's iconic dome (made famous by the film "Rebel Without a Cause" and "La La Land," among others). The road/trail meanders on a gentle grade over sage- and chaparral-covered slopes, offering worthwhile city views at every curve. The wide fire road is simple and straightforward, with no junctions to negotiate until you near the top, where a half-mile loop circles the summit. You'll reach a four-way junction just below, and north of, the summit. Turn left to walk the final few steps to the top. As flat as a pancake and about half the size of a football field, the summit of Mount Hollywood tops out at 1,625 feet in elevation. Check out the view that stretches from downtown all the way out to the ocean. The San Gabriel Mountains loom large in the background, and on the clearest days it is possible to pick out Southern California's big three peaks, far off to the east: Mount Baldy, Mount San Gorgonio, and Mount San Jacinto.

User Groups: Hikers, dogs, and horses. No mountain bikes. No wheelchair facilities.

Permits: No permits are required. Parking and access are free.

Maps: A free map is available at the park ranger station. For a topographic map, go to the USGS website to download Hollywood.

Directions: From U.S. 101 in Hollywood, take the Sunset Boulevard exit and drive east three blocks to Western Avenue. Turn left and go north on Western Avenue for 0.4 mile; the road veers right and becomes Los Feliz Boulevard. Turn left immediately on Fern Dell Drive and drive two miles (it becomes Western Canyon Road) to West Observatory Road. Turn right and drive 0.3 mile; park near the observatory. The trail begins across from the observatory at the Charlie Turner Trailhead.

Alternatively, from I-5 in Los Feliz, exit at Los Feliz Boulevard and head west. Drive 2.4 miles and turn right (north) on Fern Dell Drive. Continue as above.

Contact: Griffith Park Ranger Station, Los Angeles, 323/913-4688 or 323/913-7390, www.laparks.org.

30 BURMA ROAD TO EAGLE'S NEST

2.0 mi/1.0 hr 2 9

in Portuguese Bend Reserve on the Palos Verdes Peninsula

Map 13.1, page 683

The Palos Verdes Peninsula is laced with trails, but most are unmarked and many can only be accessed if you are a resident of one of the Peninsula's exclusive gated communities. But this trail is open to everybody, and it could easily rate as one of the most scenic in Los Angeles County. The trail is part of the 400-acre Portuguese Bend Reserve, the largest of 10 reserves that comprise the Palos Verdes Nature Preserve. It's an easy walk along a fire road to Eagle's Nest in Rancho Palos Verdes. The hike starts where Crenshaw Boulevard ends at its southernmost point. A dirt road begins here, and most people call it Burma Road or Burma Trail, although some still call it Crenshaw Extension. That name remains from the days before the 1956 Portuguese Bend landslide put an end to the developers' dreams to extend the road and build houses all over this area. The hike is simple enough: Just follow the dirt road gently downhill as you enjoy nonstop cerulean blue Catalina Channel views. If you want to get off the wide road, several narrower trails intersect with it, including Peacock Flats Trail and Ailor Trail. In about a mile you'll come to a restored coastal scrub area called Peacock Flats, named for the showy-feathered fowl that roam the neighborhoods. Climb the pine-dotted knoll on your left, known as Eagle's Nest, and marvel at the beauty of the Pacific. This makes a good turnaround spot for a two-mile round-trip, or if you prefer, you can continue wandering farther southward. Either way, you'll have a bit of an ascent to get back to the trailhead, so make sure you bring some water with you, especially on warm days.

User Groups: Hikers, mountain bikes, dogs, and horses. No wheelchair facilities.

Permits: No permits are required. Parking and access are free.

Maps: Trail maps are available for free download at www.pvplc.org.

Directions: From I-110 in Wilmington, exit at Highway 1/Pacific Coast Highway, heading west. Drive three miles to Crenshaw Boulevard and turn left (south). Drive four miles south on Crenshaw Boulevard until it ends in Rancho Palos Verdes (the nearest cross street is Burrell Lane). Park alongside the street or at Del Cerro Park and walk south along Crenshaw until it turns into a dirt road/trail.

Contact: Palos Verdes Peninsula Land Conservancy, Rolling Hills Estates, 310/541-7613, www.pvplc.org.

31 BOLSA CHICA ECOLOGICAL RESERVE

1.5 mi/0.75 hr — 1 — 8

in Huntington Beach

Map 13.1, page 683

What a dichotomy. From the footbridge over the water at Bolsa Chica Ecological Reserve, you can see mussels, minnows, egrets, cordgrass, pickleweed, and huge flocks of shorebirds swirling in unison over the sparkling waters. But just a few hundred yards away, the state beach is lined with RVs, the oil-drilling grasshoppers are doing their monotonous job, and the traffic is crawling past on Highway 1. Where would you rather be? Right. The 1.5-mile loop trail at Bolsa Chica Ecological Reserve reminds us of what our coastline is supposed to look like and who depends on it the most—the birds on the Pacific Flyway. The 530-acre reserve is a migratory rest stop, and the birds are plentiful and fascinating to watch. The trail runs along the top of a levee, providing a vantage point that's just a few feet above the water's edge. What birds will you see? Brown pelicans, widgeons, pie-billed grebes, mergansers, pintails, and terns. If you're lucky, you may even spot a few endangered species, like the Belding's savannah sparrow (an unusual bird because it can drink seawater) or the California least tern. Consider this: For years, private developers have been trying to pave over this place and build pricey homes and condominiums, but so far, the birds are winning. We're rooting for them.

If you want to hike with a trained naturalist, show up on the first Saturday of any month at 9am. Bring a jacket and binoculars and plan on getting a well-rounded education on bird identification, ecology, and endangered species.

User Groups: Hikers only. No dogs, horses, or mountain bikes. No wheelchair facilities.

Permits: No permits are required. Parking and access are free.

Maps: For a topographic map, go to the USGS website to download Seal Beach.

Directions: From I-405 in Seal Beach, exit at Seal Beach Boulevard and drive west to Highway 1. Turn south on Highway 1 and drive 4.5 miles to the Bolsa Chica Ecological Reserve entrance on the inland side of the highway, across from Bolsa Chica State Beach.

Contact: Amigos de Bolsa Chica, Huntington Beach, 714/840-1575, www.amigosdebolsachica.org.

32 TWO HARBORS TO EMERALD BAY

9.0 mi/5.0 hr 2 9

on Catalina Island

Map 13.1, page 683

If you want to take a hiking trip to Catalina Island, but you don't want your trip to be complicated or crowded with people, follow this one key instruction: Take the ferry to Two Harbors, not to Avalon. This applies whether you are going for the day or staying overnight. From the ferry drop point at Two Harbors pier, you can pick up your hiking permit and begin hiking right away on the West End Road, a dirt road that is nearly level and sticks close to the shoreline for its entire route. Head west—getting eyefuls of rocky outcrops, steep headlands, beckoning coves, and the beautiful blue Pacific—until at 1.25 miles you reach Cherry Valley and Cherry Cove. The area is named for the native Catalina cherry tree that grows there, which displays beautiful white flowers in the spring. Continue hiking on the flat dirt road, passing Howland Landing at almost four miles out. Stay far away from the plentiful No Trespassing signs there. Remain on the road until you see an obvious cutoff trail on your right leading to beautiful Emerald Bay, at 4.5 miles. Have a picnic on the gorgeous white-sand beach and ponder how amazing it is to have this fabulous island so close to Los Angeles.

Although this excursion makes a fine day trip getaway from the mainland, your best bet is to spend the night in Two Harbors (either camping or in more luxurious accommodations), then continue hiking and exploring the next day. If you're on a day trip, you'll have to be back in Two Harbors in time for the boat ride home.

User Groups: Hikers only. No dogs, horses, or mountain bikes. No wheelchair facilities.

Permits: A free Santa Catalina Island hiking permit is required and may be obtained on the day of your hike from Two Harbors Visitors Center, or in advance at www.catalinaconservancy.org. Fees are charged for the ferry from the mainland to Two Harbors.

Maps: A trail map of Catalina Island is provided when you pick up your hiking permit. For a topographic map, go to the USGS website to download Santa Catalina West.

Directions: Catalina Express provides ferry transportation to Two Harbors from San Pedro. As of September 2019, fares are approximately $75 per adult round-trip.

Contact: Two Harbors Visitor Services, Two Harbors, 310/510-0303, www.catalina.com; Santa Catalina Island Conservancy, 310/510-2595, www.catalinaconservancy.org; boat trips: Catalina Express, 310/519-1212 or 800/481-3470, www.catalinaexpress.com.

33 EMPIRE LANDING ROAD TRAIL

8.3 mi one-way/4.0 hr 2 9

on Catalina Island

Map 13.1, page 683

This spectacular one-way hiking trip on Catalina Island requires a bare minimum of planning in exchange for tremendous rewards. First, you have to arrange to take the ferry from the mainland to Avalon, Catalina's "big city." When you arrive, you must pick up your free hiking permit in town and take the shuttle bus from Avalon to Airport in the Sky. That's where your hike on the Empire Landing Road finally begins. Along its 8.3-mile length, you'll travel along the north side of the island on a curvy, up-and-down road that passes by a marble quarry, numerous coves and beaches, and fascinating rock formations. If you're lucky, you'll see an island fox, a huge bison, or maybe even a wild turkey.

When the trail ends at Two Harbors, you have three choices: Take the bus shuttle back to Avalon, camp or stay at the various lodgings in Two Harbors, or take the ferry from Two Harbors back to the mainland. For the latter two possibilities, you must plan in advance. If you want to take the ferry back to the mainland, you need to alert the ferry company that you're going in to Avalon but leaving from Two Harbors. There is no extra fee for this service, but you have to make sure you finish your hike in time to catch the last boat. One more thing to consider: When is the best time of year to visit Catalina? Unquestionably, it's spring or fall, when the weather is good and the summer crowds are nonexistent.

User Groups: Hikers only. No dogs, horses, or mountain bikes. No wheelchair facilities.

Permits: A free Santa Catalina Island hiking permit is required and may be obtained on the day of your hike from the Santa Catalina Island Conservancy, the Catalina Island Interpretive Center, or at the Catalina Airport, or in advance at www.catalinaconservancy.org. Fees are charged for the ferry from the mainland to Avalon, and for the shuttle bus from Avalon to the airport.

Maps: A trail map of Catalina Island is provided when you pick up your hiking permit. For a topographic map, go to the USGS website to download Santa Catalina.

Directions: Several companies, including Catalina Express and Catalina Flyer, provide ferry transportation to Avalon from San Pedro, Long Beach, Dana Point, and Newport Beach. As of September 2019, fares are approximately $75 per adult round-trip.

Contact: Santa Catalina Island Conservancy, 310/510-2595, www.catalinaconservancy.org; Two Harbors Visitor Services, 310/510-0303 (lodging and campgrounds), www.catalina.com (general information, permits); boat trips: Catalina Express, 310/519-1212 or 800/481-3470, www.catalinaexpress.com; Catalina Flyer, 949/673-5245, www.catalina-tickets.com; air transport: Island Express, 800/228-2566; inter-island shuttle service, 310/510-0143.

34 DEVIL'S PUNCHBOWL LOOP

1.0 mi/0.5 hr

in the Devil's Punchbowl Natural Area south of Pearblossom

Map 13.2, page 684

The Devil's Punchbowl is visual proof that you're in earthquake country, where faulting and erosion have made bizarre shapes out of ancient sedimentary rocks. They thrust and jut upward, creating vertical walls as high as 300 feet, and they look as if they're about to topple inward on each other. From the viewpoint behind the visitors center, you look down into the land of the devil: the Punchbowl, a giant abyss that is the working of the San Andreas Fault and the result of centuries of stream carving. Juniper, piñon pine, and manzanita manage to eke out a meager living amid all the sandstone. The park's easy, one-mile loop trail offers fine views into the depths of the Punchbowl. It switchbacks gently downhill to the canyon bottom and then climbs back up, passing by some of the taller rock slabs in the park. Here's a great tip: Park rangers hold full-moon hikes here once a month in the summer. Note: If you find this type of geological action fascinating, you may want to hike the park's longer trail to the dramatic Devil's Chair, a breathtaking overlook above the Punchbowl. Make sure you stop in at the nature center here at Devil's Punchbowl, where you can see its excellent display of wild birds.

User Groups: Hikers, dogs, and horses. No mountain bikes. No wheelchair facilities.

Permits: No permits are required. Parking and access are free.

Maps: Free trail maps are available at the nature center. For a topographic map, go to the USGS website to download Valyermo.

Directions: From Highway 14 near Palmdale, take the Highway 138 exit east for 16 miles to Pearblossom. Turn right on County Road N-6 (Longview Road) and drive south for 7.5 miles to the Devil's Punchbowl entrance. (The road makes several turns and changes names all the way, but all junctions are signed for the park.) From the park entrance, continue another 0.25 mile to the parking lot by the nature center. The trail begins behind the park nature center.

Contact: Devil's Punchbowl Natural Area, Pearblossom, 661/944-2743, www.devils-punchbowl.com.

35 BURKHARDT TRAIL TO THE DEVIL'S CHAIR

7.0 mi/3.5 hr 3 9

in the Devil's Punchbowl Natural Area south of Pearblossom

Map 13.2, page 684

This is one of the most interesting and enjoyable hikes in the entire Los Angeles area, although, for a lot of people, it's a long drive to get here. It's worth it even if you may not think so in the first 20 minutes or so of hiking, where the trail leaves the Devil's Punchbowl parking lot and quickly joins a boring dirt road set in rather barren terrain. Finally, after 0.9 mile of steady climbing on this uninspiring road/trail, you reach a sign for the Devil's Chair Trail, a left turnoff. Follow it and immediately you are in the pines and walking on a smoothly graded, pleasant trail. You'll cross Punchbowl Creek and enter an easy grade as you lateral across the slopes above the Devil's Punchbowl. The trail undulates gently up and down, crossing one small ravine after another. As you gradually gain elevation, you also gain views of the white rocks of the Devil's Punchbowl and the desert beyond. Two different rocky promontories, just off the trail, provide particularly imposing viewpoints.

At a junction with a trail coming in from South Fork Campground, go left and begin the final leg of your journey. Surprisingly, the final jaunt to the Devil's Chair is downhill. To be exact, it's 10 short switchbacks downhill. The last 50 yards of the path, which follow a narrow backbone ridge to the Chair itself, are so prone to erosion that the trail is encased in a tunnel of fencing. Have a seat on the Devil's Chair and enjoy this surreal scene for a while, then retrace your steps and go back up those switchbacks.

User Groups: Hikers, dogs, horses, and mountain bikes. No wheelchair facilities.

Permits: No permits are required. Parking and access are free.

Maps: Free trail maps are available at the nature center. For a topographic map, go to the USGS website to download Valyermo.

Directions: From Highway 14 near Palmdale, take the Highway 138 exit east for 16 miles to Pearblossom. Turn right on County Road N-6 (Longview Road) and drive south for 7.5 miles to the Devil's Punchbowl entrance. (The road makes several turns and changes names all the way, but all junctions are signed for the park.) From the park entrance, continue another 0.25 mile to the parking lot by the nature center. The Burkhardt Trail begins on the south side of the parking lot.

Contact: Devil's Punchbowl Natural Area, Pearblossom, 661/944-2743, www.devils-punchbowl.com.

36 COOPER CANYON FALLS

3.6 mi/2.0 hr 2 9

in San Gabriel Mountains National Monument

Map 13.2, page 684

After the snow has melted, here's a first-rate reason to make the 34-mile drive to the high country of the Angeles Crest Highway: a visit to Cooper Canyon Falls. The waterfall is set in a beautiful, 6,000-foot-elevation forest, a dependably cool place on any hot day in L.A. Start your hike north of Buckhorn Campground, at the trailhead parking lot for Burkhart Trail. The hike is a mostly downhill trip through a dense forest of big firs, cedars, and pines. There's almost no undergrowth in these woods—just conifers and big rocks. It feels as if you're in the southern Sierra Nevada, but, no, this is the San Gabriels. The Burkhart Trail laterals along the canyon slopes, high above Buckhorn Creek, then makes a left turn into Cooper Canyon and traces a long switchback downhill. At 1.75 miles from the camp, you'll reach a junction with the Pacific Crest Trail. Turn right, toward Burkhart Saddle and Eagle's Roost. It's only 300 feet to the waterfall, which drops just below the trail's edge. Some hikers choose to scramble down the steep cliff to its base, where you can stand on an island of boulders and enjoy the falls' noisy, 35-foot drop. Be sure to get here early in the year, when the stream flow is still strong. Trailhead elevation is 6,300 feet.

User Groups: Hikers, dogs, and horses. Mountain bikes are allowed on the Burkhart Trail but not on the Pacific Crest Trail. No wheelchair facilities.

Permits: No permits are required. A National Forest Adventure Pass is required for each vehicle; fees are $5 for one day or $30 for a year. Interagency access passes are also accepted.

Maps: An Angeles National Forest map is available from the U.S. Forest Service. Maps of the Angeles Front Country and High Country are available from Tom Harrison Maps. For a topographic map, go to the USGS website to download Waterman Mountain.

Directions: From I-210 in La Cañada, take Highway 2/Angeles Crest Highway northeast for 35 miles to Buckhorn Campground, on the left. It's 1.2 miles past the Mount Waterman ski lift, and just beyond Cloudburst Summit. Continue just beyond the campground to the trailhead parking lot.

Contact: Angeles National Forest, Los Angeles River Ranger District, San Fernando, 818/899-1900, www.fs.usda.gov/angeles.

37 MOUNT WATERMAN

5.6 mi/3.0 hr 2 10

in San Gabriel Mountains National Monument

Map 13.2, page 684

The peak of Mount Waterman (at 8,038 feet) is a fine destination for a moderate day hike in the San Gabriel Mountains, and the view from the summit is one you won't soon forget. The only problem that awaits is figuring out which peak is really the peak, because the top of Mount Waterman is so wide that there are three summits. From the trailhead (elevation 6,700 feet), you simply head uphill on remarkably smooth, well-graded single track. The ascent is partially shaded by a mixed pine, cedar, and fir forest. At one mile out, you'll reach a saddle where your views open wide, taking in the Mojave Desert and the San Gabriel Wilderness. Climb some more, through long switchbacks, to a junction at 2.1 miles, then turn right for the summit. It's an easy 0.6 mile to the peak. Keep your eyes peeled for Nelson Bighorn sheep, which are sometimes seen in the area. Also check out the huge sugar pine cones that are found alongside the trail. When you reach the flat top of Mount Waterman, the trail heads east and then south to the highest of Waterman's summits, atop a jumble of boulders. This spot provides the best possible view, looking out over the magnificent San Gabriel Mountains. On the clearest days, you can see all the way to 10,834-foot Mount San Jacinto, standing sentinel above Palm Springs. Total elevation gain along this trail is 1,300 feet.

User Groups: Hikers, dogs, horses, and mountain bikes. No wheelchair facilities.

Permits: No permits are required. A National Forest Adventure Pass is required for each vehicle; fees are $5 for one day or $30 for a year. Interagency access passes are also accepted.

Maps: An Angeles National Forest map is available from the U.S. Forest Service. Maps of the Angeles Front Country and High Country are available from Tom Harrison Maps. For a topographic map, go to the USGS website to download Waterman Mountain.

Directions: From I-210 in La Cañada, take Highway 2/Angeles Crest Highway northeast for 34 miles to the signed trailhead for the Mount Waterman Trail on the right (south) side of the road, east of the Mount Waterman ski lift operation and west of Buckhorn Campground.

Park in the pullout across the road from the trailhead sign.

Contact: Angeles National Forest, Los Angeles River Ranger District, San Fernando, 818/899-1900, www.fs.usda.gov/angeles.

38 MOUNT WILLIAMSON

5.0 mi/3.0 hr 3 10

in San Gabriel Mountains National Monument

Map 13.2, page 684 BEST

This summit trail feels a bit rougher and more remote than those to many other peaks in the San Gabriel Mountains, and it's famous for its steep dropoffs. But the trail's total elevation gain is only 1,600 feet, and the visual rewards are tremendous. Mount Williamson is on the north side of the Angeles Crest Highway, which means that although you are hiking in a mountain environment, you're on the desert side of the mountain. The forest on this slope is more sparse (the upper slopes are dotted with wind-sculpted Jeffrey pines), the trail is more exposed, and many of the best vistas are of the western Mojave Desert, to the north. Even if you're not in the mood to climb to the 8,214-foot summit, you can hike to a saddle at 1.9 miles out, where the Pacific Crest Trail drops down to the west. Views to the south are excellent here, with a big chunk of the San Gabriel Mountains spread out before you. From the saddle, take the summit trail on your right, heading 0.6 mile farther north on a remarkably steep grade. (A few switchbacks would be convenient here, but there are none.) Although the views have been excellent all along, nothing prepares you for the scene on top of Mount Williamson's narrow ridgeline, which offers dizzying views on both sides. The San Gabriels are on your left, and on the clearest days you can see far beyond them to the L.A. basin and the Pacific Ocean. A vast sweep of Mojave Desert is on your right, 5,000 feet below. Don't turn around at the first pointy summit you reach; follow the backbone trail a bit farther to a second and flatter summit, which is 30 feet higher. The view from here is even more extraordinary—you can look directly down into the Devil's Punchbowl and the San Andreas Fault. All in all, it's an extraordinary place.

User Groups: Hikers, dogs, and horses. No mountain bikes. No wheelchair facilities.

Permits: No permits are required. A National Forest Adventure Pass is required for each vehicle; fees are $5 for one day or $30 for a year. Interagency access passes are also accepted.

Maps: An Angeles National Forest map is available from the U.S. Forest Service. Maps of the Angeles Front Country and High Country are available from Tom Harrison Maps. For a topographic map, go to the USGS website to download Crystal Lake.

Directions: From I-210 in La Cañada, take Highway 2/Angeles Crest Highway northeast and drive 42 miles to Islip Saddle (one mile east of the tunnels). Park in the large parking lot on the north side of the road; the trail begins by the restrooms. (If you are coming from Highway 138 near Phelan or Piñon Hills, take Highway 2/Angeles Crest Highway west for 25 miles to Islip Saddle, 16 miles west of Big Pine.)

Contact: Angeles National Forest, Los Angeles River Ranger District, San Fernando, 818/899-1900, www.fs.usda.gov/angeles.

39 VINCENT GAP TO MOUNT BADEN-POWELL

8.0 mi/4.0 hr 4 10

in San Gabriel Mountains National Monument

Map 13.2, page 684

Like the climb to the summit of Mount Baldy, the climb to the summit of Mount Baden-Powell is something of a requirement for Southern California hikers. Luckily, this requirement is a little easier to attain, because the Pacific Crest Trail heading up to Mount Baden-Powell is a mere eight-mile round-trip with a 2,800-foot elevation gain. The summit of Baden-Powell is at 9,399 feet and is directly across the East Fork San Gabriel River Basin from, and slightly northwest of, Mount Baldy. As you might guess, the views from the summit are extraordinary. The summit area is also a botanist's delight, as 2,000-year-old limber pines can be found growing there. From the southwest edge of Vincent Gap, the Pacific Crest Trail leads through open forest—first oak, sugar pine, and Jeffrey pine, and as you climb, mostly lodgepole pine and occasional limber pines. The trail is extremely well maintained, with 42 switchbacks following a moderate grade all the way up. A quarter mile from the top, you leave the Pacific Crest Trail and follow the summit trail south (left). Once on top, you can see more than a vertical mile below you to the East Fork San Gabriel River Basin. Mount Baldy is of course prominent, as is the Mojave Desert, Catalina Island, Mount San Jacinto, and Mount San Gorgonio. In case you haven't heard, the British Lord Baden-Powell, for whom this peak is named, founded the Boy Scouts organization. The Scouts have placed a monument to him at the summit.

User Groups: Hikers, dogs, and horses. No mountain bikes. No wheelchair facilities.

Permits: No permits are required. A National Forest Adventure Pass is required for each vehicle; fees are $5 for one day or $30 for a year. Interagency access passes are also accepted.

Maps: An Angeles National Forest map is available from the U.S. Forest Service. An Angeles High Country map is available from Tom Harrison Maps. For topographic maps, go to the USGS website to download Crystal Lake and Mount San Antonio.

Directions: From I-210 in La Cañada, take Highway 2/Angeles Crest Highway northeast and drive 53 miles to Vincent Gap. Follow the Pacific Crest Trail uphill from the parking lot. If you are coming from Highway 138 near Phelan or Piñon Hills, take Highway 2/Angeles Crest Highway west for 15 miles to Vincent Gap, which is 5.5 miles west of Big Pines.

Contact: Angeles National Forest, Santa Clara/Mojave Rivers Ranger District, Acton, 661/269-2808, www.fs.usda.gov/angeles; Big Pines Visitors Center, 760/249-3504.

40 BIG HORN MINE

4.0 mi/2.0 hr

in San Gabriel Mountains National Monument

Map 13.2, page 684

If you want to get a good look at a piece of California history, take this easy walk to the Big Horn Mine, probably the most impressive of all Southern California mine sites. The mine was founded in 1894 by Civil War veteran Charles Tom Vincent, a Civil War veteran who discovered a rich vein of ore while hunting for Bighorn sheep. Although the mine reportedly produced as much as $200,000 in gold during its good years, roughly 1902 to 1910, neither Vincent nor anybody else ever got rich. An abundance of mine ruins remain at the site, and the trail itself is the mine's old wagon road. Follow the gated road from Vincent Gap, passing a water-filled shaft and some debris left from the cabins that housed the miners. Soon you round a bend and see the long-abandoned stamp mill building perched precariously on a hillside. Years ago hikers were able to explore this ramshackle building and walk through the mine tunnels, but now everything is gated off in the interest of safety. Be sure to obey all the "no trespassing" signs. (Rumors abound that the Forest Service intends to destroy these ruins completely, but as of late 2019, they are still intact. For updates, check with the Big Pines Visitors Center, 760/249-3504). Choose a spot nearby and pull out your lunch. From this perch at about 7,000 feet in elevation, you'll enjoy fine views across the gorge of the East Fork San Gabriel River to Mount Baldy and its sibling peaks. On your way to or from the mine site, be sure to take the 0.5-mile side trail that leads to the remains of Vincent's cabin, where he lived as a recluse for more than 40 years. The turnoff is at the Sheep Mountain Wilderness sign, just 150 yards from the trailhead.

User Groups: Hikers, dogs, and horses. No mountain bikes. No wheelchair facilities.
Permits: A free Sheep Mountain Wilderness permit is required; they are available at the trailhead. A National Forest Adventure Pass is required for each vehicle; fees are $5 for one day or $30 for a year. Interagency access passes are also accepted.
Maps: An Angeles National Forest map is available from the U.S. Forest Service. An Angeles High Country map is available from Tom Harrison Maps. For topographic maps, go to the USGS website to download Crystal Lake and Mount San Antonio.
Directions: From I-210 in La Cañada, take Highway 2/Angeles Crest Highway northeast and drive 53 miles to Vincent Gap. Park on the south side of the highway and start hiking on the gated road (not the nearby trails). If you are coming from Highway 138 near Phelan or Piñon Hills, take Highway 2/Angeles Crest Highway west for 15 miles to Vincent Gap, which is 5.5 miles west of Big Pines.
Contact: Angeles National Forest, Santa Clara/Mojave Rivers Ranger District, Acton, 661/269-2808, www.fs.usda.gov/angeles.

Fish Canyon Falls

41 FISH CANYON FALLS

5.2 mi/2.5 hr  2 10

in Angeles National Forest near Duarte

Map 13.2, page 684

Note: The devastating San Gabriel Complex Fire of 2016 damaged many sections of the Fish Canyon Trail, and as of September 2019, it is still closed. Check with the city of Duarte about future trail opening dates (www.accessduarte.com).

Fish Canyon Falls is one of the loveliest waterfalls set in one of the most beautiful canyons in the San Gabriel Mountains, and yet for many years, accessing the falls has been problematic. Many decades ago, you could hike right to the falls on an easy trail through Fish Canyon, but access to the trailhead was blocked by the expansion of a private rock quarry owned by the Azusa Rock Company (a.k.a. Vulcan Materials). For most of the 1980s and 1990s, hikers had no access at all to Fish Canyon. Then, in 1998, a three-mile-long bypass trail was created to solve the problem, but the trail was steep, loose, narrow, riddled with poison oak, and didn't have nearly enough switchbacks. For a decade afterward, hikers endured this arduous 9.4-mile round-trip trek for the chance to see the prized 80-foot-high falls. But in 2014, the Azusa Rock Company built a 0.7-mile fenced access trail that allows hikers to pass through the quarry's private property and deposits them at the old trailhead to Fish Canyon, located on adjacent Angeles National Forest land. The access trail opens at 7am daily and closes at 7pm April-September and at 5pm October-March. You must make sure that your car is out of the parking lot by closing time or it will be towed. Also, dog lovers take note: You can only bring Fido on this trail on Saturdays and Sundays.

Once you reach the back of the quarry, you

cross a bridge over Fish Creek and are walking in lovely Fish Canyon. Waterfall lovers, rejoice. The Fish Canyon Trail meanders gently uphill, sticking closely to Fish Creek and passing by the ruins of old cabins from the early 1900s. The path tops out at a high box canyon, where the waterfall is found. If the water flow is high, Fish Canyon Falls is a stunner, dropping 80 feet in four stair-stepped tiers.

User Groups: Hikers only. Dogs are allowed only on Saturdays and Sundays. No horses or mountain bikes. No wheelchair facilities.

Permits: No permits are required. Parking and access are free.

Maps: A Fish Canyon trail guide, with a topographical map, is available from the city of Duarte (and is also usually available from a signboard near the trail's start).

Directions: From the junction of I-210 and I-605 near Duarte, follow I-605 north to its end, then turn right (east) on Huntington Drive. Drive 0.6 mile and turn left on Encanto Parkway. In about a mile it turns into Fish Canyon Road; keep going until it ends. Enter through the Access Trail gate at the Azusa Rock quarry (3901 Fish Canyon Road).

Contact: City of Duarte Parks and Recreation Department, Duarte, 626/357-7931, www.accessduarte.com; Azusa Rock quarry, www.azusarock.com.

42 SAN ANTONIO FALLS

1.5 mi/1.0 hr  1 9

in San Gabriel Mountains National Monument

Map 13.2, page 684

Mount Baldy is that big mountain that you can see from almost everywhere in the Los Angeles Basin (on a clear day), and if you hike the trail to San Antonio Falls, you'll be able to see almost everywhere in the Los Angeles Basin. Trailhead elevation is 6,160 feet, a fine elevation to start at if you like clean, fresh, mountain air. For the best waterfall show, you've got to time your trip carefully for the first warm days after winter, sometimes as early as March, when the snow melts off the mountain and pours into 80-foot San Antonio Falls. By early summer, the waterfall show is over. The hike to the falls is easy, following the Mount Baldy ski lift maintenance road, which is paved and has only a slight uphill grade. At 0.7 mile, you round a sharp curve and see the falls, gracefully dropping in three tiers. If you wish, you can follow a well-worn path through loose gravel and talus to the waterfall's base, but be careful on the unstable slope. One of the best parts of this trip comes on your return walk to the trailhead. You're witness to lofty views of the far-away San Gabriel Basin as you stroll back down the road.

User Groups: Hikers, dogs, horses, and mountain bikes. No wheelchair facilities.

Permits: No permits are required. A National Forest Adventure Pass is required for each vehicle; fees are $5 for one day or $30 for a year. Interagency access passes are also accepted.

Maps: An Angeles National Forest map is available from the U.S. Forest Service. A Mount Baldy map is available from Tom Harrison Maps. For a topographic map, go to the USGS website to download Mount San Antonio.

Directions: From I-210 in Upland, take the Mountain Avenue/Mount Baldy exit and drive north for 4.3 miles (Mountain Avenue becomes Shinn Road). At a T-junction with Mount Baldy Road, turn right and drive nine miles to San Antonio Falls Road on the left, 0.3 mile past Manker Flats Campround. Park in the dirt pullouts by Falls Road and begin walking on the gated, paved road.

Contact: Angeles National Forest, San Gabriel River Ranger District, Glendora, 626/335-1251, www.fs.usda.gov/angeles; Mount Baldy Visitors Center, 909/982-2829.

43 MOUNT BALDY

13.6 mi/8.0 hr 5 10

in San Gabriel Mountains National Monument

Map 13.2, page 684 BEST

You just can't call yourself a Southern California hiker until you've climbed to the top of Mount Baldy (elevation 10,064 feet), the highest peak in the San Gabriel Mountains. The shortest and easiest route (which is neither short nor easy, with a 13.6-mile round-trip and a 3,500-foot elevation gain) starts from San Antonio Falls Road. Follow the trail to San Antonio Falls (see listing in this chapter), but from the waterfall, continue uphill on the road for another 3.5 miles to Mount Baldy Notch. Go left and follow another fire road 1.4 miles, mostly in the shade of stately conifers, to the upper end of the ski lift. At the top of the upper lift, you access the infamous Devil's Backbone, a steep and jagged ridge. Some hikers find this section of trail, with its sheer dropoffs on both sides into the Lytle Creek Canyon and San Antonio Canyon, to be quite hair-raising. Soon you'll pass the south side of Mount Harwood at 9,552 feet (really just a high bump on Baldy's ridge), and then reach a wind-blown saddle between Harwood and Baldy. A few gnarled, wind-sculpted limber pines eke out a living in this barren terrain. From the saddle, it's only a short tromp to the top, but this is the steepest stretch of the entire day. When you finally reach Baldy's rock-strewn summit, what can you see? If it's a clear day, it's the best vista in the San Gabriel Mountains. Just about everything comes into view—desert, city, ocean, the peaks of the San Bernardino Mountains, even a few high summits of the southern Sierra and Death Valley, 130 miles distant. The earlier in the season you take this hike, the better your chance for good visibility. But there's a caveat: unless you are an experienced mountaineer, don't think about making the trip until the Devil's Backbone is free of snow and ice, which is usually in late May. The Devil's Backbone stretch is extremely treacherous in icy conditions.

If you want to cut seven miles and 1,300 feet of elevation gain off your round-trip, you can ride the Mount Baldy ski lift up to Baldy Notch, rather than hiking 3.5 miles up (and then down) San Antonio Falls Road. The ski lift operates only on weekends and holidays during the hiking season, however. By the way, in case you were wondering, Mount Baldy's formal name is Mount San Antonio. "Baldy" has just been its nickname for as long as anybody can remember.

User Groups: Hikers and dogs. No horses or mountain bikes. No wheelchair facilities.

Permits: A free campfire permit is required for hikers using a backpacking stove (no open fires permitted). A National Forest Adventure Pass is required for each vehicle; fees are $5 for one day or $30 for a year. Interagency access passes are also accepted.

Maps: An Angeles National Forest map is available from the U.S. Forest Service. A Mount Baldy map is available from Tom Harrison Maps. For topographic maps, go to the USGS website to download Mount San Antonio and Telegraph Peak.

Directions: From I-210 in Upland, take the Mountain Avenue/Mount Baldy exit and drive north for 4.3 miles (Mountain Avenue becomes Shinn Road). At a T-junction with Mount Baldy Road, turn right and drive nine miles to San Antonio Falls Road on the left, 0.3 mile past Manker Flats Campround. Park in the dirt pullouts by Falls Road and begin walking on the gated, paved road.

Contact: Angeles National Forest, San Gabriel River Ranger District, Glendora, 626/335-1251, www.fs.usda.gov/angeles; Mount Baldy Visitors Center, 909/982-2829.

44 ICEHOUSE SADDLE

7.2 mi/4.0 hr 3 9

in the Cucamonga Wilderness, San Gabriel Mountains National Monument

Map 13.2, page 684

When it's wintertime in Southern California and you get the itch to throw a few snowballs, where do you go? Icehouse Canyon on Mount Baldy, of course. But Icehouse Canyon is good in the summer, too, especially if you want a hiking escape far from the smog of the Inland Empire. You can go for as long or as short as you like in the canyon—it's a great place to just set out from your car, climb until you're tired, then turn around and head back. The canyon got its name in the 1850s, when 100-pound blocks of ice were carved from its frigid stream canyon and carried by mule-drawn wagon to satisfy the thirst of the growing city of Los Angeles.

Many people don't hike very far in the canyon before picking a spot to sit and relax by the cold, clear water, but if you're looking for a destination, Icehouse Saddle at 7,580 feet is a good one, perfect for picnicking, with lovely views to the east and west. The saddle is also the site of a major trail junction, where routes lead in four directions, including the famous Three Ts Trail that travels to Timber Mountain, Telegraph Peak, and Thunder Mountain. The Icehouse Canyon Trail begins by passing a few summer cabins, some still in use and others in ruins. The trail sticks close to the stunningly clear stream that runs all the way through the canyon. The surrounding forest is a lovely mix of oak, big-cone Douglas fir, pine, fir, and cedar. At one mile in, you reach a junction with the Chapman Trail. Both the Chapman and Icehouse Canyon Trails lead to Icehouse Saddle, but the Icehouse Canyon Trail stays along the creek and gets to Icehouse Saddle sooner via a steeper grade. Stay on your trail and at 1.8 miles, you reach a Cucamonga Wilderness boundary sign, where you must fill out a free permit if you have not already done so at the Mount Baldy Visitors Center in town. From here, you have another 1.8 miles to go, with a total 2,600-foot elevation gain from the trailhead. It's an aerobic ascent for sure. You'll pass trickling Columbine Spring at 2.8 miles, then a second junction with the Chapman Trail at 3.0 miles. If you like, you can make a semi-loop back from Icehouse Saddle by following the Chapman Trail, which will make this an 8.8-mile round-trip. Along the way, the trail camp at Cedar Flats (also called Cedar Glen) offers another fine rest stop.

User Groups: Hikers, dogs, and horses. No mountain bikes. No wheelchair facilities.

Permits: A free wilderness permit is required for both day hiking and backpacking in the Cucamonga Wilderness and is available from the Mount Baldy Visitors Center or at the self-serve permit kiosk along the trail at the Cucamonga Wilderness boundary. A National Forest Adventure Pass is required for each vehicle; fees are $5 for one day or $30 for a year. Interagency access passes are also accepted.

Maps: An Angeles National Forest map is available from the U.S. Forest Service. A Mount Baldy map is available from Tom Harrison Maps. For topographic maps, go to the USGS website to download Cucamonga Peak and Telegraph Peak.

Directions: From I-210 in Upland, take the Mountain Avenue/Mount Baldy exit and drive north for 4.3 miles (Mountain Avenue becomes Shinn Road). At a T-junction with Mount Baldy Road, turn right and drive 6.4 miles, then bear right on Ice House Canyon Road. Drive 100 yards to the parking lot at the end of the road.

Contact: Angeles National Forest, San Gabriel River Ranger District, Glendora, 626/335-1251, www.fs.usda.gov/angeles; Mount Baldy Visitors Center, 909/982-2829.

45 ETIWANDA FALLS

3.0 mi/1.5 hr 

in North Etiwanda Preserve in Rancho Cucamonga

Map 13.2, page 684

There's a waterfall in Rancho Cucamonga? Why, as a matter of fact, there is. Way out there in the inner Inland Empire, where it is more often hot and dry than wet and watery, lies beautiful Etiwanda Falls, the prize of North Etiwanda Preserve. Not only that, but the preserve is also home to several endangered, threatened, and sensitive species, including the coastal California gnatcatcher, Southwestern willow flycatcher, least Bell's vireo, San Bernardino kangaroo rat, rufous-crowned sparrow, and San Diego horned lizard.

From the preserve trailhead, getting to the falls is easy. Simply hike north, following the main fire road and enjoying fine views of the high peaks above Rancho Cucamonga. At 0.3 mile from the start, you'll reach a fork with a sign pointing right for the picnic area and left for the trail. Don't go left or right; instead, stay straight, hiking around a large metal gate and staying on the fire road. From here it is another 1.2 miles to the falls, heading gently-to-moderately uphill on the rocky fire road. Ignore all the side roads and just keep heading straight. In the last half-mile you'll hike past a second metal gate, this one painted bright yellow. There is no mistaking the roar of the 40-foot cascade; the falls drop over bright-orange-colored rocks in a glorious rush of noisy whitewater.

User Groups: Hikers and horses. No dogs or mountain bikes. No wheelchair facilities.

Permits: No permits are required. Parking and access are free.

Maps: A trail map is available at the trailhead or by free download at www.specialdistricts.org.

Directions: From the junction of I-210 and I-15, take I-15 south and exit at Baseline Road. Drive 0.5 mile west on Baseline Road, then turn right (north) on Etiwanda Avenue. Drive 2.2 miles north on Etiwanda Avenue to its junction with Wilson Avenue. Bear left (west) on Wilson Avenue for about 100 yards to where it reconnects with Etiwanda Avenue, then turn right and continue on Etiwanda for one more mile until it dead-ends at the parking lot of North Etiwanda Preserve.

Contact: San Bernardino County Special Districts Department, San Bernardino, 909/387-5940, www.specialdistricts.org.

46 SEELEY CREEK TRAIL

2.0 mi/1.0 hr 2 9

in San Bernardino National Forest near Crestline

Map 13.2, page 684

To reach the start of the Seeley Creek Trail, you have to drive through a town called Valley of Enchantment, and that should tell you just about all you need to know about the area and the trail. It's beautiful up here—no, let's say it's enchanting—and although the elevation is only 4,000 feet, the conifers grow so big you'll think you're in the southern Sierra. The Seeley Creek Trail is a short and easy walk to a destination called Heart Rock, which, during periods of rain or after snowmelt, becomes Heart Rock Falls. Heart Rock is a smooth giant boulder in which nature has carved a perfect, heart-shaped bowl, about three feet deep and five feet wide. When Seeley Creek is running strong, a 25-foot waterfall spills into the heart's crown, then flows out the bottom and free falls downward. The stream flows year-round, and Heart Rock is always fascinating to see, but it's most compelling when the waterfall is flowing strong. The trail begins in a rather pedestrian fashion, along a road opposite the buildings of Seeley Camp, a Los Angeles Parks and Recreation camp. But once you walk beyond the camp boundary, the enchantment begins.

User Groups: Hikers, dogs, horses, and mountain bikes. No wheelchair facilities.

Permits: No permits are required. Parking and access are free.

Maps: A San Bernardino National Forest map is available from the U.S. Forest Service. For a topographic map, go to the USGS website to download San Bernardino North.

Directions: From I-10 near San Bernardino, take I-215 north five miles to Highway 30 east. Drive two miles east on Highway 30 and exit on Highway 18/Waterman Avenue. Drive north on Highway 18 for about 20 miles to the junction of Highways 18 and 138. Turn north on Highway 138 and drive 2.5 miles to the sign for Camp Seeley, just past the town of Valley of Enchantment. Turn left at the camp sign on Road 2N03 and take the left fork in the road (don't park in the camp parking lot). Cross the creek, which usually flows over the road, and look for the double-track trail on the right, near a sewer pipeline sign. Park alongside the road. You will be directly across the creek from the main parking lot for Camp Seeley, near the playground area.

Contact: San Bernardino National Forest, Big Bear Discovery Center, Fawnskin, 909/382-2790, www.fs.usda.gov/sbnf.

47 DEEP CREEK HOT SPRINGS

4.0 mi/2.0 hr 

in San Bernardino National Forest near Hesperia

Map 13.2, page 684

This trail is not the highlight of this trip, but its destination is. Deep Creek's hot springs are well known, well loved, and heavily visited. Although there are a few ways to hike to them, this route is the most popular simply because it's the shortest. It's called the Goat Trail for a reason—this is a no-nonsense path that leads straight down from the trailhead to the creek, and straight up on the return. The total elevation change is only 700 feet, but on a hot day, it's, well...hot. Summer temperatures can easily exceed 100°F, so most sane people visit on cool days in winter and spring. The hot springs consist of three pools alongside the creek; the hottest one is the farthest from the stream's edge. Note: The Goat Trail ends on the north side of Deep Creek, and you must ford the creek to reach the hot springs, then hike a short distance downstream. When Deep Creek is running high, this ford can be difficult, so check with the Big Bear Discovery Center before planning an early spring visit. And keep in mind that although the hot springs are located on public Forest Service land, the trailhead is not, so you have to pay a fee to park and start your hike here. If you want to access the hot springs without paying a fee, you can start your hike on the Bradford Ridge Path, which begins where Highway 173 crosses Kinley Creek. Since these hot springs are quite popular, several rules are in effect: no camping, no wood or charcoal fires, and no glass containers.

User Groups: Hikers, horses, and dogs. No mountain bikes. No wheelchair facilities.

Permits: No permits are required. A fee is charged by Bowen Ranch for crossing over their private land.

Maps: A San Bernardino National Forest map is available from the U.S. Forest Service. For a topographic map, go to the USGS website to download Lake Arrowhead.

Directions: From Cajon Pass at I-15, drive north for six miles and take the Hesperia exit. Drive east through the town of Hesperia on Main Street and turn left (east) on Rock Springs Road. Follow Rock Springs Road to its end. Turn left on Kiowa Road and drive 0.5 mile, then turn right on Roundup Way. Follow Roundup Way for 4.4 miles (it turns to dirt), then turn right on Bowen Ranch Road (dirt). Drive 2.5 miles to a fork, bear right, and drive 3.3 miles farther on Bowen Ranch Road. Stop and register at the ranch house (a fee is charged), then continue to the road's end and the parking area and trailhead.

Contact: San Bernardino National Forest, Big

Bear Discovery Center, Fawnskin, 909/382-2790, www.fs.usda.gov/sbnf.

48 TELEGRAPH CANYON AND SOUTH RIDGE LOOP

4.0 mi/2.0 hr 2 8

in Chino Hills State Park near Riverside

Map 13.2, page 684

If you don't mind sharing your walk with equestrians and mountain bikers, this loop trail in Chino Hills State Park may be just what you need to revive yourself from a day of office work, freeways, and rush-hour traffic. Start walking on the wide Telegraph Canyon Trail from near Chino Hills Campground, following a seasonal creek. You'll hike for about two miles, climbing fairly steeply in the second mile, and then loop back on the South Ridge Trail. The park is mostly grasslands and oaks, with a few wet canyon ravines providing homes for sycamore groves and wildlife. Native California walnut trees also grow here. Remember that the best time to visit the park is in winter or spring; if you come in summer, make it as early in the morning as possible. In addition to the heat, summer brings with it the infamous Inland Empire smog.

User Groups: Hikers, horses, and mountain bikes. No dogs. No wheelchair facilities.

Permits: No permits are required. A $5 day-use fee is charged per vehicle.

Maps: A map of Chino Hills State Park is available at the entrance kiosk or by free download at www.parks.ca.gov. For topographic maps, go to the USGS website to download Yorba Linda and Prado Dam.

Directions: From the junction of Highway 71 and Highway 91 near Corona, drive north on Highway 71 to Soquel Canyon Parkway. Turn left on Soquel Canyon Parkway and drive one mile to Elinvar Avenue. Turn left and drive to the end of Elinvar Avenue, at its intersection with Sapphire Road. Turn left on Sapphire Road and then right immediately at the Chino Hills State Park sign. Continue down the park road for three miles to the campground and turn into the parking area. The Telegraph Canyon Trail begins just below the campground.

Contact: Chino Hills State Park, Riverside, 951/780-6222, www.parks.ca.gov or www.chinohillsstatepark.org.

49 MORO CANYON AND RIDGE LOOP

5.2 mi/2.5 hr

in Crystal Cove State Park near Laguna Beach

Map 13.2, page 684

Moro Canyon is on the inland side of Crystal Cove State Park, and when you see how much foliage thrives here, you'll have a hard time believing that on average, only 12 inches of rain falls each year (although during the winter of 2010-2011, the park received a whopping 48 inches!). Moro Creek flows only in the wet winter season, but even in the driest summers its edges are lined with oaks, sycamores, and willows, which attract birds, small mammals, and butterflies. We managed to identify the anise swallowtail butterfly (yellow and black) and the red admiral butterfly (brown, red, and black) on one trip. Unlike the other trails on the inland side of the park, the Moro Canyon Trail is on a gentle grade, which makes it a fine route to take into the park's backcountry. The trail begins on a dirt road by the park entrance kiosk. At 1.6 miles out, turn right on the East Cut Across Trail and make a switchbacking climb up to Moro Ridge. The ascent will get your heart pumping. After a mile, turn right on the Moro Ridge Trail and follow it as it rolls along the ridge top, offering many fine ocean views. Be sure to take the short spur trail off the Moro Ridge Trail to Emerald Vista, a scenic spot for a lunch break, before heading back downhill. Then backtrack to the Moro Ridge Trail and finish out your loop by turning right on the BFI Trail (don't ask us what it stands for because we can't print it). It's pretty hard to get lost in this park; every major junction is marked with a "you are here" trail map.

User Groups: Hikers, horses, and mountain bikes. No dogs. No wheelchair facilities.

Permits: No permits are required. A $15 day-use fee is charged per vehicle.

Maps: A trail map of Crystal Cove State Park is available at the visitors center or by free download at www.parks.ca.gov. For a topographic map, go to the USGS website to download Laguna Beach.

Directions: From Corona del Mar, drive south on Highway 1 for three miles to the entrance to Crystal Cove State Park, on the inland side of the highway. Park near the ranger station; the Moro Canyon Trail begins down the park road by the entrance kiosk.

Contact: Crystal Cove State Park, Laguna Beach, 949/494-3539, www.parks.ca.gov or www.crystalcovestatepark.com.

50 BOMMER RIDGE AND BOAT CANYON ROAD

9.6 mi/5.0 hr 

in Laguna Coast Wilderness Park near Laguna Beach

Map 13.2, page 684

If you are a nature lover living in or visiting Southern California, Orange County is probably not the first place you think about when it comes to hiking. Shopping, maybe. Beach-going, definitely. But if you haven't visited Orange County's Laguna Coast Wilderness Park, you're in for a pleasant surprise. In a county largely given over to development, this 7,000-acre park contains one of the few remaining parcels of coastal sage scrub habitat. You'll smell its wonderful scent almost everywhere you walk. The park also includes the only natural lakes in Orange County.

This view-filled hike starts with a climb up Willow Canyon Road to the Bommer Ridge Trail. The ridge offers expansive vistas of neighboring sage-covered canyons and the wide blue Pacific. Connect to Boat Canyon Road and head out for more views, now of Emerald Bay, Irvine Cove, and the beaches around Laguna. You'll have to backtrack to find your way back to your car, but who wouldn't want to see this scenery all over again? On the final stretch, you can opt to take the Laurel Spur to Laurel Canyon Trail instead of the Willow Canyon Road. Many interesting rock outcrops can be seen along this stretch, plus wildflowers and plentiful birds.

If you're not up for this long hike but would still like to explore Laguna Coast Wilderness Park, the 3.5-mile Willow/Laurel Canyons loop is one of the most popular in the park. If you'd like to learn more about Laguna Coast Wilderness Park and its many trails, stop in at the James and Rosemary Nix Nature Center at the Little Sycamore Canyon Staging Area on Laguna Canyon Road. The center is open daily 9am-4pm.

User Groups: Hikers, horses, and mountain bikes. No dogs. No wheelchair facilities.

Permits: No permits are required. A $3 day-use fee is charged per vehicle.

Maps: A trail map is available at the parking area. For a topographic map, go to the USGS website to download Laguna Beach.

Directions: From I-405 in Irvine, exit south on Laguna Canyon Road. The Willow Canyon parking entrance is located 0.3 mile south of the El Toro Road intersection. Or, from Laguna Beach, drive 3.1 miles north on Laguna Canyon Road to the parking lot entrance on the left. The lot is open 8am-5pm daily.

Contact: Laguna Coast Wilderness Park, Laguna Beach, 949/923-2235, www.ocparks.com/lagunacoast or www.lagunacanyon.org.

51 HOLY JIM FALLS

2.5 mi/1.5 hr 

in Trabuco Canyon in Cleveland National Forest

Map 13.2, page 684

It seems that everybody in Orange County

knows about and likes to visit Holy Jim Falls. The waterfall and its canyon were named for a beekeeper who lived here in the 1890s—James T. Smith, better known as Cussin' Jim. Apparently he had a temper and a colorful way with language. But conservative mapmakers who plotted Trabuco Canyon in the early 20th century found Smith's nickname in bad taste, so they changed it to Holy Jim, and it remains. Whether it's because of the interesting history of the area or the beauty that it still exhibits today, the trail to Holy Jim Falls is well known and frequently walked, especially in springtime. The 2.5-mile stroll is in the cool shade along Holy Jim Creek. Start by walking down the dirt road, past some leased cabins, to the signed trailhead. There the trail turns to single track. You're surrounded by a lush canyon filled with oaks, big leaf maples, wildflowers, and even a few bracken ferns. The trail crosses the creek several times and gently gains some elevation as it heads upstream. Where the trail steepens noticeably as you pass a large, old oak tree on your left, cross the creek one final time. Instead of following the main trail as it switchbacks uphill, you'll go to the right, continuing along the stream. An easy 300-yard stream scramble brings you to the waterfall's base, and if there isn't a scout troop there eating lunch (as there was on our trip), you'll be able to listen to the sweet music of the falls.

User Groups: Hikers, dogs, horses, and mountain bikes. No wheelchair facilities.

Permits: No permits are required. A National Forest Adventure Pass is required for each vehicle; fees are $5 for one day or $30 for a year. Interagency access passes are also accepted.

Maps: A Cleveland National Forest map is available from the U.S. Forest Service. For a topographic map, go to the USGS website to download Santiago Peak.

Directions: From Laguna Hills (north of San Juan Capistrano) on I-5, exit on El Toro Road and drive east for six miles. Turn right on Live Oak Canyon Road and drive about four miles (two miles past the entrance to O'Neill Regional Park). Turn left on Trabuco Creek Road, which is an often unsigned, rocky, dirt road just past the paved Rose Canyon Road turnoff. The road is usually suitable for passenger cars. Go five miles on the dirt road to the well-signed parking area for the Holy Jim Trail. The trail leads from the left side of the parking lot.

Contact: Cleveland National Forest, Trabuco Ranger District, 951/736-1811, www.fs.usda.gov/cleveland.

52 BELL CANYON AND EAST RIDGE LOOP

5.2 mi/2.5 hr

in Ronald W. Caspers Wilderness Park

Map 13.2, page 684

Caspers is Orange County's largest public parkland, covering a whopping 8,000 acres and 42 miles of trails in the western Santa Ana Mountains. The park received a bad rap in 1986 when two children were attacked (in separate incidents) by a mountain lion. While some people may still be scared off by this terrible piece of history, many locals consider Caspers to be the best park in Orange County. Even the drive to reach it is a pleasure—a winding cruise inland from the coast, past ranches, nurseries, and long stretches of open space. The 5.2-mile Bell Canyon and East Ridge Loop is a great introduction to the park's myriad charms. Start on the East Ridge Trail across from Live Oak Campground. The initial steep climb will get your heart pumping, but in spring, you are rewarded with a colorful display of wildflowers. At any time of year you'll gain panoramic views of Bell Canyon below and the surrounding peaks and ridges of Cleveland National Forest. On clear days the town of San Juan Capistrano comes into view, as well as the coast beyond, and sometimes even San Clemente Island. After two miles on the East Ridge Trail, turn left on the Sun Rise Trail and hike 0.6 mile through grasslands and coastal sage scrub to connect to the Bell Canyon Trail (via a short stint on the Cougar Pass Trail). A left turn on the Bell Canyon Trail will lead you alongside Bell Creek and finally to a gate leading into the Old Corral Picnic Area. Here you'll find the park's often-photographed old windmill, a reminder of this fertile valley's cattle ranching days in the 1940s. From here, follow the paved road past the equestrian campground and then back to your starting point at Live Oak Campground.

User Groups: Hikers and horses. No dogs. Mountain bikes are permitted on East Ridge and Bell Canyon Trails. No wheelchair facilities.

Permits: No permits are required. A $5 day-use fee is charged per vehicle on weekends, $3 on weekdays.

Maps: Free trail maps are available at the entrance station, or you can download one at www.ocparks.com/caspers. For a topographic map, go to the USGS website to download Canada Gobernadora.

Directions: From I-5 at San Juan Capistrano, take the Ortega Highway (Highway 74) exit and drive east for 7.6 miles. The park entrance is on the left. Park near the restrooms at Live Oak Campground; East Ridge Trail begins there.

Contact: Ronald W. Caspers Wilderness Park, San Juan Capistrano, 949/923-2210, www.ocparks.com.

53 SAN JUAN LOOP TRAIL

2.1 mi/1.0 hr 2 8

in Cleveland National Forest near Lake Elsinore

Map 13.2, page 684

The San Juan Loop Trail is an easy and informative walk that serves as a good introduction to the Santa Ana Mountains. The only factor you must consider: Don't try to hike here in summer, when these mountains can feel hotter than the desert. The trailhead features a rather negative sign, which explains in doomsday-style the dangers of mountain lions, rattlesnakes, poison oak, and rugged terrain. If the sign doesn't convince you to get back in the car and go to Disneyland instead, start hiking on the loop trail, which parallels the road for its first 0.5 mile. You'll forget about the car noise as you start examining all the plant life along the trail, which includes deep red monkeyflowers, purple nightshade, and tall, spiky yuccas with their silky, milk-white flowers. Lizards dart here and there among the foliage. The terrain is dry and exposed, but thriving nonetheless. A half-mile out, you'll pass a railing and overlook above a small seasonal waterfall on San Juan Creek, which has many clear, granite-lined pools. In another 0.5 mile, you'll pass the turnoff for the Chiquito Basin Trail (a highly recommended option for those seeking a longer trip), and then you'll pass through a lovely grove of ancient oaks. The loop trail finishes out by bringing you back to the opposite side of the parking lot.

User Groups: Hikers, dogs, horses, and mountain bikes. No wheelchair facilities.

Permits: No permits are required. A National Forest Adventure Pass is required for each

San Juan Loop Trail

vehicle; fees are $5 for one day or $30 for a year. Interagency access passes are also accepted.

Maps: A Cleveland National Forest map is available from the U.S. Forest Service. For a topographic map, go to the USGS website to download Sitton Peak.

Directions: From I-5 at San Juan Capistrano, take the Ortega Highway/Highway 74 exit and drive north. In 21 miles, you'll reach the Ortega Oaks store on the right, 0.75 mile past Upper San Juan Campground. The trailhead is across the road from the store; turn left and park in the large parking lot. Start the loop trail on the right (north) side of the parking lot.

Contact: Cleveland National Forest, Trabuco Ranger District, Corona, 951/736-1811, www.fs.usda.gov/cleveland.

54 BEAR CANYON LOOP TRAIL

6.7 mi/3.5 hr

in the San Mateo Canyon Wilderness near Lake Elsinore

Map 13.2, page 684

Is it winter or spring? Is the weather cool and clear? If you've answered yes to both, this is a fine time to take a hike on the Bear Canyon Trail—either a little out-and-back trip for as far as you like, or the full 6.7-mile loop, which circles a junction called Four Corners. First, stock up on some chocolate from the candy store at the trailhead (this is why it must be a cool day; otherwise, carrying chocolate is out of the question). Set off on the trail adjacent to the store, heading into the San Mateo Canyon Wilderness and climbing gently through chaparral-covered slopes. In spring, many yuccas bloom along this stretch. Take the right fork one mile in, and in another mile, you'll reach the start of the loop; take the right branch to start. The trail has a mere 700-foot elevation gain, and in places, it offers expansive views of the San Juan Canyon. Pigeon Springs is a popular resting point, where you can find some shade among the oaks. Four Corners is 0.5 mile beyond Pigeon Springs, and there, you'll turn sharply left to loop back. If you're looking for more of a workout, you can always turn right at Four Corners to head for 3,280-foot Sitton Peak. On the clearest days, you can see up to 50 miles distant from the summit. It looks like you could take a big leap and land on Catalina Island. Sitton Peak is a 9.5-mile round-trip.

User Groups: Hikers, dogs, and horses. No mountain bikes. No wheelchair facilities.

Permits: No permits are required. A National Forest Adventure Pass is required for each vehicle; fees are $5 for one day or $30 for a year. Interagency access passes are also accepted.

Maps: A Cleveland National Forest map is available from the U.S. Forest Service. For a topographic map, go to the USGS website to download Sitton Peak.

Directions: From I-5 at San Juan Capistrano, take the Ortega Highway/Highway 74 exit and drive north. In 21 miles, you'll reach the Ortega Oaks store on the right, 0.75 mile past Upper San Juan Campground. The parking area is across the road from the store; turn left and park in the large parking lot. Cross the road to begin hiking on the Bear Canyon Trail, to the right of the store.

Contact: Cleveland National Forest, Trabuco Ranger District, Corona, 951/736-1811, www.fs.usda.gov/cleveland.

55 TENAJA FALLS

1.4 mi/1.0 hr

in the San Mateo Canyon Wilderness near Murrieta

Map 13.2, page 684

The only hard part about getting to Tenaja Falls is the long drive, but you can't miss the trailhead once you arrive. The parking lot is usually filled with cars. The trail leads from the signboard down to the creek, which is easy to cross at low water. If the water is too deep, follow a use trail upstream and cross the creek where it's narrower. Just be sure to join up with the main road again; following the streamside use trails is a needlessly difficult way to the falls. You'll hike northward on the wide road, rising out of the canyon alongside sage- and chaparral-covered hillsides. In a few minutes, you'll round a curve and be treated to a partial view of the waterfall ahead. What a sight—Tenaja Falls is huge compared to other waterfalls in Orange County, dropping 150 feet in five tiers. It's magnificent when flowing full, which is only after a period of rain, usually between December and March. Keep walking toward the waterfall; the trail deposits you at its lip. When the water is low enough, you can cross over the top of the falls to the other side of the creek, but be extremely cautious on the slippery granite if you choose to do so. Note: You can also hike to Tenaja Falls from the Tenaja trailhead (you'll pass it on your drive in), but it's a much longer, 5.4-mile one-way trek.

User Groups: Hikers, dogs, and horses. No mountain bikes. No wheelchair facilities.

Permits: No permits are required. A National Forest Adventure Pass is required for each vehicle; fees are $5 for one day or $30 for a year. Interagency access passes are also accepted.

Maps: A Cleveland National Forest map is available from the U.S. Forest Service. For a topographic map, go to the USGS website to download Sitton Peak.

Directions: From Lake Elsinore, drive south on I-15 for about 12 miles to the Clinton Keith Road exit in Murrieta. Drive south on Clinton Keith Road, which becomes Tenaja Road, for 4.5 miles. At a signed intersection with Tenaja Road, turn right and drive 4.3 miles west. Turn right on Cleveland Forest Road and drive one mile to the Tenaja trailhead. Stay straight, passing by the trailhead, and reset your odometer. Continue 4.4 miles on Road 7S04 to a hairpin turn and a parking pullout on the left.

Contact: Cleveland National Forest, Trabuco Ranger District, Corona, 951/736-1811, www.fs.usda.gov/cleveland.

56 SANTA ROSA PLATEAU ECOLOGICAL RESERVE

4.5 mi/2.5 hr 2 8

in the Santa Rosa Plateau Ecological Reserve

Map 13.2, page 684

Those volcanic-looking rocky mesas you see as you drive through the foothills along Clinton Keith Road are home to some of Southern California's last vernal pools. These are seasonal ponds that give life to endangered plants and wildflowers and provide a resting place for wintering birds. Whereas these pools are more common in the San Joaquin Valley, in Southern California they have all but vanished, which is one reason for the establishment of the Santa Rosa Plateau Ecological Reserve. Another reason is the existence of the rare Engelmann oak, a semi-deciduous species of oak that only loses its leaves during times of drought. Several fine groves of Engelmann oaks are found within the reserve's border.

If you're visiting in late winter or early spring and you just want to see the vernal pools, you can do so with a one-mile walk on the Vernal Pool Trail from a trailhead located two miles west of the reserve visitors center, on Clinton Keith Road. If you're here at any other time of the year, your best bet is to start your trip at the visitors center. If you can, show up on weekday afternoons or on Saturday morning and go on one of the ranger-led interpretive hikes (call ahead for an exact schedule). If you'd rather hike on your own, start out on the left side of the Granite Loop Trail. Connect to the Vista Grande Trail and head uphill to its junction with Monument Road. You'll pass some lovely Engelmann oaks along the way. Turn right on Monument Road, then take the left spur to the top of Monument Hill (elevation 2,046 feet), the highest point in the reserve. The views of the chaparral- and cactus-covered hills and rolling grasslands are lovely. If you arrive early in the morning before the frequent afternoon haze moves in, you'll be able to pick out classic Southern California landmarks: Mounts San

Gorgonio, San Jacinto, and Palomar; Cuyamaca Peak and Mount Woodson, in San Diego; the high summits of the San Gabriel Mountains; and yes, even the Pacific Ocean. Retrace your steps to head back, or make a semi-loop by turning left on the Tenaja Truck Trail, then right on Waterline Road.

User Groups: Hikers, horses, and mountain bikes. (Horses and mountain bikes allowed only on signed multiuse trails.) No dogs. No wheelchair facilities.

Permits: No permits are required. A $4 day-use fee is charged per adult; $3 for children 12 and under.

Maps: A trail map is available at the visitors center and at all four trailheads in the reserve. For a topographic map, go to the USGS website to download Wildomar.

Directions: From Lake Elsinore, drive south on I-15 for about 12 miles to the Clinton Keith Road exit in Murrieta. Drive west on Clinton Keith Road for four miles (past Aveneda La Cresta) to the visitors center entrance, on the left. Park near the visitors center.

Contact: Santa Rosa Plateau Ecological Reserve, Murrieta, 951/677-6951, www.rivcoparks.org.

57 GRAY'S PEAK

7.0 mi/3.5 hr

in San Bernardino National Forest near Big Bear Lake

Map 13.3, page 685

Check your calendar before you set off on this peak hike; this trail is closed from November 1 to April 1 to protect bald eagles that nest in the area. But the rest of the year, if you want to get up high and get a good look at Big Bear Lake, this trail will fit the bill. A bonus is that it is easy enough (only a 1,200-foot elevation gain) that most older children can make the trip comfortably. A negative, for some, is that this is also a popular mountain-biking trail, but the riders we saw were all very courteous to hikers. The trail starts out by heading roughly west, then joins with a dirt road. There are only two junctions to look for. Turn right at the first junction, walk about 200 yards, and then turn left to access the "official" Gray's Peak Trail. From there it is 2.75 miles to the top, with a little scrambling required in the last 0.25 mile. The summit is located at 7,920 feet, and offers inspiring views of the lake through a filter of lodgepole pines. The sound of the wind in the pines will accompany you for much of this hike. Like so many places in Big Bear, the boulder outcrops along this trail and on the summit are fascinating, and will tempt you to climb on top.

User Groups: Hikers, dogs, horses, and mountain bikes. No wheelchair facilities.

Permits: No permits are required. A National Forest Adventure Pass is required for each vehicle; fees are $5 for one day or $30 for a year. Interagency access passes are also accepted.

Maps: A San Bernardino National Forest map is available from the U.S. Forest Service. For a topographic map, go to the USGS website to download Fawnskin.

Directions: From the town of Big Bear Lake on Highway 18, take the Stanfield cutoff to the north shore of the lake, where it junctions with Highway 38. Turn left and drive 3.5 miles on Highway 38 to the Gray's Peak trailhead, on the right side of the road 0.6 mile west of the town of Fawnskin. If the parking area at the trailhead is full, you can park across the highway at Grout Bay Picnic Area.

Contact: San Bernardino National Forest, Big Bear Discovery Center, Fawnskin, 909/382-2790, www.fs.usda.gov/sbnf.

58 COUGAR CREST TRAIL TO BERTHA PEAK

6.0 mi/3.0 hr

in San Bernardino National Forest near Big Bear Lake

Map 13.3, page 685

Put on your hiking boots and prepare to climb.

That's what you have to do on the Cougar Crest Trail—gain 1,300 feet over three miles to reach Bertha Peak, elevation 8,201 feet. You can see the peak, capped with electronic relay equipment, from the trailhead parking lot. Views of the Big Bear area are spectacular along the route, and the trail is well built, making this an excellent day hike—or running path if you're a jogger. The first mile is on dirt roads in a forest of piñon and Jeffrey pines, but soon the path narrows to single track. The more you climb upward, the more you see; turn around every now and then to check out the lake and mountain views. Finally, at two miles, you reach the Pacific Crest Trail (PCT), where the grade eases considerably. Turn right and follow the PCT for 0.5 mile to a dirt road, then turn right again and climb steeply to reach Bertha's summit. Look for old, gnarled juniper trees along the route. The view from the peak includes Big Bear Lake, of course, plus Mount San Gorgonio and other high peaks and ridges, and green Holcomb Valley below you.

User Groups: Hikers, dogs, and horses. No mountain bikes. No wheelchair facilities.

Permits: No permits are required. A National Forest Adventure Pass is required for each vehicle; fees are $5 for one day or $30 for a year. Interagency access passes are also accepted.

Maps: A San Bernardino National Forest map is available from the U.S. Forest Service. For a topographic map, go to the USGS website to download Fawnskin.

Directions: From the town of Big Bear Lake on Highway 18, take the Stanfield cutoff to the north shore of the lake, where it junctions with Highway 38. Turn left and drive 1.3 miles on Highway 38 (0.5 mile past the Big Bear Ranger Station) to the Cougar Crest trailhead, on the right side of the road. If you are traveling from Fawnskin, the trailhead is 2.4 miles east of Fawnskin on Highway 38, on the left side of the road.

Contact: San Bernardino National Forest, Big Bear Discovery Center, Fawnskin, 909/382-2790, www.fs.usda.gov/sbnf.

59 WOODLAND TRAIL

1.5 mi/0.75 hr 2 8

in San Bernardino National Forest near Big Bear Lake

Map 13.3, page 685

If you're spending the weekend or the week in Big Bear, a visit to the Big Bear Discovery Center in Fawnskin will provide all the information you need about hiking, fishing, and exploring around the Big Bear area. After talking with the nice people there, take the terrific short walk on the Woodland Trail, which starts near the visitors center. You can pick up an interpretive brochure and learn all about serviceberry, yerba santa, Jeffrey and ponderosa pines, indigo bush, and piñon pines. A bonus is that on the return leg of the loop, you get great views of the lake, but you're far enough away that you don't get hit by the wind that often blows on the north side. From high points on the trail, your vista expands all the way across the lake to Big Bear City.

User Groups: Hikers, dogs, horses, and mountain bikes. No wheelchair facilities.

Permits: No permits are required. A National Forest Adventure Pass is required for each vehicle; fees are $5 for one day or $30 for a year. Interagency access passes are also accepted.

Maps: A San Bernardino National Forest map is available from the U.S. Forest Service. For a topographic map, go to the USGS website to download Fawnskin.

Directions: From the town of Big Bear Lake on Highway 18, take the Stanfield cutoff to the north shore of the lake, where it junctions with Highway 38. Turn left on Highway 38 and drive 0.5 mile to the Woodland trailhead, on the right side of the road. It's directly across the highway from the East Boat Ramp, or one mile east of the Big Bear Discovery Center.

Contact: San Bernardino National Forest, Big Bear Discovery Center, Fawnskin, 909/382-2790, www.fs.usda.gov/sbnf.

60 CHAMPION LODGEPOLE PINE

1.0 mi/0.5 hr 1 8

in San Bernardino National Forest near Big Bear Lake

Map 13.3, page 685

Let's see now. The biggest giant sequoia tree is the General Sherman Tree, in Sequoia National Park. But which is the biggest lodgepole pine tree, and where do you find it? We're delighted you asked. It's the Champion Lodgepole, located only a few miles from Big Bear Lake. The big tree is growing in a grove of world champions, the largest lodgepole pines around. What's strange is that these big guys are growing at 7,500 feet in elevation, when usually in Southern California, lodgepole pines won't grow at less than 8,000 feet. The Champion is about 400 years old, stands 112 feet tall, and has a circumference of 20 feet. After a long but enjoyable drive on a dirt road to the trailhead, you'll find the trail to the big tree is flat and easy. It follows a small stream to a junction. Turn right and walk the last few yards to the Champion, which is surrounded by a fence and situated at the edge of a pretty meadow.

User Groups: Hikers, dogs, horses, and mountain bikes. No wheelchair facilities.

Permits: No permits are required. Parking and access are free.

Maps: A San Bernardino National Forest map is available from the U.S. Forest Service. For a topographic map, go to the USGS website to download Big Bear Lake.

Directions: From the dam on the west end of Big Bear Lake, drive 3.5 miles east on Highway 18/Big Bear Boulevard to Mill Creek Road. Turn right (south) on Mill Creek Road/Forest Service Road 2N10 and follow it for five miles, through several junctions. (The road turns to dirt.) At Forest Service Road 2N11, turn right and drive one mile to the parking area. The route is well signed for the Champion Lodgepole Pine.

Contact: San Bernardino National Forest, Big Bear Discovery Center, Fawnskin, 909/382-2790, www.fs.usda.gov/sbnf.

61 CASTLE ROCK TRAIL

2.0 mi/1.0 hr 3 9

in San Bernardino National Forest near Big Bear Lake

Map 13.3, page 685

There are a couple tricky elements about this trail: There's no real parking area, just a pullout along the highway, and although the path to Castle Rock has a mere 700-foot elevation gain, it's compressed into one mile and climbs steeply right from the trailhead. The trail is smooth sand, surrounded by manzanita, big ponderosa pines, and a ton of rocks. It's located by the area of Big Bear Lake called Boulder Bay, a perfectly descriptive name. As you climb, you gain tremendous views of the lake, but you'll miss them completely unless you turn around. In about 20 minutes you'll reach a rocky overlook, which is where many people stop and pull up a granite boulder to sit on. The main trail becomes a spiderweb of trails, as people have chosen all different routes around the rocks. If you continue upward, you'll reach a saddle and then start to descend slightly. Castle Rock, which is easily distinguishable by its shape, is just to the east, off the trail as you head downhill. If you tire out before the saddle, just pick any boulder that's easy to climb and get on top to enjoy the lovely views of the lake. On one trip in late March we were treated to a lovely shower of snow flurries. Isn't Big Bear the greatest? Trailhead elevation is 6,700 feet.

User Groups: Hikers, dogs, and mountain bikes. No horses. No wheelchair facilities.

Permits: No permits are required. Parking and access are free.

Maps: A San Bernardino National Forest map is available from the U.S. Forest Service. For a topographic map, go to the USGS website to download Big Bear Lake.

Directions: From the dam on the west end of

Big Bear Lake, drive one mile east on Highway 18/Big Bear Boulevard to the signed Castle Rock trailhead, on the right (it's by the Big Bear City Limit sign). Park in the turnout on the lake side of Highway 18, about 50 yards farther east, and then walk across the road to the trailhead.

Contact: San Bernardino National Forest, Big Bear Discovery Center, Fawnskin, 909/382-2790, www.fs.usda.gov/sbnf.

62 PONDEROSA VISTA NATURE TRAIL

1.0 mi/0.5 hr 2 8

in San Bernardino National Forest near Angelus Oaks

Map 13.3, page 685 BEST

The Ponderosa Vista Nature Trail wins hands down for the trail with the corniest interpretive plaques. When you visit, you'll see what we mean. But aside from the overdone prose, everything else on this trail is first-rate, making for a great introduction to the flora and fauna of San Bernardino National Forest. You can choose between the short loop (0.3 mile) and the long loop (0.6 mile), but why not hike both? You can learn about assorted birds of the forest, such as acorn woodpeckers, redbreasted sapsuckers, and yellow-rumped warblers, as well as various trees—ponderosa pine is the most common conifer in the area, but incense cedars, black oaks, white firs, and piñon pines also grow. The highlight of the trail is an overlook point with a view across the Santa Ana River Canyon. An old photograph at the overlook shows what the canyon used to look like and explains about the building of the Rim of the World Highway in 1935. That was the same year that black bears were introduced to the area. No wonder—with the new highway, they could just get into their RVs and drive in.

User Groups: Hikers, dogs, horses, and mountain bikes. No wheelchair facilities.

Permits: No permits are required. Parking and access are free.

Maps: A San Bernardino National Forest map is available from the U.S. Forest Service. For a topographic map, go to the USGS website to download Big Bear Lake.

Directions: From I-10 at Redlands, take the Highway 38 exit and drive northeast for 25 miles to the trailhead for the Ponderosa Vista Nature Trail, on the left side of the road. If you reach the Jenks Lake turnoff, you've passed it. Park in the parking lot by the trailhead.

Contact: San Bernardino National Forest, Mill Creek Ranger Station, Mentone, 909/382-2882, www.fs.usda.gov/sbnf.

63 WHISPERING PINES TRAIL

0.5 mi/0.5 hr 2 8

in San Bernardino National Forest near Angelus Oaks

Map 13.3, page 685

Right across the road from the Ponderosa Vista Trail is the Whispering Pines Trail, another short, easy interpretive trail that is both fun and informative. Time to play *Trivial Pursuit:* This trail appeared on what television show, filmed in 1969, about a blind girl and a furry dog? If you guessed *Lassie,* you win. In the show, the girl walked this trail and read the braille interpretive displays. Anyway, this nature trail has less of a grade than the one across the highway, although it's not quite as scenic. You will see numerous pines with an incredible amount of holes drilled in them—the work of industrious acorn woodpeckers. A minus is the sound of nearby Highway 38, but the pluses are the sound of the wind in the pines and lots of squirrels and jays.

User Groups: Hikers, dogs, horses, and mountain bikes. No wheelchair facilities.

Permits: No permits are required. Parking and access are free.

Maps: A San Bernardino National Forest map is available from the U.S. Forest Service. For a topographic map, go to the USGS website to download Big Bear Lake.

Directions: From I-10 at Redlands, take the Highway 38 exit and drive northeast for 25 miles to the trailhead for the Whispering Pines Trail, on the right side of the road. If you reach the Jenks Lake turnoff, you've passed it. Park in the well-signed parking lot by the trailhead.
Contact: San Bernardino National Forest, Mill Creek Visitors Center, Mentone, 909/382-2882, www.fs.usda.gov/sbnf.

64 JENKS LAKE

1.0 mi/0.5 hr 

in San Bernardino National Forest near Angelus Oaks

Map 13.3, page 685

Much of the area near Jenks Lake was burned in the 2015 Lake Fire, but pretty little Jenks Lake was spared. If you visit on a weekday when nobody is around, you'll find it's a magical little spot of bright blue water, with Mount San Gorgonio looming in the background. As late as April, the peak is often crested with snow and the wind can whip off the surface of the small lake, creating little whitecaps. Visit Jenks Lake on a Saturday in July, however, and it's another story. The place will be packed with picnicking families, kids from nearby summer camps, and people fishing for largemouth bass, bluegill, and rainbow trout in the stocked lake. (No swimming is allowed.) No matter when you arrive, you should take the short walk around the perimeter of the lake, then begin with the nature trail that leads behind the picnic area. The south shore of the lake is the quieter side. After looping around the lake, walk to the back side of the picnic area, where you're be surprised by the vista—the canyon drops off vertically, with sheer cliffs that fall hundreds of feet. Yes, this is the Rim of the World, just like the highway of the same name. Fortunately, a railing is in place to keep you from leaning too far over the edge. Note: Hikers looking for a longer adventure can set off from either the South Fork or Forsee Creek trailheads (near Jenks Lake) and head into the San Gorgonio Wilderness. If you don't have a permit, you can always turn around when you reach the wilderness boundary.
User Groups: Hikers and dogs. No horses or mountain bikes. Some wheelchair facilities available.
Permits: No permits are required. A $5 day-use fee is charged per vehicle (the National Forest Adventure Pass does not apply here).
Maps: A San Bernardino National Forest map is available from the U.S. Forest Service. For a topographic map, go to the USGS website to download Big Bear Lake.
Directions: From I-10 at Redlands, take the Highway 38 exit and drive northeast for 27 miles to the Jenks Lake turnoff on the right. Turn right and follow Jenks Lake Road west for two miles to the parking area for the lake. Note: Jenks Lake Road continues and reconnects to Highway 38 a few miles to the east.
Contact: San Bernardino National Forest, Mill Creek Visitors Center, Mentone, 909/382-2882, www.fs.usda.gov/sbnf.

65 ASPEN GROVE TRAIL

5.0 mi/2.5 hr 

in the San Gorgonio Wilderness near Angelus Oaks

Map 13.3, page 685

This beautiful aspen grove was hit hard by the July 2015 Lake Fire, but it's recovering. This small remnant grove of quaking aspens (Populus tremuloides) is one of only two native groves outside of the Sierra Nevada Mountains. As of September 2019, the grove is open but the trailhead access road, Forest Road 1N05, is still closed due to logging activity related to the wildfire cleanup (check with the Mill Creek Ranger Station or Big Bear Discovery Center for updates on the road). This is a place you definitely want to see, especially in the autumn when the aspen leaves don their golden gorgeous golden coats. From the Aspen Grove trailhead, a short walk down a dirt road leads you into a cool and shady grove of aspen trees along Fish Creek. If you're accustomed to the aspen trees of the eastern Sierra, you'll notice that these have smaller leaves—an adaptation to the dry climate. You may be happy just hanging out right here, but if you proceed farther by crossing Fish Creek, you're in the San Gorgonio Wilderness, and you need to have a permit in your possession. The trail to the right leads to a few more aspens and then peters out. Follow the trail to your left (uphill), heading away from the creek. A pretty walk of less than two miles through a mixed conifer forest will deliver you to two meadows—first, tiny Monkey Flower Flat, and then, after crossing Fish Creek again, Lower Fish Creek Meadow.

User Groups: Hikers, dogs, and horses. No mountain bikes. No wheelchair facilities.

Permits: A free wilderness permit is required for both day hiking and backpacking and is available in advance from the Mill Creek Visitors Center. Permits can also be obtained in person at the Mill Creek Visitors Center or Barton Flats Visitors Center on Highway 38. Parking and access are free.

Maps: A San Bernardino National Forest or San Gorgonio Wilderness map is available from the U.S. Forest Service. A San Gorgonio Wilderness map is available from Tom Harrison Maps. For a topographic map, go to the USGS website to download Moonridge.

Directions: From I-10 at Redlands, take the Highway 38 exit and drive northeast for 32 miles to Forest Service Road 1N02, signed for Heart Bar Campground, Coon Creek, and Fish Creek. Turn right (south) and drive 1.25 miles to Road 1N05, then bear right. Drive 1.5 miles to the Aspen Grove trailhead, on the right. This last stretch of dirt road can sometimes be difficult for low-clearance, two-wheel-drive vehicles, depending on recent weather.

Contact: San Bernardino National Forest, Mill Creek Visitors Center, Mentone, 909/382-2882, www.fs.usda.gov/sbnf.

66 BIG FALLS

0.6 mi/0.5 hr 2 9

in Big Falls Recreation Area near Forest Falls

Map 13.3, page 685

Quick—what's the largest year-round waterfall in Southern California? Big Falls, of course. At 500 feet tall, Big Falls delivers on its name, but unfortunately it's difficult to see the waterfall's full height. That's okay, though, because the Big Falls Recreation Area is still a great destination, and the short hike to the overlook of Big Falls is a fun and easy walk. The elevation at the trailhead is just over 6,000 feet, which means the air is cool and clear. Begin hiking at the lower parking lot, below the picnic area, and set off on an unsigned path heading downstream along Mill Creek Wash. When you pass a private cabin alongside the wash, look for a good place to cross Mill Creek by rock hopping, and then do so. On the far side of the stream, pick up the trail leading uphill on the right side of Falls Creek, which is a feeder stream to Mill Creek. Hike past a small cascade on the bottom of Falls Creek, and head uphill for about five minutes to the overlook area for Big Falls. What you see is the top 40 to 50 feet of a very Yosemite-like free fall, and then some cascading water below. The huge middle part of the fall is hidden in the rocky canyon. Darn. So where can you get a better view of Big Falls? Actually, the best view is from your car window, as you drive past the last few houses along Valley of the Falls Road, shortly before entering the Big Falls Recreation Area. Along this stretch, you can see the full-length vista of Big Falls that usually appears on postcards. Another good spot is at the turnaround loop just before you enter the main parking lot for the falls.

User Groups: Hikers, dogs, horses, and mountain bikes. No wheelchair facilities.

Permits: No permits are required. A National Forest Adventure Pass is required for each vehicle; fees are $5 for one day or $30 for a year. Interagency access passes are also accepted.

Maps: A San Bernardino National Forest is

available from the U.S. Forest Service. For a topographic map, go to the USGS website to download Forest Falls.

Directions: From I-10 at Redlands, take the Highway 38 exit and drive northeast for approximately 14 miles to the intersection with Valley of the Falls Road. Bear right and continue for 4.5 miles to the Big Falls Recreation Area, past the town of Forest Falls. Park in the first parking lot on the left.

Contact: San Bernardino National Forest, Mill Creek Visitors Center, Mentone, 909/382-2882, www.fs.usda.gov/sbnf.

67 VIVIAN CREEK TRAIL TO MOUNT SAN GORGONIO

16.0 mi/1-2 days 5 10

in the San Gorgonio Wilderness near Forest Falls

Map 13.3, page 685 BEST

There are lots of ways to reach the summit of Mount San Gorgonio, the tallest mountain in Southern California, but the shortest way is on the Vivian Creek Trail. That's the good news. The bad news is that it's also the steepest way. The summit of San Gorgonio is at 11,502 feet, and the Vivian Creek trailhead is at 6,100 feet, so you can see what you're in for. Luckily, there are several camps along the way: Vivian Creek Camp at 1.2 miles, Halfway Camp at 2.5 miles, and High Creek Camp at 4.8 miles. It's an eight-mile one-way trip to the summit, and although some people hike the round-trip in a day, it's much better to take two or more days so you can enjoy yourself and not have to rush back before dark. Here's one more precautionary tale: This is the busiest trail in the wilderness. Often it is impossible to get a day-hiking or backpacking permit at the last minute, so in summertime, make a permit reservation far in advance.

The trail leaves the upper end of Big Falls Picnic Area and crosses Mill Creek Wash (be careful at this crossing; Mill Creek is subject to flash floods). On the far side, the path starts on a steep mile-long climb to the hanging valley of Vivian Creek, where Vivian Creek Falls sometimes fall. Vivian Creek Camp is located just past here on the east side of the trail. (No camping is allowed on the west side of the trail.) Vivian Creek Camp is a convenient place to camp if you've gotten a late afternoon start. The trail continues along Vivian Creek, crossing it numerous times under the shade of a mixed conifer forest, to Halfway Camp. A few more switchbacks and you cross High Creek, arriving at High Creek Camp, at 9,000 feet. High Creek Camp is famous for being a cold and windy place to spend the night, so remember to bring your earplugs. At this elevation, only lodgepole pines grow, and as you gain another 2,000 feet in elevation, even these stalwarts give way to granite. At the base of San Gorgonio's summit, you meet up with the trail from Dollar Lake Saddle. Turn right, then left at the next junction, and climb to the 11,502-foot summit of Old Greyback, as it's called. Are you exhausted? Join the party. So is everybody else who makes it this far, but what an accomplishment! Hope you brought a good map so you can identify all the major landmarks of Southern California...

User Groups: Hikers, dogs, and horses. No mountain bikes. No wheelchair facilities.

Permits: A free wilderness permit is required for both day hiking and backpacking and is available in advance from the Mill Creek Visitors Center. Permits can also be obtained in person at the Mill Creek Visitors Center or Barton Flats Visitors Center on Highway 38. A National Forest Adventure Pass is required for each vehicle; fees are $5 for one day or $30 for a year. Interagency access passes are also accepted.

Maps: A San Bernardino National Forest or San Gorgonio Wilderness map is available from the U.S. Forest Service. A San Gorgonio Wilderness map is available from Tom Harrison Maps. For topographic maps, go to the USGS website to download Forest Falls and San Gorgonio.

Directions: From I-10 at Redlands, take the Highway 38 exit and drive northeast for about 14 miles to the intersection with Valley of the Falls Road. Bear right and continue for 4.5 miles to the Big Falls Recreation Area, past the town of Forest Falls. Drive to the parking area at the end of the road and walk uphill through the picnic area on the dirt road. Cross Mill Creek Wash at the trail sign.
Contact: San Bernardino National Forest, Mill Creek Visitors Center, Mentone, 909/382-2882, www.fs.usda.gov/sbnf.

68 BLACK MOUNTAIN LOOKOUT

8.0 mi/4.0 hr 

in San Bernardino National Forest near Idyllwild

Map 13.3, page 685

The summit of Black Mountain is at 7,772 feet and this trailhead is at 5,100 feet, so you have nearly 2,700 feet of climbing to do over only four miles. Along the way, you'll pass through several ecosystems, starting in chaparral and oaks and ending up in pine and fir forest. In April and early May, the wildflowers along the route can be exceptional. From near the start, your views open up to include mighty Mount San Gorgonio, various peaks in the San Gabriel Mountains, and Banning Pass. The Black Mountain Trail departs the highway and climbs steadily for 3.6 miles, then meets up with the fire road to the lookout. Turn right at the only junction and you are there. The 360-degree summit view encompasses some of Southern California's most beautiful country, including most of the big peaks of the San Gabriel, San Jacinto, and San Bernardino Mountains. This is no L.A. city view. It may discourage you somewhat to see that so many others have come in from the opposite direction by driving to within a half-mile of the top; this is a popular trip for folks who are camped at nearby Boulder Basin and Black Mountain Campgrounds. Just remember: You earned this summit. And if you don't want to see anybody else, try hiking this trail in winter, when the road is closed and the only way to get to Black Mountain is on foot. This is also the season when visibility is at its best.
User Groups: Hikers, horses, dogs, and mountain bikes. No wheelchair facilities.
Permits: No permits are required. Parking and access are free.
Maps: A San Bernardino National Forest map is available from the U.S. Forest Service. A San Jacinto Wilderness map is available from Tom Harrison Maps. For a topographic map, go to the USGS website to download San Jacinto Peak.
Directions: From Idyllwild, drive northwest on Highway 243 for about 10 miles to the Black Mountain trailhead on the right (east) side of the highway. The trailhead is 1.3 miles south of the Vista Grande Fire Station.
Contact: San Bernardino National Forest, San Jacinto Ranger District, Idyllwild, 909/382-2921, www.fs.usda.gov/sbnf.

69 SEVEN PINES TRAIL

7.4 mi/4.0 hr 

in the San Jacinto Wilderness near Idyllwild

Map 13.3, page 685

The best thing about the Seven Pines Trail is that you can just wander as far as you please and have a good time. The mileage above reflects hiking 3.7 miles, with a 2,300-foot elevation gain, to the junction with the Deer Springs Trail, but even a mile or two on this path is enjoyable. The first mile climbs steeply through beautiful conifers and many granite boulders and then joins the beginning of the north fork of the San Jacinto River. Where the path crosses the stream, you enter a gorgeous forest of pines and incense cedars. Hanging out right here might suit you just fine, but if you want more exercise, continue uphill to Deer Springs Junction, which is also the headwaters for the

north fork. You'll cross the stream twice more on your way. Trailhead elevation is 6,320 feet.
User Groups: Hikers, horses, and dogs. No mountain bikes. No wheelchair facilities.
Permits: A free wilderness permit is required for day hiking or backpacking and is available in person or in advance by mail from the San Jacinto Ranger District. Parking and access are free.
Maps: A San Bernardino National Forest or San Jacinto Wilderness map is available from the U.S. Forest Service. A San Jacinto Wilderness map is available from Tom Harrison Maps. For a topographic map, go to the USGS website to download San Jacinto Peak.
Directions: From Idyllwild, drive northwest on Highway 243 for 5.5 miles to the right turnoff for Stone Creek, Fern Basin, Marion Mountain, and Dark Canyon Campgrounds. Turn right and drive 0.2 mile, then bear left, following the signs for Dark Canyon Campground. Continue through the campground and up the hill to reach the Seven Pines trailhead.
Contact: San Bernardino National Forest, San Jacinto Ranger District, Idyllwild, 909/382-2921, www.fs.usda.gov/sbnf.

70 DEER SPRINGS TRAIL TO SUICIDE ROCK

7.0 mi/4.0 hr 

in the San Jacinto Wilderness near Idyllwild

Map 13.3, page 685

If you're wondering how to spend a morning or an afternoon in Idyllwild, the hike to Suicide Rock will turn your visit into a trip you'll never forget. Pick up a wilderness permit and head for the trailhead, but be sure to pack some snacks and water for a little celebration at the top. Most of the work is in the first 2.4 miles to Suicide Junction, as you climb up through manzanita, ceanothus, and oaks, heading into the higher country of cedars and pines. At the junction, bear right and leave the Deer Springs Trail for the last mile to Suicide Rock, which contours on an easier grade. From the three-mile point onward, your views of Lily Rock and Tahquitz Peak are outstanding, and once you're on Suicide Rock, at 7,528 feet in elevation, you are directly across from Lily Rock's Yosemite-like chunk of white granite. You can watch clouds drift between you and the neighboring peaks, right at eye level. The view below is of the Idyllwild area—there's little in sight besides a few houses and water tanks tucked in among a vast sea of conifers.
User Groups: Hikers, dogs, and horses. No mountain bikes. No wheelchair facilities.
Permits: A free wilderness permit is required for both day hiking and backpacking and is available in person or in advance by mail from the San Jacinto Ranger District.
Maps: A San Bernardino National Forest or San Jacinto Wilderness map is available from the U.S. Forest Service. A San Jacinto Wilderness map is available from Tom Harrison Maps. For topographic maps, go to the USGS website to download San Jacinto Peak and Idyllwild.
Directions: From Idyllwild, drive northwest on Highway 243 for one mile to the Deer Springs trailhead on the right side of the road (across the highway from the Idyllwild County Park visitors center parking area).
Contact: San Bernardino National Forest, San Jacinto Ranger District, Idyllwild, 909/382-2921, www.fs.usda.gov/sbnf.

71 ERNIE MAXWELL SCENIC TRAIL

5.2 mi/2.5 hr 

in San Bernardino National Forest near Idyllwild

Map 13.3, page 685

The Ernie Maxwell Scenic Trail is the perfect route for hikers who aren't up to the climbing that is de rigueur for most trails in the Idyllwild area. With only a 600-foot elevation change on an undulating trail, even families with small children could manage this path, which leads through a lovely conifer forest. Keep in mind, however, that since you're not climbing, you will not get the spectacular views that are granted on most other trails in the area; this is a walk that is built for enjoying the close up, rather than the far off. The trail leads downhill from the start, contouring through a forest of Jeffrey, ponderosa, and coulter pines, with scattered firs and incense cedars among them. You can practice your tree identification. The trail's end is a bit of a disappointment; it simply reaches a dirt road where you turn around and hike back. Along the way, you'll see some good views of Suicide Rock and Tahquitz Peak.

User Groups: Hikers, dogs, horses, and mountain bikes. No wheelchair facilities.

Permits: No permits are required. A National Forest Adventure Pass is required for each vehicle; fees are $5 for one day or $30 for a year. Interagency access passes are also accepted.

Maps: A San Bernardino National Forest is available from the U.S. Forest Service. For a topographic map, go to the USGS website to download Idyllwild.

Directions: From Idyllwild on Highway 243, turn east on North Circle Drive in downtown, which becomes South Circle Drive, and then becomes Fern Valley Road. Follow Fern Valley Road to Humber Park. You will drive a total of 3.5 miles from downtown. The trailhead is on the right, at the lower end of the parking lot.

Contact: San Bernardino National Forest, San Jacinto Ranger District, Idyllwild, 909/382-2921, www.fs.usda.gov/sbnf.

72 DEVILS SLIDE TRAIL TO TAHQUITZ PEAK

8.4 mi/4.0 hr 3 10

in the San Jacinto Wilderness near Idyllwild

Map 13.3, page 685 BEST

The Devils Slide Trail is the premier hiking trail in the Idyllwild area, with 8,828-foot Tahquitz Peak as the favored destination, especially for hikers from out of town. The best solution to the crowds? Plan a trip before Memorial Day, after Labor Day, or any time during the week. We've hiked the trail in mid-May and saw almost nobody, but then again, it snowed on our trip.

The trail leads from Idyllwild's Humber Park on a steady but manageable uphill climb through the forest to Saddle Junction, 2.5 miles up. Once you reach the junction, head right for Tahquitz Peak. The next mile is loaded with far-reaching views of the desert below and the San Jacinto Mountains, seen from an increasingly open lodgepole pine forest. At the next junction, head right again, soon saying goodbye to the trees and hello to a stark landscape of granite. The summit is only 0.5 mile away. Tahquitz Peak has the only operating fire lookout you can hike to in the San Jacinto Ranger District, and it's sometimes staffed by volunteers. (Two other lookouts in the district are accessible by road, but not by trail.) From the lookout, which was constructed in 1938, you're offered a panoramic view of both the San Jacinto and Santa Rosa Mountains.

Note: If you want to hike to Tahquitz Peak via an alternate trail that sees fewer people, take the South Ridge Trail instead of the Devils Slide Trail. (You still need to pick up a free wilderness permit at the Idyllwild Ranger Station.) It's a 7.2-mile round-trip via the South Ridge Trail from the vicinity of Saunders Meadow Road. Be sure to hike early in the day in the summer months—this trail is even more exposed than the Devils Slide Trail.

User Groups: Hikers, dogs, and horses. No mountain bikes. No wheelchair facilities.

Permits: A free wilderness permit is required for both day hiking and backpacking and is available in person or in advance by mail from the San Jacinto Ranger District. A National Forest Adventure Pass is required for each vehicle; fees are $5 for one day or $30 for a year. Interagency access passes are also accepted.

Maps: A San Bernardino National Forest or San Jacinto Wilderness map is available from the U.S. Forest Service. A San Jacinto Wilderness map is available from Tom Harrison Maps. For topographic maps, go to the USGS website to download Idyllwild and San Jacinto Peak.

Directions: From Idyllwild on Highway 243, turn east on North Circle Drive in downtown, which becomes South Circle Drive, and then becomes Fern Valley Road. Follow Fern Valley Road to Humber Park. You will drive a total of 3.5 miles from downtown. The trailhead is on the right, at the upper end of the parking lot.

Contact: San Bernardino National Forest, San Jacinto Ranger District, Idyllwild, 909/382-2921, www.fs.usda.gov/sbnf.

SAN DIEGO AND VICINITY

Blessed with a nearly perfect year-round climate, San Diego is an ideal place to lace up your boots, and there's a lot more to see than just palm trees and sandy beaches. At San Elijo Lagoon, coastal estuaries and wetlands are preserved for wildlife and nature-lovers. On the inland side of the county, more than 100 miles of trails await at Cuyamaca Rancho State Park, including paths to 5,700-foot Stonewall Peak and 6,512-foot Cuyamaca Peak. Nearby, the Laguna Mountains offer a dramatic setting that overlooks the desert thousands of feet below. North of the Laguna-Cuyamaca range is the smaller Palomar range, where firs, pines, and cedars create a Sierra Nevada-like atmosphere. And if you're craving the coast, San Diego offers 76 miles of beaches, including those at Torrey Pines State Reserve, a popular place for sunset walks.

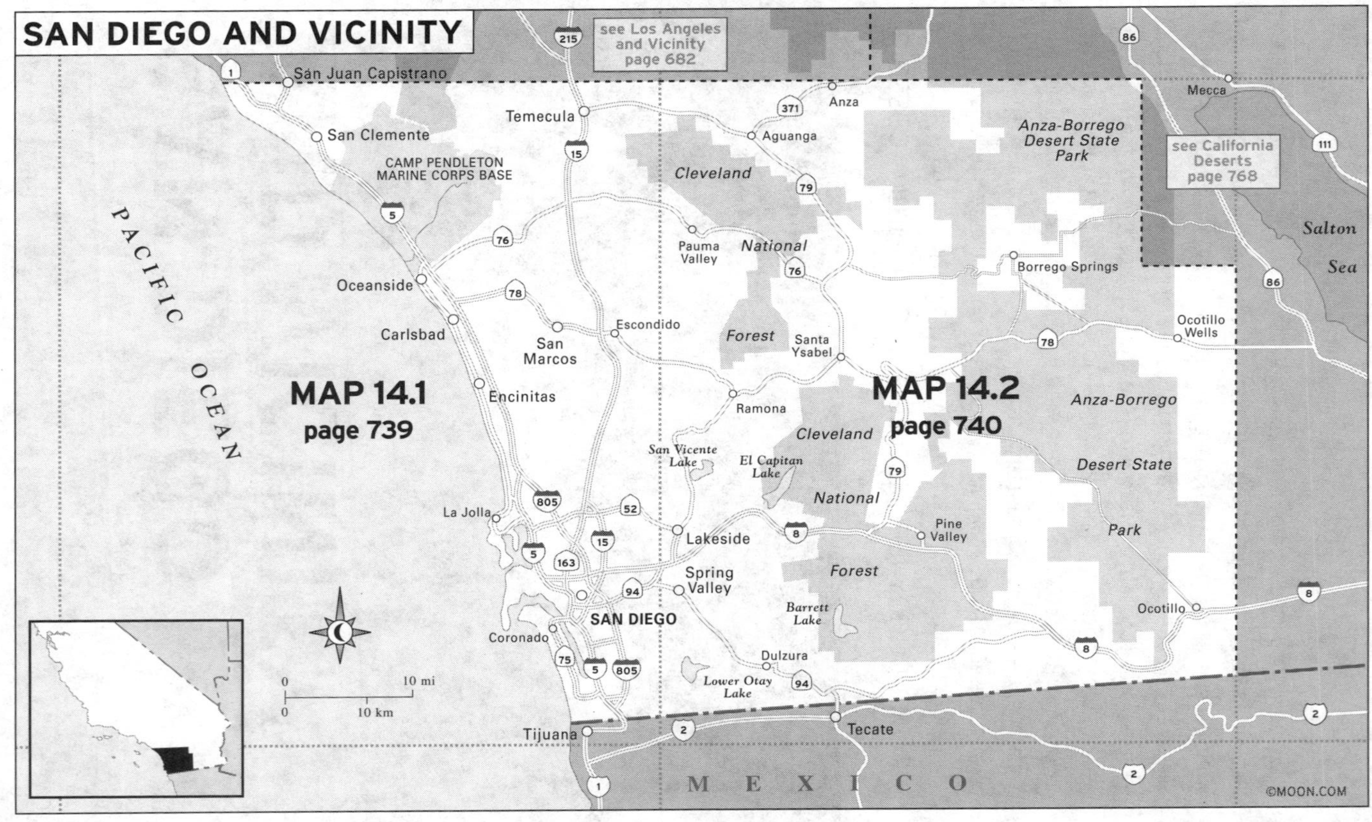
SAN DIEGO AND VICINITY
see Los Angeles and Vicinity page 682
see California Deserts page 768
PACIFIC OCEAN
MAP 14.1
page 739
MAP 14.2
page 740
San Juan Capistrano
San Clemente
CAMP PENDLETON MARINE CORPS BASE
Oceanside
Carlsbad
Encinitas
La Jolla
San Marcos
Temecula
Escondido
Coronado
SAN DIEGO
Tijuana
Spring Valley
Lakeside
San Vicente Lake
El Capitan Lake
Lower Otay Lake
Dulzura
Barrett Lake
Tecate
Ramona
Pauma Valley
Cleveland National Forest
Santa Ysabel
Aguanga
Anza
Pine Valley
Borrego Springs
Anza-Borrego Desert State Park
Ocotillo
Ocotillo Wells
Mecca
Salton Sea
MEXICO
0 10 mi
0 10 km
©MOON.COM

Map 14.1

Sites 1-19
Pages 741-753

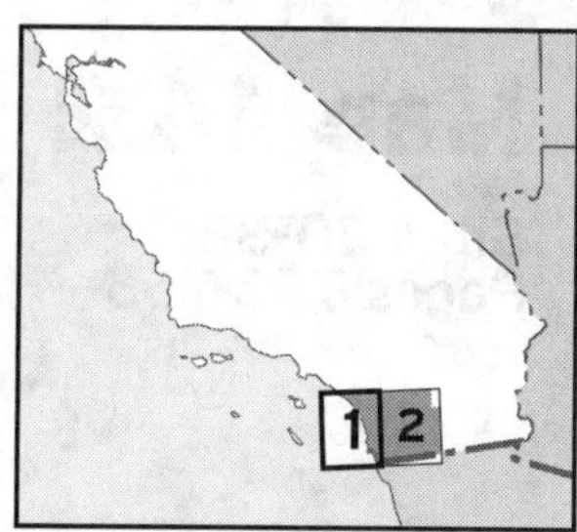

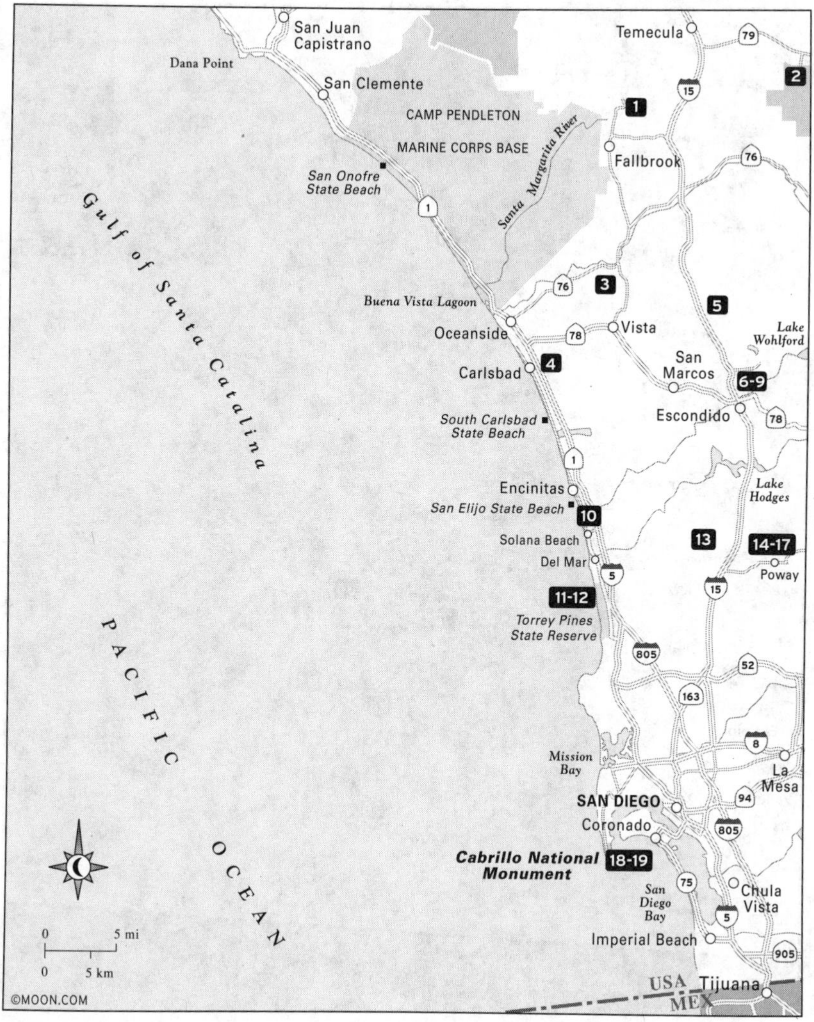

San Juan Capistrano
Temecula
Dana Point
San Clemente
CAMP PENDLETON
MARINE CORPS BASE
Santa Margarita River
Fallbrook
San Onofre State Beach
Gulf of Santa Catalina
Buena Vista Lagoon
Oceanside
Vista
Lake Wohlford
Carlsbad
San Marcos
Escondido
South Carlsbad State Beach
Encinitas
Lake Hodges
San Elijo State Beach
Solana Beach
Del Mar
Poway
Torrey Pines State Reserve
PACIFIC OCEAN
Mission Bay
La Mesa
SAN DIEGO
Coronado
Cabrillo National Monument
San Diego Bay
Chula Vista
Imperial Beach
USA
MEX
Tijuana
1 2 3 4 5 6-9 10 11-12 13 14-17 18-19
0 5 mi
0 5 km

Map 14.2

Sites 20-38
Pages 753-765

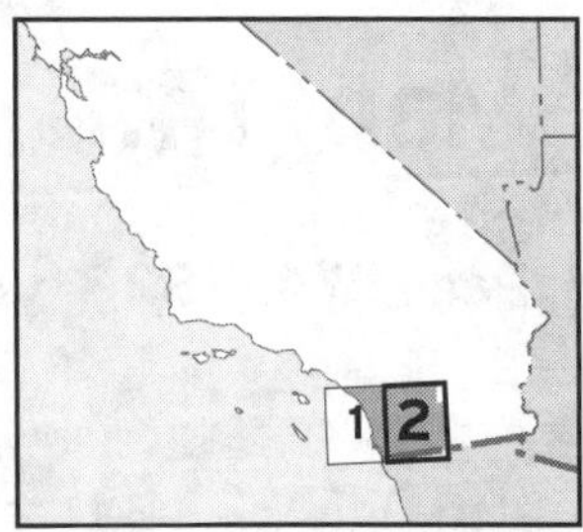

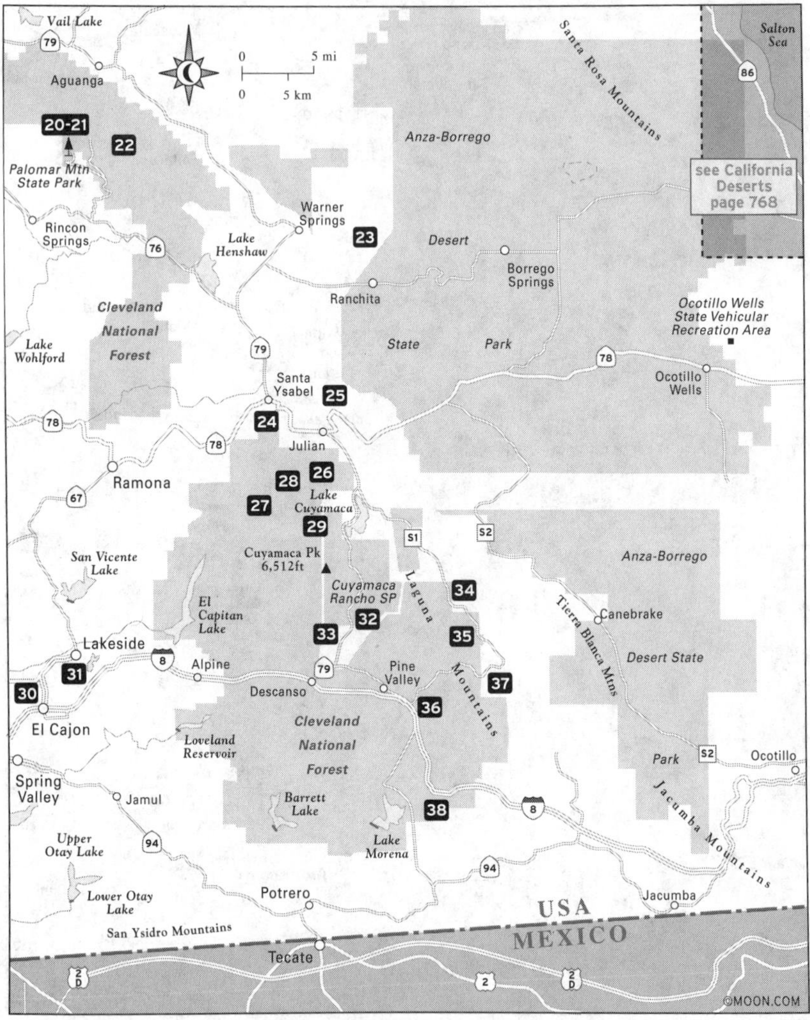

1 SANTA MARGARITA RIVER TRAIL

5.6 mi/3.0 hr 2 8

in Fallbrook

Map 14.1, page 739

A few miles north of downtown Fallbrook lies the Santa Margarita River, one of the last free-flowing rivers in Southern California. The river forms a native riparian habitat attracting many kinds of wildlife, particularly birds. There are six miles of marked trail, but the most popular walk is a 2.8-mile one-way hike from the Sandia Creek Drive trailhead. It has only a 400-foot elevation gain, so it is suitable for walkers and joggers, as well as people looking for a longer outing. An equestrian trail runs parallel to the hiking trail. There are several places where you can cross the river, but you'll have to get your feet wet; there are no bridges. First-time visitors here are amazed by the beauty of the Santa Margarita River Canyon, with its moss-covered rock outcrops, side canyons that branch off the main river, and dense forest canopy. It's like nothing you'll find anywhere else in San Diego County.

User Groups: Hikers, dogs, horses, and mountain bikes. No wheelchair facilities.

Permits: No permits are required. Parking and access are free.

Maps: For topographic maps, go to the USGS website to download Temecula and Fallbrook.

Directions: From I-15 south of Temecula, take the Mission Road (S13) exit west and drive to De Luz Road in Fallbrook. Turn north on De Luz Road and drive about 1 mile, then turn right on Sandia Creek Drive. Drive 0.5 mile to the parking lot on the right, just before the road crosses the river at Rock Mountain Drive.

Contact: Fallbrook Land Conservancy, Fallbrook, 760/728-0889, www.sdlcc.org/flc.

2 DRIPPING SPRINGS TRAIL

13.6 mi/2 days 3 8

in the Aqua Tibia Wilderness

Map 14.1, page 739

At the very northern edge of San Diego County lies the Aqua Tibia Wilderness, a land of extreme summer heat, exposed slopes, no available water sources, and thick chaparral-chamise, ceanothus, manzanita, and ribbonwood. The place appears suitable for only the most steadfast of hikers. Or so it seems. Actually, if you hike the Dripping Springs Trail in early spring, when the temperature is just right, the Aqua Tibia is a pastoral place with blooming shrubs and wildflowers, crystal-clear vistas, and flitting butterflies and bees. Trailhead elevation at Dripping Springs Campground is 1,600 feet, and the peak of Aqua Tibia Mountain is at 4,547 feet. The trail leaves the campground, crosses the rocky wash of Arroyo Seco Creek, and starts to climb. In the first three miles of trail, you get views of Vail Lake to the north and the big mountains of Southern California—San Jacinto, San Gorgonio, and San Antonio (Baldy). Another mile passes, and you can see Santiago Peak and the white dome of Palomar Observatory to the south, plus fine views of the Pacific Ocean, the Santa Rosa Plateau, and the rest of the Santa Ana Mountains. The chaparral gets taller as you go, and the trail gets steeper and narrower. When you finally near the peak of Aqua Tibia Mountain, you've climbed out of the chaparral and into oak woodland with a few scattered pines, which means—yes!—shade. Remember, hike this on a cool day in early spring, and you're in heaven. Hike it in summer, and you're in Temecula's version of hell.

User Groups: Hikers, dogs, and horses. No mountain bikes. No wheelchair facilities.

Permits: A free wilderness permit is required for overnight stays and can be obtained at the Dripping Springs station near the campground or from the Palomar Ranger District. Day users should sign the register at the trailhead.

A $5 parking fee is charged unless you have a National Forest Adventure Pass or interagency access pass.

Maps: A Cleveland National Forest map is available from the U.S. Forest Service. For a topographic map, go to the USGS website to download Vail Lake.

Directions: From I-15 in Temecula, take the Highway 79 east exit. Drive 11 miles east on Highway 79 to Dripping Springs Campground, on the right. Free parking is available outside the camp entrance. The trail begins at the south end of the campground.

Contact: Cleveland National Forest, Palomar Ranger District, Ramona, 760/788-0250, www.fs.usda.gov/cleveland.

3 GUAJOME LAKE TRAIL

3.0 mi/1.5 hr 2 7

in Guajome Regional Park near Oceanside

Map 14.1, page 739

Guajome Regional Park is home to one of the richest riparian areas of any of San Diego County's parks. The big draw is a spring-fed lake and marsh, which have enticed nearly 200 species of birds to pass sometime in the park. The waterways are also the happy home of many frogs, which you will hear but probably not see. In fact, *Guajome* means home of the frog. The park's main hiking trail leads from the parking lot and skirts the edge of mid-sized Guajome Lake, then continues up to the park's wedding gazebo and alongside Guajome Marsh. It's a popular trip for dog-walkers and families. An out-and-back trip will cover about three miles, and along the way you might see a few red-winged blackbirds, a white-faced ibis, or even the rare least Bell's vireo. Bring your binoculars. Fishing for bullheads, crappie, catfish, and sunfish is also popular at Guajome Lake. If you want to hike farther, additional trails lead into the grassland and chaparral interior areas of the park.

User Groups: Hikers, dogs, horses, and mountain bikes. No wheelchair facilities.

Permits: No permits are required. A $3 day-use fee is charged per vehicle.

Maps: A free trail map is available for download at www.sdparks.org. For a topographic map, go to the USGS website to download San Luis Rey.

Directions: From I-5 in Oceanside, take the Highway 76 exit, and drive east for seven miles to Guajome Lake Road. Turn right (south) into the park entrance.

Contact: Guajome Regional Park, Oceanside, 760/724-4489, www.sdparks.org.

4 BATIQUITOS LAGOON ECOLOGICAL RESERVE

3.2 mi/1.5 hr 1 7

near Carlsbad

Map 14.1, page 739

The trail around Batiquitos Lagoon is more of a walk than a hike, and it is only somewhat free from the nearby roar of the freeway, but nonetheless, the lagoon is one of San Diego's special places. Surrounded by I-5, a golf course, ritzy homes, and a big five-star hotel, the lagoon is a small island of nature amid a sea of development and artifice. It's a wonderful place to study the peaceful movements of birds and small animals, who go about their daily lives ignoring the surrounding chaos of human activity. This is also a great place to walk your dog after work (just be sure to keep him or her on a leash so the wildlife is not disturbed). From the end of Gabbiano Lane, walk toward the nature center, then pick up the trail that skirts along the edge of the lagoon, heading from west to east. The path runs for 1.6 miles one-way; most people just stroll as far as they please and then turn back. Four other small parking lots off Batiquitos Drive provide additional access points. While you walk, you'll have a near-guarantee of spotting herons, egrets, mudhens, mallards, teals, and other common water birds, as well as bunnies and lizards galore. Many rare birds can also be seen, including the elegant tern, marbled godwit, snowy plover, and yellow warbler.

User Groups: Hikers and dogs. No horses or mountain bikes. No wheelchair facilities.

Permits: No permits are required. Parking and access are free.

Maps: For a topographic map, go to the USGS website to download San Luis Rey.

Directions: From I-5 in Carlsbad, take the Poinsettia Lane exit and head east. Turn right on Batiquitos Drive, then bear right on Gabbiano Lane and drive to its end. Park in the small lot (there is space for six cars) or alongside the road, but do not park in front of the mailboxes.

Contact: Batiquitos Lagoon Ecological Reserve, Carlsbad, 760/931-0800, www.batiquitosfoundation.org.

5 HELLHOLE CANYON

4.8 mi/2.0 hr 3 7

Hellhole Canyon Preserve near Valley Center

Map 14.1, page 739

Hellhole Canyon Preserve seems a bit misnamed. We didn't think there was anything hellish about it, except maybe the heat on a summer afternoon. The preserve takes up 1,712 acres on the west flank of Rodriguez Mountain and is bounded by Indian reservations to the north and west. Because of the fire-adapted foliage that blankets this preserve—primarily chaparral and sage scrub plants such as redberry, manzanita, lilac, and monkey flower—the landscape recovers quickly from wildfires, which seem to occur regularly here every five to ten years. But with all this chaparral and no big trees, count on almost no shade anywhere in the preserve. From the trailhead staging area, the only choice is to head steeply downhill into the canyon on Hell Creek Trail. One mile down the trail you'll reach Hell Creek, which runs with vigor in the wet season and maintains a small trickle in the summer. Beyond the creek, the trail follows the route of the old Escondido flume. You walk alongside the rock-lined bed of this 15-mile-long canal, which was built in 1895 to transport water from the San Luis Rey River to Lake Wohlford. At 1.4 miles you reach a fork, where you can go left or right to walk a pleasant two-mile loop through rolling grasslands and chaparral, then head back up the trail the way you came. And on a hot day, that uphill return will be memorable. Ambitious hikers have the choice of continuing on a steep ascent to the summit of Rodriguez Mountain, where they will be treated to a view of the distant Pacific Ocean.

User Groups: Hikers and horses. No dogs or mountain bikes. No wheelchair facilities.

Permits: No permits are required. Parking and access are free.

Maps: A free trail map is available for download at www.sdparks.org. For an interesting hike, download a free interpretive brochure (www.hellholecanyon.org) that describes the plants seen in this preserve. For a topographic map, go to the USGS website to download Rodriguez Mountain.

Directions: From I-15 south of Temecula, take Highway 76 east for 15 miles and turn right (south) on Road S6/Valley Center Road. Drive five miles and turn left on North Lake Wohlford Road. Drive two miles and turn left on Paradise Mountain Road. Drive 3.3 miles to a T-intersection, where you turn right on Los Hermanos Ranch Road and then immediately left on Kiavo Road. Drive 0.5 mile on Kiavo Road to Santee Lane and the preserve entrance.

From Escondido and points south, take East Valley Parkway to North Lake Wohlford Road. Turn right and follow North Lake Wohlford Road for six miles to Paradise Mountain Road. Turn right on Paradise Mountain Road and follow it for 3.5 miles to Kiavo Road. Take Kiavo Road one block to Santee Lane and turn left into the preserve entrance.

Contact: Hellhole Canyon Preserve, Valley

Center, 760/742-1631, www.sdparks.org or www.hellholecanyon.org.

6 JACK CREEK NATURE TRAIL

1.0 mi/0.5 hr 

in Dixon Lake Recreation Area near Escondido

Map 14.1, page 739

If you are exceptionally lucky, it will be a rainy year in San Diego, and you will be able to see the waterfall flow along Jack Creek at Dixon Lake Recreation Area. We've only seen it trickle, but we've seen pictures of the 20-foot falls at flood, and it's quite beautiful. Nonetheless, a stroll on the 0.5-mile Jack Creek Nature Trail is good in any season, although best in winter and spring, when the hills are green and the flowers in bloom. The trail begins just inside the park entrance at the primitive road gate, and travels past a picnic area and along Jack Creek to the lake's edge. Along the way, many cute bunnies are likely to cross your path. (They are western cottontails, to be precise.) If the creek is flowing strong, be sure to take the right spur to the waterfall's base; otherwise, just go straight for the northeast side of the lake. At the water's edge, near the buoy line, the trail connects to the Sage Trail leading into Daley Ranch—a great choice if you feel like hiking farther. Many people choose instead to plunk a line in the water and see if they can catch a largemouth bass, rainbow trout, or catfish. If you do so, be sure to purchase a Dixon Lake fishing permit (a California fishing license is not required here).

User Groups: Hikers only. No dogs, horses, or mountain bikes. No wheelchair facilities.

Permits: No permits are required. A $5 day-use fee is charged per vehicle on weekends and holidays only.

Maps: For a topographic map, go to the USGS website to download Valley Center.

Directions: From Escondido, drive north on I-15 and take the El Norte Parkway exit. Drive 3.1 miles east on El Norte Parkway, turn left (north) on La Honda Drive, and drive 1.3 miles to the Dixon Lake entrance, on the right. Turn right, and after passing the kiosk, turn left and park at the Jack Creek Picnic Area.

Contact: Dixon Lake Ranger Station, Escondido, 760/839-4345, www.escondido.org.

7 CHAPARRAL INTERPRETIVE TRAIL

0.6 mi/0.5 hr 

in Dixon Lake Recreation Area near Escondido

Map 14.1, page 739

Short and sweet, the Chaparral Interpretive Trail lies on the boundary between Dixon Lake Recreation Area and 3,161-acre Daley Ranch Preserve. The trail is a great place to get an education on San Diego's natural ecology. It travels through four distinct Southern California plant communities—mixed chaparral, oak woodlands, coastal sage scrub, and a mature riparian area. Interpretive signs along the way identify the foliage you see, including Engelmann and coast live oaks, toyon, various sages, and blue-eyed grass. It is not uncommon for hikers to catch sight of a coyote or a bobcat along this trail, especially when hiking early in the morning. In addition to being an easy stroll, some of this trail is shade-covered, making it pleasant even on warm days.

User Groups: Hikers only. No dogs, horses, or mountain bikes. No wheelchair facilities.

Permits: No permits are required. A $5 day-use fee is charged per vehicle on weekends and holidays only.

Maps: For a topographic map, go to the USGS website to download Valley Center.

Directions: From Escondido, drive north on I-15 and take the El Norte Parkway exit. Drive 3.1 miles east on El Norte Parkway, turn left (north) on La Honda Drive, and drive 1.3 miles to the Dixon Lake entrance on the right. Turn right, and after passing the kiosk, turn left and park at the Jack Creek Picnic Area.

Contact: Dixon Lake Ranger Station, Escondido, 760/839-4345, www.escondido.org.

8 BERNARDO MOUNTAIN

7.2 mi/3.5 hr

by Lake Hodges near Escondido

Map 14.1, page 739

If you're spending the day anywhere near Lake Hodges, make sure you save a few hours to take this nice hike up to the summit of Bernardo Mountain. The mountain rises 900 feet above Lake Hodges and offers great views of the lake, the nearby Laguna Mountains, much of northern San Diego County, and on clear days, the Pacific Ocean and Mexico. The trail was opened to the public in 2002 as part of the partially completed Coast-to-Crest Trail, which will someday span 55 miles from the ocean at Del Mar to the San Dieguito River's source on Volcan Mountain. This section of the trail has quickly become well known to Escondido-area hikers and mountain bikers. The route begins with a less-than-promising start on a concrete path that parallels the I-15 freeway. In about 0.5 mile, the concrete turns sharply right and crosses under the freeway, and soon things start to get a whole lot better. At 1.5 miles you'll cross lovely Felicita Creek, a year-round stream that is lined with oaks and sycamores and provides an excellent place for spotting birds. In another mile you will have circled around to Bernardo Mountain's north slope, which is covered in tall chaparral. Keep heading uphill, switchbacking your way up the slope on a remarkably mellow grade, until you top out at the summit at 3.6 miles. This is a good spot to say a few words of thanks to the Nature Conservancy, the Trust for Public Land, the San Dieguito River Valley Conservancy, and the city of Escondido for purchasing this land and making it available for public use.

User Groups: Hikers, dogs, horses, or mountain bikes. No wheelchair facilities.

Permits: No permits are required. Parking and access are free.

Maps: For a topographic map, go to the USGS website to download Valley Center.

Directions: From San Diego, drive north on I-15 to south Escondido and take the Via Rancho Parkway exit east for about 100 yards. Turn right (south) at the first light on Sunset Drive. Follow Sunset Drive 0.2 mile to its end and the trailhead.

Contact: San Dieguito River Park, Escondido, 858/674-2270, www.sdrp.org.

9 RANCH HOUSE, BOULDER, AND EAST RIDGE LOOP

4.8 mi/2.5 hr

at Daley Ranch Preserve near Escondido

Map 14.1, page 739

Since its opening to the public in the late 1990s, Daley Ranch has become a favorite park of locals and visitors in the Escondido area. This 3,161-acre park contains a biologically unique landscape consisting of lush oak forests, coastal sage scrub, and native grasslands. The park also has great historical significance, being rich in Native American history as well as the home of English immigrant Robert Daley, who settled here in 1869. The Daley family farmed, raised horses, built a dairy, and later vacationed in this area until late in the 20th century, when the land was purchased by the city of Escondido. This hike follows a meandering loop around the park's redwood-constructed Ranch House. Follow the Ranch House Trail and the Boulder Loop Trail, then return on the East Ridge and Creek Crossing Trails. Along the way, you'll enjoy fine views of Escondido, pass by two small ponds, and get a look at the Daleys' impressive homestead. Pick up a park map at the trailhead; all junctions are well signed. If you'd rather not hike on your own, the park offers a wide range of naturalist-led hikes most Saturdays and Sundays.

Daley Ranch Preserve

User Groups: Hikers, dogs, horses, and mountain bikes. No wheelchair facilities.
Permits: No permits are required. Parking and access are free.
Maps: Free park maps are available at the trailhead. For a topographic map, go to the USGS website to download Valley Center.
Directions: From Escondido, drive north on I-15 and take the El Norte Parkway exit. Drive 3.1 miles east on El Norte Parkway, and turn left (north) on La Honda Drive. Drive 1 mile on La Honda Drive and park in the dirt lot on the left.
Contact: Daley Ranch Preserve, Dixon Lake Ranger Station, Escondido, 760/839-4345, www.escondido.org.

10 SAN ELIJO LAGOON

5.0 mi/2.5 hr 2 8

in Solana Beach

Map 14.1, page 739

San Elijo Lagoon Ecological Reserve is bordered by the housing developments and shopping centers of Encinitas, Solana Beach, and Rancho Santa Fe, but the lagoon's multitudes of resident and migratory birds don't seem to mind—and neither do hikers and nature lovers. When you first see it, you may find it hard to imagine enjoying a nature experience so close to the freeways and roads. Suspend your disbelief and pay a visit to the lagoon, which is a mixture of freshwater from inland creeks and saltwater from the ocean. The reserve has seven miles of hiking trails with six different trailheads, so there's a lot to explore here. The south side is a little wilder than the Manchester Avenue side, and the trails are longer, so start there. A gated fire road leads down to the lagoon from the north end of North Rios Avenue, and you can hike either right or left. Birds are abundant, especially great egrets, stilts, gulls, and godwits. Great blue herons occasionally make an appearance, and as you wander inland, you'll see many songbirds among the chaparral.

If you want to educate yourself about what you are seeing, an intelligent series of interpretive signs is displayed on the Nature Center Trail, a one-mile loop located on the north side of the lagoon (off Manchester Avenue, in Cardiff). The signs explain about saltwater and freshwater marshes, coastal sage scrub, and the wildlife living in these communities.

User Groups: Hikers and dogs. The one-mile Nature Center Trail is wheelchair-accessible. No horses or mountain bikes.

Permits: No permits are required. Parking and access are free.

Maps: A free trail map is available for download at www.sdparks.org. For a topographic map, go to the USGS website to download Encinitas.

Directions: From I-5 in Solana Beach, take the Lomas Santa Fe Drive exit and drive west to North Rios Avenue. Turn right and go 0.8 mile to the end of the road and the trailhead. Park alongside the road.

Contact: San Elijo Lagoon Ecological Reserve, Cardiff, 760/634-3026, www.sdparks.org or San Elijo Lagoon Conservancy, 760/436-3944, www.sanelijo.org.

11 GUY FLEMING LOOP TRAIL

0.75 mi/0.5 hr

in Torrey Pines State Reserve near Del Mar

Map 14.1, page 739

Torrey Pines is one of the greatest hiking destinations in San Diego, with several short but sweet trails and enough spectacular scenery to keep you coming back for more. The Guy Fleming Loop Trail is the easiest of the trails in the park, with almost no elevation change, so it's suitable for all levels of hikers. The path has great views of the Pacific Ocean, La Jolla, Del Mar, and Los Peñasquitos Marsh. If you hike the right side of the loop first, you come to the North Overlook, where you can check out the vistas, as well as San Diego's rare tree, the Torrey pine. The trail then loops around to the South Overlook, where you can sometimes see San Clemente and Catalina Islands. People frequently hold weddings at the South Overlook. If they're smart, they plan them for spring, when the wildflowers bloom along the trail.

User Groups: Hikers only. No dogs, horses, or mountain bikes. No wheelchair facilities.

Permits: No permits are required. A $12-25 day-use fee is charged per vehicle (higher fees apply April to September and on weekends year-round).

Maps: A free map of Torrey Pines State Reserve is available at the park visitors center. For a topographic map, go to the USGS website to download Del Mar.

Directions: From I-5 in Del Mar, take the Carmel Valley Road exit and drive west 1.5 miles. Turn south on Camino del Mar and drive 0.7 mile to the reserve entrance. Turn right, drive up the hill 0.7 mile, and park at the first parking area on the right, signed for the Guy Fleming Trail. If this lot is full, you can park farther up the hill, at the visitors center, and walk back down the road.

Contact: Torrey Pines State Reserve, San Diego, 858/755-2063, www.parks.ca.gov.

12 RAZOR POINT AND BEACH TRAIL LOOP

2.5 mi/1.5 hr 2 9

in Torrey Pines State Reserve near Del Mar

Map 14.1, page 739 BEST

If you can get a parking spot in the lot by the visitors center at Torrey Pines State Reserve (it's not easy on weekend afternoons), you can start hiking right away on the Razor Point Trail, cutting over to the Beach Trail from Razor Point and heading to the beach. The Razor Point Trail provides dramatic views of the reserve's eroded coastal badlands, which would look like something straight out of the desert if not for the ocean beyond. There's a spiderweb of paths, only some of which are signed, but it's fine to just wander around at random and visit as many of the overlooks as possible. Windswept Torrey pines grace the bluffs, and wildflowers bloom in the sandy soil in springtime. When

Torrey Pines State Reserve

you're in the mood, head south from Razor Point (paralleling the ocean) until you hook up with the Beach Trail, and turn right, squeezing through the narrow, steep sandstone entrance to the beach. It's great fun. A return uphill on the Beach Trail makes an excellent loop.

User Groups: Hikers only. No dogs, horses, or mountain bikes. No wheelchair facilities.

Permits: No permits are required. A $12-15 day-use fee is charged per vehicle (higher fees apply April to September and on weekends year-round).

Maps: A free map of Torrey Pines State Reserve is available at the park visitors center. For a topographic map, go to the USGS website to download Del Mar.

Directions: From I-5 in Del Mar, take the Carmel Valley Road exit and drive west for 1.5 miles. Turn south on Camino del Mar and drive 0.7 mile to the reserve entrance. Turn right, drive up the hill one mile, and park by the reserve office and visitors center. The trailhead is across the park road from the visitors center.

Contact: Torrey Pines State Reserve, San Diego, 858/755-2063, www.parks.ca.gov.

13 LOS PEÑASQUITOS CANYON

6.5 mi/3.0 hr 1 8

in Los Peñasquitos Canyon Preserve near Poway

Map 14.1, page 739

If it is winter or spring and your thoughts are turning to love, there may be no better spot in San Diego for a first date than Los Peñasquitos Canyon Preserve. The trail that runs from one end of the canyon to the other is wide and level, perfectly built for good conversation and maybe some hand-holding. When the cascades along the creek are flowing, you can find a big volcanic boulder to sit on and watch the reflections of the sky in the water. If not, there are numerous places where you could lay out a picnic blanket under a spreading oak or sycamore tree. Early in the year, the wildflowers bloom and the grasses become verdant. Can this much beauty be found so close to a large urban area? You bet. Although you can hike the trail starting from either end, the eastern trailhead near Poway is preferred, because that end of the path is more shaded. As you wander, keep watching for mileage marker 3, because soon after it, you will see a hitching post and bike rack on the right, where you can veer off the main trail and scramble down to the cascades on Los Peñasquitos Creek. Even when the stream is reduced to a trickle, the car-sized boulders in the creek are fascinating to see; they are remnants of a volcanic island chain formed underwater 140 million years ago.

User Groups: Hikers, dogs, horses, and mountain bikes. No wheelchair facilities.

Permits: No permits are required. A $3 day-use fee is charged per vehicle.

Maps: A free trail map is available for download at www.sdparks.org. For a topographic map, go to the USGS website to download Poway.

Directions: From Escondido, drive south on I-15 for 16 miles to the Mercy Road exit. Turn right (west) on Mercy Road and follow it for one mile, crossing Black Mountain Road, to the trailhead parking area.

Contact: Los Peñasquitos Canyon Preserve, San Diego, 858/484-7504, www.sdparks.org.

14 BLUE SKY ECOLOGICAL RESERVE

4.0-6.0 mi/2-3 hr

in the Blue Sky Ecological Reserve near Poway

Map 14.1, page 739

The 700-acre Blue Sky Ecological Reserve provides habitat for several rare and threatened animal and plant species, including harried San Diego humans who desperately need a place to stop and smell the flowers. The reserve is home to the San Diego horned lizard and a lovely grove of coast live oaks. It's a great place to hike on hot days in San Diego because so much of the reserve is shaded by a dense tree canopy. From the trailhead, hike along the wide, flat fire road, or head down onto the Creekside Trail, which connects back to the fire road in a short distance. Deer, rabbits, and birds of many kinds are commonly seen. Poison oak is prevalent, too, but stay on the main trails and you can easily avoid it. At about one mile, turn right on the trail to Lake Poway, a short ascent away. The lake is a fine place to catch catfish and trout or to rent a rowboat and row your hiking partner around the lake (boat rentals are available Wed.-Sun.). You can also walk the perimeter of the lake, which will add two miles and some climbing and descending to this mostly level route. Or just retrace your steps to the main trail, and head back to the trailhead for a four-mile round-trip. Another option is to continue on the main trail to the left fork for Lake Ramona. Follow the fork and you'll face a fairly steep climb up to Lake Ramona's dam, but the reward is a lovely view all the way to the Pacific Ocean.

If you enjoy hiking with a naturalist, check the reserve's website at www.poway.org/bluesky for the dates and times of free guided hikes. The trips are usually only one mile in length—just right for families with young children.

User Groups: Hikers, dogs, and horses. No mountain bikes. No wheelchair facilities.

Permits: No permits are required. Parking and access are free.

Maps: For a topographic map, go to the USGS website to download Escondido.

Directions: From I-15 near Poway, drive north to the Rancho Bernardo Road exit. Drive east for 3.5 miles on Rancho Bernardo Road/Espola Road to the reserve (on the left).

Contact: Blue Sky Ecological Reserve, 858/668-4781; City of Poway, 858/668-4400, www.poway.org.

15 MOUNT WOODSON

3.6 mi/2.0 hr 3 8

near Poway

Map 14.1, page 739

Mount Woodson is the neighborhood summit to climb for the thousands of people who live in the Poway, Scripps Ranch, and Rancho

Bernardo areas. The light-colored, rocky mountain—a favorite playground of rock climbers from all over San Diego—is always there in the background, looming over the suburbs below. If you've never seen Mount Woodson except from the bottom looking up, maybe it's time to lace up your hiking boots. The trail has a 1,500-foot elevation gain to reach the 2,894-foot peak, so you'll get in your workout for the day, but you won't be so wiped out that you can't enjoy the vistas or the fascinating rock formations you'll see along the trail. Hike on the path south of the fire station, and then follow the paved Mount Woodson Road. You'll reach the top at 1.8 miles, where a ton of electronic equipment is in place. Wander around a bit on the ridge until you find the best spot to look out over the wide blue Pacific, pick out the summits of Mount Baldy and Palomar Mountain, and then congratulate yourself for having bagged Mount Woodson's peak. If you are looking for more of a challenge on the way to Woodson's summit, you can take a longer trail (seven miles round-trip) that starts at Lake Poway. This alternate trail is the preferred route for people who can't stand hiking on pavement. The path is steep and narrow in places, and has a 2,000-foot elevation gain to the summit. It begins on the east side of Lake Poway, so from the lake's main parking lots you must walk about a half-mile around the lake (counterclockwise) to access it.

User Groups: Hikers, dogs, horses, and mountain bikes. No wheelchair facilities.

Permits: No permits are required. A $5 parking fee is charged per vehicle.

Maps: For a topographic map, go to the USGS website to download San Pasqual.

Directions: From Poway, drive east on Poway Road for 3.5 miles and turn north on Highway 67. Drive three miles to the Ramona CDF Fire Station, on the left. The trail begins by the fire station.

Contact: Lake Poway Recreation Area, Poway, 858/668-4770, www.poway.org.

16 GOODAN RANCH SYCAMORE CANYON PRESERVE

3.1-5.0 mi/1.5-2.5 hr 

in Sycamore Canyon Preserve near Poway

Map 14.1, page 739

Are you looking for a good spot to watch the sun set, but you don't feel like braving the traffic to the beach? A trip to the adjoining Goodan Ranch Sycamore Canyon Preserve could be just the ticket. The terrain is coastal sage scrub, chaparral, and oak woodland (no surprises here), but the path leads into beautiful canyons and offers wide vistas of San Diego County. The preserve's trails are well maintained and well signed, with trail maps posted at major intersections. From the parking lot, take the winding single-track trail on the left through the chaparral, heading down through Martha's Grove (a group of ancient oak trees), then out into the open grasslands. Turn right on the fire road and then right again to loop back for a 3.1-mile round-trip. If you want to hike longer, continue downhill on the Martha's Grove Trail and add on a two-mile loop around the southern half of Goodan Ranch, which is dotted with historic buildings dating back to the 1930s and year-round streams. This will give you a five-mile loop hike. Note: The preserve is also popular with mountain bikers, but the ones we met were extremely courteous to hikers.

User Groups: Hikers, dogs, horses, and mountain bikes. No wheelchair facilities.

Permits: No permits are required. Parking and access are free.

Maps: A free trail map is available for download at www.sdparks.org. For a topographic map, go to the USGS website to download San Vicente Reservoir.

Directions: From Poway drive east on Poway Road to Garden Road. Turn right, drive one mile on Garden Road, and turn right on Sycamore Canyon Road. Drive 2.5 miles to the road's end at the Goodan Staging Area.

Contact: Goodan Ranch Sycamore Canyon

Preserve, Poway, 858/513-4737, www.sdparks.org.

17 IRON MOUNTAIN

6.0 mi/3.5 hr 3 8

near Poway

Map 14.1, page 739

A well-maintained trail leads to the summit of 2,696-foot Iron Mountain, where the view of northern San Diego County is inspiring. The hike is challenging enough for some good aerobic exercise, but short enough that it can be accomplished after work on the long days of summer, assuming the day is not too hot. If you are wondering about the name "Iron Mountain," its meaning is revealed about one mile up the trail, where a side trail goes very steeply uphill to the remains of an old iron ore mine. A half-mile past this side trail is the right turnoff for the summit, which lies 1.4 miles farther. A hiker's register can usually be found on top, where most visitors are inclined to scribble a few wise words. Many comments revolve around the pointy summit's commanding view, which extends all the way to the shimmering Pacific. There are likely to be plenty of other users on this trail, including mountain bikers, hardcore joggers, and equestrians, but everybody is usually friendly. Note: This is one of two possible routes to Iron Mountain. The other route starts just a short distance north of this one at the end of Ellie Lane (just off Highway 67), and is much more challenging. Both trails offer the same reward, but the route described here is easier by far, with an elevation gain of only 1,150 feet.

User Groups: Hikers, dogs, horses, and mountain bikes. No wheelchair facilities.

Permits: No permits are required. Parking and access are free.

Maps: For a topographic map, go to the USGS website to download San Vicente Reservoir.

Directions: From Poway, drive east on Poway Road for 3.5 miles to its junction with Highway 67. The trailhead is at this junction, on the east side of Highway 67 at a small gravel parking area. Park there or alongside the road.

Contact: City of Poway, Poway, 858/668-4400, www.poway.org.

18 BAYSIDE TRAIL

2.0 mi/1.5 hr 2 10

in Cabrillo National Monument

Map 14.1, page 739

While everybody else at Cabrillo National Monument is visiting the old Point Loma Lighthouse, having their picture taken by the statue of Juan Rodríguez Cabrillo, or checking out the wonderful view of San Diego from the visitors center, you can sneak off for a hike on the Bayside Trail and find a surprising amount of solitude. Gorgeous coastal vistas will accompany that solitude, as well as an interesting lesson in native coastal vegetation. This coastal Mediterranean habitat is one of the eight most sensitive in the world.

Take the paved sidewalk trail from the parking lot to the lighthouse, where you can peer inside at the period furniture and imagine what life was like for the lighthouse keeper and his family in the 1890s. Then check out the Lighthouses of Point Loma exhibit in the Assistant Keeper's Quarters next door and the great views from the overlooks on the lighthouse's far side. After this short tour, pick up the paved road on the east side of the lighthouse, signed as the Bayside Trail. Take the left fork, which is gravel, and wind gently downhill around Point Loma, occasionally tearing your eyes away from the view so you can read the interpretive signs. If you do, you'll learn all about coastal sage scrub, local and migrating birds, and fire ecology. On every step of the trail, the whole of San Diego Bay and the Pacific Ocean are yours to survey. You'll see huge navy ships sailing out to sea, flocks of gulls following the fishing boats back into harbor, plus sailboats and jet skiers galore. The trail ends 300 feet below the statue of Cabrillo, where a sign says Trail Ends—Return by the Same Route. Darn.

User Groups: Hikers only. No dogs, horses, or mountain bikes. No wheelchair facilities.

Permits: No permits are required. A $20 entrance fee is charged per vehicle, which is good for seven days.

Maps: A free brochure and trail map of Cabrillo National Monument are available at the entrance station or visitors center. For a topographic map, go to the USGS website to download Point Loma.

Directions: From I-5 South or I-8 West in San Diego, take the Rosecrans Street exit and drive south. Staying on Rosecrans Street, you will turn right on Cañon Street and then left on Catalina Boulevard. The road ends at Cabrillo National Monument. The trail begins by the old lighthouse.

Contact: Cabrillo National Monument, San Diego, 619/557-5450, www.nps.gov/cabr.

19 CABRILLO TIDEPOOLS

1.0 mi/0.5 hr 1 10

in Cabrillo National Monument

Map 14.1, page 739 BEST

We love tidepools, and the ones at Cabrillo National Monument are some of the best in Southern California. You may want to stop in at the Cabrillo National Monument visitors center before you head straight for the tidepools. A film on tidepool life plays continually in the auditorium and the Cabrillo Store sells brochures and books on how to explore the pools and identify the various creatures that live there. Even more important, you should check your tide table before you visit (or phone the park), or else your hike may be very, very short. A fenced trail leads along the bluff tops for a few hundred feet, but then you descend to the rocky beach and walk a long stretch. (You have to stop below the coast guard station, as that area is closed to the public for restoration.) What will you see? Most likely, you'll get a peek at mussels, crabs, sea hares, barnacles, sea stars,

Carbrillo Tidepools

anemones, snails, and limpets. If you're lucky, you could see an octopus, an abalone, or a sea urchin. Is it wintertime? Why, we believe a passing gray whale just waved her flipper at you. Gray whales may be seen returning to their breeding grounds in Baja California from late December though early March.

User Groups: Hikers and dogs. No horses or mountain bikes. No wheelchair facilities.

Permits: No permits are required, unless you are traveling in a group of 10 people or more. A $20 entrance fee is charged per vehicle, which is good for seven days.

Maps: A free brochure and trail map of Cabrillo National Monument are available at the entrance station or visitors center. For a topographic map, go to the USGS website to download Point Loma.

Directions: From I-5 South or I-8 West in San Diego, take the Rosecrans Street exit and drive south. Staying on Rosecrans Street, turn right on Cañon Street, left on Catalina Boulevard, and continue to the monument entrance. After paying the entrance fee, take the right fork (immediately following the entrance station) that is signed as Tidepools Parking Area. Continue down the hill to the parking area.

Contact: Cabrillo National Monument, San Diego, 619/557-5450, www.nps.gov/cabr.

20 WEIR AND LOWER DOANE VALLEY LOOP

3.0 mi/1.5 hr

in Palomar Mountain State Park

Map 14.2, page 740

If you've never visited before, Palomar Mountain State Park is like a shock to your system—a good shock. At 5,500 feet in elevation, the air is cool, the conifers are big, and suburban sprawl seems far, far away. We kept shaking our heads in disbelief at the Sierra Nevada-like feel of the place. A good introduction to the park is this loop hike on three trails: the Doane Valley Nature Trail, the Weir Trail, and the Lower Doane Valley Trail. From the parking area at Doane Pond (which is always busy with children learning to fish), head away from Doane Pond on the trail that crosses the park road. Start your walk on the Doane Valley Nature Trail and veer left onto the Weir Trail, following pretty Doane Creek under the shade of big pines, firs, and cedars. Cross the creek about one mile out (shortly after the left fork for the Baptist Trail), then follow the Lower Doane Valley Trail as it loops back around a meadow. You'll probably see deer and mountain quail and hear many birdcalls. You'll certainly see the evidence of resident woodpeckers in the big old trees. When the trail nears Doane Valley Campground, cross the creek again and make a sharp switchback to the right, on the Doane Valley Nature Trail. The nature trail will close out your trip, bringing you back to the trailhead in 0.75 mile. As you pass the giant conifers and grassy meadows along the way, you will ask yourself again and again, "Is this really San Diego?"

User Groups: Hikers only. No dogs, horses, or mountain bikes. No wheelchair facilities.

Permits: No permits are required. A $10 day-use fee is charged per vehicle.

Maps: A map of Palomar Mountain State Park is available at the entrance station or park headquarters, or by free download at www.parks.ca.gov. For topographic maps, go to the USGS website to download Boucher Hill and Palomar Observatory.

Directions: From I-15 north of Escondido, drive east on Highway 76 for 21 miles. Turn left (north) on Road S6/South Grade Road and drive 6.5 miles to the junction with Road S7. Turn left on Road S7 and drive three miles into the park. Pay your fee at the entrance station, then continue on the park road, turn right, and drive to the parking area by Doane Pond and the school camp.

Contact: Palomar Mountain State Park, Palomar Mountain, 760/742-3462 or 760/767-5311, www.parks.ca.gov or www.friendsofpalomarsp.org.

21 BOUCHER TRAIL AND SCOTT'S CABIN LOOP

4.0 mi/2.0 hr 2 9

in Palomar Mountain State Park

Map 14.2, page 740 BEST

You may be wowed by the view of Pauma Valley from Boucher Lookout (at elevation 5,438 feet), but start walking on the Boucher Trail, and you'll be wowed even more. The trail descends from the fire lookout, passing a burn area. It crosses Nate Harrison Grade Road and heads for Cedar Grove Campground. The camp is well named; the cedars are huge and majestic here. Bear right at the fork by the campground, walk a brief stretch on the camp road, and then cross the park road to pick up the Scott's Cabin Trail, which leads to the cabin site of an 1880s homesteader. Only the base of the cabin remains—it's a rather sad-looking pile of sticks and logs. From the site, take the right fork to head back to park headquarters and Silvercrest Picnic Area. Walk to your right on the park road for a few hundred yards until you can pick up the Boucher Trail once more and walk back to the lookout. Here the Boucher Trail is the narrow trail that runs between the legs of the driving loop to the lookout. What? You say you forgot your troubles along the way? That's what happens here at Palomar Mountain.

User Groups: Hikers only. No dogs, horses, or mountain bikes. No wheelchair facilities.

Permits: No permits are required. A $1-day-use fee is charged per vehicle.

Maps: A map of Palomar State Park is available at the entrance station or park headquarters, or by free download at www.parks.ca.gov. For topographic maps, go to the USGS website to download Boucher Hill and Palomar Observatory.

Directions: From I-15 north of Escondido, drive east on Highway 76 for 21 miles. Turn left (north) on Road S6 (South Grade Road) and drive 6.5 miles to the junction with Road S7. Turn left on Road S7 and drive three miles into the park. Pay your fee at the entrance station, then continue on the park road and bear left at the sign for Boucher Lookout. Park at the lookout and begin hiking on Boucher Trail.

Contact: Palomar Mountain State Park, Palomar Mountain, 760/742-3462 or 760/767-5311, www.parks.ca.gov or www.friendsofpalomarsp.org.

22 OBSERVATORY TRAIL

4.4 mi/2.5 hr

in Cleveland National Forest on Palomar Mountain

Map 14.2, page 740

The hike to reach Palomar Observatory is far better than the drive to reach it. Even if you have absolutely no interest in astronomy, the National Recreation Trail to the observatory is just plain fun to walk. From Observatory Campground, the trail is an aerobic uphill climb, but on a well-graded, well-maintained trail with an 800-foot elevation gain. The shade is dense from oaks, pines, and cedars, and you'll find many giant-sized pine cones along the trail. At 0.5 mile, you reach an overlook platform with a lovely view of Mendenhall Valley, and then you head back into the forest to climb some more. The last stretch of trail brings you out to the observatory parking lot, where you turn right, walk through the lot and past the museum, and head straight for what looks like a big white golf ball—the 200-inch Hale telescope. Be sure to walk up the couple flights of stairs to the telescope viewing area and learn all about how the amazing gadget works. More than 100 billion galaxies like ours are within spotting range of the giant telescope. Every clear night of the year, the scope is scanning the skies in an attempt to unveil the mysteries of the universe. The astronomy museum in the neighboring building is also worth a look.

User Groups: Hikers, dogs, horses, and mountain bikes. No wheelchair facilities.

Permits: No permits are required. A $5 parking fee is charged unless you have a National

Forest Adventure Pass or interagency access pass.

Maps: A Cleveland National Forest map is available from the U.S. Forest Service. For a topographic map, go to the USGS website to download Palomar Observatory.

Directions: From I-15 north of Escondido, drive east on Highway 76 for 21 miles. Turn left (north) on Road S6 (South Grade Road) and drive 6.5 miles to the junction with Road S7, and then continue north on Road S6 for three more miles to Observatory Campground, on the right. Drive through the camp to the signed parking area for the amphitheater and trailhead.

Contact: Cleveland National Forest, Palomar Ranger District, Ramona, 760/788-0250, www.fs.usda.gov/cleveland.

23 HOT SPRINGS MOUNTAIN

10.4 mi/5.5 hr 3 9

on the Los Coyotes Indian Reservation near Warner Springs

Map 14.2, page 740

Lots of people drive all the way out to Warner Springs and hike to the summit of Hot Springs Mountain at 6,533 feet just so they can say they've climbed the highest mountain in San Diego County (even though it's a mere 21 feet taller than Cuyamaca Peak in Rancho Cuyamaca State Park). But if it's April or early May, another great reason to hike here is to see the wildflower display, which is surprisingly diverse and colorful. Autumn is also scenic; the mountain's slopes shelter dense stands of black oaks, which turn a brilliant gold in late October. Note: The entrance gate at the Los Coyotes Indian Reservation is only attended on weekends and Monday holidays, so if you plan to visit on a weekday, write or call ahead for permission to visit.

Once you've obtained your permit and map at the entrance station, you'll drive onward to the trailhead near Los Coyotes Campground (inside the reservation boundary) to start hiking on Sukat Road. The hike follows dirt roads the whole way, and the first mile is the toughest, with a 550-foot gain. At the top, you meet up with a better dirt road that runs up the south slope of Hot Springs Mountain. Turn right (west) and ascend higher along the ridgeline, passing by small flower-filled meadows interspersed among groves of Coulter pines and black oaks. There's a lot more greenery up here than you'll find in most of San Diego County.

Technically, Hot Springs Mountain has two summits, east and west, and on the latter you'll find an abandoned lookout tower that has been closed since the mid-1970s but was once used by the California Department of Forestry for spotting fires. The dilapidated old building looks precarious, like a strong wind could knock it over completely. Continue past it on a rough use trail to the eastern summit. You'll have to do a little scrambling up this chaparral-covered hill. On top is a concrete slab perched on a rock outcrop, a USGS marker, and a register where you can sign your name and read the comments of other visitors. Hot Springs Mountain's summit offers a fascinating perspective on the immense size of the Salton Sea, the surrounding desert, the Henshaw Valley, and the Pacific Ocean. The total elevation gain for this hike is 2,200 feet. Warning: Four-wheel-drive vehicles are permitted on this road/trail, so it is possible you may be passed by a few gas-guzzlers—but most of the time it's just you and the mountain.

User Groups: Hikers, dogs, horses, and mountain bikes. No wheelchair facilities.

Permits: An access permit is required and is available at the entrance gate. The entrance fee is $10 per person. The entrance gate is usually attended 8am-5pm on weekends and Monday holidays.

Maps: A trail map is provided when you pay the entrance fee. For a topographic map, go to the USGS website to download Hot Springs Mountain.

Directions: From Santa Ysabel at the junction of Highways 78 and 79, take Highway 79 north for 12 miles toward Warner Springs. Turn east (right) on Camino San Ignacio (about two miles before Warner Springs Resort). Continue for about six miles to the reservation entrance gate. You will be given a map to the trailhead (it's across from the Los Coyotes Campground sign) when you pay your entrance fee at the guardhouse.

Contact: Los Coyotes Band of Indians, Warner Springs, 760/782-0711 or 760/782-2790, www.kumeyaay.info.

24 INAJA MEMORIAL TRAIL

0.5 mi/0.5 hr 1 7

in Cleveland National Forest near Santa Ysabel

Map 14.2, page 740 BEST

At 3,200 feet in elevation, you can look down a long way into the steep canyon of the San Diego River. And that's what you do here on the Inaja Memorial National Recreation Trail, a short but interesting path that begins at the Inaja Picnic Area. The path undulates along the canyon edge, sometimes following stairs and sometimes on a gently graded trail, passing through a brushy landscape of rocks and chaparral. If you pick up an interpretive brochure at the trailhead, you can learn all about the plants that thrive in this area—live oak, scrub oak, wild lilac, toyon, manzanita, and chamise—and the geology of its granitic rocks. Yours for the taking are wide views of both the Santa Ysabel Valley and Volcan Mountain near Julian. The picnic area and trail have an interesting history: They were named to honor the 11 firefighters who lost their lives in the 60,000-acre Inaja forest fire of 1956.

User Groups: Hikers and dogs. No horses or mountain bikes. No wheelchair facilities except at the picnic area.

Permits: No permits are required. A $5 parking fee is charged unless you have a National Forest Adventure Pass or interagency access pass.

Maps: A Cleveland National Forest map is available from the U.S. Forest Service. For a topographic map, go to the USGS website to download Santa Ysabel.

Directions: From Julian, drive northwest on Highway 78/79 for six miles (to one mile south of Santa Ysabel). Inaja Picnic Area and the trailhead are on the south (left) side of the road.

Contact: Cleveland National Forest, Palomar Ranger District, Ramona, 760/788-0250, www.fs.usda.gov/cleveland.

25 FIVE OAKS TRAIL AND VOLCAN MOUNTAIN

3.2-5.4 mi/1.5-2.5 hr

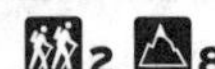

in Volcan Mountain Wilderness Preserve near Julian

Map 14.2, page 740

Volcan Mountain Wilderness Preserve is a San Diego County parkland that is open to hiking, mountain biking, and equestrians (sorry, no dogs). The first-rate Five Oaks Trail is for hikers only, and it provides a route along the lower slopes of Volcan Mountain that bypasses most of the alternate multi-use trail, a steep and unattractive fire road. To access it, follow the fire road for the first 0.4 mile, and then cut off onto Five Oaks Trail (watch for the stone steps on the right). Once on the trail, you are dwarfed by dense groves of tree-sized manzanitas. On warm days, you may feel a huge debt of gratitude for their shade. Farther along the trail, black oaks provide a cool canopy, plus a splash of rich color in the autumn. Where the foliage opens up, you'll gain glimpses of Palomar Mountain and the Anza-Borrego Desert. After 1.2 miles on the Five Oaks Trail, you reach a stone bench on a ridge with a view to the south, overlooking the Julian area.

If hiking this trail has whetted your appetite for a trip to the summit of Volcan Mountain, it's only another 1.1 mile up the fire road. The view from the top is a wide panorama from the desert to the coast. If you'd like to hike to the summit with a knowledgeable guide, free ranger-led hikes are offered on weekends once a month from April to November (call 760/765-4098).

User Groups: Hikers only. No dogs. Horses and mountain bikes are allowed on fire roads, but not Five Oaks Trail. No wheelchair facilities.

Permits: No permits are required. Parking and access are free.

Maps: A free map is available at the trailhead or by free download at www.sdparks.org. For a topographic map, go to the USGS website to download Julian.

Directions: From Julian, drive north on Farmer Road for 2.2 miles. Turn right on Wynola Road, drive 100 yards, then turn left on the continuation of Farmer Road. Drive 200 yards and park on the right side of Farmer Road by the Volcan Mountain Preserve sign.

Contact: Volcan Mountain Wilderness Preserve, Julian, 760/765-4098, www.sdparks.org.

26 DESERT VIEW AND CANYON OAK LOOP

3.5 mi/2.0 hr 2 8

in William Heise County Park near Julian

Map 14.2, page 740

William Heise County Park, a favorite of San Diego hikers, is located near Julian at 4,000 feet in elevation. The park was badly burned in 2003 and 2007 wildfires, but its oak forests and shrubs are regenerating beautifully and it's often hard to discern where the fire damage occurred. From the trailhead, start hiking through the oaks. You'll leave the Nature Trail to join the Canyon Oak Trail in 0.25 mile. Bear left on the loop, then bear left on the Desert View Trail. The route is steep, but in 0.1 mile, you reach an overlook with an expansive view of the Cuyamaca and Laguna Mountains. The trail continues upward for another 0.75 mile to a spur trail leading to a higher overlook, Glen's View. The broad vista here will surprise you—you'll spy the Anza-Borrego Desert, the Salton Sea, and even the Pacific Ocean. A makeshift scope on top of a stone monument at Glen's View helps you identify all of San Diego County's best features.

User Groups: Hikers only. No dogs, horses, or mountain bikes. No wheelchair facilities.

Permits: No permits are required. A $3 day-use fee is charged per vehicle.

Maps: A free trail map is available at the entrance station or by free download at www.sdparks.org. For a topographic map, go to the USGS website to download Julian.

Directions: From Julian, drive two miles west on Highway 78/79 and turn left (south) on Pine Hills Road. Drive two miles, turn left on Frisius Drive, and drive two more miles. Frisius Drive turns into Heise Park Road and enters the park. From the park entrance kiosk, continue straight on the park road and drive to near its end. Trail parking is located above campsite No. 64 or next to campsite No. 77. The trailhead is located near campsite No. 87 at the top of the campground.

Contact: William Heise County Park, Julian, 760/765-0650, www.sdparks.org.

27 CEDAR CREEK FALLS

4.4 mi/2.5 hr 2 9

in Cleveland National Forest near Julian

Map 14.2, page 740

Since it's a fantastic waterfall and swimming hole that's a relatively short hike from the car, Cedar Creek Falls is no secret among San Diego hikers. Word gets around fast about these kinds of great destinations. Additionally, it's easy to find: the trailhead is well signed and is a major access point for the California Riding and Hiking Trail. The only hard part is the long drive in on a dirt road (about eight miles), but it's doable for passenger cars (except immediately after the most extreme storms). Begin by hiking downhill and to the right on the wide fire road, enjoying views of the far-off San

Diego River Canyon, as well as colorful spring wildflowers on the slopes alongside the road. At 1.4 miles, look for a left fork off the main trail. It may be unsigned, but it's the first and only left turnoff you'll see. Follow it southeast, heading up and over a small saddle. When you come down the other side, you'll see two possible trail options. The left fork takes you to the top of the falls; the right fork continues down to the valley, where you turn left and head upstream to Cedar Creek Falls. It's worth taking the left fork so you can see what the waterfall looks like from above—it's like a gorgeous infinity pool with a dizzying 100-foot dropoff—but then you'll need to backtrack to this junction and take the opposite fork to access the 50-foot-wide pool at the waterfall's base. (It's too dangerous to scramble down the waterfall's cliff to the base; follow the trail instead.)

Note: If you'd like to visit this waterfall without the long drive on a dirt road, it can be accessed via another trailhead in the town of Ramona, off Thornbush Road (take San Vicente Road to Ramona Oaks Road to Cathedral Way to Thornbush Road). The trail from Ramona to Cedar Creek Falls is about five miles round-trip.

User Groups: Hikers, dogs, horses, and mountain bikes. No wheelchair facilities.

Permits: No permits are required. Parking and access are free.

Maps: A Cleveland National Forest map is available from the U.S. Forest Service. For a topographic map, go to the USGS website to download Santa Ysabel.

Directions: From Julian, drive two miles west on Highway 78/79, then turn left (south) on Pine Hills Road. In 1.5 miles, bear right on Eagle Peak Road. In 1.4 miles, bear right again, staying on Eagle Peak Road. Continue 8.2 miles on this partly paved, partly dirt road to the signed trailhead just beyond mile marker 9, at a four-way junction of roads. (The road gets a bit rough after the first four miles, but it's usually suitable for passenger cars.)

Contact: Cleveland National Forest, Palomar Ranger District, Ramona, 760/788-0250, www.fs.usda.gov/cleveland.

28 THREE SISTERS FALLS

4.0 mi/2.0 hr 3 9

in Cleveland National Forest near Julian

Map 14.2, page 740

Three Sisters Falls is a must-see for serious San Diego waterfall lovers, but the trip is not for everybody. The drive to the trailhead is fairly arduous (several miles of bumpy driving on dirt road) and the hike, although fairly short, is mercilessly steep and follows an unmaintained route, not a real trail. It's mostly downhill on the way in and mostly uphill on the way back, so save some energy for your return trip.

Start at the signboard for the Cedar Creek Trail, an old ranch road. Follow it for 0.7 mile, heading slightly uphill to a saddle where you can see and hear the falls in springtime, and then switchback down to the left for 0.4 mile until you meet up with tiny Sheep Camp Creek. Cross Sheep Camp Creek and pick up the good trail on its far side, heading right. You'll ascend slightly for 0.3 mile to a second low saddle, where once again you should be able to spot the Three Sisters in the canyon below. This visual incentive is critical, because you're about to face some remarkably steep downhill scrambling, which might be more accurately called "bouldering." Wear your best-gripping boots and bring hiking poles if you have them; the footing is loose and/or nonexistent in places. After descending a rugged 500 feet, you'll finally reach Boulder Creek. Hike, rockhop, or wade upstream for a few hundred yards to get to the base of the falls. Depending on Boulder Creek's flow, there may be several possible routes, but whatever you do, stay off the slick rock as much as possible. If you have to choose between stepping on these rocks and wading through poison oak, choose the poison oak. Really. So what's the payoff? A triple set of waterfalls on Boulder Creek, the Three Sisters creates an impressive display of white water on smooth granite. The middle fall is the tallest at about 50 feet, and the large pool at the bottom will tempt you to swim.

User Groups: Hikers, dogs, horses, and mountain bikes. No wheelchair facilities.

Permits: No permits are required. Parking and access are free.

Maps: A Cleveland National Forest map is available from the U.S. Forest Service. For a topographic map, go to the USGS website to download Cedar Creek.

Directions: From Julian, drive two miles west on Highway 78/79, then turn left (south) on Pine Hills Road. In 1.5 miles, bear right on Eagle Peak Road. In 1.4 miles, bear left (south) on Boulder Creek Road and drive 8.4 miles to a hairpin turn and junction with another dirt road. A Forest Service signboard for Cedar Creek Trail is located there. Park alongside the road and take the trail from the signboard.

From I-8 in downtown San Diego, take Highway 79 north (Descanso exit) for 1.3 miles. Turn left on Riverside Drive and drive 0.6 mile to "downtown" Descanso and its intersection of roads. Follow Oak Grove Drive 1.6 miles to Boulder Creek Road, on the right. Turn north on Boulder Creek Road and drive 13 miles on this part-paved, part-dirt road to a hairpin turn and junction with dirt Cedar Creek Road. Park alongside the road and take the trail from the signboard.

Contact: Cleveland National Forest, Palomar Ranger District, Ramona, 760/788-0250, www.fs.usda.gov/cleveland.

29 CUYAMACA PEAK TRAIL

5.2 mi/3.0 hr 2 9

in Cuyamaca Rancho State Park near Julian

Map 14.2, page 740

A 6,512-foot summit in San Diego? Yes, it's true. Cuyamaca Peak is the undisputed king of the peaks in Cuyamaca Rancho State Park, and it's just shy of being the tallest summit in the county. (Hot Springs Mountain near Warner Springs is a bit taller at 6,533 feet.) The main trail to the summit is the paved Lookout Fire Road that is closed to vehicle traffic. Normally we avoid paved trails like the plague, but this one is so pleasantly graded (1,650 feet of climbing spread out over 2.6 miles) and delivers such a fantastic 360-degree view at the top that it's worth making an exception. If you like, you can bypass some of the pavement by starting your trip on the Azalea Glen Trail from Paso Picacho Campground, then connecting to Azalea Spring Road, Conejos Trail, and finally the paved summit road. (This will add another mile to your trip.) What do you see when you attain the summit of Cuyamaca? Just about everything that surrounds San Diego: the ocean (see if you can pick out Catalina Island on the clearest days), Mexico, Mount San Jacinto, Mount San Gorgonio, Palomar Observatory, Anza-Borrego Desert, and the Salton Sea. So what does Cuayamaca mean? Roughly, it's "place beyond the rain."

User Groups: Hikers and mountain bikes. Leashed dogs are permitted on Lookout Fire Road. No horses. No wheelchair facilities.

Permits: No permits are required. A $10 day-use fee is charged per vehicle.

Maps: A map of Cuyamaca Rancho State Park is available at the entrance kiosk or by free download at www.parks.ca.gov. A more detailed map is available from Tom Harrison Maps. For a topographic map, go to the USGS website to download Cuyamaca.

Directions: From San Diego, drive east on I-8 for 40 miles to the Highway 79 exit. Drive north on Highway 79 for 11 miles and turn left into Paso Picacho Campground. Park at the day-use parking lot.

Contact: Cuyamaca Rancho State Park, Descanso, 760/765-0755, www.cuyamacasp.org or www.parks.ca.gov.

30 COWLES MOUNTAIN

3.0 mi/1.5 hr  

in Mission Trails Regional Park

Map 14.2, page 740

Mission Trails Regional Park is a playland for outdoor lovers; the visitors center alone provides enough entertainment to fill an entire afternoon. It's a huge, architecturally unique building with state-of-the-art displays, and it's better designed than many museums. If you only have time to hike one trail in the park, you may as well go for the summit of Cowles Mountain, a 1,591-foot peak with a 360-degree view of the city. They say Cowles Mountain is the highest point in San Diego, but they mean the city, not the county. Pick a cool day, because the trail is sunny and exposed, ascending through chaparral and sage scrub, and with a 951-foot elevation gain to the summit. When you reach the top and look out at the city below, consider the temporary state of all you survey compared to the rock you're standing on, which is nearly 150 million years old. If you feel like hiking some more, you can continue another 1.5 miles from Cowles Mountain Summit to Pyles Peak Summit. If you want to take a somewhat mellower grade to Cowles Mountain, you can start at the trailhead at Mesa Road. From there, it's 2.2 miles to the top.

User Groups: Hikers and dogs. No mountain bikes or horses. No wheelchair facilities.

Permits: No permits are required. Parking and access are free.

Maps: A free map of Mission Trails Regional Park is available at the visitors center. For a topographic map, go to the USGS website to download La Mesa.

Directions: From I-15 south of Poway, take Highway 52 east and exit at Mast Boulevard. Turn left on Mast Boulevard and then right on West Hills Parkway. Turn right on Mission Gorge Road, drive two miles, and then turn left on Golfcrest Drive. Follow Golfcrest Drive to its intersection with Navajo Road, where the trailhead for Cowles Mountain trailhead is located, on the left. If you wish to go to the park's visitors center first, continue past Golfcrest Drive on Mission Gorge Road and turn right at the park entrance.

Contact: Mission Trails Regional Park, San Diego, 619/668-3281, www.mtrp.org.

31 SILVERWOOD WILDLIFE SANCTUARY

1.5 mi/1.0 hr 

in the Silverwood Wildlife Sanctuary near Lakeside

Map 14.2, page 740 BEST

The Silverwood Wildlife Sanctuary, a favorite spot of San Diego bird-watchers, is managed by the San Diego Audubon Society and open to hikers on Sundays only (9am-4 pm). If it's your first visit, stop in at the Frank Gander Nature Education Center before stepping out on the trails. Exhibits focus on the process of fire ecology and how birds and animals adapt to fire. Late winter and spring are the best times to visit; wildflowers are profuse and many birds, from bluebirds to wrens, make their nests here. Binoculars are a must; more than 160 bird species have been sighted in the sanctuary, including Costas hummingbirds, various woodpeckers, flycatchers, towhees, and an abundance of songbirds. If you are new to birding, show up at 10am or 1:30pm on Sunday for a free, guided hike (Oct.-June). The Audubon Society naturalists who lead the walks are incredibly knowledgeable, and they tailor the walk to the ability of the people who attend. This is a wonderful, educational trip for bird-watchers and non-bird-watchers alike. And if you want more walking to go with your bird-watching, the sanctuary has a total of 5.7 miles of hiking trails. Many people head for the Circuit Trail, which runs along a high ridge and offers great views.

User Groups: Hikers only. No dogs, horses, or mountain bikes. No wheelchair facilities.

Permits: Hikers must sign in at the trailhead

register. Parking and access are free, but donations are gratefully accepted.

Maps: Maps are available at the trailhead register. For a topographic map, go to the USGS website to download San Vicente Reservoir.

Directions: From I-8 in San Diego, drive east to Highway 67 near El Cajon. Drive north on Highway 67 to Lakeside, where you turn right on Mapleview Street. Drive a short distance, turn left on Ashwood Street (which becomes Wildcat Canyon Road), and drive 4.8 miles to 13003 Wildcat Canyon Road.

Contact: Silverwood Wildlife Sanctuary, Lakeside, 619/443-2998, www.sandiegoaudubon.org.

32 STONEWALL PEAK TRAIL

4.0 mi/2.0 hr 2 10

in Cuyamaca Rancho State Park

Map 14.2, page 740

A great trail for first-timers to Cuyamaca Rancho State park is the Stonewall Peak Trail across from Paso Picacho Campground. Although slightly dwarfed by neighboring Cuyamaca Peak, Stonewall Peak is no slouch in the summit department: its peak towers at 5,730 feet in elevation. Stonewall Peak overlooks the site of the turn-of-the-century Stonewall Mine, as well as a large chunk of the Cuyamaca Mountains and Anza-Borrego Desert. The trail has only an 850-foot elevation gain and is remarkably well-graded. A series of multiple switchbacks whisk you to the summit on a well-graded path. The final 50 yards of trail are cut into an exposed stone ridge; granite stairs and a handrail keep you from going over the edge. The summit view is nothing short of grand, taking in all of the park, Lake Cuyamaca, and the desert far to the east. Squint hard and you can see the Palomar Observatory, Mount San Gorgonio, Mount San Jacinto, and the Salton Sea.

User Groups: Hikers only. No dogs, horses, or mountain bikes. No wheelchair facilities.

Permits: No permits are required. An $8 day-use fee is charged per vehicle.

Maps: A map of Cuyamaca Rancho State Park is available at the entrance kiosk or by free download at www.parks.ca.gov. A more detailed map is available from Tom Harrison Maps. For a topographic map, go to the USGS website to download Cuyamaca.

Directions: From San Diego, drive east on I-8 for 40 miles to the Highway 79 exit. Drive north on Highway 79 for 11 miles and turn left into Paso Picacho Campground. Park at the day-use parking lot. The trail begins across the highway from the campground.

Contact: Cuyamaca Rancho State Park, Descanso, 760/765-0755, www.cuyamaca.us or www.parks.ca.gov.

33 GREEN VALLEY FALLS

0.5-3.0 mi/0.5-1.5 hr 1 9

in Cuyamaca Rancho State Park

Map 14.2, page 740 BEST

The Green Valley area in the southern region of Cuyamaca Rancho State Park is a lush, cool oasis for park visitors. A trip to Green Valley Falls is an easy walk with a good payoff on a warm day. From the picnic area parking lot at Green Valley Campground, follow the wide fire road along the Sweetwater River to the cutoff for the falls, then hike downhill to your left. By summer, the river's cascades aren't terribly dramatic, but there are still many cool pools where you can soak your toes, as well as wide granite ledges where you can lay out a towel and lounge around on the rocks. If you feel like logging a few more miles, you can continue past the falls' cutoff to the fire road's junction with South Boundary Fire Road. Turn right and loop back via South Boundary and Arroyo Seco Fire Roads, making a 3.5-mile round-trip.

User Groups: Hikers, horses, and mountain bikes (on the fire road only). No dogs. No wheelchair facilities.

Green Valley Falls

Permits: No permits are required. An $8 day-use fee is charged per vehicle.

Maps: A map of Cuyamaca Rancho State Park is available at the entrance kiosk or by free download at www.parks.ca.gov. A more detailed map is available from Tom Harrison Maps. For a topographic map, go to the USGS website to download Cuyamaca.

Directions: From San Diego, drive east on I-8 for 40 miles to the Highway 79 exit. Drive north on Highway 79 for seven miles and turn left (west) at the sign for Green Valley Campground. Follow the signs to the picnic area. One sign points either straight ahead or to the left for the picnic area; continue straight to reach the trailhead.

Contact: Cuyamaca Rancho State Park, Descanso, 760/765-0755, www.cuyamaca.us or www.parks.ca.gov.

34 GARNET PEAK

4.4 mi/2.5 hr

in the Laguna Mountain Recreation Area

Map 14.2, page 740

The route to Garnet Peak begins on the Pacific Crest Trail (PCT) at the Penny Pines trailhead, where you can see the list of names of the good people who have donated funds to California's national forests for reforestation. Garnet Peak's magnificent summit view and the relative ease of this trail have made this a favorite of San Diego hikers. Follow the well-graded PCT to the north (left). The trail has pleasantly little elevation gain, and it hugs the Laguna Mountain rim, offering nearly continual views of Storm Canyon and the Anza-Borrego Desert. You won't see any trail signs directing you to the peak. Ignore the first two right turnoffs at 1.5 miles out (they lead to expansive overlooks, but they won't take you to the summit). Instead, turn right at the third right turnoff, signed for the Garnet Peak Trail. The trail makes a rocky ascent, but in less than a mile, you reach the jagged, 5,900-foot summit. There you're rewarded with mind-boggling views of the Anza-Borrego Desert, Palomar Observatory, Mount San Jacinto and Mount San Gorgonio, the Laguna and Cuyamaca Mountains, and on and on. On a crisp January day, we were able to spot snow-covered Mount Baldy, 90 miles to the northwest, as well. Most remarkable is that the desert floor is 5,000 feet below you, and it appears to be straight down. This summit vista can boggle your mind. Total elevation gain on the trail? A mere 500 feet. Judging by the popularity of this trail on the weekends, it might just be too easy.

User Groups: Hikers and dogs. No horses or mountain bikes. No wheelchair facilities.

Permits: No permits are required. Parking and access are free.

Maps: A Cleveland National Forest map is available from the U.S. Forest Service. A map of the Laguna Mountain Recreation Area is available from the Descanso Ranger District or the Laguna Mountain Visitors Center. For a topographic map, go to the USGS website to download Monument Peak.

Directions: From Julian, drive south on Highway 79 to the left fork for Road S1/Sunrise Scenic Byway. Bear left and drive south for about 12 miles to the Penny Pines Plantation, between mile markers 27.5 and 27.0. Park along the road.

Contact: Cleveland National Forest, Descanso Ranger District, Alpine, 619/445-6235, www.fs.usda.gov/cleveland.

35 LIGHTNING RIDGE TRAIL

1.5 mi/1.0 hr 1 8

in the Laguna Mountain Recreation Area

Map 14.2, page 740

The Lightning Ridge Trail is one of the show-and-tell trails of the Laguna Mountain Recreation Area, where you can get up high and get a clear view of how beautiful and unusual this tall, cool mountain on the edge of the desert really is. The trail is easy enough for almost any hiker to accomplish, with only 250 feet of elevation gain. It begins at a small stone monument at Laguna Campground's amphitheater parking lot and follows the edge of a meadow, making several long, sweeping switchbacks uphill through pines and oaks. Kick a few pine cones as you walk. The trail tops out at a water tank at the top of the ridge. The cement tank is uninspiring, but the view is sweet: Laguna Meadow lies directly below, a beautiful, green expanse in spring. If you time your trip for after a good season of rain, you may see a rare sight: Little Laguna Lake, in the middle of the meadow. This is the secret vanishing lake of the Laguna Mountains.

What's the best time to hike this trail? Unquestionably it's winter or spring—by Memorial Day, the meadow grasses are often dry and brown. If you're lucky, you can walk this trail on a clear winter day, when it's covered with a few inches of snow.

User Groups: Hikers and dogs. No horses or mountain bikes. No wheelchair facilities.

Permits: No permits are required. A $5 fee is charged for parking inside Laguna Campground. You can park outside the campground for free.

Maps: A Cleveland National Forest map is available from the U.S. Forest Service. A map of the Laguna Mountain Recreation Area is available from the Descanso Ranger District or the Laguna Mountain Visitors Center. For a topographic map, go to the USGS website to download Monument Peak.

Directions: From Julian, drive south on Highway 79 to the left fork for Road S1/Sunrise Scenic Byway. Bear left and drive south for approximately 13 miles to Laguna Campground, on the right, between mile markers 26.5 and 26.0. Turn right on the camp road, and drive 0.75 mile to the amphitheater parking lot. Park there and then look for the small stone monument just beyond the restrooms, on the northeast side of the parking lot. The trail begins there.

Contact: Cleveland National Forest, Descanso Ranger District, Alpine, 619/445-6235, www.fs.usda.gov/cleveland.

36 COTTONWOOD CREEK FALLS

2.0 mi/1.0 hr 2 9

in the Laguna Mountain Recreation Area

Map 14.2, page 740

If you don't have the time for the day hike to spectacular Kitchen Creek Falls, this shorter trip to nearby Cottonwood Creek Falls is a close second choice for scenic beauty. With only a one-mile downhill walk, you'll quickly be exploring the many small waterfalls and big pools along Cottonwood Creek, or happily counting the bright pink flowers on the streamside cacti. The trail is unsigned at its start, and it usually appears overgrown with brush, but after about 100 yards, the path widens, and the downhill grade becomes less steep. When you reach the canyon bottom, which takes about 15 minutes, turn sharply left and walk alongside Cottonwood Creek, heading upstream. In just a few minutes, you'll reach the first of several cascades, each about 12 feet high. Hike as far as you like, pick your favorite waterfall or pool, and have a seat alongside it.

User Groups: Hikers and dogs. No horses or mountain bikes. No wheelchair facilities.

Permits: No permits are required. Parking and access are free.

Maps: A Cleveland National Forest map is available from the U.S. Forest Service. A map of the Laguna Mountain Recreation Area is available from the Descanso Ranger District or the Laguna Mountain Visitors Center. For a topographic map, go to the USGS website to download Mount Laguna.

Directions: From San Diego, drive east on I-8 for 47 miles to the Highway S1/Sunrise Scenic Byway turnoff. Drive north on Highway S1 for about two miles to the large pullout, on the west side of the road (it has an obvious, graffiti-covered rock wall), between mile markers 15.0 and 15.5. Cross the road on foot and locate the unmarked trail at the north end of the guardrail.

Contact: Cleveland National Forest, Descanso Ranger District, Alpine, 619/445-6235, www.fs.usda.gov/cleveland.

37 DESERT VIEW NATURE TRAIL

1.2-3.0 mi/1.0-2.0 hr 

in the Laguna Mountain Recreation Area

Map 14.2, page 740

Wow, what a view. If you've never before stood on a conifer-covered mountain and looked down on the vastness of the desert, your first time is something you'll always remember. That's what you get on the Desert View Nature Trail, near the summit of Laguna Mountain. Start hiking from Burnt Rancheria Campground, heading east to meet the Pacific Crest Trail (PCT). Turn north (left) on the PCT, hiking along the mountain rim. The trail hugs the rim, which is perched on the edge of the Anza-Borrego Desert, providing fine views of the desert floor 4,000 feet below you. On a clear day you can see all the way to Salton Sea shimmering in the distance, and to the odd-looking smokestacks of Plaster City. The trail continues north to Desert View Picnic Area and returns via a loop through a shady forest of pines and oaks. When you reach a clearing 0.5 mile out, you'll find a water fountain with a plaque commemorating the great outdoors. Take the spur trail here, heading east and uphill for a short distance, for the best view of the day. If you hike the nature trail loop only, you'll have a 1.2-mile round-trip, but most people get so captivated by the views that they wind up walking a bit farther on the PCT to the north. It's so compelling, it's hard to stop.

User Groups: Hikers and dogs. No horses or mountain bikes. No wheelchair facilities.

Permits: No permits are required. A National Forest Adventure Pass is required for each vehicle; fees are $5 for one day or $30 for a year. Interagency access passes are also accepted.

Maps: A Cleveland National Forest map is available from the U.S. Forest Service. A map of the Laguna Mountain Recreation Area is available from the Descanso Ranger District or the Laguna Mountain Visitors Center. For a topographic map, go to the USGS website to download Mount Laguna.

Directions: From San Diego, drive east on I-8 for 47 miles to the Highway S1/Sunrise Scenic Byway turnoff. Drive north on Highway S1 for about 10 miles to Burnt Rancheria Campground, on the right, between mile markers 22.5 and 23.0 (near the town of Mount Laguna). Park by the amphitheater at Burnt Rancheria Campground, where the trail begins.

Contact: Cleveland National Forest, Descanso Ranger District, Alpine, 619/445-6235, www.fs.usda.gov/cleveland.

38 KITCHEN CREEK FALLS

4.5 mi/2.5 hr 3 10

in Cleveland National Forest near Pine Valley

Map 14.2, page 740

Kitchen Creek Falls is the most beautiful waterfall in San Diego, a visually stunning 150-foot drop that is hidden just a few hundred yards off the Pacific Crest Trail (PCT). Thousands of PCT hikers go right past it without even knowing it's there, although they may shake their heads and wonder where all those day hikers are heading. The hike to reach the general vicinity of the falls is quite easy, since it follows the well-graded PCT from Boulder Oaks, which crosses underneath I-8 and then climbs uphill. The total gain is only about 500 feet. The tricky part comes in finding the unmarked cutoff for Kitchen Creek Falls and then scrambling your way down steep slopes to reach its base. Here's how you do it: After 45-50 minutes of hiking, start looking carefully to your left for a narrow spur trail. You'll reach it at exactly two miles up, which for most people is about an hour of trail time. Turn left on the spur and hike a short distance to see if you're looking down on Kitchen Creek—a fairly flat stream with many good-looking pools. If you are, you're also right above the waterfall, and to reach it, you must cut down the hillside on one of many use trails, heading downstream. (Keep the creek on your right; don't cross it.) Use great caution in getting to the waterfall's base—stay on the dirt trails, and stay off the polished granite, even when it's dry. Get yourself safely to a spot where you can look up and admire the gorgeous falls, which are a series of tiered cascades that twist and turn over rounded ledges in the bedrock. Plan on staying awhile.

User Groups: Hikers and dogs. No horses or mountain bikes. No wheelchair facilities.

Permits: No permits are required. A National Forest Adventure Pass is required for each vehicle; fees are $5 for one day or $30 for a year. Interagency access passes are also accepted.

Maps: A Cleveland National Forest map is available from the U.S. Forest Service. For a topographic map, go to the USGS website to download Live Oak Springs.

Directions: From San Diego, drive east on I-8 for 50 miles to the Buckman Springs Road turnoff. Drive south on the frontage road (old Highway 8) for 2.3 miles to the Boulder Oaks Campground. Stay on the frontage road; do not turn onto Buckman Springs Road. Park at the campground, at the signed trailhead for the PCT.

Contact: Cleveland National Forest, Descanso Ranger District, Alpine, 619/445-6235, www.fs.usda.gov/cleveland.

CALIFORNIA DESERTS

This vast region of desert beauty includes soaring sand dunes, craggy mountain ranges, and below-sea-level salt flats. In Death Valley, trails lead to 700-foot-high sand dunes, colorful badlands, towering rock walls, volcanic craters, and even a waterfall. At Mojave National Preserve, hikers can climb to the summits of sand dunes or scramble through and around the volcanic cliffs at Hole-in-the-Wall. At Joshua Tree National Park, visitors explore gold-mine ruins, fan palm oases, and a wild landscape filled with jumbled boulder piles and Dr. Seuss-like Joshua trees. Even in the urban cityscape of Palm Springs, hikers can visit the Agua Caliente Indian Canyons or the Coachella Valley Preserve for a taste of "real" desert. And to the south, Anza-Borrego Desert State Park encompasses palm groves, year-round creeks, slot canyons, and badlands.

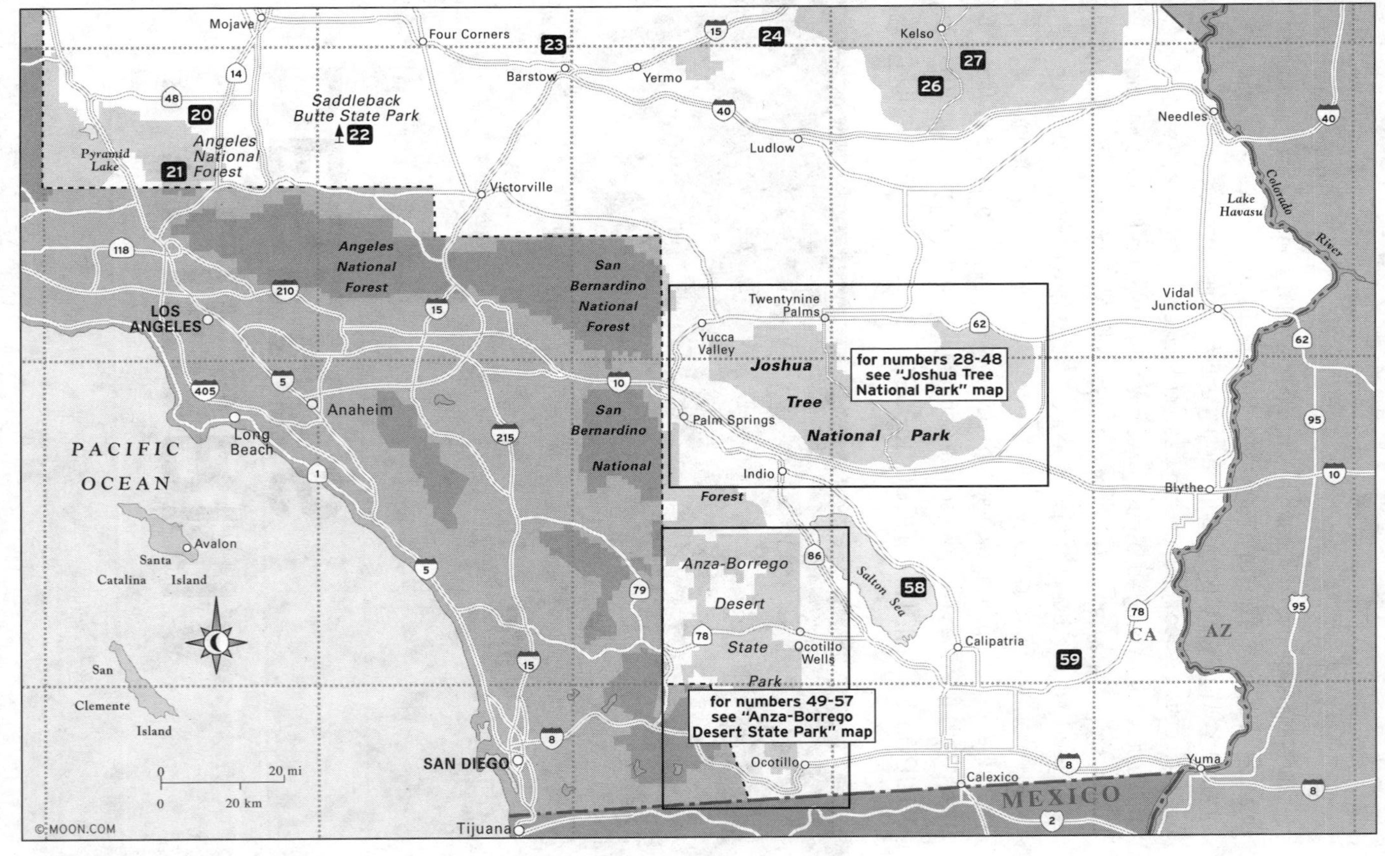
Mojave
Four Corners
23
15
24
Kelso
27
Barstow
Yermo
26
14
48
20
Saddleback Butte State Park
22
40
Needles
40
Pyramid Lake
Angeles National Forest
21
Ludlow
Victorville
Lake Havasu
Colorado River
118
Angeles National Forest
San Bernardino National Forest
210
15
LOS ANGELES
Twentynine Palms
Yucca Valley
62
Vidal Junction
62
Joshua Tree National Park
for numbers 28-48 see "Joshua Tree National Park" map
405
5
10
Anaheim
San Bernardino National Forest
Palm Springs
95
215
Long Beach
PACIFIC OCEAN
1
Indio
10
Blythe
Forest
Avalon
Santa Catalina Island
5
86
Anza-Borrego Desert State Park
Salton Sea
58
79
78
78
Ocotillo Wells
Calipatria
CA
AZ
59
95
15
San Clemente Island
for numbers 49-57 see "Anza-Borrego Desert State Park" map
8
0 20 mi
0 20 km
SAN DIEGO
Ocotillo
8
Calexico
Yuma
8
MEXICO
2
©MOON.COM
Tijuana

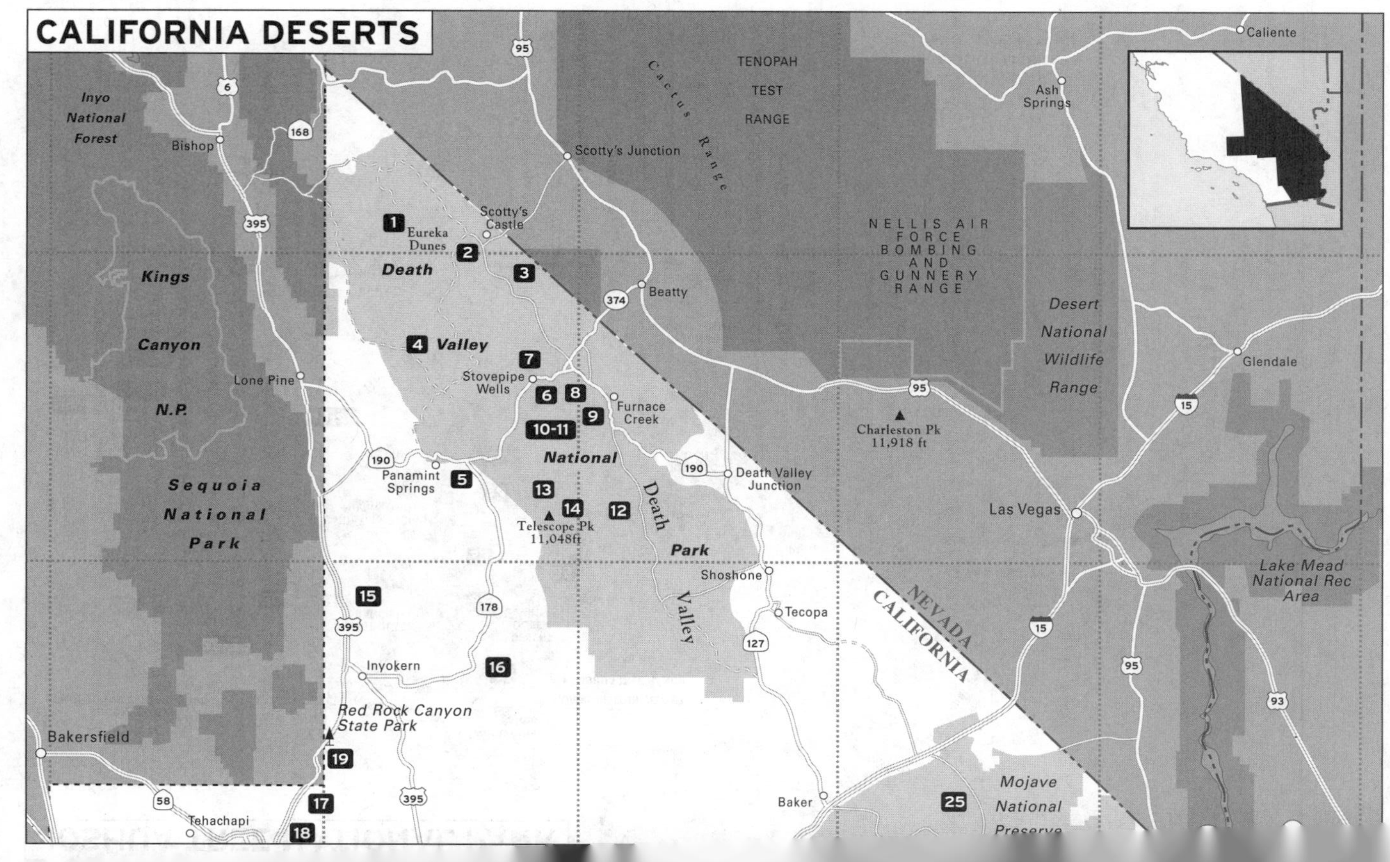
CALIFORNIA DESERTS
Inyo National Forest
Bishop
Kings Canyon N.P.
Sequoia National Park
Lone Pine
Bakersfield
Tehachapi
Red Rock Canyon State Park
Inyokern
Panamint Springs
Death Valley National Park
Eureka Dunes
Scotty's Castle
Stovepipe Wells
Furnace Creek
Telescope Pk 11,048ft
Death Valley
Shoshone
Tecopa
Baker
Death Valley Junction
Beatty
Scotty's Junction
Cactus Range
TENOPAH TEST RANGE
NELLIS AIR FORCE BOMBING AND GUNNERY RANGE
Charleston Pk 11,918 ft
Desert National Wildlife Range
Ash Springs
Caliente
Glendale
Las Vegas
Lake Mead National Rec Area
Mojave National Preserve
NEVADA
CALIFORNIA
1
2
3
4
5
6
7
8
9
10-11
12
13
14
15
16
17
18
19
25

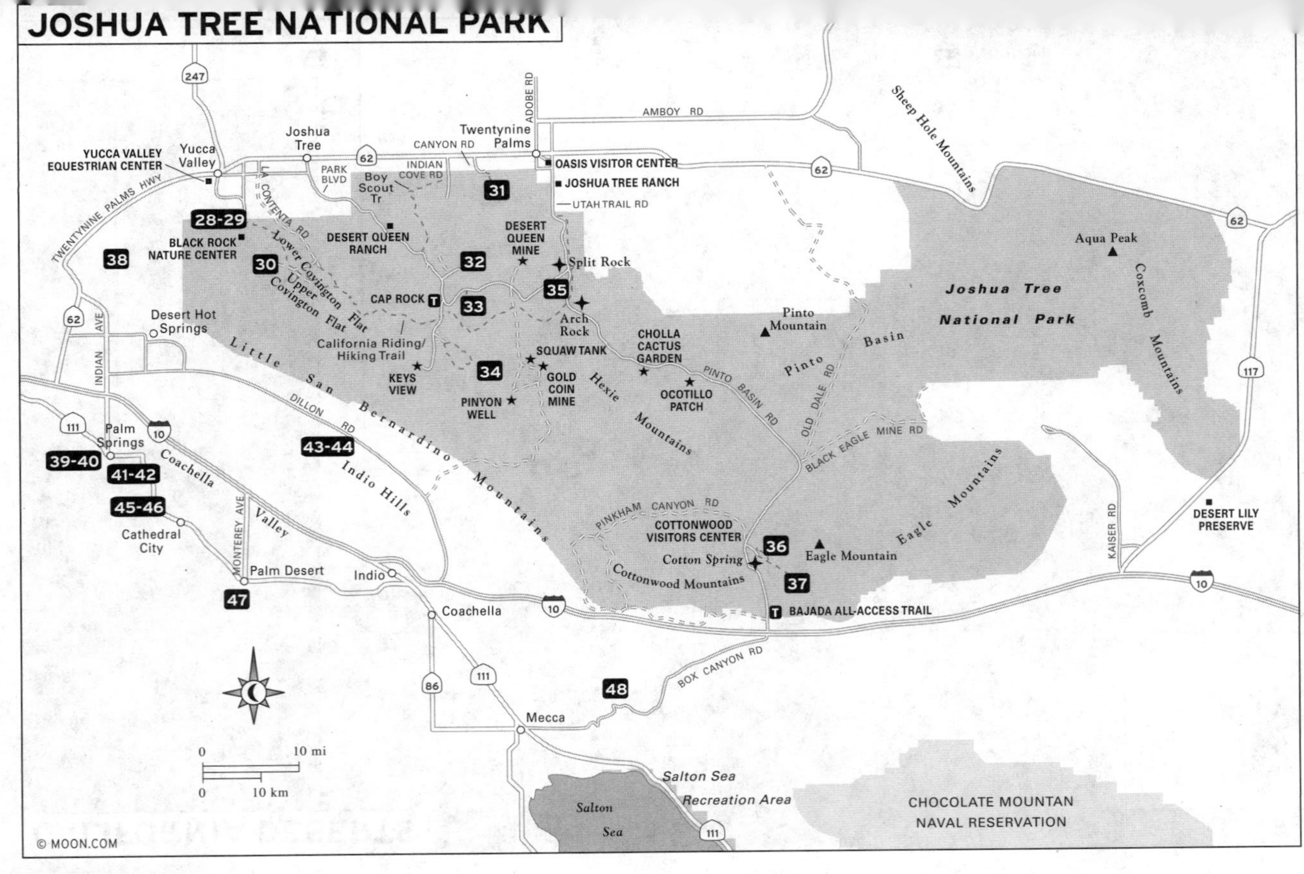
JOSHUA TREE NATIONAL PARK
YUCCA VALLEY EQUESTRIAN CENTER
Yucca Valley
TWENTYNINE PALMS HWY
Joshua Tree
PARK BLVD
Boy Scout Tr
INDIAN COVE RD
CANYON RD
Twentynine Palms
ADOBE RD
AMBOY RD
OASIS VISITOR CENTER
JOSHUA TREE RANCH
UTAH TRAIL RD
Sheep Hole Mountains
28-29
LA CONTENTA RD
BLACK ROCK NATURE CENTER
38
30
Lower Covington Flat
Upper Covington Flat
DESERT QUEEN RANCH
31
DESERT QUEEN MINE
32
Split Rock
35
CAP ROCK
33
Arch Rock
Aqua Peak
Joshua Tree National Park
Coxcomb Mountains
Pinto Mountain
Pinto Basin
Desert Hot Springs
INDIAN AVE
California Riding/Hiking Trail
SQUAW TANK
CHOLLA CACTUS GARDEN
Little San Bernardino Mountains
KEYS VIEW
34
GOLD COIN MINE
PINYON WELL
Hexie Mountains
OCOTILLO PATCH
PINTO BASIN RD
OLD DALE RD
BLACK EAGLE MINE RD
DILLON RD
Palm Springs
43-44
39-40
41-42
Coachella Valley
Indio Hills
45-46
Cathedral City
MONTEREY AVE
Palm Desert
47
Indio
Coachella
PINKHAM CANYON RD
COTTONWOOD VISITORS CENTER
Cotton Spring
Cottonwood Mountains
36
Eagle Mountain
Eagle Mountains
37
BAJADA ALL-ACCESS TRAIL
KAISER RD
DESERT LILY PRESERVE
BOX CANYON RD
48
Mecca
0 10 mi
0 10 km
Salton Sea
Salton Sea Recreation Area
CHOCOLATE MOUNTAIN NAVAL RESERVATION
© MOON.COM

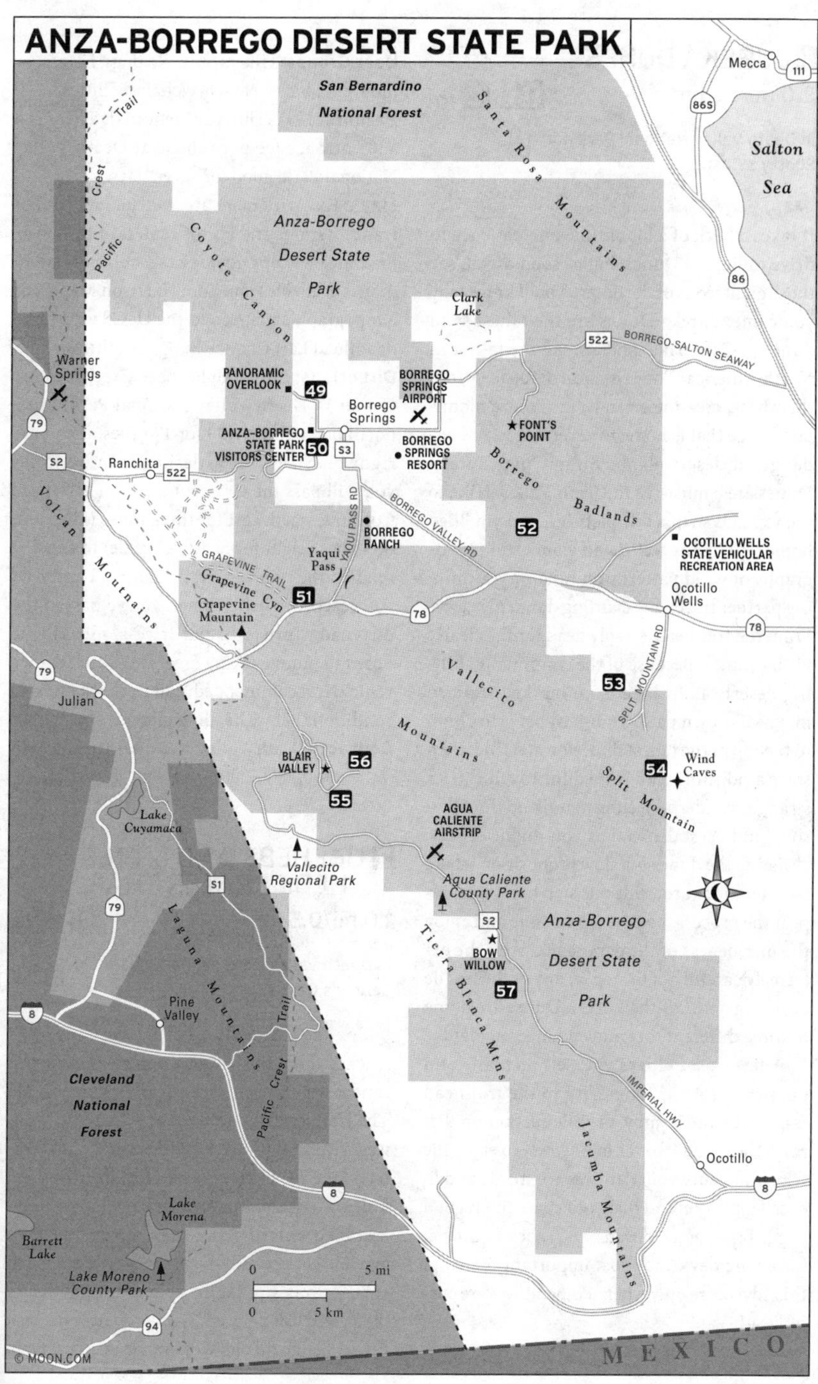
ANZA-BORREGO DESERT STATE PARK
San Bernardino National Forest
Santa Rosa Mountains
Mecca
111
86S
Salton Sea
86
Anza-Borrego Desert State Park
Coyote Canyon
Pacific Crest Trail
Clark Lake
522
BORREGO-SALTON SEAWAY
Warner Springs
79
PANORAMIC OVERLOOK
49
BORREGO SPRINGS AIRPORT
Borrego Springs
FONT'S POINT
ANZA-BORREGO STATE PARK VISITORS CENTER
50
S3
BORREGO SPRINGS RESORT
S2
Ranchita
522
Borrego Badlands
Volcan Moutnains
YAQUI PASS RD
BORREGO RANCH
BORREGO VALLEY RD
52
OCOTILLO WELLS STATE VEHICULAR RECREATION AREA
GRAPEVINE TRAIL
Yaqui Pass
Grapevine Cyn
51
Grapevine Mountain
78
Ocotillo Wells
78
79
Julian
Vallecito Mountains
53
SPLIT MOUNTAIN RD
BLAIR VALLEY
56
Wind Caves
54
Split Mountain
55
Lake Cuyamaca
AGUA CALIENTE AIRSTRIP
Vallecito Regional Park
Agua Caliente County Park
S1
79
Laguna Mountains
S2
BOW WILLOW
Tierra Blanca Mtns
Anza-Borrego Desert State Park
57
8
Pine Valley
Cleveland National Forest
IMPERIAL HWY
Jacumba Mountains
Ocotillo
8
8
Lake Morena
Barrett Lake
Lake Moreno County Park
0 5 mi
0 5 km
94
MEXICO
© MOON.COM

1 EUREKA DUNES

2.0 mi/1.0 hr

in Death Valley National Park north of Scotty's Castle

Map, page 769

It takes a heck of a lot of time and patience to drive to Eureka Dunes, but as soon as you see those giant icons of the desert, you'll know why you came. Eureka Dunes are the tallest sand dunes in California, and among the tallest in North America. They rise nearly 700 feet from their base, creating a sandy, miniature mountain range that is home to several rare and endangered desert plants. Simply put, Eureka Dunes are a must-see in Death Valley. Hike to the top and snap a few pictures, and you'll go home with many weird and wonderful photographs of wind patterns on sand or your hiking partner traversing swirling dune ridge tops. From the trailhead, simply head for the clearly visible dunes. Because of the continually shifting desert sand, there is no marked trail, so make your own path. Your best bet is to climb to the top of the tallest dune you can find, then trace a ridgeline path from dune to dune. It's a strange, wonderful feeling to walk on the silky-soft sand crystals. And as you might expect, climbing the dunes is a slow proposition—take two steps forward, slide one step back, then repeat the process. Just take your time and enjoy the uniqueness of the experience. Also, be extremely careful not to step on any of the fragile dune vegetation—the Eureka Dunes are home to three different rare and endangered plants.

A few tips: Prepare yourself mentally and physically for the long drive to the trailhead (especially the bumpy 44-mile section on dirt roads), and you'll be far more likely to enjoy the trip. Make sure your car tires are sturdy and in excellent shape, and that your spare tire is good to go. Take plenty of water and snacks with you for a long day. And most important: Attempt this adventure only when temperatures are cool in Death Valley.

User Groups: Hikers only. No dogs, horses, or mountain bikes. No wheelchair facilities.

Permits: No permits are required. There is a $30 entrance fee per vehicle at Death Valley National Park, good for seven days.

Maps: Free park maps are available at park entrance stations and visitor centers or by download at www.nps.gov/deva. A more detailed map is available from Tom Harrison Maps. For a topographic map, go to the USGS website to download Last Chance Range Southwest.

Directions: From the Furnace Creek Visitors Center in Death Valley National Park, drive north on Highway 190 for 17 miles, then bear right on Scotty's Castle Road. In 32 miles you will pass the Grapevine entrance station. Continue northwest for three miles (keep left; don't bear right for Scotty's Castle) to the dirt road on the right signed for Eureka Dunes. (If you reach Ubehebe Crater, you've passed the dirt road.) Turn right and drive 44 miles to the Eureka Dunes parking area. A high-clearance vehicle is recommended; call to check on road conditions before heading out.

Contact: Death Valley National Park, Death Valley, 760/786-3200, www.nps.gov/deva.

2 UBEHEBE AND LITTLE HEBE CRATER TRAIL

1.0 mi/0.5 hr

in Death Valley National Park near Scotty's Castle

Map, page 769

A walk along the rim of a not-so-ancient volcano is what you get on Little Hebe Crater Trail. The trail leads along Ubehebe Crater's southwest rim to Little Hebe and several older craters. Ubehebe Crater is 500 feet deep and 0.5 mile across, and was formed by volcanic activity that occurred between 300 and 1,000 years ago. Little Hebe and the other craters are much smaller but similar in appearance—mostly black and ash colored, with eroded walls that reveal a colorful blend of orange and rust from the minerals in the rock. At 0.5 mile from the trailhead, you reach a junction where you can continue straight ahead to Little Hebe Crater or just loop all the way around Ubehebe's rim. Take your pick—from the high rim of Ubehebe, it's easy to see where you're going, as well as down into the valley below, and far off to the Last Chance Range. Note: The trail surface is a mix of loose gravel and cinders, so it's a good idea to bring hiking boots or high-top shoes. A side note: Most visitors to Ubehebe Crater don't even bother with this trail. Instead, they just get out of their cars, make a beeline run for the bottom of the huge crater, and then moan and groan when they realize they have to make the steep climb back up. Go figure.

User Groups: Hikers only. No dogs, horses, or mountain bikes. No wheelchair facilities.

Permits: No permits are required. There is a $30 entrance fee per vehicle at Death Valley National Park, good for seven days.

Maps: Free park maps are available at park entrance stations and visitors centers or by download at www.nps.gov/deva. A more detailed map is available from Tom Harrison Maps. For a topographic map, go to the USGS website to download Ubehebe Crater.

Directions: From the Furnace Creek Visitors Center in Death Valley National Park, drive north on Highway 190 for 17 miles, then bear right on Scotty's Castle Road. In 32 miles you will pass the Grapevine entrance station. Continue northwest for five miles to the left turnoff to Ubehebe Crater.

Contact: Death Valley National Park, Death Valley, 760/786-3200, www.nps.gov/deva.

3 FALL CANYON

5.6 mi/3.0 hr  

in Death Valley National Park near Scotty's Castle

Map, page 769

Most park visitors take the one-way drive through Titus Canyon to see a desert canyon with giant alluvial fans and towering rock walls. But if you want to witness a similarly imposing desert scene on foot, take a hike in Titus Canyon's next-door neighbor, Fall Canyon. There is no formal trail, but the canyon walls keep you funneled in the right direction. From the parking area, hike to your left (north) on the unsigned trail. In 0.5 mile, you'll reach a wash, but its walls quickly narrow, then later widen again, then repeat the pattern. A gravel surface makes the walking a bit strenuous. Scan the walls' colorful surfaces as you walk, and you'll notice tiny arch formations and miniature caves and alcoves. At 2.8 miles, you are faced with a 20-foot dry fall, and this is where most hikers turn back. If you are experienced at rock scrambling, however, you can locate and follow a use trail on the canyon's south side to bypass the fall. After doing so, you'll enter a 0.5-mile-long, polished narrows area, which many consider to be as beautiful as the narrows in Death Valley's Mosaic Canyon.

User Groups: Hikers only. No dogs, horses, or mountain bikes. No wheelchair facilities.

Permits: No permits are required. There is a $30 entrance fee per vehicle at Death Valley National Park, good for seven days.

Maps: Free park maps are available at park entrance stations and visitors centers or by download at www.nps.gov/deva. A more detailed map is available from Tom Harrison Maps. For a topographic map, go to the USGS website to download Ubehebe Crater.

Directions: From the Furnace Creek Visitors Center in Death Valley National Park, drive north on Highway 190 for 17 miles, then bear right on Scotty's Castle Road. In 14 miles, turn right at the sign for Titus Canyon. Drive 2.7 miles to the parking area, just before Titus Canyon Road becomes a one-way road. Begin hiking to the left of Titus Canyon on a narrow, unsigned trail heading north.

Contact: Death Valley National Park, Death Valley, 760/786-3200, www.nps.gov/deva.

4 UBEHEBE PEAK

6.0 mi/3.0 hr 4 9

in Death Valley National Park

Map, page 769 BEST

Are you prepared for a long drive and then a difficult hike? If you are, the rewards on this trip are great. The climb to Ubehebe Peak would be strenuous enough if you just accounted for the steep grade, but add in the fact that this is Death Valley, and the hike becomes a butt-kicker. The long drive on dirt roads to the trailhead is enough to keep the majority of visitors away. If you decide to make the trip, be sure your car has high clearance, your tires are sturdy and in excellent shape, and your spare tire and jack are at the ready. Once you get to the trailhead, the rewards are great. Ubehebe Peak offers tremendous views of both the snowy Sierra Nevada and the desertlike Last Chance Range, as well as Racetrack and Saline Valleys. The trail is a narrow miners' route that switchbacks up and up and up, and you can be darn sure that you won't come across any shade on the way. There is no trail for the final 0.5 mile to the summit; most hikers content themselves with the view from the saddle below. (If you stop there, you won't miss out. The view is incredible, especially of the Grandstand rock formation far below, and the salt flats of the Saline Valley to the west.) Experienced climbers can make the final summit scramble. Total elevation gain is 1,900 feet; the summit is at 5,678 feet in elevation. Note: Before or after your trip, be sure to explore around the Racetrack area, where you can see the tracks of rocks that have slid along the surface of the mudflats, pushed by strong winds. To see them, drive about two miles south of this trailhead to the pullout and interpretive sign for the sliding rocks, then walk about a half-mile out on the playa. Many a fine photograph has been shot of these fascinating rock tracks.

User Groups: Hikers only. No dogs, horses, or mountain bikes. No wheelchair facilities.

Permits: No permits are required. There is a $30 entrance fee per vehicle at Death Valley National Park, good for seven days.

Teakettle Junction on the road to Ubehebe Peak

Maps: Free park maps are available at park entrance stations and visitor centers or by download at www.nps.gov/deva. A more detailed map is available from Tom Harrison Maps. For a topographic map, go to the USGS website to download Ubehebe Peak.

Directions: From the Furnace Creek Visitors Center in Death Valley National Park, drive north on Highway 190 for 17 miles, then bear right on Scotty's Castle Road. In 32 miles, you will pass the Grapevine entrance station, then continue northwest for 5.8 miles (keep left; don't bear right for Scotty's Castle). Turn right on the dirt road signed for Racetrack. Drive 20 miles on Racetrack Road. Bear right at Teakettle Junction and drive 5.9 miles to a pullout on the right side of the road, across from the large rock formation called the Grandstand. High-clearance vehicles are necessary on Racetrack Road.

Contact: Death Valley National Park, Death Valley, 760/786-3200, www.nps.gov/deva.

5 DARWIN FALLS

2.2 mi/1.0 hr

in Death Valley National Park near Panamint Springs

Map, page 769

Darwin Falls is a must-do desert hike. A waterfall in the desert is a rare and precious thing, a miracle of life in a harsh world. The trip is easy enough for young children, and although the temperatures in this area can be extreme in the summer, an early-morning start makes the short hike manageable almost year-round. Of course, be sure to carry water with you. Follow the trail into the canyon, and you'll soon see a trickle of water on the ground that grows wider and more substantial the farther you walk. You simply follow the stream, crossing it a few times, for about a mile. The canyon walls narrow, and the vegetation becomes much more lush. Just beyond a small stream-gauging station, you come to the waterfall—a 30-foot cascade tucked into a box canyon. A large cottonwood tree grows at its lip. In the spring, more than 80 species of resident and migrating birds have been sighted in this canyon. Although it may be tempting to cool off your feet in the water, park rangers request that people refrain from bathing or swimming in order to protect this rare environment that supports so many native species.

User Groups: Hikers only. No dogs, horses, or mountain bikes. No wheelchair facilities.

Permits: No permits are required. Parking and access are free.

Maps: Free park maps are available at park entrance stations and visitors centers or by download at www.nps.gov/deva. A more detailed map is available from Tom Harrison Maps. For a topographic map, go to the USGS website to download Panamint Springs.

Directions: From Lone Pine on U.S. 395, drive east on Highway 136 for 18 miles, and then continue straight on Highway 190 for 30 miles. The right (south) turnoff for Darwin Falls is exactly one mile before you reach the Panamint Springs Resort. Look for a small Darwin Falls sign and a dirt road. Turn right and drive 2.5 miles on the dirt road to a fork in the road; bear right and park at the signed trailhead. Alternatively, you can exit U.S. 395 at Olancha and Highway 190 and drive east on Highway 190 for 44 miles.

Contact: Death Valley National Park, Death Valley, 760/786-3200, www.nps.gov/deva.

6 MOSAIC CANYON

1.0 mi/0.5 hr

1 10

in Death Valley National Park near Stovepipe Wells

Map, page 769 BEST

The Mosaic Canyon hike is one of the scenic highlights of Death Valley, and it's accessible to all levels of hikers. The trail shows off plenty of colorful slickrock and polished marble as it winds its way up a narrow, high-walled canyon, which was formed by a fault zone. A rock formation called mosaic breccia—multicolored rock fragments that appear to be cemented together—is embedded in the canyon walls. The best mosaics are visible in the first 0.25 mile, making this trip rewarding even for those who don't like to hike more than a short distance.

From the trailhead, the route enters the canyon almost immediately, and the smooth marble walls close in around you. At various points, the fissure you're walking through opens wider into "rooms" bordered by marble walls, then narrows again. After 0.3 mile, the canyon walls open out to a wide alluvial fan that is not quite as interesting as the narrows area. Many people turn around here, but if you like, you can continue walking another 1.5 miles. The path ends at a dry waterfall that is too high to be scaled.

User Groups: Hikers only. No dogs, horses, or mountain bikes. No wheelchair facilities.

Permits: No permits are required. There is a $30 entrance fee per vehicle at Death Valley National Park, good for seven days.

Maps: Free park maps are available at park entrance stations and visitors centers or by download at www.nps.gov/deva. A more detailed map is available from Tom Harrison Maps. For a topographic map, go to the USGS website to download Stovepipe Wells.

Directions: From Lone Pine on U.S. 395, drive east on Highway 136 for 18 miles. Continue east on Highway 190 for approximately 60 miles to 0.25 mile west of Stovepipe Wells Village. Look for the Mosaic Canyon turnoff, on the right. If you reach Stovepipe Wells Village, you missed the turnoff. Turn right and drive 2.2 miles to the trailhead parking lot. The last two miles are rough dirt road but are usually passable by passenger cars.

Contact: Death Valley National Park, Death Valley, 760/786-3200, www.nps.gov/deva.

7 MESQUITE FLAT SAND DUNES

3.0 mi/1.0 hr 

in Death Valley National Park near Stovepipe Wells

Map, page 769

Nothing makes a better introduction to Death Valley than a visit to the 80-foot-high Mesquite Flat sand dunes, near Stovepipe Wells. No, these aren't the giant sand dunes that Death Valley is famous for; those are the Eureka Dunes. But if you've just driven into the park, this hike will convince your senses that you're really in Death Valley, a place like no place else. There is no marked trail because of the continually shifting desert sands, so you just make a beeline from the roadside parking area to the dunes. How far you wander is completely up to you. Early in the morning or right about sunset are the best times to visit because of the incredible show of color and light in the ghost-like dunes. Full-moon nights are also popular, and it's easy to imagine why. They'll have you dreaming of Arabian nights.

Note: The walk from the highway to the dunes is so short that many visitors underestimate how hot and dry this trip can be. Not only should you carry plenty of water, but avoid visiting during the hottest part of the day. There have been more than a few fatalities here, which could have easily been avoided by more careful planning.

User Groups: Hikers only. No dogs, horses, or mountain bikes. No wheelchair facilities.

Permits: No permits are required. There is a $30 entrance fee per vehicle at Death Valley National Park, good for seven days.

Maps: Free park maps are available at park entrance stations or by contacting Death Valley National Park. A more detailed map is available from Tom Harrison Maps. For a topographic map, go to the USGS website to download Stovepipe Wells.

Directions: From Lone Pine on U.S. 395, drive east on Highway 136 for 18 miles. Continue east

Mesquite Flat Sand Dunes

on Highway 190 for approximately 62 miles, past Stovepipe Wells Village, to the Mesquite Sand Dunes parking lot on the north side of Highway 190 (2.4 miles east of Stovepipe Wells).
Contact: Death Valley National Park, Death Valley, 760/786-3200, www.nps.gov/deva.

8 SALT CREEK INTERPRETIVE TRAIL

1.0 mi/0.5 hr 1 8

in Death Valley National Park

Map, page 769 BEST

Salt Creek is exactly what its name implies—a stream of saline water—and it's home to the Salt Creek pupfish, a species that lives nowhere else. The fish underwent an incredible evolutionary change in order to live in this saline creek, which was once a part of a much larger freshwater lake. The biological alteration would be roughly the same as if humans decided to drink gasoline instead of water. In the spring (usually late February and March), you can look down into Salt Creek and spot the minnow-sized pupfish swimming about. The plants along the stream are typical of California coastal wetlands—salt grass and pickleweed. Birds congregate by the stream, including great blue herons. Because the trail is on a wooden boardwalk, it is accessible to all hikers, including wheelchair users.

User Groups: Hikers and wheelchairs. No dogs, horses, or mountain bikes.

Permits: No permits are required. There is a $30 entrance fee per vehicle at Death Valley National Park, good for seven days.

Maps: Interpretive trail brochures are available at park visitors centers or at the trailhead. Free park maps are available at park entrance stations and visitors centers or by download at www.nps.gov/deva. A more detailed map is available from Tom Harrison Maps. For a topographic map, go to the USGS website to download Beatty Junction.

Directions: From the Furnace Creek Visitors Center in Death Valley National Park, drive 12 miles north on Highway 190 to the turnoff for Salt Creek. Turn left and drive 1 mile to the Salt Creek parking area.

Contact: Death Valley National Park, Death Valley, 760/786-3200, www.nps.gov/deva.

9 HARMONY BORAX WORKS AND BORAX FLATS

1.0 mi/0.5 hr 1 8

in Death Valley National Park

Map, page 769

A stroll on Harmony Borax Works Interpretive Trail, combined with a longer excursion on neighboring Borax Flats, makes an easy and interesting walk through Death Valley's history. Borax was first discovered in Death Valley in 1881, but transporting it proved difficult, because the nearest railroad was 165 miles away, in Mojave, over fierce, rugged terrain. Enterprising miners figured out the solution: Build specially designed wagons that could carry huge, extra-heavy loads pulled by teams of 20 mules. The rest, as they say, is history. The paved loop leads past examples of the 20-mule team wagons, as well as equipment used for refining borax. At the west end of the loop, you can leave the pavement and walk out to the site where Chinese laborers gathered the stuff from the salt flats. The flats are easy to walk on, with a crusty, hard surface. Eventually the trail dissipates in the mud, so when your curiosity is satisfied, just turn around and head back.

User Groups: Hikers only. No dogs, horses, or mountain bikes. No wheelchair facilities.

Permits: No permits are required. There is a $30 entrance fee per vehicle at Death Valley National Park, good for seven days.

Maps: Free park maps are available at park entrance stations and visitors centers or by download at www.nps.gov/deva. A more detailed map is available from Tom Harrison Maps. For a topographic map, go to the USGS website to download Furnace Creek.

Directions: From the Furnace Creek Visitors Center in Death Valley National Park, drive north on Highway 190 for 1.3 miles to the left turnoff for Harmony Borax Works and Mustard Canyon. Turn left, then stay to the left to reach the trailhead parking area.

Contact: Death Valley National Park, Death Valley, 760/786-3200, www.nps.gov/deva.

10 GOLDEN CANYON INTERPRETIVE TRAIL

2.0 mi/1.0 hr 1 9

in Death Valley National Park

Map, page 769

The Golden Canyon Interpretive Trail is a perfect path for first-timers in Death Valley National Park. Because the trail is so short, most people continue beyond the end of the self-guided stretch, heading deeper into Golden Canyon to Red Cathedral, 0.3 mile from the last numbered trail marker. The interpretive trail follows the path of an old road through a flat alluvial fan exhibiting a colorful array of volcanic rocks, sand, and gravel. Imagine every shade of gold you can think of—from yellow to orange to apricot. That's what you'll see here in the cliffs, which are composed of the layered remains of ancient lake beds. They're especially gorgeous near sunrise and sunset. At the final interpretive post, you can turn around and head back, or take the left fork of the trail and continue to Red Cathedral, the huge red cliff that looms in the background. Its lovely hue is caused by the weathering of rocks containing a large quantity of iron. A surprise is that by the time you reach Red Cathedral, you've gained some 300 feet in elevation—enough to provide some wide views looking back the way you came.

Note: This may be an easy walk, but it's in Death Valley, so more than a few fatalities have occurred here from people who tried to hike during the hottest part of the day in spring or fall, or worse yet, any time in the summer. Always carry plenty of water with you and avoid hiking at this low elevation when the temperature is high.

User Groups: Hikers only. No dogs, horses, or mountain bikes. No wheelchair facilities.

Permits: No permits are required. There is a $30 entrance fee per vehicle at Death Valley National Park, good for seven days.
Maps: Interpretive trail brochures are available at park visitors centers or at the trailhead. Free park maps are available at park entrance stations and visitors centers or by download at www.nps.gov/deva. A more detailed map is available from Tom Harrison Maps. For a topographic map, go to the USGS website to download Furnace Creek.
Directions: From the Furnace Creek Visitors Center in Death Valley National Park, drive southeast on Highway 190 for 1.2 miles to the right turnoff for Badwater. Bear right and drive south for two miles to the Golden Canyon parking area, on the east side of the road.
Contact: Death Valley National Park, Death Valley, 760/786-3200, www.nps.gov/deva.

11 GOWER GULCH LOOP

5.5 mi/3.0 hr 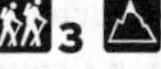 3 9

in Death Valley National Park

Map, page 769

This hike is an extension of Golden Canyon Interpretive Trail (see listing in this chapter) for slightly more experienced hikers. When you reach the last interpretive trail marker on Golden Canyon Trail, take the right fork for Gower Gulch Loop. The path is signed with small hiker symbols; watch for them as you continue your trek into the colorful badlands—deeply creased, eroded, and barren hillsides. Hike across the shoulder of Manly Beacon, a yellow sandstone hill with lovely views. At the base of Manly Beacon's south slope, you reach a junction. Turn right to loop back through Gower Gulch (the left fork leads to Zabriskie Point, a popular drive-to overlook). On your return, remember to stay in the wide main wash and keep heading downhill; this will keep you from making a wrong turn in the canyons of Gower Gulch. You'll notice white outcroppings in the rock, the raison d'être for the old borax mines still found in the area. Also look for mine adits (horizontal shafts); several are bored into the canyon walls. Eventually the canyon narrows, and the trail leads around the side of a 40-foot dry fall. The final mile of the loop parallels the highway, heading back to the mouth of Golden Canyon and its parking area.

One thing to keep in mind: Be sure to carry enough water for the few hours you'll be out on the trail. The total elevation gain is only 800 feet, but it's pretty darn hot out here.
User Groups: Hikers only. No dogs, horses, or mountain bikes. No wheelchair facilities.
Permits: No permits are required. There is a $30 entrance fee per vehicle at Death Valley National Park, good for seven days.
Maps: Free park maps are available at park entrance stations and visitors centers or by download at www.nps.gov/deva. A more detailed map is available from Tom Harrison Maps. For a topographic map, go to the USGS website to download Furnace Creek.
Directions: From the Furnace Creek Visitors Center in Death Valley National Park, drive southeast on Highway 190 for 1.2 miles to the turnoff for Badwater. Turn right and drive south for two miles to the Golden Canyon parking area, on the east side of the road.
Contact: Death Valley National Park, Death Valley, 760/786-3200, www.nps.gov/deva.

12 NATURAL BRIDGE CANYON

1.2 mi/1.0 hr  2  9

in Death Valley National Park

Map, page 769

Natural Bridge Canyon is a good spot to take a short walk and get a good taste of what Death Valley is all about. Because the canyon has an abrupt slope, the hike is not as easy as you may expect. The loose gravel surface of its floor makes walking a workout. Still, you should at least go as far as the natural bridge for which the canyon is named; it's only 0.3 mile in, or about 15 minutes from your car. The "bridge" is an imposing overhang about 40 feet high and 25 feet wide. It was formed by repeated flash flooding over thousands of years. Take a walk underneath it, then make your way up the canyon a little farther and watch other visitors walk underneath it. All the while, you can't help but ponder the amazing geologic action that has created Death Valley. If you want to go farther back into the canyon, you'll find more interesting features, such as dry waterfalls and "wax drippings," which are formed when water drips down the canyon walls and forms a type of mud. The canyon walls come together at a 15-foot dry fall 0.6 mile in, so that's your turnaround point.

User Groups: Hikers only. No dogs, horses, or mountain bikes. No wheelchair facilities.

Permits: No permits are required. There is a $30 entrance fee per vehicle at Death Valley National Park, good for seven days.

Maps: Free park maps are available at park entrance stations and visitors centers or by download at www.nps.gov/deva. A more detailed map is available from Tom Harrison Maps. For a topographic map, go to the USGS website to download Furnace Creek.

Directions: From the Furnace Creek Visitors Center in Death Valley National Park, drive southeast on Highway 190 for 1.2 miles to the right turnoff for Badwater. Bear right and drive south for 13.2 miles to the left turnoff for Natural Bridge Canyon. Turn left and drive 1.7 miles to the trailhead.

Contact: Death Valley National Park, Death Valley, 760/786-3200, www.nps.gov/deva.

13 WILDROSE PEAK TRAIL

8.4 mi/5.0 hr 3 10

in Death Valley National Park

Map, page 769 **BEST**

If it's boiling in Death Valley, you can always make the long drive out to Wildrose Canyon and begin your hike at a trailhead elevation of 6,800 feet. Get this: You'll even find trees here. Whew, what a relief—at least until you start climbing in earnest, heading for 9,064-foot Wildrose Peak. The hike begins at the 10 charcoal kilns (they look strangely like beehives) that were built in the 1870s to make charcoal for the local mines. Walk to the north end of the kilns to find the signed trail, then start climbing through scattered piñon pines and junipers. You can see far off to the Sierra, even Mount Whitney, and then as you climb higher, you can look down at Death Valley and Panamint Valley. Well-graded switchbacks make the 2,200-foot climb manageable, and the panoramic views make the energy expenditure completely worth it. If you tire out, at least try to hike the first 2.5 miles of trail, where you'll get a good dose of vistas from a saddle below the summit. The last mile to the summit is the steepest.

Note: This trail can be snowed in any time between November and May. Check with the park before making the long drive.

User Groups: Hikers and horses. No dogs or mountain bikes. No wheelchair facilities.

Permits: No permits are required. There is a $30 entrance fee per vehicle at Death Valley National Park, good for seven days.

Maps: Free park maps are available at park entrance stations and visitors centers or by download at www.nps.gov/deva. A more detailed map is available from Tom Harrison Maps. For a topographic map, go to the USGS website to download Wildrose Peak.

Directions: From Stovepipe Wells, drive west on Highway 190 for eight miles to Emigrant Canyon Road, then turn left (south). Drive 21 miles to a junction with Wildrose Canyon Road. Turn left (east) and drive seven miles to the parking area on the right, across from the Charcoal Kilns.

Note: Trailers and vehicles longer than 25 feet are prohibited on Emigrant Canyon Road; travelers with these types of vehicles should access Wildrose Canyon via Panamint Valley

Road (18 miles farther west on Highway 190 than Emigrant Canyon Road).

Contact: Death Valley National Park, Death Valley, 760/786-3200, www.nps.gov/deva.

14 TELESCOPE PEAK TRAIL

14.0 mi/9.0 hr 4 10

in Death Valley National Park

Map, page 769

The chief highlight of the long hike to the summit of Telescope Peak is this: When you get there, you can pivot around and in one long, sweeping glance take in Mount Whitney to the west and Badwater to the east. For the uninitiated, that means you're seeing the highest point in the contiguous United States and the lowest point in the Western Hemisphere from the same spot (one is ahead of you, one to your back). The other big deal about the hike is that the trailhead is at 8,000 feet, so you don't have to worry about passing out from the valley's heat. The peak (at 11,049 feet) is the highest in Death Valley National Park, and the trail to reach it is well graded and well maintained. Nonetheless, the 3,000-foot climb and the long mileage take their toll, so don't try this hike unless you're in good shape. In addition to passing piñon pines and junipers, you'll also see some ancient bristlecone pine trees once you climb above 10,000 feet. To supplement the vistas of Mount Whitney and Badwater, you are also witness to Death Valley and Panamint Valley, as well as the White Mountains to the north. It's beyond spectacular. But the climb is one heck of a workout, so be prepared.

Note: This trail can be snowed in any time between November and May. Check with the park before making the long drive.

User Groups: Hikers only. No dogs, horses, or mountain bikes. No wheelchair facilities.

Permits: No permits are required. There is a $30 entrance fee per vehicle at Death Valley National Park, good for seven days.

Maps: Free park maps are available at park entrance stations and visitors centers or by download at www.nps.gov/deva. A more detailed map is available from Tom Harrison Maps. For a topographic map, go to the USGS website to download Telescope Peak.

Directions: From Stovepipe Wells, drive west on Highway 190 for eight miles to Emigrant Canyon Road, then turn left (south). Drive 21 miles to a junction with Wildrose Canyon Road. Turn left (east) and drive nine miles to the end of Wildrose Canyon Road at Mahogany Flat Campground. The road gets very rough and steep for the last 2 miles after the charcoal kilns. High-clearance vehicles are recommended.

Note: Trailers and vehicles longer than 25 feet are prohibited on Emigrant Canyon Road; travelers with these types of vehicles should access this trailhead via Panamint Valley Road (18 miles farther west on Highway 190 than Emigrant Canyon Road).

Contact: Death Valley National Park, Death Valley, 760/786-3200, www.nps.gov/deva.

15 FOSSIL FALLS

1.0 mi/0.5 hr 1 8

off U.S. 395 north of the Highway 178 and Highway 14 junction

Map, page 769

Now don't get your hopes up and think you're going to find a waterfall way out here in the desert east of U.S. 395. There's no water to be found anywhere at Fossil Falls, but there's an excellent hike to an ancient lava field where you'll find polished and sculptured rock formations. The trail is well maintained, flat, and easy enough for children, although you don't want to hike it at high noon on a hot day. The falls look more like a giant pit or crevice in the ground, carved with beautiful water-sculpted lava formations, which were polished in the last ice age. Fossil Falls is not just appealing to geology buffs; there's something here for history buffs as well: This area was used by Native

Americans for at least 10,000 years. There are petroglyphs and rock rings adjacent to the trail. Look and enjoy, but remember that these artifacts are protected by federal law—don't touch or take them.

User Groups: Hikers and dogs. No horses or mountain bikes. No wheelchair facilities.

Permits: No permits are required. Parking and access are free.

Maps: For a topographic map, go to the USGS website to download Little Lake.

Directions: From the junction of Highway 14 and U.S. 395 near Inyokern, drive north on U.S. 395 for 20 miles to just north of Little Lake, and turn east on Cinder Road. Drive 0.6 mile, bear right at the fork, and drive another 0.6 mile to the Fossil Falls trailhead.

Contact: Bureau of Land Management, Ridgecrest Field Office, Ridgecrest, 760/384-5400, www.ca.blm.gov/ridgecrest.

16 TRONA PINNACLES

0.5 mi/0.5 hr 1 8

east of Ridgecrest and south of Trona

Map, page 769

If the Trona Pinnacles were miniaturized, they'd look like oblong-shaped lumps of modeling clay ready to be turned on a potter's wheel. They're actually tufa spires made of calcium carbonate, and the Trona Pinnacles National Natural Landmark features more than 500 of them, some as high as 140 feet. Like the tufa spires at Mono Lake, the Trona Pinnacles were formed underwater from calcium-rich springs in the days when giant Searles Lake still had water in it—probably 50,000 years ago. Now the lake bed is dry, so the tufa spires jut upward from a flat, dry plain. Yes, they're weird looking, but in a good way. If you're the kind of person who likes the weird-looking tufa formations at Mono Lake (we are), you'll enjoy this area. A 0.5-mile loop trail leads through the pinnacles, but most people just wander around at random, gazing at the strange, giant tufa spires. Wear sturdy hiking shoes—the tufa is quite sharp.

User Groups: Hikers and dogs. No horses or mountain bikes. No wheelchair facilities.

Permits: No permits are required. Parking and access are free.

Maps: A free brochure on the Trona Pinnacles is available from the Bureau of Land Management. For a topographic map, go to the USGS website to download Searles Lake.

Directions: From Ridgecrest, drive east on Highway 178 for 20 miles to the junction with Trona-Red Mountain Road. Continue on Highway 178 for 7.7 more miles to the signed right turnoff for the trailhead. (High-clearance vehicles are recommended.)

Contact: Bureau of Land Management, Ridgecrest Field Office, Ridgecrest, 760/384-5400, www.ca.blm.gov/ridgecrest.

17 DESERT TORTOISE DISCOVERY LOOP

2.0 mi/1.0 hr 1 8

in Desert Tortoise Natural Area off Highway 14 near California City

Map, page 769 BEST

The Desert Tortoise Natural Area features an easy interpretive trail that teaches visitors all about *Gopherus agassizii,* better known as the desert tortoise, California's state reptile. Don't get your heart set on seeing one, though, as the creatures are rather shy. You have to look for them, and you have to get lucky. At the preserve, you can also learn all about other desert reptiles and desert plants. A few short interpretive trails are worth strolling, but the two-mile Discovery Trail offers the best chance of seeing tortoises. Look for their burrows underneath creosote bushes, and keep your fingers crossed that one decides to pop his or her head out. Spring (usually from early March to late May) is the best time for tortoise sightings, when the wildflowers are in bloom. The tortoises like to eat them. The best tortoise fact we learned on our trip? During a sudden rainstorm, a tortoise may emerge from its burrow and drink enough water to last a full year.

User Groups: Hikers, horses, and wheelchairs. No dogs or mountain bikes.

Permits: No permits are required. Parking and access are free.

Maps: A free map to the Desert Tortoise Natural Area is available at the trailhead. For topographic maps, go to the USGS website to download California City North and Galileo Hill.

Directions: From Mojave, at the junction of Highways 58 and 14, drive northeast on Highway 14 for 4.5 miles to California City Boulevard. Drive east on California City Boulevard for nine miles to 20 Mule Team Parkway. Go east on the parkway and continue driving 1.3 miles to Randsburg-Mojave Road. Turn left (northeast) on Randsburg-Mojave Road and drive four miles to the signed parking area.

Contact: Bureau of Land Management, Ridgecrest Field Office, Ridgecrest, 760/384-5400, www.ca.blm.gov/ridgecrest.

18 RED CLIFFS

2.0 mi/1.0 hr

in Red Rock Canyon State Park off Highway 14 north of Mojave

Map, page 769

Red Cliffs Natural Preserve is a hikers-only section of Red Rock Canyon State Park, where you can walk alongside and view close-up the reddish columns of 300-foot desert cliffs and colorful eroded badlands. If you've visited some of Utah's desert parks, you'll find the similarity striking. The colors you see are caused by iron oxide, or rust, but the cliffs' myriad creases and folds have been formed by a combination of fire and water—volcanic action and the coursing flow of streams and rivers. The park lies on both sides of Highway 14, and on the Red Cliffs side, you hike on old jeep tracks, gaining views of the El Paso Mountains as you ascend. It's hard to believe that this wilderness-like desert is so close to urban Los Angeles, because when you're out here, the city seems a million miles away. At the preserve boundary 0.75 mile from the trailhead, you can continue on the jeep road into the Scenic Cliffs area, or turn around and retrace your steps. The Scenic Cliffs area is closed each year from February 1 to July 1, the nesting season for various birds of prey. To get the full Red Rock State Park experience, take this hike at sunset, spend the night in the park's Ricardo Campground, and stay up late to see the stars as you've never seen them before.

User Groups: Hikers, dogs, and horses. No mountain bikes. No wheelchair facilities.

Permits: No permits are required. A $6 day-use fee is charged per vehicle.

Maps: For a topographic map, go to the USGS website to download Cantil.

Directions: From Mojave, at the junction of Highways 58 and 14, drive northeast on Highway 14 for about 20 miles to the Red Cliffs parking area, on the right (east) side of the road.

Contact: Mojave Sector Office, Lancaster, 661/946-6092, www.parks.ca.gov, or Red Rocks Interpretive Association, https://redrockrrcia.org.

19 HAGEN CANYON NATURE TRAIL

2.0 mi/1.0 hr

in Red Rock Canyon State Park off Highway 14 north of Mojave

Map, page 769

At the edge of the El Paso Range, eroded badlands rise up from the sandy soil, their whimsical shapes sculpted by eons of wind and water. Once the home of the Kawaiisu Indians who carved petroglyphs in the vividly colored cliffs, and later a gold mining site, stagecoach stop, and backdrop for Hollywood westerns, this multi-hued collection of creased and folded sandstone buttes is the centerpiece of Red Rock Canyon State Park. If you're a television buff, you might recognize this otherworldly landscape from vintage shows like "Bonanza" and "Lost in Space." The park's cliffs have appeared in more than 100 films. Take a walk among these fascinating badland formations on the 1.2-mile Hagen Canyon Nature Trail, and you'll find photo opportunities everywhere you look. Some of the fluted cliffs look like colorful candles melting in the sun. Others have small caves or "windows," inviting children (and adults) to climb and explore. A smattering of Joshua trees adds a touch of green to the desert palette.

User Groups: Hikers, dogs, and horses. No mountain bikes. No wheelchair facilities.

Permits: No permits are required. A $6 day-use fee is charged per vehicle.

Maps: For a topographic map, go to the USGS website to download Cantil.

Directions: From Mojave, at the junction of Highways 58 and 14, drive northeast on Highway 14 for about 20 miles to the Hagen Canyon parking area, on the left (west) side of the road.

Contact: Mojave Sector Office, Lancaster, 661/946-6092, www.parks.ca.gov, or Red Rocks Interpretive Association, https://redrockrrcia.org.

20 ANTELOPE VALLEY POPPY RESERVE LOOP

2.0 mi/1.0 hr 2 9

west of Lancaster and Highway 14

Map, page 768 BEST

Our first trip to the Antelope Valley California Poppy Reserve was a wee bit disappointing. We showed up in late March, expecting to see the hillsides completely covered in bright orange flowers, but only a few straggler poppies were left, dry and shriveled from the desert wind. It was our own darn fault for poor planning. If you want to see the amazing poppy show at Antelope Valley, you simply must time your trip perfectly. The best way to do so is to call the recorded wildflower update phone line (661/724-1180) or monitor the park's website starting in late February; you'll find out exactly when the bloom is expected to be at its best. It can be anywhere from late February to late April, and it's different every year. There are several possible loop trips in the park, but the best one for poppy-watching is the North and South Poppy Loop, a combined two-mile loop that leads from the west side of the Jane S. Pinheiro Interpretive Center. Wheelchairs can access a short section of this trail. On either leg of the loop, be sure to take the cutoff trail that leads to the Tehachapi Vista Point, where you can get up high and take a look around.

User Groups: Hikers and wheelchairs. No dogs, horses, or mountain bikes.

Permits: No permits are required. A $10 day-use fee is charged per vehicle.

Maps: For a topographic map, go to the USGS website to download Del Sur.

Directions: From Lancaster on Highway 14, take the Avenue I exit and turn west on Avenue I, which becomes Lancaster Road. Drive 14 miles to the entrance to the Antelope Valley California Poppy Reserve, on the right. The trail begins by the interpretive center.

Contact: Antelope Valley California Poppy Reserve, Lancaster, 661/724-1180 or 661/724-1206, www.parks.ca.gov; Mojave Sector Office, 661/946-6092.

21 VASQUEZ ROCKS

3.0 mi/1.5 hr 2 8

in Agua Dulce

Map, page 768

In case you're wondering whether there is any "country" left near the city of Los Angeles, the park office at Vasquez Rocks Natural Area should convince you. It's a barn, complete with hay and horses. After stopping by and picking up a trail map, take a walk on the Foot Trail and get a close-up look at the bizarre tilted rock slabs that have made this place famous. (The park has been used in various TV and movie productions.) The largest rock slabs are nearly 150 feet high, and they are tilted as much as 50 degrees, jutting out at various angles toward the sky. The geologic wonders are a result of continuing earth movement along the Elkhorn Fault, which has compressed, folded, and tilted the underlying sandstone rock layers. If you think about it too much, you won't want to stand still in one place for too long. From the parking area, begin hiking on the Foot Trail through the colorful sandstone slabs, then loop back on the Pacific Crest Trail (a dirt road), which returns to the other side of the parking area.

User Groups: Hikers, dogs, horses, and mountain bikes. No wheelchair facilities.

Permits: No permits are required. Parking and access are free.

Maps: Free trail maps are available at the park office. For a topographic map, go to the USGS website to download Agua Dulce.

Directions: From the junction of I-5 and Highway 14, drive northeast on Highway 14 for 15 miles to Agua Dulce. Take the Vasquez Rocks/Escondido Canyon exit and drive north on Escondido Canyon Road for 2.2 miles to the park entrance. Continue down the dirt road to the large parking lot and picnic area, and begin hiking on the Foot Trail.

Contact: Vasquez Rocks Natural Area, Agua Dulce, 661/268-0840, http://parks.co.la.ca.us.

22 SADDLEBACK BUTTE PEAK TRAIL

3.2 mi/2.0 hr

east of Lancaster and Highway 14

Map, page 768

Saddleback Butte State Park is a 3,000-acre Joshua tree woodland, but if those funny-looking trees aren't enough to inspire you to make the trip, this hike to the summit of Saddleback Butte should do it. After a 1,000-foot climb to the 3,651-foot summit, you're rewarded with sweeping vistas of Antelope Valley, the San Gabriel Mountains, the Tehachapi Mountains, and the Mojave Desert. Make sure you've picked a cool day, then start hiking from the park campground through sand and plentiful Joshua trees, heading directly for the clearly visible peak. The first stretch of trail is nearly flat. At one mile out, a trail leads off to the left to Little Butte; ignore it, and continue straight for granite Saddleback Butte. The last 0.5 mile of trail is remarkably steep and rocky. A saddle near the summit provides excellent views. Keep going to the very top, where you can fully survey the strange surrounding landscape—the meeting place of the western Mojave Desert and the high San Gabriel Mountains.

User Groups: Hikers only. No dogs, horses, or mountain bikes. No wheelchair facilities.

Permits: No permits are required. A $6 day-use fee is charged per vehicle.

Maps: For a topographic map, go to the USGS website to download Hi Vista.

Directions: From Lancaster on Highway 14, take the 20th Street exit. Drive north on 20th Street for less than 0.5 mile, then turn right (east) on Avenue J. Drive 19 miles on Avenue J to 170th Street East. Turn right, drive one mile, and turn left on Avenue K, at the sign for the state park campground.

Contact: Saddleback Butte State Park, Lancaster, 661/727-9899 or 661/946-6092, www.parks.ca.gov.

23 OWL CANYON/ RAINBOW BASIN

4.0 mi/2.0 hr

northwest of Barstow

Map, page 768

You just never know what kind of good stuff you'll find when you travel around the state, and that's certainly true when you reach the

Rainbow Basin area north of Barstow. From the Bureau of Land Management's (BLM's) Owl Canyon Campground, you can take a four-mile round-trip hike into some colorful desert country. The well-named Rainbow Basin is made from a cornucopia of colorful sediments—deposits that were formed in lake beds 20 million years ago. The most colorful areas can be seen by taking an auto tour around the basin, but before or after you do so, you should take this hike in Owl Canyon.

The trail begins at Owl Canyon Campground in an ordinary-looking dirt-and-gravel wash. Within minutes, the canyon walls get narrower and rockier, and various colorful sediments begin to show themselves in the rock. There's so much to look at and photograph, and so many boulders and obstacles to climb over and around, that you won't be moving very fast. At 0.6 mile, look for a cave entrance on your right. If you have a flashlight, you can tunnel through it and enter a small side canyon. If you keep traveling in the main canyon, you can hike a total of two miles out. The trail ends near the base of Velvet Peak (a granite ridge), in a colorful rock bowl.

User Groups: Hikers and dogs. No horses or mountain bikes. No wheelchair facilities.

Permits: No permits are required. Parking and access are free.

Maps: For a topographic map, go to the USGS website to download Mud Hills.

Directions: From I-15 at Barstow, take the Barstow Road exit and drive north 0.8 mile. Turn left on Main Street, drive 0.2 mile, then turn right on First Avenue. Drive one mile, and you will cross over two bridges; just after the second bridge is Irwin Road. Turn left on Irwin Road and drive 5.6 miles. Turn left on Fossil Beds Road (a gravel road), and drive 2.9 miles to the access road for Owl Canyon Campground. Turn right, drive 0.3 mile, then turn right again and drive 1.6 miles to the family campground (go past the group camp). The trail begins by campsite No. 11.

Contact: Bureau of Land Management, Barstow District Office, Barstow, 760/252-6000, www.ca.blm.gov/barstow.

24 AFTON CANYON

3.0 mi/1.5 hr

east of Barstow

Map, page 768

They call Afton Canyon "the Grand Canyon of the Mojave," and although its proportions may be smaller than the other Grand Canyon, Afton is no slacker in terms of desert drama. Sheer walls of pink and red rock rise straight up, 300 feet above the Mojave River, where a thin strip of water flows almost year-round. From the campground, follow the trail east along the river, amid a surprising amount of foliage. Saltcedar trees thrive along the stream, as well as planted cottonwoods and willows, creating a protective habitat for birds and other wildlife. As you travel farther, the canyon gets more interesting. Its walls tower above you, beautifully carved and sculpted by the Mojave River in the days when it was a much bigger waterway—probably 50,000 years ago. Hike as far as you like into the canyon, then turn around and head back. A good side-trip is a visit to Pyramid Canyon, one of Afton's side canyons. Start from the campground and cross the river under the first set of railroad trestles, then head south into Pyramid Canyon. The walls slowly narrow until it becomes a classic slot canyon. In the first 0.25 mile, you can see why they call it Pyramid Canyon.

User Groups: Hikers, dogs, horses, and mountain bikes. No wheelchair facilities.

Permits: No permits are required. Parking and access are free.

Maps: For topographic maps, go to the USGS website to download Cave Mountain and Dunn.

Directions: From Barstow, drive 36 miles east on I-15 and take the Afton Road exit. Drive 3.5 miles southwest to Afton Campground (the dirt road is well graded). Park near the railroad trestles.

Contact: Bureau of Land Management, Barstow District Office, Barstow, 760/252-6000, www.ca.blm.gov/barstow.

25 TEUTONIA PEAK

4.0 mi/2.0 hr 

in the Mojave National Preserve east of Barstow

Map, page 769

Teutonia Peak, on the northeast edge of Cima Dome, is the perfect summit for geometry enthusiasts. Cima Dome's claim to distinction is its nearly symmetrical dome, a weathered geological feature that once was much higher than it is now. The dome rises 1,500 feet above the surrounding desert, covers almost 70 square miles, and spreads some 10 miles in diameter. In fact, the dome is so massive that when you're standing on top of it, you can't see it.

Nonetheless, you'll definitely know you're on top of it. The peak tops out at 5,755 feet and offers head-swiveling desert vistas. A two-mile trail ascends moderately to its summit. The first mile of trail is fairly level, leading through cacti, piñon pines, and Joshua trees, the Mojave Desert's signature plant. The Cima Dome yucca trees and the Joshua tree woodlands on the south face of the New York Mountains comprise one of the densest areas of Joshua trees in the Southwest. Some of these trees grow as tall as 25 feet and are 200 years old or more. (They're a different, bushier subspecies from the kind found in Joshua Tree National Park.)

As you walk, you can clearly see your destination, Teutonia Peak, as well as the rugged-looking New York Mountains to the south. At 1.5 miles, the final ascent begins. At 1.9 miles, you reach a saddle just shy of Teutonia's summit, where panoramic desert views are revealed. Scramble the last short stretch to reach the summit and catch your breath, enjoying the far-reaching vistas. In winter, you might not stay very long, because the wind can howl up here.

User Groups: Hikers, dogs, and horses. No mountain bikes. No wheelchair facilities.

Permits: No permits are required. Parking and access are free.

Maps: A map of Mojave National Preserve is available at the park visitors center or by download at www.nps.gov/moja. A more detailed map is available from Tom Harrison Maps. For a topographic map, go to the USGS website to download Cima Dome.

Directions: From Baker, take I-15 east for approximately 25 miles to Cima Road. Turn right (south) on Cima Road and drive 12 miles to the trailhead, on the right side of the road.

Contact: Mojave National Preserve, Barstow, 760/252-6100 or 760/252-6108, www.nps.gov/moja.

26 KELSO DUNES

3.0 mi/1.5 hr 

in the Mojave National Preserve southeast of Barstow

Map, page 768

What's the most popular place in Mojave National Preserve to watch the sun set? Unquestionably it's the Kelso Dunes, which rank second in both height and range of all the California dunes. The Kelso Dunes cover 45 square miles, reaching a height of about 650 feet. (Eureka Dunes in Death Valley are the highest at about 700 feet; the Algodones Dunes in the Imperial Valley cover the largest area, 270 square miles.) In a wet spring, desert wildflowers bloom on and around the dunes, adding brighter colors to the gold and pink sand.

Be sure to read the interesting interpretive signs at the Kelso Dunes trailhead, then walk a short distance toward the closest dunes, which are plainly visible. Constantly moving sand makes a formal trail impossible. If you climb high enough in the sand, you are rewarded with views of the surrounding desert, including the

Granite and Providence Mountains. Many people don't bother to climb to the top, though. They just plop themselves down and make sand angels or roll around on the dunes' silky surface. Another popular activity is trying to cause small sand avalanches that sometimes produce harmonic booming sounds. For this to occur, the sand must be extremely dry. Some desert lovers swear by the healing power of these vibrating noises.

User Groups: Hikers and dogs. No horses or mountain bikes. No wheelchair facilities.

Permits: No permits are required. Parking and access are free.

Maps: A map of Mojave National Preserve is available at the park visitors center or by download at www.nps.gov/moja. A more detailed map is available from Tom Harrison Maps. For a topographic map, go to the USGS website to download Kelso Dunes.

Directions: From Barstow, take I-15 east for approximately 60 miles to Baker, then turn south on Kelbaker Road and drive 42 miles, past Kelso, to the signed road on the right for Kelso Dunes. Turn right (west) and drive three miles to the dunes parking area.

If you are coming from the south on I-40, take the Kelso/Amboy exit and drive 14 miles north on Kelbaker Road to the signed road on the left for Kelso Dunes.

Contact: Mojave National Preserve, Barstow, 760/252-6100 or 760/252-6108, www.nps.gov/moja.

27 CRYSTAL SPRINGS TRAIL

1.6 mi/1.0 hr 3 9

in the Providence Mountains State Recreation Area southeast of Barstow

Map, page 768

The big draw at the Providence Mountains State Recreation Area is touring Mitchell Caverns on a guided walk, so a lot of people miss out on the excellent do-it-yourself hiking trails in the area. The Crystal Springs Trail is the best of those, leading from the visitors center uphill to a rocky overlook in the Providence Mountains. The trailhead elevation is 4,300 feet. The trail is moderately steep—it gains 700 feet over its brief length—and feels surprisingly remote compared to the parking lot full of people waiting to tour the caverns. You hike upward through Crystal Canyon, where lucky hikers sometimes see Bighorn sheep. Rocky outcrops shoot up from both sides of the trail. You'll witness a remarkable variety of high-desert foliage: piñon pines, junipers, and prickly plants galore—chollas, barrel cactus, catclaw, cliff rose, and the like. As you climb, keep turning around to check out the increasingly widening vistas. The trail ends near Crystal Springs, where you get a fine view of the surrounding desert and mountains. Then just turn around and head back downhill.

A good side-trip is to add a jaunt in the opposite direction from the visitors center. Follow the Niña Mora Overlook Trail from the park campground for 0.25 mile to an overlook of the Marble Mountains and Clipper Valley. (Note that the park is open only from 8 am to 5 pm on Fridays, Saturdays, Sundays, and holiday Mondays, so check your calendar before you drive out here.) And, of course, if you've driven all the way out here, you should sign up for a tour of Mitchell Caverns (and it's prudent to make a reservation before you go; phone 760/928-2586). The limestone caverns and their stalagmites, stalactites, and helictites are fascinating. Tours are held year-round Friday to Sunday and on holiday Mondays at 11 am and 2 pm (during the hot summer, tour time is 10 am).

User Groups: Hikers only. No dogs, horses, or mountain bikes. No wheelchair facilities.

Permits: No permits are required. A $10 day-use fee is charged per vehicle. An additional fee is charged for cavern tours ($10 adults, $9 seniors, and $5 children ages 3-16).

Maps: For a topographic map, go to the USGS website to download Fountain Peak.

Directions: From Barstow, take I-40 east for

100 miles to the exit for Essex Road, Mitchell Caverns, and Providence Mountains State Recreation Area near the town of Essex. Turn north on Essex Road and drive 15.5 miles to the Providence Mountains visitors center.

Contact: Providence Mountains State Recreation Area, Essex, 760/928-2586, www.parks.ca.gov.

28 HIGH VIEW NATURE TRAIL

1.3 mi/1.0 hr 2 8

in Joshua Tree National Park near Yucca Valley

Map, page 770

This easy trail is perfect for a clear winter morning's hike, and unlike most trails in Joshua Tree, you're unlikely to have much company here. This lack of popularity, along with its fine vistas and easy grade, are the best reasons to explore here. The trail is a loop that begins and ends at a parking area near Black Rock Canyon Campground. Pick up an interpretive brochure at the Black Rock Canyon Nature Center (you'll pass it as you drive in), and you can get a brief education on desert plants and animals as you walk. The trail undulates along, climbing a total of only 350 feet, until it reaches a high point with a lovely view of 11,502-foot Mount San Gorgonio and a less-inspiring view of the sprawling desert towns of Yucca Valley and Joshua Tree. A bench marks the spot, and there's a trail register where you can record your comments. The loop back downhill is longer and flatter than the way up. Note: The loop can also be accessed from the campground and nature center via a 0.5-mile spur trail that begins just west of the nature center.

User Groups: Hikers only. No dogs, horses, or mountain bikes. No wheelchair facilities.

Permits: No permits are required. Parking and access are free in the Black Rock Canyon area of Joshua Tree National Park.

Maps: Free park maps are available at park entrance stations and visitor centers or by download at www.nps.gov/jotr. A more detailed map is available from Tom Harrison Maps or Trails Illustrated. For a topographic map, go to the USGS website to download Yucca Valley South.

Directions: From Banning, drive east on I-10 for 16 miles to the Highway 62 exit. Turn north on Highway 62 and drive 24 miles to the town of Yucca Valley. Turn right on Joshua Lane (signed for Black Rock Canyon) and drive five miles to the entrance to Black Rock Canyon Campground. Just before the entrance, turn right on a dirt road signed for South Park Parking Area and follow it to its end at the trailhead. The parking area is just outside of the national park boundary, but the trail is inside the park.

Contact: Joshua Tree National Park, Twentynine Palms, 760/367-5500, www.nps.gov/jotr.

29 WARREN PEAK

6.0 mi/3.0 hr 3 10

in Joshua Tree National Park near Yucca Valley

Map, page 770

If you seek a less tame adventure than you get on many short trails in Joshua Tree National Park, the trip to Warren Peak might suit you well. Located in the far northwest corner of the park, the trail and its 5,103-foot summit destination feel surprisingly remote. The peak provides a terrific view of Southern California's tallest mountains, which are crowned with a mantle of snow in winter and early spring. The trail out of Black Rock Canyon Campground starts in a desert wash, with plenty of Joshua trees, piñon pines, and cholla cacti keeping you company. Keep your eyes on the trail signs, which funnel you into the correct forks in the canyon. (There are several critical turns to make.) The sandy wash narrows to a walled canyon, then broadens again. As you climb gently but steadily, you'll see junipers, oaks, and piñon pines replacing some of the lower desert flora. At about two miles out, you'll spy Warren Peak's pointy fractured rock ahead and to the right. The trail gets a bit hard to discern in places, but watch for trail ducks, and keep your eye on Warren Peak. The last 0.25 mile to the summit is steep and requires some scrambling but is easily accomplished. If it's not too windy, you'll want to stay on top of the pointy, conical peak for a while, and not just so you can read the summit register. Views of Mount San Gorgonio, Mount San Jacinto, San Gorgonio Pass, and the Mojave Desert will make your heart pound. To the southwest are Palm Springs and the Morongo and Coachella Valleys.

User Groups: Hikers only. No dogs, horses, or mountain bikes. No wheelchair facilities.

Permits: No permits are required. Parking and access are free in the Black Rock Canyon area of Joshua Tree National Park.

Maps: Free park maps are available at park entrance stations and visitors centers or by download at www.nps.gov/jotr. A more detailed map is available from Tom Harrison Maps or Trails Illustrated. For a topographic map, go to the USGS website to download Yucca Valley South.

Directions: From Banning, drive east on I-10 for 16 miles to the Highway 62 exit. Turn north on Highway 62 and drive 24 miles to the town of Yucca Valley. Turn right on Joshua Lane (signed for Black Rock Canyon) and drive five miles to the Black Rock Canyon Nature Center. Park and then walk uphill to the Black Rock Canyon trailhead, at the upper end of the campground.

Contact: Joshua Tree National Park, Twentynine Palms, 760/367-5500, www.nps.gov/jotr.

30 EUREKA PEAK

10.8 mi/6.0 hr

in Joshua Tree National Park near Yucca Valley

Map, page 770

The total elevation gain on this trip is only

Joshua trees near Warren Peak

1,500 feet to reach the summit of Eureka Peak (at 5,518 feet), but it feels more difficult than that. The problem is sand and rocks—lots of them—and the fact that the trail is hard to discern in places. However, if you're willing to put in some effort, your reward is a commanding view of the western edge of Joshua Tree National Park, as well as Mount San Jacinto and Mount San Gorgonio. Sand and snow—you see it all from here. Begin hiking on the California Riding and Hiking Trail, which you'll follow for two miles until you come to a major wash. This is where things start to get tricky; keep looking for trail markers signed as EP (for Eureka Peak) to keep you on track. Take the right fork in the wash, leaving the California Riding and Hiking Trail. In another 0.5 mile, take the next right fork into another wash. Hike through this wash for 1.7 miles to its end. A trail marker directs you to your left, heading up and over a ridge. At the top, turn right (south), hike up to a saddle, and then continue on to the south side of Eureka Peak, where there's a short path to the summit. When you get to the top, what's the only downer? You find that plenty of people have driven their cars up to the peak via a dirt road from Covington Flat. No fair. An option is to follow this road back downhill for one mile to the California Riding and Hiking Trail, turn left, and follow the trail back to your starting point. It makes a good loop trip and only adds one mile to your total distance.

User Groups: Hikers only. No dogs, horses, or mountain bikes. No wheelchair facilities.

Permits: No permits are required. Parking and access are free in the Black Rock Canyon area of Joshua Tree National Park.

Maps: Free park maps are available at park entrance stations and visitor centers or by download at www.nps.gov/jotr. A more detailed map is available from Tom Harrison Maps or Trails Illustrated. For topographic maps, go to the USGS website to download Yucca Valley South and Joshua Tree South.

Directions: From Banning, drive east on I-10 for 16 miles to the Highway 62 exit. Turn north on Highway 62 and drive 24 miles to the town of Yucca Valley. Turn right on Joshua Lane (signed for Black Rock Canyon) and drive five miles to the Black Rock Canyon Nature Center. Park at the nature center and then walk uphill to the California Riding and Hiking Trail trailhead, on the left (east) side of the campground entrance.

Contact: Joshua Tree National Park, Twentynine Palms, 760/367-5500, www.nps.gov/jotr.

31 FORTYNINE PALMS OASIS

3.0 mi/1.5 hr 2 8

in Joshua Tree National Park near Twentynine Palms

Map, page 770

The biggest surprise on the Fortynine Palms Oasis Trail is not the large and lovely grove of palm trees at the trail's end. It's that there are no Joshua trees to be found anywhere along the trail. What? No Joshua trees in this part of Joshua Tree National Park? It's true—the elevation is a bit too low for them here. Taking their place are the namesake 49 palms, of course, and lovely spring wildflowers, including huge bushes of bright yellow brittlebrush. Try to hike here in March or April, when you may get lucky and catch the red barrel cacti in bloom. Winter is another lovely season here.

The trail is an old Native American pathway, and it's well maintained and easy to follow. It winds around, climbs up and over a small ridge, and then curves around to the palm grove. First you'll see a cluster of 10 palms, and then a larger grouping a short distance away. Although you can see and hear Highway 62 and its sprawling suburban towns as you hike, once you reach the palm grove, all traces of civilization are left behind. Have a seat on a boulder to listen and watch for birds, but be sure to obey all the signs delineating where you may and may not explore. This lush, green, vibrant spot is critically important as a watering hole for

Bighorn sheep and coyotes. Birds cherish this spot, too—orioles, finches, and hummingbirds congregate here for both the trickling spring water and the palm fruits.

User Groups: Hikers only. No dogs, horses, or mountain bikes. No wheelchair facilities.

Permits: No permits are required. Parking and access are free in this area of Joshua Tree National Park.

Maps: Free park maps are available at park entrance stations and visitors centers or by download at www.nps.gov/jotr. A more detailed map is available from Tom Harrison Maps or Trails Illustrated. For a topographic map, go to the USGS website to download Queen Mountain.

Directions: From Banning, drive east on I-10 for 16 miles to the Highway 62 exit. Turn north on Highway 62 and drive 29 miles to the town of Joshua Tree. Continue east on Highway 62 for 10 miles to just west of the town of Twentynine Palms. Turn right (south) on Canyon Road, located by the High Desert Animal Hospital. Drive 1.7 miles on Canyon Road; bear left where the road forks. The pavement ends at the Fortynine Palms Oasis trailhead.

Contact: Joshua Tree National Park, Twentynine Palms, 760/367-5500, www.nps.gov/jotr.

32 BARKER DAM LOOP

1.5 mi/1.0 hr  1 8

in Joshua Tree National Park near Twentynine Palms

Map, page 770

There's a lake in the desert (well, in wet years, anyway), and it's hidden in a magical place called the Wonderland of Rocks. You can't water-ski or swim there, but you can enjoy birdwatching and photograph the reflections of odd-shaped boulders in the water's surface. The lake is formed by Barker Dam, built by cattleman C. O. Barker in 1900 to improve upon a natural boulder dam that captured rain runoff in this basin. The lake was completely dry for most of the early 21st century, but since 2017, there's been enough rain to make the lake a viable watering hole most of the year. Even if the lake is only a mirage when you visit, this short loop is still a great walk, as it also leads past many of the unique granite boulders of the Wonderland of Rocks. Rock climbers can often be seen strutting their stuff here. The trail loops back past some petroglyphs (take the short spur trail) and Indian grinding holes. If the petroglyphs seem remarkably visible and clear to you, it's because years ago a movie crew painted over them to make them more visible to the camera. For this tragic reason, the park calls these paintings the "Disney petroglyphs."

User Groups: Hikers only. No dogs, horses, or mountain bikes. No wheelchair facilities.

Permits: No permits are required. There is a $30 entrance fee per vehicle at Joshua Tree National Park, good for seven days.

Maps: Free park maps are available at park entrance stations and visitors centers or by download at www.nps.gov/jotr. A more detailed map is available from Tom Harrison Maps or Trails Illustrated. For a topographic map, go to the USGS website to download Indian Cove.

Directions: From Banning, drive east on I-10 for 16 miles to the Highway 62 exit. Turn north on Highway 62 and drive 29 miles to the town of Joshua Tree. Turn right on Park Boulevard and drive 14 miles to Hidden Valley Campground, on the left. Follow the signs for Barker Dam. Note: To reduce traffic congestion in the park, Joshua Tree operates the Roadrunner Shuttle Service from November to April. The shuttle leaves the Oasis Visitor Center in Twentynine Palms and makes stops at Ryan Mountain, Barker Dam, Hidden Valley, and other popular locations in the park's central region. The free shuttle service is optional, but recommended during peak weekends.

Contact: Joshua Tree National Park, Twentynine Palms, 760/367-5500, www.nps.gov/jotr.

33 RYAN MOUNTAIN TRAIL

3.0 mi/2.0 hr 2 10

in Joshua Tree National Park near Twentynine Palms

Map, page 770 BEST

If you hike only one trail in Joshua Tree National Park, this should be the one. Ryan Mountain (at 5,470 feet) provides what many insist is the best view in the park. You can see the Queen Valley, Wonderland of Rocks, Lost Horse Valley, Pleasant Valley, and the far-off mountains, San Gorgonio and San Jacinto. It's a complete panorama. The route travels through boulders and Joshua trees—no surprises here—on a well-maintained and easy-to-follow trail. The ascent is a bit steep—a 1,000-foot elevation gain over only 1.5 miles—but it's over with quickly, so just sweat it out. Be sure to sign the summit register and then have a seat on one of the rocks of Ryan Mountain to enjoy the view. The peak's boulders are estimated to be several hundred million years old, which gives you something to think about while you admire the vista.

User Groups: Hikers only. No dogs, horses, or mountain bikes. No wheelchair facilities.

Permits: No permits are required. There is a $30 entrance fee per vehicle at Joshua Tree National Park, good for seven days.

Maps: Free park maps are available at park entrance stations and visitors centers or by download at www.nps.gov/jotr. A more detailed map is available from Tom Harrison Maps or Trails Illustrated. For a topographic map, go to the USGS website to download Keys View.

Directions: From Banning, drive east on I-10 for 16 miles to the Highway 62 exit. Turn north on Highway 62 and drive 45 miles to Twentynine Palms and the park's visitors center. Turn right on Utah Trail Road and drive eight miles to a Y-junction. Bear right and continue for nine miles, past Sheep Pass Campground to the trailhead parking area, on the south side of the road. You can also reach the trailhead via Park Boulevard out of the town of Joshua Tree, turning left at Cap Rock Junction and continuing 2.5 miles to the trailhead. Note: To reduce traffic congestion in the park, Joshua Tree operates the Roadrunner Shuttle Service from November to April. The shuttle leaves the Oasis Visitor Center in Twentynine Palms and makes stops at Ryan Mountain, Barker Dam, Hidden Valley, and other popular locations in the park's central region. The free shuttle service is optional, but recommended during peak weekends.

Contact: Joshua Tree National Park, Twentynine Palms, 760/367-5500, www.nps.gov/jotr.

34 LOST HORSE MINE

4.2 mi/2.0 hr 2 8

in Joshua Tree National Park near Twentynine Palms

Map, page 770 BEST

You get the full desert experience on the Lost Horse Mine Trail, including spectacular mountain and valley vistas, high-desert flora, and a visit to an old gold mine. The trail (really an old road) leads uphill for 1.8 miles to Lost Horse Mine. The mine produced a gold profit at the turn of the century—9,000 ounces of gold—and is the best preserved of all the mines in the national park. Still standing are the mine's stamp mill, old building foundations, and a few open mine shafts. Continue from the mine another 0.3 mile up the old road, climbing more steeply up the ridge to wide overlooks of the Queen Valley, Lost Horse Valley, Pleasant Valley, and the eastern stretch of the national park. The summit here is 5,278 feet; turn around and retrace your steps before the trail begins to descend.

User Groups: Hikers only. No dogs, horses, or mountain bikes. No wheelchair facilities.

Permits: No permits are required. There is a $30 entrance fee per vehicle at Joshua Tree National Park, good for seven days.

Maps: Free park maps are available at park

Lost Horse Mine

entrance stations and visitors centers or by download at www.nps.gov/jotr. A more detailed map is available from Tom Harrison Maps or Trails Illustrated. For a topographic map, go to the USGS website to download Keys View.

Directions: From Banning, drive east on I-10 for 16 miles to the Highway 62 exit. Turn north on Highway 62 and drive 29 miles to the town of Joshua Tree and Park Boulevard. Turn right on Park Boulevard and drive 15.8 miles to Cap Rock junction. Bear right and drive 2.4 miles to the dirt road on the left that is signed for Lost Horse Mine. Turn left and follow the dirt road to the trailhead parking area.

Contact: Joshua Tree National Park, Twentynine Palms, 760/367-5500, www.nps.gov/jotr.

35 SKULL ROCK NATURE TRAIL

1.7 mi/1.0 hr 

in Joshua Tree National Park near Twentynine Palms

Map, page 770

Joshua Tree National Park is arguably more famous for its rock formations than it is for Joshua trees. If you want a close look at some of the park's weird and wonderful hunks of quartz monzonite, the Skull Rock Trail will provide it. The official trail is only 0.25 mile long, but if you're okay with doing a little cross-country hiking, you can easily turn it into a 1.7-mile loop. The trail provides a quick education: Interpretive signs point out paper-bag bush, turbinella oak, cholla cactus, and other desert flora. The path runs between the Skull Rock parking area and Loop E in Jumbo Rocks Campground, so you can start at either place. It winds among giant, rounded rock formations and passes by its namesake, Skull Rock. The big boulder looks loosely like what its name implies. A spiderweb of paths leads around Skull Rock; this is where everyone abandons the formal trail and starts climbing around on the smooth, rounded rock surfaces. To complete the longer loop, you must cross the park road twice, navigate an unmaintained stretch on the north side of the road, and walk a 0.5-mile stretch of the Jumbo Rocks Campground entrance road. It sounds complicated, but it's quite doable.

User Groups: Hikers only. No dogs, horses, or mountain bikes. No wheelchair facilities.

Permits: No permits are required. There is a $30 entrance fee per vehicle at Joshua Tree National Park, good for seven days.

Maps: Free park maps are available at park entrance stations and visitors centers or by download at www.nps.gov/jotr. A more detailed map is available from Tom Harrison Maps or Trails Illustrated. For a topographic map, go to the USGS website to download Malapai Hill.

Directions: From Banning, drive east on

I-10 for 16 miles to the Highway 62 exit. Turn north on Highway 62 and drive 45 miles to Twentynine Palms and the park's visitors center. Turn right on Utah Trail Road and drive eight miles to a Y-junction. Bear right and continue four miles to the trailhead parking area alongside the road shortly before the entrance to Jumbo Rocks Campground. Begin hiking on the left (south) side of the road. If you are camping at Jumbo Rocks, you can start hiking from the entrance to Loop E.

Contact: Joshua Tree National Park, Twentynine Palms, 760/367-5500, www.nps.gov/jotr.

36 MASTODON PEAK

3.0 mi/1.5 hr 2 9

in Joshua Tree National Park near Cottonwood Spring

Map, page 770 **BEST**

The Mastodon Peak Trail begins at Cottonwood Spring Oasis, a little slice of watery paradise for birds and wildlife. After a short paved section, the trail sets off in the desert sand, and after 0.5 mile, you take the left fork for Mastodon Peak. Shortly you'll pass another trail junction with the path to Cottonwood Spring Campground; stay right. The route has almost no elevation change along its route to the base of the peak. It's a pleasant, easy stroll among tall ocotillos, yucca, and smaller cacti. At the Mastodon's base, you must choose whether or not to scramble to the top; the going is steep but short. Although it's a nice trip just to hike to the peak's base and try to imagine the Mastodon's profile, it's recommended you go for the summit. The easiest route is around the back of the Mastodon, on its east side. In a few minutes you are at the top, admiring the surprisingly wide view: Not only do you see a great expanse of Joshua Tree's desert and the Eagle Mountains, but also snowcapped Mount San Jacinto and the miragelike Salton Sea shimmering in the distance some 30 miles away.

If you want to add some history to your hike, retrace your steps to the junction with the trail to Cottonwood Spring Camp. Turn right there and hike past the Mastodon Gold Mine and the Winona Mill Site. The mine was worked in the 1920s with a modicum of success. From the mill site, you don't need to backtrack to the main trail; the path loops back to the Cottonwood Spring parking area.

User Groups: Hikers only. No dogs, horses, or mountain bikes. No wheelchair facilities.

Permits: No permits are required. There is a $30 entrance fee per vehicle at Joshua Tree National Park, good for seven days.

Maps: Free park maps are available at park entrance stations and visitors centers or by download at www.nps.gov/jotr. A more detailed map is available from Tom Harrison Maps or Trails Illustrated. For a topographic map, go to the USGS website to download Cottonwood Spring.

Directions: From Indio, drive east on I-10 for approximately 25 miles. Turn north on Cottonwood Spring Road and drive seven miles to Cottonwood Spring visitors center. Turn right and drive another mile, passing the campground entrance, to the day-use parking area at Cottonwood Spring Oasis.

Contact: Joshua Tree National Park, Twentynine Palms, 760/367-5500, www.nps.gov/jotr.

37 LOST PALMS OASIS

7.5 mi/3.5 hr 2 9

in Joshua Tree National Park near Cottonwood Spring

Map, page 770 **BEST**

If the weather is cool and accommodating, and you're in the mood for a longer hike in southern Joshua Tree National Park, the Lost Palms Oasis Trail comes highly recommended. Many consider Lost Palms Oasis to be the best palm grove in Joshua Tree, and the hike to reach it has little elevation change. The trail begins at Cottonwood Spring Oasis, and for the first 0.5 mile follows the same path as the Mastodon Peak Trail. Stay straight at the junction with the trail to Mastodon Peak; continue straight through a series of washes and low ridges covered with various low-elevation desert cacti. There is no indication of the huge palm oasis until you are almost on top of it, at slightly more than three miles out. The main trail brings you to an overlook point above the palms, and a steep use trail descends 0.25 mile into the grove. Make the rugged 200-foot descent to the canyon bottom; the remoteness of the area and the lush atmosphere of the leafy palm grove make it worth the effort. The Lost Palms Oasis grove contains more than 100 palms in its main canyon. In the upper end of the canyon is a side canyon with more palms, although these are more difficult to reach.

User Groups: Hikers only. No dogs, horses, or mountain bikes. No wheelchair facilities.

Permits: No permits are required. There is a $30 entrance fee per vehicle at Joshua Tree National Park, good for seven days.

Maps: Free park maps are available at park entrance stations and visitors centers or by download at www.nps.gov/jotr. A more detailed map is available from Tom Harrison Maps or Trails Illustrated. For a topographic map, go to the USGS website to download Cottonwood Spring.

Directions: From Indio, drive east on I-10 for approximately 25 miles. Turn north on Cottonwood Spring Road and drive seven miles to Cottonwood Spring visitors center. Turn right and drive a mile, past the campground entrance, to the day-use parking area at Cottonwood Spring Oasis.

Contact: Joshua Tree National Park, Twentynine Palms, 760/367-5500, www.nps.gov/jotr.

38 BIG MORONGO CANYON LOOP

1.5 mi/1.0 hr 1 8

in the Big Morongo Canyon Preserve north of Palm Springs

Map, page 770

Big Morongo Canyon Preserve is a bird-watcher's place, plain and simple. In fact, if you're not carrying binoculars and a field book when you visit, you'll feel like a real outsider. Fortunately, you don't have to know anything about birds to have a good time. We examined the interpretive exhibit at the trailhead kiosk, and within a few minutes of hiking, we were able to spot and identify a pair of western tanagers. (And usually we can't tell a blue jay from a blue grouse.) The best bird-watching seasons are spring and fall, so time your trip for those seasons, if possible. Although a fire burned through this preserve in 2005, consuming much of the willows and riparian plants, the vegetation has grown back remarkably fast.

Start this loop from the kiosk by bearing left to connect to the Desert Willow Trail, an exposed pathway through a desert wash, then in 0.4 mile turn left again on the Yucca Ridge Trail. As you climb Yucca Ridge, you'll gain panoramic views of Big Morongo Canyon and the San Jacinto and San Gorgonio Mountains. Note the gneiss and schist rock formations along the trail; they are some of the oldest rocks in California—one to two billion years old. In 0.7 mile, connect to the Mesquite Trail and enjoy a streamside walk alongside Fremont cottonwoods and red willows that have regenerated after the 2005 fire. You may smell the distinct scent of sulfur from underground springs. Finally you'll join the Marsh Trail for the final stint back to the trailhead, following a boardwalk made of recycled plastic milk containers. If you haven't added a few species to your bird list by this point in the hike, you will now. More than 1,400 pairs of birds per square kilometer nest here annually, making the Marsh Trail a bird-watcher's paradise.

User Groups: Hikers only. No dogs, horses, or mountain bikes. Wheelchair users can follow the fully accessible Marsh Trail.

Permits: No permits are required. Parking and access are free.

Maps: For a topographic map, go to the USGS website to download Morongo Valley.

Directions: From Banning, drive east on I-10 for 16 miles to the Highway 62 exit. Turn north on Highway 62 and drive 11 miles to Morongo Valley. Look for a sign on the right for the Big Morongo Canyon Preserve (at East Drive); turn right and drive 200 yards to the preserve entrance, on the left. Trails begin at the kiosk/information center.

Contact: Big Morongo Canyon Preserve, Morongo Valley, 760/363-7190, www.bigmorongo.org.

39 AERIAL TRAMWAY TO DESERT VIEW TRAIL

2.0 mi/1.0 hr 1 10

in Mount San Jacinto State Park and Wilderness

Map, page 770

The first time you ride the Palm Springs Aerial Tramway, you realize that human beings are capable of creating miracles. In just a few minutes (which you spend gaping out the big windows at the view), you are whooshed from the desert floor, at 2,643 feet in elevation, to the Mount San Jacinto State Park and Wilderness, at 8,516 feet. From cacti to clouds, from palms to pines, and in our case, from desert heat to snow flurries. There are dozens of possible hikes from the top of the tramway, but the easiest of them all is on the Desert View Trail. Since the trail is in the state park but not in the state wilderness, you don't even need a permit—just get off the tram and start hiking. Where else for so little effort can you get expansive views of the desert and high mountain country? Not too many places.

To reach the Desert View Trail, follow the park's nature trail to the left from the back of the tram station; it joins Desert View. The vistas are awesome every step of the way, especially looking out over Palm Springs and the Indian Canyons. As you walk, be on the lookout for Cooper's hawks and yellow-rumped warblers.

Here's an insider's tip for planning your trip: The best deal on the Palm Springs Aerial Tramway is to buy the Ride and Dine Ticket (available after 4pm). For a moderate additional charge, you get a huge buffet dinner to go with your tram ride and day of exploring on the mountain. It's an incredible experience to spend the afternoon hiking, have dinner in the huge dining room as the sun goes down, and then ride the tram back downhill in the darkness.

User Groups: Hikers only. No dogs, horses, or mountain bikes. No wheelchair facilities.

Permits: No permits are required. The Palm Springs Aerial Tramway charges $26.95 per adult, $16.95 per child ages 3-10, and $24.95 for seniors ages 65 and older for a round-trip ticket to Mountain Station. Contact the Palm Springs Aerial Tramway for information about schedules, fees, and special programs.

Maps: A trail map of Mount San Jacinto State Park and Wilderness is available at the offices listed below. For a topographic map, go to the USGS website to download San Jacinto Peak.

Directions: From Banning, drive 12 miles east on I-10 and take the Highway 111/Palm Springs exit. Drive nine miles south on Highway 111 to Tramway Road, then turn right and drive 3.5 miles to the tramway parking area. Walk to the tram station, buy your ticket, and ride the tram to its end at Mountain Station. Walk out the back side of Mountain Station, follow the paved path downhill, and walk to your left for the Desert View Trail.

Contact: Mount San Jacinto State Park and Wilderness, Idyllwild, 951/659-2607, www.parks.ca.gov; Palm Springs Aerial Tramway, 888/515-8726, www.pstramway.com.

40 AERIAL TRAMWAY TO SAN JACINTO PEAK

11.6 mi/6.6 hr 3 10

in Mount San Jacinto State Park and Wilderness

Map, page 770 BEST

You could hike to 10,834-foot San Jacinto Peak the hard way, upward from Idyllwild on one of several possible trails, but then you'd miss out on the many delights of the Palm Springs Aerial Tramway and hiking through Long and Round Valleys. So take the tram instead, get your wilderness permit at the ranger station, and begin hiking on the Round Valley Trail. It switchbacks gently uphill through the pines and firs, most of the time following a creek laden with corn lilies, to reach beautiful Round Valley, at 9,100 feet. At the west end of Round Valley, you reach a Y-junction in the trail, near the seasonal ranger station. Take the left fork heading toward Wellmans Divide, with a short, steep ascent just before you reach it. The views to the north and east are inspiring, including jagged Tahquitz Peak and Red Tahquitz—a bit of foreshadowing of things to come.

At Wellmans Divide, turn right on the Deer Springs Trail. You have 2.6 miles to go, and the views stay with you the whole way. Climb northward on the granite slopes of Miller Peak, make a sharp left switchback, and head southwest to the spur trail for San Jacinto Peak. Just before you reach the summit, you'll find a handsome stone hut, built in 1933 by the Civilian Conservation Corps and still used by hikers as an overnight shelter. Take a look inside this intriguing structure, then press on to the summit, where the views are truly breathtaking. You can see just about all of Southern California, parts of Mexico and Nevada, and west to the Pacific Ocean. John Muir said that the vista from San Jacinto was "one of the most sublime spectacles seen anywhere on Earth," and he was a guy who saw a lot of vistas. Total elevation gain is 2,300 feet.

User Groups: Hikers only. No dogs, horses, or mountain bikes. No wheelchair facilities.

Permits: A free wilderness permit is required for day hiking or backpacking in the San Jacinto Wilderness and is available from the ranger station at Mountain Station. Backpackers should obtain a permit in advance by mail from Mount San Jacinto State Park and Wilderness. No permits are required. The Palm Springs Aerial Tramway charges $26.95 per adult, $16.95 per child ages 3-10, and $24.95 for seniors ages 65 and older for a round-trip ticket to Mountain Station. Contact the Palm Springs Aerial Tramway for information about schedules, fees, and special programs.

Maps: A trail map of Mount San Jacinto State Park and Wilderness is available at the offices listed below. A map of the San Jacinto Wilderness is available from Tom Harrison Maps. For a topographic map, go to the USGS website to download San Jacinto Peak.

Directions: From Banning, drive 12 miles east on I-10 and take the Highway 111/Palm Springs exit. Drive nine miles south on Highway 111 to Tramway Road, then turn right and drive 3.5 miles to the tramway parking area. Walk to the tram station, buy your ticket, and ride the tram to its end, at Mountain Station. Walk out the back side of Mountain Station, follow the paved path downhill, and head right (west) for a few hundred yards to the ranger station. Get a day-hiking permit and continue hiking on the well-signed trail heading for Round Valley.

Contact: Mount San Jacinto State Park and Wilderness, Idyllwild, 951/659-2607, www.parks.ca.gov; Palm Springs Aerial Tramway, 888/515-8726, www.pstramway.com.

41 MURRAY CANYON TRAIL

4.0 mi/2.0 hr 2 9

on the Agua Caliente Indian Reservation in Palm Springs

Map, page 770

If you think Palm Springs is all tennis courts,

golf courses, and beauty parlors, you haven't been to the Indian Canyons off South Palm Canyon Drive. The Indian Canyons—Palm, Andreas, and Murray—are what's left of the old Palm Springs. They're wide-open stretches of desert, with red rock, fan palms, sulfur streams, barrel cactus, Bighorn sheep, and broad vistas of surprising color and beauty. The Murray Canyon Trail is an excellent exploration of this area, beginning at the picnic grounds between Murray and Andreas Canyons. The trail is well-packed sand and is clearly marked along the way. After an initial wide-open desert stretch, you enter Murray Canyon, which narrows and twists and turns, so you never see where you're going until you come around the next bend. The stream you've been following begins to exhibit a stronger flow, and the streamside reeds, grasses, palm trees, and wild grapes intensify their growth accordingly. If you're a fan of red rock, you'll love the 100-foot-tall slanted rock outcrops and cliffs. After passing a left fork for the Coffman Trail, climb up and over a small waterfall in Murray Canyon, staying on the left side of the stream. In another 0.25 mile, you'll reach a larger set of falls. These falls block any possible further progress but provide many good pools for swimming and granite shelves for picnicking. Birders, keep on the alert for a possible sighting of the endangered Least Bells Vireo, which nests in this canyon.

One thing to keep in mind when you visit Murray Canyon, or any of the Indian Canyons: Make sure you check what time the park gates are closing for the day, and then make sure you finish your hike so your car is out of the parking lot by closing time. Show up 15 minutes late, and you can have a real problem on your hands. (Guess how we know.)

User Groups: Hikers and horses. No dogs or mountain bikes. No wheelchair facilities.

Permits: No permits are required. A $9 day-use fee is charged per adult, $7 for seniors 62 and older and students with ID, and $5 for children ages 6-12.

Maps: A brochure and trail map are available at the entrance kiosk. For topographic maps, go to the USGS website to download Palm Springs and Cathedral City.

Directions: From Palm Springs, drive south through the center of town on Highway 111/Palm Canyon Drive and take the right fork signed for South Palm Canyon Drive. Drive 2.8 miles, bearing right at the sign for Palm Canyon/Andreas Canyon. Stop at the entrance toll gate, drive about 200 yards, and turn right for Murray Canyon. Drive past the Andreas Canyon trailhead and continue to Murray Canyon Picnic Area, a mile from the entrance kiosk.

Contact: Indian Canyons Visitors Center, 760/323-6018, www.theindiancanyons.com.

42 TAHQUITZ CANYON

2.0 mi/1.0 hr 1 10

on the Agua Caliente Indian Reservation in Palm Springs

Map, page 770 **BEST**

Just about everything in Palm Springs has a legend behind it, and Tahquitz Canyon (pronounced TAW-kits) is no exception. Named for an Agua Caliente Indian shaman who abused his powers and was banished from his tribe, Tahquitz Canyon is a spectacular outdoor museum of desert flora and fauna. Yet the curse of Tahquitz remains so powerful that even today, some local tribe members refuse to venture into the evil shaman's rock-studded canyon.

Not so for the thousands of Palm Springs visitors who have hiked here since Tahquitz Canyon's public reopening in 1999. After years of abuse by raucous, partying crowds in the 1960s and 1970s, the canyon was closed to public access for more than two decades. The Agua Caliente Indians, owners of this land, went to great pains to clean out all the garbage, graffiti, and debris and to restore this desert canyon to its native state. Now visitors can hike on their own or join a ranger-guided walk along this easy trail through the canyon to the base of its 60-foot waterfall. Movie buffs will recognize the showering falls as the entrance to the land of Shangri-La in Frank Capra's 1937 film *Lost Horizon*. Tahquitz's other treasures include plentiful bird life, Indian rock art, and lush stands of desert lavender, mesquite, and creosote. Don't miss a trip to this unique place; it is sure to be the highlight of your visit to Palm Springs.

User Groups: Hikers only. No dogs, horses, or mountain bikes. No wheelchair facilities.

Permits: Entrance fees are $12.50 per adult and $6 for children ages 6-12. Reservations are recommended for guided hikes, which are held October-June (8am, 10am, noon, and 2pm) and in summer at 8 am only. You may hike on your own 7:30am-5pm daily, but you must enter the preserve by 3:30 pm. From July-September, the canyon is usually open only Friday-Sunday.

Maps: For topographic maps, go to the USGS website to download Palm Springs and Cathedral City.

Directions: From Palm Springs, drive south through the center of town on Highway 111/ Palm Canyon Drive and turn right on Mesquite Avenue. Drive 0.5 mile to the Tahquitz Canyon visitors center.

Contact: Tahquitz Canyon Visitors Center, Palm Springs, 760/416-7044, www.tahquitzcanyon.com.

43 MCCALLUM POND AND MOON CANYON LOOP

3.9 mi/2.0 hr 2 9

in Coachella Valley Preserve

Map, page 770

On the Coachella Valley's north side, seismic activity has forced underground water to the surface, creating wetlands, marshes, and ponds at the 17,000-acre Coachella Valley Preserve. The water nourishes groves of California fan palms—thousands of them. Start your exploration on the McCallum Trail at the visitors center, a 1930s log cabin constructed from palm trunks. A raised wooden walkway winds though a grove of venerable, thick-skirted palms—a breathtaking contrast to the surrounding desert. Hum a few bars of "Midnight at the Oasis" as you walk under these cool, leafy palms, some 150 years old. Soon the trail opens out to a sandy wash that leads to the McCallum Grove, where skirted palms stand sentry over a tranquil pond. Wander around its perimeter, then head uphill on Moon Canyon Trail to gain a ridgetop view of the surrounding Indio Hills. As you walk, keep your eyes out for the Coachella Valley fringe-toed lizard, a sand-colored lizard with fringes on its toes. This endangered lizard, which makes its home here and nowhere else, was the impetus for the creation of this preserve.

User Groups: Hikers only. No dogs, horses, or mountain bikes. No wheelchair facilities.

Permits: No permits are required. Parking and access are free.

Maps: Trail maps are available at the preserve visitors center.

Directions: From Palm Springs at the junction of Highway 111 and East Ramon Road, head east on Ramon Road for 9.5 miles, then turn left on Thousand Palms Canyon Road. Drive two miles and park in the Coachella Valley Preserve parking area on the left.

Contact: Coachella Valley Preserve, Thousand Palms, 760/343-2733 or 760/343-1234, www.coachellavalleypreserve.org.

44 PUSHWALLA PALMS

5.2 mi/2.5 hr 2 9

in Coachella Valley Preserve

Map, page 770

At Coachella Valley Preserve, the desert landscape is bisected by the San Andreas Fault, which has created numerous springs that pop up from underground. These spring-fed oases provide palm seeds with the water they need to germinate, giving rise to a number of palm groves. More than 1,000 palms rise like leafy mirages in this spectacular place. In each grove, you'll find a lush, shady spot that provides nourishment and shelter for a variety of desert creatures, from owls to bats to chuckwallas. To get away from the preserve's busy visitors center area, follow the trail to the Pushwalla Palm grove, which starts at the parking lot and then leads across the road, heading for an obvious ridge. Follow the trail up the ridge, gaining better views with every footstep. Time your trip for the few weeks of spring when the desert wildflowers are in full bloom, and you'll find this path lined with the bright yellow blossoms of desert gold. Most of the Coachella Valley comes into view as you ascend. At about 1.5 miles, the trail tops out on a wide mesa, then drops steeply downhill to the oasis. Near the bottom of the descent is a trail junction; go left for Pushwalla Palms. Once you're under the leafy shade of these magnificent trees, you won't want to leave.

User Groups: Hikers only. No dogs, horses, or mountain bikes. No wheelchair facilities.

Permits: No permits are required. Parking and access are free.

Maps: Trail maps are available at the preserve visitors center.

Directions: From Palm Springs at the junction of Highway 111 and East Ramon Road, head east on Ramon Road for 9.5 miles, then turn left on Thousand Palms Canyon Road. Drive two miles and park in the Coachella Valley Preserve parking area on the left.

Contact: Coachella Valley Preserve, Thousand Palms, 760/343-2733 or 760/343-1234, www.coachellavalleypreserve.org.

45 LYKKEN TRAIL

4.5 mi/2.0-3.0 hr

in the Santa Rosa and San Jacinto Mountains National Monument

Map, page 770

Many desert hikes are on the flat side, and sometimes you feel like exercising your lungs with a solid climb. When that mood strikes you, do what hundreds of weekend exercisers do in Palm Springs: head for the Lykken Trail, which climbs high above downtown and offers a glorious desert and city view. Just remember to bring plenty of water because this trail is shadeless and often hot, even in the middle of winter. Lykken Trail follows the baseline of Mount San Jacinto, roughly paralleling Palm Canyon Drive, for about nine miles (there's a section of trail missing in the middle, but you can make the connection by walking on city streets). Several trailheads provide access to the trail, all of them in or near downtown Palm Springs. From the end of West Mesquite Avenue, you can jump on the trail's southern stretch and make an aerobic ascent to a point high above Tahquitz Canyon, where picnic tables mark a high overlook. It's views, views, views all the way, and it's not uncommon to see Bighorn sheep along the trail. An out-and-back trip is about 4.5 miles. Or start at the Ramon Road trailhead, following the Lykken Trail north for about 1.5 miles to a junction with the Museum Trail. As you climb, your perspective widens to encompass a 180-degree cityscape studded with thousands of green palm trees. Turn right at an obvious fork marked by a four-foot-high rock pile, then start your descent on Museum Trail. The path drops a merciless 1,000 feet in 1.2 miles, then bottoms out at the Palm Springs Art Museum parking lot. Walk one block east to Palm Canyon Drive, then turn right to saunter back to Ramon Road. Just try to make it back to the car without stopping for eggs Benedict and Bloody Marys. Note: The Lykken Trail makes a great nighttime hike in the warmer months of the year, when you can enjoy the sparkling city lights from high above. If you hike at night, don't forget your headlamp so you can watch for sidewinders and rattlesnakes, which tend to come out in the evening.

User Groups: Hikers and dogs. No horses or mountain bikes. No wheelchair facilities.

Permits: No permits are required. Parking and access are free.

Maps: Free trail maps are available at the Santa Rosa and San Jacinto Mountains National Monument Visitors Center.

Directions: From Highway 111 in downtown Palm Springs, turn south onto South Palm Canyon Drive, then right (west) on Ramon Road. Drive 0.6 mile to the road's end and trailhead. The West Mesquite Avenue trailhead is 0.5 mile south near Belardo Road.

Contact: Santa Rosa and San Jacinto Mountains National Monument Visitors Center, Palm Desert, 760/862-9984, www.blm.gov/ca.

46 GARSTIN TRAIL TO MURRAY HILL

8.0 mi / 4.0 hr

in the Santa Rosa and San Jacinto Mountains National Monument

Map, page 770

Palm Springs' highest summit is unfairly named. Murray Hill's pyramid shape pokes into the sky above the Coachella Valley, demanding a 2,200-foot climb to the top. It's a rightful peak, not a hill. Pick a cool winter day for your ascent—the cactus-and-rock terrain offers no relief from the unrelenting desert sun, even in winter. Start your trip on Garstin Trail, switchbacking quickly and steeply uphill in 1.2 miles, expanding your vista over Palm Springs' lush golf courses, azure swimming pools, and mid-century modern mansions. Spiny barrel cactus pop up alongside the path. Gain the ridge at a major trail fork; veer right to stay on Garstin and soon join Wildhorse Trail. Wildhorse ascends first steeply, then more moderately, for two miles to connect with Clara Burgess Trail, which winds up to Murray Hill's summit. The pointy pinnacle offers a 360-degree view, with the Salton Sea shimmering in the south and snowcapped Mount San Jacinto framing the west. A few picnic tables provide a perfect place for a view-filled lunch. Clink your water bottles together to honor the peak's namesake, Dr. Welwood Murray, an 1880s Palm Springs pioneer.

User Groups: Hikers only. No dogs, horses or mountain bikes. No wheelchair facilities.

Permits: No permits are required. Parking and access are free.

Maps: Free trail maps are available at the Santa Rosa and San Jacinto Mountains National Monument Visitors Center.

Directions: From Highway 111 in downtown Palm Springs, turn south onto South Palm Canyon Drive. On the south end of town, turn left on Bogert Trail, drive 0.9 mile, and turn left on Barona Road. Park in the cul-de-sac.

Contact: Santa Rosa and San Jacinto Mountains National Monument Visitors Center, Palm Desert, 760/862-9984, www.blm.gov/ca.

47 ART SMITH TRAIL

6.0 mi/3.5 hr

in the Santa Rosa and San Jacinto Mountains National Monument

Map, page 770

You can hike as far as you like on the Art Smith Trail, but most people just settle for an out-and-back of a few miles. The entire trail is eight miles one-way, and if you can arrange a car shuttle, that trek would make a fine day. If not, just follow this trail for its first couple of miles to a leafy green palm oasis, enjoy a rest in the shade, and then retrace your steps. If you're a fan of desert flora, you'll really enjoy all the plant life on this trail, especially the chubby round barrel cactus and stately ocotillos. The trail climbs pretty steeply for the first 0.5 mile, then the grade mellows out somewhat. At 1.2 miles you pass a junction with Hopalong Cassidy Trail; stay left on Art Smith Trail and reach the top of the climb soon thereafter. A much easier mile leads you to the first palm oasis, and although it contains a few shady palms, keep going for another 0.6 mile to the next oasis, which is larger and healthier looking. As you sit among these lovely palms and cool your heels in the few pools of water, you may find yourself wondering about Art Smith. He was the president of a local equestrian club and a tireless advocate for trails in the Coachella Valley.

User Groups: Hikers only. No dogs, horses, or mountain bikes. No wheelchair facilities.

Permits: No permits are required. Parking and access are free.

Maps: Free trail maps are available at the Santa Rosa and San Jacinto Mountains National Monument Visitors Center.

Directions: From the junction of Highway 111 and Highway 74 in Palm Desert, turn south on Highway 74. Drive four miles to the Art Smith Trailhead on the right, just past (and across the road from) the Santa Rosa and San Jacinto Mountains National Monument Visitors Center.

Contact: Santa Rosa and San Jacinto Mountains National Monument Visitors Center, Palm Desert, 760/862-9984, www.blm.gov/ca.

48 LADDER CANYON AND BIG PAINTED CANYON LOOP

5.0 mi/2.5 hr 3 9

in the Mecca Hills Wilderness

Map, page 770 **BEST**

With an elevation below sea level, the Mecca Hills region is full of geological treasures, and they're easy to see on a 5-mile loop up Ladder Canyon and back down Big Painted Canyon. Both canyons are aptly named. Big Painted Canyon awes and delights with its extraordinary geology and colorful mineral deposits in hues of rose, pink, red, purple and green. Ladder Canyon is pure theme-park-style fun. Ordinarily, most would-be explorers would be stymied by slick walls, giant boulders, and dry waterfalls, but thanks to a series of metal ladders that are placed at all the tricky spots, even casual hikers negotiate this slot canyon. You ascend a ladder, squeeze through a narrow slot between pink and gold sandstone walls, duck your head under a boulder, then climb up another ladder and repeat. (The ladders are maintained by a group of local volunteers, but you should always assess their sturdiness before climbing or descending.) To connect the two canyons, a trail travels about one mile along the rim above them. This high mesa is an extraordinary place, especially in spring. The moonscape-like landscape, lined with sparse gravel, is punctuated by hundreds of towering ocotillo plants that frame a long-distance view of the Salton Sea, shimmering to the south.

User Groups: Hikers only. No dogs, horses, or mountain bikes. No wheelchair facilities.

Permits: No permits are required. Parking and access are free.

Maps: Download a map of Mecca Hills Wilderness at www.blm.gov/ca.

Directions: In the town of Mecca, take 66th Avenue east for about 4 miles; it will change names to Box Canyon Road. Turn left at the sign for Painted Canyon Road. Follow this dirt road for 3.5 miles to the trailhead. Unless a recent severe storm has damaged the road, it is usually passable by passenger cars.

Contact: Bureau of Land Management Palm Springs South Coast Field Office, 760/833-7100, www.blm.gov/ca.

49 MAIDENHAIR FALLS AND HELLHOLE CANYON

5.6 mi/3.0 hr

in Anza-Borrego Desert State Park near Hellhole Canyon

Map, page 771

If you have taken the hike to Borrego Palm Canyon Falls and found that it suited your taste for desert adventure, this trip to Maidenhair Falls is a more challenging path to a slightly bigger and more dramatic desert waterfall. Stop in at the park's visitors center before you begin, and pick up a handout with trail directions. Also remember to be prepared for a longer excursion in the desert (bring tons of extra water, and cover your head with a light-colored hat). Your destination is a 20-foot waterfall with a walled backdrop of maidenhair ferns and mosses. The route to reach it travels from Highway S22 south of the visitors center into the mouth of Hellhole Canyon. Begin on the California Riding and Hiking Trail for the first 200 yards and turn right. You'll pass a few fan palms, myriad cacti, some odd-shaped rocks, and Native American grinding holes along the route. Cottonwoods grow in places along the stream. Maidenhair Falls is a bit tricky to find, tucked into a narrow canyon corner, but with luck, there will be enough water running in the stream to clue you in to its location.

User Groups: Hikers only. No dogs, horses, or mountain bikes. No wheelchair facilities.

Permits: No permits are required. Parking and access are free.

Maps: Maps and brochures are available at the park's visitors center, or by free download at www.parks.ca.gov. An Anza-Borrego Desert State Park map is also available from Tom Harrison Maps or Wilderness Press. For a topographic map, go to the USGS website to download Tubb Canyon.

Directions: From Julian, drive east on Highway 78 for approximately 19 miles to Highway S3/Yaqui Pass Road. Turn left (north) on Highway S3/Yaqui Pass Road and drive for 12 miles to Borrego Springs. Turn left on Highway S22/Palm Canyon Drive and drive one mile to the signed junction just before the park's visitors center. Turn left and drive 0.75 mile to the large parking lot on the west side of the road.

Contact: Anza-Borrego Desert State Park, Borrego Springs, 760/767-5311; visitors center, 760/767-4205, www.parks.ca.gov.

50 BORREGO PALM CANYON

3.0 mi/1.5 hr 2 9

in Anza-Borrego Desert State Park near Borrego Springs

Map, page 771 BEST

The hike to Borrego Palm Canyon Falls is only 1.5 miles long, but it feels like a trip from the desert to the tropics. You start out in a sandy, rocky, open wash, sweating it out among cacti and ocotillo, and you end up in a shady oasis of fan palms, dipping your feet in the pool of a boulder-choked waterfall. If you haven't visited this special place in recent years, you may be surprised at how much has changed. A series of severe rainstorms and flash floods in the canyon in the years between 2003 and 2010 have wiped out a large number of palms and left their trunks scattered all over the canyon floor, wedged under large boulders, and stacked on top of one another. (One rainstorm was so intense that it created a wall of water 30 feet high and 100 feet wide, which sent witnesses running for their lives. Meanwhile, not a single drop of rain fell in the town of Borrego Springs, only three miles away. Such are the vagaries of desert storms.) On a sunny, calm day, it's hard to imagine the destruction that rain in the desert can cause, but the evidence is all around you in this canyon.

The trip begins on the Borrego Palm Canyon Trail from the state park campground; make sure you top off your water bottles before you start walking. If you pick up an interpretive brochure at the park's visitors center, you can identify the array of desert plants that grow along the trail, including cheesebush, brittle-bush, catclaw (ouch!), and chuparosa. In about 0.5 mile, you're suddenly surprised by the sight of bright green, leafy palm trees up ahead. Borrego Palm Canyon is the largest of more than 25 groves in the park. Go toward the palms, and in a few minutes, you'll be nestled in their shade, listening to the desert wind rustle their fronds. This first grove is not as large as it used to be, but it still has about 20 mature palms. Small, three- to five-foot palm trees are growing up in the aftermath of the destruction. Follow the trail a little farther, and you'll reach a 12-foot waterfall that streams over giant boulders and forms a large, sandy pool. Listen and watch for bird life—more than 80 migratory species use this oasis as a watering stop. Bighorn sheep also come here to drink, especially during dawn and dusk.

For your return trip, follow the well-marked "Alternate Trail" back to the campground, which follows a slightly longer, more meandering route through the wash.

User Groups: Hikers only. No dogs, horses, or mountain bikes. No wheelchair facilities.

Permits: No permits are required. An $10 day-use fee is charged per vehicle (the fee applies only in the visitors center parking lot or trailhead by the campground).

Maps: Maps and brochures are available at the park's visitors center, or by free download at www.parks.ca.gov. An Anza-Borrego Desert State Park map is also available from Tom Harrison Maps or Wilderness Press. For a topographic map, go to the USGS website to download Borrego Palm Canyon.

Directions: From Julian, drive east on Highway 78 for approximately 19 miles to Highway S3/Yaqui Pass Road. Turn left (north) on Highway S3/Yaqui Pass Road and drive 12 miles to Borrego Springs. Turn left on Highway S22/Palm Canyon Drive and drive one mile to the signed junction just before the park's visitors center. Turn right and drive one mile to Borrego Palm Canyon Campground. The trailhead is at the west end.

Contact: Anza-Borrego Desert State Park, Borrego Springs, 760/767-5311, www.parks.ca.gov; visitors center, 760/767-4205.

51 CACTUS LOOP AND YAQUI WELL

2.6 mi/1.5 hr

in Anza-Borrego Desert State Park near Tamarisk Grove

Map, page 771

The Cactus Loop and Yaqui Well Trails are two separate nature trails at Anza-Borrego Desert State Park, but since they're right beside each other, you may as well hike both. The Cactus Loop Trail is a one-mile loop, and more hilly than you may expect from a nature trail. It shows off seven kinds of cacti, including barrel, hedgehog, fishhook, beavertail, and cholla. Visitors often spot chuckwallas and other lizards scurrying among the spiny plants. The Yaqui Well Trail climbs for 0.8 mile among cacti, ocotillo, and cholla to a mesquite grove, and then reaches Yaqui Well. In a small circle around this seep, a tremendous variety of greenery grows, including mesquite and false desert willow, given life by the year-round presence of water. Desert birds show up here, particularly colorful hummingbirds. If you're in the mood for more desert education, drive five miles east of Tamarisk Grove to the short little loop trail at the Narrows. It's packed with a lot of geologic punch; you'll get a big lesson in geological processes, from faulting and landslides to erosion and earthquakes.

User Groups: Hikers only. No dogs, horses, or mountain bikes. No wheelchair facilities.

Permits: No permits are required. Parking and access are free.
Maps: Maps and brochures are available at the park's visitors center, or by free download at www.parks.ca.gov. An Anza-Borrego Desert State Park map is also available from Tom Harrison Maps or Wilderness Press. For a topographic map, go to the USGS website to download Borrego Sink.
Directions: From Julian, drive east on Highway 78 for 19 miles to Tamarisk Grove Campground at Road S3. The trailheads for the Cactus Loop and Yaqui Well Trails are opposite the camp entrance off Road S3.
Contact: Anza-Borrego Desert State Park, Borrego Springs, 760/767-5311; visitors center, 760/767-4205, www.parks.ca.gov.

52 THE SLOT

1.5 mi/1.0 hr 2 10

in Anza-Borrego Desert State Park

Map, page 771 BEST

This short hike is a winner for just about anybody—families, couples, photographers, and even people who don't really like to hike. This narrow siltsone canyon, simply called The Slot, is sheer entertainment of the type you'd expect to find at Disneyland, except that this place was made by Mother Nature. From the parking area, simply descend into the slot canyon—the large crevice that lies below you. There are usually plenty of footprints showing the best possible route to enter The Slot, and once you have accomplished this, the rest of the hike is extremely easy. Hike to your left (slightly downhill) and you'll soon notice the canyon becoming increasingly narrow. You will need to squeeze through walls that are sometimes no more than shoulder-width apart. The colors of the pink and tan siltstone, with the blue desert sky above, make for interesting photographs. About 0.7 mile from the start, you'll pass underneath a boulder bridge that is precariously lodged in a narrow gap. A few hundred yards beyond, the canyon widens and the trail meets up with a jeep road. Simply retrace your steps from here, enjoying the magic of this slot canyon all over again.
User Groups: Hikers only. No dogs, horses, or mountain bikes. No wheelchair facilities.
Permits: No permits are required. Parking and access are free.
Maps: Maps and brochures are available at the park's visitors center, or by free download at www.parks.ca.gov. An Anza-Borrego Desert State Park map is also available from Tom Harrison Maps or Wilderness Press.
Directions: From Christmas Circle in Borrego Springs, drive 11.5 miles southwest on Borrego Springs Road. Turn left on Route 78 East and drive 1.5 miles to mile marker 87.2. Turn north on the unmarked Butte Pass Road (a dirt road that is very easy to miss). Drive one mile up this dirt road to a fork, where you bear left. Continue another mile to the parking area for The Slot. If the road is particularly rutted, low-clearance vehicles should stop and park 0.25 mile from the trailhead.
Contact: Anza-Borrego Desert State Park, Borrego Springs, 760/767-5311, www.parks.ca.gov; visitors center, 760/767-4205.

53 ELEPHANT TREE TRAIL

1.5 mi/1.0 hr 1 7

in Anza-Borrego Desert State Park near Split Mountain

Map, page 771

It's not just the odd-looking elephant tree that you get to see on this trail, but also many of the common flora of Anza-Borrego Desert—creosote bush, burroweed, indigo bush, barrel cactus, ocotillo, catclaw, cholla, smoke tree... There's enough desert-plant identification to do to keep you busy quizzing your hiking partner all day. But it's the single elephant tree on the loop that steals the show, with its crinkled, folded "skin" on its trunk. The tree is an odd patchwork of colors (yellowish bark, blue

Elephant Tree Trail

berries, and orange twigs) and its bark has a very evocative odor, something like a spicy air freshener. The Elephant Tree Trail used to feature several elephant trees, but all but this one lone specimen have died. It is located near the end of the loop. If possible, time your trip for late winter or early spring, when the ocotillos sprout brilliant red plumes and the pink sand verbenas bloom.

User Groups: Hikers only. No dogs, horses, or mountain bikes. No wheelchair facilities.

Permits: No permits are required. Parking and access are free.

Maps: Maps and brochures are available at the park's visitors center, or by free download at www.parks.ca.gov. An Anza-Borrego Desert State Park map is also available from Tom Harrison Maps or Wilderness Press. For a topographic map, go to the USGS website to download Harper Canyon.

Directions: From Julian, drive east on Highway 78 for 35 miles to Ocotillo Wells. Turn south on Split Mountain Road and drive 5.8 miles to the right turnoff that is signed for Elephant Trees. Turn right and drive 0.8 mile on a rough, dirt road to the trailhead.

Contact: Anza-Borrego Desert State Park, Borrego Springs, 760/767-5311; visitors center, 760/767-4205, www.parks.ca.gov.

54 WIND CAVES

1.5 mi/1.0 hr 1 7

in Anza-Borrego Desert State Park near Split Mountain

Map, page 771

Get a close look at Anza-Borrego's amazing geology at the Wind Caves off Split Mountain Road, near Ocotillo Wells. The 4.3-mile dirt road to the trailhead is best suited for four-wheel-drive vehicles, but it's a spectacular trip through tall, colorful canyon walls, formed by layered sediments from ancient lakebeds. Anza-Borrego's geologic story revolves around water: Fossilized sea shells prove that most of this desert was once submerged under both tropical waters from the Gulf of California and fresh water from the Colorado River. Animals like sea turtles and sharks once swam in what is now parched desert. The scenic drive is reward enough, but once you reach the trailhead, a steep 0.75-mile hike provides sweeping views of a prominently striped mud hill formation known as Elephant Knees and the Carrizo Badlands and deposits you at the sandstone Wind Caves, where you'll want to spend some time clambering around and exploring. It's easy to see why early Native Americans used these "holes in the rock" as natural shelters. Many of the alcoves are large enough for a small family.

User Groups: Hikers only. No dogs, horses, or mountain bikes. No wheelchair facilities.

Permits: No permits are required. Parking and access are free.

Maps: Maps and brochures are available at the park's visitors center, or by free download at www.parks.ca.gov. An Anza-Borrego Desert State Park map is also available from Tom Harrison Maps or Wilderness Press. For a topographic map, go to the USGS website to download Harper Canyon.

Directions: From Julian, drive east on Highway 78 for 35 miles to Ocotillo Wells. Turn south on Split Mountain Road and drive 10 miles to a signed right turn for Fish Creek Wash and Wind Caves. Turn right and drive 4.3 miles on rough dirt road to the trailhead (on the left, just beyond the wash's narrowest stretch).

Contact: Anza-Borrego Desert State Park, Borrego Springs, 760/767-5311; visitors center, 760/767-4205, www.parks.ca.gov.

55 GHOST MOUNTAIN

2.0 mi/1.0 hr

in Anza-Borrego Desert State Park near Blair Valley

Map, page 771

When most people imagine a life of living off the land, they instinctively think of doing so in a place where water is plentiful. Not so with Marshal South, who, in the 1930s, chose Ghost Mountain, in the Anza-Borrego Desert. South and his wife built an adobe home atop the mountain and lived there with their children for more than 15 years. The family tried to live simply, attempting to survive in the spartan style of early Native Americans. Sadly, South's wife eventually tired of the rugged desert life and her husband's odd idealism, and the family split up.

The Ghost Mountain Trail climbs through a series of steep switchbacks to the remains of the South homesite, which includes a few partial walls, an old mattress frame, and some assorted cisterns and barrels used for storing precious water. The destination is worthwhile not just because the sight of it sparks your imagination, but also because of the lovely, 360-degree desert views you gain as you ascend Ghost Mountain. When you stand on the top on a clear, cool day, you can almost imagine why South chose this remote homesite.

Remember that Blair Valley and Ghost Mountain are higher in elevation than other parts of the park. Not only does this make them cooler spots for hiking, but it also means that a wide variety of desert plant life grows here. The ocotillos and yuccas put on a spectacular show in early spring.

User Groups: Hikers only. No dogs, horses, or mountain bikes. No wheelchair facilities.

Permits: No permits are required. Parking and access are free.

Maps: Maps and brochures are available at the park's visitors center, or by free download at www.parks.ca.gov. An Anza-Borrego Desert State Park map is also available from Tom Harrison Maps or Wilderness Press. For a topographic map, go to the USGS website to download Earthquake Valley.

Directions: From Julian, drive east on Highway 78 for 12 miles to Road S2, turn south, and drive six miles to the left turnoff for Blair Valley Camp. Turn left (east), drive 1.4 miles on a dirt road, and then bear right at the fork. Drive another 1.6 miles, bear right again, and drive 0.5 mile to the Ghost Mountain/Marshal South Home trailhead.

Contact: Anza-Borrego Desert State Park, Borrego Springs, 760/767-5311; visitors center, 760/767-4205, www.parks.ca.gov.

56 PICTOGRAPH TRAIL

2.0 mi/1.0 hr 2 9

in Anza-Borrego Desert State Park near Blair Valley

Map, page 771

Although a Native American rock-art site is the destination of this trip, the Pictograph Trail comes with a bonus: an inspiring overlook of the Vallecito Mountains from the brink of a dry waterfall. It's a desert vista that's hard to forget. The path begins at the Pictograph trailhead and wanders through huge granite boulders. First you go through a dry wash and then climb up a ridge. At 0.5 mile out, you begin to descend. At 0.75 mile, you'll find some pictographs, painted in red and yellow pigments by the nomadic Kumeyaay Indians. (Look for the pictographs on the side of a large boulder on the right side of the trail.) The slightly faded geometric designs were made with natural pigments and are estimated to be 2,000 years old. Continue farther on the trail, and the canyon narrows dramatically until its walls come together at the brink of a dry waterfall more than 150 feet tall. From its edge the panoramic view is stunning, both of the steep dropoff and the far-off mountains and valley.

User Groups: Hikers only. No dogs, horses, or mountain bikes. No wheelchair facilities.

Permits: No permits are required. Parking and access are free.

Maps: Maps and brochures are available at the park's visitors center, or by free download at www.parks.ca.gov. An Anza-Borrego Desert State Park map is also available from Tom Harrison Maps or Wilderness Press. For a topographic map, go to the USGS website to download Earthquake Valley.

Directions: From Julian, drive east on Highway 78 for 12 miles to Road S2, turn south, and drive six miles to the left turnoff for Blair Valley Camp. Turn left (east), drive 1.4 miles on a dirt road, and then bear right at the fork. Drive another 1.6 miles and bear left at the next fork. In 0.25 mile, bear left again. Continue two more miles to the end of the road, at the Pictograph trailhead.

Contact: Anza-Borrego Desert State Park, Borrego Springs, 760/767-5311; visitors center, 760/767-4205, www.parks.ca.gov.

57 MOUNTAIN PALM SPRINGS CANYON

2.0-5.0 mi/2-3 hr 1 9

in Anza-Borrego Desert State Park near Bow Willow

Map, page 771

Although the groves of fan palms in Mountain Palm Springs Canyon are not as large as in Borrego Palm Canyon, they're still beautiful and popular with park visitors. The palm oases, fed by underground springs and shaded by the magnificent fan palms, create a haven for plants and wildlife, as well as for hikers looking for a cool and pleasant place to spend the day. If you visit in early winter when the palms bear their fruit (dates), you may find so many birds singing in the palms that you can hardly hear yourself think. Look for the pretty hooded oriole in particular, which builds its nest on the underside of palm fronds.

Six distinct palm groves grow in Mountain Palm Springs Canyon, as well as occasional elephant trees; you can visit some or all of the groves in one walk. The route begins in a rocky arroyo, but it becomes more trail-like in short order. The first grove of trees, Pygmy Grove at 0.5 mile, has been burned. The second grove, Southwest Grove at 1.0 mile, is larger and prettier. Most hikers turn back here for a two-mile round-trip, but if you are carrying a map and in the mood for an adventure (and a few extra miles of cross-country walking), take the right fork just before you enter Southwest Grove and head uphill to an elephant tree, where an indistinct footpath heads off to the Surprise Canyon Grove. From Surprise Canyon, go to your left to see Palm Grove Bowl—it's a natural bowl that is ringed with more than 100 palm trees. Return to Surprise Canyon and loop back to your starting point, passing by North Grove on the way. Or retrace your steps to Southwest Grove and head uphill for 0.6 mile to Torote Bowl. There are some good elephant tree specimens there.

User Groups: Hikers only. No dogs, horses, or mountain bikes. No wheelchair facilities.

Permits: No permits are required. Parking and access are free.

Maps: Maps and brochures are available at the park's visitors center, or by free download at www.parks.ca.gov. An Anza-Borrego Desert State Park map is also available from Tom Harrison Maps or Wilderness Press. For a topographic map, go to the USGS website to download Sweeney Pass.

Directions: From Julian, drive east on Highway 78 for 12 miles to Road S2, turn south, and drive 29 miles to the Mountain Palm Springs Campground entrance road, on the right. Turn right and drive straight for 0.6 mile (don't take any of the campsite turnoffs) to the parking area by a stone marker for Mountain Palm Springs Canyon.

Contact: Anza-Borrego Desert State Park, Borrego Springs, 760/767-5311, www.parks.ca.gov; visitors center, 760/767-4205.

58 ROCK HILL TRAIL

2.0 mi/1.5 hr 

on the east shore of the Salton Sea near Calipatria

Map, page 768

If it's wintertime—anywhere from December to February—it's a good time to pay a visit to the Salton Sea National Wildlife Refuge (now called the Sonny Bono Salton Sea National Wildlife Refuge, after the 1970s singer-turned-politician), one of the lowest places in the United States, at 228 feet below sea level. Winter is the only season when the area isn't blistering hot, and it's also the time that peak populations of birds are gathered at the refuge. The Rock Hill Trail, one of two trails at the refuge, gets hiked by approximately 40,000 bird-watchers a year. From the observation platform behind the visitors center, the path heads out along a levee and then abruptly climbs to a hill above the Salton Sea. It's a great place to watch the pelicans dive and to shake your head in wonder at the immense size of the saline Salton Sea. The sea was formed from 1905 to 1907, when a series of artificial dams on the Colorado River burst their seams. Its water has become increasingly saline over the years due to agricultural runoff, evaporation, and the lack of a replenishing freshwater supply.

Although fish do not fare well in the changing waters of the Salton Sea, bird lovers find plenty to cheer about. In addition to seeing the plentiful waterfowl that spend the winter in the saltwater and freshwater marshes—geese of many kinds, mergansers, widgeons, and teals—hikers might spot an endangered species such as the Yuma clapper rail or peregrine falcon, or even a burrowing owl. Wintering snow geese and Ross geese are also big attractions along this trail. They are seen in great numbers every December.

User Groups: Hikers only. No dogs, horses, or mountain bikes. No wheelchair facilities.

Permits: No permits are required. Parking and access are free.

Maps: A free map of the refuge is available at the visitors center. For a topographic map, go to the USGS website to download Niland.

Directions: From Indio, drive south on Highway 111 for approximately 50 miles to the turnoff for Sinclair Road, which is four miles south of Niland. (If you reach Calipatria, you've gone too far.) Turn right on Sinclair Road and drive six miles to the Salton Sea National

Wildlife Refuge visitors center, located at the intersection of Sinclair Road and Gentry Road.
Contact: Sonny Bono Salton Sea National Wildlife Refuge, Calipatria, 760/348-5278, www.fws.gov.

59 NORTH ALGODONES DUNES WILDERNESS

1.0 mi/1.0 hr 2 8

east of Brawley and south of the Salton Sea

Map, page 768

The Algodones Dunes could best be described as an ocean of sand. They are located in the far southeast corner of California, amid a whole lot of...well, to be honest, nothing. Still, this is a unique and fragile place, where a massive dune system covers more than 1,000 square miles. It's the largest (in breadth, not height) dune system in the United States. In between the dunes lie flat basins in which desert willow, smoke trees, and mesquite flourish, and rare reptiles, such as the desert tortoise and fringe-toed lizard, make their homes. The dunes are divided into two areas, a large section south of Hwy. 78 that is open to OHVs and a smaller section north of Hwy. 78 that is protected as the Algodones Dunes Wilderness Area. Nature lovers head to the wilderness area, where the dunes rise to heights of 350 feet and stretch over a five-mile-wide expanse. You can wander around as much as you like, but since walking in sand is a tiring experience, you probably won't wander very far. (There are no formal trails across the dunes because of the continually shifting sands.) Mostly, this is a place to visit to gain a glimpse into a rare, special world comprised entirely of sand and sky.

User Groups: Hikers, dogs, and horses. No mountain bikes. No wheelchair facilities.

Permits: No permits are required. Parking and access are free.

Maps: A brochure and trail map are available from the Bureau of Land Management (BLM) office listed below. For a topographic map, go to the USGS website to download Niland.

Directions: From Brawley, drive east on Highway 78 for 26 miles. The wilderness area lies on the north side of the highway, but it is illegal to park alongside the road. Instead, take the turnoff for Ted Kipf Road (also signed as Niland-Glamis Road) to access the dunes.

Contact: Bureau of Land Management, El Centro Field Office, El Centro, 760/337-4400, www.blm.gov.

Index

M

T

XYZ

Acknowledgments

The following park rangers, interpretive specialists, park aides, public information specialists, and field scouts reviewed the listings in this edition for the following areas:

U.S. FOREST SERVICE

Eldorado National Forest: Jennifer Chapman, Dustin Bell, Rebecca Shufelt, Charis Parker Humboldt-Toiyabe National Forest: Tiffany Holloway, Erica Hopp

Klamath National Forest: Joshua Veal

Lake Tahoe Basin Management Unit: Heather Noel; field scout Sabrina Young, field scout Tom Hedtke

Lassen National Forest: Kevin Sweeney

Mendocino National Forest: Sandra Punky Moore

Modoc National Forest: Ken Sandusky, Suzanna Johnson, Sally Carter

Plumas National Forest: Lee Anne Schramel, Jason Lynn

Shasta-Trinity National Forest: Josef Orosz, Carol Underhill, Carolyn Napper; field scout Tom Hesseldenz

Six Rivers National Forest: Douglas Winn, Bridget Litten, Karenda Dean, Jeff Marszal

Stanislaus National Forest: Diana Fredlund, Joel Silverman

Tahoe National Forest: Joseph Flannery; field scout Robert Stienstra, Jr.

CALIFORNIA DEPARTMENT OF PARKS AND RECREATION

Sacramento Headquarters: Adeline Yee

Bay Area Headquarters: Karen Barrett, Neill Fogarty

Mount Diablo: Carmen Clintas

Santa Cruz/San Mateo District: Stan Kopacz, Barbara Morris, Mike Merritt, Kate Brandon, Bill Wolcott, Phil Bergman, Scott Sipes, Terry Kiser

Marin District: Nick Turner, Natasha Gilchrist, Carmen Cintas

Mendocino: Tracy Weisberg

South Yuba: Marc Weatherbee

Plumas/Eureka: Matt Green

CALIFORNIA DEPARTMENT OF FISH AND WILDLIFE

Sacramento Headquarters: Peter Tira, Patrick Foy

NATIONAL PARKS AND RECREATION AREAS

Golden Gate National Recreation Area: Charlie Strickfaden

Lassen Volcanic National Park: Kevin Sweeney

Lava Beds National Monument: Angel Sutton

Point Reyes National Seashore: Jennifer Stock; field scout John Dell'Osso

Redwood National and State Parks: Candace Tinkler, Greg Little

Smith River National Recreation Area: Douglas Winn, Bridget Litten, Karenda Dean; field scout Michael Furniss

Whiskeytown National Recreation Area: Josh Hoines

BUREAU OF LAND MANAGEMENT

King Range: Sandra Miles
Ukiah District: Serena Baker

REGIONAL PARKS AND OPEN SPACE

East Bay Regional Park District: Dave Mason; field scouts Ned MacKay, Shelly Lewis, Joe DiDonato, Lisa Brodtmann, Bridget Calvey, Josh Carlson, Fred Cortopassi, Steven Donnelly, Wayne Gilfillan, Sonya Gomez, Ashley Grenier, Sergio Huerta, David Kendall, Monique Looney, Chris Lyall, Matt McDonell, Sarah Miracle-Kyte, Joseph Murdach, Christopher Newey, Terry Noonan, Beverly Ortiz, Mark Pearson, Scott Possin, Jim Rutledge, Mark Taylor, David Vance, Dave Weaver, Gordon Willey, David Zuckermann

Marin Municipal Water District: Ann Vallee, Don Wicks, Matt Cerkel

Marin County Parks: Rosemary Passantino, Brian Sanford, Ari Golan; past edition: Bill Hogan

Midpeninsula Regional Open Space District: Leigh Ann Gessner, Korrine Skinner, Brandon Downing; field scout Shelly Lewis

San Mateo County Parks: Carla Schoof

Santa Clara County Parks: Tamara Clark, Laurel Anderson, Marina Hinestrosa; field scout Robert Stienstra Jr., field scout Janet Tuttle

Sonoma County Regional Parks: field scout Michael Pechner

Loch Lomond Recreation Area: David Brooks

Pacific Gas & Electric Company: Paula Forgi
Arcata Marsh Interpretive Center:. Denise Homer

Sonoma County Parks: Donna LaGraffe; field scout Michael Pechner

City of Ferndale: Frances Scalvini

Photo Credits

Title page photo: Tom Stienstra; page 3 © Tom Stienstra; page 4 © Ann Marie Brown; page 11 © Tom Stienstra; page 20 © Ann Marie Brown; page 24 © Sabrina Young; page 27 © Ann Marie Brown; page 31 © Sabrina Young; page 33 © Ann Marie Brown; page 34 © Tom Stienstra; page 37 © Ann Marie Brown; page 43 © Ann Marie Brown; page 46 © Tom Stienstra; page 51 © Tom Stienstra; page 65© Tom Stienstra; page 77 © Tom Stienstra; page 81 © Tom Stienstra; page 92 © Tom Stienstra; page 104 © Tom Stienstra; page 108 © Tom Stienstra; page 126 © Tom Stienstra; page 129 © Ann Marie Brown; page 136 © Tom Stienstra; page 141 © Tom Stienstra; page 153 © Tom Stienstra; page 157 © Tom Stienstra; page 171 © Ann Marie Brown; page 181 © Sabrina Young; page 187 © Ann Marie Brown; page 188 © Ann Marie Brown; page 197 © Tom Stienstra; page 203 © Tom Stienstra; page 208 © Tom Stienstra; page 211 © Ann Marie Brown; page 227 © Tom Stienstra; page 246 © Tom Stienstra; page 262 © Tom Stienstra; page 268 © Tom Stienstra; page 287 © Ann Marie Brown; page 301 © Tom Stienstra; page 304 © Tom Stienstra; page 351 © Tom Stienstra; page 357 © Tom Stienstra; page 388 © Tom Stienstra; page 397 © Tom Stienstra; page 437 © Ann Marie Brown; page 442 © Ann Marie Brown; page 449 © Ann Marie Brown; page 455 © Ann Marie Brown; page 458 © Ann Marie Brown; page 463 © Ann Marie Brown; page 467 © Ann Marie Brown; page 481 © Ann Marie Brown; page 503 © Ann Marie Brown; page 519 © Ann Marie Brown; page 526 © Ann Marie Brown; page 535 © Ann Marie Brown; page 538 © Ann Marie Brown; page 547 © Ann Marie Brown; page 557 © Ann Marie Brown; page 578 © Ann Marie Brown; page 588 © Ann Marie Brown; page 595© Ann Marie Brown; page 599 © Ann Marie Brown; page 610 © Ann Marie Brown; page 639 © Ann Marie Brown; page 657 © Ann Marie Brown; page 287 © Sabrina Young; page 681 © Ann Marie Brown; page 687 © Ann Marie Brown; page 690 © Ann Marie Brown; page 701 © Ann Marie Brown; page 714 © Ann Marie Brown; page 723 © Ann Marie Brown; page 737 © Ann Marie Brown; page 746 © Sabrina Young; page 748 © Ann Marie Brown; page 752 © Ann Marie Brown; page 762 © Ann Marie Brown; page 767 © Ann Marie Brown; page 774 © Ann Marie Brown; page 777 © Ann Marie Brown; page 790 © Ann Marie Brown; page 794 © Ann Marie Brown; page 807 © Ann Marie Brown